Art of Our Century

The Story of Western Art 1900 to the Present

Under the Direction of

JEAN-LOUIS FERRIER

With the Collaboration of

YANN LE PICHON

**English Translation
Under the Direction of**

WALTER D. GLANZE

Longman

Longman Group UK Limited
Longman House, Burnt Mill, Harlow,
Essex CM20 2JE, England
and Associated Companies throughout the world.

Originally published under the title *L'Aventure de l'Art au XXe Siècle*
in France in 1988 by Éditions du Chêne

Published in North America by Prentice Hall Editions, an imprint of Prentice Hall Press,
in 1989.

First published in the United Kingdom in 1990 by Longman Group UK Limited.

ISBN: 0-582-00037-8

Printed in Switzerland on the presses of Weber, in Bienne.

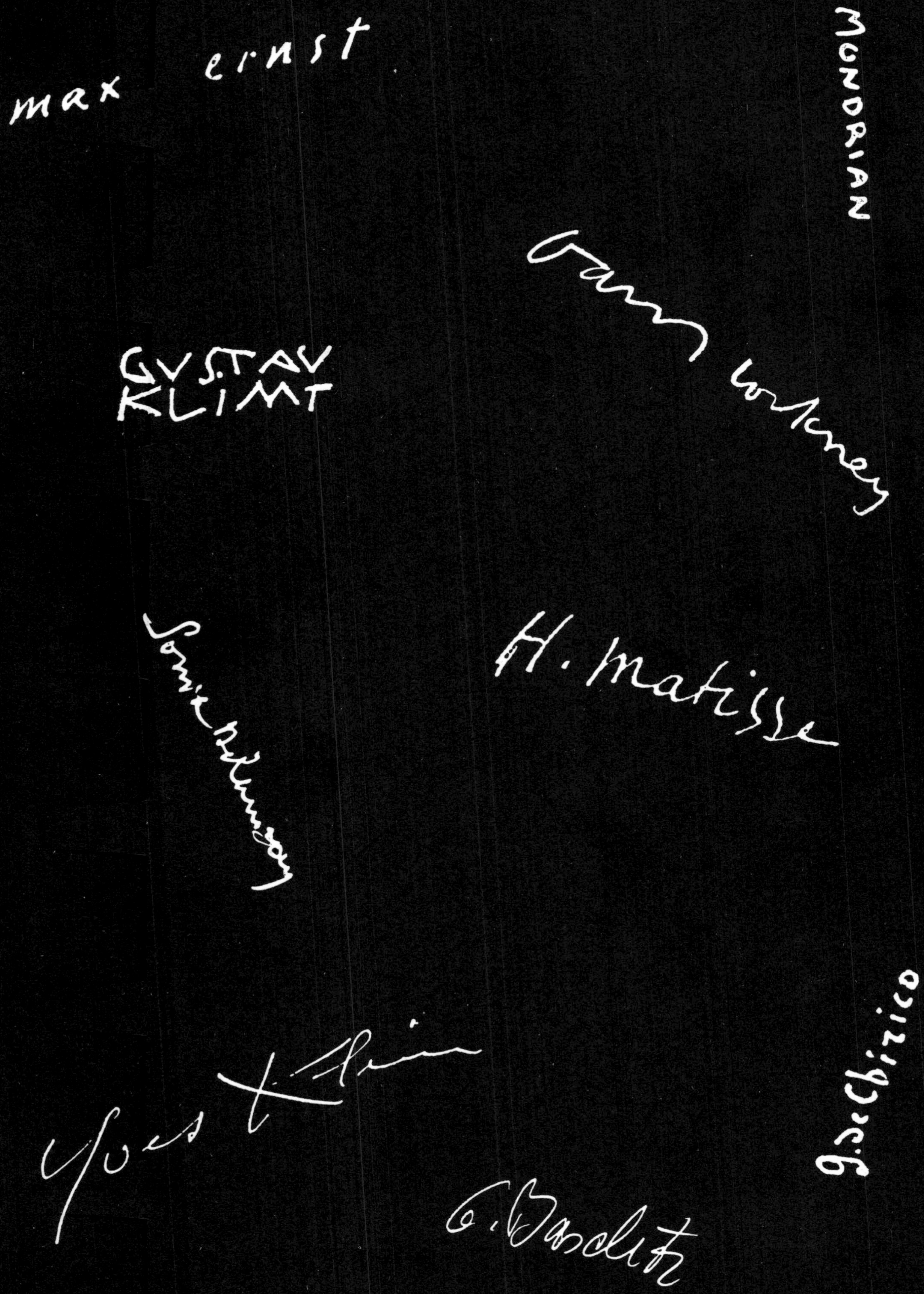

max ernst.

MONDRIAN

GVSTAV
KLIMT

David Hockney

Sonia Delaunay

H. Matisse

Yves Klein

G.deChirico

G. Baselitz

Art of Our Century

C O N T E N T S

P R E F A C E

To understand what truly occurred during a given period, it is necessary to summarize facts, to review them. This is an established habit of the best writers: William Shakespeare, Agatha Christie, Georges Simenon. Perhaps even God keeps a record book to remember what has taken place in various places at various times. Because it is condensed, such a summary can be more expressive and more meaningful than long descriptions of phenomena, stories, and anecdotes, interpretations and hypotheses. We have only to read over such an inventory, with no additional commentary, to see how strange our century is, how empty and aimless certain years have been, as if to hide their basic lack of interest behind a screen of pseudo-events, and how rich other years are, amazingly full of decisive events that occurred in a brief time period. The year of the Battle of Verdun, 1916, is one of these years, marking both the birth of Dada and the advent of Suprematism, two crucial ideas that will dominate the world of art as our century draws toward its close.

It is easier to be certain of the important elements of the first half of the century than to be certain of what is important in our half of the century. If the two ideas that were to dominate the century were born yesterday, would we be aware of it? It is unlikely. But reading this book gives one the feeling that such ideas exist. It is a stimulating, optimistic account. And its optimism is founded on facts, on the fireworks of intellectual and emotional discoveries, on an idea of what constitutes novelty, expressed through examples that are utterly amazing.

Evolutionism, the supreme ruler of science, has recently been the subject of dispute in artistic culture. People have begun to question whether something is better by definition if it is new. Nonetheless, the notion of newness is still very much alive, and the idea that discovery is a triumph of the mind is nowhere near its demise. What other criteria of quality do we have aside from novelty? Perhaps some criteria that involve quantity? Or is quality what attracts the attention of the greatest number of people for the greatest number of reasons? Is that the multifaceted surface from which each glance is reflected in an entirely original manner? The sheer number of facts condensed in this book might serve as the basis for answers to such questions. Indeed, using an absolute numerical criterion would mean using the highest degree of simplicity in art, as our century shows by example in Brancusi's sculpture, or in the painting of Malevich or Mondrian.

A few brief articles, ten or fifteen annotations, with the precision and concision typical of this book, can give the reader's imagination as good an idea of the times as could long dissertations in which our interest would become lost in a flood of details. That is why accounts such as this one are stimulating and useful in many situations: for the beginner, of course, who is seeking a general view, but also for those who already know (or think they know) that overview, for there are connections and relationships that conventional history and art books cannot make apparent amidst the mass of their information. And this book will serve well as a daily tool to answer our perpetual question: When exactly did it happen?

The amount of labor, of research, of analysis behind such a book is enormous. Only the incredible wealth of the art of this century can explain why it was completed at all. If this compact history of art did not have the accuracy of the very best works, it would leave us with a bitter, artificial aftertaste. But this is not just a substitute for those best works—it is the condensation of a passion expressed in its most immediate form.

A book such as this leaves a great deal to the imagination: What might have happened? What did happen between the lines? Behind what we already know? Watching the imaginary parade of artists who will pioneer the major ideas of our century, we can understand, for example, how small the active artistic community has really been, how close the contact was among the Fauves, the Cubists, and the Surrealists during the century's most decisive years, when these artists saw each other almost daily. It is a lesson to discover to what point the artistic scene of our own times was rigorously prepared for, by how many impassioned discussions and by how much work day after day in the studios. It is a lesson, for we must admit that relatively little that is new has been born beyond the periphery of this major art. It seems that, at least until very recently, the most important changes have been produced by almost daily encounters among different creative artists with similar preoccupations. A book such as this cannot, by definition, give us much information on the years to come. All we can know of the future is that, on the basis of our experience, it is sure to be a surprise for us. This work shows us who we already have become, because it tells us where we have come from.

PONTUS HULTEN

I N T R O D U C T I O N

A CENTURY OF RUPTURES

The revolution of modern art has frequently been compared to the revolution that took place in Italy during the Renaissance. Just as the artists of that time launched paintings, sculpture, and architecture down a path that diverged from medieval ideas, the artists of the beginning of our century broke with rules transmitted by their predecessors. Like the Renaissance artists, the artists of our century expressed new needs in accord with the knowledge of the new period, establishing a figurative system that was progressively more distinct from, then opposite to, the old one. Like they did, in short, the artists of our century changed thought patterns and sensibilities.

All this was already quite clear when Fauvism was born in 1905, the year when everything began. Let us review the facts. Matisse and his friends, Derain, Vlaminck, and Marquet, principally concerned with the primordial role they felt appropriate to assign to color, aroused hostility, mockery, and incomprehension at the Salon d'Automne. The gallery where they exhibited their works also housed a small, traditionally made bust, enthroned on a pedestal in a corner of the room. This unexpected juxtaposition must have struck the critic Louis Vauxcelles, who in the supplement of *Gil Blas,* published on October 17, stated, "The candor of this bust is a surprise amidst the surrounding orgy of pure colors; it is Donatello amongst the wild beasts"—in French, the "fauves." The comment seems equally provoked by one of Henri Rousseau's works being shown at the same Salon: a lion in the act of devouring an antelope in a dreamlike jungle.

The term "Cage of the Fauves" came up and spread rapidly throughout Paris. Impressionism, Gauguin, Cézanne, and Van Gogh were at that time far from being accepted, only by a handful of young avant-garde artists. Expressionism, for its part, was beginning to appear in Germany. These are the first fissures in the century—nothing will ever again be as it was before.

The decisive rupture, however, came in 1907, and it was to be the work of one man: Picasso. The famous painter was twenty-six years old, and lived in poverty in the Bateau-Lavoir, in Montmartre. He had made himself known to a small number of art lovers with his melancholy canvases from his blue period and rose period. But then he suddenly broke with his own past in a large, overwhelming composition, inspired simultaneously by African art and Iberian sculpture: *Les demoiselles d'Avignon.* Picasso had been a child prodigy, and after a time the tradition inherited from the Renaissance held no more secrets for him. Either he could repeat himself ad nauseam, or else he could choose to begin all over, which is what he did.

The reactions of Apollinaire, Braque, and other friends were disastrous. But there was one exception: The poet André Salmon was to note a short time later: "These are bare problems, numbers written in white on the blackboard. It is the clearly enunciated statement of equation painting." This judgment was later corroborated by Jean Paulhan, who, in writing on Cubism the year after *Demoiselles,* commented, "Instead of the how, the why. Perhaps even further: What is the world, after all, and what is it made of?"

Traditional art, we know, despite great disparities among schools, has as it's principal goal to reproduce the visible world with the maximum amount of *vraisemblance,* notably by means of perspective, the bit and bridle of painting according to Leonardo da Vinci. It gives an objective vision of beings and things just as the experimental method in the last century rendered a positive and restrictive conception of reality. But with the help of the theory of relativity and quantum mechanics, the exact sciences soon discovered that this vision was untrue both in the infinitely great dimension and in the infinitely small. And so the indeterminism of matter, and even a new form of spirituality, arose. There would be no more grandiose canvases, no more historical painting, gone are the luncheons on the grass, the sunset. Instead of the how, we are shown the why of everything: Artistic avant-gardes tirelessly, endlessly ask that question.

The most significant artist in this regard was Wassili Kandinsky, who in 1910 became the first artist to create an abstract watercolor. "For me, the splitting of the atom was as if the whole world had split, and suddenly thick walls crumbled. Everything was soft, uncertain, vacillating. It would not have astonished me to see a stone melt in the air and evaporate," he wrote. Others were equally affected—Picasso and Braque by the splitting of the atom, Duchamp by the mathematical speculation on infinite space, Malevich and Mondrian by everything involving philosophical rigor. Sculpture and architecture were soon to enter the fray. Modern art was born.

A CENTURY OF CONTINUITY

But what can be seen as clearly as a series of ruptures over the course of the century is a continuity. And in Matisse's work, first of all. When the great Fauve created the two versions of *Dance* for the Barnes Foundation in 1932 and 1933, he constantly kept the painting of Giotto in mind, particularly the frescoes of the chapel of the Arena in Padua. These fascinated him. Then came the paper cutouts toward the end of his life. Here he practiced direct cutting of color, without a preliminary drawing, just as a sculptor might attack stone. The cutouts definitively resolved the problem of volume and line that had already opposed Leonardo to Botticelli.

The same may be said of Bonnard, who jotted notes on "the day's costume," and who sought to show in his paintings what one might take in at a glance upon entering a room. He attempted to push Impressionism to its utmost consequences, pressing, sliding, moving, ever so slightly at times, beyond a simple questioning of the past.

The idea of continuity leads to the idea of flowering, and so it, too, becomes, in this century, creative and innovative.

The idea of continuity inspires the grouping together of everything that might, from decade to decade, be part of, be recognizable in, the New Objectivity in Germany, the quarrel of Realism in France, the New Figuration the world over.

That same idea differentiates itself as much from the noisy avant-gardes as from late-blooming Socialist Realism, which adopted the foolish goal of stopping time in art. This grand idea included artists as diverse as Otto Dix, Kokoschka, Bacon, Giacometti, Pignon. Their attitude is in no way passive in relation to the reality they accepted and experienced, while Abstractionism often eluded it or ignored it. And Picasso returned to it quite naturally in the second half of his work, once the years of negation and destruction were over.

Many works seem abstract or abstruse because we do not know how to read them. "The dialogue with nature remains for the artist a condition sine qua non," declared Klee. "He, too, is human; the artist is himself nature, a bit of nature in nature's kingdom." But Klee is also innovative in that he was never content to reproduce form but sought to penetrate the function of this nature, never taking his eyes from it. The forest is not the same for the woodchopper, the casual walker, or the berry gatherer. The one judges the thickness and health of the foliage, the other pays attention to the odor it gives off, the third is sensitive to the thickets and bushes. "The blossoming of an apple tree, its roots, the rise of the sap, the trunk, a cut showing the growth rings, the flower, its structure, its sexual functions, the fruit, the envelope protecting its seeds. A complex of states of growth," Klee continued in his notebook. Never had painters explored the visible world so closely. That, too, was part of the revolution of modern art.

Although on an entirely different level, the Surrealists, those inveterate scandal makers, also belong pictorially to continuity. Dali explained how he had tried to give in his paintings an "instant color photograph, that you could hold in your hands, of superfine images" rising out of the depths of our personal or collective subconscious. His craft is classic, as academic as that of Magritte or Tanguy.

Surrealism does indeed "place the umbrella and the sewing machine on the dissecting table," playing on unusual juxtapositions and comparisons. But the objective elements of which these juxtapositions are composed must be immediately identifiable if they are to attain their goal, which is to trouble our gaze. This is the imagery of our dreams, our obsessions, our hallucinations. And what are we to think of Hyperrealism, which emerged fifty years later, as if to contradict abstract art at the very moment when that art had entered into our daily visual habits? Histories of art do not seem to have taken sufficient note that the same century produced artists as divergent as Mondrian and Dali, Duchamp and Bacon, Kandinsky and Goings or Estes, each of equal stature.

Then came the final avatar of continuity: the recent Transavantgarde. Who would have imagined that, as we approach the end of the century, the very notion of the avant-garde would be devalued, abandoned, to the extent that scandal as the impetus of cultural and social change is now inoperative? First in Italy, amongst associates of the critic Achille Bonito Oliva, then throughout Europe and the United States, artists such as Chia, Garouste, Kiefer, or Schnabel have unhesitatingly returned to traditional craftsmanship, reintroducing oil painting, charcoal, pastels, glazes, and varnishes, along with personal sensitivity and ancestral myths.

A CENTURY OF DARING

This passing of avant-gardes does not, however, prevent our century from having been one of great daring, including every imaginable audacious act: Duchamp, in 1917, sent his *Fountain*, a urinal placed on a pedestal, as a sculpture to the Salon of Independents of New York; in 1954, Jasper Johns completed a painting that was an exact copy of the American flag; in 1976, Christo drafted an army of engineers and students to erect an ephemeral fabric wall twenty-five miles long on the California coast, and in 1985 he wrapped the Pont-Neuf in Paris for a three-week period.

Duchamp's first gesture of daring dates, in fact, from 1913: The wheel and frame of a bicycle fastened to a stool was his first "ready-made," its purpose to attack the work of art mounted on its perpetual pedestal. It was a challenge: The artist chose a manufactured object and signed it. "The ready-made is located in a zero zone of the mind," explained the Mexican poet and essayist Octavio Paz. "It is a date with nobody for the purpose of noncontemplation." Then came Arman's piled objects, composed of assemblages of every possible nature: violins, gas masks, tools, shoes, boat anchors; César's Compressions: cars and motorcycles reduced to cubes; Arte Povera's rocks in natural states, and piles of coal. Or an Ash Can museum. Never had anything like this been seen.

If Picasso, Braque, Kandinsky, and Mondrian reinvented painting, they had never gone as far as placing it in doubt. With Duchamp—and ever since Duchamp—the very question of art has been asked. Now that everything can be art, what is art? And even: Does art exist? And, if it exists, in what form should it then make itself evident?

The Futurism that inspired Duchamp to create his *Nude Descending a Staircase* had opened the way. When subscribers of the sensible newspaper *Le Figaro* opened their daily edition on February 20, 1909, they could scarcely believe their eyes. There, on the front page, they discovered a *Manifesto*, signed by one Filippo Tommaso Marinetti, who truly transgressed all limits. "A racing car, its trunk decorated with large pipes like a serpent with explosive breath, a roaring automobile that seems to run over a hail of bullets, is more beautiful than the *Victory of Samothrace*," he had the effrontery to state. And there was more: The same text glorifies war, according to him the only method of hygiene the world has, exalts contempt for females, demands the demolition of libraries and museums. Futurist painting, proceeding in large part from Cubism, was not very creative. But with Futurism, the invective and the insult substituted for the first time for esthetic discourse. The artist goes on stage, went out into the street, fought with his fists for his ideas. It was, even before Dada, supreme daring.

But what does the future bring? To the indeterminism of matter and to spiritualist openings came the response of war in the age of technology and its consequent nihilism. Before launching the Battle of Verdun in the dawn of February 21, 1916, the Germans had placed a canon every thirty-three feet over thirty-seven miles of the front, so that when they opened fire, there was suddenly nothing but a gigantic flame from one end of the horizon to the other. The earth shook beneath the soldiers. Eight million dead in the First World War, forty million during the Second World War—difficult even for the most inattentive of people to continue painting at an easel in the silence of the studio. Hans Prinzhorn, as early as 1922, wondered about the plastic creativity of mental patients, already a fascinating subject for Klee, and later for Dubuffet, who studied it under the concept of Art Brut in the 1940s. It marked the emergence of the irrational, of madness in art, after rationalism had proved its impotence.

All the Dadaisms, Neodadaisms, Neoneodadaisms proceeded, more or less, from there. Yves Klein, who, on April 28, 1958, exhibited empty space at the Iris Clert Gallery; Tinguely, who blew up a sculpture in the garden of the Museum of Modern Art in New York; or Beuys, his face covered with gold powder, who sat explaining art to a dead rabbit for three hours—they all proceeded from that impetus. Now and forever, the daring gesture, the showman artist, the shaman artist, or better yet, "the anartist," to use Hélène Parmelin's term.

A GOLDEN CENTURY

The term Golden Century, as everyone knows, is usually reserved for the seventeenth century in Spain to express the exceptional richness of its art. But how much richer, in our century, modern art is.

Let us briefly retrace its adventurous path: 1905, Fauvism and Expressionism; 1908, Cubism; 1915, Suprematism; 1916, Dadaism; 1917, Neoplasticism; 1924, Surrealism. Then, pausing briefly to catch its breath, the adventure continues: 1948, Cobra; 1950, Abstract Expressionism; 1956, Pop Art; 1960, New Realism; 1963, New Figuration; 1967, Conceptual Art, Arte Povera, and Land Art; 1980, Transavantgarde. And studding its path all the while are illustrious names: Picasso, Matisse, Duchamp, Malevich, Mondrian, of course; but also Léger, Delaunay, Dufy, Soutine, Hopper, Dali, Magritte, Miró, Dubuffet, Pollock, Fautrier, Jorn, Tàpies, Rauschenberg, Johns, Warhol, Lichtenstein, Monet . . .

Monet? Absolutely. Monet, who died in 1926. When Clemenceau unveiled the *Waterlilies* the following year at the Orangerie in Paris, the principal constituent movements of the century are already history. But what was exhibited was much more than the masterpiece of Impressionism. It was no longer simply a question of the reflection of the sun on water, but of the flaming of light, as if, through the viewpoint of an almost total abstraction, a world of atoms ceaselessly recreated itself under our eyes in the only mural painting of totally new conception executed since Delacroix's decorations.

Examples abound. On July 25, 1909, Blériot completed the first aerial crossing of the English Channel. The event—before Lindbergh—startled imaginations. A twenty-four-year-old artist, Robert Delaunay, was carried away by the exploit. A new adherent to Cubism, he created Inobjective Painting in 1925, and two years later came the miracle: a huge canvas entitled *Homage to Blériot.* "Simultaneous solar disk. Forms. Creation of the constructive disk. Solar fireworks. Depth and life of the sun. Constructive mobility of the solar spectrum; birth, fire, evolution of planes. Everything is round shapes: sun, earth, horizons, plenitude of intense life, of poetry that one cannot verbalize—a Rimbaldism. The motor on the canvas. Solar force and force of the earth," he wrote in his notebooks. Not only was the break with the Renaissance complete, but a system of color forms was established, which, beyond Blériot, expressed the era of supersonic aviation and the conquest of space.

"When I see a Léger, I am happy," Apollinaire used to say. He might have said the same of Delaunay, and of all those after him who brought into their works their fascination with the modern world: of Vasarely, whose plastic vocabulary reached the level of our planetary conscience; or of Mathieu, who introduced speed into painting, simultaneously liberating the universe from signs; of Warhol, who brought the joys and excitement of our consumer society into the museum; of Lichtenstein, who sought in the comic strip pictorial and moral values capable of transcribing our new myths into urban civilization, just as Courbet, in another time, calqued onto the almanac prints of Franche-Comté the rural Realism of *A Burial at Ornans.*

This activity has created such a furor that sociologists and estheticians on all sides speak of a crisis of figurative values, as if, from the moment Picasso executed the admirable and terrible *Demoiselles d'Avignon* in 1907, everything became ruptures, breaks, quests, and wanderings. Now, as the year 2000 dawns—it is enough to thumb through this book to be convinced of it—the notion that the art of our century is obscure and inaccessible seems false. If Brancusi's *Birds* have lost their feathers, they do nonetheless soar toward the mind. And who would dare challenge the idea that the mathematical rigor of Pevsner's sculptures arises from a sublime, new Classicism?

"ART OF OUR CENTURY"

While histories and encyclopedias of art proceed by chapters and articles, this work is put together, on the contrary, like a newspaper, recording the essential events as they happen each year. It selects across eighty-nine years, from 1900 to the present, the most noteworthy of art news from the domains of painting, sculpture, and architecture. Thus we see how, one by one, the great movements that founded modern art were constituted, what ideas drove their creators, what difficulties they encountered before they were established. Other important events parade through the reader's imagination: the Armory Show, which, in 1913, revealed those movements to America; the creation of the Museum of Modern Art in New York by three generous donors; and the desperate struggles of the Russian avant-garde against Stalinism and those of the German avant-garde against Hitler.

One also discovers the principal locations of creativity for the art of our century: the Bateau-Lavoir, La Ruche, and Montparnasse, all in Paris; the Bauhaus in Weimar, then in Dessau; Black Mountain College and the Chelsea Hotel in the United States. We are also witness to the lives of the great collectors, such as Alfred C. Barnes, who, in 1923, purchased one hundred paintings from Soutine in a single transaction. We are introduced to the great merchants: Vollard, Kahnweiler, Peggy Guggenheim, Leo Castelli. We are present at the major auctions that permit the art market to develop. One can begin reading on any page, at either end of the book. It is utterly riveting.

But this is in no way a simple chronicle in which everything is included and neutralized. The main points are there: Each year includes a long opening article, often accompanied by excerpts from manifestoes, writings, or declarations by artists. Shorter articles and a yearly page of brief news favor rapid reading.

The numerous anecdotes are recounted not so much for what they are as for the amount of explanation and significance they contain. For it is not true that discourses on art must be incomprehensible. We are willing to bet that everything can be demonstrated, retraced, and explained in a century that was—and still is—exciting and, in the final analysis, coherent, from beginning to end.

The book has a clear, accessible style, inspired by information from a variety of sources. The tone of a period is brought back to us by the reproduction of the great manifestoes of this century, and by excerpts from theoretical works by artists, historians, and philosophers such as Freud, Klee, and McLuhan.

JEAN-LOUIS FERRIER

• The structural concept of *Art of Our Century* is a chronological presentation of eighty-nine chapters, one chapter each for the years 1900 through 1988.

• Each year is introduced by a brief editorial, followed by an overview of that chapter.

• The field of art is put in larger context through two features: The first page of each year lists events in other cultural areas—literature, theater, music, and motion pictures. And each decade is preceded by a two-page spread in which important developments in the arts are juxtaposed year by year with other great events of the decade—in literature, music and theater, motion pictures, science and technology, and politics and daily life.

• Many of the principal articles are connected by a system of references. For example, the article on Kandinsky in 1910 refers to other major Kandinsky articles, in 1911, 1926, 1927, and 1944.

• Other sources of reference are the appendix Artworks Reproduced or Discussed and the General Index of subjects and names. The reader thus has three ways of seeking reference to a particular topic.

• In addition, there are two appendixes that put much of the general information in specific contexts: the Selected Movements (twenty-nine of the more than three hundred movements and tendencies that are discussed in this work) and the Selected Biographies (one hundred and twelve of the greatest creators of modern art, chosen from among ten times this number of artists who are treated in this work).

• Each article is written as though it originated within the respective year it appears in this book. Consequently, when Charles-Édouard Jeanneret is mentioned in 1916, it is without reference to Le Corbusier, the name he assumed in 1920; Prague is in Austria-Hungary until 1919, when Czechoslovakia was created; Leningrad is called Petrograd from 1914 to 1924 and St. Petersburg until 1914, etc. (But note that in captions, which give the artwork's current location, the name is, for example, Leningrad throughout.) Likewise, monetary values, especially the franc and the dollar, are those of the respective year, often differing vastly from what they are today.

• Some museums may be referred to by their common abbreviations, especially CNAC (Centre National d'Art Contemporain, in Paris); CNAP (Centre National des Arts Plastiques, in Paris); LACMA (Los Angeles County Museum of Art, in Los Angeles); MNAM (Musée National d'Art Moderne, in Paris); MOCA (Museum of Contemporary Art, in Los Angeles); MOMA (Museum of Modern Art, in New York). Also note Beaubourg = Georges Pomidou Center (located at the Rue Beaubourg, in Paris).

• In preparing the English-language edition of this work, the names of works of art were rendered in a form that is customary in English-speaking countries; for example, we translate Duchamp's *Nude Descending a Staircase*, but we retain Picasso's *Les demoiselles d'Avignon*. Some works have been known by different names throughout the decades, and sometimes they were renamed by their creators; but to avoid confusion, this edition is consistent in the use of any names of artworks—of which more than 1,700 are mentioned.

W.D.G.

It all begins in 1905. In Paris, Fauvism bursts noisily into the Salon d'Automne, and the demise of Bouguereau sounds the death knell of academic painting. The same year witnesses the birth of Expressionism, with the formation of Die Brücke in Dresden. From now on, there will be no break in activity. Cubism in 1908, with Picasso and Braque; Futurism in 1909, setting the trend of

1900

	1900	**1901**	**1902**	**1903**	**1904**
ARTS	• Paris World's Fair • Monet exhibits his first *Waterlilies*	• Birth of the School of Nancy • Death of Arnold Böcklin	• Otto Wagner's building for *Die Zeit* in Vienna • Grand Toulouse-Lautrec retrospective	• Death of Gauguin • Birth of the Vienna Ateliers	• Picasso moves into the Bateau-Lavoir • Triumphal Cézanne show at the Salon d'Automne
LITERATURE	• *Le rire* by Henri Bergson • *Lord Jim* by Joseph Conrad • *The Interpretation of Dreams* by Sigmund Freud	• *The Buddenbrooks* by Thomas Mann • *Kim* by Richard Kipling • *The Octopus* by Frank Norris	• Accidental death of Émile Zola • *The Immoralist* by André Gide	• First session of the Académie Goncourt • *The Call of the Wild* by Jack London • *Man and Superman* by George Bernard Shaw	• *The Late Mathias Pascal* by Luigi Pirandello
MUSIC AND THEATER	• *Tosca* by Giacomo Puccini in Rome	• *Jeux d'eaux* by Maurice Ravel in Paris • *Russalka* by Antonin Dvorak in Prague • Death of Giuseppe Verdi	• *Pelleas and Melisande* by Claude Debussy in Paris • *Cathleen ni Houlihan* by W. B. Yeats in Dublin	• *Pelleas and Melisande* by Arnold Schönberg • Oscar Hammerstein builds the Manhattan Opera House	• *Madama Butterfly* by Giacomo Puccini • *The Cherry Orchard* by Anton Chekhov
MOTION PICTURES	• *Cinderella* by Georges Méliès	• *The Little Doctor*, a British film	• *Voyage to the Moon* by Georges Méliès • *Salomé* by Oskar Messter	• *The Great Train Robbery*, 12 minutes: the longest film so far	• *The Damnation of Faust*, a French film
SCIENCE AND TECHNOLOGY	• Max Planck states his quantum theory • Flight of the first zeppelin	• First wireless telegraphic message, by Marconi, from Cornwall to Newfoundland • First motor-driven bicycles	• Aswan Dam opened	• First powered flight, by Orville and Wilbur Wright • Nobel prize to Marie Curie and Henri Becquerel for their radium research	• Construction of Panama Canal begins • Invention of offset printing • Pavlov is awarded the Nobel prize
POLITICS AND DAILY LIFE	• Boxer Revolt in China • Creation of the Commonwealth of Australia • The Cake Walk is the most popular dance in America	• Death of Queen Victoria • Theodore Roosevelt becomes President	• Volcano destroys the town of St. Pierre on Martinique	• First motor taxis in London • First crossing of the United States coast-to-coast by automobile (65 days)	• Russo-Japanese War (the first use of trenches) • Entente Cordiale between France and England • Paris Conference on White Slave Trade

1909

the pugnacious manifesto—in just four years, the first revolution of modern art is set in motion. That revolution is preceded, or accompanied, by the death of its great percursors: Gauguin dies in 1903, Cézanne in 1906. As the World's Fair of 1900 pauses for a moment on the threshold between the past and the future, the new century declares itself a fighter resolved to win.

1905	1906	1907	1908	1909
• The Fauves at the Salon d'Automne • Birth of Die Brücke in Dresden	• Death of Cézanne • Discovery of African art • Russian artists at the Salon d'Automne	• *Les demoiselles d'Avignon* by Picasso • *Danae* by Klimt	• Birth of Cubism	• Birth of Futurism
• *Three Essays on the Theory of Sexuality* by Sigmund Freud • *The Blue Angel* by Heinrich Mann	• Death of Ibsen • *The Jungle* by Upton Sinclair • *The Four Million* by O. Henry	• *Creative Evolution* by Henri Bergson • *White Fang* by Jack London	• *Mother* by Maxim Gorki • *L'enchanteur pourrissant* by Guillaume Apollinaire • *Three Lives* by Gertrude Stein	• *Exultations* by Ezra Pound • *The Notebooks of Malte Laurids Brigge* by Rainer Maria Rilke
• *La mer* by Claude Debussy in Paris • *Salomé* by Richard Strauss in Vienna • Belasco produces *The Girl of the Golden West*, in Pittsburgh	• *Spanish Rhapsody* by Maurice Ravel • Mozart Festival in Salzburg	• Gustav Mahler becomes director of the Metropolitan Opera of New York • The first *Ziegfeld Follies*, in New York • Death of Edvard Grieg	• *Boris Godunov* by Modest Mussorgsky • *Fireworks* by Igor Stravinsky	• The Russian Ballet in Paris • *Erwartung* by Arnold Schönberg
• First regular movie theater, in Pittsburgh	• *Humorous Phases of a Funny Face* by J. Stuart Blackton, one of the first films using animation	• *Twenty Thousand Leagues under the Sea* by Georges Melies • *Skating* by Max Linder	• *The Last Days of Pompeii* by Arturo Ambrosio • The first animation films by Émile Kohl	• The first newsreels • The first movie star: Mary Pickford
• Albert Einstein establishes the Special Theory of Relativity	• First radio program of voice and music, by R. A. Fessenden, in the United States • Identification and arrest of "Typhoid Mary"	• Slow-motion filming invented, by August Musger • Louis Lumière invents color photography	• Ford produces the first Model T • Invention of the battle tank • Hermann Minkowski's four-dimensional geometry	• First flight across the English Channel, by Louis Blériot • Robert E. Perry reaches or at least comes very close to the North Pole
• Japanese victory over Russia • Formation of the Canadian provinces Saskatchewan and Alberta	• U.S. troops occupy Cuba • Alfred Dreyfus rehabilitated • Earthquake in San Francisco, killing 700	• Oklahoma becomes the 46th state • First daily comic strip (*Mr. Mutt*, later *Mutt and Jeff*)	• Earthquake in Calabria and Sicily, killing 150,000 • Foundation of Tel Aviv • Women's-rights demonstrations in London	• Lenin publishes *Materialism and Empiric Criticism* • London hairdresses give the first permanent waves

1900
SUMMARY

In Paris, the Belle Époque asserts itself dramatically at the World's Fair. The city is packed with crowds enthralled with the opulent art dominating Paris, its streets, and the entrances to the newly constructed metro. The moment of triumph has finally come for the Impressionists, painters of happiness, who now attract to the City of Light countless other artists, such as young Picasso, seduced by the euphoric hedonism of the times. In the same year, Rodin displays a Promethean humanism on the panels of his Gates of Hell. Freud discovers in dreams a rebellion of repressed sexual instincts. And Nietzsche's death is a reminder of his declaration that man's greatness lies only in his "will to power" and in his capacity for invention.

WORLD'S FAIR

The World's Fair on the Champ-de-Mars
Paul Cézanne Finally Recognized
Paul Guimard: His Strange Metro Entrances

ENCOUNTERS AND INFLUENCES

Mary Cassatt Exports Impressionism
Japanism and the Nabis

GREAT MASTERS

Monet Exhibits His Garden

DEVELOPMENTS

Munch: the Dance of Despair
The Russians Discover the Jugendstil

ART NEWS

The Painter of the American Landscape Dies
The Transparencies of the MacClurg Building
Closer to Zola Than to Rodin
Picasso Takes the Prize
Polemic on Sacré-Coeur
In Brief

WRITINGS AND THEORIES

Dreams According to Freud
Thus Saw Ruskin
Thus Spoke Nietzsche

LITERATURE

FRANCE
Charles Péguy launches Les cahiers de la quinzaine.
  The philosopher Henri Bergson publishes a seminal book, Le rire.
  The English writer Oscar Wilde dies in Paris, a refugee in France after his prison term.
  Paul Claudel publishes Connaissance de l'est, *a collection of prose poems from his stay in East Asia.*

GREAT BRITAIN
Publication of Lord Jim *by Joseph Conrad.*

THEATER

FRANCE
Edmond Rostand's L'aiglon *is a great success, with Sarah Bernhardt and Lucien Guitry.*
  At the Théâtre Antoine, Jules Renard produces his latest work, Poil de carotte.

SWEDEN
Premiere of August Strindberg's The Dance of Death.

MUSIC

FRANCE
The young composer Claude Débussy has his first success with Nocturnes.
  Performance of Louise *by Gustave Charpentier.*

ITALY
Premiere of Tosca *by Giacomo Puccini.*

AUGUSTE RODIN:
THE GATES OF HELL. 1900. Paris.
Musée d'Orsay

A Promethean humanism.

14

THE WORLD'S FAIR ON THE CHAMP-DE-MARS

PARIS

The twentieth century opens with a World's Fair, which lasts two hundred days and attracts almost fifty million visitors to its eighty-three thousand exhibits on the Champ-de-Mars. Many visitors carry "photographic cameras," a new social phenomenon, which—along with the increase in the printing of postcards—plays an important role in popularizing the arts, particularly painting.

These vistors from all over the world, many wearing straw hats and flower-patterned veils, are impressed by the baroque and Art Nouveau pavilions that have invaded the Champ-de-Mars, which is now connected to the Champs-Élysées by a grand cast-iron bridge, framed by spirited horses and dedicated to Czar Alexander III.

From both sides of the Avenue Nicolas II, the recently built Grand Palais and Petit Palais look like sumptuous temples of art, to which an arts and sciences pavilion has been added. On the Left Bank of the Seine and across from the Louvre, the Orsay railroad station seems to

echo the theme. The painter Édouard Detaille notes in his diary: "At noon they took me to the Quai d'Orsay. The railroad station is superb and looks like a Beaux-Arts palace, and the Beaux-Arts palace looks like a railroad station, so I suggest that the architect Laloux interchange them, if there is still time to do so."

In the Petit Palais, almost five thousand works of art "from the beginning to 1800" are exhibited and admired by the crowds. In the Grand Palais, there is a "centennial" exhibit of French art climaxing with the Impressionist period. Despite their disappointment at being unable to participate in the "decennial" exhibit that complements this show, the Impressionists are finally having their official triumph: Bazille, Boudin, Degas, Guillaumin, Lebourg, Lépine, Manet, Monet, Morisot, Pissarro, Renoir, Seurat, and Sisley are well represented and increasingly admired.

Orientalist Léon Gérôme, a member of the Institute, tries to prevent President Lubet from entering the Impressionist room.

Orsay railroad station.

He stands before the door with arms outstretched: "Stop, Mr. President, this is France's shame." But the Impressionists, so disparaged in the past, enjoy popular acceptance. With the diffractions of their dazzling colors they cross the threshold to this century with brilliance.

The great sculptor Auguste Rodin, looking like a wizard with his flowing beard, chooses at the age of sixty and at the height of his fame to show one hundred and fifty of his sculptures in a

separate, personal pavilion built at his own expense at the Place de l'Alma. He had had doubts as to his reception, and now revels in the success predicted by his friend Claude Monet in the preface to the catalog. The museums of Copenhagen, Hamburg, Dresden, Budapest, and even Philadelphia are snatching up Rodin's sensuous and tormented works. For this personal exhibit, Rodin decides to complete his interminable plaster assembly *The Gates of Hell*. The

AT THE CENTENNIAL EXHIBITION OF FRENCH ART, THE IMPRESSIONISTS ARE FINALLY HAVING THEIR OFFICIAL TRIUMPH

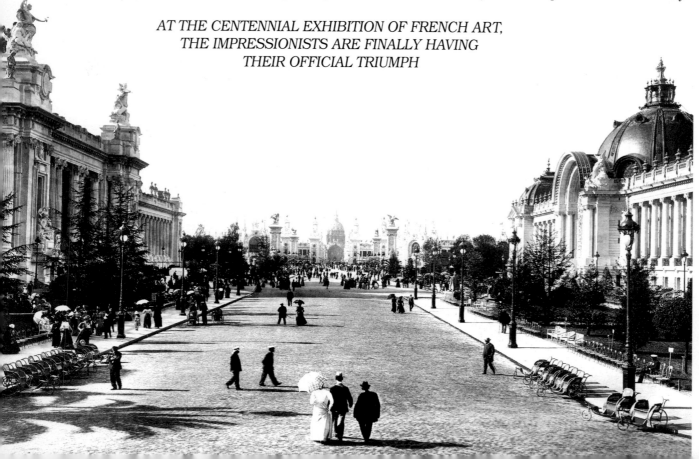

General view of the World's Fair: to the right, the Grand Palais; to the left, the Petit Palais; in the background, the Alexander III Bridge.

PAUL CÉZANNE FINALLY RECOGNIZED

work had been commissioned by the government in 1880 for the Museum of Decorative Arts, which was to be built at the present site of the Orsay railroad station. It was with the assistance of his model and pupil, Camille Claudel, the sister of the dramatist who wrote the *Tête d'or* (golden head), that Rodin created his *Gates*. He was inspired by Dante's *Inferno*, Ovid's *Metamorphoses*, and Baudelaire's *Flowers of Evil*—a veritable matrix where most of the groups of the *Gates* were born and shaped.

"But it still isn't finished," many reproached Rodin. The sculptor answered: "Are the French cathedrals finished?" These overwhelming *Gates of Hell*, to which despairing but loving figures cling, convulsed and split apart, might easily stop the affected progress of the type of academic sculpture that lingers everywhere at the exhibits on the Champ-de-Mars and which is more reminiscent of the art of the nineteenth century than of the century that has just begun.

Nevertheless, an ambience of modernity reigns. It is created by the use and the exploitation of several impressive new techniques. Apart from a dramatic accident, namely, the collapse of a concrete footbridge that caused the death of a dozen people, the visitors are delighted by the exhibits. They are thrilled by the development of electricity, to which one of the largest palaces, lit by more than ten thousand bulbs, is dedicated. They are fascinated by the first moving sidewalk; it is called "the street of the future." But above all they appear to be seduced by cinematography. The films of Louis Lumière are projected on a huge screen. He became famous last year when he completed the Photorama in which the continuous images of "panning" are preserved on a single plate.

The inventor Raoul Grimoin-Sanson has created a Cinéorama for the World's Fair. It offers viewers the incredible sight of panoramic views taken from a balloon. Some enthusiastic reporters already call photography a new art: The Seventh Art!

PAUL CÉZANNE: APPLES AND ORANGES. 1895-1900. Paris. Musée d'Orsay

Paris. Among the Impressionists that are exhibited, thanks to Paul Gallimard and Roger Marx, at the Centennial, the most intriguing figure is Paul Cézanne, who occupies a place of honor with three of his works. "He's very much in vogue, it's extraordinary," writes Pissarro to his son Lucien. Cézanne, now sixty-one, and suffering from diabetes, is living in retirement at Aix-en-Provence.

PAUL GUIMARD: HIS STRANGE METRO ENTRANCES

Paul Guimard: metro entrance at the Bastille.

"Very simple and very elegant, these little pavilions created by Monsieur Guimard are all of iron, ceramics, and glass. Airy like champagne," said *Le Figaro* of February 1.

MARY CASSATT EXPORTS IMPRESSIONISM

PARIS

The most Parisian of American painters is back. Since her return from the United States last March, Mary Cassatt of Pittsburgh has been dividing her time between her apartment on the Rue de Marignan and her castle in Beaufresne, in the Oise department. It seems that at the age of fifty-six this friend of the Impressionists—and an Impressionist herself—has decided to build a bridge between American collectors and French painters. She is placing her knowledge of art at the service of rich amateurs in the New World. It has been a long time since Miss Cassatt began to

study at the Beaux-Arts Institute and at the Louvre. She was twenty-two. Her determined work and her talent were rewarded a year later, in 1868, when her *Mandolin Player* was accepted by the Salon of French artists.

It is Degas to whom she owes her entry to the Impressionists. One afternoon in 1877, Degas visited her studio and, impressed with her work, invited her to participate in the Salon des Indépendants; two years later, she exhibited there. When she returned to the United States in the fall of 1898, she was an established artist. She renewed acquaintances in the financial and industrial world. Her brother Alexander was president of the Pennsylvania Railroad. Mary also resumed her friendship with Louisine Waldron Elder, who had married Henry O'Havenmeyer. Thanks to such patrons, Mary Cassatt became an effective adviser in the formation of large collections of paintings in the United States.

MARY CASSATT:
MOTHER AND CHILD.
Paris. Musée d'Orsay

JAPANISM AND THE NABIS

PARIS

Tadamasa Hayashi, general commissioner of the Japanese art section at the World's Fair, thought he should relegate Japanese prints to second place. He supposed that interest in the prints was quiescent. But Manet, Toulouse-Lautrec, Van Gogh, and Gauguin found inspiration for their graphic and pictorial works in such prints. Jules Claretie declared thirty years ago that "Japan is a teacher"—and this influence has not changed to this day. An example is the decorative inventions of Art Nouveau, which are best illustrated by the vases of Gallé.

The continued Japanese influence can be seen above all in the creations of artists who, under the name of Nabis—meaning "prophets" in Hebrew—met in 1888 to simplify art and thus sublimate it and give it universal

validity. Seeking to recall "the flavor of primitive emotions," they have paid special attention to "Japanese fabrics." They are impressed by the arabesque stylization and the use of pure colors as flat tints for the fabrics. Bonnard, Denis, Maillol, Ranson, Sérusier, Vallotton, and Vuillard (whom the Natanson brothers got together for their *Revue blanche*) remain doubtlessly the most fervent adherents of Japanism. The "very Japanist Nabi," as Pierre Bonnard was nicknamed, demonstrates this in his lithographic illustrations of Verlaine's poems *Parallèlement*, which he created this year at the request of the art dealer Ambroise Vollard.

ÉDOUARD VUILLARD:
LA RAVAUDEUSE. 1891.
Paris. Musée d'Orsay

Photograph of Monet in his garden at Giverny.

CLAUDE MONET:
WATERLILIES. 1900.
Paris. Musée d'Orsay

MONET EXHIBITS HIS GARDEN

PARIS

Twenty-two paintings with a barely identifiable theme. Painted during the last five years. Bursts of color, burning light, reflection, transparency. The Claude Monet exhibit at the Durand-Ruel gallery from November 22 to December 15 includes his most daring work yet: the waterlilies in the garden.

When Monet settled in his house in Giverny in 1883—he had first seen it from the train running from Vernon to Gisors and was immediately captivated—it was merely a charming building with pink walls amid an apple orchard. He transformed the orchard into a valley of peonies, lilies, and foxglove; five gardeners planted according to the season. In 1893 he bought a marshy lot on the other side of the railroad track and had a pond dug. Waterlilies soon bloomed. Together with the arched Japanese bridge uniting the two shores, the aquatic plants with broad flat floating leaves and showy flowers are dazzling visitors to the Durand-Ruel gallery.

Some fascinating history accompanies this masterpiece. When Monet asked the mayor of Giverny for authorization to dig in his garden and install a sluice so that he could capture the water of the Epte that flows alongside, he had to deal with hostility of some villagers. Washerwomen who used this tiny tributary of the Seine to do their laundry were concerned that Monet's proposed changes would reduce the flow of the Epte. Others feared that the exotic plants Monet planned to grow there would poison the cattle drinking downstream. Was it his usual country outfit of heavy boots and poacher's hat that worked a miracle with the people of Giverny? The artist did get what he wanted, fortunately.

Monet's Japanese bridge, inspired by Hiroshige's *One Hundred Famous Sites in Edo*, has a good location in the exhibition at Durand-Ruel. It is not just the bridge, of course, but the yellow, white, red, and purple waterlilies that Monet renders as so many lively touches, quickly put on canvas. He also had rendered a gamut of rare flowers, delivered to him from Japan through Tamada Hayashi, a Japanese dealer and collector living in Paris.

The time of ridicule and penury is happily over. At the age of sixty, Monet enjoys success, and his prices keep rising: One of his masterpieces, *The Bridge at Argenteuil*, brought 21,000 francs three years ago at the Vever sale, to the great surprise of the artist who wondered how anyone would bet such a large sum on him. Throughout this summer, he has triumphed at the centennial of French art at the World's Fair. So much so that it seems that all of Impressionism is now winning, although critics once saw nothing in it but "palette scrapings."

(See also 1919 and 1927.)

MUNCH: THE DANCE OF DESPAIR

CHRISTIANIA

At the independents' exhibition three years ago, the Norwegian painter Edvard Munch stunned the public with his "anguished Expressionism" in his *Eighteen Pictures from the Modern Life of the Soul,* a series also shown under the title *The Frieze of Life.*

This year, he is exhibiting a large canvas, *The Dance of Life,* as a synthesis of works shown in 1897. The same obsessions display even greater tension. Three emblematic figures crystallize his idea of woman. At the left, a blonde figure in white, the virgin, icon of purity and inaccessible innocence. At the right, the nocturnal mother, stiff and resigned to her fate, a suffering, mute servant. Between these static figures is a red vampire woman, leading a man in her perverse dance; she is the incarnation of devouring sensuality and fatal seduction. In the background, couples dance joylessly under a setting sun. The silhouette recalls a withdrawing Messiah, unseasonable or unable to warm frozen despair.

EDVARD MUNCH:
THE DANCE OF LIFE. 1900.
Oslo. National Gallery

THE RUSSIANS DISCOVER THE JUGENDSTIL

MOSCOW

In January and February last year, Russians discovered Art Nouveau. The Society for Encouragement of the Arts presented a panorama of current works of art.

The German variant of Art Nouveau, the Jugendstil, had been only a vague notion for the Russians. They knew only Julius Diez, and mainly from his drawings in the magazine *Jugend* (youth). The exhibit at the Secession in Munich, which opened in February in the rooms of the Stroganov School, is a revelation to the Russians.

The Secession of Munich is primarily Franz von Stuck. Confronted with his painting *Sin,* the critic P. N. Gay was seized with admiration. Serge Glagol, on the other hand, is reserved: The Jugendstil is "pretentious symbolism." Glagol favors modern tendencies. Is the Munich Secession academic? For partisans of the avant-garde, its favorable reception by the Moscow middle class is a negative factor. Differences of opinion about the Munich Secession reflect current ambivalence in Moscow. Connoisseurs wonder whether the Munich School or Paris will reign. Stuck or Cézanne, these are the stakes. The enemies of the academy have their francs on Cézanne.

The Painter of the American Landscape Dies

For twenty years, Frederick Church had been practically forgotten. His grandiloquent style having ceased to please, he passes away on April 7 in almost total solitude. And yet, more than any other painter, he had been adulated in Europe as well as in the United States. Born in Hartford, Connecticut, in 1826, he knew better than anyone how to paint the American landscape in vast and detailed compositions. Virgin nature, whether arid or luxuriant, seemed to him the grandiose sign of the divine presence. He was the first American artist to paint the Andes Mountains. He was seventy-four when he died.

The Transparencies of the MacClurg Building

At 218 South Wabash Avenue in Chicago, the MacClurg Building raises its large glass bays—eight floors of them—which make the building transparent. Conceived by William Holabird and Martin Roche, the structure is part of a program of office buildings undertaken betwen 1887 and 1889 by the two architects, who belong to the Chicago School, which is known throughout the United States and Europe. They were pupils of W. Le Baron Jenney, whose sober and effective esthetic they adopt. The MacClurg Building is a perfect example of the new American architecture.

Closer to Zola Than to Rodin

Constantin Meunier, one of the masters of Realism in Belgium, has always been the interpreter of the working life he discovered in the mines and factories of the "black country." Painter and sculptor, he gives endless expression to people at their work, their creative acts, their slavery, their revolts. *The Harvest and the Earth*, the high relief he now completes, is a project that will leave its mark. Closer to Zola, with whom he shares a descriptive preciseness, than to Rodin, we find him, at age sixty-nine, at the height of his artistic glory.

PABLO PICASSO:
THE PAINTER ARRIVES IN PARIS. 1900.
Private Collection

Picasso Takes the Prize

Just after he arrived in Paris for the centennial of the Grand Palais, where one of his canvases figures in the Spanish selection, Pablo Ruiz y Picasso, nineteen years old, wins a comfortable contract: 150 francs a month offered him by his compatriot, the art dealer Pedro Manach. The dealer had already launched several Catalan painters living in Paris, such as Nonell, Canals, and Pichot, and has sold an appreciable number of paintings. The overwhelmed young artist created a very Parisian first canvas, *Le Moulin de la Galette*, immediately acquired by an impassioned collector. Now he signs his works P. R. Picasso, opting for his mother's name. But his success does not prevent him from returning to Barcelona to his family, to which he remains very attached.

Polemic on Sacré-Coeur

The Parisians are divided into two camps: the faithful who climb the difficult stairs of Montmartre to pray, and the scoffers who laugh till they cry at the mention of the "five Roman-Byzantine suppositories" by the architect Paul Abadie. The Basilica of Sacré-Coeur de Jésus had been built on the very spot where the insurrection of the 1871 Commune had begun, so that the place could be purified and the blood spilled in the event washed away. Constructed by means of a national subscription, voted in 1873, the scaffolding had been in place for almost twenty years. The Parisians object mostly to the extreme heaviness of the building and of its cupolas.

IN BRIEF...

GERMANY
Wassili Kandinsky and Paul Klee are students of Franz von Stuck at the Royal Academy in Munich.

SPAIN
First Pablo Picasso exhibition in Barcelona: 150 drawings are hung on the walls of Els Quatre Gats, a renowned café, a gathering place for the artistic youth of the town.

UNITED STATES
In New York, the French sculptor Auguste Bartholdi erects a group called Washington and La Fayette, *which is a replica of the one in Paris.*

FRANCE
The large retrospective of the Belgian painter Alfred Stevens, organized at the Beaux-Arts Academy, enjoys great success.

The Revue blanche *features a Georges Seurat retrospective, organized by Félix Fénéon.*

The art dealer Ambroise Vollard publishes an edition of Paul Verlaine's Parallèlement, *illustrated by Pierre Bonnard. He intends to continue publishing art books.*

The church of Sacré-Coeur at Montmartre, in Paris.

THUS SAW RUSKIN

He became, said Marcel Proust, "the spiritual adviser of his time." Venerated in all of Europe as an art historian endowed with a remarkable mastery of the English language, John Ruskin, born in London in 1819, died at his estate of Brantwood, Cumberland, on January 20, after having devoted a good part of his wealth to the creation of museums and cultural societies. He formalized his concept of architecture in his book *The Seven Lamps of Architecture*, an excerpt of which follows.

. . . I believe architecture must be the beginning of arts, and that the others must follow her in their time and order; and I think the prosperity of our schools of painting and sculpture, in which no one will deny the life, though many the health, depends upon that of our architecture. I think that all will languish until that takes the lead, and (this I do not think, but I proclaim as confidently as I would assert the necessity, for the safety of society, of an understood and strongly administered legal government) our architecture will languish, and that in the very dust, until the first principle of common sense be manfully obeyed, and a universal system of form and workmanship be everywhere adopted and enforced . . .

This severity must be singular, therefore, in the case of that art, above all others, whose productions are the most vast and the most common; which requires for its practice the cooperation of bodies of men, and for its perfection the perseverance of successive generations. And taking into account also what we have before so often observed of Architecture, her continual influence over the emotions of daily life, and her realism, as opposed to the two sister arts which are in comparison but the picturing of stories and of dreams, we might beforehand expect that we should find her healthy state and action dependent on far more severe laws than theirs: that the license which they extend to the workings of individual mind would be withdrawn by her; and that, in assertion of the relations which she holds with all that is universally important to man, she would set forth, by her own majestic subjection, some likeness of that on which man's social happiness and power depend. We might, therefore, without the light of experience, conclude, that Architecture never could flourish except when it was subjected to a national law as strict and as minutely authoritative as the laws

John Ruskin.

which regulate religion, policy, and social relations; nay, even more authoritative than these, because both capable of more enforcement, as over more passive matter; and needing more enforcement, as the purest type not of one law or another, but of the common authority of all . . . and that chance rests on the bare possibility of obtaining the consent, both of architects and of the public, to choose a style, and to use it universally.

JOHN RUSKIN
The Seven Lamps of Architecture
(Excerpt)

DREAMS ACCORDING TO FREUD

VIENNA

Will psychology become a science? Five years ago, Alfred Binet founded the magazine *L'année psychologique* in Paris, and a year later a Congress of Psychology was held in Munich.

Research into the hidden recesses of the soul is the talk of the town. Scientists are not lagging far behind the Symbolists who, after reading Schopenhauer and his disciple Eduard von Hartmann, have had many dreams about the unconscious.

Sigmund Freud, a forty-four-year-old Viennese neurologist and psychiatrist, is interpreting dreams, his key to unlocking the subconscious.

In the Bible, the eleventh and the favorite son of Jacob's twelve sons, interprets dreams and is made governor of all the lands of Egypt by the Pharaoh. Is Freud taking his Hebrew progenitor as a model? In his controversial book *The Interpretation of Dreams* he declares that a dream has meaning in spite of apparent incoherence; it is "in the image of the past."

There are dreams that all people have. Freud says they are wish fulfillments, with a profound sexual impulse of infantile origin. Often repressed by moral prohibitions, these wishes find an outlet in expressions of fantasy. It is the way the libido, or sexual drive, releases itself.

Freud has abandoned the term "psychology" and coined the word "psychoanalysis." *The Interpretation of Dreams* is being met with silence, although his editor had bet on a subterfuge: He dated the work "1900," thinking that it would arouse more interest with the beginning of the new century, even though it was available in bookstores last November.

(See also 1910, 1924, 1938.)

THUS SPOKE NIETZSCHE

Professor of Greek philology in Basel, admirer of Schopenhauer and Wagner, the German philosopher Friedrich Nietzsche became the composer's close friend but broke loose from his estheticism, thus rejecting art as a means of escape. The refusal of the life-will annihilates, according to him, the vital instinct. He opposes to the Greek art and harmonious order, as symbolized by Apollo, the ecstatic art that aspires to the universality to which Dionysos appeals. He exalts, against the values of knowledge, those of life, and launches the myth of the "Superman." More than a philosophy of being, his thought is that of the "perhaps" and of the faith in "eternal return." Having become demented in 1889, Nietzsche, cared for by his sister, died in Weimar on August 25, at the age of fifty-six.

Art sets the aspects of this changing world, it is eternization, will to overcome the gradual change. It is not history but art that expresses the real life. Art realizes what nature has wanted and attempted, it completes her imperfect sketches. This is why the world is justifiable only as an esthetic phenomenon . . .

In order to have art, in order to have any action or any esthetic contemplation at all, a preliminary physiological condition is indispensable: ecstasy.

Twilight of the Idols

Art makes us think about states of animal vigor . . . it is a raising of life feeling, a life stimulant . . . The effect of a work of art, that is, of the proper state to create a work of art, is the perfection of being, is completion, is a step toward profusion.

The Will to Power

The greatness of the artist is not measured by the "beautiful feelings" he arouses but by the degree it takes to approach the grand style. This style has this in common with great passion, that it disdains to please, that it forgets to persuade, that it commands, that it wants to master the chaos of the self. That it wants to compel its chaos to become form, to become logic, simple, without ambiguity, mathematics, law: There lies the great ambition.

Human, All-Too-Human

Happiness is not the goal, the feeling of power is. An immense strength in man and in humanity wants to exert itself, wants to create; it is a continuous chain of explosions that do not aim at happiness at all . . .

All my truths to me are bleeding truths. To create suffering for oneself and for others to render them capable of the highest life, the victor's life, that would be my goal . . .

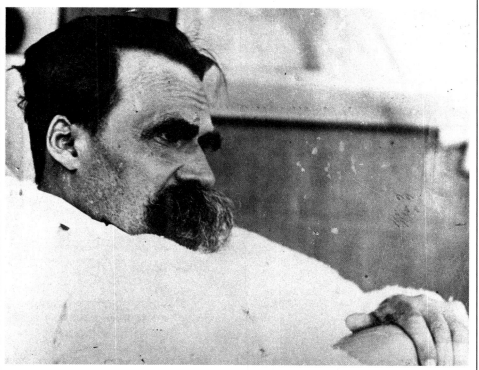

Friedrich Nietzsche.

Never have I found the woman by whom I would like to have children, except this one woman that I love: I love you, oh eternity! I love you, oh eternity!

Thus Spoke Zarathustra

We will have taken a great step in esthetics when we will have attained not only the intellectual conviction but the intimate certitude that evolution in art is linked to the dualism of the Apollinian spirit and of the Dionysian spirit, in the same way that procreation depends on the duality of the sexes whose perpetual struggle is uninterrupted except for ephemeral reconciliations . . . To understand this antagonism, let us first imagine it as represented by the two esthetic worlds of dream and ecstasy.

The Birth of Tragedy

While Gauguin affirms the necessity of "establishing the right to dare to do all" and sculpts his House of Pleasure, every architect, sculptor, and painter dreams of liberating life and stylizing it in Art Nouveau. They have all been won over to the movement by the Nabis, a group of artists who declare that nothing must escape their grasp. Apartment houses and stores, private homes and gardens, furniture, vases, dishes and glassware, everything will bear the modernizing touch of the movement. Art becomes decorative, and in this regard the School of Nancy works wonders. Still, one master landscape artist, the tireless Cézanne, continues to scrutinize nature, and labors at painting countless views of it.

1901
SUMMARY

DINING-ROOM SET BY ÉMILE GALLÉ AND VASES BY CLÉMENT MASSIER.
The craftsman's skill at the service of a refined esthetic.

THE MARVELS OF THE SCHOOL OF NANCY

NANCY

"My roots are at the bottom of the trees" is the maxim of the group of young artists whom Émile Gallé is assembling in his school in Nancy as part of a "provincial alliance of industrial arts." Most art magazines have announced its formation and publish its by-laws, which are based on his faith in "art for everyone." He wants to organize a center of regional creativity rooted in Lorraine. Above all, the fifty-year-old aims at uniting the arts with industry so as to promote the combination as widely as possible.

Gallé was strengthened by the success of his exhibits of flower vases, a sensation at the 1878 World's Fair, and of his "talking furniture," at the 1889 World's Fair. He surrounds himself with creative people whose vocation he inspires with an esthetic based on a "confrontation with the outdoors." The best known of the disciples are the glass blower August Daum, the cabinetmakers Eugène Vallin and Louis Majorelle, the architect Émile André, and Victor Prouvé, a childhood friend and the "propagandist" of the group.

Gallé is the French leader of the feud that developed in the 1880s, and he stimulated internationally a Neogothic style and a Japanizing renovation in architecture and the decorative arts. It is flourishing under several names: "Liberty" in Great Britain, "Tiffany Style" in the United States, "Jugendstil" in Germany, and "Modern Style" in Belgium and France. "Art Nouveau" is also coming into vogue in the City of Light. The description is taken from the name of the store opened five years ago in Paris by Samuel Bing, a fervent admirer of Japanese prints. Gallé was then associated with his father in a mirror-and-glass business, "where the love of flowers reigned as a hereditary passion." Gallé, specializing in botany and in glass chemistry, integrated his naturalist's inspi-

Group of glasses and vases by Émile Gallé.

ration and glass expertise with ravishing, sinuous decorations.

Profiting from the exquisite work of the glaziers Karl Koepping in Berlin and Louis C. Tiffany in New York, Gallé uses blown and crackled glass techniques to apply painted, gilded, and enameled decorations and enchanting inlays. He plays with a range of colors, the deepest blue and light green and shades of brown, which create marvels between layers of glass.

Like the late William Morris, the eminent Victorian and social reformer, who dedicated most of his sixty-two years to embellishing the home by the creation of

the first furniture, accessories, and decorator store in London, in 1861, Émile Gallé wishes to use his institution in Nancy to transform the frame of daily life. He wants to abolish the distinction between major and minor arts and arrive at a "social art" that he would popularize by active participation in exhibits.

In his school in Nancy, Gallé plans to train workers to develop all branches of the decorative arts. They will use the latest technical advances to produce the most common household objects in quantity at a good price—and with a rare esthetic quality. His friend, the master

cabinetmaker Louis Majorelle crafts slim, elegant furniture, usually of acacia wood, with decorations of waterlilies or orchids, which are the equal of their Chinese or Japanese models. He attaches to small inlaid and lacquered furniture pieces gilded bronze decorations, with emphasis on curves and trefoils.

Though inspired by Far Eastern art, the works of the School of Nancy have a French quality. They seek to have us "listen to the sweet language of the forest of Lorraine, which their works secretly speak."

INVITATION TO TRAVEL

PARIS

"This iron and steam palace needed a sumptuous sitting room, and it received one yesterday," the *Petit Parisien* of April 2 says. "It is retrograde, reactionary, and scandalous," writes another paper, as it defends Art Nouveau. The site that arouses equal admiration from one party and disgust from another is the gilded restaurant in the Lyon railroad station, opened on April 7 by President Loubet. It is the design of Marius Toudoire, who was also the architect of the station. The Paris-Lyon-Mediterranean railroad company wanted to endow the station with a unique brilliance.

The restaurant is sumptuous. It looks more like a casino than a restaurant in a railroad station. The stucco worker Édouard Lefebvre composed a veritable décor in round moldings. They show off the brightly colored paintings that adorn the restaurant, the great hall, and the two entrances. The painter Toudoire directed thirty other prominent artists to represent the cities and regions through which the railroad line runs. Paul Berthier painted Grenoble; Paul Sain,

The restaurant at the Lyon railroad station.

Avignon; Paul Buffet, Sousse. The crowning glory was entrusted to the most experienced: Dubufe, Maignan, and Flameng. The three large cities of the network, Paris, Lyon, and Marseille, are celebrated on the ceiling of

the gilded hall in a Naturalistic and allegorical style. The ceiling of the great hall depicts the grape harvests of Bourgogne (Maignan) and the gathering of citrus fruit in Nice (Gervex).

But it is the new restaurant,

above all, that is an invitation to travel, to soak up luxurious scenery where the sky is always clear, the sea always blue, and where the women are always beautiful and elegant.

LAVIROTTE: 29 AVENUE RAPP

Building created by Jules Lavirotte on Avenue Rapp. "To make a façade into a visual event . . ."

PARIS

First Prize for the façade competition organized by the City of Paris went this year to the building that the architect Jules Lavirotte of Lyon recently finished at 29 Avenue Rapp. Lavirotte's is particularly significant, for it is a departure from the excessive reticence of Haussmann in modern architecture. It is characterized by bold decoration. There are feminine figures of the Baroque caryatids, and luxurious organic convex and concave curves of Art Nouveau, now

familiar because of the subway entrances designed by Hector Guimard, who is also from Lyon.

A plant décor frames the entrance like an illuminated design around an initial letter. It ascends the façade, curling around the blind arch and hugging the balconies, then separating at the top of the building. Lavirotte is beautifully served by the ceramist Alexandre Bigot, who created the elements of the decor in high relief and bas-relief. The façade is of an exceptional pictorial virtuosity.

27

ARNOLD BÖCKLIN: THE ISLAND OF THE DEAD.
1880. Leipzig. Museum der bildenden Künste

BÖCKLIN LANDS ON THE ISLAND OF THE DEAD

FIESOLE

The Swiss painter Arnold Böcklin, who chose to live out his life in Italy, has at last set foot on this dark Island of the Dead. Fiesole had haunted him so much that he painted five almost identical versions of it. He is seventy-four years old and obsessed by death. "Death," in fact, is represented on his visionary, unfinished frescoes *War* and *Pestilence,* which display astonishing, evocative power in strange, fantastic visions of a symbolic character with allusions to mythology. The character of unreality in his workmanship earned him the nickname "the creator of magic paintings."

Born in Basel, Böcklin freed himself from the traditions of Swiss painting in the sense understood by Gottfried Keller, who wanted to paint "real scenery really idealized, or ideal landscapes made real." Böcklin worked first in Düsseldorf, from

1845 to 1847, with Johann-Wilhelm Schirmer, a landscape artist considered sublime. He moved on to Brussels and Antwerp, where he studied the seventeenth-century Flemish painters, and returned to Switzerland, where he worked in the Geneva studio of the landscape artist Alexandre Calame. At the age of twenty-one, he arrived in Paris in the midst of the revolution of 1848. Later in Basel, he formed a friendship with the historian Jakob Burckhardt, who was responsible for initiating Böcklin into the art of the Italian Renaissance.

Böcklin was sensitive to the serene atmosphere of the surroundings of Basel, but simultaneously influenced by the German philosopher Friedrich

Nietzsche. He sought to depict forces unleashed by natural elements. Fascinated by the earthy mythology of antiquity, he moved to Rome for eight years. On his return to Germany, he became popular among art

HE WAS HAUNTED SO MUCH BY THIS DARK ISLAND THAT HE PAINTED FIVE ALMOST IDENTICAL VERSIONS

lovers mainly through the admiration of his patron, Count Schack. He was appointed professor at the Art Academy in Weimar, where he taught for two years, from 1860 to 1862.

This artist "without a fatherland" eventually was attracted to Italy again, and he began his famous *Island of the Dead,* a title discovered by an art dealer, Franz Gürlit. Böcklin called it a "dream painting." It is his most symbolic, even most visionary painting. Perhaps he was inspired by the island of Ischia,

or by San Michele, the island cemetery of Venice. It is the archetypal vision of the irrevocable Last Voyage. Charon's boat glides over the silent black waters of the Styx towards cliffs that are open like heavy, dark wings. The white figure of death, wrapped in a shroud, looms in contrast with dark cypress branches which will encircle him in their mystery.

The *Island of the Dead* transforms the public's curiosity in Böcklin into celebrity. His obsessive attraction to the supernatural and his dramatic Realism show the artist to be the heir of German Romanticism and the prestigious descendant of a Caspar David Friedrich who, however, had never forgotten the lesson in polychromy of Nicolas Poussin. The fame of Böcklin is fading. The trends in painting make his style too literary. His coal-black waters are death itself, compared with the glittering ponds of Monsieur Monet.

PICASSO LOSES HIS BEST FRIEND

PARIS

Hearing that his friend Casagemas had committed suicide over a love affair, Pablo Picasso is deeply confused. Suicide! Why? He does not understand!

He was spending the winter in Madrid, where he heard of the death of his painter friend with whom he had moved to Paris. Carlos Casagemas had fallen in love with Germaine Gargallo, a woman of easy virtue who had been his model. She did not reciprocate his feelings. On Sunday, February 17, the dramatic climax came in the Hippodrome, a restaurant at 128 Boulevard de Clichy.

Casagemas, who for some time had been drinking to excess, had invited Germaine, her sister Odette, and three Spanish comrades to dinner. Taciturn by nature, he was also nervous and boisterous that evening. Toward the end of the meal, he placed several envelopes on the table: One was addressed to the police chief. He whipped a pistol out of a pocket, aimed it at Germaine, yelled "This is for you!," and fired. He put the gun to his head and cried out, "This is for me!" Miraculously, Germaine was not hurt, but the bewitched suitor collapsed with a fatal wound. He died later in the evening in the Bichat hospital.

Upon his return to Paris in June, Picasso made several paintings of Casagemas on his deathbed—Casagemas with his familiar black hair, long nose, receding chin, but with his eyes closed. The most accomplished of these works is the *The Burial of Casagemas (Evocation)*, a medium-size vertical canvas of about 5 X 3 feet.

The Burial of Casagemas, as is Picasso's wont when undertaking a major work, was preceded by several preparatory drawings. They show a crowd of men, women, and children deep in thought around a reclining body. Some of the drawings include light and shade; others appear to be simple, quick sketches. They prefigure the

PABLO PICASSO: THE BURIAL OF CASAGEMAS. (EVOCATION)
1901. Private Collection

lower part of the painting. In this way, they are like some paintings by El Greco, *the Adoration of the Name of Jesus*, for instance. Picasso's canvas is divided into two parts—earth and heaven. The body of Casagemas is surrounded by Spanish-looking, weeping figures in long dark cloaks. Paradise is populated with earthy houris with large, heavy legs, one of whom is helping the arrival mount a horse.

The dominant motif is that of maternity, which is represented by a woman who is preceded by two little angels, symbols of life and renewal.

The influence of El Greco is not limited to the two-tier organization of the motif. It is also manifest in the manner in which the work is painted. During his winter's stay in Madrid, Picasso made a day trip to Toledo. He saw *The Burial of the Count of*

Orgaz in the church of San Tome, a fabulous funereal symphony, with its serene clarity arranged on a bright, sad palette of blacks, whites, and gold. In Picasso's *Burial of Casagemas*, we find the same drama, the same relief, but with an intense sensuality.

Among the nude houris offered by Picasso for the joys of Paradise for his deceased friend, two wear black stockings and a third, red ones. These are, of course, allusions to the residents of the brothels celebrated by Toulouse-Lautrec.

Picasso admires Lautrec. He appreciates his compatriot Isidro Nonell's caustic humor. He is fond of the Swiss Théophile-Alexandre Steinlen, who is famous for drawings and posters that stigmatize human misery. If Picasso often saw such misery and denounced it, he assumes in this *Burial* an air of hauteur as never before. Casagemas, who came from a rich family, had been in a naval academy before taking up art, less by vocation, apparently, than because of a taste for the artist's freedoms. He conducted unusual experiments, such as "fried drawings": He plunged sketches into a pan of boiling oil in order to obtain unforeseen results.

Picasso's passion for his art is of an entirely different kind. He has painted since childhood in Malaga. The grandiose evocation of Casagemas' burial signaled a first mature step, at the age of twenty. He has used canvases as screens in his studio, to hide some of the disorder. But they did not fail to find buyers soon.

(See also 1904, 1905, 1907, 1909, 1912, 1921, 1937, 1945, 1946, 1948, 1953, 1954, 1958, 1973).

DERAIN AND VLAMINCK IN CHATOU

CHATOU

There are some favored spots that—when enhanced by painters captivated by their charms—remain in the memory of those who make them into great places of art. This is the case of the charming community of Chatou, on the shores of the Seine west of Paris. Because a railroad connects Paris to Port Marly, Chatou is one of the favored meeting places of the Impressionists. Courbet placed his *Ladies on the Shore of the Seine* there in 1856. Not far away, on the island of Croissy, near the spa Grenouillère, Monet and Renoir invented the inklings of Impressionism in 1869. Most important, Auguste Renoir liked to come with good friends to the inn of Father Fournaise, who rented out canoes and sailboats; in 1881, Renoir painted there his *Déjeuner des canotiers*. A bucolic spot on the water—and a gastronomic attraction—Chatou also enchanted authors like Flaubert, Zola, and Maupassant.

André Derain and Maurice de Vlaminck, two young men and great admirers of the Impressionists who have now deserted Chatou, decided to walk in the steps of their illustrious predecessors and, full of enthusiasm, to work there together to reinvent landscape painting. Last year, they rented a studio in an abandoned restaurant adjacent to the inn of Father Fournaise. André Derain was born in Chatou itself, twenty-one years ago, the son of a baker; he attended the Carrière Academy and is a Neoimpressionist. His friend Maurice de Vlaminck a giant and four years his senior, who is a bicycle racer, a violinist, and an anarchist newspaperman. He became passionate about painting when he discovered Monet. At the recent Van Gogh retrospective at Bernheim-Jeune, he was introduced to Matisse by Derain. They all shared an admiration for the instinctive power of the Dutchman who had loved the environs of Chatou.

Landing site at the Pont de Chatou.

MAURICE DENIS PAYS HOMAGE TO CÉZANNE

MAURICE DENIS: HOMAGE TO CÉZANNE. 1900. Paris. Musée d'Orsay

Paris. "Cézanne's example teaches us to transform sensory elements into works of art," says Maurice Denis, who exhibits his *Homage to Cézanne* at the Nationale des Beaux-Arts. He painted it last year. Standing around a still life by the master of Aix are, from left to right, Redon, Vuillard, Mellerio, Vollard, Denis, Sérusier, Ranson, Bonnard, and Madame Denis.

Curious Monsieur Vollard

What strange taste! Having dared to exhibit the shocking Cézanne six years ago, Ambroise Vollard repeats the offense now with the nudes of Pablo Picasso, a twenty-year-old Spaniard. A Creole born on the island of Réunion, Vollard is a very curious art dealer. His gallery on Rue Laffitte looks more like a Middle Eastern marketplace than an exhibition space. So Picasso is perfectly at home there. The violence of his canvases, the expression of suffering that emanates from them, are in the greatest possible contrast to the lovely pale-and-pink-toned exposures of flesh that enchant the "true" amateurs of art and that can currently be enjoyed at the Salon.

AUGUSTE RENOIR: PORTRAIT OF AMBROISE VOLLARD. Paris. Bibliothèque Nationale

When Adolf Loos Becomes an Interior Decorator

In 1896, the Viennese architect Adolf Loos, thirty-three years old, had expressed his horror of decorative excesses in the magazine *Ver Sacrum*. In the same year, the spare style of his Goldmann & Salatsch store had caused a great uproar. But now he seems to have watered down his wine. The furnishing of the Turnowsky house at 19 Wohllebengasse, Vienna 4, which he has just completed, is both traditional and Classical. Craftsmen have used wild cherry to create corner living rooms with an angled banquette and a little oval table, easy chairs, and comfortable seating. As if going from the avant-garde to bourgeois taste were a matter of getting up and changing places.

Marquet's Hard Times

Albert Marquet, former pupil at Gustave Moreau's studio at the Beaux-Arts with Matisse and Rouault, exhibits for the first time at the Salon des Indépendants. At the age of twenty-six, he is one of the hopes of the new generation with his landscapes of high color. But these are hard times. To make a living, Marquet paints bad opera scenery with loud colors for Jambon the decorator, in exchange for a few francs a day.

Kandinsky the Leader

At the age of thirty-five, Wassili Kandinsky quits Franz von Stuck's painting class at the Munich Academy, and founds the Phalanx, a group whose purpose is to organize exhibits informing the public about "the art of tomorrow." The members will also develop a way of teaching painting that will use new methods having nothing to do with academic teaching, which is limited, as everyone knows, to drawing from models and copying old plaster casts. Combining the useful with the pleasant, the spiritually minded Kandinsky plans, moreover, to take his pupils on bicycle tours so that they can visit the famous Bavarian churches, for, he says, "visiting churches in Moscow during my youth had been very profitable for me."

WASSILI KANDINSKY: THE SLUICE. 1901. Munich. Lenbachhaus, Städtische Galerie

Hodler: The Explosion of "Springtime"

Ferdinand Hodler, the painter from Bern, triumphs this year at the exhibition of the Viennese Secession with one of the freshest of his works in terms of conception and fabrication. *Springtime* is an allegory of the birth of desire in the image of two adolescents. To the advantage of a subject that awakens all the romantic poetry and the taboos linked to the problems of sexuality, Hodler has been able to place his gift as a painter in the service of a change in mentality that asserts itself more each day. Fruit of his maturity—Hodler is forty-six—*Springtime* asks the same questions as does the art of Edvard Munch, in a language both different and curiously similar.

PAUL GAUGUIN:
THE HOUSE OF PLEASURE. 1901.
Paris. Musée d'Orsay

GAUGUIN SCULPTS THE HOUSE OF PLEASURE

ATUANA

Not wanting to believe that Maori culture had completely disappeared from Polynesia and that that beautiful race did not "save anything at all from its beautiful splendor," Paul Gauguin leaves Tahiti on September 10 for the faraway Marquesas. He settles on the island of Hiva Oa, also called Dominique, in Atuana, where he buys a five-thousand-square-foot lot near the girls' school of the Roman Catholic mission. Although he is in ill health, he supervises the building of a house from his own drawings. It is built on piles and closed with bamboo shutters and covered with coconut branches, and measures 20 x 42 feet.

Around the door to Gauguin's room, the "master of the tropics" sculpts two wooden panels in the form of a portico in the Maori tradition. The left panel reads, "Be mysterious." The right panel reads, "Love and you will be happy." The archway reads, "House of Pleasure." The messages are intentionally provocative—the parishioners of Monsignor Martin and the police have taken a dislike to the Frenchman and nicknamed him the "rascal."

As a sculptor (as well as a painter), he appreciates the geometric forms and intricate stylizations of "the very advanced decorative arts" of Oceania, whose "tikis" and traditional objects he seeks out and studies: bowls and plates, war clubs, pendants and jewelry. Gauguin feels that his ultimate task is to "go back to the source, to humanity in its infancy."

BOURDELLE RECOVERS BEETHOVEN

ANTOINE BOURDELLE:
BEETHOVEN. 1901. Paris.
Private Collection

PARIS

Rodin's favorite pupil, Antoine Bourdelle, who last year founded a school of sculpture with the master, has returned once again to the work that has haunted him since 1888: the bust of Beethoven. Convinced that if art must "contain the heart" it should also "let the hand tremble," the music-loving Bourdelle has the most exuberant admiration for the composer of the Ninth Symphony. He tries to show the tumult of the music in the genius's tormented head which he fashions with hands that indeed tremble.

This sculptor is passionate and courageous. He says that his inspiration is of peasant origin. "As a child in Montauban, I was fascinated by my father's work; he made solid country-style furniture. I believe that cutting wood for a hopper or a stool taught me the balance of construction."

VICTOR HORTA'S LASH OF THE WHIP

BRUSSELS

Large stores all over the world are trying to project a public image of progress and modernity associated with the avant-garde. This explains why Victor Horta, the bold forty-year-old architect who was born in Ghent, has been chosen to design the new Innovation department store in Brussels, where he had studied at the Art Institute.

Horta has demonstrated the potential of building with iron and the possibilities of decoration. He uses iron with rare virtuosity, in an anthology of forms of the "lash of the whip" line, as he calls his style. The line is based on a thorough analysis of plant morphology, which Horta synthesizes in a masterly interpretation. Nervous and flexible, it is used everywhere in the design for balconies and balustrades and in decorative iron-

work which embellishes the building. It is apparent also in functional parts, such as the clearly visible posts and structural portions that support the floors and the internal galleries.

It is the triple pediment rising above the iron and glass façade of the Brussels store that could be considered the bravura piece. The curves and countercurves of the "lash of the whip" line are developed into stone flowers. The viewer may neglect the paradox: Iron and glass surfaces support the volume of stone, contrary to architecture's towering history.

Horta, who worked with the Neoclassicist architect Alphonse Balat before striking out on his own, has had many successes. His House of the People, also in Brussels, was the first demonstration of the possibilities of iron in a monumental program.

Victor Horta: the Innovation department store in Brussels.

THE HOUSE ON THE PRAIRIE

ILLINOIS

In February and again in July, the American architect Frank Lloyd Wright, thirty-two years old, published innovative plans for a house in the *Ladies' Home Journal*. These plans have been executed in a house that Wright built for the Willits family in Highland Park, Illinois. Wright trained with the celebrated Louis Sullivan before opening his own office, in Chicago, in 1893. Since then, he has designed several private homes. With the Willits House, Wright has created a new kind of house. Above the full-length ground floor is the smaller upper story. Horizontal lines are emphasized by the lines of the concrete basement, dark wood-

en bands, windows set in a straight row, the slightly sloping roof. When he planned the Willits House, Wright no doubt recalled his visit to the Colombian exhibit in the Chicago World's Fair of 1893. At that

Frank Lloyd Wright: Willits House at Highland Park, Illinois.

exhibit, there was a small-scale copy of the Ho-O-Den Temple, the Japanese pavilion. In the Willits house, Wright reproduced the cruciform ground plan and the concept of an interior where division into separate rooms no

longer exists, except in the upper story, where the bedrooms are. Like the Japanese temple, which was oriented around the "tokonoma," or the sanctuary, the Willits House is organized around the fireplace in the American pioneer tradition. A single room consists of an entrance and a hallway on the right, the living room in front, the dining room and veranda on the left, the service areas and the kitchen in the rear.

Wright calls his creation "a town house on the prairie," because he wants it integrated with its environment. The basement of Willits House extends into a terrace garden and serves as a transition between the house and the outdoors.

Henri de Toulouse-Lautrec passes from this world too soon. But today, there can be no doubt that, through his models from Montmartre, he had already said all there was to say. Life may be an absurd game, but art is no luxury. It is a witness, a confession, the expression of the self. Benedetto Croce, the Italian philosopher, concurs. In his critique of the imitation of nature, he considers art to be the primary form of mental activity, purely intuitive. As a reaction against the naturalist positivism of his time, he publishes Esthetics As a Science of Expression, an essay in which he states that the creative act is the exterior manifestation of a state of mind. What else do Klimt and Klinger imply when they pay homage to Beethoven with such dramatic sensuality?

1902

SUMMARY

LITERATURE

UNITED STATES
Publication of James Joyce's novel The Wings of the Sea Gull.

FRANCE
Accidental death of Émile Zola at sixty-two.
   André Gide publishes The Immoralist *at the Mercure de France, at his own expense.*

THEATER

GERMANY
Frank Wedekind produces Pandora's Box.

IRELAND
In Dublin, performance of Cathleen ni Houlihan *by W. B. Yeats.*

RUSSIA
Stanislavsky produces Gorky's The Underworld.

MUSIC

FRANCE
Gabriel Faure composes Eight Short Pieces.
   The premiere of Pelleas and Melisande *by Claude Débussy at the Opéra Comique arouses much controversy.*

MOTION PICTURES

FRANCE
Georges Méliès shows his film Voyage to the Moon: *the first science-fiction film, of 16 minutes.*

HENRI DE TOULOUSE-LAUTREC:
THE FEMALE CLOWN CHA-U-KAO.
1895. Paris. Musée d'Orsay

TOULOUSE-LAUTREC: THE MIDGET WHO BECAME A GIANT

PARIS

Death last September has made a giant out of Henri de Toulouse-Lautrec, a "ridiculous little man whose deformity is reflected in each of his drawings," according to Goncourt. This broken, limping "midget" foundered in the irrational evasions of alcohol and in the illusory consolations of prostitutes. At the age of thirty-seven, emaciated and shriveled up, he died in the arms of his devoted mother at the family home in Malromé, in the Gironde.

Sharing the opinions of the masters, the poet André Rivoire states, "When the public knows the work that Henri de Toulouse-Lautrec always guarded so jealously from it, it will understand what the world of art has lost with his premature death; it will also see what it has gained from the frantic life that hastened this death." Fervent young artists, such as the Nabis painters and Steinlen, Valadon, and Picasso, admire and imitate the graphic vigor and severity of Lautrec's lithographs and forceful posters, the vibrant nervousness of his raw touch, the virulence of his colors, the boldness of his Japanizing compositions.

Lautrec moved away from the Impressionists around 1895. He

Toulouse-Lautrec with one of his models.

FERVENT YOUNG ARTISTS ALREADY ADMIRE AND IMITATE THE GRAPHIC VIGOR AND THE VIRULENCE OF HIS COLORS

joined the Nabis and the *Revue blanche* founded by the Natanson brothers and remained hostile to Expressionist theory. He was as Realist as they come. Drawing must be forceful. It must seize the allure and the characteristic traits of the model. Color is needed only to render the atmosphere in which the drawing appears. Concentrating on night, on scenes and stages of shows in Montmartre and on artificial gas and electric light, Lautrec demonstrates an

almost malevolent boldness in the use of pure colors parodying the subject.

Through Lautrec, Expressionist humanism can be understood. It is a caricature that bears the imprint of the compassion of the painter, who in the case of Lautrec was the most complex and least duped by prostitutes and nocturnal highlifers, by the riffraff and the frenzied population of Montmartre and Batignolles. "Ah, Lautrec, we can see that you belong to the building!" Degas exclaimed, when he first gazed on the paintings of the Moulin de la Galette and the Moulin Rouge nearly a decade ago. More than Manet, Renoir, Degas, or even Van Gogh, this deformed

aristocrat, who was just over four feet tall, knew how to adapt to the spirit of the people of the Butte—the Butte, which reduces life to its simplest expression, does away with everything that complicates it and, continually finding bacchic hallucinations in drunkenness, transforms disdain into indulgence and mixes gaiety with sarcasm.

Lautrec coined strong words, as well as brush strokes, about these evils: "He looks like a sole, with eyes on the same side of the head," he said about a dancer; "This one," he said of a drunk, "looks as though he were coming with wine from the cave." He was a student of Princeteau, Bonnat, and Cormon, who had been influenced by Daumier, Forain, and Degas. He succeeded during the *belle époque*: He reconciled art with the street and its diversions, the cabarets, the "café-concerts." He became a painter with a cutting edge.

Tristan Bernard says that

Lautrec's eyes belonged only to Lautrec, but that his look was so piercing that he dominated all others. More than five thousand drawings since childhood, four hundred and forty prints and posters, two hundred and seventy-five watercolors, and seven hundred and thirty-seven oil paintings—that is the prodigious output he left to Countess Toulouse-Lautrec, who wants to will them to the Luxembourg, that so academic museum. In view of the reticence of the museum's directors, the art historian Maurice Joyant (a childhood friend of the painter who always encouraged him, especially during his detoxification cure three years ago, to take his chalks and brushes in hand again and make a fascinating series on the circus, where humor conflicts with bitterness) sought, with the help of a young cousin of the painter, Gabriel Tapié de Céleyran, to have them taken to the Albi Museum instead.

TOULOUSE-LAUTREC THE POSTER PAINTER

PARIS

"Silence, gentlemen! The great painter Toulouse-Lautrec is coming in with his girlfriends and a guy I don't know." So sang out Aristide Bruant one night in his cabaret in Montmartre. It reflected the ironic and at the same time cordial tone of Bruant's relationship with the painter of his poster portrait.

The poster was so popular that when Bruant went to the Ambassadeurs, in 1892, he demanded that his friend be commissioned for the new poster. The songster of "the little people" used a biting tone in his sar-donic poems; his attraction for lowlife men and loose women had a decisive influence on Lautrec, who did not spare them the arrows or the consolation of his chalks and oils.

The same style characterizes the lively, sharp drawings of Toulouse-Lautrec's posters. They demonstrate his dynamism, which has made advertising an art. He knew how to profit from what he had learned in the Chinese shadow theater Chat-Noir (black cat) and from Japanese prints. He made stylized silhouettes of sparse detail and simplified space, and enhanced the force of color with sections in flat tints. And he brought celebrity to his friends Bruant, La Goulue, Valentin le Desosse, Jane Avril, and Mademoiselle Eglantine.

HENRI DE TOULOUSE-LAUTREC: YVETTE GUILBERT GREETING HER AUDIENCE. 1894. Albi. Musée Toulouse-Lautrec

MADEMOISELLE GUILBERT ENTERS

PARIS

Yvette Guilbert made her debut, in 1892, at the Concert-Parisien, a cabaret in the Saint-Denis suburb, and became the darling of Paris within eight days. She was twenty-three years old, with black-gloved, predatory hands and a sphinx-like body. Henri de Toulouse-Lautrec depicted her in drawings, paintings, and posters. He conveyed the intangible: the way the great entertainer inimitably articulated each syllable, aimed directly at each listener, from her tongue, from her throat. His drawing describes not so much what he sees as what he writes with a quick gesture: some traits, a spot of color on the canvas or on paper—the work is done.

There is an affinity between the cutting voice of Yvette Guilbert and the cutting line of Toulouse-Lautrec. Mademoiselle Guilbert greets the public, her dress and curtain in green, her hair red, her face barely sketched in. It is a Lautrec masterpiece. But when the singer saw the album of sixteen lithographs, with text by Gustav Geffroy, she saw herself as ugly and she considered suing the artist for damages. She changed her mind.

HENRI DE TOULOUSE-LAUTREC: ARISTIDE BRUANT. 1892. London. Victoria and Albert Museum

THOMAS EAKINS ELECTED TO THE ACADEMY

PHILADELPHIA

At the age of fifty-eight, Thomas Eakins, long a controversial figure, has finally been elected to the National Academy of Design. The honor crowns a magisterial work, including some of the most important works of the American Realist school.

Eakins was born in Philadelphia and studied in Paris with Gérôme and Bonnat. He was profoundly influenced by a trip to Spain, where the discovery of Ribera and particularly Velásquez proved a revelation. They left an imprint on all his work. Back in the States, he painted landscapes reflecting his interest in the outdoors, hunting, and nature. He allied himself with the poet Walt Whitman, who said of him, "Eakins is not a painter, he is a force." This force collided with the American mentality of prudishness at the 1875 show of his most famous painting, the *Gross Clinic*.

Inspired by Rembrandt's

THOMAS EAKINS: WILL SCHUSTER AND A BLACK MAN GO RAIL HUNTING. 1876. New Haven. Yale University Art Gallery

Anatomy Lesson, this painting shows a physician operating on a patient's leg. It generated a scandal.

Eakins's troubles did not end there. In 1886, he was forced to

resign from his position as director of the Pennsylvania Academy of Fine Arts, because he recommended the study of the male nude, a scandalous position according to Puritan mentality.

AMERICAN PAINTING IN MOURNING

ALBERT BIERSTADT: LAKE TAHOE. 1868. Cambridge, Massachusetts. Harvard University, Fogg Art Museum

UNITED STATES

American art has lost two painters this year who typified the end of the last century: Albert Bierstadt and John Twachtman.

Bierstadt was born in New England and died at the age of seventy-two. He made painting American landscapes a worthy occupation. He was famous for his large works, such as *Lake Tahoe* (1868), and paid homage to its innumerable natural marvels. From the Appalachian Mountains to the meandering Mississippi River, from the glaciers of the Rockies to the deserts of Colorado, he searched farther for what civilization had left of untouched, harmonious, original nature.

Bierstadt was close in spirit to the German Romantics and above all to the cosmic spirit of the New England poet Henry

David Thoreau, author of *Walden*. He imprinted his work with a mystical Naturalism. He saw in the grandiose landscapes manifest signs of God and His blessing on the New World.

Twachtman was born in Cincinnati, Ohio, and died in Gloucester, Massachusetts, at the age of seventy-nine. He was one of the first, and most brilliant, representatives of American Impressionism. He studied at the Julian Academy in Paris. His works, influenced by American Luminists, are distinguished by their musical quality and attention to the decorative nature of composition. It is a delicate network of fine lines that gives his works, such as *The White Bridge* or *Hemlock Pool*, the fresh vibrating subtlety of light. They come very close to the goal sought by the Neoimpressionists.

Stunning Fireworks

The opening of the First International Exhibition of Modern Decorative Art takes place in Turin from April to November. The exhibition brings together the various avantgarde expressions of Art Nouveau, marking the triumph of this movement. Beside the Italians, also present are the Austrians, Belgians, British, French, and Germans. While it is spectacular, the exhibition reveals nonetheless some deep, opposing currents. Above all, it is a stunning display of fireworks that just might herald the blossoming of the international decorative movement.

130 Francs for a Matisse

Can Madame Matisse, who runs a dress shop on the Rue de Châteaudun, stop worrying about where the next meal is coming from? The enterprising art dealer Berthe Weill, who opened a gallery with the slogan "Make way for the young generation" in December last year, has, in fact, just sold one of Henri Matisse's canvases for 130 francs. The artist, a former notary's clerk, abandoned everything in order to paint, following the example of Gauguin, whom he admires. He leads a hard life. Berthe Weill was deeply moved by the minuscule maid's room where the couple lived, a room, she said, that was just the width of a bed.

Homage to the God Beethoven

Max Klinger, renowned Symbolist artist from Leipzig, has created a sculpture of Beethoven. In *L'Européen* of October 11, Guillaume Apollinaire could write this about the work: "I had already seen this sort of colored-marble Jupiter last winter in Vienna. It was considered a masterpiece. The discussions that have been going on for over a year do not improve it in my opinion." The artists of the Viennese Secession are of a completely different opinion than Apollinaire on the value of this Beethoven. That is why they transformed this year's pavilion of the Secession into a sort of temple to celebrate Klinger celebrating Beethoven. Gustav Klimt personally associated himself with this "work of total art" by creating an allegorical frieze in three parts in which art appears as the means of liberating people from the anguish and suffering of life.

Rodin Salutes Aristide Maillol

It is a good year for Aristide Maillol. Ambroise Vollard presented his first one-man exhibition composed of twenty-two sculptures and eleven tapestries. The exhibition is more a *succès d'estime* than a financial success, but Maillol is now recognized as an artist with a future. The painters and writers of the *Revue blanche*, such as André Gide, Alfred Jarry, Pierre Bonnard, Édouard Vuillard, and Maurice Denis, give him fervent support—Octave Mirabeau bought several small pieces from him—and Rodin says of his *Leda*: "I do not know in all of modern sculpture a piece that is as absolutely beautiful." It seems that *The Mediterranean*, just begun, promises to be an utter masterpiece.

A Large Private Collection Is Opened to the Public

Are we witnessing the slow move of private collections toward public ones? Four years ago, the Dutuit endowment formed the initial contribution for the museum in the Petit Palais with a collection that has no equal, including artists from Daumier to Courbet, and now the opening of the Folkwang Museum in Hagen, Germany, is announced. The moving force behind it is the Belgian architect Henry Van de Velde, invited by the Grand Duke of Weimar the year before. The museum, opened on July 19, houses the collection of the art patron Karl Ernst Osthaus. Van de Velde has always fought for modern art, so the new museum will be decidedly oriented toward the present and the future.

MAX KLINGER: BEETHOVEN. 1902. Leipzig. Stadtmuseum

"L'Assiette au Beurre"

Where can you find drawings by Steinlen, Ibels, or Willette at a good price? Where do penniless painters, such as Van Dongen and Soffici, place their drawings so they can make a bit of money? At the *Assiette au Beurre*, of course! Now wrapping up its first year in existence, this satirical journal publishes one edition after the other, decidedly outclassing its competitors with *L'argent* by Kupka in January, *La vie facile* by Villon in February, and Vallotton's *Crime and Punishment* in March. If they lack the virtuosity of Cappiello or Rabier, these young painters still deliver a mean blow.

Flatiron Building, New York.

OTTO WAGNER'S *DIE ZEIT*

Since September 26, Vienna has become richer through a journalistic and artistic attraction: the dispatch office of the newspaper *Die Zeit* by the famous architect Otto Wagner. Stylized Gothic letters ornating the façade, prominent light bulbs, aluminum door with silvery highlights—the overall technological effect is complete. Wagner again demonstrates the needs of contemporary life: economy and functionality. Executed in the absolute purity of the style that is his . . .

OTTO WAGNER: MODEL FOR THE DISPATCH OFFICE OF THE DAILY *DIE ZEIT*. 1902

CHICAGO TO NEW YORK

NEW YORK
Since the great fire of 1871, which raged for three days, the construction of Chicago has taken on a new look. Fireproof steel permits the erection of tall structures. The planet now has skyscrapers. There are elevators, electricity, and gas on all floors and façades that no longer have to help hold up the structure and thus are open to lights. A stylistic revival is here.

The guiding light? Daniel Hudson Burnham, a corpulent fifty-six-year-old moustached architect, a pioneer in the use of reinforced metal. He dreams of making "Chicago so beautiful that it will surpass Paris." He proposes concepts dear to Baron Haussmann: large axes, vast urban compositions, the generalized use of stone, the alignment of cornices, the planting of trees in the streets—without abandoning American gigantism. New York beckons his talent.

His last construction, the Flatiron Building, pierces the Manhattan sky like the prow of an immense ship. It soars nineteen stories at the busy confluence of Broadway, Fifth Avenue, and 23rd Street. Construction required an underlying metal scaffolding. The revetment and the ornamentation give it an air of Haussmann-like architecture, in spite of the height, and it is a tourist attraction. Burnham was construction director for the 1893 World's Fair in Chicago, where he discovered the styles of the different national pavilions.

BENEDETTO CROCE: CRITIQUE OF THE IMITATION OF NATURE

At forty-six years old, the great Italian philosopher and essayist Benedetto Croce is coming to grips with art. Already his *History Contemplated under the Concept of Art Alone,* published in 1893, revealed an audacious spirit refusing both the idealism stemming from Hegel and a down-to-earth positivism. In his *Esthetics,* which is currently being published in Milan, he approached the problem from the other end—with the idea that any artistic creation is an intuitive unit of form and content, but with close links to history. The excerpt that follows is an illustration of his theses: Croce rejects the idea that the artist could be satisfied with the imitation of nature.

The proposition that art is "imitation of nature" has several meanings. These three words have sometimes affirmed or defined truths, sometimes supported errors, and, more often, expressed no thought in particular. We arrive at a scientifically legitimate meaning if "imitation" is understood as "representation" or "intuition" of nature, a form of knowledge. And if it is this that one means, setting off the spiritual nature of the process, then another proposition becomes legitimate: namely, that art is "idealization" or an "idealizing imitation" of nature. But if by imitation of nature it is understood that art furnishes mechanical reproductions, more or less perfect duplicates of natural objects, before which the same tumult of impressions is renewed that is produced by the other natural objects, then the proposition is obviously erroneous. The painted wax statues that simulate living beings and before which we step back disconcerted in wax museums, do not give us any esthetic intuitions. "Illusion" and the "hallucination" have nothing to do with the quiet mastery of artistic intuition. If an artist paints the spectacle of a wax museum, if a burlesque actor skillfully pretends to be a lifeless statue, we see again spiritual work and artistic intuition. Even a photograph, if it has something artistic, has it to the extent that it represents, at least partly, the photographer's intuition, his point of view, the pose and the situation he did his utmost to select . . . And if it is not entirely art, it is because the natural element remains more or less undeletable and unsubordinated. Which photograph, and I think of the best, could give us total satisfaction? Is there a single one in which an artist wouldn't make one or several changes, retouching, removing, or adding something?

The theme or the content cannot be dealt with through epithets of praise or of condemnation. When art critics note that a theme is "poorly chosen," in cases where this remark may be justified, it is not really a matter of blaming the "choice of the theme" (which would be absurd) but the manner in which the artist has treated it, thus a matter of blaming the inappropriate expression that results from unresolved contradictions. And when the same critics, before a work they proclaim to be artistically perfect, rebel against the theme or the content as "unworthy of art" and blamable, we can only advise the critics to leave the artist in peace. Artists can only be inspired by what has made an impression on them; and one would have to make changes in the ambient nature or in society to make these impressions disappear. If ugliness would disappear from the world, if in its place universal virtue and felicity would set in, then artists would no longer express perverted and pessimistic feelings, only calm, innocence, and joy—Arcadians of a true Arcadia. But as long as ugliness, pain, and depravity impose themselves upon the artist, their expression comes out . . .

BENEDETTO CROCE
Esthetics As a Science of Expression and
General Linguistics *(Excerpt)*

MEDARDO ROSSO:
MADAME X. 1896.
Galleria Internazionale
d'Arte Moderna

**Art is idealization or an
idealizing imitation
of nature.**

Death comes to two of the greatest masters of the late nineteenth century. If Gauguin owed a great deal to Pissarro, who had initiated him into Impressionism, he angered the master when he renounced Pissarro's descriptive Naturalism in favor of the primitive and sacred Symbolism of the "savages." His death in Oceania, making him a legend, seems to vindicate him. "It is what is within that we must see," advised the author of Noa Noa. This reinteriorization gives free rein to the expression of the inner self, as Camille Claudel shows through sculpture, and Gustav Klimt with his gilded frescoes.

1903

S U M M A R Y

GREAT MASTERS

Gauguin Becomes a Legend
In Gauguin's Words
Perfumed *Noa Noa*

DEVELOPMENTS

Gustav Klimt Accused of Pornography
Establishment of the Vienna Ateliers

ART NEWS

The "Firemen" Set St. Petersburg on Fire
Rouault's Holy Sisters
The Secession in Deep Trouble
Iron and Glass Architecture on the Rue de Réaumur
Perret, Architect in Concrete
In Brief

OBITUARIES

Good bye to Whistler
Pissarro, the Painter of Painters

MASTERWORKS

The Despair of Camille Claudel

LITERATURE

AUSTRIA-HUNGARY
Final issue of the magazine Ver Sacrum.

UNITED STATES
Jack London begins his writing career with The Call of the Wild.

FRANCE
First session of the Académie Goncourt. Publication of The Life of Beethoven *by Romain Rolland.*

GREAT BRITAIN
Publication of The Ambassadors *by the American author Henry James and of* Typhoon *by Joseph Conrad.*

ITALY
Benedetto Croce founds the magazine Critica.

MUSIC

AUSTRIA-HUNGARY
Arnold Schönberg composes Pelleas and Melisande.
  Béla Bartók begins the composition of his opera Kossuth.

UNITED STATES
The famous Italian tenor Caruso debuts at the New York Metropolitan Opera.

FRANCE
Erik Satie composes the piano piece Trois morceaux en forme de poire *for four hands.*

RUSSIA
Sergei Rachmaninoff performs his Variations on a Theme by Chopin.

OTHER PERFORMANCES

FRANCE
In Paris, Isadora Duncan creates the Danses-Idylles.

PAUL GAUGUIN:
THE WHITE HORSE. 1898. Paris.
Musée d'Orsay

Portrait of Paul Gauguin.

PAUL GAUGUIN:
AND THE GOLD OF THEIR BODIES . . .
1901. Paris. Musée d'Orsay

GAUGUIN BECOMES A LEGEND

MARQUESAS ISLANDS
Paul Gauguin, the master of the school of Pont-Aven venerated by the Nabis, a friend of Pissarro, Degas, Émile Bernard, and Van Gogh, the most fervent admirer of Cézanne, the unfortunate founder of the solitary "Tropical Studio" in Tahiti, dies in poverty at the age of fifty-five, in Atuana, on the island of Hiva Oa, to which he retired two years ago.

He had been greatly affected by a sentence of three months in jail for injuring policemen. He isolated himself in his home, which he called the "House of Pleasure," for eight days. Suffering fainting fits, he hailed a neighbor, the old Marquesian Tioka, and asked him to bring Pastor Vernier. The pastor found Gauguin in great pain. The

painter did not know whether it was day or night; he was delirious. Gauguin died of a broken blood vessel. The bishop of the Marquesas, Monsignor Martin, whom Gauguin had hated because the bishop reproached him for ogling the young girls in

HE WANTED MOST OF ALL TO REDISCOVER THE SUGGESTIVE AND INTERNALIZED FORCE OF PRIMITIVE ART

the bishop's school, had the Frenchman buried in the Catholic cemetery, then wrote to his congregation: "Nothing of interest happened here other than the sudden death of a sad personage named Gauguin, a famous artist, enemy of God and of all that is honest."

The "House of Pleasure" was

put up for sale, and there was an auction in Papeete of Gauguin's work. The clerk of the registry office asked the painter Le Moine to help prepare the inventory. They threw into the trash, according to Le Moine's confession, a large number of "drawings, sketches, outlines of statues that showed not the mind of a genius, but a dirty mind." The painting representing *Pont-Aven in Snow*, which Gauguin had brought on his last trip from France, in 1895, was presented the wrong way up by the auctioneer, who maliciously called it *Niagara Falls*. Victor Ségalen, a

navy doctor, bought it for the price of a loaf of bread: a mere seven francs.

At the end of the year, eight canvases were shown at the First Salon d'Automne. Ambroise Vollard is a rare art dealer—he appreciates the painter: He has thirty-six Breton and Tahitian canvases, including the *La belle Angèle* and his masterpiece, *Whence Do We Come? What Are We? Where Are We Going?* He plans to organize a show of Gauguin's paintings and drawings on the anniversary of his disappearance. He has asked Gauguin's last faithful friend, the painter Georges-Daniel de Monfreid, to buy up as many works as possible.

Mette Gauguin, who had taken refuge with her children in Copenhagen in 1885, and had

had no further dealings with her husband, is informed of his death and tries to recover the canvases. She confesses she does not know their value. The tight circle of Gauguin's admirers, of whom the chief were the Symbolist poets (including Mallarmé, who admired him for being able to "put so much mystery in so much brightness"), had become enlarged after the zeal of Mallarmé had presented him as an innovating genius.

Gauguin was a sailor and a stockbroker, and was trained in Impressionism by Camille Pissarro. From 1886, he devoted himself exclusively to painting. He worked in Pont-Aven, then Martinique. In 1888, he embarked, at the age of forty, on candid, colorful Symbolism. Under the influence of Émile Bernard and Japanese prints, he invented a pictorial technique distinct from the atomized dispersions of Neoimpressionist Pointillism, namely "cloisonné" (partitioned) and "synthetist" (flat sections of bright colors). His *Vision after the Sermon* is the technique's most striking manifestation.

Gauguin wanted to inaugurate "the right to dare everything," affirming that "in order to do something new, we must go back to the source, to humanity in its infancy." He pursued this Primitivism with the descendants of the ancient Maori. In his last letters, he observed that what was inimitable in his work was his motto "In spite of me the savage." He looked always for a lost paradise and a happy beyond. The painter of the *Yellow Christ* and of a Tahitian Virgin Mary, the *Orana Maria*, wanted, above all, to find again the suggestive, internalized power of primitive Egyptian, Greek, Peruvian, and Khmer art, which he used as models for his paintings of nonchalant Tahitian women.

Having once written that glory is an empty work, a "vain reward," he preferred his legend and died in penury.

(See also 1901.)

IN GAUGUIN'S WORDS

Heard from Mallarmé about my pictures from Tahiti, "It is extraordinary that one can put so much mystery in so much brightness."

I am strong because I am never led astray by others and do what is in me.

On the whole, in painting, one should look more for suggestion than for description.

Color, which is vibration, just as music, is able to attain what is most general and yet most vague in nature: its interior force.

Basically, painting is like humans, mortal but always living in a struggle with matter.
I have tried to make everything breathe in this painting: belief, passive suffering, religious and primitive style, and the great nature with its scream.

Color is in itself enigmatic in the feelings it gives us, it can logically be used only enigmatically, to give us the musical feelings that follow from color, from its own nature, from its interior, mysterious, enigmatic strength. With the help of wise harmony we create the symbol.

Pure color! Everything must be sacrificed to it.

The artist must take nature's elements and create a new element.

What matters is that which is today, and which will open the course of art in the twentieth century.

PERFUMED "NOA NOA"

"For sixty days, I have been longing to reach this desired land . . ." Thus begins the beautiful report by Paul Gauguin of his first trip to Tahiti (June 8, 1891, to June 14, 1893). He entitled it *Noa Noa*, a Tahitian expression evoking aphrodisiac perfumes. He used sharply outlined paintings, photographs, and original wood carvings to illustrate this autobiographical text, full of exotic characters and ethnologic references to the beliefs of the descendants of the Maori. Upon his return to Paris, he proposed that the Symbolist poet Charles Morice supplement the book with his poems, make an art book of the whole. Morice did so, but his gently emphatic poems are in contrast to the savage text of Gauguin, the keen ethnologist of Oceanians.

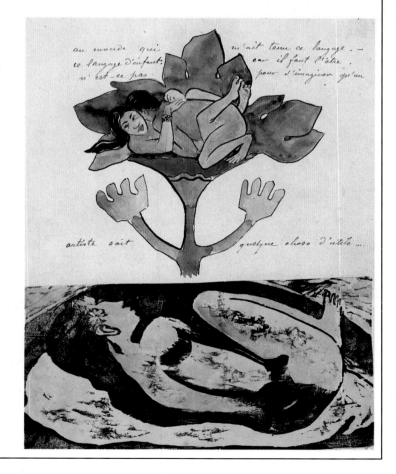

PAUL GAUGUIN:
PAIRING, NOA-NOA. 1894-1895.
Paris. Louvre

GUSTAV KLIMT ACCUSED OF PORNOGRAPHY

GUSTAV KLIMT: JUDITH AND HOLOFERNES. 1903.
Vienna. Österreichische Galerie

VIENNA

After the exhibition last year of the *Beethoven Frieze*, Klimt continues to triumph—and to scandalize. He is the controversial king of the Viennese Secession. The sketches of frescoes commissioned for the great hall of the university are at the center of arguments, conversations, and rumors. He symbolizes *Medicine, Philosophy,* and *Law* in his own manner. It is mainly this last work, shown for the first time, that feeds the polemics.

The distressed antagonists, the same people who are alarmed at the accents of Mahler and at the research of Dr. Freud into the secret chambers of the soul, reproach Klimt for the excessive and, they say, sickly sensuality of his art. The argument may really be about the general conception of the work and its composition. They led to the ministerial decision, approved by most of the public but not unexpectedly protested by the artist, to exhibit his frescoes in the Modern Stadtgalerie rather than in the university as had been planned.

His composition *Law* places the values of good and evil on the same plane while emphasizing the contrast be-tween the severe rigidity of the institution and the soft curves of error. This moral ambiguity is unacceptable to the Viennese bourgeoisie. At stake is the conflict between a hymn to life celebrating the cosmic universality of the erotic impulse and the surrounding hypocrisies. The latter forced the artist to resign from his position of president of the Secession.

More and more people are discovering the greatest painter and innovator in Austria in a long time. Many of his portraits integrate fine layers of gold to emphasize a magic, subtle preciousness. On a trip last year to Ravenna, he was struck by the sumptuous mosaics of Saint Apolline and Saint Vital. Their splendor led the Byzantines to mystical asceticism. For Klimt, it became an invitation to voluptuous ecstasies.

ESTABLISHMENT OF THE VIENNA ATELIERS

VIENNA

As soon as the journal *Ver Sacrum* (the sacred spring), an organ of the Viennese Secession, ceased publication, a new association was born: the Wiener Werkstätte, or Vienna Ateliers. It results from the ideas of two former collaborators on *Ver Sacrum,* the architect Josef Hoffmann and the graphic artist Koloman Moser.

Two years ago, at the Secessionist exhibition, Hoffmann and Moser discovered the Arts and Crafts Movement, specifically the work of the Britons Mackintosh and Ashbee, who championed the functional use of art and thus opposed the academic tradition. They are bringing about a renaissance of applied arts, which in their eyes are equal in rank to painting, sculpture, or architecture.

The Vienna Ateliers are being launched with the backing of the financier Fritz Waerndorfer. Moser is as gifted in wall decoration and stained glass as in graphic arts; Hoffmann is interested in furniture and jewelry, in addition to his architectural profession. They intend to have artists make objects used in daily life. They insist that craftsmanship preserve the quality of manufacture.

The "Firemen" Set St. Petersburg on Fire

Since the "Centennial" of the 1900 World's Fair, where Corot, Manet, and Monet were a revelation for visitors, Impressionism has acquired an international reputation. Unfortunately, that does not stop the academic French painters from spreading their mediocre creations all over the world. Proof of this is the current exhibition of French art in St. Petersburg. A jury placed under the joint presidency of Bouguereau and Carolus-Duran has made the selection for the exhibit, so that the whole show is given over to the reactionary painters known as "Pompiers" (firemen). It is true that painters such as Meissonier, Detaille, and others are still well-known in Russia. Living art is not defended when these artists are exported.

Rouault's Holy Sisters

Rouault is Christian. And it is from a Christian point of view that he looks upon the sin and misery of this world. His recent series dedicated to Sisters, if it bears some relationship to the style of Toulouse-Lautrec, is especially close to Dostoevski and Léon Bloy. Soldier's girls, tarts from the Longue Peine suburb, women addicted to drink who lope through dark streets, the ensemble reaches the limit of what is bearable. But at the same time, it depicts the daughters of Jerusalem around Veronica bearing the image of the Holy Face. "Deep inside the impure or heartless creature lies Jesus," says Rouault, as his art miraculously shows.

The Secession in Deep Trouble

Emperor William II had intervened the year before to condemn the Secessionists of Berlin and to defend an academic and moralizing esthetic. Max Liebermann opposed the Emperor's statements, and some twenty resignations resulted from this intervention. From then on, polemics took control. A conflict, not devoid of antisemitism, is exposed between those in power, assisted by representatives of the most sclerotic

ERNEST MEISSONIER:
THE SIEGE OF PARIS. 1870-1871. Paris. Musée d'Orsay

tradition, and the partisans of a kind of modern art that is an adventure. Thus, Max Liebermann cannot be congratulated enough for his statement: "It is not the most powerful of princes but the artist alone who shows art the path to follow. What is new, admittedly, often appears incomprehensible. Nevertheless, taking the risk of being wrong, we dare to show what is innovative."

Iron and Glass Architecture on the Rue de Réaumur

Baron Schilde opens his new industrial premises at 124 Rue de Réaumur in Paris. The work of the architect Georges Chédanne, the construction is almost entirely of metal, and is inspired by Art Nouveau without having its excesses. To combat the monotony of the façades, Chédanne played on the transparencies of iron and glass. And inspired by his prestigious elder, Gustave Eiffel, he realized a true ironwork masterpiece whose smallest details are visible. This use of iron as a means of plastic expression in a block of offices is an important first.

Perret, Architect in Concrete

Up to now, architects were loath to use reinforced cement, preferring stone instead, and only engineers, for the past fifteen years, had had recourse to it in their building. So the apartment building put up by Auguste Perret at 25 Rue Franklin in Paris is the first of its kind. It is a revolution in the art of building that was made possible by the fact that the architect was his own client. With his brother Gustave he acquired the land on which his apartment house was put up, and he opens his office there on the ground floor.

Auguste Perret: building on the Rue Franklin in Paris.

CAMILLE PISSARRO: SELF-PORTRAIT. 1873. Paris. Musée d'Orsay

PISSARRO, THE PAINTER OF PAINTERS

PARIS

Camille Pissarro is dead at the age of seventy-three. "The painter of painters" had moved to the Boulevard Morland in order to put the Austerlitz Bridge on canvas. Almost all of his colleagues considered him their master or inspiration. He had proclaimed in the Nouvelle Athènes restaurant, where they met after the war of 1870, that it would be necessary to burn down the Louvre and the Art Institute before they could present their "sensation."

Mary Cassatt states that Pissarro was such a good teacher that "he could have taught the stones to draw correctly." Cézanne was occasionally a pupil of the "humble and colossal Pissarro." Pissarro was modest but eager, sectarian with regard to the Symbolists and his former pupil Paul Gauguin, and he suffered a long lack of recognition.

The oldest of the great Impressionists, Pissarro remained attentive to the young. He did not hesitate to support the divisive theses of Georges Seurat in an encounter with his pupil Paul Sig-nac, in 1885. That did not prevent him, on finding the Pointilllist method fastidious over a longer period, from returning to his former method after three or four years of Neoimpressionist work. In his last years, Pissarro pursued, alone, the vibrant path of his vocation as a landscape painter that he had discovered in the Antilles, the islands of his birth.

GOOD-BYE TO WHISTLER

LONDON

The American painter James Whistler is dead. He was born in 1834 in Massachusetts and was intended for the army. He quit the military and became a painter. He moved to Paris, where he was influenced by Gustav Courbet. Presently, he distanced himself from the spokesman of Realism in favor of a lighter manner marked by Impressionism and Japanese subtlety. *The Piano*, rejected for the Paris exhibition of 1859, was shown successfully in London the following year. Whistler was inspired by the London fog to do a series of engravings. His portraits were of a sensitive melancholy mood. He once told a model who was tired, "Look at me for a few more minutes and you will look at yourself for all time."

JAMES WHISTLER:
MRS. FREDERICK R. LEYLAND. 1873.
New York. Frick Collection

THE DESPAIR OF CAMILLE CLAUDEL

PARIS

Camille Claudel's group *Maturity*, a poignant allegory of her break with Auguste Rodin, is exhibited in the Salon of French artists in its final version. It was cast last year by her friend, Captain Tissier. It is an autobiographical work. She is naked, and "pleading" with Rodin, who is being dragged away by his mistress Rose Beuret. It is a final farewell to her former lover, whom she now hates.

Claudel refused last year to consent to a joint exhibition with Rodin in Prague. She said, "Let him pretend that I am under his protection and make people believe that my work is due to his inspiration; I would have some chances at success there that would revert to him. But I am not in a mood to let myself be mocked any longer by this sly fox." While she is buried in solitude, Rodin revels in glory. He is commander of the Legion of Honor, and exhibits in the National Arts Club in New York and three books about him appear, including one by Rainer Maria Rilke.

Why did Claudel come to detest the great Rodin, for whom she was student, model, inspiration, and mistress from 1883 until a rupture occurred in 1893? She was the oldest daughter of a receiver of stamp duties in Aisne, where she was born thirty-nine years ago, the sister of the poet and diplomat Paul Claudel. She was a sculptor from an early age. She convinced her father to move the family to Paris, enabling her to follow her precocious vocation. She registered with the Colarossi School and was counseled by the sculptor Alfred Boucher, who recommended her to Rodin because she seemed to have similar gifts. Rodin fell in love with her, engaged her as practitioner, became her secret lover, and made an admirable first portrait of her called *Aurora*. She collaborated in many of the figures of the *Gates of Hell*; evidence of her tormented inspiration can be discerned.

In 1886 and 1887, she sculpted an admirable bust of Rodin and a head of her brother Paul Claudel as a "young Roman."

CAMILLE CLAUDEL:
MATURITY. 1899-1903.
Paris. Musée d'Orsay

Paul accompanied her to Mallarmé's Tuesday meetings, where she met Claude Debussy, who fell in love with her. When she exhibited her famous *Waltz* in

*"I SHOWED HER
WHERE TO FIND GOLD,
BUT THE GOLD SHE FINDS IS HERS"*

1893, the composer bought it, and never separated from it. It is one of the most characteristic masterpieces of her genius; it is animated by a spirituality that her brother admired.

Camille Claudel showed signs

of paranoia after the split with Rodin. On May 10, 1894, Edmond de Goncourt noted in his diary that the rupture had taken place and that Rodin was

very upset, crying to his friends about the loss of his "Egeria." Camille, who had had one or even two abortions, had demanded that he renounce his liaison with his former mistress Rose. He would not do it, and

moved to Meudon, where in 1894 he bought the Villa des Brillants. Rumor has it that Camille was seen hidden in nearby bushes there. Rodin esteems her and wants to help her. He has said, "I showed her where to find gold, but the gold she finds is hers." But this is not the opinion of most art critics, who, as Roman Rolland wrote in the *Revue de Paris*, believe that she is only "a caricature of Rodin's genius." Camille has isolated herself in her studio on the Quai Bourbon and neglects herself to such an extent that her family is concerned. How will it all end?

Three sacred places in the world of art cast a spell over three painters in search of themselves. Mount Sainte-Victoire enthralls Cézanne, the old master from Aix, who analyzes the mountain's structure under shimmering light. Saint-Tropez brings Matisse back to Signac, whose divisionist technique he now applies to the Mediterranean composition of Luxe, calme et volupté. Montmartre is claimed by Picasso, who brings his gang of friends to the Bateau-Lavoir. While Gérôme's burial in the cemetery at Montmartre is a requiem for academic Orientalist painting, the simultaneous deaths of Eadweard Muybridge the photographer and Étienne Jules Marey the physiologist draw attention to "chronophotography."

1904

S U M M A R Y

AVANT-GARDE

Picasso Moves into the Bateau-Lavoir
Picasso Distinguishes Himself at Berthe Weill's

DEVELOPMENTS

The Gustave Moreau Museum Is One Year Old
Matisse Signs *Luxe, Calme et Volupté*

MASTERWORKS

Cézanne at Mount Sainte-Victoire

ART AND THE EAST

Vroubel the Byzantine
The End of Orientalism

ART NEWS

The Phalanx Disbands
Van Dongen Is Adopted by the Critics
Fantin-Latour's Immortal Flowers
Degas and the Outdoors
"La Peau de l'Ours"
Brancusi, the Pedestrian of Paris
In Brief

ART AND SCIENCE

Marey, Muybridge . . . and Movement

ARCHITECTURE

Sullivan's Department Stores
Liberty in Mourning

PABLO PICASSO:
WOMAN WITH CROW
(Margot of the Lapin Agile).1904.
Toledo, Ohio. Museum of Art

PICASSO MOVES INTO THE BATEAU-LAVOIR

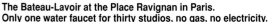
The Bateau-Lavoir at the Place Ravignan in Paris.
Only one water faucet for thirty studios, no gas, no electricity.

Pablo Picasso.

MONTMARTRE

A single water faucet, rusted and encrusted, for almost thirty studios, no gas, no electricity, façades of disjointed planks that drip water and let the winter wind whip through, a creaking staircase, permanent odors of cat dung and urine. This is where Pablo Picasso, twenty-three years old, settles on May 6, definitively it seems after three previous brief stays in Paris, in 1900, 1901, and 1902.

How did the artist come to settle in an area frequented by scoundrels and beggars, poor people and prostitutes, so unsafe that he never goes out in the evening without a firearm? There is no doubt that the reputation of the Butte had something to do with it. It's been home to many painters, from Van Gogh to Toulouse-Lautrec.

Picasso is renting the former studio of Paco Diurio for fifteen francs a month. Diurio, a

Basque, decided to isolate himself in a small hut in the area. Picasso bought for eight francs the furniture of the sculptor Pablo Gargallo: an army cot, a mattress, a table, a chair, and a wash basin. It was all moved to the studio on a handcart by

HE PAINTS AT NIGHT BY THE LIGHT OF A CANDLE THAT HE HOLDS IN HIS HAND. HIS CANVAS IS FLAT ON THE FLOOR

Picasso and his friend Manolo and a hired street urchin.

The Bateau-Lavoir—the "washing boat"—owes its name to the poet Max Jacob. He baptized it by analogy with the boats in which the washerwomen come to do their laundry along the rivers; these boats are misshapen and are unsteady like the building. It is also called the "House of the Trapper," because a Canadian trapper is said to have lived there. The strange

building has been a resort of cursed artists since Maxime Maufra (a friend of Paul Gauguin and a member of the Pont-Aven school) lived there a few years ago. The house is on a steep slope. It has a single story on the side of the Rue de Ravignan, where its entrance is located at number 13, and five stories on the other side, so that one enters there from the top of the slope.

Picasso's studio is at the end of a passage leading from the entrance. It is relatively spacious, although his friends call it "the maid's room." He paints at night, by the light of a kerosene lamp or of a candle that he holds in his hand. His canvas is flat on the floor. He does not like to be disturbed in the morning. The

janitor, a Madame Coudray, a Daumier-style gossip, polices his rest, awakening him only when a buyer comes. "Monsieur Picasso, you can open, this man means business."

As soon as Picasso was settled in the Bateau-Lavoir, he painted the *Woman with Crow*. It is related, as are all his works, to meetings or events that struck him. This crow fascinated him when he saw it hopping from table to table in the Lapin-Agile, the cabaret where the art students of Montmartre spend their evenings joking and smoking. The woman is Marguerite Luc, called Margot, the daughter-in-law of Frédé, the owner of the Lapin-Agile. She bends her pale face toward the bird, which she is petting with a slender hand and long fingers.

This painting is another of his works with a moving intensity to which he holds the secret. It belongs in the blue period, begun three years ago—like *Célestine,* an old woman whose left eye is veiled by cataracts, painted early in the year in Barcelona, and *The Couple,* a recent canvas, in which two people leaning at a table symbolize the misery of life.

One can discern changes in his paintings. It is not only because he lives in Montmartre or that his studio is the stopping-off point for Spanish artists in Paris. The cultural environment is less exalted than that of Barcelona, where he spent his adolescence. The stimulant for change is a young woman, Fernande Olivier.

Elegant and sensuous, she occupies all of Picasso's thoughts. He is proud to have a companion at whom people look as soon as they enter Azon on the Rue de Ravignan, or Vernin on the Rue Cavalotti, the restaurants frequented by bohemians. Fernande is health and youth incarnate. She takes the artist away from both the doubtful, easy models who keep Montmartre painters busy and the brothels. His passion is evidenced in several drawings and sketches of the young woman. They depict her arrogant breast, her majestic carriage, an immense hat with feathers.

Is Picasso happy? He dreams. In spite of the decrepitude of the place, he sets up housekeeping with Fernande. He is pathologically jealous. Blue is the color of death. Other colors might appear in his work.

(See also 1901, 1904, 1905, 1907, 1909, 1912, 1921, 1937, 1945, 1946, 1948, 1953, 1954, 1958, 1973.)

PICASSO DISTINGUISHES HIMSELF AT BERTHE WEILL'S

PARIS
He wanted *The Madman* to be there, for he is one of the persons in Picasso's drama. The great attraction at the group show, which features painters like Picabia, Dufy, or Girieud, is the overwhelming talent of Picasso. The show opened on October 24 at the Berthe Weill gallery, on the Rue Victor-Massé. Picasso's work was done shortly before the artist settled in the Bateau-Lavoir. He seems to have been inspired by a well-known starving beggar in Barcelona, who appears in several of his drawings.

We can see in this painting the influence of Isidro Nonell, the great Catalan painter who is a few years older than Picasso, and of the young essayist Eugenio d'Ors. The fifteen paintings that Nonell exhibited in the Sala Parès two years ago impressed Picasso. In his eyes, they depicted losers in the battle of life and Eugenio d'Ors echoed the feeling in a long accusatory essay in the magazine *Pel y Ploma* after the exhibition. Picasso's painting is far from having a merely emotional or sentimental source. If he multiplies the unfortunates, the ragamuffins, it is in order to pose a stark question to society. That is why Picasso wanted *The Madman* to appear at Berthe Weill's.

PABLO PICASSO:
THE MADMAN. 1904.
Barcelona. Museo Picasso

THE GUSTAVE MOREAU MUSEUM IS ONE YEAR OLD

GUSTAVE MOREAU: ROUGH SKETCH — **Was Moreau an inspired precursor?**

PARIS

Will the public finally find its way to the Gustave Moreau Museum? The painter, who died in 1898 of stomach cancer, bequeathed to Paris at the age of seventy-two, his town house and its contents at 14 Rue de La Rochefoucauld, on the condition that they be used to perpetuate his work.

It was a poisoned gift. There has never been a private museum in France. In addition, some of the conservators and artists who were consulted on the matter of accepting Moreau's bequest found that there were too many sketches and outlines. They had to wait until passage of a law for the donation to be ratified by the authorities; creation of the museum was conditioned on payment by Henri Rupp, Moreau's friend and universal heir, of his own share of the estate, estimated at 470,000 francs, assuring operation of the museum.

The Gustave Moreau Museum opened in January. It exhibits eight hundred paintings, three hundred and fifty watercolors, and about five thousand drawings. Many items were inspired by Symbolism or mythology or heavily modernistic experiments.

The artist, whose turn-of-the-century eclecticism was often criticized, created compositions like *Oedipus and the Sphinx* and *Les prétendants,* which pushed tradition to its extreme limits. He was a genius, foreshadowing future trends, as evidenced by his severe *Hélène à la porte de Scée* and even more so by his controversial "palettes" which, fifteen years ago, presaged what seems to be an entirely new path for painters: spots of color rubbed on the canvas. For the last six years of his life, Moreau taught at the Art Institute. He was an exceptional teacher, and was adored by his students. One was Georges Rouault, who became close to Moreau and is the conservator of this first private museum in the country.

HENRI MATISSE: LUXE, CALME ET VOLUPTÉ. 1904-1905. Paris. MNAM

MATISSE SIGNS "LUXE, CALME ET VOLUPTÉ"

SAINT-TROPEZ

Popularized by Guy de Maupassant, who wrote a beautiful story about it in 1888, this little port attracted the painter Paul Signac. He landed there in his yacht *Olympia*, named in honor of Manet's work. He invited his Neoimpressionist friends Luce and Cross to his house, "La Hune" (the top). This summer, he invites Henri Matisse to his joyous "painting competitions." Matisse is amazed at the South, and falls under the spell of Saint-Tropez. He is influenced by his friend's "divisionism," and paints a large canvas with a title reflecting its euphoric inspiration: *Luxe, calme et volupté.* Signac is enchanted and expects to buy it.

CÉZANNE AT MOUNT SAINTE-VICTOIRE

PARIS

Cézanne, who is so unpopular in his native Aix-en-Provence that children throw stones at him in the street, is having a belated triumph at the Salon d'Automne. A whole room is given over to him. It is filled with his leaning bottles, concave apples, and stocky bathers with barely outlined shapes. All the young painters, led by Pablo Picasso, go to the Grand Palais to see the unheard-of boldness of the man who, according to some critics, has defective vision. The old master of Aix gives an unkindly reception to the enthusiastic painters who see him in his studio on the Chemin des Lauves, outside Aix. He has been despised so long that he believes they are sent by his enemies to mock him with exaggerated praise. Émile Bernard traveled to Aix-en-Provence on his return from Egypt to ask Cézanne about his art. Bernard publishes a report of their conversations about theory in the July issue of the magazine *Occident:* Cézanne tries to explain how he went beyond Impressionism. He says that nature must be penetrated in depth, its internal dimensions rendered; this is why he believes it is absolutely necessary to introduce a sufficient amount of blue color into light vibrations represented by reds and yellows—they make us feel the air.

While listing some processes that may enlarge the field of vision, Cézanne warns against

PAUL CÉZANNE: MOUNT SAINTE-VICTOIRE. 1904-1906. Basel. Kunstmuseum

TO PENETRATE NATURE IN DEPTH, TO RENDER ITS INTERNAL DIMENSION

overly intellectual systematizing. The artist must be wary of a literary spirit that can turn the painter from the path: "The entire study of nature may lose itself too long in intangible speculation."

His own path is beautiful. It has been correctly followed towards this exploration, which is as perceptive as it is persever-

ing. In his drawings, watercolors, and oils, Cézanne keeps walking around Mount Sainte-Victoire in order to see it from various angles and, it can be said, from all seams. He pays heed to the successive atmo-spheric phenomena on its summits and in its valleys, its faults and folds, with the changing hours and seasons. He looks at the mountain from Tholonet Road, from the Château-Noir forest, from the village of Saint-Marc. It is probably from the height of the Lauves that he has the most profound feeling of embracing it, of obtaining a

fuller, more "abstract" view.

No painter has shown so much love for a mountain, with the possible exception of Japanese artists for Fujiyama. In spite of the sovereign and unique disdain that Cézanne has for the "Japanese craze," his study of a mountain that he wishes to conquer, regardless of cost, recalls the Japanese prints, specifically the thirty-six views of Mount Fuji by Hokusai.

This prophet is without honor in his own country! Cézanne is happy with the friendship and admiration of the poet Joachim Gasquet, who was enthusiastic about the *Sainte-Victoire au grand pin*, shown at the Salon of the Friends of Art in Aix in 1896. But he is dismayed by compatriots whom he calls ignorant and

"bums." One of them, Louis Gautier, has written a mocking poem on Sainte-Victoire. It ends as follows: "If nature were what this painter believes it to be, this hasty painting would be enough for her glory."

The residents of Aix are not the only people who have the prerogative of such incomprehension. Last year, Henri Rochefort published a venomous article in the *Intransigeant*, under the title of "Love for Ugliness," about the Zola collection—the novelist owned ten works made by the young Cézanne.

(See also 1906.)

VROUBEL THE BYZANTINE

MOSCOW

Did Mikhail Aleksandrovich Vroubel—he was born in Omsk in 1856—want to be embodied in his last work, *The Fallen Angel*, which was directly inspired by Lermontov, and in the descendants of the Satanic heroes of the English poets John Milton and William Blake?

This work, combining reality and vision, irresistibly recalls a painting he completed four years ago: *The Swan Princess*. There is the influence of Byzantine art so dear to Vroubel which, as he says, differs profoundly from the art of the Italian Renaissance because its essence resides in ornamental order. The effect of fantasy is clearly accentuated in the two paintings by the decorative character of some of the details, like the feathers that form the angel's bedding as well as the princess's arm.

The immense solitude of Vroubel's subjects is his own. He is increasingly the prisoner of a mental illness. It cuts him off from reality and all possible communication, except for painting, into which he plunges with heroic and desperate energy.

Considered for two decades by the critic Répine as one of the greatest spirits of new Russian art, Vroubel is a member of the group called "The World of Art," formed in 1890 by the artist and decorator Alexander Benois and enlivened by Sergei de Diaghilev.

MIKHAIL VROUBEL: THE SWAN PRINCESS. 1900. Moscow. Tretiakow Gallery

THE END OF ORIENTALISM

PARIS

Jean-Léon Gérôme, the most famous Orientalist painter, dies on January 10 at the age of almost eighty while preparing to go to Monte Carlo with his friend Bonnat. He was one of the last "Pompiers" (firemen) hostile to the Impressionists—he called them "damn jokers." He fought a last battle against their "trash," vainly trying to prevent their show at the Luxembourg.

The requiem mass and burial in the Montmartre cemetery of this esteemed officer of the Legion of Honor were attended by the most important personages in government and the arts. He leaves to his wife and their four daughters a considerable estate; it is estimated at over a million francs. There are many paintings and sculptures and a fantastic set of accessories, arms, and disguises he used for composing the vividly colored paintings he showed for fifty-seven years in the Salon. His reputation in Europe and America is due to his unusual facility in rendering the "local color" of his historic, orientalizing reportage. His Realism is no longer in vogue, having been supplanted by photography. He survives his fame.

JEAN-LÉON GÉRÔME: THE PRISONER. 1861. Nantes. Musée des Beaux-Arts

The Phalanx Disbands

The Phalanx Group, founded three years ago by Wassili Kandinsky, has not overcome its financial difficulties. The number of pupils not being sufficient, the school created by Phalanx had already been closed at the end of the previous year. Now it will stop its exhibits. Like the Secessionists of Berlin, the Munich group had as its goal making foreign art better known, so that Germany could pull out of its provincialism. In four years, twelve exhibitions were devoted notably to Monet, Signac, and Toulouse-Lautrec.

Van Dongen Is Adopted by the Critics

Invariably wearing sandals and socks with holes worn through them so that his toes stick out, blond-bearded, a mocking look on his face, handsome Kees Van Dongen is the darling of Montmartre, where he has been living for three years, having left his native Holland. But he is also a painter, and a good painter. His first exhibition with Matisse in Paris at the Vollard gallery on the Rue Laffitte from November 15 to November 24 attracted the interest of the critics. The well-known Félix Fénéon prefaced the exhibition, but the public is not interested. They find his bright-colored canvases too aggressive.

Fantin-Latour's Immortal Flowers

A friend of Manet, and of the Impressionists whose group portrait he painted, Henri Fantin-Latour dies on August 25 in Buré in the department of Orme without having become a member of the shocking movement. In fact, he insisted above all on total liberty. His friendships, however, rendered him suspect to the very academic jury of the Salon, and for that reason he never received any reward, despite the submissions he sent in with obstinate regularity. Not terribly intrigued by the human face, he had devoted himself to still-life paintings of flowers and fruits. Each season, he sent representatives to London to sell his pictures of elegant bouquets that had established his reputation across the Channel. His best-selling specialty is the exquisitely charming roses he painted.

Degas and the Outdoors

Against all expectations, Degas has agreed to spend two weeks at the estate of his dear friend Henri Rouart in La Queue-en-Brie because his doctors have advised him to get some fresh air. But he would not renounce studio painting, turning his back to the window. To those who express their surprise, he reveals his secret: "From time to time, I take a look through the coach-door window." For, according to him, if one wishes to learn how to paint, one must copy the masters and not nature. That is how he recently answered the mother of a young artist: "So young and so sincere before nature! Madame, he is lost."

"La Peau de l'Ours"

An original and complicated idea! André Level, a young financier who is also a lover of art, along with a few friends, has just formed an association with the purpose of establishing a mutually owned collection of paintings. The association is called "La Peau de l'Ours" (the bearskin). Its members collectively buy works by young painters, which are to be sold at public auction within ten years. Each member will make a contribution of 200 francs a year for a share, and the acquired works will be assigned by drawing lots. If the occasion arises, the profits will be divided among the members of the association and the artists from whom the works were bought. The first acquisitions: Picasso, Matisse, Braque, Marquet, and still more. Balance sheet to appear in ten years.

Brancusi, the Pedestrian of Paris

Leaving Munich, where the teaching of fine arts seemed too much like Bucharest, Constantin Brancusi comes to Paris on foot. "I went along country roads," he recounts, "I roamed the forests, and I sang of my joy and happiness. In the villages, the peasants welcomed me with open arms. They saw very well that I was one of them." At the age of seven, Brancusi was a shepherd in the Carpathian Mountains. He knew plants, animals, and stars before learning the alphabet. At the age of thirty he arrives at the Beaux-Arts Academy in Paris. At night, he is a dishwasher to earn enough money to eat. In his studio, at 16 Place Dauphine on the sixth floor, are nothing but a few pieces of furniture. And on the wall, written in red, this thought: "Do not forget that you are an artist! Do not lose your courage, fear nothing, you will succeed."

HENRI FANTIN-LATOUR: FLOWERS AND FRUIT. 1865. Paris. Musée d'Orsay

MAREY, MUYBRIDGE...

ÉTIENNE JULES MAREY:
SEA GULLS IN FLIGHT. 1887.
Beaune. Musée E. J. Maret et
des Beaux-Arts

This strange bronze sculpture evokes
successive images of a flying bird.

...AND MOVEMENT

ENGLAND-FRANCE

One was an Englishman who emigrated to the United States, a photographer of genius, Eadweard Muybridge. The other was a French physician, physiologist, and professor at the Collège de France, Étienne Jules Marey. They both die at the age of seventy-four, less than a fortnight apart: Muybridge on May 5, in Kingston-on-Thames, his native town, and Marey on May 15, in Paris. They will be remembered as the first men to pierce the mysteries of animal and human locomotion, about which almost nothing was known before their investigations.

Muybridge's photography is famous in Europe and America. In 1872, the millionaire governor of California, Lelan Stanford, who had a stable of race horses in Palo Alto, asked him to do some picture-taking for him. Stanford argued with another millionaire horse lover, Fred McCrellish, who did not believe that a trotting or galloping horse lifts all four of its hoofs off the ground simultaneously. Stanford had read an article by Dr. Marey that described the oscillograph that enabled him to discover that a horse's legs move in an entirely unexpected way. He invited Muybridge to photograph the phenomenon. Muybridge obliged, making several series of chronophotographs proving that Marey was correct.

THE FIRST MEN TO PIERCE THE MYSTERIES OF ANIMAL AND HUMAN LOCOMOTION

One fine day, the painter Ernest Meissonier realized, after looking at Muybridge's photos, that he himself had been mistaken in his interpretation of the movements of a horse. He built a course and let himself be pulled by a fast horse. He observed and drew the gallop of the animal running before his eyes. But Marey's camera demonstrated that the naked eye cannot see what a machine sees. Meissonier was such a conscientious professional he repainted the caval-

ry in his *Battle of Friedland*, one of his largest paintings.

Marey also revealed how birds fly. After studying various bodily movements for medical information, such as the heart rhythm, the quiver of muscles, and ventilation in the lung, he perfected a photographic flash, enabling him to make twelve photographs every second. He was able to make successive pictures of birds in flight. The result was his curious bronze statues concretizing these images.

The greatest achievement of Marey and Muybridge was doubtless the demonstration of human locomotion. Muybridge worked at the University of Pennsylvania starting in the spring of 1884. He worked on more than a hundred thousand photographs of the most diverse activities. They included nude men and women running, jump-

ing, boxing, and throwing water on one another.

Marey had the idea, at the physiological station in the Parc des Princes, where he conducted experiments, of dressing a runner entirely in black, from head to toe. He photographed him against a black background, so that the pictures show only the silvery bands and points traced along the man's body and legs. Spectral diagrams show the lines articulating, bending, opening, and separating.

Marey, the publisher of many specialized publications, collected his main research for a work in 1894 called *Movement*, intended for the public at large. He explained his work clearly, from the flight of birds to the thrust of waves on a beach. If Muybridge was a poet of images, Marey was a scientist who expected to be able to contribute to the knowledge of life and the universe.

(See also 1909.)

SULLIVAN'S DEPARTMENT STORES

CHICAGO

Louis Sullivan is one of the great modern American architects. His most important works are in Chicago. His Auditorium Building made him famous at the age of thirty-three.

Sullivan is a theoretician. In his writings and in his architecture he expresses his search for Functionalism, which he summarizes in his famous dictum, "Form follows function," to which he adds that everything created by nature has a structure and a form; that the exterior foreshadows the interior, and that this appearance is the sign that differentiates things from one another and from us. Sullivan strives to liberate architecture from everything that is superfluous. He reduces his buildings to a set of masses, proportions, and articulations.

Compensating for his extreme rigor, he exhibits an exuberant interior decor.

The (apparently) contradictory traits of Sullivan's style are seen again in the Schlessinger and Mayer stores.

Richly decorated iron panels of the first two floors contrast with the geometric purity of the whole. But the architect emphasizes horizontal line; his new façades differ from his tall buildings in both Saint Louis and New York.

In Sullivan's eyes, each building must have its own personality. It is not interchangeable. He says that the building must be a proud and arrogant thing, down to its last detail, without a single dissonant line. It is difficult to give a more precise definition of the Functionalism so dear to new American architecture.

Frédéric Bartholdi: the Statue of Liberty.

Louis Sullivan: Schlessinger department store in Chicago.

LIBERTY IN MOURNING

PARIS

Frédéric Auguste Bartholdi dies at the age of seventy. The sculptor had left his native town of Colmar after the annexation of Alsace-Lorraine. He never forgot those lost provinces, whose heroic resistance he symbolized in the monumental rock, *The Lion of Belfort*. He was greatly affected by the war and left France. He visited the United States and conceived the idea of a monument to American independence. On his return to France, he worked to set up a national subscription. The French people would donate a statue to the American people, who would pay for construction of the pedestal. Bartholdi, having chosen to symbolize Liberty, was inspired by *La liberté guidant le peuple (Liberty guiding the people)* by Delacroix. He transformed the exalted heroine into the guardian of the American Constitution. Gustave Eiffel contributed the statue's metal scaffolding. After a twenty-six-day crossing of the Atlantic Ocean on the *Isère, La liberté éclairant le monde (Liberty lighting the world)* was given a triumphal reception on its arrival in New York. It was dedicated in New York Harbor in 1886.

The death of William Bourguereau, pope of the "Pompiers," is symbolic of this year. Modern art bursts into bloom with two avant-garde schools, the Fauves in Paris, and Die Brücke in Dresden. The former creates a sensation at the Third Salon d'Automne, where their gallery is named the Cage aux fauves (the cage of wild beasts), after the loud, violent colors of their canvases. Matisse, Derain, Manguin, Rouault, Valtat rival each other to be the most daring in the exhibition. As for Die Brücke, the four German students who founded this movement hope to launch a revolt against refinement and rationalism in favor of the authentic expression of their strongest creative impulses.

1905

S U M M A R Y

AVANT-GARDE

The Cage of the Fauves at the Salon d'Automne
Four Students Launch Die Brücke
The Posthumous Fame of Van Gogh

ARCHITECTURE

The Garden City by Tony Garnier
The Masterstroke of the Samaritaine

ART NEWS

Controversy over Arnold Böcklin
Klee Discovers the Louvre
African Art at the Café
Stieglitz, 291 Fifth Avenue
A Work of Art with a Span of 167 Feet
A Good Giant at La Ruche
In Brief

DEVELOPMENTS

Picasso Changes from Blue to Pink
Apollinaire on Picasso

OBITUARIES

Bouguereau, the Pope of the "Pompiers," Is Gone

LITERATURE

GERMANY
Heinrich Mann publishes The Blue Angel (Professor Unrath).

AUSTRIA-HUNGARY
Publication of Three Essays on the Theory of Sexuality *by Sigmund Freud.*

FRANCE
Jules Verne, whose work has enjoyed great success, dies in Amiens.
    The recently established Prix Femina is awarded to Romain Rolland for his novel Jean-Christophe.

RUSSIA
Publication of Feodor Sologoub's novel The Petty Demon.

MUSIC

GERMANY
Performance of Salomé *by Richard Strauss, from Oscar Wilde's text.*

AUSTRIA-HUNGARY
Premiere of the operetta The Merry Widow *by Franz Lehár.*

SPAIN
Manuel de Falla wins the opera-competition award of Madrid for Life Is Short.

FRANCE
Maurice Ravel completes his piano piece Mirrors.
    At Concert Lamoureux, Claude Debussy's La mer *is booed by the audience and the critics.*

HENRI MATISSE:
WOMAN WITH A HAT. 1905.
Private Collection

THE CAGE OF THE FAUVES AT THE SALON D'AUTOMNE

HENRI ROUSSEAU: THE HUNGRY LION. 1905. Basel. Kunstmuseum

PARIS

The Third Salon d'Automne, presided over by Auguste Renoir and Eugène Carrière, opens on October 18 in the Grand Palais, on the Champs-Élysées. It closes on November 25. In addition to two retrospectives of Ingres and Manet, the show has one thousand six hundred and thirty-six works by living artists, proving it is indeed taking up the slack of the Salon des Indépendants created in Paris in 1884. Elie Faure in his preface to the catalog writes, "The show is fortunate in grouping together young energies that the beautiful, overly troubled, and scattered manifestations of the Indépendants could not present to us. These golden banners are due the exhibition of the liveliest efforts accomplished by French artists during the past thirty years." The renowned art historian launches this appeal to the public, which is intrigued by the novelties: "We must have the freedom and the will to understand a new language."

It is a very lively language, in fact. Such artists in one room: Henri Matisse with his brightly colored *Woman with a Hat* and his *Sailors* bursting with vivid colors; Derain with his joyful, crude *View of Collioure;* Manguin with a solar *Siesta;* Valtat with outrageously purplish *Sailors;* Vlaminck with *Valley of the Seine at Marly,* looking like a

beautiful mirage; or Puy with a *Stroll under the Pines,* with violent pictorial effects. The room creates a scandal. "A pot of paint has been thrown in the public's face," writes Camille Mauclair, the critic of *Le Figaro.* Faced with a lovely *Torso of a Child,* the ultraconservative Louis Vauxcelles utters this rather picturesque remark: "Donatello among wild beasts!"

The same commentary is issued in the *Gil Blas* in an article about Matisse's *Woman with a Hat:* He states that the presentation "would have the fate of a Christian virgin delivered up to wild beasts in a Roman circus."

The idea of a circus was no doubt suggested to him by the *Forains* and the *Prostitutes* of Rouault, who also dressed them in eccentric colors. The idea of "wild beasts" was inspired by a forceful painting by Henri Rousseau: *The Hungry Lion Jumps on the Antelope, Devours It, the Panther Anxiously Waits for the Moment When It Can Have Its Share . . . Sunset.*

The great naive painter was nicknamed "Rousseau the Customs Officer" by Alfred Jarry

"A POT OF PAINT HAS BEEN THROWN IN THE PUBLIC'S FACE"

because he worked in the Paris customs office. He was inspired to paint his animal subjects in a large jungle by the photograph of a lioness and an antelope made by the taxidermist Quentin in 1889 for the inauguration of the zoological gallery of the Museum of Natural History in Paris. Contrary to what is being said, Rousseau did not journey to Mexico in order to paint his exotic flora, but to the tropical section of the Jardin des Plantes (botanic garden in Paris), whose

ANDRÉ DERAIN: VIEW OF COLLIOURE. 1905. Paris. MNAM

ERNST LUDWIG KIRCHNER: SELF-PORTRAIT WITH PIPE. 1905. Private Collection

magical atmosphere plunged him "into revery."

Exquisitely primitive and marvelously poetic, the large painting in front of which Rousseau proudly stands guard is such a sensation that the magazine *Illustration* of November 4 reproduces it along with paintings by Matisse, Manguin, Derain, Guérin, Valtat, Puy, Vuillard, Rouault and underneath *The Bathers* by Paul Cézanne, who is represented by ten paintings from the Provence, one of which is the sparkling *Paysage à l'Estaque*. There are two Russian painters from Munich, Kandinsky and Jawlensky.

We bet that the nickname "Wild Beasts"—*Fauves*—chosen by Vauxcelles for the most original of the exhibitors will become popular.

Their solar and thick colors, burning and bleeding, spreading out as if from the effect of violent blows, seem to try to attack Impressionist and Pointillist art.

Looking at Pierre Bonnard, utterly unconcerned, and represented in another room in the fall show, the spectator can have the impression that the painters in this "wild-animal cage" have decided to seize the lion's share in the sudden evolution of art that seeks to go beyond Impressionism and burst it open just as public taste is reconciling to it.

Like Cézanne, who in his solitude wants to attain a "stern grandeur" of creation or rather a more structured recreation, these "Fauves" seem to be tired of the atomized dispersions of their predecessors and may want to be bold enough to give colors their maximum chance to impress the public forcibly, with a clarion call.

The Third Salon d'Automne? A show as amazing as it is clashing in color. No doubt it will be discussed for a long time!

FOUR STUDENTS LAUNCH DIE BRÜCKE

DRESDEN

Die Brücke (the bridge) is the meaningful name of both the transition to the creative act and of the tie between the creators. It is chosen by four students at the Technical Academy of Dresden to designate their new movement. It refuses to be a school in the academic sense of the word. The young men want to attract to their movement "all the factors of revolution and ferment," which break with the Academism, Berlin Impressionism, and Art Nouveau.

The four are Ernst Ludwig Kirchner, a twenty-four-year-old student of architecture, who does mostly wood carvings; Erich Heckel, who prefers sculpture; Karl Schmidt-Rottluff, who has chosen lithography; and Fritz Bleyl, a painter. Each initiates the others in the technique he knows best.

THE POSTHUMOUS FAME OF VAN GOGH

VINCENT VAN GOGH: SELF-PORTRAIT WITH GRAY FELT HAT. 1887. Amsterdam. Van Gogh Museum

AMSTERDAM

Four hundred and seventy-three works by Vincent Van Gogh—including seventy-four canvases—are presented to the Stedelijk Museum by the widow of his dear brother, Theo. This is a great success, unfortunately posthumously, for poor Vincent, who wrote in an unfinished letter, "I am risking my life in my work, and half my reason is gone." The success of the retrospective is due precisely to his passion and to the delirious character of his febrile touch. The painters of the "wild-animal cage"—the "Fauves"—of the Salon d'Automne and the Flemish and German Expressionists salute Van Gogh as the prophet of their ardor, their torments, and their exaltation.

THE GARDEN CITY BY TONY GARNIER

LYON

An industrial city, with fifty percent of its surface green, heated by cheap electricity! This is the project that Tony Garnier, thirty-six years old, newly appointed architect for the town of Lyon, brings back from Rome, where he boarded, from 1899 to 1904, at the Villa Medici. As a student at an art institute, first in Lyon, then in Paris, Garnier frequents the studio of Julien Guadet, to whom he owes several of his ideas. Unlike today's anarchic urban concentrations, his city separates working from residential areas and pedestrian malls from automobile roads. It has roof terraces, arcades, squares, and streets with trees, an underground railroad station, an airport, and sports appurtenances. Each neighborhood will house thirty-five thousand people. He has placed the whole on half-flat, half-hilly terrain in the bend of a river, like his native city.

During the Dreyfus affair, during his student days in Paris, Garnier was close to the radical-socialist circles of Jaurès and Zola. He drew from them the certainty that the new century would see the marriage of town

Tony Garnier: sketch for the Garden City project.

and industry—not only that, but the conviction that in a socialist society humans will be able to enjoy a good life. He therefore does not include in his project any police stations, prisons, barracks, or churches—they have become entirely unnecessary.

The material he envisages is reinforced concrete. This also is revolutionary. Until now, it has been used only for rare utilitarian edifices. Concrete permits the introduction of a free plan, with all that means of new architectural possibilities. And yet Garnier is not really breaking with tradition.

Garnier also brings back from Rome a reconstruction of Tusculum and some drawings of Roman monuments, reflecting his interest in ancient architecture. The roof terraces are Mediterranean reminiscences. His municipal center is a modern version of an agora where citizens can meet, as in antiquity. If his project for a stadium includes imposing monumental entrances, it is because it will house popular events and ceremonies as well as athletic competitions.

When plans for the "Industrial City" were shown last year at the Beaux-Arts Academy of Paris, the journal *Construction Lyonnaise* emphasized the industrial and commercial aspect of Garnier's plan: metallurgical and textile plants, mulberry farming, silkworm raising, a river port—all equipped with "the most modern hygienic installations." After viewing the show, the mayor of Lyon, Édouard Herriot, became enthusiastic over Garnier's innovative project, and decided to appoint him to the position he occupies today.

Tony Garnier: sketch for the Garden City project.

THE MASTER-STROKE OF THE SAMARITAINE

PARIS

Will the "Samar" style of Frantz Jourdain dethrone the "Metro" style of Hector Guimard? More and more Parisians come every day to admire the splendid façade of the department store La Samaritaine on the Rue de la Monnaie.

Jourdain integrates immense ceramic panels with the metal structure of the building. The floral décor enlivens the glass bays with brilliant colors. The sparseness of style differs from that of Hector Guimard, who is more baroque, more flamboyant in his work, which claims kinship with the Naturalism dear to Viollet-le-Duc and Ruskin.

The fifty-eight-year-old Jourdain is an enemy of traditionalism and a partisan of the synthesis of the arts. Two years ago, he was one of the founders of the Salon d'Automne, which this year revealed "Fauvism" to the public. He is a journalist, a pamphleteer, a polemicist, a novelist, and a friend of Goncourt, Monet, Renoir, Rodin, and Zola.

Controversy over Arnold Böcklin

Henry Thode, professor of art history at the University of Heidelberg, publishes a book with the names of two painters as the title: *Hans Thoma and Arnold Böcklin.* In the book, he attacks Julius Meier-Graefe, cofounder of the magazine *Pan* and the man who introduced Impressionism to Germany as well as the author of a small work, *The Böcklin Case*, in which he argues that the Swiss painter, who died four years earlier, led German art to an impasse. Thode, a partisan of religious, moral, and patriotic art, could not accept this point of view. On the contrary, he celebrates Böcklin's ties to Nordic mysticism, as well as his aspiration to the unity of "the sky and the earth, the clouds and the sea."

Klee Discovers the Louvre

Accompanied by his friends Hans Bloesch and Louis Moilliet, the painter Paul Klee made his first visit to Paris from May 31 to June 13. He toured the Louvre where he admired Leonardo da Vinci, that "revolutionary in the modulation of color values," as well as Rembrandt and Goya. Curiously, though, the young artist from Bern—he is twenty-six—did not attempt to contact either Picasso or Matisse, and it seems he was not interested in Cézanne. On the other hand, he leaves full of enthusiasm after a production of *The Barber of Seville* at the Théâtre Sarah Bernhardt.

African Art at the Café

Maurice de Vlaminck discovered African art in a café in Argenteuil one scorching hot summer afternoon. He was painting by the Seine, and when the sun got too hot, he went to the corner bistro. Immediately his glance was drawn to three loudly colored statuettes enthroned on a shelf behind the counter. Seeing his interest, the owner ended up making him a gift of the three statuettes. "They are as beautiful as the *Venus of Milo*," exclaimed his friend André Derain when he showed them to him.

Stieglitz, 291 Fifth Avenue

Opening of "The Little Gallery of the Photo-Secession" at 291 Fifth Avenue in New York. The labor of the photographers Alfred Stieglitz and Edward Steichen, who is also a painter, it follows the success of the magazine *Camera Work*, founded by Stieglitz two years earlier. The choice of the term "Photo-Secession" recalls the inclination of the modern artists in Germany and Austria who called themselves Secessionists in order to emphasize their break with the academic tradition. Stieglitz and Steichen believe that photography, contrary to current opinion, is an art. Over dinner in the famous restaurant Mouquin's, meeting place of New York artists, where they had met some friends who were also Secessionists, they decided to open their gallery.

A Work of Art with a Span of 167 Feet

The latest realization of the Swiss engineer Robert Maillart: a bridge 167 feet long over the Rhine at Tavanasa in the canton of Grisons. Built of monolithic concrete, it puts an end to the traditional technique of constructing a roadway supported by weight-bearing arches, which are replaced here by the organic fusion of the roadway itself, the arc, and the reinforcing wall following a coherent system. Maillart is the inventor of this system that makes his bridges works of art of an exceptional elegance. Born in Bern in 1872, he had already attracted notice four years earlier with his Zuoz Bridge in the Engadine, built according to the same idea, but of smaller proportions.

A Good Giant at La Ruche

Over six feet tall, eighty years old, strong as an ox, Fernand Léger moves into La Ruche at 2 Passage Dantzig, near the Vaugirard slaughterhouses. The former wine pavilion at the 1889 World's Fair, La Ruche (The Beehive) owes its name to its workshops in the form of alveoli, grouped around a central rotunda. It houses a multitude of marginal artists, like the Bateau-Lavoir in Montmartre, and like it, is stripped of all comforts. After studying architecture at Caen, and making appearances at Art Deco where he passed the entry competition, Léger is a good giant who practices an emphatic Impressionism. To make a living, he exercises various crafts.

Robert Maillart: bridge over the Rhine, at Tavanasa.

PICASSO CHANGES FROM BLUE TO PINK

PARIS

Some of the thirty paintings he shows in February and March in the Serrurier gallery, on the Boulevard Haussmann, lead one to guess that Pablo Picasso has reached a more serene period in his life. Pink tints of what seems to be dawn are beginning to succeed the blue, melancholy mists of the passage of a "dark night." Perhaps a sudden shower and a kitten are enough to produce this change . . .

At the height of summer last year, the painter on his way to his studio, in the Bateau-Lavoir, picked up a kitten during a thunderstorm and met an opulent young woman, Fernande Olivier, who was drawing water from the only faucet in his wobbly building. He offers her the kitten, engages her in conversation, invites her to his studio. They see each other regularly. Early this year, she comes to live with him. It seems to have salubrious effects on his morale. It must be why his figures have lost their pale tint, their frightened and morose looks. There are no more alcoholics, beggars, fools, or drug-addicted prostitutes. There are clowns instead.

Around last Christmas, he goes to see Father Santol, who directs a charity home on the Avenue de la Motte-Piquet, and sees the circus installed on the Esplanade des Invalides, as it is each year during the holidays. Since then, the jugglers have set up their circus and performed their tricks on his canvas. Picasso goes regularly to see the circus in Montmartre, and finds the ambience of the last works of Toulouse-Lautrec, whom he admires and whose circus lithographs are now published.

Is his newly found relationship with circus denizens the reason he continues to paint them? Like them, he is an immigrant artist, a nomad who must continually create to live. It would explain

PABLO PICASSO: BOY WITH A PIPE. 1905. New York. Private Collection

APOLLINAIRE ON PICASSO

It has been said about Picasso that his works give evidence of a precocious disenchantment.

I believe the contrary.

Everything enchants him, and his undeniable talent seems to me to be at the service of a fantasy that mixes precisely the delicious and the horrible, the abject and the delicate.

His Naturalism, in love with accuracy, is coupled with this mysticism, which in Spain lies at the bottom of the least religious souls. It is known that Castelar was carrying a rosary in his pocket, and even if Picasso is not very religious, he still retains, I am sure, a sublimated worship of Saint Theresa or Saint Isidore.

In Rome, at Carnival time, there are masks (Harlequin, Columbine, or cuoca francese) who in the morning, after an orgy sometimes ending with a murder, go to St. Peter to kiss the worn toe of the statue of the prince of the Apostles.

These are beings who would enchant Picasso.

Under the bright rags of his slender acrobats, one really feels the young people of the working class, fickle, sly, deft, poor, and lying. His mothers wring thin hands, the kind of hands one often sees among young mothers of the working class, and his naked women show the pubic hair disdained by traditional painters, and which is the shield of Western modesty.

GUILLAUME APOLLINAIRE
Les peintres cubists *(Excerpt)*

why he is shown dressed in a harlequin suit in the cabaret Au Lapin Agile, one of the loveliest paintings in the show.

The exhibition has had quite some success, and has given Guillaume Apollinaire reason to write a laudatory piece on Picasso's art. The two men met some weeks before through the sculptor Manolo, another Spanish artist living in Paris. Max Jacob, André Salmon, and Picasso now meet so often in Picasso's studio in the Bateau-Lavoire that Picasso has written above his door "Meeting Place of Poets."

After the exhibition, Picasso spends two months, June and July, in Schoorl, near Alkmaar, in Holland, on the invitation of his friend, the writer Tom Shilperoort. He describes his departure: "I had no money, neither did Max Jacob. He went to the janitor. He came back with 20 francs. I had a satchel and put my paints in it. The brushes did not fit in; I broke the handles and left." Even more than the famous Dutch light, he discovers volumes of bodies in Schoorl. The time of the puny anatomies of Barcelona, of the emaciated bodies of his blue period, is long gone. His *Hollandaise à la coiffe* testifies to his interest in rounded shapes.

Is it possible that less than a year ago Picasso asked for a donation at the Rue de la Motte-Piquet? His material life has changed in a way that was not predictable. Gertrude and Leo Stein, two American art lovers in Paris, buy two of his paintings, *Woman with Fan* and *Young Woman with Flower Basket*. It is said that Miss Stein is so enchanted with his work that she is considering asking him to do her portrait.

(See also 1901, 1904, 1907, 1909, 1912, 1921, 1937, 1945, 1946, 1948, 1953, 1954, 1958, 1973.)

BOUGUEREAU, THE POPE OF THE "POMPIERS," IS GONE

PARIS

The Religious Bulletin of the Diocese of La Rochelle et Saintes of August 26 reports how remorsefully and piously the glorious painter William Bouguereau, officer of the Legion of Honor since 1903, departed this life. Stretching out trembling hands to receive extreme unction, he says to the priest who attends him on his deathbed, "I condemn what was done for the announcing the death of this friend of Cabanel and Gérôme, admires the voluptuous models of Bouguereau's celebrated *Birth of Venus*. The painter sells it to the government in 1879 for 15,000 francs, a handsome amount. It becomes the star attraction of the Luxembourg. The painting, measuring 10 x 7 feet, is one of the most typical specimens of academic art of the second half of the last century.

WILL THE ART OF THE "POPE OF THE POMPIERS" SURVIVE HIS DEATH?

world and its vanities." The diocesan bulletin reports his last words, "Amen! Amen!," adding "Perhaps at that moment the great artist saw the sweet Madonnas he painted so beautifully in their glory bowing to him. They came to announce that Heaven had forgiven him."

The many titles to fame of this painter are beyond counting. After winning his second Grand Prize of Rome, in 1850, for his academic *Zenobia Found by the Shepherds*, he is awarded medals, chairmanships, and honors that celebrate European painting at the end of the century.

The honor that flatters him most was election to the Beaux-Arts Academy, on January 8, 1876, and the loud argument there with Léon Bonnat: "This was the only public honor I ardently wished for!"

Henri Rousseau, who "experienced a profound emotion" in Inspired by *La Source* of the late Ingres, Bouguereau bathes his voluptuous models in a humid atmosphere, sending his most fervent followers into ecstasy. The sensual abandon of Venus's companions in the muscular arms of virile Tritons is crowned by a moving cluster of Cupids, in an evanescent pink, like the nipples of the goddess.

The master, acknowledged as such by most of his students at the Beaux-Arts Academy and at the Julian Academy, where he taught until his death at the age of eighty, had only a single failure, his pupil Henri Matisse. Meticulous, well groomed, clearly careful of his appearance, Bouguereau criticized Matisse mercilessly: "You are wiping your charcoal with your finger? That's what a careless man does. Take a little rag. And start by drawing the lovely plaster casts we have hanging on the

WILLIAM BOUGUEREAU: THE BIRTH OF VENUS. 1876. Paris. Musée d'Orsay

studio walls for your edification. Then you will show your work to an experienced person: He will correct you . . . You still have to learn perspective, but first of all we have to have a pencil for you that will not slip from your fingers.

No, really, you will never be able to draw correctly."

Matisse was made dizzy by the "empty perfection" of such lessons, and was enchanted when Bouguereau threw him out of the studio. He went for advice to Gustave Moreau. Then to Bonnat. It appears that Bonnat thought, "This boy is dangerous; he has to leave here as quickly as possible!"

But now there is so much talk about this Matisse! And many young painters are wondering if the art of the "Pope of the Pompiers," of the conventional artists, will survive his death.

What will come of *Remords d'Oreste, Famille indigente, Nymphes et leurs satyres, Charités, Premier deuil, Idylles enfantines,* or *Jeunesse de Bacchus*?

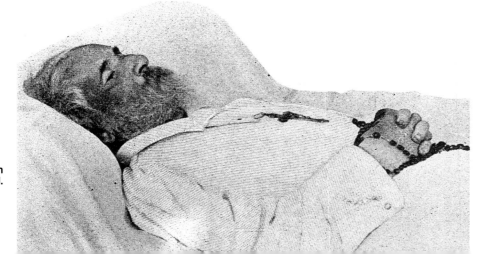

William Bouguereau on his deathbed.

There are visible signs of an evolution in thought. Luncheon on the Grass. scandalously rejected by the Salon of 1863 and considered the first sign of modern art, enters the Louvre. Rodin's formidable The Thinker is installed in front of the Pantheon. The admiration of young painters for Cézanne as a prophet waxes greater with the death of the artist in the Provence. Conservatism yields to the spirit of the search for a daring renewal of inspiration. Gauguin's message has come across: The arts of primitive peoples will regenerate us. Suddenly, African art fascinates the Fauves, as well as Picasso and Braque. For their part, the architects are moving ahead. In Vienna, Adolf Loos kills ornamentation, while Otto Wagner purifies architectural lines.

1906
S U M M A R Y

LITERATURE

GERMANY
Rainer Maria Rilke publishes a collection of poems, the Book of Pictures.
  Gerhart Hauptmann publishes his play And Pipa Dances.

AUSTRIA-HUNGARY
Publication of Young Törless, *a novel by Robert Musil.*

FRANCE
Publication of Propos *by Alain, and of Georges Sorel's* Reflections on Violence, *a very successful book, concerned with anarchistic activities.*

NORWAY
Death of Henrik Ibsen, the great playwright.

SWEDEN
Selma Lagerlöf publishes The Adventures of Niels Holgerson.

MUSIC

FRANCE
Maurice Ravel has completed his Spanish Rhapsody.

MOTION PICTURES

UNITED STATES
J. Stuart Blackton, a pioneer of American cinematography, produces Humorous Phases of a Funny Face, *one of the first films using animation.*

PAUL CÉZANNE:
SELF-PORTRAIT.
1879-1882. Paris.
Musée d'Orsay

THE LAST HOUR OF CÉZANNE

AIX-EN-PROVENCE
In September, Paul Cézanne writes to Émile Bernard, "I am old and sick and I promised myself to die painting . . ." This vow of the master of Aix was fulfilled: He dies on October 22, a victim, at the age of sixty-seven, of his passion for painting.

A few days earlier, a violent storm knocks him down while he is painting *Le Cabanon de*

fascinated by the mountain, and compared himself, in a letter to Vollard, to Moses looking at the Promised Land. He confessed with enthusiasm: "I breathe the virginity of the world. I feel colored by all the shades of the infinite. I am one with my painting. We are a rainbow-colored chaos." A marvelously structured chaos that evokes the admiration of young painters

HE APPROACHES AN ALMOST ABSTRACT RECOMPOSITION OF NATURE

Jourdan in his beloved countryside near Aix; he is carried home in a laundryman's cart. The next day he decides to resume the portrait of his gardener, Vallier. It is the last painting he works on. He is exhausted by the effort, and lies down again. He finds the stamina to write a last letter to his supplier. He orders "burnt lake."

He is buried in the cemetery of Aix. Mount Sainte-Victoire is visible. It had haunted the painter, who wanted to "penetrate its geologic foundations." He was

like the Fauves, Picasso, Braque, and Matisse. But it upset some art critics, like Camille Mauclair. "The name of Cézanne," he said, "will remain attached to the most memorable joke in the art of these last fifteen years." Actually, Cézanne confided to one of his young admirers, "Perhaps I came too soon; I was a painter of your generation rather than of mine." What was his boldness? How did he go beyond the Impressionism of his friends, Monet, Renoir, Pissarro, and Guillaumin, whom he joined in

PAUL CÉZANNE: THE GARDENER. 1906. Zurich. Fondation Buhrle

PAUL CÉZANNE: LE CABANON DE JOURDAN. 1906. Basel. Kunstmuseum

admiring Manet? Cézanne had come up, hirsute and wild, from the South, to meet his friends in the Café Guerbois on the Avenue de Clichy or in the restaurant Nouvelle Athènes.

The originality of the "Cézanne vision" comes from one of his statements: "For us humans, nature exists more inside than on the surface." Paul Gauguin, whom Cézanne blamed for having "stolen his little sensation," said of him, "A man of the South, he spends entire days on the summit of the mountain reading Virgil and looking at the sky. His horizons are thus high, his blues are very intense, and his reds vibrate stunningly."

Nothing made Cézanne more sarcastic than what he called "flat painting." Trying to make his vibrant colors more powerful by matching them with "constructive touches," he went to work in the countryside. In 1883, when he was painting the seashore at Estaque, he came to understand that the rhythm of modulations had to be organized geometrically, "like a playing card," he would say to Pissarro. He gradually treated his landscapes, his still lifes, his male and female "bathers" and his portraits in layers, to the point where the art critic Gustave Geoffroy saw in them, in his analysis written for *Vie artistique,* "the intoxication of a man who tries to reproduce the feeling within the restricted space of his canvases."

Cézanne saw in art "a harmony paralleling nature." He pushes this idea of painting to its extreme. During his last period, he approaches an almost abstract recomposition of nature. This message is being considered by some young painters who might well want to put it into practice. When Cézanne said, "I think of the landscape inside myself, and I am its conscience," it was no doubt because he was the opposite of a theoretician, the head of a school. He was a misanthrope, with only one passion: painting. He said to his son Paul that a formula is perfect only when it is "adequate to the character and grandeur of the subject being interpreted."

Profoundly moved by Mount Sainte-Victoire, he preferred to capture it at the end of the day, when the sun puts its "intelligent smile" on its wild slopes and its inaccessible summit. That was the "hour of Cézanne," the hour of his happiness.

(See also 1904.)

IN CÉZANNE'S WORDS

You surely know that there is only one painter in the world, and it's me . . .

The tints are the strength of a painting.

There is one minute of that world that passes! To paint it in its reality! and forget everything for that.

I am the pioneer of the artistic route that I have discovered.

When color reaches its greatest richness, form reaches its plenitude.

In art everything is theory, developed and applied in contact with nature.

Will I arrive at the goal I have sought and pursued for so long? . . . I thus continue my studies . . . I always study with nature, and I seem to progress so slowly.

For the artist, to see is to conceive, and to conceive is to compose.

For the artist is not aware of his emotions, the way the bird modulates his sounds: He composes!

One does not paint souls, one paints bodies . . .

Paul Cézanne with his painting *The Great Bathers.*

The coloring feelings that give light are causes of abstractions that do not allow me to cover my canvas or to pursue the outlining of objects—the contact points are tenuous and delicate, and it follows that my painting stays incomplete.

As a painter, I become more lucid facing nature, but at home, the concretization of my feelings is always very painful . . . Here, near the river, the motives are manifold, the same subject seen under a different angle becomes a study object of the most intense interest and so variable that I believe I could be kept busy for months without changing my place, just by leaning down sometimes more to the right, sometimes more to the left.

There is a color logic . . . The painter must obey it and nothing else.

Never the brain's logic; if he succumbs to it, he is lost. Always the logic of the eyes. If he feels correctly, he will think correctly.

Painting is, first of all, optical. That's where the material of our art is: in what our eyes think. Nature, when we respect her, always tells us what she means.

We are an iridescent chaos.

Nature must be treated through the cylinder, the sphere, the cone, the whole placed in perspective.

FOUR AMERICANS IN PARIS

PARIS

Gertrude Stein and her brothers, Leo and Michael, and Michael's wife, Sarah, settle on the Rue de Fleurus and the Rue Madame. Their salons are frequented by all the painters in Paris and by poets and writers from Europe and America.

Last year, they began supporting French artists: Michael and Sarah concentrate almost exclusively on Henri Matisse. Leo and Gertrude at first buy the splendid portrait of *Madame Cézanne in an Armchair* by Paul Cézanne, then a canvas by Matisse, *The Woman with a Hat,* which was quite a sensation at the Salon d'Automne last year.

Every American visiting Paris owes it to himself to visit the Steins. There one may meet Matisse and his wife, Picasso and Fernande Olivier, and so

many others. Gertrude Stein introduces Picasso to Matisse. The Steins return to San Francisco, California, after the earthquake and the great fire that ravages the city on April 18 and 19: They carry with them the first works by Matisse ever seen in the United States.

The Stein's collection is enriched with Picasso's portrait of Gertrude. She poses more than eighty times. She takes the bus at the Odeon, she travels across Paris to the icy studio in the Bateau-Lavoir. Picasso paints while Fernande reads the fables of La Fontaine aloud. In the spring, he erases the face because he is not satisfied with it. It was only in the autumn, upon his return from Gosal, that in Gertrude's absence he paints the final portrait—of which, it is said, she is very fond. It is inspired by African art and by Spanish sculpture.

PABLO PICASSO:
PORTRAIT OF GERTRUDE STEIN. 1906.
New York. Metropolitan Museum of Art

A FAUVE ON THE HILL

MONTMARTRE

The twenty-nine-year-old Dutch painter Kees Van Dongen, recently threw in his lot with Fauvism with great enthusiasm. He seems to be less interested in the views on the shores of the Seine or in the landscape around Collioure than in the human figure, more specifically women's faces.

His recent move is doubtlessly made for a reason. Having lived in Paris since 1897, he moves from Girardon, a blind alley where he lived with his wife, Gus, and their daughter, Dolly, to 13 Rue de Ravignan, that well-known set of wobbly studios known among artists as the Bateau-Lavoir. He is Picasso's neighbor and makes use of the opportunity to paint the portrait of the lovely Fernande Olivier, Picasso's companion.

His new portraits are remark-

KEES VAN DONGEN: PORTRAIT OF MADEMOISELLE BORDENAVE. 1905. Private Collection

ably different from his previous portraits. His painting of Marie Krall, of the Antoine Theater, prompts the critic Louis Vauxcelles to note its intense treatment and somber manner. In the *Portrait of Mademoiselle Bordenave,* there are no more cheeks scarred with yellow, green, vermilion, or Prussian blue, no more jet-black hair or immense eyes and a harshly outlined mouth. It is true that the *Woman with a Hat,* which Matisse showed in last year's Salon d'Automne, set the stage. Van Dongen pushes harsh sensuality even further.

After his arrival in Paris from Delfshaven, near Rotterdam, where he was born in 1877, Van Dongen does seemingly everything: a strongman at Les Halles, house painter, sketch artist on café terraces, caricaturist for satirical papers. His portraits are beginning to attract customers. The fact that his neighbor Pablo Picasso admires the portrait of Olivier is of no small importance.

AFRICAN ART CASTS A SPELL ON ARTISTS

PARIS

A new passion has conquered the world of the young artists who are always ready to admire primitive values. The passion is African art. It is almost everywhere in Paris—in the museum at the Trocadero, where Dr. Hamy assembles large collections, in the Vieux Rouet, and in Father Heymann's store, the main supplier, which collectors have nicknamed "the slave trade on the Rue de Rennes." The doors of studios are open to receive statuettes, masks, and fetishes, which the painters and sculptors treat like idols and show to one another secretly. They see in African art the beginning of an answer to their own questions.

Who started this fad? Vlaminck asserts that he was the first to receive the revelation of African statuary. But it was Paul Gauguin, who was captivated by Oceanian art, who paved the way, as is demonstrated by the retrospective of his work at the current Salon d'Automne. In one moment he assimilated everything that modern creators can take from their far-away inspiration. It is said that Derain became convinced of the importance of primitive art when he saw the Gauguin collection; he is in love with African art.

Matisse discovers African sculpture with his friends Vlaminck and Derain. It has a more profound effect on the leader of the Fauves than on his two friends. In several of Matisse's recent works the religious tradition of African art and its purity of line respond to the development of his formal search.

On the other hand, Picasso is sensitive to the supernatural in these statuettes. Initially, they seem to him to be just "fetishes." It is said that he fell under their spell one evening when he was invited, with Matisse, to Gertrude Stein's for dinner at the Rue de Fleurus. Matisse brought along a small statue that had particularly struck him that afternoon in Heymann's store. Picasso did not take his eyes off it all evening. The next day, the poet André Salmon visited him at the Bateau-Lavoir and saw several drawings on the floor that he had made during the night—they were based on the model of the statue that had fascinated him so.

The final extensions of Impressionism—Postimpressionism, Cézanne—have demonstrated the desire of avant-garde artists to go further in the search for artistic renewal. With the entrance on the scene of African art, a break seems to have occurred that would take them even further away from the traditional art of the past.

(See also 1984.)

GREBO MASK.
Paris. Musée Picasso

73

THE RUSSIANS AT THE SALON D'AUTOMNE

PARIS

Twelve rooms in the Grand Palais decorated by Léon Bakst are placed at the disposal of fifty-three Russian artists for the Salon d'Automne. The collection is gigantic: Seven hundred and fifty works are shown. Sergei de Diaghilev made the selection.

The St. Petersburg painters, led by Alexander Benois, concentrate on the exaltation of the past or on theater decor. The art of the Muscovites (Grabar's landscapes, Maliavin's portraits of peasant girls) is more colorful. A specially promising talent is shown by Mikhail Larionov. He is only twenty-five years old and has participated in all avantgarde events in Moscow since 1900. His 1905 *Landscape* shows the obvious influence of the Fauves in the use of a range of pure colors.

Parisian critics are not enthusiastic over this Russian art. But they acknowledge the greatness of Vroubel, for whom an entire room has been reserved. Somov also has an entire room.

Vroubel has been in a sanitarium for four years. He is fifty years old. He mixes reality with fantasy and gives life and flesh to his visions.

MIKHAIL LARIONOV: LANDSCAPE. 1905. Paris. MNAM

Dedication of *The Thinker* by Rodin in front of the Pantheon.

"THE THINKER" BEFORE THE PANTHEON

PARIS

A surprising, mundane ceremony is held: Madame Segond-Weber, whose white peplum flies around her under the impulse of her grandiloquent gestures, recites a poem by Victor Hugo. On April 21, Rodin's *The Thinker* is enthroned in front of the columns of the Pantheon in the presence of the artist, who is visibly moved. The statue he designed for the center of the lintel of his *Gates of Hell* symbolizes the poet's power of concentration: the creator thinking of his work. It was shown for the first time to the International Society of London two years ago, when it was enlarged in plaster. It was so denigrated by critics that the author Gabriel Mourey decided to launch a public subscription in protest. It brought in 15,000 francs and made it possible to offer the bronze casting to Paris. Few on the municipal council approve of the inauguration. One of the councilmen, Monsieur Lampué, is disgusted, and protests against "this Pithecanthropus who dishonors the noble portico of our national Pantheon." The obstinate *Thinker* is not revolutionary. He is reminiscent of the statues of *Lorenzo de Medici* and *Moses* by Michelangelo.

Death of a Martyr Painter

Half paralyzed, incapable of speaking after an operation for throat cancer, Eugène Carrière could communicate only in writing with his loved ones. To a friend who came to wish him a happy New Year, he responded by drawing a coffin. He died on March 27, surrounded by his family. Of his sober palette and his domestic subject matter showing dimly lit interiors, the frightful Degas had said: "Well! They've been smoking in the children's room again!" Yet this was a grand artist with a fine soul and a work of infinite sensitivity, who was falsely categorized by the public and by critics as one of the presumptuous "Pompier" painters.

A Soul beneath the Vault of the Grand Palais

An unexpected discovery at the Salon d'Automne where the largest exhibition of Russian art to have been seen as yet in Paris is being presented: the tempera paintings on cardboard by the Lithuanian painter Mikhalous Ciurlionis. Born in Vilnyus in 1875, Ciurlionis is convinced of the omnipotence of the soul. He paints fantastic architecture and musical impressions situated at the limits of abstraction and Symbolism. A peculiar characteristic of Ciurlionis' work is that his favorite tonalities are the same ones described by the philosopher Rudolf Steiner in his book *Theosophy,* published two years ago in Berlin, as being constituent elements in the aura of spiritually receptive beings. He has just begun a series of works devoted to the signs of the zodiac.

Picasso in a Panic over Typhoid Fever

Pablo Picasso and his beautiful, opulent companion, Fernande Olivier, put an abrupt end to their summer stay in Gosol, an eagle's nest in the heart of the Pyrenees, accessible only on muleback. The cause of their brusque departure: a case of typhoid fever contracted by the daughter of the innkeeper at whose place they are staying. Picasso had gone to Gosol on a sort of pilgrimage to the source after two years of Parisian life, sharing the simple life of the peasants and drawing their rough features. But illness has always panicked him, and so Fernande and he return to their home in the Bateau-Lavoir at the beginning of August, completely exhausted.

The First Modern Painting Enters the Louvre

An outstanding donation! With the accord of his children, the great collector of Impressionist painting Étienne Moreau-Nélaton has decided to make a gift of thirty pieces to the State. These will be temporarily placed in the Museum of Decorative Arts. Painter, historian of Corot, Daubigny, Delacroix, Fantin-Latour, Millet, and Manet, whose catalogue of engravings he publishes this year, the generous, forty-seven-year-old donor above all merits praise for serving the French on a silver platter the famous *Luncheon on the Grass* they so deplored just a short time before. The hue and cry raised by Édouard Manet's painting in 1863 at the Salon des Refusés is already nothing more than a bad memory. With its Realist openness, it is now considered one of the principal masterpieces prophesying modern art.

Juan Gris Moves to the Bateau-Lavoir

Sixteen francs! With 16 francs in his pocket, José Vitoriano Gonzáles, called Juan Gris—nineteen years old—has realized his dream: He has found a place to live in Paris, where he arrived at the end of September from Madrid. His sister, Antonieta, helped him with his plan. They sold all they owned, including José Vitoriano's bed and mattress, so that they could pay for the train ticket. The increasing fame of his compatriot Picasso drew Gris to the Bateau-Lavoir on the Rue de Ravignan where he has found a place to live. He makes the rounds of the editing offices of illustrated papers hoping to sell his drawings, but without much success. On the walls of his studio: columns of figures scrawled in charcoal. This is how he keeps an account of how much he owes his grocer, who agrees to feed him on credit.

IN BRIEF...

GERMANY
Curt Hermann organizes a Neoimpressionist section at the Secession show.
   Edvard Munch designs the sets for Ibsen's Ghosts.
   In Cologne, the architect Peter Behrens builds the concert hall of the Gardens of Flora.

UNITED STATES
The great American Impressionist Childe Hassam is awarded the Carnegie prize.
   Major architects are commissioned to build churches: Unity Church in Oak Park, Illinois, is built by F. L. Wright, and Goodhue begins the construction of St. Thomas in New York.
   Lyonel Feininger creates a series of comic strips for the Chicago Sunday Times.

FRANCE
The dealer Ambroise Vollard buys all of Maurice de Vlaminck's paintings.

RUSSIA
Exhibition of works by Alexei von Jawlensky, organized by Serge de Diaghilev.

ÉDOUARD MANET: LUNCHEON ON THE GRASS. 1862. Paris. Musée d'Orsay

ADOLF LOOS: ORNAMENT IS A CRIME

Adolf Loos, born in 1870, is unquestionably a talented architect, but he is disliked in Vienna. It is true that it is his own fault. In 1898, in the Secessionist magazine *Ver Sacrum,* he attacked vehemently the academic style of the buildings of Vienna's circular boulevard, the famous Ring. A little later, he expressed his disagreement with the spirit of Secession. Today, concerned with severity and rationality in furniture design, he denounces ornamentation. The following excerpt is from his *Wohnungswanderungen,* a work to which he has just put the finishing touches and for which he seeks a publisher. Relying on self-promotion, proudly remaining outside of any group, he invites the public to visit houses that were furnished or decorated according to his advice.

MACKINTOSH:
CHAIR. 1901. England

For two years, there has been talk about bankruptcy of modern interior decoration. Some consider a return to older styles. And as remedy, the Biedermeier is prescribed.

In Germany, the modern movement is called Jugendstil. We call it Secession. Both designations have become terms of insult.

Nearly ten years ago, in a series of articles, I warned against these styles. I said one should furnish one's home neither in one of the old styles nor in one of these new ones, but in a truly modern way.

At the time, I was expressing a minority opinion. A small minority: I was in fact a minority of one.

Our modern creations were treated with contempt, by artists as well as by the authorities. I suggested that it was not really necessary to elaborate the style principles of our time since we already have this style. Our machines, our clothing, our carriages and their horses, our glass and metal objects, and everything, everything that has escaped the architects' sabotage is modern. As for woodwork, it has had to be supplied to architects on a contract basis for the last fifty years. But it was a worthwhile effort to keep woodwork away from the fancy goods so favored by architects.

Nothing prevented us from setting up modern interior decorating. The path to it was simple. Certain objects made by carpenters, and those who worked with wood, had escaped the architect. It was merely a matter of gathering them and using their shapes for similar purposes. To serve cigars, there are the boxes paraded by bellboys in Viennese restaurants. There are ice-cream containers for everything that is "pastry with ice cream" in the cafés. In stores, glass show-cases serve as furniture. Metal trimmings intended for locks are also used in the manufacturing of trunks.

We had cabinet work that was modern. But something that required the help of architects was absent, namely, ornamentation. Since older furniture had ornaments and profiles that were cut and inlaid, and since the modern woodworker was incapable of designing any, the architect took advantage of him. The woodworker's lack of ability can be explained by the fact that he is a modern man. The architect, on the other hand, is capable because he is not modern. The modern man, as I already suggested ten years ago, is no longer able to produce an ornament. The products of our modern culture offer no ornaments. Trunk manufacturers, leather workers, tailors, and machine manufacturers don't know about ornament.

What makes our culture grand is its inability to create new ornaments. The evolution of humanity goes hand in hand with the ordinary object's moving away from embellishment. Our artists working in applied arts may object as much as they want: for civilized humans, a nontatooed face is more beautiful than a tatooed one, even if the tatoo were done by Kolo Moser.

ADOLF LOOS
Wohnungswanderungen
(Excerpt)

PERRET REVEALS CONCRETE

PARIS

How to build a garage? By erecting a building as revolutionary as cars are to carriages! It appears that this is the idea for the garage at 51 Rue de Ponthieu being completed by Auguste Perret. The façade reveals a reinforced concrete skeleton. What a consecration of the material invented in 1867 by Georges Monnier, who used it at first to make flower boxes. It must be pointed out that the business of Auguste Perret's father was one of the earliest to turn to concrete.

This is not Perret's first use of the material. He made a building at 25 bis Rue Franklin with a concrete structure covered with sandstone elements. In the builder's garage at Rue Ponthieu, the façade is not a support as in traditional structures, but itself is supported by columns, allowing glass bays to fill the whole surface. The columns rise from the ground to a slender slab that juts out at the top like a cornice. The row of small windows at the top floor resembles a frieze.

The large glass surface illuminates the central passageway of the garage. Due to the lightness of the beams and the concrete poles, the interior is almost as light and as open as if the building were of metal. To facilitate the arrangement of cars and to avoid right-angle parking, the partitions on the ground floor are angled rather than perpendicular to the walls. Cars reach upper floors on an ingenious system of elevators and movable platforms. So much sophistication for something that, after all, is only a garage? Let it be remembered that cars have been exhibited in the Grand Palais like works of art since 1901.

Auguste Perret: garage at 51 Rue de Ponthieu, Paris.

WAGNER STRIPS ARCHITECTURE

Otto Wagner: interior of the Savings Bank in Vienna.

VIENNA

No more embellishments and volutes! A fifty-five-year-old architect, Otto Wagner, is sweeping out the historicist tradition to which he belonged. He now exposes the façades of the new Postal Savings Bank and clothes them with—modernity. Located near the Ring, the sumptuous boulevard of the city's upper classes, the building surprises the onlooker with its simple volume and large, clean surfaces. But the building does not lack the monumentality appropriate to its function.

The recent Wagnerian method of attaching large marble plaques with aluminum nails to a simple brick construction adds an esthetic effect to speed and economy in building. "What is not practical can never be beautiful" is a saying to Otto Wagner's liking. The dispatch office of the daily *Die Zeit* has already proved that the functional orientation of the building, defined according to the exigencies of the times, cannot be hidden any longer behind architecture that clings to tradition. Functionality has now become style!

Who can cavil that the nails, an original decoration in the façade, have no real constructive function? This architect, enamored of modernity, uses the symbolic meaning of new materials and recent technologies to create a modern architectural language. The summit of his art is attained in the banking floor, where glass and aluminum predominate. From the delicate vaulted glasswork reflected in the lighted floor panels, to the aluminum revetment of the pillars and the totemic heating columns, everything is sheer technical elegance combined with artistic sensitivity.

What could be a better image for the Savings Bank than that of effectiveness and sober wealth, enhanced by the accents of the future?

From the noisy Bateau-Lavoir in Montmartre comes a jolt of energy when twenty-six-year-old Pablo Picasso paints Les demoiselles d'Avignon, *a difficult canvas of large dimensions that seems destined to chart the course of the future. At the same time in Vienna, Gustav Klimt paints his most famous picture,* Danae, *pushing tradition to the limits of its possibilities for renewal. Primitivism, with its robust health and bluntness, counters the refinements of art and psychoanalysis. Picasso is probably more revolutionary than Klimt, who is nineteen years his senior. But perhaps the painting of the past has not had its final say.*

1907

S U M M A R Y

AVANT-GARDE

Les demoiselles d'Avignon: Picasso's Shot
Picasso Subjugated by Fetishes
Reporting from the Museum at the Trocadero

MASTERWORKS

The Irradiations of Gustav Klimt

ART NEWS

Duchamp Gets the Jokers on His Side
Berthe Weill's Troubles
The Engraved Works of Beardsley
The Dreamlike Vision of Henri Rousseau
Did Her Picture Kill Paula Modersohn-Becker?
In Brief

SCULPTURE

A Shout in the Studio
Derain's Cubic Man

ARCHITECTURE

Olbrich: the Marriage Tower

LITERATURE

UNITED STATES
Jack London becomes a celebrity with the publication of White Fang.
William James publishes Pragmatism.

FRANCE
Publication of two important books: Henri Bergson's Creative Evolution *and Léon Blum's controversial* About Marriage.

SWEDEN
Rudyard Kipling is awarded the Nobel prize in literature.

MUSIC

UNITED STATES
Gustav Mahler becomes director of the New York Metropolitan Opera.

FRANCE
Premiere of Histoires naturelles *by Maurice Ravel.*

NORWAY
Edvard Grieg dies in Bergen. His best-known works are Norwegian Dances *and* Peer Gynt.

THEATER

IRELAND
J. M. Synge's The Playboy of the Western World *is performed at the Abbey Theater in Dublin and causes a riot.*

POLAND
Performance of The Judges *by the painter and playwright Stanislaw Wyspianski.*

MOTION PICTURES

FRANCE
Georges Méliès produces Twenty Thousand Leagues under the Sea, *from Jules Verne's work, while Max Linder produces* Skating.

PABLO PICASSO:
LES DEMOISELLES D'AVIGNON.
1907. New York. MOMA

PABLO PICASSO: STUDY FOR LES DEMOISELLES D'AVIGNON. 1907. Philadelphia. Museum of Art

JEAN-DOMINIQUE INGRES:
THE TURKISH BATH. 1862.
Paris. Louvre

"LES DEMOISELLES D'AVIGNON":
PICASSO'S SHOT

PARIS

His suicide seems inevitable. At night, he is alone and distressed in the streets of Montmartre. His friends say that they would not be at all surprised to find him one fine morning hanging from his easel next to his impossible painting—from the window of his studio.

"It's as if you wanted to feed us scraps and give us gasoline to drink to make us spit fire!" That is what Braque would say after seeing the painting. Matisse demands revenge, because its maker, the twenty-six-year-old Pablo Picasso, still living at the Bateau-Lavoir, has dishonored art.

The impossible picture was born of the artist's memory of Barcelona: prostitutes standing at the entrance to a brothel on the Carrera d'Avinyo, a hot street in the Barrio Gotico, a mere stone's throw from where

he lived. Thence its title: *Les demoiselles d'Avignon.*

It is its overall brutality that evokes the condemnation of Braque and Matisse and even of the poet Guillaume Apollinaire, who has been the spokesman for and the defender of the painter;

"IT'S AS IF YOU WANTED TO FEED US SCRAPS AND GIVE US GASOLINE TO DRINK TO MAKE US SPIT FIRE!"

Apollinaire calls it "the philosophic brothel" of Picasso, as if the tradition of the masters had been overthrown and turned into derision, as if ancient and modern values had crumbled suddenly, struck dead before our eyes.

Les demoiselles d'Avignon, with its prostitutes who seem to have been sketched with large strokes of a hatchet, with their narrow gaze, their enormous

feet, in fact emits an aura of brutality and savagery quite exceptional in the history of Western art. In his first sketches, Picasso placed in the midst of prostitutes a sailor and a soldier carrying a skull in the outstretched arm. But he feared falling into moralizing symbolism and reduced his composition to the five menacing ghouls who so repel his friends.

The painting was made during two periods of intense work, in February and July, after his discovery of African art in the museum at the Trocadero. Another of its sources seems to be Spanish sculpture, which he saw among the recent acquisitions of the Louvre and from

which he took the hemstitched eyes and the rather heavy jaws. Another influence may have been Gosol, a village in the hot sun above the valley of Andorra, accessible only by mule, where he isolated himself last summer with his companion, Fernande Olivier. He shared the life of the peasants, hunting with them, tramping the mountain trails while listening to their legends. He was inspired to paint figures with undershot jaws, low foreheads, and large flat faces in the shape of diamonds and triangles in copper-covered beige.

The painting seems also to be a response to *The Great Bathers* by Cézanne and even more so to the *Turkish Bath* by Jean-Dominique Ingres shown at the Salon d'Automne two years ago. Picasso wanted to form a contrast. The Ingres was inspired by the hot baths of Adrianople. Amid dreamlike architecture,

PICASSO SUBJUGATED BY FETISHES

Ingres' bathers are goddesses with skin of opaline whiteness. They are covered only by their hair, strewn with pearls and ribbons, which falls on their shoulders. It is the most beautiful case of indiscreet jewels ever.

In *Les demoiselles d'Avignon*, Picasso went from oriental splendor to a brothel in the Barrio Gotico. His naked prostitutes shoot their gaze on the customer and appear as bitter as gasoline. With noses like cheese wedges, large pointed knees, and immense feet, the angular creatures attack the eye like acid.

Why did Picasso go so far in destroying the human figure? The canvases of his admirable blue and pink periods show a world of young pregnant women, gaunt ballerinas, half-starved acrobats, old men in rags, people moving, people walking on roads leading nowhere—they have already alienated the public. Now dislocating the perspective inherited from the Renaissance, he breaks the back of idealization. It is as if his figures were planks in a fence through which the eye fixes the void!

Les demoiselles d'Avignon is a barbarous caricature of the flesh. "That's interesting, my boy, you should be a caricaturist," the famous critic Félix Fénélon, drawn by fame to the Bateau-Lavoir, would have said. It is a painting that breaks totally with the past. It could well open an entirely new path for art.

What will be the fate of this canvas? In view of the lack of his friends' enthusiasm, Picasso has rolled up his work and relegated it to a corner in his studio. There is an exception—the Steins, Gertrude and Leo, like it.

(See also 1904, 1905, 1909, 1912, 1921, 1927, 1937, 1945, 1946, 1948, 1953, 1954, 1958, 1973.)

"One speaks always of the Africans' influence on me. What to do? All of us, we used to love the fetishes. Van Gogh said: Japanese art, we all had it in common. With us, it is the Africans. But they have no more influence on me than on Matisse. Or on Derain. For them, the masks were sculptures like any others. When Matisse showed me his first African head, he talked about Egyptian art.

"When I went to the Trocadero, it was disgusting. A flea market. The odor. I was all alone. I wanted to go away. I did not leave. I stayed. I stayed. I understood that it was very important: Something was happening to me, wasn't it?

The masks! They were not sculptures like the others. Not at all. They were magical things. And why not the Egyptians, the Chaldeans? We did not notice it. They were primitives, not magics. The Africans, they were intercessors, a word that I learned then and have known since that time. Against anything; against unknown, threatening spirits. I was still looking at the fetishes. I understood: Me too, I am against everything. Me too, I think everything is unknown, is the enemy! Everything! Not the details—like women, children, animals, tobacco, gambling . . . But the whole thing! I understood what it was used for, this sculpture, by the Africans. Why sculpt like that and not otherwise. They were not Cubists, however, Cubism did not exist then. Surely some guy had invented the models and some guys had imitated them, tradition, you see. But all these fetishes, they served for the same thing. They were weapons. To help people stop being subjects of the spirits, to become independent. Tools. If we give the spirits a shape, we become independent. Spirits, the subconscious (but that was not yet a subject of conversation), emotion, it's all the same thing. I understood why I was a painter. All alone in this ghastly museum, with masks, red-skinned dolls, dusty mannequins. Les demoiselles d'Avignon must have arrived on that day, but not at all because of the shapes: because it was my first canvas of exorcism, yes!"

Reported by ANDRÉ MALRAUX
in La tête d'obsidienne

PABLO PICASSO: STUDY FOR LES DEMOISELLES D'AVIGNON. 1907. Basel. Galerie Beyeler

REPORTING FROM THE MUSEUM AT THE TROCADERO

PARIS

In spite of the laudable effort of Dr. Hamy, the founder in 1878 of the Ethnographic Museum at the Trocadero, the household and ritual objects and the works of art brought in from the colonies and various scientific missions to America, Africa, and Oceania are not well treated there. The collections are covered with dust and arranged without order or clarity. The boxes in which they arrive are transformed hastily into show cases. But poetry also arises out of this prodigious chaos, from the magical character of weapons, hunting and fishing instruments, jewelry, masks, fetishes. They give an impression of the supernatural. Strange place, this museum. Picasso, looking for renewal, was overwhelmed by it.

THE IRRADIATIONS OF GUSTAV KLIMT

VIENNA

Deprived of a showroom since he left the Secession two years ago, Gustav Klimt intends to take advantage of the opening of new rooms set up by the architect Joseph Hoffmann and participate in the Kunstschau (art show) to be held next year. (Seventy-nine artists, from all schools, will participate.) He will present works that mark the zenith of his painting on a gold background.

This Viennese artist is the son of a craftsman gilder to whom he owes his attraction to the regal effects of this unalterable metal. It fascinated him in the Ravenna mosaics. At forty-six years of age, he has reached maturity with two masterpieces, *The Kiss* and *Danae.*

The paintings are sensual and refined, perfectly expressive of his original artistic method of applying the ornamental tendencies of Art Nouveau to erotic subjects. It is easy to find in his work a certain influence of traditional painters, and also a Symbolism that is Dionysian, Byzantine, and Rococo all at once.

Klimt believes that creators must be redeemers who, delighting in the dramatic powerlessness they share with all mortals, transcend the ephemeral character of amorous fusion to the sublime quenching of desire. Through their creative energy, they connect with the oldest myths of humanity. Perfecting them in art, they resolve their enigma: the infinite power of love. He says that he is moved by an irresistible sympathy for "the sufferings of humanity in all its weakness." It is a compassion that can be compared to that of the mystics for the Passion of Christ. Teresa of Avila said, "The pain is so strong that it makes me groan and is accompanied by so much pleasure that I would like it never to stop."

Danae is a classical theme of Western art, appearing even in Roman art before its revival in the Italian Renaissance. But

GUSTAV KLIMT: DANAE. 1907. Salzburg. Galerie Welz

Klimt's ecstatic *Danae,* who receives the leaven of heaven from the chief god, makes it an entirely new theme.

There is a good reason why the artist chose this myth. It no doubt was recalled to memory by the *Danae* of the academic painter Léon Comerre. Danae, the only daughter of the king of Argos, is locked up by her father in a tower guarded by fierce dogs, because the oracle predicted that he would not have sons and that he would be killed by his grandson. Madly in love with this prisoner, Zeus succeeds in impregnating her by showering

his divine seed over her in the form of a golden rain. She bears a son, Perseus. Gustav Klimt shows her to us wrapped in silken veils, in a contracted fetal position, painfully concentrated but sensuously overcome by divine irradiations. It is a painting that symbolizes the supernatural inspiration the artist must have in order to transmit this *femme fatale* to painting. His is a power of sublimation and fecundity!

By a magnificent play of interlaced gilded scrolls and the juxtaposition of stylized geometric forms that recall Byzantine

mosaics, Klimt was able to express the intertwining and amorous interpenetration of the lovers in *The Kiss.* Abstract symbols amplify the almost sacred mystery through simplification. In this way, he succeeds in giving an eternal dimension to his work, which may appear primitive and religious due to the absence of perspective and the elimination of shadows.

(See also 1918.)

Duchamp Gets the Jokers on His Side

Marcel Duchamp starts off well at the age of twenty at the first Salon des Humoristes. The Salon was created by Félix Juven, editor of the magazine *Le rire*, and its preview took place on May 25 at the Palais de Glace. Young Marcel exhibits five drawings there, and one of them, *Les toiles de X*, charms the public with its caption: "They aren't even good enough to f . . . in the bathroom." As if everyone were delighted that art had turned into a form of derision.

Berthe Weill's Troubles

Matisse is beginning to make a name for himself; Dufy is doing so very slowly; for Derain and Vlaminck, times are still hard. The group, exhibited two or three times a year now by Berthe Weill in her gallery on the Rue Victor Massé, gives her many worries. The artists themselves are not always tolerant. "Oh, no! We want nothing to do with that little young man who keeps trying to sneak in with us. Put him in the next room if you want him here," thundered Matisse on the subject of Dufy the year before. Still more unpleasant, the partisans of tradition come into the gallery to insult Berthe Weill, and sometimes threaten her with their fists.

AUBREY BEARDSLEY: WOMAN IN THE MOON. 1894

The Engraved Works of Beardsley

Nine years after his death, Aubrey Beardsley is given the honors of the gallery Shirleys in Paris, where his engraved works are presented. Considered "decadent" and very "fin de siècle," he quickly gained international renown, and decisively influenced the development of Art Nouveau. At the end of his brief life—Beardsley died of tuberculosis in 1898 at the age of twenty-six—his highly stylized technique became more Rococo, notably in his illustration of *The Rape of the Lock* by Pope, as can be noted here.

HENRI ROUSSEAU: THE SNAKE CHARMER. 1907. Paris. Musée d'Orsay

The Dreamlike Vision of Henri Rousseau

On a chair next to his large painting *The Snake Charmer*, which he exhibits at the Fifth Salon d'Automne from September 30 to October 22, a sad Henri Rousseau keeps watch over his mysterious composition, commissioned by Robert Delaunay's mother on her return from a trip to India. Frantz Jourdain, president of the Salon, in fact has relegated Rousseau to a small area dedicated to the decorative arts, where he sits behind a curtain. "Poor, naive Henri, whom they wanted to make famous two years ago, is now relegated to the wine cellar," writes the critic Arsène Alexandre in *Le Figaro*.

Did Her Picture Kill Paula Modersohn-Becker?

Born in Dresden in 1876, Paula Modersohn-Becker, the wife of the painter Otto Modersohn, was known in French art circles for having attended classes at the Beaux-Arts Academy in Paris. A friend of Cézanne, Gauguin, and Sérusier, she wanted to overcome the Impressionist heritage she found in her work. Among her last paintings is *Mother and Child*, in which she rediscovers almost archaic ways of expressing the simple joy of motherhood. A cruel irony of fate, Paula Modersohn-Becker died on November 21, after the birth of her child.

A SHOUT IN THE STUDIO

HENRI MATISSE:
RECLINING NUDE I. 1907

PARIS

A shout in the studio! And drama! History does not say that it concerns the *Reclining Nude I*, Henri Matisse's largest piece of the last two years, but the fact is that one of his sculptures falls down with the clay still fresh. The collapse smashes the head and the arm. Fortunately, the accident is not beyond repair. While Matisse is "choked by the accident," the damage is found to be less serious than thought and it is repaired within a day.

The great Fauve liked to say that he "uses clay to rest from painting." But if sculpture is simply a relaxation, would his feeling be so intense that he has to walk the banks of the Seine to calm down? The influence of Rodin on Matisse the sculptor seems at least equal to that of Cézanne on Matisse the painter, for Matisse seeks in sculpture the relationships of masses and in his painting he finds light from the relationships of colors.

Michelangelo said that a statue is beautiful only if it is thrown down a mountain and reaches the bottom undamaged. Does Matisse know this celebrated remark? Perhaps this is the unconscious reason for his dismay. For, like Michelangelo, he wants his art to be characterized primarily by the solidity of its form, its monumentality.

DERAIN'S CUBIC MAN

PARIS

André Derain leaves Chatou and moves to 22 Rue de Tourlaque in Montmartre. He visits Picasso and the whole art colony in the Bateau-Lavoir. He is one of the most important painters of this generation. The art dealer Daniel-Henry Kahnweiler makes a contract with him. Derain now tries his hand at sculpture. *Sitting Man* belongs to a series of figures cut from the same stone. The sober sculptures emphasize the search for volume simplified to the extreme and powerfully defined. This is similar to the present preoccupation in painting. They also evoke African art. It is evident they are inspired by it. Under the direct influence of primitive art, with which he and others have been familiar for a year, he is directing himself to an intellectual path. In the artist's studio are enormous blocks in the process of being trimmed. What esthetic surprise is the artist preparing?

ANDRÉ DERAIN: SITTING MAN. 1907. Front and back

OLBRICH: THE MARRIAGE TOWER

DARMSTADT

Nuptial box or marriage tower 160 feet high? The dignitaries of the Grand Duchy of Hesse-Darmstadt have decided, after difficult bargaining, that it is a marriage tower. The decision is made easier by the fact that the architect, Joseph Maria Olbrich, waived his fee.

The tower was the ardent wish of the person whose marriage on February 5, 1905, it commemorates and who receives it as a gift: His Highness Ernst-Ludwig, Grand Duke of Hesse and close friend of Olbrich. "It must rise above the city, visible from afar," he is said to have stated, raising his hand as if taking an oath when he learns of the happy decision. It is even reported in the *Darmstädter Tagblatt* that the gesture inspires Olbrich to shape his roof of greenish copper into five fingers symbolizing the union of the Grand Duke.

After fifteen months, the tower will be finished and inaugurated next May. It is already rising above the Matildenhöhe, where it crowns the new city of artists promoted by the Grand Duke, who wants to adorn his capital with flourishing arts, celebrating the glory of his reign.

When the then thirty-two-year-old Olbrich was summoned in 1899, Vienna lost the former assistant of Otto Wagner, one of the creators of the Jugendstil and the genial builder of the pavilion of the Secession. But in Darmstadt, where a strong bond of friendship soon united Olbrich and the Grand Duke, the Duke allowed the architect to realize his dream: creating on virgin terrain a whole world planned to the last detail, where "streets, gardens, tables, easy chairs, chandeliers, spoons" would all be made in the same spirit.

The Grand Duke has made the artists' city of Darmstadt into a little island of gaiety and charm, where each house is a complete work of art, individualized according to the sensibility of the occupants. There are seven houses in all. One was designed by Peter Behrens. It neighbors the Ernst Ludwig House, a one-story building that contains a meeting room and the studios.

The marriage tower is Olbrich's most recent and most personal work. He is the "poet among architects," according to Otto Wagner's formula of praise. While the individual houses of the artists' city are still under the sign of the Jugendstil, the tower grandly rises in its vertical mass, in contrast with the horizontal Ernst Ludwig House. It is made of brick and stone, very simple, without functional mawkishness, thanks to the architect's inexhaustible imagination.

Joseph Maria Olbrich: Marriage Tower in Darmstadt.

The marriage tower will not be used as a residence but as the commemoration of the ducal couple and the town. When he was summoned by the Grand Duke, Olbrich was accused of favoritism and rejected as a foreigner. But since then, things have changed: He is flattered by the residents of Darmstadt. They are proud of the gift that promises to be a monument—a viewing point and a modern example of architecture.

Louis Vauxcelles, critic for Gil Blas, gives Cubism a birth certificate, baptizing the new school and its break with the rules of art that had been laid down in the Renaissance. Picasso had made the first breakthrough the year before with Les demoiselles d'Avignon. *Now Braque, rejected by the Salon d'Automne, takes up the challenge in his exhibition at the Kahnweiler gallery. In an important article, Matisse explains his concept of color, while Worringer discourses on abstraction. Henri Rousseau is welcomed by the avant-garde at the Bateau-Lavoir. As the century gets under way, Paris has established itself as the capital of modern art.*

1908

SUMMARY

LITERATURE

SPAIN
Publication of Blood and Soul *by Blasco Ibañez.*

FRANCE
Guillaume Apollinaire publishes L'enchanteur pourrissant, *with wood engravings by Derain.*

GREAT BRITAIN
G. K. Chesterton publishes his novel The Man Who Was Thursday.

ITALY
Maxim Gorki, living in exile on Capri, publishes Mother.

SWITZERLAND
Robert Walser publishes The Institute Benjamenta, *in German.*

MUSIC

FRANCE
In Paris, staging of Boris Godunov *by Modest Mussorgsky, produced by Sergei de Diaghilev, with a brilliant performance by Feodor Chaliapine.*
   Florent Schmitt composes Quintet for Piano and Strings.

RUSSIA
Stravinsky, having just completed his Fireworks, *meets Sergei de Diaghilev.*

GEORGES BRAQUE:
HOUSES AT L'ESTAQUE. 1908.
Bern. Kunstmuseum

Georges Braque playing the concertina in his studio.

GEORGES BRAQUE:
BATHING WOMAN. 1907-1908.
Private Collection

GEORGES BRAQUE'S GREAT BREACH

PARIS

The six paintings sent by twenty-six-year-old Georges Braque to the Salon d'Automne, are all refused. Matisse and Guérin are on the jury and are permitted to disregard the decision for one painting. They "fished out" two, but the offended artist withdrew all six of his paintings.

When the Salon d'Automne was created five years ago by the architect Frantz Jourdain, the painter Georges d'Espagnat, and the *Mercure de France* critic Ivanohé Rambosson, its purpose was both to render homage to the great artists rejected at the end of the century and to give young artists a place to exhibit. Henri de Toulouse-Lautrec, Auguste Renoir, and Odilon Redon each had a retrospective of some thirty paintings there in 1904. Cézanne had two exhibitions, in 1904 and last year. They were so striking that they have already modified the path of young painters. Fauvism was born there three years ago amidst sarcasms. Have we returned to the blindness of the Salon that officially refused Manet's *Luncheon on the Grass* in 1863?

The Braques baffled everyone. The canvases bear no resemblance to Fauvism. They are somewhat like Cézanne's closely intertwined cubes, cones, and cylinders.

Could it be the realization of Cézanne's greatness that Braque spends the summer in Estaque, near Marseille, where the master of Aix created some of his most astonishing works? Among the refused paintings are his *Houses at l'Estaque* reduced to hieratic volumes of ocher paint that leave no doubt as to their origin. Another influence on Braque is Picasso's *Les demoiselles d'Avignon*, even though he was horrified by the "hacked-up" women when he discovered them last year at the Bateau-Lavoir. But he was also deeply moved, and he soon made a large *Nude*, also among the refused works.

The paintings are seen in November, together with other Braques, at the Kahnweiler gallery, a boutique measuring 13 x 13 feet, at 28 Rue Vignon, in the Madeleine neighborhood.

Daniel-Henry Kahnweiler opened his gallery a year and a half ago. He is the son of a family of German-Jewish bankers who destined him for the stock exchange, in his words "a profession as stupid as they come." His intention is to " . . . let the public admire painters it doesn't know and for whom one must open a path." Shaken by *Demoiselles* when he saw it in Picasso's studio, Kahnweiler visits Braque a little before he leaves for Estaque. He is shocked by the attitude of the jury at the Salon d'Automne and proposes an exhibition to the painter. Kahnweiler entrusts the foreword of the catalogue to Guillaume Apollinaire, who is known for supporting avant-garde painting. He is abundant with praise: "Here is Georges Braque. He leads an admirable life. He passionately strives toward beauty, and he reaches it seemingly without effort . . . His spirit willingly caused the sunset of reality, and here he is, plastically creating a universal renewal, in himself and around himself." Under the dithyramb of this literary genre, Apollinaire reaches the core of things. As much as Picasso is a torn Spaniard bearing the tragic sense of life inside himself, the Frenchman Braque is measured and well-balanced. Born in Havre, the son of an artisan, he loves "good workmanship" and the "well-done." He lives on the Rue Lepic, in Montmartre, but is not a bohemian. He is a kind of "controller" who, rather than dismantling the visible, prefers to reconstruct it geometrically and rhythmically.

Matisse, asked by the critic Louis Vauxcelles what the works refused by the Salon d'Automne look like, answers, "Braque sent a painting made out of little cubes." To make himself understood properly, Matisse draws on a piece of paper, in a few seconds, two cubes reproducing the *Houses at l'Estaque*. His words do not fall on deaf ears. Reviewing the exhibition of the Kahnweiler gallery for *Gil Blas*, Vauxcelles writes, in essence, "Monsieur Braque is a very daring young man. The example set by Picasso and Derain made him fearless. He reduces everything, places, figures, and houses, to geometrical diagrams, to cubes." Author three years ago of the word "Fauvism," this devil of a man certainly knows how to turn out a formula.

(See also 1912, 1953, 1963.)

MECISLAS GOLDBERG: THE GEOMETRY OF THE SOUL

Rebuilding the intellect of the line—this, according to his own words, is the goal Mecislas Goldberg pursues in his work *La morale des lignes* (the morale of lines). His research was inspired by the work of the designer and caricaturist André Rouveyre, a close friend of Matisse and Apollinaire. But what Goldberg says in his book has a more general significance. Written in 1904 and published late that year, it is at the core of contemporary issues, and only his premature death from pulmonary tuberculosis has prevented Goldberg from being the great critic of Cubism. We give the following excerpt to render homage to Goldberg.

We are not yet aware of the mathematical formulas of plastic art, but we can catch a glimpse of certain indelible laws by analyzing significant works, and by applying to them the historic law, the intellectual law, and the sentimental law.

Even when dipping into geometry, one finds precious instructions of esthetic constructions. I am not speaking here of architecture; in this art, nobody would deny the value of lines, of angles, and of curves.

But the mere inspection of a propeller, of an ellipse, of a trajectory, of a cylinder or cone, or of a tangent and its relations suggests ideas of an esthetic that is solid, independent from fleeting sentimentality, from momentary emotion: "The section of a turn-

PABLO PICASSO: FOREST ROAD. 1908

ing cone by a parallel plane in a generator is a parabola, but the section of a cylinder and a turning cone by a plane that meets all points of contact is an ellipse."

The two laws, when applied to the mystery of the flesh, adapted to the rules of stereochemistry and of embryogeny by combining physics and biology, create the form, the face that becomes the "mirror of the soul" to some of us, and a principle of esthetics to others . . .

All living architecture, like the acoustical chord, has its knots, its rests, it has its polarization centers, and its essential intersections, in the same way that the cross section of a tunnel is "generally" elliptical or oval, or that the arch of bridges is cylindrical, that the arch of suspension bridges is a parabola, that the span of the Pantheon established by Rondelet is made of big arches (elongated ellipsoid, spherical arch, a catenary system), that the arch of the Pantheon in Rome is hemispheric, and that the curve of the cranium, the arch of the mouth, and thousand other curves, junctions, and crossings of the human architecture establish the general character of matter as well as the character of the species, the race, and the personality.

Look at the peasant of the Beauce with his arched back, his great nasal curves, his gnarled limbs and compare him with the stocky Breton or the mountain dweller: You must bow to the geometric law that denounces, so to speak, the plasticity of forms, their relations, their usage, their duration.

MECISLAS GOLDBERG
La morale des lignes *(Excerpts)*

THE BANQUET AT THE BATEAU-LAVOIR

MONTMARTRE

"We are the two greatest painters of our time, you in the Egyptian vein, I in the modern style." It was this peremptory declaration that Henri Rousseau—nicknamed "Le Douanier Rousseau" by Alfred Jarry, because Rousseau had worked as a customs clerk in Paris—salutes, with all the authority of his sixty-four years, his twenty-seven-year-old host, Pablo Picasso. Indeed, at the beginning of November, the Spanish painter, who met Rousseau through the poet Guillaume Apollinaire, gives a grand banquet in his honor in his studio at the Bateau-Lavoir.

What a liquor-flowing, wild, unreal party! Picasso's best friends are there: Georges Braque, the poets Max Jacob, André Salmon, and Apollinaire, the young painter Marie Laurencin, the critic Maurice Raynal, the sculptor Auguste Agéro, the Americans Gertrude and Leo Stein, and some other happy rascals already quite drunk on arrival. Because of the general intoxication, it is difficult to get an exact recount of the party. The brouhaha is at its peak when Rousseau knocks at the door like a ghost.

He wears a large soft-brimmed hat and carries a walking stick in his left hand and his violin in his right. Uptight and intimidated, he is nonetheless enchanted to see so many lit-up lanterns surrounding his painting. It is a huge portrait of his second wife, Joséphine, bought some time before by a flabbergasted Picasso, who discovered it in the Montmartre secondhand shop of Père Soulier. The painting could have inspired *Les demoiselles d'Avignon,* whose hieratic shapes and terracotta colors prompt the comparison to Egyptian art. During the meal, Rousseau decides to play a valse of his own composition called *Clémence,* dedicated to his second ex-wife. Playing with quasi-mystical fervor, he doesn't feel

HENRI ROUSSEAU: PORTRAIT OF A WOMAN. 1895

At the banquet, this picture, which Picasso had found and bought in a secondhand shop, was solemnly surrounded by lanterns.

the candle wax that is trickling on his head and forming, in the words of Fernande Olivier, Picasso's lover, a small but extremely funny pyramid.

Then he sings his favorite song, "Ay! Ay! Ay! What a toothache I've got." Apollinaire declaims a poem in his honor, improvised on a paper napkin, telling of Aztec landscapes, monkeys, mangoes, and pineapple. It ends with the words "The paint-

ings you paint, you live them in Mexico," meant to stress the strangeness of the paintings.

It is a fantasy of the painter, who claims that during his military service in 1867 he took part in the Mexican campaign and saw the jungles that inspired his exuberant vegetal compositions. The truth is quite different. Not only did he not take part in the expedition by Napoleon III to save Emperor Maximilian, but it

was in the hothouses of the Jardin des Plantes of Paris that he found the inspiration for his highly poetic virgin woods: the woods of the *Tiger Struggling with Buffalo.* It is shown at the Salon des Indépendants from March 19 to May 2. Besides, Rousseau takes great pains to hide the fact that he found his animal subjects in an illustrated version of a children's album of savage beasts.

Unfortunately, the critics are unanimous. They make a fool out of the gentle Rousseau. "This dramatic scene," writes the critic of *La République Française,* "takes place in India: On a tin-plate painted green, a cat skin is drying up, while a horn protrudes from a blackish heap. All this is in a metallic forest . . ."

Amazingly, Rousseau seems to take these insults for compliments. He pastes this criticism from *Le Matin* in his scrapbook: "To crown our merriment, the divine Rousseau, who imagines a fight between a buffalo and a panther as striped as his *Soccer Players,* hanging not far away! Come on, vain spiteful people, shut up, stop blaspheming. Henri Rousseau is a modern Giotto!"

On the other hand, Picasso and some of his friends have deep respect, which shows under the merry casualness of their reception for this astonishing master who produces an ingeniously simple art and whose coloristic genius and perfect honesty they admire. Called, more or less ironically, a "primitive," Henri Rousseau is one, indeed, both as a man and a painter. This is what the Steins think; they drive him home, to his modest studio-domicile at 2 bis Rue Perrel in the neighborhood of Plaisance. The American Max Weber admires Rousseau enormously and thinks of introducing him in the United States.

(See also 1905 and 1910.)

POMPON'S GOOSE

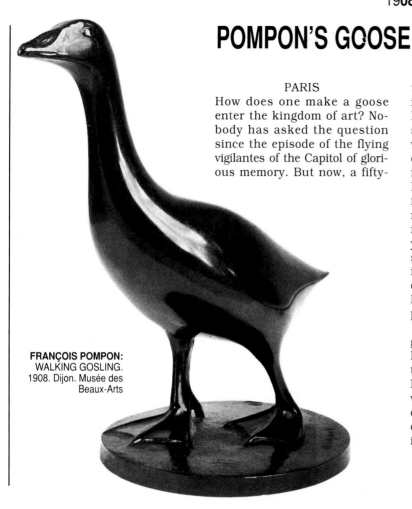

FRANÇOIS POMPON:
WALKING GOSLING.
1908. Dijon. Musée des
Beaux-Arts

PARIS

How does one make a goose enter the kingdom of art? Nobody has asked the question since the episode of the flying vigilantes of the Capitol of glorious memory. But now, a fifty-three-year-old artist specializing in the rendition of animals, François Pompon, has found a solution. During the day he works as an assistant for celebrities in order to make a living. He has worked for Auguste Rodin, laboring over the small figures of *The Gates of Hell.* At night he is his own man, sculpting in his own right. He saw a young goose swinging down a sunny path and understood that in order to grasp the figure cut out by light he had to eliminate his too-realistic models and simplify volumes.

Born in Saulieu, in Bourgogne, in 1855, Pompon came to Paris in 1875 after studying at the Beaux-Arts Academy of Dijon. He became dissatisfied with academia and tried to introduce life into his work by an extreme simplification of form. It is an approach to the liking of his colleague Constantin Brancusi, who declares that "The more he is truthful to nature, the more he feels he is 'making corpses.'"

At the Salon of 1888, Pompon shows *Cosette,* inspired by Victor Hugo's *Les Misérables.* In 1892, increasingly interested in backyard animals, which he observes all around his studio, he does *A Newborn Chick.* Distancing himself from Barye's Romanticism, he finds his own style this year with the *Walking Gosling.* The artist discards anatomic details which, by causing stationary and mutilating shadows, cancel all deep truth.

This goose, smooth like the egg she will never lay, causes some to smile and intrigues others, who forget that in Rome the goose was a sacred animal dedicated to Juno, Jupiter's wife, goddess of the sky.

THE STONE KISS

PARIS

Brancusi, who two years ago refused to work with Auguste Rodin because, he says, "Nothing grows in the shade of big trees," performs by cutting directly into a calcar block, a work of an almost revolutionary originality, which he names *The Kiss.* Extremely minimalistic and stylized, the sculpture represents the half busts of a man and a woman literally joined in one compact entity. It has, with its symbolism, its will of symmetry, and the simplicity and purity of its lines, the characteristics of both Romanian folk art and primitive idols.

The "shepherd of the Carpathian mountains," as he likes to describe himself, Brancusi is pervaded by the vigorous folk art of his native country. But undoubtedly he also saw at the Salon d'Automne of 1906 the Gauguin retrospective of his work from Tahiti and last year the *Sitting Man* that André Derain exhibited at the Kahnweiler gallery, a direct-cut, compact, stylized sculpture. In *Prayer,* an allegoric figure of a woman, destined for the tomb of a Romanian notable, Brancusi rejects all trace of Academicism. He tries to clean out the shape as much as possible and charge it with symbols.

It is in his studio on the Rue Montparnasse, where he made the *Prayer,* that he is visited by Apollinaire, Léger, and Marcel Duchamp, and that he sculpts *The Kiss.* The work rejects Classicism, and undoubtedly will become the starting point of a completely new conception of sculpture.

CONSTANTIN BRANCUSI: THE KISS.
1908. Paris. MNAM

FÉLIX VALLOTTON: THE ABDUCTION OF EUROPA. 1908

THE ABDUCTION OF EUROPA

PARIS

"I prepared for the Salon d'Automne *The Abduction of Europa*, which I think is quite good," Félix Vallotton writes to his brother Paul at the end of May. The forty-three-year-old Swiss painter is at the peak of his glory. His engraving work is known worldwide, and his paintings sell well. Since his marriage to Gabrielle Rodrigues-Henriques, daughter of an art dealer for the Bernheim company, he has left forever his anarchist friends of the Nabis circle and lives a bourgeois life.

If his mode of living becomes tame, his painting becomes more provocative. In September, at the Salon d'Automne, his *Abduction of Europa* is a sensation. "One admires it while gritting one's teeth. It is very unpleasant and very powerful," critic Louis Vauxcelles writes in *Gil Blas*. Indeed, the irony of the painter demythifies the Homeric figures. Vallotton boasts that he painted the bull by copying the illustration from the Larousse dictionary. But the force of the painting comes from its absence of perspective.

The Abduction of Europa appears to be thumbing its nose at humanistic tradition.

THE ASH CAN SCHOOL HAS A SHOW

NEW YORK

An important exhibition opens at the Macbeth Gallery on February 3. Eight painters grouped appropriately under the name The Eight exhibit together for the first time. This is an exhibition-manifesto for these artists, who already are known to some extent. The critics are harsh. They call them the Ash Can School, because the artists rebel against the conventional style dictated by the almighty Pennsylvania Academy where several of them studied. They want a sheerly American painting, expressing and describing contemporary reality.

Four used to be artist-reporters. Encouraged by their leader, Robert Henri, they are fond of unexpected street scenes and accidents, small facts of existence. They form a heterogeneous group, because their common trait is the desire to paint the city, but they do so in diversified styles. In Henri's opinion, spontaneity is the mark of a good painting. This explains the group's somewhat hasty style. Henri shares his taste for

MAURICE PRENDERGAST: CENTRAL PARK. 1901. New York. Whitney Museum

the picturesque with his friends. His street urchins show the vivacity of which he is so fond in Frans Hals. *The Laughing Boy* is hung at the entrance of the exhibition like a sign for The Eight.

William Glackens, an admirer of Renoir, paints people strolling in Central Park, the women in their graceful attire. John Sloan preserves his reporter's verve when he shows a crowd in front of the barber's shop: *Hairdress-*

er's Window is typical of his rapid stroke and popular subject. Nightlife and its mirage attract Everett Shinn. Maurice Prendergast loves the beaches and the parks of New York. Ernest Lawson paints the outskirts of the city and the port in a style resembling Impressionism. Arthur B. Davis, with his dream scenes, unicorns, and young women, is closer to the Symbolism that seduced Ameri-

cans at the end of the last century.

It is a colorful exhibition, and the critics do not omit underlining the "dissonances of these eight orchestras with different tuning." Crowds show up at the opening. The exhibition moves on to Philadelphia and to eight other American cities.

Moscow Finally Gets to See the French Avant-Garde

La toison d'or, a Symbolist magazine, was founded in 1906 by the art dealer Nicolas Riabouchinski. Since then, it has encouraged artistic and literary exchanges between France and Russia, the responsibility for French news having been delegated to Alexandre Mercereau, a twenty-four-year-old poet. This year in *La toison d'or,* the young man published a series of Charles Morice's studies on "the new tendencies in French art." Most important, he organized the first exhibition sponsored by the magazine in Moscow. The exhibition attempts to emphasize the characteristics common to French painting and painting by young Russians. An excellent panorama of painting in France from Impressionism to contemporary times is on view, including almost all the members of the Nabis group, the Fauves (with several of the canvases that caused an uproar at the 1905 Salon d'Automne), Braque, and Rouault. On the Russian side of the exhibit, Larionov stands out, with about twenty works influenced by Vuillard, Bonnard, and Gontcharova.

Cappiello Puts on a Happy Face

A man who can draw, a caricaturist, Italian, Parisian by adoption, and, above all, a poster artist! At the mere age of thirty-three, Cappiello is no longer a beginner. Born in 1875 in Leghorn, where he showed early signs of a taste for observation and a certain flair, his sure sense of decoration has already made him one of the current masters of the poster. The one he has just secretly made for Thermogen Cotton, its character probably inspired by the fire-eaters that perform on the boulevards Saturday evenings, is a model of its kind. To be successful, a poster has to be lively, funny, effective, so that it catches your eye at first glance. Cappiello is in magnificent possession of all these qualities. And that distinguishes him from the mass of poster artists who are, alas, too literary and, most often, too wordy.

Modigliani at the Salon des Indépendants

Among the 6,701 works at the Salon de Indépendants, which takes place again this year at Cours-la-Reine under the direction of its new president Paul Signac, there are four paintings and a fabulous drawing by a young Italian, twenty-four-year-old Amedeo Modigliani. It seems that it is on the advice of one of his admirers, Doctor Alexandre, whom he met in the autumn of 1907, that Modigliani agreed to present his works. From a middle-class Jewish family in Leghorn, Modigliani, who showed signs of his calling at a young age, was encouraged by his mother. He studied at the academies in Florence and Venice, and has been living in Paris for two years.

LEONETTO CAPPIELLO: THE THERMOGEN. 1908. Paris. Bibliothèque Nationale

Richard Gerstl Commits Suicide

On November 4, a relatively unknown painter—he had never exhibited—killed himself. He was a friend of the composer Arnold Schönberg, and it is even said that his impossible love for Schönberg's wife is the cause of his suicide. His name was Richard Gerstl, he was born in Vienna in 1883, and had studied in that city at the Beaux-Arts Academy. Gerstl painted mostly landscapes and portraits whose thick layering recalls the German Impressionists Max Liebermann and Lovis Corinth. The manner in which he killed himself has jolted his friends: facing a mirror, Gerstl tied a cord around his neck and plunged a knife into his heart. They believe he will continue to be known as one of the best Viennese artists of the early part of the century.

Adolf Loos Against Crime

Is it because of his three-year stay in the United States between 1893 and 1896 that the architect Adolf Loos discovered the innovations of the young Chicago School? In any case, the fact is that his essay *Ornament Is Crime* stirs the stagnant waters of Viennese architecture. Relying on the purist arguments of Louis Sullivan and the functionalist doctrine of Otto Wagner, Loos attempts to show that the ornamentalism of Art Nouveau so dear to the Viennese Secession is not suited for our culture, an architecture stripped of ornament being in his opinion the sign of clear thinking and of a high level of civilization. He feels that the renunciation of all decor is inevitable. Son of a mason, born in Brünn in 1870, Adolf Loos is thirty-eight years old.

WILHELM WORRINGER: ABSTRACTION AND EMPATHY

Wilhelm Worringer is a young art historian, born in 1881 in Aachen. He studied art history at the Universities of Freiburg, Berlin, and Munich. But he wrote his doctoral dissertation at the University of Bern: *Abstraction and Empathy*. The work became famous overnight with avant-garde artists in Germany. Opposing the "antinatural" style of Gothic art to the Naturalism of the Renaissance, he addresses implicitly the same problem as that of the avant-garde, namely, that of the conditions under which abstraction is possible.

EGYPTIAN BAS-RELIEF. About 2400 B.C. Leiden. Rijksmuseum van Oudheden

Let us recapitulate: The original artistic impulse has nothing to do with imitation of nature. This impulse is in search of pure abstraction as the sole possibility of finding rest amidst the confusion and obscurity of the image of the world, and it creates a geometric abstraction starting with itself, in a purely instinctive manner. It is the realized expression, and the sole expression conceivable for man, of the emancipation from any arbitrariness and any temporality of the image of the world. But soon this impulse tends to rip out the individual thing from the exterior world, which retains as its main interest its obscure and disconcerting connection with this outside world, and so tries to get closer to it through artistic restitution of its material individuality, to purify this individual thing of everything that is life and temporality in it, to make it as much as pos-

sible independent both from the surrounding world and from the subject of contemplation, which does not want to enjoy in it the vitality that is common to both, but the necessity and the legitimacy where this impulse can find refuge from its connection with ordinary life, in the only abstraction to which it can aspire and which it can attain. Restitution of the finite material individuality is both important and possible underneath the surface boundaries but also in the intermingling of artistic presentation with the rigid world of the crystalo-geometric: namely, the two solutions that we could observe. Anyone who understands his own solutions in the light of all their presuppositions can no longer speak of "these charming childish mumblings of stylization."

Now, all these momentums that we have just analyzed, and which revealed themselves as so many aspects of the need for abstraction, are what our definition wants to gather and summarize with the help of the notion of "style," and what it wants to oppose as such to any Naturalism that results from the need for Einfühlung (empathy).

Because the need for Einfühlung and the need for abstraction appeared to us as the two poles of man's artistic sensitivity in as much that it can be the object of pure esthetic appreciation. These two needs are antithetical, they exclude each other, and the history of art never ceases to display the continual confrontation between the two tendencies.

WILHELM WORRINGER
Abstraction and Empathy *(Excerpt)*

HENRI MATISSE: THE PRIMACY OF COLOR

The man who was the head of the Fauves at the Salon d'Automne of 1905, was called "the doctor" or "the professor" by the young painters, because of his small gold-framed spectacles. Born in 1869 in Cateau-Cambrésis, twelve years before Picasso and Léger, thirteen years before Braque, he inspires respect owed to an elder. Though not much inclined toward theory, he can speak with great insight about his work. In any case, he agreed to reveal a few of his thoughts on pictorial creation for the Christmas issue of *La grande revue*. The perpetual novelty and the perpetual simplicity of his view can be seen in the excerpts that follow.

HENRI MATISSE:
HARMONY IN RED. 1908.
Leningrad. Hermitage Museum

For me, expression does not reside in the passion that bursts forth on a face or that asserts itself through a violent movement. Expression is in the overall arrangement of my painting: the space occupied by the bodies, the empty spaces around them, the proportions, all of this plays a part. Composition is the art of arranging in a decorative manner the various elements at the painter's disposal to express his feelings. In a painting, each part will be visible and will play its proper role, be it a principal or a secondary one. Everything that has no usefulness in the painting is therefore harmful. A painting comprises an overall harmony: Any superfluous detail would steal, in the mind of the spectator, the place of another detail that is essential . . .

Suppose I have to paint a woman's body: First I give it grace, charm, then it is necessary to give it something more. I am going to condense the meaning of this body by seeking its essential lines. The charm will be less apparent at first, but it will emerge in the end from the new image that I will have obtained and which will have a wider meaning, a more fully human one. The charm will be less prominent, because it is not truly characteristic, but it exists nevertheless, contained in the general concept of my forms.

A painting must carry inside itself its total meaning and must impose it on the spectator before he is even aware of the subject. When I see the Giotto frescoes in Padova, I don't worry about which scene of Christ's life I have before my eyes, I understand the feeling that is emerging from it, for it exists in the lines, the composition, and the color, and the title can only confirm my impression. . .

HENRI MATISSE
Remarks on Painting (*Excerpts*)

Another jolt of energy comes with Marinetti's Futurist Manifesto, published on the front page of Le Figaro's February 20 edition, marking the appearance of the invective in the arts. From now on the direction of painting will be Futurist—rovocative and lampoonist. The movement seems to put the century on a track and in a mood that neither Fauvism nor Cubism, distracted at first by problems of a pictorial nature, could have foreseen. But Futurism is not all there is. Bourdelle, at the age of forty-six, turns out to be the successor to the great Rodin, while in Vienna a brilliant young artist by the name of Egon Schiele makes his debut.

1909

SUMMARY

AVANT-GARDE

Marinetti Brings Boxing to Art

MANIFESTO

Marinetti: Futurist Manifesto

DEVELOPMENTS

Bourdelle Has High Ambitions
Chauchard Deceived

ART NEWS

Henri Rousseau Is Saved by the Monkeys
Egon Schiele Revolts Against His Teachers
Léon Brakst Starts the Dance
The Laethem Group
Mondrian's Burning Tree
In Brief

PORTRAITS

Fernande's Metamorphoses

ARCHITECTURE

Mackintosh Builds the Art Academy

ÉTIENNE-JULES MAREY:
SUCCESSIVE IMAGES OF A RUNNER.
1886. Beaune
Musée E.-J. Marey et
des Beaux-Arts

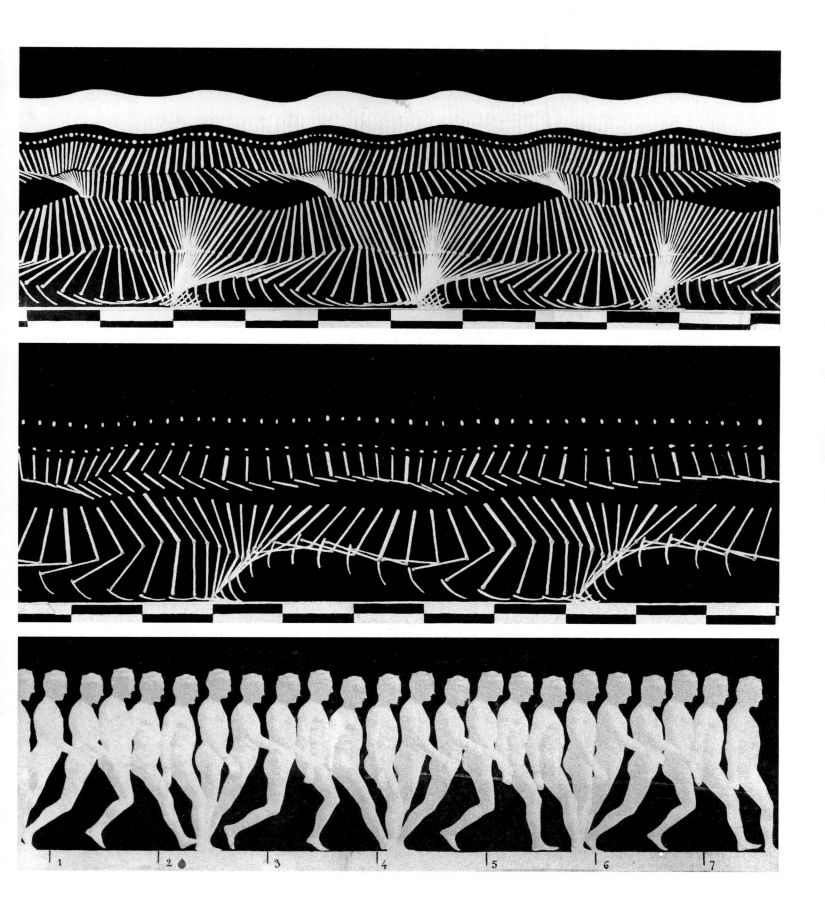

MARINETTI BRINGS BOXING TO ART

PARIS

The readers of *Le Figaro* do not believe their eyes. Indeed, under the title "Futurist Manifesto," the daily paper reserves its first page of February 20 for the lucubrations of a little-known Italian poet, Filippo Tomasso Marinetti. What the thirty-three-year-old Marinetti writes is truly stupefying: A roaring car is more beautiful than the *Victory of Samothrace* . . . war is the only hygiene of life . . . libraries and museums ought to be destroyed. Can one stand back and accept anarchism, immoralism, provocation, and, in one word, stupidity? The letters of protest flood the office of *Le Figaro*.

In truth, the elegant and rich Marinetti is not that little known after all. He had his first literary success in 1898 with a poem, *The Old Sailors*, that was highly praised by Catulle Mendès and declaimed by the great Sarah Bernhardt. Four years ago, he wrote a "hilarious" tragedy, *Le roi Bombance* (the feasting king), a deeply pessimistic Rabelaisian farce whose central character is Saint Decay, "a terrifying ghost born of the pestilential fumes arising from the ponds of the past."

Filippo Tommaso Marinetti was born in Alexandria, where his father was a business lawyer. After being spoiled by a Sudanese nanny, he went to the secondary school of Saint-

Filippo Tommaso Marinetti, theoretician of Futurism, in his car.

François-Xavier, a local Jesuit institution. He surrendered to his father's desire and got a law degree at the University of Genoa, then later dedicated himself to a literary career. For support, he chose a Parisian newspaper rather than one in Rome or Milan because, in his eyes, Paris is the capital of modern art and French the universal language of culture.

His manifesto inaugurates a new genre: boxing in artistic struggle. In Futurism, the poet, the artist gets on stage, incites to mutiny, practices insult and provocation, and addresses society with subversive violence: "The main thing in a manifesto is precise accusation, well-defined insult." It undoubtedly was not by chance that Marinetti took the numbering of his paragraphs, so as to better pound on spirits, from Marx's and Engels'

Communist Manifesto. Shaken last fall by Picasso's and Braque's Cubism, readers of *Le Figaro* are now shocked.

Cubism was never expected to be a movement with a program, a doctrine leader. Before the word was minted by the critic Louis Vauxcelles, who wasn't precisely a fan of the young artists, Picasso and Braque didn't even know they were Cubists, and they still don't.

Eadweard Muybridge: photographs of a horseman in motion.

MARINETTI: FUTURIST MANIFESTO

Their common endeavor is a lengthy work of disassembly and assembly, analysis and synthesis of the elements of the visible world—marking the breach with traditional figurative art.

Marinetti, in turn, is a mouthpiece. Painters such as Giacomo Balla, Carlo Carrà, Gino Severini, and Luigi Russolo, who understand his message, still have not found the system of forms that allow them to translate Marinetti's ardent speeches. Five years ago, Boccioni painted a canvas showing a car being chased by fox-hunting dogs, but in the most constrained style. Severini makes landscapes that look like Millet's *Angelus* in Pointillism. Does this really represent the future?

Until now, only chronophotography has been able to unveil the secrets of movement. The Englishman Eadweard Muybridge's photos were the first, about twenty years ago, to show that a horse trots by throwing one leg forward. A French scientist, Étienne Jules Marey, painted lines and white dots on the head, arms, and legs of a walking person clad in black in order to make, through chronophotography, a diagram of human motion that cannot be seen with the naked eye.

Impressed, in spite of what they say, by the Cubist revolution and its temerity, are Futurist painters going to ask chronophotography to open the way for them? For the time being, the ardent Marinetti would like to preach the prohibition of spaghetti. He says that the abuse of pasta makes Italians stupid and prevents the renovation of Venice, exhausted by century-long pleasures. People whisper that he would like to build factories around Saint Mark, burn the gondolas, and fill in the channels with the rubble from the old palaces!

(See also 1912, 1914, 1915, 1919.)

1. We want to sing the love of danger, the habit of energy and of temerity.

2. The essential elements of our poetry will be courage, daring, and revolt.

3. Literature having until now magnified a pensive immobility, ecstasy, and sleep, we want to exalt the aggressive movement, the insomnia, the double-time march, the somersault, the slap in the face, and the punch.

4. We declare that the splendor of the world has been enriched with a new beauty: the beauty of speed. A racing car, its trunk decorated with large pipes like snakes with an explosive breath . . . a roaring automobile that gives the impression it is running on a hail of bullets, is more beautiful than The Victory of Samothrace.

5. We want to praise the man who holds the steering wheel, whose ideal column goes through the Earth, which itself is launched in the circuit of its orbit.

6. The poet must exert himself with warmth, brilliance, and lavishness in order to increase the enthusiastic fervor of primordial elements.

7. There is no beauty except in struggling. No masterpiece without an aggresive character. Poetry must be a violent assault against unknown forces to summon them to lie down before man.

8. We are on the extreme promontory of the centuries! . . . What good is there in looking back as long as we have to bash in the mysterious doors of the Impossible! Time and Space died yesterday. We already live in the absolute, since we have already created ominipresent speed.

9. We want to glorify war—the sole hygiene in the world—militarism, patriotism, the destructive gesture of the anarchists, the beautiful ideas that kill, and a contempt for the female.

10. We want to demolish the museums, the libraries, fight moralism, feminism, and all the opportunistic and utilitarian cowardices.

11. We will sing the great crowds agitated by work, pleasure, or revolt: the multicolor and polyphonic undertows of revolutions in the modern capitals; the vibration by night of the arsenals and the job sites under their violent electric moons; gluttonous railroad stations, swallowers of smoking snakes; bridges jumping like gymnasts crossing the

diabolical cutlery of sunny rivers; adventurous steamships sniffing the horizon; locomotives with their large breastplate, fidgeting on the rails, like enormous steel horses tied up with long pipes; and the gliding flight of airplanes whose propellers have flappings of flags and clappings of a enthusiastic crowd.

It is in Italy that we launch this proclamation of tumbling and incendiary violence,

Front-page of the *Le Figaro* **with the Futurist Manifesto.**

through which we are founding this Futurism because we want to free Italy from its gangrene of professors, archaeologists, guides, and antique dealers.

Italy has been for too long the great market of the secondhand dealer. We want to rid it of the unnumerable museums that cover it with innumerable cemeteries.

Museums, cemeteries . . . Really identical in their sinister contact of bodies that do not know themselves.

FILIPPO TOMMASO MARINETTI
Excerpt from the proclamation published
in *Le Figaro* of February 20

BOURDELLE HAS HIGH AMBITIONS

PARIS

Antoine Bourdelle, who has exhibited regularly at the National Art Exhibition since 1891, is known to the public at large. They admired an ensemble of impressive sculptures at his first one-man exhibition, in 1905, at the gallery Hebrard, Rue Royale. Torn between contemporary subjects and the attraction that antiquity has for him, Bourdelle chose the topic of Hercules preparing to unleash his invisible arrow and kill the birds of Stymphalus. This rendition in bronze of Hercules' sixth labor allows the artist to show the admirable mastery he has reached. In an attitude of extreme tension, the hero leans on a rock in a swaying movement that both acquires balance and translates coiled strength. The powerful composition exceeds the myth, in order to evoke the virile force of man. Bourdelle thinks of exhibiting his *Hercules the Archer* at the next Salon.

He is busy with an art pervaded by his own meditation and ignores the cafés and social life. He thinks only about his art. He rises early, and never leaves his studio at 16 Impasse du Maine. It is full of sculptures, some finished, some still rough, with plaster blocks awaiting to be processed. There are numerous drawings and sketches. Assistant to Rodin for fifteen years, Bourdelle this year pursues his career all by himself. At the age of forty-six, he is considered by the master of Meudon as his spiritual heir. He honors Rodin's confidence and keeps his promises. Bourdelle proves his profound personality, and appears to be the best sculptor of his generation.

Antoine Bourdelle with his *Hercules the Archer*.

CHAUCHARD DECEIVED

PARIS

The founder of the Galeries du Louvre, the famous Chauchard, gathered for ten years, in his luxurious house on the Avenue Velasquez, the works of the most celebrated artists of his time. He died on June 10.

He was known for two passions. The first was collecting art works prized by the Salon. The second, less well known, was planning his own funeral. He had decided all the details of the procession, linking art with his death. He wanted it to be a symbolic apotheosis. His best friends were to follow the casket, each carrying one of his favorite paintings. Georges Leygues was to lead the march, carrying the *Angelus* by Millet. Unfortunately, the bitterness that erupted when his will was opened did not allow Chauchard's deepest wishes to be executed.

The employees of the Galeries du Louvre believed they would be Chauchard's heirs. But he used to say, all the time, "I will leave everything to the Louvre," and he did. He even willed the *Angelus* to the Louvre. The employees received nothing. His friend Leygues received fifteen million gold francs, and his butler, one million. The employees, considering themselves insulted parties, decided to boo the funeral procession. They followed it, shouting, hurling abuse, throwing projectiles, as far as the Place de la Bastille. There, such confusion reigned that the police had to intervene. So, the illustrious Chauchard in his gold cloth shroud was hastily deposited in his mausoleum at the Père Lachaise cemetery, amid booing and affronts.

Henri Rousseau Is Saved by the Monkeys

A cheat out of the kindness of his heart, a liar out of the goodness of his soul, Henri Julien Félix Rousseau, nicknamed the Douanier (the customs clerk), accused of fraud and convicted in criminal court on January 9, owes the fact that he was not sent to prison to his painting. Two years earlier, he had been involved in a case of forgery to help a friend who he believed was a victim of the Bank of France. The affair brought him to la Santé and now gets him a sentence of two years of solitary confinement with remission and a fine of 100 francs. If, in the end, the sentence is light, it is because his lawyer had the idea of showing the court *Les deux farceurs*, a painting by Rousseau depicting two monkeys drinking a bottle of milk against a jungle background. The painting made the jury laugh, and Rousseau was saved.

Egon Schiele Revolts Against His Teachers

June 17 marks the founding of the Neue Kunst Group at the Pisko gallery on Schwarzenbergerplatz in Vienna. The initiator of it is a nineteen-year-old fellow, Egon Schiele, the most gifted painter of the new Viennese generation, according to Gustave Klimt. A third-year student at the academy, Schiele had drawn up, along with some friends, a list of complaints, including a demand for greater student freedom, which gets him expelled from the school in April. The Art Nouveau group, of which he was elected president, numbers fifteen members, including the musician Arthur Löwenstein, the painters Anton Peschka, Erwin Osen, and Hans Böhler, as well as the actor, poet, and painter Paris von Gütersloh.

Léon Bakst Starts the Dance

The choreography is by Fokine, the music is by Arenski, the scenery and costumes are by Bakst: To the theme of *Cleopatra,* the all-new troop of the Russian Ballet founded by Sergei de Diaghilev has decided to break with the tried and true. A daring and penniless patron, Diaghilev has always been a lover of art, which explains why he called on his compatriot, fifty-three-year-old Léon Bakst, an ardent propagandist of modern art in Russia, for this first ballet. Bakst is an elegant, refined eclectic, and one finds this kind of eclecticism appearing in his scenery and costumes for *Cleopatra.*

The Laethem Group

Laethem-Saint-Martin is a village near Gand that has already seen the emergence of an artists' community at the turn of the century with the painters Gustave Van De Woestijne and Albert Servaes and the sculptor George Minne. More recently, a new group has formed, including Frits Van den Berghe, Gust and Léon De Smet, all painters and all from Gand, as well as the writer P. G. Van Hecke. With Constant Permeke, who is from Anvers, this second Laethem Group made a valuable recruit.

PIET MONDRIAN: THE RED TREE. 1909. The Hague. Gemeentemuseum

Mondrian's Burning Tree

Long a painter of cows and prairies, Piet Mondriaan has just created a masterpiece: *The Red Tree,* bare on a blue background, which immediately propels the painter at the age of forty-one to the front rank of contemporary artists. In January, with his friends Cornelius Spoor and Jan Sluyters, he had a stunning exhibition at the municipal museum of Amsterdam. He had always said he would drop one of the two *a's* in his last name when he found his true personality. It now seems to have happened. His canvas is, in fact, signed "Mondrian"—with one *a.*

LÉON BAKST: PROGRAM COVER. 1909. Paris. Opera

PABLO PICASSO: WOMAN'S HEAD. 1909. Paris. Musée Picasso

Two images of Fernande Olivier by Picasso, compared with her photograph, above.

PABLO PICASSO : PORTRAIT OF FERNANDE. 1909. Düsseldorf. Kunstsammlung

FERNANDE'S METAMORPHOSES

PARIS

An unquestionable sign of social promotion: Picasso leaves the shaky Bateau-Lavoir in September and installs himself in a bourgeois building on the Boulevard de Clichy. It is there that the now famous Spanish painter makes his first Cubist sculptures, three-dimensional transpositions of his pictorial research. The most remarkable among his sculptures is *Woman's Head*, a portrait of Fernande Olivier, his companion since 1904. It is cast in bronze and was made on the basis of numerous charcoal sketches brought back from the artist's recent stay in Horta de Ebro, in Catalogna.

For some years, Picasso has been preparing his audience for an art that refuses to appeal to a familiar reality. His sculpture allows him to perfect his visual investigations. Indeed, *Woman's Head* offers a fragmentation of plans in a multiplication of surfaces, equivalent to as many viewpoints as possible. Since *Les demoiselles d'Avignon*, the painter tries to find other means of expressing perspective while continuing the study of volumes. A perfect knowledge of primitive art, especially of Iberic sculpture, as well as his recent discovery of African Art, are not unrelated to all this.

African sculpture joins the lesson received from Cézanne, and Picasso is not the only interested artist. Vlaminck, Derain, Matisse, Braque, and others also seem to find their inspiration in it. In a first stage, Picasso borrows its instinctive, even compulsive, character, combining it with the powerful symbolism that he has put in his paintings for the last two years.

However, *Woman's Head* goes beyond African or Iberic models

A FRAGMENTATION OF PLANS IN A MULTIPLICATION OF SURFACES, EQUIVALENT TO AS MANY VIEWPOINTS AS POSSIBLE

and appears as an innovative work. An important series of paintings done last year—*Standing Nude, Three Women, Forest Road,* and several still lifes—put him on this path. A palette reduced to browns, grays, and greens, a quasi-formal calligraphy, inspire him to try his hand at sculpture. He tried an ensemble of small statues in wood and some in plaster. One can see the artist's concern to distribute and multiply the play of light on an irregular surface. What an evolution since the first bust of Fernande, made in 1906! It was a portrait with a concentrated and collected expression, with perfect, almost classical, volumes.

In this latest sculpture, Picasso succumbs to his frenetic desire for demolition. He tortures the human figure with such enthusiasm that he compels the viewer to move, to walk around the work in order to reconstruct, out of the many ridges and flat and disassembled plans, a face, *the* face of the beloved woman.

(See also 1904, 1905, 1907, 1910, 1911, 1912, 1913, 1921, 1927, 1937, 1945, 1946, 1948, 1953, 1954, 1958, 1973.)

MACKINTOSH BUILDS THE ART ACADEMY

GLASGOW

The new Art Academy of Glasgow, the construction of which started a dozen years ago, is finally completed! This great Scottish port can now be proud to have one of the best architectural achievements thus far in this new century. It is already the center of an original artistic school, whose "leader" is the very same architect who built the Academy: Charles Rennie Mackintosh, forty-one years old and one of Glasgow's citizens.

Son of a police officer, Mackintosh befriended Herbert MacNair at the Academy, and they in turn befriended the sisters Margaret and Frances MacDonald, whom he and MacNair marry.

In 1895, the men had the idea of founding a "Group of the Four," influenced by William Morris, one of the fathers of the Arts and Crafts Movement, whose intention was to differentiate local art from the European Art Nouveau: The goal of the Group of the Four was to promote decoration as a legitimate art and give it a new style, the simplest and clearest possible. The Four distinguished themselves as early as 1896, when they presented their first work in London, at the Arts and Crafts Exhibitions Society. But they

decorative arts, won the competition organized for the construction of a new Art Academy. Work started immediately but had to be interrupted in 1899 because of lack of money. It resumed in 1907.

Three of the four sides of the building are constructed of local gray granite. The fourth is made of brick. The main staircase and the museum hall on the second

THE ONLY THING THAT COUNTS IS THE EMPHASIS ON STRUCTURAL ARTICULATION

met with a lack of comprehension from traditional critics, who were disconcerted by the right angles and the light-colored wood of the furniture.

Hired by the Honey and Keppie agency, Mackintosh, equally interested in architecture and

floor, to which the staircase leads, are lit by a glass panel. They thus serve as a "light well," as was conceived by Horta, the Belgian architect, creator of the Innovation department stores in Brussels, in 1901.

In 1907, when renovation

work on the Art Academy was under way, Mackintosh takes the opportunity to redesign the library wing. His style has evolved. The high bay windows, the lights they introduce into the library and the vertical momentum they lend to the walls, mark a breach with the three other façades of the school.

The interior of the library establishes the absolute reign of the straight line. Mackintosh abandons all metallic decorations. The only thing that counts is the Japanese-style emphasis on structural articulations.

Mackintosh is considered the leader of Art Nouveau in England, where he imposes, together with his Four, the logical harmonization of architectural conception, geometrical, without ornaments, and rigorously designed, strict furniture.

Beaux-Arts School at Glasgow, built by Mackintosh (1897-1909).

This is the most important decade of the century. Despite the war, avant-garde movements spring up one after another throughout Europe. Kandinsky paints the first abstract watercolor in 1910, and establishes the Blue Rider the next year. In 1912, Delaunay's Inobjective Painting appears, followed by the Metaphysical Painting of Georgio de Chirico and Suprematism in 1915. Dada is born in 1916, Neoplasti-

	1910	1911	1912	1913	1914
ARTS	• Kandinsky paints the first abstract watercolor • *Dance* and *Music* by Matisse	• The Blue Rider in Munich • Kandinsky publishes *About the Spiritual in Art*	• Delaunay creates Inobjective art • The Futurists exhibit in Paris	• America discovers modern art at the Armory Show • Duchamp's first "ready-made": *Bicycle Wheel*	• *Güell Park* by Gaudí in Barcelona • Delaunay paints *Homage to Blériot*
LITERATURE	• Death of Tolstoy • *Five Great Odes* by Paul Claudel	• *Éloges* by Saint-John Perse • *Bestiary* by Guillaume Apollinaire	• *The Tidings Brought to Mary* by Paul Claudel • *Death in Venice* by Thomas Mann	• The first volume of *Remembrance of Things Past* by Marcel Proust • *Totem and Taboo* by Sigmund Freud • *Le grand Meaulnes* by Alain-Fournier	• *Les caves du Vatican (Lafcadio's Adventures)* by André Gide • *Dubliners* by James Joyce
MUSIC AND THEATER	• *L'oiseau de feu* by Igor Stravinsky in Paris • *Der Rosenkavalier* by Richard Strauss in Vienna • Gustav Mahler's *Second Symphony*	• Igor Stravinsky's *Petrouchka* with the Russian Ballet • Death of Gustav Mahler	• *Prélude à l'apres-midi d'un faune* by Claude Debussy, performed by the Russian Ballet • *Pierrot lunaire* by Arnold Schönberg in Berlin • *Daphnis and Chloe* by Maurice Ravel	• The scandal of Stravinsky's *Rite of Spring* at the Théâtre des Champs-Élysées	• *Toward the Flame* by Aleksandre Scriabin • Irving Berlin's *Watch Your Step*
MOTION PICTURES	• *A Child of the Ghetto* (United States); *Hamlet* (Denmark); *Lucrezia Borgia* (Italy)	• *Anna Karenina* (Russia); *The Abyss* (Denmark); *Pinocchio* (Italy)	• *War and Peace* (Russia); *Quo Vadis* (Italy)	• *Fantomas* by Louis Feuillade • The first Charlie Chaplin films	• Charlie Chaplin in *Making a Living* • *Cabiria* by Giovanni Pastrone
SCIENCE AND TECHNOLOGY	• Charcot's expedition to Antarctica aboard the *Pourquoi pas?* • First crystal-set radio transmission in the United States	• Amundsen reaches the South Pole • Rutherford's theory of atomic structure	• Kasimir Funk coins the term "vitamin" • *Introduction to Psychoanalysis* by Sigmund Freud	• First household refrigerator, in Chicago • Ford introduces new assembly-line techniques • Grand Central Terminal in New York is completed	• First use of radium to treat cancer, in London • Panama Canal opens
POLITICS AND DAILY LIFE	• Death of Edward VII, succeeded by George V • Japan annexes Korea • The Union of South Africa is established	• Revolution in Central China • American-Japanese and Anglo-Japanese commercial treaties	• The *Titanic* sinks on her maiden voyage • Arizona and New Mexico join the United States	• Balkan War; Treaty of Bucharest	• War: invasion of Belgium and France; French victory at the Marne; German victory over Russia at Tannenberg

1919

cism in 1917, and the Bauhaus movement in 1919. Meanwhile, an event of considerable importance occurs in 1913. At the Armory Show in New York, and later in Chicago and Boston, America discovers, to its utter wonder and scandal, the great founders of modern art, from Matisse to Picasso and Duchamp, of whom the nation had been arrogantly ignorant until then.

1915	1916	1917	1918	1919
• Birth of Metaphysical Painting • *Suprematist Manifesto* by Malevich	• Birth of Dada at the Cabaret Voltaire in Zurich	• Mondrian creates Neoplasticism • Death of Rodin	• Deaths of Gustav Klimt, Egon Schiele, and Otto Wagner • *White Square on White* by Malevich	• The Bauhaus is created • Death of Auguste Renoir
• Romain Rolland is awarded Nobel prize in literature and publishes *Above the Battle* • *A Spoon River Anthology* by Edgar Lee Masters	• *Leu feu* by Henri Barbusse • *Le cornet à dés* by Max Jacob • *The Metamorphosis* by Franz Kafka	• *La jeune parque* by Paul Valéry • First issue of Pierre Reverdy's *Nord-Sud* • *Prufrock and Other Observations* by T. S. Eliot	• *The Decline of the West* by Oswald Spengler • *Calligrammes* by Apollinaire, who dies before its publication • *The Twelve* by Aleksandr Blok	• *Les champs magnétiques* by André Breton and Philippe Soupault • *Winesburg, Ohio* by Sherwood Anderson
• Manuel de Falla's *Love the Magician* in Madrid • Classic New Orleans jazz in bloom	• *Scythian Suite* by Sergey Prokofiev in Petrograd	• *The Story of a Solder* by Ramuz and Stravinsky • *The Breasts of Tiresias* by Guillaume Apollinaire • *To Each His Truth* by Luigi Pirandello	• Death of Claude Debussy • *Duke Bluebeard's Castle* by Béla Bartók in Budapest • *Mystery-Bouffe* by Mayakovski in Petrograd	• *The Three-Cornered Hat*, ballet by Manuel de Falla, with stage design by Picasso • *Le mondain merveilleux* by Béla Bartók
• *The Birth of a Nation* by D. W. Griffith • *The Vampires* by Louis Feuillade	• *Intolerance* by D. W. Griffith	• *The Immigrant* with Charlie Chaplin • First Buster Keaton films	• Abel Gance's pacifist film *J'accuse* • *Plastic Counterpoint* by Viking Eggeling	• *The Cabinet of Dr. Caligari* by Robert Wiene • *Madame du Barry* by Ernst Lubitsch
• Ford produces the one-millionth car • First transcontinental telephone call, New York-San Francisco (between Bell and Watson)	• First British tanks fight in the Battle of the Somme	• First recording of a jazz concert, in the United States • 100-inch reflecting telescope, at Mount Wilson	• Max Planck is awarded Nobel prize in physics for his quantum theory	• Obervations of solar eclipse confirm Einstein's theory of relativity
• War: French offensive in the Champagne; defeat of the Allies at the Dardanelles; sinking of the *Lusitania*	• War: Battle of Verdun; naval engagement at Jutland • Margaret Sanger helps establish the first birth-control clinic	• America enters the war • Russian Revolution	• Armistice, on November 11 • Execution of the Czar and his family • Treaty of Brest-Litovsk • End of the Austro-Hungarian Empire	• Treaty of Versailles • Establishment of the Weimar Republic • Formation of the League of Nations

A year of revolution! Acts of great iconoclastic daring come from all sides. After the dramatic birth of Fauvism in 1905, art of the twentieth century now makes great strides toward its liberation from realistic representation, the laws of classical perspective, and Cartesian logic. Art suddenly takes off in the direction of pure abstraction with Kandinsky, of planned abstraction with Kupka, of analytical Cubism with Picasso and Braque, of the destructuralization of forms with Léger and Delaunay, of absolute stylization with Matisse, and of naive oneirism with Henri Rousseau. At the same time, Freud, writing on the hallucinations of Leonardo da Vinci, discovers the determining role played by flashes of the unconscious in artistic inspiration.

1910
SUMMARY

MUSIC

AUSTRIA-HUNGARY
Richard Strauss composes Der Rosenkavalier, *with a libretto by Hugo von Hoffmannsthal.*

FRANCE
Triumphant performance of L'oiseau de feu, *which brings fame to the twenty-eight-year-old Russian composer Igor Stravinsky and to Sergei de Diaghilev's ballet.*
Premiere of the Second Symphony *by Gustav Mahler under the direction of the composer, who was practically unknown in France.*

LITERATURE

AUSTRIA-HUNGARY
Rainer Maria Rilke publishes The Diary of My Other Self.

UNITED STATES
Ezra Pound publishes The Spirit of Romance.

FRANCE
Publication of African Impressions *by Raymond Roussel,* Mystère de la charité de Jeanne d'Art *by Charles Péguy, and* Five Great Odes *by Paul Claudel.*

INDIA
Rabindranath Tagore publishes Lyrical Offering.

ITALY
Benedetto Croce publishes Problems in Esthetics.

WASSILI KANDINSKY:
ABSTRACT WATERCOLOR (DETAIL).
1910. Paris. MNAM

WASSILI KANDINKSY: ABSTRACT WATERCOLOR. 1910. Paris. MNAM
The direct expression of our inner world.

Kandinsky in Munich 1909.

KANDINSKY:
THE FIRST ABSTRACT WATERCOLOR

MUNICH

The event is important: Wassily Kandinsky, forty-six—born in Moscow on December 4, 1866—has painted the first abstract watercolor. He goes beyond Expressionism, beyond Cubism, beyond Futurism. In his eyes, this is not an attempt or an experiment without a tomorrow but a need of the time, engaging all forms of art.

It is worthwhile retracing the manner in which the artist came to this abstraction. There is a funny story that he has been telling his friends: It was two years ago, toward dusk, that Kandinksy went to his studio, still under the impression of a day spent painting the landscape. Suddenly he saw, leaning against the wall, a painting of extreme beauty, composed of shapes and colors whose meaning he could not grasp. Who could have put it there during his absence, a masterpiece like that? Then, approaching it, he solved the riddle: It was one of his paintings, lying on its side. At that moment he knew with certainty it was figurative presentation that had done damage to his way of painting.

Already in his works of the latest years, in Murnau, in the Bavarian Alps where he spent his summers, Kandinsky had made his subjects—the church in Murnau, mountains, groups of trees, fields—explode with color. And he was already then searching for what he found today: an internalized art like music. He is sure that painting can have the same power and intensity as music.

Besides the story of the canvas lying on its side, two other events in his life seem to have played a role. In 1885, during the exhibition of French Impressionists in Moscow, he was fascinated by Monet's *Haystack*, one of a series of paintings showing haystacks around his property of Giverny consumed by light. It was the discovery of a quasi-abstract painting. This was followed by a haunting question: Why wouldn't painters, one day, succeed in painting freely, with pure shapes and colors?

The same year, a performance of *Lohengrin* at the Court theater confirmed his feelings. Kandinsky likes to remember how, while listening to Wagner, he saw wild lines appearing before his eyes; how the violins, the deep basses and wind instruments, mentally evoked for him the entire gamut of colors; how a whole complex of tensions rose in his soul. Twenty-five years later, it was these recollections and fascinations that he succeeded in translating into painting for the first time.

Perhaps Kandinsky would have never taken the great step, however, had he not read Worringer's *Abstraction and Empathy*, the brilliant 1907 essay by a young art historian popular in Germany in avant-garde circles.

"The tendency toward abstraction is the consequence of man's deep turmoil in confronting the world," writes Worringer. "Ruined by the presumption to know, modern man finds himself as helpless as primitive man before the image of the world."

Our ancestral image of reality, once believed to be based on immutable laws, was shaken by modern science. Kandinsky was deeply impressed. Having learned that the atom itself was divisible, reality seemed so weak on its bases that he wouldn't have been surprised to see rocks melt into thin air and disappear. Thus, for him there would be no other truths than those we discover inside ourselves, sustained by what he calls the "principle of inner need."

Kandinsky, whose influence on the Neue Künstlervereinigung (the New Artists' Association of Munich) is clear, considers that ". . . all means are sacred if they are necessary to one's inner self." He is working on an essay whose title he has already chosen: *About the Spiritual in Art and Especially in Painting*, for which he is looking for a daring publisher. An extract has already appeared in Russia.

It will be a demanding work, showing the concern for spirituality underlying the artist's conception, raising questions on the relationship between shape and colors, which are viewed less in their perceptive dimension and more in their possibility of affecting the soul.

Does his watercolor open a new path for artistic creation? Made out of spirals and spots that act on the eye by their sheer energy, it is an advance over his oil paintings which, although enigmatically titled "compositions," have not until now passed the stage of allusive figuration. We are awaiting the next painting to form an opinion.

However, there is reason to believe that one should see in this watercolor a decisive step forward, which Gauguin was the first to wish for when he declared not long ago: "Pure color, we must sacrifice everything to it!"

(See also 1911, 1926, 1927, 1944.)

KUPKA PLANS COLOR

PARIS

Frantisek Kupka has invented a new pictorial technique by planning color in a special way. The technique involves a superposition of prismatic colors by vertical planes. Thus, he shows unparalleled originality this year, perhaps equaling Kandinsky's abstract watercolor. Unlike the latter, our Czech artist actually starts out with figurative subjects, which he tries to filter progressively until they become transparent. He goes from the warmest to the coldest shades, and preferably finds his inspiration in women's attitudes, bathing women, women picking fruit or looking in the mirror.

Kupka, born in 1871, arrived in Paris in the spring of 1895, and went to live in Montmartre. In 1905, he moved to Puteaux, where Jacques Villon was his studio neighbor. In 1906 he showed his *Autumn Sun* at the Salon d'Automne. He soon became enthralled by the reverberations of light on calm waters. Then he tried to render decomposed movement, like Marey in his chronophotographies. This is how he came to paint his *Plans par couleur* (planes by color), which are a culmination of his previous studies.

The interference of his elliptic shapes and vertical zones of transparent color shows a desire for clairvoyance and, undoubtedly, the search for a kind of divination of the world, of cosmic visions, which, if he persevered, could make him the first truly abstract painter. It is clear that Kupka who two years ago was heavily influenced by archaic Greek art in his series of engravings for Aeschylus' Prometheus takes large steps towards chromatic abstraction. What an evolution, within a few years, from his first posters and caricatures!

FRANTISEK KUPKA: PLANS POUR COULEURS. 1910. Paris. MNAM
The interference of prismatic colors.

ABSTRACT ART: WAGER OR REVOLUTION?

MUNICH

Everybody in artistic circles is wondering: Is abstract art a futureless wager or, on the contrary, a completely new way of painting, with a precise goal —namely, the direct expression on canvas of the interior world, which is infinitely vaster than the visible world?

On the "wager" side, the editor of the *Münchner Neueste Nachrichten* comments on the current exhibition of the Neue Künstlervereinigung, chaired by Kandinsky: "It's one of two things: Either most of the members of this society are incurably demented, or we are dealing with a gang of unscrupulous bluffers, who are perfectly aware of our time's hunger for sensational events and are trying to exploit the situation."

On the "pictorial revolution" side, there is the entire European avant-garde. Indeed, abstraction doesn't only go a long way back, but could also be the logical path of development for twentieth-century art. It comes directly from Impressionism and Postimpressionism, Fauvism, and Cubism, to the extent that these schools break with traditional figurative values. And, before these, there was Turner, whose last paintings are but a conflagration of sunlight, and even the ornamental abstraction of the primitives. Already Gauguin painted a green horse, Cézanne reduced his *Mount Sainte-Victoire* to large colored surfaces, and Van Gogh made his blue faces and yellow skies.

No doubt, the future will tell that abstract art has infinite possibilities for renewal. For is there anything more monotonous than the miles of landscapes, still lifes, and insipid nudes spelling out their eternal boredom in the official salons, compared with an art rooted in the yet unexplored abysses of the spirit?

VOLLARD HACKED UP BY PICASSO

PARIS

How far will Picasso go? We already know that he is capable of dismembering women's bodies, as in *Les demoiselles d'Avignon*, or cutting guitars and pitchers down to crumbs, but now he is taking up the human face. More specifically, the face of his dealer, Ambroise Vollard.

The work was exhibited last week, on Rue Laffite, in the gallery of the colorful art dealer. What was it? Was the canvas hung upside down? What on earth could this assembly of sharp angles resembling glass shards represent? The public couldn't believe what it saw.

They say that truth comes out of the mouths of babes. The solution of the enigma was given by a little boy of four, who visited the gallery quite often, and who was there with his art-loving father. Stepping suddenly up to the painting and pointing at it with his little hand, he shouted: "That's Vollard!" Undoubtedly, it took the eye of a child to recognize the resemblance that the eye of an adult, too used to conventions, couldn't see.

Picasso, pushing Analytical Cubism to its limits, painted his two other art dealers, Wilhelm Uhde and Daniel-Henry Kahnweiler, in portraits that were also barely recognizable.

Vollard had his portrait done by many of his artists, including Cézanne, Maurice Denis, Bonnard, and Renoir, who all retained his various psychological features: One after the other, they showed the astute, mistrusting side of the potbellied man.

Picasso painted something entirely different. Certainly he did not forget that less than ten years ago Vollard had refused him the price of a railway ticket to Barcelona in exchange for a roll of canvases from the blue period. But Cubism, through its cutting up and dismantling of the image, opened up for him the universal side of the human being. And so we got something like a philosophical portrait, one that makes us think of Socrates, with the face of Silenus, meditating with closed eyes.

PABLO PICASSO: PORTRAIT OF AMBROISE VOLLARD. 1910. Moscow. Pushkin Museum

LÉGER EXECUTES THE WOODS

FERNAND LÉGER: NUDES IN THE FOREST. 1910.
Otterlo. Kröller-Müller Museum

PARIS

Fernand Léger, appearing as a self-taught marginal person, says, while contemplating the work of his friends from the Bateau-Lavoir: "They are above events; I gather everything in the street." He likes scrap iron, pieces of corrugated tin, metal tubes, and people from the suburbs. He reveals a social vocation: The man who works and suffers acquired in his eyes a plastic dimension that he fills with power and modernism. Thinking about *Les demoiselles d'Avignon*, painted three years ago by Picasso, he created *Nudes in the Forest*. Into this

original theme he tried to transcribe the sum of his research. The purple naked bodies of the woodcutters stand in a landscape made up of cut-up cylindrical cones. There is perfect identity between the man's torso and the trunk of the tree, between the man's arms and the logs. Human, vegetable, and mineral fragments intermingle to create a geometrical landscape that is a homage to Cézanne, whom he calls "the true primitive of a new art," and to Henri Rousseau, whom he admires for the extreme simplicity of his poetical vision.

DELAUNAY BREAKS THE EIFFEL TOWER

PARIS

"Robert shouldn't have broken the Eiffel Tower. . ." Reportedly, these were the last words uttered by Henri Rousseau on September 2, before he died of gangrene at the Necker Hospital.

His admirer Robert Delaunay was one of the seven people who followed the coffin of the gentle "Douanier." "The Tower," as Delaunay, twenty-five calls it, is the center of a series on which he is working. He disarticulated the tower in order to redeem its aerial element, cut it up and tilted it to render its nine hundred eighty feet of vertigo. No art formula known until today could solve the case of the Eiffel Tower. Realism made it look small; the old Italian laws of perspective made it thinner. That's why Delaunay ended up adopting ten points of view and fifteen field depths: One part is seen from above, another part from below, while the houses around it are taken from the right, the left, with a bird's-eye view.

The writer Blaise Cendrars may have been the originator of the "Tower" series. Returning from Chartres at the beginning of the year, he fell out of his car and broke his shinbone at the entrance of the Park Saint-Cloud. Transported to the Palais Hotel, he stayed there immobilized, for twenty-eight days; from his bed, he could see the Eiffel Tower looming over Paris. His friend Delaunay, who came to keep him company almost every day, was thrilled by the perspectives he could find. He made a lot of sketches and even brought his paint box.

The influence of Seurat, on the other hand, also played a part. Among his latest paintings was a small Pointillist canvas showing the Eiffel Tower, in which he applied Chevreul's theory of simultaneous contrasts, also adopted by Delaunay in his first paintings. And—is it a simple coincidence?—Chevreul was in love with the Eiffel Tower. Every day during its construction, he had has carriage drive him to the Champ-de-Mars to see the progress of the work, which he was lucky enough to see finished before he died at the age of one hundred and three, in 1889.

ROBERT DELAUNAY: EIFFEL TOWER. 1910. Basel. Kunstmuseum

A NAIL IN THE PAINTING

L'ESTAQUE

Is it because he learned decorative painting, completely opposed to any metaphysical speculation, or is it simply because he is French? Be that as it may, the fact remains that in the midst of the Analytical Cubist era Georges Braque has retained his taste for the concrete.

His latest paintings, like those of his friend Picasso, approximate abstraction. Broken violins, pitchers cut up into their multiple facets, fragments of various objects such as palettes, glasses, pianos, music scores that seem to float in space—the subjects of all these compositions are difficult to recognize. One doesn't know which way to hang them.

Yet, two of his recent paintings, *Violin and Palette* and *Jug and Violin* have, at the top, a nail painted in *trompe l'oeil* with its shadow projected onto the canvas as though it were there to hang the painting.

Another innovation: A third recent still life, *Le Pyrogene,* contains a pipe and a folded newspaper bearing the four capital letters GIL B (for *Gil Blas,* the title the newspaper). Already in *The School of Athens* Raphael used printed letters on the backs of the *Timeaus* and the *Ethics* that Plato and Aristotle carry under their arms, so as to characterize the two Greek philosophers. Braque used a long-obsolete technique, but he gave it new significance.

Indeed, Cubism, which originated with Cézanne and his concern with discerning the geometrical structure of reality under its elusive appearance, paradoxically broke this structure to pieces. Somehow, it had to reestablish its connection with the visible: thus the famous nail and the letters, which are signs as well as means of recognition.

Could Cubism be the latest Mannerism? Is it greedy for ambiguities, false indications, false appearances? Or must we see in Braque's nail a form of irony, perhaps even sarcasm, for the theoretical and intellectual aspect of Cubism? If an artist brings nothing new, he is accused of being old-fashioned; if he does bring something new, he is called a revolutionary. It seems that Braque wanted to reconcile the new and the old.

WINSLOW HOMER: BREEZING UP. 1876. Washington. National Gallery

WINSLOW HOMER HAS LEFT US

UNITED STATES

Winslow Homer, painter and watercolorist, died on September 29 in Prout's Neck, Maine. He was born in Boston in 1836. His vigorous Realistic work will undoubtedly remain as one of the most important bodies of American painting of the end of the nineteenth century. His most famous paintings and watercolors are tumultuous scenes evoking, above all, the life of sailors, such as *The Life Line, The Fog Warning,* and *The Gulf Stream.* He had the skill of capturing the ever-changing movement and luminosity of the sky in Maine, where he lived after spending two years in Tynemonth, a little fishing port in England. In his compositions, which had a certain degree of pathos, he tried to express man's fight against the elements; but at the end of his life, he was also influenced by the mirages of Japanese prints.

PROTESTS AT THE SECESSION

BERLIN

The Secession ("Sezession"), created eleven years ago as a reaction against official art, is suffering a crisis. Its members completely disagree with the attitude of its selection jury who rejected the group Die Brücke (The Bridge) for its exposition this year. Indeed, the jury rejected the work of Heckel, Kirchner, Pechstein, Nolde, and Schmidt-Rottluff, all members of the famous Dresden group.

During its general assembly, some attacked Max Liebermann, a supporter of French Impressionism, and art dealer Paul Cassirer, whom they accused of being dictatorial. As a sign of opposition, Beckmann, known for his objectivity, and Leo von König were elected to the managing committee. But this election did not solve the conflict among the members of Die Brücke. That's why a New Secession was created on the initiative of Max Pechstein. Its first group show took place in May, under the title "Works of those rejected by the Berlin Secession."

Since then, a deep conflict has arisen between Nolde and Liebermann. The former was expelled from the Secession, to which he belonged even though he was a member of the New Secession. Indeed, he had sent an insulting letter to Liebermann, telling him that he was incompetent because he was senile. The latter, deeply upset (he is sixty-three years old), quit and was replaced by Corinth.

CROSS ENHANCES THE IRIDESCENCE OF THE SEA

LE LAVANDOU

Certain names predispose toward painting. Such was the case of Henri-Edmond Delacroix (meaning literally "of the cross"), who chose the pseudonym of Cross in order to avoid confusion with the great Romantic painter, and who died recently at the age of sixty-four. In his adolescence he was a student of Carolus-Duran, who was from Lille like he himself and who influenced his early work.

However, in 1884, when he was twenty-eight, Cross adopted Neoimpressionism. With Seurat and Signac, he was one of the founders of the Salon des Indépendants and became its vice-president in 1891. He most-ly painted Mediterranean landscapes, such as *Plage du Midi* (beach in the South of France), 1892, or *Mother Playing with Her Child*, painted later and owned by Félix Fénéon.

Cross' painting was light, iridescent, sunny; it used the Pointillist technique with a personal touch, with largely spaced strokes of light colors.

The painter lived in the South of France since 1891, when he went there to cure his rheumatism. His friends followed. Fascinated by the brilliance of the colors of sunlight, Cross was one of the precursors of Fauvism, linked to Matisse. The latter came to work with him, in Var, during the summer of 1904 and the next winter composed *Luxe, calme et volupté*, a title taken from a poem by the French poet Charles Baudelaire and one of his rare Pointillist paintings.

The freedom of Cross' paint-ings assured his success. His works reflected a lyrical analysis of light, a euphoria especially present in the artist's pagan mythological subjects.

HENRI-EDMOND CROSS: THE GOLDEN ISLAND. 1891-1892. Paris. Musée d'Orsay

HENRI MATISSE: DANCE. 1910. Leningrad. Hermitage Museum

"The blue of the sky, the pink of the bodies, the green of the hill . . ." **(Henri Matisse).**

THE WILD FARANDOLE OF HENRI MATISSE

PARIS

The French are paradoxical people: They don't like Henri Matisse, the most French of all painters. In turn, his two Russian collectors, Sergei Ivanovich Chtchoukin and Ivan Morosov, both industrialists from Moscow, are wild about his painting.

Currently one can admire at the Salon d'Automne two compositions of the artist, *Dance* and *Music*, commissioned by Chtchoukin for the decoration of his house. The artist worked hard on them for a year in his studio of Issy-les-Moulineaux. Both compositions are large: 8 1/2 x 19 feet.

After making the first sketches, Matisse explained them to critic Étienne Charles: "I can imagine the visitor entering: The second floor is before him. After his effort to climb the stairs, he needs to be refreshed. That's why the first panel will represent a dance on the top of a hill . . . I'll do it with the simplest means, those that allow the painter to express his inner vision most efficiently. We achieve the highest serenity by the simplification of ideas and by plastic means."

Dance repeats a round appearing in the background of *La joie de vivre*, exhibited by

Matisse four years ago at the Salon des Indépendants. With its hand-holding bodies, it evokes the morning of the earth. But it has a concision never pushed so far before. Reduced to their essential lines, the five characters hold hands in a rhythmical dance, executed in three colors only: the blue of the sky, the pink of the bodies, the green of the hill. This taste for the music of lines and colors seems to stem from Matisse's interest in Muslim art, which exceeds all others in joining spirituality and sensuality. But he is also very sensitive to Gauguin's exoticism and hieratic

Symbolism. He discovered Gauguin's Tahitian works as early as 1905. Gustave Moreau, who was his teacher, prophetically said to him: "You will be the simplifier of painting." Today, Henri Matisse is searching for a soaring simplicity able to "offer modern man an altogether classic delight."

With this remarkably harmonious *Dance*, Henri Matisse has indeed achieved perfect rhythmical unity, with a modern dynamism that presages a new style, made up of violence and purification.

(See also 1905, 1908, 1916, 1933, 1951, 1954.)

113

Félix Nadar, as seen by his son and successor.

NADAR THE "FAKE-TOGRAPHER"

PARIS

"He was a good-hearted man," Claude Monet said about him. Félix Nadar, a man always ready to help political, scientific, or artistic revolutions, has died at the age of ninety.

His true name was Félix Tournachon. He was at one and the same time a journalist, novelist, cartoonist, painter, balloon pilot, and, above all, photographer. He was born in 1820, in a family of typographers from Lyon who had come to live in Paris. In 1858 he made the first aerial photograph from a balloon, above Petit-Bicêtre, and, three year later, the first underground photograph using electricity, in the catacombs of Paris. He also was the inventor of photographic portrait: His portraits of Baudelaire, Victor Hugo, Clemenceau, and Jules Verne are pure masterpieces of psychology.

But painting earned him his glory. From April 15 to May 15 1874, his red-painted studio (red was his favorite color) at 35 Boulevard des Capucines, sheltered the Anonymous Society of Painters, Sculptors, and Engravers, rejected by all galleries and museums. There were three hundred paintings by thirty artists (among whom were Monet, Degas, Sisley, Renoir, Boudin, Cézanne, and Berthe Morisot), called "palette scrapings" by the critics; but this collection was the foundation stone of the Impressionist school.

Nadar's studio was a lively place where he loved to receive his friends, who included writers, artists, musicians, and the like. "I am a painter too," he said to Degas one day. In his suburban accent, Degas answered: "Come on! Fake artist, fake painter, fake-tographer!"

A DONKEY BECOMES HEAD OF A SCHOOL

PARIS

For a month now, Parisians have been floating in boats in a Paris as romantic as Venice. It must have been the contemplation of the flooded canallike streets that gave three young art students, Roland Dorgelès, Pierre Girieud, and André Warnod, the idea of naming *Sunset on the Adriatic*, a painting given star billing at the current Salon des Indépendants.

The three pranksters convinced Frédé, the owner of the cabaret *Le Lapin Agile*, to lend them his donkey, Aliboron.

The animal was placed before a haycock in the middle of the street. The three accomplices alternatively dipped its tail in various pots of paint, and the donkey smeared a canvas placed under its rear. A dauntless observer wrote down, amidst the cheering of the crowd, every tail stroke painted by master Aliboron. When the donkey got tired of this exercise, the work was signed Joachim-Raphaël Boronali (an anagram of Aliboron), "Italian painter," then entered and deposited at the Salon des Indépendants.

The beans were spilled the day of the opening by an article written by Dorgelès in *Le Matin*, titled "A Donkey Becomes Head of a School."

BORONALI: SUNSET ON THE ADRIATIC. 1910

Odessa's International Salon

Since last year, the city of Odessa has been arranging an annual exhibition where foreign artists are represented. The initiative for the exhibition came from the sculptor Vladimir Izdebeski. The first exhibition had brought together works by several Frenchmen, including Braque, Bonnard, Gleizes, Matisse, Henri Rousseau, Signac, and Vuillard. The Italian artist Balla represented the new Futurist movement. The second exhibition has just been held, with paintings by the Russians Larionov, Gontcharova, Bourliouk (the two brothers, David and Vladimir), Kandinsky, and Jawlensky. The only foreigner this year is the German Gabriele Münter.

Frank Lloyd Wright in Fiesole

The most romantic of the American architects, Frank Lloyd Wright, has decided to reconcile theory with practice. At the age of forty-three, he has left his wife and six children and gone to Italy, where he is staying with Mrs. Cheney, the wife of one of his clients. Living in Fiesole the majority of the time, he claims he admires the painters and architects of the Renaissance, whom he studies and hopes to equal. A large exhibit of his works in Berlin is also announced.

A New Berlin Magazine

A new magazine, *Der Sturm* (the storm), is born on March 3, and it is meant to be part of the new spirit evident for some time now in Berlin's literary and artistic circles. Its editor, Herwarth Walden, known as a musician and talented leader under his real name of Georg Lewin, hopes to spread knowledge of the so-called avantgarde movements such as Fauvism, Cubism, and Futurism. His ultimate goal is to publish texts by writers, poets, and painters, as well as black-and-white and color illustrations.

The Valet de Carreau in Moscow

The year ends on a lovely note for the avant-garde, thanks to the Valet de Carreau exhibition. Besides the well-known painters Larionov, Gontcharova, and the

NATALIA GONTCHAROVA: HAYMAKING. 1910. Paris. Private Collection

Bourliouk brothers, works by promising artists are shown: Malevich, who had come to Moscow in 1905, and who is exhibiting for the first time outside official salons, and Lentoulov, expelled from school last year because his artistic conceptions were judged to be too "Cézannian." Lentoulov's brother-in-law is responsible for financing the exhibition. Seeing its success, Lentoulov is already thinking about new shows to come for the Valet de Carreau.

How Far Will Functionalism Go?

The architect Peter Behrens, born in Hamburg in 1868, and now forty-two years old, seems to be afraid of nothing. With its metal framework and large glass bays, devoid of all ornamentation, his building for AEG, the German electric company located in Berlin, is revolutionary on all scores. Influenced in the beginning by Art Nouveau, Behrens now seems to be trying to orient himself in a completely different direction.

Gaudí's Casa Milá

The Catalan architect Antonio Gaudí has just completed the Casa Milá in Barcelona. He had begun it five years earlier. Nick-

named the "Pedrera," this apartment building with its undulating, organic shapes is a perfect incarnation of the Art Nouveau style that Gaudí has pushed to the limits of the irrational. A peculiar characteristic is the apartment building's chimneys, abstract structures recalling phantoms that swim up from the depths of dreams. In 1883, Gaudí, as everyone knows, had laid the first stone of la Sagrada Familia (the Holy Family), a cathedral comparable to the sacred buildings of the Middle Ages, and he now announces that Güell Park, overlooking the city, is almost completed.

AEG factory in Berlin, built by Peter Behrens.

GENTLE ROUSSEAU: AN ABSOLUTE DREAMER

PARIS

Henri Rousseau, nicknamed Le Douanier (the customs clerk), was buried in the common grave at the Bagneux cemetery on September 4. Seven people were there, among them Paul Signac and Robert Delaunay. He was sixty-six years old.

Born in Laval on May 21, 1844, he worked as a minor clerk at the Customs House of Paris, dabbling in painting on Sundays. In 1893 he decided to retire in order to dedicate himself to his art. He had nine children, of whom seven died in their infancy, and two wives, Clémence, for whom he composed a waltz, and Joséphine.

Henri Rousseau used to paint in the morning. In the afternoon, he took off the gray shirt that protected his clothes and put away his palette. Then he received groups of young pupils whom he taught the rudiments of music to round out his meager pension.

In the evening, he sometimes played his violin on street corners, or presided at literary and musical gatherings at home. He exhibited at the Salon des Indépendants and the Salon d'Automne, said that he would gladly "finish" Cezanne's paintings, detested Matisse's, and admired Bouguereau and Gérôme.

He called himself a painter of nature, "this beautiful and great nature whom any honest painter should worship," and, indeed, made beautiful landscapes on the banks of the Seine with its solitary fishermen in their boats. He also liked to paint the acacias in the Bois de Boulogne.

His most fabulous paintings are based on copies from book and catalog illustrations, such as *The Sleeping Gipsy*, representing a circus lion and a fashion plate put together. His gibbons, langurs, and apes of all descriptions come from an album printed by the Galeries Lafayette. Rousseau placed his subjects in the luminous vegetation that he had seen at the Jardin des Plantes (botanical garden) where, with the complicity of a gardener, he entered the hothouses, becoming intoxicated by their heavy fragrance. Rousseau painted his waking dreams.

Fate made Alfred Jarry introduce Rousseau to the art avant-garde. He was twenty, Rousseau almost fifty; they had met in 1894, at the Indépendants, in front of a terrifying painting, *La Guerre* (the war).

The author of *Ubu roi* introduced him to Apollinaire, who introduced him to Picasso, another painter who was very impressed by the marvelous candor of Rousseau's oneiric paintings. That year he only exhibited one painting at the Salon des Indépendants, and that was *The Dream*, showing a naked woman reclining on a Louis-Philippe sofa in the middle of a tropical forest, upon which he begged Apollinaire to defend him against the jeers of the public and critics.

(See also 1905, and 1908.)

HENRI ROUSSEAU: THE DREAM. 1910. New York. MOMA

Rousseau's last painting, shown at the Salon des Indépendants in 1910.

SIGMUND FREUD ANALYZES ART

Fifty-four years old, Sigmund Freud the neurologist and psychiatrist, who practices in Vienna, where his theories on the role of sexuality in dreams and psychopathological behavior are beginning to found a school (he succeeded this year in creating the International Psychoanalytical Association), attempts to apply these theories in a profound study of a Leonardo da Vinci painting, *The Holy Virgin, Child, and St. Anne*. This essay was published by Deuticke under the title *A Childhood Recollection of Leonardo da Vinci*. Freud analyzes, for the first time, the influence of the sexual instinct on pictorial creation. By examining Leonardo's childhood emotions, he argues that Leonardo in fact sublimated these emotions in his works. He believes he can discover, in the Holy Virgin's dress in this painting, the shape of a vulture that would be the indirect expression of an "oral" fantasy of the infant in love with his mother—the infant being Leonardo himself. According to Freud, art may be a substitute expression of repressions of infantile sexual desires.

To my knowledge, only once has Leonardo introduced in his scientific writings some facts about his childhood. Where he speaks of the flight of the vulture, he interrupts himself suddenly to follow a recollection from his early childhood: "I seem to be destined to concern myself particularly with the vulture, for one of my first childhood recollections was that while I was still in the cradle a vulture came to me, opened my mouth with his tail, and hit me several times with this tail between the lips." This scene is probably not an actual recollection but was created later in Leonardo's mind . . .

The intuition of the relationship between his scholarly investigations and the history of his childhood made him later exclaim that he had always intended to thoroughly study the problem of the flight of birds because he had been visited by a vulture while still in the cradle.

What someone believes to recall from his childhood is not a matter of indifference. In general, priceless testimonies are hidden here, affecting the most important traits of his psychic development.

An observation of daily life shows us that most people succeed in putting significant parts of their instinctive sexual forces in the service of their occupational activity. The sexual instinct is particularly appropriate to such relationships because of its ability to sublimate, that is, to abandon its immediate goal in favor of nonsexual and possibly higher goals . . . Let us simply state this fact: The artist's creative work derives from his sexual desires. And we shall recall what Vasari said of Leonardo's beginnings: smiling women's heads and beautiful little boys, that is, representations of the first objects on which his sexuality would become fixed . . .

Having reached the zenith of his life, in his

fifties, at that age where men's libido often attempts a renewed energetic activity, Leonardo undergoes a new evolution. Still deeper layers of his soul are revived; but this kind of regression favors his art, which was in the process of declining. He meets the woman who awakens in him the recollection of the happy and sensually ecstatic smile of his mother, and under the influence of this recollection he recovers the inspiration that guided his first artistic work when he was shaping smiling women's heads. He paints the Mona Lisa, St. Anne, *and the series of paintings characterized by the enigma of their smile . . . Thanks to his older erotic emotions, he once more triumphs over the inhibition that had been hampering his art . . . Artistic talent and the capacity for work being closely tied to sublimation, we must admit, though, that the essence of the artistic function remains psychoanalytically inaccessible . . . The contours of the determinations of our personal life—stemming from "necessities" of our constitution or from "accidents" of our childhood—may still be unexplored in their dimensions, but we must no longer doubt the importance of the first years of our childhood. We still have too little respect for Nature, which, according to the sibylline words of Leonardo, words that foreshadow those of Hamlet, "is full of infinite reasons that are beyond our experience." Each human being, each of us, answers to one among the endless number of attempts through which these "reasons" of Nature's strive toward existence.*

SIGMUND FREUD
A Childhood Recollection
of Leonardo da Vinci
(Excerpt)

Freud discovered the outline of a vulture in this painting (when looked at sideways).

LEONARDO DA VINCI:
THE HOLY VIRGIN, CHILD,
AND ST. ANNE. About 1508-1510.
Paris. Louvre

Decidedly, abstraction does not sit well even with the artists of the avant-garde. The exhibition of the Blue Rider in Munich comes about when Kandinsky's peers reject one of his canvases, Composition 5. At the same time in Paris, however, Cubism makes great strides. The moment seems near when everyone will be producing Cubist canvases, risking the creation of a modern Academicism. Sculpture and architecture, meanwhile, are off in new directions. But perhaps the event of the year takes the form of a fascinating news item: At the moment when public opinion is focused on the disappearance of the Mona Lisa, the poet Guillaume Apollinaire is arrested for involuntary concealment after his secretary steals several Iberian statuettes from the Louvre.

1911

S U M M A R Y

AVANT-GARDE

**The Blue Rider Charges
Kandinsky: Three Mystical Necessities
Klee between Van Gogh and Voltaire
Polemic over French Art**

MOVEMENTS

Is Cubism Becoming Academic?

DEVELOPMENTS

**Guillaume Apollinaire Is Accused
The Trio of Puteaux**

ART NEWS

**Antoine Bourdelle Makes Isadora Dance
Cubism in Prague
The Day of Glory for the Pompiers
The Death of Fritz von Uhde
Henri Matisse's Fury
In Brief**

SCULPTURE

**Archipenko Makes Shapes Obey
Gargallo Cuts Metal**

ARCHITECTURE

All the Arts in One Palace

FRANZ MARC:
BLUE HORSE. 1911.
Bern. Kunstmuseum

THE BLUE RIDER CHARGES

MUNICH

Two years ago, when the Tannhäuser gallery organized the first exhibition of the New Artists' Association, the important daily *Münchner Neueste Nachrichten* accused most of the members of being "incurable madmen" or "shameless charlatans." These madmen were Kandinsky, Jawlensky, Marianne Werefkin, Erbslöh, Kanoldt, Kubin. Today, the painters themselves are in conflict.

Indeed, after months of bickering, the breach came at the beginning of December, when the jury of the third exhibition of the Association refused one of Kandinsky's paintings, *Composition V*, because it was too abstract. Rumor has it that Otto Fischer, one of Kandinsky's opponents, declared that "a painting without a subject is absurd." This remark is absurd itself; we know the painter's constant anxiety and intellectual demands when he ventured outside the beaten path of figurative art. The proof is his essay *About the Spiritual in Art and Especially in Painting*, recently published by Piper Verlag.

So Kandinsky, the cofounder of the New Artists' Association, ended up by storming out and creating a competitive exhibition, with Franz Marc and other artists who disagreed.

A SHARED SPIRITUAL QUEST RATHER THAN A SHARED PROGRAM

This show opened at the Tannhäuser gallery on December 18, in a hall adjoining the third exhibition of the Association. The paintings, not many of them, are collectively called "The Blue Rider." The name was found by Kandinsky and Marc while they were drinking coffee in Marc's house in Sindelsdorf: The two painters happen to love blue, riders, and horses.

Is the Blue Rider more than a random name? In spite of their common concerns, the artists' inspiration is so varied that the exhibition, unlike Futurism or even Cubism or Fauvism, doesn't show any schoollike esthetics. Kandinsky put together the work of some of his friends; a *Self-Portrait* and two *Visions* of the Austrian composer Arnold Schönberg, who is less revolutionary in his painting than in his music; six paintings of his companion Gabrielle Münter, among which is a *Still Life with St. George,* painted in folk-art style; and, as a posthumous homage, two drawings of Eugen von Kahler, who died on December 13 in Prague.

On the other hand, Kandinsky invited some foreigners: the brothers Bourliouk and Natalia Gontcharova from Russia, Robert Delaunay and Henri Rousseau (from whom he wants to buy a painting) from France. Franz Marc did the same, which explains the presence of the

WASSILI KANDINSKY:
SKETCH WITH HORSEMAN. 1911.
Paris. Collection Flinker

ERICH HECKEL:
YOUNG GIRL STANDING.
1910. Bern. Private Collection

KANDINSKY: THREE MYSTICAL NECESSITIES

animal painter Jean Bloé Niestlé, who is not that new, but also of some real innovators like Campendonck or Macke.

So, this exhibition, in which one would vainly try to find a program, has no orientation, no guidelines, and no unity. It was to be expected, since Franz Marc was quoted to have made up this slogan: "Let's rid ourselves of all progams!" In turn, Kandinsky, with his *Composition V*, demands the right to dare anything, provided the painting is nourished by what he calls "the principle of inner necessity."

Apparently, there is no close relationship between the two creators of the Blue Rider. Kandinsky's painting is a search for the absolute. He writes in his essay that, in his eyes, colors speak less to the spectator's sensitivity than to his soul because they come from the depths of the being. As early as 1903 he had a painting in which a rider clad in a blue cape gallops on a white horse through a romantic fall landscape; undoubtedly, this painting was in his mind when, with Franz Marc, he gave the new movement its name.

In turn, Franz Marc seems less "advanced" than Kandinsky who, at forty-five, is fourteen years older. Until now, Marc has dedicated himself almost exclusively to paintings of animals: yellow cows, yellow, red, or blue horses, deer and a dog in the snow. He is seeking a pantheistic union with nature. And perhaps this is what brings him close to Kandinsky, rather than his style.

The publication of an *Almanac of the Blue Rider* was announced for next year. It will contain the reproduction of some of the exhibited works and theoretical studies. In spite of the disagreements, this *Almanac* should reveal what kind of modernism these painters have in common. (See also 1908, 1910, 1926, 1944.)

It has not been easy for Wassili Kandinsky to find a publisher for his essay *About the Spiritual in Art and Especially in Painting,* which he had been working on for several years. As its title suggests, the book is a reflection on the relationship of the mind and artistic activity, a relationship that is at the core of the abstraction that Kandinsky originated last year with a watercolor made of nothing but strokes and spots. Piper Verlag in Munich published the book. It has just come out, yet it is so much in demand that the publisher is already planning a second edition.

WASSILI KANDINSKY: POETRY. 1911. Rotterdam. Boymans Museum

This interior necessity is in fact based on three mystical necessities:

1. Every artist, as creator, must learn to express what is personally characteristic. (The element of the personality.)

2. Every artist, as a child of his era, must express what is characteristic of this age. (The element of style in its interior value, consisting of the language of the times and the language of the people.)

3. Every artist, as servant of the art, must express that which is characteristic of art generally. (The element of pure and eternal art, found among all human beings, among all peoples and at all times, and which appears in the work of all artists of all nations and in all ages and which does not obey, as essential element of art, any law of space or time.)

Through the first two elements, the spiritual eye sees the third one bared. We then realize that the "rough" sculpted column of an Indian temple is animated by the same soul as any living work of our time.

The element of pure and eternal art alone will keep its value. Instead of weakening its power, time will increase it ceaselessly by giving it new strength. The more a "present" work possesses the elements that are particular to the artist and his century, the more easily the work will find access to the souls of its contemporaries. The more the eternal and pure element dominates in it, the more the two other elements will seem hidden, and the more the work will thus have difficulty in finding access to the soul of its contemporaries. Sometimes it takes centuries for this pure sound finally to reach the soul of humanity.

It can therefore be said that it is the preponderance of the third element that is an index of the splendor of a work of art and the greatness of the artist.

WASSILI KANDINSKY
About the Spiritual in Art
and Especially in Painting *(Excerpt)*

PAUL KLEE: SELF-PORTRAIT. 1911. Switzerland. Private Collection

KLEE BETWEEN VAN GOGH AND VOLTAIRE

MUNICH

Paul Klee's *Self-Portrait,* although made in ink, shows the deep psychological and esthetic affinities of the artist with Vincent Van Gogh. And with good reason. At thirty-three, Klee feels he is an accursed artist. Living in Munich since 1906, and encouraged by some friends and critics, he thought of exhibiting at Brackl or Tannhäuser, the most active art dealers of the Bavarian capital. But both of them doubt his commercial value. And if Tannhäuser ended up by proposing an exhibition of some thirty paintings, it was unfortunately in an unacceptable corridor.

However, since he decided not to let himself succumb to depression, Klee started the illustration of *Candide.* He had been thinking of this project for some time, because he loves "Father Voltaire's" manner of never complaining, and he is seduced by the extreme econo-my of *Candide's* language. He would like, therefore, to be able to achieve Voltairian economy in the engravings he is doing now, with their larvalike figures playing like marionettes the bitter comedy of lucidity.

Klee reads Voltaire in the original. And not only Voltaire, but also Molière, Corneille, Racine, and Shakespeare, and the great Greek and Roman classics. Born in Müncherbuchsee, near Bern, in 1879, in a family of musicians, he is an excellent violinist; if he chose painting over music, it was because he thought painting was less advanced than music and he could "push it forward a little."

After successful Gymnasium studies in Bern, he came to Munich and studied with Knirr, who is the director of a private preparatory school. Then he studied at the art academy, in the class of Franz von Stuck. Afterwards, like any young man who destines himself for art, he made a one-year voyage to Italy. But he was not well-liked because of the Primitivism of his paintings, and also because they look like children's drawings and even like the art of the mentally ill that can be seen in the large collection of the Waldau hospital; in fact, he confesses that he often likes that kind of art better than museum art.

Klee believes that a painter must be a poet, nature lover, and philosopher at the same time. He has the same obsession as Goethe, whom he knows quite well, namely the idea of a primeval form, rich with all real or possible worlds, mineral, vegetal, animal, spiritual. Hence his dual interest in children's drawings and the graphic expression of the mentally ill. And he has not forgotten that poor Vincent Van Gogh was also hospitalized in a psychiatric ward.

There is at least one painter, in Munich, Wassili Kandinsky, who understands Klee's total originality. Unfortunately, the two met too late for Kandinsky to invite Klee to the Blue Rider exhibition that opened on December 18 at the same Tannhäuser gallery. But Kandinsky plans a second exhibition of the group for next March. Klee will be invited, probably with his engravings for *Candide.* And that's a promise!

POLEMIC OVER FRENCH ART

Carl Vinnen, the traditional painter, publishes, at Diedrichs publishers in Jena, a Protest of German Artists. The cause of this protest is the acquisition of a Van Gogh painting by the art gallery of Bremen. Vinnen thus indirectly attacks the activities of those museum directors whom he considers irresponsible. Among his targets is Hugo von Tschudi, who opened the National Gallery of Berlin to modern art. (The emperor fired Tschudi for this policy.) More generally, Vinnen denounces the invasion of the German art scene by Frenchmen. But he got a massive reply through a collective effort directed by Franz Marc called "German and French Art." It expresses Marc's opposition to Vinnen's chauvinist approach.

IS CUBISM BECOMING ACADEMIC?

PARIS

On Friday, April 21, the XXVIIth Salon des Indépendants opened at Quai d'Orsay. Over four hundred new members enrich the numbers of this important event, which by statute has neither jury nor prizes. Cubism has its own following, this being its first collective manifestation. But when the public discovers the work of Gleizes, Lhote, Metzinger, Delaunay, Le Fauconnier, Archipenko, a huge scandal breaks out, not unlike the commotion caused not long ago by Fauvism.

The critics lash out with unaccumstomed fervor, speaking of "cube masters," and even Apollinaire seems uneasy. He writes in the *Intransigeant*: "Here, Metzinger is the only adept of Cubism properly speaking. The pleasantness of his work proves that this discipline is not incompatible with reality." Writing about Fernand Léger, whose *Nudes in the Forest* is at the core of the polemic, the poet shows his anxiety, although he underscores the artist's talent and force: "Mr. Fernand Léger has the most inhuman accent in this exhibition hall. His art is difficult. He creates, if we dare say the word, cylinder painting, and does not hesitate to give his composition the savage look of piled-up tires." But these lines give us the key of his uneasiness: "We will speak later about Picasso's influence on the development of such a new art."

Undoubtedly, what bothers him, and many others, is Picasso's and Braque's absence from the event; as everybody knows, they are the founders of Cubism and continue to incarnate its spirit. Instead of the true Cubists, only their followers exhibit in this salon, those whom people start calling the *cubisteurs* (cubisters). Apollinaire, Salmond, Raynal, and a few other advanced critics feel that this is not Cubism but its

GEORGES BRAQUE: A PORTUGUESE. 1911. Basel. Kunstmuseum

ROGER DE LA FRESNAYE: THE CUIRASSIER. 1910. Paris. MNAM.

caricature, its parody, and almost its Academicism.

The large *Cuirassier* presented by Roger de La Fresnaye is the most significant in this sense. While pretending to find its inspiration in Cubism, nothing could be more different from it. First of all, the choice of an epic subject is the antithesis of the ascetic mood of Picasso and Braque. The only goal of these artists is to reconsider the means of representation of an object in the space of the painting; La Fresnaye, by the exalted dynamics of his composition and the simplification of plans, tries to express heroism and turn his *Cuirassier*, directly inspired by Géricault's, into a universal symbol of courage. How could one fail to see that this is the spirit of old art itself, only adorned with the feathers of modernism?

Could this be the end of the Cubist adventure, a mere style pretension, used by other painters as a comfortable yet audacious recipe? No. Because, at the same time as their followers show their art, Picasso and Braque continue their exploration of the intimacy of objects at Céret, where they work in seclusion.

(See also 1908, 1909, 1910, 1912, 1913.)

GUILLAUME APOLLINAIRE IS ACCUSED

PARIS

On August 21, France learned about the disappearance of the *Mona Lisa*, stolen by a mysterious thief. He left only the frame and the protective glass before which one morning Roland Dorgelès came to shave himself to protest against the reflections it caused on the canvas. And the day after the theft Apollinaire published in the *Intransigeant* a virulent article denouncing the negligence of the guards. One must say that he has good reason to complain. Four years ago, his secretary, Géry Piéret, needing money, had stolen from the Louvre two Iberian statuettes that he immediately had sold to Picasso. Their Primitivism, together with African sculpture, was the origin of *Les demoiselles d'Avignon*.

Now, the incredible secretary did it again. On the mantelpiece of Apollinaire's living room was a third statuette. Was it bravado? Provocation? Géry Piéret, in a letter to the police, accused himself of the theft of the *Mona Lisa*.

A distressed Apollinaire rushed to inform his friend Picasso, and they both decided to get rid of the incriminating statuettes by throwing them into the Seine. But after wandering around all night, they returned to the painter's studio, on the Boulevard de Clichy, without having found the heart to do it.

So Apollinaire thought of another solution: return the statuettes, anonymously, through the newspaper *Paris-Journal*. The art critic André Salmon, also the poet's friend, writes there. But the police took it very badly. *Paris-Journal* invited its readers to see the statuettes, exhibited in the lobby of the newspaper. Worse yet, it published a series of interviews with the "mysterious thief."

André Salmon's indiscretion? Anyway, the next day Parisians learned about the arrest of Mr. Guillaume Kostrowitski, known in the world of letters as Apollinaire. Interrogated by the police, the poet did not take long in admitting that he sheltered the accused, his secretary, Géry Piéret. Indicted for receiving and concealing stolen goods, Apollinaire was incarcerated in the prison of La Santé. Only for a few days though, because his brilliant counsel, José Théry, did not take long in getting him out, although Picasso, summoned, refused to testify in his favor.

In his cell, Apollinaire meditated about these casual words of Géry Piéret to Marie Laurencin, "I'm going to the Louvre, Madam, do you need anything?"

Guillaume Apollinaire.

THE TRIO OF PUTEAUX

PUTEAUX

Among other qualities, future art historians will have to have precise cartographic knowledge. This century is only eleven years old, and yet one feels that its artistic adventure will be read as a list of proper names. Artists' names, of course, but also towns, neighborhoods, streets, cafés. Puteaux, for instance.

Strange "masses" take place in this grim suburb northeast of Paris, where people talk of mathematics, the golden number, and the fourth dimension.

Every Sunday, strange worshipers leave the capital city and meet in the studio of two brothers, two artists, who at the end of last century left their Normandy and their notary of a

The three brothers Duchamp.

father to embrace their religion: art, painting. The Duchamp brothers—Jacques, who took the name of Villon in homage to the poet, and Raymond (Duchamp-Villon)—surrounded themselves with the cream of the current avant-garde of art and poetry: Apollinaire, Ribemont-Dessaignes, Gleizes, Léger, Picabia. However, the most mysterious character of the group seems to be the youngest Villon brother: Marcel Duchamp. He is twenty-four and paints. Like his older brothers, he is influenced by Fauvism and Cubism, but his recent paintings, especially the *Portrait of Chess Players*, shows an iconoclastic sense of humor.

Antoine Bourdelle Makes Isadora Dance

Paris. Having received the commission on July 31 for the sculptured trim of the façade and atrium of the future Théâtre des Champs-Élysées, for which he is also to execute some frescoes, Antoine Bourdelle, who has just turned fifty, hopes to surpass himself. Drawing on Greek mythology for his subject matter, and mainly interested in expressing the art of the dance, he has chosen Isadora Duncan, the famous thirty-three-year-old dancer, as his model, because she herself was inspired by ancient Greek dances in her "free" choreographies. The image of an unrestrained woman dancing on air, she will be represented in the allegory of a *Nude in Flight*, which delights her.

Cubism in Prague

A group of young Prague artists, all Cubists or sympathizers with the movement, has just left the Mánes Art Society to form the Plasticians Group. The painters involved are Vincenc Benes, Josef Capek, Emil Filla, Bohumil Kubista, Antonin Procházka, and Václav Spála. The group also includes writers such as Karel Capek, sculptors such as the brilliant Otto Gutfreund, and architects such as Vlastislav Hofman and Pavel Janak. The greatest originality of this group lies in the fact that, without renouncing Cubism's formal victories, it remains very attached to literary themes, as proven by Procházka's *Prometheus,* Benes' *Suzanne in the Bath*, and Gutfreund's *Hamlet*. All of them hope to exhibit their work beside the international avant-garde, so they await the arrival of works by Picasso, Derain, Friesz, Kirchner, and Heckel in Prague.

The Day of Glory for the Pompiers

On May 1, surrounded by members of the Republican Guard, high-held swords, potted plants, top hats, and outfits by the great designers of the day, President Fallières along with Monsieur Dujardin-Beaumetz, undersecre-

ANTOINE BOURDELLE: SKETCH OF ISADORA DUNCAN, DANCING

tary of state for the Beaux-Arts, opened the Salon des Artistes Français at the Grand Palais. The entire art world is there: Gabriel Ferrier, Cormon, Rochegrosse, Bonnat, Azéma, and many others. The critics sing endless praises, the public flocks to the event. The Classicism of tradition against the mystifications of the innovating Fauves and Cubists: That is worth going to see. It was the day of glory for the members of the Institute, the winners of the Prix de Rome, the gold, silver, and bronze medalists. "Something like the July 14 of painting and sculpture," people read in the *Revue des beaux-arts.*

The Death of Fritz von Uhde

An eminent member of the Munich Secession, Fritz von Uhde, dies. He had been one of the first outdoor painters, a follower of Courbet. Then he tried to paint the Gospel: Mary, poor daughter of a peasant, leaning on a snow-covered fence, waiting for Joseph. Or Jesus taking a meal at the table of a modest family of craftspeople. But to the church his religious naturalism smelled slightly of sulphur. So Fritz von Uhde was not buried with all the honors ordinarily accorded a well-known artist.

Henri Matisse's Fury

Arriving in Collioure where he spends the summer months every year, Henri Matisse discovered the word "Kub" written in enormous letters on the walls of the house he had rented for the season. Convinced that the Cubists had instigated this to make fun of him, he fell into a terrible fit of anger. But why indeed would the Cubists have gone all the way to the Mediterranean coast to taunt him? In fact, it was all nothing but a sign for a popular food product, put up by an advertising company. But the great Fauve, infuriated, will hear none of it. His vacation, he says, is ruined.

IN BRIEF...

AUSTRIA-HUNGARY
Twenty-five paintings by Oskar Kokoschka are shown in the Hagenbund exhibition in Vienna; they are the object of violent criticism.

FRANCE
The Camondo estate brings to the Louvre paintings by Degas, Renoir, Cézanne, Monet, Manet, and Van Gogh.

Pablo Picasso executes four etchings for Max Jacob's Saint Matorel.

Odilon Redon completes the decoration of the library of the Cistercian monastery at Font-froide in the Languedoc.

Raoul Dufy ventures into fabric designing for the couturier Paul Poiret.

GREAT BRITAIN
Roger Fry organizes a second international Postimpressionist exhibition at the Grafton Galleries.

NORWAY
At the Christiania museum, a retrospective of Edvard Munch features 101 paintings.

SWEDEN
The critic Adolf Andenberg organizes an exhibition of the works of Carl Hill, who has just died.

ARCHIPENKO MAKES SHAPES OBEY

ALEXANDER ARCHIPENKO:
DRAPED WOMAN. 1911.
Paris. MNAM

PARIS

What force and daring in Alexander Archipenko's sculptures! Since he exhibited last year at the Salon d'Automne, this sculptor has not stopped causing scandal. His style is close to what Cubism and Futurism are in painting, but it is impossible to define him by the mere influence of a movement.

He was born in 1887, the son of an engineer, and studied

To begin with, he is preoccupied with volume and the relations between masses. In this respect, he could well be even more extremist than his peers in modern sculpture, Brancusi and Duchamp-Villon, who, like himself, are members of the Section d'Or (golden section).

But his main concern is vacuum, which has the force of the absent object and thus creates volume. He says this subject has

THE VACUUM HAS THE FORCE OF THE ABSENT OBJECT AND THUS CREATES VOLUME

mathematics. He is enthralled by the relationship between science and art. He came to Paris from Kiev in 1908, and lived at 2 La Ruche, in Montparnasse, formerly the wine pavilion of the 1889 World's Fair, now an artists' studio. He works there alone, and studies ancient Greek art at the Louvre rather than the Art Academy; he cannot stand the latter's academic teaching. For the same reason he disliked his teachers at the art academy of his native town. Finally, they expelled him.

Since his first Parisian works, he freed himself from Rodin's influence, which can be seen in his work presented in Moscow in 1906. His current style prevailed, making him, at twenty-four, one of the leaders of avant-garde sculpture.

always been of interest to him.

However, even though simplification and an emptying of volumes are the mark of his sculpture, he still thinks that the figurative should be prevalent. In spite of the mathematical rigor of his art, the female body has a large place in Archipenko's universe; he likes to reminisce about the ancient Slavic stone idols that pervaded his childhood in the Ukraine. Consequently, in a work such as *Draped Woman* there is an echo of the traditional topic of motherhood. This alone is enough to differentiate him from the Cubists, with their pulverized violins and guitars, as well as from the Futurists, with their love for automobile speed and modernism.

GARGALLO CUTS METAL

BARCELONA-PARIS

Pablo Gargallo is not a native Catalan (he was born in Maella, in Aragon, in 1881), but he has lived since childhood in Barcelona and has studied there. Between 1899 and 1900 he frequented the famous café Els Quatre Gats, where Nonell, Picasso, and many other artists used to meet. In 1903 he went to

Paris, where he kept company with Max Jacob, Manolo, and of course Picasso. Back in Barcelona, he made stone sculptures, friezes, and bas-reliefs for theaters and for the Saint-Paul hospital. In 1907, during a short stay in Paris, he produced his first work of cut metal, a small *Mask with a Hair Strand*. But it was only in 1911 that he decid-

ed to exploit fully this special technique. Gargallo had observed the work of Catalan ironworkers, but only in order to do something entirely different: The masks and characters he cuts in *repoussé* copper, as well as metal wire and ribbons, are a new path for sculpture, using wire, concave surfaces, holes, and empty spaces.

Stoclet Palace: exterior.

Stoclet Palace: interior.

ALL THE ARTS IN ONE PALACE

BRUSSELS

Everything is now completed! Since 1905, Austrian architect Josef Hoffmann has been working hard. But what satisfaction! He could finally see a dream come true: a building conceived as a "total art work."

One can admire this building in a residential area. The ensemble is so noble that it was christened the Stoclet Palace, after the name of its owners and alluding to the great mansions of the Italian Renaissance.

How did an Austrian architect get to build in Brussels? It is an amazing story. In 1903, Belgian industrialist Adolphe Stoclet traveled to Austria with his wife. One day, in Vienna, they saw a wonderful villa. They asked to visit it and, their enthusiasm

growing, wanted to meet the architect, Josef Hoffmann, of whom they had never heard. After their meeting, Mr. and Mrs. Stoclet commissioned him to build their private house in Brussels.

Josef Hoffmann designed the building as a complex of cubic elements with various sizes. The main part was given monumental proportions. A tower was erected there. At the top, in each of the four corners, the bronze figure of an athlete was installed.

Except for this ornament, Hoffmann was totally faithful to the Functionalism he had proposed. He obeyed the principle that all shapes must be governed by the overall plan.

On the exterior, the walls were

covered in white Norwegian marble squares. This technical procedure was already used by Otto Wagner, another famous architect from Vienna. Inside, the Stoclet palace also has marble, as well as frescoes executed by the Vienna Ateliers after cartoons by Klimt. But the owners keep the secret regarding interior decoration and will not let visitors in for art's sake! So nobody has actually seen the interior fittings so far.

Still, it is known that the furniture, lighting fixtures, and carpets were also designed by Hoffmann. He even decided on the kind of cylinder-shaped trees and plants that adorn the garden together with the fountains.

Hoffmann founded the Vienna Ateliers with Koloman Moser in

1903, and they rapidly gained a worldwide reputation. They created a modern high-quality craftmanship compatible with today's architecture.

The rejection of ornamentation, under the pretext of faithfulness to the truth of structures and materials, has often led architecture to a detrimental dryness. This is not the case in Brussels. The Stoclet Palace is already considered by the enlightened public as one of the great successes of architecture in recent years. It is comparable to Italian Renaissance palaces, precisely as its happy owner wanted it.

The Inobjective Painting of Robert Delaunay is born at the same time the Futurists hold their first exhibition in Paris. After years of uncertainty, history seems to have turned a page, for it is difficult to imagine what might prompt art to return to the rules and principles of the past. For its part, Cubism, labeled and codified by Gleizes and Metzinger in their work About Cubism, displays a tendency toward becoming a way of doing, except when seen in the art of its creators. When an unknown, Marc Chagall, arrives on the banks of the Seine from his native Russia, the Section d'Or (golden section) of the Duchamp-Villon brothers seems to offer the greatest promise for the future.

1912
S U M M A R Y

AVANT-GARDE

Delaunay: the Appearance of Nonobjective Art
From the Notebooks of Robert Delaunay

CUBISM

The Simultaneous Collages of Braque and Picasso

WRITINGS AND THEORIES

Gleizes and Metzinger: Objects Are Formed in the Mind

DEVELOPMENTS

The Buzzing of the Beehive

ART NEWS

The Divine Proportion of the Golden Section
Death of a Painter of Battle Scenes
Valentine Is Overcome by Lewdness
Uncle Bernhard's Bounty
In Brief

POLEMIC

Schiele Imprisoned for Pornography
Germany Consecrates Modern Art

EXHIBITIONS

The Futurists Conquer Paris

LITERATURE

GERMANY
Thomas Mann publishes Death in Venice.
   Gottfried Benn publishes a book of poetry, Morgue.

FRANCE
Publication of Paul Claudel's The Tidings Brought to Mary.

GREAT BRITAIN
Publication of Pygmalion *by George Bernard Shaw.*

SWEDEN
Death of August Strindberg.

MUSIC

GERMANY
Arnold Schönberg composes the suite Pierrot lunaire, *the first work in which atonal notation is used.*

MOTION PICTURES

DENMARK
Danish filmmaking reaches an apogee with Blue Blood *by Glückstadt.*

UNITED STATES
Mack Sennet founds the Keystone Company.

FRANCE
Méliès produces The Conquest of the Pole.

OTHER PERFORMANCES

FRANCE
Paris remains under the spell of the Russian Ballet, and of Maurice Ravel's Daphnis and Chloe *and Claude Débussy's* Prélude à l'après-midi d'un faune. *In the latter, Nijinsky's performance shocks conservative viewers.*

ROBERT DELAUNAY:
DISK. 1912. Connecticut.
Private Collection

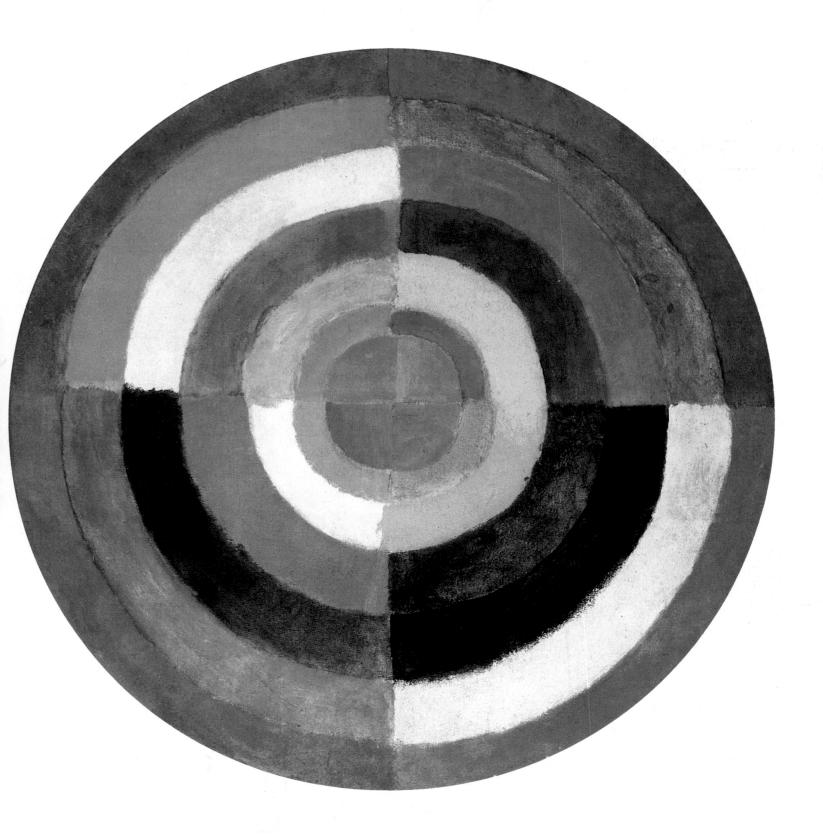

DELAUNAY: THE APPEARANCE OF NONOBJECTIVE ART

PARIS

One day, not being able to give his yellow the brightness of Veronese or Rubens, Delacroix sent for a cab to take him to the Louvre, to have a close look at the real thing. It was around 1830. At the time, Paris had canary-yellow cabs that one could hire, and that was what Delacroix was brought. To his great surprise, he saw something that he had never noticed before, namely, that the yellow of the cab produced violet in the shadow. He immediately returned to his studio and experimented with the phenomenon. So shadow could be violet, or blue, or green . . . Modern art was born. And, more remotely, nonobjective art.

So far Robert Delaunay has fragmented the Eiffel Tower in the Cubist manner of breaking up guitars and pitchers. Now his innovative gifts appear in the *Disk*, a recent round canvas that

his painter friends consider with displeasure. Compared with this, even the *City of Paris*, a large composition much commented upon at the latest Salon des Indépendants, seems already a thing of the past, in spite of its brightly colored alveoli breaking up the figures.

TO EXPRESS THROUGH PURE COLOR THE NEW EXPERIENCES OF OUR TECHNOLOGICAL SOCIETY

Everything started at the beginning of the year, when the artist thought of a painting based only on color contrasts, in which color would be both the theme and the structure of the painting at the same time. Delaunay isolated himself in a room where he hermetically closed the blinds. Then, with a drill, he made a little round hole in the blinds, and studied, decomposed, and analyzed the

sun ray that filtered through. By studying sunlight, he found unsuspected sources of emotion, outside any objective representation. The result was his series titled *Windows*, sometimes mirroring polychrome prisms, sometimes made shinier with pulverized lapis-lazuli.

Yet, in the *Windows,* in spite of their great novelty, he keeps the Cubist grille that cuts up the surface of the painting with horizontal and vertical lines crossing at straight angles. In the *Disk*, Delaunay went further: He freed himself of the Cubist grille. Here, surfaces roll around each other and appear in a circular pattern and in contrasts.

Delaunay's bedside book, the same as that of Seurat and his

friends some years ago, is a thick volume with an interminable title: *De la loi du contraste simultané des couleurs et de l'assortiment des objects colorés considérés d'après cette loi dans ses rapports avec la peinture* (the law of simultaneous contrast and matching of colored objects considered in light of this law and its relationship with painting), by Michel-Eugène Chevreul. He was a chemist at the Gobelin manufacturing plant and died in 1887, at the age of 103.

The artist was deeply influenced by a passage where Chevreul explains that "putting a color on a canvas doesn't only mean coloring the place touched by the brush; it also means coloring the surrounding space with the complementary color." The consequence is that "a red circle is surrounded by a slight green aura, which weakens as it goes further away; a yellow circle

ROBERT DELAUNAY
CITY OF PARIS. 1910-1912
Paris. MNAM

is surrounded by a violet aura and vice versa."

However, there is another origin, too. In 1909, Delaunay did a few paintings inside the Saint-Séverin church. He curved the sky-bound pillars and deepened the vault, which opened up and seemed to explode. But the main thing happened on the ground where the stained-glass windows projected their colored shapes that moved and became alive with the movements of the sun. At the foot of the pillars the small polychrome circle appeared. The flamboyance of the gothic rose showed the artist his way. And, undoubtedly, the rose also made him find the cosmic symbol he was seeking.

In 1906-1907, Delaunay had already painted a Neoimpressionistic *Landscape with Disk*. In the middle, there was a blind sun represented as an unpainted spot where the canvas showed; he did not know how to do it otherwise. Under the nave of Saint-Séverin he found what he missed then: the nucleus of fire capable of bringing it to life. Not only that, but in today's *Disk* there is nothing left that could recall a landscape, from the trees and plants visible in front to the horizon closing the space.

Unlike Kandinsky's abstraction, which is supported by a spiritualist reflection, Delaunay's nonobjective art is an attempt to create a new type of Realism, capable of expressing, through pure color, the new experiences awaiting us in the technological and industrial society of the future, such as aviation and automobile travel. Cubism already smashed our old vision, followed by Futurism which wonders how to paint speed. With his *Disk*, Delaunay would like to have created "the shape" that best expresses our modern reality. All this at the age of twenty-seven.

(See also 1914, 1937, 1941.)

ROBERT DELAUNAY: WINDOWS SIMULTANEOUSLY OPENED. 1912. London. Tate Gallery

FROM THE NOTEBOOKS OF ROBERT DELAUNAY

Realism is for all the arts the eternal quality that must decide about the beauty, its duration, and what is adequate for it.

In the field of painting, let us seek the purity of the means or the purest means for the expression of the purest beauty.

"Simultaneous contrast" assures the dynamism of the colors along with their construction in the painting, and it is the strongest mean of expression of reality . . .

We are coming to a purely expressive art of painting, outside of any bygone, archaic, geometric style, an art becoming plastic, not serving any other cause than to translate human nature more flexibly in its inspiration towards beauty (not literature, or technique, or process).

The first painting was just a line that surrounded the shadow of a man projected by the light of the sun on the ground.

But we have come a long way from that "image"—we have light (light colors, dark colors, their complements, their intervals, and their simultaneity), and all the shades of color are issued from our intelligence to create harmony.

Without subject, no resource: This, however, does not mean a literary subject, that is, an anecdotal subject. In painting, the subject is all plastic and results from sight and must be the pure expression of human nature.

The eternal subject is found in nature itself: the inspiration and the clear vision that belong to the wise who discover the most beautiful and the strongest limitations.

Notes on the Construction
of the Reality of Pure Painting

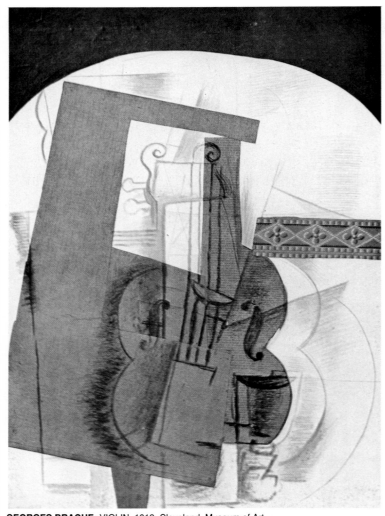

GEORGES BRAQUE: VIOLIN. 1912. Cleveland. Museum of Art

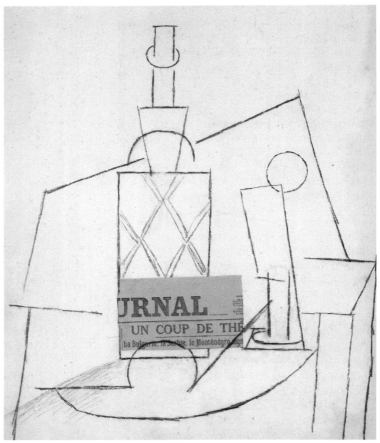

PABLO PICASSO: BOTTLE AND NEWSPAPER ON A TABLE. 1912. Paris. MNAM

THE SIMULTANEOUS COLLAGES OF BRAQUE AND PICASSO

PARIS

Are Braque and Picasso cutting up the future with their bold scissors? They cut, and then paste on canvas, large shapes in modest paper patterned as fake wood or fake marble. For a year already, Braque has been adding stenciled letters to his paintings, the kind used by movers to mark their boxes. Like the nails Braque used to paint in *trompe l'oeil* on the top of some of his Analytical Cubist paintings, perhaps it is a means of indicating which way to hang the picture. But above all he wants to prove that beauty can be created with the most modest means. At the same time he tries to imitate various materials in *trompe l'oeil,* a technique he learned to perfection in the studio of his father the house painter.

Today, however, a new step is made. No more illusion. Braque and Picasso add pieces of the real thing to their paintings. How did the idea come to them? Here is the story: The two inseparable friends spent the summer in Sorgues, Braque and his wife, Marcelle, in the villa Bel-Ami, Picasso and his new companion, Eva, at the Clochettes. One day in September, Braque went to Avignon and saw a roll of imitation-wood paper in the window of an art-supply store. He bought it. He then cut a few squares out of it, pasted them on cardboard and sketched with charcoal a fruit bowl, grapes, and a glass. The first collage was born. He showed it to Picasso. Later on, Picasso, who returned to Paris first, sent him a significant letter in his French-Catalan lingo, "My dear friend Braque, I am using your latest paperistic dust-catching technique . . ." because for years the two had worked together and shared their research and discoveries.

What, then, is the role of these "paperistic" procedures? Wood-imitating paper or the pieces of upholstery binding reintroduce color while freeing the work from drawing. Space is reestablished through these appliqués, which stress the cohesion of the shape and the consistency of the painting. It is a synthetic painting resulting from a rigorous analytical process and illegible because of its abstraction.

Traditional painters used to imitate crystal or lace. Braque and Picasso, in turn, use the raw materials of our environment. After fake-wood paper, they started to cut newspapers, with news items and varied typographical styles. It is as though they wanted to introduce our naked reality into their work.

(See also 1908, 1909, 1910, 1911, 1913.)

GLEIZES AND METZINGER: OBJECTS ARE FORMED IN THE MIND

Four years after its birth, Cubism has found its first theoreticians. They are two painters, Albert Gleizes, thirty-one years old, and Jean Metzinger, twenty-nine years old. Braque likes to say that Picasso and he shared "thoughts." Here, to the contrary, Cubism is analyzed, explained, legitimized. As if it were a matter of convincing the public and the critics who have remained hostile. Even if Gleizes and Metzinger are not themselves the founders of the new movement, their work is of immediate interest, as we can see from the following excerpt.

There is nothing real outside of us, there is nothing real except the coincidence of a feeling and an individual mental direction. We are not likely to doubt the existence of the objects that impress our senses. But we cannot be certain about the images they make appear in our mind.

So we are surprised when well-meaning critics explain the remarkable difference between the shapes attributed to nature and those of contemporary painting through the will to represent things not as they appear but as they are. How are they? According to these critics, the object has an absolute and essential shape, and in order to free this shape we would eliminate the traditional light and shade and perspective. What simplicity! An object does not have one absolute shape, it has several, it has as many as it has planes in a range of meaning. The one dealt with by these writers adapts itself, as if by miracle, to geometrical forms. Geometry is a science, painting is an art. The geometer measures, the painter relishes. The absolute of the one is inevitably the relative of the other. Too bad if logic is offended. Does logic ever prevent wine from having different degrees of perfection in the chemist's test tube and in the drinker's glass?

We laugh out loud when we think of all the novices who expiate their literal understanding of the remarks of a Cubist and their faith in absolute truth by laboriously placing side by side the six faces of a cube and both ears of a model seen in profile.

Does it follow that we should, like the Impressionists, rely on sensitivity only? By no means. We are seeking the essential, but we are seeking it in our personality and not in the kind of meticulous eternity that mathematicians and philosophers may have planned . . .

It is not surprising that those who are strangers to painting do not immediately share our assurance; but that they get irritated does not make sense. Should the painter do his work backward, to satisfy them and give back to objects the ordinary appearance that he is destined to strip away?

Because the object is truly transubstantiated, even the most experienced eye has difficulty discovering it, and a great charm results. The picture that reveals itself only slowly seems to wait to be questioned —almost as though it reserved an infinity of answers to an infinity of questions.

ALBERT GLEIZES AND JEAN METZINGER
About Cubism *(Excerpt)*

JEAN METZINGER: WOMAN WITH GREEN DRESS. 1912. Paris. Musée d'Art Moderne de la Ville

La Ruche at night.

MARC CHAGALL:
TO RUSSIA, TO DONKEYS,
AND TO OTHERS. 1911.
Paris. MNAM

THE BUZZING OF THE BEEHIVE

PARIS

Marc Chagall, twenty-five, a Russian painter, came to "La Ruche" (the beehive) at the beginning of the year. Two years ago, he arrived in Paris, attracted by the cultural brilliance of the city that had reached him in his native town of Vitebsk.

La Ruche, in the middle of Montparnasse, is a strange building. It owes its name to its alveolar row of studios and its fervent creative atmosphere. It was partly built by Gustave Eiffel's team for the 1900 World's Fair, then torn down. Sculptor Alfred Boucher had it disassembled, then rebuilt at 2 Passage Dantzig, in the 15th *arrondissement*, to shelter artists.

Sculpture studios are on the ground floor, while painters are located on the second and third floors. La Ruche is so big that it can accommodate one hundred and forty tenants. There is even a three-hundred-seat theater. Richer artists inhabit the warmer stone parts of the building; the others have to make do with the freezing glass-and-steel rotunda. Chagall is among the latter. But he is warmed up by his friendship with the other dwellers: his compatriots Archipenko and Soutine, who paints huge pieces of meat hung up in his studio; the painters Léger, Modigliani, and André Lhote; the poet Blaise Cendrars; the Marxist journalist and playwright Anatoli Lunacharski, who often meets Lenin at the Restaurant de la Rotonde for endless political chats.

Chagall was born in 1887, in a very religious Jewish family, in a region of Russia widely marked by rich and poetic Hasidic folklore. In spite of the ritual taboo and his family's opposition, he was attracted to painting early. He studied in St. Petersburg, with Léon Bakst, an innovative spirit who made his students

*IN THE ALVEOLAR ROW OF STUDIOS,
A FERVENT CREATIVE ATMOSPHERE*

discover modern art. Thanks to Bakst's encouragement and the generous offer of a small pension by a lawyer named Vinaver, Chagall decided to come to Paris. Every month he goes to the post office to withdraw the 120 francs sent by his Maecenas; when the clerk asks, "Paper or gold?" he invariably answers, "Paper, in gold it's too little."

He lives in such poverty that he paints on tablecloths, bedsheets, and even torn-up night shirts. His studio is filled with stretchers, egg shells, bread crusts, and remainders of herring, which he divides in two lots, eating the head one day and the tail the next. Night after night he works by the light of a kerosene lamp. At sunrise, he hears the lowing of the cows killed at the neighboring slaughterhouse of Vaugirard.

These cows appear in his paintings, blue, yellow, green. At a time when Cubism is becoming a pervasive theory, daring modern art and sweet tradition melt together in Chagall's work.

(See also 1931.)

The Divine Proportion of the Golden Section

The first exhibition of the Section d'Or (golden section) group took place at the La Boétie gallery during the entire month of October. The public was shown two hundred Cubist canvases by thirty-one artists, even without the participation of Picasso and Braque, who do not exhibit outside the Kahnweiler gallery, where they are shown exclusively. Among the most notable are Léger, Gleizes, Metzinger, Gris, Duchamp, Duchamp-Villon, Villon, Lhote, La Fresnaye, Marcoussis, and Archipenko. This exhibition has a didactic character, and what was only suspected can now be verified: Four years after its birth, Cubism has entered a theoretical phase. That is essentially due to the Duchamp-Villon brothers, who bring together several artists on Sunday afternoons at Jacques Villon's studio in Puteaux under the sign of the Section d'Or.

Death of a Painter of Battle Scenes

Édouard Detaille, the painter of battle scenes, died in Paris on December 24. He died the death of generals, in his bed and fast asleep. He was sixty-four years old. An uncompromising patriot, profoundly marked by France's defeat in 1870—the dramatic renderings that he painted of that event had contributed a great deal to making him famous—and a pupil of Meissonier, considered to be too talented for the Salon competitions by the age of twenty-one, he had dedicated all his work to French military glory. Heads of state and foreign rulers spoke to him as they would to a military man. In 1884 even the Tsar had invited him to attend important maneuvers in Russia. Invited to visit Paris in 1910, King Edward VII of England confided to him, "I'm not happy about this, but I have to go to Berlin to see my nephew. He is quite mad; you won't escape war." Maybe it is because he died in his sleep that his masterpiece is an oneiric painting: *The Dream* shows soldiers sleeping on the bare ground dreaming of glory.

Valentine Is Overcome by Lewdness

Lewdness is a force because it excites strong people to release their energy, and therefore to keep renewing it. Lamartine's grandniece, Valentine de Saint-Point, a thirty-seven-year-old poetess who generally goes about in a red dressing gown, confirms this thought. With her sensuous mouth and enormous green eyes, she declaims her *Woman's Futurist Manifesto* in the Salle Gaveau in Paris on June 27, and provokes quite an uproar. Whistles, howls, cries, the desired effect of scandal has been immensely successful. One question from an older gentleman quite beside himself: "At what age, madam, should we teach our daughters lewdness?" Fortunately, bodyguards, Futurists themselves, were there to protect her against the outraged.

IN BRIEF...

GERMANY
In Berlin, Kandinsky retrospective at the gallery Der Sturm, which opened recently.

BELGIUM
The nine panels of Emil Nolde's Life of Christ, shown at the World's Fair, create a scandal.

UNITED STATES/FRANCE
Durand-Ruel exhibits simultaneously at their New York and Paris galleries works by Auguste Renoir, which are met with great success.

FRANCE
At Bernheim gallery, Claude Monet shows twenty-nine views of Venice, a city he discovered a few years ago.
After thirty-three years of hard work, the mailman Cheval has just completed his Ideal Palace, built almost entirely with pebbles.

GREAT BRITAIN
The Stafford Gallery in London holds the first Picasso exhibition in Great Britain.

RUSSIA
Mikhail Larionov organizes he exhibition "Donkey's Tail" in Moscow, including works by Kazimir Malevich.

MARCEL DUCHAMP: THE KING AND QUEEN SURROUNDED BY SWIFT NUDES. 1912. Philadelphia. Museum of Art

Uncle Bernhard's Bounty

Art needs patrons. The publication of the *Almanac of the Blue Rider* by Piper Verlag in Munich in mid-May would not have been possible without Bernhard Koehler, who gave 3,000 marks to cover publication costs. Koehler is a rich Berlin industrialist, the uncle of the wife of August Macke, initiator of modern art. Besides works by Cézanne, Manet, and Monet, his collection includes paintings by Kandinsky, Gabriele Münter, Campendonk, and Delaunay. The year before, he had acquired, on Macke's advice, El Greco's *Saint John.* "Without his helping hand," believes Kandinsky, who knows what he is talking about, "the *Blue Rider* would have remained a dream."

SCHIELE IMPRISONED FOR PORNOGRAPHY

GERMANY CONSECRATES MODERN ART

NEULENGBACH

Painter Egon Schiele was arrested on April 13 by the police of Neulengbach (Lower Austria), where he has frequently stayed since last year. A certain Mossig, a retired navy officer, has accused him of having seduced his daughter, Tatjana-Georgette-Anna, an enticing young person

FINALLY SOME RELIEF FROM MY SUFFERING! FINALLY SOME PAPER, A PENCIL, BRUSHES AND PAINTS!

of fourteen. In addition, he was accused of having pornographic drawings lying around his studio while very young models posed for him.

The artist, who had thought that he had found a working haven in Neulengbach, is actually a victim of provincial lack of understanding for modern art. It is true that Schiele makes erotic drawings of adolescent girls, or paints them in watercolor, and it is also true that the girls let their nudity show. But although his works express the troubled beginnings of sexuality, their exceptional artistic quality saves them from the sin of pornography. Regarding the accusation of corrupting a minor, what else can it be but the fantasy of an overprotective father?

Schiele is quite bitter about the injustice of the accusations. "Finally! Finally! Finally! Finally some relief from suffering! Finally some paper, a pencil, brushes and paints, to draw and write with. The torture of these wild hours, vague, cruel, endless, shapeless, gray monotonous hours when I had to live deprived of everything, robbed of everything, between these four naked cold walls, like an animal." Schiele wrote this on April 16, after receiving the painting materials he had been incessantly asking for.

Born on June 12, 1890, in Tully, a small town on the Danube, about 40 miles from Vienna, Schiele is the sixth child of an Austrian railway clerk. He showed precocious talent for

drawing and, after mediocre secondary studies, enrolled in the Art Academy of Vienna. He was expelled in 1909 because he rebelled against the old-fashioned teaching of Christian Griepenkerl, who directed painting classes. The same year, he was discovered by Gustav Klimt, who invited him to exhibit four paintings at the Internationale Kunstschau Wien. He gained instant recognition.

Understandably so. His drawings and paintings are free from any pose and grandiloquence. They translate profound feelings, show extreme virtuosity, a rare sense of color, and an acute sense of execution. Their composition is incisive, nervous, refined, sometimes Expressionistic and desperate.

After twenty-seven days of detention, Schiele was tried on May 7 by the judge of Sankt Polten, a neighboring town to which he had been transferred. The judge symbolically burned one of the incriminating drawings and imposed a fine, but acquitted him of the main accusation: corruption of a minor. He probably was sensitive to the seriousness and talent of a twenty-two-year-old genius.

EGON SCHIELE: CHILD LYING ON HER BELLY. 1911. United States. Private Collection

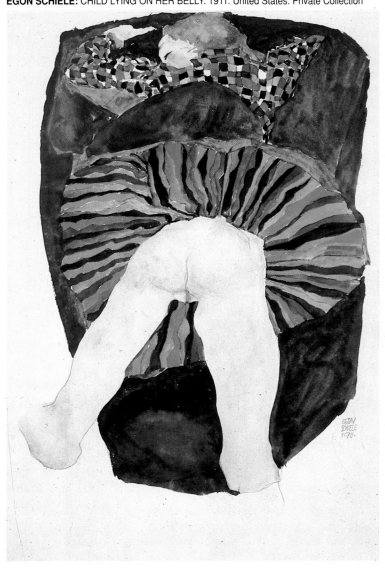

COLOGNE

The brand-new exhibition hall is the host of the Sonderbund (special association), which proposes a kind of retrospective of modern art since 1905.

The first impression is that of a homage to Van Gogh. With over one hundred paintings, he occupies three halls, which are the axis of the exhibition. On the left are other halls for Cézanne, Gauguin, Picasso, and the Neoimpressionists (Cross, Signac). On the right is a corner for the Norwegian Munch, and the rest is for Germany. At the end of the axis are stained-glass panels painted by Heckel and Kirchner. Thus Van Gogh seems to have been symbolically placed between the art of Germanic and Latin countries. Since the organizer thinks Expressionism is universally loved, he reserved it a place of choice. Members of Die Brücke and the Blue Rider are also present.

A savage, imaginative, visionary, Kokoschka surprised visitors. His Austrian compatriot Egon Schiele, little known in Germany, also raised much interest with his nudes.

The novelty, as compared with previous exhibitions of the Sonderbund, is the opening to Germans. Certain critics complain that it did not have beneficial results, and speak of an invasion of mediocre artists. But the group of Rhenish Expressionists is represented respectably with the cousins August and Helmut Macke, Carlo Mense, and Hans Thuar.

THE FUTURISTS CONQUER PARIS

PARIS

The Futurists show their work for the first time at the Bernheim-Jeune gallery in February. This exhibition is considered the artistic event of the season. The press, echoing the public, has varied reactions to it, but the crowds keep coming. As a prelude to this exhibition, Umberto Boccioni and his group published last year in Milan the *Technical Manifesto of Futurist Painting,* in which they reiterated their avant-garde position. The manifesto was first commented upon by the French papers *Excelsior, Paris-Journal,* and *L'Intransigeant.*

The Futurist exhibition, which wants to be a direct expression of modern life and the rejection of harmony and good taste, does not hide its controversial, even provocative, character. The preface of its catalogue is yet another manifesto where the five Italian protagonists, Filippo Tommaso Marinetti, Umberto Boccioni, Gino Severini, Carlo Carrà, and Luigi Russolo reiterate their principles.

This group of thirty-eight paintings could be exhibited thanks to the joint efforts of the eminent French writer and art critic Félix Féneon and Gino Severini, who has lived in Paris, in a studio in Impasse Guelma, since 1906. Severini went to Rome and suggested to his compatriots to exhibit at Bernheim-Jeune. Boccioni accepted immediately, aware of the impact of a Paris exhibition for the international spreading of Futurism. Marinetti accepted, too. For the same reason, three years ago, he

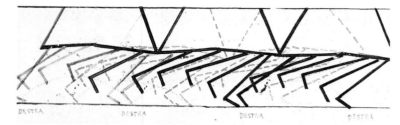

GIACOMO BALLA: SKETCH FOR YOUNG GIRL RUNNING ON A BALCONY

GIACOMO BALLA: YOUNG GIRL RUNNING ON A BALCONY. 1912. Milan. Civica Galleria d'Arte Moderna.

Futurists.

had published his manifesto in *Le Figaro,* thus becoming the founder, theoretician, and mouthpiece of the movement.

Severini, who is a friend of Picasso, Braque, and Juan Gris, brought his Italian friends to their studios. There they met the poets Max Jacob, André Salmon, and Guillaume Apollinaire. The artists' studios, fruitful and privileged places for exchanges, became laboratories where young artists share their views in a way that is stimulating and profitable for each of them. Conversations go on strong, continued at the café. Boccioni, in turn, met the sculptors Archipenko, Brancusi, and Duchamp-Villon.

The exhibition is next scheduled to be shown in London, Berlin, Brussels, The Hague, and Amsterdam. One great absence though: Giacomo Balla, the only signatory of the *Technical Manifesto of Futurist Painting* who refused to come. One regrets his absence even more when one thinks that his *Young Girl Running on a Balcony* and the preliminary drawings for this work clearly demonstrate the sources of Futurist painting. Seurat's Neoimpressionism is another source, from which it takes tone division; a third one would be chronophotography, which lends it the linear analysis of movement.

(See also 1909, 1914, 1915, 1919.)

An event of considerable importance occurs when the United States discovers modern art. Until now, American painting had been traditionalist as well as provincial. The Armory Show exhibition comes as a shock. For the first time, viewers in New York, then Chicago and Philadelphia, can see the entire body of modern painting from Cézanne to Picasso and Duchamp. But Russia also shows signs of life with Malevich. In Paris, Guillaume Apollinaire publishes his Esthetic Meditations, and by retracing the steps of Cubism's initiators he gives the movement its letters of nobility.

1913
S U M M A R Y

EVENTS

The Armory Show: Modern Art Discovers America
Matisse at the Stake
Opinions and Testimonies

SCANDALS

The Rite of Spring

ART NEWS

From Tokyo to Montparnasse
Camille Claudel Is Confined in an Institution
Six Feet Long for a Poem
The Rayonist Manifesto
In Brief

AVANT-GARDE

Malevich Provokes St. Petersburg
Juan Gris's Warning

WRITINGS AND THEORIES

Apollinaire Explains Cubism

LITERATURE

AUSTRIA-HUNGARY
In Vienna, Edmund Husserl publishes Introduction to Pure Phenomenology.

FRANCE
Beginning of a new series of books called Les soirées de Paris *under the direction of Guillaume Apollinaire, who also publishes* Alcools, *a collection of his poems.*
    Marcel Proust publishes Remembrance of Things Past.

ITALY
Soffici and Papini found the avant-garde magazine Lacerba *in Florence.*

SWEDEN
The Nobel price in literature is awarded to the Indian poet Rabindranath Tagore.

MUSIC

FRANCE
Performance of the ballet Jeux *by Claude Débussy, starring Nijinsky.*
    Performance of Festin de l'araignée *by Albert Roussel.*

MOTION PICTURES

DENMARK
Reconstruction of the Titanic *in the film* Atlantis *by Blom.*
    Glückstadt produces The Island of the Dead, *inspired by Arnold Böcklin's painting.*

UNITED STATES
Success of Mack Sennett and the Fatty series.

FRANCE
Louis Feuillade produces Fantomas, *and Émile Cohl creates an animated film,* Le Baron de Crac.

MARCEL DUCHAMP:
NUDE DESCENDING A STAIRCASE, NO. 2. 1912. Philadelphia. Museum of Art

The best exhibited painting at the Armory Show in New York. One critic saw in it "an explosion in a brick factory."

THE ARMORY SHOW: MODERN ART DISCOVERS AMERICA

At the Armory Show.

CONSTANTIN BRANCUSI:
MADEMOISELLE POGANY, VERSION I.
1912-1913. Paris. MNAM

NEW YORK

Nobody doubts the success of the Armory Show any longer. By mid-March, one hundred thousand visitors have seen it. It was there that the Metropolitan Museum bought a painting by Cézanne, the first ever to be acquired by an American museum. On February 17, the day of the inauguration, four thousand people visited the show. Still, two weeks passed before the

museum? There is none in New York. That was why a huge building designed for military drill by a regimental armory was finally chosen.

Last year, the Sonderbund exhibition took place in Cologne. Walt Kuhn and Arthur B. Davies, the two organizers of the Armory Show, ordered the catalogue. They were enthralled by its freedom, novelty, and creative invention. Walt Kuhn

A HUNDRED THOUSAND VISITORS AT A SHOCKING EXHIBITION

public began to flock to the armory of the 69th infantry regiment, on 25th Street and Lexington Avenue and rented from Colonel Conley, commander of the regiment, for $4,000.

The idea of a modern-art exhibition was the inspiration of several independent artists following an exhibition organized by photographer Alfred Stieglitz, who was the first to show Picasso and Matisse in New York. European avant-garde art was practically unknown in New York. Impressionist or Postimpressionist painters such as Monet, Van Gogh, and Gauguin were also completely unknown. But where would they find an exhibition space large enough for their purpose outside of a

immediately traveled to Cologne, then to Paris, where Arthur B. Davies joined him.

They were helped by the famous art dealer Ambroise Vollard, and by Walter Pach, who divides his time between the United States and France and who has just finished the American translation of Delacroix's *Journal.* They met Marcel Duchamp, Brancusi, and Picabia. This was only a few months ago; they had certainly wasted no time.

Although only one-third of the one thousand six hundred exhibited works are European, they attract the public's and the critic's attention most, because they are the most revolutionary. "I had this totally old-fashioned idea that portraits should represent their model, seascapes the sea, and landscapes nature," writes Julian Street in *Everybody's Magazine*. The same critic, speaking of the most important painting of the exhibition,

Nude Descending a Staircase by Duchamp, professes to have thought that it represented "an explosion in a brick factory."

The former President Theodore Roosevelt, who came on a private visit, peremptorily exclaimed, "This is not art!" As to Matisse's painting, it is thought "indecent" or "epileptic" by those who do not understand that the artist never intended to ridicule the human figure but rather to express it through color.

These varied reactions show the total novelty of the art exhibited at the Armory Show: Matisse, of course, but also Cubists and Futurists shown in a common exhibition hall, which some refer to as a "chamber of horrors." In this hall, where representatives of hostile yet complementary movements meet, one can see the main breach with the past. Both movements are engaged in a fierce battle with the object: Their paintings are nothing but broken guitars and violins, prismatic constructions, slashing of traditional space, in an attempt to make speed and the fourth dimension visible. The great tenor Enrico Caruso, who also came to see the Armory Show, was for once voiceless.

Another significant event was the showing of forty paintings or drawings by Odilon Redon who, although French, is little known in France. Walt Kuhn discovered his work at the Sonderbund in Cologne and decided to dedicate a complete hall to him at his own risk. No artist has ever gone so far in the exploration of his ghosts and dreams, perhaps with the exception of Henri Rousseau.

After New York, the Armory Show goes to Boston and Chicago, where it will probably attract the same comments and passion. It was decided—the exhibition wasn't placed in an armory for nothing—that on the closing evening there would be a parade with trumpets and drums in the green-plant-decorated halls of the 69th regiment, to celebrate the event. A brass band for art. Modern art will have conquered America with a flourish.

MATISSE AT THE STAKE

CHICAGO

In spite of some discordant voices, a great many people in New York's artistic circles received the Armory Show with interest and enthusiasm, since it made them discover modern art. Nevertheless, the professors and students of the Chicago Art School showed a backward and arrogant traditionalism. On April 16, the day of the closing of the exhibition, Matisse, Brancusi, and Walter Pach were burned in effigy; two copies of the work of the great Fauvist artist were reduced to ashes in the presence of a demented crowd on Michigan Avenue.

It is easy to understand Walt Kuhn's anger and disgust. He bluntly expresses his feelings in a letter to his friend and coorganizer of the Armory Show, Arthur B. Davies, who remained in New York. He explains how he had to stop professors who, at the exhibition, incited their students without even trying to understand the works they saw. In his opinion, the lynchers and organizers of autos-da-fé are nothing but vulgar louts.

HENRI MATISSE: THE RED STUDIO. 1911. New York. MOMA

OPINIONS AND TESTIMONIES

Until this exhibit, Americans knew nothing of this movement except through the works of certain young artists who went to France to immerse themselves deliberately in this new environment. But most of them were weak imitators. It seems that they were struck by the extravagance of the French painters and sculptors, extravagance of which they rendered only a pale reflection, missing the strength of the original works. Consequently, the public received the production of these disciples with a smile, incapable of recognizing that they wanted to be taken seriously.

Frederick James Gregg: Harper's Weekly, *February 15*

This is not amusing, it is dismaying and disheartening. The other day, someone attributed to me the statement that the human race was nearing insanity. I never said that, but if anyone is trying to convince me that this is "the modern art," and that it is representative of our time, I would be obliged to think that statement is true.

Kenyon Cox: Harper's Weekly, *March 15*

Most often, the impression this exhibit leaves with the artist or the layman, even the most intelligent, is that the work presented is not only a radical break with the past but is a subversive questioning of art itself as it has been conceived and recognized until the present time. That there is a break with preceding forms, this I admit, but as for being subversive, I can only offer my personal conviction that it is not.

Walter Pach: For and Against

THE RITE OF SPRING

PARIS

Immediately after its inauguration, the Théâtre des Champs-Élysées was the stage of a new scandal; the first was when almost everybody in Paris protested against its architecture by Perret and its sculptured decorations by Bourdelle.

On May 29, the theater celebrated the Grande Saison de Printemps (great spring season) with the Russian Ballet in *The Rite of Spring* by Igor Stravinsky. With this production, Gabriel Astruc, founder and director of the theater, provoked a storm that shows no signs of calming.

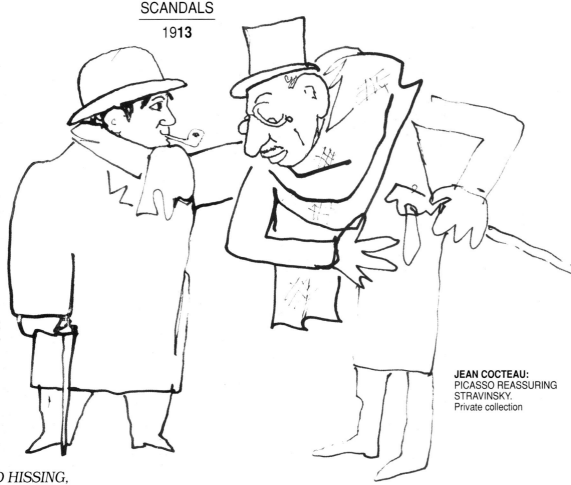

JEAN COCTEAU:
PICASSO REASSURING STRAVINSKY.
Private collection

SHRIEKING AND HISSING, THE SPECTATORS WERE OVERCOME WITH FRENZY

The Théâtre des Champs-Élysées.

Igor Stravinsky's dissonant orchestration and the savage, furious choreography entrusted by Diaghilev to Nijinski caused a wave of indignation to sweep through the greater part of the audience.

In the wings, deeply distressed, the inseparable Nijinski and Diaghilev demanded that the curtain be drawn. Astruc, bent over his balcony, shaking his fist at the frenzied public, shouted at the top of his lungs, "Listen first! Hiss later . . ." But his trembling voice could not drown the shrieks and the hissing of the raging spectators. And when the ballet ended on the "Scenes of Pagan Russia," the entire theater was overcome with frenzy. Even Bourdelle's daring frescoes of the atrium, Maurice Denis's compositions, the lighting fixtures by Bagnès and Perrassy seemed to partake in the madness.

Indeed, the composer has pushed to the limit the accumulation of metric and harmonic innovations that lend his score a terrifying force, and transform it into a "summary of modern art," as Jean Cocteau said.

It is known that Stravinsky composed *The Rite* in Clarens, on the banks of Lake Leman. He had already worked there on *Petrouchka*. In 1909, his *Fireworks*, playing in St. Petersburg, had interested Diaghilev, who commissioned *L'oiseau de feu* (the firebird).

Stravinsky has had a good relationship with the Russian Ballet ever since. Their collaboration culminated with this erotic explosion, reminiscent of Bourdelle's metopes. In fact, one of them, *La danse*, was inspired by Isadora Duncan and Nijinsky himself.

While Bourdelle regrets that he had so little time for his frieze and tablets, he is thrilled to have worked so well with the architect. He agrees with Perret that "the legitimate place of architectural sculpture is in those parts of the monument where architecture does not play a role."

From Tokyo to Montparnasse

After a forty-five-day crossing aboard the Mishima Maru, the painter Tsugouharu Foujita arrived in Paris via Marseille. One of his first visits was Picasso's place at 5 Rue Schoelcher, where he was taken by the Chilean painter Ortiz de Zarate, whom he had met in Montparnasse. It seems, however, that Picasso's Cubist efforts enchanted Foujita less than the few canvases by Henri Rousseau that Picasso owns. Various Montparnasse circles, always hungry for exoticism, entertained Foujita as soon as he arrived. It is still not known whether he came to find himself or lose himself.

Camille Claudel Is Confined in an Institution

For some time now, lovely Camille Claudel, sister of the poet and emulator of the great Rodin, has no longer been seen in Paris. She had been Rodin's pupil, assistant, source of inspiration, and lover. She had definitively broken off with him in 1894, and lived alone, avoiding people, dedicated to her work. But illness began to take its toll. Becoming increasingly neurotic, she would no longer leave her constantly shut-tered studio on the Île Saint-Louis except at night. At the age of forty-eight, she is confined, on Monday, March 10, to the Ville-Evrard Asylum a "systematic persecution delirium, based mainly on interpretations and fibbing."

Six Feet Long for a Poem

A brilliant vertical road map that draws the reader's eye simultaneously into a chromatic dance and the music of words, *The Prose of the Trans-Siberian* is the first livre-objet (object-book).

The colors are by Sonia Delaunay, after a poem by Blaise Cendrars. And, as a novelty, the same text is set in ten different typefaces. The seasoned poet is overcome: "Madame Delaunay has made such a pretty book that my poem is more colorful than my life. That makes me happy. All the more so because this book is six feet long. And still more so because the whole publication is as tall as the Eiffel Tower."

Camille Claudel with one of her works.

SONIA DELAUNAY: THE PROSE OF THE TRANS-SIBERIAN. 1913. Paris. MNAM

IN BRIEF...

GERMANY
In Berlin, the gallery Der Sturm shows works by Archipenko.
Walter Gropius has been commissioned to design the interior of sleeping cars.
First Salon d'Automne in Germany organized by Walden with Léger, Delaunay, and several Futurists.
Emil Nolde embarks for the Pacific Ocean with the scientific expedition of Külz-Leber.

FRANCE
American Synchromists appear in the Salon des Indépendants.
The La Boétie gallery displays sculptures by Boccioni.

GREAT BRITAIN
Creation of the London Group, following the Camden Town Group, which, last year, had decorated a fashionable cabaret, the Cave of the Golden Calf.

ITALY
Russolo and the Futurist group publish a manifesto: The Art of Noises, *a combination of the sounds of cars, tramways, factories, and the like.*

The Rayonist Manifesto

Written two years ago, the *Rayonist Manifesto* now appears in Moscow, coupled with the exhibition "The Target," the first big Rayonist group show. The manifesto's author, painter Mikhail Larionov, who was struck by the illuminations of Turner's last paintings, which he saw in London in 1906, conceives of forms as if they were bundles of crossed lines like light rays. "We needed to find a point of departure," he explains, "from which painting could fully become itself, while maintaining the stimulus of real life." Among the followers of Rayonism are Kyril Zdanevich, Michel Le Dentu, Alexandre Chevchenko, Natalia Gontcharova, and of course Mikhail Larionov himself.

JUAN GRIS'S WARNING

CÉRET

"Picasso's gang" makes waves among the population of the small town of Vallespir, where Picasso and his friends Braque, Gris, and Max Jacob spend the summer. At the Grand Café and Chez Armand, where one can feast for forty centimes, everybody speaks about the licentious behavior of the Parisian artists and their companions, who walk around in daring outfits with their legs bare. Yet the Cubists came here for a rest cure of silence and meditation. The atmosphere of Céret allows them to think and renew themselves.

Juan Gris, remembering his taste for the exact sciences, rejects the abandonment of color and shape, and remodels the Cubist approach. Braque and Picasso have for the past two years pushed the analysis and decomposition of objects to their abstract limits. Gris reminds them with good reason that the destruction of the objective world must always be a necessary premise of its stylistic recomposition.

These are the subjects that are discussed at the Grand Café and Chez Armand. Isn't it paradoxical that the most theory-minded among them warns against the dangers of pushing theory too far?

KAZIMIR MALEVICH: THE WOODCUTTER. 1911. Amsterdam. Stedelijk Museum

JUAN GRIS: STILL LIFE WITH BOOK.1913. Paris. MNAM

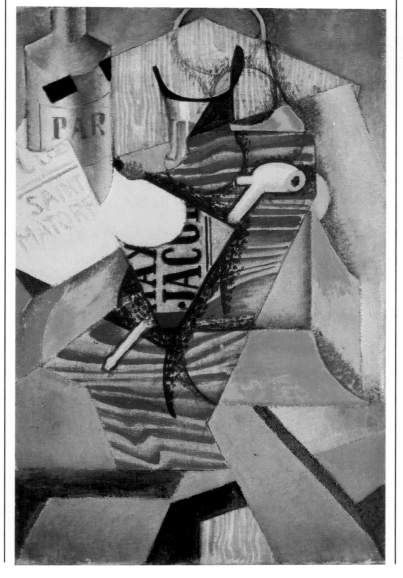

MALEVICH PROVOKES ST. PETERSBURG

ST. PETERSBURG

The painter Kazimir Malevich, born in Kiev in 1878 and the leader of young Russian artists, has been involved since 1909 in the most daring pictorial experiments. At the exhibition of the Young Artists' Union, which opened in St. Petersburg at the beginning of this winter, he vigorously showed his leadership.

In his *Woodcutter* one of his most beautiful paintings, which he calls "a dynamic arrangement," he turns his peasant subject into a robot with aggressive volumes that seem to move. He is interested in the relationship between pure shapes and their surrounding space, and seeks an internal tension that makes his paintings vibrate. "Here is an artist," said his friend Natalia Gontcharova, "who skips steps in art evolution." The strange thing is that, although he adopted a Cubism close to Léger's, he insists that his roots are in the Russian people's Primitivism. Lately, he and Gontcharova have become interested in the prehistoric stone sculptures found in the south of Russia. He thinks "a return to the land" is needed!

APOLLINAIRE EXPLAINS CUBISM

For several years, poet and art critic Guillaume Apollinaire has been the main defender of the avant-garde. Regular contributor to the *Intransigeant,* he created his own magazine, *Les soirées de Paris* (Paris evenings) of which he is the manager. It is not by chance that his book *The Cubist Painters, Esthetic Meditations* borrows its subtitle from the *Metaphysical Meditations* by Descartes. Apollinaire attempts, on the one hand, a classification of the various tendencies of Cubism, from Picasso and Braque to Léger, Marie Laurencin, Delaunay, Gleizes, and Metzinger, and, on the other hand, an exploration of what it is that opposes today's art to the traditional one. But it remains the work of a writer, or the work of a philosopher, rather than the work of a theoretician of art.

Many of the new painters only paint pictures without a real subject. And catalogues often designate things and people without characterizing them.

Just as there are people named Legros ("the fat one") who are very thin and people by the name of LeBlond who have brown hair, I have seen canvases titled "solitude" but showing several characters.

One still condescends sometimes to using words vaguely explanatory such as portrait, landscape, still life; but many young painters prefer the general term "painting."

These painters, if they still observe nature, no longer imitate it and carefully avoid the representation of scenes observed in nature.

Resemblance no longer has any importance, for everything is sacrificed by the artist to the truths and necessities of a higher nature that he assumes without really discovering it. The subject no longer counts, or it counts for very little.

Modern art generally rejects most of the means to please that were implemented by the great artists of yore.

If the goal of painting is still what it used to be—to please the eye—the viewer henceforth has to learn to find another pleasure than the traditional pleasure that can be found in the contemplation of nature.

One thus moves toward an entirely new art, an art that will be to traditional painting what music is to literature.

It will be pure painting, the way music is pure literature.

The music lover, when listening to a concert, experiences a different order of joy than what he feels by listening to natural noises such as the murmuring of a brook, the whistling of the wind in a forest, or the harmonies of human language founded on reason.

FERNAND LÉGER: STAIRWAY. 1913. Zurich. Kunstmuseum

In the same way, the new painters will give their admirers artistic sensations that result from the harmony of shocking lights.

GUILLAUME APOLLINAIRE
The Cubist Painters
(Excerpt)

1914

For art, the first consequence of the declaration of war is the disbanding of the members of Europe's avant-garde. Among the French, Braque, Léger, Duchamp-Villon, Kupka, and Czaky, along with numerous others, respond to the draft. The Spaniard Pablo Picasso, whose country does not go to war, is left virtually alone in Paris.

In Germany, the consequences are similar: August Macke, Franz Marc, Max Ernst, and Otto Dix also leave for the front lines. In the meantime, in Italy, which remains neutral, Futurism, led by the ardent Filippo Tommaso Marinetti, continues to cut capers. By no means does any of this signify that modern art is threatened. The sudden appearance of Giorgio de Chirico seems bound to result in chimeric, new perspectives in art.

SUMMARY

AVANT-GARDE

Giorgio de Chirico Transcribes Dreams
Schopenhauer: the Dream as Metaphysics
Hartley's Flags
The Synchromists Have a Show

MASTERWORKS

Robert Delaunay in the Sky

ENVIRONMENTS

The Baroque Décor of Güell Park

ART NEWS

The Sale of the Bearskin
Larionov and Gontcharova at the Paul Guillaume Gallery
Macke is Killed at Perthes-sur-Hurlus
Cubism Is Defeated by the War
In Brief

WRITINGS AND THEORIES

Boccioni: Futurism and Time-Space

SCULPTURE

Where Does Sculpture Stand Today?

GIORGIO DE CHIRICO:
PREMONITORY PORTRAIT OF
GUILLAUME APOLLINAIRE. 1914.
Paris.MNAM

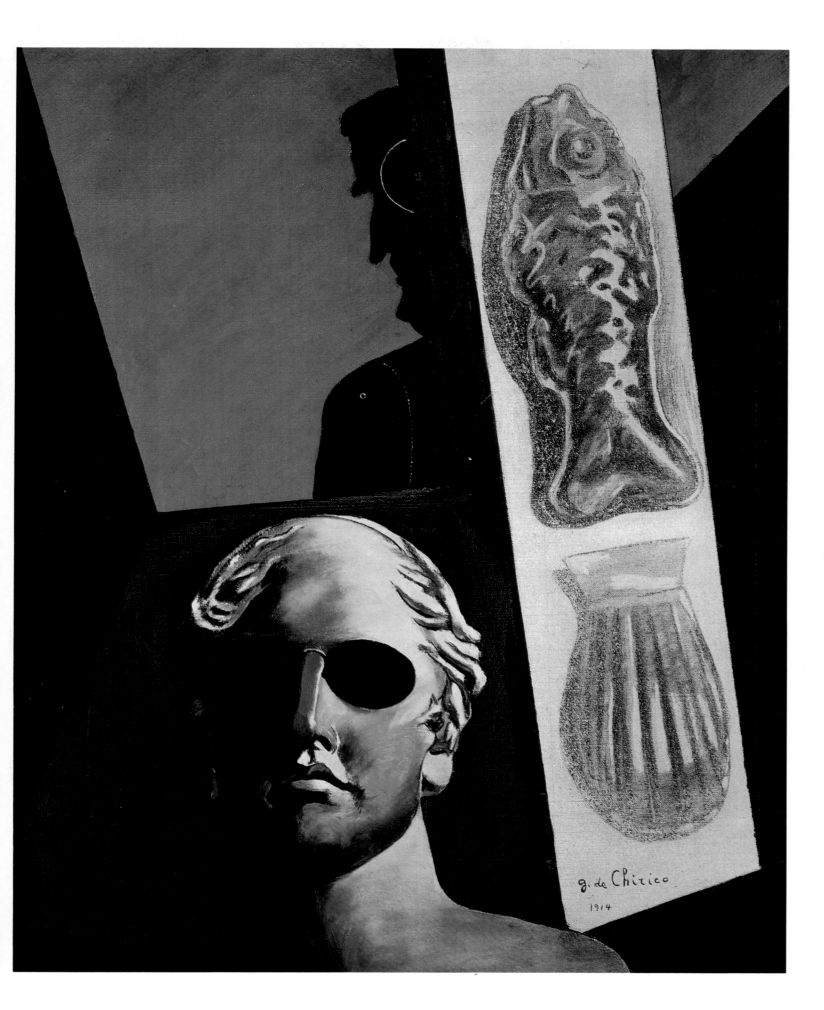

GIORGIO DE CHIRICO TRANSCRIBES DREAMS

PARIS

The painter of railway stations! That is what Picasso calls Giorgio de Chirico since he saw his paintings, inspired by the Montparnasse railway station, last year at the Salon des Indépendants. De Chirico is also a painter who is not influenced by Cubism, Fauvism, or Impressionism. "His originality is new enough to be welcomed," writes Apollinaire.

De Chirico resembles no other painter. He came from Florence to Paris with his mother on July 14, 1911, to join his brother Andrea, a musician known under the name of Alberto Savinio.

His father was an engineer; he worked for a company that built railways. Giorgio was born on July 11, 1888, in Volo, Thessaly, and studied at the Polytechnical Institute of Athens. After his father's death in 1905, he studied art in Munich: the Art Academy, the revelation of Arnold Böcklin, Max Klinger, the German romanticists, visionary painting—enough of a background to gain him a special place in art circles.

He recently exhibited some thirty paintings in his studio, at 115 Rue Notre-Dame-des-Champs. The young art dealer Paul Guillaume, who has just opened a gallery on the Rue du Faubourg Saint-Honoré, gave him a contract. For a monthly salary of 120 francs the painter supplies the dealer with six paintings a month; each painting is thus worth 20 francs. It is next to nothing, but de Chirico seems satisfied.

"De Chirico's painting is not painting as we understand it today. It could be defined as dream writing. Through almost infinite rows of arcades and façades, large straight lines, overgrown masses of simple colors, almost funeral-like light and dark spaces, he expresses the feeling of vastness, solitude, immobility, stagnation, awak-

GIORGIO DE CHIRICO: ENIGMA OF A DAY. 1913. London. Private Collection

ened by the remembrance of certain scenes in our almost-dormant soul." So writes Ardengo Soffici in a recent issue of the magazine *Lacerba.*

The enigmatic immensity of the Montparnasse railway station, prolonged by its endless shadow on a fall afternoon, inspired de Chirico. However, he is far from being a mere painter of railway stations. Florence,

Rome, and especially Turin, where he stopped for a few days on his way to Paris, are at the core of his art. "In Turin, everything is an apparition. You go out to a square and find yourself facing a stone man who looks at you with that stare that only statues have." In Turin, on the Carlo-Alberto square, Nietzsche had run, at the moment of succumbing to insanity, to hug a

horse abused by its owner. Like Nietzsche, de Chirico is a nihilist. Like Nietzsche, he believes in premonitions, secret signs, fatal circumstances. He, too, is convinced of the spiritual decadence of our society. Perhaps that is the source of empty mysterious squares, of clocks showing noon at two in the afternoon in his paintings.

De Chirico's originality stems

from his long rapport with philosophers: Nietzsche, but also Kant, Schopenhauer, and Weininger. Soon after his arrival in Paris, he endlessly read and scribbled poems in Schopenhauer's *Essay on Ideas and Miscellaneous Pieces.* The French edition of the book appeared two years ago. In it, dreams, hallucinations, second sight, and visions are considered the black diamond of thought. At the same time, the Viennese Otto Wein-inger confirmed the artist's belief that "psychic phenomena are more real than physical phenomena."

But his reading of the philosophers does not prevent his painting from drawing its effects out of casual encounters. On the contrary. The target encircling the poet's temple in his recent *Premonitory Portrait of Guillaume Apollinaire* reflects his irritation at seeing the pseudointellectual entourage of the poet smoke clay pipes, similar to those used for target shooting at fairs. The red rubber glove nailed to a board in *Song of Love* was bought at the household appliance section of a department store.

Giorgio de Chirico says he will soon leave. He cannot stay long anywhere. Since his arrival, he considers Paris the city of cities; a kind of Athens in the time of Pericles, which anyone deserving the name of "artist" must experience. He finds a beneficial environment here: Apollinaire, Brancusi, whose influence can be seen in the heads of his models, Picasso, whom he respects, Derain, whom he abhors, Max Jacob, Blaise Cendrars, Modigliani. "A metaphysical city," is what he calls Paris.

(See also 1926 and 1978.)

SCHOPENHAUER: THE DREAM AS METAPHYSICS

It is an unexpected Schopenhauer that is revealed in his short *Essay on Phenomena.* The publication is dated 1850, but it was translated into French only two years ago. It covers dreams, apparitions, hallucinations, somnambulism, occultism—subjects that are considered unworthy of philosophy but in which the author sees metaphysical significance. This work has been a veritable revelation for Giorgio de Chirico. The following passages are from this essay—note the strangeness of Schopenhauer's tone.

To pretend to see dreams as simple plays of thought, simple images of fantasy, is to show a lack of reflection or integrity, for, clearly, they are different. Mere fantasy products are weak, languishing, incomplete, partial, and short-lived; one can hardly fix them in memory for more than a second. Even the most vivid game of fantasy cannot in any way compare to the palpable reality that a dream places before our eyes. Our faculty of representation in dreams exceeds infinitely that of our imagination; each intuitive object reveals a truth, an achievement, a logical universality that extends to the most essential inner properties, as does reality itself, whereas fantasy remains far away. For that matter, our faculty of representation would procure us the most marvelous paintings if we could only choose the subject of our dreams . . .

Experience teaches us moreover that the dream organ, which in general functions with ordinary light sleep as well with deep "hypnotic" sleep, can occasionally work in the awakened brain, too; that is, the eye with which we see dreams is able to open up when we are awake. The figures that then appear before us are so fallaciously similar to those that enter the brain through the senses that the one may be mistaken for the other . . . A figure appearing in this way will be given—depending on its origin—the name of hallucination, of vision, of second sight, or of apparition . . .

Such phenomena are a sure refutation not only of materialism but of the naturalism that I have described as being physics placed on the throne of metaphysics. They demonstrate that the order of nature, which one tries to see as absolute and unique, is purely phenomenal and consequently purely superficial and that its base is founded on the essence of things themselves, independent of its laws. The phenomena in question are, at least from a philosophical point of view, doubtlessly the most important among the facts that experience offers us. It is every scholar's duty to study them thoroughly . . .*

ARTHUR SCHOPENHAUER
Essay on Phenomena
and Miscellaneous Pieces
(Excerpts)

GIORGIO DE CHIRICO:
SONG OF LOVE. 1914. New York. MOMA

THE SYNCHROMISTS HAVE A SHOW

MARDSEN HARTLEY: PORTRAIT OF A GERMAN OFFICER. 1914. New York. Metropolitan Museum of Art

NEW YORK

Synchromism was revealed last year at the Armory Show. It is again in the center of New York's artistic news, thanks to an exhibition dedicated by the Caroll Gallery to the work of MacDonald-Wright. The artist is absent, since he did not think it necessary to return to the United States for the event.

With Morgan Russel, who lives and works in Paris, he created Synchromism two years ago. Inspired by Neoimpressionism (which in turn arose from the works of Chevreul, Helmholtz, and Roods on color), Synchromism considers all forms only from the standpoint of their color relationships. In this sense, it is close to Delaunay. In his series of *Windows* Delaunay was the first to try to replace traditional perspective with a new system, using color shapes to express modern life. Macdonald-Wright came to Paris in 1907 form Charlottesville, Virginia, where he was born in 1890. But Synchromism was born in 1912 from his decisive meeting with Morgan Russel, who was four years his senior. In general, their paintings are abstract. They are made of simple geometric forms, triangles, circles, or portions of circles in bright colors, creating a feeling of vibrant visual mobility. The two painters, who are close to Delaunay, Matisse, and Apollinaire, participate in the Salon des Indépendants and the Salon d'Automne.

MORGAN RUSSEL: SYNCHROMY IN BLUE AND VIOLET (STUDY). 1913. Minneapolis. Private Collection

HARTLEY'S FLAGS

BERLIN

Remaining in Germany despite the declaration of war, Mardsen Hartley is one of the best current New York painters, although he is not well known to the public. Born in 1877 in Maine, where he likes to spend his summers, he broke with American Naturalist tradition. His landscapes of circa 1908 were influenced by the Italian Neoimpressionist Segantini.

Alfred Stieglitz gave him his first solo exhibition at the Gallery 291, in 1909, and initiated him in contemporary art. The artists spent hours studying Stieglitz's exhibitions of Matisse and Picasso in his gallery in 1910 and 1911. Thanks to Stieglitz's financial support, Hartley was able to go to Europe, where he has spent the past two years studying European art.

In Paris, he was first attracted by Cubism and Fauvism. However, French art seemed too intellectual for this tormented soul who, on the contrary, was deeply touched by Expressionism. He currently paints in bright colors, as in the *Portrait of a German Officer*, based on symbols and badges found in German flags and uniforms. In Munich, Hartley was warmly met by Kandinsky and Marc. They discussed at length the spiritual principles of the Blue Rider, which made him become more and more abstract. In Paris, Hartley participated in the cosmopolitan evenings offered by Gertrude Stein.

ROBERT DELAUNAY IN THE SKY

PARIS

The event took place five years ago, on Sunday, July 25, 1909. Louis Blériot landed his monoplane, *Blériot XI*, on the golf green at Dover, two steps from Shakespeare's cliff, the scene of King Lear's madness. Thirty-two minutes earlier, Blériot had departed from Baraques, a village on a huge flat field near Calais. He achieved the first crossing of the English Channel with a "heavier-than-air" device.

Five years later, this event found its painter: Robert Delaunay, age twenty-nine. The 8 X 8 foot painting dedicated to the first crossing of the Channel is simply called *Homage to Blériot* and bears a dedication, "First solar disks simultaneously formed for the great constructor Blériot 1914."

Until now, many a painting had shown the fabulous feat. Undersecretary of State Dujardin-Beaumetz had commissioned the academic painter François Thévenot to produce a very descriptive official painting, in which Blériot's plane flies over Dover. But Delaunay wanted to do something entirely different.

His *Homage* is made of large concentric colored circles and some smaller ones, which make it almost abstract. When one looks closely, one can see, in the center of the circles, the wheels and the propeller of *Blériot XI*,

ROBERT DELAUNAY: HOMAGE TO BLÉRIOT. 1914. Basel. Kunstmuseum

Louis Blériot in his airplane.

and tiny mechanics at work. At the top of the composition there is the biplane of the Wright brothers, the other aviation heroes. Two years ago, Delaunay painted a first *Disk* in which colors were applied in circles and opposed by sharp contrast. Here they are multiplied, giving an intense feeling of visual mobility, a shifting of air and light, the suggestion of space gained by a moving mechanical engine.

The other artists who wanted to express Blériot's exploit sought psychological detail. Delaunay painted a solar fireworks as the only means to glorify the conquest of the air. He put the engine in the painting.

On October 14, 1909, with its wings folded against the fuselage and accompanied by the Republican Guard, Blériot's monoplane was taken from the Gare du Nord (railway station) to the Conservatory of Arts and Crafts in midst of general fanfare. Thus today Delaunay celebrates our new heroes.

(See also 1912, 1937, 1941.)

Güell Park.

THE BAROQUE DÉCOR OF GÜELL PARK

BARCELONA

After fourteen years of work, Güell Park is still unfinished! It was interrupted by the death of the very wealthy Count Eusebio Güell, who had commissioned it, giving full freedom to the architect, Antoni Gaudí y Cornet, to express his dreams on the slopes of Montana Pelada, north of Barcelona. Fifty villas, only two of which were built, concert halls, conference halls, restaurants, and schools should have been built on a 37-acre site that is not very appropriate for city planning. The project was an unprecedented attempt to incorporate architecture into nature within a city garden.

The part that was completed, however, shows the functional and, at the same time, totally dreamlike mood of the project. Gaudí showed his talents as city planner, architect, sculptor, ceramist, and colorist in his con-cern to retrieve the spirit of synthesis of times long past.

In Gaudí's eyes, "only a poetic universe is fit to be inhabited, because it is the only universe permitting imagination to manifest itself." Indeed, everything here was used to make symbols reflect shapes: pillars evoking caryatides or repeating the heli-coidal forms of surrounding trees, terrace walls simulating a palm-tree forest complete with carob trees, brooms, and fir trees added to the existing vegetation. In the labryinth of Güell Park, everything shows relentless ornamental extravagance and folly.

The exuberant entrance fence is surrounded by two pavilions with sinuous lines. Inside, the visitor doesn't stop being surprised and discovering new things. First, he goes up a wide staircase. The staircase is surrounded by a wall covered with white ceramic. On one banister, there is a prehistoric-looking animal covered with blue, green, and ocher mosaics. Soon, the staircase divides into two parts around fountains decorated with a series of animals made of blue, green, and ocher mosaics with a fossilized appearance. Then, on both sides, there are huge terraces paved with chesslike tiles contrasting with the surrounding overdecoration. Beyond that, serving as an outdoor theater, is a somewhat wide esplanade. Around it there is an endless bench, decorated with a mosaic made with porcelain shards, imitating the movement of a wave.

All this does not mean that Gaudí did not respect architectural laws. On the contrary, he pushed them to an extreme refinement. Since 1883 he has been the director of the Sagrada Familia site, the only cathedral built in our time. As in the recently finished Colonia Güell chapel of Santa Colona de Cervelló, he experiments with a great invention: the reversed vault without flying buttresses. Nothing from the fantasy of his walking promenades to the doric temple with the vertigo-inducing inclined pillars, serving as a roofed market, nothing would have been possible without a perfect technique. In this sense, Gaudí's structures evoke the technique of baroque buildings. These are still numerous in Catalonia and represent a permanent reference for Gaudí.

Gaudí, now sixty-two, is the most famous Spanish architect. Some see in him the master of Art Nouveau. But perhaps he is, first of all, an exceptional visionary genius. His art perfectly agrees with technical forces as well as with the forces of nature. *(See also 1926.)*

The Sale of the Bearskin

When it was created in 1904 at the instigation of the young financier André Level, La Peau de l'Ours (the bearskin) had as a goal to put together a mutually owned collection of modern paintings. The works acquired over the past ten years by the members of the association were put up for sale on March 2 at the Hôtel Drouot. The collection included one hundred and forty-five works by sixty artists, among them a dozen Picassos, five Matisses, four Utrillos, and three Rouaults, as well as canvases by Van Gogh, Bonnard, and Gauguin. *The Jugglers* by Picasso was sold to the Munich dealer Tannhäuser for the record amount of 11,500 francs.

Larionov and Gontcharova at the Paul Guillaume Gallery

In June, there is an exhibition of Larionov and Gontcharova at the Paul Guillaume gallery at 6 Rue de Mirosmenil. In the preface to the catalog, Apollinaire shows himself to be an ardent defender of Rayonism, created the year before in Moscow by Larionov. "The work of art, such as it is conceived of by Larionov and the Rayonists in the plastic arts or in Russian literature, is like a magnet on which all surrounding life converges," he writes. Rayonism aims in effect at fixing the light rays reflected off the surfaces of objects by means of color, instead of by means of the objects themselves. However, Gontcharova differs from Larionov in her subject matter, which is inspired by modern life in a manner closer to Futurism, though she, too, is a Rayonist. They are both thirty-three years old, and hope to settle in Paris.

Cubism Is Defeated by the War

Is Cubism dead, done in by the declaration of war? The general call to arms has scattered its troops. Braque received his marching orders in Sorgues, where he was on vacation. Léger left on August 2 as a soldier in the corps of engineers. La Fresnaye signed up for the infantry. And with them, Villon, Gleizes, Duchamp-Villon, Csaky, and still others are joining up, as are their eternal defenders, Salmon, Warnod, Raynal, Apollinaire, Cendrars. Only the antimilitarist Pablo Picasso, whose country has not gone to war, stays behind in Paris. Very disoriented, he thinks about taking up new avenues of creativity, to the point that his enemies accuse him of trying to leave Cubism before it abandons him.

AUGUSTE MACKE: THREESOME PROMENADE. 1914. Lugano. Thyssen Bornemisza Collection

Macke Is Killed at Perthes-sur-Hurlus

Drafted on August 8, August Macke was killed on the front at Champagne six weeks later at Perthes-sur-Hurlus. He was twenty-seven years old. A pupil at the Academy of Fine Arts in Düsseldorf, he was a passionate admirer of the Impressionists, and had made several trips to Paris, notably with his wife's uncle, the industrialist and collector Bernhard Koehler. Influenced first by Matisse, then by Cubism, he subsequently found himself friends with Franz Marc in 1910, which associated him with the Blue Rider. Later on, he exalted nature, although he did not have the metaphysical preoccupations of a Franz Marc. A stay in Tunis with Paul Klee in April of this year had completely changed him: He brought back watercolors and hundreds of drawings. He leaves more than two hundred paintings.

MIKHAIL LARIONOV: COMPOSITION. 1913. Paris. MNAM

IN BRIEF...

GERMANY
In Berlin, Herwarth Walden presents a retrospective of Marc Chagall.

In Munich, founding of the New Secession with the participation of Klee, Jawlensky, Beckmann, and Kokoschka.

UNITED STATES
First one-man exhibition of Brancusi in New York, at Gallery 291.

GREAT BRITAIN
Publication in London of the English Futurist Manifesto Vital English Art, *by Marinetti and C. Nevinson.*

ITALY
Exhibition of Probitas, an Antifuturist group.

Publication of Sant'Elia's Manifesto of Futurist Architecture *and of his drawings of the* New City.

BOCCIONI: FUTURISM AND TIME-SPACE

Futurist Painting and Sculpture was almost entirely written last year, but it could not be published before this March. Boccioni gathered in it mainly the articles he had published in the review *Lacerba*. The following excerpt, however, abandons the polemic tone for explanation and theory.

The Cubist's attempt at a picture fails because it is based on the involution of a discovery of Cézanne's and not on the logical definition process of an evolution. But now the Futurist discovery of recollection and feeling intervenes in the construction of the modern painting.

It is a matter of uniting the concept of space, to which Cubism limits itself, with the concept of time. It is a matter of finding a construction in which the two concepts of space and time are balanced out for the resolution of emotions. It is a matter not only of building objects that are enriched and renewed through the contribution of tactile knowledge and accidental vision, but of creating a plastic environment in which the objects can develop all their emotive plastic potentiality. It is a matter, in fact, of adding to the objective plastic renewal of the French a subjective plastic renewal, of creating consequently a new emotive evaluation that springs forth from the plastic potentiality characteristic of the object. And as the emotive plastic values of the objects vary as much as the objects, that is, infinitely, it is necessary to react to this kind of Impressionism, which we will call ethical, and which until today has made us accumulate and analyze inefficent, unnecessary, dissimilar plastic elements in a single picture. It is necessary to create a discipline that coordinates and gives to each element of the picture its own proper function.

This discipline, as I said before, is not fixed but intuitive, and it obeys the mysterious necessity of the picture, it obeys its composition. Once we have accepted the picture as a hierarchy of plastic values, a new hori-zon opens before us. It is the Impressionist revolution channeled into the dynamic order of Futurism. We are approaching the plastic state of mind. Therefore, the concepts of speed, copenetration, simultaneity through which we Futurists interpret things, make us unite in a single picture the plastic values that struck us yesterday, or a year ago, and the values that push us to look for the brush today and to go to work . . .

UMBERTO BOCCIONI:
Futurist Painting and Sculpture
(Excerpt)

UMBERTO BOCCIONI:
UNIQUE SHAPE OF CONTINUITY
IN SPACE. 1913.
Rome. Private Collection

WHERE DOES SCULPTURE STAND TODAY?

Sculpture is trying to find itself. One could even think it *is* finding itself. In the sense that the boldest among the artists seem to want to shed "the straightjacket of Analytical Cubism" and deal anew with reality itself—close attention to its poetic resonances in isolation should reveal its value. The assembled compositions by Braque, Picasso, and Gris have already their followers and imitators. And what's more, it seems that *any* object, from now on, can be raised to the rank of a work of art. That's revolution.

RAYMOND DUCHAMP-VILLON:
GRAND HORSE. 1913. Paris. MNAM

PABLO PICASSO:
ABSINTHE GLASS.
1914. Paris. MNAM

This work, created in spring, is a veritable "still life" in painted and sand-sprinkled bronze, with a real spoon, the kind that is used for melting sugar into absinthe. It is indicative of Picasso's evolution toward Synthetic Cubism, which we could see already in his paintings that include paper collages and small objects.

"The power of the machine forces itself on us, and it is hard to imagine living beings without it," Duchamp-Villon wrote to a friend. With this *Grand Horse,* which he made in 1 1/2-foot-high plaster for the Salon d'Automne, the artist wants to express "the form of superior dynamism" in movement.

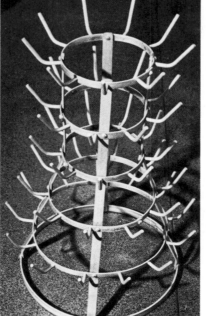

MARCEL DUCHAMP:
BOTTLE RACK. 1913.
Paris. MNAM

Ever since his adolescence, Marcel Duchamp wanted to do *art sec*—Dry Art—and last year he proclaimed that any common, manufactured object can be raised to the rank of art through the mere choice by an artist. For example, this bottle rack, which he had bought at a town-hall bazaar.

Suprematism will go farther than Cubism, farther than Futurism, farther than all the avant-garde movements put together, declares a thirty-six-year-old giant, Kazimir Malevich. And he is probably not far off. His theories and ideas call into question every artistic creation, shake every work of art to its foundation. In Paris, nothing new is happening except for some scuffles among a few artists-in-hiding on the sidewalks of the cafés in Montparnasse. But when Italy enters the war on the side of the Allies, the entire Futurist group immediately signs up, delighted to go to battle against their long-time enemy, the Austro-Hungarian Empire.

1915

S U M M A R Y

AVANT-GARDE

The Suprematism of Malevich

MANIFESTO

Malevich: the Search for the Absolute

DEVELOPMENTS

**Stieglitz Founds the Magazine *291*
Picabia and Duchamp in the United States**

ART NEWS

**An Artist Exhibits Artists
Kokoschka Is Wounded at the Front
Jacob Epstein's Jackhammer Man
The Military Adopts Cubism
The Painter of Storms
In Brief**

ART AND THE WAR

**Artists on all Fronts
Steinlen Flies to the Aid of the Poilus
The Futurists Volunteer**

KAZIMIR MALEVICH:
SUPREMATISM. 1915.
Amsterdam. Stedelijk Museum

THE SUPREMATISM OF MALEVICH

PETROGRAD

Since the end of the last century, avant-gardes in art in Europe and in Russia have been following an accelerated rhythm. Symbolism, Expressionism, Fauvism, Cubism, Futurism, Rayonism . . . And here is a new tendency that is still more innovative: Suprematism. But although the avant-gardes succeed one another, they do not necessarily resemble each other, except on one point: their common desire to eliminate their competitors.

from this experience. To understand the permanent restlessness in Russian intellectual circles, it is necessary not to overlook the ideological and political background from which it developed at the end of the nineteenth century. It is impossible to judge today the activities of a painter like Malevich if the history of Russian nihilism, for example, is not taken into consideration.

What did the anarchist and revolutionary groups want? To

KAZIMIR MALEVICH: AN ENGLISHMAN IN MOSCOW. 1914.
Amsterdam. Stedelijk Museum

THE ATTEMPT TO EMBODY THE ABSOLUTE IN A PURIFIED PAINTING

The exhibition held in Petrograd in December under the title "0,10" offered us a good sample of the rivalry driving avant-garde artists. There was the unexpected spectacle of two exhibitors coming to blows to settle their differences. The altercation was violent; it was necessary to separate the enraged individuals. Who were they? On the right was the tall and thin Tatlin, and on the left an over-excited giant, the head of the new movement, Kazimir Malevich.

The latter was not unknown in Russian art circles. He arrived in Moscow in 1905 and participated in the revolutionary events in December. His revolutionary fervor was unquestionably derived

remake totally the society of their time. To destroy everything and return it all to point zero. What does the master think of Suprematism today? To destroy the old art, to build a new art over its ruins, and to elevate the latter to its highest level. "Quickly cast off the damaged skin of the centuries," Malevich prescribed. "Suprematism is the beginning of a new civilization." Further: "I tell all of you to reject love, reject estheticisms, throw away the baggage of wisdom, because your wisdom is insignificant and ridiculous in the new civilization. I have untied the knots of wisdom and liberated the consciousness of colors."

But what are these inflamma-

The 0,10 exhibition.

tory declarations really trying to say? How can conceptual utopias of this type be embodied in particular works?

Malevich did not just fall from a sky of pure ideas. He had a past as an artist. His first characteristic works date from 1908. These were figurative paintings in which individuals embodied the great symbols of humanity. Many of the scenes painted were inspired by rural life. The monumental character of the figures, as in *Woman with Buckets and Child* of 1910, the geometric treatment of planes, the color contrast, as in *The Return of the*

Harvests of 1911, provide evidence that Malevich paid careful attention to old paintings (especially Byzantine icons) and modern works: Cézanne, Matisse, Picasso, Léger, Larionov, Gontcharova.

This year, however, after a series of so-called "alogical" paintings, in which he accumulated representations of incongruous objects on the same canvas, visually jumping from one subject to another, the artist opted for abstraction, choosing to bring it to its final consequences. He then determined to launch his bomb, the *Suprema-*

tist *Manifesto*, and his torpedoes, thirty-five completely abstract works. The most surprising of them, the one closest to a zero degree of painting, was a *Black Square on White*. According to Malevich, the elementary contrast of black and white releases a universal energy; all past, present, and future paintings are summarized in this opposition and are consumed there. There is something of Savonarola in this mystic iconoclast, who responds more to the dizziness of his speech than to the width of his targets.

If Cubists or Futurists, as revolutionary as they were, created a new repertory of forms capable of expressing the world in which we live today, they did not for a moment doubt the legitimacy of the painting they wanted only to revitalize. But even the possibility of painting is questioned by Malevich. Not only are his paintings abstract, like those of Kandinsky, but they are radical: They no longer make any exterior, interior, physical, or mental reference. The time of art presented as metaphysical has come, so that it is impossible to determine which is the most important of its pictures or writings.

The high-spirited giant must have needed courage to push the frontiers of creation back so far, and this was not the first time that the desire to attain the absolute would lead to the edge of Nothing.

The public and the critics, of course, ridiculed the Petrograd exhibition. Malevich and his disciples consoled themselves by recalling that Manet and Cézanne had also been derided. The possibility is not excluded that the *White Square on Black*, because of the way in which it is being questioned, will join *Luncheon on the Grass* and *Mount Sainte-Victoire* in the pantheon of the history of art. *(See also 1918 and 1935.)*

MALEVICH: THE SEARCH FOR THE ABSOLUTE

All past and recent painting before Suprematism (as sculpture, verbal art, music) has been subjugated by the shapes of nature, waiting to be liberated, to speak in its own language, independent of reason, common sense, logic, philosophy, psychology, laws of causality, and technological changes.

It was a Babel in the world of art.

The art of painting, the art of sculpture, and verbal art were until now a camel loaded with a jumble of odalisques, Egyptian and Persian emperors, Salomes, princes, princesses with their beloved mutts, hunts, and the lewdness of Venuses.

botanists, zoologists, archaeologists, engineers, but there were no creative painters.

There was no painting constituting its own goal, there was no creation. Painting a composition showing a debauched woman cannot be called creation.

Nor is it possible to see the idealization in Greek statues as creation, for there was only a desire to improve the subjective Me.

Nor can we consider as creation the paintings that have an excessiveness of real shapes: icon painting by Giotto, Gauguin, etc., nor mere copies of nature.

Creation exists only where paintings pre-

KAZIMIR MALEVICH:
BLACK SQUARE ON WHITE.
1913. Leningrad.
Russian Museum

Up to now, there have been no pictorial attempts proper, that is, without constant recourse to reality.

Painting was a necktie on the starched shirt of a gentleman and a pink corset stretched over the inflated abdomen of a fat lady.

Painting is the esthetic side of the object, but it has never been original, has never been its own goal. Painters were examining magistrates, police officers who wrote out assorted reports on spoiled merchandise, on thefts, on murders, and on bums.

Painters were also attorneys, happy storytellers of anecdotes, psychologists,

sent shapes that take nothing from what has been created in nature, but which proceed from pictorial matter, neither repeating nor modifying the original forms of nature's objects . . .

KAZIMIR MALEVICH
From Cubism to Suprematism
(Excerpt)

STIEGLITZ FOUNDS THE MAGAZINE "291"

MAN RAY: PORTRAIT OF ALFRED STIEGLITZ. 1912-1913. New Haven. Yale University

NEW YORK

Alfred Stieglitz, Marius de Zayas, and Francis Picabia have founded the magazine 291 this year. Picabia arrived in New York for the first time in 1913 for the Armory Show. Marcel Duchamp, whose *Nude Descending a Staircase* was the most controversial painting of the exhibition, landed on the American continent only this year. Both have been associated with the photographer Alfred Stieglitz and the group of artists he supports. Stieglitz naturally gave his new magazine the name of the celebrated avant-garde gallery that he opened in 1905.

This magazine was inspired by *Les soirées de Paris*, published under the editorship of Guillaume Apollinaire from November 1913 to August 1914. It was also in the spirit of *Camera Work*, which Stieglitz was publishing since 1903, and which, too, was a very experimental magazine. The first issue of 291 contained original drawings by Picabia, belonging to his series of unreal images that had provocative titles such as *Here She Is* or *Portrait of a Young American in the Nude*. That first issue also contained picture symbols by Guillaume Apollinaire, typographic compositions by Marius de Zayas, and poems by Stieglitz. 291 is a free magazine unlike any other in existence in the world at this time.

Stieglitz thinks that his new magazine will help his gallery regain its vitality. It is interesting to compare the exhibitions he organized this year with 291, since both demonstrate the same open-mindedness. He exhibited Francis Picabia, John Marin, the sculptor Elie Nadelmann, and works by children.

PICABIA AND DUCHAMP IN THE UNITED STATES

NEW YORK

The war which at first promised to be brief is turning into a drawn-out affair. It is still too soon to predict the economic and human consequences. On the other hand, the terrible conflict could very well aid art and restore its vigor. There is actually nothing more revitalizing than trips abroad by painters. Two of the more turbulent avant-garde artists, Francis Picabia and Marcel Duchamp, found the atmosphere in Paris intolerable, and they decided to go into exile.

The confrontation between modern European art and the New World had explosive effects two years ago, when the Armory Show was staged. It now turns out that the scandal has given way to a healthy rivalry among artists. In any event, Duchamp and Picabia were welcomed in New York as the most celebrated representatives of contemporary French culture. Press conferences and interviews followed one after another at a feverish pace. The madness of New York life did not arrest the creative power of the two participants.

Duchamp is laboring on a work that has been planned for some time, *The Bride Stripped Bare by Her Bachelors,* also called *Large Glass.* He has made his first American "registration object," a snow shovel, a type of work to which he gave the special name of "ready-made." Picabia is painting strange mechanical designs. His *Very Rare Picture upon the Earth* is a joyous farewell to the spirit of seriousness.

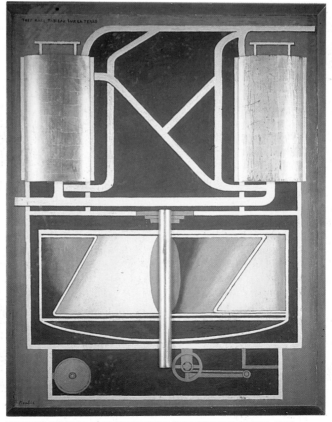

FRANCIS PICABIA: VERY RARE PICTURE UPON THE EARTH. 1915. Venice. Peggy Guggenheim Collection

An Artist Exhibits Artists

Gertrude Vanderbilt Whitney, herself a sculptor, founds the Friends of Young Artists, an association whose purpose is to give talented young people the chance to exhibit without having to overcome the often insurmountable obstacle of a jury or a selection process. She has already shown the work of a few of her friends in her McDougal Alley studio in Greenwich Village, but she plans to develop her new and unselfish organization as far as possible.

Kokoschka Is Wounded at the Front

With a bullet wound in his head and a bayonet wound in his lung, the twenty-nine-year-old painter Oskar Kokoschka was gravely hurt on August 29 during an attack near Luck on the Galician front. O.K., as his friends call him, had signed up with the Austrian dragoons after his break with the lovely Alma Mahler, widow of the musician Gustav Mahler. He had met her one evening in the living room at the home of friends, and took her off to an adjoining room where she sang, just for him, "The Death of Isolde" before asking him to paint her portrait. Dreadful Oskar had fallen hopelessly in love with her at that very moment.

Jacob Epstein's Jackhammer Man

A sensation at the London Group's exhibition, the thirty-five-year-old sculptor Jacob Epstein presents his *Rock Drill* this year. It is a work symbolizing the triumph and power of mechanized man. In fact, *Rock Drill* shows the stylized bust of a worker mounted on a jackhammer, which is in turn held in place by a tripod. Epstein at first planned to attach the jackhammer to a pneumatic system to make it move. But he decided against that, preferring instead to capture the observer's attention solely with his disturbing masked quasi-robot.

The Military Adopts Cubism

Cubism, as everyone knows, alters perspective and breaks up objects. That much can be seen in any recent painting by Picasso, Braque, Gleizes, or Metzinger. So the military has quickly understood how to take advantage of the movement. They have created camouflage units whose work proceeds directly along the lines of Cubist painting. Nothing better, in fact, for hiding a cannon or a truck from the enemy's view than to visually break up the large objects with pieces of green, brown, and gray material. Coming upon a convoy of heavy artillery on the Boulevard Raspail, Picasso was happily surprised. "We are the ones who invented that!" he called out to Gertrude Stein who was with him, delighted to see Cubism adopted by the army.

The Painter of Storms

The news of a storm over the Channel or the North Sea sent Francis Tattegrain into a swoon. He would immediately rush to the train station, armed with his painting equipment, so he could go see the angry elements close up. Infatuated with the sea, he painted it, in fact, in all its states, especially when the waves were whipped up by the wind. Respectful of Realism, he would scrupulously reconstitute storms in his paintings, creating seascapes that were impressive for their truth, lacking only the sound of the surf and the spray. On January 1, he died at the age of sixty-three in the town of Arras.

JACOB EPSTEIN:
ROCK DRILL. 1913-1914.
London. Tate Gallery

ARTISTS ON ALL FRONTS

OTTO DIX: ARTILLERY. 1914. Düssseldorf. Kunstmuseum

PARIS-BERLIN

The great devourer of men swallowed them like so many other artists, this war whose key word is general mobilization. "I accept being only a man, something of an animal, and a puny and weak person who laughs at this enormity and has no other concern and admires only men who retain their self-control," wrote gunboat operator Derain to his friend Vlaminck, a factory worker on the home front, on April 15 of this year.

There were actually few who escaped the ordeal, like Matisse because of his age, Picasso because of his nationality, or Duchamp on account of his health. And so off they went . . . Like Braque, whose works were being shown in Dresden and Berlin at the moment of the declaration of war, and who was wounded in the head at the Artois front on May 11 and had to be trepanned. And Léger who, mobilized into the engineer corps, drew sketches from life.

On the German side, Corporal Max Ernst was transferred to a quieter post, and Dragoon Oskar Kokoschka was seriously wounded in an attack near Luck, in Galicia, while Franz Marc mourned for his friend August Mack, killed on September 26 of last year, and Kirchner, victim of a nervous breakdown, is today in a sanatorium.

As for the Russians, Kandinsky and Jawlensky left Germany for Moscow, and Chagall, who reached Vitebsk several weeks before the outbreak of hostilities, is currently occupying a post in the Petrograd section.

However, there were also those who answered the call although nothing compelled them to do so. Kisling and Kupka thus enlisted in the Czech Legion. Soutine, who enrolled in the "army of workers," was soon discharged because of his health, as was Modigliani. There were also those who just wanted a good fight, and in the first rank of these appeared the Futurists, who unreservedly applauded the entry of Italy into war with the Austro-Hungarian Empire.

STEINLEN FLIES TO THE AID OF THE POILUS

FRANCE

In his *Sketches from the War,* Théophile Alexandre Steinlen uses his engraver's talent to denounce war. He arranges the soldiers on the battlefront or on the platforms of railroad stations as they leave wives and children. He is moved by the distress of the most affected peoples: the Belgians and the Serbs, in particular. But the mordancy of his design, reminiscent of Daumier, does not hinder in any way the expression of the emotion that transpires under the sobriety of his Realism.

This popular, veristic illustrator was born in Lausanne, in 1859, and landed in Montmartre at the age of twenty-two. He collaborated on the *Chat noir, Gil Blas, Mirliton, Rire,* and *Assiette au beurre* before founding *Les humoristes* with Forain four years ago. Steinlen uses his experience as a caricaturist and a creator of posters full of verve to create one of the most valiant *Marseillaises* ever sketched.

THÉOPHILE STEINLEN: THE MARSEILLAISE

THE FUTURISTS VOLUNTEER

The Futurists at the front.

ITALY

The slogan "War, the only therapy of the world" appeared in the *Manifesto of Futurism* in 1909. It was under this warlike title that Marinetti had just republished in Milan, in Italian, the book that recently appeared in French under the less belligerent title of *Futurism*. It declared straight out, "We consider obsolete and discardable the hypothesis of an amicable blending of the nations, and we accept only a single hygienic therapy for the world: war." No one applauded the entry of Italy into the conflict as much as the Futurists. Marinetti, Boccioni, Carrà, Sant'Elia, and their friends gladly donned uniforms. Actually, an internal war had been dividing their own ranks since a short time earlier.

The Futurist group from Florence was the most original extension of Italian Futurism since 1913, with writers like Giovanni Papini and Aldo Palazzeschi and painters like Ardengo Soffici, Ottone Rosai, the very young Primo Conti, and, keeping at a distance, Alberto Magnelli and the Argentinian Emilio Pettoruti. Their magazine *Lacerba*, in which a number of articles by Boccioni and word pictures about liberty appeared, will remain as one of the principal organs of the movement. Following some friction in 1914, the publication of the pamphlet *Futurism and Marinettism* in February of this year, signed by the three founders of *Lacerba*, marked the break with Marinetti. They reproached him wholesale with "the cult of ignorance, descriptive Naturalism, schoolboy propaganda, messianic optimism, militarism, chauvinism, secular religiosity, and contempt for women." They mocked him for preferring René Ghil over Rimbaud, Gustave Kahn over Laforgue, Signac over Renoir, and De Groux over Matisse.

It is generally true that the *Lacerba* group was more far-sighted in its esthetic options, but they were no less aggressive than the opposition. Speaking in Rome on February 21, 1913, Papini surpassed Marinetti and Boccioni in bravado: "I have always loved to break windows and put down others; there are famous skulls in Italy that still exhibit the livid bumps of my stone throws." At the end of the same year, when he himself had joined *Lacerba* in Futurism, Papini reaffirmed: "I am a Futurist because Futurism represents a love of risks and of dangers . . ." This was the same tone of invective and derision found in January 1914 in the *Manifesto against Pain* by Palazzeschi: "Scoundrels! Cowards! Milksops! Dawdlers! Latecomers! . . . Look death in the face and it will give you something to laugh about for the rest of your life."

When war broke out in Europe last year, the Florentine Futurists were no less militant than Marinetti in wanting Italy to enter the war; finally their country, joining the Allied camp, declared war against the Austro-Hungarian Empire on May 23 of this year. Considering that a major objective had been achieved, Papini and Soffici immediately suspended publication of *Lacerba* in order to enlist. Like their friends in the Marinetti group, they wanted to be able to express their aggressiveness by bearing arms.

(See also 1909, 1912, 1914, 1919.)

GINO SEVERINI: CANNONS IN ACTION. 1915. Milan. Private Collection

Who could have foreseen that from neutral, softspoken Switzerland the winds of revolt would waft into the middle of a burning Europe? In the dawn of February 21, as the bloodiest battle in history breaks out at Verdun, rebellious artists of every nationality gather at the Cabaret Voltaire in Zurich. Under the name of Dada they proclaim an innovation of comparable proportions: the right of art to dare to do everything. It is the main event of the year, if not for two deplorable, war-related deaths among the Italian Futurists. Umberto Boccioni is killed in a fall from his horse at Sorte, near Verona; Sant'Elia is cut down in an attack at the front at Trieste before he has the opportunity to produce any works of importance. His plans were full of the promise of a great visionary architect.

1916

S U M M A R Y

LITERATURE

GERMANY
Franz Kafka publishes
The Metamorphosis.

UNITED STATES
Jack London commits suicide in Glen Ellen, California, at age 40.

FRANCE
Henri Barbusse is awarded the Prix Goncourt for Le feu.
  Max Jacob publishes his collected prose poems in Le cornet à dés.

GREAT BRITAIN
Publication of Daedalus *by James Joyce.*
  Death of Henry James, the American-born British novelist.

MUSIC

UNITED STATES
The French composer Edgar Varèse moves to the United States.

RUSSIA
Sergey Prokofiev's Scythian Suite *in Petrograd scandalizes the public.*

MOTION PICTURES

UNITED STATES
D. W. Griffith's film Intolerance *is a commercial flop.*

JEAN ARP:
HEAD OF TZARA. 1916.
Geneva, Musée d'Art et d'Histoire

DADA SPRINGS UP AT THE CABARET VOLTAIRE

ZURICH

The sight of a cannon every thirty feet for forty miles was one never seen before. When the German troops launched the battle of Verdun at dawn on February 21, Allied fliers reported that the horizon was one long line of fire. Then the ground began to tremble under the explosion of shells. Sixty thousand victims of the slaughter fell in a single day.

While Europe is undergoing the horrors of war, Switzerland, in the center of the conflict, is watching others fight. In Zurich, a handful of young people from several countries do not hesitate to proclaim loudly that there is something better to do than kill each other. They meet every night at the Cabaret Voltaire at Spiegelgasse 1, a narrow paved alley in the old city. And there, far from the battlefields, they recite, sing, and organize dance exhibitions under the enigmatic name of Dada, to the amazement of the well-meaning Protestant citizens from the banks of the Limmat River.

A demobilized German, Hugo Ball, who is simultaneously a poet, stage producer, anarchist, Catholic, mystic, and pacifist, founded the Cabaret Voltaire with his companion Emmy Hennings, who, like himself, is an immigrant from Germany. They were joined by the Alsatian Jean Arp, who had no desire to die for the Kaiser, and by Sophie Taeuber, a teacher at the School of Decorative Arts in Zurich. Because her school prohibits appearances on stage at Spiegelgasse under penalty of dismissal, she participates in shows with her face hidden by a mask. There are others: the poet Richard Huelsenbeck and two Romanians, the painter Marcel Janco and Tristan Tzara. At twenty years of age, Tzara is the youngest of them all. His father has sent him to Switzerland to study engineering at the State Polytechnical School, but his only passion is for poetry.

The opening ceremonies of the Cabaret Voltaire were held on February 5, shortly before the beginning of the battle of Verdun. Artists and students from both sides, revolutionaries in exile, passing tourists, international swindlers, faith healers, spies, and other questionable characters were on hand to witness a spectacle such as had never been seen before. After February 5, the Dadaist evenings of the Cabaret Voltaire never stopped attracting a captivated public.

One of the exciting events was the Great Sabbath, hosted by Arp, Tzara, Janco, Ball, and their colleagues. Laughter and shouts from the spectators were responses to the sighs of love, the outbreaks of hiccups, the sound-effect poems composed of "wa-was" and "meows" coming from the stage. There was a large drum to support the proceedings. Also, a handsome demonstration of "phonetism" presented by Hugo Ball in "Karawane": "Jolifanto bambla o bambla, grossiga m'pfa habla horem egega goramen . . ." The anarchist poet was sliding around for the occasion in a large geometric cardboard form. There was also the simultaneous recitation of "The admiral is looking for a house to rent," which combined the German voice of Huelsenbeck, the English of Janco, and the French of Tzara, with musical support from whistles.

Elsewhere in Europe, on all fronts, there were the voices of the generals in their different

MARCEL JANCO: CABARET VOLTAIRE. 1916

On stage, from left to right: Hugo Ball (at the piano), TristanTzara, Jean Arp, Richard Huelsenbeck, Marcel Janco, Emmy Hennings, Friedrich Glauser.

TRISTAN TZARA:
MR. ANTIPYRINE'S MANIFESTO

languages, sending the generation of young to be killed with cracks of gunfire and the thunder of cannon. This was not very different from what was going on at the Cabaret Voltaire, except for the slight difference that the outcries and noises there were a denunciation of the war.

Dada is, in effect, a revolt. Tristan Tzara is thus able to proclaim in the *Manifesto of Mr. Antipyrin*: "Art is not serious." To denounce dangerous choices in a society too sure of itself and at the same time to put on trial all arts that have hitherto failed in their task of creating values capable of launching the mind in new directions, that is what all the members of Dada want to be understood by their evening follies in Zurich.

The name of the movement appeared for the first time in June in the first issue of *Cabaret Voltaire*. The founders of the cabaret did not dream at the outset of grouping themselves together under a common label. However, Hugo Ball very soon developed the idea of collecting and unifying the different activities of their faithful painter, poet, and sculptor friends of Spiegelgasse.

The story is that in April, wanting to find a pseudonym for one of his dancers, he opened a French-German dictionary at random in order to stimulate his imagination, the way others open the Bible to find a rule of conduct there. He opened it at the beginning of the letter "D," and since his index finger was passing over the word "dada," Huelsenbeck, who was watching what he was doing, suddenly understood what could be done with such a term. Too providential to be the pseudonym of a young woman, it could be the baptismal name of their as-yet-unnamed movement. The hobbyhorse (French, *dada*) of the language of children thus became a rallying sign against the absurdity of massacres.
(See also 1920 and 1924.)

Dada is our intensity: it erects the bayonets without consequence to the Sumatral head of the German baby; Dada is life without slippers or parallel; which is for and against unity and decidedly against the future; we know wisely that our brains will become cosy cushions, that out antidogmatism is just as elitist as the civil servant and that we are not free and shout for liberty; harsh necessity without discipline or morals and we spit on humanity.

became a whale, the children were running till they were out of breath.

Then came the great ambassadors of feeling who cry out historically together:

Psychology Psychology ho ho
Science Science Science
Vive la France
We are not naive
We are successive

Arp, Tzara, and Richer in Zurich.

Dada remains within the European framework of weaknesses, it is still shit, but from now on we want to shit in many colors to decorate the zoological garden of the art of all the flags of consulates.

We are circus directors and we whistle among the winds of the fairs, among convents, prostitution, theaters, realities, restaurants, ho ho bang bang . . .

Dada is not madness, or wisdom, or irony, look at me, kind bourgeois.

Art was a shell game, children putting together words that have a bell at the end, then crying and shouting the stanza, and putting boots on dolls and the stanza became queen to die a little and the queen

We are exclusive
We are not simple
And we know how to talk
about intelligence.

But us, Dada, we don't share their views, for art is not serious, I tell you, and if we show the crime so we can learnedly say ven-ti-lat-or, it is to please us, gentle listener, I love you so much, I assure you, and I adore you.

TRISTAN TZARA
Mr. Antipyrine's
Manifesto *(Excerpt)*
Zurich, July 14, 1916

THE LESSON OF MATISSE

PAUL GUILLAUME EXHIBITS DERAIN

HENRI MATISSE: PIANO LESSON. 1916. New York. MOMA

This great *Piano Lesson* that Matisse composed in his studio at 19 Quai Saint-Michel in Paris, is a rigorous and harmonious graphic and pictorial lesson, rich in symbolic signs. A polysemous masterpiece! First of all, it is an antiwar painting. In fact, it depicts his son Pierre, whom he forced to take up music and who was delighted to escape its rigors through the mobilization. Matisse regretted this and shows him in the painting as a younger child, with the piano lesson imposed on him. He is studying to the rhythm of the metronome, whose pyramidal form is registered on his forehead and in the triangle of green light from the window. Surfaces of geometric colors are seen, a method showing the influence of Juan Gris, who was at Collioure at the beginning of the war. They shade the arabesques of the stand amplified by those of the balcony. A melodious rhythm which is interpreted by the boy under the severe surveillance of two effigies as he dutifully plays some Bach or Mozart.

PARIS
An unexpected consequence of the unending war our country is fighting against Germany is the first individual exhibition of André Derain, organized from October 15 to 21 by the young art dealer Paul Guillaume at his apartment. The confidential nature of this limited exhibition was desirable because the artists had been mobilized since the beginning of hostilities and had fought through heavy artillery on the Somme, Verdun, and Aisne fronts.

This exhibition of ten canvases, ten drawings, and ten engravings by Derain, all works done before 1914, is important for the painter and the life of French art. The exhibition is accompanied by an illustrated catalogue published for the occasion. It begins with a preface by Guillaume Apollinaire, himself in military service. He wrote a short time before being wounded by a bullet in the temple on March 17: "After youthful wildness, Derain has turned to balance and restraint. His art is now stamped with the expressive grandeur that could be called classical-antique." This introduction is followed by tributes by Blaise Cendrars, Max Jacob, and Pierre Reverdy, all admirers and friends united for this grand premiere.

The public in Paris remembered the wild canvases that a group of young painters, including Derain, had exhibited at the Salon d'Automne of 1905. Since 1909, however, one could discern a return to form as well as a more austere palette in the paintings of Derain. They are hieratic pictures influenced by Cubism, in which a great drive for composition is observed.

The artist became acquainted with the young dealer while on leave, at the suggestion of Apollinaire and Max Jacob. Paul Guillaume was looking for works capable of attracting the attention of wealthy Americans passing through Paris.

The Turkish Villa

The painter Charles-Édouard Jeanneret, who at the age of twenty-nine dreams of being another Ingres, seems destined to make a name for himself in the field of architecture. As a trial run, the villa he completes for the industrialist Anatole Schwab in Chaux-de-Fonds, Switzerland, is the work of a master. With its flat roof, its walls that function as membranes, its well-balanced outlines, the house at 167 Rue du Doubs is ultramodern. But no one is a prophet in his own country. The house in the pine forest was barely up when the stunned residents of Chaux-de-Fonds baptized it "the Turkish villa."

Apollinaire Has His Skull Trepanned

In a wooded area at the front at Aisnes, Second Lieutenant Guillaume Apollinaire was struck by shrapnel from an exploding 150-shell on March 17. Shrapnel penetrated Apollinaire's helmet and made a star-shaped hole in his temple, just as de Chirico had foreseen in his 1914 portrait. Surgeons had to drill into Apollinaire's skull, and Picasso, who came to console him at Val-de-Grâce, sketched the portrait of his bandaged head with a few infallible strokes. Under the title *Assassinated Poet*, his friends published a volume of his poetry and organized a banquet in his honor on December 31. "A star of blood crowns me forever," he says to them in a pensive moment.

The Death of Franz Marc at Verdun

Franz Marc, who had volunteered for duty out of patriotism, falls on March 4 at Verdun. He was thirty-six years old. In its March edition, the magazine *Der Sturm* pays homage to him on its first page with an article by the editor, Herwath Walden. Deploring the collapse of spiritual values in the modern world, Marc wanted to replace defunct religion with art. His work was a pantheist search for communion with nature, and he frequently used pure colors in his palette for symbolic meaning. In 1911, he had created the Blue Rider with Kandinsky in Munich.

PABLO PICASSO: APOLLINAIRE TREPANNED. 1916

Death of a Seer in Painting

A contemporary of the Impressionists and of the Pompiers painters, Odilon Redon dies on July 6 in Paris. He occupied a special place in the history of art. He applied himself to the task of "putting the logic of the visible in the service of the invisible," as he wrote. Discovering the mysteries of the infinitely small thanks to the microscope of the botanist Armand Clavaud, his pastels, charcoal drawings, and sketches marked French painting with a visionary dimension. Redon did not participate in contemporary movements, though the Nabis were his friends and he influenced Gauguin and Émile Bernard. Maurice Denis wrote: "He was the ideal of the young Symbolist generation, our Mallarmé."

ODILON REDON: DREAM. 1904. Fribourg. Private Collection

BOCCIONI KILLED BY HIS HORSE

VERONA

The Italian painter and sculptor Umberto Boccioni died on August 17 following a fall from his horse during a military exercise at Sorte, near Verona. He was only thirty-four years old. He was a supporter of Futurism, with which he was connected since meeting Marinetti in 1910.

Boccioni was then creating portraits inspired by Pelliza and Previati. When he painted a window overlooking the Grand Canal, he was careful to include the small bouquet of flowers. He signed the *Technical Manifesto of Futurist Sculpture* in 1912, which was followed in 1913 by two masterpieces, *Development of a Bottle in Space* and *Unique Shape of Continuity in Space*, showing the movement of a walking man. This placed him in the first rank of contemporary sculpture. He declared, "A valve that is opened and closed creates a rhythm that is as attractive as, but infinitely more novel than, that of an eyelid."

On the other hand, he wanted

"to destroy the pretended nobility of marble and bronze" through the use of multiple materials: "glass, cardboard, cement, concrete, hair, leather, fabrics, mirrors," and even "electric light." The result is his "polymaterial" creations, such as his *Dynamism of a Racehorse*.

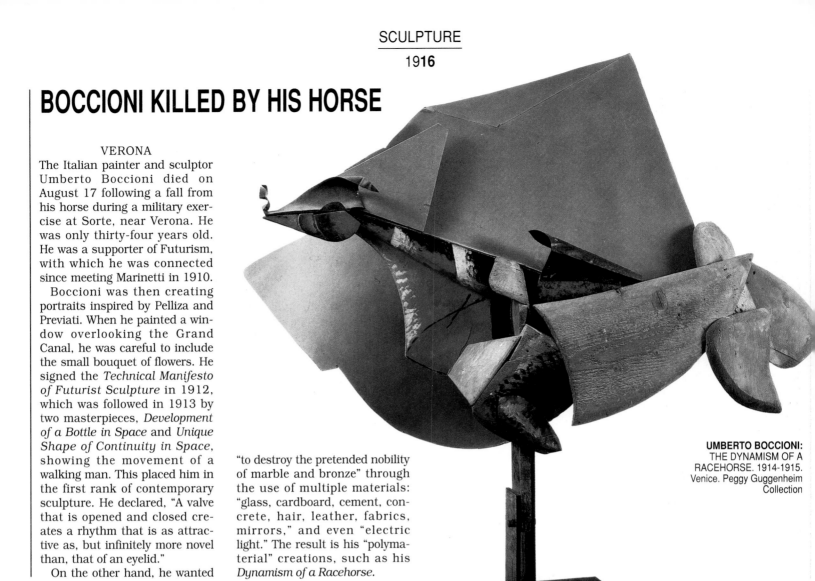

UMBERTO BOCCIONI:
THE DYNAMISM OF A RACEHORSE. 1914-1915.
Venice. Peggy Guggenheim Collection

THE SMALL CONSTRUCTIONS OF HENRI LAURENS

HENRI LAURENS:
SMALL CONSTRUCTION. 1915.
Paris. MNAM

PARIS

Since last year, and in parallel with his pasted papers, Henri Laurens has been creating small constructions made of wood and multicolored plaster in geometric forms that deal with nature "in terms of spheres, cylinders, and cones," as Cézanne had recommended to him.

It was the painter Georges Braque who introduced Cubism to Laurens who, until then, in the words of his wife Marthe,

had been working alone and "in anxiety." The two artists had become acquainted in Montmartre. Laurens, born in Paris in 1885 and a master stoneworker by trade, had set himself up in modest circumstances in 1902. The two men became close friends, and Braque, who was then in his full Cubist period and in collaboration with Picasso, gave the sculptor a long description of his revolutionary concept of pictorial space.

Profoundly impressed, Laurens gradually oriented his work toward Cubism, and every small structure or head or bottle that he created after the clowns and

dancers of the previous year was the application to sculpture and projection into space of the Cubist idea of simultaneously representing all surfaces of an object. Composed of geometric elements assembled in a planned order with contrasting paints and colors, these constructions were made to be viewed from different angles while retaining their unity.

Picasso had already attempted to create constructions in three dimensions in 1912, but one could say that Cubist sculpture was actually born with Laurens, whose constructions were more elaborate and more finished.

THIS WAS THE ARCHITECTURE OF THE FUTURE

TRIESTE

Antonio Sant'Elia died in combat in the defense of Triest last October 10, at the age of twenty-eight. Sant'Elia left us many large projects but unfortunately very few finished architectural creations.

Born at Como on April 30, 1888, he studied at the city industrial school and obtained his diploma as a master worker in 1905. He then worked in the technical services of the city of Milan, and he attended the Brera School from 1909 to 1911. He designed a small house decorated with bas-reliefs made of wrought iron and multicolored mosaics—the Villa Elisi. Built in the vicinity of Como, it is almost his only completed structure. It was not yet a representative indication of the innovative character of his art because it still shows the influence of the Italian interpretation of the floral style of the Viennese Secession of Otto Wagner. In 1912, on his return to Milan, he worked on various projects, especially for the central railway station of the capital of Lombardy and the Monza cemetery. During the same year, he met up with the Milanese avant-garde artists, with whom he later founded the New Tendency group.

From then on, his numerous drawings revealed his real stature. At the first exhibition of the New Tendency in May 1914, Sant'Elia presented his designs for the "New City," a futuristic city: monumental buildings, with outside elevators and mechanical stairways, crossed by bridges and galleries, with airplane runways over tunnels, intersected by underground railroads. These designs, of high plastic quality, presenting an intense dynamism, offer a revolutionary vision of the city of the future.

The architect, in fact, wanted to be a town planner; the new vertical town planning by Sant' Elia went far beyond the vision of American cities with their isolated skyscrapers deprived of organic connection with an overall structure. His city was to be completely developed around a strongly structured architectonic system with connections on several intersecting vertical levels. The walks for pedestrians and the roads and paths traced indispensable relationships to the harmonious dynamism of the future city.

It was probably also in 1914 that Sant'Elia met Marinetti and the Futurists, whose concerns were close to his. He signed the *Manifesto of Futurist Architecture* in July, where he stated that our sensitivity ". . . is enriched by a taste for light and practical forms, for the provisional and for speed," and that "... our houses will not last as long as we do, each generation having to build its own." Designs of his future city, accompanying his manifesto, appeared in the August issue of the Futurist magazine *Lacerba.*

In his fabulous projects, Sant'Elia gave free rein to his visionary imagination, which could not be held in check by any contingency. We should point out that, apart from his Futurist vision, Sant'Elia dedicated himself to professional activities on behalf of Secessionism. Sant'Elia was designing not for the purpose of proposing precise projections, but to affirm his concept of a utopian city.

Following the example of other Futurists, he enlisted in the Italian army in July. He was decorated for valor and commissioned a second lieutenant. The architect of the future died fighting against Austria-Hungary on the Isonzo front.

ANTONIO SANT'ELIA:
NEW CITY (STUDY). 1914.
Private Collection

Another avant-garde movement springs up in Holland, a nation spared by the war. *Piet Mondrian and Théo Van Doesburg publish the first edition of the magazine* De Stijl. *At the same time, they establish Abstract Geometric painting on a spiritualistic foundation. During this time, Marcel Duchamp causes an uproar when he sends a urinal, baptized* Fountain, *the most provocative of the "Ready-Mades" he has produced up to now, to the Independents of New York. With the death of Auguste Rodin, the history of art turns a prestigious page.*

1917

S U M M A R Y

AVANT-GARDE

Mondrian Creates Neoplasticism

MANIFESTO

Mondrian: a Purified Esthetic Form

DEVELOPMENTS

Modigliani: the Scandal of the Nudes
The Last Breath of Auguste Rodin

ART NEWS

A Party for Georges Braque
Alfred Stieglitz Closes His Gallery
Carolus-Duran: Velásquez Hadn't Heard Him
Picabia Founds the Magazine *391*
The Arnsberg Salon
In Brief

DEVELOPMENTS

Léger: *The Game of Cards*
The Great *Parade* Brawl

SCANDALS

Marcel Duchamp, the Great Disturber
The Richard Mutt Case

LITERATURE

AUSTRIA-HUNGARY
Sigmund Freud publishes Introduction to Psychoanalysis.

FRANCE
Publication of the first issue of the magazine Nord-Sud, *under the direction of Pierre Reverdy.*
   Paul Valéry publishes La jeune parque.

GREAT BRITAIN
Publication of The Wild Swans at Coole *by W. B. Yeats.*

MUSIC

ITALY
In Bologna, Ottorino Respighi composes The Fountains of Rome.
   Premiere of Stravinsky's Fireworks *in Rome, with a stage design by Balla.*

SWITZERLAND
Performance, before a selected audience, of The Story of a Soldier *by Ramuz, with music by Igor Stravinsky.*
   Ferruccio Busoni creates Turandot *in Zurich.*

THEATER

ITALY
Performance of Luigi Pirandell'o's To Each His Truth.

MOTION PICTURES

UNITED STATES
Premiere of the Chaplin film The Immigrant.
   Maurice Tourneur completes the film Poor Little Rich Girl, *with Mary Pickford.*

SWEDEN
Sjöström produces The Outlaws.

PIET MONDRIAN:
COLOR PLANES IN OVAL (PAINTING III).
1914. Amsterdam. Stedelijk Museum

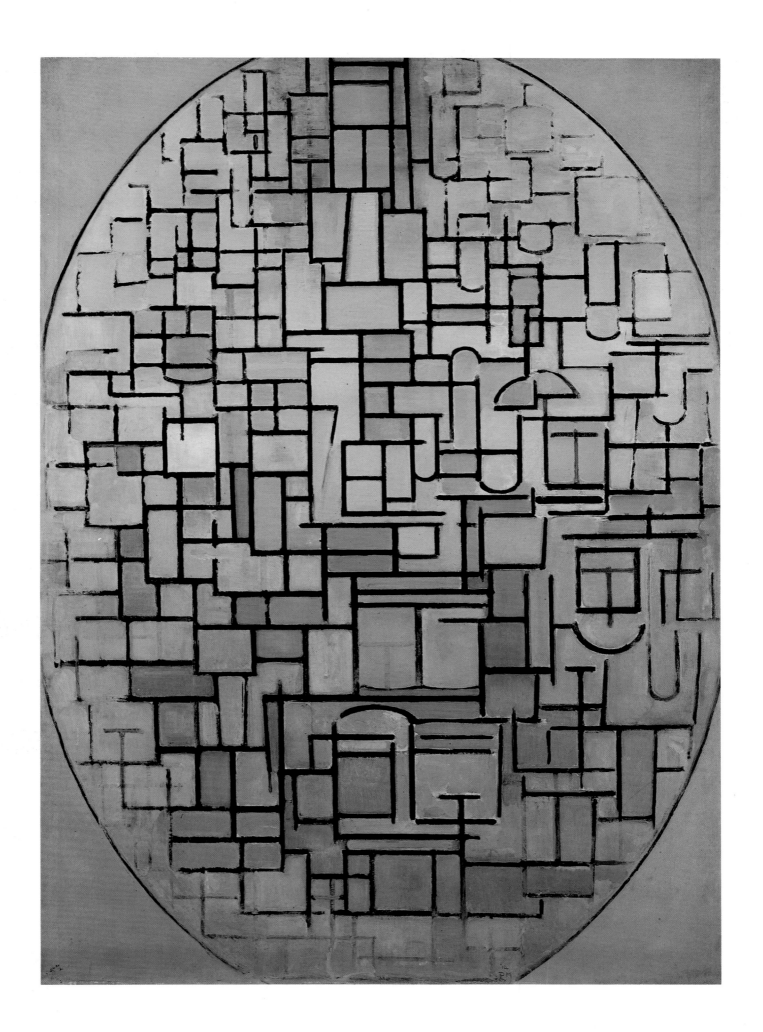

MONDRIAN CREATES NEOPLASTICISM

LEIDEN

Since they became acquainted two years ago, Théo Van Doesburg has been encouraging Mondrian to start an art magazine. Mondrian is forty-five years old, and Van Doesburg is eleven years younger. He began to go along reluctantly, believing that the time for such an enterprise was not ripe and that the dis-

A CONTROLLABLE PRECISION, A CONSCIOUS PENETRATION OF REALITY, AN EXACT BEAUTY

semination of innovative ideas could develop only slowly. However, the enterprising spirit of Van Doesburg eventually swept him along, and from then on the matter was a foregone conclusion. "This small magazine would like to provide a contribution to the development of the new esthetics. It would like to make new developments in the plastic arts accessible to modern people," the first issue of the publication declared. It appeared this October, and it is titled *De Stijl* (the style).

The groups around these two men include the painters Bart Van der Leck and Vilmos Huszar, a Hungarian who has settled in Holland, the Belgian sculptor and painter Georges Vantongerloo, and three Dutch architects, Olud, Wils, and Van't Hoff. The group and the magazine propose to disseminate theories and research concerning Neoplasticism, whose principles began to be expounded by Mondrian from this first issue.

To a great extent Neoplasticism developed from the shock felt by artists on viewing the Cubist works that Picasso and Braque had sent to Amsterdam for the Modern Kunstring exhibition in 1911. Their discovery reinforced their convictions, which were directed toward simplification of plastic means and toward reducing the diversity of what is visible to a small number of signs. Mondrian had until then remained in the shadows, painting windmills, purple

undergrowth, and the wet open country and skies of his native country according to Dutch landscape traditions. Convinced of the importance of Cubism, however, he broke with his own past and went to Paris, where he lived from 1912 to 1914 and participated in the Salons des Indépendants before being detained in Holland by the declaration of war. He spent the summer there three years ago. With the tenacity of the Dutch, who had wrestled two-fifths of their land from the sea, he then undertook to pull nature away from the overflowing of its luxuriance to subject it solely to the discipline of the spirit. During his years in Paris, he simplified

forms, summarized, condensed, and sacrificed the individual to the universal and subordinated the details or adornments to the sole desire of expressing the essential. Gradually he reduced the visible world to the elementary rules of its formal grammar.

Cubism, however, was not the only source for Mondrian. The *Great Initiates,* by Édouard Schuré, which he read when it appeared in 1889, impressed him greatly, and the writings of the theosophist M.H.J. Schoenmaekers were to become decisive. According to Schoenmaekers, ". . . the artist is a mystic to the degree that he contemplates living reality." He defined style as ". . . the general in spite of the particular," and he believed that the new theosophical image of the world should lead to " . . . a controllable precision, a conscious penetration of reality, an exact beauty." The concepts cen-

tral to the concerns of the De Stijl movement led its members to the most rigorous abstraction and to restriction to the lines most obvious to the senses, the vertical and the horizontal. Thus, in the most recent seascape by Mondrian, titled simply *Composition,* the artist reduces the tarred breakwaters protecting Walcheren Island to a forest of black crosses.

To the members of De Stijl, abstraction is a moral necessity rather than an esthetic principle. According to Mondrian and his colleagues, it is neither more nor less than delivering the world from tragedy. It is an effect or efflux generated from particular and individual visions achieved by dominating an objective and consequently arriving at a universal plastic language intended to prepare for the advent of a better world.

It is this utopian perspective that attracts the creators—poets, architects, sculptors—associated with the group and the magazine. They want to simplify vision in order to simplify life, to cleanse reality from its natural impurities and its accidental disorders, to end the adoration of nature. Where are they heading? Van Doesburg is already claiming in connection with the interplay of verticals and horizontals that perpendiculars to oblique lines are more suitable for expressing the dynamism of the reality in which we are now living. Whereas Picasso and Braque are content to shatter the image of the visible on their Cubist canvases, they want to reconstruct it.

For this reason, in picture after picture, they are attempting to perfect with "a controllable precision" the geometric framework suitable for creating a spiritual Esperanto of the visible for use by modern man.

(See also 1945.)

THÉO VAN DOESBURG:
SUCCESSIVE ABSTRACTION OF A NATURALISTIC SUBJECT: THE COW. 1916. New York. MOMA

MONDRIAN:
A PURIFIED ESTHETIC FORM

The life of the cultured person of today gradually turns away from natural things to become more and more an abstract life.

With natural (exterior) things becoming more and more automatic, we see our vital attention concentrate more and more on interior things. The life of the really modern person is neither purely materialistic nor purely sentimental. Rather, it manifests itself as an autonomous life of a human mind, conscious of itself.

The modern human—even though a unity of body, soul, and mind—shows us a changed conscience: All expressions of life appear under another aspect, I mean under a more positively abstract aspect.

The same applies to art. Art will become the product of another duality in humans: the product of a cultured exteriority and a more conscious, deeper interiority. As a pure representation of the human mind, art will express itself in a purified esthetic form, that is, abstractly.

The really modern artist feels consciously the abstraction in the experience of beauty, he recognizes that the sense of the beautiful is cosmic, universal. The corollary of this conscious recognition is the abstract plastic, the individual adhering to what is universal.

The new plastic art thus cannot take the shape of natural or concrete representation, which, it is true, always indicates the universal to a certain extent or at least harbors it. This new plastic art will not adorn itself with the things that are characteristic of particularization, that is, with natural form and natural color. On the contrary, it must find its expression in the abstraction from any form and color, that is, in the straight line and in the clearly defined primary color.

These means of universal expression were discovered in modern painting through the advance of a progressive and logical abstraction of form and color. Once found, we saw the appearance of the exact representation of bare relationships and the essential, fundamental fact of any plastic experience of the beautiful.

PIET MONDRIAN: COMPOSITION NO. 10. 1915. Otterlo. Kröller-Müller Museum

The new plastic art is therefore an esthetic relationship accurately presented. The artist of today creates it, in painting, as a consequence of any plastic art of the past, and he does this best in painting, because painting is the art that is the least tied to contingencies. Modern life in its entirety, getting deeper, can see itself reflected purely in the art of painting.

PIET MONDRIAN
De Stijl, No. 1 *(Excerpt)*

MODIGLIANI: THE SCANDAL OF THE NUDES

PARIS

The police of the 18th *arrondissement* were rather free with their hands when they confiscated pictures and drawings by Modigliani after the *vernissage* on December 3 at the Berthe Weill gallery at 50 Rue Taitbout. Acting on complaints, they confiscated several nude paintings by the Italian painter "because they were offensive to modesty." One of them, for which the brief text by the poet Blaise Cendrars in the program praised "the coming and going of passion," had this derisive slogan: "The matter should be told!" Amedeo Modigliani, who had taken as his motto, "Your actual duty is that of saving your dream," was nevertheless floating in success. His scandalous nudes were witness to this; he fell very much in love in April with a student from the Colarossi School, Jeanne Hébuterne, with whom he is living on Rue de la Grande-Chaumière.

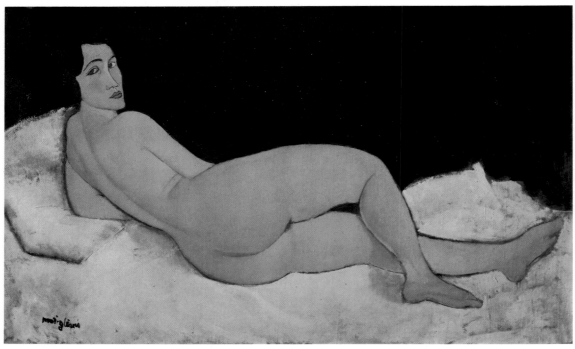

AMEDEO MODIGLIANI: GREAT NUDE RECLINING. 1917. Private Collection

THE LAST BREATH OF AUGUSTE RODIN

MEUDON
"And it is said that Puvis de Chavannes is not beautiful!" This was the last pronouncement by Auguste Rodin, who breathed his last words at the age of sixty-seven. He died at his "Villa des Brillants" on November 17 as a result of pulmonary congestion. He died shortly after the death of his "old mistress," Rose Beuret, whom he finally decided to marry on January 29, after fifty-two years of living together, on his own part often unfaithfully. The famous sculptor of *The Kiss* was certainly a man with a profusion of women in his bronzes or of metamorphoses in his marbles. Having lost his memory toward the end, although not his best keepsake, he came to demand of Rose where his wife was: "No, not you; the one who remained in Paris." He was still thinking about Camille Claudel twenty-five years after their separation. The creator of *The Gates of Hell, The Burghers of Calais, Balzac*, and so many busts of enamored women rests beside his legitimate wife in his garden beneath the bronze statue of his *Thinker*. He left his assets and collections to the French state in 1916.

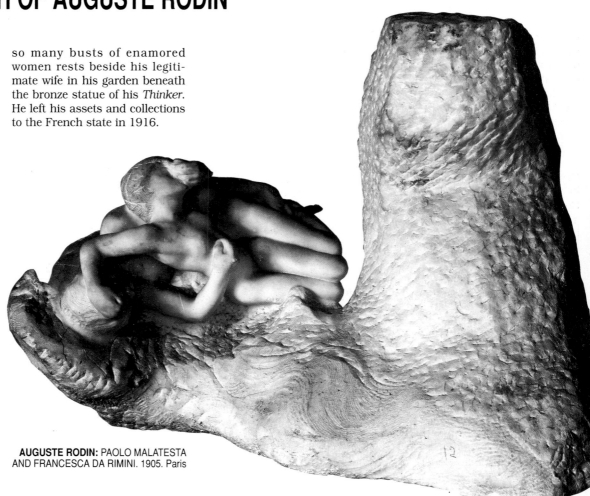

AUGUSTE RODIN: PAOLO MALATESTA AND FRANCESCA DA RIMINI. 1905. Paris

A Party for Georges Braque

On May 11, 1915, Georges Braque, who was serving in the infantry, was seriously wounded in the head during an attack at Carency in the Artois region. Hospitalized for a long period after being operated on for head injuries, he convalesced in Sorgues, then returned to Paris in January. To celebrate his recovery, his two army citations, and his discharge from the service, his friends Juan Gris and Henri Laurens organized a banquet on January 15. During the course of the party, the poet Pierre Reverdy read some very moving poetry. Having invented Cubism with Picasso, Braque has now decided to invent Braque, and he returns to still-life compositions.

Alfred Stieglitz Closes His Gallery

The man who had been "a bridge between Europe and the United States" closes Gallery 291 in New York. There, since 1905, America had seen Picasso, Braque, Matisse, Brancusi, and, quite recently, the Italian Futurists Gino Severini and other artists of the international avant-garde. The last exhibition of the "biggest small room in the world" had been devoted to the American Georgia O'Keeffe. Stieglitz had discovered her drawings a year ago. "At last, the force of a woman's work on paper," he had exclaimed.

Carolus-Duran: Velásquez Hadn't Heard Him

He gave his first name as Carolus, and people called him the capering Carolus-Duran. Charles Auguste Émile Durand, alias Carolus-Duran, died on February 18 in Paris. Having been one of the young artists who gathered around Manet at the Salon des Refusés in 1863, he traveled to Italy and Spain before finding success as a society portrait artist. His *Woman with Glove,* for which he received the gold medal at the Salon of 1879, had opened the doors of fortune to him. He identified himself with the master of Spain's Golden Century, and when he began a portrait, he had the habit of crying out: "Help me,

Velásquez!" To which one of his elegant models made the comment: "I believe, sir, that your servant did not hear you!"

Picabia Founds Magazine "391"

Is it a carbon copy of *291,* Alfred Stieglitz's magazine, which ceased publication several months ago because of financial difficulties? Not quite. If the format, idea, and typography of *391* are plagiarized from the famous New York magazine, its contents are quite different. It was started by Francis Picabia in Barcelona, where he now lives, and the first edition appeared on January 15. He has invited Arthur Cravan, the boxer-poet, Marie Laurencin, Maximilien Gauthier, and Olga Sackaroff, among others, to submit contributions. Their tone is the very same as that of Dada: nihilistic, cold, ironic, and destructive, similar on all accounts to the provocations of Tristan Tzara and his friends at the Cabaret Voltaire in Zurich.

CAROLUS-DURAN:
MADEMOISELLE CROIZETTE. 1873.
Tourcoing. Musée des Beaux-Arts

The Arensberg Salon

The importance of Alfred Stieglitz and his friends is well known in the American art world. But another circle has been competing with his for the last three years: Walter and Louise Arensberg's salon. Arensberg, who has a vast cultural background, was first smitten by modern art at the Armory Show. He was living in Boston at the time, and visited the exhibit on its very last day. He was so deeply affected by it that he decided, on his return, to take his entire family and move to New York, so that he could be closer to the avant-garde that was beginning to form. Since that time, their living room is an evening meeting place for artists and poets, including Marcel Duchamp, who had lived with the Arensbergs when he first arrived in New York four years earlier.

LÉGER: THE GAME OF CARDS

VILLEPINTE

A 75-millimeter cannon breech probably taught him more than all the museums of the world. We believe so because Fernand Léger, mobilized into the engineer corps since the onset of hostilities, was gassed at Verdun one sunny morning. He owes his masterpiece, *The Game of Cards*, a large canvas, to the war.

He painted it at Villepinte Hospital, in the suburbs of Paris, where he was recovering from burns in his lungs. The painting depicts men playing cards in the trench between attacks. It is perhaps an involuntary homage to Cézanne, who dealt with the same subject. The difference, however, is that the players, French soldiers, are disjointed robots here, dehumanized like the steel of helmets and shells.

The Game of Cards originated from drawings made from life and sent from the front to his wife, Jeanne. They apparently

FERNAND LÉGER:
THE GAME OF CARDS. 1917. Otterlo.
Kröller-Müller Museum

did not please the esthetes who stayed peacefully in Paris, which enraged Léger. "To all those fatheads who ask whether I am or still will be a Cubist upon returning, you may tell them that more now than ever. There is nothing more Cubist than a war like this one, which divides a man more or less neatly into several pieces and sends him to the four points of the compass."

Before leaving for the front, Léger tended toward abstraction.

This is now finished. He now emulates Paolo Ucello, who painted his masterpiece at the battle of San Romano.

THE GREAT "PARADE" BRAWL

PARIS

"The three Boches" was how the major Parisian press, shocked by the opening of *Parade* on May 18 at the Châtelet Theater, characterized Cocteau, Picasso, and Satie, who had collaborated with Diaghilev in composing and presenting that "realistic ballet." "To Berlin!," "slackers!," "opium smokers!," cried out the horrified spectators, who were injured and beaten all the way to the orchestra pit. One very worthy

PABLO PICASSO:
CURTAIN FOR
"PARADE." 1917.
Paris. MNAM

gentleman shouted, "If I had known it was so beastly, I never would have taken the children!"

What was the cause of such a brawl? The young poet Jean Cocteau! Dreaming, in fact, " . . . of extending the Cubist guitars of Picasso into music," Cocteau had been "concocting" a seditious project for some time: to convince the artist to plan out and paint the curtain, decoration, and costumes of a ballet whose plot he had proposed to the musician Erik Satie. It was " . . . a burlesque scene played at the door of a traveling theater for the purpose of attracting the public." In love with Olga Kokhlova, one of the dancers of the Russian Ballet, Pablo Picasso went along with the concept, like Satie, who included siren and typewriter sounds in his cacophonic music. Although *Parade* chased the public away, Apollinaire did not hesitate to predict the future success of "this type of Surrealism."

MARCEL DUCHAMP, THE GREAT DISTURBER

NEW YORK

The enemy of Academicism struck once more. This time, he did not choose the painters of the Salon des Indépendants of Paris as his target but the jury of Independents of New York, to which he belonged, as the height of irony. After having shocked the entire New York art world four years ago at the Armory Show with his explosive *Nude Descending a Staircase*, Marcel Duchamp decided to backslide and to once again send out a challenge.

For the first exhibit of the Society of Independents, Duchamp sent a very unusual sculptured piece anonymously: an enameled pottery piece called *Fountain*, signed R. Mutt, the name of a New York manufacturer of sanitary equipment. The said *Fountain* was actually a urinal, which the officials hastened to hide behind a partition for the duration of the exhibition. Needless to say, it was dismissed by the jury.

Putting aside the provocation—the schoolboy wish to shock the bourgeoisie by a simple strategy—let us attempt to understand the meaning of this gesture by the artist. It is known that this was not Duchamp's first attempt to transform a common object into a work of art. The last of the Villon brothers had invented the "ready-made" in Paris in 1913, a *Bicycle Wheel* mounted on a stool. There was later the *Bottle Rack* with the trademark Hérisson in 1914, bought at the Hôtel de Ville bazaar.

The idea of using a lowly, crude material to be transformed into a precious or artistic object is not entirely original. Cubists have already accustomed us to this type of alchemy with their paste-ups. It is known that Picasso was the first to execute impressive mountings suggesting mandolins or guitars by means of roughly cut wooden boards so as to reach the limits of art. But Duchamp, who wanted to be a radical, pushed the

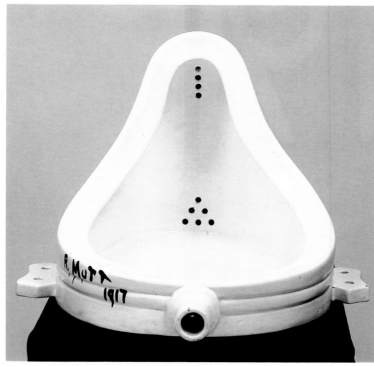

MARCEL DUCHAMP: FOUNTAIN. 1917. Paris. MNAM

THE RICHARD MUTT CASE (OPEN LETTER TO THE AMERICANS)

Following the rejection of his *Fountain* by the jury of the Independents of New York, Marcel Duchamp wrote the letter that can be read below. It was published in the first issue of *The Blind Man*, a small magazine created by Duchamp and a few of his friends. Richard Mutt is the name of a New York manufacturer of bathroom fixtures.

Apparently any artist having paid six dollars can exhibit. Mr. Richard Mutt sent a fountain. Without discussion, his shipment disappeared and was never shown. What was the basis for refusing Mr. Mutt's fountain?

1. Some claimed that it was immoral, vulgar.

2. Others that it was plagiarism—a simple bathroom fixture.

Now, Mr. Mutt's fountain is not immoral. It is an accessory that one can see every day in plumber's windows.

Whether Mr. Mutt has made the fountain with his own hands or not is without importance. He chose it. He has taken an ordinary element of existence and has displayed it in such a manner that the utilitarian meaning disappears under the new title and the new point of view—he has created a new thought for this object.

As for the plumbing argument, it is absurd: The only works of art produced by America are its plumbing fixtures and its bridges.

logic of appropriating real objects to extremes. Beyond rejecting the traditional concepts of painting and sculpture, his manufactured objects have a value of intellectual challenge rather than artistic sublimation. What is important, according to Duchamp, is " . . . to register a ready-made object," that is, to set the date, hour, and minute it will be selected in advance, as a sort of rendezvous.

The ready-made is a kick applied to a work of art on its traditional pedestal and at the same time a critique of taste and an intellectual cleansing. It is an application of the indifference principle, since concepts of beauty and ugliness are without meaning here. However, the choice of a ready-made object is not a simple matter, contrary to what one might think.

"It is necessary to arrive at selecting an object," confides Duchamp, "with the idea of not being impressed by this object on the basis of enjoyment of any order." One must enter a zero zone of the sensibility and the spirit. "However, it is difficult to select an object that absolutely does not interest you, not only on the day on which you select it but always, and which does not have any chance of becoming attractive or beautiful and which is neither pleasant to look at nor particularly ugly."

Is this true of his *Fountain*? Duchamp passes a little beyond his own rules with it. The function of the object deprives it of a harmless character. The desire to be shocking is obvious. This explains the Pavlovian reflex of the jury of Independents.

However, it is said that Duchamp has been dreaming of other provocations in the past and now. Like the naming of a "reciprocal ready-made," which would consist, for example, of using a Rembrandt painting as an ironing board. If he carries out this new project, he unquestionably risks seriously perturbing the museum curators.

(See also 1913, 1923, 1968.)

1918

S U M M A R Y

Just when it seemed that the bloodshed in Europe was almost at an end, another scourge, the Spanish flu, attacks. During the night of October 31, it took the life of Egon Schiele, who, at the age of twenty-eight, was the most promising artist of the Vienna School. His master and admirer Gustav Klimt dies, as well as the architect Otto Wagner, and Koloman Moser, founder of the Vienna Ateliers. In Soviet Russia, meanwhile, difficulties arise among artists of the avant-garde who disagree on the form and content of revolutionary art. Malevich, confident of a totally new beginning—political, artistic, and metaphysical—produces a painting composed solely of a white square painted on a white background.

MOURNING

The Vienna School Is Decimated
Apollinaire Mourned by His Friends
Apollinaire Talks about Art

DEVELOPMENTS

Father Victory Visits Monet
132,000 Francs for Dancers

ART NEWS

The First Issue of *Valori plastici*
The Birth of Purism
The Founding of the Group of November
War Plunges Modern Sculpture into Mourning
If God Were a Machine
In Brief

ART AND THE REVOLUTION

Chagall: Art in the Street
The Limits of Suprematism
Masterpieces for the People
Kandinsky the Official

GUSTAV KLIMT:
ROSEBUSHES
UNDER TREES. 1905.
Paris. Musée d'Orsay

EGON SCHIELE:
SELF-PORTRAIT WITH SPREAD
FINGERS. 1911. Vienna. Historisches Museum

EGON SCHIELE:
KNEELING GIRL PULLING HER
CLOTHES UP. 1910.
Private Collection

THE VIENNA SCHOOL IS DECIMATED

VIENNA

What heavy losses in this capital, which had become the "European crossroads of arts and thought"! Defender of Expressionism and destroyer of the "military spirit" that he believes victimizes our world, the Viennese writer Karl Kraus declares, "This is the end of a world!" Not to mention the collapse of the Austro-Hungarian Empire and the Hapsburg dynasty, three great artists were lost to Vienna this year, in addition to the Marxist doctrinaire Victor Adler, the photographer Hugo Henneberg, the painter Gustav Klimt, the graphic artist Koloman Moser, and the architect Otto Wagner. Finally, a friend of Klimt, Egon Schiele, twenty-eight, twenty of whose paintings had been enthusiastically received at the 49th Exhibition of the Secession, died on October 31 of the Spanish flu, three days after his wife Edith passed away from the same disease. His passing has endangered the survival of the famous

Secession, which had already been imperiled in 1905 by the resignation of Klimt and his colleagues, especially Moser and Wagner.

Taking eighteen of his colleagues with him, on May 25, 1897, Klimt had left the Künstlerhaus (the official artists' center founded in Vienna in 1861). They had decided to found an association of the "Viennese

FOR EACH CENTURY ITS ART, FOR ART ITS FREEDOM

Artists of the Austrian Secession." Klimt was named president. This group has had a new exhibition hall since 1898, designed in the Art Nouveau style, or *Jugendstit* by Joseph-Maria Olbrich, an assistant to Otto Wagner. Its portal contained this motto: "For each century its art, for art its freedom." Klimt prepared the picture poster for their exhibition. Symbolizing the triumphal struggle of youth against barbarism, it

represented Theseus bringing down the Minotaur. The group founded a monthly journal the same year, *Ver Sacrum*, which was published up to 1903. Wishing to liberate themselves from the restraints of social, political, and therefore esthetic conservatism, they wanted to provide art with a more extensive vocation than merely painting and to extend it to all decorative arts. They also decided to pay close attention to new discoveries by foreign artists. Gustav Klimt came to be the most striking personality of this new school in Vienna, which admired the Symbolism of his allegorical friezes, whose sacred eroticism created a scandal. Admirers of his work saw in these friezes magnificent

stylized illustrations of the duality of Eros and Thanatos, of Love and Death.

Koloman Moser, nicknamed "Kolo," is unquestionably the one who, by "the sprightly lightness of his imagination" (as one of his friends put it), best accomplished the group's dream of a total union of life and art, an example of which they wanted to provide in their designs of stained-glass windows for the Am Steinhof church at the request of Otto Wagner. To create, produce, and promote works of art accessible to everyone, they established, in 1903, the Vienna Ateliers, together with Joseph Hoffmann. Their profits were to be distributed to all associates. Otto Wagner distinguished himself in 1894 by his inaugural speech at the School of Architecture of the Academy of Fine Arts. This paper was published the following year under the title

Moderne Architektur. It was republished four times until 1914. He abandoned ornamentation, rationalized spatial concepts, and made abundant use of steel and glass. A professor until 1915, he had a great influence on his students, in whom he inculcated the new Functionalism of modern architecture.

One of the great original features of this Vienna School, which set an example first of all in Germany and then elsewhere in Europe, was precisely the interdisciplinarity that the exchanges among the branches of the Secession made possible. It should be borne in mind that although Gustav Klimt, its main driving force, was a partisan of the cult of absolute beauty, he maintained a still greater faith in the freedom of artists. Having been able to understand the flamboyant language of the "young savage" Kokoschka, he knew how to approach the neurotic cruelty of Schiele, whom he welcomed enthusiastically in 1908. "Young people first of all destroy what is already in existence. However, I don't resent them, because that's just the way it is," he declared, trusting their novel ambitions.

This master, so thoroughly imbued with pure esthetics, was not mistaken in supporting Egon Schiele, the implacable Expressionist of exaggerated eroticism, the portraitist more tormented than Vincent Van Gogh had been, to whom he owed much of his art. Schiele was a painstaking analyst of morbid emotions of the soul beneath vibrations of flesh in terror. Only recently did he divest himself of the disturbing feverishness of his obsessions. His *Trees* of 1917 and his rural landscapes became purified images by a man who, although still young, seemed to want to achieve serenity. European painting went into mourning after the death of Schiele, because it was hard to think of any artist in his generation who could be compared to him. It is tragic that he died at the very moment his oil painting began to show a mastery that is comparable to that of his watercolors and drawings.

APOLLINAIRE MOURNED BY HIS FRIENDS

PARIS

Guillaume Apollinaire died on November 9 at 202 Boulevard Saint-Germain, where he had been living since 1913 following his separation from Marie Laurencin. He died at thirty-three, not directly because of the war, in which he had been wounded, but from the Spanish flu. As some sort of irony, he had just written an item for *L'Europe nouvelle*, November 2, in which he lamented the death of a young poet, Justin-Franz Simon, a victim of that epidemic, which has been ravaging all Europe. His funeral was held at Saint-Thomas d'Aquin on November 13, and his body was taken to Père-Lachaise for burial. At the head of the funeral cortege walked his mother, Madame de Kostrowitzky, and the woman he married in May, "the beautiful Russian" Jacqueline. Serge Férat and Max Jacob walked beside the two women. Jacob wrote to one of his friends that evening: "Truly, neither successes by my friends nor those of victorious France can ever restore what this death has caused to wither away in me. At this point, I don't know what is to become of my life."

The procession, included Pierre Mac Orlan, Picasso and his wife Olga, Léautaud, Cendrars, Léger, and Derain and his wife.

MARIE LAURENCIN: GROUP OF ARTISTS. 1908. Baltimore. Museum of Art

APOLLINAIRE TALKS ABOUT ART

"Braque does not owe anything anymore to what surrounds him. His mind has voluntarily caused a twilight of reality, and now a universal renaissance is being worked out plastically inside himself and outside himself."

"Neither Boccioni nor Severini are without talent. However, they did not understand Cubist painting properly, and their mistakes have made them set up in Italy a kind of dispersion art; a popular, loud art."

"It will perhaps be reserved to an artist as

devoid of esthetic concerns and as preoccupied with energy as Marcel Duchamp, to reconcile art and the people."

"Is this art deep rather than elevated? It cannot get by without the observation of nature and acts upon us as familiarly as nature." (With regard to Picasso)

"The art of Mademoiselle Laurencin tends to become pure arabesque, humanized by the observation of nature."

FATHER VICTORY VISITS MONET

EDGAR DEGAS:
FOUR DANCERS. About 1899.
Washington, D.C. National Gallery of Art

132,000 FRANCS FOR DANCERS

PARIS

Edgar Degas died on September 26 of last year. His name has reached the height of artistic popularity. At four sales from March to December, collectors were able to purchase not only works by the master but also the canvases of other painters that he had put together in a very attractive collection. Degas began to make acquisitions quite early, but he had to relinquish them after the bankruptcy that ruined his family in 1878. At the end of the 1890s, however, he resumed his purchases from the dealer Ambroise Vollard or at galleries or from artists such as Suzanne Valadon.

Degas was accustomed to saying, "Anyone who can live only in the contemplation of himself is unfortunate." He had considered placing his collection in a museum, but his intention remained a dream. His aversion to the managements of museums like the Louvre and the Luxembourg and his increasing unconcern as he was growing older prevented him from taking the steps necessary for achieving such a project. He ended up leaving all his assets to his brother René and the four surviving children of his sister Marguerite.

The characteristic complexity of Degas is seen in the choice of pictures he collected at his home at 6 Boulevard de Clichy. Ingres and Delacroix, El Greco and Van Gogh, David and Cézanne, Millet and Mary Cassatt were neighbors on his walls. As could have been expected, the Degas sales were a great success. On March 26 and 27 at the Georges Petit gallery, El Greco triumphed with his *St. Ildefonso*, which was sold for 82,000 francs. The newspaper *Le Siècle* maliciously pointed out that it had formerly been bought for 20 francs by Millet.

Among modern paintings, Manet went the highest with his *Portrait of Madam Manet on a Couch* for 62,000 francs. At the sale of May 6 to 8, it was learned that the *Grand portrait de famille* of Manet had been withdrawn, the picture having been purchased by the Louvre for a price of 400,000 francs.

It was with his paintings of dancers that Degas reached his highest peaks, especially with his *Four Dancers* (132,000 francs) and Mademoiselle Fiacre in *Ballet de la source* (80,000 francs). The last two sales, that of November 22 to 23 and the one held from December 11 to 13, saw the purchase of two paintings, *Repasseuses* and the *Portrait of Diego Martelli*.

Adding to these sales those that will take place next year, it can be expected that the proceeds from these sales will exceed twelve million francs.

GIVERNY

A very emotional and decisive meeting held at Giverny will certainly be considered one of the greatest moments in the history of art in the twentieth century. Georges Clémenceau, who at the end of this year of triumph is called by the French "Father Victory," has paid a visit to his old friend Claude Monet after the armistice celebrations. He decided to bring to fruition a project that he is greatly interested in and which he had already discussed with the famous painter. In honor of the peace, Monet is offering the French government a series of "large decorations" inspired by his garden, whose aquatic and floral themes had caught his Dionysian eye for many years. The paintings show mauve, pearl-colored, or pink waterlilies, weeping willows, tufts of agapanthus, and moving reflections of the sky, in which the hesitant shadows of clouds mix with those of rings of roses and the Japanese bridge.

In Clémenceau's opinion, such magic pictures merit a prestigious frame. Monet was very pleased to select the Museum of Decorative Arts, in which fourteen of his works have already been placed, donated by Moreau-Nélaton. The painter, who values the admiring but frank friendship of his neighbor —Clémenceau owns a house at Bernouville, close to Giverny —and was greatly touched by the moral support given him after the death of his wife, Alice, in 1911 and his son, Jean, in 1914, gave his consent because " . . . this is the only way available to me to participate in the victory," as he told Clémenceau.

He has such confidence in him that he wanted Clémenceau himself to select the panels. To paint them, he had an immense additional shop built two years ago, which he is dedicating completely to this vast project.

The First Issue of "Valori Plastici"

Enthusiastically encouraged by Carlo Carrà, Mario Broglio, who is also a painter and art critic, has just established the magazine *Valori plastici* in Rome. The first issue opens with Carrà's painting *L'ovale des apparitions* and a text written by the painter, effectively announcing the priority the magazine plans to give to "metaphysical painting," the principal reaction for the time being against Futurism and in favor of a return to figurative art. Among his contributors are Giorgio de Chirico and his brother Savinio, De Pisis, and Arturo Martini.

The Birth of Purism

At Éditions des Commentaires, a manifesto is published, signed by Amédée Ozenfant and Charles-Édouard Jenneret. Ozenfant, a thirty-two-year-old painter, is editor of the magazine *L'élan*. Jeanneret, a year younger, is also a painter, although up to now he has been known principally as an architect. Their work forms the basis for a new theory, "Purism," which aims at making harmonious contact between esthetics and the civilization of machines. Purism is to succeed "Cu-Cubism," which has become a new Academicism, according to Jeanneret. From December 15 until December 28, they exhibited their paintings jointly—harsh still-life compositions—at the Thomas gallery in Paris.

The Founding of the Group of November

The founders of the Group of November want a political art that throws everything old overboard and joins the people. Its instigators in Berlin are essentially the painters Max Pechstein and Georg Tappert. In their first pamphlet, they state: "The future of art and the seriousness underlying the moment oblige us, the revolutionaries of the mind—Expressionists, Cubists, Futurists—to form a close association."

War Plunges Modern Sculpture into Mourning

Fallen on the field of honor, victim of murderous insanity, as was his friend La Fresnaye, Raymond Duchamp-Villon, brother of Jacques Villon and Marcel Duchamp, died in Cannes on October 7, a little more than a month before the armistice. The cause of death was an interminable case of typhoid fever, contracted on the Champagne front. In 1912 he had been the initiator of the revolutionary Cubist house, exhibited at the Salon d'Automne. But Duchamp-Villon's principal work will always be his *Grand Horse*, whose sparseness and modernism makes him the equal of Brancusi and Boccioni. Raymond Duchamp-Villon, exempt from service, had signed up as a member of the medical auxiliary. He was forty-two at the time of his death.

If God Were a Machine

Dead at the age of thirty-eight, Morton Livingstone Schamberg was one of very few American artists who could be called a Dadaist. Influenced very early by nascent European abstract art, Schamberg found his style when he met Picabia and Marcel Duchamp at the home of the collector Walter Arensberg in New York. Inspired by industrial forms, the work of Schamberg is cold in appearance, yet it has an irony and a deadpan humor. He is especially known for his sculpture *God*, created in 1918, one of the first examples of Dada sculpture in the United States. It is made of a siphon mounted on a miter box, and symbolizes the veneration of his compatriots for the machine.

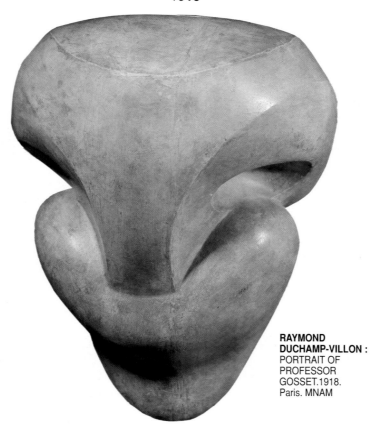

RAYMOND DUCHAMP-VILLON : PORTRAIT OF PROFESSOR GOSSET.1918. Paris. MNAM

MORTON SCHAMBERG: GOD. 1918. Philadelphia. Museum of Art

CHAGALL: ART IN THE STREET

VITEBSK

What does Marc Chagall know about Marxism? That "Marx was a Jew and that he had a long white beard." This is the reason why the members of the Vitebsk Soviet find that his paintings do not correspond to their artistic doctrine.

He had an ingenious idea for joyfully celebrating the first anniversary of the Revolution on October 25: to decorate the streets of his native city with streamers. He requested young and old—schoolchildren, students, building painters—to transfer a dozen sketches he created to large sheets.

By the anniversary date the spectacle was imposing: Multicolored animals were balanced above a dazzled throng, inflated by the wind of the Revolution. However, they were no sooner aloft when Chagall declared: "Don't ask me why I paint in blue and green and why a calf is seen in the belly of the cow." Voices were raised, questioning whether Karl Marx would have agreed to cows being painted green. And perhaps it would have been better to make blouses useful for workers from the miles of fabric used for making the streamers.

His friend Anatoli Vassilievich Lunacharski, people's commissar of public instruction, commissioned Chagall to establish an art school in Vitebsk. Somberly dressed, a leather briefcase under his arm, the artist had the perfect appearance of a Soviet functionary.

When he requested subsidies for his school, a functionary replied, "What do you think, Comrade Chagall: Which is more important, emergency repairs of the bridge or money for your school?" Marx was a Jew, like Chagall, and he had a long beard, but it appears that Chagall did not take after him for long in his revolutionary post.

MARC CHAGALL: THE WATER CARRIER. 1911. Private Collection

THE LIMITS OF SUPREMATISM

In this first postrevolutionary year, the enthusiasm of the avant-garde artists reaches great heights. These artists find themselves finally recognized and engaged in their role of trying to change the world. But Kazimir Malevich, going his own way, pursues his quest of radical Supremacist abstraction. He submitted fifteen paintings to the Tenth State Exhibition, which opened in December, including his *White Square on White*. In the catalogue he says: "I have cracked the links and the limitations of color. I want you to plunge into whiteness . . . and to swim in this infinity."

KAZIMIR MALEVICH: WHITE SQUARE ON WHITE. 1918. New York. MOMA

MASTERPIECES FOR THE PEOPLE

KANDINSKY THE OFFICIAL

MOSCOW

Sergei Ivanovich Shchukin, a brilliant businessman, philosopher, and art historian, had always said that his fabulous collection of modern paintings would go to the Russian people. He had even specifically willed it to the Tretiakow gallery after his death. But now that the new masters of the Kremlin are deciding matters in their current nationalization, several hundreds of paintings by Van Gogh, Cézanne, Gauguin, Degas, and Matisse, as well as more than fifty Picassos from his blue and pink periods, have been thrown together in one solid mass!

Born in Moscow in 1851 into a family that had been conducting industrial and commercial affairs since the eighteenth century, Shchukin studied in Germany, Finland, and St. Petersburg. Interested in philosophical matters, he founded the Institute of Philosophy in Moscow. He lived in Paris for part of the year and was acquainted with the work of Rodin, Huysmans, Degas, and Renoir. He began collecting Impressionist works in 1897, after which his friend Feodor Botkin took him to see works by Monet at the Durand-Ruel gallery. After that he never stopped.

The masterpieces of the nationalized collection include *Mount Sainte-Victoire* by Cézanne, *The Arenas of Arles* by Van Gogh, *Fruit Harvest* by Gauguin, all exceptional paintings, and especially *Dance* and *Music* by Matisse, two large compositions 8 1/2 x 19 feet in size, which were commissioned in 1909 to decorate the stairway of the Trubetskoi Palace, Shchukin's Moscow residence. He opened it to the public every Sunday, so that artists, students, critics, and art lovers from Moscow could be in contact with the latest trends in modern art sooner than they could have been in Paris.

Shchukin induced another large-scale Russian collector, Ivan Morosov, also a manufacturer, to become interested in modern art. The Morosov collection, almost seven hundred paintings, includes works by Vroubel, Chagall, Larionov, Gontcharova, and, from France, Gauguin, Picasso, Monet, Cézanne, Pissarro, Vuillard, Derain, Marquet, and Vlaminck. It was also open to the public on Sunday morning. At this time, it continues to belong to Morosov. Bonnard and Maurice Denis have decorated the palace in which their works still appear. But for how long? It will also be nationalized, and this should take place soon. A date has been given: May 1 of next year.

MOSCOW

Kandinsky returned to Moscow when war was declared and agreed to become a member of the plastic-arts department. Tatlin asked him to accept the post; he had been sent by Lunacharski, the popular education commissar in charge of revolutionary art. Having been assured that he would have no contact with politics, Kandinsky agreed to serve his country. He is also a professor at the state Art Institute. In each of the functions, he is so overloaded with work that he has little time for painting. He created only six paintings this year. He is trying not to fall into the daily rut of bureaucracy, and he does not want to impose creative ideas in all areas. During his rare moments of leisure, he translated his autobiography, *Regards sur le passé*, into Russian. The book has just appeared. Plans are to have him establish a Museum of Pictorial Culture in Moscow and new museums in the provinces. He is actively supported in his activities by his young wife, Nina de Andreevsky, the daughter of a general, whom he married in February.

PABLO PICASSO:
TWO CLOWNS. 1901.
Moscow. Pushkin Museum

The architect Walter Gropius founds the Weimar Bauhaus, which he hopes to make into a revolutionary communal school. The sort of teaching it would foster would be original in that it would not dissociate courses on theory from studio work, so that each student would become a builder of the cathedrals of the future. As for Italy, it looks back to its recent past: The Futurists, who had so valiantly fought against the Austro-Hungarian Empire, are honored with a retrospective exhibited in the principal cities of Italy. It is the end of an era and the beginning of a new one that promises hope as well as hardship.

1919

S U M M A R Y

AVANT-GARDE

The Bauhaus Wants to Invent the Future
The Bauhaus Manifesto
Grosz: Dehumanized Man
Hausmann: Robot Sculpture

EXHIBITIONS

Italy Consecrates the Futurists

WRITINGS AND THEORIES

Severini: the Example in the Tradition

DEVELOPMENTS

"I Am Still Making Progress," Declares Renoir
The Mirbeau Sale

ART NEWS

Survage and Colored Rhythm
Marcel Duchamp's Eyes Aren't Cold
The Omega Studios Close
A Museum Advertises
In Brief

WRITINGS AND THEORIES

Witkiewicz: Metaphysics of Art

LITERATURE

GERMANY
Franz Kafka publishes In the Penal Colony.

UNITED STATES
Man Ray founds the magazine TNT.

FRANCE
André Breton and Philippe Soupault edit Les champs magnétiques—*they invent Automatic Writing—for the magazine* Littérature, *which they have founded with Louis Aragon.*
    The Prix Goncourt is awarded to Marcel Proust for Within a Budding Grove.

GREAT BRITAIN
Sherwood Anderson publishes Winesburg, Ohio.
    Bertrand Russell publishes Introduction to Mathematical Philosophy.

MUSIC

FRANCE
At the soirées "Lyre et Palette," Ricardo Vines creates Perpetual Motion *by Francis Poulenc, dedicated to the painter Valentine Gross.*

HUNGARY
Béla Bartók composes the music to the pantomime Le mondain merveilleux.

MOTION PICTURES

GERMANY
Robert Wiene creates The Cabinet of Dr. Caligari, *which introduces Expressionism to cinematography. Ernst Lubitsch produces* Madame du Barry, *featuring Pola Negri.*

UNITED STATES
Foundation of United Artists. Stars are Chaplin, Griffith, Pickford, and Fairbanks.

JOHANNES ITTEN:
CHROMATIC SQUARES

The squares on the facing page are from an introductory course taught by Johannes Itten at the Bauhaus. They were meant as exercises to acquaint the students with color complements.

THE BAUHAUS WANTS TO INVENT THE FUTURE

WEIMAR

A school called the Bauhaus has just been opened in Weimar, while the delegates gathered in the theater are still debating the type of democracy the future Germany should have. This small provincial town, which has a population of only 40,000, is a cultural focal point. Goethe, Schiller, and Liszt lived here, and their influences are still felt in the city. It is expected that the Bauhaus will stir up a great deal of dust in the art world.

The teachers of the former School of Plastic Arts, it was said, would not be able to adapt themselves to the program of the Bauhaus. Gropius intends to break with academic education. He wants to return to the ideals of the builders of cathedrals in the Middle Ages, to found a "working community." He has already acquired a solid reputation at the age of thirty-six. The research office he founded with his colleague Adolf Meyer developed, among other achieve-

RELEARNING OF COMMUNITY LIFE, AN INITIATION INTO ALL ARTISTIC DISCIPLINES

"Bauhaus" means literally a "construction building." The term was chosen by the architect Walter Gropius, the founder and director of the school. The school was officially presented to the public on April 23. It results from the merging of two already existing establishments, the School of Arts and Trades, directed until 1914 by the Belgian architect Henry Van de Velde, and the School of Plastic Arts, a more traditional, academic, institution.

Ill-wishers predicted that this marriage would not take place.

ments, the plans for the Fagus factory in 1910. This was an innovative construction in glass and steel. Gropius believes that the Bauhaus, born out of the political upheavals in Germany, will be a revolutionary school. The program, as presented in a document of several pages, is surely so. These pages, in the form of a manifesto signed by Gropius himself and those who run the school, are introduced by a wood engraving by Lyonel Feininger—a cathedral adorned by five-pointed stars: *The Cathedral of the Future*, prophetically

Johannes Itten.

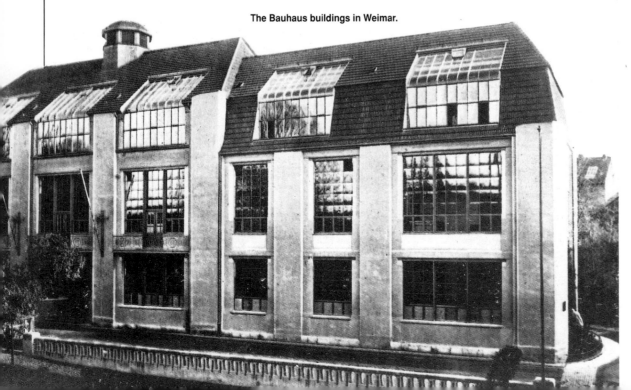

The Bauhaus buildings in Weimar.

announced by Gropius, a promise of the "total art" that should embody architecture. This will not be taught as such at the Bauhaus, but it will be prepared for by lavish training as the ultimate goal and its culmination.

The instruction provided is not connected with required courses. Discussions among teachers and students will be of fundamental importance. Two categories of teachers will be called on to transmit their experiences to the students, who will then create their synthesis: on the one hand, "masters of form," who will be artists, and, on the other hand, "shop masters," who will be artisans.

Gropius believes that manual work is of primary importance. In order for students to become well acquainted with the intrinsic qualities of the materials used. There will be shops dedicated to working with wood, metal, stone, glass, and, of course, paint. He wants the artisan to become again an artist, and on the other hand for the artist to rediscover the virtues of artisanal work.

Will this program be respected? This is very doubtful under the current conditions. The Bauhaus has two hundred and seven students, a hundred and one girls and a hundred and six boys. They were accepted for admission on the basis of work presented—no diplomas were required. Unfortunately, there are too few shops, and money is lacking for setting up new ones. Only the lithography, printing, and bookbinding shops are able to function.

It is believed that Gropius intends to propose to famous artists that they become "masters of form" at the Bauhaus. He has thus considered Paul Klee. But as of now, at the beginning of September, only two known artists have been engaged: the American Lyonel Feininger and the Swiss Johannes Itten. The latter previously taught painting in Vienna and will teach the introductory course at the Bauhaus. The students at the Bauhaus do not expect to be initiated directly into architecture. They will first have to acquire basic knowledge of construction art. Training at the Bauhaus will be based on a relearning of community life and initiation into all artistic disciplines. The student should free himself from conventions that hamper his creative capacities. Gropius' dream is that of making the students inventors of new forms adapted to their social function.

But will German society evolve in the direction hoped for by Gropius? At the moment, it is not only the work of the architect that is impossible in Germany, because of the lack of raw materials, but also collaboration among artisans, industrialists, and artists, due to general conditions of hardship.

(See also 1927, 1932, 1933, 1937.)

THE BAUHAUS MANIFESTO

The final goal of any plastic activity is the building! To decorate it was once the most noble task of the plastic arts; they belonged intimately to the component parts of the great art of architecture. Today, they delight in an autonomy that may, again, lead to a collaboration among all creative artists.

Architects, painters, and sculptors must relearn to know and understand the complex form of the construction as a whole and in its element: Then their works will be filled again with the architectonic spirit that they lost in the art of the drawing room.

The old art schools could not achieve this unity, and, anyway, how could they have done it—art being unteachable. They must turn again to workshops. The universe of model draftsmen and of those who work in the applied arts, a universe where one limits oneself to drawing and painting, must finally rediscover the universe of building. When the young man who feels the call for plastic creativity first learns a trade, as in the old

Walter Gropius.

days, then the unproductive artist will no longer be doomed to unfinished works, for he will have a trade, a capacity to excel in something.

Architects, sculptors, painters, all of us, we must return to manual work! For there is no "professional art." There is no basic difference between the artist and the artisan. The artist is just an elevated version of the artisan. Thank heaven, during rare moments of light that are beyond his control, art flourishes unconsciously from the work of his hands, but the knowledge of the basics of his work is indispensable to any artist. It is the source of all creative production.

Let us therefore form a new union of artisans, free of the arrogance that led to a separation of classes and built a wall of arrogance between artisans and artists! Let's have the will to do it, let's conceive and achieve together the construction of a future that will unite everything: architecture, sculpture, and painting in a single formation, and that one day will rise toward heaven, the shining symbol of a new faith.

WALTER GROPIUS
The Bauhaus Manifesto *(Excerpt)*

LYONEL FEININGER:
THE CATHEDRAL OF THE FUTURE. 1919.
Berlin. Bauhaus-Archiv
Cover of the Bauhaus Manifesto (wood engraving).

ITALY CONSECRATES THE FUTURISTS

GIACOMO BALLA: AUTOMOBILE SPEED + LIGHT + NOISE. 1913. Zurich. Kunsthaus

MILAN

Sixty-eight artists were exhibited from March 11 to the end of April at the National Futurist Exhibition. Their works were later shown in Genoa and Florence. This development is mainly due to the desire of Italian Futurists to regain their dynamism, which had been halted by the war and by the deaths of two of its leading spirits.

The period of upheaval had claimed the painter and sculptor Umberto Boccioni, who died in Verona at age thirty-three, and the architect Antonio Sant'Elia, thirty-one years old, who disappeared near Montefalcone, on the Trieste front. In his *Manifesto of Futurist Architecture* Sant'Elia had declared on July 11, 1914, that "The basic characteristic of Futurist architecture will be transitoriness. Objects last for a shorter time than we do. Each generation should manufacture its own city." He could do no better than reject addiction to the past and affirm adopting modernism, characterized by dynamism, mechanization, speed, and violence, without which the arts lose all vitality and even their reason for being.

Although a Futurism that would return to traditional pictorial means had been praised in 1917, Gino Severini does not abandon Futurist taste for machines. In *Le Mercure de France* of January 1, he expresses his belief that "the process of building a machine is analogous to the process of creating a work of art." Because the goal of the artist is not esthetics but life itself, he is concerned with reality. His work should make reality "more alive, more intense, and more true than the actual objects." He should not represent them but reconstruct them.

It is not without boldness that Marinetti, the main founder of the movement, writes in a tract released at the beginning of March, "Futurism, born in Milan eleven years ago, has influenced the entire world through thousands of exhibitions, conferences, and concerts. It has created innumerable different Futurisms according to the requirements of the field." Its most recent claim to distinction, he believes, is that of having influenced Italian political life by public pronouncements of revolutionary, anticlerical, and antimoralist patriotism and of having organized the first demonstration against Austria in Milan on September 15, 1914. "Italian Futurism," he declares, "is the spirit of the new generation that battled against the Austro-Hungarian Empire and victoriously destroyed it." He is convinced that "Futurists are disseminators of courage and champions of liberty!"

While the exhibition in Milan was being held, Marinetti participated in the foundation of the "Faces of Combat." He rallied to the political program of Mussolini. Perhaps he tried thus to regain control of a movement that had moved away from his control a short time earlier: Giacomo Balla was outstanding in Milan. With his compositions imbued with lyrical sensuality, he knew how to express the ephemeral character of sensory phenomena. And Fortunato Depero was able to create a sensation with his puppets and his "rubber devils."

Futurists want to be sorcerers' apprentices from whom nothing, save life, escapes!

(See also 1909, 1912, 1914, 1915, 1916, 1929.)

LUIGI RUSSOLO: THE DYNAMISM OF AN AUTOMOBILE. 1912-1913. Paris. MNAM

SEVERINI: THE EXAMPLE IN THE TRADITION

Like many other artists, Gino Severini felt, with the prolongation of the war, a lack of proportion between his art and the terrible reality. He searched in several directions—mechanical animation of the work of art or return to figurative presentation. We are reproducing here, at a time when Italy consecrates Futurism, his remarks on the evolution of this movement, as published in *Le Mercure de France* under the title "Avant-Garde Painting 1917."

I don't intend to impose any restrictions on subject choice; I just want it understood that the familiar objects that surround us, and which we use all the time, constitute "modern subjects" and that it is not necessary to rack one's brain in search for "subjects" —which would necessarily be inspired by intellectual preferences of a more or less philosophical nature, rather than by a purely plastic sense or by a desire to do nothing but paint.

Precision, rhythm, the brutality of machines and their movements have no doubt led us to a new Realism that we can express without painting locomotives.

All the efforts of avant-garde painters aim at the expression of this new Realism which I defined in the preceding article, Ideist Realism, adopting Remy de Gourmont's apt expression.

The obsession to penetrate, to conquer by all means the sense of the real, to identify with life in all fibers of our body, is at the base of our search and at the base of the esthetics of all times.

In this general context can be found the origins of our precise and geometrical constructions, of our applications of assorted materials on canvas, such as fabric, glass, paper, and of all the futile attempts that unfortunately were poorly understood or systematized.

In my personal search, I went as far as combining mobile surfaces of cardboard and paper that can be rotated and moved sidewise. From there, it was a small step to use motors or other mechanical forces.

But we all have now abandoned these means to reach Realism and movement in a painting, as well as the relation between "quantities" of colors and the position of lines—only exclusively pictorial means must convey the feeling of the real that we are striving for.

For the era of reactions through "ism" is finished, and from the created works a kind of collective esthetics changes gradually,

GINO SEVERINI:
BLUE DANCER.
1912. Milan.
Collection Mattioli

the result of the combined efforts of many artists. This does not necessarily mean a renunciation of the personality because, as we see in the example of plastic art to this day, originality may have had a collective esthetic basis.

GINO SEVERINI
Le Mercure de France

"I AM STILL MAKING PROGRESS," DECLARES RENOIR

CAGNES

On the evening of December 2, before going to bed in his room in the Villa des Collettes, Auguste Renoir, who had come down with pulmonary congestion at age seventy-eight, called for a sheet of paper and a pencil. He wanted to draw a vase, but he was exhausted. At 2 a.m. the next day, ". . . he died without suffering," his son Jean wrote to Durand-Ruel, who had successfully arranged an exhibition in his gallery in New York of the most distinguished and most brilliant Impressionists.

All of Renoir is revealed in this last gesture of a hand which, tightened by his crippling rheumatism, was reaching for a pencil that he could not pick up! This successful painter had lived for the pleasure of calling up sun-filled landscapes, wide-awake flowers, pulpy fruit—a fruit dish overflowing with apples, grapes, and figs was one of his last paintings—and especially young women. He told Matisse, who had come from Nice to visit him, that they are ". . . the supreme feat of God."

In 1908, Renoir moved into the wooden studio that he had had built among the centuries-old olive trees on the grounds of his villa. There he created a large painting, *The Great Bathers*. His three sons, Pierre, Jean, and Claude, considered donating it to the state since Renoir considered it to be a "culmination" and "a good springboard for future research."

Irresistibly inspired by his model Dédée, a "superb Russian," with whom Jean was in love, he showed her reclining nude in two different poses in a vibrant Provençal landscape. In this composition, dedicated to the "eternal woman," Renoir wanted her to fill the canvas "until it cracks."

Extending the undulating vastness of forms, and enhancing their flamboyant color, including vivid red—because he had found that his tints faded in time—Renoir abandoned himself to the euphoria of sensual fullness and color. "I am still making progress," he declared, entranced. "I am still successful, and I will not die before I achieve my masterpiece."

In spite of his paralyzing infirmities, the amazing Renoir proved himself more enthusiastic than ever for these overflowing bathers, whose flowering, youthful physical charms he has reproduced so well.

In his old age, this son of Boucher and Fragonard rejoined his grandfather Rubens!

After having been welcomed at the Louvre in his wheelchair like a king last August, he wanted to make a car trip to Chatou to the inn of Father Fournaise. It was there that in 1881 he painted the famous *Déjeuner des canotiers*, radiant with his love for his future wife, Aline Charigot. With his twisted fist he then wiped away the tears blurring the recollection of one of his dearest memories.

AUGUSTE RENOIR: THE GREAT BATHERS. 1918. Paris. Musée d'Orsay

THE MIRBEAU SALE

PARIS

Octave Mirbeau died more than two years ago. The sale of his collection of paintings on February 24 was a reminder of his role in the artistic life of France. He who had used his satirical verve for pitiless indictments against the clergy and society, keenly defended the artists he loved. The author of the *Journal d'une femme de chambre* was also the author of articles celebrating Impressionism. He deeply admired Cézanne, Van Gogh, Monet, Pissarro, and Renoir. He owned several of their paintings.

In accordance with the wishes of her husband, Madame Mirbeau began transforming their house at Cheverchement, in which he wrote most of his works, into a country resort for writers, painters, and sculptors whom fate had treated unkindly. To assure the functioning of such a home, it became necessary to sell the collection of Octave Mirbeau.

The proceeds from that sale amounted to 418,000 francs. Three of the eight paintings by Cézanne that the writer owned went for substantial prices.

Cézanne's *Self-Portrait* brought 25,000 francs, Manet's *Luncheon on the Grass* went for 13,000 francs. The highest-priced painting in the sale was *L'Estaque* by Braque, at 41,000 francs. The two Van Goghs, *Father Tanguy* and *Still Life with Fish*, sold for 20,200 and 15,000 francs respectively. The *Bust of Mirbeau* by Rodin went for only 5,000 francs. A low bid for one about whom Mirbeau wrote: "He will be viewed as the greatest reformer of the art of statuary, which finds in him a model of movement and passion."

Survage and Colored Rhythm

"You would think you were present at the creation of the world," says Blaise Cendrars in an article in *La rose rouge* on Léopold Survage's invention. According to the poet, Survage has already completed over two hundred sketches representing colored abstract forms as part of the composition of a film he calls *Colored Rhythm*. In fact, encouraged by Apollinaire and Picasso as early as 1913, Survage has been working on the project since before the war. In 1914, he tried to take out a patent on his colored rhythm, and to interest the Gaumont firm in it. He published a theoretical article in *Les soirées de Paris*, and then came the war. So, while waiting for a patron to materialize, he has returned to painting pictures.

Marcel Duchamp's Eyes Aren't Cold

Having popularized certain objects of daily use, such as bottle carriers, hat racks, and toilet bowls, as works of art and baptizing them "ready-mades," Marcel Duchamp prays for the creation of an "inverted ready-made." This would consist of taking, say, a painting by Rembrandt and using it as an ironing board. Lacking a Rembrandt, he is content for the moment with putting a mustache on a reproduction of the *Mona Lisa*, and naming the travesty L.H.O.O.Q., with his characteristic slyness. It seems he and his paint brush are waiting for a curator with sufficient courage to hand over the authentic *Mona Lisa* from the Louvre so that he can finally realize his fantasy.

The Omega Studios Close

Art critic, but mainly painter and decorator, Roger Fry was hoping for a revival of the applied arts in England, and especially for their enrichment from the experiences of the most daring young artists. To this end, he founded the Omega Studios in London with Duncan Grant and Vanessa Bell in 1912. It was a hallowed spot for inventiveness, where the fine arts could rub elbows with embroidery, ceramics, bookbinding, and clothing design; where the sculptor Gaudier-Brzeska could make objects carved out of wood and

LÉOPOLD SURVAGE: VILLEFRANCHE-SUR-MER. 1915. Paris. MNAM

Wadsworth the painter could design printed textiles. But the war has killed off one, mobilized the other, and turned away the public, all having a cruel effect on Omega, which has had to shut its doors this year.

A Museum Advertises

Andry-Farcy, "heavy on the hairpiece, light on knowledge, and devoid of talent," according to his furious adversaries, was named curator of the Musée de Grenoble this autumn. His first move was to cover a wall near the train station with posters telling foreign tourists "Stay in Grenoble one day more and visit the Musée Art Gallery, one of the most beautiful in France." Painter, poster artist, journalist, collector, and overweight, he is the creator of a comical character who resembles him very much and appears in his advertisements, which seems to some to be incompatible with his position. He is nonetheless an ardent defender of modern art.

STAY IN GRENOBLE 1 DAY MORE and VISIT the MUSÉE ART GALLERY one of the most Beautiful IN FRANCE

Advertisement for the Musée de Grenoble.

GROSZ: DEHUMANIZED MAN

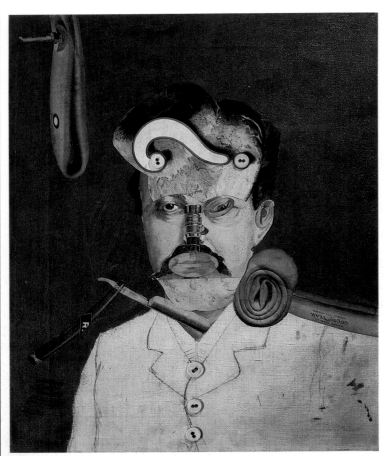

GEORGE GROSZ: REMEMBER UNCLE AUGUST, THE UNHAPPY INVENTOR
(A VICTIM OF SOCIETY). 1919. Paris. MNAM

BERLIN

George Grosz, a young Berlin artist and a great sensation in this first postwar year, has attacked his Uncle August. The ungrateful nephew has cut out, assembled, and glued detached pieces and buttons on his portrait. In short, he has amused himself dadaistically in disfiguring it with a great deal of irony and a feeling for the grotesque.

Since his years of study at the Academy of Fine Arts in Dresden, acid has been flowing in the veins of the young man. How did he come to detest his compatriots to that extent? He judges and condemns German society for its sadism, and very soon his vitriolic pencil is striking the crawling vermin of the large city, a place that always fascinates him. Tall and slender, a dandy in appearance, he expresses his hatred and deep mistrust of the German type, " . . . with low forehead and with thick neck."

Born in Berlin in 1893, he returned from Dresden to settle there in 1911. A cruel satirist from his very beginnings—he worked for *Ulk* (joke), the satirical supplement of the *Berliner Tageblatt*—he never stopped taking aim at the petit bourgeoisie and the military, which he represented with the face of a pig. Under the influence of Dada his sharpness became still more pitiless. A victim of society, a freak with mouth closed by a false mouth and rendered stupid by a brain in question-mark form, and with a knife at the throat, Uncle August is classified in the category of human machines molded by the global war.

Germans are not the only victims of Grosz. "Hardness and clarity in doing evil! There is enough minor music to put one to sleep!" He applies these words to ". . . insipid French painters like Cézanne and Picasso."

HAUSMANN: ROBOT SCULPTURE

BERLIN

Raoul Hausmann is a theoretician, poet, pamphleteer, provocateur, photographer (he is the inventor of photomontage), and, above all, a "dadasoph," according to the nickname his friends have given him. This ironical thirty-year-old Viennese was in fact the cofounder of the Dada club of Berlin with Richard Huelsenbeck last year. He has just completed a sculpture whose title is significant: *The Spirit of Our Age (Mechanical Head).* Since it is composed of objects borrowed from daily life, this sculpture is the very symbol of antiart. Hausmann has attached to a wig holder a purse, a pliable goblet, a fragment of metric tape, a wooden ruler, the number 22, and a jewel case. These different objects were chosen by

him as emblems of the petit bourgeois spirit, which is uncompromisingly opposed by Dada.

In a violent manifesto in January against the Weimar Republic, Hausmann denounced traditional values: "I announce the world of Dada! I laugh at science and culture, those assurances of a society condemned to death!" Before founding the journal *Der Dada* in June, he had already published a 1916 journal of anarchist tendencies, *Die freie Strasse* (the free street), with the poet Franz Jung.

Although the influences of Boccioni and Giorgio de Chirico are unquestionable, Hausmann's *Head* is nevertheless novel. It does not represent a celebration of our scientific and industrial society, but its condemnation .

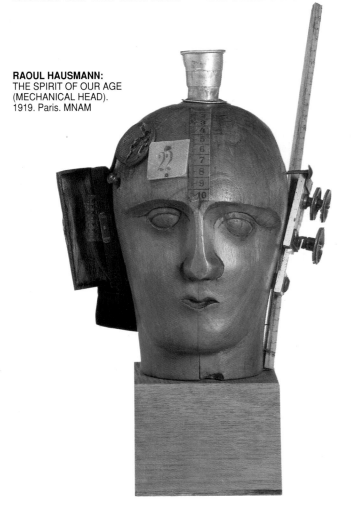

RAOUL HAUSMANN:
THE SPIRIT OF OUR AGE
(MECHANICAL HEAD).
1919. Paris. MNAM

WITKIEWICZ: METAPHYSICS OF ART

A deeply pessimistic mind, and a philosopher, playwright, and painter, thirty-four-year-old Stanislaw Ignacy Witkiewicz is the theoretician of the pure form. His essay *Les formes nouvelles en peinture et les malentendus qui en decoulent* (the new forms in painting and the misunderstandings that derive from them) puts the metaphysics of art in perspective. Sometimes called "confused and verbose," this essay is, however, of an unequaled richness—lyrical, explanatory, scathing with irony. The passage that follows underlines what is tragic in the existence of any artist, but also emphasize the permanence of art.

The artwork must be born, excuse the grotesque expression, from the most vivid tripes of the individual, yet freed to the utmost from this viscerality in the end. That's the recipe, but it is difficult to apply.

Through which terrible detours shouldn't the artist err, which abysses shouldn't he cross, enduring incomprehension, the contempt and the laughter of "connoisseurs," before he reaches his own style, which will be imitated by the horde of art jackals—buffoons or exploitive businessmen—once he has conquered the terrible fortress where the eternal Mystery reigns. The genuine artist does not follow the beaten paths, he is always on the wrong track, even though the only right and unique one, his, seems to be determined in advance. Therefore, one should be amazed, while traveling these paths that are lacerated, bitten to shreds, among the black depths of the Mystery, that the first one who ventured into it, when all around were virgin forests bristling with dangers—anguish, lies, madness, helplessness, disgust—did not miserably perish. Alas, too often we admire all this once the show is over, this sometimes sordid, sometimes sublime tragedy that is the artist's life. Actually, his life is often just a sum of senseless events, generally absurd and illogical events, because his life is not governed by clear goals, such as fortune, success, or scientific truth, not even by the incarnation of some precise idea, but by a brutal force in whose hands the artist writhes in convulsions as though he were a victim of tetanus or strychnine poisoning. This implacable force is the necessity to communicate to other human beings, in the guise of the beautiful, the monstrosity of solitary existence in a boundless universe, a universe that itself is the sole and tragic beauty of this existence. How come, then, the result is so meager, after the poor artist has lived through such horrible adventures?

STANISLAW WITKIEWICZ:
MULTIPLE SELF-PORTRAIT IN RUSSIAN UNIFORM. 1915

Art is a field where the lie cannot, under any condition, lead to positive results. Utilitarian values, with the exception of very primitive ones, change constantly, but what was truth in art in ancient Egypt or ancient China is still truth to us, and will remain so as long as democratization and mechanization will not turn us into automatons incapable of experiencing the metaphysical.

STANISLAW WITKIEWICZ
Les formes nouvelles en peinture et les malentendus qui en decoulent *(Excerpt)*

This decade witnesses three major events in art. In 1924, the official birth of Surrealism in André Breton's circle introduces psychoanalysis to art. In 1927, Monet's Waterlilies is unveiled at the Orangerie. And three generous women found New York's Museum of Modern Art in 1929. In the domain of architecture, a wild spree of

	1920	1921	1922	1923	1924
ARTS	• Death of Modigliani • Dada exhibition at the Winter Brasserie in Cologne	• The Kahnweiler Sale • Picasso's *Three Musicians*	• Prinzhorn reveals the art of the mentally ill • Chagall and Kandinsky leave Russia for Germany	• *The Bride Stripped Bare by Her Bachelors* by Duchamp • Albert C. Barnes buys 100 paintings from Soutine	• Birth of Surrealism • Death of Mailman Cheval
LITERATURE	• *The Theory of the Novel* by György Lukács • *Chérie* by Colette • *Le cimetière marin* by Paul Valéry	• *Suzanne and the Pacific* by Jean Giraudoux • *Si le grain ne meurt* by André Gide	• *Ulysses* by James Joyce • *Babbitt* by Sinclair Lewis	• W. B. Yeats is awarded Nobel prize in literature • *Sonnets to Orpheus* by Rainer Maria Rilke	• *Anabase* by Saint-John Perse • *A Passage to India* by E. M. Forster • *The Magic Mountain* by Thomas Mann • Deaths of Franz Kafka and Joseph Conrad
MUSIC AND THEATER	• First Salzburg Festival • *Pulcinella* by Igor Stravinsky	• *The Eiffel Tower Wedding Party*, a ballet by Jean Cocteau • *King David* by Arthur Honegger • *Six Characters in Search of an Author* by Luigi Pirandello	• *Triadic Ballet* by Oscar Schlemmer • First recording by Louis Armstrong with the King Oliver Orchestra in Chicago	• James P. Johnson creates the Charleston • *Knock* by Jules Romains • *Cœur à gaz* by Tristan Tzara	• *Rhapsody in Blue* by George Gershwin • Diaghilev's *Blue Train* in Paris
MOTION PICTURES	• *The Phantom Carriage* by Victor Sjöström • *The Sign of Zorro* by Fred Niblo • *Dr. Jekyll and Mr. Hyde* by John Robertson	• *The Kid* with Charlie Chaplin • *The Wheel* by Abel Gance • *Dream Street* by D. W. Griffith	• *Nosferatu* by F. W. Murnau • *Dr. Mabuse, the Gambler* by Fritz Lang • *Cops* by Buster Keaton	• Greta Garbo's film debut, in *Gösta Berling* • Erich von Stroheim's *The Raptors*	• *Mechanical Ballet* by Fernand Léger • *The Navigator* by Buster Keaton • *The Ten Commandments* by Cecil B. De Mille
SCIENCE AND TECHNOLOGY	• Hermann Rorschach develops his ink-blot test • The structure of the Milky Way is demonstrated by Max Wolf, through photography	• Discovery of insulin • Development of B-C-G tuberculosis vaccine • Albert Einstein is awarded Nobel prize in physics	• Discovery of vitamin E • Niels Bohr is awarded Nobel prize in physics	• Discovery of diphtheria vaccination • Process for sound motion pictures demonstrated by Lee de Forest	• Willem Einthoven is awarded Nobel prize in medicine for his work in electrocardiography • First use of insecticides
POLITICS AND DAILY LIFE	• The 19th Amendment gives American women the right to vote • Gandhi launches his civil-disobedience campaign in India	• Sacco and Vanzetti are found guilty of murder • Hitler's Brown Shirts (S.A.) begin to terrorize their opponents	• The Irish Free State is proclaimed • Mussolini forms a Fascist government • Emily Post publishes *Etiquette*	• The first birth-control clinic is founded, in New York • Hitler makes an unsuccessful coup d'état • John Maynard Keynes publishes *A Tract on Monetary Reform*	• Lenin dies, and Stalin forms a "troika" with Zinoviev and Kamenev • Hitler, in prison, writes *Mein Kampf*

1929

activity includes the publication of *Le Corbusier's* Vers une architecture, bringing the author instant fame, as well as the festive inauguration of Walter Gropius' new Bauhaus structures in Dessau in 1927. Elie Faure publishes The Spirit of Forms, *a vast synthesis concluding his famous* History of Art.

	1925	**1926**	**1927**	**1928**	**1929**
	• International Exhibition of Modern Decorative and Industrial Arts in Paris • Birth of the New Objectivity	• Death of Antoni Gaudí • Exhibit of Max Ernst's frottages in Paris	• Monet's *Waterlilies* at the Orangerie • Inauguration of the Bauhaus in Dessau • Death of Juan Gris	• *Surrealism and Painting* by André Breton • Miró in Holland	• Inauguration of MOMA in New York • Dali conquers Paris
	• *The Great Gatsby* by F. Scott Fitzgerald • Posthumous publication of Franz Kafka's *The Trial* • *Le paysan de Paris* by Louis Aragon	• *Under the Sun of Satan* by Georges Bernanos • *The Seven Pillars of Wisdom* by T. E. Lawrence • *Capital of Pain* by Paul Eluard • Death of Rainer Maria Rilke	• *Being and Time* by Martin Heidegger • *The Spirit of Forms* by Elie Faure • *Men Without Women* by Ernest Hemingway • Henri Bergson is awarded Nobel prize in literature	• *Lady Chatterley's Lover* by D.H. Lawrence • *Les conquérants* by André Malraux • *The Gypsy Ballads* by Federico García Lorca	• *A Farewell to Arms* by Ernest Hemingway • *All Quiet on the Western Front* by Erich Maria Remarque • *The Time of Indifference* by Alberto Moravia
	• *Wozzeck* by Alban Berg in Berlin • *L'enfant et les sortilèges* by Ravel, with libretto by Colette	• *First Symphony* by Dmitri Shostakovich • *Turandot* by Giacomo Puccini, conducted by Toscanini	• Duke Ellington at the Cotton Club in Harlem	• *Bolero* by Maurice Ravel • *The Threepenny Opera* by Bertolt Brecht with music by Kurt Weill • *An American in Paris* by George Gershwin	• *Marius* by Marcel Pagnol • Death of Sergei de Diaghilev
	• *Battleship Potemkin* by Sergei Eisenstein • *The Joyless Street* by G. W. Pabst • *The Gold Rush* with Charlie Chaplin • Debut of the Laurel and Hardy team	• *Metropolis* by Fritz Lang • *Nana* by Jean Renoir • Death of Rudolph Valentino	• *Napoleon* by Abel Gance • *The Jazz Singer* by Alan Crosland, with Al Jolson	• *The Passion of Joan of Arc* by Carl Theodor Dreyer • *Loulou* by G. W. Pabst • Walt Disney creates Mickey Mouse	• *Hallelujah!* by King Vidor • *Un chien andalou* by Luis Buñuel and Salvador Dali • The "talkies" begin to replace silent films
	• First television transmission in Great Britain	• The first 16-millimeter film produced by Kodak • New stellar theory by James Jeans	• Ivan Petrovich Pavlov publishes *Conditioned Reflexes* • Ford produces its 15-millionth Model T	• Alexander Fleming discovers penicillin • H. Geiger and W. Müller invent the Geiger counter	• Einstein proposes a unified field theory • Louis de Broglie is awarded Nobel prize in physics for discovering the wave nature of electrons
	• Leon Trotsky loses his powerful position in Russia • First solar eclipse in New York in 300 years	• Hirohito becomes emperor of Japan, succeeding Yoshihito • Gene Tunney becomes heavyweight champion, succeeding Jack Dempsey	• Lindbergh's solo flight from New York to Paris • Civil war in China	• Amelia Earhart is the first woman to fly across the Atlantic • 65 countries sign the Kellog-Briand Pact, outlawing war	• Black Friday at the New York Stock Exchange • Leon Trotsky is banned from the USSR

On January 24 of this disturbing and disturbed year, Modigliani dies, to be followed the next day by his companion Jeanne Hébuterne, who commits suicide. He leaves behind a brilliant body of work, brusquely cut short. Meanwhile, in Cologne, Max Ernst and Baargeld, who have been chased out of the Museum of Decorative Arts, exhibit their Dadaist works in the back room of the Winter Brasserie. The location becomes a mecca in a disputatious Europe. Is this a foreshadowing of events to come? In Soviet Russia's Moscow, the sculptors Gabo and Pevsner launch their Realist Manifesto, laying the foundation for their newly created movement, Constructivism.

1920
SUMMARY

GREAT MASTERS

Modigliani's Accursed Life
A Sculptor of Primitive Effigies
Opinions on Modigliani

DEVELOPMENTS

Expressionist Aftereffects of the War

WRITINGS AND THEORIES

Paul Klee: the Creative Confession

POLEMIC

The Scandal of the Winter Brasserie

ART NEWS

Georgio de Chirico, Pictor Classicus
Dada the Reformer
Dreier and Duchamp Create the Société Anonyme
Ozenfant and Jeanneret Found L'esprit nouveau
Tzara Awaited Like the Messiah
In Brief

SCULPTURE

Marcel Duchamp, Sorcerer's Apprentice
Tatlin: Monument for the Third International

MANIFESTO

Gabo and Pevsner: Constructivism

LITERATURE

GREAT BRITAIN
Ezra Pound publishes Instigations.

AUSTRIA
The Hungarian philosopher György Lukács publishes, in German, The Theory of the Novel.

FRANCE
Paul Valéry publishes his poem Le cimetière marin.
Colette publishes Chéri.

MUSIC

GERMANY
The first Salzburg Festival opens with the medieval play Jedermann, *in an adaptation by Hugo von Hofmannsthal, directed by Max Reinhardt.*

UNITED STATES
Charles Ives publishes the Concord Sonata, *at his own expense.*

FRANCE
Premiere of Igor Stravinsky's ballet Pulcinella, *with choreography by Massine, with stage design by Picasso.*

RUSSIA
First concert of factory sirens in Petrograd.

GERMANY
Paul Wegener creates The Golem.

MOTION PICTURES

UNITED STATES
Great success of two films: Dr. Jekyll and Mr. Hyde *by John Robertson, with John Barrymore, and* The Sign of Zorro *by Fred Niblo, with Douglas Fairbanks.*
Premiere of Pat Sullivan's cartoon Fritz the Cat.

SWEDEN
Victor Sjöström creates The Phantom Carriage, *from a novel by Selma Lagerlöf.*

AMEDEO MODIGLIANI:
PORTRAIT OF JEANNE HÉBUTERNE.
1919. Private Collection

MODIGLIANI'S ACCURSED LIFE

PARIS

The friends of "Modi" are bewildered! Hardly had the death of their dear Amedeo been announced to them, when a second thunderbolt struck. Jeanne Hébuterne, his companion, pregnant with their second child, leaps from the window of her parents' apartment and is crushed on the sidewalk.

"His health began to deteriorate," he also wrote him. "My advice to go immediately to a sanitarium in Switzerland was fruitless. He treated me as an enemy at that moment and replied, Don't moralize! He was a child of the stars, and reality did not exist for him." Amedeo, who had returned seven months ago from the Riviera, where he had

"HE WAS A CHILD OF THE STARS, AND REALITY DID NOT EXIST FOR HIM"

Modigliani died at Charity Hospital at 9 p.m. on January 21, and Jeanne took her life at 4 a.m. the next day.

Emmanuele, the painter's brother, sends a telegram from Italy: "Bury him like a prince!" The funeral ceremonies are arranged by Kisling. Léopold Zborowski, a merchant and a fervent admirer of Modigliani, has a long telephone conversation with Emmanuele to ask him what is to be done with little Jeanne Modigliani, a charming infant fourteen months old, who had been assigned a wet nurse by her parents. He told him how much her father had loved her and that he had gone to see her a short time before his death.

gone with Jeanne Hébuterne for a rest, was seized with a creative fever. He began to produce a series of admirable portraits of people around him, audaciously designing and creating his unique self-portrait with an exhausted face.

He wrote on the preparatory drawing of his last work, a portrait of the Greek musician Mario Varvogli, "Il Novo Anno. Hic incipit vita nova." (The new year. The new life begins here.) Before succumbing to tubercu-

AMEDEO MODIGLIANI: RED HEAD. 1915. Paris. MNAM

lar meningitis, he murmurs, "Dear, Italy." His last wish was to return to his native Italy.

The fourth child of Jewish parents—a Romanian broker and a tender and intelligent mother of Marseillaise and Tunisian origin, Amedeo was born in Leghorn, on July 12, 1884. During the summer of 1895, Eugenia Modigliani writes in her diary that Amedeo, who suffers from severe pleurisy, acts like a spoiled

child. She asks herself, " . . . what is in this chrysalis? Perhaps an artist?" The boy gives up his studies at age fourteen to attend the studio of Micheli, himself a student of Fattori, one of the main "Macchiaioli," who, having abandoned their characteristic spots, end up preferring broad, flat tints.

Amedeo registers at the Free School du Nu in Florence, in 1902, then at a school in Venice, from where he writes to a friend that he has received ". . . the most valuable education of my life." He sees his chance and hastened to Montmartre in the winter of 1906. His studio, close to the Bateau-Lavoir, makes it possible to meet "the Picasso band." On Picasso's portrait he writes the significant word "savoir!" (know!). In turn, Picasso observes ironically about this ham-actor boy, who recites

Modigliani.

A SCULPTOR OF PRIMITIVE EFFIGIES

Annunzio and Dante and who hangs out with disreputable painters, "It is strange, he has never been interested in the Boulevard Saint-Denis, only in Montparnasse."

Close to Kisling and Survage, Amedeo shares with Soutine and Utrillo their indulgence in alcohol and their attraction to opium. He detests Cocteau, and makes a caricatural portrait of him. "Apart from Picasso and Max Jacob, he distrusts the entire world," the British poet Beatrice Hastings declares. Modigliani's passionate and stormy affair with the poet stimulates his painting. He is encouraged by the art dealer Paul Guillaume and in 1915 begins a series of large nudes, working with professional models. They sit stretched out on vermilion and dark red couches. Their orange bodies are reproduced with a single explosive discharge of a sensuality imprinted with morbidity, leading to hesitation between desire and contemplation. His plastic spirit seems inspired under the effect of narcotics.

Influenced at first by Paul Cézanne in his portraits of the *Cellist* and the *Beggar,* Modigliani discovers the spellbinding power of African art, thanks to Picasso's *Demoiselles d'Avignon.* However, he does not forget the Gothic lessons of Simone Martini and the Renaissance lessons of Botticelli, from whom he borrows the aristocratic elongation of his "swan women." He dreams of the expressive vacuity of the orbits of African masks. This soberly psychological portrait artist shades the eyes of most of his subjects with blue and gray lines. He makes the viewer understand that if man is speechless in what he perceives he does not see what arouses him: his internal dream, which saves him from earthly misfortunes.

(See also 1908 and 1917.)

PARIS

From 1910 to 1912, Amedeo Modigliani dedicates himself almost exclusively to sculpture, creating about thirty effigies in stone, increasingly hieratic and elongated. The faces, female for the most part, clearly show the influence of African masks, without excluding an indirect reference to Etruscan sculpture in his first works and a Gothic influence later.

He presents seven sculptures in the studio of his friend Amedeo de Souza-Cardoso in 1911 and eight in the Tenth Salon d'Automne in 1912. He then abandons these physically exhausting experiences. Their spiritual inspiration also might have been exhausted. It was perfected at the side of Constantine Brancusi at Falguière, where he had rejoined him after coming down from Montmartre.

Modigliani is introduced to the Romanian sculptor by Dr. Paul Alexandre, who owns a large collection of Baoulé sculptures from the Ivory Coast. His preparatory charcoal sketches clearly show that the sorcery of African art still fascinates the attentive Italian, ever since his first meetings with Picasso.

Brancusi expertly assists Modigliani in his constructive work. Stripped to the essentials, the work is inspired by the African statues: a "direct cutting" of forms reduced to the essentials of their totem power. In 1908 he had given us a powerful example of rare simplicity and solid symbolism with his work *The Kiss.*

While confronting his subject, Modigliani reacts like Brancusi to the academic or Rodinesque virtuosity of the model in the primitiveness of his stone creations. However, he knows how to refine it by accentuating vertical lines defining the isosceles triangle of the face and the ridge of the nose, which he prolongs in exaggerated style from above by fissured superciliary arches to tiny mouths reduced to dumb stupor. He gives the impression of faces that are dedicated to contemplation of an eternal religious peace.

AMEDEO MODIGLIANI:
FEMALE HEAD. 1912-1913.
Paris. MNAM

OPINIONS ON MODIGLIANI

Today Amédée, my dearest friend, rests at the Père-Lachaise cemetery covered with flowers according to your will and ours. All the artistic youth has staged a triumphal funeral ceremony affected by emotion for the most gifted artist of our time.
  Letter from Léopold Zborowski, *January 31, 1920,* to Emmanuele Modigliani, *the painter's brother*

Without a doubt, many of his nudes are too uniformly of this apricot hue that was the fashion and which made warm and nostalgic fruits of so many young women's faces. But don't you prefer this Far Eastern color—oh, patina of opium!—to the eczematous roses so many painters continually inflict on us?
  Gustave Coquiot. Les Indépendants, *1920*

I observed Modigliani draw. His sharp sense of nuance makes him mold an arm joint, or the innocent curve of a young breast. He contains in a hardly perceptible stroke an entire architecture, supports the light bulge of an abdomen, extends a motion up to the very soul, makes it live . . . I would like to express my admiration for the drawings of Modigliani. In them the style is all grace . . .
  Francis Carco. "Modigliani," in L'Éventail, *July 15, 1919*

He never ceased being a gentleman.
  Charles-Albert Cingria

His haughty aristocratic soul will float among us for a long time in the shimmering of his beautifully variegated rags and tatters.
  Paul Guillaume

EXPRESSIONIST AFTEREFFECTS OF THE WAR

ALSODARMSTADT
Could Expressionism be dead? Dead, like so many of its supporters, on the field of honor? The art critic and historian Wilhelm Hausenstein believes it is, whereas the public that rejected it at the beginning flocks to the important exhibition of German Expressionism at the Kunsthalle (art hall) from June 10 to September 30. The many paintings represent important personalities from Die Brücke and the Blue Rider, also Barlach, Kokoschka, and Karl Hofer, as well as the septuagenarian Christian Rohlfs, an early Expressionist, and even Picasso, Braque, and Vlaminck—showing the relationship of Expressionism with Paris, which had never been done before on this scale.

The triumph of Expressionism began while the World War was in full rage, when the dealer Paul Cassirer took the initiative by giving full space to the paintings that had been rejected in 1917 at the summer exhibition of the Berlin Secession.

The old guard from Die Brücke, about forty in number, had abandoned the trenches to immerse themselves in nature again. The exhibition shows them freed from internal visions. Their landscapes are always greatly colored. Pure instinct is abandoned in favor of more profound reflection. Since moving to Davos as a patient, Kirchner, who has never been fond of large cities, devotes himself to Swiss landscapes. For their part, Heckel, Mueller, and Schmidt-

KARL SCHMIDT-ROTTLUFF:
CONVERSATION
ABOUT DEATH. 1920.
Munich. Staatsgalerie
Moderner Kunst

OTTO DIX:
DISABLED SOLDIERS
IN A CARD GAME. 1920.
Private Collection

Rottluff impart more severity to their compositions, in forms they now simplify.

Pechstein, who preaches "the unity of the people and art," may be the only one who has not changed. His paintings are more irrational and more dramatic than ever, like the explosive and violent paintings of George Grosz, who represents the rising generation, or Otto Dix, who is not represented at all at the exhibition.

The spirit of disability the war created inspires him to create a cycle of four paintings. Their jumble of prostheses, roller tables, and nightmarish heads is all but unbearable. "Another man arises from these long and dangerous exercises of domination over his person . . . especially with the wish to question for the future . . . more deeply, more severely, more tenaciously, more unkindly . . . Confidence in life has been lost." Would Nietzsche, a faithful companion of young Expressionist combatants at the front, have wondered at what point these lines would someday apply to people in their twenties and thirties—while older people may have returned from the war more serene?

(See also 1905, 1911, 1912, 1916.)

PAUL KLEE: THE CREATIVE CONFESSION

Called by Gropius to the Weimar Bauhaus, where he will teach as of the beginning of next year, Paul Klee, at forty-one years of age, is on the threshold of celebrity. Whether it is a matter of the plastic mechanics of a painting, or its formal agents, or its metaphysical significance, he is always at the core of pictorial creation. His thought, as much as his painting, is poetic and lapidary. He just published, in the magazine *Tribüne der Kunst und der Zeit* in Berlin, "The Creative Confession," his most important writing so far. A particularly significant passage follows.

Let's develop this; with a topographic map, let's make a little trip in the country of Better Knowledge. From the neutral position, propulsion of the first act of mobility (the line). Shortly thereafter, stop to catch your breath (broken line or, in the case of repeated stops, articulated line). Look backward on the distance covered (countermovement). Mental evaluation of the distance covered and the remaining stretch (cluster of lines). A river creates an obstacle, so one takes a boat (undulating movement). Upstream, one might find a bridge (series of arches). On the other bank, encounter with a spiritual brother who wishes also to go where Better Knowledge is located. Full of joy, we feel like one at first (convergence), but little by little differences spring up (layout separated by two lines). A certain agitation on one side and on the other (expression, dynamism, and psyche of the line).

We are crossing a plowed field (surface crossed by lines), then a thick forest. My companion has gone astray, searches and describes suddenly the conventional movement of the hound. I don't possess all my self-control either; the approaches to a new river are covered with fog (spatial element). It will soon lift. Basket workers are going home in a horse-drawn cart (wheel). With them a child with the most amusing small curls (movement in spiral form). Then night falls while the temperature becomes more oppressive (spatial element). Lightning on the horizon (zigzag lines). True, above our heads stars are still shining (seedlings of points). The first stage is finally reached. Before going to sleep, many things reemerge as recollections, because this tiny trip abounds in impressions.

The most diversified lines. Spots. Soft touches. Smooth surfaces. Soft. Streaked. Undulating movement. Hampered movement. Articulated. Countermovement. Braiding. Weaving. Mason's work. Overlap-

PAUL KLEE: NIGHT FLOWERS. 1918.
Essen. Folkwang Museum

ping. Solo. Several voices. Line about to lose itself. To recover strength (dynamism).

Happy regularity of the first trip; then the annoyances, the nerves! Trembling contained, small consoleding caresses of the breeze. Before the storm, assault of horseflies. Furor, murder. Intuition as guiding wire even in the twilight and where the bushes are thickest. Lightning, threatening reminder of a temperature chart. The one of a sick child . . . a very long time ago . . .

PAUL KLEE
The Creative Confession *(Excerpt)*

THE SCANDAL OF THE WINTER BRASSERIE

COLOGNE

Will the urinal of Marcel Duchamp have rivals? It is known that Duchamp sent a urinal that he called *Fountain* to the first show of the Society of Independents in New York in 1917, which rejected it. The implement made another entry into art three years later at the Winter Brasserie, now one of the higher places of the Rhineland avant-garde.

Here are the facts. The Artists Association of Cologne organizes a nonjury exhibition in the hall of the Museum of Decorative Arts, on the Hanse Boulevard. However, the museum curator, who was recently appointed, is indignant at the entries of Baargeld and Max Ernst. After a heated discussion between the museum management and the Association, these entries are judged undesirable, and consequently withdrawn.

This leads the two banned artists to rent an inner room, partially exposed to rain, from the owner of the Winter Brasserie for the exhibition of their Dadaist works. The placard announces: "Here is Dada Baargeld, the well-loved. Here is Dada Max Ernst, the feared." And as an olfactorily symbolic sign, visitors can enter this

ONE COLLAGE INCLUDED PART OF ALBRECHT DÜER'S ADAM AND EVE. THE POLICE CONSIDERED IT PORNOGRAPHIC!

inner room only through the men's room, with its urinals.

However, this passage is worth the trouble. Ernst chains a hatchet to one of his sculptures to make it easier for visitors to destroy it. For his part, Baargeld presents an aquarium called *Fluidoskeptryk*, whose reddened water partly conceals an alarm clock, a head of hair, and a wooden hand. The aquarium is broken on the *vernissage* day by a girl dressed for first communion, after she recites verses judged obscene by the spectators. A bloody liquid spreads over the floor.

Max Ernst was born on April 2, 1891, in Brühl, a town in the vicinity of Cologne. His father, an amateur painter of still lifes and religious subjects, earning him a local reputation in religious circles, was a teacher in a school for deaf-mutes. His mother, Louise, née Kopp, a pretty, bright-eyed woman, had a natural sense of humor. The boy got up secretly one night to follow, barefoot, the railroad line thast passed his parents' house to see where the rails met the horizon. He was taken back home by family friends who ran into him at a crossing. He became a painter after studying literature at Bonn University. His visit to a clinic for mental patients, where he discovered figurines made from bread crumbs by one of the inmates, convinced him to explore the vague territories at the edge of madness.

He participated in the First German Salon d'Automne in 1913, and then the war erupted. He was in the field artillery for four years, the "great filth," which he turned away from for Dada after the armistice.

His comrade, Baargeld, a pseudonym (which literally means "cash" or "ready money"), is the son of a Cologne banker. He is one of the founders of the Rhineland Communist party. He managed a newspaper of the extreme left, *Der Ventilator*, for one year. It has now been banned by British occupation authorities. He is one of the artists who give German Dadaism its revolutionary color.

Ernst and Baargeld place drawings and lithographs to be taken free of charge at the entrance to the inner room of the Winter Brasserie, but do not find takers, even at that "price." However, one sheet is seized by the police. It supplies a pretext for closing the exhibition, according to an affidavit by Ernst's uncle who is a public prosecutor in Cologne. The work seized is a collage, one of whose elements is cut from the engraving *Adam and Eve* by Albrecht Dürer. It is considered pornographic.

Dürer pornographic! When the truth of the matter is cleared up, the embarrassed authorities are obliged to lift their ban, but the accused work is not returned to the show.

Max Ernst's father is furious. He writes to his son: "I curse you. You have dishonored us."

(See also 1916.)

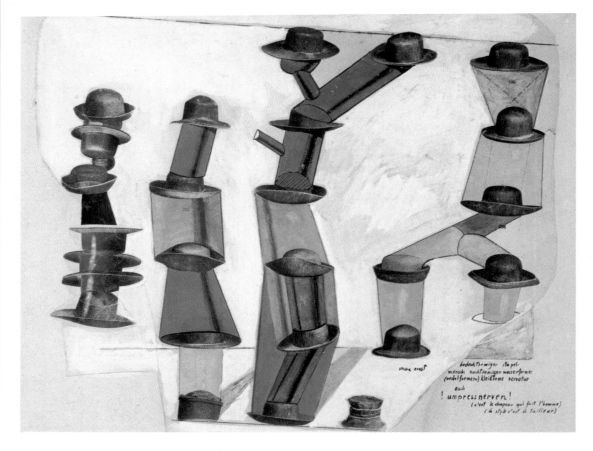

MAX ERNST:
THE HAT MAKES
THE MAN. 1920.
New York. MOMA

Georgio de Chirico, Pictor Classicus

At the age of thirty-two, Giorgio de Chirico, brilliant initiator of metaphysical painting, reverts to Classicism. Behind his change is a visit to the Villa Borghese Museum in Rome last year. As he stood before a work by Titian, overwhelmed by admiration, he had a sudden revelation of great art. Tongues of fire lapped around him, while outside the resounding call of a trumpet announced a resurrection. Since then, de Chirico has copied several works by Lotto, Michelangelo, and Raphael, so that his technique can absorb the teachings of the old masters. From now on, he will sign his paintings "Pictor Classicus."

Dada the Reformer

Dada has its first international fair at the Otto Burchard gallery in Berlin. The exhibition opened on June 5, with one hundred and fourteen paintings, collages, and art objects by Max Ernst, Otto Dix, Raoul Hausmann, Hannah Höch, George Grosz, and Rudolf Schlichter, among others. Hanging from the gallery ceiling, a mannequin, dressed in the uniform of a German police officer, holds a sign, "Hanged by the Revolution." In addition, Hausmann has written a fourteen-point manifesto, *What Is Dada and What Does It Want in Germany?* The document is a mixture of apparently serious suggestions for social reform and absurd proposals for making the world more Dadaist. Among his proposals, Hausmann calls for churches to be used to hold Dada demonstrations.

Mademoiselle Dreier and Duchamp Create the Société Anonyme

The banner of the Société Anonyme, designed by Man Ray, waves proudly over 47th Street in New York. The Société Anonyme is a collection of modern art put together by painter Katherine Dreier and Marcel Duchamp, who believe that artists, not critics, should control discourse on art. The Society will not limit its activities to exhibitions. Its library welcomes anyone interested in contemporary art; it will organize

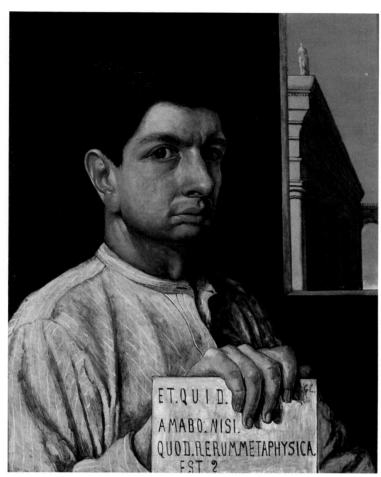

GIORGIO DE CHIRICO: SELF-PORTRAIT. 1920. Munich. Staatsgalerie Moderner Kunst

lectures and colloquia. Worthy of note is the fact that the fabulously wealthy Mademoiselle Dreier voted against the *Fountain,* a urinal that Duchamp sent to the Independents of New York three years ago. But that was before the artist explained his objectives to her.

Ozenfant and Jeanneret Found "L'esprit nouveau"

The first issue of the magazine *L'esprit nouveau,* created by the painters Amédée Ozenfant and Charles-Édouard Jeanneret and the poet Paul Dermée, is available in bookstores as of October 15. The magazine will spread a constructive spirit in pictorial, architectural, sociological, technical, scientific, and literary domains. Ozenfant and Jeanneret, who is named president and chief executive officer, will be responsible for the editing, proofreading, illustration, production, and administration of the magazine. So that he

can reserve the use of his name for his painting, Jeanneret will write articles on architecture under the pseudonym of Le Corbusier-Saugnier, after Le Corbusier, a maternal grandfather's family name. In the very first issue, he calls to order "Their Honors the Architects," making them aware of the esthetic of the machine while reminding them of the eternal laws of the art of building. Among intended contributors are the esthetician Victor Basch, André Salmon, Adolf Loos, Jean Cocteau, Gino Severini, and Elie Faure.

Tzara Awaited Like the Messiah

At the end of last year, the poet Tristan Tzara moved to Paris from Zurich, where he had created the Dada movement in 1916 when he was only twenty years old. The Parisian poets of the younger generation, André Breton, Philippe Soupault, and Louis Aragon, who

have been holding meetings since January to discuss their magazine *Littérature,* await Tzara as if he were the Messiah. Now that the war is over, they decide it is time to take up arms against patriotism, nationalism, and the bourgeoisie. Having won over Zurich, New York, and Berlin, will Dada appeal to Paris? Its destructive diatribes already seem slightly out of phase. One wonders when a true revolution in thought will actually come about.

MARCEL DUCHAMP, SORCERER'S APPRENTICE

NEW YORK

Man Ray killed in Marcel Duchamp's first-floor apartment at West 73rd Street? America almost lost one of its most promising artists. Man Ray was helping Duchamp develop an optical apparatus he invented, consisting of glass plates rotating around an axis and driven by a small motor, when the sudden acceleration caused the glass to break into pieces that almost decapitated him.

When Duchamp's machine rotates (it was repaired, its defects eliminated), there is no sign that he could harbor murderous ideas. It is apparently one of the most peaceable works he has produced. Its five glass plates of unequal dimensions, on which white and black lines are traced, form large continuous circles of perfect geometry by rotation. Since youth, the artist has been attracted by what he calls "amusing science." This work is unquestionably the one that has best satisfied his "engineering" side.

Duchamp has never concealed the fact that he meant "to free himself from the physical aspect of painting," especially because he "was fed up with the expression 'foolish like a painter.'" It is no accident that the last painting he made, at the insistence of his friend Katherine Dreier, is significantly titled *Tu m'* (approximately, "You . . . me"). On the other hand, to the extent that his optical machine acts on the eye's ability to retain an image for a fraction of a second after its disappearance, it fully satisfies his desire for immateriality.

Duchamp feels strongly that painting and sculpture are incapable of rivaling the beauty implicit in technical objects, which are refined more and more every day. In a letter, Léger reports on a visit to the Salon

MARCEL DUCHAMP: ROTATIVE GLASS PLATES. 1920. New Haven. Yale University Art Gallery

Motorized optical device: Five glass plates with black designs form continuous circles when turning on a motor-driven axis.

d'Aviation in the company of Brancusi and Duchamp at the outbreak of the war. "Marcel was a dry type with something elusive about him. He walked among the engines and propellers without saying a word. He suddenly said to Brancusi, 'Painting is finished! What can be done better than this propeller? Can you do this?'"

Movement has always interested Duchamp. This is the case in his *Coffee Mill* of 1911, in which the crank is seen at several points in its circuit. It is also present in his *Nude Descending a Staircase*, which created a scandal at the Armory Show two years later. However, movement here is only suggested, as with the Futurists. But with his *Rotative Glass Plates* the artist introduces a novelty: actual movement in a work of art.

European artists did not end up "Dadaizing"—Duchamp's *Rotative* may very well be the signal for a reconciliation with the machine age.

(See also 1913, 1917, 1923, 1968.)

TATLIN: MONUMENT FOR THE THIRD INTERNATIONAL

Vladimir Tatlin posing with his Monument.

This monument for the Third international by Vladimir Tatlin—is it sculpture or architecture? As sculpture: This monumental project is meant to have a height of more than 1,300 feet and draws on the Russian sculptor's research in which art and technology are combined. As architecture: The three suspended volumes within the metal structure that turn on their axes are actually assembly rooms.

GABO AND PEVSNER: CONSTRUCTIVISM

Two sculptors, the thirty-year-old Nahum Gabo and his brother, the thirty-four-year-old Anton Pevsner, have decided to reconstruct art on an entirely new basis, in agreement with the society in which we live today. Even Cubism and Futurism do not break really with the past, in their eyes. The text that follows is the center section of their *Realist Manifesto*, printed in Moscow on August 5 by the 2nd state printing plant. The reader will find it to be a bewildered hymn to science and technology.

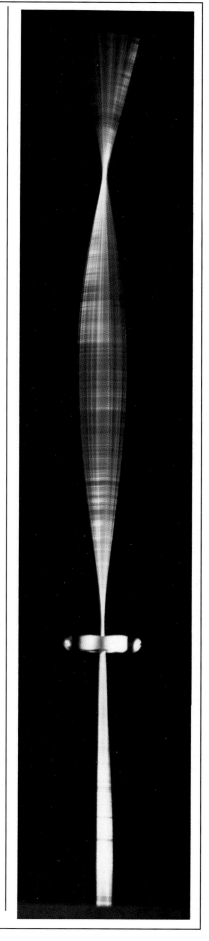

We proclaim: For us, space and time are born today. Space and time: the only forms where life is built, the only forms, therefore, where art should be erected.

States, political and economic systems, die under the push of the centuries; ideas crumble, but life is robust; it grows and cannot be ripped up, and time is continuous in life's true duration. Who will show us more efficient forms? Which great human will give us more solid foundations? Which genius will conceive for us a legend more elating than the prosaic story that is called life?

The fulfillment of our perception of the world under the aspects of space and time: that is the only goal of our plastic creation.

And we do not measure our work by the yardstick of beauty, we do not weigh it on the scales of tenderness and feeling. The plumb line in hand, the look accurate as a ruler, the mind rigid as a compass, we are building our works as the universe builds. This is why, when we represent objects, we are tearing up the labels their owners gave them, everything that is accidental and local, leaving them with just their essence and their permanence, to bring out the rhythm of the forces that hide in them.

1. In painting, we repudiate color as a pictorial element. Color is the idealized and optical face of the objects. The exterior impression is superficial. Color is accidental and has nothing in common with the internal content of bodies.

We proclaim that the tone of bodies, that is, their material substance absorbing the light, is their sole pictorial reality.

2. We deny the line its graphic value. In the real life of the bodies, there is nothing graphic. The line is only an accidental trace that humans leave on objects. It has no connection to essential life and to the permanent structure of things. The line is a merely graphic, illustrative, decorative element.

We acknowledge the line only as the direction of static forces that are hidden in the objects, and of their rhythms.

3. We disown volume as a plastic form of space. One cannot measure space by volumes just as one cannot measure a liquid in inches. Look at our real space: What is it if not a continuous depth?

We proclaim depth as the unique plastic form of space.

4. We disown, in sculpture, mass as a sculptural element. Every engineer knows that the static forces of solids, their material resistance, are not a function of their mass. Example: the rail, the buttress, the beam . . . But you sculptors of any trend and any nuance, you always cling to the old prejudice according to which it is impossible to free volume from mass. Like this: We take four planes and we make of them the same volume that we would make with a mass of one hundred pounds.

We thus restore to sculpture the line as direction, which prejudice had stolen from it. This way, we affirm in sculpture depth, the unique form of space.

5. We repudiate: the millennial error inherited from Egyptian art: static rhythms seen as the sole elements of plastic creation.

We proclaim a new element in plastic arts: the kinetic rhythms, which are essential forms of our perception of real time . . .

Art is called upon to accompany man everywhere where his tireless life takes place and acts: at the workbench, at the office, at work, at rest, and at leisure; work days and holidays, at home and on the road, so that the flame of life does not go out in man.

PEVSNER AND GABO
Realist Manifesto *(Excerpts)*

NAHUM GABO: KINETIC SCULPTURE. 1920. London. Tate Gallery

The French government fails in its most basic artistic duty: It renounces its right to preemption of the Kahnweiler estate, sequestered during the war because of the art dealer's German nationality. France loses an unanticipated opportunity to renew the collections in its national museums. But if Cubism is almost squelched, given the excessive number of canvases thrown onto the market, Picasso is not prevented from giving the movement its crowning glory: two simultaneous versions of *Three Musicians*. In the domain of architecture, the great innovation of the year appears to be *Mies van der Rohe's tower of the future,* a skyscraper with curved glass walls, which capture and give off light.

1921
S U M M A R Y

EVENTS

The Government Gives Up Its Masterworks
Where Does Cubist Sculpture Stand?
Portrait of an Art Dealer

DEVELOPMENTS

Picabia Persists and Signs
The Happiness of Vlaminck

ART NEWS

The Bauhaus Sends for Paul Klee
Dufy between Dream and Reality
The Poet of Sleep Dies
Marinetti's Latest Find
In Brief

MASTERWORKS

Picasso's Serene Music

ARCHITECTURE

Mies van der Rohe Invents the Tower of the Future
Mendelsohn: e=mc²

LITERATURE

GERMANY
Bertolt Brecht publishes
In the Jungle of Cities.

FRANCE
Death of the playwright Georges Feydeau.
  Publication of Suzanne and the Pacific *by Jean Giraudoux and* Si le grain ne meurt *by André Gide.*

ITALY
Publication of Luigi Pirandello's Six Characters in Search of an Author.

SWEDEN
Anatole France is awarded the Nobel prize.

MUSIC

GERMANY
Paul Hindemith creates, in Frankfurt, Murderer, Hope of Women, *based on the text by the painter Oskar Kokoschka.*

FRANCE
The Swedish Ballet performs The Eiffel Tower Wedding Party *by Jean Cocteau, with music by the Group of Six.*

SWITZERLAND
Premiere of Arthur Honegger's King David *at Mézières.*

MOTION PICTURES

GERMANY
Hans Richter creates Rhythm 21.

UNITED STATES
Premiere of The Kid *with Charlie Chaplin and* Dream Street *by D. W. Griffith.*

GEORGES BRAQUE:
MAN WITH A GUITAR. 1914.
Paris. MNAM

THE GOVERNMENT GIVES UP ITS MASTERWORKS

KEES VAN DONGEN: PORTRAIT OF KAHNWEILER. 1907.
Geneva. Musée du Petit-Palais

FERNAND LÉGER: WOMAN IN BLUE. 1912. Basel. Kunstmuseum

PARIS

The first two Kahnweiler auctions take place on June 13-14 and on November 17 at the Drouot mansion. When the war was declared, the dealer of the Rue Vignon—who now has a gallery in the Rue d'Astorg—left Paris for Rome and Bern. Like his compatriot Wilhelm Uhde, he learns of the seizure of his assets at the onset of the conflict. Article 297 of the Treaty of Versailles gives France the right to liquidate the confiscated assets of German subjects. On October 7, 1919, Parliament passes a law regulating the formalities of such liquidations. Though the law may be perfectly suitable for liquidations of industrial and commercial companies, it should not have been meant to include the art market.

The works of art in Kahnweiler's possession pose a particu-larly delicate problem because the collection includes 1,500 paintings, watercolors, and prints representative of contemporary art. Three hundred and sixty-five are sold at the first two auctions: Fifty-seven Braques, sixty-three Derains, twenty-four Grises, seventeen Légers, seventy-two Picassos, thirty-three Van Dongens, ninety-nine Vlamincks, plus a number of gouaches and drawings—the dispersion of the fabulous treasure underscores the enormity of neglect on the part of the ministries involved.

Paul Léon, director of the Beaux-Arts Academy, simply neglects the possibility of suspending the liquidation of artistic works or the right of preemption on the part of the government, which could have bought a large part of the works at a good price. The national

museums pass up an excellent opportunity for expansion and renewal. As a matter of fact, they are not even represented at the auction. Because the Beaux-Arts Academy is sinking deeper and deeper into the defense of reactionary values, it views the Cubists as nothing more than "Boches" or Bolsheviks."

On top of that, the Rosenbergs—Paul and Léonce—who usually are enlightened dealers, now focus on the tame and watered-down Cubism of imitators. They are wary of the smell of scandal that continues to emanate from pre-1914 canvases. Not only do the pair push cir-

cumspection and caution to the point of not buying anything at the two auctions: Léonce—a catalog and assessment expert —plays the role of liquidator.

Braque, affected by the world conflict, can no longer bear seeing paintings assessed below their value just because they flood the market. After hitting Léonce Rosenberg in the stomach and breaking his walking stick on "that bastard" in the Drouot exhibition room before the auction even starts, the painter goes into such a rage that nothing can bring him back to reason except the intervention of two policemen, who drag him off to the station under the astonished eyes of the audience.

The incident illustrates the disappointment felt by artists for whom Kahnweiler was the principal buyer before the war. Kahn weiler, himself, had neither the inclination nor the courage to attend his own liquidation. Nevertheless, under the name of "Grassat," he founds a small association which includes his friend Hermann Rupf, the German dealer Alfred Flechtheim, and his brother Gustave. Because funds at his disposal are scarce, he has to limit himself to the purchase of a few canvases by Léger, Gris, Derain, Van Dongen, and Vlaminck that no one else wants.

But even if the painters have good reason to complain about the collapse of prices—Braque's *Man with a Guitar* sold for as little as 2,400 francs and Léger's *Woman in Blue* for 2,500 francs—they do not, paradoxically, end up as losers. Indeed, the low prices allow a number of dealers, especially from abroad, to buy large numbers of their paintings, some of which wind up in major international collections. The painters' images are greatly enhanced, contrary to the intention of the adversaries.

Paul Léon himself is responsible for the negligence on the part of the government—he does not meet the obligations of his office. His attitude is not one of innocence. He is a worldly, sleek talker who assumes this attitude to win over the Academy and the members of the Institute, to which he is eager to be elected.

The liquidation of the Uhde collection last year brought in 168,000 francs, while expectations were for 100,000 francs. The two Kahnweiler auctions confirm the tendency—they bring in, respectively, 216,335 francs and 175,215 francs. There are predictions that there will be great interest in the next two auctions. This belies Franz Jourdain, who was inspired by the declaration of war to utter this cry of stupidity: "Finally, Cubism is screwed."

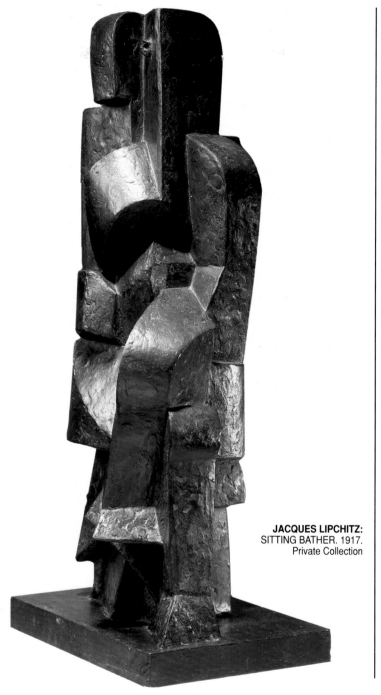

JACQUES LIPCHITZ:
SITTING BATHER. 1917.
Private Collection

WHERE DOES CUBIST SCULPTURE STAND?

PARIS

With Ossip Zadkine, Henri Laurens, Raymond Duchamp-Villon, Archipenko, and Jacques Lipchitz, Cubism recently has gone to its limits in the domain of sculpture. Long ago, the first constructions by Pablo Picasso laid down the foundations of the new sculptural grammar: polychromy, integration of varied materials, and especially the rhythmic use of planes and the appearance of forms through "latticework." As with painting, Cubist sculpture is essentially dedicated to the relationship between objects and space. This is evident in the fact that equal space is given to the volumes and the voids that separate them. The influence of Italian Futurism, mainly of Boccioni, has led the Cubist sculptors, particularly Duchamp-Villon and Jacques Lipchitz, to work with dynamic forms. In the work of Lipchitz, the planes are cleverly deployed according to a rhythmic "verticality," a development of the volumes around their axis. Archipenko and Laurens explore the possibilities of the dialectic of concave and convex forms. Zadkine introduces lyricism, sometimes of a baroque nature. Above all, Cubist sculpture remains the area where perspectives opened up by Cubist painting find application.

PORTRAIT OF AN ART DEALER

PARIS

Notwithstanding the injustice that strikes him, Daniel-Henry Kahnweiler does not hesistate to regain confidence. He knows that art does not go away and is convinced that "it is great painters that make great dealers." After all, he is only thirty-seven years old. He was twenty-three when he opened an art gallery at 28 Rue Vignon.

This young German Jew, born in Mannheim on June 25, 1884, to a family of bankers, discovers painting at the Museum of Karlsruhe. Passionate about art, he is captivated in 1903 by Cézanne and the Fauves. In 1907 he decides to become an art dealer in Paris. On the advice of his compatriot Wilhelm Uhde, he pays a visit to Pablo Picasso to see *Les demoiselles d'Avignon.*

From his first glance, he knows that a new era in painting is being heralded. He meets again the next day with Picasso, and they are together from then on.

He now reestablishes himself in the old stables in the Rue d'Astorg and starts looking after the most beautiful thoroughbreds of the "stable" over which he presides—the Cubists. Picasso and Gris are his favorites.

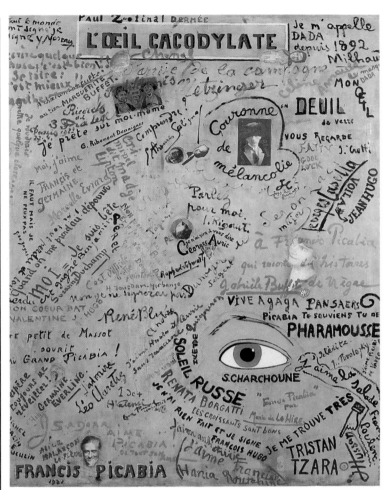

FRANCIS PICABIA: CACODYLIC EYE. 1921. Paris. MNAM

PICABIA PERSISTS AND SIGNS

PARIS

"Dada will live forever! And I will remain Francis Picabia!" Isn't the enthusiasm of the most turbulent of the Dadaists merely a façade? On May 11, in *Comœdia*, Picabia announces that he wants to break with the group that had started to form around him in the previous year. The friendship and perfect understanding between Tzara and Picabia has started to fray; the warm ambience of the early days in Zurich has made room for suspicion and envy. Gone is the wonderful harmony of those Sundays in the Rue Émile-Augier, where Aragon, Éluard, Auric, Ribemont-Dessaignes, Crotti, and others would gather. It is Cocteau who finds the right words to sum up the situation. Running into Picabia, who is suffering from herpes ophthalmicus, he declares, "After a long illness, Picabia is cured. I actually saw Dada come out of his eyes."

Cured? Probably. Of Dada? Less likely. If there was ever an artist who does not give an inch in terms of his rebellions and provocations, it is certainly Picabia. Witness the—collective—painting *Cacodylic Eye*, that he signed himself and had signed by his friends. Faithful to his principle that "Art with a capital A is everywhere," and considering that (according to him) the value of a painting depends on the signature, Picabia makes a simple calcuation: the more signatures, the more the painting is worth. Accordingly, he places around the painting of an eye—his eye, after a treatment with sodium cacodylate—the initials and jokes of his friends. Milhaud, Poulenc, Jean Hugo, Pansaers, Soupault, Péret, and dozens of others contributed their graffiti and quips. There is no doubt about it: Dada is not dead.

THE HAPPINESS OF VLAMINCK

PARIS

The people in Paris are very familiar with the imposing figure of Maurice de Vlaminck. At the moment, the artist participates in a show at the Bernheim-Jeune gallery, where his self-portrait is surrounded by works of the greatest contemporary painters. The portrait is successful with those who appreciate its vigor and sparseness.

At the age of forty-five, Vlaminck has depicted himself without flattery, though not without humor, that is, with the characteristic lucidity of a man who manages to impress. He is duly famous. Since his prestigious show two years ago at the Druet gallery, he has established himself as one of the major figures in French painting. The words written by Gustave Goeffroy in the introduction to the catalogue have been confirmed: "An ever more pronounced return to expressive painting, a continuous development of a particular sensitivity expressed in forms that are rough and summary in overall effect . . ."

Vlaminck is blessed by fate. He has bought a house for 10,000 francs in Valmondois after selling a number of paintings to the Swedish dealer Halversen, in 1919, and has vacated his studio in the Rue du Départ. He is remarried, to Berthe Combe, who bears him a girl, his fourth; he has three girls from his first marriage, to Suzanne Berly. He is a famous, rich, happy painter whose talent is generally recognized. Vlaminck's life destroys the myth of the artist rejected by society.

Vlaminck with his Self-Portrait.

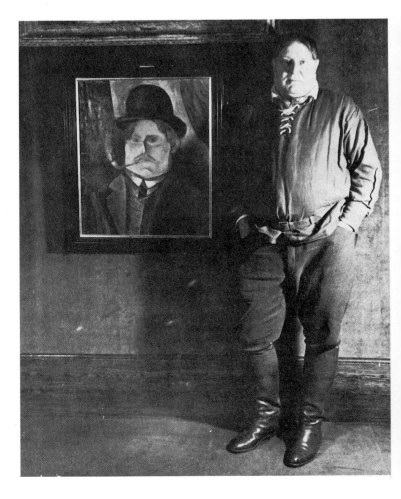

The Bauhaus Sends for Paul Klee

In October of last year, a telegram caught Klee by surprise in Ascona, Italian Switzerland, where he was staying with friends Jawlensky and Marianne von Werefkin. "My dear Paul Klee," reads the message, "we unanimously invite you to accept a chair at the Bauhaus in Weimar." It was signed by Walter Gropius, director of the famous school, as well as by several professors, including Lyonel Feininger and Johannes Itten. The Bauhaus' declared goal is to combine fine arts and applied arts in an integral whole. After taking up his duties at the beginning of January, Klee, who is at his prime at the age of forty-two, will teach the grammar of forms.

Dufy between Dream and Reality

The painter from Normandy, Raoul Dufy, now forty-four, has discovered the warm colors of the Provence in Vence, and is establishing himself as one of the greatest colorists of the times. His views of Vence, exhibited at the Bernheim-Jeune gallery, are proof of the fact, as are seven fabrics he presents at the Salon des Artists Décorateurs. Encouraged by the designer Paul Poiret, over the past ten years, he has been involved in printing textile designs. He has set up a studio on the Boulevard de Clichy, where he now creates arabesque patterns of fruits and flowers to decorate his fabrics.

The Poet of Sleep Dies

A glass of punch and an opera chandelier shone more brightly to his eye than the sun. When Fernand Khnopff dies in Brussels on November 12 at the age of sixty-three, the whole decadent and Symbolist era dies, too. With him disappear the fashions of Wagneromania, a belief in the occult, absinthe, and a cast of stars, including Joséphin Péladan, Khnopff's close friend who would dress up like Nebuchadnezzar and call himself the sandwich man of the hereafter. In his paintings, women are depicted as souls, and landscapes are induced dreams, as if the artist worked with his eyes closed. He had basically been a forgotten man for the past twenty years.

Marinetti's Latest Find

To attract attention, the passionate founder of Futurism, Filippo Tommaso Marinetti, who had his own armored car built at the end of the war, has become a sculptor. The poet has freely expressed his objections to the haphazard accumulation of miscellaneous junk. The work he now shows is meant to be touched by viewers. Its principal components are a cheese grater, a sponge, a piece of cork, and various pieces of fabric nailed to a cardboard backing. The cheese grater is probably a message aimed at his compatriots whose flabbiness he explains by their abuse of pasta and Parmesan. Closer to Dada than to Futurism, the work is mysteriously named *Paris-Sudan*.

FILIPPO TOMMASO MARINETTI: PARIS-SUDAN. 1921. Private Collection

RAOUL DUFY: VENCE SCENERY. 1920. Private Collection

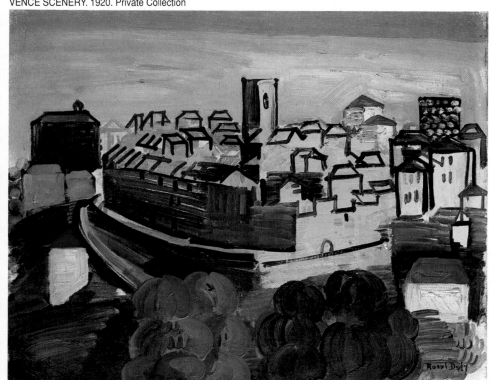

PICASSO'S SERENE MUSIC

FONTAINEBLEAU

Cubism is dead, long live Cubism! At a time when Picasso, now rich and famous, seems to have abandoned Cubism, he gives it its masterpiece, *Three Musicians,* in two simultaneous versions, each measuring about 6 1/2 x 7 feet.

While he spends the summer at Fontainebleau, where he has rented a villa with his wife, Olga, and his son Paulo, born on February 4, to give the baby some fresh country air, he performs one of those sudden reversals of which he seems to know so well. The rare visitors privileged enough to enter his studio

can't believe their eyes. In recent years, he had become everyone's painter, having returned to traditional subjects and techniques. All of a sudden, he seems to be back in the front lines of modernity.

Inspired by Italian comedy, both versions of the canvas show a Pierrot, a Harlequin, and a monk—all three musicians, larger than life, standing in back of a table. One of the paintings, the second, is more involved, more elaborate than the first, which pushes the art of painting to a degree of purity rarely achieved.

With its large brown, ocher, blue, and ivory-white areas,

which overlap and are juxtaposed at the same time, the setting is worthy of Velásquez or Zurbarán, as the dark sonorities remind us. What are the three people doing? Pierrot plays the clarinet, Harlequin the guitar, and the monk has a music sheet on his knees. Under the table lies a wolfhound with a wide-open mouth. But these paper-thin figures do not belong to the world of the living. They are masks, effigies nailed down by the play of light and shadow on the stage of eternity.

Picasso undoubtedly remembers the costumes from *Parade,* painted in 1917, where he broke

up the bodies of the dancers by means of geometric shapes. Now he has raised Synthetic Cubism to the peak of its creative tension, forcing it to reconstruct something visible from the mere formal intentions of the artist.

Another source of surprise for Picasso's visitors lies in the fact that next to the two versions of the *Three Musicians,* the Fontainebleau studio contains a painting that is the exact opposite. It depicts a trio of female giants with immense legs and feet, matte complexions and wide-spread eyes—*Three Women at the Fountain.*

PABLO PICASSO: THREE MUSICIANS. 1921. New York. MOMA

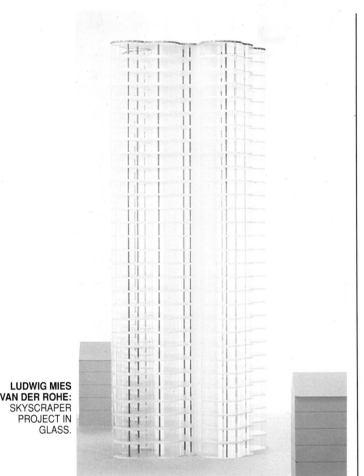

LUDWIG MIES VAN DER ROHE: SKYSCRAPER PROJECT IN GLASS.

MIES VAN DER ROHE INVENTS THE TOWER OF THE FUTURE

BERLIN

Transparent architecture? This revolutionary idea has become reality, thanks to Ludwig Mies van der Rohe and his "glass skyscraper" project, which is striking in its extreme lightness and simplicity.

Mies' development is far from ordinary. Because his real name, Ludwig Mies, did not please him—Mies in German means miserable, poor, wretched—he added his mother's maiden name. He was born in 1886. His father was a stonecutter. He discovers architecture while contemplating the aerial vaults of the cathedral of Aachen, his hometown. He works for a stucco expert, moving up from messenger to draftsman, active in all styles: "Louis Quatorze in the morning, Renaissance at night."

In 1908, in Berlin, he enters the Behrens studio with Walter Gropius. He is influenced by Behren's Neoclassicism. In the project of a skyscraper consisting of a metal skeleton and a glass envelope, his style finds its expression. The transparent building challenges the concept of materiality and reveals its structure. The façades, traditionally bearing-walls, are transformed into glass walls, while the skeleton supports the floors.

The birth of the curtain wall signifies a break with traditional walls. The architecture is purified. rendered naked. Glass replaces stone or concrete. He discovers new possibilities based on the play of reflection and no longer on the effects of light and shadow.

MENDELSOHN: e=mc²

ALLENSTEIN

From now on, Albert Einstein will have his tower and Expressionism its masterpiece. Erich Mendelsohn completes the construction in Prussia of what is to become the astronomical laboratory for the founder of the theory of relativity. It is the first major work by the thirty-four-year-old architect, who studied in Munich, where he sought the company of the painters of the Blue Rider.

The origins of Mendelsohn's tower were a series of sketches made at the Russian front. He wrote to a friend, "My sketches are nothing but notes, outlines of fugitive visions, although they appear immediately as entities because of their nature as buildings." The year was 1917.

In 1919, he exhibits his sketches at the gallery of Paul Cassirer in Berlin. In the same year, he starts building the Einstein Tower, pursuing a dream that has haunted him for years. The body of the tower rises from the ground and soars like a fluid mass. The cement envelope underscores the play of light on the protuberances and hollow parts. Originally, Mendelsohn wanted to use reinforced concrete, which would have freed him entirely from the constraints of right angles and the vertical alignment of floors. For technical reasons, only the substructure and the upper part are in concrete. The rest is in brick coated with a layer of mortar.

The Einstein Tower is also a remarkable tool. The light from the cosmos is captured, then reflected by the telescope and projected on spectrographic instruments in the lower part.

The Einstein Tower by Mendelsohn in Allenstein.

The event of the year is the publication in Heidelberg of a book by Hans Prinzhorn, *Die Bildnerei der Geisteskranken, which deals with plastic art of the mentally ill. As early as 1912, Klee had taken an interest in the drawings and paintings of the insane. But with Prinzhorn, a philosopher, psychotherapist, and art historian, the art of the insane makes an erudite entry into contemporary culture. Meanwhile, artists flock to Montparnasse from the four corners of the earth, and fill the sidewalk cafés and give wild parties.*
All this is in distinct contrast to the order reigning in Moscow, where the Russian avant-garde is brought into line under the guise of restoring equilibrium and sanity to the workers.

1922

S U M M A R Y

WRITINGS AND THEORIES

Prinzhorn Discloses the Art of the Mentally Ill
Prinzhorn: a Schizophrenic Impression of the World

DEVELOPMENTS

Kokoschka's Crime
André Lhote Opens an Academy

ART NEWS

Uccello Lives Again on the Walls of Mexico
Kandinsky Leaves Russia
The Justified Anger of "Mister Punch"
The Belgians Are Busy
Man Ray Creates "Rayographs"
In Brief

ART AND TRADITION

The Return of the Beautiful Craft
Daily Life in Montparnasse

ART AND THE REVOLUTION

Abstract Art Forbidden in the Soviet Union

ANONYMOUS:
MAN'S HEAD

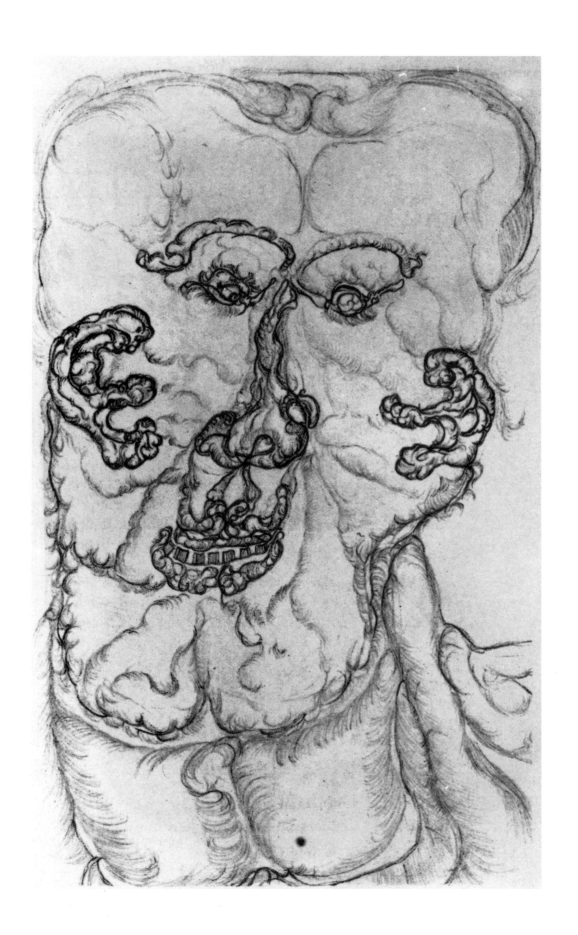

PRINZHORN DISCLOSES THE ART OF THE MENTALLY ILL

HEIDELBERG

Klee noticed that geniuses are sometimes locked up behind the walls of our asylums. In 1912, he wrote in the magazine *Die Alpen,* "The works of the alienated should be taken more seriously than all the museums of fine arts together, if we want to reform art today. In order not to rely on archaic techniques, we have to reach higher." However, there was no reference work that offered a scientific basis for what, until now, was derived only from intuition.

Such a work has just now been published by Springer Verlag under the title *Die Bildnerei der Geisteskranken*, which can be translated, roughly, as "the creative imagery of the mentally ill." The author is Hans Prinzhorn, a thirty-six-year-old man of many talents. He is a psychotherapist, a philosopher, an art historian, and a baritone blessed with a beautiful voice. Since January 30, 1919, he has worked as an assistant to Professor Wilmanns at the psychiatric clinic of Heidelberg. In two and a half years of hard work, he has gathered about five thousand drawings, paintings, and sculptures of schizophrenics. This collection constitutes the basis of his book.

Unusual artists! There is August Neter, fifty-four years old, who saw in a cloud the creative witch of the world. There is

ANONYMOUS:
HOLY PERSON.
Heidelberg. Prinzhorn
Collection

ANONYMOUS:
MARVELOUS SHEPHERD.
Heidelberg. Prinzhorn Collection

"A CAPACITY THAT LIVES IN EVERYONE BUT WHICH USUALLY REMAINS LATENT OR ATROPHIES"

Franz Pohl, a fine ironworker of fifty-eight who, assuming he was personally attacked, understood "he's crazy" instead of "he has arrived" when the conductor announced the last stop of the streetcar that took him home every night. The cry caused Pohl to fly into dark rages which led to his confinement. There is Heinrich Welz, a thirty-nine-year-old baron with a doctorate in law, who is not satisfied with creating paintings by the exercise of his will alone. He engages in strange rotations to overcome gravity. All of these individuals have been hospitalized for several years for schizophrenia. All draw their inspiration from the abysses of art.

Prinzhorn warns the reader from the onset that he is not the first researcher who has been interested in the artistic pursuits of the mentally ill. He mentions, among others, the Italian psychiatrist Cesare Lombroso and the French author Marcel Réja, who prepared the way at the end of the previous century and the beginning of this century. The innovative aspect of Prinzhorn's approach to the book, however, is that he never uses the works of the patients for diagnostic purposes. On the contrary, he asks the question why mentally sound persons have an esthetic interest in the works of alienated people, and he outlines a reply: Clandestinely and with absurd means, they express "a capacity that lives in everyone but which usually remains latent or atrophies." This is true to the extent that there is often a striking similarity between what they produce and what many contemporary artists actually experience.

Indeed, the hallucinatory *Skirt Metamorphoses* by August Neter resembles the collages of Max Ernst. The enigmatic and at the same time precise curves of Heinrich Welz evoke Marcel Duchamp's sketches for his "bachelor machines." The Austrian painter and draftsman Alfred Kubin, who visits the Heidelberg collection in February, does not hesitate to write about Franz Pohl in the magazine *Kunstblatt;* "My strongest impression is that of the oils and crayon drawings of an ironworker living at the Emmendingen asylum." "The innate inventive power points to a master of the highest order."

Prinzhorn also talks as a sociologist, and concludes: "This affinity for the 'schizophrenic' world is essentially the same affinity that twenty years ago explored forms of expression and experiences from the worlds of the child and the primitive—in protest against the tentacular rationalism of past generations, in which the best saw themselves as suffocating." "The best" refers to Klee, Kandinsky, Picasso, Matisse, and especially Gaugin, who was the first to express enthusiasm for Primitivism. As the book appears, it becomes the topic of discussion in the German and European avant-garde.

PRINZHORN: A SCHIZOPHRENIC IMPRESSION OF THE WORLD

The first work to consider the drawings, paintings, and sculptures of the mentally ill as such, without any clinical concern, Hans Prinzhorn's *Die Bildnerei der Geisteskranken*, is already seen as a classic on the matter. Klee and Kandinsky included it in their libraries at the Bauhaus in Weimar, where, as in other places, it gave rise to lively and profound discussions on the origin and direction of artistic creation. An excerpt from the concluding part follows.

It is a surprising fact that the relationship between the sensations of schizophrenia and the sensations that are manifest in contemporary art has to be evoked in the same terms. But when making this observation, we also must establish the differences between the two, which is not a difficult task. With the schizophrenic, the experience is like destiny. He becomes detached from the world of the senses and is torn apart as if he were the victim of a cruel and unavoidable fate against which he often wages a long struggle, before surrendering and gradually feeling at home in his autistic world, enriched by delirium. With the contemporary artist, the detachment from reality, familiar and even courted as of late, is also the result of an experience, but this detachment is more or less the effect of judgment and resolution. It is the result of the sorrowful awakening of an individual for whom traditional ties with the world have become unbearable.

We do not want to devote further attention to the disintegration of the impression of the traditional world, from which this eccentric attitude develops in an often grandiose manner and still more often through something like a convulsive distortion. At any rate, this phenomenon is not simply a product of Expressionism, as some shortsighted people would apparently still have us believe. On the contrary, Expressionism is an interpretation of this disintegration, an attempt to put it to use. If we set aside the confusion of manifestos and try to grasp the idea that serves as stimulus and which continually leads to new exaltations, we find a burning desire of inspired creation, the kind that would exist among primitive peoples and which we know from the great eras of cultures. Here we touch upon the ill side of our time, its tragedy and its distortions.

However little attention we may pay to contemporary forms of expression, we discover everywhere, in the plastic arts as in the various literary genres, a series of tendencies that would reach their highest pitch only in a true schizophrenic. Our intention, however, is not to find signs of mental illness in these forms of expression. We simply sense throughout these forms an affinity for particularities we recognize as distinctive characteristics of schizophrenics. This explains the kinship among the works of our collection, and the fascination they evoke.

This affinity for the "schizophrenic" world is essentially the same affinity that twenty years ago explored forms of expression and experiences from the worlds of the child and the primitive—in protest against the tentacular rationalism of past generations, in which the best saw themselves as suffocating.

HANS PRINZHORN
Die Bildnerei der
Geisteskranken *(Excerpt)*

ANONYMOUS:
MAN IN A
STRAITJACKET.
Heidelberg.
Prinzhorn Collection

KOKOSCHKA'S CRIME

OSKAR KOKOSCHKA:
MAN AND PUPPET.
1922. Berlin.
Staatliches Museum

DRESDEN

Could a professor from the Academy of Fine Arts be a murderer? This is what the Dresden police, called to the scene, considered for a moment. A young woman lies beheaded in the yard, surrounded by cries, at the break of day following a festive night. The police check the evidence . . . the victim is a doll.

That morning, the painter Kokoschka exorcises his past at the age of thirty-six. Never having succeeded in accepting the rupture with Alma Mahler in 1915, and having joined the war hoping to die of heartbreak, he has a life-size doll made in the image of his beloved. To dress it as elegantly as Alma herself, he buys lingerie and dresses from the best couturiers in Paris. He keeps her at his side at all times. He takes her for rides in his carriage on sunny days. He even hires, rumor has it, a box for her at the Opera.

Enough is enough. After making abundant drawings and paintings of Alma, he is cured of his unhappy passion. To celebrate his new position as professor, he installs a chamber orchestra in a fountain, and arranges for torches, champagne, and numerous guests. At dawn, Kokoschka fractures the skull of the doll with a bottle of red wine. It is the end of a crazy night, when everyone is drunk.

ANDRÉ LHOTE OPENS AN ACADEMY

PARIS

His taste for discussions on esthetics and his militant defense of the Cubist cause make André Lhote a natural as a professor of painting. Accordingly, he has opened an academy, at the end of a street in the Montparnasse quarter, the Rue du Départ. Yet another academy, peevish people say, in an area where there are already plenty!

Dozens of young men and women assiduously attend his weekly class to profit from his lessons. Ascending a staircase, which is as steep as a ladder, they arrive in a large room where the silence is impressive. The comments and advice of the master are absorbed with concentrated attention. Lhote, an excellent pedagogue, closely follows the work of each student and repeats, whenever necessary, the explanations he dispenses so generously. Though he exercises great authority over the class, his ideas are in harmony with those of his students.

It is not the first time that Lhote has worked as a professor. In 1918, he started teaching at the Académie de Notre-Dame-des-Champs. He stayed for two years, then a year ago joined the Modern Academy at 240 Boulevard Raspail, where he continues to teach to this day. In 1917, Lhote participated in the creation of the Synthetic Cubism group with Braque, Maria Blanchard, and Metzinger, all supported by the art dealer Léonce Rosenberg. The following year, he submitted articles to the *Nouvelle revue française*, as a fervent defender of the group and its theories. Lhote has also announced a series of speeches in France and abroad. And he plans monographs on Corot and Seurat.

His students benefit from his immense cultural knowledge and especially from his qualities as a painter, which were recognized following his show in 1920 at the Druet gallery. Lhote teaches—from a life model—how to give predominance to the mass by multiplying the points of view, and how to use a limited palette with flat colors. In a few years, a new generation of young talents may emerge from this nursery.

ANDRÉ LHOTE: RUGBY.
1917. Paris. MNAM

Uccello Lives Again on the Walls of Mexico

Jean Charlot, a young Frenchman, is the first artist to have completed one of the frescoes in Mexico's ambitious mural program, established by José Vasconcelos, minister of public education. In the main stairway of the National Preparatory School of Mexico, Charlot, just off the boat from France, has completed *The Massacre in the Great Temple*, inspired by an incident in the conquest of Mexico. The fresco is a direct descendant of both pre-Columbian mural art and modern artists such as Matisse and Léger. But perhaps most striking is the solid geometric structure of *The Massacre* that relates it to Uccello's *Battle of San Romano*.

Kandinsky Leaves Russia

Is it the end of the revolutionary spring in Russia? Wassili Kandinsky, founder of the Academy of Arts where he occupied the position of vice-president, has decided to leave his country. He is neither a Marxist nor a Communist, so Pjotr Kogan, a proclaimed Marxist, is named president in his place. Kandinsky had taken an active role in popularizing the arts after the Revolution had begun, creating twenty-two provincial museums. The story goes that three peasants wandered into his last exhibition in Moscow by mistake. When they saw his paintings, they commented, "We don't understand a thing, but they make us feel as if we're in a church." A dangerous sentiment, shared, no doubt, by the atheist masters of the regime. Kandinsky leaves for Weimar, Germany, where Walter Gropius has invited him to teach at the Bauhaus.

The Justified Anger of "Mister Punch"

An incident at the Salon d'Automne in Paris: This year, Robert Delaunay is exhibiting *Manège of Pigs*, one of his most important works since the famous *Homage to Blériot*, painted in 1914. The painting of a carnival merry-go-round is composed of multicolored circles that seem to spin in space.

ROBERT DELAUNAY:
MANEGE OF PIGS.
1922. Paris. MNAM

To show that the work has nothing to do with the easel painting people hang on their apartment walls, Delaunay exhibited it flat on the floor, something Georges Rouault failed to appreciate when he walked over the painting and insulted the artist. The irascible Delaunay, nicknamed "Monsieur coup de poing" (Mr. Punch) by his friends, almost pulverized him, but his wife, Sonia, intervened before the incident got out of hand.

The Belgians Are Busy

New magazines are flooding Belgium. *Salopes,* with snappy illustrations and text by Paul Joostens, makes its first appearance in Anvers, following Paul Van Ostaijen's *Bezette Stad*, illustrated by Oscar Jespers. Besides these two excellent publications there are *Sélection,* with its Expressionist tendencies, and *Le disque vert* (the green disk), more literary in tone. Also newcomers are the Anvers magazine *Het Overzicht*, under the poet Michel Seuphor and the painter Jozef Peeters, and the Brussels magazine *7 Arts*. Two friends, Victor Servranckx and René Magritte, announce their manifesto on "Pure Art."

Man Ray Creates "Rayographs"

The album published by the American painter and photographer Man Ray under the title *Champs délicieux* (delicious fields) with a preface by Tristan Tzara is due to fortunate circumstances. At Ray's Paris home at the Hôtel des Écoles on the Rue Delambre, the artist had laid some keys, cotton balls, and bits of string on pieces of light-sensitive paper, inadvertently left exposed to light. The result was a world of mysterious, shadowy visions. The artist developed the process, and called these new works "rayographs," a kind of dark print of reality.

THE RETURN OF THE BEAUTIFUL CRAFT

PARIS

Since the end of the war, there has been a return to Naturalism by numerous painters. The time of innovations and scandalous experiments appears to have come to an end. Everyone seems conscious of the fact that theories alone are not sufficient to complete a work. The artist returns to tradition, in order to find a solid and sure basis. From Picasso to Braque, by way of all of yesterday's followers of Cubism—Derain, Bissière, Dufy, Hayden—who knows how many others execute the reversal. They are united by a passion which they raise to the level of "the beautiful craft." Evidence is provided by exhibits of "Young French Painting," first at the Manzi-Joyant gallery, later in various cities in France.

ANDRÉ DERAIN:
KITCHEN TABLE. Paris
Musée de l'Orangerie

DAILY LIFE IN MONTPARNASSE

PARIS

Montparnasse is celebrating. People are still far from having satisfied their hunger for pleasure, light, and waste, reborn at the time of the armistice, after four years of austerity.

Fascinated artists and refugees make Montparnasse the end of their wanderings. The area changes practically overnight, retaining little of its former character. It is Montparnasse that for the longest time was quiet and rural, with farms and orchards, and with numerous stables and coachhouses for the horses and carriages of the Parisian transportation system. Now, as soon as the stables become empty, they are transformed into studios for painters and sculptors.

Every day, bars, hotels, cafés, dance halls, and restaurants are opened, but the artists prefer to gather at the Dôme or La Rotonde around a café crème, the fashionable drink of the day. Even before the war, they gathered here to discuss the future of art or to dwell on their misery, rubbing elbows with Germans, Scandinavians, and exiled Bolsheviks. Today, more and more pleasure seekers hang out with the artists and a cosmopolitan fauna, including Pascin, Foujita, Soutine, Léger, Zadkine, Diego Rivera, Kisling, Marcoussis, Van Dongen, Krémègne, Derain, Othon Friesz, Cendrars, Max Jacob, Salmon, and Cocteau. Picasso is not often seen. He is living like a bourgeois on the Rue La Boétie. The same is true for Vlaminck, who likes the countryside better than Paris. Chagall doesn't appear at all. He is in Berlin, trying to retrieve some of his canvases.

At the Dôme, but especially at La Rotonde, a young, carefree, well-built woman, Kiki, is often seen. She is a model for Kisling, Foujita, and Derain. She has a tumultuous love affair with Man Ray, an artist from Philadelphia, who is close to Marcel Duchamp, whom he got to know in New York City. When Man Ray arrived in Paris in 1920, he was welcomed by the Dadaists. He bought a large camera and photographs the paintings of Braque and Picasso and others.

Disappointed by the Puritanism that prevails in the United States, Americans are arriving here in ever-larger numbers to look for anticonformism, a carefree life, the exchange of ideas and . . . alcohol, which is no longer available at home because of Prohibition. Two young arrivals are a sportswriter for the *Toronto Star,* Ernest Hemingway, and the poet Ezra Pound. Each newcomer has the duty to visit Gertrude Stein, the intimidating doyenne of the Americans in Paris. She arrived here in 1904, and in 1906 Picasso painted her portrait. Even more numerous than the citizens from the New World are the Jews from Central Europe and Russia, who started to arrive in waves even before the war. They are building a reputation. The celebrations, which often involve costume parties, are becoming more and more numerous and boisterous. They are held at Bal Bullier or at an artist's lucky enough to have a large studio, as Pascin does. The extraordinary atmosphere of freedom that prevails in Montparnasse attracts thousands of people. This area may, like Montmartre, be invaded by tourists.

ABSTRACT ART FORBIDDEN IN THE SOVIET UNION

MOSCOW

The Russian capital is swept clean. After the economic restructuring (NEP) that started a year ago, the authorities have decided to put order in what seems to be the only area that still escapes their control—the world of art. Both Trotsky and Lenin bang their fists on the

WHAT ARE THE NEW GUIDELINES? CREATE A REALISM GEARED TOWARD THE PEOPLE

table. In *Marxism and Futurism* Trotsky accuses the advocates of the avant-garde of "idealism." Lenin expresses his severe doubts about modern art: "I don't understand anything about it, and it doesn't give me any pleasure."

Censorship is again imposed, Lunacharski, the people's commissar for public instruction, who once cast a sympathetic eye on the new trends, now objects to Futurism, which he claims "is detested by the Proletariat."

In this context, "Futurism" refers to all innovative movements, including Suprematism and Constructivism, not just Futurism. In this sense, the term has virtually been abandoned by the artists. Lunacharski creates confusion by reminding the Russian avant-garde of the Fascist components of Italian Futurism. However, the Russian avant-garde has always marched on the side of the Revolution, which today's authorities seem to have forgotten. Since the early years of the century, the avant-garde has developed solid roots. The artistic life in Petrograd, then St. Petersburg, was lively. Moscow had been a focus for all of European art. Russian artists visited the Western capitals and returned with a harvest of ideas. For Malevich, "Cubism and Futurism were revolutionary art movements that preceded the Revolution in the economic and political life." With the advent of Bolshevism, the creators fully adhered to the

program of the Revolution. They viewed themselves as active participants in social movements.

Since 1918, the old art schools have been replaced and avant-gardists appointed to head the new institutions. At IZO (the art department of the commissariat of public instruction), Rozanova is put in charge of museography.

At Inkhouk (the Institute of Artistic Culture), Kandinsky occupies himself with the ties between the search for form and its social application. The onset of the Revolution sees the blossoming of Propaganda Art (agitprop), its mission to erect temporary structures for festivals and celebrations, to create temporary decorations, to put the idea of a synthesis of the arts to practical use. Abstractionism finds its place as a matter of course; for example, for Lissitsky, who designs platforms and posters, it is necessary to give the people simple and recognizable forms.

The authorities are attacking Abstractionism for "being too removed from the people." Three years ago, Lenin gained permission to close down *The Art of the Commune*, the official organ of the avant-garde. This was followed by the dissolution of the Proletkult. Last year, Lenin did not hesitate to talk about reeducating the intellectuals. In recent months, the attacks have doubled in intensity, and they have

changed in nature. The authorities not only want to impose a function upon the arts, they criticize its very essence.

What are the new guidelines? Lenin's tastes are known. They are expressed in the program of the Association of Revolutionary Painters, established in February: A Realism geared toward the people, refreshed with new themes. Labor, the economy of the country, and the Revolution are glorified. New names appear in the foreground, for example, Kisselis and Guerassimov. Interest is aimed at those rejecting a formal approach. If these tendencies persist, the risk exists of a general deterioration in artistic creation in a country that has enjoyed of a richness without precedence.

(See also 1930 and 1935.)

ALEXANDRE GUERASSIMOV: MASTER OF THE HEATH. 1918. Moscow. Tretiakow Gallery

The year turns out to be exceptionally fortunate for Soutine. The great American collector Albert C. Barnes, who comes specifically to visit the artist in his studio at La Ruche, buys one hundred canvases from him at a time. Perhaps even more important is the position taken by Marcel Duchamp, who declares "definitively incomplete" his major work,* The Bride Stripped Bare by Her Bachelors. *Begun in 1912, the painting does in fact emphasize the dual notion of completion and incompletion in a work of art. Manet had first proposed the notion in 1863, when his* Luncheon on the Grass *introduced into modern art the concept of the "Sketch Style," poorly understood at the time.

1923

SUMMARY

AVANT-GARDE

The Bride's Secret
Marcel Duchamp: the Unfinished Masterpiece
Gaston de Pawlowsky: the Fourth Dimension

DEVELOPMENTS

Barnes Buys Soutine

ART NEWS

Steinlen, Witness of the Pitiless *Belle Époque*
Fourth and Final Stage of the Kahnweiler Liquidation
Gustave Eiffel: the Orphan Tower
Léger Makes the Swedish Ballet Dance
The Evening Dada Died
In Brief

ARCHITECTURE

A Holy Chapel in Concrete
Wright, Resistance to Earthquakes

WRITINGS AND THEORIES

Le Corbusier: Guidelines

LITERATURE

AUSTRIA
Rainer Maria Rilke publishes Sonnets to Orpheus.

UNITED STATES
Wallace Stevens publishes Harmonium.
E.E. Cummings publishes Tulips and Chimneys.

ITALY
Publication of Italo Svevo's novel The Confessions of Zeno.

SWEDEN
The Irish writer W. B. Yeats is awarded the Nobel prize.

MUSIC

UNITED STATES
James P. Johnson creates a new syncopated sound, the Charleston.
Bix Beiderbecke forms a jazz band in Chicago.

MOTION PICTURES

GERMANY
Viking Eggeling shows his Diagonal Symphony *in Berlin.*

UNITED STATES
Premiere of Erich von Stroheim's The Raptors.

SWEDEN
Greta Garbo's debut, in Mauritz Stiller's Gösta Berling.

OTHER PERFORMANCES

FRANCE
Premiere of Knock *by Jules Romains, with Louis Jouvet.*
Performance of Tristan Tzara's Cœur à gaz *at the Club du Faubourg.*

IRELAND
Premiere of The Shadow of a Gunman *by Sean O'Casey.*

MARCEL DUCHAMP:
THE BRIDE STRIPPED BARE BY HER BACHELORS (LARGE GLASS). 1915-1923. Philadelphia. Museum of Art

THE BRIDE'S SECRET

To the unprepared viewer *The Bride Stripped Bare by Her Bachelors* may seem difficult to understand at first, yet it follows a strict symbolism. This symbolism is concerned with events in Duchamp's childhood, but also, and mainly, with general archetypes. In many ways, this work stems from a mystical and alchemic inspiration, and this is, precisely, its secret. The diagram below lists its principal themes.

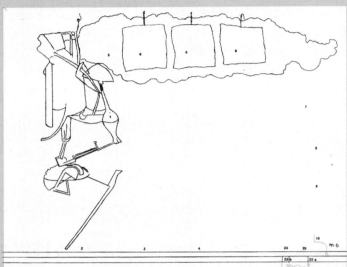

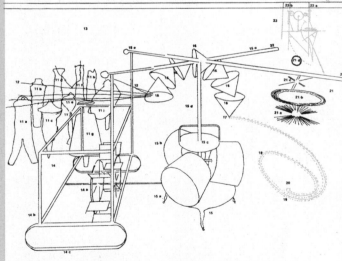

THE BRIDE'S DOMAIN (upper glass panel)
1. The Bride. 2. The Bride's clothes. 3. Cooler. 4. Horizon. 5. Inscription from above (Milky Way). 6. Air-draft piston (or filament). 7. Nine shoots. 8. Area where shadows are cast. 9. Area where the image of the sculpture of droplets is reflected. 10. Gravity handler.

THE BACHELORS' DOMAIN (lower glass panel)
11. Nine male-like molds (or Eros Matrices that form the cemetery of uniforms and liveries). 11a-11i. The nine Bachelors. 12. Capillary vessels. 13. Waterfall area. 14. Water mill. 14a. Drive wheel of the mill. 14b. Chariot. 14c. Slide. 15. Chocolate grinder. 15a. Chassis Louis Quinze. 15b. Roller. 15c. Cravat. 15d. Bayonet. 15e. Scissors. 16. Sieve. 17. Butterfly-pump area. 18. Toboggan. 19. Area with three splashes. 20. Free weights with nine holes. 21. Oculist witnesses. 21a-21c. Oculist's charts. 21d. Site where a lens should have been. 22. Fighting log. 23. Boxing match. 23a. First ram. 23b. Second ram. 24. Area with a sculpture of droplets. 25. Area of the Wilson-Lincoln effect.

MARCEL DUCHAMP: THE UNFINISHED MASTERPIECE

NEW YORK

When is a painting or a piece of sculpture finished? Because artists like Manet, Matisse, and Picasso have been placing less emphasis on the beauty of a nude or the passion on a face compared with the direct expression of forms and colors, no one really knows. Even Michelangelo, during the Renaissance, left the bodies in his "Slaves" as sketches, to better illustrate the struggle of man against matter. Now Marcel Duchamp declares "definitely unfinished" his most ambitious work, *The Bride Stripped Bare by Her Bachelors.*

The work was started around 1912, after Duchamp had been inspired by reading the *Journey in the Land of the Fourth Dimension* by Gaston de Pavlovsky, a series of brief philosophical tales describing what happens when a person ventures outside of the three-dimensional world. Pavlovsky was the director of *Comoedia*, a daily dedicated mainly to the theater in which since 1908 he published the tales that were to become his book. At the time, speculation on the fourth dimension was extremely fashionable amongst the public. Duchamp was natu-

rally sensitive to this, as were his brothers, Jacques Villon and Raymond Duchamp-Villon, who had a particular interest in such problems, as did all those who, from Gleizes to Metzinger, attended the Sunday gatherings of the Puteaux group.

Duchamp's work is large—9 feet high, 5 1/2 feet wide—and consists of two juxtaposed parts. The top part contains mainly the frightening carcass of a kind of praying mantis which represents the bride. The lower part contains several elements, such as a group of nine male-like molds symbolizing the bachelors. The painting's main claim to originality is undoubtedly the fact that the motifs are enclosed behind two glass panes, which caused it also be to called *Large Glass*, no doubt in consideration of the length of its original title.

The use of glass is of major importance to the artist. In reference to Pavlovsky, the intention was to show, in three dimensions, an antiworld with N dimensions. Everyone knows how perspective makes it possible to create the illusion of depth on a flat surface, that is, a third dimension. This is true for all of traditional painting, from Piero

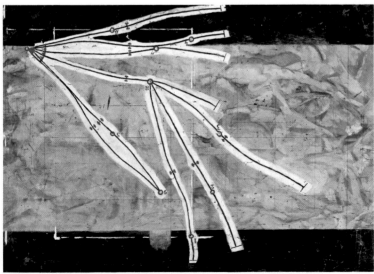

MARCEL DUCHAMP: NETWORK OF STOPPAGES. 1914. New York. Private Collection

GASTON DE PAWLOWSKY: THE FOURTH DIMENSION

Gaston de Pawlowsky's *Journey in the Land of the Fourth Dimension*, published in 1912 while Duchamp was beginning work on his *Large Glass*, is preceded by a long theoretical preface in which the author explains his philosophical thinking. The postulation by modern science of the notion of N-dimensional spaces, which seems to find a rational basis in the laws of relativity, would, according to him, give rise to new metaphysical and spiritual laws. These are some of the reflections of this preface, which we have chosen to present below, despite their difficult reading because of the importance they held for Marcel Duchamp at the time.

della Francesca to Titian and Velázquez. A traditional painting will often give the impression of "plunging" into the wall on which it hangs.

But the *Large Glass* is different, in the sense that it is not a painting, nor is it a piece of sculpture. Its transparency renders it inseparable from both the site it occupies and the space that surrounds it unless it is hung from a wall like a painting. Enigmatic elements mix with and are superimposed on the surrounding environment, creating the notion that it could be a projection with four dimensions into our reality which, apparently, has only three.

Pavlovsky defined the fourth dimension as "the necessary symbol of an unknown without which the known could not exist." He had a platonic and even spiritual concept of what is real. To this, Duchamp adds doubt and irony. This means that he never accorded the visible world the breadth of reality.

Sometimes *The Bride Stripped Bare By Her Bachelors* is compared to the stained-glass windows of Gothic churches. Besides the fact that the subject matter is totally different—there are no saints, no biblical figures in Duchamp, only a man-eater who taunts her suitors—in the church windows the polychromatic play of the pieces of glass changing with the course of the sun reveal the splendor of God to the faithful. By contrast, this *Large Glass*—created in our times, when the sky is empty —can only represent a search for meaning. This is the main reason, it seems, that the work is impossible to complete.

(See also 1913, 1917, 1920, 1968.)

What is meant by "the fourth dimension"?

It is the necessary symbol of an unknown without which the known could not exist. The fourth dimension in our world of three dimensions is the variable whose existence is indispensable in any equation of the human spirit but whose quality fades when one attempts to assign it a particular value...

The fourth dimension is that unknown without which the known could not exist.

This eternal aspect of being, this immutable movement of thought, this permanent criticism of transitory forms, this perpetual crack of the whip that keeps the conscious world from crystallizing and falling asleep, this unknown that must always accompany the known as a complement, this fourth measure without which the other three could not integrally account for the Universe, this is what we call, for lack of a better word, the fourth dimension . . .

The fourth dimension represents the artistic side of life.

Thus, it is the role of the fourth dimension to complete our awareness of the Universe, to symbolize this immense, active, imponderable, immeasurable, and mysterious domain of art that we could never divorce from a general conception of the Universe without omitting the raison d'être of that Universe, its evolution, and its goal.

GASTON DE PAWLOWSKY
Journey in the Land
of the Fourth Dimension
(Excerpts from the preface)

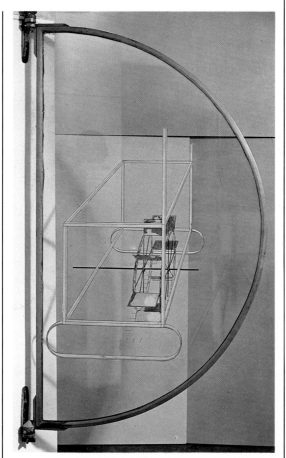

MARCEL DUCHAMP: GLIDER CONTAINING A WATER MILL IN NEIGHBORING METALS. 1913-1915. Philadelphia. Museum of Art

BARNES BUYS SOUTINE

PARIS

Argyrol, a medication consisting of silver salts, is the cornerstone of the fortune of an American chemist, Albert C. Barnes, who builds up a magnificent collection of paintings.

He decides to house his collection in his own museum, in Merion, near Philadelphia. He hires the French architect Philippe Cret to oversee construction and hopes to open it next year to students.

He won't let journalists in or museum curators, about whom he never stops raging. "Those people," he claims, "talk about painting like an eighty-year-old talks from hearsay about a wedding night."

Barnes is furious with the poor reception given by critics at the exhibit at the Pennsylvania Academy to seventy-five of the paintings he brought back from Paris at the beginning of the year. He possesses works of the Barbizon School, the Ash Can School, and major Impressionists and Postimpressionists. His French advisor, Paul Guillaume, takes him to Zborovski, Chaim Soutine's dealer. Barnes is overwhelmed, and he winds up buying about one hundred Soutines.

Barnes is not satisfied with having bought all the paintings held by Zborovski, and insists on meeting Soutine, who has brought back from long stays in the south—particularly in Ceret and in Cagnes—a large number of paintings that he has the intention of destroying.

Barnes buys most of the canvases in the studio, then tells Soutine, "Now go and change, I'm taking you to dinner." "But I have nothing else to wear," Soutine says. "Never mind," Barnes responds, "We'll buy a suit on the way."

What a break! For the first time, Soutine can picture an end to the miserable life he has been leading since his arrival in Paris ten years ago. He is the son of a modest Jewish tailor, from Smilovich, near the Lithuanian city of Minsk. In July 1913, he

arrives via Russia, first at the Cité Falguière, then at La Ruche.

Soutine is happy to find compatriots, Kokoine and Krémègne, who introduce him to Chagall. But he feels closest to Modigliani, with whom he spends several late nights drinking in Montparnasse.

Soutine is fascinated and influenced by paintings in the Louvre by Goya, El Greco, and

FOR THE FIRST TIME SOUTINE CAN PICTURE AN END TO THE MISERABLE LIFE HE HAS BEEN LEADING SINCE HIS ARRIVAL IN PARIS TEN YEARS AGO

Chaim Soutine.

Barnes' discovery of Soutine is a turning point in the painter's life; his work seems to develop toward new themes, with still lifes assuming special importance.

Rembrandt. But his feeling of impotence before the deep compassion expressed by those painters pushes him toward a violent and at times hallucinatory Expressionism.

Buried in his studio, he paints furiously. He does not hesitate to destroy with even greater fury the decomposing fruits of his pictorial frenzies. The miserable fowl, the wilting gladioli, the ugly children not only bear witness to the poverty in which he has been living, they are the imperious projections of an angst-ridden visionary.

This apparently sloppy painter is in fact concerned about the execution of his paintings, to the point of wishing he would not have to use the same brushes twice. Thanks to the admiration he has evoked in Barnes, he will be able to do this.

Steinlen, Witness of the Pitiless Belle Époque

Friend of the poor and oppressed, Théophile Alexandre Steinlen died at the age of sixty-four on November 14 in Paris. Born in Lausanne, Switzerland, he had dedicated himself to painting, posters, drawing, illustration, and caricature, all with equal talent. When Picasso first stayed in Paris in 1901, Steinlen was one of the few members of the older generation he went to see. He admired the tragic sense of daily life in Steinlen's work, and was deeply influenced by it. Not everything is of uniform quality in his work, but Steinlen will remain the lucid witness of the pitiless *Belle Époque*.

Fourth and Final Stage of the Kahnweiler Liquidation

The fourth and final sale of the Kahnweiler estate takes place on May 7 and 8 at the Hôtel Drouot. It makes a profit of 227,662 francs. Among the items on the auction block are forty-six works by Braque, thirty-six by Derain, twenty-six by Gris, eighteen by Léger, fifty by Picasso, and ninety-two by Vlaminck. This one-day sale is the fourth, and comes after those held in 1921 and 1922. The large number of works thrown onto the market at one time as a result of these sales had already dangerously lowered prices. This sale ends the liquidation of the Cubist dealer's possessions, seized by the government during the war because of Kahnweiler's German nationality. The dealer was able to buy back very few of the confiscated paintings, and comes out of the affair a penniless man.

Gustave Eiffel: the Orphan Tower

Guy de Maupassant, who hated the tower, would have lunch on its second floor because, he said, that was the only place in town where he could not see it. The Eiffel Tower was attacked incessantly while it was being built between August 1887 and March 1889. Its critics, believing in their own good taste, called for the destruction of the "disgusting column of bolts and sheet metal." By the time its brilliant builder dies on December 27 at the venerable age of ninety-one, it had become the very symbol of the city of Paris, its praises sung by painters as well as poets who made it famous. Eiffel, an engineer who was determined to be original, had understood that metal construction would be a problem as long as heavy, fragile cast iron was used. He had built his tower by assembling iron girders prefabricated in the factory, as he had already done with his two other masterpieces—the Maria-Pia Bridge near Porto, and the Garabit viaduct.

Léger Makes the Swedish Ballet Dance

With its African theme by Blaise Cendrars, percussive music by Darius Milhaud, and curtain, sets, and costumes by Fernand Léger, *The Creation of the World* is a great new success for the Swedish Ballet. Under the direction of Rolf de Maré and his dancer Jean Börlin, the corps was discovered three years ago at the Théâtre des Champs-Élysées, when they were performing *La nuit de la Saint-Jean* with sets and costumes by Nils Dardel and a poster by Paul Colin. Then came *L'homme et son désir*, which Claudel set in Brazil, again with Léger's participation, and *Skating Ring* in a sports setting by Canudo, with music by Arthur Honegger. Now the public witnesses the glorification of this ballet.

The Evening Dada Died

According to its organizer, the Russian poet Iliazd, also known as Ilia Zdanevich, *La soirée du coeur à barbe* on July 6 at the Théâtre Michel was supposed to reconcile Breton and Tzara, who had been separated by theoretical and personal quarrels since the beginning of last year. But the evening ended up in a brawl. Instead of the announced play by Tzara, Breton got up on stage and attacked his erstwhile friends with blows of his cane. The audience responded. Éluard was roughed up, and everyone entered the fray. By the end of the evening the entire hall was in disarray, and one person had an arm broken. Poor Iliazd must accept the obvious: This time, the Dada spirit is truly dead.

Gustave Eiffel on his Tower.

The church at Raincy by Auguste Perret.

A HOLY CHAPEL IN CONCRETE

LE RAINCY

Built in thirteen months for the town of Raincy, in the Department of Seine-Saint-Denis, the Church of Our Lady is immediately christened "the Holy Chapel in Concrete." The entire undertaking was a bet! Last year, the local priest consulted Auguste Perret about building a church. He had only 300,000 francs. The lowest bid amounted to 1,800,000 francs. The architect accepted the financial challenge, and added an artistic one. He wanted to prove that concrete is the most economical material. He wanted to show that it can be beautiful as well. With the Théâtre des Champs-Élysées, built in 1913, Perret had given concrete its nobility. Ten years later, he gives it God's seal, thanks to the church's vertical lightness and its horizontal, omnipresent luminosity.

The plan of Notre-Dame-du-Raincy is classical. It consists of an apse and side aisles, and a nave whose vaulted roof is supported only by very light columns with vertical fluting. Here lies the real advantage of concrete: It does not require the use of expensive and heavy masses to support the structure. The lateral walls and the façade are prefabricated screens made of perforated concrete. A large number of round, rectangular, and diamond-shaped apertures bring light into the church through windows that have been designed and colored by Maurice Denis with soft, polychromatic light.

Perret has recreated the bright vertical sweep of great Gothic structures. It is astonishing that his interior columns measure only a little more than one foot in diameter. The joyous luminosity in which the entire church is bathed is impressive. It was one of the architect's principal goals. He wanted the parishioners to be able to read the texts of the liturgy and the canticles. Paradoxically, the Neoclassical agnostic gets along very well with the advocate of the prophets, Maurice Denis, who says, "Above all, I want to make sure that in my life as an artist I will never have to mourn for my dignity as a Christian." He claims that "works of art lighten up under the shine of the altar." The architect had better build a religious structure!

Still, Auguste Perret is far from getting full support. People are not pleased with the steeple. It is considered too "geometric." It is a sheaf of columns that becomes more slender as it rises in stages toward the cross that dominates it. Perhaps he put more rigor into it than sacred enthusiasm.

WRIGHT, RESISTANCE TO EARTHQUAKES

TOKYO

Tokyo, the great metropolis with five million inhabitants, lies in ashes. An earthquake followed by a fire kills more than 150,000 people in September. One man can pride himself on having saved human lives—Frank Lloyd Wright. Last year, the great American architect completed the construction of one of the few buildings in Tokyo that resisted both calamities—the Imperial Hotel.

Since his flight to Europe, Wright has had his share of trials—in particular, the fire at his house, Taliesin. Scarcity of commissions and his financial difficulties took him to Japan, where in 1915 he is given the contract to build the Imperial Hotel. He introduces the cross-shaped plan of prairie houses, freely adapting it to the Oriental style. The main original feature is the fact that it is earthquake-proof. A slab rests on piles driven into the spongy subsoil—piles that act like the fingers of a waiter carrying a tray. Thanks to this flexibility, the structure absorbs quakes. There was considerable doubt about the effectiveness of the system, but now there is proof that it works. The owner of the Imperial Hotel writes to Wright to congratulate him for having saved the lives of many schoolchildren who sought refuge at the hotel.

The Imperial Hotel in Tokyo
by Frank Lloyd Wright.

LE CORBUSIER: GUIDELINES

A Swiss painter, architect, and cofounder with Amédée Ozenfant of the review *L'esprit nouveau*, Charles-Édouard Jeanneret published a firebrand of a book under the pseudonym Le Corbusier. Released as a Crès edition, this work made the author famous at the young age of thirty-six. The book, entitled *Vers une architecture* (toward an architecture), gave a thrashing to all that directly or indirectly hindered the art of construction from making its entrance into the scientific and industrial society in which we now live. Le Corbusier, while being a fervent upholder of Functionalism, held no disdain for the eternal laws of architecture. A portion of a chapter devoted to guidelines appears below.

Architecture is the first manifestation of man creating his universe. He does this in the image of nature, in observance of the laws of nature, laws that govern our nature and our universe. The laws of weight, statics, and dynamics are enforced by a reduction to the absurd: either hold or collapse.

A sovereign determinism can be seen in natural creations, giving them the effect of balance and reason. Objects are seen as infinitely modulated, evolutionary, varied, and unitary.

The primordial laws of physics are simple and few in number. The laws of morality are simple and few in number.

Contemporary man planes a board perfectly with a planing machine in a few seconds. Previously, man planed a board fairly well with a plane. Primitive man did a very poor job by striking a board with a silex or a knife. Primitive man used a modulus and guidelines to make his task easier. The Greeks, the Egyptians, Michelangelo, and Blondel used lines and outlines to correct their works and to satisfy their artistic sense and mathematical thinking. Contemporary man, using nothing at all, builds the Boulevard Raspail. He then proclaims that he is a liberated poet and that his instincts alone are enough. However, he expresses himself only by artificial means learned in schools. He is an unchained lyric poet with an iron collar around his neck, someone who knows things, but things that he has neither invented nor mastered, who has during his education lost that candid and important childlike energy that makes one constantly ask "Why?"

A guideline is a protection against the arbitrary. It is the crucial test by which any work done ardently gains legitimacy. It is the student's way of checking his answers, the logician's proof of his thesis.

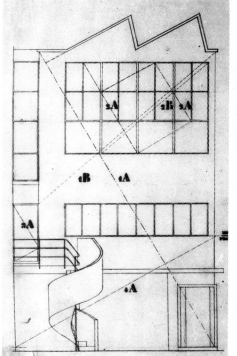

Sketch and photograph of the house Le Corbusier built for Amédée Ozenfant.

A guideline is a spiritual appeasement that leads to a search for ingenious and harmonious relations. It confers eurhythmy to the work.

A guideline gives the work a mathematical aspect and a benign sense of order. Setting a guideline determines the fundamental geometry of the work, defining, therefore, one of its fundamental impressions. Setting a guideline is one of the decisive moments of inspiration, one of the main operations of architecture.

LE CORBUSIER
Vers une architecture *(Excerpts)*

A turning point in the century comes with the publication of the **Surrealist Manifesto** *by André Breton, a birth certificate for the movement of the same name. The nihilism of the Dadaist revolt, born in Zurich's Cabaret Voltaire while the Battle of Verdun raged on, is done for. Breton and his circle call for dreams, the unconscious, the marvelous. With the support of Freud and Lautréamont, the time has come ,for an intellec-tual revolution that is to change our lives. Even* Léger's **Mechanical Ballet,** *where for the first time common objects play the role of movie stars, and Diaghilev's highly unusual* **Blue Train** *have an air of the past about them in comparison. Meanwhile, at the Sorbonne, Juan Gris gives a widely publicized lecture on the relationship between art and science.*

1924

SUMMARY

AVANT-GARDE

Surrealism: the Unconscious Enters Art
André Breton: What Is Surrealism?

PERFORMANCES

Francis Picabia Doesn't Open
Acting Objects
A Train for the Avant-Garde

DEVELOPMENTS

Paul Klee's Puppets
First Chagall Exhibit in Paris

ART NEWS

Baranoff-Rossiné's Color Piano
Archipenko Archipainter
The Quatre Bleus Set Out to Conquer America
Doucet's *Demoiselles*
In Brief

PORTRAITS

The Last Dream of Mailman Cheval

WRITINGS AND THEORIES

Juan Gris: Art Is a Science

MAX ERNST:
THE ELEPHANT OF CELEBES. 1921.
London. Tate Gallery

SURREALISM: THE UNCONSCIOUS ENTERS ART

MAX ERNST: AU RENDEZ-VOUS DES AMIS. 1922. Cologne. Wallraf-Richartz Museum

Max Ernst is a former Dadaist. Among others, he initiated the famous scandals at the 1920 exhibition which were organized in the back room of the Winter Brasserie in Cologne. He is a German citizen forbidden to stay in France, but he crosses the border with the passport of Éluard, who came to visit him in his fief. He may also be the creator of the first Surrealist painting, *The Elephant of Celebes*, produced four years ago, two before the movement came into being. The painting shows a big potbellied animal, half animal, half machine, resembling at the same time a pachyderm and a cast-iron pot. With its very low horizon and fish swimming in the sky, the painting was inspired by the Metaphysical Painting of de Chirico and by a childhood memory—a slightly

ANDRÉ MASSON:
AUTOMATIC DRAWING

PARIS

They could easily be mistaken for a bunch of happy friends having a party. They are young, they are noisy, they have their fixed meeting places—certain cafés like the Grillon and the Cyrano on the Place Blanche. They go to circuses and popular movie theaters, they insult priests, they bathe naked in fountains, and they practice free love . . . Who could imagine that

born. They needed a program. Now they have one. André Breton's *Surrealist Manifesto*, which appears in bookshops in October, gives the movement its theoretical basis. It has a program and a permanent office, the Bureau of Surrealist Research, and a journal, *The Surrealist Revolution.*

Indeed, the days of fun are over, the days of schoolboy jokes and intellectual irresponsibili-

DADA WAS A REBELLION. SURREALISM WANTS TO BE A REVOLUTION

these troublemakers, who prefer to hang out in bad places and to indulge in the most stupid spectacles, rather than to attend the Salons where the intellect reigns, are—though they deny it—the cream of the literary and artistic elite of today?

They founded the group, then needed a name. In 1917, Apollinaire talked about the "surreal" in a letter to a friend. The word fit perfectly. Surrealism was

ty—the days of Dada. Because Dada was rebellion and Surrealism wants to be a revolution with its own philosophical masters, that is, Marx, Freud, Lautréamont, Dostoevski, of which Max Ernst has painted a group portrait that includes Breton, and Aragon, Éluard, Desnos, Crevel, Soupault, Benjamin Peret . . . They are all driven by a great purpose: a will to change the life of society.

ANDRÉ BRETON: WHAT IS SURREALISM?

MAX ERNST:
UBU IMPERATOR.
1923. Paris.
MNAM

salacious song about an elephant with a big behind from the islands of Celebes, sung by him and his friends on the way to school to annoy the bourgeois. Since the beginning of the century, Freud's theories of the unconscious and the libido and his dream interpretation had utterly changed the image man has of himself. But they had not yet touched the contemporary art movements. In his Manifesto, Breton makes up for lost time when he appeals to sleeping philosophers since reason solves only the lesser problems. The time has come for the rule of the irrational, hypnosis, hallucinations, artificial sleep, and Automatism.

In the field of Automatism, Breton and Soupault have ex-perimented for the last three years, *Magnetic Fields* being the result. André Masson who returned from the war psychologically bruised by what he saw at Chemin des Dames, creates the first Automatic Drawing. While Max Ernst plays with unusual combinations—elephant and cast-iron pot—painted meticulously, Masson, having created a void inside himself, throws a network of lines on the paper. A world emerges of wrecks and hybrids that seem incapable of joining the living.

Like the Dadaists, the Surrealists are angry young men, totally disgusted by world conflict. In their eyes, not only the traditional morality is bankrupt but also the arts, literature, science, philosophy, and politics—all must be rethought on a different basis. Madness, childhood, clairvoyance, the supernatural—these are the wide-open spaces they want to explore in their desire to "dive into the unknown to find something new," as stated by their master, Apollinaire. *(See also 1926, 1928, 1934, 1938, 1941, 1942.)*

Surrealism, noun: *Pure psychic Automatism by which one undertakes to express, verbally, in writing, or by any other form, the true functioning of thought. It is dictated by thought, without any control by force of reason, and without any concern of an esthetic or moral order . . .*

Surrealism is based on the belief in the superior reality of certain forms of association that have been overlooked, in the supreme power of the dream, and in the detached game played by thought. It tends to ruin definitively all other psychic mechanisms and substitute itself for them in the resolution of the principal problems of life . . .

Childhood perhaps most closely approaches "true life." This is the stage of life beyond which man possesses nothing more than his pass and a few complimentary tickets, where everything competes for the effective and risk-free possession of one's self. Surrealism seems to make these aspects of childhood viable again. It is as if one was once again running to one's safety or to one's

doom. One relives a precious terror in the shadows. Thank God it's still only Purgatory. With a shudder, one crosses what the occultists call the "dangerous countrysides." My steps draw the attention of monsters waiting in ambush. They are still not too ill-willed toward me, and I am not lost, because I fear them. Here are "the elephants with women's heads and the winged lions." Soupault and I tremble at their sight. Here is the "soluble fish" that still frightens me a little . . .

Anything can be used to arrive at the desired suddenness in certain associations. The papiers collés of Picasso and Braque have the same value as the introduction of a commonplace in a passage of a most refined literary style. You may even assemble as freely as possible headlines and fragments of headlines taken from newspapers, and (observing, if you will, the rules of syntax) use that as the title of a poem . . .

Surrealist Manifesto *(Excerpts)*

Marcel Duchamp and Madame René Clair
as Adam and Eve, photographed by Man Ray.

ACTING OBJECTS

PARIS

Household utensils such as ladles, pots, and salad bowls have become movie actors! It seems unthinkable. Yet, they are the first to fill the parts in the *Mechanical Ballet*, Fernand Léger's short feature film. Léger has always been interested in mass-produced items. "I am a Classicist, my point of departure is the pure object," he states, marking his difference with the romantic Pablo Picasso. Besides Henri Rousseau, his favorite painters are David and Poussin. Now the objects that figure in his paintings have started to move in a rhythmic fashion.

The premiere is a major event. The film has no plot, and was made without a script. Man Ray and Dudley Murphy were the cinematographers. Georges Antheil composed the score. Léger did the rest. The *Mechanical Ballet* proceeds rhythmically. It plays on fragments of reality, which, when seen in isolation, take on an amazing quality. The close-ups are obsessive: Details magnified one hundred times function as flat color surfaces, and slow motion creates shadows on reliefs. Léger has been a movie fan ever since Apollinaire made him see Charlie Chaplin while on military leave in 1916. He was struck by Abel Gance's *The Wheel:* "Mobile images are presented like a tableau." His *Ballet* is above all a painter's film. He prefers the motion of a crank arm by far to that of an eyelash or a smile. Gloria Swanson, better watch out!

FRANCIS PICABIA DOESN'T OPEN

PARIS

It was almost called "*Relâche doesn't open.*" On the night of the premiere, November 27, at the Théâtre des Champs-Élysées, the Paris elite anxiously waits in line in front of doors that, strangely enough, remain closed. People in evening clothes have come to watch the performance of the first "instantaneous ballet," created by Picabia and Erik Satie, two personalities of the artistic avant-garde. An aura of scandal surrounds the event. The principal dancer of the troupe, Jean Borlin, is bedridden, completely exhausted from the rehearsals!

The choreography of the Swedish Ballet was perfect. The project started more than a year ago. It originated when Blaise Cendrars proposed to draw up a scenario and Picabia agreed to take care of the backdrops and Satie composed the musical score. Cendrars abandoned the project, and Picabia took on the entire show.

Finally, *Relâche* (meaning "intermission" but also "suspension of performance")—a ballet in two acts, with a cinematographic interlude by René Clair —starts with a three-day delay. "You will see a very beautiful woman, a very handsome man. . . and bright lights," Picabia announces, and he adds, "*Relâche* is eternal motion." The posters warn the public, in typical Dada fashion: "Above all, don't forget to bring dark glasses and cotton to plug your ears. Come and whistle." The organizers do sell whistles at the theater. But the public refrains. Well-behaved, they sit through Satie's adventures while he scales the gargoyles of Notre Dame and fires a cannon. They barely see Marcel Duchamp and Madame Clair appear naked on stage for a brief instant, forming a living picture after Cranach's *Adam and Eve*, holding hands while wearing the simplest of outfits!

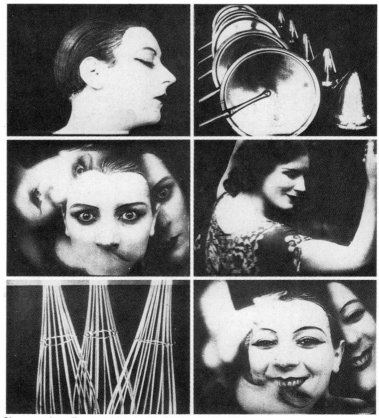

Close-ups from Fernand Léger's film *Mechanical Ballet*.

A TRAIN FOR THE AVANT-GARDE

Photograph of the show *The Blue Train*.

PARIS

The success of *The Blue Train*'s premiere on June 20 at the Théâtre des Champs-Élysées marks a new, euphoric direction, characteristic of the Roaring Twenties, for Diaghilev's Russian Ballet. Until then, the focus was primarily on aggressive artists of the avant-garde. Evidence was provided by the explosive and provocative choreography and backdrops for *Prélude à l'après-midi d'un faune*, *The Rite of Spring*, and *Parade*; all three scandalized the Parisians.

This time, Diaghilev takes them on a joyful holiday in the most seductive of express trains, seductive because it links Paris and the French Riviera. It is also the most luxurious—decorative work signed by René Prou, accessories by René Lalique. It discharges hordes of travelers bent on pleasure and relaxation onto Mediterranean beaches, which are greatly in vogue. With the theme in mind, the director of the Russian Ballet asks Cocteau to write the libretto of a "danced operetta," for which Bonisclava Nijinska, Nijinski's sister, writes the choreography. It is based on a musical score by a thirty-two-year-old composer, Darius Milhaud. The great Cubist sculptor Henri Laurens, who is thirty-nine years old, designs the backdrops for *The Blue Train* in the style of his constructions that originated with Synthetic Cubism. By means of irregularly truncated beach cabins, he humorously evokes a beach that will soon be overwhelmed by searchers for earthly delights.

Contrary to Laurens, who has never seen the sea, Cocteau puts his knowledge of beach games, fashion, and the sports of tennis and golf to good use. He creates a Beau Gosse, who because of his gymnastic fireworks will seduce "tarts" and "gigolos."

Gabrielle Chanel, a friend of both Diaghilev and Cocteau, is put in charge of costumes. She is delighted to move from the theater—where she has designed beautiful costumes adapted from Sophocles for Cocteau's ballet *Antigone*. Cocteau says, "I picked the greatest couturiere of our time because I cannot imagine Oedipus' daughters poorly dressed." The thirty-one-year-old couturiere feels at home cutting the sports outfits for the heroes of *The Blue Train*. They are costumes of knit fabrics, a fashion she launched and enjoys wearing. They brighten the stage with their lively colors. The dancer Solokova wears a bathing suit in pink knitwear. Indeed, Chanel particularly appreciates

PABLO PICASSO: THE RACE. 1922. Paris. Musée Picasso

these fabrics developed in the middle of the previous century and rendered popular by the World's Fairs of 1889 and 1900. Knits fit her designs and her suits, which she wants to be lightweight, to "free the women" wearing them.

Pablo Picasso is greatly impressed by the effect of the proscenium curtain, which bears an enlarged reproduction of his painting *The Race* (two women running on a beach), painted four years ago, in Dinard. A Fanfare, composed by the musician Georges Auric, heralds the appearance of the superb curtain. Picasso is also the creator of the illustrations in the program, drawn in a few pencil strokes with great, almost Hellenic, command.

PAUL KLEE'S PUPPETS

WEIMAR

Since 1916, when the painter Paul Klee started a puppet theater for his son Felix's ninth birthday, he has designed over fifty hand puppets, each one more amazing than the next.

First there were Mister Death, Guignol, Gretl (Guignol's wife), Sepperl (his buddy), the Devil, and the Policeman. Klee made the heads of painted plaster and the costumes with pieces of cloth snatched from his wife, Lily, and sewn on her machine. Between the living room and the bedroom, he installed a small theater, with a backdrop of a village with a church steeple bearing an immense clock. With great pleasure, smoking his pipe and petting the cat, he attends the comical exploits of the puppets manipulated by Felix. Little by little, Paul Klee starts to use eclectic elements for the heads, for example, nutshells, buttons from pants, pieces of fur, feathers, an electrical socket, bones, and even a horseshoe. New puppets are born since his settlement in Weimar, including a Young Peasant Woman, a Crowned Poet, Mister Duck, and a Buddhist Monk.

Klee is carried away by these singular, weird, even unsettling creatures to such an extent that he starts sculpting some for himself. All are made of disparate objects that catch his eye.

Six years ago, he created a remarkable piece of sculpture with chunks of brick polished by the Lech River and discovered during a walk near Augsburg. This is how he invents a powerful bull, planted squarely on outspread legs, and a big ship with a large iron smokestack.

What a spirit! Capable of any form of imagination! He seems only interested in the source of things, in their virginal birth, in their primordial gestation. "Art does not produce the visible," he states, "art makes visible." Accordingly, for his inaugural course at the Bauhaus in 1920,

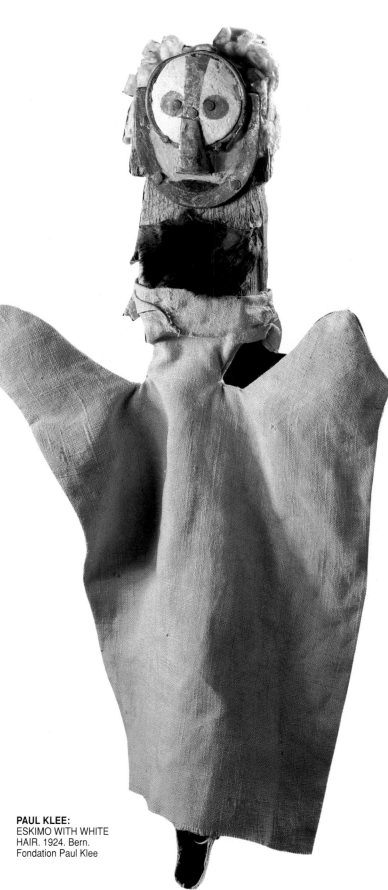

PAUL KLEE:
ESKIMO WITH WHITE
HAIR. 1924. Bern.
Fondation Paul Klee

he surprises his students by telling them about the encounter of two planets that, having left their orbits, collide and explode. "Draw what happens then!" Klee orders.

During a six-week trip in Sicily, to Taormina and Mazzaro, he visits Gela, where his favorite playwright, Aeschylus, died in 456 B.C. He meditates for a long while in the amphitheater of Syracuse. For Klee, art is a marvel like the theater. Endowed with the freshness of a child, it deserves the nickname "the Enchanted."

FIRST CHAGALL EXHIBIT IN PARIS

PARIS

The Barbazange-Hodebert gallery presents a retrospective of the work of Marc Chagall.

Violin players march over the roofs. Railway men leave their tracks in the sky. A rabbi carries his double on his head. Everything dances in a whirlwind of colors. The motifs of his paintings are deeply rooted in his Russian-Jewish origins. After nine years in Russia and Germany, he returns to Paris, where he lived from 1910 to 1914. Jewish legends and popular imagery are transcended. The naiveté of his paintings is only superficial. When looking at a Chagall painting, one feels his spirit carried to broader regions of eternal symbols and poetic wonders. The canvases can be read like humorous tales. He was close to the Cubists, who appreciated his work during his first stay in Paris, but Chagall does not adhere to any school of painting. It may be the secret of his originality and freshness.

VLADIMIR BARANOFF-ROSSINÉ:
OPTOPHONIC PIANO AND DISK. 1915-1923.
Paris. Private Collection

Baranoff-Rossiné's Color Piano

At the Bolshoi Theater in Moscow, Vladimir Baranoff-Rossiné unveils his optophonic piano, having registered the patent for it on December 8 of last year. Elaborating on one of Scriabin's ideas, Baranoff-Rossiné's invention permits the synchronized projection of colors and music. It consists of a keyboard, the keys of which activate a multicolored disk, creating the possibility for numerous compositions. When he was a member of the Russian colony in Paris before the Revolution of October, in 1915, Baranoff-Rossiné was named "French Futurist" by Apollinaire. There is no doubt that his invention offers a response to the challenge of expressing movement in painting, an issue the Italian Futurists have taken seriously.

Archipenko Archipainter

"Archipainting" is the latest invention of the sculptor Alexander Archipenko. Created in New York, where he moved last year, archipainting consists of canvases set in motion by cleverly concealed motors. Born in Kiev in 1887, Archipenko had gone to Paris in 1908 and, along with Laurens, had been a leading Cubist sculptor there. The visual animation of his works had always interested him. He had perforated them with holes, used glass, wood, or metal in them, or, in the case of his sculpture-paintings, added color. Is his bold revival due to his living in America? In any case, his archipainting pushes the limits further and further.

The "Quatre Bleus" Set Out To Conquer America

How does one find buyers? On the suggestion of their friend Galka Scheyer, now living in Los Angeles, artists Kandinsky, Klee, Feininger, and Jawlensky have formed the Quatre Bleus (the four blues), an association designed to publicize their works. Life has become uncomfortable in Germany. Galoping inflation has taken over, and for the three professors at the Bauhaus the salary is not sufficient to make ends meet. Under their new collective name they hope to become better known in the United States, and to hold exhibits that will help them sell their paintings to American collectors, since European takers are hard to find.

Doucet's "Demoiselles"

Picasso is sold on credit. *Les demoiselles d'Avignon,* painted at the Bateau-Lavoir in 1907, a work Picasso refused to sell until recently, considering it incomplete, has been bought by the clothing designer and art collector Jacques Doucet on the advice of André Breton. In December of last year, the price of sale was set at 25,000 francs, payable in twelve monthly installments, of which the last was paid in November.

LYONEL FEININGER:
ARCHITECTURE II. 1921.
Lugano. Thyssen-Bornemisza Collection

THE LAST DREAM OF MAILMAN CHEVAL

HAUTERIVES

Mailman Ferdinand Cheval dies on August 19, at the age of eighty-eight, after a life filled with mail deliveries and, even more so, with the construction of a strange "palace." He intended it to be his grave, but an administrative decision prevents his ashes from resting there. He is buried, instead, at the Hauterives cemetery, in a modest mausoleum, which he built.

On the walls of his ideal palace, Cheval wrote with pride, "As a peasant son, I want to live and die to prove that in my class there are men of genius and energy." He needed energy. "Ten thousand days of work, ninety-three thousand hours, thirty-three years of trial." In 1879, to mark the birth of his daughter, he started building the "Source of Life," a fountain of shells and a grotto of stone, consisting of pebbles gathered haphazardly along the nineteen miles of his daily mail route. That's how it all started. More than thirty years later, this unusual monument is complete, the work of a tireless man of whom everyone said, "He's a fool who fills his garden with stones."

The small rural bureaucrat was certainly not a fool. He was a man driven by a consuming curiosity and a boundless admiration for the explorers and great scientists of his time. On his route, he dreams. In his spare time, he builds a universe that is the sum of his dreams. He calls it "The Temple of Nature,"

Ferdinand Cheval's extraordinary palace of pebbles and seashells.

the Druids and Assyrians, Angkor and its lianas, Polynesia with its decorative flowers and coral—everything is present, compact and condensed within the range of his eye. It is a

the oversized character of his undertaking. This structure of a height of 46 feet, a length of 82 feet, a width of 46 feet, holding one thousand cubic feet of stone and cement, contains all the sumptuous fantasies of one of those simple men who undoubtedly are not as simple as many are bound to think.

He was neither an architect nor a mason. All alone he had to resolve innumerable technical problems. He had the occasional help of a retired friend, Joseph Cardier. In one of his numerous notebooks, Cheval writes, "From dream to reality, the distance is great. Never having touched the trowel of a mason, nor the chisel of a sharper, I was absolutely ignorant of all the rules of architecture." It is not without legiti-

mate pride that he engraves the following words on the façade of his palace: "Everything you see, passerby, is the work of a peasant. From a dream, I derived the queen of the world."

By the time his palace is completed, the townspeople no longer consider him crazy. Since 1896, the sign at the entrance to the village has read: "One is not allowed to pass through Hauterives without visiting the work of patience and good taste of the mailman." Many visitors wanted to have their picture taken in front of the masterpiece, in the company of the artist. Naturally, they want him to wear his mailman's cap.

As Cheval's posthumous glory grows, the Surrealists see in him one of their great forerunners.

> *"EVERYTHING YOU SEE, PASSERBY, IS THE WORK OF A PEASANT. FROM A DREAM, I DERIVED THE QUEEN OF THE WORLD"*

or "The Tomb of Silence and Endless Rest." It has dragons, chimeras, stone phoenixes, enormous caryatides, and sphinxes stranger than those in Egypt. Because he cannot travel the world, Cheval decides to build his own compact version of it. All that he has guessed or imagined about the planet —Aztec monuments, steles from

cathedral erected in the name of his faith in himself and in humankind.

Cheval puts all his knowledge into it, his geography, his morality, his mythology. He creates it as he would write an intimate diary, a diary about his passions and fantasies. He inscribes it with all his slogans and sayings. Smug wisdom often clashes with

JUAN GRIS: ART IS A SCIENCE

On May 15, in the Michelet Amphitheater at the Sorbonne, Juan Gris gave a lecture to the Groupe d'Études Philosophiques et Scientifiques, founded by Dr. Allendy. The lecture, entitled "The Possibilities of Painting," was covered in its entirety by the *Transatlantic Review* in its June issue, and significant portions of it were published in Spanish in the September issue of *Alfar*. In the passage reprinted below, Gris contrasts architecture, a single and indivisible entity, with construction, which, according to him, was completely lacking in homogeneity. As the reader will realize, it serves as an excellent introduction to the work of this great Cubist.

All construction in the natural world, whether it be organic or inorganic, is architecture. The molecular structure of a body, in distinguishing it from other bodies, gives it its individuality. The phenomenon of crystallization offers beautiful examples of natural architecture, since the bodies always crystallize in the same volume and form. Oxygen and hydrogen combine in certain proportions to provide a certain quantity of new molecules, a quantity dependent on the quantities of the elements that were combined, no more and no less. Thus, one realizes the synthesis of water in its quality and its quantity. This is a chemical architecture, a true architecture, since the result of this combination has a unity, a homogeneity, and chemical proportions that are completely different from those of its constituent elements. It has a new individuality. But, mixing water with wine, for example, is only a construction. The result has no new chemical properties, no unity, no homogeneity, and no individuality. In short, it is not synthesis . . .

An architectural entity cannot be dismantled into pieces where each piece would maintain autonomy or a separate life. An isolated fragment of architecture can only be a bizarre and detached piece having no existence outside of the place where it belongs. Thus, construction is but an imitation of architecture. The technique of painting is an example of colored, flat architecture and not construction. This is so by virtue of the relationship between the colors and the forms that contain these colors.

One may now say that if esthetics is the collection of relationships between the painter and the external world, relationships that lead to the subject matter of the painting, technique is the collection of relationships between the forms and the colors that they contain, and between the colored forms themselves. This is composition, which leads to the picture . . .

Each form in a picture should perform

three functions: one by virtue of the element that it represents, another by virtue of the color that it contains, and still another by virtue of the other forms which, together with it, make up the totality of the picture. In other words, it must respond to an esthetic, it must have an absolute value in the system of architectural relations, and it must have a relative value in the particular architecture of the picture.

JUAN GRIS
The Possibilities of Painting *(Excerpts)*

JUAN GRIS:
GLASS, NEWSPAPER, AND BOTTLE. 1912-1914. London. Private Collection

The Art Deco style is made official when a large exhibition on the banks of the Seine brings together architecture, painting, furniture, fashion design, and jewelry. In Paris, flounces and frills go out of style, as a joie de vivre in the times and a confidence in the future takes over. All this is in distinct contrast to Germany, recovering from the war with great difficulty. The artists who gather at Darmstadt around the New Objectivity, such as Otto Dix and George Grosz, express, on the contrary, the dark side of urban life. Its despair and corruption is expressed in aggressive, barely presentable canvases.

1925

S U M M A R Y

ART DECO

Art Deco Turns Its Back to the Past
The Overlapping Dresses of Sonia Delaunay
The Futurist Vests of Depero
Raoul Dufy, Decorator
Fashion Designer Poiret Sells His Paintings

ART NEWS

Pierre Bonnard Surrounded by Light
The Death of Sargent
The War Kills La Fresnaye
The Scandal of the Saint-Pol Roux Banquet
Duchamp Rewarded at Last
In Brief

DEVELOPMENTS

Hitler, a Mediocre Painter
Lovis Corinth, a Great Painter

EXHIBITIONS

Birth of the New Objectivity

LITERATURE

AUSTRIA
Posthumous publication of Franz Kafka's The Trial.

UNITED STATES
F. Scott Fitzgerald's novel The Great Gatsby *is well received by the critics but with little interest by the public.*
   Publication of Manhattan Transfer *by John Dos Passos.*

FRANCE
Louis Aragon pulbishes Le paysan de Paris.

MUSIC

GERMANY
Arnold Schönberg succeeds Ferruccio Busoni as professor at the Kunstakademie, pursuing his dodecaphonic studies.
   Alban Berg's Wozzeck is performed with great success at the Berlin Opera.

UNITED STATES
First recordings of Louis Armstrong with Bessie Smith.

FRANCE
Creation of L'enfant et les sortilèges *by Maurice Ravel, with a libretto by Colette.*

MOTION PICTURES

GERMANY
G. W. Pabst films The Joyless Street.

UNITED STATES
Premiere of Charlie Chaplin's The Gold Rush.
   Hal Roach creates the Laurel and Hardy team.

RUSSIA
Premiere of Sergei Eisenstein's Battleship Potemkin.

Art Deco interior. "Swollen" chest of drawers with sharkskin effect by André Groult. Painting by Marie Laurencin.

ART DECO TURNS ITS BACK ON THE PAST

PARIS

The President of the Republic, Gaston Doumergue, surrounded by four thousand guests, inaugurates the International Exhibition of Modern Decorative and Industrial Arts. The exhibition is held for five months at the Esplanade des Invalides, the Alexandre III Bridge, and the area around the Grand Palais and the Petit Palais.

Since 1911, the Society of Artists-Decorators (SAD) has pushed for this exhibit, which was also delayed by the Great War. The exhibition is on, but the Society is not a participant. It is thought that the commercial objectives that the general commissary, Senator Fernand David, intends to give the exhibition, will turn away from its artistic vocation. The press tends to agree. The principal architect, Charles Plumet, sixty-four years old, the designer of the four massive towers framing the panorama of the Invalides, wants to be "modern" rather

Panoramic view of the International Exhibition.

The Pavilion of the New Spirit.

than "contemporary." Nevertheless, some critics remark that the exhibition, whose purpose is the creation of "an alliance between art and industry," does not lack in ambiguity.

Indeed, freed from accessories, the enemy of decorum, the exhibit does not completely adhere to its principle. In the May issue of *L'amour de l'art*, the architect Auguste Perret remarks, "Decorative art should be suppressed. I'd like to know who brought these two words together, art and decorative. It is a monstrosity! Where there is true art, there is no need for decoration . . ." This is also the opinion of Le Corbusier. In his study on *L'art décoratif d'aujourd'hui*, the architect remarks, "To state the truth, decorative art is tooling." According to him, a house must be a "machine to live in," a place to engage in "putting order in the present time." He thinks of "building" as a biological act, not as an "esthetic process." His Pavilion of the New Spirit consists solely of standardized elements. It contains appropriate

cabinets, not bulky furniture. Paintings by Braque, Juan Gris, Ozenfant, and Picasso hang from the walls.

However, Le Corbusier evokes nothing but sarcasm. Even Perret, who is chairman of the international jury, exclaims, "It's idiotic! It doesn't work—there is no architecture." On the other hand, he joins Le Corbusier, Hoffmann, as well as Mallet-Stevens—the Cubist architect of the French Tourism and Embassy Pavilion—in admiring the brilliant USSR pavilion constructed by Constantin Melnikov of glass, steel, and wood painted red and white. The pavilion is the talk of the town, though many object to the arrangement of autonomous triangular spaces laid out at an angle around a pylon bearing the Soviet arms.

The painter Albert Gleizes pays it a compliment in the *Bulletin de la vie artistique:* "This pavilion stands in contrast to its surroundings, whose appearance is encumbered by embellishments." It is "in agreement with its function . . ."

Really modern and rational

constructions and designs are rare, therefore singular. There is, for example, the Lyon Pavilion designed by Tony Garnier. And "the trees" in reinforced concrete, daringly "geometricized" by the brothers Joël and Jean Martel. These contrast with the taste for *trompe l'oeil* where the stylized rose triumphs, and with bombastic Neoclassicism.

In reality, fashion plays a big part. There is every reason to think that the event will bear the passing mark of an infatuation with Art Deco: the furniture, the objets d'art, the clothes. The library desk presented in the *French Embassy* by Pierre Chareau is the most original. While simplifying forms to their extreme, he emphasizes their function. He gives his furniture a geometric style to render it more visually effective.

Nicknamed the "Riesener of Art Deco," Jacques-Émile Ruhlmann combines a remarkable technical virtuosity with the most refined elegance. He triumphs at the *Hôtel du Collectionneur* built by Pierre Patout, one of the inventors of the "ocean-liner style." He gives his highly architectural furniture very pure qualities, especially by means of fine and elegant spindle legs.

Paul Iribe is the inventor of the rose bouquet that becomes the symbol of Art Deco—the "Iribe rose." For his part, René Lalique, the goldsmith of glass, astounds the public with the large luminous fountain and the numerous pieces of molded glass adorning his pavilion.

Notwithstanding the contradictions and ambiguities, the exhibition at the Esplanade des Invalides resolutely turns its back on the frills of the *Belle Époque.* It loves the present and has faith in the future. It is sufficient to create a style—the Art Deco style.

Overlapping dresses by Sonia Delaunay.

THE OVERLAPPING DRESSES OF SONIA DELAUNAY

PARIS
The fashionable crowd of Paris gathers before the doors of the Boutique Simultanée. The boutique is installed for the length of the Exhibition of Decorative Arts on the Alexandre III Bridge, for the presentation of the collections of Sonia Delaunay and Jacques Heim.

The evening gowns, city coats, and sports clothes cut from the overlapping fabrics of Sonia Delaunay have bright colors and bold shapes, which are indeed attention-getters.

Sonia Terk, wife of Robert Delaunay, made a name for herself in 1913 with the illustration of *The Prose of the Trans-Siberian* by Blaise Cendrars. Since then, she has pursued her artistic activities and her career as a fabric designer. Her first work in textile dates back to 1911. It was also her first abstract creation. A blanket for her newborn son, Charles, it is an assembly of pieces of fabric of various bright colors in the tradition of the Ukraine, where she was born forty years ago.

Sonia Delaunay plays with the colors of her fabrics as she does with the colors of her paintings. She abandons traditional decorative motifs in fabrics—floral or other—and is interested in color only. But she does more than just transpose the results of her research on overlapping color contrasts onto fabric. In her hands, a dress or a coat becomes architectural compositions in space, governed by color. She creates a fabric while thinking of its practical application. The linkage, composition, and balance of shapes are all part of the esthetics of her creations.

The best fashion houses in Paris endorse Sonia Delaunay's designs. A trip to the Boutique Simultanée convinces many people that from now on it will be

THE FUTURIST VESTS OF DEPERO

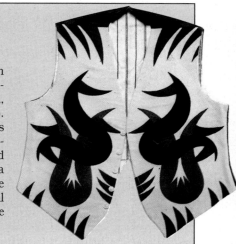

Following the dandies of Milan and Bologna, Parisian society can applaud the launching of the showy Futurist vests. They were presented at the top of the Eiffel Tower by Philippo Tommaso Marinetti, founder of Futurism, Guglielmo Jannelli, and Fortunato Depero. Depero designed and made the vests in order to introduce into this sad article of modern man's clothing a little of the fantasy of the doublet of yore. They are tailored in lively colored fabrics and decorated with elegant geometric designs, and are worn with a white shirt and a black bow tie. Depero, whose paintings, collages, and posters are characterized by volumetric figures that express a sort of mechanical fairyland, also makes toys, puppets, and theatrical costumes. He

RAOUL DUFY, DECORATOR

PARIS

A wonderful barge is moored along the banks of the Seine. It may be the most luxurious boat ever carried by the waters of the river. Flanked by two other barges, it participates in the International Exhibition of Decorative Arts. The barges, named *Amour, Délices,* and *Orgues,* are on loan from Paul Poiret, the great Parisian fashion designer, who has asked Raoul Dufy to decorate them. Fourteen wall hangings conceived by the master give the vessel the appearance of a great reception hall.

This is not the first time that Poiret and Dufy have collaborated. In 1911, the designer and the painter formed a partnership to establish, on the Boulevard de Clichy, a fabric-printing studio in order to give new life to the textile industry. The venture has made Dufy famous in the indus-

try and has allowed him to work as a designer for the great silk merchants Bianchini and Ferrier, for whom he creates several hundred designs.

Dufy makes fabrics explode. He renews their color schemes through the use of the ultra-bright tones of his Fauve palette.

RAOUL DUFY: TISSU. 1920. Paris. Musée des Arts Décoratifs

He revolutionizes the printing methods on fabric by using discharge techniques on cotton —techniques formerly used only on silk. This technique results in new effects allowing him to use this approach as an artist.

Dufy's wall hangings reflect the themes of his paintings.

They include maritime scenes of his childhood in Le Havre, sea mythology, and horse races, as in *Mannequins de Poiret aux courses.* Dufy renders a beautiful token of his respect to the Maecenases who allow him to exercise his talent as a designer and to renew the art of textile.

Paul Poiret and the tailor Christian.

FASHION DESIGNER POIRET SELLS HIS PAINTINGS

PARIS

The Drouot Mansion is the site of an artistic event on September 18. The prestigious collection of modern paintings of fashion designer Paul Poiret is put up for auction. Before the sale, he used to exhibit the collection in his private mansion on the Rue d'Antin. It consists mainly of works reflecting the friendships between Poiret and numerous painters. A portrait of the collector by his friend André Derain is bought by Monsieur Hansel for 8,000 francs.

A glance at the catalogue attests to the high quality and prestige of the collection. Presided over by the expert Georges Bernheim, the sale is a great success. The stars are Derain, Van Dongen, Matisse, Marquet, Dufy, and La Fresnaye, whose

paintings all sell for high prices. The admirers do not hesitate to raise the stakes beyond the predicted amounts.

Two canvases by Picasso, *Still Life* and *Harlequin,* find buyers at 11,200 francs and 11,500 francs, respectively. A portrait of Max Jacob by Modigliani sells for 10,500 francs. Utrillo's *Church of Saint-Denis* goes for 19,000 francs. The greatest triumph is reserved for Dunoyer de Segonzac, Poiret's friend whom he had six paintings by; *The Drinkers* draws the highest price of all, 90,100 francs.

Poiret sells his collection because of financial difficulties incurred by the very expensive redecoration of his barges *Amour, Délices,* and *Orgues* on the occasion of the Exhibition of Decorative Arts.

Pierre Bonnard Surrounded by Light

The delicate health of his wife Martha convinced Bonnard to move to Cannet in the Midi, just north of Cannes. He has bought a small house, and is surrounded by the diffuse yet blinding light he loves. His canvases depict scenes of everyday life, such as an outdoor evening party or bath time. He covers the walls of his studio with lengths of canvas, which he cuts only when he completes a picture. Thus he has a free hand, unconstrained by format. With his move to Cannet, new horizons are open to him. At the age of fifty-eight, he is the most subtle of the modern painters.

The Death of Sargent

Just when the Museum of Fine Arts in Boston is holding a retrospective of his work, John Singer Sargent, the American painter, dies in London where he has made his home. Born in 1856 in Florence to a cosmopolitan family, he had studied in Rome, Florence, and Paris. A friend of Monet, who had influenced him, Sargent showed an innovative mind in his outdoor studies and country scenes, as well as in his very fine watercolors, which he painted during his travels. But he owed his fame mainly to his portraits of high society in Boston and London. He was fifty-nine when he died.

The War Kills La Fresnaye

Of fragile health, too much so for the kind of life he was leading, Roger de La Fresnaye died in Grasse on November 27, of tuberculosis, which he contracted in 1918 at the front. He was born in Le Mans in 1885, and showed an early predilection for drawing. After attending the Julian Academy, then the Ranson Academy, he was a visible participant in the Cubist movement. *Artillery* of 1911, *The Conquest of the Air* of 1913, and *Sitting Man* or *The Architect* of 1914 are important works in which color plays a predominant role. At the end of his all too brief life, La Fresnaye had returned to a kind of Classicism. He was forty when he died.

The Scandal of the Saint-Pol Roux Banquet

The banquet organized on July 2 at la Closerie des Lilas to honor the poet Saint-Pol Roux, whom the Surrealists consider an influence, ended up in a free-for-all. Rachide, the once famous author of *Monsieur Venus*, started the fray when he declared in a voice loud enough for all to hear that "a French woman could not marry a German man." It was a well-known fact that the Surrealists were pro-German. André Breton threw his napkin in Rachide's face, calling him "a soldier's girl." Then Philippe Soupault, swinging from a chandelier, swept the dishes from the table. Finally, Michel Leiris, yelling "Down with France" from the window overlooking the Boulevard Montparnasse, was invited to present himself to the chief of police and explain what had happened, after he barely escaped a lynch mob.

Duchamp Rewarded at Last

His enduring patience was finally rewarded. On September 11, at the conclusion of the third French chess championship in Nice, Marcel Duchamp was finally crowned with the enviable title of "master" by the French Chess Federation. Duchamp had designed the poster for the championship, a renewal—though a single work does not a habit make—of pictorial activities he had ceased in 1918. He was a mediocre player, but chess had always been a form of mental cleansing for him. His new title rewarded his persistence. In addition, he also completed his second optic machine, *Rotative Demi-sphere,* which the clothing designer and collector Jacques Doucet bought with the promise of not lending it to any exhibition.

ROGER DE LA FRESNAYE: SITTING MAN OR THE ARCHITECT. 1914. Paris. MNAM

HITLER, A MEDIOCRE PAINTER

ADOLF HITLER: FINDING SHELTER AT FOURNES. 1915 (on the front line)

MUNICH

No one, of course, knows if prison ever makes a man better. Otherwise, Hitler might have made amends after his incarceration following the failed Munich putsch of two years ago, and the world might have been spared the publication of *Mein Kampf*. The book is nothing more than a virulent "settling of accounts," the embellished autobiography of a talentless painter who goes from watercolors to politics in the way people change machine guns. Hitler continued to believe in his artistic genius when the Vienna Academy of Fine Arts refused to enroll him in 1907. He had a knack for drawing, especially architectural, and he often painted views of the Austrian capital after postcards. But painstakingly executed detail is not necessarily the mark of genius. The sale to tourists of village squares and of town halls to newly married couples provided him with only a meager income. The former guest of night shelters in Vienna now attracts more people with his inflamed rhetoric than with his little pictures.

LOVIS CORINTH, A GREAT PAINTER

ZANDVOORT

Lovis Corinth always loved the Flemish painters. When he left Berlin, he headed for the Netherlands, where he planned to study the paintings of Frans Hals and Rembrandt. He died there at the age of sixty-seven. He never fully recovered from a stroke in 1911, and fought his handicap by pouring energy into painting. He was clearly an example of courage.

He studied in Munich, then lived in Paris from 1884 to 1887. At the Julian Academy he executed many studies of nudes. He attended classes of Bouguereau. Luckily, he did not adhere to the conventionalism of his teacher. On his return to Germany, he painted landscapes, still lifes, and portraits in a realistic vein.

In 1900, he settled in Berlin and participated in the activities of the Secession, becoming president in 1911. But he always remained independent of associations and movements. He claimed that his only ambition was to raise German art to a very high level. That meant ridding it of the cult of the local soil, opening it up to foreign painting, and basing it on continually creative work rather than on imitation. In that context, he had the audacity to occasionally deal with trite subjects, to show that they could be treated with originality. The most typical example of this is his *Great Martyr* of 1907. The naked body of Christ on the cross seems to cry out its pain and to reach, in tension, to another world. Those below who watch him represent the vulgar, barely involved masses.

If his total work seems somewhat disparate, it is because it is the work of an artist who cannot be classified. He received an academic education, but his drawings and paintings bear witness to the fact that he mainly obeyed what he felt in his heart should be expressed. Along with Liebermann and Slevogt, Corinth is the most characteristic representative of German Impressionism.

LOVIS CORINTH: WALCHENSEE. 1912.
Munich. Neue Pinakothek

BIRTH OF THE NEW OBJECTIVITY

MANNHEIM

In Germany, a new generation of painters is being rightly acclaimed. Gustav Hartlaub, director of the Kunsthalle in Mannheim and a major promoter of contemporary movements, organizes the first retrospective of young German painting. He calls it "the New Objectivity." Thirty-two artists with one hundred and twenty-four works are gathered under this banner.

What brings them together is the return to painstaking representation and traditional workmanship, as well as a common stylized coldness on which Hartlaub bases his designation. Yet, there are considerable differences in conviction and inspiration. On the one hand, there are painters like Kanoldt, Mense, or Schrimpf whose frozen still lifes and landscapes float between the real and the unreal, showing a great affinity with the Italian Valori Plastici. On the other hand, some painters impress with their Verism, which is imbued with political and social engagement.

They denounce and accuse, they spit the evil of the world back into its face. Besides Schlichter, Hubbuch, Scholz, and the independent Max Beckmann, the most virulent among them are Dix and Grosz, the focus of all attention. Their canvases show disgusting women with fat thighs and bellies and men with terrifying faces—all despairing and desperate. They unsheathe the weapon of their cynicism to cry out about the misery of the underworld, the unemployed, the prostitutes. Their portraits may be spoofs or caricatures, but they reveal the sharpness and lucidity of their power of observation.

Three years ago, Hartlaub revealed the dualism between "Verists" and "Classicists" in a survey in *Kunstblatt* that announced in a questioning way: "A new Naturalism?" Already, divergent sensitivities and convictions were pushing some to confront a world that others were fleeing to seek refuge in dreams.

OTTO DIX:
PORTRAIT OF JOHANNA
EY. 1924. Düsseldorf.
Kunstmuseum

The exterior signs of Realism are all they have in common.

The visitor to the Kunsthalle realizes that at a time when this New Objectivity is affirming itself, Expressionism is running out of breath. The survivors of the great era of intense excitement lost most of their strength during the war. After a short interlude in the world of Dadaism, their successors are casting a sharp eye on the sad reality of everyday life. What a contrast with the spontaneity of Heckel, Schmidt-Rottluff, and others like them. But at a closer look, the New Objectivity is not so objective. The neutral Realism of Leibl and Courbet belongs to the past, because today we face other realms of emotion.

This is an exhibition with a program of painters without a program. Still, Hartlaub must be given credit for bringing together the most dynamic creators on the contemporary German art scene. Mannheim is worth the detour—for the sake of the "New Objectivity."

(See also 1920 and 1932.)

From Barcelona comes news of the death of a great architect, Antoni Gaudí, crushed by a tram. He leaves behind the incomplete Sagrada Familia, the cathedral on which he had been working since 1884. It is distinct from everything we see in the architecture of today, whether it embraces Functionalism on a large scale or a small one. Is Gaudí's design a resurgence of the past? Max Ernst's rubbings (frottages), on the other hand, are an innovation opening a new route to Automatism. His Natural History, published by Jeanne Bucher, will push hallucination to its limits, adding a superb page to the history of Surrealism.

1926

SUMMARY

LITERATURE

FRANCE
Georgres Bernanos publishes Under the Sun of Satan.
Publication of two poetry collections: Georgia *by Philippe Soupault and* Capital of Pain *by Paul Éluard.*

GREAT BRITAIN
T. E. Lawrence publishes The Seven Pillars of Wisdom, *and D. H. Lawrence publishes* The Plumed Serpent.

SWITZERLAND
Death of Rainer Maria Rilke, who during his long stay in France was Rodin's private secretary.

MUSIC

ITALY
Under the direction of Arturo Toscanini, Giacomo Puccini's Turandot *is performed at the Scala in Milan.*

RUSSIA
Premiere in Moscow of Dmitri Shostakovich's First Symphony.

MOTION PICTURES

GERMANY
Fritz Lang's Expressionist film Metropolis *is launched with an unusual publicity campaign.*
Premiere of F. W. Murnau's Faust.

UNITED STATES
Death of the actor Rudolph Valentino. His last film, The Sheik's Son, *is a great success.*
Premiere of Don Juan *with John Barrymore.*

FRANCE
Premiere of Nana *by Jean Renoir.*

ANTONI GAUDÍ:
GÜELL PARK (DETAIL)

Detail of the Casa Batlló in Barcelona.

ANTONI GAUDÍ ENTERS ETERNITY

Antoni Gaudí in the Corpus Christi procession in Barcelona, 1924.

BARCELONA

A senseless traffic accident robs architecture of one of its greatest creators, Antoni Gaudí y Cornet. He is hit by a streetcar in the streets of Barcelona on June 7 and dies three days later at the Hospital of the Holy Cross.

Gaudí was born in Reus, near Tarragona, on June 25, 1852. Soon after entering the Barcelona School of Architecture, he has to accept various jobs to make a living while he continues his university studies. His first personal achievements occur in 1877-1878—the waterfall of the Citadel Park in Barcelona and the Casa Vicens.

Gaudí was a complete artist, as passionate about the various arts, town planning, sculpture, music, and mathematics as about architecture itself. He was closely involved in the circles of the Catalan Renaissance, which exalts the Gothic style and popular traditions. His genius was recognized early on by the more enlightened of his compatriots,

who commissioned many works.

His principal Maecenas was Eusebio Güell, an industrialist. For him, Gaudí created impressive works, such as the Güell Palace built in Barcelona between 1885 and 1889, complete with interior decoration and furniture; the Colonia Güell in Santa Colonna de Cervello, with its chapel with inclined columns; the famous Güell Park in Barcelona, which took from 1901 to 1914 to construct; and the Finca of the Güell family, erected in 1887. Gaudí's hand is seen in Catalonia, Tangiers, and Cadiz, among other cities. He made the Episcopal Palace of Astorga and—in the very center of Barcelona—two superb buildings on the Passeig de Gracia: Casa Batlló and Casa Milá, or "La Pedrera."

The latter, built between 1906 and 1910, for Pere Milá i Campas, was not nicknamed "La Pedrera," the stone quarry, for nothing. It is a fantastic structure that appears to be modeled

out of earth and stucco. It bears testimony to Gaudí's horror of right angles. The rhythm of the building is perfectly adapted to the surrounding space, to the point that at first sight one does not realize the boldness of the project and the exceptional decorative elements—iron work, pieces of sculpture, and ceramics—all perfectly integrated in the architecture. The originality of the work does not lie in the use of materials, which are traditional. Instead it lies in the design itself, with the free and modern plan, with the seductive mixture of functionality and ornamental excess, which, for example, turns the chimneys into immense figures from the dream of a demented demiurge.

Since 1884, Gaudí worked with a small team (the architects Berenguer, Jujol, and Rubió, and the painter Aleix Clapes) on what was to be his major work, the Sagrada Familia. To this Gothic basilica, started in 1876 by the architect Francisco de

Paula del Villar, the deeply religious Gaudí unceasingly dedicated all his energy and genius. The façade reveals the evolution of Gaudí's art over the course of the years. This incredible project, launched as a challenge to time itself, can only be compared to the great inspiration that drove the builders of cathedrals in the Middle Ages. At the same time, it bears witness to the humility of a great artist who sometimes might have come across—wrongly so—as a megalomaniac.

The Sagrada Familia was never finished, but Gaudí leaves behind a large number of plans, models, and drawings, which should make it possible to continue the colossal and majestic undertaking.

(See also 1914.)

FORMS AND SYMBOLS

BARCELONA
Legend appropriately turns Gaudí into a dreamer. His accidental death seems to confirm this, as do some of the claims in which he gladly presented himself as a man with instinctive skills. A man operating with the automatism that is so cherished by today's Surrealists, a man who considers it sufficient "to know whether a thing must be higher or lower, flatter or more curved. It's merely a matter of the gift of vision and I, luckily, can see." Yet, Gaudí was also a man with deep roots in his native country, in his time, and in a tradition that he vigorously prolonged. He pushed far ahead as the Futurist he was without perhaps realizing it.

If their training had not been so different, the death of Gaudí

A column-bearing tortoise at the Nativity façade of the Sagrada Familia in Barcelona.

could evoke the name of that amateur of genius who died two years ago, mailman Cheval, who built a stupendous palace and tomb for himself. Both men shared certain features in their overall work, and in the details, for example, a preference for animal and plant forms, for inscriptions, and for recycled materials. However, Cheval's trashy verses cannot possibly be compared to the formulas decorating the towers of the Sagrada Familia, nor Cheval's gathering of pebbles to the studied use of ceramic shards in Güell Park.

Moreover, the animal and plant forms used by Gaudí are not merely decorative. Erected as pinnacle turrets or slapped against walls, they preside over the profound movement of the structure. From leaves, a system of vaults and corbeling is born in Güell Park. Ramps yield to the configuration of the Sagrada Familia. From the scaly unevenness of some saurian, the tile coating of the Casa Batlló emerges. Gaudí designed a system as a function of mechanical and architectural engineering. His work is anything but the creations of an autodidact.

His long and wide-ranging studies are revealed in his first projects. Medieval art—the Viol-

let-le-Duc angle, for example—marks the Episcopal Palace of Astorga. Moorish art prevails in the forms and colors of the Casa Vicens. His work also shows traces of African architecture. Other elements are reminiscent of factories. The inspiration Gaudí found in native Catalan traditions should never be underestimated—his slanted columns and famous parabolic vaults are derived from the traditional Catalan "revoltó." The ample use of ironwork in balconies is a reminder that no other craftsmen can work iron as well as they do in Catalonia.

The animal and plant forms are not sentimentalized. They generate new forms. They carry with them a whole world of symbols in which mythology, and probably psychoanalysis, are reflected, as in the turtle bearing a column. Gaudí is a painter, sculptor, and poet as well as an architect. And what the architect leaves to the decorator, he takes, molds, reveals, sublimates. Chimney pipes by Gaudí are actual structures of a rare shape and ornamental value.

Plan for a façade of the Sagrada Familia.

BRETON VERSUS DE CHIRICO

PARIS

André Breton, betrayed, hurt, and outraged, mourns a "lost genius"—Giorgio de Chirico, the founder of Metaphysical Painting, whom Breton further accuses of being a "nasty influence." The pretext for the rupture is the June exhibition by the painter at Paul Guillaume, sponsored by the American collector Albert C. Barnes. Breton does not like the show, but he blames the painter even more for having participated in February and March in the first manifestation of the Novecento, in Milan, on the invitation of Margherita Sarfatti, Mussolini's advisor in matters of art.

It looks, indeed, as if de Chirico, who is thirty-six years old, has suddenly changed his ways. No longer does he paint sweeping lightning grazing the horizon, or deserted railroad stations and squares. He is now infatuated with Raphael and Tintoretto, whose works he copies in order to unveil their secrets. After his break with Breton, he declares that he no longer "wants to associate with the Surrealists, who are stupid and hostile."

Perhaps a renewal rather than a change may be at hand. It is indeed true that de Chirico has changed his manner of painting. The large surfaces of bold colors have been replaced with thousands of nuances created by small brush strokes. It is not only his Classicistic *Achilles* submitted for the Novecento that remains a total enigma. What about the horses, now one of his favorite themes? If Breton were willing to remove his blinkers, he would agree that it is difficult to find more disturbing horses in the entire history of painting.

GIORGIO DE CHIRICO: ORIENTAL HORSES. 1926. Private Collection

The Surrealists to Have a Place of Their Own

The Galerie Surréaliste opens on March 26 in Paris with an exhibition of works by Man Ray, including his "rayographs," and primitive objects from Oceania on loan from the collections of Breton, Éluard, and Aragon, as well as various Parisian art collectors. The gallery, under the direction of Roland Tual, is located at 16 Rue Jacques-Callot, in premises formerly occupied by the offices of the magazine *Clarté*, known to have Communist sympathies. The Surrealist exhibition at the Pierre gallery last December enjoyed a *succès d'estime*, and spawned the idea of the gallery. The catalogue of the current exhibition is composed entirely of sentences about birds. "Birds of the law, shatter like glass on the eyelash of birds" (Robert Desnos), or "So here is the white bird in the temple of the fire-colored hag" (Diderot), and "I saw then that at the sound of a bell a nun who had put a pox on the bird of the Dispensary was stuffed into a wine barrel" (Giorgio Baffo).

The Galerie Surréaliste at the Rue Jacques-Callot in Paris.

Cendrars Exhibits Brazil

Chauvinistic and poorly informed as Europeans are, they generally think that the few talented Latin American artists live either in Mexico or in Paris with the Uruguayans Torrès-García and Barradas, the Argentinian Pettoruti, and the Cubans Abela and Enríquez. But Modern Art Week in São Paolo in 1922 was an event that drew from the entire continent, thanks to painters such as Annita Malfatti, Vicente Monteiro, and Di Cavalcanti. Ever impressed with novelty, Blaise Cendrars went to see for himself. At the Galerie Percier in Paris, he is now exhibiting the Brazilian art of Tarsila do Amaral. These paintings reveal a solidly built, brilliantly colored world of black women and pine trees, factories and bridges, a renewal in modernity.

Mondrian Defends the Charleston

A theosophist as well as a painter, Piet Mondrian is a talented modern-dance enthusiast, and practices every Sunday. When the Parisian correspondent of *De Telegraph*, an Amsterdam newspaper, comes to interview him in his studio at 26 Rue du Départ, Mondrian does not hesitate to express his contempt for Holland. The Charleston is now forbidden there, considered too obscene a dance. "How can this athletic dance be forbidden?" Not only are Charleston dancers separated by considerable distance, they move so fast that they have little time to be amorous. Standing before the red phonograph he uses to practice with, Mondrian swears he will never set foot in his native country again if the Charleston continues to be forbidden.

Adolf Loos Builds for Tristan Tzara

Having come to Paris three years ago, the fifty-six-year-old Austrian architect Adolf Loos, celebrated author of *Ornament Is Crime*, published in 1908, has built a private house on the Avenue Junot for the poet Tristan Tzara. Loos' tenets are well known: Form is attractive when it expresses function and so constitutes an integral whole. It is in this spirit that he conceived of Tzara's house, in diametric opposition to Dada, a movement that Tzara helped found in 1916. In 1910, Loos had built the Steiner house in Vienna, one of the first private dwellings made entirely of reinforced concrete and stripped of all decoration.

Tristan Tzara's house, built by Adolf Loos.

MAX ERNST: NATURAL HISTORIES

The boards of his Natural History, which Max Ernst presented at the gallery of Jeanne Bucher, included an entire universe of mysterious pampas, fantastic monsters, and battles of hybrid animals. They were arrived at by a new procedure, the rubbing—frottage—of various elements, such as leaves and their nervures, the unraveled edges of sackcloth, and fragments of spare objects. The resulting images were both obsessive and hallucinatory. It was almost by chance that the artist discovered this procedure, thereby renewing the Automatism so dear to the Surrealists. He explains below the strange circumstances of this occurence.

Botticelli did not like landscapes and thought they were a genre deserving "short and mediocre investigation." He also said, scornfully, that "if one threw a sponge soaked in different colors against a wall, the trace left would be seen as a beautiful landscape." This drew a severe admonition from his colleague Leonardo da Vinci: "In order to be universal and please different tastes, a composition must be made to include some areas of darkness and others of soft penumbra. In my view, it is not to be frowned upon if, on certain occasions, you stop to contemplate traces on walls, in ashes, in clouds, or in rivers. And if you examine them closely, you will discover admirable inventions that the painter may, with his genius, use to compose battles of animals and humans, landscapes or monsters, demons and other fantastic things that will do honor " . . .

On August 10, 1925, an intolerable visual obsession made me discover the technical means that enabled me to put Leonardo's lesson into practice in a very broad manner. Starting from a childhood memory in which a panel of false mahogany across from my bed provoked a vision in my mind while I was half asleep, and, being in an inn by the sea during a rainfall, I became obsessed and irritated with the patterns of grooves in the floor, accentuated by thousands of washings. I decided to investigate the meaning of this obsession and, to aid my meditative and hallucinatory faculties, I made a series of drawings from the floorboards by randomly putting sheets of paper over them and rubbing graphite against the sheets. Closely examining the drawings obtained, the dark areas and others, I was surprised by the sudden intensification of my visionary faculties and the haunting succession of contradictory images superimposing each other with a persistence and speed that may be characteristic of the fleeting memories of a romance . . .

The fact must be stressed that drawings

MAX ERNST: THE STALLION AND THE BRIDE OF THE WIND (ON WOOD) 1926. Paris. Bibliothèque Nationale

so obtained gradually lose, through a sequence of suggestions and transmutations that arise spontaneously—as happens with hypnagogic images—the character of the matter being investigated (the wood, for example) to take on the form of unexpectedly precise images, so as to reveal, probably, the initial cause of the obsession or to reproduce a semblance of that cause . . .

This rubbing procedure relies therefore on nothing more than an intensification of the irritability of the faculties of the mind by appropriate technical means, excluding any conscious mental conduction (through reason, taste, or morals), reducing to an extreme degree the active role of the one who has thus far been called the "author" of the work. Consequently, this procedure proves to be the true equivalent of what is already known as Automatic Writing. The author participates as a spectator, indifferent or passionately involved, of the birth of his work and observes the stages of its development.

MAX ERNST
The History of a Natural History
(Excerpts)

WASSILI KANDINSKY: PAINTING AND MUSIC

While *About the Spiritual in Art,* in 1911, questioned the objectives of painting, it is with the means that Kandinsky concerned himself in *Point, Line, Plane,* recently in bookstores. The work, an outcome of his teaching at the Bauhaus, contains a portion of his course material. No other artist, besides Klee, concerned himself so significantly with the grammar of forms. In the passage below, Kandinsky compares painting and music.

The line, like the point, is used in other arts besides painting. It has a character that lends itself to a more or less precise application in the language of the other arts.

We all know what a melodic line is. Most musical instruments correspond to a linear character. The volume of the sound of the various instruments corresponds to the thickness of the line. The violin, the flute, and the piccolo produce a very thin line. Moving on to a thicker line, produced by the viola and the clarinette, we eventually reach the thickest line, produced by the deepest sounds of the double bass and the tuba.

Besides its size, the color of the line also depends on the particular color of the various instruments.

The organ is a typically linear instrument, just as the piano corresponds to the idea of the point.

It can be observed that, in music, the line represents the predominant means of expression. As in painting, it asserts itself by its volume and length. In both arts, the problem of time and space is a separate theme, and their separation has led to a timorous attitude in which the notions of time-space and space-time have been too divided. The degrees of intensity from pianissimo to fortissimo can find their equivalent in the increase or decrease in the size of the line, or its degree of clarity. The pressure exerted on the bow corresponds precisely to the pressure exerted in producing a point.

It is particularly interesting and significant that current musicographic representation, that is, standard musical notation, is nothing more than various combinations of points and lines. The length, however, is only discernible by the color of the point (black and white only, which leads to a restriction of means), and the number of quaver lines. In the same way, the height of the sound is measured in lines, with the five horizontal lines of the staff serving as a base. It is enlightening to note that the conciseness and simplicity of the means of

WASSILI KANDINSKY: COMPOSITION IN GREEN. 1923. Private Collection

transcription enable the most complicated sonorities to be conveyed in clear language to the initiated eye, or directly to the ear. These two characteristics are a source of temptation for the other arts, and it is understandable that a proper form of notation is sought for painting and dance. Even here, there is only one road to follow, that of analysis of the basic elements in order to arrive ultimately at an adequate graphic expression.

WASSILI KANDINSKY
Point, Line, Plane *(Excerpt)*

Two events of capital importance are Clemenceau's installation of the **Waterlilies** at the Orangerie, and the opening of the Bauhaus in Dessau. Monet's **Waterlilies,** as much by its theme as by its revolutionary conception of space, totally renews mural art as it had been practiced since the Renaissance. The Bauhaus, finally installed in a house of glass, built by its architect-director Walter Gropius, attracts attention from avant-garde circles around the world.
Then comes the tragic death of Juan Gris at the early age of forty-six, carried off by an attack of uremia. When we add to these events the publication of Elie Faure's **The Spirit of Forms,** the concluding and crowning work in his monumental **History of Art,** it is understandable why some years seem more important than others.

GREAT MASTERS

The *Waterlilies* Invade the Orangerie
Clemenceau Talks about Monet
Opinions on the *Waterlilies*
The Clear Lesson of Juan Gris

WRITINGS AND THEORIES

Elie Faure: the Spirit of Forms

AVANT-GARDE

Picasso's Sacred Monsters
The Montparnos underneath La Coupole

ART NEWS

Malevich in the West
The Aubette's Obliques
Arthur Dove at Stieglitz' Place
Courteline Sells His Museum of Horrors
André Masson Makes Sand Talk
The Corbusiers Are Immortalized by Bauchant
In Brief

SCHOOLS

The Bauhaus within Its Own Walls
Bauhaus Design

LITERATURE

GERMANY
The young philosopher Martin Heidegger publishes Being and Time.
Hermann Hesse publishes Steppenwolf.

UNITED STATES
Publication of Ernest Hemingway's Men without Women.

SWEDEN
The French philosopher Henri Bergson is awarded the Nobel prize in literature.

RUSSIA
Yevgeny Zamyatin is officially accused for having We, *his cruelly prophetic novel, published abroad.*

MUSIC

UNITED STATES
Duke Ellington is the star attraction at the Cotton Club in Harlem, and records Black and Tan Fantasy.

FRANCE
Premiere of the ballet La chatte *with music by Henri Sauguet and design by the brothers Nahum Gabo and Anton Pevsner.*

MOTION PICTURES

UNITED STATES
Premiere of The Jazz Singer *by Alan Crosland, with Al Jolson.*

FRANCE
Abel Gance's film Napoleon *creates a sensation at the Paris Opera because of its projection on triple screens, its fast-paced montage, and the mobility of the cameras.*

CLAUDE MONET:
WATERLILIES (DETAIL: SUNSET).
1914-1926. Paris. Musée de l'Orangerie

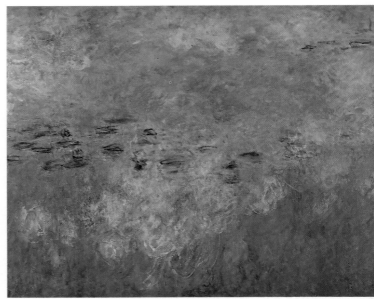

CLAUDE MONET: WATERLILIES (DETAIL). 1914-1926. Paris. Musée de l'Orangerie

THE "WATERLILIES" INVADE THE ORANGERIE

PARIS

Claude Monet, who died last December, at the age of eighty-six, in his home in Giverny, did not live to see the realization of his ultimate dream, maintained with the help of his friend Georges Clemenceau: the inauguration in a national museum of his "Grand Decorations" of waterlilies—his pictorial apotheosis! The inauguration takes place March 17 in the two large oval rooms of the Orangerie des Tuileries in the presence of both

The iridescent evocation of the waterlilies of Giverny consists of nineteen panels of 6 1/2 x 14 feet, two panels of 6 1/2 x 7 feet, and one panel of 6 1/2 x 20 feet, backed with canvas and linked in the oval rooms of the Orangerie. Eight compositions—four per room—form a harmonious unit. They cover a total of three hundred linear feet. According to the terms of the agreement signed by Monet and the government on April 12, 1922, the themes are "Clouds," "Morning," "Green Re-

homage to the creator of the *Waterlilies:* "Claude Monet, at the end of his long life, after having studied all the different motifs that nature creates with color effects in reply to light, has addressed the most docile, the most penetrable element—water —which is at the same time transparent, iridescent, and reflective. Thanks to water, he has become the painter of what

we cannot see. He addresses that invisible spiritual surface that separates light from reflection. Airy azure captive of liquid azure . . . Color rises from the bottom of the water in clouds, in whirlpools."

These circular views, these plant, floral, aqueous, subaqueous, and celestial views plunge the spectator into the contemplation of abyssal beauty.

"THE AIRY AZURE IS CAPTIVE OF THE LIQUID AZURE.
COLOR RISES FROM THE BOTTOM
OF THE WATER IN CLOUDS"

the minister of public education and fine arts, Édouard Herriot, and the director of the Beaux-Arts and member of the Institute, Paul Léon. There were few others in attendance. When Clemenceau returns in June for his personal pleasure, he states with regret that "there was absolutely nobody else" there. However, Monet has the admiration of art critics, including René Jean, who describes Monet as the "Raphael of water."

flections," "Setting Sun," "Willows," and "Reflections of Trees."

Monet's colors are obtained with finely crushed pigments bonded with oil. The colors search for one another, mix and blend with one another, in a deeply peaceful symphony that evolves subtly from white, light pink, and golden yellow to light green, dark green, ultramarine, dark blue, and cobalt blue.

The poet Paul Claudel, after his visit to the Orangerie, pays

Claude Monet at his studio in Giverny.

CLAUDE MONET: WATERLILIES (DETAIL). 1914-1926. Paris. Musée de l'Orangerie

CLEMENCEAU TALKS ABOUT MONET

Monet is the only painter who dared to push Impressionism all the way to the heavenly abstraction that haunted him day and night at the end of his life.

He admirably completed his long and patient search around the "lily pond" that he created in his garden at Giverny in 1893. His *Waterlily* series actually consists of dozens and dozens of paintings on which he started to work seriously thirty-two years ago. They were shown for the first time in 1900, at Durand-Ruel. What stubbornness! What discouragements, too.

Victim of a cataract, Monet did not submit to surgery for several years. In the last months of 1922, he "locked himself up" so he could finish his masterpiece. When he realized that the loss of sight had led him to damage some panels, he destroyed them. Finally, encouraged by Clemenceau, he underwent surgery in 1923, and took up painting again, though he thought at times that he was "finished."

"Monet is an eye, but what an eye," Cézanne said. It is the eye of a Cyclops who was already contemplating the waters of the Styx, which would return him to the amniotic happiness of his origins. In the meantime, the Seine continues to flow by his gardens at the Orangerie.

(See also 1900.)

PARIS
In recent years, Georges Clemenceau has been writing notes and comments on Claude Monet and his work, for a book that will be published next year. Here are a few excerpts:

"Monet has never had any kind of 'poetry' or theory that could hold back his brush. He decided that truth lay in what he saw, and he applied himself tirelessly to reproduce what he saw. Nothing else. It's enough."

"I simply want to say that he has made us take a major step toward an emotional representation of the world and its components, thanks to light distributions that correspond to the vibrating shadows that science has taught us to notice."

"Water attracted Monet's brush—the sea, the Seine, the limpid sleeping surface where the pink and white corollas of waterlilies create effects of quicksilver . . ."

"The aspiration of Infinity supported by the most subtle sensations of a tangible reality merging, from reflection to reflection, with the most supreme nuances of the imperceptible—that is the subject of the *Waterlilies!*"

"What a picture! A field of water with flowers and leaves intermingled with flames from the sun, with repercussions from both the screen of the sky and the mirror of the water."

OPINIONS ON THE "WATERLILIES"

Reflections in the fog and reflections in the waters, the unreal showing through the real, blended and united with it, the entire great mystery surrounding us is transformed by the painter. All that unites us in this atmosphere of objects, this is the domain from which Claude Monet, benign genius, points out riches for our enjoyment.

René Jean,
Comoedia, *December 6, 1926*

Monet seeks to become intoxicated by the abundant wine of the air, the light, the flowers, and still more light. Through his use of color, he has undeniably conquered every fleeting object that can be conquered. *He has taken changing appearances and made them permanent, trying to grasp all of nature's faces at every moment.*

Arsène Alexandre,
Le Figaro, *December 10, 1926*

The gardens of Giverny were a palette prepared by Monet himself. One month it was bright yellow, saffron colored, orange, and nasturtium as all the Earth's gold shades offered themselves to his eyes. The following month, by a wave of the wand, all the blue shades rose from the ground.

Jacques des Gachons,
Le National *December 19, 1926*

THE CLEAR LESSON OF JUAN GRIS

BOULOGNE-SUR-SEINE
The fragile health of Juan Gris, who suffered violent asthma attacks during his winter stay in Hyères, gets the better of the courageous serenity of his last years: During this time he perfected his "Conceptual Painting," as Guillaume Apollinaire defined his harmonious Cubism. After

But it was entirely an interior battle, modest like Gris—the French word for gray—which Gris chose as his pseudonym in 1906 when he left Madrid to live permanently in Paris. (His real name was José Victoriano González.)

The testament of this painter, even more French by adoption than his great friend Picasso,

HE WANTED TO BRING CUBISM TO PERFECTION, TO MAKE IT ABSOLUTE ART

suffering terribly—in his pain, he cries out "a square chest wants to take over my round chest"—he succumbs during a uremia attack, at 11 o'clock at night on May 11, surrounded by his wife, Josette, his son, Georges, and his great friends and neighbors, the Kahnweilers. He dies in his home at 8 Rue de la Mairie, in Boulogne-sur-Seine, and is buried two days later. He was forty years old.

An enormous wreath of flowers bears the anonymous inscription: "To Juan Gris, from his friends in battle." In fact, his exemplary life was a struggle to master his art more and more.

can be found entirely in his work. His work was always supported, encouraged, and promoted by his faithful dealer, Kahnweiler. Gris, who called Kahnweiler "Cavélère," met him in 1907 at the Bateau-Lavoir, where Gris occupied a dilapidated studio. In 1922, Kahnweiler installed him near his own house in Boulogne. Conducting Gris's funeral, with Jacques Lipchitz, Picasso, and Raynal present, he remarked, "He was one of the noblest artists who ever lived on this earth."

Of all the Cubists, only Gris remained faithful to the rigor of that particular pictorial disci-

JUAN GRIS: WOMAN. 1915-1917. Basel. Private Collection

Juan Gris with his wife.

pline, probably one of the most revolutionary in the history of painting. He wanted to bring Cubism to its perfection, to make it absolute art. In 1912, Apollinaire defined Gris' consuming ambition in his summary in *L'intransigeant* regarding the Salon des Indépendants, where Gris presented his *Homage to Picasso.* "His mission could be called "integral Cubism." Gris was perceptive as well as sensitive. He managed to describe his lesson in a few clear formulas. In the February 1921 issue of *Esprit nouveau,* he explained, "Cézanne makes a bottle into a cylinder, I take the cylinder to create something individual of a special type; from a cylinder, I make a bottle." It is

what he called "qualifying" objects, as an adjective qualifies a noun. He pointed out that his method was not inductive but deductive, "because the pictorial relationships between colored shapes suggest to me certain special relationships between elements of an imagined reality." He concluded: "It is as my own spectator that I derive the subject of my painting."

Indeed, his restructured still lifes, his sparse ballet backdrops for Diaghilev, his introverted geometric portraits exhibit a distinguished, classical quality.

(See also 1924.)

ELIE FAURE: THE SPIRIT OF FORMS

The Spirit of Forms is the final volume of the famous *History of Art*, a crowning achievement for Elie Faure. But whereas most of the History follows the centuries in chronological order, jumping from civilization to civilization and bringing the continents together, this final volume touches upon the heart of artistic creation. The author compares the metallic structure of the Eiffel Tower to the flying buttresses of Notre Dame, a tortoise shell to the Freyssinnet dirigible hangars at Orly airport in Paris. In these passages, art is seen as having arisen with the dawn of life itself.

For those who seek in the world of forms a general architecture that draws a powerful poetic aspect from functional logic, obvious analogies are all that is needed. Poussin, like Homer before him, saw the trunk of a palm tree in the torso of a young woman and compared it to the columns of the Maison Carrée of Nîmes. Delacroix made similar observations with regard to trees, leaves, and patterns made by water in the sand. The Écrits de Carrière include a very informative lecture on this matter, given at the Galerie Ostéologique of the Museum, where the bare skeletons of animals appear. Observe the harmonious construction of each of them, the bones moving in their sockets, bony levers being pulled by weight or by the movement of muscles, the intricate interweavings and pivots of the vertebrae, the pelvis vessel that carries the intestines, the consistency of the bony framework entrusted with the task of balancing and transmitting pressure, and all this apparatus being lifeless matter, but so animated by imperceptible functional processes serving the purpose of walking, grasping, chewing, flying, swimming, and maintaining the profound and elastic movements of the heart and lungs. Compare all the varieties present in this forest of skeletons, from the most gigantic dinosaurs before the Deluge to the smallest reptile or bird. Discover the same forms and proportions within the shell protecting this monster as huge as an oak tree and this minuscule insect no larger than a bud . . .

Universal form is built on a single basis. It can be discovered anywhere. Poor indeed is the one who, for example, fails to see in a human or animal skull not only a well-ordered countryside with hills and valleys, rivers, internal movements, geological unity, and rhythm, but also a perfect sculpture with its asymmetrical balance, its silent planes, its fleeting lines, its expressive projections, and its sinuous and pure profiles. And when man and his devices appear on the Earth, is it by chance that his weapon is similar to an animal's horn or defensive appendage? . . . Is it by chance that a submarine resembles a fish, that an airplane resembles a bird or a giant insect, that a boiler or a sewer resembles a person's entrails, that a motor resembles a beating heart? . . . There is between the mind and the motives that are constantly shaping and drawing it to seek nourishment and security, a prevailing and benign view that intelligence picks up where imitation of an object leaves off, and that invention ends where the object is forgotten. Tintoretto's outline of Paradise, where everything is living forms, resembles the mind just as much as the Parthenon or an automobile, where everything is abstract formulas.

ELIE FAURE
The Spirit of Forms *(Excerpts)*

Fossil head of a triceratops dinosaur (Paris, Jardin des Plantes).
" . . . a perfect sculpture with its asymmetrical balance, silent planes, fleeting lines, expressive projections, and sinuous and pure profiles"

PICASSO'S SACRED MONSTERS

PARIS

Is it a result of the tension of ten years of living together that has crept into the relationship between Picasso and his wife, Olga? Or is it the fact that he is approaching his fiftieth birthday—a sign of old age, which the painter fears so much? Or is it the resurgence of Spanish painters, from Ribera to Goya, who have always been fascinated with painting monsters?

At any rate, since a summer stay in Cannes, Picasso has painted a series of small canvases in which he seems to find a wicked and perverse pleasure in dismantling the female anatomy. Never before, not even in his strongest Cubist experiments, has he pushed the disfiguration of visible elements this far. The disfiguration is all the more obvious and shocking because it centers exclusively, almost sadistically, on the female body. It is not possible that his remote contacts with Surrealism have led the painter to this game of butchery? Like the Surrealists, he does explore the depths of basic eroticism and analyzes desire without the slightest concession to sentimentality.

But it seems that Picasso, above all, has a personal reason for pushing his favorite game to extremes—it is the investigation of all the combinations of the interchangeable signals that are for him the elements of reality: Even, and especially, if they are the organs and limbs of the human body, female in his case. He exploits and delves into the sources of organic ambiguities—particularly concentrating on the mouth and the female sex organs—thereby diving into the center of one of the oldest and most forceful fantasies of humankind. We should not really be surprised, considering to what extent sexual appetites have always been at the epicenter of Picasso's artistic creation.

PABLO PICASSO: FACE. About 1927. Paris. MNAM

THE MONTPARNOS UNDERNEATH LA COUPOLE

PARIS

There is no doubt that the location was predestined. Under Louis XVI, it was the site of the Pressoir farm, which included the last fifteen acres of cultivated vineyards within the enclosure of the farmer-general of revenues. On December 20, a cold night, the restaurant La Coupole is inaugurated there.

No one had ever seen this many people on the Boulevard du Montparnasse. A crowd of artists bubbling with delight devour ten thousand canapes, three thousand hard-boiled eggs, one thousand hot sausages, and eight hundred pies. Fifteen hundred bottles of champagne supplied by Mumm are consumed before midnight and more have to be found quickly. Among the celebrities are Vlaminck, Foujita, Cocteau, Pierre Benoît, Henri Béraud, and Blaise Cendrars. At five o'clock in the morning, the police force evacuates the last guests, who regret that the festivities are over so early.

La Coupole is the work of the architects Lebouc and Solvay. Its name is derived from a cupola of glass panes crowning the center of the building. Its inside columns are decorated by various painters, including Léger, Kisling, Savin, and Marie Vassilieff, whose painting on two columns shows the writer Georges Duhamel playing the flute. These painters also attended the festivities, and were paid mainly in food and drinks.

La Coupole replaces a warehouse place for lumber and coal, which had begun to look anachronistic in a developed area. The joint owners, Messrs. Fraux and Lafon, were the managers of the Dôme from 1924 to 1926, located next door. It was their idea to build a large complex containing a restaurant, a bar, and a room in the basement for dancing.

Not that long ago, Montparnasse was a quiet place, occupied mainly by the hangars and stables of the Parisian omnibuses. La Coupole is the symbol of the new Montparnasse.

Malevich in the West

With Lunacharski's help, Kazimir Malevich is on a three-month trip, accompanied by a large selection of his works. He spent March in Warsaw, where he exhibited at the Hotel Polonia and was enthusiastically welcomed by a public that the poet Tadeusz Peiper and the Kobro-Strzeminskis had prepared. He spent the next two months in Berlin, where a retrospective of his work was held, showing his Cubist-Futurist period, his Alogical period, and the Suprematist period. He even discussed plans for a film with Richter. At the invitation of Gropius, he visited the Bauhaus in Dessau, where a collection of his writings will be published in German later this year.

The Aubette's Obliques

The painter Théo Van Doesburg has completed the abstract geometric multicolored decoration of the Aubette, a dance hall in Strasbourg. Basically, the decoration is a play on oblique lines. Van Doesburg recently ended his friendship with Piet Mondrian, who doubted that slanted lines were compatible with Neoplasticism. According to Mondrian, Neoplasticism is founded solely on intersecting horizontal and vertical lines, which alone can translate the struggle of spiritual forces. For his part, Van Doesburg sees slanted lines as the very expression of modern life. Hans Arp and Sophie Taeuber also helped decorate the dance hall.

Arthur Dove at Stieglitz's Place

Arthur Dove announces a one-man exhibition at the Intimate Gallery, where Alfred Stieglitz has shown so many modern artists. Born in 1880 in Canandaigua, New York, he was the first American artist, in 1910, to practice abstraction. Now he is making collages of flowers, leaves, and miscellaneous objects. His *Portrait of Alfred Stieglitz* was done for this exhibit, and includes photographic lenses and a clock spring.

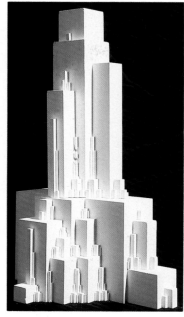

KAZIMIR MALEVICH: GOTA 2. 1923. Paris. MNAM

Courteline Sells His Museum of Horrors

At Bertheim's at the end of November, the author of *Les gaietés de l'escadron* exhibited his collection of badly painted pictures from the Flea Market. He called the collection "museum of simple labor" when he did not call it his "museum of horrors". The humorist, who had already made a name for himself by buying and reselling Rousseau's *Portrait of Pierre Loti,* is delighted with the *succès de curiosité* that greeted the sale. Five canvases were bought at prices ranging from 10,000 to 20,000 francs. The catalogue, with a preface by the associate curator of the Luxembourg Museum, included thirty-two entries with ironic comments by Georges Courteline himself.

André Masson Makes Sand Talk

Creator of the first Automatic Drawing three years ago, André Masson is an innovator once again. He had wondered for some time how he could introduce Automatism into painting, since oils and paint brush hardly allow rapid execution. He found the solution to his problem at the beach while contemplating a sandy shore. As soon as he got home, he placed an unprepared canvas on the floor of his studio, sprinkled it with drops of glue, then covered it with sand. When it dried, the sand clung only to the spots where glue had dropped. The result is this new possibility of "drawing" the material world.

The Corbusiers Are Immortalized by Bauchant

Le Corbusier asked André Bauchant, whose paintings he collects, to do a portrait of him and his wife. The architect had discovered Bauchant's work at the preview of the Salon d'Automne of 1921, where the artist was watching over his own work and whispering to visitors: "This is by Bauchant." Bauchant, plant-nursery owner in Touraine, began painting when he returned from war, a ruined man whose wife had become insane. Self-taught, he applies his theories of plant cultivation to art. He always begins his pictures at the bottom and works up. "A plant lives on roots alone. Everything is in the base. If it is solid, your picture will live." Aside from landscapes and portraits, Bauchant also paints mythological scenes. At the age of forty-four, he is an outstanding colorist.

IN BRIEF...

GERMANY
Edvard Munch exhibition at the National Galerie.
First exhibition of James Ensor in Germany.
Nolde jubilee exhibition at the Arnold gallery.

UNITED STATES
Matisse is awarded the Carnegie prize in Pittsburgh.
Richard Buckminster Fuller devises the "Dymaxion" house, a "living-machine," conceived for a futuristic way of life.

FRANCE
First exhibition in Paris of Alberto Savinio, at the Bernheim gallery.
At the Hôtel de la Plage, in Le Pouldu, in Brittany, mural paintings executed around 1889 by Gauguin, Meyer de Hann, and their friends are discovered under layers of wallpaper. They have been bought by an American art lover.
The Belgian Surrealist René Magritte moves to Paris.
Georges Rouault completes the engraving of his Miserere, fifty-eight large plates.

CZECHOSLOVAKIA
In Prague, Toyen and Styrsky found Artificialism, which is imbued with Surrealism.

ANDRÉ MASSON: DEAD HORSES. 1927. Paris. MNAM

From left to right: Wassili Kandinsky and Nina, his wife,
Georg Muche, Paul Klee, and Walter Gropius.

A party at the Bauhaus.

THE BAUHAUS WITHIN ITS OWN WALLS

DESSAU

The Bauhaus used to be housed in Weimar, in the shadows of Goethe and Schiller. Unfortunately, the fame it acquired among the international intellectual elite, especially through the exhibition of its work in 1923, could not guarantee its survival. With the new elections, the local and regional power fell into the hands of rightists, who did not want a school described everywhere as "revolutionary."

But the school did not close its doors. It simply moved. Various towns and cities offered their hospitality. Among those, the director Walter Gropius chose Dessau, a town managed by a mayor who was a Social Democrat. He offered to build a new school according to Bauhaus plans and to commission the construction of several hundred popular housing units in Torten, in the suburbs. The work by which the school had to prove itself, and which was missing in Weimar, is guaranteed for several years.

The new Bauhaus is now finished. It was inaugurated last

December in the presence of a thousand guests from Germany and abroad. The real opening of the school, however, takes place at the beginning of this year.

Dessau is three hours from Berlin by train. It is a city of workers, with about seventy thousand inhabitants. Most men work in the mechanical, chemical, and aeronautic industries.

From a distance, the Bauhaus buildings look like white cubes

NOW THE BAUHAUS CAN FULFILL ITS MISSION: TO TRAIN THE CREATORS OF THE FUTURE

set on a desolate piece of land. Upon a closer look, the visitor is struck by their transparent quality. The complex consists of three main parts linked by two passageways.

Modern materials are available to the students, especially in the printing shop, where all forms of typography are possible. Posters, advertising brochures, the school paper, and so on, are printed there. Herbert Bayer, a former student in Weimar, is in charge. He insists that the shop produce

original work. A page designed according to his advice draws attention immediately: There are no capitals, and all the characters are of the same size.

Another novelty is the creation of a program for training architects. Gropius puts Hannes Meyer, a thirty-eight-year-old Swiss architect, in charge. He is a devotee of the latest techniques and materials, as well as of the science of building itself.

Marcel Breuer, originally from Weimar, like Herbert Bayer, presides over another important shop, woodworking. It doesn't produce much wood furniture. It is a place where chairs are designed for sale to certain companies where they will be mass-produced. Mass production has already started: Breuer's latest invention, chairs and armchairs of nickel-plated steel, are being turned out in a well-known Berlin furniture company, Lengyel & Company.

Painting classes have not disappeared. Kandinsky and Paul Klee both participate in an introductory class for first-year students, organized primarily by Josef Albers, who succeeded Johannes Itten. Kandinksy initiates them into "shapes, lines, areas, and colors," while Klee proposes his reflections on "relationships between lines, areas, and forms." The artists are available to anyone who wants to practice painting.

The Bauhaus celebrations in Weimar were famous, and now they are in Dessau. They are even better. There is a jazz orchestra equal to the best in Germany. Moreover, though the theater is not used for teaching, Oskar Schlemmer is the creative force behind a drama workshop in which about ten students participate on a regular basis.

The Bauhaus is on the right path. The future is there, it has been launched.

(See also 1919, 1932, 1933, 1937.)

BAUHAUS DESIGN

Mass production of everyday objects poses a different set of problems than the creation of handcrafted items. Their stereotyped repetitiveness saturates the environment of our offices, living rooms, kitchens, etc. Bauhaus has reconciled industrial production with art by turning out functional yet esthetically attractive pieces.

Armchair of nickel-plated steel from a 1925 design by Marcel Breuer. Breuer is the head of the furniture workshop. This armchair, the first of its kind, was mass-produced in 1926 in Berlin.

Extendable wall lamp of iron and brass, made in 1923 by K.J. Jucker. This lamp is characteristic of the Weimar Bauhaus. The metal workshop was headed by Moholy-Nagy, whose goal was to encourage the creation of functional models. This piece is a student's attempt to combine a new mechanism with an appropriate form.

Aerial view of Walter Gropius' Dessau Bauhaus. Bottom right: classrooms. Top: workshops and housing. The two perpendicular passageways contain a theater, conference room, and dining hall.

269

Surrealism gambles and wins. Created four years earlier by André Breton and his circle, it is now a word on everyone's lips, an image before everyone's eyes. In fact, the movement is granted letters of nobility by all the artists, Miró, Max Ernst, Tanguy, Masson. This is unexpected since, at its inception, the movement cast itself in a literary role. That was why Breton had written his brilliant essay, Surrealism and Painting. *Sculpture is also doing well. The work of González and Gargallo, replacing bronze with punched, soldered metal, opens the medium to new possibilities for integrating and enlivening space.*

1928

SUMMARY

SURREALISM

Miró's Metamorphosis of Tradition
André Breton: the Savage Eye
Surrealist Games
How to Play "Exquisite Cadavers"
The Tribulations of Max Ernst
The Surrealists in the French Communist Party

DEVELOPMENTS

Witkiewicz: the Portrait Factory

ART NEWS

Kurt Schwitters' Strange *Commerz*
"Unism" Is Officially Born
The Painters of the Sacred Heart
Twenty-Two Works by Matisse on the Auction Block
In Brief

SCULPTURE

Gargallo Makes Metal into a Noble Material
González Renews His Friendship with Picasso
The Stylized Coupling of Giacometti
Duchamp Buys 22 Pieces of Sculpture by Brancusi

LITERATURE

SPAIN
Federico García Lorca gains fame with his Gypsy Ballads.

FRANCE
André Malraux publishes Les conquérants.
   André Breton publishes Nadja.

MUSIC

UNITED STATES
Premiere of George Gershwin's An American in Paris.

FRANCE
Maurice Ravel's Bolero *meets with immediate success.*
   Performance of The Threepenny Opera *by Bertolt Brecht with music by Kurt Weill.*

THEATER

FRANCE
Roger Vitrac's Surrealist play Victor ou les enfants au pouvoir *is received negatively during its performance at the Théâtre des Champs-Élysées.*

MOTION PICTURES

GERMANY
G. W. Pabst creates Loulou.

UNITED STATES
Walt Disney creates the first Mickey Mouse films.

FRANCE
Premiere of Carl Theodor Dreyer's The Passion of Joan of Arc, *with Renée Falconetti.*
   Germaine Dulac creates, from a scenario by Antonin Artaud, La coquille et le clergyman.

JOAN MIRÓ:
DUTCH INTERIOR I. 1928.
New York. MOMA

JOAN MIRÓ:
DUTCH INTERIOR II. 1928.
Venice. Peggy Guggenheim Collection

JAN STEEN:
THE CAT'S DANCING LESSON. 1674.
Amsterdam. Rijksmuseum

MIRÓ'S METAMORPHOSIS OF TRADITION

PARIS

After returning from a fifteen-day trip to the Netherlands, the Catalan painter Juan Miró dedicates his summer to the painting of three "Interiors" inspired by works of the Dutch masters. He had brought back reproductions on postcards. Having once set his compositions in celestial and interstellar spaces, and having freed his subjects of all weight, he has come back to earth. But he has not renounced the irrealism of the Surrealist influence or the total poetic license that characterizes the enchanted atmosphere and the phantasmagoric gaiety of his visions. He

achieves his art, not just in any way, but by referring to the most Naturalistic style of painting in existence—the Dutch. His variations on Jan Steen's oil painting on wood at the Amsterdam Rijksmuseum, entitled *The Cat's Dancing Lesson,* are significant in this respect. He derived a series of detailed studies from it, and succeeded in transposing his dreams to a solid surface. He did it all with such an exceptional sense of metamorphosis that all the original objects and persons can be found and recognized—inside out, so to speak.

Miró reveals such a genius for transmutation that it is won-

dered if his eye resembles that of a fly. Miró, himself, during one of his many diligent visits to the Louvre, noticed in Dutch paintings a "little point" that in his words went "tack! like a fly's eye." It is that eye, equipped with thousands of facets, that he focuses on the subdued spaces of tradition, analyzing their self-generating components.

With his Dutch models, he is right on target. Not that he has any iconoclastic inclination to blow up the figurative and realistic order of traditional painting in an aggressive way. But he has such a capacity for humor, fantasy, and poetic creativity that

an anecdote that touches him becomes a marvelous adventure of the spirit without bounds, without restrictions other than his freedom to stray.

The chair in Jan Steen's painting, the coffeepot, and the napkin on the table to the right are pared down. The man and the woman playing the hobo, as well as the cat, become moon-shaped. The woman to the left moves like an enormous carnival mask. The lute on the wall is turned around. The dog is transformed into a fantastic animal from whose belly a snake unfolds and encircles the entire scene.

One of the characteristics of

Miró's art is his ability to reduce or amplify in exaggerated ways any item of reality. His experiments of the summer are all the more surprising, because he seems to want to go back to a descriptive form of painting. At the same time he wants to take advantage of the new rhythmic, twirling, and spiraling possibilities with which he pulls the viewer irresistibly into his unusual mental space.

Miró is a "fellow traveler" rather than a "militant" of Surrealism. His fierce attachment to independence renders him cautious with regard to the authoritarianism of André Breton. Nevertheless, he is undoubtedly one of the painters who most strongly experience the imperative necessity for a total reversal of form and for an absolute liberation of artistic invention.

The spontaneity of his painting is different from the rigid automatism of André Breton. The latter, by the way, is greatly torn between his admiration for Miró, "maybe the most Surrealist of all of us," and the annoyance he feels with regard to the freedom the artist protects for himself vis-à-vis Surrealist rules.

Miró is a man of culture. He knows that art has as much to do with art as with the painter himself and his time. He also knows that there is no spontaneous expression of creativity, there is only a stirring to action! The proof lies here. It is the intimate Realism of the Dutch masters that stimulates Miró into creating masterpieces of imaginative virtuosity.

On the other hand, it is striking to see that Miró succumbs to the drunkenness of his metamorphoses or to the euphoria of his insolent "color compositions" only after periods of restraint and intense concentration. Before his encounter with Surrealism, he had gone through a period of what he called "Precisionism" and "Detailism." At the age of thirty-five, Miró through his attention to Dutch tradition

ANDRÉ BRETON: THE SAVAGE EYE

At the time of its inception four years ago, Surrealism was primarily a literary movement. But, before long, painters such as Max Ernst, André Masson, Yves Tanguy, and Joan Miró, who shared similar preoccupations regarding dreams, Automatism, and the unconscious, became involved in it. The questions raised by their participation moved André Breton to write *Surrealism and Paintings*. The work had a profound impact on the avant-garde. It is written in a lively, scathing, and often partial style. The excerpt below is taken from it.

One can, under the pretense of having to jump off a bridge, learn to swim by hanging increasingly large rocks from one's neck. After all, no one has bothered to weigh them. One can also, for example, learn to draw a sword skillfully, even if only to say at the appropriate moment "here is my card," and be assured the battlefield is of one's choosing. I must concede that, on his battlefield, Miró is unbeatable. No one comes as close to associating the unassociable as he does, nonchalantly shattering what we dare not break.

The cicada, scanning the fields of southern France with his eyes as big as saucers, offers his cruel song as the sole accompaniment to this traveler who, not knowing where he is headed, continues all the more hurriedly. This cicada is the ambiguous, delicious, and disconcerting genie that proceeds before Miró, introducing him to the higher powers with whom the great primitives have had little to do. Perhaps he alone is the necessary talisman, the indispensable fetish that Miró has brought with him on his trip in order to keep from losing his way. Through this creature, he has learned that the Earth shoots nothing more than wretched snails' antennae toward the sky, that the air is an open window to rockets and huge mustaches, that, to speak reverentially, one must say "Open the parenthesis, life; close the parenthesis," that, literally, "Our hearts hang together from the same tree," that the mouth of the smoker is but a part of the smoke, and that the ghost of the sun, a good omen for painting, announces his entry like any other ghost, by the noise of clanging chains.

I must emphasize that Miró ought not to have conceived such a delirious pride, that he ought not to have trusted himself alone,

however gifted he may be, however faithful inspiration has been for him thus far, however original his manner may be, to take the unchanging elements or appearance and establish the conditions for a balance that overwhelms the observer. Delirium has nothing to do with this. Pure imagination alone is the master of what it appropriates from day to day, and Miró ought not forget he is only the instrument of that imagination. His work, whether he likes it or not, involves a certain number of general notions to which others adhere. It would be useless to hold these notions, in their current state, as simple, subjective concepts incapable of taking on a new, objective reality independent of the consciousness that conceived them. I submit that Miró has other concerns besides providing free pleasure for the eyes and mind of the casual observer.

ANDRÉ BRETON
Surrealism and Painting *(Excerpt)*

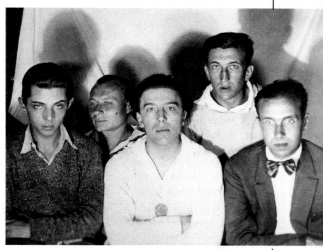

From left to right: Georges Malkine, André Masson, André Breton, Max Morise, Georges Neveux.

SURREALIST GAMES

PARIS

The regulars who hang out at the Cyrano, near the Moulin Rouge, are intrigued by the strange games in which André Breton and his friends indulge.

Challenging the "sleeping philosophers" in his *Surrealist Manifesto,* Breton is convinced that logical processes no longer apply today, except for solutions to secondary problems. He takes issue with the novel, which has become the favorite literary genre. It is without interest, because in his opinion authors do nothing in the course of the pages but add the nothingness of the characters to the nothing-ness of the descriptions.

He believes that there exists a "Surrealist usage" of the lan-guage. "Surrealism is available to all unconsciousness," individ-ual or collective.

The games in which he and his friends indulge are intended to free them from the weight of reason. They include the "Exquisite Cadavres," the game of Questions and Answers and its derivative, If and When?, Automatic Conversations, and Hypnotic Sleep.

Besides Exquisite Cadavres, the richest and most complex game, Questions and Answers also yields surprising results. It is played by two people. Each has to write a question on a piece of paper. The response, also in writing, is made without having read the question.

Examples from the sessions between Breton and Benjamin Peret:

What is a day?

A woman who bathes naked when night falls.

What is suicide?

Several sets of deafening bells.

What is rape?

The love of speed.

Anyone can do as well. Poetry is created by objective haphaz-ardness, the way Monsieur Jourdain wrote prose. Without even knowing!

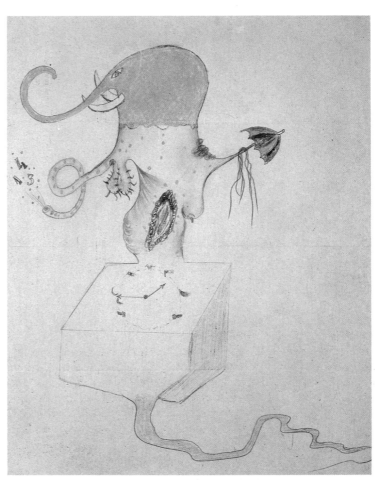

ANDRÉ BRETON, YVES TANGUY, MARCEL DUCHAMP, MAX MORISE: EXQUISITE CADAVER. AROUND 1926. Private Collection

HOW TO PLAY "EXQUISITE CADAVRES"

Sit five to a table. Each player takes a sheet of paper and writes down an article and an adjec-tive, hiding it from the other players. The paper is then folded so as to conceal the words, and each player passes the paper to the player on his right. (At the end of the game, each sheet of paper will have been passed to all five players, thus return-ing to its original spot.)

Then, each player writes down a noun, which the unknown adjective modifies. Once again, after folding the paper a second time to conceal the noun, each player passes the paper to his right while receiving the paper from his left. The process is repeated for a verb, for a second adjective, then for a second noun to serve as the object of the sen-tence. The papers are then unfolded, and, after making the necessary grammatical adjustments, the players read the resulting sentences. The first sentence obtained by this procedure is a classic example, from which the game got its name: The exquisite cadaver will drink the new wine.

The game will not necessarily be successful on the first try, since the sentences obtained will sometimes be banal or uninteresting. But some tries will bring excellent sentences. For example:

The Senegalese oyster will eat the tricolored bread. The wounded women make the blond-haired guillotine. The endless sex goes to bed with the orthodox tongue.

Try it yourself, keeping in mind that a little patience is needed. After playing the game for about an hour, you will have delightfully funny and strange sentences. The same technique can be used to draw a person, piece by piece. But this requires a certain artistic ability.

After Georges Hugnet

MAX ERNST:
MAN, WOMAN'S ENEMY, OR MAN,
WOMAN'S BEST FRIEND. 1927.
Basel. Fondation Emmanuel Hoffman

MAX ERNST: THE HOLY VIRGIN CHASTISING
THE INFANT JESUS BEFORE THREE WITNESSES,
ANDRÉ BRETON, PAUL ÉLUARD, AND THE ARTIST.
1926. Cologne. Private Collection

THE TRIBULATIONS OF MAX ERNST

COLOGNE

The incorrigible Max Ernst continues to be in the news. At the Salon des Indépendants two years ago, a card was tacked to his canvas *The Holy Virgin Chastising the Infant Jesus before Three Witness, André Breton, Paul Éluard, and the Artist,* bearing the words "Protest of Catholic artists." Today, it is the Cologne clergy who are agitating.

They have not only succeeded in closing the exhibition where the painting was on show, but after an introduction by the archbishop himself, the faithful in the cathedral, including the artist's father, Philipp Ernst, repeated three times "Pfui! Pfui! Pfui!," thereby pronouncing the excommunication of Phillip the artist.

Max Ernst is no more concerned by this than by the occasional threats of excommunication uttered against him by André Breton, the "pope" of Surrealism, who thinks Ernst is no longer "walking the line" since his participation—also two years ago—in Diaghilev's ballet *Romeo and Juliette.* After his *Natural History,* created by means of frottage, Ernst has applied frottage to oil painting with surprising results from every point of view. His recent paintings shine with black forests of desire, nights of wild love, horses in summer, walls and oceans without end.

THE SURREALISTS IN THE FRENCH COMMUNIST PARTY

PARIS

Will they join? Won't they? The back-and-forth hesitation has lasted several years. Certainly, the Surrealists are convinced that revolutionizing art and overthrowing society go hand in hand. But the crucial question confronting the most radical among them was whether to join the French Communist party, the only political organization in their eyes representing the interests of the working class for emancipation.

Doesn't the fact of joining mean the alienation of one's freedom, the subjugation of art to narrowly political imperatives? On the other hand, doesn't a refusal indicate the behavior of "revolutionary phrasemongers," of "petit-bourgeois idealists?" The debate has been waged since 1925 between the journal of Communist intellectuals, *Clarté,* and *La révolution surréaliste.* In January last year, *the* step was taken—the last resistance fell in the struggle between pure metaphysical rebellion and political engagement. Following Naville and Péret, Aragon, Éluard, Unik, and Breton have joined the Communist party. Breton is active within the cell of the workers of Gaz de France.

Breton is now accused by puritans in the Communist party of promoting the work of a pornographic painter, André Masson, whose drawings swing wildly between libido and Automatism. Is the affair losing ardor? Are Marxism and Surrealism an unnatural couple?

WITKIEWICZ: THE PORTRAIT FACTORY

ZAKOPANE

Manet's reply to a lady who did not recognize herself in the portrait she had commissioned is famous. At his wit's end, the painter allegedly replied, "Well, there's nothing left but to try to look like the painting!"

It is in an effort to counter this kind of complaint that the Polish painter Stanislaw Ignacy Witkiewicz decides to draw up strict rules for the Portrait Company he established three years ago. Paragraph three stipulates that all criticism on the part of the model is excluded: "We insist in particular on this paragraph because nothing is more difficult than keeping the client from making perfectly superfluous comments."

Was the artist making fun of the commercialization and depersonalization of art in modern society? Should there be seen in his factory, in the fact that portraits have become mass-produced items, a reply to Duchamp's "ready-mades"? At any rate, the manner in which the rules and regulations describe the different types of portraits available is closer to a commercial brochure than to a treatise on painting.

There is no room for artistic softness. The execution will be "careful," even "painstaking," in order to favor the embellishment of the flesh parts. A more jarring execution may search for the model's character and sometimes approach the level of caricature, adding a touch of "demonism" to the female face. Sometimes the emphasis is on "the arbitrary psychological interpretation according to the willingness of the company." Practical requirements complete the rules and regulations: The company will determine the background of the painting; portraits with open necks will costs "one third more"; sales prices vary between 100 and 350 zlotys, depending on methods used in production.

With Witkiewicz, there is

STANISLAW IGNACY WITKIEWICZ: PORTRAIT. 1926. Private Collection

always a pervading nihilism even a feeling of failure, despite his exceptional precociousness. He is a philosopher, playwright, and painter all at once. He wrote his first play at the age of eight, after reading Shakespeare. He wrote his first philosophical essay at the age of eighteen. A family friend, a disciple of Freud, introduced him to psychoanalysis at a young age. But it was his father, a painter himself, who wanted to be his mentor; he may have been wrong, however, in teaching him that Naturalism was the only way.

When Witkiewicz discovers Gauguin, in 1904, and meets Picasso during a dinner at Gertrude Stein's, in 1908, he has the terrible impression that he will never be able to paint again. He asks the question, "Why didn't *I* invent all of that?"

From 1914, Marcel Duchamp realized that the traditional paths of art were condemned. He buys a bottle rack at the town-hall bazaar and exhibits it as a piece of sculpture, with the certainty that in this domain no one would do better. In its own way, Witkiewicz's company also signals a farewell to painting. But will he be able to make his mark? The artist is forty-three and has few clients.

(See also 1919.)

Kurt Schwitters' Strange "Commerz"

A big event at the Grosse Kunstausstellung in Berlin: Kurt Schwitters exhibits forty-four of his works there, proving that he is a strange man. Born in Hanover in 1887, Schwitters made himself famous with his collages of found paper and his Relief Paintings, composed of all kinds of debris, such as pieces of wood, old springs, and wheels of broken-down baby carriages. The word *merz* which he uses to designate his works, is a fragment of the German word *Commerz* (commerce), which he cut out of a bank ad. He has been working on *Merzbau,* a construction made of a collection of the most peculiar objects imaginable.

"Unism" Is Officially Born

It is even more radical than Suprematism. In Warsaw, the Polish painter Wladyslaw Strzeminsky publishes a brochure in which he proclaims "the absolute objectivity of the work of art." An engineer, then an officer in the Russian army, he was one of Malevich's disciples before he became Constructivism's publicist in Poland. His canvases eliminate all traces of association, emotion, and symbol, leaving only pictorial unity. HIghly rigorous and extremely simple, his paintings have no subject other than the play of forms, lines, and colors on a two-dimensional surface. The intransigence of Strzeminsky's conceptions places him, at the age of thirty-five, in the forefront of European Geometric Abstractionism.

The Painters of the Sacred Heart

The German art critic Wilhem Uhde, friend and admirer of Henri Rousseau, organizes an astonishing exhibition at the 4 Chemins gallery. The exhibit includes self-taught painters whose candor and sincere faith in instinctive art inspired Uhde to call the show Painters of the Sacred Heart. Especially surprising are some gaudy still-life compositions, canvases invaded by flowers that defy the laws of perspective. The paintings are signed by S. Louis, who turns out to be Séraphine Louis, a former cleaning lady Uhde had employed when he stayed in Senlis. He assures the public that the "saintliness of her heart is responsible for her genius."

SÉRAPHINE:
THE RED TREE. 1928.
Paris. MNAM

Twenty-Two Works by Matisse on the Auction Block

On June 14 at the Drouot mansion, Master Lair-Dubreuil dispersed Dr. Soubies' fine collection of modern painting. Those who attended were not disappointed. The record sale price was drawn by Cézanne's *Young Man with a Cap,* which was sold for 360,000 francs. Not to be forgotten, the *Symphony in White* by Renoir brought 221,100 francs. Also auctioned off were works by Bonnard, Braque, Derain, and Van Dongen. But the real event of the day was the offering of twenty-two works by Matisse, including the *Odalisque with Blue Screen,* which sold for 217,000 francs, and *The Yellow Dress,* which sold for 230,000 francs. The total for the sale amounted to 3,142,000 francs. Contemporary art is sailing in fair winds.

WLADYSLAW STRZEMINSKY:
ARCHITECTONIC COMPOSITION. 1928.
Lodz. Sztuki Museum

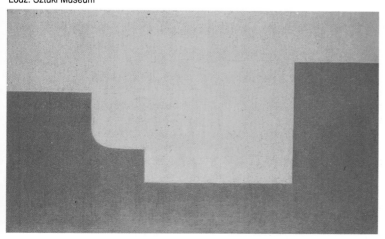

GARGALLO MAKES METAL INTO A NOBLE MATERIAL

PARIS

The picadors triumph in the art arena. Five different picadors are born in the hands of a magician with metal—Pablo Gargallo. He suffers from seeing his creations move to the gallery of Georges Bernheim, so he starts all over again. His work is constantly renewed, invariably successful.

However, life was not always easy for this artist from Aragon. He often had to sacrifice his art to the requirements of commissions. He lives in Barcelona and in Paris, where he arrived for the first time in 1903, at the age of twenty-two.

Gargallo has found his vocation in metal. He forges and he welds. After sculpting in stone, he practices *repoussé*. To have more control of the metal, he starts shearing and cutting it. The year is 1907, it is his first attempt at working with copper, *Petit masque à la mèche*. He uses the same idea in *Masque aux petits cheveux*, in 1911. The figurines mark the beginning of sheet-metal work, of cutouts and fitting. Having worked metal for sixteen years, Gargallo no longer hesitates to tackle thicker and heavier pieces with the aid of soldering techniques which his close friend González suggested to him.

Parallel to his studies in metal cutting, Gargallo has pursued the use of feminine shapes, making hollow and full forms interact with great virtuosity.

Perhaps it was financial trouble that led him to sculpting in metal rather than in any other material. With a simple piece of sheet metal, which he folds, cuts, chases, and welds, he creates fullness out of a void, convexity out of concave shapes. His *Maternity*, in 1922, consists entirely of concave shapes—contrary to the images usually associated with the subject. A cheek brushed by light is suggested by means of an empty space cut by a line. Gargallo reverses the traditional language of sculpture, but always in the service of life and humankind and in a manner that does not in any way reek of the artificial.

JULIO GONZÁLEZ:
POINTED HEAD. 1927.
Paris. MNAM

GONZÁLEZ RENEWS HIS FRIENDSHIP WITH PICASSO

PARIS

Maybe it is Picasso—a compatriot with whom Julio González appears to have started an interesting relationship—that imparts his sculpture with a new life, leading it gradually to a synthesis of forms. Though inspired by nature, González's work in metal is close to abstract art.

Metalwork no longer holds any secrets for this son of a goldsmith who was born in Barcelona in 1876. He continues to work as a craftsman besides his sculpting activities. His artistic work started in 1910 with *repoussé* portraits in metal and with ceramic figurines. As a worker at the Renault factory during the war, he learned the technique of soldering. The method produces results later on, when he starts using iron.

Having finally discovered his medium, he has completed a series of cut-out masks, which are variations on his head theme, interpreted in a style of great expressive power.

His pieces of sculpture are made of sheet metal or scrap metal, welded and cut as if by a draftsman. This may be explained by the fact that he studied drawing in Barcelona. For some time now, his pieces seem to be reaching a new level, through the evocation of the art of a draftsman attempting to conquer space.

PABLO GARGALLO:
THE PICADOR. 1928. Paris.
Private Collection

THE STYLIZED COUPLING OF GIACOMETTI

PARIS

For several months now Alberto Giacometti has been installed in a new studio on the Rue Hippolyte-Maindron. The year has mainly been marked by his meetings with André Masson, Michel Leiris, and Joan Miró.

These meetings—in which there was also an encounter with Alexander Calder—have influenced Giacometti. It is evident in his "open sculpture" series, which is often marked by an Expressionism that is tragic, simplified, and visionary in its density. These pieces are, he claims, "shapes in space, constructions that are open and aerated to let the mud out." The sculptures, which often approach hallucination, tend toward a purified manifestation of extreme feelings. For example, *Man and Woman* is a veritable incarnation of rape, or the sadistic dimension of a love relationship. The man is no more than the brutal erection of a desire "with the knife drawn." The woman is a troubling concavity, and trembling between acceptance and refusal. The forms are arched against each other in a motion that is not an embrace but a dance of death. They count less than the space separating them, or the event uniting them.

Man and Woman is the embodiment of bewilderment, the perpetuation of tension, the arrested apposition of aggression and evasion. All of this undoubtedly constitutes its dynamism, and the fascination it evokes. Giacometti has freed himself of concerns about volume to focus better on the question of empty space, which is conceived as the place and the time of a drama, a tragic scene, a pedestal for signs of intensity or mystery. For these reasons, this piece is one of the most striking illustrations of the meeting between Giacometti and Surrealism, for it explores man's most radical passions.

ALBERTO GIACOMETTI:
MAN AND WOMAN. 1928.
Paris. MNAM

MARCEL DUCHAMP BUYS 22 PIECES BY BRANCUSI

Brancusi in his workshop.

NEW YORK

Is Marcel Duchamp thinking about becoming a collector? He negotiated the acquisition of twenty-two pieces of sculpture by Constantin Brancusi once owned by the late John Quinn.

The New Yorker, who died in 1924, was a great admirer of Brancusi, and had bought numerous works by the sculptor, including *Fish* and *Mademoiselle Pogany.* In October, the first auction of the Quinn collection takes place. The second sale, which will include more sculptures by Brancusi, is scheduled for the beginning of next year, in New York.

Duchamp, a long-time friend of Brancusi, happens to be in New York, so Brancusi asks him to buy back those pieces before the sale takes place. He is afraid that some might not exceed $200 or $300, though his work is going for much more.

So Duchamp negotiates the reacquisition of the twenty-two pieces for $8,000. But Duchamp is not the only buyer. The inheritance from his parents, who passed away recently, is not sufficient. He decides to establishes a consortium with Mrs. Charles Rumsey and his friend Henri Pierre Roche, and they divide the purchased works among themselves.

Duchamp also takes advantage of the opportunity to buy back, before the sale, three of his own paintings: *Study for Nude Descending a Staircase, The Chess Players,* and *À propos de jeune soeur.* This coming fall and winter will remain linked in Duchamp's memory to Brancusi. The painter is getting ready to leave New York for Chicago. There he will prepare a Brancusi exhibit, to be held at the Arts Club from January 14 to 18.

New York now possesses its *Museum of Modern Art, not only catching up to Paris, but outdistancing it. Paris has no museum like it. Its remote origin is the Armory Show of 1913, where America discovered all the avant-garde movements in Europe at a single glance. The museum's director, Alfred Barr, is only twenty-seven years old. He proposes a new kind of museum that will welcome established masters as well as open its doors to new artists. In the annals of museum history, it is a revolution. Meanwhile other major events are occurring in Paris. Max Ernst invents the Collage Novel when he publishes The 100-Headed Woman. Above all, there is the debut of a twenty-five-year-old genius, Salvador Felipe Jacinto Dali, whose film and independent exhibition are sensational events.*

1929 SUMMARY

MUSEUMS

New York Inaugurates Its Museum of Modern Art
The People behind MOMA

AVANT-GARDE

Demuth: the Era of the Machine
Georgia O'Keeffe Paints New York

ART NEWS

Hugh Ferris's Dreams of Stone
Raymond Loewy Launches the Industrial Esthetic
Max Ernst Creates the First Collage Novel
The Big Game
The Defense League for German Culture
In Brief

SURREALISM

Salvador Dali Enters the Scene

EXHIBITIONS

A New Objectivity in the Italian Style?

EDWARD HOPPER:
HOUSE BY THE RAILROAD. 1925.
New York. MOMA

NEW YORK INAUGURATES ITS MUSEUM OF MODERN ART

NEW YORK

In an autumn characterized by great economic and financial uncertainty, faith in American art is rekindled by the inauguration of the Museum of Modern Art. On November 8, barely ten days after the stock-market crash, this first-class cultural event attracts the attention of art fans.

TO CONSERVE COLLECTIONS OF ESTABLISHED WORKS BUT ALSO TO OPEN ITS DOORS TO UNKNOWN ARTISTS

The new museum owes its existence to the determination and persistence of three remarkable women: Miss Lillie Bliss, Mrs. Cornelius Sullivan, and Mrs. John Rockefeller. They themselves are collectors, and wish to give the American public the possibility of discovering modern art—something no American museum had done. Their initiative ends up arousing an initial interest that owes its vigor to the active enthusiasm of Alfred Stieglitz.

It is Stieglitz who, from the beginning of the century, has supported, exhibited, and revealed the few American artists active in the avant-garde. He has done so through the publication of the journals *Camera Work* and *291* and by opening the Gallery 291, the Intimate Gallery, and An American Place. It is the passion with which Stieglitz encourages new forms of expression that gives faith to artists, collectors, and dealers alike. From the interest he aroused, the famous Armory Show was born in New York in 1913. It brought Americans all of modern art at once—from Cézanne to Picasso to Duchamp—and led to so many vocations. The Armory Show was housed in an army barracks—which explains its name—located at the corner of Lexington Avenue and 25th Street. It was leased for the occasion, because there were almost no exhibition spaces available in the city.

The enthusiasm generated led to the creation of several galleries, such as the Modern Gallery of Marius de Zayas, and to the formation of major collections, such as those of Walter Arensberg, Albert Barnes, Lillie Bliss, and John Quinn.

The need for the Museum of Modern Art is especially strong in view of the fact that artistic circles rarely favor modern art.

In 1921, when Miss Bliss, assisted by her friend the painter Arthur B. Davies, persuaded the Metropolitan Museum of Art to organize its first exhibit of modern art—it ranged from the Impressionists to Picasso before his Cubist period—it was so poorly received by the press—notwithstanding the careful selection of the works shown—that the experiment was never repeated. Today, historians and critics are amazed by the newly created museum. If its function is the conservation of established works, its mission is also to open its doors to unknown artists.

Alfred H. Barr, Jr., the young director who will have to solve the apparent contradiction, is well equipped to do so. Indeed, he is one of the few Americans who have seen for themselves a number of the contemporary experiments taking place in Europe. He went to the Soviet Union and met with a number of Constructivist artists, and discovered the new cultural policies. In Holland, he met with the members of De Stijl movement. In Germany, he was taken by the Bauhaus in Dessau; he considers it a "fabulous institution."

At the age of twenty-seven, Barr is exceptionally well educated. At Wellesley College, he created the first university course on twentieth-century art in the United States. The course deals with painting and sculpture, and with film, photography, architecture, industrial design, music, and the theater. He wants to develop a similar program for his museum—it would be modeled after the Bauhaus—even if he is able to execute his ambitious project only step by step.

For the time being, the museum's own collection is modest. It contains one major Edward Hopper, *House by the Railroad*, which was given to the museum after its opening; a piece in bronze by Maillol, *Île de France*; one Picasso; a few rare works by Charles Burchfield and Kenneth Miller; as well as some prints and drawings.

The opening exhibition enjoys success. It is dedicated to Cézanne, Gauguin, Seurat, and Van Gogh. It attracts close to 50,000 visitors in five weeks, in spite of its cramped quarters on the twelfth floor of a building at 730 Fifth Avenue.

The second exhibit promises to be more adventurous. It will be dedicated to living American artists, including John Marin, Georgia O'Keeffe, Max Weber, John Sloan, Charles Demuth, Lyonel Feininger, Charles Burchfield, and Edward Hopper. All in all, it is a promising debut. In the coming months and years, sponsors should begin to contribute generously.

At the time of its inauguration, the museum was on the twelfth floor at 730 Fifth Avenue. As it expanded, it moved to 11 West 53rd Street in 1932.

THE PEOPLE BEHIND MOMA

New York's Museum of Modern Art has three benefactors: Miss Lillie P. Bliss, Mrs. Cornelius J. Sullivan, and Mrs. John D. Rockefeller, Jr. They have put MOMA in the hands of its first curator, Alfred H. Barr, Jr.

Miss Lillie P. Bliss

Sister of a textile manufacturer who was a secretary of the interior, Miss Bliss is at the helm of an important collection of Postimpressionist and contemporary art. She became interested through her friend, the painter Arthur B. Davies, one of the organizers of the Armory Show of 1913. Together, they convinced the Metropolitan Museum of Art to organize its first modern art exhibit in 1921.

The Museum's Curator, Alfred H. Barr, Jr.

During the winter of 1928-1929, Miss Bliss and Mrs. Rockefeller visited Egypt and discussed the creation of a museum of modern art. Upon their return to New York, they shared their idea with Mrs. Sullivan. The three women got to work and, with the help of a professor of museology at Harvard, were able to persuade one of his former students to accept the position of curator. Alfred H. Barr, Jr., is only twenty-seven years old.

Mrs. Cornelius J. Sullivan

Born in Indianapolis, Mary Quinn taught art history in New York when she married Cornelius J. Sullivan, an attorney, bibliophile, and art lover. He was friends with John Quinn, a collector of modern art who guided him in purchasing works at the Armory Show. These works became the foundation of his own private collection.

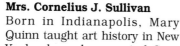

Mrs. John D. Rockefeller, Jr.

It was through her father, Senator Nelson W. Aldrich of Rhode Island, a knowledgeable collector of art who took her along on trips to Europe, that Mrs. Rockefeller acquired her taste for modern art. She was touched by Van Gogh's difficult life, and believed that a museum of modern art would bring recognition to contemporary artists.

GEORGIA O'KEEFFE PAINTS NEW YORK

CHARLES DEMUTH: MY EGYPT. 1927. New York. Whitney Museum

NEW YORK

For the first time, Georgia O'Keeffe is showing the New York public her urban landscapes: "I live on Lexington Avenue, in a two-room apartment on the thirtieth floor. I've never lived so high before, and I'm all excited. I have started painting New York. My first painting is *New York with Moon.*"

Georgia O'Keeffe was born in Sun Prairie, Wisconsin, in 1887. She attended classes at the Art Students League in New York. When Alfred Stieglitz saw her work, he exclaimed, "Finally a woman painter." In 1916 and 1917, he showed, in his Gallery 291, a splendid series of her abstract drawings and watercolors which a friend of the artist had taken to him without her knowledge.

During those years, she painted many landscapes, often close to abstracts, as for example the beautiful series *Light Coming on the Plains.* She tried to find a correspondence between the shapes and lights of nature and her emotions. Stieglitz encouraged her, and showed her work. They were married in 1924.

In her new work, she opposes natural and artificial light, churches and buildings, and plays out all the contrasts of the big city with photographic precision and an austere approach to surfaces. *Radiator Building, New York Night*, and *Shelton Hotel* are works of great purity which may be compared to those of the Precisionists.

(See also 1917 and 1988.)

DEMUTH: THE ERA OF THE MACHINE

NEW YORK

Charles Demuth has been associated with Precisionism for several years, especially because of his extreme rigor, which is evident in the exhibition at Alfred Stieglitz's Intimate Gallery from April 29 to May 15.

Demuth was born in Pennsylvania in 1883, and studied in France. However, it was on his return to the United States, and under the influence of John Marin, that he started to be interested in contemporary pictorial ways of expression. He begins by illustrating the works of his favorite authors, Zola, Balzac, Henry James, Edgar Poe, Wedekind. During a stay in Bermuda, in 1916-1917, he finds his own style. It is an original adaptation of Cubism, which is particularly successful in his watercolors of barns, trees, and architectural elements, all executed with great delicacy.

The Tower reveals his new interest in the urban and industrial landscape of America, which Demuth renders in a pure, geometric fashion. He consciously tries to create an original American style, and the titles of his recent work occasionally make ironic allusions to the need to find a language that will counterbalance the influence of Europe. *The Incense of a New Church*, from 1921, or *My Egypt*, from 1927, suggest that new values must be found in the era of the machine.

This objective undoubtedly explains both the cold and impersonal character of his most ambitious paintings and his taste for the colonial architecture of Pennsylvania, whose simple lines underscore the restraint found in the paintings.

GEORGIA O'KEEFFE: SHELTON HOTEL, NEW YORK, NO. 1. 1926. New York. Kennedy Galleries

Hugh Ferriss's Dreams of Stone

He is a professional proofreader of skyscrapers. A specialist in the painting of buildings, Hugh Ferriss has just published *The Metropolis of Tomorrow*. The work includes fifty illustrations accompanied by explanatory texts, and shows an imaginary city, which could be Manhattan. But if Ferriss, who hopes to make New York a new Athens, presents his stone dreams to architects, he refrains from building them himself. Using the constraints imposed by the zoning law of 1916 as a basis, his work is limited to exploring the infinite formal and psychological repertoire of possibilities contained in the framework of this legal code. His architectural creations, with their pyramids, needles, and severely angled profiles against *clair-obscur* backgrounds, are reminiscent of Sant'Elia's Futurist projects.

Raymond Loewy Launches the Industrial Esthetic

The thirty-six-year-old industrial designer Raymond Loewy has just completed a grand premiere in the United States. Called in as a consultant by Sigmund Gestetner, an office-furniture manufacturer, Loewy has transformed a disgraceful copying apparatus into a compact and elegant machine. An engineer and former fashion designer, Loewy hopes to combat the habitual mediocrity of industrial mass-produced products by introducing the idea of functional beauty. His trial run is a masterpiece. Since the Gestetner copier has gotten its new personality, its sales have skyrocketed.

Max Ernst Creates the First Collage Novel

The 100-Headed Woman by Max Ernst, with a preface by André Breton, is published at the Éditions du Carrefour in Paris. The work was completed in two weeks, when the artist was confined to bed by illness on a farm in the Ardèche region. The publication is a "Collage Novel," juxtapositions of bits of prints cut out of old magazines. The resulting compositions are dramatic, amusing,

HUGH FERRISS: PHILOSOPHY. 1928. New York. Columbia University

shocking, and erotic. The artist put Titans with laundresses, naked women in gigantic pipe organs, and the Eternal Father on a staircase. He himself made up the captions for these illustrations. According to the author, paste is not enough to make a collage. What is needed is a pair of very sharp scissors. And above all, a sense of the marvelous, which Ernst certainly possesses.

The Big Game

René Daumal and Roger Gilbert-Lecomte, publishers of the magazine *Le grand jeu* (the big game), refuge for many dissident Surrealists, have organized an exhibition at the Galerie Bonaparte. Worthy of note are drawings by Maurice Henry, photos by Arthur Harfaux, and especially the dreamlike paintings of the Czech Joseph Sima. André Breton suspects this will be competition for Surrealism, and is displeased.

The Defense League for German Culture

In May 1928, the newspapers announced the founding of the Defense League for German Culture, with an offensive program of resistance to the decline in traditional values. Behind the formation of the Defense League is the Nazi ideologue, Alfred Rosenberg, who has the support of two teachers, well known for their militant racism: the anthropologist Hans F.K. Günther and the architect and writer Schultze-Naumburg. Established in Weimar and Munich, its first public demonstration took place in Munich on February 25. In the great auditorium of the university, Othmar Spann, professor of law in Vienna, lectured on the crisis of contemporary culture.

IN BRIEF...

GERMANY
Marcel Duchamp visits Wassili Kandinsky in Dessau.
   Paul Klee and Max Ernst have exhibitions at the Flechtheim gallery in Berlin.

BELGIUM
Major James Ensor exhibition in the Palais des Beaux-Arts in Brussels.

UNITED STATES
Henri Matisse, who is very much in favor in America, is awarded the first prize at the International Exhibition in Pittsburgh.

FRANCE
Georges Rouault designs sets and costumes for Diaghilev's ballet The Prodigal Son with music by Sergey Prokofiev.
   The erection of a monument to Cézanne by Aristide Maillol in the gardens of the Tuileries provokes protests from some critics, notably Camille Mauclair.
   With Amédée Ozenfant, Fernand Léger opens the Académie Moderne.
   André Derain has exhibitions at the Paul Guillaume gallery and various towns in Germany.
   Exhibition of contemporary German painters and engravers, mainly Dix, Corinth, and Hofer.

GREAT BRITAIN
The Goupil Gallery shows works by Aristide Maillol.

POLAND
Establishment of the "a.r." group in Lodz, with the painters Strzeminsky and Stazewski and the sculptor Kobro.

SWITZERLAND
At the Kunsthaus in Zurich, an exhibition called "Anstrake and Surrealist Painting and Sculpture."

SALVADOR DALI: THE GREAT MASTURBATOR. 1929. Private Collection

SALVADOR DALI ENTERS THE SCENE

PARIS

Toward the end of the year, a young hidalgo with fiery black eyes and a mane of anthracite conquers Paris with a movie and an exhibition. Born in 1904, in Figueras, a small town in northern Catalonia, he is a precocious, and ambitious, young man. He puts his considerable analytical intellect to the service of a permanent desire to provoke. He is cultivated. He has seen all of modern art. He has tried everything. He has digested everything. Impressionism and Fauvism no longer hold any secrets from him. He has looked for inspiration in the Italian Metaphysical school. He has painted in the Futurist style and in the Cubist style.

The world of cinema has had its abstract movies, its Cubist movie, even its Dada film, *Entr'acte.* Thanks to Dali, it now has its Surrealist movie, *Un chien andalou* (an Andalusian dog). Dali wrote the script;

another Spaniard, Luis Buñuel, directed.

The montage is the essence of the seventh art. No one besides Dali is as well equipped for Surrealist esthetics, which, as is well known, is founded on the famous phrase by Lautréamont: "Beautiful as the chance meeting upon a dissecting table of a sewing machine and an umbrella." In the movie screened from October 1 to December 23 at Studio 28, there is no umbrella, no sewing machine, but there are seminarians, pumpkins, a grand piano, and putrefied donkeys. The objective of the two acolytes is to plunge a dagger into the heart of artistic and sophisticated Paris, and to let the intellectual blood flow. They certainly succeed.

To achieve their purpose, Dali and Buñuel create horrifying scenes. They use, for example, a mask without a mouth, another mask where the mouth has been replaced with pubic hair, a cut

hand, a razor blade slicing a calf's eye which in the film looks like the eye of a young woman, nests of ants, a naked woman carrying two sea urchins under her arms. The few people who witnessed some of the scenes

being filmed have not recovered. They saw how Dali—shaken with spasms—emptied the eye sockets of the rotten donkeys with scissors, how he clipped the jaws to uncover their teeth, as if to confirm that he had overdosed on ether, as rumor has it.

Because one success never stands on its own, a large crowd —attracted by the flavor of scandal—works its way into the first Paris exhibition of the Catalan painter. It opens at the Goemans gallery on November 20. In his desire to hit hard, Dali chooses unsettling works, whose titles alone speak for themselves: *Le jeu lugubre* (the ominous game), *Les plaisirs illuminés* (illuminated desires), *The Great Masturbator*. The latter is probably one of the wildest paintings made in the last years. The pliant forms, the biological swarming, the sulfurous eroticism, and the monstrous figures express the anxiety of the whole world. Perhaps the visitors are most struck by Dali's virtuosity. He is indeed the greatest creator of Surrealist images.

In art, horror has the particular effect of inciting laughter. The public laughs in front of Dali's canvases. It laughs at the screening of *Un chien andalou.* Is this what a contemporary prophet looks like? An artist who makes people laugh by announcing future catastrophes? If this is the case, Dali is a new Jeremiah.

A scene from the film *Un chien andalou.*

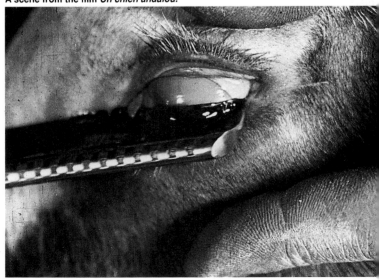

A NEW OBJECTIVITY IN THE ITALIAN STYLE?

ROME

After the careful arrangements of planes and angles of Cubism, after the thistles and whirlpools of Futurism, at the start of the twenties it looked as if the plas-

THE FUTURISTS, DISENCHANTED BY THE WAR, TURN TO TRADITION

tic arts would move closer to an ever-greater Abstractionism. But in reaction, artists almost everywhere are engaged in Realistic figurative painting, each for a different reason.

The signal was given in Paris by Picasso. Even before the end of the war, he began to draw in the figurative tradition. Painters such as Severini and La Fresnaye followed suit, giving satisfaction to painters who, like Marquet and Derain, never fully abandoned reality.

In Germany, under the banner of the New Objectivity, former Expressionists and Dadaists regrouped, for example, Otto Dix, George Grosz, Conrad Felixmüller.

However, it is in Italy that the setting is most suitable for a return to order. The regime of the Fascist masters started out by allying itself with the Futurism of Marinetti, Balla, Prampolini, and others, who spontaneously had supported the cause. Soon, however, the Fascists came to prefer the art of the traditional craftsmen. They want people and things to be immediately recognizable. The Italian artistic context lends itself all the more to this, because de Chirico was an impressive influence.

Indeed, he always respected the laws of conventional perspective for the creation of unusually static urban landscapes and disturbing still lifes—at the opposite spectrum of Cubism and Futurism. Far from being derived from the New Objectivity in Germany, a large part of new Italian painting comes from de Chirico. From 1911 to 1915, he lived in Paris,

before being called back to Italy for military service. In Ferrara, he finds Carlo Carrà, whom he helps to redirect the art of painting. This leads to the development of "Metaphysical Painting."

De Chirico and Carrà are joined for a time by De Pisis, Morandi, Sironi, and Alberto Savinio, de Chirico's brother.

Their experience and apparent disenchantment with untimely modernity, dragged in by the war, plays a major role in the former Futurists, return to tradition—Soffici, Conti, Rossi, Dudreville, and especially Sironi. The latter establishes himself as one of the masters of the new trend and often curiously close to Permeke. Since 1922, Sironi has been a contributor to the Fascist newspaper *Il Popolo d'Italia.* His detractors amuse themselves by finding a resemblance between the profile of the women in his *Solitude* and Mussolini's profile.

As a founding member, in 1922, of the Novecento move-

ment, which stands for the return to old Roman values, Sironi creates paintings with a quite personal poetry. His work is aimed essentially at showing, in nostalgic or dramatic visions, the loneliness of modern man and the tragic grandeur of the time. Sironi favors somber colors and sad spaces crossed by pallid shades. He possesses a great artistic sensitivity and a fine craftsmanship, which, notwithstanding the misuse of social themes, saves his work from the militant Realism so dear to the Duce and his friends.

(See also 1914 and 1925.)

MARIO SIRONI: SOLITUDE. 1916. Rome. Galleria Nazionale d'Arte Moderna

Mayakovski's suicide in 1930 and Malevich's death in 1935 mark turning points in the decline of the avant-garde in the USSR, as well as the end of hopes aroused among Soviet artists by the October Revolution. In Germany, moreover, Hitler's hold on power is apparent in the too-famous exhibitions of "degenerate art".

	1930	**1931**	**1932**	**1933**	**1934**
ARTS	• Moholy-Nagy's "Space-Light Modulator" exhibited in Paris	• Birth of Abstraction-Creation • Le Corbusier's Villa Savoye • Chagall in Palestine	• Frank Lloyd Wright creates Taliesin • *The War* by Otto Dix	• *Dance* by Matisse, at the Barnes Foundation • Edward Hopper at MOMA • Hitler closes the Bauhaus	• Dali faces a Surrealist tribunal • *The Green Box* by Duchamp • "Machine Art" at MOMA
LITERATURE	• Suicide of Vladimir Mayakovski • *Poems* by W. H. Auden • *The Revolt of the Masses* by José Ortega y Gasset	• *Night Flight* by Antoine de Saint-Exupéry • *ABC of Reading* by Ezra Pound • *Sanctuary* by William Faulkner	• *Journey to the End of Night* by Louis-Ferdinand Céline • *Tobacco Road* by Erksine Caldwell • *Young Lonigan* by James T. Farrell	• *La condition humaine (Man's Fate)* by André Malraux • *The Blood Wedding* by Federico García Lorca • James Joyce's *Ulysses* is allowed into the United States	• *Tropic of Cancer* by Henry Miller • Luigi Pirandello is awarded Nobel prize in literature
MUSIC AND THEATER	• *The Rise and Fall of the City of Mahagonny* by Bertolt Brecht and Kurt Weill	• *Mourning Becomes Electra* by Eugene O'Neill	• Hofmannsthal's *Jedermann* produced by Max Reinhardt	• Sergey Prokofiev returns to the USSR	• George Balanchine establishes his ballet academy
MOTION PICTURES	• *The Golden Age* by Luis Buñuel and Salvador Dali • *The Blue Angel* by Joseph von Sternheim • *Animal Crackers* with the Marx Brothers	• *City Lights* with Charlie Chaplin • *Frankenstein* with Boris Karloff	• First Venice Film Festival • *Scarface* by Howard Hawks	• *King Kong* by Schoedsack and Cooper • *The Invisible Man* by James Whale • Fritz Lang flees Germany	• *It Happened One Night* by Frank Capra • *The Scarlet Empress* by Josef von Sternberg
SCIENCE AND TECHNOLOGY	• C. W. Tombaugh discovers the planet Pluto • First transatlantic air-mail service	• Auguste Piccard makes a balloon ascent to a height of one mile	• Discovery of the positron (C.D. Anderson) and the neutron (James Chadwick) • Discovery of vitamin D	• Paul Dirac and Erwin Schrödinger are awarded Nobel prize in physics for their work on atomic energy	• *Recent Advances in Vaccine and Serum Therapy* by Alexander Fleming
POLITICS AND DAILY LIFE	• U.S. Congress creates Veterans Administration • France begins building the Maginot line	• The first woman, Hattie T. Caraway, is elected to the U.S. Senate • *The Star-Spangled Banner* becomes the American national anthem	• Franklin D. Roosevelt is elected President • The Lindbergh baby is kidnapped • Amelia Earhart is the first woman to fly solo across the Atlantic	• Hitler is appointed German Chancellor • Roosevelt launches the New Deal	• "Night of the Long Knives" in Germany • F.B.I. shoots John Dillinger, "Public Enemy No. 1"

1939

These exhibitions aim to destroy the most creative works in modern art. But France lives on despite the ideological storm raging in Europe. The International Exposition of 1937 in Paris attempts to create in our century a synthesis of the arts of painting, sculpture, and architecture. Meanwhile Picasso's Guernica addresses the artist's letter of bereavement to civilization.

1935	1936	1937	1938	1939
• Death of Malevich • Exhibition of abstract art at the Whitney Museum in New York • Hitler attacks modern art	• The Roosevelt Administration creates the WPA, helping many unemployed artists • Controversy over Realism in France	• *Guernica* by Picasso • Exhibition of "degenerate art" in Germany	• International Exhibition of Surrealism in Paris • Brancusi's sculptures at Targu Jiu	• Hitler's sale of "degenerate art" in Lucerne • Matta exports Surrealism to the United States • Morandi at the Third Quadrennial in Rome
• *Murder in the Cathedral* by T. S. Eliot • *Tortilla Flat* by John Steinbeck • Penguin in London launches the paperback	• *Gone with the Wind* by Margaret Mitchell • Federico García Lorca killed by Franco's militia	• *Man's Hope* by André Malraux • *Ferdydurke* by Witold Gombrowicz	• *La nausée* by Jean-Paul Sartre	• *Finnigan's Wake* by James Joyce • *The Grapes of Wrath* by John Steinbeck
• Death of Alban Berg • *Porgy and Bess* by George Gershwin • Début of Count Basie's orchestra	• *Music for Strings, Percussion, and Celesta* by Béla Bartók • *Carmina Burana* by Carl Orff	• Death of Maurice Ravel • Death of George Gershwin • Performance of *Lulu* by Alban Berg	• First jazz concert at Carnegie Hall	• *Ondine* by Jean Giraudoux • Igor Stravinsky moves to the United States
• *The Informer* by John Ford • *The 39 Steps* by Alfred Hitchcock	• *A Night at the Opera* with the Marx Brothers • *Modern Times* with Charlie Chaplin	• *La grande illusion* by Jean Renoir • *Snow White and the Seven Dwarfs* by Walt Disney	• *Alexander Nevski* by Sergei Eisenstein • *Hôtel du Nord* by Marcel Carné	• *Gone with the Wind* by Victor Fleming • *The Rules of the Game* by Jean Renoir • *Stagecoach* by John Ford
• Development of the Richter scale • Irène and Frédéric Joliot-Curie are awarded Nobel prize in chemistry	• Completion of the Boulder Dam on the Colorado River • First regular television broadcast in Germany	• Frank Whittle builds the first jet engine • Wallace H. Carothers patents nylon • The Golden Gate Bridge opens	• First atomic fission, in Copenhagen • Albert Einstein and Leopold Infeld publish *The Evolution of Physics*	• Death of Sigmund Freud in London • An important new pesticide: DDT
• Italian troops invade Ethiopia • The German anti-Nazi author Carl von Ossietzky is awarded the Nobel peace prize	• Beginning of the Spanish Civil War • Abdication of Edward VIII • Olympic games held in Berlin	• Japan invades China • International Exposition in Paris • Amelia Earhart is lost on a Pacific flight	• Hitler annexes Austria, his native country • Anti-Jewish legislation enacted in Italy • 40-hour work week established in the United States	• Hitler and Stalin sign a nonaggression pact; German troops invade Poland; France and Great Britain declare war • Nylon stockings appear on the market

As much as the dramatic suicide of Mayakovski, Guerassimov's devastating official portrait of Lenin seems to toll the bell for the Russian avant-garde movements. In the October Revolution, the artists thought they had seen the dawn of a new era that would grant the right to dare to do anything. But all that is over. Soviet art is to be academic, socialist, Realist, or not at all. It is to address itself to the people, in accordance with the decisions of the new masters of the Kremlin. In the meantime, Montparnasse enjoys itself as if nothing were happening. Kees Van Dongen's wild parties draw everyone who is anyone in the Paris art world. The newspapers are full of gossip from these parties.

1930

S U M M A R Y

ART AND POLITICS

The Death of Mayakovski
The Russian Avant-Garde in Exile

ART AND SOCIETY

Marin Fascinated by Manhattan
American Gothic

DEVELOPMENTS

An Evening at the Van Dongen Residence

EXHIBITIONS

Belgium Exhibits Permeke
Gromaire in the United States

ART NEWS

Matisse the Sculptor
Delvaux Astonished by the Spitzner Museum
The Circle and Square Mobilizes against Surrealism
Death of a Montparnassian
Max Ernst Creates a Scene at the Showing
of *The Golden Age*
In Brief

SCULPTURE

Moholy-Nagy's Space-Light Modulator
Calder Plays Circus

WRITINGS AND THEORIES

Louis Aragon: Scissors and Paper

ALEXANDRE GERASSIMOV: LENIN. 1930. Moscow. Lenin Museum

Left: Vladimir Mayakovski. Photograph by Alexandre Rodchenko.

Right: Rodchenko in a self-designed "Constructivist" vest.

THE DEATH OF MAYAKOVSKI

MOSCOW

Vladimir Mayakovski is dead at the age of thirty-seven. He committed suicide on April 14 by shooting a bullet through his heart. Who attaches importance to this news item? Some Russians, and some French Surrealists, including André Breton, who published in the *Révolution surréaliste* an article entitled "The boat of love has crashed against life," a line from the poem in which Mayakovski said goodbye to the world.

Mayakovski was the figurehead of the entire Russian avant-garde for almost twenty years. He was a defender of literature and the plastic arts—he saw them as closely bound in the struggle for a new esthetic and a new society. For him, art and society were linked. They had to be linked or they would lose their reason for being. They

had to be linked to "change the world," so that the world would not repeat the same errors with complacency. Mayakovski was a revolutionary from the depths of his soul.

*CONSTRUCTIVISM TURNS
INTO FORCED CONSTRUCTIVISM.
ORDERS OF THE LEADERS
REPLACE "SOCIAL CONTROL"*

He had been educated as a painter. In 1911, through the intermediary of Bourliouk, he came into contact with men who, like he himself, would incarnate Russian Futurism: the poets Khlebnikov, Krutshenykh, and Kamenski, as well as the painters Matiushin, Malevich, Tatlin, Olga Rozanova, and, of course, Larionov and Gontcharova.

Russian Futurism is above all

an adventure for decrying bourgeois customs and overthrowing its esthetic preferences. From the start, the members were on the side of the 1917 Revolution. In his autobiography, Mayakovski writes, "October. Should one adhere or not? The question did not arise for me or for the other Futurists in Moscow. It was my Revolution."

All of the Russian Futurists, writers as well as artists, put themselves at the service of a revolution they had called for. Mayakovski exalts it in his poems. He makes posters and propaganda drawings, by himself or with the help of Rod-

chenko. He writes and draws constantly in the years following Lenin's rise to power, without consideration for the modesty or the ingratitude of the subject matter. All the artists, even the strict Malevich, put their talents at the service of harsh everyday reality. It seems to them that the renewal of society will go hand in hand with the renewal of art; since the advent of Futurism, this has been their double goal. Malevich writes: "Cubism and Futurism were revolutionary art forms announcing the Revolution in the political and economic life in 1917." Now it is a matter of building up that new life.

Russian Constructivism affirms its will to properly serve the largest possible number of people. Tatlin and Rodchenko design clothing and functional furniture. Malevich designs models for earthenware. Didn't

THE RUSSIAN AVANT-GARDE IN EXILE

Mayakovski state in 1918: "We don't need an art mausoleum for the worship of dead works, we need living factories of the human spirit—in the streets, in the factories, in the workshops, and in the homes of the workers." He conducts symphonies of factory sirens.

From 1923 to 1925, Mayakovski directs the journal *Lef*, the paper of Constructivism. He has the help of some old Futurists and of newcomers like the painter Varvara Stepanova and the filmmakers Dziga Vertov and Sergei Eisenstein.

Their activities are supported by the organization "Proletkult," which provides them with regular work, thanks to contacts with industry, particularly unions. The artists design logos, slogans, and posters and create interiors and furniture for workers' circles.

When *New Lef* appears, in 1927, policy is clearly different. Fiction is rejected in favor of reportage, easel painting is condemned in favor of applied art, because "social control" must prevail over any other consideration. Constructivism turns into forced Constructivism. Orders of the leaders eventually replace "social control." One must adapt, or disappear in silence. Some of Mayakovski's old companions withdraw quietly—Krutshenykh, for example.

Mayakovski believes in adjustment. He continues to work with all his strength—lectures, theater, commissioned works, drawings—without renouncing more personal endeavors. But the public still does not understand his work, and some of his envious colleagues sabotage his actions under the pretext of proletarian art and literature. Exhaustion, discouragement, and a personal drama—which is considered crucial—lead him to take his life. With his suicide, an era is finished, maybe even an era of hope.

(See also 1918 and 1922.)

Though art in the USSR is on the way to normalization, some artists still prefer exile, in order to accomplish their creative work with full independence. The first ones left home about ten years ago, before the borders were closed definitively, as they are today.

One of the first to emigrate was Ivan Pugny. He was co-founder with Malevich of Suprematism and, in 1918, was appointed professor at the Academy of Fine Arts in Leningrad, before being invited by Marc Chagall to teach at Chagall's academy in Vitebsk. He believed that Russia was in chaos. There was no way to get a visa in the midst of the civil war. He started his wanderings by crossing the frozen Gulf of Finland under the beams of the Kronstadt spotlights. He reached Berlin, where he lived until 1925, then settled in Paris, where he had a number of exhibitions. His research centers on painting, and his technique is close to the Parisian School.

Chagall is chased from Vitebsk by Malevich at a time when Abstractionism is fashionable. He flees Propaganda Art and obtains authorization, in 1922, to leave for Berlin. Since the autumn of 1923, he lives in Paris, where his art seems to develops naturally.

Kandinsky occupied the post of vice-president of the Academy of Artistic Sciences in Moscow, which he established in 1921. When the situation deteriorates, he, too, departs for Berlin. He becomes professor at the Bauhaus, first in Weimar, then in Dessau, where he continues his work and in 1926 publishes *Point, Line, and Plane*. His shows—one of which was held this year at Galerie de France —are successful. In 1928 he receives German citizenship.

The sculpting brothers Gabo and Pevsner were also professors. Their *Realist Manifesto*, the source of Constructivism, was posted on the walls of Moscow two year ago. But then Gabo's workshop was closed down. In 1922 he leaves for Berlin. His brother joins him the following year. Pevsner now lives in Paris, where his art is hailed, and he is a French citizen.

By traveling first to Berlin and then to Paris, the Russian artists have renewed their talents. The war and the Revolution had forced them to develop original work in isolation within the borders of their country. Victimized, they went looking for the space needed for their art. They found it in exile. It was a fortunate opportunity for them, as their creations show. It is also symbolic of their tragedy.

WASSILI KANDINSKY: THE GREAT GATE OF KIEV. 1928. Paris. MNAM

MARIN FASCINATED BY MANHATTAN

NEW YORK

John Marin exhibits at Alfred Stieglitz's new gallery, An American Place. He shows a number of watercolors made in New Mexico dating as early as the twenties. Marin has always been warmly encouraged and supported by Stieglitz, who organizes individual shows for him. Marin showed at the Intimate Gallery, which Stieglitz opened

They depict the dynamism of New York and its great architectural works, such as the Manhattan Bridge, the Woolworth Building, and Grand Central Terminal. On the occasion of one of his shows, Marin writes in *Camera Work*: "I see great forces at work, great movements, great buildings and small buildings, great masses pulling small masses . . . I hear the sound of

"I SEE GREAT FORCES AT WORK . . . I HEAR LOUD MUSIC RINGING"

after he had closed the Gallery 291 in 1917.

Marin spends long periods away from New York, and comes back fascinated. "The entire city is alive; the buildings, the people, everything is alive; and the more they move me, the more I feel they are alive," he wrote in 1913 in a letter to Stieglitz.

In his paintings of New York, Marin aims for a personal synthesis between the spontaneous colors of the Fauves and the formal strictness of Cubism. They are urban landscapes of an almost metaphorical quality.

these confrontations and I hear loud music ringing."

In January, the critic Lloyd Goodrich—notwithstanding his reservations regarding the composition of some canvases—recognizes in *The Arts* that Marin can "express everything in a unique, intense, poignant moment," in accordance with "the feverish rhythm, the always alert conscience" of New York life. This is why Stieglitz gives the artist his full support. At the age of sixty, Marin is among the rare American artists of international significance.

JOHN MARIN:
LOWER MANHATTAN. 1922.
New York. MOMA

AMERICAN GOTHIC

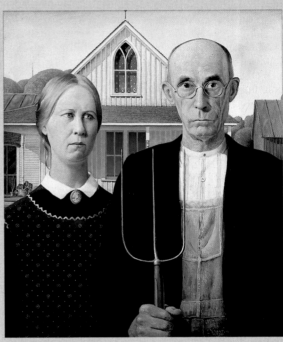

GRANT WOOD: AMERICAN GOTHIC. 1930. Chicago. Art Institute

CHICAGO

This feeds the nostalgia everyone enjoys! Sometimes a painting is sufficient to savor its perfume . . .

The Middle West, in the heart of America, is one of the least intellectually active regions. The novels by Sinclair Lewis confirm the image of a lethargic way of living. It is the exact opposite of cosmopolitan and sophisticated New York.

Recently there have been cultural developments "out there," and at the annual event of the Art Institute of Chicago the jury grants the first prize to a painting by Grant Wood, *American Gothic.*

Wood is surprised and delighted by the popular success of his painting, which has been purchased by the Society of Friends of the Museum. But reactions differ. Certain critics condemn it for being condescending, even ridiculing the nation's past. Others say it perfectly depicts the pioneer virtues of America.

The painter claims that his intention was not to satirize, but there is a touch of charming irony in the painting. In his eyes, *American Gothic* is a portrait full of the tenderness of the towns in Iowa where he grew up. The house in the background actually exists, in Eldon, a tiny town in the southern part of the state. Built in 1880, it is typical of what is called Carpenter Gothic, a simple and somewhat severe style.

Wanting to emphasize the vertical lines of the composition, Wood depicted two "American Gothic people," according to his own words. The woman is his sister, Nan. Because he wanted to make her a symbolic figure of his ancestors, he arranged her hair and dressed her like women whose posture and clothing he studied in the family album. The man with the hayfork is a dentist from Cedar Rapids.

AN EVENING AT THE VAN DONGEN RESIDENCE

PARIS

The receptions-cum-shows organized every Monday from Easter to Pentecost in his splendid residence at 5 Rue Lamber by the Dutch painter Kees Van Dongen are a wild success. "There is nothing more sophisticated, more Parisian, more 'the latest thing,' than the inaugural reception. From the top of the house to the bottom, the portraits are lined up along the walls. They live there," reports the art writer Paul Gsell, who creates a mimesis whereby the models look at their images and wind up resembling them.

Portraits of society women hang next to those of naked dancers. There are paintings of famous politicians, of clients of Maxim's, and of vacationers at Deauville—Mademoiselle Vix of the Opera, the minister Joseph Caillaux, the Countess Cassati, the film artist Mona Lils, the art dealer Paul Guillaume—many other celebrities.

Van Dongen seduces his guests as much by the sumptuousness of his celebrations as by the luxurious decoration of his house. Many remember the first "fêtes mouvementées," extravagant costume balls held in 1914 in his large studio at 33 Rue Denfert-Rochereau. All those who count were there. The critic André Warnod reported that "the painter receives his friends with naked torso, wearing large soft-colored pants, his hair and beard interspersed with little bows of pink ribbon." The fashion designer Paul Poiret triumphed as a Roman emperor.

The company with which Van Dongen surrounds himself leads a busy life, thirsty for pleasure, and hungry for shiny luxuries. He is the faithful and living image of that life. It has been said that he has created a new type of woman. Van Dongen has always cultivated women in colorful ways, from prostitutes in Rotterdam and demimondaines in Montmartre to the "gente

KEES VAN DONGEN: THE ARCHANGEL'S TANGO. 1930. Nice. Musée des Beaux-Arts Jules Chéret

parisienne" who has her portrait painted. She admires Van Dongen for being able to do it in four or five sessions. "A woman," he explains, "is like a flower that one picks and throws away. At other times, it is all of earth and all of heaven; it is the fire of life, it is the spouse, and also the lover, it is forgetting oneself in voluptuousness."

The liveliness of the colors and the freedom of expression, the insolence of his bold and naked figures—they caused a scandal at the Salon d'Automne in 1913—this poise and lack of def-

erence contribute to Van Dongen's success as a painter. He has become a celebrity while maintaining the Fauve and Expressionist audacity of his youth. He was one of the first followers of Fauvism and sent drawings to the 1908 exhibit of Die Brücke.

Around 1913, Van Dongen, in the company of his favorite model, Countess Cassati, begins to move deliberately in the direction of society life, of which he is now the impertinent observer. In 1916, he is seduced by the "divine" Leo Jasmy. He decides

to live with her in a private mansion in the Bois de Boulogne, at 29 Villa Saïd. His wife is left behind in The Netherlands—the war, you know. He dedicates himself to the "big screwballs of Paris dancing the foxtrot." He becomes, in a sense, prisoner of those wild years of which he is the "historiographic" painter.

His painting *The Archangel's Tango* has humor and fantasy, and provides evidence of the extravagance that to a large extent constitutes the seductive quality of this artist.

BELGIUM EXHIBITS PERMEKE

CONSTANT PERMEKE:
THE PORT OF OSTEND. 1921.
Brussels. Mussées Royaux des Beaux-Arts

BRUSSELS

To paint one hundred different seascapes, all of the same format! That was the challenge that Constant Permeke accepted from a dealer. In all, five hundred of his paintings are exhibited at the Palais des Expositions, starting February 12.

Permeke, the son of the painter Hendrik Permeke, now eighty-six years old, spent his childhood in Antwerp and Ostend, Belgium, before entering the Academy of Fine Arts in Ghent in 1904. During the war, Permeke was severely injured during the siege of Antwerp. He was evacuated to Great Britain, where he made large paintings of figures, for example, *The Stranger, The Butcher,* and *The Cider Drinker.* He is one of the most remarkable representatives of Flemish Expressionism, though earlier he was under the influence of Symbolism. For five years, from 1919 to 1924, Per-

meke favored both seascapes and landscapes. The earth extends like an immense ocean under the sky, creating a feeling of the infinite. The landscape he knows so well is the wide plain of maritime Flanders, where he settled last year on the proceeds from his one hundred seascapes. Permeke bought land in Jabbeke, a small town off the road from Brugge to the coast. He had the architect Piet Van der Voort build a house, De Vier Winden (the four winds), but it is mainly of his own design. It is a massive brick cube, and looks rather severe. In a large studio, Permeke paints peasants, who have replaced fishermen in recent works. He paints them in groups or as isolated figures, working or resting, but always as straight as trees.

Permeke celebrates life. He does away with all stylistic idiosyncrasies. Therein lies the unity and the strength of his work.

GROMAIRE IN THE UNITED STATES

NEW YORK

As his reputation in France grows, Marcel Gromaire leaves for the United States. At the age of thirty-eight, the painter has his first New York show, at the Valentine Dudensing Gallery. The French public admired his first canvases in 1911, at the Salon des Indépendants. He showed six works, though he was only nineteen. He was influenced by Matisse, who also made him realize the importance of Cézanne.

Gromaire was greatly affected by the war. He was in uniform for four years, and was injured at the Somme. One of his masterpieces issued from the ordeal is *The War.* It was completed five years ago and established his name with the general public.

As early as 1920, the collector Maurice Girardin (who felt strongly about the work of

Georges Rouault) noticed Gromaire and made sure that he would be the painter's exclusive dealer. Gromaire's work was not affected by the Cubist or abstract revolutions. He continued his search for figurative expression with the use of only a few colors as one of his characteristic features.

The artist is productive. Paintings have succeeded one another, *Woman Fixing Her Stocking, Sunday in the Suburbs, Smugglers.* They express a sensuality and a carnal presence.

The Americans will admire this artist who likes to use all the techniques and the materials at his disposal: oils, of course, and also watercolors, drawings, and etchings. His naked figures, his peasants, his card players, and his soldiers provide evidence of a style that can be designated as Expressive Realism.

Matisse the Sculptor

Matisse is not only a great painter, he is also an exceptional sculptor. His "Backs" series, begun in 1909, has now been completed with his fourth and final masterpiece on the same theme. The manner in which the female body is reduced to a totality of connected masses gives it a monumental dimension. It was already known that Matisse was an exceptional colorist and a very subtle draftsman. Now his sculptures, too, demonstrate that he can express sensuality with perfect economy of means.

Delvaux Astonished by the Spitzner Museum

Paul Delvaux, thirty-three years old, has just made an astonishing discovery: the Spitzner Museum, which is now at the Brussels Fair. Created in the middle of the last century by a so-called Dr. Spitzner, it is a traveling museum unique in Europe. Among the curiosities to be seen in it are a child's head preserved in a glass jar and a collection of anatomical wax models representing various venereal diseases, including the effects of syphilis. The masterpiece of the museum is a mechanical figure of Venus sleeping in a glass case. Delvaux thinks that his art will be changed by it.

The Circle and Square Mobilizes against Surrealism

Led by Michel Seuphor and the painter Torrès-García, a group of artists calling themselves the Circle and Square established a journal and organized an exhibition at Gallery 23. Their aim was to organize artists of the Constructivist school against Surrealism. The members include Léger, Kandinsky, Pevsner, Arp, Gorin, and Prampolini. On opening day, Seuphor recited poems with his face hidden behind a mask made by the sculptor German Cueto, while Russolo played the "russolophone."

Death of a Montparnassian

An American painter of Bulgarian origin, Julius Pinkas, also known

HENRI MATISSE:
FEMALE BACK IV.
1930. Paris. MNAM

as Jules Pascin, committed suicide on June 2. Pascin came to Paris in 1905, and was one of the most original figures of Montparnasse, where he led a life of pleasure. He enjoyed painting nude young girls, whom he let play in his studio, using pale tones outlined in charcoal. Intensely restless with a nonchalant appearance, his health was ruined by alcoholism. He was forty-five years old.

Max Ernst Creates a Scene at the Showing of "The Golden Age"

Chairs and windows were smashed, fistfights broke out, stink bombs were thrown, and bottles of Indian ink were hurled against the screen! The showing of *The Golden Age*, the new movie by Luis Buñuel and Salvador Dali, at Studio 28, Rue Tholozé, resulted in a brawl. Max Ernst, wearing messy clothes and an old hat, led the out-

laws. But after seeing a blind man abused, a dog run over, and a son killed by his father, it appeared that it was the two filmmakers' lack of respect for religion that provoked the spectators' anger. It caused them to react against "the systematic poisoning of French society and youth."

Max Ernst as a bandit in *The Golden Age*.

Alexander Calder "plays" with his *Circus.*

CALDER PLAYS CIRCUS

PARIS

Each evening the most imaginative American artist in Montparnasse puts on a circus performance for his friends' enjoyment which might make the Fratellinis jealous.

A world of acrobats and of clowns has issued from the magic fingers of Alexander Calder, who has worked on the production for four years. His are the most diverse of materials: cutouts from wood, rubber, fabric, and metal wire.

The origins of the circus can be traced to drawings made in 1925 to illustrate the sports section of a newspaper. Preparing a report on the circus, Calder spend fifteen days with circus performers. His drawings, which run on in continuous lines, contain the idea of metal wire!

It is hard to imagine that this circus-happy craftsman, sporting a roll of wire on a shoulder and tweezers in a hand, almost became a serious engineer after

his brilliant studies in the United States, where he was born in 1898. Maybe he inherited his bohemian nature—which caused him to abandon everything to study drawing—from his father, A. Sterling Calder, who is also a well-known sculptor.

Calder arrived in Paris four years ago. To pay for his trip, he helped paint the ship. His first Parisian show took place last year at the Binet gallery.

When looking at his first works, a development is apparent: The metal wire that he imposed upon the sculptures now dictates its own rules to the artist. Where wire was once a simple modeling tool, it has now become an autonomous element. *The Circus* is animated. But beyond the game, a sculptural element enters the picture.

His audience includes Pascin, Man Ray, Desnos, and the famous Kiki of Montparnasse. They all go to see the circus at their friend's home.

MOHOLY-NAGY'S SPACE-LIGHT MODULATOR

PARIS

The *Modulateur lumière-espace*—the *Space-Light Modulator*—of László Moholy-Nagy attracts the attention of visitors at the Salon des Artistes Décorateurs, at the Grand Palais. This sculpture in glass and metal, which is animated by a motor, meets a specific requirement: It captures light and the composition of light, and shows its power to modulate space and time.

For this thirty-seven-year-old Hungarian, light has been a concern since 1917, when he dedicated a poem to it—his artistic career was thus foreshadowed. After moving to Vienna and, in 1920, to Berlin, he joined the Constructivists and was interested in form and motion. Moholy-Nagy taught at the Bauhaus until 1928. The photograms that he designed there contain signs of the search that leads to the "modulator."

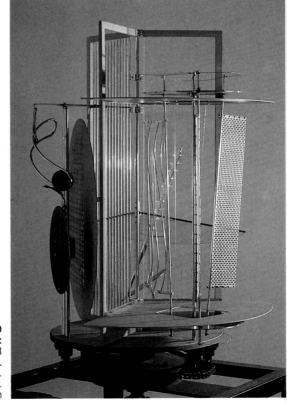

LÁSZLÓ MOHOLY-NAGY: LIGHT PROP FOR AN ELECTRICAL STAGE. 1922-1930. Eindhoven. Van Abbe Museum

LOUIS ARAGON: SCISSORS AND PAPER

Is collage a type of painting or, rather, an entirely new genre with its own meaning and particular problems? It is in response to this question that Louis Aragon wrote *La peinture au défi*, which served as the preface to a catalogue for an exposition at the Galerie Gaemans in which several artists dealt with this theme. As expected, Aragon sees collage as a well-defined technique that is more direct and more intellectual than oil painting because it plays almost relentlessly on the tensions of the mind. The passages below are typical of the tone of his essay.

It is a curious fact that, even today, almost no one seems to take note of a unique activity, the consequences of which have not yet been felt, an activity to which people have been devoting themselves lately in a systematic manner that may be more characteristic of magicians than painters. It raises questions regarding personality, talent, artistic property, and it challenges all sorts of ideas that make themselves at home in the minds of idiots. I am speaking of what, for reasons of simplicity, we call collage, even though the use of paste is but one characteristic of this technique, and not even an essential one . . .

When and where did collage first appear? I believe, in spite of what the early Dadaists might say, that credit must be given to Max Ernst, at least with regard to the forms of collage that are the most removed from the Cubists' papier collé (pasted paper), that is, photographic collage and collage of illustrations. Initially, collage tended to enjoy a generalized practice, and German Dadaist publications, in particular, contained works signed by at least ten authors. But the procedure owed its success more to surprise than to a need to express one's self at any price. Before long, the use of collage was limited to a few individuals, and the entire atmosphere surrounding collage at that time was undoubtedly tied in with the thinking of Max Ernst, and Max Ernst alone. Meanwhile, German Dadaists were divided by serious problems. It is known that they were disunited by social problems during the Revolution of 1917, and that their work came to an end with the failure of the Revolution and growing inflation. At that time, many sought to solve the problem of the uselessness of art by adapting artistic means to propogandist ends. This was how collage gave birth to photomontages, as they were called in Russia and central Europe, and the Constructivists, in particular, made use of them. It would not be right

to overlook a phenomenon that, although disdained by purist painters, represents a major movement in contemporary painting and which is primarily a symptom of the quest for meaning, a current characteristic of evolving human thought . . .

All the painters that can be called Surrealist, not an insignificant group, have dealt with collage at one time or another. If many of these works are closer to papier collé than they are to the collages of Max Ernst, involving nothing more than a modification of the canvas, they are nevertheless significant, and they arise at decisive moments in the evolution of pictorial art . . .

This procedure is an innovation, and it is pure foolishness to greet it in a blasé manner. For what use are colors now? A pair of scissors and some paper can take the place of a palette, and they do not put one back in school, as a palette does . . .

Thought is not a sport. It cannot be the pretext for small successes that draw applause. It is not detached. It is not the activity of isolated individuals. The discoveries of all of us bring about the evolution of each of us. If, at a given moment, this or that thing happens, it is not without consequences. And, if painting is no longer what it once was, painters must become aware of this. Those who do not should not be surprised if they are seen as artisans who, at great expense, make products that are rendered useless by the mere reflections of a few contemporaries.

LOUIS ARAGON
La peinture au défi *(Excerpts)*

MAX ERNST:
THE 100-HEADED WOMAN.
1929. Houston.
Ménil Collection

Chagall's image of places in the Bible, Chagall recounting the story of his life: The moment of poetry in painting has come. Indeed, this artist has known all the avant-garde movements, Cubist and Surrealist. Moreover, he was part of the Russian Revolution, hoping to bring art into the streets. Today he remains a poet and a great painter. This year sees another accomplishment, that of the shocking Le Corbusier, whose Villa Savoye in Poissy is known as the most beautiful poem ever built. The Americans steal the spotlight with their gigantic construction. With a height of 1,250 feet, the Empire State Building is now the tallest structure in the world, beating the Eiffel Tower by two hundred feet.

1931

S U M M A R Y

GREAT MASTERS

Chagall in Search of Himself
Marc Chagall: How I Became a Painter

DEVELOPMENTS

The Abstraction-Creation Group
Inauguration of the Whitney Museum

ART NEWS

Death of Forain
Dr. Dalsace's Glass House
Paris and German Art
Fromn Literature to Sculpture
In Brief

ARCHITECTURE

The House Built on Pillars Named Le Corbusier
The Empire State Building Enters the Ball

LITERATURE

UNITED STATES
William Faulkner gains fame with his Sanctuary.
    Ezra Pound publishes his ABC of Reading.

FRANCE
Antoine de Saint-Exupéry's Night Flight *is an immense success.*

THEATER

UNITED STATES
Premiere of Eugene O'Neill's Mourning Becomes Electra.

MUSIC

MEXICO
Premiere of Grand Horse, *the first modern Mexican ballet, with music by Carlos Chávez, and with settings and costumes by Diego Rivera.*

MOTION PICTURES

GERMANY
Premiere of the psychological suspense film The Cursed One *by Fritz Lange, with Peter Lorre.*

UNITED STATES
Two remarkable films are City Lights *with Charlie Chaplin and* Frankenstein *by James Whale, with Boris Karloff.*

MARC CHAGALL:
THE THREE ANGELS ARE RECEIVED BY ABRAHAM. 1931.
Nice. Musée National Chagall

MARC CHAGALL:
MOSES RECEIVES THE TEN COMMANDMENTS. 1931.
Nice. Musée National Chagall

MARC CHAGALL:
NOAH RELEASES THE DOVE. 1931.
Nice. Musée National Chagall

CHAGALL IN SEARCH OF HIMSELF

PARIS

Because Ambroise Vollard asked him to make illustrations from the Old Testament, so he could finally "dream the Bible with open eyes," Marc Chagall goes to Palestine in February, with his wife, Bella, and their daughter, Ida. During the trip, Chagall is able to have many lengthy discussions with the poets Bialik and Edmond Fleg. (Fleg, in an essay published in 1928, *Why I Am Jewish*, explained why he returned to traditional Judaism and why he fostered different views of the Jewish mystique.) There were themes that Chagall immediately began to illustrate. He illustrates an ecstatic Moses receiving the Tablets of the Law from Heaven, Noah releasing the dove, and the supper offered by old Abraham to the three messengers of God under the oak

"THE AIR OF ISRAEL MAKES ONE WISE. WE HAVE VERY OLD TRADITIONS"

tree as his wife, Sara, laughs when the three tell her she will beget a son, old as she is. Chagall remembered Rublev's icon *The Three Angels*, but Chagall shows the angels from behind, giving more importance to their wings. Together with friends, the Chagalls visit Alexandria, Cairo, and the pyramids. From Beirut on, they travel by land. In Tel Aviv, they are greeted by Mayor Dizengoff, who had invited the painter the year before in Paris to place the first stone of the museum that he had built there.

Chagall paints all around Jerusalem: near Rachel's tomb, and the Wailing Wall. He goes to Safed, where he paints in a glowing ambience the interiors of the synagogues. These works, documentary in nature, are on the whole full of sunlit euphoria. Even when he is in fear of being taken up by the "picturesque character" of Palestine, he is impressed with the triumphant but silent light of the country, its unanswerable peace.

"The air of the land of Israel makes one wise; we have very old traditions," the Russian painter states upon his return to Paris. He recounts his pilgrimage in *L'intransigeant* of June 8. He leaves for a vacation in the village of Malsane, in the pine-covered mountains of Dauphiné, where he works with much enthusiasm on the plates of the Bible. *Ma vie* (my life) is published by Stock, an autobiography translated from Russian by Bella Chagall, with thirty-two designs from the painter's youth. At forty-four years of age, he is supported by Vollard and seems very happy. His setbacks in his native land are no more than a bad memory.

Returning from Russia, and finding himself in Berlin in 1922, Chagall receives word from Blaise Cendrars: "Come back to Paris, you are a celebrity, and Vollard is awaiting you." In the spring of 1923, art dealers ask him to make some illustrations for Gogol's *Dead Souls*. From this tragic novel-poem he makes eighty-four engravings, which he offers to the Tretiakow Gallery in Moscow, in 1927, with the following dedication: "With all the love that a Russian painter has for his country."

In 1925, Vollard asks Chagall to make illustrations for about one hundred of La Fontaine's fables, saying that no one other than Chagall could adopt "the esthetic of La Fontaine, sometimes ingenious and subtle, realistic and fanciful." Profoundly intuitive, the art dealer clearly understands that this painter, Russian-Jewish, attached from his childhood in Vitebsk to the Hebrew tradition of the East, can express "all that is specifically Oriental in the storyteller's sources: Aesop, Hindi, Persian, Arab, Chinese contours, it was from them that he took his inspiration."

It was for these same reasons that Vollard trusted Chagall with the prestigious project of translating the Book of Books into images. What an incredible story, that of the "chosen people!" The first engravings, not less perspicacious in their description than the Jews who are visionaries in the evocation of their mission, are of singularly spiritual richness. They are scrupulously true to the passages of the Bible that he now depicts. He shows great insight but also great tenacity in bringing his copper work to perfection. No less original than Rembrandt and Goya, with whom he is familiar, Chagall begins his new inspirational mood.

(See also 1918.)

MARC CHAGALL: HOW I BECAME A PAINTER

In 1914, Chagall started writing his life story in Russian while confined to his home country by warfare and, later, by the October Revolution. These writings appeared in a volume entitled *Ma vie* (my life), which included fourteen etchings and dry-point illustrations. In the passage below, Chagall explains the circumstances surrounding his becoming a painter.

Here is what happened to me in a junior high school art class. A classmate who happened to be an old hand at drawing and who was always bothering me showed me a drawing he had made on a sheet of tissue paper, a picture of a smoker taken from a copy of Niwa.

I was thrown into disarray and told him to leave me alone.

My memory is a bit foggy, but I recall being enraged that such a picture could be done by the hand of this simpleton and not my own.

A sudden, violent impulse took hold of me. I ran to the library, found a copy of Niwa *and began copying a portrait of Anton Rubenstein, the composer, captivated by his wrinkled face. I worked on other illustrations, including a Greek design, and I might have also done some drawings from my imagination.*

I collected my work, took it home, and hung it on the walls in my bedroom.

I was familiar with common, unpretentious words and phrases. But a fantastic, literary, otherworldly term like "artist," if I had heard it before

at all, it would not have been in my home town.

It was so removed from us!

On my own, I would never have found the audacity to utter the word.

One day, a schoolmate came to visit and, seeing the drawings in my bedroom, exclaimed, "Say, you're a real artist, aren't you?"

"An artist, what's that?," I asked. "Who's an artist? Could it be that . . . I mean, am I . . . ?"

He left without saying any more on the matter.

Once he was gone, I remembered having seen a large sign in town, like the ones one sees hanging in front of boutiques, that read "Pènne's School of Painting and Drawing."

I thought, "This is my destiny. All I have to do now is register in this school and become an artist."

And so ended forever my mother's dream of seeing her son become a clerk, an accountant, or, at best, a well-established photographer.

MARC CHAGALL
Ma vie *(Excerpts)*

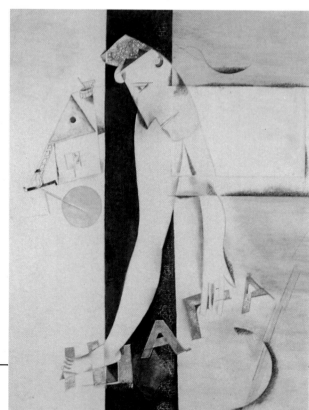

MARC CHAGALL:
UNTITLED. 1918.
Chagall's Private
Collection

THE ABSTRACTION-CREATION GROUP

PARIS

Montparnasse, where one finds on the terrace of the Dôme restaurant all of those representatives who are well known in the field of true abstracts, has well and good become the capital of abstract art. Now a new movement is born, the Abstraction-Creation group, created on February 15 from the ruins of the Circle and Square group, which lasted just about a year, from the autumn of 1929 to the summer of 1930.

Among the numerous members of the dissolved group who join immediately with the founders of Abstraction-Creation are Jean Hélion, Jean Arp, Robert Delaunay, Franz Kupka, Albert Gleizes, Georges Valmier, and Léon Tutundjian. The president is Auguste Herbin. The vice-president is the Flemish painter Georges Vantongerloo, who came on the board soon after the recent disappearance of

Théo Van Doesburg. The movement again takes up the ideas expounded with the previous group in its *Manifesto of Concrete Art*, published last year. These are the proposals.

1. Art is universal.
2. Works of art should be conceived totally from within before being put down. One should not obtain formal ideas from nature, or sensuality, or sentimentality. We wish to exclude lyricism, dramatism, symbolism, etc.
3. A painting should be constructed with pure plastic components, that is to say, with planes and colors; consequently, the painting will have no other significance except itself.
4. The construction of a painting, as well as of its components, should be simple and visually controllable.
5. The technique should be mechanical, that is to say, exact, Antiimpressionist.
6. Strive for clarity.

These rules are taken up and followed by members of Abstraction-Creation, who ratify the undertakings of the protagonists of "Concrete Art," but then find themselves unable to bring out a second edition of their magazine.

Abstraction-Creation is not only the heir of Concrete Art but also that of Circle and Square, which was founded by the Uruguayan painter Joaquín Torrès-Garcia and the Belgian art critic Michel Seuphor. Last year, they organized a unique art show at the Galerie 23 (Rue La Boétie) on April 18. Forty-six artists presented one hundred and thirty of their works. Circle and Square and Concrete Art defend themselves in the matter of constructive and geometric art over that of Surrealism and the Naturalist academicians. It would appear that differences of opinion are in fact a matter of differences in individual personalities.

INAUGURATION OF THE WHITNEY MUSEUM

NEW YORK

The Whitney Museum of American Art opens its doors on November 18 on 8th Street, in downtown Manhattan. Gertrude Vanderbilt Whitney presents her collection of more than five hundred works of American art. Since 1907, when Mrs. Whitney started her "sculptor atelier" in Greenwich Village, she has encouraged young artists, then exhibited their works. The Whitney Museum follows the Whitney Studio Club, which exhibited from 1916 to 1930 the pioneers of American art—John Sloan, Stuart Davis, Edward Hopper, William Glackens, Reuben Nakian, Reginald Marsh, Ernest Lawson, Walter Kuhn, Charles Demuth, and many others.

Mrs. Whitney explains to journalists why she created her museum. "The essential purpose of the institution will not be limited to serving as a repository for American artists of the past. As long as there have been museums, contemporary artists have had great difficulty getting past the front doors. Museums have always had the habit of waiting until a painter or a sculptor has become officially well-known before accepting his works inside their sacred environments. This is totally the opposite of what the Whitney Museum does." Besides the exhibitions she organizes, Mrs. Whitney purchases works from "her" stable, thus increasing her collection at a rapid pace. This year, she acquires about one hundred works from other artists, too, which means that the Whitney Museum is not solely a reflection of her personal taste.

There is an entire complex to be admired on 8th Street. It reflects a powerful example of twentieth-century American art.

JEAN HÉLION:
COMPOSITION. 1930. Paris.
Private Collection

Death of Forain

"I have had good fortune, I have always been happy," the celebrated painter Jean-Louis Forain recently confessed. Forain died in Paris on July 11, in his seventy-ninth year. The son of a house painter, he was the student of Gérôme and Carpeaux, the friend of Rimbaud, and undoubtedly the life of the party of the café Nouvelle Athènes, where he became the friend of Degas. His first satirical drawings appeared in 1876 in *Le scapin et la cravache;* then he contributed to a number of newspapers, including *Le Figaro.* In creating *Le fifre* in 1889 he attempted to "show everyday life, the humor in some sorrows and the sadness in some pleasures." An Impressionist in the style of Degas, he tended toward a violent Expressionism.

JEAN-LOUIS FORAIN: WOMAN LEANING ON HER ELBOW. Paris. Private Collection

Dr. Dalsace's Glass House

There is a new Crystal Palace on the Rue Saint-Guillaume in Paris, hidden behind Haussmann's stone buildings and designed by the architect Pierre Chareau. This glass house, which has three levels, is enclosed in the two stories of a small mansion. The principal innovation is the use of glass panes with concave lenses as façades, which make it possible, with the aid of projectors placed outside, at night, to create light similar to daylight. The use of movable partitions makes the interior space infinitely modifiable.

Paris and German Art

The gallery La Renaissance is showing works by the German Beckmann. The Austrian Kokoschka may be seen at the gallery Georges-Petit. Both have their origins in Expressionism, and now seem to have attained a maturity that makes them sure values in European art. Are they also sure values for French art? Nothing is less certain. In March, when the gallery Bonjean organized an exhibition of contemporary German painters, Germain Bazin wrote in *L'amour de l'art:* "Nothing is stranger and more for-eign to the French soul than this art which reveals a nervous and anguished Germany . . ." Among these painters was the Austrian Kokoschka.

From Literature to Sculpture

It was predictable that André Breton would sooner or later try his hand at the plastic arts, as Marinetti, the founder of Futurism, did before him. He has begun to create symbolic objects having the most surrealistic effect. Similar to Duchamp's "ready-mades," which we know consist of taking a bottle rack or a urinal and declaring them works of art, Breton's are different, however, in that they are montages playing on unusual juxtapositions. Valentine Hugo and Salvador Dali also construct such objects. The idea is to put a glass of milk in a woman's shoe or place a bicycle seat in the midst of foliage, so as to connect aspects of everyday reality with threads drawn from the bizarre.

ANDRÉ BRETON: SURREALIST OBJECT WITH SYMBOLIC FUNCTION. 1931. Paris. Private Collection

LE CORBUSIER: VILLA SAVOYE IN POISSY. 1931

THE HOUSE BUILT ON PILLARS NAMED LE CORBUSIER

POISSY

A house built on pillars—the plan was inspired by the minimal steering radius of a car—that is what the much criticized Le Corbusier created for Monsieur and Madame Savoye and their son Roger. The Savoyes own a magnificent park of seventeen acres surrounded by a forest in Poissy. They want to live in the country, eighteen miles from Paris. Upon arriving by motor at the villa, the chauffeur goes under the pillars, circles around the ground level of the house, and drops off his passengers without untoward maneuver right at the front door, then drives right into the garage via the same path. Nothing like it has ever been seen before.

The Savoyes are ideal clients for an architect. With no preconceived ideas, they had no precise plan in mind, but they knew the Church villa in Ville-d'Avary built by Le Corbusier two years earlier. They liked it very much,

and they decided to put total trust in the architect.

Construction was not without serious financial problems. Like all rich people, the Savoyes know their arithmetic. When the project was first presented in October 1928, the estimate of 785,000 francs was above and

THE SUSPENDED GARDEN TO WHICH SLIDING GLASS WALLS OPEN

beyond what they intended to spend on a country home. When they were presented with a second scheme, then a third, they didn't want them either. Finally, a variant of the first proposal was put forth with an intentionally underestimated amount of 558,690 francs. Le Corbusier and his associate, Pierre Jeanneret, ended up doing the house for 815,000 francs.

Nevertheless, the villa, into which the Savoyes moved in the spring, with the painting scarce-

ly dry, was very much to the owners' liking. The ideas were dear to Le Corbusier: the suspended garden to which sliding glass walls open, flooding the center of the house with bright sunlight, or the terraced roof with its solarium, sheltered from the wind by a thin wall of con-

crete, accessible by a gentle sloping ramp, with long rectangular bays puncturing the façade.

Le Corbusier wanted the elevated residence open to the four horizons, allowing the Savoyes to admire the surrounding trees and fields. Contrary to traditional construction, he did not give preference to any one of its parts—after all, front, back, and sides were not defined as such, each being something of the other three at the same time.

In spite of the fame that came to Le Corbusier upon the publication of *Vers une architecture*, in 1923, in which he lashed out at the academicians, he had, until now, built little. Construction of the immense palace of Centrosoyus in Moscow, commanded by the commissar of the people for light industry, was all the time interfered with by Soviet red tape, to such a point that the architect started to talk about the only thing of his that had been a success until now (but not without some coyness), that is, a moored barge in front of the Louvre. He had rebuilt its interior so it could serve as a night shelter for the Salvation Army. But the Villa Savoye is soon followed by the Swiss Pavilion at the Cité Universitaire, on the Boulevard Jourdan. The Pavilion looks like an immense nave launched into space by six pairs of coupled pilings.

(See also 1923, 1943, 1952, 1965.)

THE EMPIRE STATE BUILDING ENTERS THE BALL

NEW YORK

The economical and financial crisis that has been going on for two years does not stop the artistic milieu of New York from amusing themselves, nor the building contractors from building. In January, the architects profit from attending the annual fine-arts ball by making and wearing costumes of their respective buildings. All was in the fashion of Manhattan, including two new skyscrapers that have recently been put up: the Chrysler tower and the Empire State Building, the world's tallest structure.

Banks, newspapers, fashion—everything for now and for the future—is concentrated in Manhattan. But the small island is not extendable. To remedy the lack of space, buildings have been soaring since 1902. In 1911, one hundred floors were built. The buildings have the same rectangle, floor by floor, as the plots on which they were built, and the streets are transformed into corridors.

But when construction of the Equitable Building, immense yet compact, cut off light to the nearby buildings, rentals of apartments slumped. So the zoning law passed in 1916 revolutionized the architecture of skyscrapers: The size of the first floor is authorized up to a certain height; beyond that, the building has to go up with recessed floors.

More and more elevated buildings go up—yesterday, the Chrysler Tower, today, the Empire State Building and its eighty-six floors, topped by a Zeppelin mooring. Its 1,250 feet surpass the height of the Eiffel Tower by two hundred feet!

Now John D. Rockefeller, the millionaire, has a project in mind: a gigantic complex that will take years to complete.

At the fine-arts ball, the architects seemed to want to rub elbows with the heroes of the moment, such as William Van Allen, who displayed the shiny stars of his Chrysler building.

Empire State Building, in New York, 1931.

Architects of Manhattan stage the ballet *Skyline of New York*, their creations serving as masks and disguises.

Two versions of history, two visions of the world: At the very moment when Frank Lloyd Wright announces the establishment of a school in Wisconsin where he will train artisan-architects in accordance with the rules of rural American tradition, Otto Dix is putting the finishing touches on a polyptych he calls War. *The work, inspired by Dürer, gives dramatic expression to the ransom Europe has paid to death. Mexico takes its place between these two traditions, its Muralism an attempt to reconcile art and revolution. In a return to their origins, the Mexicans try to break with easel art. Perhaps this is the end of art for art's sake, so deeply does each artist feel the need to be in touch with the public once again, after long years of study that had often been elitist.*

1932

SUMMARY

ARCHITECTURE

**In Wright's Word
Frank Lloyd Wright: Talesien—a School of Nature**

ART AND HISTORY

The Mexican Muralists

MASTERWORKS

The Great War of Otto Dix

DEVELOPMENTS

**The Strauss Sale, Unexpected Bids
Creation of the Union of Soviet Artists**

ART NEWS

**Last Issue of *Der Sturm*
Duchamp Plays Chess by Telephone
Lachaise's Giant Woman
Torrès-Garcìa Leaves Paris
The Axe Falls on the Bauhaus
In Brief**

SCULPTURE

**Gabo's Columns
Calder's Mobiles**

WRITINGS AND THEORIES

**Carl Gustav Jung: Picasso Says Good-bye
to the Higher World**

LITERATURE

UNITED STATES
Tobacco Road *by Erskine Caldwell and* Young Lonigan *by James T. Farrell bring their authors public recognition.*

FRANCE
Louis-Ferdinand Céline is awarded the Prix Renaudot for his Journey to the End of Night.

GREAT BRITAIN
The novelist and essayist Aldous Huxley publishes Brave New World, *a pessimistic and disturbing vision of the future.*
T. S. Eliot's Selected Essays 1917-1932 *establish him as a major critic of the era.*

MUSIC

FRANCE
Maurice Ravel composes Piano Concerto in D Major.

MOTION PICTURES

BELGIUM
Joris Ivens and Henri Storck create a documentary of a strike, Borinage, *despite police orders to desist.*

UNITED STATES
Howard Hawks films Scarface.

ITALY
First Venice Film Festival.

OTHER PERFORMANCES

MONACO
Wassili Basil and René Blum found the Ballet of Monte Carlo, formed in part from Diaghilev's troupe.

Frank Lloyd Wright: plan for layout and extension of his Taliesin Fellowship Complex, 1932.

Frank Lloyd Wright.

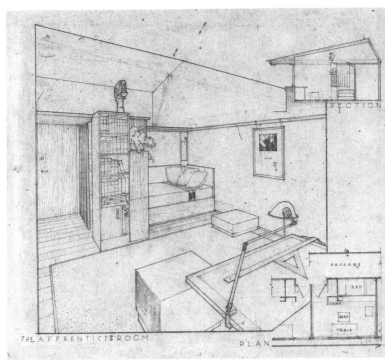

Wright's design for the apprentices' rooms.

WRIGHT CREATES A COMMUNITY

SPRING GREEN, WISCONSIN Mr. and Mrs. Frank Lloyd Wright announce the establishment of a foundation, the Taliesin Fellowship. It is the concretization and the culmination of the thoughts and experiences of a lifetime. At sixty-six years of age, Wright is without doubt the most important, the most innovative architect in the United States in this century. This foundation is a new stage in his personal growth.

He is famous for accomplishments such as the Prairie houses, the Imperial Hotel in Tokyo, a perfectly earthquake-resistant construction which held remarkably well during the terrible earth tremors of 1923, and his dwellings of precast concrete in California. He is indeed an impressive inventor of shapes, but wishes to be known as a philosopher. He was raised by his mother (an amazing person open to new ideas), who followed the very liberal principles of the German educator Friedrich Fröbel—the revolutionary inventor

of the "children's play garden," the "kindergarten," Fröbel, believed, above all, in spontaneous expression and education through play. During the long summer months passed with his family in Spring Green, Wright must have felt the unity of man

HIS POINT OF VIEW
IS DIAMETRICALLY OPPOSED TO
THAT EXPOUNDED BY LE CORBUSIER

with nature and that of the architecture of the farms, the chapels, the dwellings with human life. He found the confirmation and development of these sentiments in the writings of the New England philosopher Ralph Waldo Emerson, one of the great thinkers of the nineteenth century in the United States: For Emerson, the soul (contrary to the dogmas of the church) is the supreme judge in matters of spirituality. Even today, Emerson's ideas resound. His appeal to American students

of 1837 was called a declaration of intellectual independence of America. It preceded, by ten years, Emerson's establishment of Brook Farm, a community that brought together many of his disciples, such as Nathaniel Hawthorne and Henry Thoreau.

It was endowed with the notions of "transcendentalism," a poetic mysticism. It was one of many utopias developing in the United States. It is a tradition into which the Taliesin Fellowship fits. Its idealism can be compared to that of the Shakers of New England and the Fourierist Phalanstery of Wisconsin.

The name itself, Taliesin, reflects the spirit in which Wright's personal project takes shape. Taliesin was the name of a Welsh bard (Wright loves to recall his Welsh origins) who

sang about the wonders of arts. The word means "shining countenance." Taliesin, located at the summit of a hill overlooking the Wisconsin River, was the "face," the crown of one of Wright's favorite places where he went as a small child to gather spring flowers in the first timid sunlight of March, with snow still on the pastures. Built in 1911 on ground that was given to him by his mother, Taliesin I became the architect's personal home. An atelier and a farm were added. Of harmonious proportions, and built with local stone, the residence quickly became famous. But it was destroyed in 1914 during a criminally tragic fire in which his companion Mamah Bortwich and her children died. It was rebuilt, then destroyed again by fire in 1925, then rebuilt again.

It is here that Frank and Olgivanna, his third wife, want to open a school of architecture where ambition can go beyond that of merely acquiring a profession. If the Wrights give the name of Taliesin Fellowship to their project, it is because they wish to emphasize human relationships and philosophical concerns. The have established a program for young apprentice architects who reside and work at the site, dividing their time between architectural design, work on the farm, and construction of new buildings for Taliesin III. This work-study program attracts many young students who read Wright's autobiography, a remarkable document that expounds his philosophies, the foundations of his works, and the often solitary progress of a man with exceptional vision.

During this period of economical depression, Wright offers the students a community in which they can cut stones, chop wood, cultivate the land, and design far from towns where destitution prevails.

On the other hand, he publishes a lengthy article, "Broadacre City: an Architect's Vision," in The New York Times, in which he presents his concept of a new town, simultaneously criticizing the programs of urban concentration that are often defended today. His point of view is diametrically opposed to that expounded in the same newspaper by Le Corbusier about his plans for a Cartesian green city. According to Wright, Broadacre City would be a community organically born out of the era of the machine. It would extend over an immense area, integrating connected roads, services, and places of work, all working in harmony with nature: "Lovely homes with parks and gardens that also serve as small farms, integrating the wonders of nature of our splendid landscapes within immense spacious towns of the near future."

It is to the future that the Taliesin Fellowship apprentices are working. While awaiting the construction of new buildings, they are lodged within the abandoned school, starting their work there, and developing their skills while transforming the school.

(See also 1946.)

IN WRIGHT'S WORDS

"The man is still an iconoclast!" Whispered indignation. Perhaps. But, I wish they would dub me "radical," and let me go home. A good word "radical"? How know life unless through knowledge of the "root"?

And it was unthinkable that any house should be put on that beloved hill. I knew well by now that no house should ever be on any hill or on anything. It should be of the hill, belonging to it, so hill and house could live together each the happier for the other. That was the way everything found round about it was naturally managed, except when man did something. When he added his mite he became imitative and ugly. Why? Was there no natural house? I had proved, I felt, that there was, and now I, too, wanted a natural house to live in myself. I scanned the hills of the region where the rock came cropping out in strata to suggest buildings.

This undated photograph showing "apprentices" at work seems to have been taken after 1932. But it demonstrates the spirit in which Wright conceived of the training of future architects.

How quiet and strong the rock-ledge masses looked with the dark red cedars and white birches, there, above the green slopes.

Yes, there must be a natural house, not natural as caves and log cabins were natural but native in spirit and making, with all that architecture had meant whenever it was alive in times past. Nothing at all that I had ever seen would do.

But there was a house that hill might marry and live happily with ever after. I fully intended to find it.

Architecture, after all, I have learned, or before all, I should say, is no less a weaving and a fabric than the trees. And as anyone might see, a beech tree is a beech tree. It isn't trying to be an oak.

Another fall, another winter, another spring, another summer, and late in 1915, Taliesin the II stood in the place of the first. A more reposeful and finer one. Not a "chastened" Taliesin. No, rather up in arms declining the popular Mosaic-Isaian idea of "punishment" as unworthy of the sacrifice demanded and taken there.

Its "elevation" for me now is the modeling of the hills, the weaving and the fabric that clings to them, the look of it all in tender green or covered with snow or in full glow of summer that bursts into the glorious blaze of autumn. I still feel myself as much a part of it as the trees and birds and bees, and red barns, or as the animals are, for that matter.

Not so many dreams of the future? Moments of anguish? Oh yes—but not of regret. I am enjoying more, day by day, the eternity that is now, realizing, at last, that it is now and that it only divides yesterday from tomorrow.

Taliesin! When I am away from it, like some rubber band, stretched out but ready to snap back immediately, the pull is relaxed or released, I get back to it, happy to be home again.

THE MEXICAN MURALISTS

MEXICO

If it is the role of art to bear witness to the vitality of the spirit of the people by offering a lyrical and poetic vision in language they understand, then the great Mexican Muralists should all be well rewarded by the revolution and the esthetic adventure of the era. In contrast with the Soviet artists, who need to bend to the canons of official Realism, Diego Rivera, José Clemente Orozco, and David Alfaro Siqueiros are able to create an art of the streets, both original and rooted in the ancestral culture of the Mexican people.

Their history merits being told. In 1919, Siqueiros is sent to Europe with a captain's commission. Passing through New York, he had important discussions with his friend Orozco. In Paris, he hurried to see Rivera who, after a Cubist period, had returned to figurative work, strongly influenced by the powerful creations of the "popular"

engraver Posada. Siqueiros and Rivera went to Italy for a study trip. The Tintorettos from the Venetian School of San Rocco, the frescoes of Fra Angelico of Florence, and the Sistine Chapel at the Vatican prompted them to reflect on what could become, in their own country, art that everybody could understand.

AN ART OF THE STREETS, BOTH ORIGINAL AND ROOTED IN THE ANCESTRAL CULTURE OF THE MEXICAN PEOPLE

In 1921, Minister Vasconcelos commissioned these artists, on their return to Mexico, to decorate some public buildings. Other painters became enthusiastic. Among them were Alva de la Canal, Fernando Leal, Fermin Revueltas, Xavier Guerrero, the Guatemalan Carlos Merida, and the Frenchman Jean Charlot.

The most splendid work of this mural renaissance was done by Rivera, between 1923 and 1928.

He made gigantic compositions for the National Palace and the Cortés Palace at Cuernavaca, and painted one hundred and twenty-four frescoes on the walls of an ancient monastery that had become the Ministry of Education; immense areas of lyrical, satirical, epic paintings, solidly constructed and colored with wisdom. Orozco, Rivera's elder by three years, leaves, notably on the walls of the National Preparatory School, his message which is sometimes less caricatural, more lyrical, more abstract than Rivera's. Siqueiros shows, in *The Elements*, that he is an extraordinary virtuoso of design, expressing a developed sense of protest.

Did Rivera monopolize the scene too much? Did the other painters keep up? The fact is

that five years ago there was a general dispersion of artists. Siqueiros dedicated himself to political activism, which landed him in prison for a year. Orozco left for the United States. Charlot joined an archaeological team in the Yucatán. The recent new members, such as O'Higgins and Tamayo—more sensitive to European influences than their elders—do not make up for the departure of the older artists.

The experience continues in the United States through painters like Biddle and Benton, or their students, such as Jackson Pollock. Orozco paints a fresco in California and undertakes a large mural in Hanover, New Hampshire. Siqueiros works in Los Angeles. Rivera is keeping himself busy in Detroit. Where and how far will he go? The sometimes revolutionary themes of the Mexicans are judged as somewhat disturbing in the United States.

DIEGO RIVERA:
ZAPATA. 1929-1930.
Cuernavaca.
Cortés Palace

27

OTTO DIX:
THE WAR. 1929-1932.
Dresden. Stadtmuseum

THE GREAT WAR OF OTTO DIX

DRESDEN

Having joined up voluntarily, Otto Dix saw the war from the front lines, both in Belgium and in France. He was with the artillery. The experience has never left him. He had wanted to know it, to get the full impact in his body of feeling fear in its most realistic form. But he had no idea that it would become his obsession.

War had taken over the creative part of the painter's mind, trained by the principles of the New Objectivity. Today, he is forty-three years of age. His inspiration comes from scenes of soldiers and carnage. Added to charcoal sketches made in the field are compositions, patiently studied and elaborated at length.

From 1920 to 1923, he painted *The Trench*. Soldiers look like moles, slimy with mud. The painting created a scandal. The director of the museum in Cologne who had bought it gave it back to the seller, the art dealer Nierendorf. *The Trench* was then shown in many German towns, in group exhibitions organized by the "Never Again a War" movement.

In 1924, his war continues: Under this title, Dix recollected and published twenty sketches relating to his experiences as a soldier. It was a horror movie that he had lived through.

The last years have been a sort of truce for Otto Dix. His children were born, Nelly and Ursus. He painted them in various portraits. Then once again back to anxiety attacks, the dread of death, the nightmares of war: In 1930, he finished *Melancholy*. This year, *Vanitas*. And under the influence of Dürer and medieval works he painted a triptych, which took him two years. The composition seems like a parody of an altar piece: *The War*.

In fact, the "triptych" has *four* sections. On the left: the departure of the soldier in the misty dawn; in the middle: slaughter in the trenches; on the right: Dix himself as a soldier, dragging a

WHILE NAZIS MARCHED IN THE STREETS, HE PAINTED WAR IN ALL ITS ATROCITY

comrade to save him. (The panels are large: the center panel 7 x 7 feet, the side panels each 7 x 3 1/2 feet.) Underneath the middle panel (and measuring 7 x 2 feet) is a depiction of the last phase of the day, the sleep of restoration for the soldiers who did battle.

Many sketches and watercolors were done previous to the completion of the composition. Dix worked painstakingly. Represented is the passion of the soldier. War is in the background, with all the things experienced by the soldier. It is a universe full of dementia and violent destruction.

At a time when nationalism in Germany reigned supreme, and Nazis marched in the streets, Dix painted war in all its reality, its intrinsic nature, the atrocity of it, the stupidity of it all.

In 1923, in the magazine *Das Kunstblatt*, Carl Einstein remarked on the arrogant and repulsive paintings of his colleague Otto Dix, on their often sordid and oppressive aspects. "Dix," he wrote, "paints all that is true, and by doing so, demeans it, without the pathos of those idiots who beautify everything."

In his *Art of the Twentieth Century*, which came out last year, the same Einstein rounded off his judgment of Dix by saying that he *is* a painter who, thanks to a "meticulous technique", brings forth "a painting that is demoniacal in nature."

THE STRAUSS SALE: UNEXPECTED BIDS

AUGUSTE RENOIR: PORTRAIT OF RICHARD WAGNER. 1882. Paris. Musée d'Orsay

It was precisely 2:30 p.m. on December 15, at the gallery Georges Petit, 2 Rue de Sèze, when the sale of the Jules Strauss collection began. During the preceding two days, the public and art connoisseurs were able to admire the eighty-five pastels, watercolors, sketches, and paintings of the remarkable collection.

The auctioneers of the prestigious sale were Henri Baudoin and Alphonse Bellier. The record bid was the portrait of *Madame Berthe Morisot in Sleeves*, a painting done by Manet in his atelier in the Rue Goyat during the winter of 1868-1869. A London art lover, Turner, paid 360,000 francs. The works by Monet that were sold were *Les pins parasols au cap d'Antibes* (111,000 francs), *Les filets au parc de Pourville* (122,000 francs), and *Antibes, vue des jardins de la Salis* (205,000 francs). Works of Renoir were popular, too: *Portraits of children, The Bather,* and *Le jardin d'essai à Alger* (173.000 francs). But the painting that caused a sensation was without a doubt Renoir's *Portrait of Richard Wagner.* This work, dated January 15, 1881, was bought for the sum of 257,000 francs. *Ballet* by Degas was bought for 105,000 francs, and his *Départ de la course* went for 174,000 francs.

Although Jules Strauss was especially interested in Impressionist painters and their friends, there were two beautiful Delacroix paintings: *Mademoiselle Rose* (116,000 francs) and *Christ on the Cross* (140,000 francs). But this account would be incomplete without mentioning the Boudin and de Jongkind watercolors, the paintings by Courbet, Gauguin, Bonnard, and de Marquet, and the pastels of Roussel and Whistler. The organizers of the sale need not have feared for the financial success of the venture. The most optimistic prediction was for about 3,000,000 francs. The estimate was low because the total sales turned out to be 3,540,000 francs.

CREATION OF THE UNION OF SOVIET ARTISTS

A decree of the central committee of the Soviet Communist party suspends all avant-garde artistic associations and creates a single organization with a subsidiary in each state. The date of promulgation is April 23. The Union of Soviet Painters is under direct control of the Party. At the same time, a writers union, a composers union, and an architects union are created. The Academy of Arts is put under the direction of Isaak Brodski.

According to official terminology, "the liquidation of the exploiting classes in the Soviet Union, and the moral unification and solid politics of the Soviet society are proof of the pointlessness of the existence of associations in art and literature." This means the end of the avant-garde groups.

After Stalin came to power, the situation became more and more critical. From readjusting itself to being self-critical, the avant-garde magazine *Lef* had to quit. Two years ago, Malevich was detained for two weeks before being released because of poor health. The arrests of the intellectuals and poets are too many to count.

In whose name? For these past several years, the spirit that animates the cultural politics of the country has been known: Gorki, the ideologist of "social truth," justifies the new Academism through its being "popular," saying it will respond to the demands of a new and larger public who, in a socialist country, has the right to have its own art. But in all truth, it is unlikely that there are genuinely popular works among the current productions.

Last Issue of "Der Sturm"

The Berlin journal *Der Sturm*, founded in 1910 and directed by Herwarth Walden since its inception, has announced that it is ceasing publication. An entire epoch dies with it. The whole international avant-garde movement, from Futurists to Constructivists, was warmly received by it. Since 1931, after the bankruptcy of its publisher, *Der Sturm* has had serious financial difficulties. Walden sought support in vain. In the third issue of 1932, which is the last, bitterness pierces the irony: "We are going to vote. The German people are becoming politicized. Always and only when they vote. Considering that this popular celebration occurs more rarely than the carnival, preparations and excitement are even greater. The intellectuals, in particular, have gotten people talking and talking about them. However, outside of the carnival period, they are fundamentally apolitical . "

Duchamp Plays Chess by Telephone

Since he gave up painting in 1918, Marcel Duchamp has become an avid chess player, a game to which he has devoted an increasingly large part of his time. After being appointed a delegate to the International Chess Federation, he played two games by telephone with Buenos Aires from the Caïssa Club in Paris on May 26 and 27. He is also working on the French translation of Eugene Znosko-Borovsky's book *How to Open a Chess Game*, which is to be published in the *Cahiers de l'échiquier français* next year.

Lachaise's Giant Woman

The sculptor Gaston Lachaise has just finished his *Standing Woman*, 6 1/2 feet in height, showing a powerful, amply-formed nude, a Baudelairian giant between a prehistoric Venus and a Hindu goddess. The work was inspired by Isabel Dutaud Nagle, a Canadian ten years his senior, with whom he left his native Paris for America in December 1905. Lachaise was twenty-three years old at the time. A rare example of esthetic fidelity,

he has used Isabel Dutaud Nagle as the sole model for his numerous and increasingly spectacular female figures.

Torrès-García Leaves Paris

The Uruguayan Joaquín Torrès-García is leaving for Madrid and dreams of returning to his country. Born in 1878, he studied in Barcelona and created his first work there. He worked with Gaudí and painted frescoes influenced by Puvis de Chavannes. By 1918, however, he had become almost abstract, beginning to construct his pictures according to an original system of signs: schematic people, animals, boats, clocks, or anchors in increasingly delicate colors. Seven years ago in Paris, Torrès-García founded the Circle and Square with Michel Seuphor. The breakup of this group and financial difficulties made him decide to leave.

The Axe Falls on the Bauhaus

Ludwig Mies van der Rohe, who replaced Hannes Meyer as director of the Bauhaus, has done what was asked of him: He has restored order, and in particular has dissolved the Communist cell. He has therefore fulfilled his contract. But now the municipality of Dessau, where the Nazis have become influential, wants even more—it demands the closing of the school. A local newspaper explains why on July 8: One of the most representative "Judeo-Marxist" places must disappear from the "German land." On August 22, the axe falls: The Bauhaus must get out of Dessau. The decision has been made by a vote of twenty to five.

Man Ray and Marcel Duchamp playing chess in *Entr'acte*

OSKAR SCHLEMMER: THE BAUHAUS STAIRCASE. 1932. New York. MOMA

GABO'S COLUMNS

PARIS

Nahum Gabo abandons the meetings held in the café at Nollendorf Place in Berlin for the impassioned debates of the Abstraction-Creation group in the Avenue Wagram in Paris. As a result, the Russian sculptor has met up with his brother Anton Pevsner and becomes a member of a new melting pot of Geometric Abstraction.

Artistic complicity had already brought them together in Paris in 1924, for the exhibition at the gallery Percier, and for the creation of the designs and costumes in metal and transparent material for Diaghilev's ballet *La chatte* (the cat). In Berlin, during the past ten years, Gabo has circulated his ideas behind the *Realist Manifesto*, and in the *Charter of Constructivism*, drafted with Pevsner, they were posted on the walls in Moscow during the hot August of 1920.

Faithful to his tenets, he orients his work toward the creation of architectural pieces

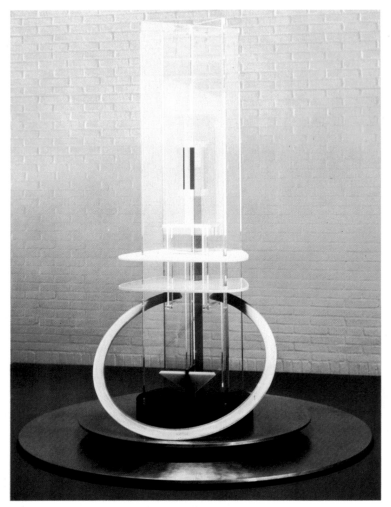

NAHUM GABO: COLUMN. 1923. London. Tate Gallery

called *Tower* or *Monument for an Aerodrome*. Even more astonishing are his *Columns*. One is reproduced in this year's album of Abstraction-Creation. Its shape can be discerned by looking through the sculpture at the point where it diffracts into a multidirectional network formed by transparent glass planes that are held by slim metallic rods. By transferring the weight of the opaque materials that make up the inert volume, Gabo produces a dynamic sculpture in which simple vectors indicate depth, while crisscrossing geometric figures amplify the space in such a way that the emptiness becomes tangible.

Sculpture, since ancient Greece, has been mainly concerned with expression, with description, with lyricism—even in Rodin. Now Gabo, more than anyone else, turns his back to the past, in perfect accord with our scientific and technological society and its different needs.

CALDER'S MOBILES

PARIS

At the Vignon Gallery, directed by Marie Cuttoli, strange sculptures, resembling engines, are shown. They are by Alexander Calder, an American who was in the news for his miniature circus performances in Montparnasse some years ago.

This time, it's many strange objects, about thirty in all, in wire and bits of iron. Fifteen are put in motion when tiny electric motors are triggered by the artist or by a visitor. Metallic, and very brightly colored, the forms are balanced at the ends of iron wires. The sculptures represent the current phase of the artist. After a visit to Mon-

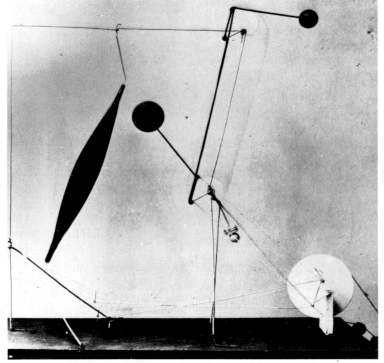

ALEXANDER CALDER: HORIZONTAL MOBILE. 1932

drian's studio, Calder wrote, "I wish to make a Mondrian that moves." Calder has now joined Delaunay, Hélion, Arp, and Pevsner in Abstraction-Creation.

Marcel Duchamp proposed that Calder call these articulated engines "mobiles," recalling the two meanings of the term, movement and motive: Calder eagerly took up the description.

Certain critics, barely familiar with Calder's native tongue, speak of "automobile art." One of them even reaches the point of calling one of the objects a "gearshift." A lot more ridicule than this is needed to discourage the jovial Calder. At the *vernissage*, he could be seen tightening up the belts, or greasing stubborn gears. Even if these first mobiles are open to improvement, Calder never loses his sense of humor.

CARL GUSTAV JUNG: PICASSO SAYS GOOD-BYE TO THE HIGHER WORLD

Professor Carl Gustav Jung, a disciple of Freud before coming to challenge some of his doctrines, was the initiator of depth psychology, which distinguishes itself from Freudian psychoanalysis by the primordial importance that it attaches to the notion of the collective unconscious. As a psychiatrist, he claimed that Picasso's work echoed the schizophrenia of the contemporary world. He was critical of the Picasso exhibition that was held at the Kunstmuseum in Zurich from September 11 to October 30, because, according to him, art should raise the soul. Still, Jung goes to the very heart of Picasso's inspiration. The passages below were taken from an article in the *Neue Zürcher Zeitung*.

For nearly twenty years, I have concerned myself with the expression of mental processes in pictorial form. This is why I am able to observe Picasso's works from a professional standpoint. On the basis of my experience, I can state that the problems addressed in Picasso's art are in all respects analogous to those that afflict my patients . . .

Nonobjective art will essentially look internally for its subjects. This internal source must not be confused with consciousness, since the latter involves the reproduction of images of objects, these images generally having to take on an appearance that is commonly expected. But the objects dealt with by Picasso are presented under a completely different appearance than what one would expect. In fact, the appearance is so different that we no longer even have the impression of dealing with objects of external experience.

The resulting work certainly makes use of forms and figures of the day, but also gives indication of a hidden meaning and therefore has a symbolic aspect. Thus, Picasso begins with paintings that are still objective and done in shades of blue, the blue of the night, the blue of the moonlight on the water, and the blue of Tuat of Hell in Egyptian mythology. The artist dies, and his soul wanders to the beyond. The life of the day clings to him, and a woman and an infant come to warn him. If the day is represented to him by a woman, the night is also; this is what in psychology is called the light soul and the dark soul (anima). The dark soul waits for him, reaching out to him in the blue penumbra, raising a pathological notion. The changes of colors introduce us to Hell. Objectivity is bound to die, as expressed by the dismal masterpiece of the young prostitute suffering from tuberculosis and syphilis. The motif of the prostitute appears at the moment of entrance into the beyond, when he, now a dead soul, meets other dead souls. And when I say "he," I mean that personality in Picasso that experiences Hell as its destiny, the man who does not turn toward the world of the day but who finds himself led helplessly toward the dark, who does not adhere to the acknowledged ideals of goodness and beauty, but, rather, to the demonic attractions of evil and ugliness, who thrives among the antichristian and Mephistophelian individuals of today, who gives rise to visions of the end of the world, this world of the daylight being engulfed by the clouds of Hades, decomposing and finally dissolving in an earthquake as the ground falls apart into fragments, rifts, and rubble. Picasso and his exhibitions are a phenomenon of our epoch, as are the twenty-eight thousand people who have viewed his work.

PABLO PICASSO:
WOMAN IN AN
ARMCHAIR. 1929.
Paris. Musée Picasso

CARL GUSTAV JUNG
"Picasso" (Excerpt)

Matisse turns out to be a brilliant Muralist. He creates two successive versions of his Dance for the Barnes Foundation in Merion, near Philadelphia. The works shatter his reputation as an Intimist artist, and tie him to the great fresco artists of the Italian Renaissance, though his approach is totally different. Curiously, it is from the United States that Intimism, restlessness, and strangeness come to us this year. A thorough retrospective of the works of Edward Hopper reveal on another level an artist of the highest caliber. American art had seemed to be only regionalist in extent, but this is not the case as it turns out. And when Hitler closes the Bauhaus, German artists seek refuge in ever greater numbers across the Atlantic. So it is that Josef Albers is named professor at Black Mountain College. Is the future fleeing the Old World?

1933

SUMMARY

GREAT MASTERS

Henri Matisse—Master of Mural Art
The Swan of Mallarmé

AVANT-GARDE

Stuart Davis: the Dynamism of the City
Socialist Painting in America

EXHIBITIONS

The Silences of Edward Hopper
Art and Politics
The Nazis Kill Off German Culture

ART NEWS

The *Minotaur* Is Founded
Objects from the Vautheret Collection Sold in Paris
Josef Albers at Black Mountain
Magnelli in Florence and Paris
Grosz in America
In Brief

SCULPTURE

Kurt Schwitters Constructs His Labyrinth
Henry Moore—Professor in Chelsea

WRITINGS AND THEORIES

Fernand Léger: the Beauty of the Wall

HENRI MATISSE:
DANCE 1 (CENTER PANEL).
1931-1932.
Paris. MNAM

HENRI MATISSE—MASTER OF MURAL ART

HENRI MATISSE: DANCE 1. 1931-1932. Paris. MNAM

NICE

Henri Matisse takes the waters and some rest at Abano near Venice. He also gets treatment from the frescoes in Padua, where he is taken every afternoon to contemplate the works of Giotto in the chapel of the Arena. At the end of May, this renowned painter, who is sixty-four years old, had returned very tired from an exhausting three years in the United States.

pieces of glass situated behind three French windows and separated by two pendants. Matisse hesitated, but Barnes was able to talk him into it.

Shortly after his return to the Côte d'Azur, Matisse rented an abandoned movie theater at 8 Rue Désiré-Niel in Nice. It was large enough for him to create work on a life-size scale.

After experimenting with many preliminary sketches, he could

interrupting pendants. Matisse did not want to correct his work. All he could do was to start all over again. It took another year of hard work.

The two versions recalled the *Dance* that Matisse had created in 1910 for a palace in Moscow belonging to Sergei Ivanovich Chtchoukin. But in the new *Dance* everything is much more monumental, more reduced to essentials, more integrated with

architecture. Matisse explained to the journalist Dorothy Duddley just before his departure from America: "Treat my decoration as one more misplaced painting. My aim was to translate painting into architecture — fresco as the equivalent of cement and stone."

The first version of *Dance* is perfectly beautiful, with its six immense paintings of nudes gravitating in space. The second

TO TRANSLATE PAINTING INTO ARCHITECTURE — FRESCO AS THE EQUIVALENT OF CEMENT AND STONE

In September 1930, as a member of the awards committee of the Carnegie prize and its awardee in 1927, the painter was invited to Pittsburgh. He took advantage of the occasion to stop off in Merion, near Philadelphia, at the residence of Albert C. Barnes, the foremost American collector of his works. Barnes asked the Frenchman to paint a mural for the main hall of his Foundation. It had been built in 1922 by the French architect Philippe Cret. Matisse's task was not easy, because it involved decorating three large

be found on top of a bench or up a ladder, armed with a charcoal pencil fixed to a long stick of bamboo, tracing the pieces in grand strokes. He worked like this for several months. He placed eleven tints of colored paper across the surface in a checkerboard pattern, finally arriving at an arrangement that totally pleased him.

The composition, of about 500 square feet (43 feet in length and 11 feet in height), was devoted to the theme of the dance. But an error had slipped through in measuring the widths of the

HENRI MATISSE: STUDIES FOR DANCE 1. 1931-1932. Nice. Musée Matisse

THE SWAN OF MALLARMÉ

version, hanging in the Barnes Foundation, is no less perfect. "When I am about to get the blues, I put myself back into balance by thinking about the total success of these panels," he wrote to his friend Simon Bussy. In fact, *Dance in Merion* is an admirable arrangement of rose, gray, blue, and black, displaying the grace of the very large nudes (eight this time) that, the artist asserts, seem on the verge of breaking a frenzied ring, ready to go onto other revels.

He overcame two principal difficulties. He was faced with the fact that the green of the grass and the foliage of the trees, except in winter, cover up the view of the sky in the direction in which the three French windows face the park of the Foundation. The second problem was that other works of art are shown in the main hall, such as *Les poseuses* by Seurat and Cézanne's *Bathers*.

Matisse, who does not like to abandon his canvases and paint-brushes, has traveled a great deal recently. In the footsteps of Gauguin he made the long trip to the South Sea Islands. He went to the United States—to New York—which gave him the most powerful "physical" experiences of his life. He dreamed of creating a work with the dimensions of the skies of Tahiti *and* of the American continent. Barnes gave him the opportunity to make the dream a reality.

And the first version of *Dance*? Normally, it would go to a Parisian museum. But the most French of all French painters is little appreciated in his own country. The critic Florent Fels, who actually knew Matisse's work quite well, wrote two years ago that it was "painting of little skill." The two versions of *Dance* should convince everyone that Matisse is one of the day's great masters of mural art.

(See also 1905, 1908, 1910, 1916, 1951, 1954.)

PARIS

At the same time that Albert C. Barnes asked Matisse to decorate his Foundation, the publisher Albert Skira commissioned Matisse to illustrate the *Poems* of Mallarmé. The artist understood the two tasks could complement each other. Just as *Dance*, an immense museum fresco, was not conceived merely to decorate some architecture, the sketches should not be limited to illustrating the contents. A book is like an architectural space. Each page is a wall that both closes and opens at the same time. The cover and its contents enclose, but the sketches liberate. Matisse thus wanted to follow the traditions of the Byzantine or the Paleo-Christian books. Just as the old masters' frescoes cover the whole surface of the wall, the design invades the entire space of the paper. No blank space, no margins, or more precisely, blank space and margins lassoed into the design. The illustration, in its rapport with letters and words, plays the role of space and margins.

Matisse shows that he was not only extremely aware of the theme in the text he was illustrating, but also of its rhythm. One perceives a profound affinity between Mallarmé and Matisse. The poet, too, was concerned about the spatial arrangement of his poems on the pages. As with Matisse, the thematics of the Golden Age were familiar to him. Matisse's obsession with the love of life and happiness had become even stronger since his trip to Tahiti in 1931, and he now saw his work on Mallarmé as a logical sequel to his stay in the South Sea Islands. His choice of poems is a testimony to the fact. The strongest images that Matisse brought back were of sea birds. They can be found in *Brise marine* (sea breeze). *L'après-midi d'un faune* (the afternoon gambols of a faun) allowed the painter to rejoin his cherished nymphs, temporarily abandoned for Merion. But a nymph always has a swan to be afraid of. The swan Matisse created for this book, in the contained violence of his sexual symbolism, reveals what an inspired artist can add to Mallarmé's poetry.

HENRI MATISSE:
THE SWAN. 1932.
Paris. Bibliothèque
Nationale

STUART DAVIS: THE DYNAMISM OF THE CITY

NEW YORK

One of the discoveries at the exhibition of mural art organized by the Museum of Modern Art, from May 23 to June 22, was clearly Stuart Davis, who last year had done an enormous fresco for Radio City Music Hall.

It is a certain sentiment for cities and towns that Davis expresses so well in his recent works—through the parceling out of forms, the vivacity and gaiety of colors, the fantasy of the letters he incorporates, and the jazz rhythm so typically American.

Born in Philadelphia, in 1894, Davis was, at an early age, in contact with the most prestigious Realist painters of the time. His father was artistic director of the *Philadelphia Press*, where four of the famous "Eight" who formed the Ash Can School worked. At the age of sixteen, Davis went to New York to study under Robert Henri. He showed five watercolors at the Armory Show. He also began working for the Socialist paper *The Masses*.

Then Davis removed himself from the Realism of "The Eight." A painting such as *Odol* showed the extent to which he had learned from Cubism, as well as the pleasure with which he could enrich an abstract structure with the typographic games that seem to be omnipresent in American life.

From the beginning, Davis was exhibited and encouraged by Gertrude Vanderbilt Whitney, who financed his trip to France in 1928. It was on his return that he rediscovered the impersonal and gigantic universe of the American city.

BEN SHAHN: THE PASSION OF SACCO AND VANZETTI. 1931-1932. New York. Whitney Museum

Homage to the two anarchists executed in 1927—a scandalous event to intellectuals around the world.

STUART DAVIS: ODOL. 1924. New York. Andrew Crispo Gallery

SOCIALIST PAINTING IN AMERICA

NEW YORK

American artists show the aftereffects of the Depression: the poverty, and the "revolution" it created. Many forms of Realism deal with the poverty that is to be found in all towns. Urban Realism is the city's version of regionalism; actually, it is its reverse, for there is little to be praised in life at this moment.

After 1931, Realism is vigorously defended by the Art Students League, under the direction of John Sloan, who publishes some designs in the Socialist paper *The Masses*. Urban Realists depict, in an unimaginative style, towns and their streets swarming with dealers, idlers, beggars, and the unemployed. The artists are interested mainly in the popular district of Union Square at 14th Street (from which they formed the name "Fourteenth Street Realists"). This is where they have their studios.

Social Realists are themselves more openly controversial, and militant. They are influenced by the New Objectivity from Germany. Ben Shahn, more than others, has emerged as an important artist since he showed in April 1932, at the Downtown Gallery, his twenty-three gouaches on the tribulations of Sacco and Vanzetti. This year, he shows another fifteen gouaches on the sentencing of the California trade unionist Tom Mooney. The front cover of the catalogue of the exhibition is done by Diego Rivera, who asks Shahn to collaborate with him on the fresco he is making at Rockefeller Center: *Man at the Crossroads.*

THE SILENCES OF EDWARD HOPPER

NEW YORK

A beautiful retrospective of the works of Edward Hopper opens at the Museum of Modern Art in November. There are twenty-five canvases, thirty-seven watercolors, and eleven engravings.

Hopper is one of the foremost American painters. He best depicts the Depression era of the American people, a depression so bad that hope seems to be at the other end of the universe. He is different from other regional painters, such as Thomas Hart Benton, Grant Wood, and John Curry. He does not depict local culture, or the ancestral virtues of the pioneers. It is the very soul of America that appears in his art. The sluggishness and the melancholy of some of his paintings are similar to those of the Sinclair Lewis novel *Main Street*, full of the solitude without horizon that seems to hover over small towns.

Edward Hopper was born in Nyack, New York, in 1882. In New York City, he was the student of some of the most famous Realists of the century: Robert Henri, William Merritt Chase, and Kenneth Hayes Miller. He made two visits to Paris. He resides at Washington Square in New York, and he spends his summers in Maine or Massachusetts.

This retrospective confirms the importance of Hopper in American art. His engravings are personal and very romantic, and he reveals in his design the qualities of an artist who, for a long time, earned his living as a magazine illustrator. But above all, it is his canvases that reach out with their dreamlike atmosphere. Hopper's subjects are almost always about silence: deserted seascapes, lighthouses against an immense blue sky, houses closed after the summer season, little houses where nothing disturbs an oppressive tranquillity. In 1928, Hopper wrote *Charles Burchfield, American*, describing the painting of his friend. It is, in fact, his own creation that Hopper displays to the world: "From what is, to an average artist, boredom with everyday life in a little provincial town, he was able to extract a quality that one could call poetic, romantic, and lyrical."

Modern Art director Alfred Barr writes in the catalogue of the retrospective: "Hopper, in spite of his Realism, is a master of the pictorial drama. But his actors are seldom human: The houses and the streets are not peopled with humans, but with fireplugs, street lamps, barbers' signs, and telegraph poles."

One of the most beautiful paintings in the exhibition is *House by the Railroad*, made in 1925. The subject is a strange and isolated house. Another characteristic painting is *Room in Brooklyn*: The bare floors, the nudity of the decor, and, above all, the light that invades the work—all accentuate solitude and immobility.

This clear, sometimes harsh, light may be the strongest point in Hopper's work. It appears in his restaurant interiors, in anonymous cafeterias, and in hotel rooms, where everything seems to be waiting, as if somebody is passing through without knowing where he wants to go.

EDWARD HOPPER:
ROOM IN BROOKLYN.
1932. Boston.
Museum of Fine Arts

THE NAZIS KILL OFF GERMAN CULTURE

Book burning at the Opera Place in Berlin, May 10, 1933.

BERLIN

The director of the Bauhaus, Ludwig Mies van der Rohe, decides in July to dissolve the celebrated school in order not to submit artistic freedom to the demands of the Nazi administration. It is the disastrous and inevitable outcome of repeated attacks by Nazi authorities on an institution that they had called "a home of cultural Bolshevism." On April 11, the Brown Shirts had invaded the Bauhaus complex, which was situated in an abandoned factory in Berlin, after it left Dessau.

Thirty-two students were taken in for questioning. The press announced the seizure of "a lot of illegal propaganda material" having to do with the German Communist party.

Under such contrived pretexts, the destruction of German culture has begun. It really started

Nazi ideals. Many great artists, such as Dix, Klee, Beckmann, and Baumeister, are chased from their professorships. There are prohibitions for political and racial reasons: Professionals are refused the right to practice for having any personal interest outside Nazi rule. They are under surveillance by a Chamber of Culture. The untoward outlook on freedom of creation is accentuated by the iconoclastic madness that has its grip on the new masters of the Fatherland.

Art labeled "degenerate" is stowed away in the cellars of museums or exposed to the mockery of the public in "chambers of horrors," organized by the "Defense League for German Culture." Book burning, organized by the Minister of Propaganda, Joseph Goebbels, occurs in all German university towns. Thousands of works bearing the

*A CLIMATE OF POGROM,
LEAVING THE CULTURAL ARTERIES
OF THE NATION WITHOUT BLOOD*

when Hitler assumed power in January. Throughout Germany, Brown Shirt fanatics systematically persecute "Jewish elements" and persons considered "politically suspect." The Prussian Academy of Arts was "purified" in February after the attempt by two of its members (Käthe Kollwitz and Heinrich Mann) to form a left front of artists against National Socialism. Its former honorary president, Max Liebermann, said in a commentary, "I can no longer eat because I'd vomit."

Since April, a new law has resulted in the dismissal of twenty-five of the best directors of museums. They were replaced with state employees, steeped in

names of Tucholsky, Kästner, Freud, Marx, and many others go up in smoke for being "nonconformist to the spirit of the new Germany."

To this progressive stifling of intellectual life, to this climate of pogrom, is added the enormous exodus of people, leaving the cultural arteries of the nation without blood. Campendonk, Kandinsky, Klee, Haussmann, Grosz, and Heartfield become exiles. Many left-wing intellectuals die in concentration camps.

We are reminded that, more than one hundred years ago, Heinrich Heine warned, "Where there is burning of books, there is also the burning of man!"

(See also 1935, 1939, 1942.)

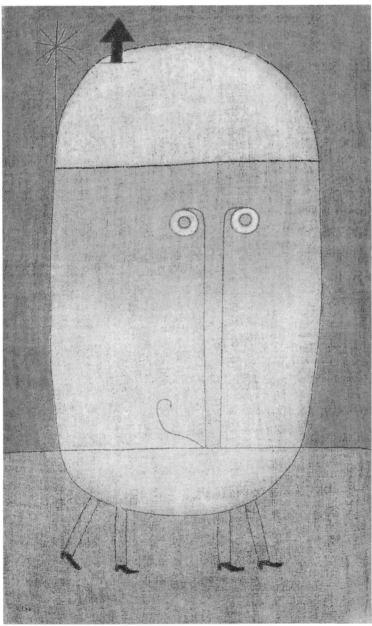

PAUL KLEE: THE MASK OF FEAR. 1932. New York. MOMA

The "Minotaur" Is Founded

Picasso wanted it to be called *Le balai* (the broom) because the new journal proposed by publisher Albert Skira was to clean out the stables of art. But it was given the more mysterious name of *Minotaur*, a myth dear to the Surrealists' subconscious. The first issue is largely devoted to Picasso, who designed the cover. In it may be found his recent drawings inspired by Grünewald's *Crucifixion*. This issue also includes an article by André Breton, "Picasso in His Element," which describes his heretofore little-known sculpture and is accompanied by previously unpublished photos by Brassaï, his favorite photographer.

Objects from the Vautheret Collection Sold in Paris

The Lyonnaise industrialist Étienne Vautheret was a man of taste. The auction of thirty-four paintings from his collections on June 16 at the Salle Drouot is the ultimate proof of this. The total amount of the sale reached 2,277,109 francs. This is hardly surprising; there were no less than twenty Renoirs among the works at auction, including *Nude on a Green Pillow*, acquired for 171,000 francs, *The Little Painter* (143,000 francs), and even *Les roses au rideau bleu* (106,000 francs). Renoir was in good company; there were paintings by Monet, Bonnard, and Utrillo, including five of Utrillo's most beautiful paintings, created between 1912 and 1915. Seurat, Corot, and Puvis de Chavannes also triumphed.

Josef Albers at Black Mountain

At forty-five years of age, the painter Josef Albers is beginning a new career in the United States after the Nazis' closing of the Bauhaus, where he was the youngest professor. As successor to Johannes Itten, he taught the introductory course in the famous school, helping to extend its fame well beyond the borders of Germany. In 1924, Albers created his first glass pictures with pieces of broken bottles, arranged like pieces of a stained-glass window. Then his compositions became both more geometric and more

PABLO PICASSO: FEMALE BUST. 1932. Paris. Musée Picasso

visual. In fact, the artist uses light as a physical means of causing an element of chance to intervene in the painting. He is to direct the art department of Black Mountain College in North Carolina, bringing his theoretical and pedagogical experience from the Bauhaus. He is thinking of experimenting, with his students, on optical illusions, relations between the second and third dimensions, false perspective, and the instability of surfaces.

Magnelli in Florence and Paris

The gallery Bellini in Florence is presenting the second exhibition of Alberto Magnelli in his native city. In 1931 Magnelli settled in Paris, where he is now better known than in Italy. In 1914 the Florentine Futurists would have welcomed him, but Magnelli preferred to remain outside of any group. Although in 1918 he was a full-fledged Abstractionist, in the twenties he returned to representational, almost metaphysical, painting. After abandoning painting in discouragement for almost two years, he returned to it in 1931. Since then, he has also continued work on sketches of "stones," begun in Florence.

Grosz in America

At forty years of age, George Grosz has realized an old dream; he is becoming an American! Last year at the invitation of the Art Students League of New York, he spent several months in the United States. But this time he has emigrated for good. Fascinated by America since childhood, in 1916 he drew *Memories of New York* without ever having been there. A year later, in the journal *Jugend* (youth), he published *Song of Gold Prospectors*, with the line "America!!! The Future!!!" This American future is now in the present. Was it a political decision? Not really. He has not resigned himself to accepting the stagnation into which Germany has been plunged; the situation does not seem to him to be a cheerful environment in which to paint. But it is a personal choice. He wants to begin a new life.

HENRY MOORE— PROFESSOR IN CHELSEA

LONDON

At thirty-five years of age, Henry Moore, who has been teaching at the Chelsea School of Art for a year, has finally been recognized as the major hope for British sculpture.

He spent his childhood in Yorkshire, where he was born in 1898 and where his father was a miner. He was destined to be a schoolteacher. He was gassed during the war, and was eligible for a scholarship to the Leeds School of Fine Arts and then to the Royal College of Art. He journeyed to Italy and Paris in 1925, then began teaching sculpting in various schools.

Moore found his creative force

HENRY MOORE: COMPOSITION. 1933. London. British Council Collection

in primitive and pre-Colombian art. In an England where the tradition of sculpture in regard to the pictorial is almost nonexistent, his first exhibition, in 1928, received only moderate acclaim. But in 1933, he is the main attraction at the Leicester Galleries, and his reception by the public is very warm. No doubt the public had heard Epstein when he said, "Henry Moore is of vital importance to the future of sculpture in England."

Moore's first sculptures represent compact forms, owing their strength to heaviness and density. He forms in them free openings, using hollows as well as swellings. Within this space, a mass charged with humanity takes life, and his reclining figures, mothers and children, become integrated with nature. The genius changes the human figure into monumental landscapes.

KURT SCHWITTERS CONSTRUCTS HIS LABYRINTH

HANOVER

For ten years, at 5 Waldhausstrasse, Kurt Schwitters has been constructing his incredible *Merzbau.* The magazine published by Abstraction-Creation, a group to which Schwitters has belonged from its inception last year, publishes a series of photos of *Merzbau* in its most recent edition. This architecture, christened by its creator first *The Column,* then *The Cathedral of Erotic Misery,* started off as a tall column in the artist's old studio and developed into a labyrinth. It held, in its sprawling tentacles, an array of heteroclitic and strange objects: mementos from the lives of Schwitters and his friends. For those who discover here Ludwig Mies van der Rohe's pencil or Sophie Taeuber-Arp's brassiere,

it is a veritable lost-and-found department. The violence emanating from the erotic "grottoes" that are included makes a tender soul quiver with fear; seen are cut-up and tomato-sauce-painted remains of the victim of a sadistic crime, and other horrible things of this nature.

In perpetual development, *Merzbau* is far from being just a humoristic temple à la Grand Guignol puppet shows. In the last three years, it has become a stern-looking construction, with unadulterated forms and sharp angles, evoking, according to Schwitters, "a Cubist painting or a Gothic architecture." Schwitters works even more intensely toward what he considers "a total work of art" that he knows he will—on principle—never finish. Is it, in his eyes, a refuge from the threats of the outside world? He reduces Hitler to a mere effigy. Is this enough to protect him?

KURT SCHWITTERS: THE FIRST MERZBAU. 1923-1933. Hanover. Kunstmuseum

FERNAND LÉGER: THE BEAUTY OF THE WALL

Fernand Léger gave a noteworthy lecture at the Kunstmuseum in Zurich: *"The Wall, the Architect, the Painter."* Mural painting is one of the battlehorses of this artist, who claims that, in our highly charged, machinelike, and collective society, easel painting is no longer as important as it once was. He reproaches architects for not adequately entrusting painters with the task of producing polychrome, decorative works needed to bring art down from its lofty status. In the passage below, he explains his thinking on a problem that is central to current discussions on art.

It would seem that the amounts you architects are now working with "cannot be reduced any further."

People always eat the same amount of food, get the same amount of sleep, and live and die in roughly the same amount of time.

They want amounts they can live with. The problem is a profoundly human one, especially when dealing with averages. One begins to feel the weight of constraints and necessities. If you destroy, you must soon come up with an "equivalent substitute."

Between the new architectural tendencies and the average urban living situation, a continuum is needed to fill a dangerous gap, a point through which the worst reactions can penetrate and find a basis for developing.

There is no denying that the elites have followed you. This is easy enough to see. But the others, the average ones, cannot follow. You went on in stylish fashion, your heads held high with a disdainful expression on your faces, toward an admirable ideal. But, in your haste to attain this absolute beauty, you should have taken the time to look behind you.

You should stop and ask yourself how long this other group, lagging behind you and out of breath, can "keep pace with your rhythm" and this new "living standard."

Out of pride, you have refrained from calling the painter, who has been waiting at the bottom of the stairs. However, this brave, modest individual, overwhelmed by your elegance, would have been useful in filling in the gap between your theoretical concept and human constraints . . .

A three-way alliance is needed between "the wall, the architect, and the painter." You had an opportunity to make such a union, but you abandoned your companion, and that break-off has caused some difficulties. A violent reaction has arisen that we must "all fight together."

You wanted to arrange colors yourselves. In our epoch, where specialization prevails, this kind of thinking is a serious mistake.

FERNAND LÉGER:
COMPOSITION WITH
THREE FIGURES.
1932. Paris. MNAM

A carpenter does not forge iron. What right do you have to arrange colors?

Color is a vital, essential element, "like fire and water." Reds and blues are useful raw commodities, like wheat. Were you architects not aware of this? Colors are like steak, and just as necessary.

It deserves repeating that color is essential; "one cannot live without it." But whose job is it to arrange this color? It is our job, the painters'. You have tried to do it. You have planned the adding of tones. This is no longer the question. The implications have become broader. Our job is to work with colors in close collaboration with you.

Our cathedrals are the product of intelligent and sensible collaborations. They are the doing of many hands. We should renew this contract.

FERNAND LÉGER
The Wall, the Architect,
the Painter *(Excerpts)*

Cover that anamorphic buttock, I can't bear to look at it! Salvador Dali has been the subject of endless talk since he burst onto center stage of the international art scene five years earlier. This time, he has enraged André Breton at the Salon des Indépendants by showing a large painting of Lenin kneeling, shirt flapping in the breeze, his buttock pitifully distorted. Dali appears before a Surrealist tribunal, but is not disowned by the movement. Everyone no doubt vaguely understood that the artist was playing the role of court jester, and he alone dared to say aloud what the others could only think to themselves. What a contrast with the discretion of Mark Tobey, who goes off to the Orient to replenish his spirits, or of Lewis Mumford, who links technology and civilization. The Americans see the doors of the future open before them.

1934

S U M M A R Y

SURREALISM

The Breton Tribunal
Une semaine de bonté

SOURCES AND INSPIRATIONS

Tobey, a New Orientalist

ART NEWS

Masson in Spain
The Filiform Art of Hans Hartung
The Scandal of *The Street*
Bellmer's Strange *Doll*
The Rockefeller Center Affair
In Brief

DESIGN

Loewy: the Beauty of the Cold
The Machine Enters MOMA

WRITINGS AND THEORIES

Lewis Mumford: Art and Technology

LITERATURE

FRANCE
Publication of René Char's poetry collection Le marteau sans maitre *(the hammer with no master) and Jean Giono's* The Song of the World.

Henry Miller's Tropic of Cancer *is published in Paris by an English publisher, with a preface by Anaïs Nin.*

POLAND
Bruno Schulz publishes his first writing, The Street of Crocodiles.

MUSIC

FRANCE
Foundation of the Hot Club of France, with Djano Reinhardt.

MOTION PICTURES

UNITED STATES
Josef von Sternberg films The Scarlet Empress *with Marlene Dietrich.*

FRANCE
Premiere of L'Atalante *by Jean Vigo and* Angèle *by Marcel Pagnol.*

OTHER PERFORMANCES

UNITED STATES
The choreographer George Balanchine establishes a ballet academy, with mainly young American dancers.

SALVADOR DALI:
THE ENIGMA OF WILLIAM TELL.
1933. Paris. Private Collection

THE BRETON TRIBUNAL

PARIS

Since he joined the French Communist party, André Breton has been touchy on doctrine. He was displeased when one of the members of the Surrealist group, the undisciplined Catalan painter Salvador Dali, exhibited at the Salon des Indépendants a large painting seriously attacking the revolutionary cause.

The painting *The Enigma of William Tell* shows Lenin kneeling, with a floppy cap, his shirt untidy, and an "anamorphic, breadlike, and flaccid" buttock supported by a crutch. Breton can't stand that buttock. With some of his admirers, he goes to the Grand Palais with the intent of tearing the offending painting with his cane . . . But Dali had hung it so high that the invaders gave up their punitive operation.

However, Dali receives a summons to appear at 9 p.m. on February 5 in Breton's studio, which is also Breton's residence, at 42 Rue Fontaine: "Agenda: Dali having committed, on several occasions, counterrevolutionary acts tending to glorify Hitler's Fascism, we the undersigned propose, despite his statement of January 25, to expel him from the Surrealist

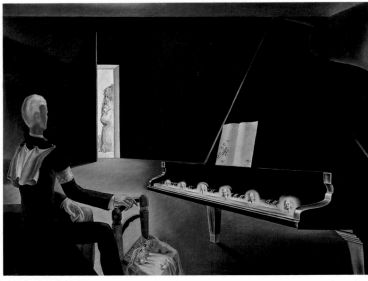

SALVADOR DALI: PARTIAL HALLUCINATION: SIX IMAGES OF LENIN ON A PIANO. 1931. Paris. MNAM

group as a Fascist element and to fight him by all means." On January 25, Dali had seemed to make amends, but now, taking into account the anamorphic buttock, it was too much! The declaration was signed by Brauner, Ernst, Hérold, Hugnet, Oppenheim, Péret, and Tanguy, as well as Breton.

At the appointed time, Dali shows up dressed in an overly large camel-hair coat, shoes without laces, and a thermometer under his tongue. He is preceded by his wife, Gala. The petitioners are there already. Breton defines his grievances against Dali, who replies in a dodgy way. He feigns surprise, uses trickery, loses a sock, gets excited, invokes the Surrealist credo, then pulls from a pocket a long speech written in the afternoon, which is read by an attendee who does not have a thermometer under his tongue.

Says Georges Hugnet: "From the irrational accessory store of his mythology, Dali brandished at random the old Hitlerian nurse, the cannibalism of objects, the great masturbator, the lamb chop and the rock lobster whose flesh and bone constitute striking contrasts, the succulence of the Hitlerian breast pierced by I don't know what nurse's pin symbolizing childhood memories, the exquisiteness of Hitler's soft flesh and mustache, his photo deciphered in an egg plate . . ."

Moreover, in the name of Surrealism, Dali approves Hitler's persecutions, glorifies murder in Sade and the infatuation with horror pushed to the imaginary in Lautréamont. Imploring his listeners to be consistent, Dali presents Hitler as a sort of genial Cecil B. De Mille of massacre and killings.

Dressed in green, Breton paces up and down his studio, his friends curious to hear him. It is perhaps the first time that he has met a Surrealist who follows his principles to their logical conclusions, and the circumstances require him to rise up and prevent him from going further. Constantly moving his pipe, with a mouth reflecting bitter hatred, and with unctuous and jerky language, he brutally expresses the feelings of anxiety and anger prevailing in the assembly. His lucidity is uncertain, his Marxism shaken at its base. He refers to Lenin's buttock, hoping he can get Dali to confess to political treason.

But Dali replies that his painting is an expression of Total Surrealism. He has depicted his dreams in detail and with a scrupulous accuracy: "Therefore, my dear Breton, if I dream of you tonight, if I dream that you and I are in an intimate position, I will not hesitate tomorrow morning to paint that scene in instantaneous colors

Dali and Gala in their Parisian studio, at the Villa Seurat.

and by hand." It was flabbergasting. Brandishing two episcopal fingers, Breton, both flattered and intimidated, issues an exhortation: "I do not advise you to do that, my friend!"

These facts, too, are reported by Hugnet. Sweating, Dali takes off his overcoat and jacket. The sweater he wears makes him look abnormally big. With disheveled hair, stumbling, still in his unlaced shoes, he takes off a first, a second, then a third, and finally a . . . seventh sweater, which he throws before Breton. Naked to the waist, on one knee, Dali takes hold Breton's hand to kiss it and beg his pardon.

It was getting late. The members of the Surrealist tribunal had spoken in turns and now were interested only in going back home. Breton is still begging Dali to give up his views on Hitler. The session adjourns without a decision. Perhaps because they finally acknowledged, after hearing Dali's delirious impromptu speech, that *The Enigma of William Tell* was not so much an attack against the charismatic leader of the Soviet Revolution as the expression of a fantasm of the father eating the child, the little Dali who was about to be eaten alive by a malicious father.

On the following day, February 6, the Republic is threatened. The Croix de Feu tries to cross the Concorde Bridge in order to seize the House of Representatives. Everywhere, throughout Paris, buses are overturned and burn in the streets. On February 9, an illegal Communist demonstration is repressed with force.

Violence, fanaticism, ideological delirium, insults, and shouting fills the streets. The year starts badly. Things are getting serious. The Surrealists no longer talk of expelling Dali.

(See also 1924, 1926, 1928, 1929, 1934, 1935, 1936, 1938, 1941, 1942, 1961, 1968, 1974, 1979.)

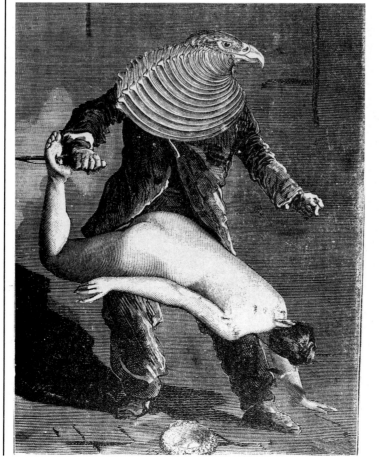

"UNE SEMAINE DE BONTÉ"

PARIS

After *The 100-Headed Woman* (1929) and *The Dream of a Little Girl Who Wanted To Enter Carmel* (1930), Max Ernst publishes with Jeanne Bucher the most successful of his Collage Novels: *Une semaine de bonté ou les sept éléments capitaux* (a week of kindness or the seven capital elements).

Ernst gives up legends and lets images speak for themselves. The result is striking. It appears as if the artist drew the illustrations himself. His inspiration came from Gustave Doré's illustrations, which he reinterprets and distorts by introducing odd elements cut from various books and newspapers he has read. When the elements are gathered, the layout is photoengraved, eliminating all traces of gluing. Ernst defines his collages as an "alchemy of the visual image," made to solidify his hallucinations.

In *Une semaine de bonté* the process leads to an upsetting of the Bible's cosmogony. The "novel" recounts the myth of the world's creation in a week, but the elements involved in *this* creation are the seven deadly sins. Each set of images shows a day of the week, which corresponds to an element. For example, Wednesday is dedicated to blood. Oedipus, a pirate with the head of a bird of prey, commits a variety of crimes: kidnapping, rape, and murder.

Intellectually close to Automatic Writing, the collage, however, requires dedication and patience. The artist makes the point: "If it is the feathers that make the plumage, then the glue does not make the collage."

MAX ERNST: UNE SEMAINE DE BONTÉ. 1934. PARIS. Gallery Jeanne Bucher (Top: Second Notebook, Monday, "L'eau"; bottom: Fourth Notebook, Wednesday, "Oedipe")

TOBEY, A NEW ORIENTALIST

SEATTLE

Return of Orientalism? Eugène Delacroix was looking for the Orient when he arrived in Morocco in 1832. And if Vincent Van Gogh decided in February 1888 to settle in Arles, it was because, in his opinion, the light of the Provence is similar to that of Hokusai. At the beginning of spring, he wrote to his brother, Théo: "You know I feel as if I were in Japan!"

Now the American painter Mark Tobey is attracted by the Orient. He goes to China with the British ceramist Bernard Leach, then to Tokyo, where he spends a month in a Zen monastery studying calligraphy, writing poems, and meditating.

Born in 1890, in Centerville, Wisconsin, Tobey has traveled extensively in Europe and the Middle East. In his thirties, he took advantage of a stay in Haiti to convert to the Baha'i religion. He moved to Paris but was disappointed with the city, and spent seven years in England. In Mexico, he met the choreographer Martha Graham and the painter Marsden Hartley. He went back to China, this time to be with the painter Ting Kwei, with whom he had become acquainted in the United States.

It was in Seattle, where Tobey lived in 1923, that he was first attracted by the art of the Far East. The discovery confirmed his increasing doubts about Western painting. For several years, he was in opposition both to the Euclidian tridimensional conception of space inherited from the Italian Renaissance and to the Objectivism issuing from that conception, prompted as he was by a violent desire to break and disintegrate shapes. Perhaps Ting Kwei is responsible for his new "orientation."

In New York, Ting Kwei once stopped Tobey in front of an aquarium in a shop window and asked why Western artists paint only dead fish and why their paintings look like holes in a wall.

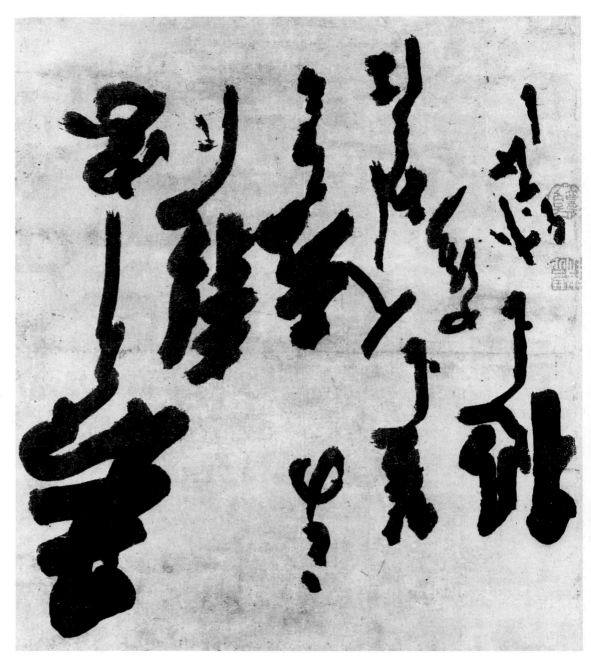

HUKUIN: LOYAL TO HIS PRINCE. Japanese calligraphy of the 18th century. Paris. Galerie Josette Ostier

Ting Kwei taught the American the Chinese art of the brush. He initiated him in the attributes of fox hair, goat hair, mink hair, and rat mustache. He showed him how to hollow the palm of a hand and to calligraph without resting on his arm so that the ink works when the brush touches the paper. A monk in Tokyo explained to Tobey the universal significance of the uninterrupted course of the calligraphic line in space.

Back from the Far East, Tobey makes a drawing entitled *Broadway Norm* with an open and fast line, drawn in one stroke.

The blooming cherry trees of Van Gogh were painted in one stroke. Calligraphy is like the sudden release of the branch, freed from an overload of snow, or like the deer's paw when it leaps. It does not cavitate or pierce the space. It lives like a fish in water. It looks for that click of the mind. All these are things that an experienced eye can see in Tobey's art.

(See also 1944 and 1961.)

Masson in Spain

Long attracted by the colors and bullfights of Spain, André Masson has settled in Tossa de Mar. He has come to travel about in the country—Montserrat impressed him—and especially to work. Among his rare visitors are Leiris and Limbour, who share his lack of enthusiasm for Surrealism. He paints strange pictures of insects and disturbing harvest scenes, which are new to his art. The social agitation shaking the country and the demonstrations he has seen in Barcelona have obviously contributed to the violence that dominates his new works. The artist, who introduced Automatic Writing into the art of painting in 1924, has returned to a more traditional technique and conception: Today he is concerned primarily with metamorphoses. The cruelty of Spain is, in his eyes, the tragic conscience of Europe. The present circumstances will not contradict him.

The Filiform Art of Hans Hartung

At thirty years of age, Hans Hartung has made his mark on art. Plays of lines and blobs, his recent works are both completely abstract and essentially filiform. Influenced by Analytical Cubism, Hartung has retained less of the attachment to reality of earlier works by Picasso and Braque in the years immediately preceding the World War, than he has of their freedom and novelty. Since he was a child, the painter has been interested in astronomy. He loves to tell how, one stormy night, he succeeded in conquering the fear of lightning that his grandmother had communicated to him. Hartung's art, in fact, is more related to the telluric or electrical forces of nature than to the undulation of a hill or a landscape. But he does not limit himself to a renewal of themes in painting. Above all, he is abstract. That is, he has decided to catch the eye of the observer through pictorial elements alone.

The Scandal of "The Street"

A scandal has broken out at the gallery Pierre where paintings by Count Balthazar Klossowski de Rola, also known as Balthus, are being shown. *The Street*, a large painting showing two people in shadows who seem to be living a separate existence, shocked the visitors by its heavy, threatening, hallucinatory qualities. Balthus, who was never part of a Surrealist group, shows similarities to the eighteenth-century painter Johann Heinrich Füssli, whose canvases emphasize the mysteries of desire. A skillful, cultivated artist with an almost traditional technique, Balthus is one of those who, bored with "isms," has decided to turn his back on the avant-garde. He is twenty-six years old.

BALTHUS: THE STREET. 1933. New York. MOMA

Bellmer's Strange "Doll"

The sixth issue of the journal *Minotaur* devotes two pages of photographs to the delirious variations of the *Doll* of Hans Bellmer. He lives in Berlin and is thirty-two years old. Before Hitler came to power, he was a publicist, but he decided that while the Nazis were in power in Germany, he would "do no work useful to society." Having heard of the *Minotaur*, he

HANS HARTUNG: T-1934-11. 1934. Private Collection

sent a selection of photos of his strange child to the journal. Made from detachable parts that can be changed at will, Bellmer's *Doll* can be alternately a skeleton of rods and sheathing, a disjointed body with its limbs connected by ball joints, or a lewd torso with budding breasts. Not for puritanical minds.

The Rockefeller Center Affair

Diego Rivera, assisted by Ben Shahn and Louise Nevelson, has spent the past year working on a vast fresco for the Rockefeller Center in New York. However, it offended many and was soon covered up with decorative designs. Here are the facts: The work, which showed human science and technology extending its benefits to agriculture, industry, and medicine, prominently displayed a very recognizable likeness of Lenin as one of the recipients of these benefits. This seems to have been the worst possible provocation. A violent campaign pro and con broke out in the American press, but Rivera refused to make any changes. He is philosophical about it, and expects to redo his fresco in Mexico.

LOEWY: THE BEAUTY OF THE COLD

RAYMOND LOEWY: REFRIGERATOR

NEW YORK

"As beautiful as a refrigerator!" A few months ago, this expression would have amused American women. It is no longer the case. The man responsible for the change is a French designer who has been living in the United States since 1919: Raymond Loewy, forty-three years old, elegant, with a small mustache.

Loewy thinks that beauty sells easily, and demonstrates it with the Sears Coldpost refrigerator he completely transformed. The former model was a sort of shoe box "decorated" with moldings and perched on top of four nondescript match sticks. Loewy's functional, refined model causes sales to jump from 65,000 units to 270,000 units per year.

The refrigerator is like a luxury car. The door handle opens with a minimum of pressure, a convenience when one returns from grocery shopping loaded with bundles. Loewy replaces the chrome-plated metal of the old rust-prone trays with aluminum. What housekeeper can resist? Best of all, the new model does not sell for a higher price than the outmoded one.

Five years ago, Loewy had a runaway success with the Gestetner copier. Success continues with the Sears Coldpost.

THE MACHINE ENTERS MOMA

NEW YORK

A fabulous exhibition called Machine Art opens at the Museum of Modern Art on March 6. Organized by the young architect Philip Johnson, it contains an assortment of more than four hundred industrial objects. Propellers, giant springs, stoves, safes, furniture, lamps, cash registers . . . and all sorts of machines and appliances. If their use is mysterious to the layman, he can still admire the shape, the material, and the finish as he would familiar works of art. The entire space of the small MOMA is invaded by the most functional and beautiful products of modern industry.

Alfred Barr, the young director of the Museum, stresses the perfect Classicism of these objects when he quotes, in the catalogue, Plato's definition of the absolute beauty of geometry. But the practical aspect of American life is not missing. The catalogue mentions the prices and the major points of sale of the objects lent by department stores and companies such as United States Steel and Westinghouse Electric. The exhibition is favorably received by *The New York Times*, in fact by the entire press, and will have an impact on the evolution of taste.

**Installation of
Machine Art at MOMA.**

LEWIS MUMFORD: ART AND TECHNOLOGY

The early printers hesitated to let the type speak for itself. They thought machine ornaments were better than no ornaments, whereas they should have realized that a certain chastity of statement, a certain reserve and underemphasis, is characteristic of good machine art; it is the function itself that addresses us, and the esthetic appeal must always be within the compass of a rational judgment . . .

As a result of our mechanical reproductive processes, we are now creating a special race of people: people whom one may call art-consumers. From earliest youth they are trained to conduct the normal activities of living within the sound of the radio and the sight of the television screen; and to make the fullest use of our other facilities for reproduction, they are taken, in all big cities at least, in troops and legions through the art galleries and museums, so that they may be conditioned, with equal passivity, to the sight of pictures. The intimate experiences, the firsthand activities, upon which all the arts must be based, are thrust out of consciousness: the docile victims of this system are never given enough time alone to be aware of their own impulses or their inner promptings, to indulge in even so much as a daydream without the aid of a radio program or a motion picture; so, too, they lack even the skill of the amateur to attune themselves more closely to the work of art . . .

Expressive art, just in proportion to its value and significance, must be precious, difficult, occasional, in a word aristocratic. It is better to look at a real work of art once a year, or even once in a lifetime, and really see it, really feel it, really assimilate it, than to have a reproduction of it hanging before one continually. I may never, for example, see the Ajanta cave paintings. From reproductions, as well as from travelers who have been in India, I well know that these paintings are worth seeing; and if ever I make the journey I expect to carry away a unique impression, reinforced by the strange faces, the different languages and customs, I shall meet on my pilgrimage. But better a few short hours in the cave, in direct contact with the work of art itself, than a lifetime in looking at the most admirable reproductions. Though here, as in many other places, I shall be grateful for the

Marc Chagall painting his wife, Bella.

mechanical reproduction, I shall never deceive myself by fancying that it is more than a hint and a promise of the original work . . .

Unless we can turn the water itself into wine, so that everyone may partake of the real thing, there is in fact no miracle, and nothing worth celebrating in the marriage of art and technics. On the other hand, if we establish this personal discipline, this purposeful selectivity, then nothing that the machine offers us, in any department, need embarrass us.

LEWIS MUMFORD
Art and Technics (*Excerpt*)

The game is over in the Soviet Union. With the death of fifty-seven-year-old Kazimir Malevich, mystic initiator of Suprematism in 1915, the unlimited hope the avant-garde artists had placed in the October Revolution is definitively extinguished. Mayakovski had already committed suicide five years earlier, emptied of hope. But when Moscow opens its first three subway stations, with their excess of garlands and Promethean myths, new cult images are put into place. Hitler, for his part, becomes a greater and greater threat to creative artists. His ideas on art and culture are chilling. How far can the shivering Western democracies carry their resistance? Night comes to Europe.

1935

S U M M A R Y

LITERATURE

UNITED STATES
John Steinbeck becomes known through his novel Tortilla Flat.

FRANCE
Suicide of René Crevel; he was an active member of the Surrealist group.
    Jean Giraudoux's play La guerre de Troie n'aura pas lieu (Tiger at the Gates).

GREECE
Posthumous publication of the poems of Constantin Cavafis.

MUSIC

AUSTRIA
Death of Alban Berg, who just completed his concerto In Memory of an Angel. *His opera* Lulu *remains unfinished.*

UNITED STATES
Premiere of George Gershwin's opera Porgy and Bess.
    Debut of Count Basie's orchestra at the Reno Club in Kansas City.

MOTION PICTURES

UNITED STATES
Premiere of John Ford's The Informer.
    Mutiny on the Bounty *with Clark Gable and Charles Laughton wins the Academy Award.*

FRANCE
Two funny films: Fantôme à vendre *by René Clair and* La kermesse heroïque *by Jacques Feyder.*

GREAT BRITAIN
Alfred Hitchcock produces The 39 Steps.

KAZIMIR MALEVICH:
RUNNING MAN.
1933-1934. Paris. MNAM

Malevich's coffin.

Funeral procession on Nevski Perspective in Leningrad.

MALEVICH'S DESPERATE DEATH

LENINGRAD

"I myself withdrew to a field that is new to me, that of thought, and, to the extent of my possibilities, I will state what I see in the infinite space of the human brain." This is the prophetic conclusion of an essay written by Kazimir Malevich on December 15, 1920 as an introduction to the special issue of thirty-four Suprematist drawings—dominated by crosses—from the lithographic presses of Vitebsk. Malevich was the director of the school of art founded by Marc Chagall and called Unovis.

The text now seems a testament by the Russian revolutionary painter, who had inherited from his Polish mother a mysticism demonstrated by this thirst for the ultimate. Hadn't he designed and painted with Suprematist patterns the cross-shaped coffin into which he is placed forever on May 15, having died of cancer in his fifty-seventh year, and in which he is buried after a funeral procession on Nevski Perspective?

It is sufficient to read his own definitions of Suprematism, presented in a *Manifesto* published on the occasion of the "Tenth State Exhibition" in Moscow, in the winter of 1918-1919, to be convinced that he gave a preeminent place and universal value to art. Malevich said: "A surface forming a square was at the origin of Suprematism, of the new Realism of color in the form of an abstract creation . . . With regard to abstract painting as a whole, I would like to point out that Suprematism is not concerned with specific objects or themes but, more generally, with pure abstraction without any qualification whatsoever."

Trying to distance himself fully from any "pictorial mixture," and desiring to reach infinite space, beyond any "utilitarian art," Malevich launched an impassioned, if not enlightened, plea:

"I broke the blue links and the limits of color. Delve into the whiteness, pilot comrades, next to me, and swim in the infinite space. I erected the semaphore of Suprematism. I crushed the borders of the colored sky beneath my feet, I took them down and made them into a bag in which I threw the colors. Swim! The free and white sea, the infinite lies in front of you."

More than a painter, more than an architect who worked on drawings of idealized architecture—the "Arkhitektoniki" —Malevich was a remarkable theoretician and writer. "The pen is more acute than the brush," Malevich said, trying to win as many followers as possible in order to form a militant front that could make art triumph as the ultimate stage of a different life, "where the houses of the new person will be located in space, the earth being a mere intermediate station for him."

As early as 1917, Rozanova, Rodchenko, Oudaltsova, Klioun,

KAZIMIR MALEVICH:
BLACK CROSS ON WHITE.
1915. Paris. MNAM

and Pougny had become his principal followers. Furthermore, one of his most faithful collaborators, El Lissitsky, convinced like his mentor that Suprematism must "move its center of gravity toward architecture," would exert an influence in Germany, especially in the Bauhaus.

But in 1928, which was the end of the new economic policy launched by Lenin in 1921, the general centralization of the administration, accompanied by a return to Academicism on the artistic scene, isolates Malevich. He was considered a "dreaming philospher," and he became the victim of police harassment. In 1930, he was arrested because of his contacts in Germany, where he was invited to exhibit. Presently released, he thanked his friends for having destroyed the documents and manuscripts that could have been used against him. More prudent, he foredated his paintings, made small architectural models, and, returning to figurative art, dedicated himself to family portraits.

The revolutionary dynamics that, in his opinion, were the opportunity for man to attain his power of harmonization with the universe turned against him. But, enclosed in his Suprematist coffin and led to his grave by a pickup truck, whose front end is decorated with a black square on a white square, he becomes a symbol of emancipation for artists. Didn't he say, "Working on Suprematism, I found out that its forms have nothing in common with the techniques of the earth's surface"? In the arrangement of his purely colored signs, which intersect or reject one another, he tried to collect that energy that can accomplish "pure action." After a black square, the "sign of economy," a red square was to give "the signal of the Revolution" in order to reach "the white square as pure movement."

(See also 1915 and 1918.)

IN MALEVICH'S WORDS

My philosophy: raze old cities and towns every fifty years, banish nature from the domain of art, abolish love and sincerity in art, but under no circumstances stem the living source of mankind (war).

The most precious elements in pictorial creation are color and texture; they are the pictorial essence the subject has always killed.

Why not wear the dress of your grandfathers, before whose powdered portraits you swoon in admiration?

The square is not a subconscious form. It is the creation of intuitive reason . . . the face of Art Nouveau! The square is a vivid and majestic newborn . . . the first step of pure creation in art . . . before it, there was naive disfigurement and copies of nature.

I metamorphosed into zero forms, I went beyond zero to creation, that is, to Suprematism, the new pictorial Realism, the nonobjective creation.

Before us stretches the abyss, free and white. Before us stretches infinity.

Painting has been long outdated, and the painter himself is a notion from the past.

Our studios are no longer producing paintings, they are building life forms; these will no longer be paintings but projects that will become living things.

Analysis will prove that things do not exist, but that their infinite exists in the same time, the "nothing" and the "something" at once.

THE NEW IMAGES OF THE CULT

MOSCOW

Who's afraid of free art? It is a question that harasses everyone who follows artistic movements in the Soviet Union today. Socialist Realism, which asserts a close relation between artistic expression and ideological expression, actually seems to spread a dangerous sclerosis within art. This is demonstrated by the latest realizations of the regime: the Intourist head office built by Joltovski three years ago, and the Moscow subway. The Komsomolskaya station clearly illustrates the avenue chosen by Soviet architecture: the celebration of the regime, the party, the nation. In the service of that exaltation, marbles, statues, colonnades, and mosaics represent Lenin the god on the rostrum. As early as five years ago, Vopra, the union of proletarian artists, launched its attacks against modernists in the name of Socialist Realism. Last year, the creation of the new Academy of Architecture finalized standardization. The country of the Revolution has given birth to the most conformist art.

The Komsomolskaya subway station in Moscow.

SHEELER AND PRECISION

DETROIT

For less than a decade, a small number of American painters have been making a peculiar return to a Realism with clear angles and frank luminosity. Preston Dickinson, George Ault, and Ralston Crawford belong to this new category of Realists. But their immediate predecessors are not forgotten: Georgia O'Keeffe, Charles Demuth, and, before them all, the unobtrusive Charles Sheeler, who has recently emerged at the forefront of recent events on the artistic scene.

The main reason why Sheeler became a photographer in 1912 was to earn his living. He was then twenty-five years old. That livelihood soon influenced his painting, giving him unsettling precision of outline and centering. Encouraged by his friend Marius de Zayas, Sheeler was among the first to exhibit paintings and photographs together. He is seen in Detroit in company with the landscape painter Charles Burchfield. This seems like bad company for the latter, who is made out to be no more than a naturalist.

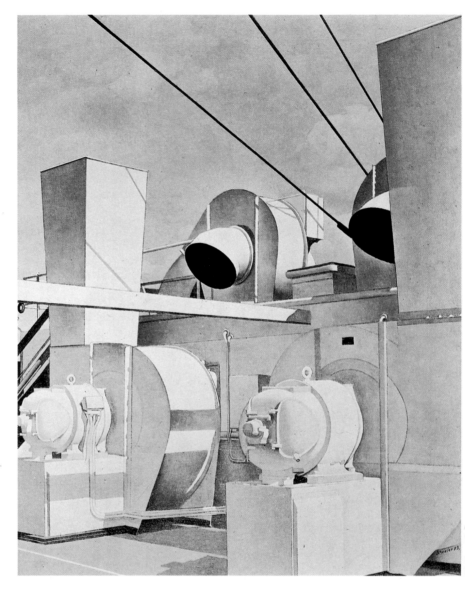

CHARLES SHEELER: UPPER DECK. 1929. Cambridge. Harvard University. Fogg Art Museum

KANDINSKY MEETS MARINETTI

PARIS

Few years go by without Italian Futurists giving the French public an exhibition accompanied by one more manifesto. But even the startling *Manifesto of Aeropainting* of 1929 raised only moderate interest. This year thus witnesses a special effort by Futurists, many of whom are exhibiting at the Salon d'Automne of Lyon and the gallery Bernheim in Paris.

In Lyon one can see paintings by Fillia, Tullio Crali, Nicola Duilgheroff, Gerardo Dottori: many aircrafts and, of course, the portrait of Marshal Balbo, the minister of air.

On the *vernissage* day at the Bernheim, a photographer catches Marinetti, imperious, imperial, reviewing his troops of Aeropainters under the quizzing eyes of a smiling couple: Nina and Wassili Kandinsky. Strange meeting! It would be interesting to know what the Futurist master and the master of abstraction said to each other. Unfortunately, this photo is the only witness of the encounter.

Marinetti at an exhibition of Italian Futurists at Bernheim-Jeune in Paris on April 4, 1935. Kandinsky is second from right.

Cassandre and "The Normandie"

How to create the advertising image of the fastest and most luxurious ocean liner in the world? After several futile attempts, the poster designer Adolphe Jean-Marie Mouron, better known as Cassandre, went to Le Havre to get a close-up look at the *Normandie*. Setting out in a little row-boat, he rowed around the ship. The result was a poster in which the viewer is looking up at an immense hull, creating a feeling of vertigo. The *Normandie* left Le Havre on May 29 with 3,500 persons on board. When it arrived in New York on June 3, it had broken the speed record for the North Atlantic crossing, winning the blue ribbon.

American Abstractionists Organize

The first major exhibition of American abstract art took place in the studio of the sculptor Ibram Lassaw in New York. The participants, who include some who took part in the 1913 Armory Show, are talking about forming an association. They have already found a name: AAA, American Abstract Artists. The future association will have the aim of encouraging abstract art in all its forms, although the founding members especially favor the geometric and Cubist styles, where they tend to follow the nonobjective avant-garde. They also hope to make themselves better known to the museums and to the public.

Death of a Precisionist

We have learned of the death of Charles Demuth in Lancaster, Pennsylvania, the city of his birth. His urban and industrial landscapes, which express America's faith in its power, made him a leader of the Precisionist movement. Always attentive to the intellectual environment of his age as well as to the New York skyline, Demuth also leaves us symbolic portraits of his artist friends, such as Marsden Hartley or Georgia O'Keeffe. In his last years, he had returned to watercolor, which he employed with a feeling that his other paintings sometimes lacked. He was fifty-two years old.

CASSANDRE:
THE NORMANDIE. 1935. Paris.
Musée de l'Affiche et de la Publicité

ALBERTO GIACOMETTI:
THE SURREALIST TABLE. 1933.
PARIS. MNAM

Giacometti Breaks with Surrealism

At the end of last year, Alberto Giacometti broke with Surrealism, although he is its most inspired and talented sculptor. According to him, his Surrealist works were only "worthless masturbations that should be thrown out." He is credited, however, with some exemplary successes, such as *L'heure des traces* or *The Surrealist Table*, from which emerge a hand and the head of a partially veiled woman. A Swiss national, born in 1901 in Stampa, a little village in the Grisons, he came to Paris in 1923 and met the Surrealists in 1930. Now he wants "to put in place" the human figure and sketches throughout the day from the busts of his brother Diego.

ADOLF HITLER AGAINST THE CORRUPTERS OF ART

The struggle against cultural decadence was one of the main themes of *Mein Kampf* when Hitler outlined his program for government in the 1920s. For the two years he has been in power, he has increased his threats and intimidation directed toward avant-garde artists. Today, however, he has decided the time has come to proclaim all his directives on art. For this he has chosen the Nazi Party Congress in Nuremberg, the glorification of Hitlerism. Below is an excerpt from his speech where he firmly states what he thinks of modern art.

Hitler making a speech.

Here is a revolution that sweeps a country and strives to foster a lofty new culture. And this is a good thing! With all the grievances we had to settle with the criminals of culture, we are still far from bringing these corrupters to justice. One thing has always been clear: Under no circumstances will we allow ourselves to argue endlessly with these persons who, if we can go by their work, are idiots or con men. Yes, we have always seen most of the actions of the leaders of these Erostrateses of culture as crimes.

Art must be the messenger of noble and beautiful things, of all that is natural and healthy. No sacrifice will have been too great in achieving this goal. If the effort fails, every penny spent must be regretted. For this art will not be an element of health, of reconstruction and renewal, but a sign of deterioration and decadence. What we see under the pretext of "the cult of the primitive" is not the expression of an innocent, naive soul, but totally corrupt and morbid depravity.

Anyone who wants to excuse the paintings and sculptures—to take particularly crude examples—of our Dadaists, Cubists, and Futurists, or our pretentious Impressionists, while referring to Primitivism in the form of expression, has really no idea of the function of art, which is not to remind mankind of its deterioration, but rather to counter it with the eternally beautiful and healthy. If this type of corruption of art is allowed to express the "primitive" in the sentiment of a people, then our own people for centuries has not waited for such barbarisms of art to be well aware of "primitivism" . . .

Our sympathy and respect go only to those who have had the courage, in other areas as well, to resist the riffraff and not draw upon their references in Bolshevik

delirium and to those who, having faith in their mission, have fought for it with a brave heart, openly and honorably.

We do not want to be told that we should not reject the idea that art has the function of serving reality, and that, consequently, in the domain of its observation and representation, art must not only depict that which is pleasant but unpleasant as well, not only beauty but ugliness. Indeed, art has always depicted the tragic problems of life and has always shown in its creations the tension between good and evil in their useful and harmful manifestations. But one should not allow harm to triumph just to prove the necessity of the useful. It is not the function of art to grovel in the dirt for dirt's sake, to depict mankind in a state of decomposition, to draw idiots to symbolize the rites of maternity, and to show twisted buffoons as symbols of virility.

And don't talk to me about "threat to artistic freedom"! Just as one does not allow a criminal to kill his fellow man, without thought of restricting his freedom, one does not grant anyone the freedom to use his sordid imagination to kill the soul of a people.

SALVADOR DALI: THE PARANOIAC-CRITICAL METHOD

What makes Salvador Dali run? Since his appearance on the forefront of the Paris art scene, he has been running—even leaping. In his brief but scathing *Conquest of the Irrational*, just published by Éditions Surréalistes, he attempts to establish Surrealism, in his opinion a shaky concept, on more solid terms. Starting with paranoia, the subject of the young psychiatrist Jacques Lacan's doctoral thesis in 1932, Dali refines his idea of a paranoiac-critical method which he first had in 1929. The following excerpt describes this idea.

Paranoia: *mental disorder of interpretive association characterized by systematic delusions.* Paranoiac-critical activity: *spontaneous method of irrational knowledge based on the interpretive-critical association of manic phenomena.*

Paranoiac-critical activity no longer sees Surrealistic phenomena and images in an isolated manner, but rather as a coherent group of systematic and significant relationships. In contrast to the passive, impartial, contemplative, and esthetic attitude of irrational phenomena stands the active, systematic, organizational and cognizant attitude of these same phenomena, considered as associative, partial, and significant events in the authentic domain of our immediate and practical experience of life.

It is the systematic-interpretive organization of the sensational, experimental, Surrealistic, scattered, narcissistic material. The Surrealistic events of the day: nocturnal pollution, the false memory, the dream, the daytime fantasy, the concrete transformation of the nocturnal phosphene into a hypnagogic image, or of the waking phosphene into an objective image, the nutritive caprice, intrauterine claims, amorphic hysteria, the voluntary retention of urine, the involuntary retention of insomnia, the fortuitous image of exclusive exhibitionism, inaction, the manic address, the regional sneeze, the anal wheelbarrow, the minimal error, Lilliputian malaise, the supernormal physiological state, the painting one has stopped painting, the painting one is painting, the territorial phone call, "the disturbing image," etc., etc., all that, I say, and a thousand other instantaneous or successive solicitations, revealing a minimum of irrational intentionality or, on the contrary, a minimum of suspicious phenomenal nullity, are associated through the mechanisms of the precise apparatus of paranoiac-critical activity in an indestructible manic-interpretive system of political problems, paralytic images, more or less mammalian issues playing the role of an obsessing idea. Paranoiac-critical activity organizes and objectifies in an exclusive manner the unlimited and unknown possibilities of systematic association of subjective and objective phenomena that come to us as irrational solicitations, to the exclusive favor of the obsessive idea. Paranoiac-critical activity discovers by this method new and objective "significations" of the irrational and allows the manic world itself to move tangibly into the realm of reality.

SALVADOR DALI
The Conquest of the Irrational *(Excerpt)*

SALVADOR DALI: THE KNIGHT OF DEATH. 1935. Paris. Private Collection

Two movements stand diametrically opposed in the art of the day. On the one hand, proponents of Realism in Paris argue with each other over what this approach to art should look like, how it should address itself to the people. In the United States, the creation of the WPA by the Roosevelt Administration poses the same problems for artists. On the other hand, abstract art perpetuates the avant-garde movements of the beginning of the century, and Surrealism triumphs in London, where it is given its first international exhibition. Once again, Salvador Dali sets everyone on their heels. His exceptional Premonition of Civil War *is* surely the first great masterpiece of Surrealist painting, as well as a gripping evocation of the fratricidal combat destroying Spain.

1936

SUMMARY

ART AND SOCIETY

The Quarrel with Realism
America—Land of Art Patronage

MUSEUMS

From Cubism to Abstract Art
Fantastic Art Comes to the MOMA

DEVELOPMENTS

England Discovers Surrealism
Sutherland on Exhibit

ART NEWS

Picasso, Director of the Prado
Lurçat at the Gobelins
Artaud and the Indians
The Golden Gate
Siqueiros, Pollock, and the Pictorial Accident
In Brief

SURREALISM

Max Ernst Paints Echo, the Nymph
Magritte Shows at Julien Levy

MASTERWORKS

Dali Haunted by the Civil War

ALBERT MARQUET:
THE PONT-NEUF AT NIGHT. 1935.
Paris. MNAM

THE QUARREL WITH REALISM

MARCEL GROMAIRE: UNEMPLOYED. 1936. Private Collection

ANDRÉ LHOTE: BUSTE DE FEMME NUE. Paris. Musée d'Art Moderne de la Ville

PARIS

Fauvism, Cubism, Futurism, abstract art—have they suddenly become outdated notions? Before and immediately after the World War, there was a feeling of a break with the past. There was the impression that the world must be totally made over, that there be a new world. Now, movements that so far were avant-garde seem destined to recur outside of a social reality to which they no longer correspond. Even though the public still is far from having assimilated their language . . .

lost in the abstraction." Gone is the time when, in 1930, he thought that collage seemed to render painting useless. A defector from Surrealism, of which he was one of the founders, he now does not disapprove of the political portraits by Guerassimov celebrating the new masters of the Kremlin—now that he is a member of the French Communist party.

It should not be held against Professor André Lhote when he preaches "the return of the man who violently demands that a smoker be at the end of the eter-

SHOULD ART RETURN TO REALISM TO BE ACCESSIBLE TO THE PEOPLE?

Focusing on this crucial question was a debate, held in June, around the time the Popular Front won the elections for the Chamber of Deputies and the Spanish Civil War introduced violence to Europe.

The debate: two days of ardent discussions at La Maison de la Culture under the title "The Quarrel with Realism." Lurçat, Gromaire, Aragon, Léger, Le Corbusier, Lhote, and Cassou are the key participating artists. Les Éditions Sociales Internationales will publish the papers in July.

The magazine *Commune* began the inquiry last year by asking the question "Wither painting?" It approached some thirty artists, among them Signac—who died shortly thereafter—Derain, Delaunay, and Giacometti. Earlier, the Forces Nouvelles group had extolled "the return to drawing, the return to traditional conscientious work in fervent contact with nature." Today the discussion is on a larger scale.

Aragon expressed himself with utter frankness: "Painters have become, even the greatest among them, genuine ignoramuses. They want their paintings less and less to depict, to signify something. They have gone overboard in reveling in style, or in the medium. They got

nal Cubist pipe." But there is a danger in the Social Realism celebrated by Aragon. For is there much difference between Hitler's Germany, where esthetic crimes mean prison, and the USSR, where writers and artists must convert to Socialist Realism, decreed by the Stalinist regime?

The purported obligation of the artist to speak to the people could well mask a desire for propaganda. Thus Léger opposes to Socialist Realism the idea of a new Realism that would abandon nothing of the conquests of modern art: "The new Realism has its origin in modern life itself, in the influence of manufactured and geometric objects, in a transposition of the imagined and the real, which are joined and tangled up, but from which has been banished all literary sentimentalism, all drama that stems from poetic or bookish perspectives."

From there it is only a step to the affirmation of the primacy of mural art: "Painting, in basing itself on the object, also has a social nature. It becomes accessible to all and can be used in schools, stadiums, and public monuments, etc." The step is taken quickly not only by Léger but also by Delaunay, who wants to "make revolution in walls," and, naturally, by Le Corbusier.

It is in the street, in fact, that art can speak to the multitudes, not in the intimacy of museums. It has to speak with a loud voice. "Mural art is the big problem today. It is painting intimately bound to life. It will meet face to face with crowds, with everyday objects or artistic ones. It will have to stand up under all changing or artificial lights," Léger says. To which Le Corbusier adds that the city must be rethought according to "architectural polychromy." They all agree: Popular judgment is warped by traditional upbringing. A worker will never dress in bad taste, and he knows how to appreciate the beauty of a piston or a bicycle, but he remains strangely backward when confronted with art. This must change!

The almost constant reference is Courbet, whose Socialist Realism remains the standard. But France was, in his time, an agrarian country in which three out of four people made their living from the soil. Things have changed. "What is Realism? What is reality?" asks Gromaire. "Reality is not only that which is in the grasp of our hand, within the sight of our eye, it is also what is within the grasp of our mind, and what is not yet within its grasp."

The pictorial responses, of course, are manifold. And all contribute something good. The best may well come from Albert Marquet, who did not participate in the formal discussions. He announces an exhibit in December, at the gallery Druet. And those who have seen in his studio his most recent work, *The Pont-Neuf at Night*, speak of it as a masterpiece expressing our new reality.

THOMAS HART BENTON: CITY LIFE. 1930. New York. New School for Social Research

AMERICA—LAND OF ART PATRONAGE

UNITED STATES

Art patronage, which has developed since 1933, has made over the artistic landscape of America.

The Crash of 1929 worsened the fate of American artists, who already had difficulties making themselves known in a country where work comes before art and leisure-time activities. Painters have long been part of the lot of poor people. They are all victims of the Crash, lengthening the waiting lines in soup kitchens.

The largest part of the help, by far, comes from the federal government. It was President Franklin D. Roosevelt who decided last year to put an end to artistic poverty by introducing a government program of aid to the most deprived artists. This action program, attached to the Works Project Administration (WPA), includes the distribution of regularly scheduled subsidies and purchase orders for artists. An art critic and former museum curator, Holger Cahill is the head of the WPA.

The WPA succeeds in coming to the aid of thousands of artists. On the walls of government office buildings everywhere in the country, paintings and decors blossom. In Washington, the mural at the Department of Justice is made by Broadman Robinson. Post offices are also the site of many.

Local painters work at the local level. The quality of subsidized works (several thousand in all) is uneven. Government patronage does not ban abstract art but favors conventional styles. A few artists, nevertheless, distinguish themselves from the pack; in particular, Arshile Gorky, whose mural *Aviation: Change of Shapes Subjected to Aerodynamic Constraints*, made up of ten juxtaposed canvases for Newark Airport, in New Jersey, remains close to abstraction. Painters espouse, in general, themes that directly depict reality: poverty, injustice, economic crisis. Thomas Hart Benton, Ben Shahn, Grant Wood, and many other artists benefit

from this miraculous help. They practice their art on subjects close to what can be termed Social Realism.

Aid also extends to photographers. Under the direction of the Farmers Aid Agency, they crisscross the country and bring home gripping scenes of rural poverty. Architects entrusted with the conception of housing projects, writers, musicians —they, too, share in the federal munificence.

Creative artists from all walks of life and from all over hold a convention. They define their concept of the role of the artist in society. They decide that they owe it to themselves to defend culture against "Fascism and the Crash." Strangely enough, this smacks of Soviet Socialist Realism. This is an unforeseen extension of the policy of the President, who now expresses his concern that we might see "young enthusiasts beginning to paint Lenin's face on the Department of Justice."

FROM CUBISM TO ABSTRACT ART

NEW YORK

A prestigious exhibition is organized at the Museum of Modern Art under the theme "Cubism and Abstract Art." In the preface of the catalogue, Alfred Barr, the Museum director, explains that the exhibit was conceived as a historical synthesis, a general retrospective, brushing aside at once all spirit of controversy. No American artist is represented. It is European art that reigns as master. There also is an absence of many recent works, but there are some beautiful compositions by Miró dating from 1933 and a magnificent *Head* by Julio González. Some beautiful paintings by Piet Mondrian bear witness to his productiveness during the last twenty years.

It is primarily on the historic aspect of abstract art, going through Cubism, Futurism, and Constructivism, that the accent is placed. "It was over twenty years ago that the first purely abstract paintings were created," Barr writes in the catalogue. "Many of the final phases in the development of abstract art were reached before the last war." Whatever the case may be, there is renewed interest in the subject, as much in New York as in various European countries. Ten years ago, it was said in all quarters that abstract art was dead! But, in a few years, it will be time to organize an exhibition of abstract art of the thirties to show the contemporary works being produced in London, Barcelona, Prague, Warsaw, Milan, Madrid, Paris, and other centers of creative activity.

This exhibition is also a trib-ute to those who were the pioneers of abstract art, like Alfred Stieglitz or Katherine Dreier, who, as early as 1920, had created through her Société Anonyme innumerable exhibitions of European abstract art. It was well before the founding, in 1929, of the Museum of Modern Art.

"Cubism and Abstract Art" presents the two main currents in abstract art: One is intellectual, geometrical, essentially coming out of Cubism; the other is lyrical and optimistic, which developed from Matisse and the Fauves to Kandinsky. Also represented, through architectural renderings or applied art, are the German Bauhaus, Dutch Neoplasticism, French Purism, and Russian Suprematism and Constructivism.

The pages dedicated by Alfred Barr to "Abstract Art and Politics" are read with interest. He underlines, in particular, the connections between Futurism and Fascism, Surrealism and Communism. He reminds the reader that for the Nazi regime, abstract art is "Kunstbolschevismus," and that nine of the artists represented in the exhibition (Kandinsky, for instance), have left Germany in the last three years. "This essay and this exhibition" he concludes, "could well be dedicated to these painters of squares and circles, as well as to the architects influenced by them, who had to suffer from the philistines in power."

(See also 1908, 1910, 1915, 1917.)

JUAN GRIS: STILL LIFE ON A CHAIR. 1917. Paris. MNAM

PIET MONDRIAN: COMPOSITION 7. 1913. New York. Guggenheim Museum

FANTASTIC ART COMES TO THE MOMA

NEW YORK

For museums, too, there are exceptional vintage years. Thus, 1936 will remain a telling date in the young history of the Museum of Modern Art, familiarly called MOMA. Founded in 1929 and managed by the young art historian Alfred H. Barr, Jr., the museum presents two major exhibitions in the space of a few months. The first in the spring, "Cubism and Abstract Art," allowed visitors to discover the great names and the trends of modern painting. Since the beginning of December and until the end of January next year, an exhibition on Fantastic Art, Dada, and Surrealism is being held. The exhibits are the fruit of one plan: to present in an objective way the principal movements of modern art.

However, the current exhibit goes back further. It follows, chronologically, the history of the fantastic and the marvelous in European and American art over five centuries. It particular-ly shows how the fantastic was one of the predominant veins in medieval art. There are scenes of Hell and the Apocalypse, and illustrations of miracles accomplished by saints. There is also art from the beginning of Romanticism.

From the terrifying prisons by Piranesi to the nightmares of Füssli, from Blake to Goya, the visitor understands rapidly that

TELLING THE HISTORY OF FANTASTIC ART AND EXPANDING THE PERMANENT COLLECTION

there exists a history of Fantastic Art. This art can also be architecture, as is proven by the section devoted to this discipline, with photographs of the palace built by the mailman Cheval in Hauterives, of the Casa Milà by Gaudí, or the metro stations by Guimard.

Yet, the most important works are those of the Dadaists and Surrealists, and of their friends. De Chirico, Tanguy, Ernst, Picasso, Duchamp, Klee, Kandinsky, Chagall, and many others are joined by a common fascination with the irrational, the spontaneous, the marvelous.

Beyond presenting works of so-far unknown artists to the American public, the organizers pursue another goal: enriching the collections of MOMA. When the museum celebrated its fifth anniversary two years ago, Barr pleaded for the constitution of a solid permanent collection, underlining the risk of seeing the museum transform itself into an art gallery.

In direct line with this policy, and thanks to the gifts of benefactors, MOMA has decided upon the purchase of several of the works displayed this year. Three superb reliefs by Jean Arp are acquired; also, a canvas entitled *The Nostalgia for the Infinite,* by Giorgio de Chirico, the major influence on Surrealist painting. Several works by Max Ernst will be the property of MOMA: among them, *Two Children Threatened by a Nightingale* and *La bicyclette graminée garnit de grelots les grisons grivelés et les échinodermes courbant l'échine pour quêter des caresses.* From Miró, the museum purchases *Person Throwing a Stone at a Bird,* made in 1926. And it purchases one of Tanguy's most famous paintings, *Mommy, Daddy Is Hurt,* a canvas made in 1927. The most unusual acquisition is probably *Breakfast in Fur,* by Meret Oppenheim.

All the works acquired—thanks especially to funds allocated by Mrs. Rockefeller—come just in time to broaden the collections at MOMA. Americans can now contemplate living art year-round: the Museum of Modern Art, at 11 West 53rd Street in New York.

MERET OPPENHEIM: OBJECT: BREAKFAST IN FUR. 1936. New York. MOMA

ENGLAND DISCOVERS SURREALISM

LONDON

Roland Penrose, whom the founder of Surrealism, André Breton, describes as "Surrealist in friendship," can be satisfied. On June 11, the first major international Surrealist show ever held in Great Britain opened at the New Burlington Galleries.

The London public has had adequate time to prepare itself for a shock. In 1933 and in 1934, Miró and Dali presented a vast range of their works in the best galleries in the British capital. But this time, thanks to Penrose, who prepared this display with frequent trips to Paris, the English Surrealists mobilize the bulk of their troops in huge halls where museum paintings by Picasso, de Chirico, Miró, Ernst, Dali, Klee, Magritte, Man Ray, Picabia, and Duchamp are shown side by side with the sculptures of Moore, Giacometti, Arp, Brancusi, or Calder, and with remarkable works of primitive and insane art.

Breton and Éluard come to lend a hand to their British friends. They speak in French to an overwhelmed and astonished audience. But the chief attraction of the presentation is the appearance of Dali dressed up as a helmeted deep-sea diver. Through his helmet, the Catalan painter reads an extravagant account of his life and of his love for Gala, his companion. But when Dali shows bizarre signs of agitation, someone thinks to unscrew the helmet—in the nick of time. Instead of delivering a Surrealist pantomime, Dali was well on the way to suffocating.

Thousands of people parade through the New Burlington Galleries. So many, in fact, that Penrose, the treasurer, delightedly deposits substantial sums of money every night.

ROLAND PENROSE: THE LAST VOYAGE OF CAPTAIN COOK. 1936. London. Private Collection

GRAHAM SUTHERLAND: RED TREE. 1936. B.P. International PLC

SUTHERLAND ON EXHIBIT

LONDON

The International Surrealist Show, which takes place during the months of June and July in the New Burlington Galleries, introduces the young London painter Graham Sutherland, who is represented with his two oils on canvas. He is a discovery.

Invited by Roland Penrose, the organizer of the show, Sutherland admits to never having thought of himself as a Surrealist. He does not like it when painters arbitrarily juxtaposes images.

Sutherland is thirty-three years old. He has long devoted himself to drawing and etching. He exhibited for the first time eleven years ago, and was immediately elected to the Royal Society of Etchers. In 1930, he was appointed professor of etching at the Chelsea Art School. In 1932, he started working in painting proper. The desertion of American etching collectors during the Depression makes it difficult for an etcher to survive.

Picasso, Director of the Prado

After the first fighting broke out in Spain on July 19, many Spaniards in Paris become alarmed and knock on Pablo Picasso's door. Whose side would he take, Franco's or the Republicans'? He immediately chooses to oppose Franco. President Manuel Azaña therefore proposes that he become director of the great Madrid museum, the Prado, where he had, as an adolescent, made excellent copies of Velázquez. It is a symbolic gesture, which Picasso accepts with pride, although the paintings of the famous museum have been moved to a safe place. "It is extraordinary! I am the director of an empty museum."

Lurçat at the Gobelins

For the first time the Gobelins Museum has commissioned a design from Jean Lurçat, on the theme *The Illusions of Icarus* (10 x 17 1/2 feet). Since 1915, Lurçat has tenaciously struggled to revive the medieval traditions of the craft of "lisse" and to return tapestry to its original purpose of wall decoration. He eliminates perspective and the three-dimensional effects more appropriate to painting, uses yarns sparingly, employing only a limited range of clear but warm tones, and works with a looser woof. A painter-poet, Lurçat manipulates a complex universe where nature and humanity are magically intertwined.

Artaud and the Indians

The Surrealist poet Antonin Artaud has just spent several months in Mexico. Determined to "flee European civilization," he wound up spending some time among the Tarahumara Indians. But he also devoted himself to lecturing and to writing articles for local newspapers. In his opinion, Surrealism must be surpassed; that is why the only artist whom he felt he should speak about was Balthus. Among the Mexican artists, Artaud has accepted only the painter Maria Izquierdo, because he recognizes in her "a truly Indian inspiration." In fact, only the Indians have not disappointed Antonin Artaud.

The Golden Gate

In November, L. S. Moissieff's Bay Bridge was opened, connecting San Francisco to Oakland. It is a suspension bridge in several sections, with two levels for cars and trains. But people are impatiently awaiting the opening next May of J. B. Strauss' spectacular Golden Gate Bridge. Its construction will have taken a little more than four years, and its central span is 4,200 feet long. Despite its exceptional length, it is suspended from only two cables, three feet in diameter, on two metal towers 744 feet high. The legendary site of the Golden Gate is in the heart of the earthquake zone of the Pacific coast, and the construction of it was especially sensitive.

Siqueiros, Pollock, and the Pictorial Accident

Siqueiros, like Orozco and Rivera, is glad to return to work in the United States, despite official rebuffs, as he finds an attentive public among American artists. When he opened an "experimental studio" in New York, young artists, such as Jackson Pollock, soon joined. For Pollock, Thomas Hart Benton's technique remains static, whereas the program of exploration that Siqueiros calls the "Pictorial Accident" promises more spontaneity; the splashes and trickling paint hold many possibilities to exploit.

The Golden Gate Bridge in San Francisco.

MAX ERNST PAINTS ECHO, THE NYMPH

PARIS

Max Ernst is always where you least expect him. During the show "Fantastic Art, Dada, and Surrealism" at New York's Museum of Modern Art, which makes official his collages and his frottages, he devotes himself here in Paris to a new technique: decalcomania! Never has his painting been so hallucinatory, so imaginative, so feverish.

Decalcomania was invented by his friend, the painter Oscar Dominguez. It consists of the controlled use of ink blots or crushed paint, as can be seen in *The Nymph Echo,* a painting that seems to spring from a childhood memory. "Adolescence has those bursts of enthusiasm toward great moments of soli-

MAX ERNST: THE NYMPH ECHO. 1936. New York. MOMA

tude," he states. "The mind soothes itself, and the senses catch their breath before the fight." In reply to a prayer, *The Nymph Echo* came to him.

The mysteries of the forest have always attracted the painter. But it is not enough for him that the forests be savage and impenetrable, secular, swarming, careless, ferocious, fervent, pleasant, or without yesterday or tomorrow. Like the heavy vegetation of *The Nymph Echo,* they are all this at once. There is a forest for the woodcutter, another for the stroller, yet another for the insect.

Even though the frottages, or rubbings, express what is seen unconsciously, the decalcomania of Max Ernst plunges to the abyss of basic life. If the beetle could paint, this is how it would show us the leaves strewn on the carpet of its forest.

MAGRITTE SHOWS AT JULIEN LEVY

NEW YORK

The United States welcomes the first showing of the works of the Belgian Surrealist painter René Magritte. The event assumes capital importance for the world of painting. From January 3 to January 20, the Julien Levy Gallery shows a group of paintings and drawings presented by a friend and compatriot of the painter, Paul Nougé, in the company of a poem by Paul Éluard, translated by Man Ray: "Stairs of the Eye." At the age of thirty-eight, Magritte asserts himself as one of the most visible painters of the young European pictorial avant-garde. Canvases such as *The Key to Dreams* or *Perpetual Motion* are admirable examples.

The shock he experienced when discovering, in 1925, Metaphysical Painting by Giorgio de Chirico led Magritte in a

RENÉ MAGRITTE: THE KEY TO DREAMS. 1930. Paris. Private Collection

direction he has not since left. His style defines itself immediately: legible workmanship and perfect mastery of the technical problems suggesting *trompe l'oeil.* He stages everyday images, which he manipulates in order to extract the hidden meaning. "An object makes you think there are others behind it," he proclaims in one of his first writings, "Words and Images," published by *La Révolution Surréaliste* in December 1929.

Magritte admits his undisguised passion for the work of Edgar Allan Poe. It is reflected in his *Man with Newspaper* and *The Red Model.* This repertoire of familiar objects, these commonplace scenes, trigger the mystery. But at the same time, the artist tricks us—making us forget even the painting itself—through his innate aptitude for a magic that belongs to him alone.

DALI HAUNTED BY THE CIVIL WAR

PARIS

Salvador Dali finishes one of his most fantastic and frightening compositions. When he found himself in Barcelona two years ago for a show, he had to suddenly leave the city. It was the scene of violent armed groups, and a dangerous climate reigned. It is not surprising that Dali, once back in Paris, translates onto canvas an anguish unfortunately very legitimate.

Above an arid, ravaged land, before a background of sky invaded by apocalyptic smoke, a huge human body rends itself, quarters itself, strangles itself, grimaces with pain and madness. A monstrous hand crushes a breast. Some fingers, a foot, a tongue convulse themselves. It could be an Expressionist painting, if the Surrealist touch were not present. Discreet presence, but all the more surprising: a

few beans lie on the earth like turds. The work has as its title *Soft Construction with Boiled Beans*. But it is the subtitle that attracts attention: *Premonition of Civil War*. At the time Dali was completing the painting, the feeling dominant in Spain was that the civil war was a major risk. The young Spanish Republic was threatened on the left and on the right.

The situation has worsened

considerably. Since July, a terrible drama has been playing itself out in this tragic land. This is what this painting conveys with an uncommonly expressive force, giving, by the same token, a masterpiece to Surrealist painting.

(See also 1929, 1934, 1935, 1938, 1961, 1968, 1974, 1979.)

SALVADOR DALI:
SOFT CONSTRUCTION WITH BOILED BEANS (PREMONITION OF CIVIL WAR). 1936. Philadelphia. Museum of Art

This is the year of paradoxes. Guernica, created by Picasso for the Spanish Pavilion at the International Exposition in Paris, tolls the bell for civilization. But at the same time, at the same exposition, Sonia and Robert Delaunay rediscover, by a different path, the synthesis of the arts cherished by the Renaissance, where architecture, sculpture, and painting were joined as one. While Paris is parading in its finery, the drama of the day seems to be in Munich, where there is an exhibit of "degenerate art," at Hitler's request. The exhibit displays everything that is most creative in modern art, from Gauguin and Cézanne to Klee, who has gone to Bern where he lies gravely ill.

1937

S U M M A R Y

MASTERWORKS

Picasso Paints *Guernica*
Paul Éluard: Victory of Guernica

THE INTERNATIONAL EXPOSITION

Trying To Conjure the Future
The Delaunays Hire 50 Unemployed Artists
***La fée électricité*: the Largest Painting in the World**
The Palace of Light

ART AND POLITICS

Hitler: German Art versus Modern Art

ENCOUNTERS AND INFLUENCES

Klee Acknowledged by His Peers
Kandinsky Meets His Friend Klee

ART NEWS

Matisse Inaugurates the First Issue of *Verve*
The Masters of Independent Art
A House in the Trees
The New Bauhaus in Chicago
In Brief

EXHIBITIONS

The Popular Masters of Reality

WRITINGS AND THEORIES

Walter Benjamin: Art Has Lost Its Aura

LITERATURE

FRANCE
André Malraux writes the novel Man's Hope *on the Spanish Civil War, in which he participates.*

POLAND
Witold Gombrowicz publishes his novel Ferdydurke.

MUSIC

UNITED STATES
Death of George Gershwin at the age of thirty-nine.
The avant-garde composer John Cage creates Construction in Metal *with the dancer Merce Cunningham.*

FRANCE
Death of Maurice Ravel.

SWITZERLAND
Performance of Alban Berg's opera Lulu *in Zurich, two years after Berg's death.*

THEATER

UNITED STATES
Premiere of John Steinbeck's Of Mice and Men.

MOTION PICTURES

UNITED STATES
Walt Disney creates Snow White and the Seven Dwarfs, *his first long animated film.*

FRANCE
Jean Renoir shows one of his best films, La grande illusion.
Premiere of Marcel Carné's Drôle de drame.

PABLO PICASSO:
GUERNICA (DETAIL). 1937.
Madrid. Prado

354

PABLO PICASSO: GUERNICA. 1937. Madrid. Prado

PICASSO PAINTS "GUERNICA"

PARIS

At the beginning of June, a little over a month after its official opening, the Spanish Pavilion at the International Exposition receives the large mural composition commissioned last winter to Pablo Picasso by the Spanish Republican government.

Poet José Bergamin, cultural attaché at the Spanish embassy in Paris, had contacted the famous painter to obtain his agreement, for the symbolic sum of 150,000 francs. No subject was imposed on him: He was only asked to make it large and powerful.

After two difficult years, both on personal and artistic levels, Picasso told his dealer and friend, Daniel-Henry Kahnweiler, that he wanted to paint a canvas that would express the century, not just his own life. However, once he had the opportunity, he paced the floor in his studio on the Rue des Grands-Augustins. Only when the terrifying news of the Guernica bombardment arrived was he able to set to work.

The small Basque town on the Biscaya gulf was largely destroyed on Monday, April 26, by Junker 52 and Heinkel 51 planes of the Condor Legion, on General Franco's order. Hitler is proud of this legion, which provides air support for Franco's troops. The bombing of civilians was meant to demoralize the enemy. There were one thousand six hundred and fifty-four dead and eight hundred and eighty-nine wounded, mostly old people, women, and children.

After seeing three photographs of the massacre on the front page of *Ce Soir*, on May 1, Picasso starts the first work for his painting. Some sixty sketches and drawings show a mother running with her dead child, a wounded horse, a bull's head, a woman falling into the burning ruins of her house, broken faces. André Malraux visits on his return from a speaking tour to the United States, where he tried to raise money for Spanish Republicans. The drawings are aligned at the foot of a huge white canvas, measuring 11 1/2 x 24 1/2 feet. Pointing his finger at them, Picasso said, "I would like them to crawl up on the canvas, like roaches."

Thanks to photographs taken by Dora Maar, the artist's current companion, the various stages of the composition can be traced. The preparatory sketches and drawings are assembled in order. They are colored, but the painting is black, gray, and white. Asked why, Picasso, annoyed, answers that he "didn't have time to finish it." It is said that the poet Paul Éluard, who closely followed the elaboration of the painting, assured Picasso that it was fine the way it was.

Undoubtedly, the truth is dif-

Picasso working on *Guernica*.

PAUL ÉLUARD: VICTORY OF GUERNICA

Translated by Wallace Fowlie

ferent. In order to express the bloodshed, the painter makes a large red tear cut from cardboard, which he tries to pin on each of the characters. He changes his mind; it seems unnecessary. *Guernica* is black, gray, and white, like the photos of the massacre sent from Spain by telephoto, and like the huge black and white headlines announcing the killing in the papers.

There are no bombs or planes in *Guernica,* only women writhing in pain under the glare of an electric sun. The horse with its hip pierced by a lance, in the center of the composition, is the symbol of the innocent, mortally wounded victims. The bull on the left derives from bullfights; their cruelty has always fascinated Picasso. The figures come from Cubism, with its dismemberment of people and things, and from his more recent period of "metamorphoses," in which the painter turns the human figure inside out like a glove. Still, the painting is full of the presence of technical war and the noise of machine guns. Blinding white light evokes that of incendiary bombs.

Guernica is much more than a painting of the present moment. It shows the disaster of our society. At the exhibition, visitors walk in front of the huge painting. Some, moved by the fratricide that is tearing up Spain, weep. Others, young painters, are most amazed by its expression of violence. Perhaps the future will remember "Victory of Guernica," a poem by Paul Éluard, which acts as a dedication to the painting.

(See also 1904, 1905, 1907, 1909, 1912, 1921, 1927, 1937, 1945, 1946, 1948, 1953, 1954, 1958, 1973.)

1
Beautiful world of huts
Of mines and fields

2
Good faces in the fire good faces in the cold
In refusals in nights in name calling in blows

3
Faces good for everything
Here is the void looking at you
Your death will be an example

4
Death a heart thrown backwards

5
They made you pay for the bread
The sky earth water sleep
And the misery
Of your life.

6
They claimed they wanted good minds
They rationed the strong and judged the imbeciles
Gave alms divided a penny in halves
They bowed before corpses
They vied in politeness

7
They persevere they exaggerate they are not of our world

8
Women and children have the same treasure
Of green leaves of spring and pure milk
And time
In their pure eyes

9
Women and children have the same treasure
In their eyes
Men defend it as best they can

10
Women and children have the same red roses
In their eyes
Each one shows his blood

11
The fear and courage of living and dying
Death so hard and so easy

12
Men for whom this treasure was sung
Men for whom this treasure was wasted

13
Real men for whom despair
Feeds the devouring fire of hope
Let us open together the last bud of the future

14
Pariahs death earth and hideousness
Of our enemies have the monotonous
Color of our night
We will triumph over them.

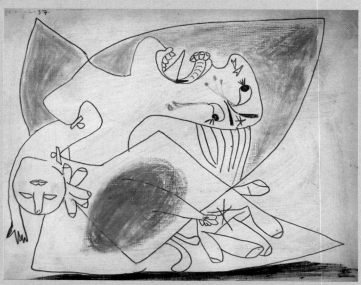

PABLO PICASSO:
MOTHER WITH HER DEAD CHILD.
1937. Madrid. Prado
(Preparatory sketch for *Guernica*)

TRYING TO CONJURE THE FUTURE

PARIS

President Albert Lebrun inaugurates a prestigious event, still in the making. The International Exposition of the arts and technology of modern life is ready a month later, in June. Unfortunately, several strikes and a negative social climate, together with growing international tension, cruelly deny the peaceful mission of this event. On its one hundred hectares, spread along both banks of the Seine, it shows "everything that unites people, and nothing that separates them."

On both sides of the Trocadero, the Russian and German Pavilions, spectacular symbols of ideological confrontation between nations, seem to defy each other. The eagle crowning the pavilion of the Third Reich, 180 feet high, throws piercing glances at the 110-foot-high muscled couple brandishing the hammer and sickle over the Soviet building.

Trainloads of material, brought from the other side of the Rhine River, are needed for the steel-and-stone monster designed by Albert Speer, Hit-

The Russian Pavilion at the International Exposition.

The German Pavilion at the International Exposition.

ler's architect and minister of equipment. For months, German workers labor to finish the building before the scheduled opening.

The USSR makes a similar effort. The building, 525 feet long, designed by Iofan, has a marble-covered façade bearing the dates 1917-1937; it seems to signify that the history of the country started only twenty years ago, and that there was no Russia before the Revolution.

The most enlightening fact, so to speak, is the architectural poverty of the two buildings. This cheap and demagogic Neoclassicism makes it difficult to believe that not long ago Germany was the country of the Bauhaus, and Russia the center of Constructivism.

In a pompously artificial movie-set decor, the Italian Pavilion reminds the visitor of the luxuries of ancient Rome.

In contrast, the Spanish Pavil-

ion bears the burden of its real tragedy, the civil war that ravages the country. Its masterpiece is *Guernica*, a huge painting by Picasso, made after the destruction of the Basque town.

Fifty-two countries are represented in this exhibition, which, in a sense, remodels the face of Paris: The mammoth Trocadero was replaced by the Palais de Chaillot with its terraces facing the Eiffel Tower, the Champ-de-Mars, and the École Militaire. The discreet Museum of Public Works is more original than the Tokyo Palace, its neighbor on the Avenue du Président Wilson. However, France, with its obvious Neoclassicism, is not much more innovative than the other countries. Amidst all the traditionalism, a few buildings stand out, such as the Air Palace, decorated by the Delaunays, and the Pavilion of Light, designed by Mallet-Stevens.

The Air Palace at the International Exposition, decorated by the Delaunays.

THE DELAUNAYS HIRE 50 UNEMPLOYED ARTISTS

PARIS

Leon Blum, head of government of the Front Populaire, who wants the avant-garde to be present at the International Exposition, entrusts the decoration of the Air Palace and the Railways Palace to Robert and Sonia Delaunay, on the condition they hire fifty unemployed artists. The task is immense: For the Air Palace, an 840 sq. ft. painting; for the Railways Palace, a 19,000 sq. ft. composition, plus a 1,600 sq. ft. panel and ten huge bas-reliefs. Nothing like this has been done since the Renaissance, when painters, sculptors, and architects joined their efforts in a building seen as a synthesis of all arts.

During March and April, the artists live and work together in a garage at the Porte Champerret. Among them, some young, some less so: Bissière, Manessier, Bertholle, Survage, and many others. There, they paint huge canvases: an ensemble of colored rhythms, a joyful hymn to modern man's adventure.

For the Railways Palace, Sonia Delaunay creates various murals. Among them, *Voyages lointains* (far journeys), two large compositions for the staircases, each measuring 2,400 sq. ft. For the same palace, Robert Delaunay works on the four pillars of the grand hall, 30 feet high, decorating them with a series of monumental "infinite rhythms." They contain elements taken from the railway's universe: wheels, gears, signal panels, even the dial of a clock, all intermingled.

At the beginning of the century, when the Lyon railway station was decorated, painters displayed the cities where the traveler would stop on the Paris-Lyon-Marseilles run and the regions he would cross, such as the vineyards of Bourgogne and the Rhône Valley. Today, the Delaunays deliberately eliminate the trivial details to concentrate on the impression of movement, vibrations, and speed.

The Air Palace, built on the

THE DELAUNAYS ELIMINATE TRIVIAL DETAILS TO CONCENTRATE ON MOVEMENT AND SPEED

Esplanade des Invalides, two steps from the Alexander III Bridge, is revolutionary.

Robert Delaunay was the genius who initiated Inobjective Painting in 1912, replacing traditional linear perspective with a play of colored circles. The artist intended not so much to achieve spiritual abstraction, like Kandinsky before him, but rather to create something entirely different, namely a Realism capable of fully expressing the scientific and technical society in which man is to live from now on. In the cockpit-shaped Air Palace, Delaunay lends architectural proportions to his conception. A circular catwalk allows the visitor to go out in space and find himself next to two fighter planes, suspended at unequal heights amidst large chromatic circles. The illusion of aerial evolution is complete.

Curiously, in spite of his two successful versions of the *Dance*, painted for the Barnes Foundation in the United States between 1931 and 1933, Matisse gets no commission. He visits the Delaunays at Porte Champerret and is enthusiastic. Their works are among the best achievements of the exhibition.

(See also 1912, 1914, 1941.)

"LA FÉE ÉLECTRICITÉ": THE LARGEST PAINTING IN THE WORLD

PARIS

Two hundred feet by three hundred and sixty feet, *La fée électricité* is the largest painting in the world. Everyone who contributed to the discovery of electricity is illustrated: Archimedes; Leonardo da Vinci; Otto von Guericke, who built the first electric-friction machine; Zénobe Gramme, a genius who invented the dynamo; Bernouilli; Watt; and Edison . . . in all, one hundred and ten personalities, standing among waterfalls, power plants, and turbines. In order to paint them, Raoul Dufy asks members of the Comédie Française to pose for him in his studio at Saint-Ouen. A complete success! Visitors to the International Exposition gather in crowds before the huge fresco. They admire the heroes of the modern world the way people admired the saints in churches in the Middle Ages. There is a difference: Dufy writes the name under each image so that everyone can identify them—something that wasn't necessary for the saints.

RAOUL DUFY: LA FÉE ÉLECTRICITÉ. 1937. Paris. MNAM

THE PALACE OF LIGHT

PARIS

The largest spark in the world, the largest movie screen in the world, and now the largest painting in the world. The Palace of Light is the centerpiece of the International Exposition. The architect is Robert Mallet-Stevens, whose participation in the International Exhibition of Decorative Arts of 1925 was very well received.

Situated at the axis of the Champ-de-Mars, the palace gives it perspective with its large curved wall, measuring 2,000 feet and covered with small pearls, which in the evening permits open-air projection of the first movies to be made in Cinemascope, a procedure developed by Professor Chrétien. Another feature: Against hidden walls, painted in three shades of yellow, and with a black bottom, a 23-foot-long spark lights up at regular intervals above a pond. Visitors pack themselves all around it. At the last moment, the brand-new Ouessant projector was placed beside the building. It is the most powerful in the world, and its quadruple rays sweep the roofs of the capital at night.

Inside the pavilion, the same gigantic proportions fill the eye. The curved lobby is decorated with a huge fresco by Raoul Dufy, a homage to the pioneers of electricity. Before it there is a 500,000-volt circuit breaker, a world record of power.

Mallet-Stevens, who is a promoter of Functionalism, has, however, a sense of proportion. In addition to the Palace of Light, he has built the Brazilian pavilion of coffee, the pavilion of tobacco, and the pavilions of hygiene and solidarity.

The Electricity Pavilion at the International Exposition, designed by Mallet-Stevens.

HITLER: GERMAN ART VERSUS MODERN ART

MUNICH

No sooner have the Berlin Olympic games ended than a new farce takes place. On July 18, Adolf Hitler inaugurates the First Great Exhibition of German Art. On hand are dignitaries of the National Socialist Party, and millions are glued to their radios.

This frustrated watercolorist who, in his own opinion, would have been another Michelangelo had fate not made him *Führer*, plays his favorite role: judge of "degenerate art" and rescuer of German culture. Intoxicated with anger, he announces a pitiless purging policy "against the last elements of our cultural perversion." He calls modern artists criminals and fools, and threatens them with prison, psychiatric hospitals, and sterilization—the only appropriate treatment for artists who see the sky green and the grass blue.

Several times since 1933, the masters of the Third Reich have expressed their intention of renewing the creative spirit of the nation and destroying the alleged Bolshevik spirit of art. Today, the time bomb they planted four years ago explodes with a double impact.

On the one hand, "a new type of human, of striking beauty" bursts with health and evokes the simple life: peasant families, idyllic mother-child scenes, bucolic landscapes; in short, a warming up of the leftovers of nineteenth-century genre painting. These painters show a rare capacity to escape to an imaginary idyllic world, remote from social reality. All this takes place at the German House of the Arts, the first monumental architecture of the new Germany and a true, strong-pillared kitsch palazzo of Nazism.

On the other hand, the so-called degenerate art is relegated to a plaster warehouse under the decrepit arcades of Hofgarten. Under poor lighting, seven hundred and thirty works are piled up in small halls, partitioned so that the largest possible number of "horrors" can be hung. It was a systematic robbery, ordered by Goebbels in twenty-five museums, and carried out by Adolf Ziegler, "official artist of Germany," shortly before the exhibition. Among the one hundred twelve condemned artists are Klee, Kokoschka, Picasso, Beckmann, Max Ernst, the Expressionists of the Die Brücke such as Kirschner and Nolde, Abstractionists like Kandinsky, Verists including Grosz or Dix, and Jewish painters such as Chagall, Meidner, or Freundlich.

The government asks for the opinion of the people, which is methodically channeled. The Nazi press announces "a morgue of suicides, fools, freaks, and imbeciles in their coffins." Access to the exhibition is forbidden to minors. However, over forty thousand visitors, three times more than for the Great Exhibition of German Art, stand in line, before doors that open only every three minutes. Some are simply eager for thrills; and to ridicule. Some are there for the miraculous discovery of a still unknown art. For most, it is the last opportunity to see what they love . . . But nobody reacts with indifference.

(See also 1933, 1935, 1939, 1942.)

MARTIN AMORBACH:
DIE AUSSAAT. 1937

"A new type of human, of striking beauty."

Hitler inaugurates the First Great Exhibition of German Art.

KLEE ACKNOWLEDGED BY HIS PEERS

BERN

There is a long line of visitors to see Paul Klee in the modest three-room apartment where he lives with his wife, on the third floor at 6 Kistlerweg. He moved there four years ago when he returned to Switzerland to escape Hitler's regime.

Georges Braque, who lives in Basel, comes to see him in the spring. Klee, who for two years has suffered from bronchitis, with lung and heart complications, hesitates to receive him. They talk for four hours. Kirchner comes from Frauenkirch, he wants Klee to come and rest in Grisons, but Klee refuses, fearing to interrupt his work.

Pablo Picasso comes in November. They had never met, although for years they were both friends of the art dealer Daniel-Henry Kahnweiler. Picasso spends a long time looking at the artist's portfolios. His spontaneous enthusiasm brings much joy to Klee, who considers Picasso the greatest painter alive. Few words are spoken, but it means great support at a time when one hundred and two of his works have been confiscated by the Nazis, seventeen of them the target of the spectators' anger at the "degenerate art" exhibition in Munich.

PAUL KLEE:
ROTE SÄULEN
VORBEIZIEHEND.
1928.
Private Collection

KANDINSKY MEETS HIS FRIEND KLEE

WASSILI KANDINSKY:
SUR LES POINTES.
1928. Paris. MNAM

BERN

Kandinsky wants Paul Klee to go to Paris to see Dr. Soulié de Morant, the famous acupuncturist who cured Kandinsky's wife from the headaches she had had since childhood. But Klee is too weak for a long trip, and his condition becomes worse.

When Kandinsky comes to Bern for his exhibition at the Kunsthalle, he is grief-stricken. His former colleague from the Bauhaus is a shadow of himself. Painfully, Klee shuffles from hall to hall, leaning on his wife's arm and having to sit down to look at the paintings.

In 1933, when the famous school was closed, Kandinsky moved to Neuilly, to an apartment found for him by Marcel Duchamp on the bank of the Seine because he wanted to have the river under his windows. Since then, he has achieved a superior synthesis of his art. In his own words, it is a connection between the brain and the heart, technique and intuition, a symbiosis with scientific thinking.

The Nazis confiscated fifty-seven of Kandinsky's "degenerate" works. But the public went to Kunsthalle from all corners of Europe. They came in homage to the initiator of modern art, but also to see his latest paintings, which may be colder than his earlier work but are charged with spirituality.

Matisse Inaugurates the First Issue of "Verve"

Executed with the greatest care in the studios of Fernand Mourlot, the cover of the first issue of *Verve*, a journal published in December by the art lover Éfstratios Eleftheriades, also known as Teriade, shows a beautiful lithograph by Matisse—a drawing of a nude in motion, placed on a background of blue, black, and red rectangles. This major artistic and literary publication, supported by Americans who have bought 15,000 copies, intends to be very eclectic and includes articles by Maurice Heine on "The Blood of Martyrs" and by John Dos Passos on "Fire," as well as Judith Cladel on Maillol. Admirable photographs by Man Ray and Cartier-Bresson also appear in it.

The Masters of Independent Art

Who are these "masters of independent art" being exhibited at the Petit Palais? One might think that with painters such as Goerg, Coubine, or Waroquier the organizers are proposing figures who are declining because they do not belong to any group. However, it is more a question of the Parisian School in its entirety and of everything that is not official art. For one reason or another, they have included those who have continued Neoimpressionism, from Signac to Desvalliers, Intimists such as Bonnard and Vuillard, many Fauves from Matisse to Valtat, and Cubists from Picasso to Marcoussis. The principal merit of the exhibition is that it draws attention to artists who have recently died before attaining fame, such as Emmanuel Gondouin and Maria Blanchard. The former died in 1934, the latter in 1932 at the age of fifty-one. Both were products of Cubism, and had developed individual styles before illness carried them off.

A House in the Trees

The Kaufmann House, called "House at the Waterfall," in Bear Run, Pennsylvania, is nearing completion. Its construction began last year. Its creator is Frank Lloyd Wright, one of the most celebrated contemporary architects, who is very attached to the idea of integrating architecture with nature. His principles include breaking up the idea of the façade, the dislocation of masses, and the liberation of space. Will the Kaufmanns, who love the outdoors, appreciate their unique residence? Its conception is entirely new: waterfalls, walls of bonded stones, large bay windows, wide concrete terraces, a stairway erected over water, tall trees amidst masses of rocks; everything happening as if there were no longer any difference between outdoors and indoors. For the first time in history, architecture and nature are integrated into a single entity. This success no doubt originated in a childhood dream of living among trees.

The New Bauhaus in Chicago

Did the Nazis kill the Bauhaus when they decided to close it in April 1933? It seems not, since it is now being revived in the United States! Albers has been teaching at Black Mountain College for the past four years, and this year Gropius became Professor of Architecture at Harvard. Now Moholy-Nagy arrived from England in July to open a new Bauhaus in Chicago. The opening took place October 18. The teaching is organized after the Dessau model. After a two-year introductory course, the students choose to work in one of six workshops. At the end of five or six years of studies, they will be able to think of themselves as being educated in architecture. Moholy-Nagy is hoping for students who wish to acquire a general culture; he has added a science curriculum. It seems that the most important problem remains: recruitment. At present, there are few young people who dare to undertake the experience.

IN BRIEF...

BRAZIL
Answering a call from Costa and Niemeyer, Le Corbusier goes to Brazil to study the plans of the future city Brasilia.

CUBA
Eduardo Abela founds an institute of painting in Havana.

FRANCE
At the Galerie la Pléiade, first exhibition of Henri Michaux, a Belgian poet who is getting more and more into painting.

Otto Wols, a German painter and photographer, is nominated official photographer of the International Exposition in Paris.

GREAT BRITAIN
Ben Nicholson and Nahum Gabo publish the review Circle.

JAPAN
International Surrealist exhibition in Tokyo, organized by Éluard, Hugnet, Penrose, Takiguchi, Yamanaka.

FRANK LLOYD WRIGHT: THE KAUFMANN HOUSE. 1936. Bear Run, Pennsylvania

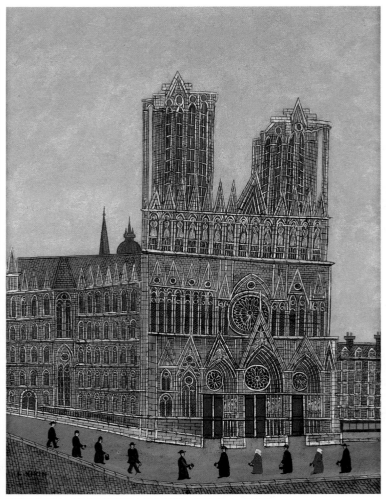

LOUIS VIVIN: THE CATHEDRAL OF REIMS. 1923. Paris. MNAM

CAMILLE BOMBOIS: SACRÉ-CŒUR. 1932. Paris. MNAM

THE POPULAR MASTERS OF REALITY

PARIS

They have been called, not without some contempt, "Sunday painters," "sacred-heart painters," "instinctive," or "naive." Now they are officially acknowledged and praised under the pompous name of "Popular Masters of Reality." The initiative belongs to the curator of the Grenoble Museum, Andry-Farcy, with the assistance of the museum's chief talent scout, Sonia Delaunay's former husband, the art dealer Wilhelm Uhde. During early fall, they proudly show almost two hundred naive paintings, including one by Henri Rousseau. The exhibition is held at Salle Royale, 11 Rue Royale, in Paris, cosponsored by the City of Paris. In November, most of the exhibition travels to the Kunsthaus in Zurich. On Octo-

ber 12, art critic Maximilien Gauthier founds an association of friends of Henri Rousseau, chaired by Albert Sarrault.

The exhibition is visited by Parisian society, which is moved and intrigued at the same time. In the catalogue, Gauthier notes that the Cubists and their friends are first in admiring

Rousseau's influence on modern art is taken seriously.

His poetic genius somewhat outshines the ingenuous charm of the eight other painters. But the public is moved by their marvelous sincerity. The exhibition contains thirty-five ineffable landscapes of Paris and its suburbs by Louis Vivin, a former

THESE SO-CALLED NAIVE PAINTERS ARE ACKNOWLEDGED OFFICIALLY AND PRAISED

Henri Rousseau, for "realizing in a naive way what they had searched for in an intellectual manner." Without doubt, this is Rousseau's first great public triumph. Some of the paintings are from the biggest collections: from Vollard, Kahnweiler, Paul Guillaume, even Kandinsky.

postman who died last year at the age of seventy-five; works by Camille Bombois, a former fair artist discovered by Uhde in the streets of Montmartre in 1922; André Bauchant, seventy-four years old, whose allegoric peasant paintings have roots in his work in a hothouse; Maurice

Utrillo, son of Suzanne Valadon, with twenty-four paintings, including the beautiful painting The Lapin Agile in Snow. Also exhibited are Dominique Peyronnet, the erstwhile lithographer, who is seventy-five years old; still lifes with delirious flowers by Séraphine Louis, a housekeeper who became insane and was hospitalized a few years ago; Jean Éve, a former customs clerk, who is thirty-seven years old; Adolf Dietrich, a Swiss woodcutter, who is sixty years old; and René Rimbert, a forty-one-year-old postman.

The appeal of the naive is inescapable—the purity and the simplicity of their painting charms the public.

WALTER BENJAMIN: ART HAS LOST ITS AURA

Walter Benjamin is the innovative and original author of numerous essays on art and literature in relation to society. Last year he gave the *Zeitschrift für Soziale Forschung*, which had taken refuge in Paris and was published by Alcan, a short study entitled "The Work of Art in the Age of Mechanical Reproducibility." He then reworked and transformed the manuscript. This is a passage from the reworked text. It deals with what Benjamin calls the aura of the work of art and what becomes of it in our society, where everything can be easily reproduced. His viewpoint in many ways renews interpretation of works of art.

We can sum up all these failings by going back to the notion of aura to say: In the age of techniques of reproduction, what is harmed in the work of art is its aura. This process is symptomatic; its significance goes beyond the artistic domain. We could say, in general, that techniques of reproduction detach the object reproduced from tradition. These techniques, by increasing the number of copies, substitute a phenomenon of mass production for an event that occurred only once. By allowing the reproduction to be seen or heard under any condition, the techniques give the reproduction a current relevance. These two processes lead to a weakening of the transmitted reality, a weakening of tradition, which is the counterpart of the crisis currently affecting humanity; they are closely linked to the mass movements of today.

The uniqueness of the work of art is identical to its integration in the group of relationships called tradition. This tradition is itself undoubtedly a living reality, and extremely changeable. An ancient statue of Venus, for example, belonged to another tradition and was, for the Greeks, an object of worship, whereas the clergy of the Middle Age saw it as an evil idol. But there was a common element in these contradictions: Both the Greeks and the medievals saw Venus as unique, and felt her aura. In its beginnings, worship expressed the inclusion of the work of art in the group of traditional relationships. We know that the earliest works of art were made for ritual, magical first, then religious. Now, it is a fact of decisive importance that a work of art can only lose its aura if there remains in it no trace of its ritual function. In other words, the unique value of the "authentic" work of art is based upon this ritual that originally was

the basis of its ancient usefulness. However great the number of intermediaries, this fundamental link is still recognizable as a secularized ritual through the cult of beauty, even in its most profane forms. The cult of beauty, born during the Renaissance and predominant over the course of three centuries, still holds today the recognizable mark of its origins, in spite of the first serious threat to its existence. When the first truly revolutionary reproduction technique, photography, contemporary to the beginnings of socialism, appeared, artists felt the approach of a crisis, which no one, one hundred years later, can deny. They reacted by professing "art for art's sake," that is, the theology of art. This doctrine led directly to a negative theology: A "pure" art was created that refused not only to play any essential role, but to subject itself to the conditions that an objective project always imposes . . .

In order to study the work of art in the age of techniques of reproduction, we must remain very aware of this group of relationships. They bring to light a fact that is truly decisive, one appearing for the first time in the history of the world: the emancipation of the work of art in relation to its parasitic existence as a part in ritual. More and more works of art are being made for the express purpose of being reproduced.

WALTER BENJAMIN
The Work of Art in the Age of Mechanical
Reproducibility *(Excerpts)*

Is it a huge joke or an unprecedented affirmation of artistic liberty? The International Exhibition of Surrealism in Paris pushes provocation further than ever before. And Dali dashes off to London where Freud has at last agreed to see him. The contrast with Brancusi's monumental work in Targu Jiu in his native Romania is striking. Composed of three large elements, the Table of Silence, *the* Gate of the Kiss, *and especially the* Endless Column, *125 feet high, the work is the affirmation in our troubled times of the loftiest idea of art, as well as the appearance of an entirely new idea of the environment.*

1938

S U M M A R Y

LITERATURE

CHILE
The poet Pablo Neruda publishes Spain in the Heart, *inspired by his impressions of the Spanish Civil War.*

FRANCE
Publication of Jean-Paul Sartre's La nausée.
Christian Zervos publishes a History of Contemporary Art, *and Henri Focillon, his important work on* The Art of the West.

MUSIC

UNITED STATES
First jazz concert at Carnegie Hall, with the orchestras of Benny Goodman and Count Basie.

MOTION PICTURES

GERMANY
Leni Riefenstahl gains fame with her spectacular film on the Olympic games, The Gods of the Stadium.

FRANCE
Marcel Carné creates two films, Hôtel du Nord *and* Le quai des brumes.

RUSSIA
Sergei Eisenstein films Alexander Nevski.

RADIO

UNITED STATES
Orson Welles creates panic when announcing a Martian landing in his radio adaptation of The War of the Worlds *by H. G. Wells.*

At the International Exhibition of Surrealism.

A GRAND CELEBRATION OF SURREALISM

PARIS

Everybody who is somebody in the world of art and literature is in their evening clothes, waiting for Enigmarelle, the son of Frankenstein! It is January 17, the opening of the fantasmagoric International Exhibition of Surrealism, at the Beaux-Arts Gallery, Faubourg Saint-Honoré.

The visitors cannot believe their eyes. For a long time, Surrealists have wanted to organize an event that would put an end to the eternal hanging of paintings on the anonymous walls of a gallery, a salon, a museum. For the benefit of *their* work, they want surroundings that would be a creation in their own right, expressing *their* idea, *their* dreams. They all cooperated: Max Ernst, Kurt Seligmann, Man Ray, André Masson, and Oscar Domínguez, under the supervision of Marcel Duchamp as "voluntary technician." It is a howling success.

The first shock is received at the entrance: Salvador Dali's *Taxi pluvieux* (rainy taxi).

It is an old jalopy, in which the artist placed two mannequins: a driver with a dogfish head and, in the back seat, a crazy blonde in evening gown, sitting among lettuce and endives, under a pipe system unleashing a violent spray. Besides green plants in the taxi, there are two hundred happy snails thriving in the rain.

The gallery is entered through Surrealist Street, a long corridor where twenty mannequins are being dressed or undressed by twenty artists. Among the most striking: André Masson's, its head imprisoned in a wicker cage; Maurice Henry's, its head caught in a cotton cloud; Max Ernst's, a widow in a naughty black short dress stepping on a man sprawled on the floor; Man Ray's, a weeping woman shedding large crystal tears, her hair decorated with clay pipes.

On the walls of the corridor are blue enamel plaques bearing the names of historic streets in white letters: Rue de la Vieille-Lanterne, where Gérard de Ner-

SALVADOR DALI:
LE TAXI PLUVIEUX
1938. Paris. Galeri des Beaux-Arts

Mannequin of Maurice Henry at
the International Exhibition of Surrealism.

val committed suicide; Rue Vivienne, where Lautréamont used to live; and the names of invented streets: Rue de la Transfusion de Sang (blood-transfusion street), Rue aux Lèvres (lip street), and Rue Albert-Tison, after a fictitious character.

The exhibition halls contain the works of over sixty Surrealists from various countries. But the environment draws more attention than the paintings. The glass windows of the central hall are covered by Duchamp with twelve hundred coal sacks suspended next to one another. In a fold of the softly rippled floor, covered with dead leaves, is a shiny pond with waterlilies and reeds. In the corners of the room are four huge beds, smartly covered with satin quilts. In the middle, heating is provided by an iron stove like the ones used in winter on the terraces of Parisian cafés.

The whole thing would have been the most horrendous mixture of odds and ends, were it not for humorous glorification of the values dear to Surrealists: woman, the beauty of the flesh, erotic fantasies, and the relationship between love and revolution, which is particularly close to André Breton's heart.

Breton will soon go to Mexico, to meet Trotsky, the historical Communist leader of the Russian Revolution, who symbolizes opposition to Stalin. In Surrealist circles, one even speaks of a jointly signed manifesto that would define "an independent revolutionary art." That should make the press shut up. From left to right, it reviews the exhibition with sarcasm, derision, and insults. In a Europe devoured by two cancers, Hitlerism and Stalinism, both equally dictatorial in art as well as in politics, the Surrealists' provocation is sending the world a message of freedom.

The evening of the opening, everyone waits in vain for Enigmarelle, who was supposed to cross the exhibition at half past midnight. Hélène Vanel dances around the pond—and in it—to the steps of a dance called "L'acte manqué" (the futile action) in order to pass the time. But Enigmarelle does not come. Neither does Dali, who left on a train for London to see Sigmund Freud. Was Dali, perhaps, supposed to incarnate, "in false flesh and bones," the authentic descendant of Frankenstein? No one will ever know!

(See also 1924, 1926, 1928, 1938, 1941, 1942.)

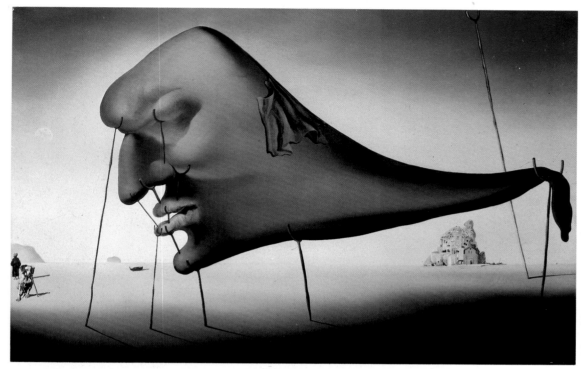

SALVADOR DALI: SLEEP. 1937. Edward James Foundation

DALI MEETS FREUD

LONDON

On the one side, the father of psychoanalysis. On the other side, the *enfant terrible* of Surrealism, the perfecter of the method called "critical paranoia." How could they not meet, one day or another? The event takes place on July 19, in Freud's new home. The Austrian writer Stefan Zweig takes Dali to the Good Doctor, recently ransomed from the Nazis in Vienna and spirited to Paris, then here.

On the one side, an old gentleman, weakened by disease (cancer) and deeply affected by his flight and exile. On the other side, facing the man who says he has discovered the secret of dreams and the life of the unconscious, the Spanish prankster. He is the most active and inventive of the Surrealists, to whom he has brought new energy and an extremely fruitful method of analysis.

Dali's interest in the mental illness called paranoia had intrigued a young disciple of Freud's, Dr. Jacques Lacan. Dali and Lacan had met to share their experiences. In Dali's opinion, critical paranoia is a method of gaining knowledge "based on critical and systematic objective research of delirious associations and interpretations." Poetry practices this method based on spontaneity and irrationalism. Painting is even more appropriate for the purpose.

Freud, who is busy with his work on Moses and the religious phenomenon, is said to have told Dali: "In classic paintings, I look for the subconscious; in Surrealist works, I look for the conscious element." The witticism is amusing and significant. Dali uses it to declare, against his peers, that if they didn't watch out Surrealism would become a "dead doctrine" and a "sect." Freud speaks of "sublimation" in art. No word could please Dali more. In his noncritical paranoia, he claims to be the incarnation of sublimity.

REACTIONS

An international Surrealist exhibit opened yesterday on the Rue du Faubourg Saint-Honoré. The artists presented oddly dressed mannequins, which are, to say the least, whimsical. André Masson's model sported the "hat of an elegant woman." We hope that elegant women will not become Surrealists!
L'Humanité, January 18

All that is for the future, and while Monsieur Chautemps is trying to form the 104th government of a perfectly realistic Republic, we would like something serious to chew on. So I'm off to Maxim's where I'll meet esthetes for whom the "tangible visit of a nightmare" is food for thought only. Here's a Surrealist image for you: a stomach pondering its fate.
Candide, January 20

ÉDOUARD
VUILLARD:
PORTRAIT OF KER
XAVIER ROUSSEL.
Paris. Musée
d'Art Moderne
de la Ville

THE VUILLARD TRADITION

VUILLARD AS MURALIST

GENEVA
The French government donates a series of large decorative works for the Assembly Hall of the League of Nations Palace. The works on the topic of peace are commissioned to Maurice Denis, Roger Chastel, Ker Xavier Roussel, and Édouard Vuillard. The latter, in spite of his old age, has the courage to spend long hours perched on scaffolding to illustrate the subject taken from Delacroix and Puvis de Chavannes: *Peace, Protectress of the Muses.* Vuillard learned mural work when he painted the topic of *Comedy* for the Palais de Chaillot last year. In Geneva, he uses an unfamiliar repertory. He is an Intimist artist, but here he tackles allegory. His muses have rather conventional poses, but he is true to his style in the plantlike column that decorates the landscape where a youthful group is frolicking.

PARIS
The Museum of Decorative Arts, at the Marsan Pavilion, organizes an anniversary exhibition of Édouard Vuillard—he has painted for fifty years. His life is closely linked to that of his dear friend Ker Xavier Roussel, who lived in his house for a long time and married his sister Marie. Roussel turned the twenty-year-old Vuillard away from his military career and directed him to the École Libre des Gobelins, where Professor Maillart corrected drawings free of charge. Vuillard later enrolled at the Julian Academy, where he drew remarkable academic pieces, which he signed "Vuillard, student of Mr. Gérôme," the famous conventional painter. He found

there his former mates from the Lycée Condorcet, especially Maurice Denis, and he met Paul Sérusier, Émile Bernard, and then Paul Gauguin. He abandoned his somber Realism in the style of Chardin and adopted the ideas of his friends of the Pont-Aven group. His painting was a perfect illustration of the theories of Maurice Denis. He became a member of the Nabi movement, which, since 1888, has included such diversified personalities as Bonnard, Maillol, and Vallotton.

Vuillard had his first solo show forty-seven years ago, in the Rue des Martyrs, at the offices of the *Revue blanche*, a magazine created two months earlier by Thadée Natanson. Vuillard illus-

trated this Nabi magazine, in which he was called the "Zouave." His art remained traditional, with truthful and precise, but sensitive, observations. He rarely used pure chromatic ranges: broken grays, white, and greens were dominant. He used the decorative resources of Nabi art, thus learning to "furnish space to saturation." He made decorations for Paul Desmarais, a cousin of the Natansons, in 1892; then for Claude Anet, in 1898. These works showed how well he knew how to mix the Nabi synthetical style with his own taste for analysis. He also worked on prints, assimilating the Japanese style and adding a subtle sense of dream, freshness, and introversion.

At the end of 1900, Vuillard met Lucie Hessel, wife of an art dealer, and fell in love with her. She lived with him until her death, in 1928, often posing for him. Their meeting marked a turning point in his art, which used to be very personal. From Hessel on, he sought reality in the passing instant. For him, the depth of things was to be found on their surface. He painted with glue; he played expertly with the "muddy matter" that he brought to life with his brush. He gave appearances a parallel life, as though it were the expression of a double personality.

"His art was familiar and charming. The spirit replaces sublimity," said Apollinaire, who respected Vuillard.

Breton in Mexico

André Breton is spending some time in Mexico visiting Diego Rivera and Frida Kahlo. Other guests at their country home include Leon Trotsky and his wife. The Surrealist poet has often met the exiled Russian revolutionary. The three of them—the poet, the painter, and the revolutionary—have published a manifesto, *For an Independent Revolutionary Art*, calling for "the artist's unshaking fidelity to his inner self" against politics and esthetics that would repress him. The painters Montenegro, Merida, and Best Maugard were seen at the banquet held by Mexican intellectuals in Breton's honor.

The Box

Marcel Duchamp has published his "complete works" in the form of a portable museum entitled *The Box*. It consists of sixty-nine reproductions of his paintings and drawings, four reduced-size "ready-mades," four pages of text, and a celluloid replica of *The Bride Stripped Bare by Her Bachelors*. Each box also includes an original and the name of the recipient. The first "printing" will be conservative: twenty copies. But the artist anticipates future printings in keeping with the demand.

Death of Suzanne Valadon

Although she had long lived in Montmartre, Suzanne Valadon, who died April 7 in her seventy-third year, retained an almost virile robustness from her peasant origins, as well as her love of nature and flowers. A model and close friend of Puvis de Chavannes, Henner, and Renoir, and the mistress of Toulouse-Lautrec, the mother of Maurice Utrillo was encouraged to paint by these artists and by Apollinaire, who admired her blasé nudes. Her best friend, Dégas, did not hesitate to testify that "this devil is a genius at drawing."

Kirchner's Suicide

Ernest Ludwig Kirchner committed suicide at Frauenkirch, Switzerland. He was one of the founders of the Expressionist group Die Brücke in Dresden. But since the 1920s, his painting had become rather Cubist. Only the wood engravings that he created to illustrate certain books, such as Georg Heym's *Umbra Vitae* in 1924, continued to testify to a strong and original talent. In 1937, the Nazis confiscated six hundred and thirty-nine of his works, and displayed twenty-five of his paintings at the exhibition of "degenerate art" in Munich. Inasmuch as he was already suffering from tuberculosis and had become neurasthenic, these events contributed to his suicide.

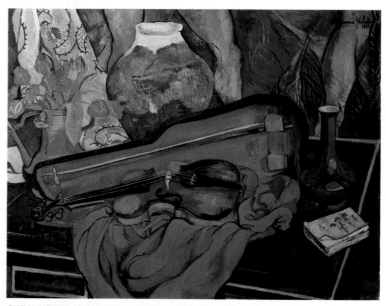

SUZANNE VALADON: STILL LIFE WITH VIOLIN CASE. 1923. Paris. Musée d'Orsay

"Guernica" in London

On the initiative of Roland Penrose, *Guernica* was exhibited at the New Burlington Galleries from October 4 through 29, then at Whitechapel Gallery where Major Clement Attlee, leader of the opposition Labor Party, gave an opening speech. Supporters of Franco sent to Burlington Galleries, on behalf of their side, Zuloaga's enormous painting glorifying the defenders of the Alcazar in Toledo. But whereas a large crowd, affected by the destruction of the little Basque town last year, came to see *Guernica*, the hall where Zuloaga's work was shown was—to Penrose's immense satisfaction—rarely visited, except by some cats.

IN BRIEF...

UNITED STATES
The Mexican painter Ruffino Tamayo decides to settle in New York.

FRANCE
Leaving his job as a teacher at the Ranson Academy, Roger Bissière has decided to return to his native town, Villeréal, in the Lot-et-Garonne.

GREAT BRITAIN
At the London Gallery, two exhibitions worth mentioning: René Magritte and Max Ernst.

THE NETHERLANDS
Exhibition of abstract art at the Stedelijk Museum in Amsterdam.

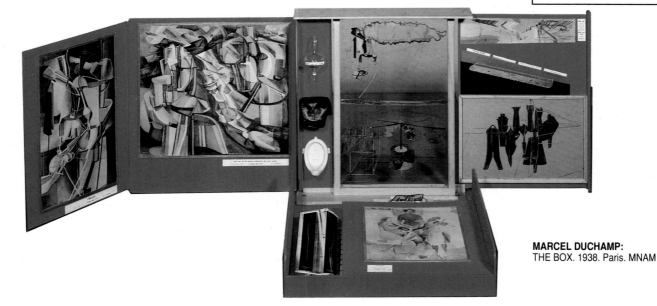

MARCEL DUCHAMP:
THE BOX. 1938. Paris. MNAM

GROPIUS IN THE UNITED STATES

HARVARD

First England, now the United States. The German architect Walter Gropius emigrates once more, after a three-year collaboration with Maxwell Fry. Since April 1, the founder of the Bauhaus has been teaching at Harvard University. His task is difficult: The Graduate School of Design follows an academic line in architecture, so he encounters much opposition, even from modern architects. The German master gets into the habit of visiting his students' worktables twice a week, and, even though he doesn't talk much, his truthful attention encourages individual initiative and contributes to opening up imaginations.

The Lincoln House, Massachusetts, by Gropius.

KRÖLLER-MÜLLER: A MUSEUM IN A PARK

OTTERLO

Twelve miles from Arnheim, capital of the province of Gueldre, southeast of Amsterdam, the Kröller-Müller Museum opens its gates on July 13. It is located in the middle of the Hooge Veluwe National Park, bought three years ago by Mrs. Hélène Kröller-Müller. In the midst of a huge reserve of unspoiled nature (134,000 acres of forest, inhabited by deer and sheep), it holds an exceptional art collection.

Mrs. Müller, wife of the successful Dutch businessman Anton Kröller, wants to create an artistic environment where nature, art, and architecture can mix harmoniously. After rejecting the plans of Ludwig Mies van der Rohe, then Berlage's, she and her husband choose those of the Belgian architect Henry Van de Velde. The construction of the small building with perfect proportions is sponsored by the Dutch government, after Mrs. Kröller donates her collections. She is the director of the museum. The building allows only a partial exhibition of the collection, but the works will be continuously changed. Her purchases are guided by the eminent art critic H. P. Bremmer, and range from the fifteenth century to the twentieth.

Especially noteworthy is the Van Gogh collection. There are some eighty-seven paintings and over one hundred and fifty drawings, bought when the painter was still practically unknown. But the visitor drawn to Otterlo by the work of this artist will also admire numerous Impressionist and Cubist works, as well as the twentieth-century Dutch School. Piet Mondrian is the representative of its most daring abstract trend.

The day will come when the park will contain sculptures: In this landscape of trees and sky, the slightest elevation seems to be waiting for a sculpture or a geometrical figure to which it can serve as a pedestal.

The Kröller-Müller Museum.

BRANCUSI BUILDS IN HIS NATIVE TOWN

TARGU JIU

The monumental ensemble made by Constantin Brancusi in the memory of the "heroes of the region, who died during the war 1914-1918" was solemnly inaugurated in Romania, in the native region of the sculptor, in late October. The project had been commissioned three years ago by the wife of the Romanian prime minister, Mrs. Tatarascu, and the National Women's League of Gorj. The same year, Brancusi, who had been living in France since 1904, and who was becoming known in Europe and the United States, made the model of the *Gate of the Kiss*. This is one of the three elements of the ensemble, the others

being *Endless Column* and *Table of Silence*. The monument was at first to be of one piece. But Brancusi wanted to create an ensemble. He was inspired by the landscape, rediscovered during a trip to Targu Jiu in 1937, and decided to distribute harmoniously three works on a 3,000-foot axis perpendicular to the Jiu River. *The Table of Silence* is placed along the river; next to a park, the *Gate of the Kiss*. Finally, next to the Church Saint-Pierre and Saint-Paul, on a circular piazza, is placed the *Endless Column*.

Brancusi did not invent the shapes of these three sculptures for the occasion. He had known them for a long time. In 1916, he

conceived an "inifinite column" made of rhomboidal elements which can be multiplied indefinitely. Based on that work, he made, in 1920, a column with nine elements of old oak; it looks like a smaller one sculpted in 1918 for the decoration of a garden in Voulangis, not far from Paris. In Targu Jiu, the engineer Stefan Georgescu, helping to build the column, encountered huge technical difficulties. The structure is almost 100 feet high and weighs nineteen tons. Its fifteen elements and two semielements in cast metal coated with gilded brass are "piled up" on a steel skeleton. The work took from October last year to July of this year.

The topic of the kiss appeared in a work of 1908. Brancusi repeated and transformed it three times: once for a gravestone, once in a column, and between 1933 and 1937 in a project for a meditation temple for the Maharaja of Indore.

Made of Bampotok travertine, the gate is composed of two pillars, with the theme of the kiss on their four faces, and a transverse beam where the theme appears forty times in all. Its dimensions, calculated by the golden number, are 16.83 feet in height, 21.16 feet in length, and 5.54 feet in width.

The *Table of Silence* (seven feet in diameter) is also made of Bampotok limestone. It consists of two superposed circular stones and is surrounded by twelve stools made of two hemispheres each. It has the rustic simplicity of the furniture that Brancusi has always made for himself.

Rigorous and powerful, this monumental ensemble is enthusiastically received by the Romanians, who love Brancusi more and more.

(See also 1957.)

At Targu Jiu, in Romania, the *Endless Column*, the *Gate of the Kiss*, and the *Table of Silence* by Constantin Bracusi.

Hitler has decided to strike a final blow to modern art, selling off its masterpieces, seized in Germany, at an auction organized in the neutral territory of Lucerne, Switzerland. The contrast with the attitude of Mussolini, much less a traditionalist than his friend the Nazi dictator, is striking. The proof comes at the Third Quadrennial of Rome where homage is rendered to the Bolognese Giorgio Morandi, whose art and attitude relate him in no way whatsoever to Fascism.

The single comic note is Utrillo's dispute with American customs. In Poland, the suicide of Witkiewicz, who was unable to withstand the combined attack on his country by the Soviet Union and Germany, is made public.

1939

S U M M A R Y

ART AND POLITICS

Hitler Pilfers Modern Art
Speer: the Plans for Greater Berlin

AVANT-GARDE

Matta Exports Europe
Cornell's Strange Boxes

GREAT MASTERS

The Affair of the Postcards

DEVELOPMENTS

The New MOMA
Death of an Art Dealer

ART NEWS

Robert Maillart's Parabolic Vault
The Vitalists Burn Hitler in Effigy
The Suicide of Witkiewicz
Ernst Is Interned
Braque Exhibition in the United States
In Brief

EXHIBITIONS

Is Morandi a Great Painter?

WRITINGS AND THEORIES

André Lhote: What Is a Landscape?

LITERATURE

ITALY
Giuseppe Ungaretti collects his poems in The Life of a Man.

GREAT BRITAIN
Sigmund Freud dies in London, where he had fled from Vienna, escaping the Nazis.
  Louis MacNeice publishes the long poem Autumn Journal, *a comment on the contemporary sociopolitical scene.*

SWITZERLAND
Publication of James Joyce's Finnigan's Wake, *which disappoints the critics.*

MUSIC

UNITED STATES
Igor Stravinsky lectures at Harvard University, and stays in the United States.
  Coleman Hawkins records Body and Soul, *after staying in Europe for several years.*

THEATER

FRANCE
Premiere of Jean Giraudoux's Ondine, *directed and performed by Louis Jouvet.*

MOTION PICTURES

UNITED STATES
Premiere of Gone with the Wind *by Victor Fleming (and others), and of* Stagecoach *by John Ford.*

FRANCE
Jean Renoir films The Rules of the Game.

GEORGE GROSZ: THE BIG CITY.
1916-1917. Lugano.
Thyssen-Bornemisza Collection

HITLER PILFERS MODERN ART

LUCERNE

The Black Friday of German museums starts at 2:15 p.m. on June 30, at The Grand Hôtel National of Lucerne, two months before war is declared. In the heart of neutral, businesslike Switzerland, the gallery Theodor Fischer organizes the auction of "paintings and sculptures by modern masters originating from German museums."

This apparently innocent title hides a sinister pilferage of art to the benefit of Nazi Germany. Since his ascension to power, in 1933, Hitler has declared this art "degenerate." Nobody ignores this fact among the three hundred and fifty collectors, art dealers, and museum curators and directors who hasten here from the whole world. Also, nobody ignores the fact that the money raised in the auction goes straight to the *Führer's* strongboxes, in the face of the assurances that the former owners of the works will be compensated.

PABLO PICASSO: THE SOLER FAMILY. 1903. Liège. Musée de Liège

ERNST BARLACH:
THE AVENGER. 1922.
Cologne. Ludwig Museum

But love for art, or rather for the celebrity of some of the thirtynine artists represented, is stronger than any moral or political consideration.

Besides the incontestable masterpieces by the foreigners Matisse, Picasso, Chagall, Van Gogh, and Ensor, there are works by the great German avant-gardists: Klee, Marc, Beckmann, and Grosz, some of the stars of Expressionism. The one hundred and twenty works bought are indeed tempting, but how can anyone forget the scandalous circumstances of their presence in Lucerne? They came after a noisy Nazi pilferage of German museums intended for the "degenerate art" exhibition in Munich two years ago, sanctioned by a new law.

The atmosphere of the auction

hall is pervaded by macabre euphoria.

A self-portrait by Van Gogh is taken to the United States by Frankfurter, the director of *Art News* magazine, who pays the highest price of the day: 175,000 Swiss francs. Otto Mueller breaks the record of the lowest price with 260 francs.

While many works are bought by private collectors, several museums take the opportunity to complete their collections. The representative of the future Museum of Modern Art of Liège buys works by Gauguin and Ensor, and a large traditional 1903 painting by Picasso, *The Soler Family,* for 36,000 Swiss francs. (It is difficult to say why the Picasso was seized.) Georg Schmidt, the new director of the Kunstmuseum of Bale, bought six works, among them *Rabbi* by Chagall. Through Karl Buchholz, the Berlin art dealer, Schmidt has direct access to the warehouse of confiscated works, which allows him to buy cheaply *The Betrothed of the Wind,* one of Kokoschka's masterpieces, and twelve other paintings. Many important works are sold "under the table" after the Lucerne auction, where eighty-four works are sold for half a million Swiss francs.

There is something painful in the auction, even though one can interpret the conduct of the buyers as an act of rescue from Nazi barbarism. It is a pity, though, that their greed was such that they paid no heed to the exiled German artists who had called for a boycott of the sale.

There is a terrifying piece of news from Berlin: Some five thousand works, considered "nonsalable," are burned in barracks there on March 20— *before* the auction of Lucerne. A final solution, as it were, adopted by a frustrated watercolorist who becomes a dictator, to exterminate modern art in the Germany of his fantasmagorias.

(See also 1933, 1935, 1937, 1942.)

The Reich Chancellery in Berlin. A modernized Berlin will be the most gigantic among the four "cities of the *Führer*," the other three being modern Munich, Nuremberg, and Linz.

SPEER: THE PLANS FOR GREATER BERLIN

BERLIN

For the fiftieth birthday of the *Führer*, the architect Albert Speer presents him with the first part of the East-West axis of Berlin. This candelabra-lit five-mile stretch runs from the Brandenburg Gate to Adolf Hitler Place. It is a preview of the mammoth remodeling planned for the capital.

The *Führer* has had for some time the dream of building "Germania," an impressive European metropolis, the capital that National Socialist Germany deserves. On January 30, 1937, the fourth anniversary of his conquest of power, Hitler appointed Speer "general inspector of buildings for the renovation of the capital of the Reich." The then thirty-two-year-old architect was the natural choice, thanks to his innate sense of crowd psychology. Speer becomes well known when he organizes Nazi ceremonies at Nuremberg and builds his "Dome of Lights." It was he who planned the German Pavilion at the International Exposition in Paris two years ago, as well as the temporary chancellery in Berlin. The favor of the master of Germany opens unlimited horizons.

In his later plans for Berlin, Speer designs five circular avenues with a radial net of secondary routes: From east to west and from north to south, a gigantic network of arteries, approximately thirty miles long, crosses Berlin. In the center of the stretch between the south and north railroad stations will be a triumphal road on which ministries and other government buildings of the Reich will be built. Like its Parisian model, the Champs-Élysées, which Hitler intends to surpass, this avenue will be decorated with a triumphal arc to be designed by Speer. In the center, a grand square will contain the ideological center of the political and military power, with Hitler's palace and the new chancellery. This vast space will be dominat-ed by the colossal mass of a Great Hall. In it, a hundred and fifty thousand people, moved by their own numbers, will be able to listen to the dictator's fiery speeches.

Fascinated by the personality of his protector, Speer shows genuine architectural and planning talent in adapting himself to Hitler's political manipulation of architecture. Oversized buildings, an expression of Hitlerian megalomania, are the symbol of the oppressive National Socialist power. Neoclassic style, with its simple but massive shapes, represents the eternal values of official State and "Kultur".

However, aside from the partial enlargement of the west artery, everything is still a project. After the beginning of hostilities with France and England on September 3, and the recent ban of "construction not useful for war," will Hitler's architectural dream have to be postponed until a victorious peace is achieved?

MATTA EXPORTS EUROPE

NEW YORK

The most deeply impressed is the art dealer Julien Levy. "Matta came into my gallery self-assured, exuberant, and elusive. He showed me a portfolio of explosive pencil drawings. For me, he is by far the best among the young Surrealists," Levy declares, after proposing a one-man exhibition. Levy has one of the top galleries on Madison Avenue. Roberto Matta Echaurren, simply called Matta, may well have signed a pact with success.

He came to New York in October. Born in Chiloé, Chile, in 1902, he spent a few years in France, England, and Italy, enriching his experience. Architect by trade, he worked in Le Corbusier's studio; three years ago, on Dali's advice, he met André Breton.

Breton examined his drawings and told Matta bluntly: "You are a Surrealist." The young man knew nothing about Surrealism,

ROBERTO MATTA: COMPOSITION. 1939. Lugano. Thyssen-Bornemisza Collection

but somehow felt he had found what he had been looking for "like the turtle who comes out of the egg in the middle of the desert and starts crawling toward the sea . . ." Matta became friends with Breton and Tanguy, then set out for New York, and took Surrealism along.

Today, American painting is divided into two camps: regionalists, in reaction to European currents, and modernists such as Stuart Davis, engaged in Cubism.

Matta, introduced into New York artistic circles on Breton's recom-

mendation, imposes himself as an apostle of Automatism. He feels close to many artists of his age who are trying to escape the constraints of Cubism, such as Jackson Pollock, Arshile Gorky, and Robert Motherwell.

JOSEPH CORNELL: FORTUNETELLING PARROT. 1937-1938. Venice. Peggy Guggenheim Collection

CORNELL'S STRANGE BOXES

NEW YORK

The artistic year in New York ends with a large solo exhibition by Joseph Cornell at the Julien Levy Gallery, which specializes in Surrealism.

Cornell's objects are Surrealist in the manner of Max Ernst's collages. In fact, Cornell got the idea of his "collage sculptures" and "constructions" in 1931, when he discovered, at the same gallery, Ernst's work *The 100-Headed Woman*.

More often than not, he makes boxes containing several manufactured items: mirrors, pipes, Renaissance figures, a sky map,

hotel cards, and painted paper, mixed in subtle compositions and treated with great manual ability. Objects discovered in souvenir shops and old newspapers may be artificially aged, polished, or given patina, because the artist is attentive to the esthetic effects produced by various materials. A New York critic describes the exhibition as a "holiday toy store for sophisticated pleasure."

Indeed, at the age of thirty-six, this solitary esthete has refinement. In spite of his adhesion to Surrealism, he has no black humor or aggressiveness. His fragile objects, joined together by the discreet complicity of a poetic moment, seem to be as withdrawn as their creator.

THE AFFAIR OF THE POSTCARDS

NEW YORK

The last act of "the Utrillo affair" is played. The owners of the Carmine Gallery, which exhibited forty works by Utrillo, from February 13 to March 4, are condemned to pay an additional duty in order to take the paintings out of customs. Because the paintings were inspired by postcards, the American authorities classify them as manufactured items, and therefore do not allow their duty-free import. From the customs point of view, the paintings must be treated as reproductions.

This interpretation, a curious one to say the least, scandalizes artistic circles and causes several interventions. At the age of fifty-six, and at the peak of glory, Utrillo experiences a revival of the polemic that injured his pride a few years ago. When he became famous after his exhibition at the gallery Paul Guillaume in 1922, some people, out of envy, argued that he copied postcards and therefore could not be considered a professional artist. His mother, Suzanne Valadon, faced the accusers: "My son produced masterpieces by inspiring himself from postcards; others think they produce masterpieces, but all they do is postcards."

The painter stopped working in this manner several years ago because inquisitive people approached him and sometimes made him so furious that he ended up at the police station. He started to use black and white photographs instead. Postcards served only to refresh his memory. For early phases of a painting he used a ruler, a compass, a plumb line, and a square. "With these things, one cannot make a mistake," he says. Anyway, it is obvious that the result has nothing to do with mere copying!

The great New York exhibition attracts a crowd of collectors and curious people, who come to see the work of the "cursed painter." The exhibition follows Utrillo's evolution: the beginnings with the "Montmagny period," from 1903 to 1907, the "white period" up to 1916, then a more colorful stage. Utrillo remains faithful to Montmartre, to the melancholic suburbs north of Paris, and to country churches. He also takes the visitor to Bretagne and to Corsica, where he was staying with his mother. He now seems to have a stable period. He has been married to Lucie Pauwels for four years and lives in Vésinet.

The art dealer Paul Pétridès signed an exclusivity contract with him in 1936. Has he found his peaceful haven?

AMERICAN CUSTOMS AUTHORITIES CLASSIFIED UTRILLO'S WORKS AS "MANUFACTURED ITEMS"

MAURICE UTRILLO:
RUE SAINT-VINCENT. 1910.
Switzerland. Private Collection

THE NEW MOMA

NEW YORK

The spectacular new Museum of Modern Art opens on May 10. It is an aluminum-and-glass six-story building, surprisingly subtle and luminous, of the international style celebrated by MOMA in its famous 1932 exhibition organized by the young architect Philip Johnson.

The new MOMA is built by the architects Philip Goodwin and Edward Stone. Its first exhibition, "Art of Our Time," is as spectacular as the building itself. It is a splendid demonstration of the director Alfred Barr's ambition to present all living arts of our time, regardless of style. There are sections for painting, sculpture, architecture, and industrial design, and also for cinema and photography. The opening is the culmination of ten years of courageous policy applied during a bleak period in the history of the United States.

At its creation ten years ago, the museum had almost no permanent collection. Now it owns first-class works due to the generous donations of Miss Lillie P. Bliss, Mrs. John D. Rockefeller, and Mrs. Simon Guggenheim, as well as to wise acquisitions. Among this year's purchases: a historic painting, *Les demoiselles d'Avignon*, by Pablo Picasso, purchased after two years of negotiations with the dealer Seligmann, for $28,000. *Les*

demoiselles was painted by the artist in his Montmartre studio in 1907; due to its wholly new treatment of space and the human figure, it is one of the founding works of modern art.

At MOMA, it joins other masterpieces, including works by Matisse, Kandinsky, and Henri Rousseau, turning the museum into one of the centers of twentieth-century art.

The trustees of the Museum of Modern Art in New York with *Les demoiselles d'Avignon*. From left to right: J.H. Whitney, Mrs. W.T. Emmet, A. Conger Goodyear, N.A. Rockefeller, Mrs. J. Sheppard, E. Ford, and Mrs. J. Parkinson.

DEATH OF AN ART DEALER

VERSAILLES

The art world is in mourning. On June 22, Ambroise Vollard dies in Versailles, after a car accident. A true artist among art dealers is no more.

He was not one of those dealers who jump on the customer. On the contrary, he received art lovers in his gallery at the Rue Lafitte with a passive, somnolent look. But, in spite of the tired stare of a man who keeps odd hours, he was a remarkable salesman, who would surreptitiously steer the client toward the work of one of his friends.

His friends? They were named Cézanne, Henri Rousseau, Rodin, Maillol, Bonnard, Picasso, Matisse. Besides being an art dealer, Vollard was an art publisher. He sponsored Bonnard's illustrations of Baudelaire's *Fleurs du mal* and Chagall's for *The Fables of La Fontaine*.

He wrote sometimes. Two years ago, he published *The Memoirs of an Art Dealer*, a book of anecdotes that takes the reader on a tour of the studios of his friends in Montmartre and Montparnasse. The greatest painters have made portraits of him. Thus, thanks to Renoir, Cé-zanne, Bonnard and Picasso, we can remember this man with his high bold forehead and a nose that made him look like a sleepy Socrates. Vollard was a sphinx, an enigma, and a shrewd man at the same time. He was born in Saint-Denis-de-la-Réunion and went to Paris for his studies. He dies at the age of seventy-one.

Robert Maillart's Parabolic Vault

The leading attraction of the Swiss National Exhibition in Zurich was Robert Maillart's cement pavilion with its ultrathin parabolic vault. It is the realization of a lifelong architectural objective in that it is based on the continuity of structure to which Maillart has devoted his work. As early as 1908, he had patented his *pilier-champignon* (mushroom-pillar) system, in which the pillar is organically integrated into the slab it supports, functioning as a floor. Maillart is famous for the bridges he has built in Alpine valleys. He is now sixty-seven years old.

The Vitalists Burn Hitler in Effigy

The Vitalists, a new group of artistic and literary innovators, held a banquet chaired by Maurice de Vlaminck at the restaurant Les Compagnons du Tour de France at 16 Rue des Quatre-Vents in Paris. On this occasion they burned a portrait of Adolf Hitler, "an art critic who considers himself qualified, as a former house painter, to state that all the artists of the French school—Braque, Derain, Gauguin, Laurencin, Valadon, Kisling, Matisse . . . are degenerates."

The Suicide of Witkiewicz

Stanislaw Ignacy Witkiewicz, also known as Witkacy, committed suicide at Jeziora in Poland. Painter, philosopher, and dramatist, Witkiewicz was one of Poland's most famous artists. In addition to Realistic works, he leaves portraits of Expressionistic inspiration approaching Automatism, which were often created under the influence of drugs. A pessimist about the future of Western civilization, he was unable to bear the final blow when the Soviet forces attacked his country on September 18, joining the armies of Hitler's Germany. He was fifty-four years old.

Ernst Is Interned

During the last Great War, France mistakenly arrested the artists who had come to defend it, such as the American Cummings and the Czech Kubista. Now, with the new war, it treats as enemies those who had expected to find a refuge there, because they are of German origin. Max Ernst, who was living very peacefully in Saint-Martin d'Ardèche with the English painter Leonora Carrington, was arrested and taken to the concentration camp of Milles near Aix, where he found among the prisoners other creative people such as the writer Walter Hasenclever and the painter Hans Bellmer. The camp includes a former brickyard where Ernst and Bellmer have managed to make drawings with makeshift means at their disposal, amidst dust and Kafkaesque shadows. The poet Paul Éluard has protested to President Albert Sarraut.

Braque Exhibition in the United States

Who is the greatest, Braque or Picasso? It is difficult, if not impossible, to decide this today. They have both had highly successful exhibitions devoted to their works in the United States. Unlike Picasso, Braque practices an art of equilibrium, of craftsmanlike restraint, of continuity. The two great artists of the period, who at the beginning of the century created Cubism together, are now placed in opposition. "Braque the inspector," they called him then—a title that is even more fitting today.

The cement pavilion by Robert Maillart with its parabolic vault.

GEORGES BRAQUE: LARGE GUERIDON. 1929. Washington, D.C. Philips Collection

GIORGIO MORANDI: STILL LIFE. 1929-1930. Milan. Private Collection

IS MORANDI A GREAT PAINTER?

ROME

The Third National Art Quadrennnial is on, at the Exhibition Palace. Founded in 1931 by the Italian government within the framework of its art-acquisition policy, this salon encompasses all trends, from Futurism to Metaphysical Painting. Noteworthy is that it includes a retrospective of the Bolognese painter Giorgio Morandi. He is not much known to the public, although he was honored with the exhibition prize twice, in 1931 and in 1935.

The artist exhibits forty-two paintings, two drawings, and twelve etchings, which bring him the second prize for painting. The first prize goes to the painter Bruno Saetti. The prize causes a controversy, which turns into the "Morandi case." The critics take sides. The press echoes their declarations. What claims are there against the painter? Some people doubt that others are ready to grant him a place in the pantheon of Italian contemporary art.

The renowned critic Roberto Longhi, in his first class of the 1934–1935 season at Bologna University, acknowledged that Morandi is "one of the best living painters of Italy." Morandi is also admired by his colleague Arnold Beccaria, who wrote numerous praising articles in the Milan magazine *Corrente* and the first monograph about his work. In turn, the detractors abound in arguments against his paintings: In their eyes, they are too simple and without interest. In the *Corriere Padano,* of Ferrara, Osvaldo Licini and Carlo Belli speak ironically of the "small soundproof gray room" (an allusion to Morandi's palette), where the works are "all the same, disciplined, correct, and well aligned."

Uninterested in controversies, Morandi paints. Discreet, in contemplation and silence, he chooses his subjects from his familiar atmosphere and does not modify in any way his inspiration or his use of time. His paintings and engravings are done in his studio in Bologna, in the Via Fondazza, where he lives with his three sisters, Anna, Dina, and Maria-Teresa, and in Grizzana, on the hills of Emilia, where he owns a house. Philosophically, Morandi thinks the future will tell.

(See also 1945.)

ANDRÉ LHOTE: WHAT IS A LANDSCAPE?

André Lhote, who is both a painter and a professor, has become over the years one of the most listened-to theorists of modern art, especially concerned with maintaining a balance with tradition. His *Traité du paysage* (treatise on the landscape), published by Floury, is a model of its kind. The eternal rules of painting are recalled on each page, and many illustrations are used and presented as the brake and the rudder of any pictorial creation. Lhote's ideas are important to this era, which has, since the turn of the century, seen wave after wave of avant-garde artists, now trying to redefine themselves. Below are essential passages from the *Traité*.

Which laws must a work of art obey in order to achieve dignified expression while escaping sloppy sentimentality? What profound requirements must a work of art fulfill? Spirits such as Poussin and Seurat who are specifically Latin, who favor impartial speculation and who have temperaments complex enough to quickly give life to the images in their minds, apply definite rules to their art. From the fifteenth century to the end of the Renaissance, intelligent thinkers undertook to examine their feelings or view of the world using line and color, and reflected on the surest means of soliciting or maintaining the respect of others. Even while intending to express their emotions, they calculated the power of certain groupings of lines or blending of colors to cast a spell. They quickly realized that the eye was a tyrant that demanded to be both stimulated by the variety of elements used and reassured by a few well-placed resemblances: Before a surface divided into fragments of different orientations, a crumpled piece of paper, for instance, the eye panics, unable to follow lines that are not unified by any obvious law; the eye soon tires of such a view. In contrast, before a surface divided by a too-obvious law, such as a tiled floor or a gate, the eye is insufficiently stimulated and remains indifferent. Contrary to what the profane believes, the essence of art is not to limit nature but to represent, under the pretext of imitation, pure plastic elements: measures, directions, ornaments, lights, values, colors, matter, distributed and organized according to the demands of the laws of nature. Once this has been done, the artist does not cease to be dependent upon nature; but rather than meanly imitating its accidents, he imitates its laws . . .

Those who study the forms of nature know that plastic manifestations such as air and water currents, the structure of seashells or plants, etc., contain the most beautiful share of these elements, which are both stimulating and reassuring. From then on, the art of drawing and painting, which depends on the art of the senses, finds its laws in morphology. It was not an unreasonable gesture on the part of the Moderns to listen to the lesson of the Africans and Polynesians, for "primitive" people who live side by side with the forms of nature, who follow its rhythms, who physically feel its repercussions, spontaneously find the combination of those forms that are the most vivid. These delegates of natural forces have much to teach the "civilized" peoples who are prisoners of the inhuman machine.

ANDRÉ LHOTE
Traité du paysage *(Excerpts)*

André Lhote in his studio.

1940

	1940	1941	1942	1943	1944
ARTS	• Death of Paul Klee • Léger and Mondrian in New York	• Death of Robert Delaunay • Exhibition of Young French Painters at the gallery Braun in Paris	• Arno Breker exhibits at the Musée de l'Orangerie in Paris • Peggy Guggenheim opens the gallery Art of This Century in New York	• Fautrier, in hiding, paints his series of *Hostages* • First exhibition of Jackson Pollock in New York	• Deaths of Kandinsky in Paris and Mondrian in New York • First exhibition of Dubuffet, at the gallery Drouin • First exhibition of Vasarely, at Denise René's gallery
LITERATURE	• *For Whom the Bell Tolls* by Ernest Hemingway • *Native Son* by Richard Wright • *On the Marble Cliffs* by Ernst Jünger	• Death of James Joyce	• *The Myth of Sisyphus* by Albert Camus • *Le parti pris des choses* by Francis Ponge • *The Skin of Our Teeth* by Thornton Wilder	• *Being and Nothingness* by Jean-Paul Sartre • *The Little Prince* by Antoine de Saint-Exupéry	• *Kaputt* by Curzio Malaparte • Max Jacob dies in the Drancy Camp • Death of Jean Giraudoux
MUSIC AND THEATER	• *Medea* by Darius Milhaud • *Microcosm* by Béla Bartók	• *Quatuor pour la fin des temps* by Olivier Messiaen • *Le vin herbé* by Frank Martin	• *Rodeo* by Aaron Copland • Popular songs in the United States include *White Christmas* (Irving Berlin) and *Praise the Lord and Pass the Ammunition*	• *The Satin Slipper* by Paul Claudel at the Comédie Française • Death of Max Reinhardt in New York	• *Désir attrapé par la queue* by Picasso is read by Picasso, Jean-Paul Sartre, and Michel Leiris
MOTION PICTURES	• *The Great Dictator* with Charlie Chaplin	• *The Maltese Falcon* by John Huston • *Citizen Kane* by Orson Welles	• *The Evening Visitors* by Marcel Carné and Jacques Prévert • *To Be or Not To Be* by Ernst Lubitsch • *Obsession* by Luchino Visconti	• *Le corbeau* by Henri-Georges Clouzot • *Casablanca* by Michael Curtiz • *Shadow of a Doubt* by Alfred Hitchcock	• *Henry V* by Laurence Olivier • *Lifeboat* by Alfred Hitchcock
SCIENCE AND TECHNOLOGY	• Edwin McMillan and Philip Abelson discover neptunium, the first transuranic element • First successful helicopter flight, in the United States	• Intensive atomic research under the code name "Manhattan Project" begins in the United States	• Enrico Fermi splits the atom in Chicago • Henry J. Kaiser develops techniques for building 10,000-ton Liberty ships in four days	• Discovery of streptomycin by Waksman and Schatz • Henrik Dam and E. A. Doisy are awarded Nobel prize in medicine for discovery of vitamin K	• Quinine is synthesized • Otto Hahn is awarded Nobel prize in chemistry
POLITICS AND DAILY LIFE	• Defeat of France; General de Gaulle appeals to the nation • Discovery of the caves of Lascaux	• Germany attacks the USSR • Japan attacks Pearl Harbor • Hitler declares war on the United States	• Battle of Midway • The German armies are stopped at Stalingrad	• Surrender of German armies at Stalingrad • Warsaw Ghetto Revolt • Tehran Conference	• Landing of the Allies in Normandy; liberation of Paris and Rome; German retreat in Russia; American offensive in the Pacific

1949

avant-garde artists: Arshile Gorky, Pollock, and Rothko in New York; Fontana in Buenos Aires; Dubuffet, Wols, Mathieu, Vasarely, and Bazaine in Paris. And the creation of the Cobra movement in 1948 brings together Danish, Belgian, and Dutch artists. The war takes us into a new period. The adventure of art in the second half of the century begins.

1945	1946	1947	1948	1949
• Mondrian retrospective at MOMA • First Salon de Mai, with an homage to Bissière • *Charnel House* by Picasso	• Léger, Chagall, Breton go to the United States • Lucio Fontana publishes the *White Manifesto* • *La joie de vivre* by Picasso	• Opening of the Musée National d'Art Moderne in Paris • Death of Bonnard	• Birth of the Cobra movement • Opening of the school Subject of the Artists in New York • Deaths of Kurt Schwitters and Arshile Gorky	• Moore retrospective at the Musée National d'Art Moderne • Death of James Ensor in Ostend
• Death of Paul Valéry • *Christ Stopped at Eboli* by Carlo Levi • *L'homme foudroyé* by Blaise Cendrars	• *Zorba the Greek* by Nikos Kazantzakis • *The Death of Virgil* by Hermann Broch • *Paterson* by William Carlos Williams	• André Gide is awarded Nobel prize in literature • *The Plague* by Albert Camus • *Doctor Faustus* by Thomas Mann • *A Streetcar Named Desire* by Tennessee Williams	• *Pisan Cantos* by Ezra Pound • *The Naked and the Dead* by Norman Mailer	• *The Second Sex* by Simone de Beauvoir • *1984* by George Orwell • *Death of a Salesman* by Arthur Miller
• *Caligula* by Albert Camus, with Gérard Philipe • Deaths of Anton Webern and Béla Bartók	• *The Victors* and *The Respectful Prostitute* by Jean-Paul Sartre		• *Dirty Hands* by Jean-Paul Sartre • First international jazz festival at Antibes	• Death of Richard Strauss • *Sonatas and Interludes* by John Cage • Bertolt Brecht founds the Berliner Ensemble
• "Rome, Open City" by Roberto Rossellini • *Children of Paradise* by Marcel Carné and Jacques Prévert	• First film festival at Cannes • *Beauty and the Beast* by Jean Cocteau • *Ivan the Terrible* by Sergei Eisenstein	• *Monsieur Verdoux* with Charlie Chaplin • *Quai des Orfèvres* by Henri-Georges Clouzot	• "Witch hunt" in Hollywood • *The Treasure of the Sierra Madre* by John Huston • *The Red Shoes* by Michael Powell • *The Bicycle Thief* by Vittorio De Sica	• *The Third Man* by Carol Reed • *Orphée* by Jean Cocteau
• First atomic bomb detonated, in New Mexico • Fleming, Florey, and Chain are awarded Nobel prize in medicine for the discovery of penicillin	• First electronic computer, at the University of Pennsylvania • Atomic bomb tests at Bikini • Chester Carlson invents the xerography process	• A U.S. airplane is the first to break the sound barrier	• Invention of the transistor • *Sexual Behavior in the Human Male* by Alfred C. Kinsey	• A guided missile reaches 250 miles, the highest altitude so far • The USSR tests its first atom bomb
• Germany surrenders; Hiroshima and Nagasaki are bombed; Japan surrenders • Yalta and Potsdam Conferences • United Nations chartered, in San Francisco	• Nuremberg Tribunal; verdicts include death sentence for twelve top Nazis	• The *Exodus* incident • India becomes independent	• Assassination of Gandhi • Proclamation of the state of Israel • Berlin blockade • Marshall Plan • Beginning of the Cold War	• Foundation of the People's Republic of China under Mao Tse-tung • The Republic of Eire is proclaimed in Dublin • North Atlantic Treaty is signed

A great painter perishes. Paul Klee succumbs to cardiac arrest in his native Switzerland, where he had withdrawn to escape Nazism. Do we understand today the importance of this solitary and brilliant artist who tried so hard to reveal the hidden forces of being? Living artists, for their part, are alarmed at the rapidity of France's defeat in the face of Hitler's troops, and many of them who had moved there to flee Nazism wonder what is to become of them. To help them emigrate, the United States immediately establishes CAS, and sends a young volunteer, Varian Fry, to Marseilles. He has already been contacted by some of the artists.

1940

S U M M A R Y

GREAT MASTERS

He Listened to the World Vibrate
In Klee's Words

ART AND THE WAR

Munch Refuses to Collaborate
Moore under the Bombs

ART NEWS

Loewy Refurbishes Lucky Strike
An American in Marseilles
Foujita, War Correspondent
Rockefeller Center Transforms Manhattan
Artists in the Face of War
In Brief

MURAL ART

Lurçat Revives Tapestry

WRITINGS AND THEORIES

Jean-Paul Sartre: the Real and the Imaginary

LITERATURE

UNITED STATES
Ernest Hemingway publishes For Whom the Bell Tolls.
 Richard Wright publishes Native Son.

GREAT BRITAIN
Dylan Thomas publishes Portrait of the Artist As a Young Dog.

ITALY
Publication of The Desert of the Tartars *by Dino Buzzati.*

MUSIC

FRANCE
Performance of the opera Medea *by Darius Milhaud, with sets and costumes by André Masson.*

GREAT BRITAIN
Publication of 153 pieces for piano of Béla Bartók's Microcosm.

ITALY
Premiere of Luigi Dallapiccola's opera Night Flight *in Florence, inspired by Saint-Exupéry's novel.*

MOTION PICTURES

UNITED STATES
Charlie Chaplin parodies Hitler in The Great Dictator.
 The blend of classical music and animation in Walt Disney's Fantasia *is not appreciated by the public.*

PAUL KLEE
SENECIO. 1922
Basel. Kunstmuseur

**Paul Klee with his cat,
Bimbo; in Bern, fall 1935.**

PAUL KLEE: FLORENTINE VILLAS. 1926. Paris. MNAM

HE LISTENED TO THE
WORLD VIBRATE

LOCARNO

At the Sant'Agnese Clinic of Muralto-Locarno, sixty-one-year-old Paul Klee dies of cardiac paralysis six weeks after France, whose language he spoke and whose literature he admired, capitulates to Hitler. Klee was born in Switzerland but spent much of his life in Germany.

It sometimes happens that individual and collective destinies coincide. He was thrust into one of the darkest nights known in the history of humanity. Fate would have it that the illness that devoured the artist for five years was aggravated by yet another fatal illness, which

was affecting Germany. Three years before Klee's death, the exhibit of "degenerate art" organized by the Nazis opened in Munich, the city where Klee had lived for many years. It included seventeen Klees.

Such a demonstration of diabolical force probably did not astonish inordinately the man who combined in his work the impulses toward life with those toward death that work in the human unconscious.

During the months preceding his death, Klee painted angels and demons. The titles of his last drawings and paintings are premonitions: *Early Suffering, Explosion of Fear, Death and*

Fire. In the latter, death appears as a blue skull, casting whitish reflections onto a dark red background. Death, fire, metamorphosis, possible resurrection . . . Before death carries him away, Klee works on a final lunar *Still Life*: a green coffeepot, three vases, and a statuette in lovely gray-violet tones on a pedestal table. He never gets to sign it.

As he was alone in his last agony, Klee had been alone in his life as a painter. Even his duties as a professor, first at the Bauhaus in Weimar, which he joined in 1921, then for a short period at the Academy of Fine Arts in Düsseldorf, did not succeed in fracturing his solitude.

This may be why his work is one of the most original and most unclassifiable of the century. It passes through movements, schools, and styles without being affected by them. At a time when what was being advanced was formal research, strict abstraction, the large format, and the will to reach not individuals but groups, indeed mobs, the work of Klee can seem only like the height of incongruity.

Is this really a painter's work? These very small formats? These apparently childish drawings? These curious hieroglyphics? The bizarre titles: *Senecio, Florentine Villas, Le gris et la côte?* A preoccupation with rhythms, which is more like a musician's than a painter's?

Everyone knows the famous sentence that begins his *Creative Confession*, an essay written in 1920: "Art does not reproduce the visible, it makes visible." A seer and a thief of fire, this is what the painter must be. Only by the powers of painting are "the forces that have created and create the world" brought to light. His first drawings consisted of fine hatchings or complex strokes. Threadlike and labyrinthine, they evoked imaginary cities, uncanny architectures, aerial or underwater landscapes inhabited by disquieting creatures—they explore the hidden recesses of creation. Then quickly, color appears, subdued, bright, charged with a mysterious energy: lilacs and light yellows, mauves, liquid blues, and pinks enhanced by ideograms and signs whose meaning offers itself for decoding while at the same time concealing itself. Klee's work is one of the most enigmatic that exist: All that is unformed, unstable, on the threshold of metamorphosis is caught in the implacable snares of his drawing. All that is firm, solid, rooted is as though submitted to a slight neutronic bombardment of color that allows only the substance of things to subsist.

Lothar Schreyer, his colleague at the second Bauhaus, in Dessau, tells the following story. One day, he hears scraping and tapping noises and sounds of falling coming from the studio that Klee occupies above his own. Fearing that Fritzi, the artist's legendary cat, might be sharpening his claws on his master's works, Schreyer leaps up the steps, four by four, opens the door without knocking and sees . . . Klee, distraught, going from one painting to another, adding a touch of color here, a scratching there, a scarcely visible nuance of an erasing elsewhere.

Is it sufficiently realized that the world is no longer the same since Klee pinned it onto his mysterious little pieces of canvas, paper, and cardboard?

(See also 1911, 1920, 1924, 1937, 1987.)

IN KLEE'S WORDS

In a painting, houses set on their sides do not collapse, just as a tree does not need to bloom or man to breathe.

In the beginning, there is the act, but even before that, there is the idea. And, since infinity has no set beginning, like a circle, being without beginning and end, one must admit the primacy of the idea.

In other times, one depicted the visible things on earth, things one enjoyed, or would have enjoyed, seeing. Today, the relativity of the visible has become obvious, and we agree to see only one particular example in the totality of the universe, inhabited by innumerable latent truths.

Art is an image of creation. It is a symbol, just as the earth is a symbol of the cosmos.

What we are seeking is not form but function.

The work of art is first and foremost genesis, and its history may be briefly represented as a spark shot mysteriously from some unknown source that sets the spirit on fire, sets the hand in motion, and, transmitting itself like movement to matter, becomes the work of art.

Form is the end, death. Formation is life.

It is no one's idea to demand that a tree form its branches on the model of its roots. Everyone agrees that the top is not simply a reflection of the bottom. It is evident that different functions existing in different orders have serious dissimilarities.

A sleeping man, the circulation of the blood, breathing measured in the lungs, the delicate functioning of the kidneys, and in the head a world of dreams regarding the powers of destiny: a group of functions joined in rest.

All Faustian tendencies are unknown to me. I occupy an original point in creation, a distant point where I imagine formulas for humans, animals, plants, for the earth and the rocks, for water, air, all the cyclical forces.

It is certain that one does not lie down with demons: The tension of their presence is too strong.

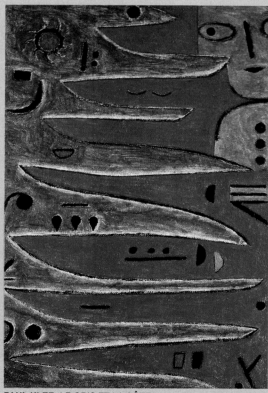

PAUL KLEE: LE GRIS ET LA CÔTE. 1938. Bern

MUNCH REFUSES TO COLLABORATE

EKELY

Edvard Munch cannot be labeled a Germanophobe. Quite the contrary, Germany was the Norwegian's "second country" during long visits between 1892 and 1908. But since the invasion in April of his native land by Nazi troops, he has refused, as do many of his countrymen, any and all collaboration with the invaders. Indeed, he rejects energetically a proposal to participate in the "cultural advisory council" set up by the Quisling government under the boot of the occupier.

It must be said that Munch's relations with the Third Reich deteriorated slowly. In 1933, Hitler's minister of propaganda, Joseph Goebbels, still communicated "best wishes to the great Nordic artist in the name of German artists" on his seventieth birthday. But four years later, a Nazi commission confiscated eighty-two of Munch's works from museums and public collections and the painter was stamped as a "degenerate artist." In the three years that followed, art dealers in Berlin and Munich sold off Munches at cut-rate.

Munch lent his support to another "degenerate artist," the young German painter Ernst Wilhelm Nay, who was thus able to spend holidays in Norway.

Munch, nearing eighty years of age, is living in his winter studio at Ekely, removed from the world, but suffering from an illness of the eyes. At any moment, the order to evacuate could chase him from his home.

Suffering from anguish all his life, Munch discovers a strange calm when faced with this situation, fraught with real danger. To Pola Gauguin, Paul's son, he confides during a recent visit: "Don't you understand that all the ghosts are buried away in a hole facing this single great ghost?" It is as though Nazism has become the liberating agent of his soul.

EDVARD MUNCH: YOUNG WOMEN ON A BRIDGE. London. Christie's

MOORE UNDER THE BOMBS

LONDON

The bombs that fall on the capital of the United Kingdom do not spare Henry Moore. His studio is seriously damaged, and he himself has to take up residence outside the city. But if Moore, a combatant in the First World War, is no longer young enough to take up arms, he is nonetheless concerned, and returns often to London as official artist of the troops.

His notebook under his arm, Moore covers the subway stops where his fellow countrymen take refuge each night to escape the bombings. He derives hallucinatory sketches that evoke a Goya or a Jacques Callot. In his watercolors and chalk drawings of human forms stretched out on the platforms an atmosphere of unreality prevails.

HENRY MOORE: AIR-RAID SHELTER SKETCH BOOK. 1940-1941. Henry Moore Foundation

Loewy Refurbishes Lucky Strike

George Washington Hill, the president of American Tobacco, is highly satisfied. In March, he went to see the designer Raymond Loewy to ask him to improve the Lucky Strike cigarette packet. Loewy replaced its dark green color with a light surface. He also placed the brand's distinctive red circle on both sides of the packet, which up to now was only on one side. In its new dress, the Lucky Strike packet looks smarter. Knowing that everything Loewy touches turns to gold, a strong increase in sales is expected.

An American in Marseilles

Varian Fry, thirty-two years old, has volunteered to represent the CAS—the Centre Americain de Secours (American rescue center)—in Marseilles. In 1935, in Berlin, Fry witnessed a roundup of Jews and does not want to pass up the chance to save some of the potential victims of Nazism who have recently fled to France. Last autumn, he opened an office in a small apartment on the Rue Grignan. The purpose of the CAS is to arrange for secret emigration of threatened intellectuals and artists to the United States. Requests are pouring in.

Foujita, War Correspondent

Foujita, the most talented of the Japanese who love Paris, left the City of Light on May 23, just before the invasion of France by Nazi forces. He is now a war correspondent for the imperial government of Tokyo. In August, he exhibited a dozen canvases at the Salon Nika, before his new duties took him to Manchuria, where he witnessed the battle of Nororhan on the Russian-Manchurian border. He then returned to Tokyo, where he participated in the exhibition commemorating the 2,600th anniversary of the Empire of the Rising Sun.

Rockefeller Center Transforms Manhattan

After nine years of work, Rockefeller Center has been completed. Situated in the heart of Manhattan,

The old Lucky Strike Pack.

the center is comprised of a group of fourteen buildings, including the RCA Building. It is the work of the architect Raymond Hood, who unfortunately died before construction was completed. His lamelliform style breaks with the old type of skyscraper, which merely imitated the Gothic tower or extended the Hausmannian apartment house to forty stories. The buildings making up this new center, which introduce urbanism on a grand scale into the city of today, in the age of parkways and bus terminals, are transforming the New York skyline.

Artists in the Face of War

Herbert Read wrote recently that art does not serve as "consolation or inspiration in a time of universal horror and despair." That is why, as at the time of the war of 1914-1918, the British have organized the "War Artists Scheme," under the direction of art historian Kenneth Clark. The artists have each been assigned individual tasks: Paul Nash is at the Air Ministry, his son John at the Royal Navy, and Stanley Spencer at the Port Glasgow naval shipyards. John Piper and Graham Sutherland are painting the bombed-out ruins. The most impressive is certainly Paul Nash, who paints airplane carcasses washed up on the beaches with the same visionary touch as he painted the trenches and devastated countryside of the war of 1914.

RCA Building, Rockefeller Center, New York.

JEAN LURÇAT:
AFGHAN HOUND.
1938. Aubusson.
Musée de la Tapisserie

LURÇAT REVIVES TAPESTRY

AUBUSSON

In September of last year, when Hitler and Stalin invaded Poland, Guillaume Janneau, manager of the Gobelin and Beauvais factories that had withdrawn to Aubusson, commissions Jean Lurçat to do four large tapestry cartoons on the theme of the four seasons. In collaboration with Marcel Gromaire and Pierre Dubreuil, Lurçat's task is to make them on the spot with the factory foremen and the workers. He is also to watch over the production of the hangings, each of which is to measure 170 square feet. More than twenty tapestries are woven since the beginning of the year, in spite of the variety of conflicts on the continent.

For a long time, the painter and engraver has been fascinated by mural art. Lurçat was twenty-seven years old when his mother produced his first tapestries with canvas stitch. When his work grew in scale, he confided his compositions, as well as the cartoon *The Storm*, to the Hennebert studios, canvas specialists in Toulon. *The Storm* was the first of Lurçat's works woven with a smooth nap. He learned an important lesson from the experience: to copy a painting faithfully in wool is an error because the very technique of tapestry is thus not used as a medium of original creation.

It was in Aubusson two years ago that Lurçat met François Tabard, one of the youngest heads of one of the oldest workshops in the city: From father to son, the Tabard firm has been weaving since 1637. Tabard is convinced that in order to revive tapestry, wall hangings adapted to the age must be created. Lurçat decides to create a large

TO COPY A PAINTING FAITHFULLY IN WOOL IS AN ERROR . . . HE MUST BEGIN WITH THE WOOL ITSELF, NOT WITH TUBES OF PAINT

piece, *Harvests*. Eager to be initiated into the rudiments of weaving, he even sits down at the loom.

At the same time, he discovers the *Apocalypse* of Angers during a trip. The beauty, the rhythm of the scenes, the arrangement of the crowds, the monumental structures dazzle him. He notices the restrained palette, the large stitched weaving, the simplified design. In addition, *Apocalypse* moves him as a warning against the misfortunes of an impending war . . . Lurçat goes back to Aubusson in shock over the vision. *Harvests* is already off the looms. He is dismayed: The wools dyed according to the gouached cartoon capture the intended tones only approximately.

Lurçat understands that he must begin with the wool itself, not with tubes of paint. Among the skeins, he henceforth chooses the yellows, blues, and grays he needs. He gives them numbers, which helps to determine a cartoon that is not painted but calibrated according to the nuances of the material. A saving of dyes. Production time is cut down. Wool stocks are abolished. All this lowers the cost.

Today, the Aubusson workshops live again. Lurçat is revolutionizing tapestry.

JEAN-PAUL SARTRE: THE REAL AND THE IMAGINARY

Jean-Paul Sartre, a young philosophy teacher at the Lycée du Havre, is not a complete unknown. Two years ago, his novel *La nausée* (nausea) was published, and a collection of short stories entitled *The Wall* came out last year. Both works attracted the attention of the literary world. His latest work, *The Imaginary*, has just been published by Gallimard's scholarly Bibliothèque des Idées collection. It is not easy reading. Sartre deals with the formation of the image-producing conscience. Beloware passages relevant to artistic activity, in which the author describes how we construct images.

When I look at a drawing, my gaze contains all the human intentions that produced that drawing. Someone drew those lines to make a picture of a runner. This picture undoubtedly needs my consciousness to be viewed as such. But the artist knew that, even counted on it; he asked for our participation when he drew those black lines. It should not be thought that I first see these lines as simply lines, and then as parts of a picture. In our perception itself, the lines are representative. Look through a sketchbook: You might not necessarily grasp the sense of each line, but you will know that each one represents something and that this is the very reason for its existence. Thus, the capacity to represent is a real quality of those lines, one that I sense along with their size and shape. You might say that this is simple knowledge. A cube is also knowledge: I cannot see simultaneously its six sides. Yet when I look at this piece of wood, it is a cube that I see. Any imagery of the consciousness produced by this drawing is thus built on a real position of existence that preceded it and which motivates it on the level of perception, even if this consciousness itself could establish its object as nonexistent, or simply neutralize the existential thesis . . .

When we interpret a stain on the tablecloth or a swirl in the wallpaper, we are not really giving these forms representative properties. In reality, the stain represents nothing; when I see it, I see it only as a stain, such that when I move to the level of imagery the intuitive basis of my image is nothing that had previously appeared in my perception.

There are two possibilities: In one, we move our eyes freely without forethought, and we consider the outline of a stain as we will, following the order that pleases us, seeing arbitrary relationships in this or that part in an overall movement that draws us in no particular way. This is what happens when we are sick in bed with nothing to do: Our eyes roam over the wallpaper. Sometimes a shape emerges out of the swirls, that is, with these eye movements we see a somewhat coherent grouping. My eyes trace a path that remains outlined in the wallpaper, and I say to myself: It is a crouching man, a bouquet, a dog. That is, out of these free movements, I set up a hypothesis, I give the shape that appeared a representative value. Most of the time, I don't expect to see a whole image, but something crystallizes suddenly. "It looks like part of a bouquet, the top of a face," etc. This knowledge has incorporated itself into my eye movements and directs them: Now I know how to finish the image, I know what to look for.

Or, a certain shape appears by itself and invites the eye to follow it . . .

Once again the shape is only suggested: We can hardly make out the forehead and the eye, but we already know it is the head of an African man. We finish it ourselves by reaching an agreement between the real givens of perception (the swirls on the wallpaper) and the creative spontaneity of our movements. Thus we will find the nose, mouth, and chin ourselves.

JEAN-PAUL SARTRE
The Imaginary (Excerpts)

PAUL KLEE:
TANZT ENTSETZEN

Artists react in one of three ways to the reality of Nazism triumphant. There are those like Vlaminck, who, for various reasons, come to terms with the Occupation and even go to Germany. Others, such as Max Ernst or Masson, gather in Marseilles on the Côte d'Azur, in the liberated zone, and await their visa for the United States. And then there are those who decide to stay put but are already organizing themselves in anticipation of an artistic and intellectual resistance. The latter is the case for the so-called painters "of French tradition," who exhibit their work at the gallery Braun, under the leadership of Lapicque and Bazaine. As for Kokoschka, in exile in London since 1938, he tirelessly fulminates against Nazi barbarism under the hail of Luftwaffe bombs.

1941

S U M M A R Y

ART AND HISTORY

Kokoschka's Long Wandering
Nolde Banned by the Nazis
Front-Line Art at the Jeu de Paume

DEVELOPMENTS

Life in "Visa-Hope Villa"

ART NEWS

The Death of Jawlensky
Donation by the Société Anonyme to Yale
The Second Death of Émile Bernard
Roland Penrose, the Camouflager
Enthusiasm for Dali in New York
In Brief

ART UNDER THE OCCUPATION

The End of a Great Solitaire
French Artists Visit Germany
Young French Painters Exhibit

LITERATURE

ARGENTINA
Jorge Luis Borges publishes Fictions.

FRANCE
With the publication of Le crève-cœur, *Louis Aragon returns to a classical verse form.*

GREAT BRITAIN
In Darkness at Noon *, the Hungarian-born author Arthur Koestler denounces the inhumanity of Communism.*

MUSIC

GERMANY
Olivier Messiaen composes—in a concentration camp— Quatuor pour la fin des temps.

GREAT BRITAIN
The oratorio A Child of Our Time, *a pacifist manifesto by Michael Tippett, is prohibited by the courts.*

MOTION PICTURES

UNITED STATES
Premieres of The Maltese Falcon *by John Huston and* Citizen Kane *by Orson Welles.*

FRANCE
Premiere of Remorque *by Jean Grémillon.*

THEATER

FRANCE
Louis Jouvet and his troupe leave for a tour of South America.

OSKAR KOKOSCHKA:
THE RED EGG AND THE PARTITION OF EUROPE. 1940-1941. Private Collection

KOKOSCHKA'S LONG WANDERING

LONDON

His friends called him the "Pullman painter," because of the nights that Oskar Kokoschka spent in railway sleeping cars tirelessly crisscrossing Europe. His ordeal is over now. His companion, Olga Palkovskà, whom he met in Prague, where he had taken refuge in 1934, before the rise of Nazism, convinced him to leave Czechoslovakia for London after the French and British agreements in Munich on September 39, 1938 abandoned his country to Hitler.

These retreats on the part of democracies before the Third Reich provoked profound bitterness from Kokoschka, and from this bitterness was born last winter an accusatory painting, *The Red Egg*, which he had originally entitled *The Axes*. Depicted are the four great European powers: Germany with Hitler; Italy with Mussolini; France with a cat sporting the national insignia; and Great Britain with the British lion, his tail coiled in

OSKAR KOKOSCHKA: THE BETROTHED OF THE WIND. 1914. Basel. Kunstmuseum

the form of a British pound. All four are grouped around a table, ready to devour a roasted chicken: Czechoslovakia, which succeeds in escaping, leaving a red egg in a platter. By associating the four countries in this manner, the artist wished to demonstrate that each in its way, and all together, contributed to the ruin of Czechoslovakia, whose capital, Prague, is seen in flames in the background. The duplicity of France and England is accentuated by the inscription "In Pace Munich."

Born in Pöchlarn, Austria, on March 1, 1886, Kokoschka spent his apprenticeship years in Vienna, the city of Freud, Klimt, Schönberg, Adolf Loos, Gustav Mahler . . . all of them spirits eminently intolerable to the Hitlerian esthetic. In 1937, he was still able to display his work in the Austrian capital. Yet that same year, four hundred and seventeen of his works were removed from rooms of German museums and confiscated by the Nazis, but the famous exhibit of "degenerate art" honored him more than enough. Two years later, one of his masterpieces, *The Bethrothed of the Wind*, born of his tempestuous love affair with Alma Mahler, the musician's widow, was part of the Luzerne sale of paintings seized from the German museums and acquired by the Kunstmuseum in Basel.

The Nazis would not forgive him for intervening to defend Max Liebermann, who had resigned, in May 1933, from the Prussian Academy of Fine Arts because of the officializing of antisemitism. Kokoschka had paid homage to him in an open letter to Dr. Goebbels in the

OSKAR KOKOSCHKA: DOUBLE PORTRAIT. 1919. Rotterdam. Boymans Van Beuningen Museum

Frankfurter Zeitung. Not yet completely Nazified, the newspaper had the audacity to publish it.

In Prague, he painted mainly landscapes. The view from his window of the Moldau River inspired him a great deal. Sixteen paintings date from that period. The magic of Prague dictated one last painting, which was produced in London—hence its title: *Nostalgia.*

Having abandoned his chair of professor of drawing at Dresden's Academy of Fine Arts, the painter found that Prague represented the possibility of survival because of the immediate interest the art dealer Hugo Feigl showed in him. Feigl put him in contact with the president of the country, Jan Mazaryk, and Kokoschka painted his portrait. A change might have taken place in Kokoschka. He had never been concerned about politics.

Worried about the ever-more arrogant power of the Nazi dictatorship, the democrat Kokoschka wished to express his moral convictions. In Mazaryk, he wanted to depict the symbol of resistance to Hitler. He explained himself in an interview published in September 1935 by the *Prager Tagblatt*: "I want to do a historical painting, a painting that can be shown in the schools so that children may understand that patriotic tasks, just like personal duties, can be united in the service of humanism."

The same year, he intervened publicly to condemn the Italian invasion of Ethiopia. In 1936, he supported the defense of Republican Spain. In London, he was named honorary president of the Free German Cultural League, which gathered together German-speaking intellectuals and artists who had emigrated.

In his exile here in the British capital, which is heavily bombed by the *Luftwaffe,* he is all the less able to forget the continent, set on fire and bloodied. In these conditions, how are idyllic paintings executed? But, then, it is true that idylls never attracted Kokoschka very much.

(See also 1918, 1922, 1931, 1980.)

NOLDE BANNED BY THE NAZIS

BERLIN

Among the painters of the Expressionist generation, Emil Nolde occupies a special place. First of all, because of his age he practically belongs to the previous generation: He was born in 1867, the same year as Käthe Kollwitz. And like Kollwitz, he could have turned toward the pervading atmosphere of Naturalism. Secondly, this die-hard individualist, who joined Die Brücke for a short time beginning in 1906, paradoxically was an early Nazi sympathizer. He himself claimed that he had been one of the first members of the National Socialist Party. On August 18, 1934, his signature was still included in the Nazi newspaper *Der Völkische Beobachter,* at the bottom of an appeal to give all powers to Hitler after Hindenburg's death.

Since May 1933, however, Nolde has been attacked in the press, just like all modern painters. The Nazi ideologue Alfred Rosenberg, in *Der Völkische Beobachter* of July 7, 1933, did not deny Nolde a certain gift: He assessed Nolde's maritime landscapes as having strength. But he judged his portraits to be "negroid."

A few critics tried to defend Nolde's painting as being faithful to the Nordic ideal. But in the 1937 exhibition in Munich dedicated to so-called "degenerate art," Nolde suffered the same fate as the painters generally labeled Expressionist.

In August, he is excluded from the plastic arts section of the Chamber of Culture. Which means, to put it plainly, he no longer has the right to show his work or to make professional claims as a painter.

Moreover, he receives an official letter from the Chamber of Culture declaring that his works cannot belong to the "National-Socialist patrimony." More precisely, he finds himself considered a "non-German" painter: an extraordinary disgrace for Nolde, who drew his inspiration from "Germanity"!

EMIL NOLDE: YOUNG COUPLE. 1931-1935. Lugano. Thyssen-Bornemisza Collection

FRONT-LINE ART AT THE JEU DE PAUME

PARIS

Since June 1940, war painting has become a favored genre in Nazi Germany. German victories must be illustrated and glorified. Combatants must be urged to show themselves as heroes.

Furthermore, soldiers are encouraged to translate their front-line experiences into drawings or paintings. *Signal,* a Nazi weekly published in French, regularly makes room for these amateur artists. The pictures provide evidence that the Nazi regime is favorable, even in wartime, to the development of highly cultural leisure activities. This is an extension of propagandistic promotion sponsored by the leisure organization *Kraft durch Freude* (strength through joy).

Thus, Nazi Germany now takes charge of obtaining exhibit space for these "soldier artists." In Paris, the Jeu de Paume Museum is requisitioned to show works, principally drawings and watercolors, produced by soldiers of the *Wehrmacht.* The title is "Kunst der Front" (front-line art).

The exhibit consists of portraits, landscapes, and war scenes—completely unoriginal—the most mediocre result of what academic art and Sunday painting, with an assiduous technique, can produce.

LIFE IN "VISA-HOPE VILLA"

MARSEILLES

On March 25, André Breton, his wife, Jacqueline, his daughter Aube, and Victor Serge and his son Vlady sail aboard the *Capitaine Paul Lemerle*, a dilapidated

IT DIDN'T TAKE BRETON LONG TO ORGANIZE HIS COURT. EVERY SUNDAY, THE SURREALISTS PLAYED THEIR FAVORITE GAMES

cargo ship on which three hundred passengers are piled one on top of the other. On March 31, André Masson and his wife leave Marseilles aboard the *Carimare*. Their destination: New York, by way of the coasts of Africa and Martinique—the promised land.

If they are able to leave Marshal Pétain's France, which is under the boot of the Nazis, it is thanks to Varian Fry, a thirty-three-year-old American who came to Vichy France on August 23 of last year as a representative of CAS, the American rescue center. The rapidity with which France was defeated surprised everyone in the United States. Quickly understood were the dangers with which Article 19 of the Armistice Convention threatened antinazi politicians, artists, and intellectuals. They must be moved to the United States. Which is why Varian Fry came to Marseilles. He stayed in the Hôtel Splendid, then settled into a small apartment on the Rue Grignan, which serves as his reception office.

Fry had considered traveling all over the country by bicycle in order to contact potential exiles, but the news of his presence and of his mission spread so quickly that such candidates immediately presented themselves en masse. In order to house them, he rented a building with eighteen rooms located in the middle of a park. This villa, Air-Bel, is on the Marseilles-Toulon railroad line, one hour from La Canebière.

It didn't take Breton long to organize his court. A number of Surrealists are in the area, some having fled the occupied zone, others waiting for a visa. Every

Sunday, there were gatherings at Air-Bel. They always got around to games: making collages, "Exquisite cadavres," question-and-answer games, riddles, the truth game. Among the regulars were many painters: Victor Brauner, Oscar Domínguez, Max Ernst, Jacques Hérold, Wilfredo Lam, Hans Bellmer, and Masson. Among the writers were the ever-faithful Benjamin Péret, rebels such as René Char and Tristan Tzara, and passersby such as Arthur Adamov.

Two of the best moments were an exhibit of paintings by Max Ernst, which were hung from the plane trees in the park—several were bought by Peggy Guggenheim, who was passing through—and an auction of paintings with the actor Sylvain Itkine in the role of auctioneer. But if the Air-Bel villa is to remain part of the history of art, it will be thanks to the invention of a card game. The idea for it was Jacques Hérold's. The traditional figures are replaced by those of heroes dear to the unconscious of the Surrealists. The players drew lots: Brauner had Hegel and Hélène Smith assigned to him; Breton had Paracelsus. The Dream was shared by Domínguez and Lam; Ernst got Sancho Villa and the Ace of Love.

Not everyone can or wishes to leave France. The latest news is that Breton, after a stopover in Fort-de-France, where he is sub-jected to the harassments of the Vichy government, makes it safely to New York. So does Masson. An irony of fate: The United States refuses entrance to Victor Serge, he who had baptized Air-Bel villa "Visa-Hope Villa"; he is too marked by a revolutionary past. He sails on to Cuba.

For his part, Max Ernst leaves for Lisbon. On July 14, he flies with Peggy Guggenheim to New York's LaGuardia Airport on a Pan American World Airways clipper. As for Varian Fry: After a year of clandestine action, which arranges for the passage of more than one thousand refugees into the United States, he is turned away by Vichy as an "undesirable foreigner" and at the end of August is conducted to the Spanish border.

Tenants at the Villa Air-Bel. In the foreground is Wilfredo Lam with his wife; at the extreme left, Oscar Domínguez; behind them, at the right in profile, André Breton; and above him, Jacques Hérold.

The Death of Jawlensky

In 1896, Jawlensky left his native Russia for Germany. With his compatriot Kandinsky, he took part in the exhibitions of the Blue Rider. Except for the war years, which he spent in Switzerland, the major achievements of his career took place in Germany. In 1921 he settled in Wiesbaden, where he died recently, on March 25. In 1929, he suffered an attack of arthritis. Since then, almost paralyzed in both arms, he stubbornly continued to paint in solitude and contemplation. "Art," he loved to repeat, "is a yearning for God."

Donation by the Société Anonyme to Yale

Katherine Dreier has given to Yale University the famous collection of the Société Anonyme, which she founded in 1920 with Marcel Duchamp. The purpose of the Société Anonyme, over the past twenty years, was more to promote contemporary art in the United States than to collect works. These high-quality works display a cross section of the most important European and American artists of our period. They include, most notably, Albers, Archipenko, Arp, Brancusi, Braque, Calder, Chagall, de Chirico, Dove, Ernst, Kandinsky, Léger, Matisse, Mondrian, and Picasso, as well as a large number of lesser-known artists whom Miss Dreier wished to encourage.

The Second Death of Émile Bernard

Émile Bernard, the inventor—with Paul Gauguin in 1888—of Cloisonné Synthetism, died April 16 at the age of seventy-three in his studio on Quai Bourbon. It is his second death because, as Cézanne remarked: "He absolutely turns his back on what he develops in his writings." Even Van Gogh, who had so admired his young audacious work at Pont-Aven, begged him to become himself again. But, jealous of Gauguin's success, Émile Bernard had regressed into pompous Academicism.

ALEXEI VON JAWLENSKY: MATURITY. Around 1912. Munich. Städtische Galerie

Roland Penrose, the Camouflager

Soon after the defeat of France, the painter Roland Penrose, who organized the Surrealist exhibition in London in 1936, among other shows, was mobilized as an instructor of camouflage. In addition to the use of Cubism to break up forms visually, he teaches young recruits to smear their faces with cow dung, so as to conceal them from the eyes of the enemy. He has also been asked to test a greenish ointment made by a cosmetics firm. He coated the body of his friend, the beautiful and restless Lee Miller, who then became invisible against the landscape.

Enthusiasm for Dali in New York

An exhibit of the works of Salvador Dali is being held at the Julien Levy Gallery. Just before the French defeat in June 1940, the *enfant terrible* of Surrealism was among the first European artists to be exiled to the United States. He was already well known there, as he had visited several times. He sailed from Lisbon, accompanied by his wife, Gala. The exhibition, which has attracted a good crowd, displays his recent war "with eyes filled with infinite deaths," which he painted last year.

Gala and Dali with *The Face of War*, at the Julien Levy Gallery in New York.

THE END OF A GREAT SOLITAIRE

MONTPELLIER

Robert Delaunay died of the complications of cancer in Montpellier, where he retired after the French defeat. He was fifty-six years old. A generous, quick-tempered man—his colleagues had nicknamed him "Mister Punch"—he was, above all, one of the best contemporary painters. He initiated Inobjective Painting in 1912. He felt that it was the only art capable of expressing the entirely new world of the machine age.

Close to Cubism when he started out, he became known for his series on the Eiffel Tower, which his friend Rousseau, on his deathbed, accused him of having reduced to pieces. Then came his *Windows Simultaneously Opened*, which prefigure his nonobjective period.

His masterpiece is his *Homage to Blériot* of 1914, about which he wrote in his *Cahiers* (notebooks): "Constructive mobility of the solar spectrum; opening, fire, evolution of the airplane. Everything is round, sun, earth, horizon, fullness of intense life, of poetry that cannot be verbalized—life à la Rimbaud. The motor in the painting. Solar strength and force of the earth."

It is hard to believe that there has never been an official Delaunay retrospective in France. But at the International Exposition of 1937, he was entrusted with the decoration of the Air Palace and the Railways Palace, provided he used fifty unemployed painters. It was one of the times in this century when the synthesis of the arts, like during the Renaissance, reappeared in France, although on a very different basis. It was also his last important work. Illness made it difficult, if not impossible, for him to continue working normally.

ROBERT DELAUNAY:
RHYTHM I. 1940. Paris.
Musée d'Art Moderne de la Ville

FRENCH ARTISTS VISIT GERMANY

PARIS-BERLIN

Nazi Germany is trying to please French intellectuals. There are still some who, after the September exhibit called "The Jew and France" and in spite of the execution of hostages or "terrorists," respond favorably to the "charm" offensives.

Were the French artists who were invited on a study trip to Germany promised that their cooperation would facilitate the release of prisoners? Rumors circulate to that effect. Maurice Denis, however, declines the invitation, as do Bonnard and Matisse, who are also invited; they understand the role that the Nazis want them to play.

Some others do not consider the invitation a problem. The painters Derain, Van Dongen, Dunoyer de Segonzac, Friesz, and Vlaminck and the sculptors Belmondo, Bouchard, Despiau, Landowski, and Lejeune meet German artists and visit studios and exhibits. They attend many official luncheons. One is presided over by that extraordinary art lover, Field Marshal Göring.

The French artists are chaperoned by the sculptor Arno Breker, who conceived the idea of the trip, which he organized with Otto Abetz, the German ambassador to Paris. Breker believes that such exchanges can lead to better mutual acquaintance.

Despiau, Friesz, Segonzac, Van Dogen, and Derain as part of a delegation of French painters and sculptors about to leave for Germany.

YOUNG FRENCH PAINTERS EXHIBIT

PARIS

On May 10, at the gallery Braun, an exhibit opens that scarcely attracts the attention of the occupying Germans: "Twenty Young Painters in the French Tradition." The event, through the combined efforts of one of the painters, Jean Bazaine, and the director of Chêne publications, André Lejard, gathers together Beaudin, Berçot, Bertholle, Bores, Coutaud, Desnoyer, Gischia, Lapicque, Lasne, Lautrec, Legueult, Le Moal, Manessier, Marchand, Édouard Pignon, Suzanne Roger, Singier, Tal-Coat, and Walch.

At the opening, two officers of the German Propaganda-Staffel come into the gallery, look around, and leave without saying a word. Even though the works presented had nothing to do with Nazi esthetics (certain ones, close to being abstract, and very vivid in color, had some similarities to so-called "degenerate art"), the use of the expression "French tradition"—during these times of helpless confusion when people search the past for formulas that would lead to putting the nation right again—must have calmed down the censors. It is true that the exhibit benefits from the support of Young France, an association that was "official," but so antiauthority that its existence seems threatened, and which includes among its members Bazaine, Manessier, and Lautrec. All hold dear the Personalism of Emmanuel Mounier who, since 1934, has been against any form of indoctrination of art, and advocates the individual liberty of the artist as essential.

The model to which most of these young painters relate is not any tradition extolled by Vichy but the "authentic" tradition of medieval art and particularly of Roman art. This means a rejection of the linear perspective inherited from the Renaissance, the adoption of stained-glass windows, compartmentalized enamels, and tapestries from the Middle Ages. But it includes also lessons drawn from Fauvism and from Cubism, which, although more recent, are equally an integral part of our pictorial tradition.

Lapicque, an engineer, a physicist, and the author of a 1938 thesis on *"The Optic of the Eye and the Vision of Contours,"* a musician as well, but especially a magnificent painter, discovered that—contrary to the classical law, but according to stained-glass windows, tapestries, medieval enamels, or Rouen faience of the eighteenth century—it is the color blue that must be used for static objects in the foreground, and red, orange, or yellow in moving backgrounds, such as sky or water.

He has been putting his discoveries into practice since 1939, on canvases of great originality, and on the verge of abstraction. Over red and gold backgrounds, a blue grille stands out. Last year, deeply distressed by the defeat and the invasion, he had painted *Saint Catherine of Fierbois* and *Joan of Arc Crossing the Loire River*. Of a resolutely modern construction, this *Joan of Arc*, whose forms have the hardness of armor, incarnates combat against the invader. The red and the blue, besides their spatial functions, are allied to the white of the canvas and thus create the French national colors. The painting's subject prevents it from being part of the exhibit. But *The Maritime Vocation*, which is very close to *Joan of Arc*, represents the artist at Braun's, and astounds the Young Painters. Has not Lapicque given in it the principles of a novel type of representation?

CHARLES LAPICQUE: JOAN OF ARC CROSSING THE LOIRE RIVER. 1940. Paris. Palais de Tokyo

Thanks to Arno Breker, Adolf Hitler's favorite sculptor, Vichy France is dishonored. A large retrospective of his Hellenizing, academic art opens at the Jeu de Paume in Paris, with the blessing of those in that country who have chosen to live on their knees. While Picasso and Braque symbolize both modernity and the refusal to compromise with the Occupation, several great artists of the early part of the century, such as Léger and Mondrian, have left for the United States. There they have joined the Surrealists, who, like Max Ernst, have fled into exile in large numbers. Barely settled on the other side of the Atlantic, Ernst had painted a vast canvas, and gave it the unequivocal title Europe after the Rain.

1942

S U M M A R Y

ART AND HISTORY

Nazi Art Conquers Paris
The Biennale under the Sign of War
The Judgment of Paris

GREAT MASTERS

The *Patience* of Braque
Picasso's *Aubade*: Enigma or Parody

ART NEWS

The Disappearance of Baranoff-Rossiné
Death of González
The Foundation of VVV
Artists in Exile
Opening of the Musée National d'Art Moderne
In Brief

ART IN EXILE

New York, a European Capital
Peggy Guggenheim Shows the Surrealists

MASTERWORKS

Max Ernst Paints *Europe after the Rain*

ARNO BREKER:
COMRADES (DETAIL)

Exhibition of the German sculptor Arno Breker at the Musée de l'Orangerie.

NAZI ART CONQUERS PARIS

PARIS

From May 15 to 30, an exhibition at the Musée de l'Orangerie presents the works of the most famous of Nazi Germany's sculptors, Arno Breker. The cream of Paris society is present at the opening. Arletty, Sacha Guitry, Paul Morand, Jacques Chardonne, Jean Cocteau, and Serge Lifar—the art world of France's Vichy government does not miss the event. The official character of the exhibition can only encourage the regulars of elegant Parisian evenings to attend. Otherwise, they would risk being suspected of sympathizing with the "terrorists."

Breker lived in Paris from 1927 to 1934. He attended the Grande Chaumière studio. Thanks to his friendship with the Nazi minister of armaments, the architect Albert Speer, he returns to Paris with the honors of a celebrated artist. His reception is the occasion of a veritable diplomatic ceremonial. He receives a letter of congratulation from Marshal Pétain, and President Laval organizes a luncheon at the Hôtel Matignon.

Ultimately, Breker appears to be a pawn in the collaboration policy between France and Germany. All the "collaborationists" bring along their speeches. The minister of education, Abel Bonnard, opens the exhibition by paying homage to this "sculptor of heroes" that the times called for. The secretary of state, Jacques Benoist-Méchin, exalts Hitler as the protector of the arts, and he gives thanks to the war for having "fertilized the creative power" of Breker.

A committee of honor set up to sponsor the exhibition is quite an exceptional gesture. It includes the sculptors Paul Belmondo, Henri Bouchard, Charles Despiau, Paul Landowski, and Louis Lejeune, and the painters Derain, Van Dongen, Dunoyer de Segonzac, Friesz, Legueult, Oudot, and Vlaminck. A monograph by Despiau, including one hundred and twenty photographs, is put up for sale for the occasion.

From all sides, the significance of Breker's art is clearly indicated. It is monumental art which, ever since the Nazis came to power in Germany, has served to illustrate the ideological orientation of the Third Reich. In his

ARNO BREKER: SITTING YOUNG WOMAN

preface to the exhibition's catalogue, the art critic Jean-Marc Campagne emphasizes that Breker "has been esteemed worthy of forging the image of German youth," a youth that believes in strength. In like manner, Despiau speaks of a "virile" art that aspires to exalt "strength, physical health."

Such is what the Third Reich asks of Breker. It is understandable that he conforms, to the extent that obedience procures money and success. He would probably still be leading the bohemian life if Albert Speer, at the time general commissioner for the renovation of Berlin, had not in 1938 commissioned two monumental statues for the new chancellery.

Breker is forty-two years old. He has made his choice with total awareness: While modern painters are forbidden to show their works, he decides to give Germany, in his sculptures, the image of its Nazi aspirations.

To him, Greek tradition is merely the easiest medium for conveying the "values" extolled by the Third Reich.

The figures of his monumental sculptures are not simply representative of an academic art. They are perverted Academicism, pushed toward a didactic Symbolism. More muscular than the athletes of Greek antiquity, more taut than necessary to go to the limits of their capacity, his *Torch Bearer*, his *Man of Action*, and his *Thinker* make sure that everyone receives the message. Breker draws from tradition only the formulas that immobilize it, not the imagination that could enrich it.

During a trip to Florence, before he came to Paris in 1927, he was overwhelmed by his discovery of Michelangelo. Subsequently, he was nurtured by French sculpture as represented by Rodin, Bourdelle, and Maillol. A talented technician, he used the experience he had acquired to transform Nazi soldiers into heroes like those of antiquity, but usually clothing them in grandiloquent ideas rather than in their military uniforms.

(See also 1933, 1935, 1937, 1939.)

THE BIENNALE UNDER THE SIGN OF WAR

VENICE

Once sought after everywhere, the Biennale is no longer anything but a German-Italian coproduction, which four countries have joined: Spain, Hungary, and neutral Sweden and Switzerland. Italian predominance is obvious: Out of 3,560 works, 2,520 are Italian. Since 1928, Antonio Maraini, secretary general of the exhibition, has wanted to reduce foreign participation. His goal has finally been realized.

Even if the war has not suspended this important artistic event, it invades the pavilions of the Biennale in this peaceful city of the Doges. The pavilions of the enemy nations shelter a presentation of the Italian army. Official portraits, stylized scenes of combat, and representations of military installations are side by side. The air force called on painters such as Tullio Crali, Tato, and Dottori and the almost abstract painter Enrico Prampolini to carry out its section! Their idolatrous iconography of machinery and aviation reflects the warlike interests of the regime. The dynamic aviator panoramas, looking like documentary films, exalt the glorious deeds of the Italian air force. Thus these painters become the eulogists of Italian nationalism and of Mussolini.

Unlike the Third Reich, whose section reflects the academic precepts of National Socialist Realism, the Fascist regime knows how to put modern artistic styles at the service of propaganda, without decreeing an offical style.

In other pavilions, the traditionalism of mythological scenes and social portraits abounds. There are a few dancers and hunting scenes. Remarkable all the same are the rooms devoted to de Pisis and to de Chirico, who remains a great painter in spite of his apparent return to Academicism.

This exhibition, which glorifies the Rome-Berlin Axis, has considerable ideological value in this third year of the war. In spite of the material difficulties about which Maraini complains in the preface to the catalogue, the exhibition aims at affirming the cultural mission of Italy in the face of the "destructive barbarism" of the enemy. The Biennale is an instrument of Fascist propaganda.

THE FASCIST GOVERNMENT KNOWS HOW TO PUT MODERN ARTISTIC STYLES AT THE SERVICE OF PROPAGANDA, WITHOUT DECREEING AN OFFICIAL STYLE

"THE JUDGMENT OF PARIS"

The art of the Third Reich abounds in female nudes. Designated procreaters or women of pleasure under the heavy gaze of a Nazi Paris, they are Aryan from their hair to their nipples. They symbolize the new cult of beauty and of racial purity—the central dogma of National Socialism. The platitude of the compositions is equaled only by the uniformity and the repetition of an Academicism inherited from the nineteenth century. The gifts of the official artists reside more in their fidelity to the ideological line defined by Hitler than in their esthetic invention. New German art, conceived for eternity, is an endless bore.

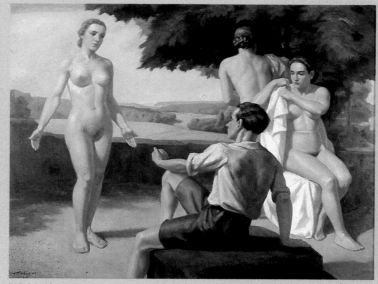

IVO SALIGER: THE JUDGMENT OF PARIS. 1939. Property of RFA

THE "PATIENCE" OF BRAQUE

GEORGES BRAQUE: PATIENCE. 1942. Lausanne. Private Collection

PARIS

Morose because of the war, a recluse in his studio at Montsouris Park, Georges Braque paints denuded little pictures, such as *Bread* and *Fish*. They are the fruits of these times of scarcity. Then he begins to attack a strange subject, which proceeds from his moral preoccupations and from the austerity to which he is constrained. It's about a woman who, enclosed within a stifling universe of fractured and overlapping spaces, dreams, but without being able to escape the still lifes that seem to hold her prisoner. He entitles his composition *Patience*.

After a period of sumptuous ornamental syntheses, animated and with clear, bright colors, whose objects and human figures seem to evolve into a state of weightlessness, Braque has since the beginning of the war been addicted to introspection and meditation, as though he has taken for his own this thought of Buffon's: "Genius is only a long patience."

Disproportionately elongated, the bust of the symbolic figure rises toward a double face, supported by an arm as rigid as a column; the other arm is stretched out in black curls. Two spaces coexist in the canvas: The first is tactile and totally vibrating; the second is directed in flight toward the window which opens out onto the night.

A few cards scattered by a skeletal hand, an abandoned chessboard, the solitary bottle of sherry, and above all the lost, faraway gaze: Everything suggests desolate waiting, the confused helplessness that the German occupation seems to have provoked in the soul of the painter. The anguish that wells up from the composition is, nevertheless, surpassed by the spiritual density of the inspiration. Never has Braque been so serious. Didn't he once say, "If painting doesn't disquiet, what is it?"

PICASSO'S "AUBADE": ENIGMA OR PARODY

PARIS

Since autumn 1940, Pablo Picasso, now sixty-one years old, has been living and working in his studio on the Rue des Grands-Augustins, where he painted *Guernica* in 1937. Dora Maar, his new companion, is by his side. During this time of war, the couple does not travel, with the exception of a few escapades to Royan. It is a period of fruitful work for the artist, who paints and draws tirelessly and has begun to sculpt again.

From this important ensemble of genres emerges a painting of large dimensions (6 1/2 x 8 1/2 feet) of undeniable pictorial quality and whose subject is utterly new. Entitled *Aubade*, the canvas is dated May 4. A young nude woman stretches out on a sofa. A female guitar player is to her right. At the left bottom corner, a picture frame fallen to the floor recalls drawings executed in September a year ago in which this motif appeared. It is easy to reconstruct the genesis of the work. Picasso loves to carry out series, exhausting all variations and plastic possibilities, duly signing each drawing and painting. *Aubade* was preceded by a series of drawings, dated May 1941, of a reclining, sleeping half-nude woman. In August, he gave her a companion, a discreet voyeuse. The theme was modified in September—the painter and his model become feminine figures. This year, the painter becomes a

PABLO PICASSO: AUBADE. 1942. Paris. MNAM

guitarist. The scene remains no less enigmatic. Is it about an "odalisque as slave"? Treated with the broken, dislocated spaces to which the painter has accustomed the viewer, this is one of his most disconcerting works. A feeling of parody, one of Picasso's usual tricks, should not be put out of mind. Light humor is distilled in this somber and tragic period.

The Disappearance of Baranoff-Rossiné

In these times of confusion and terror, it is noted that some artists suddenly lack appeal. This is what has happened to the painter and sculptor Vladimir Baranoff-Rossiné. He had worked in Paris from 1910 to 1917, then again in Russia until 1925, when he permanently established himself in Paris. He pursued his experiments with light and movement, which had always fascinated him. What has happened to the creator of the "optophonic piano," which combined sounds and colors? We have lost sight of him. Nobody knows!

Death of González

One of the greatest sculptors of our time, Julio González, died in Arcueil, where he lived; he was sixty-six years old. The originator of iron sculpture in 1927, he used oxyacetylene welding, which he had learned in the Renault factory during the First World War. Skillful at beating, forging, riveting, soldering, and embossing metal, he was both an imaginative spirit and a dedicated artisan. His best-known work is the monumental *Montserrat,* which he created for the Spanish Pavilion at the International Exposition in 1937.

The Foundation of "VVV"

Three V's, for Victory over the forces of death now unleashed across the planet, Victory over the exploitation of man by man, and Victory over the enslavement of the soul. The issue of the magazine *VVV* appeared in June. Max Ernst, editorial consultant, designed the cover. The director of the publication is David Hare, because of his American nationality. In this first issue, Breton has published an article of rebellion, "Prolegomenon to a Third Surrealist Manifesto or Not." The birth of the journal coincides with the arrival in New York of Marcel Duchamp, who has also been associated with the editorial committee.

VLADIMIR BARANOFF-ROSSINÉ: UNTITLED. 1938

JULIO GONZÁLEZ: MASK OF MONTSERRAT, SCREAMING. 1941-1942. Paris. MNAM

Artists in Exile

With the assistance of André Breton, the Pierre Matisse Gallery is giving an exhibition on "Artists in Exile" in New York, March 3 to 28. Side by side in the pages of the catalogue are Matta, Ossip Zadkine, Yves Tanguy, Max Ernst, Marc Chagall, Fernand Léger, André Breton, Piet Mondrian, André Masson, Ozenfant, Lipchitz, Berman, Tchelitchev, and Seligmann. It is apparent that the difficult conditions of exile have made the diverse origins and the conflicting esthetic and political views among these artists take on lesser importance. The exhibition places before the New York public an excellent summary of what the Parisian School was at the time war broke out.

Opening of the Musée National d'Art Moderne

Mr. Louis Hautecœur, General Secretary for Fine Arts, did not wish to wait for better times to open the new Musée National d'Art Moderne (national museum of modern art) at the Tokyo Palace built for the 1937 International Exposition. Only a third of the rooms were open, and the twenty Vuillard paintings belonging to the collections have not been displayed out of concern for their safety. But canvases of Valloton, Poncelet, and Brianchon can be seen, which are a good example of the spirit in which, for the past dozen years, acquisitions have been made in view of this opening.

NEW YORK, A EUROPEAN CAPITAL

NEW YORK

They arrived one after the other. Painters, sculptors, musicians, filmmakers, poets. The first to move here encouraged their friends to follow. Exile brings forth solidarity. All of them were famous in Europe. Now they are here, reunited in a cosmopolitan colony that counts among its ranks the richest artistic talents of the old continent: George Grosz, the expressionist painter; Kisling, the wily old resident of Montparnasse; Zadkine, Mondrian, Léger, Ozenfant, Chagall, Gropius, Moholy-Nagy, Mies van der Rohe, the musicians Milhaud and Schönberg, the dramatic author Bertolt Brecht, the filmmaker Fritz Lang, and Surrealists—the last wave of immigrants: Max Ernst, Tanguy, Breton, Duchamp, Masson, and others.

All had fled a Europe set on fire and bloodied by Hitler. For some of them, migration had gotten under way at the beginning of the century. They left various countries, and relocated in Paris, where the artistic life was experiencing tremendous excitement. The defeat of France, the occupation of the country by Nazi troops, the anti-semitic persecutions forced many to pick up their belongings once again and leave their adoptive country. The French joined them to get to New York, the city that had become, in these sad times, the symbol of liberty.

If American artists have without reticence, even often in a brotherly manner, received the refugees of art, the New York galleries, on the other hand, for the most part turn up their noses at these inspirational "stars," who are judged to be too European. There are also problems of communication: Few of the European artists speak American English. It is not surprising to learn that these people in exile miss the cafés of Pigalle and Montparnasse. Lucky ones have found a job, generally teaching at a college.

Artists exiled in New York. From left to right, first row: Matta, Zadkine, Tanguy, Ernst, Chagall, Léger; second row: Breton, Mondrian, Masson, Ozenfant, Lipchitz, Tchelitchev; back row: Seligmann and Berman.

PEGGY GUGGENHEIM SHOWS THE SURREALISTS

NEW YORK

Duchamp at the beginning of autumn organizes the exhibit entitled "First Papers of Surrealism." Peggy Guggenheim then opens her gallery, Art of this Century, to the Surrealists. An architect, Frederick Kiesler, organizes the space where Tanguy, Duchamp, Matta, Ernst, Masson, and Man Ray are shown. The paintings are hung in a corridor resembling a subway tunnel. In fact, every two minutes, the noise of a train makes the partitions tremble, and the lights of the gallery begin to blink. The American artists who attend the opening in large numbers are surprised by the décor of the staging. It does not prevent them from looking at the works very attentively.

Surrealist exhibition in New York.

MAX ERNST: EUROPE AFTER THE RAIN, II. 1940-1942. Hartford. Atheneum Museum

MAX ERNST PAINTS "EUROPE AFTER THE RAIN"

NEW YORK

"Bonito! Bonito!" If Max Ernst finally manages to get to the United States and completes *Europe after the Rain,* one of his masterpieces, it is thanks, curiously, to the customs officers at the train station in Champblanc, a village in the Pyrenees, at the Spanish border.

The artist was detained there by the stationmaster, a Frenchman with the responsibility of verifying the exit visas of travelers. He found Ernst's to be a little suspicious and confiscated his passport. The artist was asked to go to the customs room, where he had to open his valises. At the very moment that Ernst expected to be turned back, he heard the customs officers say: "Bonito! Bonito!" They had just uncovered rolled canvases that left them in a state of admiration. The stationmaster, in awe as well, declared while returning Ernst's passport, "Monsieur, I adore talent. Monsier, you have a lot of talent. I

admire it." Ernst once again took his seat in the train taking him to the safety of Spain.

If his works please so much, it is because they belong to his recent, so-called decalcomania period. Children know the procedure well. It consists of spreading more-or-less-diluted black ink on a sheet of white paper, covering the sheet of paper with another sheet, then applying unequal pressure on them with a hand, thus obtaining a thousand nuances. Victor Hugo had had recourse to this procedure in some of his wash drawings. Oscar Domínguez rediscovered it and transmitted it to Max Ernst, who had the idea of trying the experiment with sufficiently fluid oil paints. The result was immediately astonishing.

It has been five years since the artist became a decalist. He owes to the process an entire flowering of lichens and mosses, of old veined trees, of somber sea rocks. But never before had he used it with as

much mystery as in *Europe after the Rain.*

The painting, of average dimensions (it measures about 2 x 3 feet), was begun in 1940, then taken up several more times in Marseilles, at the Air-Bel villa, where the artist lived while waiting to leave France, then again in Princeton, New Jersey, where he settled down after marrying Peggy Guggenheim. This is the second canvas that the artist devoted to the same subject. It is presented as a desolate landscape, mixing people, rocks, trees, and various architectural structures, all struck by an internal cataclysm that ate away their substance. It is a world of destroyed temples and eroded palaces, a world in which a few anamorphic humans, breathing polluted air, can scarcely survive.

The first version is quite different. It depicts a geographical map of Europe, deformed in every direction, a little like medieval maps on which coasts

are not accurately made. This second version is more bizarre, more inhuman, desperate: Like frottages, or rubbings, a process to which the artist owes the plates of his *Natural History* and his mythical *Forests,* the decals reveal a hallucinatory Automatism. But never before had Ernst pushed hallucination to this point of nervous tension. *Europe after the Rain, II* is the image of a world in ruins, seen from the abysses within humans.

Ernst has exhibits in New York, Chicago, and New Orleans, but his painting does not have appeal. Only the young painters demonstrate enthusiasm. But with just as much admiration as the stationmaster in Champblanc, Gypsy Rose Lee, the queen of New York striptease, for want of the dramatic *Europe after the Rain,* buys another, more pleasing decal, and asks the artist to paint her portrait, please.

(See also 1924, 1926, 1928, 1936, 1941, 1976.)

The national honor has been saved. With the series Hostages, painted in hiding by Fautrier in the old Chateaubriand home where he has taken refuge from the Gestapo, the Resistance has found its artist. Never before has a modern artist showed wounds, bruised sores, bloody flesh with such anguish. And in another act of bravura, Picasso, whose works the Nazis sanction in exhibitions of "degenerate art" throughout Europe, is one of the few people to accompany the remains of Soutine, a Jew, to the cemetery. Le Corbusier engages in resistance as well, but in his own way. His **Conversation with Students of the Schools of Architecture** *challenges the Neoclassical values upheld by the Occupation.*

1943

S U M M A R Y

AVANT-GARDE

Fautrier or the Flesh of Hostages
An Unknown Named Pollock

DEVELOPMENTS

Color above All
Picasso Buries Soutine

ART NEWS

Dubuffet in the Metro
The Wehrmacht Imitates the Bauhaus
Otto Freundlich Is Assassinated
Picasso, a Toreador and Bicyclist
The *Merzbau* Is Destroyed by Bombs
In Brief

WRITINGS AND THEORIES

Le Corbusier: Where Does Architecture Stand?
Henri Focillon: the Life of Forms

LITERATURE

FRANCE
André Frenaud's collection of poems, Les rois mages *(the three wise men from the East) enjoys great popularity.*
Antoine de Saint-Exupéry publishes Flight to Arras *and, illustrated by the author,* The Little Prince.

GREAT BRITAIN
T. S. Eliot publishes Four Quartets.

THEATER

UNITED STATES
Death of Max Reinhardt in New York. After a distinguished career as director of the Deutsches Theater in Berlin and founder of the Salzburg Festival, he devoted himself to motion pictures after his emigration to America.

FRANCE
Jean-Louis Barrault produces, at the Comédie Française, The Satin Slipper *by Paul Claudel; the play had been considered unstageable, but now enjoys a triumphal success.*
At the Théâtre de la Cité, Charles Dullin produces Jean-Paul Sartre's first play, The Flies.

MOTION PICTURES

UNITED STATES
Alfred Hitchcock films Shadow of a Doubt.
Casablanca by Michael Curtiz is immediately popular.

FRANCE
Premiere of Le corbeau *by Henri-Georges Clouzot.*

JEAN FAUTRIER:
SMALL HOSTAGE NO. 2. 1943
Paris. Private Collection

FAUTRIER OR THE FLESH OF HOSTAGES

CHÂTENAY-MALABRY

A child prodigy, at the age of thirteen he was accepted by the Royal Academy of London where, after the death of his father, his mother had taken him. Now forty-five, Jean Fautrier is the honor of French painting while so many artists are siding with the Nazi occupiers.

Here are the facts: Fautrier passes mail to the Resistance. His friend, the writer Jean Paulhan, warns him to go into hiding with no delay, because the Gestapo is looking for him. Paulhan gives Fautrier an address: the hospital of Dr. Savoureux, in Châtenay-Malabry, which takes in exhausted intellectuals. The hospital occupies the house in the Vallée aux Loups in which Chateaubriand lived from 1807 to 1817. It is there that Fautrier begins, in total secrecy, a series of paintings devoted to the painful theme of hostages.

The studio that Dr. Savoureux makes available to the artist is at the back of a garden and, in fact, occupies the upper floor of the Velleda tower in which Chateaubriand wrote *The Martyrs*. From that tower, Fautrier can hear German trucks rumbling along a byroad that leads to the wood of elms where the hostages they are transporting will be shot. He can hear the noise of bullets reverberating through the clusters of trees. It is intolerable. His works thus are less the image of the tortured, such as exist in great number in painting, as the moving imprint or trace they leave on the soul.

The paintings appear as substances that sometimes are heightened by drawings in either gentle or violent tones, carried to lyrical heights and as removed from abstract art as from representational art. They are not bodies, but open and bloody wounds, bruised injuries, greenish or reddish flesh in states of decomposition. There was a bygone era in which painters were required to depict historical events: the barricades of the

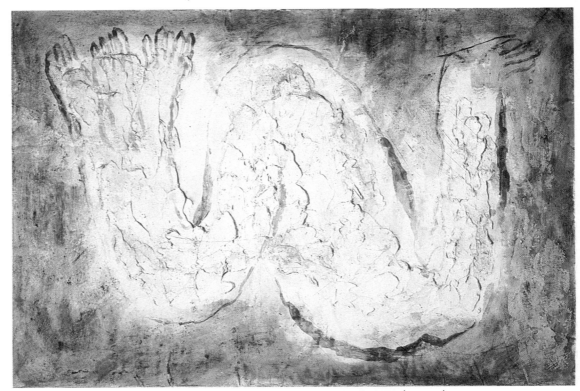

JEAN FAUTRIER: L'ÉCORCHÉ. 1942. Paris. Private Collection

Commune, the coronation of Napoleon, the first ball gown. And even Picasso's *Guernica* is an ultimate massacre of the innocents themselves. In Fautrier, on the other hand, there remain only packs of nerves, cut while still alive, a moment of tragic release into which the artist throws his instinct.

Fautrier would never have achieved such results if he remained faithful to oil painting and the easel. For quite some time, he has been working flat on the floor, using pastes, colored powders, and a variety of inks. He prefers paper to canvas, backing it later to allow for better adhesion. He begins by priming his paper with a coating of Spanish white and glue, which constitutes less a background than a sort of "field" with a hard crust, uneven on the inside and from which he extracts his substances and floats his images. The images can stretch out or overflow as they like; they can contract or open exactly like a living material.

Fautrier had his first exhibit in

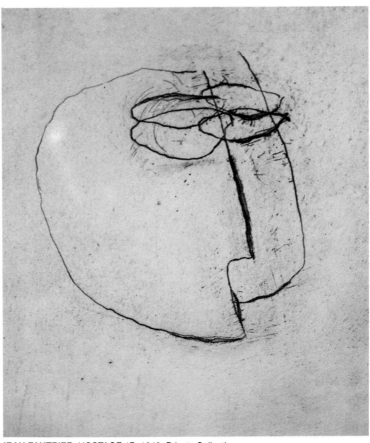

JEAN FAUTRIER: HOSTAGE 1B. 1943. Private Collection

AN UNKNOWN NAMED POLLOCK

1921, in a garage. Jeanne Castel, who was to become a famous art dealer, had met him at a painter's gathering. He was dressed in gray, he kept away from the others, and he suggested a young Dominican. Madame Castel, who thought he was a bit pale, advised him to drink cod-liver oil. She decided to exhibit ten of his canvases in the garage of her husband, Marcel Castel. The critics did not deign to attend, for fear of getting dirty. But his painting already translated a tragic sense of life.

In 1927, Louis Vauxcelles, who coined the word Fauvism, then the word Cubism, wrote: "This odd Fautrier whose exhibition has just opened at Georges Bernheim's is a unique painter. What he does resembles nothing that is known. This somber, moving art conceals a fierce soul."

To which André Malraux adds, in 1933: "In several of his canvases, the subject becomes a pretext to a dense and powerful writing. We have here a temperament that is rich, with an almost constant tragic resonance, probably due to the very nature of the artist, but also to his two-fold search: To push the intensity of color to its extreme and to capture the essence by dint of sacrifices." At the time, Fautrier was painting "abominable things," such as animals with disjointed thighs and bursting entrails. Present already was his fascination with defilement, prefiguring today's *Hostages*.

In *The Martyrs* Chateaubriand relates in epic style the deeds of the first Christians. When Fautrier unveils his paintings, it is seen that he, too, is pursuing a celebration of torture, but by completely different means. The Nazi who rolls by under Fautrier's windows, now ever more nervous because he can feel the hour of defeat approaching, does not suspect that right under his nose a destitute painter, sought by the police, is in the process of depicting, in a series of canvases snatched from destiny, the martyrology of France refound.

(See also 1964.)

NEW YORK

Peggy Guggenheim presents the painter Jackson Pollock for the first time in her gallery, Art of this Century, November 9 to 27. Born in Cody, Wyoming, the artist is thirty-one years old. He has been living in New York for thirteen years. Fourteen canvases of enormous power are shown, and James Johnson Sweeney has written the presentation text. "Pollock's talent," he says, "is volcanic. He is fire, outpouring, indiscipline. He bursts with a not yet crystalized mineral extravagance. He is sumptuous, explosive, troubling."

Very few people agree, however, that such talent is found in the young Pollock. The critic Clement Greenberg is one of the few people to understand his language and to take up his defense. He writes in the periodical *The Nation*: " . . . He is the equivalent, even if it is in a negative and somewhat impotent manner, of that American chiaroscuro dominated by Melville, Hawthorne, and Poe, and which Blakelock and Ryder have best rendered in painting." About two of the most important pieces in the exhibition, Greenberg writes: "*Guardians of the Secret*, like *Male and Female*, zigzags between the intensity of an easel painting and the sweetness of mural paintings." As for Sweeney, he ends his review by asserting that "among the young painters of our time, Jackson Pollock, by his exuberance, his independence, and his innate sensitivity, holds the promise of an exceptional future."

Still very young, Pollock has linked himself to the small number of American painters who are the most progressive—such as Stuart Davis, Arshile Gorky, Rothko, De Kooning—before becoming interested, through Picasso and Masson, in the forces of the unconscious, either personal or collective. His paintings depict the bird of dreams, or the Roman she-wolf, or Pasiphaë, but in a style closer to Automatic Writing than to representative description. He is influenced by aboriginal art from the American East and by the murals that have come out of the Mexican revolution, each one located on the fertile terrain of archetype and mythology. Peggy Guggenheim has commissioned from Pollock a huge mural work, to be twenty-three feet long. Marcel Duchamp has suggested to the artist that he execute it on canvas so that Miss Guggenheim may take it along in case she one day moves to another home.

(See also 1952 and 1956.)

JACKSON POLLOCK:
THE MOON WOMAN
CUTS THE CIRCLE.
Around 1943.
Paris. MNAM

CHAIM SOUTINE: HOUSE ON CRETE. 1919-1920. Private Collection

PICASSO BURIES SOUTINE

PARIS

During a brief ceremony at the Montparnasse cemetery, the painter Chaim Soutine is buried on August 11 at three o'clock in the afternoon. Under the beautiful sky of a summer day, homage is paid by Marie-Berthe Aurenche, his companion since 1940 and the former wife of Max Ernst; Gerda Groth, a German Jew whom Soutine called Mademoiselle Garde and who shared his life between 1937 and 1940; and Cocteau and Picasso who, defying the most elementary rule of security, do not fear being seen at the burial of a Russian Jew.

Soutine, tortured, anguished, the victim of all sorts of excesses dating from his first years in Paris, settling here in 1911, had for many years been suffering from a stomach ulcer. The ulcer became perforated during his stay in a village in Touraine,

Champigny-sur-Veude, where he had been hiding from the Nazis with Mademoiselle Aurenche. After a long and painful return to Paris, he is operated on. He dies the morning of August 9 without regaining consciousness. He is fifty years old.

After the ultrarich American art collector Albert C. Barnes had in a single stroke acquired a hundred of his paintings in 1923, Soutine rapidly enjoyed a certain amount of fame. Critics and art lovers were filled with enthusiasm for him—Georges Charensol and Waldemar Georges, for example, and the art historian Elie Faure, who devoted a monograph to him in 1929. The art lovers Madeleine and Marcellin Castaing invited him to spend summers on their property near Chartres from 1931 to 1935. Obsessed by the poverty that he had known only

too well, Soutine had a curious relationship to money. He conducted himself like a miser, but with bizarre whims. He refused to own two pairs of shoes, and stayed at home when his only pair had to be resoled. On the other hand, he collected beautiful light-gray felt halts for which he paid a great deal of money!

Rarely happy with himself, he would buy back or swap his old canvases for new ones, then would destroy them. He also lacerated recent works with which he was not entirely satisfied. He was fascinated with Rembrandt, and made two lightning visits to Holland to see his paintings in the Rijksmuseum.

In the roar of the war, his death goes all but unperceived. But his works are sought after. There is no doubt that a great artist has been extinguished.

(See also 1923.)

COLOR ABOVE ALL

SAINT-GERMAIN-EN-LAYE Just as his last illustration work, Paul Claudel's *The Tidings Brought to Mary*, was being edited, the painter, writer on art, and originator of the Nabi movement, Maurice Denis, is crushed, at the age of seventy-three, by a truck whose headlights suddenly blind him. He dies on November 13 in his large house in Prieuré and is buried, according to his wishes, in the white layman's robe of the Dominican order.

He was nicknamed the "Nabi of the beautiful icons," so strongly was his art —marked by the influences of things Japanese and by Gauguin—tinted by a tender mysticism derived from the Italian Primitives. In 1919, Denis founded the Ateliers of Sacred Art, along with Desvallières and Rouault. We owe to him numerous religious decorations found in chapels, churches, and basilicas, as well as in public buildings: the Théâtre des Champs-Élysées, the Petit Palais, the Senate, the Palais de Chaillot.

His themes of privileged inspiration were the exaltation of familial love (he had eight children by his two wives) and Christian faith. Evidence are his illustrations of Verlaine and of the *Imitation of Jesus Christ*, commissioned by Vollard, or paintings such as *The Catholic Mystery* and *Easter Morning*.

In 1890, he was the author of one of the founding statements of modern painting: "It is to be remembered that a painting, before being a war horse, a nude woman, or any old anecdote, is essentially a flat surface filled with colors arranged in a certain order." Later, returning in part to the audacity of his youth, he wanted to institute "a New Classical order."

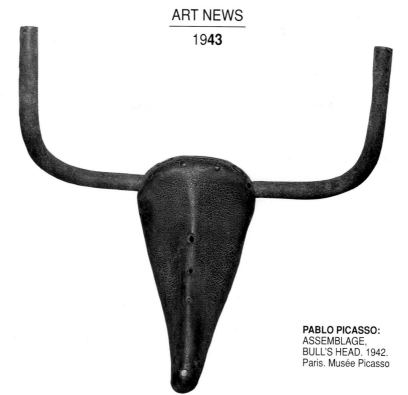

PABLO PICASSO: ASSEMBLAGE, BULL'S HEAD. 1942. Paris. Musée Picasso

Dubuffet in the Metro

Jean Dubuffet, forty-two years old, who, unhappy with his work, twice gave up painting for the wine business, has completed a series on passengers in the metro. They are simple drawings of men and women in funny hats, squeezed like sardines in a can, with huge noses in the middle of their faces, in garish contrasting colors skillfully placed on canvas or paper. The artist, who has always had an ambition to paint "man in a business suit" hopes to develop this theme further, for his personal pleasure, into a little album composed of lithographs, whose text will be written by his friend and admirer, the writer Jean Paulhan.

The Wehrmacht Imitates the Bauhaus

Military people definitely like modern art better than civilians! Previously, during the First World War, camouflage was born from the abhorred Cubism, which was particularly successful at interrupting angles and breaking up masses. Now, the Atlantic Wall constructed by the Nazis to protect the continent from an Allied invasion permits more than one comparison with the principles governing the avant-garde builders: on the architectural level, in economy of form, and in the use of concrete. The *Wehrmacht* is imitating the Bauhaus that Hitler closed when he came to power.

Otto Freundlich Is Assassinated

The sculpture *The New Man* by Otto Freundlich had the questionable honor of gracing the cover of the catalogue of the 1937 exhibition of "degenerate art" in Munich. Was it the pioneer of abstract art—he was one of the best colorists—the sculptor, or the man who came to the aid of those detained in Hitler's concentration camps that the Nazis had it in for? In any case, he was arrested on February 21 at Saint-Martin-de-Fenouillet, a hamlet in the Pyrénées-Orientales where he was hiding. Freundlich was immediately deported to Poland. He died on March 9 at the Lublin-Maidanek camp, at sixty-five years of age.

Picasso, a Toreador and Bicyclist

Picasso is a god who creates a world out of nothing! It was, no doubt, to maintain this well-established reputation that the artist recently created his *Assemblage, Bull's Head* by simply assembling a bicycle seat and a set of rusty handlebars. The idea came to him in a fraction of a second, when he discovered them in a scrap heap. The artist merely soldered them together, as he has often done with other objects from the trash. But this time he is thinking of casting his unusual montage in bronze, without in any way eliminating the form of the seat or the handlebars. He believes this is a necessary condition, so that his *Head* will not lose any of its effect of surprise or mystery.

IN BRIEF...

GERMANY
Death of Oskar Schlemmer, at Baden-Baden. Professor at the Bauhaus from 1920 to 1929, he was involved in sculpture and theater.

UNITED STATES
In New York, Alexander Calder retrospective at MOMA, and exhibition "Art in Progress" where the Large Glass of Duchamp is celebrated for the first time.
  Clifford Still takes his place as head of the San Francisco School, with an exhibition at the City Museum.

FRANCE
In the Galerie de France in Paris, exhibition "Twelve Painters of Today," including Albert Manessier, Léon Gischia, Jean Bazaine, Gustave Singier, and Édouard Pignon.
  Nicolas de Staël settles in Paris, where he suffers enormous financial difficulties; Jeanne Bucher buys his canvases and drawings.

NORWAY
Death of the sculptor Gustav Vigeland in Oslo.

SWITZERLAND
Death of the painter Sophie Taeuber-Arp in Zurich. Accident or suicide?

The "Merzbau" Is Destroyed by Bombs

On the night of October 8, an Allied bombardment of Hanover destroyed Kurt Schwitters' *Merzbau*. Its tentacles had invaded eight rooms of his house when he left to take refuge in Norway in 1937. The force of despair made him then begin a new construction, which the Nazi invasion of that country forced him to abandon. Today Schwitters lives in a small house in a London suburb. In light of the announcement of the destruction of the first *Merzbau* and the forced abandonment of the second, will he have the strength to begin his life's work again?

One of the blockhouses of the German Atlantic Wall, at Saint-Brévin-l'Océan.

LE CORBUSIER:
WHERE DOES ARCHITECTURE STAND?

How to reconstruct France? The war was not yet over when Le Corbusier shared his inner thoughts with architecture students, at their request, on October 18, 1942, on the occasion of an epoch-making lecture. Below are passages from this lecture, published just now by Denoël under the title *Conversations with Students of the School of Architecture*. In it, the great architect goes over some of the ideas he holds dear on the art of building. We should note that as someone who was strongly opposed by the people of his generation, he sends his message to young people, who, in his eyes, are alone capable of taking up the architectural and urban revolution toward which he has long worked.

In no other age has a society been as helpless as ours, for it has lost and broken off the contact between its physical lifestyle and the natural elements of its spiritual conduct. Severance of contact between ends and means, absence of a line of conduct. In building, lack of restraint is at its peak, for a Byzantine spirit deprives reasonable ends of the most prodigious means of achievement civilization has ever known. At the hour of his greatest material power, man is deprived of views . . .

The tasks that beckon our mechanized society are immense here in France, as they are in the whole world.

We must reconstruct departments ravaged by war, but that is nothing. Hasn't the country for a long time had to construct itself, reconstruct itself, reconstitute itself as cells are reconstituted in tissue or families in households, through new generations, thus acting out the eternal play of life?

Alas! We were sound asleep and our country was covered over with dust . . .

Outside—in the universe, taking place at the same time, were the conquests and ravages of a technical revolution whose philosophical conclusion would assuredly come to pass at the fateful hour. This revolution of consciousness that awaits us.

We see values that are centuries old, millenia old, cracking, even crumbling. The speed of automation was spreading new information to every part of the territory. Natural relationships were violated and man, in some sense, made unnatural, abandoning his traditional ways, losing his footing, accumulating horrors all around him, the result of his lowered social status: his dwelling, his street, his city, his suburb, his countryside. A new and encroaching, filthy, funny, boorish, cruel, and ugly built-up area, sullying countryside, cities, and hearts.

Le Corbusier.

Everything has been accomplished, taken to the worst extremes—a consummated catastrophe. The man of these past hundred years, by turns sublime and base, has strewn the ground with the detritus of his acts. Architecture is dying out, another is being born! . . .

A page is turning; this page that is turning is you, the young people of this unprecedented era, who will cover the blank flyleaf with a flowering of grandeur and intimacy.

LE CORBUSIER
Conversations with Students of the
School of Architecture *(Excerpts)*

HENRI FOCILLON: THE LIFE OF FORMS

A professor at the Sorbonne and later at the Collège de France, Henri Focillon died at the age of sixty-two in the United States where he had been teaching an archaeology course at Yale University since 1940. An art historian, he had written major works on Romanesque sculpture and nineteenth- and twentieth-century European painting. In the United States, Focillon worked for the cause of Free France, energetically fighting with the word and with the pen for what he hoped would soon be a victory by the Allies. As a way of paying tribute to both the scholar and the man, below we are printing excerpts from his most famous book, *La vie des formes* (the life of forms), an essay on methodology and on doctrine that was first published in 1934.

At a time when we are considering the question of the life of forms in matter, we are not separating one notion from the other, and if we use two terms it is not to endow an abstractionist process with objective reality but rather to bring out the constant, indissoluble, irreducible character of de facto harmony. Hence, form does not act as a superior principle that fashions a passive mass, for we can consider that matter imposes its own form on form. Indeed, the question is not one of matter and of form in themselves but of matters in the plural, numerous, complex, changing, having an appearance and weight, issuing from nature but not natural.

A number of principles can be derived from what we have just stated. The first is that matters have a certain calling or, if you will, a certain formal mission. They have a consistency, a color, a texture. They are form and, as such, they call on, limit, or develop the life of artistic forms. They are chosen not only because they are convenient to work with or, to the extent that art serves needs in life, because it is a good thing to use them, but also because they lend themselves to a particular treatment, because they impart certain effects. Hence their form, in its utter crudeness, provokes, suggests, propagates other forms, and, to use a seemingly contradictory expression, because they liberate them according to their law. But we should note without further ado that this formal vocation is not a blind determinism, for—and now we come to the second point—these matters, so appropriately characterized, so suggestive and even so demanding of art forms, over which they exert a kind of attraction, are, in turn, profoundly changed by them.

Thus the matters of art and the matters of nature are divorced from each other, even if they are bound up by strict formal convention. We see a new order setting in. There are two distinct reigns, even without bringing in techniques and production. The wood of the statue is no longer the wood of the tree; sculpted marble is no longer marble from the quarry; gold that is cast and hammered out is a metal without precedent; the brick that is baked and constructed bears no relationship to clay from the claypit. Color, texture, and all the values that affect the visual sense of touch have changed. Surfaceless things, hidden behind the bark, buried in the mountain, trapped in the nugget, submerged in the mud, have separated from chaos, acquired an epidermis, adhered to space, and taken in light that fashions them in its turn . . . The visible life of matter has been transformed . . .

We are reminded of what Flaubert said about the Parthenon—"black as ebony." Perhaps by that he meant an absolute quality—the absolute on a scale that dominates matter and which even transforms it, or simply the stern authority of an indestructible thought. But the Parthenon is in marble, and this is extremely important, so that the cement tambours that respectful restoration has interspersed among the columns could seem no less cruel than mutilation. Is it not strange that a volume could change, according to whether it takes shape in marble, bronze, wood, according to whether it is painted in distemper or oil, engraved with the burin or lithographed? Do we not risk confusing epidermal and surface properties, which can be easily changed, with others that are more general and constant? No, the truth is that volumes, in their various states, are not the same, as they depend on the light that shapes them, that brings out their fullness or hollowness and makes the surface the expression of a relative density . . .

HENRI FOCILLON
La vie des formes (Excerpts)

1944

SUMMARY

Kandinsky leaves this world a few months after the Liberation. He was seventy-eight at the time, and had been the creator of the first abstract watercolor in 1910. And Mondrian dies in New York, where he had sought refuge. With these two deaths, a page in twentieth-century art turns, at the same time that abstract art puts its mark on the world. But already other quests, other names are appearing: Dubuffet, Vasarely, and in the United States Baziotes, Motherwell, and Tobey, whose work is validated after Jackson Pollock had suddenly erupted onto the international art scene in the preceding year.

GREAT MASTERS

Kandinsky: with Closed Eyes
In Kandinsky's Words

DEVELOPMENTS

The *Harmony* of Maillol Will Remain Incomplete
The New Beginning of the Indépendants

ART NEWS

Sartre Plays Picasso
The Third Reich Will Not Get Its Paintings
Norman Rockwell Contributes to the War Effort
Pollock the Engraver
The Death of Munch
In Brief

AVANT-GARDE

The Automatism of Motherwell
Tobey Exhibits the "All-Overs"
Dubuffet Jostles the Human Face
Vasarely Exhibits at a Hat Shop

KANDINSKY: WITH CLOSED EYES

NEUILLY-SUR-SEINE
Wassili Kandinsky is dead. He was seventy-eight years old. He had celebrated a birthday on December 3. On the thirteenth, the state of his health declined, and that very evening he passed away gently, without suffering. Ever since March, he had difficulty taking the familiar walk that every afternoon after his nap had taken him to the Bois de Boulogne. At first, he barely paid attention to it, but then he was stricken with arteriosclerosis, and his illness worsened.

Under the Occupation, the American Embassy on several occasions urged him to go to the United States. But he had become a French citizen in 1939, and he intended to remain in France. He loved Paris, even if Paris had not loved him very much.

Indeed, it can not be said that Kandinsky, who was born in Moscow in 1866 and became a naturalized German, was received with open arms when he took refuge in France in July 1933.

Hitler had barely come to power when he began to fulminate against modern artists, labeling them demented criminals. Ludwig Mies van der Rohe, the last director of the Bauhaus, where Kandinsky had been teaching the grammar of forms, received imperative instructions from the Nazi police: "You must turn out Kandinsky, he is dangerous for us due to his spirit." It was Marcel Duchamp who found a little apartment for the painter and his wife, on the seventh floor of a building under construction in Neuilly on the bank of the Seine. Kandinsky wanted an expanse of water under his windows.

Tall, wearing narrow-rimmed glasses, reserved without being shy, he took a visitor's hand, plunged his half-closed eyes into the visitor's the first time he received him in his studio, and murmured after a long silence, "Now I know you!" Is that what was displeasing? The artist, in any case, was received coldly by the Parisian avant-garde for the reason that the Parisians liked

WASSILI KANDINSKY: LANDSCAPE WITH TOWER. 1908. Paris. MNAM

nothing, or almost nothing, outside of the late Cubism that Gleizes and Metzinger had duly curbed with rules and precepts. Kandinsky was already recognized internationally, though his abstraction was disconcerting.

Between Kandinsky and his colleagues, as well as between him and those who became his dealers, the dialogue was as between deaf people. It is so to this day.

His widow, Nina, confides: "He possessed the rare talent of being able to represent in his mind the world of his paintings, with their colors and their forms, exactly as he later set them down on canvas." It is possible that many of these colors and forms, particularly those belonging to his last period, their myriads of rings swarming across the surface of the work, proceed from the phosphenes, both circular and luminous, that are at times impressed on the eyeball when the eyelids are lowered. This seer, who scrutinized his visitor from half-closed eyes, would have painted in his last years what he was seeing with closed eyes.

It must not be concluded that Kandinsky outright turned his back on external reality. In Murnau, where he spent his vacations in the beginning of the century, he painted admirable landscapes of the Bavarian Alps. He was forty-four years old when he completed his first abstract watercolor. Discounting his apprenticeship years, there are two great periods that can be seen in his work. The first, in the wake of his abstract watercolor, runs the gamut from superabundance to romantic vehemence. Some of these can-

WASSILI KANDINSKY:
LAST JUDGMENT. 1912.
Paris. MNAM

vases, such as the *Last Judgment* and especially *Composition 3* (springtime) and *Composition 4* (summer), are superb. A second period, featuring strict geometrical entanglements, is colder, more calculating. It began around 1925, while Kandinsky was teaching at the Bauhaus, and is sustained through the rest of his life, leading to an ultimate profundity.

"Of all the arts, abstract painting is the most difficult," he said. "It demands that you know how to draw well, that you have a heightened sensitivity for composition and for colors, and that you be a true poet. This last is essential." And in his most important book, *About the Spiritual in Art,* published thirty-three years ago, he judges that painting is nothing if it doesn't express what he called "the principle of internal necessity."

There exist two conceptions of color, for the most part opposed to each another. One of them, purely retinal, was put forward by Newton. It rests on the simultaneous play of complementary colors (blue, red, yellow) and contrasting colors. It is found in the Inobjective Painting of Delaunay, who uses it to express the dynamism of modern life. This conception is the daughter of the exact sciences. The second conception comes from Goethe and addresses the soul. It is this second that is found from beginning to end in Kandinsky, inscribed between two metaphysical "nothings," black and white.

Indeed, all of this scarcely addresses a Cartesian and materialistic France. Kandinsky believed in the imminent arrival of spiritualism. At the very moment he passes away, Paris has just been liberated. Even if it is true that the war is not over, Hitler was right: Kandinsky remains dangerous because of his spirit, so much does it seem today that he is the true bearer of the future.

(See also 1908, 1910, 1911, 1926, 1927.)

IN KANDINSKY'S WORDS

Each period of a civilizaton creates an art that is specific in it and which we will never see reborn. To try to revive the principles of art of past centuries can lead only to the production of stillborn works.

Those who hunger for illumination, those who see, remain on the fringe. They are derided, they are treated as mad. But these few rare souls resist and are vigilant. They have an obscure need for spiritual life, for knowledge, for progress.

All methods are sacred if they are internally necessary. All methods are sins if they are not justified by internal necessity.

The artist who allows his gifts to go unused is a lazy slave.

If, from today on, we set about cutting all of our links with nature, tearing ourselves from her, unhesitatingly and with no possibility of turning back, contenting ourselves exclusively with combining pure color with a freely invented form, the works that we would create would be ornamental, geometrical, and at first glance very little different from a tie or a rug.

The true work of art is born from the "artist": a mysterious, enigmatic, and mystical creation. It detaches itself from him, it acquires an autonomous life, becomes a personality, an independent subject, animated with a spiritual breath, the living subject of a real existence of being.

Painting is an art, and art in its entirety is not a goalless creation flowing into nothingness. It is a power whose goal must be to develop and to refine the human soul.

The artist is not a "Sunday child" for whom everything immediately succeeds. He does not have the right to live without duty. The task that is assigned to him is painful; often, it is a heavy cross for him to bear.

White rings like a silence that suddenly could be understood. It is a "nothing" full of juvenile joy or, to put it better, a "nothing" before all beginnings. Thus, perhaps, resonated the earth, white and cold, during the days of the glacial era.

Like a "nothing" without possibility, like a dead "nothing" after the death of the sun, like an eternal silence, without a future, without even the hope of a future, black resonates internally.

WASSILI KANDINSKY:
THE BLUE OF THE SKY.
1940. Paris. MNAM

THE "HARMONY" OF MAILLOL WILL REMAIN INCOMPLETE

BANYULS-SUR-MER

Aristide Maillol dies in a car accident on September 24 in Banyuls, where he was born on December 8, 1861. He leaves unfinished the sculpture of a standing nude that he had entitled *Harmony.* The title characterizes his entire work. Rodin pointed out to Octave Mirbeau: "Do you know why Maillol's work is so fine? Because it doesn't engage your curiosity." The author of *The Gates of Hell,* toward the end of his life, during a visit he paid Maillol in his studio, declared to him: "Maillol, when I am dead, you will replace me." Conscious that his work, like that of Michelangelo, was marked by a pervading despair, Rodin was thus expressing nostalgia for the sensual and peaceful equilibrium of the Greek order, of which Maillol was precisely the heir. "His art is nude and ingenuous," said Maurice Denis of his friend who had joined the Nabi movement.

Maillol was at first a painter, encouraged by Gauguin, whom he had met, in 1892, through their mutual friend Daniel de Monfreid. The next year, he created a tapestry workshop in Banyuls, but had to give up his miniature creations because he was ruining his eyes. It was in 1900 that he began to devote himself to sculpture, with a talent immediately appreciated by Ambroise Vollard.

Maillol moves to Marly-le-Roi in 1903 and two years later enjoys his first success, with his *Mediterranean* at the Salon d'Automne.

Such a supple manner of modeling forms could only impress Auguste Renoir, who discovered his own vocation as a sculptor while watching Maillol execute a bust in Cagnes in 1907. Whether Maillol baptizes his figures *Venus, Pomona, Île-de-France,* or *Leda,* he pays homage to women by transmitting "the kiss" that he said he had "received from Greece."

ARISTIDE MAILLOL:
STATUE AT THE JARDIN
DES TUILERIES.
1906. Paris

THE NEW BEGINNING OF THE INDÉPENDANTS

PARIS

Paris could not celebrate her liberation only by singing and dancing. Art had to have a role as well. The Salon d'Automne becomes simultaneously that of the Liberation, exhibiting from October 6 to November 5 works by Villon, de Staël, Léger, Gromaire, Braque, Delvaux —and seventy-four canvases and five sculptures by Picasso. An entire gallery of the Palais des Beaux-Arts is reserved to the genius about whom Louis Parrot wrote in *Les lettres françaises,* on October 7: "It is only just that the artists of Paris who helped bring about the liberation of the capital have thought to pay homage to the painter who has most effectively symbolized the spirit of the Resistance." Since *Guernica* (1937), the public had not seen any more works by Picasso. More significantly, this is the first time that the artist participates in a Salon.

But after the surprise comes the scandal. The public had forgotten about the style of painting that contorts, dislocates, swells, and dismembers the human body. Canvases such as *Aubade, La femme à l'artichaut,* or *La chaise aux glaïeuls* stir up violent reactions. It is necessary to put together a team of painters and students to protect the artist's works. The National Committee of Writers protests in a motion signed notably by Louis Aragon, Paul Éluard, François Mauriac, Paul Valéry, Jean-Paul Sartre, and Georges Duhamel. Paris is free again.

Reunion in Picasso's studio after the reading of his play *Le désir attrapé par la queue*. From left to right, standing: Dr. Lacan, Cécile Éluard, Pierre Reverdy, Louise Leiris, Zanie Campan, Picasso, Valentine Hugo, Simone de Beauvoir; sitting: Jean-Paul Sartre, Albert Camus, and Jean Aubier.

IN BRIEF...

GERMANY
Publication of the Scholtz report, which lists 21,903 objects of art that have been confiscated by the Nazi authorities.

BELGIUM
Exhibition of one hundred canvases by Paul Delvaux at the Palais des Beaux-Art in Brussels.

UNITED STATES
At the MOMA, "Twelve Contemporary Painters," including several canvases by Jackson Pollock.
  The sculptor Ossip Zadkine settles near Tuscon in Arizona.

FRANCE
Henri Matisse illustrates Pasiphaë by Henry de Montherlant.
  At the gallery l'Esquisse, "Abstract Paintings" with Domela, Magnelli, Kandinsky, de Staël.

SWITZERLAND
Exhibition "Concrete Art" in Basel, organized by Max Bill, painter, sculptor, and professor of industrial esthetics in Zurich.

Sartre Plays Picasso

Le désir attrapé par la queue (desire caught by the tail), the Surrealistic play written by Picasso, without grammar or syntax, during a frigid January three years ago, has been presented with an ideal cast. In the principal roles were: Jean-Paul Sartre, Round Piece; Simone de Beauvoir, the Kitchen; Raymond Queneau, the Onion; Michel Leiris, the Big Foot; Dora Maar, Thin Anguish; Germaine Hugnet, Fat Anguish; Zanie Campan, the Tart . . . The reading of the play took place on March 19, in the apartment of Zette and Michel Leiris on the Quai des Grands-Augustins. Albert Camus was responsible for introducing the characters, announcing the acts and describing the décor. The audience was impressed by the artist's talent for comedy.

The Third Reich Will Not Get Its Paintings

In August an action of the SNCF (the French national railroad) narrowly prevented a final pillage by the occupiers. One hundred and forty-eight cases with paintings confiscated from Jewish collections—Cézannes, Gauguins, Degases, Braques, Modiglianis, Picassos, and other works by great modern artists considered "degenerate" in the Reich—were to be shipped to a warehouse in Czechoslovakia, to be sold to finance the Nazi war machine. However, the boxcars never left the Parisian region thanks to a series of simulated technical accidents. The timely arrival of Leclerc's army made it possible to return them to their point of departure, the Jeu de Paume Museum, while waiting to return them to their owners.

Norman Rockwell Contributes to the War Effort

All America is familiar with Rockwell's subjects: daily life, adolescents reading newspapers, Boy Scout camping, a tramp grilling his hot dogs . . . The contribution he is now making to the war effort is effective. His posters *The Four Freedoms,* illustrating the objectives of President Roosevelt, are in everyone's mind. In 1916 he did his first *Saturday Evening Post* cover. Since that time, he has provided illustrations for it more than three hundred times. His clean and descriptive style and his characteristic manner of grasping significant detail explain his unfailing popularity.

Pollock the Engraver

The many artists who passed through the engraving studio of S. W. Hayter since its establishment in 1927 at 17 Rue Campagne-Première found there a friend to whom nothing about engraving was unknown. Fleeing the war, Hayter came to New York in 1940 and opened his Studio 17 there. American artists did not snub him. That is how Jackson Pollock came to be initiated into the techniques of engraving. It is said that the experiments of Masson, who also works with Hayter, impressed him. Working with the chisel and the Automatism it permits appear to interest Pollock to the point where he wants to spend several months doing nothing but engraving.

The Death of Munch

Edvard Munch died in Ekely on January 23, full of anger on seeing his country occupied by the Germans. He was the painter who had the most influence on the principal German artistic movement of this century, Expressionism. He has bequeathed his work to the city of Oslo. His old Swedish friend Hilma af Klint, one year his senior, followed him to the grave. She is leaving her work to the Swedish town of Jarna, on condition that nothing be shown for twenty years. She had exhibited Munch in her Stockholm studio beginning in 1894, at the time she herself was executing Automatic Paintings and drawings under the influence of theosophy.

THE AUTO-MATISM OF MOTHERWELL

NEW YORK

Robert Motherwell, one of the American painters closest to the Surrealist group here, has been experimenting with the techniques of Automatism.

At the University of Stanford, in California, he discovers and is in awe of the collection of the works of Matisse that Michael and Sarah Stein put together when they lived in Paris.

The speech that André Malraux in 1937 devoted to the war in Spain strongly impresses Motherwell and proves to be a determining factor in orienting his future work. It stimulates the interest that this particularly cultivated artist showed during several trips to Europe. The New York milieu of exiled Surrealists, including Duchamp, Ernst, Lam, Masson, Tanguy, and Breton, fully appreciates Motherwell, although they reproach his painting for being too "abstract" for their tastes.

Robert Motherwell and Jackson Pollock are introduced to each other by the painter William Baziotes, who knew Pollock when they were both working for the WPA, created by the

ROBERT MOTHERWELL: PANCHO VILLA, DEAD AND ALIVE. 1943. New York. MOMA

A PARTICULARLY CULTIVATED ARTIST SHOWING GREAT INTEREST IN EUROPEAN ART

Roosevelt Administration for unemployed culturists during the Depression. The three painters intend to bring together a group of young artists who would collaborate on what the Surrealists call "Automatism." The project is never completed, but Motherwell, Pollock, and Baziotes, as well as their wives, begin to write "Automatic" poems together, each one writing a line in turn, the whole then assembled without a logical order, a little in the style of "Exquisite Cadavers."

In Pollock's studio, Motherwell and Pollock make their first collages. Motherwell, on the advice of Baziotes and Matta, invites Jackson Pollock to participate in the exhibition "First Papers of Surrealism," organized two years ago by the Surrealists. Pollock, who doesn't care for group activities, refuses to join.

Motherwell's writing, which has appeared in the magazine *VVV* and in *The Document of Modern Art,* of which he is the director, reflects the passions and preoccupations of contemporary artists.

The Museum of Modern Art is the first museum to buy a Motherwell. It is an important painting: *Pancho Villa, Dead and Alive.* Peggy Guggenheim organizes the first one-man exhibition of Motherwell, in her gallery, Art of this Century.

TOBEY EXHIBITS THE "ALL-OVERS"

NEW YORK

This year marks an anniversary and a date for Mark Tobey. Ten years ago, he took his first trip to the Orient. This April, his first one-man exhibition is held.

The nineteen works retrace the decade. Tobey wove his canvases with semiautomatic "White Writing." The infinite order of the world is evoked by an inextricable network of vibrionic lines and signs. From *Broadway Norm,* the first example of "White Writing," which dates from 1935, to the recent works, the public grasps the suppleness of Tobey's processes and his indifference concerning the walls erected between abstraction and representation.

Through the diversity of his works, accomplished in a descriptive or purely rhythmical style, Tobey tries to express what the content of reality is to him: a movement woven into the deepest dimension of time. His ambition is to lose all individuality, so that his work will be pure invitation to meditation. It is the principle of the "All-Over" style.

Although the composition of a painting is traditionally conceived as a construction of parts linked to one another by the vehicle of perspective, the space of the "All-Overs" is indivisible. It is facilitated by his tendency to be monochromatic. The representation acquires, on the other hand, a force accentuated by the continual evolution of arabesques, with no movement from top to bottom, only convergences toward the center. From this point, the eye reaches the depth of the work, perhaps even more: the heart of all reality.

Tobey's canvases are thus situated beyond simple lyrical abstraction. Perhaps "abstract icons" is the apt description.

DUBUFFET JOSTLES THE HUMAN FACE

PARIS

The first conspicuous exhibition of liberated Paris is that of an unknown artist at the gallery Drouin. He is Jean Dubuffet. His paintings, which resemble children's drawings in their deliberate clumsiness, provoke a scandal of the kind that hasn't been seen for a long time. The gallery receives anonymous letters, the guest book is covered with insults. To say the least, no electricity is passing between Jean Dubuffet and the public.

The artist is endowed with solid artistic knowledge, having attended the Beaux-Arts School in Le Havre. He went back to painting only two years ago, at the age of forty-one, after two abortive attempts. (He had made a career as a wine merchant.) Exempted by his family's fortune from the need to sell his paint-

JEAN DUBUFFET: COUNTRY HOUSE. 1944. Private Collection

ings, he has only to follow his own desires. He plays with awkward forms, with graffiti, with scribbling, with crude materials. He rediscovers the origin of art. His works recall a child's drawing and stress the importance, for Dubuffet, of the works of the mentally ill, which he collects ardently and to which he was sensitized notably by the book that Hans Prinzhorn devoted to the subject in 1922.

Dubuffet has his admirers. His friends Georges Limbour and Jean Paulhan appreciate his painting. He is preparing illustrations for a collection by the poet Francis Ponge. In spite of the simplicity of Dubuffet's themes (the metro, Paris, daily life), his anticultural will is not accepted. He wishes to remain, he says, a "common man," but—and this is no small paradox—the common man himself does not recognize him.

(See also 1945, 1961, 1973, 1985.)

VASARELY EXHIBITS AT A HAT SHOP

PARIS

Inaugurated in June, closed during the Liberation, the exhibition of graphic works and drawings by Victor Vasarely reopens its doors in the autumn on the third floor of 124 Rue La Boétie, in the apartment of Denise René, a milliner, who transformed it into a painting gallery for the occasion.

Thirty-two years old, Vasarely was trained at the Budapest Bauhaus, the branch of the famous institution created by the painter Alexander Bortnyik. He settled in Paris in 1930 and, to earn his living, did advertising work, mainly for Havas and for Draeger in Montrouge, where he discovered airbrushing.

A virtuoso of *trompe l'oeil*, he

is mainly fascinated by optical effects. These are found in the exhibition in his *Harlequins*, his *Zebras, Échiquiers*. All play on the ambiguity of form and content, binary contrasts and reversible images. *Heads* is traced on the surfaces of a cube seen in axonometric perspective, alternatively concave and in relief. He also paints on cellophane, superimposing several sheets in order to obtain a multidimensional effect of depth through transparency.

Vasarely's work has been well received. But he is reproached for not being really in the realm of painting. The artist replies that his productions are conceived as the opposite of easel paintings, rather as partitions that can be repeated infinitely.
(See also 1955 and 1969.)

VICTOR VASARELY: GRAPHIC STUDY IN AXONOMETRIC PERSPECTIVE. 1934. Gordes. Musée Didactique Victor Vasarely

Mondrian, who died the previous year, is given the retrospective refused to him during his lifetime in New York's Museum of Modern Art. This signifies international recognition of the person who, with Malevich, was the great initiator of Abstract Geometric painting. Also in the United States, Peggy Guggenheim introduces a new painter, Mark Rothko, whom she exhibits in her gallery Art of This Century. In France, the Salon de Mai is created, and Picasso follows Guernica with Charnel House, inspired by the horror of the concentration camps, discovered after the defeat of Nazi Germany.

1945

SUMMARY

GREAT MASTERS

The Posthumous Victory of Mondrian
In Mondrian's Words

EXHIBITIONS

Morandi in Florence
Rothko at Art of This Century

ART NEWS

Fautrier Exhibits *Hostages*
Creation of the Salon de Mai
Hans Grundig in Moscow
Denise René Opens a Gallery
In Brief

ART AND HISTORY

Picasso: the Horror of the Camps

WRITINGS AND THEORIES

Jean Dubuffet: For Art Brut

LITERATURE

FRANCE
Death of Paul Valéry.
Robert Brasillach is sentenced to death and executed.
Foundation of the magazine Les temps modernes *by Jean-Paul Sartre.*
Publication of Blaise Cendrars's collection of memoirs, L'homme foudroyé.
Maurice Merleau-Ponty publishes the existentialist work Phenomenology of Perception.

ITALY
Carlo Levi's Christ Stopped at Eboli *brings him worldwide recognition.*

MUSIC

AUSTRIA
The composer Anton Webern is killed by an American soldier on sentry duty.

UNITED STATES
Death of the Hungarian composer Béla Bartók. The funeral is paid for by the New York Society of Composers.

THEATER

FRANCE
Homage to Jean Giraudoux with the performance of The Madwoman of Chaillot.
Shakespeare's Hamlet *is performed by the Renaud-Barrault troupe in the translation by André Gide, with sets by André Masson.*

PIET MONDRIAN:
VICTORY BOOGIE-WOOGIE. 1943-1944.
Connecticut. Private Collection

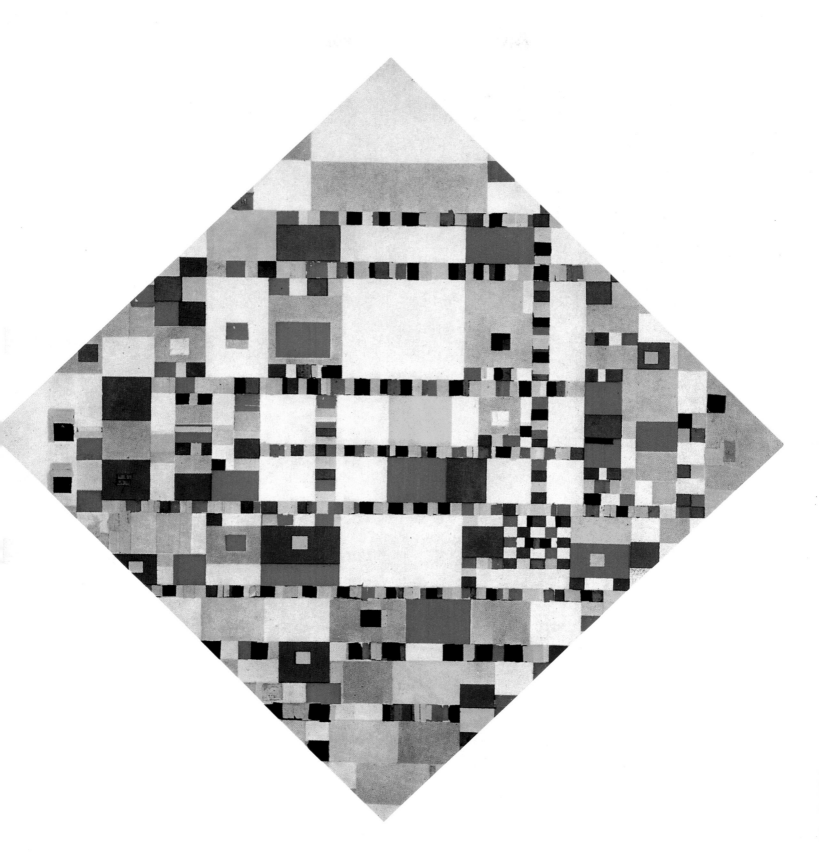

THE POSTHUMOUS VICTORY OF MONDRIAN

NEW YORK

He loved New York. He arrived here on October 3, 1940, from London, where he had moved two years earlier, to flee the Nazi air raids that were making a hell of the English capital. In the evening he liked to take walks around Rockefeller Center. The geometry of the lighted windows seemed like his paintings to him. His last works are images of New York. And it is New York that will hand him the triumph that Paris had always refused him.

The retrospective of Mondrian's works that can be seen at the Museum of Modern Art is the first that has ever been devoted to him, and it occurs one year after his death. Mondrian died of pneumonia at Murray Hill Hospital on February 1, 1944, at the age of seventy-two.

His friend, the painter and poet Michel Seuphor, remembers: "During the twenty-three years he spent in Paris, he never had a single one-man show. He was distinguished by something else, and it was enough for him

PIET MONDRIAN: STILL LIFE WITH GINGER II. 1912. The Hague. Gemeentemuseum

Piet Mondrian in his study.

to be recognized by a small number of people. I think of the gatherings of friends on Friday nights in a little café on the Quai Voltaire, then at the Closerie des Lilas, which Robert Delaunay invaded with his noisy and candid verbosity. Mondrian listened and did not speak; without refusing to be sociable, he was simultaneously present and absent. To an outside observer, he may have appeared to be the least significant person at these gatherings of important personalities. But I don't think a single one of us did not experience his transcendent presence as support."

In 1917, Mondrian, as we know, originated Plasticism, an art of total clarity and strict economy of materials which, together with the Suprematism of Malevich, is the source of Geometric Abstraction. Formerly, in his native Holland, Mon-

drian had been a landscape painter. It was the impact of Cubism on his mind, with the liberation that it means in regard to objective reality, that revealed him to himself. Are the works of the great Cubists, such as Picasso and Braque, still measured alongside nineteenth-century painting, whereas those of Mondrian begin a new era? It is not impossible. It would appear that the essential is elsewhere: It is in the fact that this man, whose works culminate painting by an extreme of rigor, is also the man who wanted to destroy it.

There was something of the theosophist in Mondrian, and more than that, something of the mystic. For him, it was not a question of creating a new style that would come to be joined to all the other preexisting ones, but to have art pass into life and become useless from the moment that life itself, which he prophesized, would become a work of art for each one of us. This is the meaning of the horizontal-vertical rhythm that appears everywhere in his paintings and in which he saw the foundation and the essence of everything. And this was the reason as well for the reduction of his palette to the primary colors exclusively, accompanied by black and white. He wanted his canvases to be the icons of a city of the future, their goal being —by the fact that they were exemplary—to prepare its coming.

This explains the silence and the solemnity of Mondrian's works. Rarely has art been more ascetic. In 1924, the artist broke away from Théo Van Doesburg, who reproached him for his austerity and maintained that the slanted line at a 45-degree incline better corresponded to the dynamism of modern man. An admirable quarrel for painters! One that opposed two ways of being, two visions of the world, two beliefs, and two metaphysics.

But the slanted line is not the only thing that Mondrian had excluded from his paintings. Quite early, he had also suppressed curves and all greens because they reminded him of trees, which he loathed. He denied neither the omnipresence of nature, of which the Impressionists before him had made an object of delight, nor of matter; but they were a passage in which he saw mere chaos.

Perhaps right there is the secret of his inordinate love for New York, so very vertical and tossing her geometrical order toward the sky. His last compositions, *Broadway Boogie-Woogie* and *Victory Boogie-Woogie*, where the black grille henceforth disappears to make room for a quadrature of red, yellow, and blue squares, seem to be a hymn to the joy of living, as one can discover at the MOMA exhibition.

In order to survive, Mondrian had been a painter of flowers on porcelain for practically his whole life. Perhaps this also explains his hatred of nature. He is buried in Cypress Hill Cemetery where the rows of rectangular tombstones, set on level ground, evoke his paintings.

(See also 1917.)

IN MONDRIAN'S WORDS

In order to approach the spiritual in art, we will make as little use as possible of reality, because reality is opposed to the spiritual. Hence, there is a logical explanation for elementary forms. As these forms are abstract, we find ourselves in the presence of an abstract art.

Like religion, Art is superhuman and cultivates the superhuman element in man, and it is consequently a means of human evolution.

To consider relationships solely by creating them and attempting to balance them in art and in life is the lofty task of our day; it is a way of preparing for the future.

Freed of any utilitarian limitation, plastic art must not only keep pace with human progress, it must even stay ahead of it.

Everything is composed by relation and reciprocity. Color exists only through another color, dimension is defined by another

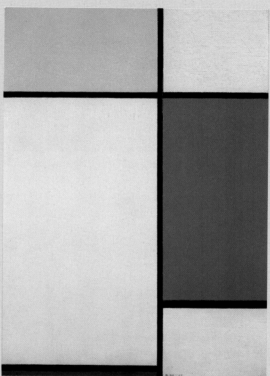

PIET MONDRIAN:
COMPOSITION. 1927.
Private Collection

Neither life nor art can be brought into being if we consider the spirit alone. Or matter alone. The unity of the two makes creation.

The universal can be expressed in pure manner only when the particular does not obstruct our path. Only then can universal consciousness (in other words, intuition), which is at the origin of all art, be rendered directly, giving birth to a purified artistic expression.

Neoplasticism depicts a precise order. It depicts equity, because equivalence in the composition of plastic forms indicates to everyone that equal but nonetheless different rights have been assigned.

dimension, there is no position except in opposition to another position. Form and color have found their proper use: From now on, they will be nothing but "plastic" means of expression and will no longer dominate in the work as they did in the past.

Neutral line, color, and form, "in other words, elements that have the appearance of something familiar," are established as a means of general expression. As these means represent the highest degree of simplification, young people are the ones who must preserve them, determine their composition, and establish them according to their nature.

MORANDI IN FLORENCE

ITALY

Giorgio Morandi is currently being honored by two simultaneous exhibitions, one in Florence at the Galleria dei Fiore from April 21 to May 3, and the other in Rome at the Galleria La Palma in April and May. His country has barely come out of the ordeal it suffered during the international conflict, and everyone is hoping for a refound liberty. With liberty, the polemics aroused by the esthetic position adopted by the artist are revived. After being arrested for acts of resistance, Morandi was obliged to keep out of sight. His arrest was followed by the rapid liberation of June 1943, along with his friends and intellectual defenders from Bologna, Roberto Longhi, Carlo Ludovico, Ragghianti, and Cesare Gnudi. Morandi has now withdrawn to Grizzana in the Bolognese Apenines, and

GIORGIO MORANDI: STILL LIFE. 1920. Milan. Private Collection

there, all alone, he never stops painting, drawing, and engraving.

We owe the exhibition in Florence to his lifelong friend Roberto Longhi, the historian and art critic. In Florence as in Rome, the collection of works covers the period from 1915 up to pieces completed just now. We find again that very personal universe, stripped of all trivial detail, composed of silence and of meditation, and denounced by his detractors. Today that universe appears to be symbolic of Morandi's moral commitment during the war: Detached from external events, he distances himself from the world.

The most recent works are particularly revealing of this attitude. In his still lifes, he uses familiar objects and multiplies their combinations. What captivates him are the relationships established between these mute accessories and the space arranged between them that animates the composition.

(See also 1939.)

ROTHKO AT ART OF THIS CENTURY

NEW YORK

Peggy Guggenheim has invited Mark Rothko to exhibit in the gallery that she created in 1942 and which immediately became the home of the Surrealists in exile. Born in Russia in 1903 and having emigrated to Oregon with his family at the age of ten, Rothko has been living in New York since 1925 and has already participated in numerous activities of New York artists. In 1936 and 1937, he worked in the programs of the Federal Art Project, designed to employ artists during the Depression. There he began important friendships with other artists, who were often living as he was, isolated in an American environment unreceptive to contemporary art.

The exhibition, which runs from January 9 to February 4, shows that Rothko has moved

MARK ROTHKO: HIERARCHICAL BIRDS. 1944. Washington, D.C. National Gallery of Art

away from the representative style that characterized his work up to the beginning of the forties, and we see that with the Surrealists he has found a vision that corresponds to his own search. In a radio program in 1943, Rothko expressed the necessity, in a period of upheaval such as ours, of finding a new language. For artists can no longer speak their anguish and their hopes in face of the contemporary world in the styles available to them. And he declared: "If our titles recall myths familiar from the time of antiquity, it is because we had to use eternal symbols to express fundamental feelings. They are the symbols of the primitive fears and motivations of man . . ."

Among the fifteen paintings now exhibited are *The Sacrifice of Iphigenia, The Syrian Bull, The Birth of the Cephalopods,* and *Omens of the Bird Gods.* All have free references to mythology. The horizontal organization of a space in which the abstract elements are in suspension is quite original, although it evokes somewhat that of Joan Miró.

ROGER BISSIÈRE:
BLACK VENUS. 1945.
Paris. MNAM

Fautrier Exhibits "Hostages"

Jean Fautrier is showing his major series *Hostages* at the gallery Drouin, with a catalogue prefaced by André Malraux. The *Hostages* were painted by the artist during the Occupation, in Chateaubriand's house in the Vallée aux Loups at Châtenay-Malabry, where he had taken refuge to escape the Gestapo. The works are the ultimate in Abstraction, but at the same time no one has ever succeeded in showing so penetratingly bruises, wounds, or living and decomposing flesh. It is not representational painting in that nothing is identifiable or descriptive. But at the same time, Fautrier's abstraction rejoins reality in deep and invisible areas.

Creation of the Salon de Mai

From May 29 to June 29, the gallery Maurs at 3 Avenue Matignon will be the home of a new salon, the Salon de Mai. It brings together fifty-eight painters, engravers, and sculptors and twenty-eight poets and writers. Its conception goes back to the end of 1943 when, in the back room of a modest café on the Rue Dauphine, a small group of hopeful artists met at the suggestion of Gaston Diehl. The participants represent the new generation of artists. No specific esthetic policy has been chosen; there is a beautiful eclecticism going from representation to Surrealism and abstraction. In addition to the homage rendered to the painter Roger Bissière, there are works by Labisse, Le Moal, Manessier, Gruber, Fougeron, Pignon, Prassinos, Singier, Nicolas de Staël, Tal Coat. The Salon de Mai is the salon of renewal, and it is being welcomed enthusiastically.

Hans Grundig in Moscow

Defamed for his politically aware art, Hans Grundig, a Verist painter of the New Objectivity, lived under the terror of National Socialism. In 1939, the racial insanity separated him from his Jewish wife, the painter Léa Grundig, who was forced to emigrate to Palestine. After spending five years in concentration camps, he followed the Red Army with three hundred other deportees sent to the front. He is now in Moscow, where he awaits his return to Germany.

Denise René Opens a Gallery

Denise René who, last year, emptied her milliner's workshop to exhibit the graphic works of Vasarely, is opening a gallery of paintings at 124 Rue La Boétie. The first exhibition will be the works of Max Ernst belonging to Paul Éluard. Also planned are a presentation of paintings by Lhote and his students, then a group show entitled "From Ingres to the Present," with drawings by the master of Montauban as well as canvases by Juan Gris, Modigliani, and Pablo Picasso. Denise René, however, does not want to stop there. She is seeking to create her own stable of artists, painters that she likes and wishes to promote.

PABLO PICASSO: CHARNEL HOUSE. 1944. New York. MOMA

PICASSO: THE HORROR OF THE CAMPS

PARIS

A sequel to *Guernica*! This is what Picasso painted over the course of last winter and the spring of this year. We are dealing with a painting of large dimensions (over 6 x 8 feet) entitled *Charnel House*, black, gray, and white like *Guernica* and for the same reasons. He, like others, was inspired by the photographs in the newspapers that—now the defeat of Hitler is confirmed—reveal the unbelievable to all eyes: the dead of Auschwitz, Buchenwald, Dachau, Ravensbrück, innocent victims of the most enormous attempt at extermination.

Did Picasso have any knowledge of the pitiless and final struggle for life waged among the prisoners in the gas chambers? And did he know about the pyramids of human bodies found there, formed as the sturdier ones among the victims hoisted themselves up onto the weaker ones, seeking a residue of breathable air near the ceiling in their crazed hope of escaping asphyxiation? His *Charnel House* in any case depicts a pyramid of three cadavers composed of a man, a woman, and a child piled on the floor of an empty room with the door ajar.

The heap that the three bodies form is curiously topped by a still life of large dimensions consisting of a casserole and a wine pitcher. One is at first taken aback by this amalgam of disproportionate elements, then everything becomes clear. Picasso, once again, wanted to avoid the too-literal detail, and in order to do this, he employed unusual parallels in order to mix the themes, to deform space, as in dreams, and to give the appearance of a nightmare to reality.

Only recently, unable to prevent the officers of the Nazi Kommandantur from visiting him in his studio on the Rue des Grands-Augustins, Picasso distributed to them, at the moment of their departure, postcards reproducing *Guernica*. He had written these words on them: "Emportez! Souvenir! Souvenir!" ("Take it! Souvenir! Souvenir!") And to the German soldier who offered him coal in these times of hardship, he retorted, declining the offer: "A Spaniard is never cold!"

Today, *Charnel House* makes one shiver. If *Guernica* prefigured modern warfare waged with technical weapons, we have here its result: white death. So atrocious that it marks a fatal threshold on which the idea of humanity stumbles.

JEAN DUBUFFET: FOR ART BRUT

The painters of the new generation have a dual problem to resolve: breaking away not only from the influence of tradition as did the great creators of modern art at the beginning of the century, but also from the influence of these very modern artists. Indeed, it is not easy to be innovative after Picasso, Matisse, Klee, or Kandinsky. That led Dubuffet to reflections on art in which he gives full recognition to ordinary accidents that have been carefully neglected or dismissed such as aberrations, formless formations, manifestations of chance. He proposes exploring new and unknown territories. The thoughts that follow afford a glimpse of his *Notes aux fins lettrés* (notes for literate purposes), to be published early next year by Gallimard.

STARTING FROM THE FORMLESS

The point of departure is the surface that must come alive—the canvas or sheet of paper—and the first splash of color or ink we put on it: the effect, the adventure that results. This spot, as we enrich and orient it, must guide the work. A painting is not built like a house, using the architect's reference points, but rather with our backs to the result—gropingly, as we back away! Alchemist, you will not discover how to make gold by looking at gold. Run to your retorts, boil some urine, watch, avidly watch the lead, that is where your task lies. And you, painter, splashes of color, splashes and outlines, look at your palettes and your rags, the keys you are seeking are there.

ABERRATIONS

Aberrations, too, must be represented in the chorus of the work of art. Why not have aberrations? Are they not human faculties? As such, are they not more or less abundantly part of the psychic mechanism of every human being? Will they not lead to the most precious discoveries? Does not art begin with aberrations? What exactly is an aberration? Isn't living one of them?

MAKE THE MATERIAL COME ALIVE

Man's thought takes off, it takes shape. It becomes sand, oil. It becomes a spatula, a scraper. It becomes the idea of oil or of the scraper. But at the same time, the scraper retains its own nature, and so it scrapes wildly and awkwardly without rhyme or reason and slips and scrapes next to the desired spot, slips out of our hand and sideways. And oil, too, preserves its nature, and so it flows and dries—so poorly, and so slowly that we become furious—and dries so unevenly too.

MAKING DO

It is only human to rely on chance. To refuse to draw from it what we can is illogical, it is

JEAN DUBUFFET: ARCHETYPES. 1945

self-satisfaction and foolishness. The camper who lights a fire lays his hand on what happens to be around, the twigs within his grasp, uses the wind, with sand makes a spot for a fire, if there even is any sand, otherwise with stones, if he finds them.

JEAN DUBUFFET
Prospectus aux amateurs de tous genres
(prospectus for all types of amateurs)
(Excerpts)

On his return to Paris, Léger loudly declares that America is an endless continent, and that Europe, badly wounded, must now come to terms with her. This does not prevent Matisse, now close to eighty, from finding a second youth, nor does it stop Picasso, at work in the Château Grimaldi in Antibes, from finally knowing *la joie de vivre*. But what is to become of the young European painters, now that everyone has recognized the damage Hitlerism has done to art? Meanwhile, in Buenos Aires, Fontana's White Manifesto makes its debut, and an extraordinary forger, Hans Van Meegeren, is brought to trial for having made false Vermeers during the war.

1946

S U M M A R Y

GREAT MASTERS

America Is a World without Limits
Fernand Léger: New York
Homage to Edvard Munch
Matisse Rediscovers the Splendor of His Youth
Picasso Bucolic and in Love

DEVELOPMENTS

Are the Forged Vermeers Forged Van Meegerens?
She Did End Up Looking Like Her Portrait

ART NEWS

André Breton Brings Back Indian Art
Rouault versus the Vollard Heirs
De Chirico versus de Chirico
Exhibitions in London
In Brief

AVANT-GARDE

Lucio Fontana: the White Manifesto

ARCHITECTURE

The Spiral-Shaped Museum of Frank Lloyd Wright
The Astonishing Prefabricated Houses of Jean Prouvé

FERNAND LÉGER:
BLACK DIVERS. 1944.
Paris. MNAM

FERNAND LÉGER:
LA GRANDE JULIE. 1945.
New York. MOMA

contortions, and whirlings of Michelangelo's ceiling in the Sistine Chapel. But a head, an arm, a leg flitting about and being found again on a vertical plane among footprints, or stretched out, elongated, thickened, disarticulated—these compositions without moderation and without direction are things he brought with him from the United States.

It's not that we can speak of an "American period" of Léger. His principal acquisitions, such as free-floating objects or the fragmentation of space, come from the thirties, and even further back, from the Cubists, when, as a respectful disciple of Cézanne, he reduced a Normandy landscape or a still life to an interlocking of cones, cubes, and cylinders. But the fact of living and working in a machine-oriented society, which has always appealed to him, has led him to maturity.

Indeed, Léger found a world of upheaval in the United States, of mass-produced objects that were neat and precise, of agricultural machines in the fields that were as beautiful as butterflies and even, paradoxically, cyclists who were all the more magnified in that they moved along in large bunches over highways that were deserted because of gas rationing.

Other paintings resulted, among them *La grande Julie,*

AMERICA IS A WORLD WITHOUT LIMITS

PARIS
In the very last days of the year that has just gone by, Léger returns from his five-year exile in the United States. The man who has always had the gift of turning a phrase doesn't have sufficient words to express his enthusiasm in an interview for the newspaper *Arts Spectacles*: "It's not a country, it's a world. There, everything is limitless. You find yourself before a power in motion with reserves of strength whose end cannot even be conceived of. An unbelievable vitality, perpetual motion . . ."

He comes back with forty or so canvases, about a third of what he painted during his stay: "I am bringing back very recent works . . . I was struck by the intensity of contrasts, of movement. This

is what I sought to express in painting. I want to translate the character of the human body evolving in space with no point of contact with the earth. I arrived at this by studying the movements of divers who throw themselves into the water from very high up. This fascinated me. You will see what I have done. In order to express movement, I have also taken cyclists as a theme, handsome guys and beautiful girls in red, yellow, and green sweaters."

Actually, his *Divers* derive from young dock workers diving into the oily waters of the port of Marseilles as seen from the ship that was ready to carry him to New York in October 1940. And they probably also originate from the powerful musculatures,

Fernand Léger in his New York study, 1942.

one of his masterpieces, painted shortly before he left New York. The painting depicts a young woman holding a flower in one hand and her bicycle with the other. She is young, healthy, without mystery, a carrier of the future. She is the anti-*Mona Lisa*, in opposition to the universally celebrated painting of Leonardo da Vinci, which is troubled and emotional and which represents everything that Léger hates most in painting.

However, if he is a painter of technological civilization (even at the beginning, Picasso was already calling him the "tubist"), Léger has never been a reporter or an illustrator. "It has never amused me to copy a machine. I invent images of machines, just as others invent landscapes from their imagination. The mechanical element is not a bias or an attitude for me, but a means of arriving at giving a sensation of force and power." Each artist possesses a weapon that permits him to brutalize tradition. Léger's weapon is to paint paintings that, independent of their subject, attract the eye as does a beautiful car.

In New York, Léger was able to exhibit every year, whereas in France he is far from being recognized as the equal of Braque or Matisse. He still remembers his participation in the Salon des Indépendants, "the great, ugly, and beautiful Salon" to which, trembling, he brought his first works at the age of twenty. During his years of poverty, at La Ruche, he ate cat meat and painted forged Corots to survive. Invited to Yale University as a part-time lecturer in 1940, Léger was bestowed with glory and honor by America. Why on earth did he come back?

(See also 1917, 1933, 1955.)

FERNAND LÉGER: NEW YORK

Before he lived there, from 1940 to 1945, Fernand Léger had been in the United States once, from September to December 1931, visiting New York and Chicago. He was fifty years old. His work may have been far from completed, but his style was for the most part set. However, he discovered across the Atlantic a mechanized civilization that fascinated him and at which he could only have guessed in the Old World. His discovery of New York was dazzling, as he wrote on his return for the periodical *Cahiers d'art* (art notebooks). Here is an excerpt.

The most colossal sight in the world. No film, no photograph, no journalist account could lessen the amazement of New York by night, seen from the fortieth floor. This city has been able to withstand all attempts to rob it of its glamor, all the curious people who have tried to describe it, to copy it. It retains its freshness, its unpredictability, its sense of amazement for the traveler who sees it for the first time.

The steamer, moving slowly, gently changes perspectives: We look for the Statue of Liberty, the gift from France. It is a tiny, unassuming statuette, forgotten in the middle of the port before this bold, vertical new continent. We cannot see her, in vain she raises her arm as high as she can. It is useless. Like a night light, she casts a bit of light on enormous moving objects, forms that, indifferent and majestic, cover her with their shadow.

Amazing country, where the houses are taller than the churches, where the window washers are millionaires, where they organize football matches between prisoners and the police!

New York, transparent, translucent New York, blue, red, yellow buildings! An extraordinarily enchanting spectacle, the light given off by Edison pierces all this and pulverized the structures.

The ethnic neighborhoods are wonderful at any time of day. There is a rawness, such a richness of raw materials. Russian, Jewish, Italian, Chinese neighborhoods. Third Avenue on Saturday night is like Marseille!

Pink hats for the Negroes. Shop windows where you will see a bicycle suspended over a dozen eggs, stuck in order in green sand.

Plucked chickens, suspended against the light, presented against a dark background—the dance of death!

FERNAND LÉGER
New York (Excerpt). Paris. 1931

FERNAND LÉGER:
FAREWELL, NEW YORK.
1946. Paris. MNAM

HOMAGE TO EDVARD MUNCH

EDVARD MUNCH: THE CRY. 1893. Oslo. National Gallery

OSLO

In 1944 Norway lost one of its greatest artists, the painter Edvard Munch, who alone exercised an international influence. This year a retrospective pays homage to him.

Born on December 12, 1863, into a family of physicians, Munch had a childhood darkened by the premature death of his mother when he was five years old and the death of his sister Sophie when he was thirteen. All his life, fear of illness dictated to him very peculiar and very strict rules of conduct. Thus he always avoided playing sports out of fear of wetting his feet. And if anyone had the misfortune of telling him that he didn't look too well, he immediately went to bed. He detested hyacinths and apartment plants because their scent reminded him of the odor of death. He never attended a burial.

His love affairs in the Bohemian circles of Oslo and Berlin marked his relationships with women in a definitive way. He thus depicts woman as having a vamp's features, robbing man of his independence, his strength, and his art, and then leading him to the grave.

His way of using pure color in order to create dissonance and of crunching features have had a considerable influence on Nordic art. His works are inscribed in the progression of Symbolist art works, which they extend by very different means. He is a painter of the soul who exposes nerves. The Modern Art Museum of Oslo, which today is commemorating him, presents a thousand paintings and an equal number of wood engravings. Brought together are the paintings of his youth, rich in sensuality, such as *Jealousy* or *The Kiss* and especially *The Cry*, his most famous canvas, which dates from 1893 and announces, by the figure holding his head with his two hands and its explosion of colors, the anguish of Expressionism.

MATISSE REDISCOVERS THE SPLENDOR OF HIS YOUTH

VENCE

Henri Matisse, who has gone back to Vence, is putting the finishing touches on a series of cutout papers for *Jazz*, an album that Tériade is to publish.

In his old age, he is also rediscovering the beginnings of his activity as a painter. At the age of twenty, he was operated on for appendicitis, which was at the time a serious illness, and during the long convalescence following his operation, he suddenly decided to devote himself to painting. And he decided this in the strangest manner.

His hospital neighbor, in the next bed, had received a game of patience, which consisted of cutting out colored figures that were then pasted on a backing so as to make of them a screen. Matisse got so interested in this

game that he asked his parents to get one for him, and as soon as he was better, he went to enroll in a school of fine arts.

For *Jazz*, he is devoting himself to cutouts of the same sort. The process he has perfected is the following: He covers sheets of paper with a fine layer of gouache, and then cuts with scissors into their surfaces, with no preliminary drawing, various elements that he assembles afterwards on other sheets in order to arrive at compositions that are flat colored surfaces.

Ever since Fauvism in 1905, Matisse has sought the method that would permit him to synthesize volume and line. As he says it himself, the technique of glued papers permits him "to sculpt color." And, thanks to his artistic maturity, his first fin-

HENRI MATISSE: JAZZ. CUTOUT XII: WOMAN SWIMMING IN THE AQUARIUM. 1943-1946. Paris. MNAM

ished works in this area seem destined to lead him toward a major accomplishment. He confides his impressions to a notebook: "Have your spirit pass into your hand, and not your hand into your spirit."

Alongside *Jazz*, Matisse envisions the decoration of a chapel in Vence as a sign of gratitude

toward the nuns who cared for him during the war. This chapel will include stained-glass windows issuing from his practice of working with cutout papers, and several murals in ceramic with black lines on a white background depicting a Way of the Cross, which the artist wishes to be totally tragic and bare.

PABLO PICASSO: LA JOIE DE VIVRE. 1946. Antibes. Musée Picasso

PICASSO BUCOLIC AND IN LOVE

ANTIBES

For four months, Picasso has once again settled down on the Côte d'Azur. Dor de la Souchère, a Latin professor in Cannes and the curator of the Château Grimaldi, which has been converted into a museum, proposed to the artist in search of a studio to come and work in the unoccupied upper rooms of the château. Between September and December, he completes about thirty paintings there, all of large dimensions and all marked by a tumultuous and infectious euphoria.

This period will probably one day be considered the "anti-*Guernica*" period. This tragic event, in which an entire civil population perished, had inspired in Picasso an immense composition, wherein his indignation was expressed in a cry. And since that time, his work was to remain totally impregnated by that "atmosphere of murder and barbarity."

In his Antibes canvases the artist seems, on the contrary, to abandon his past, at least for a while. At this time, he is paint-ing compositions in which the favorite subjects of classical antiquity are scattered about, engaged in the most youthful of liberties. An entire world of dancing or reclining nymphs, centaurs pawing the ground, endearing goats and deer, fauns, shameless satyrs, and triton musicians, evolve on the canvas

*LEAVING THE MOOD
OF TRAGEDY BEHIND, HE CREATES AN ENTIRE
WORLD OF JOYOUS NYMPHS AND FAUNS*

in unbridled rhythms. The masterpiece of all of this is *La joie de vivre*, a panel with a very elongated format, measuring 4 x 8 feet, grouping together the ensemble of his themes in a wild bacchanal.

Around them, in the form of still lifes, are fish, octopuses, sea urchins, or else lemons, eggplants, bunches of grapes bought at the Antibes market, not to mention the traditional guitar, which duplicates the wittiest of his graphic works.

The works are executed for the most part with deck paint on fibrocement plates or, when Picasso is in the heat of creation, on old canvases from the museum's stock of paintings lacking any great artistic value. Thus, ever the iconoclast and readily facetious, he used the very official portrait of a highly placed Antibes personality who had been a governor in Lebanon and was depicted in formal dress, as a prop for a lascivious faun, not without first adding, so insiders whisper, some very personal accessories.

Picasso rediscovered his former taste for metamorphoses, which he had had in the thirties when he would transform his mistresses into troubling or luxurious vegetation. But this time his old pessimism seems to have disappeared as if by magic. One might say that he is drawing and painting, just as has often happened to him, for his friends or his children. He seems to be freed from all anguish. He is a human, Picasso, who seems not to know despair, as if he had never encountered it.

He creates a mythology that is a close relative of that of the Helladic period, but with a modern inspiration as much on the level of the transformation of his mythical characters as on that of their total freedom of execution.

One figure is characteristic of this new vein of painting, namely an inspired woman, a sort of priestess of joy who dances in the company of goats, while the luminous sun of the Mediterranean has replaced the black sun of the Spanish Civil War.

The fact that Françoise Gilot, an enterprising and seductive young woman who had come to ask him for painting lessons during the German occupation, has recently moved in with Picasso, who is now sixty-five years old, could not be unrelated to his new source of inspiration.

(See also 1904, 1905, 1907, 1909, 1912, 1921, 1927, 1937, 1945, 1948, 1953, 1954, 1958, 1973.)

ARE THE FORGED VERMEERS FORGED VAN MEEGERENS?

HANS VAN MEEGEREN: THE LAST SUPPER. Private Collection

THE NETHERLANDS

In 1937 a painting by Vermeer depicting *The Pilgrims of Emmaus* appeared on the French market. Today the painting is housed at the Boymans Museum, which acquired it for the price of 550,000 florins. The sum had been gathered by the city of Rotterdam, the Rembrandt Society, and a Dr. Bredius, a Vermeer specialist.

In the beginning of September 1945, an unknown painter, Hans Van Meegeren, declared that he was the creator of the alleged masterpiece and of a series of paintings on religious subjects that he had executed at the beginning of the war. Among the latter was *The Last Supper*, in which Christ is seen in the midst of his disciples—one of the paintings that convinced Dr. Bredius that Vermeer had

indeed produced paintings inspired by the Bible.

To demonstrate the veracity of his claims, Van Meegeren undertook the execution, under the surveillance of judges and experts, of a painting to be supposedly his sixth forged Vermeer, entitled *Jesus and the Scholars*. In this manner he accepted the challenge to compete with Ver-

meer while once again becoming himself. But in this public demonstration he could not do better than to give Jesus the common face of a movie star.

Forgers, as we know, proceed by enlargements and juxtapositions of authentic fragments. Van Meegeren, sensitive to the relation of yellow and blue in Vermeer, and having discovered

the artist's blue, based his forged paintings on this relation.

However, is the work executed under surveillance from the same hand as the others? A number of collectors and critics strongly doubt it. They reject Van Meegeren's claims, saying that on the technical and material level they are not proven by the facts.

SHE DID END UP LOOKING LIKE HER PORTRAIT

Gertrude Stein in 1906 (Baltimore, Museum of Art).

PARIS

In August, in a depopulated vacationing Paris, the death of Gertrude Stein, the great American writer who had chosen to live in France, went practically unnoticed. She, who was one of Picasso's prestigious models (his *Portrait,* painted in 1906, was one of the first pre-Cubist works), was herself an important lover of art.

In the avant-garde milieus in the beginning of the century, she exercised an influence analogous to that of a Madame de Staël in another time, perpetuating the tradition of the salons. She was the friend and patron of Picasso, Braque, Derain, and Matisse, all of whom she bought numerous works from.

Very impressed by *Les demoiselles d'Avignon,* which she saw in the course of its development

in Picasso's studio in the Bateau-Lavoir in Montmartre, she wrote: "Each masterpiece has come into the world with a dose of ugliness in it. This ugliness is the sign that the creator is saying a new thing in a new way." This is a thoroughly remarkable judgment by comparison with that of Apollinaire and Braque who, at the same time, were critical of the painting, which shocked them by its absolute originality. Her portrait, which required ninety modeling sessions at Picasso's, approximated African masks. In her surprise, she pointed out to the painter that it scarcely resembled her. Picasso is supposed to have answered that she had nothing to worry about, because she and her portrait would end up by coming together.

André Breton
Brings Back Indian Art

André Breton, who has been living in the United States with his wife, Elisa, since 1941, has recently returned to France. In his luggage are Indian sculptures worthy of the greatest collections. Indian art, which developed in a cultural and social context totally different from ours, has many artistic values in common with the African sculpture admired by the Cubists at the beginning of the century. It has the same lack of ostentation, the same creative force, the same sadness, the same feeling of simplicity and monumentality. The pieces brought back by Breton are priceless. The pope of Surrealism had settled in the "Village," the New York Saint-Germain-des-Prés, and had become an announcer of the Voice of America, for which his friend, the painter Amédée Ozenfant, was an editor. He says he is very worried about the Stalinists' suppression of French painting and literature.

NORTH AMERICAN INDIAN MASK.
Ottawa. Musée National de l'Homme

IN BRIEF...

UNITED STATES
Death of Lázló Moholy-Nagy, creator in Chicago of the New Bauhaus. He was fifty-one.

Toulouse-Lautrec retrospective at the Metropolitan Museum of New York.

FRANCE
Auguste Perret begins the reconstruction of the city of Le Havre, largely destroyed in the bombardments of 1944.

Opening in Paris of the gallery Maeght with a Henri Matisse exhibition.

Death in Paris of the painter Henri Le Fauconnier, largely forgotten. His canvas Abundance *was a sensation among the Cubists in 1911.*

War, a famous painting by Henri Rousseau, enters the Louvre.

The ex-Futurist Gino Severini comes back to Paris after spending ten years in Italy and Switzerland.

THE NETHERLANDS
Triumph of Vincent Van Gogh at the Stedelijk Museum of Amsterdam.

Rouault versus
the Vollard Heirs

The painter Georges Rouault is taking legal action against the heirs of Ambroise Vollard—the famous art dealer who died in 1939—to prevent them from disposing of eight hundred and fourteen canvases that he "neither finished nor signed." The artist claims the right to repossess his works, which were "in progress" at the time of the dealer's decease. These canvases, found in the studio that Vollard had placed at his disposal, were only, according to Rouault, rough sketches of works not completed. He reproaches the Vollard heirs for disposing of his canvases as they see fit. Will the court agree with Rouault and authorize him to burn, before an officer of the court, the three hundred and fourteen unfinished canvases that he considers "too far from his concept of perfection"?

De Chirico versus de Chirico

On June 18 an exhibition of works by Giorgio de Chirico belonging to a private collection opened in Paris. On July 17, the painter sent a registered letter stating that of the nineteen exhibited paintings of which he had received photos he recognized only four as authentic. The exhibition was soon dismantled. But there is the question as to whether the paintings are really fakes or whether de Chirico has refused to recognize paintings he considers inferior as being from his hand. The latest maneuver by the artist who rediscovered the technique of the Renaissance painters—and signs paintings "Pictor Classicus"—gives reason to disconcert even its author!

Exhibitions in London

One hundred and thirty paintings, drawings, and engravings by Paul Klee, created between 1903 and 1940, will start the year at the National Gallery in London, which is taking the place of the Tate Gallery, severely damaged by German air raids during the war. The paper shortage has prevented the publication of a catalogue comparable to that published in 1941 by the Museum of Modern Art in New York. The Tate Gallery has announced its reopening in a few months with a major exhibition of American art.

PAUL KLEE:
PATHOS II.
1937. Paris.
MNAM

LUCIO FONTANA: THE WHITE MANIFESTO

Lucio Fontana was born in 1899 in Rosario Santa Fe, Argentina, of Italian parents. He received his training at the Brera School in Milan; then, as an avant-garde sculptor, he became interested in very diverse techniques, looking for new forms of plastic expression through the use of such materials as ceramics, porcelain, concrete, and phosphorescent materials. After using figurative language marked by acute Expressionism, he has made his current doctrine: "Free Abstractionism versus absolute Abstractionism." Fontana exhibited many times in Italy before returning to Argentina in 1939. His *White Manifesto*, which he is publishing now in Buenos Aires in collaboration with a group of students, has been widely hailed.

Art is in a latent period. There is a force that man cannot express. We express it literally in this manifesto. We therefore ask all the world's scientists, who are aware of the fact that art is a vital necessity of the species, to devote part of their research to the discovery of the luminous and malleable substance and instruments that will produce sounds with which to develop four-dimensional art. We will submit the necessary reference materials to the researchers. Ideas cannot be rejected. They are to be found in the form of seeds in society, and thinkers and artists express them. Each thing arises out of necessity and is valid for its time. Plastic art consisted of ideal representations of familiar forms, of images that one made real in an ideal sense. The viewer imagined one object after the other, he imagined the muscles and the clothes represented.

Today, experimental knowledge is replacing knowledge based on images. We are aware of a world that exists and which is self-explanatory and which cannot be changed by our ideas . . . Materialism rooted in all consciousnesses demands an art with values all its own. Far removed from those representations that are today a farce. The people of this century, forged in materialism, have become insensitive to the representation of familiar forms and to the narration of experiences that are repeated over and over . . .

We are calling for a change in the very essence and in the form. We are calling for painting, sculpture, poetry, music to be transcended. We need an art that is more in harmony with the requirements of a new spirit . . .

The artistic era of paralytic colors and forms has come to an end. Man is becoming more and more insensitive to frozen images that lack a sense of vitality. Immobile ancient images no longer satisfy the desires

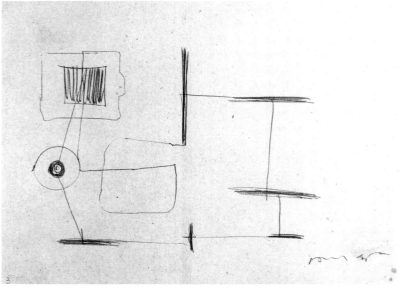

LUCIO FONTANA:
SPATIAL IDEA. 1946.
Paris. MNAM

of the new man schooled in the necessity for action, in complicity with automation that forces him into constant dynamism. The esthetic of organic movement is replacing the esthetic feebleness of frozen forms.

Invoking this transformation that has taken place in human nature and the psychic and intellectual changes in all human relationships and activities, we are abandoning the use of familiar art forms and are beginning to develop an art based on the unity of time and space . . . We conceive of the synthesis as a sum of psychic elements: color, sound, movement, time, space, making up a physical and psychic unity. Color, the element of space, sound, the element of time, and movement that develops in time and space, are the fundamental forms of the new art, which comprises the four dimensions of existence—time and space.

LUCIO FONTANA
White Manifesto 1946 (Spacialism)
(Excerpt)

THE SPIRAL-SHAPED MUSEUM OF FRANK LLOYD WRIGHT

NEW YORK

The American architect Frank Lloyd Wright is working on the project of a revolutionary museum whose scale model he has presented to the press. Essentially, this museum will consist of an inclined plane of four thousand feet, coiling up to a height of six floors, in the shape of a logarithmic spiral. Its structure will consist of two tangential spirals. The longest, whose slope will be the gentlest, will constitute the gallery proper, where the works will be exhibited. The shorter spiral will allow one to pass from one level to the other. An elevator cage will occupy the point of tangency of the two spirals. It is to be something like a gigantic snail, hollowed out in the middle by a funnel-shaped well. The dome of the new museum will be translucent, and a perpetual light will blend natural lighting with artificial lighting. The birth name of this spiral will be: the Guggenheim Museum.

Frank Lloyd Wright with the model of his Guggenheim Museum.

THE ASTONISHING PREFABRICATED HOUSES OF JEAN PROUVÉ

Prefabricated houses by Jean Prouvé for victims in Lorraine in 1944-1945.

FRANCE

The destruction due to the war has put the problems of prefabrication at the head of the list of topics in the field of architecture. Thus the architect Jean Prouvé has just taken out of its wrappers the project of a house, produced in a factory and delivered ready to be set up.

His first such research goes back to the thirties, when Citroën began to manufacture auto bodies completely out of steel. The result for Prouvé today is an individual house, of medium size, capable of being assembled in three or four hours, and disassembled in fewer than two hours by three untrained people.

The assemblage can be done without screws, by the simple fitting of panels, floorboards, façades, and roofing. To insure insulation and water- and airtightness, the panels are made out of sheet metal of double thickness with a sheet of asbestos glued to them and an air mattress reinforced with glass wool. Prouvé's house offers the comfortable and solid living conditions of minimal housing. Nevertheless, the constraints of space obliged him to rethink the entire interior arrangement: vertically sliding windows, movable tables, beds, and storage space.

Jean Prouvé, who originally worked in wrought iron, is simultaneously an architect, a craftsman, and an engineer. Each one of his productions obeys the demands of style, while at the same time brilliantly solving the problems of resistance of materials and manufacturing. At the heart of his work is the "constructive idea," which does not turn its back on a Functionalism inherited from the Bauhaus but makes an effort to reconcile it with the needs of the greatest number of people.

1947

SUMMARY

Pierre Bonnard, another of painting's giants, perishes at the age of eighty in Cannet. Filled with a desire to push Impressionism to its ultimate consequences, and considered at times a traditionalist for that reason, he is, on the contrary, youth itself. Along with Vuillard, his friend, he takes his place in the Musée National d'Art Moderne, which makes its debut in Paris after its doors had opened a crack in 1942. For the occasion, Picasso makes a gift to the French nation of ten important canvases, including his recent still life Enameled Saucepan. *Finally, a revelation comes with Wols, who pushes lyric abstraction to its grating extremes.*

GREAT MASTERS

**Bonnard, the Magician of Light
In Bonnard's Words
Opinions on Bonnard**

DEVELOPMENTS

**Twelve Million Francs for the Fénéon Collection
Max Bill, with No Inside or Outside**

ART NEWS

**The Stained-Glass Windows of Bréseux
Art and Economics in Poland
Hartung at the Gallery Lydia Conti
International Exhibition of Surrealism
Neutra's Desert House
In Brief**

AVANT-GARDE

**Wols at the Galerie Drouin
Art of This Century Closes Its Doors**

MUSEUMS

Paris Gets Its Museum of Modern Art

PIERRE BONNARD:
ALMOND TREE IN BLOOM. 1946.
Paris. MNAM

444

PIERRE BONNARD: NUDE IN A BATHTUB. 1936. Paris. Petit Palais

BONNARD, THE MAGICIAN OF LIGHT

CANNES

Pierre Bonnard died in Cannes on January 23 at the age of eighty in his villa, the "Bosquet," where he had been living since 1925. His death, like his life, was of an exemplary discretion. A few scant lines at the bottom of a newspaper was all that announced the disappearance of a man who had become one of the most important of French painters. Since the death of his wife, Marthe, in 1942, Bonnard had been leading a very solitary existence. Her death had affected him greatly and had marked a sensitive turning in the evolution of his work.

This painter of exuberant nature, of light, this pagan who manifested a solar penchant for the sensual beauties of the feminine body, this Uranian in love with the skies and the water, this lyrical orchestrator of color,

Pierre Bonnard painting in Cannet.

had come face to face with pain and sadness. Before losing the woman who was also his favorite model, the war had already touched him. In a letter to Matisse, his neighbor from Cimiez, he confided that for him painting was no longer anything but a "work of consolation." But if his work had acquired a new seriousness, it had retained nonetheless a somptuous vividness, and it manifested a freedom, an audacity—notably in the arbitrary use of colors—that leaves far behind it the formal innovations of the younger generation.

But to say "arbitrary" does not mean that Bonnard was inattentive to reality, or that like the Fauvists he offered sacrifices to the idol of pure painting. On the contrary, few artists have been as preoccupied as he with the slightest nuances of light, with the fine variation of tones to which a leaf or the edge of a cloud or the silky surface of a skin may be submitted. The world painted by Bonnard has something of a world at its beginning, a world that has not yet undergone assaults of evil, that "civilization" has not yet sullied, a world such as it must have appeared to the gaze of the first innocent and awestruck human being.

This is the gaze, in any case, with which Bonnard looked at

woman, at the body of woman. The old legend of original sin has been forgotten, Eve has been cleansed of her act. Here she is again naked and shameless at her toilette, with iridescent skin, a discreet blazon of rediscovered femininity, finally eternal.

Bonnard painted directly onto canvas in rolls, which he pinned onto the wall. He only cut it into the final size when he had finished his work. Thus he avoided any predetermined framing and enlarged his work along with the development of his field of vision. He was seeking to "depict what one sees when one suddenly penetrates a room with a single step." This was his way of having us sit at his table or installing us next to Marie in the intimacy of her bathroom.

He was so sensitive to changes in the visible that every day, in his notebook, he took down climatic variations: "fine," "cloudy," "wind," "rain and sun," "cloudy beauty," embellishing his notations for rough sketches of a dog, face, or mast of a boat. Then he specified: "When the weather is sunny but cool, there is vermilion in the orangy shadows." What he described was the clothing that the day wears. For around half a century, this was the point of departure of each of the artist's landscapes.

But it is probably in the self-portraits that Bonnard's art attains its maximum intensity. Few painters have scrutinized themselves with as little self-satisfaction. In the last self-portraits, the habitually light, rapid, turbulent paintbrush is transformed into a cutting and precise scalpel. Bonnard, at the end of his life, liked to repeat this statement of Delacroix's: "One never paints violently enough."

His last painting, an *Almond Tree in Bloom*, pushes perceptive hallucination to the limits. Those who saw only a latter-day Impressionist in this independent man, always on the fringe of the movements of his time, will discover the vastness of his genius tomorrow.

(See also 1925.)

IN BONNARD'S WORDS

There are few people who know how to see, to see well, to see fully. If they knew how to look, they would understand painting better.

Drawing is sensation. Color is reasoning.

The painting is a series of dots that are linked together and end up forming the object, the piece over which the eye wanders without any snags.

The object is not to paint life. The object is to make painting come alive.

Color does not embellish the drawing, it strenghtens it.

The main subject is the surface, which has its color, its laws, over and above the objects.

He who sings is not always happy.

I am only beginning to understand. We must start everything all over.

I hope that my painting will hold up, without cracking. I would like to land before the young people in the year 2000 with the wings of butterflies.

PIERRE BONNARD: THE YELLOW BOAT. 1938. New York. Private Collection

OPINIONS ON BONNARD

Does Bonnard paint the world? I rather think he witnesses the birth of the world, the sudden and miraculous birth of objects and characters. Before him, the universe is newborn. Before him the universe emerges, little by little, continuously. Bonnard had closed his eyes. he is opening them. Not only does he have eyes. He has a mind and a heart, the ancient mind, and the ancient heart of contemporary man. He does not spurn the suggestions of his mind and his heart. But first the sight, the miraculous sight of beings and things coming out of limbo. The world before him is turning from nothingness into life.
LÉON WERTH. Cahiers d'aujourd'hui. *1919*

Often, people refused to see him as anything but fanciful. That is understandable. For the most severe and least subtle censor cannot help but smile when he sees a cat stretching, so caressingly! Or a dog scratching itself or watching, head cocked. And can he suppress a smile if he even considers Bonnard's characters, often so funny, so amusing! But this fancifulness that has never left him, and perhaps even less so now, is not all there is to Bonnard's talent. There is a certain melancholy about him.
CHARLES TERRASSE. Bonnard. *1927*

TWELVE MILLION FRANCS FOR THE FÉNÉON COLLECTION

PARIS

Three weeks before the sale of the collection of Félix Fénéon, the famous writer and great collector of the Neoimpressionists, whose ardent defender he was, the Louvre has acquired four important works of Seurat in good condition: a study for his great painting *Les poseuses,* a pencil study for *Circus* (up to then, the Louvre possessed only the canvas, left incompleted in 1891), and two charcoal drawings, one produced in 1883 and the other in 1887.

In return for these acquisitions, the museum management has agreed to grant every opportunity for purchasing to amateurs and to foreign museums, thus departing from the usual pattern followed for the exportation of art works, in order to contribute to the influence of Seurat in the world. The management is equally committed to not exploiting its rights to preempt the market rate at auctions.

Though deprived of these four masterpieces, the Fénéon collection nevertheless remains exceptionally rich. Seurat is represented in it by nine charcoal drawings, Paul Signac by several watercolors and six canvases, and Henri-Edmond Cross by some landscapes. The sales were announced as a capital event and took in a total of about twelve million francs.

Two charcoal drawings of Georges Seurat, *The Black Horse* and *Twilight,* were sold for 215,000 and 310,000 francs respectively; *Suburbs,* a Pointillist masterpiece, went for 1,300,000 francs, and *Forest Edge in Springtime,* for 505,000 francs. A canvas by Matisse, *Tulips and Daisies,* produced in 1905, sold for 740,000 francs; a nude by Modigliani for 527,000 francs; a canvas by Cross for 295,000 francs; a painting by Vuillard for 300,000 francs; a Bonnard painting for 360,000 francs. *The Model and Her Painter* by Bonnard (which in 1941 could find no one to take it for more than 6,000 francs) was bid up to 81,000 francs.

Félix Fénéon, who had established the *catalogue raisonné* of Seurat's works over a period of ten years, died in Châtenay-Malabry in 1944 at the age of eighty-three. Upon the death of his wife, Fanny, who willed all of her possessions to the University of Paris on the condition that the university establish a literary prize named after Fénéon, the decision was made to put the collection up for sale.

Jean Paulhan, another critic, has said of him: "In a hundred years, we have probably had only one critic, and that is Fénéon."

MAX BILL, WITH NO INSIDE OR OUTSIDE

ZURICH

About the project of *Continuity* by Max Bill, a monument that is to be erected in Zurich, Robert Le Ricolais, the great specialist of pliable structures, writes: "The inside is equivalent to the outside, because infinity symbolized by a reversed eight turns on itself like a worm to prove that the wrong side is the right side. Shape doesn't take space, but space is controlled by shape. The mind is lost in an endless eddy like liquid under the blades of a propeller. You throw your glove into the air, it falls back on the other side, filled with the infinite." Indeed, the monument is based on the principle of the famous and mysterious Möbius strip or band, which, in contradiction to Euclid, possesses only a single surface and a single edge. A sculptor and painter from Zurich, Max Bill, at the age of thirty-nine, is a former student of the Dessau Bauhaus, where he studied from 1927 to 1929. He then participated in the Circle and Square group. Standing before his sculptures, one's first tendency is to classify them among the productions of abstract art. This would be wrong! He specifically attacks the currently much abused tendency of categorizing a large proportion of modern art under the concept of abstraction. One could almost qualify all art, even realistic art, as abstract, he explains, since it results from a process of selection and reduction of reality. Even before the war, as an admirer of Mondrian and Théo Van Doesburg, Bill wanted an art that depended solely on colors, light, and movement, and which combined all these elements. No more deforming or transforming of nature, but rather the search for a harmony, according to a formal quest possessing its own logic. For Max Bill, sculpture must take mathematics into account. According to him, the primary element of every plastic work resides in geometry.

Mixing science and art, what a sacrilegious fantasy. When *Continuity* is erected in Zurich, one may be sure that there will be no lack of arguments for or against this monument.

MAX BILL:
CONTINUITY. 1947.
Paris. MNAM

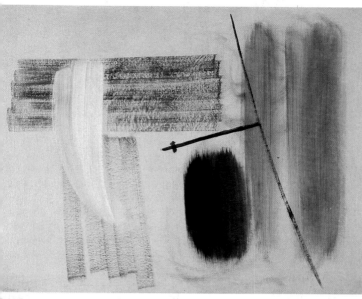

HANS HARTUNG: T-1947-28. 1947. Private Collection

had been noticed last year at the Salon de Mai and at the Salon des Réalités Nouvelles.

International Exhibition of Surrealism

The International Exhibition of Surrealism has opened at the gallery Maeght. Twenty-four nations are represented by some ninety artists, painters, sculptors, and poets, including Tanguy, Ernst, Miró, Toyen, and Arp. An outstanding catalogue introduces them. Visitors must undergo a test before entering the room devoted to Marcel Duchamp: Several curtains of rain falling from the ceiling into mossy drains discourage the visitor from entering the initiation room. Believers and nonbelievers resign themselves to getting wet.

Neutra's Desert House

In the desert of Palm Springs, California, Richard Neutra has completed one of his major works, the Kaufmann House. The availability of large panes of glass has given him an opportunity to apply some of his favorite principles: a wide opening on the landscape and the interpenetration of interior and exterior spaces. Its open plan and strong horizontals give this desert house the appearance of a pavilion floating in the landscape, whose harshness forms a striking contrast with the building and the swimming pool that adjoins it.

The Stained-Glass Windows of Bréseux

The movement to renew sacred art with abstract art is now well under way. An important step has just been taken, thanks to the open mind of a priest in the diocese of Besançon, the Canon Ledeur, who became, at the Liberation, the leader of the new diocesan commission on sacred art. The canon has turned to a painter still little known to the general public, Alfred Manessier, thirty-six years old, who has just received an order for two windows for the choir of the church in the hamlet of Bréseux, which is located in the commune Maîche, in the Jura.

Hartung at the Gallery Lydia Conti

Abstract art, which has never had a great success in Paris, returns to us today thanks to an artist of German origin who lost a leg fighting Nazism. He is Hans Hartung, forty-three years old. The artist is an excellent calligrapher whose paintings are composed of spots and marks that act directly on feelings, and are removed from any representation, allusive or otherwise. The human gesture, however, is never entirely devoid of feeling; the works of Hartung evoke a galactic universe of explosions and dissociations diametrically opposed to the cold abstraction of artists such as Dewasne or Herbin. His power and refinement

Art and Economics in Poland

Poland is awakening to the democratization of cultural values. The press is promoting the idea of beauty for every day and everybody, a slogan referring to raising the esthetic level of everyday objects. Stimulating industrial and artisanal production is becoming an essential concern in this war-torn country. The leaders of the new government organization intend to give a prominent place and a new role to the plastic arts.

RICHARD J. NEUTRA: KAUFMANN HOUSE. 1946-1947. Palm Springs, California

WOLS AT THE GALERIE DROUIN

ART OF THIS CENTURY CLOSES ITS DOORS

PARIS

Wols is almost famous and yet perfectly unknown. Many who believed that they were attending his first one-man show were actually at his second. The first, which took place in this same gallery two years ago, included only gouaches and watercolors.

Wols, whose real name is Wolfgang Schulze, was born in Berlin in 1913 and changed his name to escape from his austere bourgeois family, as well as from the authority of a father who was Chancellor of Saxony. It was the death of his father that decided his break with his family and country; at the same time he cemented new alliances, as between art and alcohol.

Settled in Paris since 1932, Wols earns his living through photography and by giving German lessons. His watercolors and his gouaches are sheer enchantments, extraordinarily light-filled visions. The influence of Klee is obvious. Like Klee, he takes refuge in the spirit and paradise of a childhood that he had never wanted to renounce. But as for his paintings, they contain something much more somber. They are kinds of soliloquies, obeying his psychic Automatism and following the meanderings of his imagination. Critics, whether they like or dislike him, speak a great deal about "spot painting." His spots make of him, along with Hartung, Jackson Pollock, and others, a veritable leader.

Wols explained his vision of the world to a woman friend by showing her a crack in the sidewalk. "I don't know what I am. I am a microbe . . . Look at that crack. It is like one of my drawings. It's a living thing. It will grow. It will change every day like a flower . . . It was created by the only force that is real."

We are not very far from Jean-Paul Sartre, who was sensitive to this artist's work. For the moment, Wols is living in a minuscule hotel room and is working without an easel, practically without light, and with very little money.

ALFRED WOLS: BLUE GRENADE. 1946. Paris. MNAM

JACKSON POLLOCK: CIRCUMCISION. 1946. Venice. Peggy Guggenheim Collection

NEW YORK

People will regret that the famous gallery Art of This Century, which Peggy Guggenheim opened in 1942 and which was, during these crucial years for American art, a meeting place for everything that New York had in young talent, ceases to exist.

Peggy Guggenheim had gathered a jury of Marcel Duchamp, Piet Mondrian, Howard Putzel, and the three top experts of the Museum of Modern Art to help her select forty paintings from among those of the younger generation of American painters. The names that distinguished this first exhibition included those of Jackson Pollock, Robert Motherwell, and William Baziotes. In the years that followed, she devoted one-man shows to these three painters, and did the same for Clyfford Still and Mark Rothko and others. She also made a contract with Jackson Pollock that gave him a living while he was still an unknown.

During Jackson Pollock's first one-man exhibition at Art of This Century, Alfred Barr bought *The She Wolf* for the Museum of Modern Art, and during Pollock's 1945 exhibition, Clement Greenberg declared that Jackson Pollock was "the most powerful artist of his generation and perhaps the greatest since Miró." Since 1943, Pollock has become the main attraction of the gallery, to the point that certain artists left Art of This Century and went to Samuel Kootz who had recently opened a gallery nearby.

Nevertheless, Art of This Century was the general headquarters of the Surrealists in exile: Max Ernst, whom Peggy Guggenheim had married, André Breton, André Masson, Tanguy, Matta. Peggy Guggenheim describes its turbulent life in her autobiography, *Out of This Century*, published last year.

PARIS GETS ITS MUSEUM OF MODERN ART

PARIS

So hoped for by Parisians and Frenchmen who regretted finding contemporary works of art only in private galleries, the Musée National d'Art Moderne—which in 1942 had opened its doors at the Palais de Tokyo to reveal only one-third of its rooms—is finally fully accessible to the public.

WORKS THAT ARE CONTEMPORARY BUT NOT REALLY REPRESENTATIVE OF THE GREAT MOVEMENTS OF OUR CENTURY

Inaugurating the opening celebration for the three thousand paintings that the government had been buying or receiving as donations for fifty years, the new curator of the museum, Jean Cassou, a writer who was a member of the Resistance and to whom we owe brilliant studies on El Greco and Picasso, announced: "Paris is henceforth endowed with a museum in which the public will be able to follow the development of those schools and movements that give so much prestige to French art and to the Parisian School."

Together with the director of the Musée des Beaux-Arts, Robert Rey, Cassou fully intends, in fact, to provide the museum with a program of exhibitions and acquisitions that would allow it to evolve in its own time. He is more than a little proud of admiration for ten works by Picasso created since 1925, almost all of which Picasso donated to him. Until now, the only work by Picasso that could be found in a national collection was his *Portrait of Gustave Coquiot*, a canvas from his youth that is hardly representative of his painting. "Picasso is Spanish, but his glory is French," he affirms. "These ten works represent some of his most daring and most remarkable periods."

The museum includes beautiful paintings by Vuillard, Bonnard, Matisse (who is the muse-

um's painter of honor), Léger, La Fresnaye, Bissière, Villon . . . The critics praise such choices but have a sterner view of the collection as a whole and point out serious gaps. Thus Jacques Lassaigne writes: "To speak frankly, only the first twenty-two rooms of the ground floor deserve to be called a museum. The basement, where the works

that could not be admitted into the earlier classification have been discreetly grouped under the names of various Salons, provides, along with the academic rooms, a kind of foil and an example of the errors in which official art buyers have reveled for decades."

He judges that their greatest

The Musée National d'Art Moderne in Paris.

difficulty lies "in comprehending the great movements in the history of contemporary art." In fact, it is regrettable that one cannot find, with the exception of Robert Delaunay's *City of*

Paris, the most remarkable works of movements as important as Fauvism, Cubism, Futurism, and Surrealism, not to mention Dadaism and Abstractionism.

PABLO PICASSO: ENAMELED SAUCEPAN. 1945. Paris. MNAM

One of the ten works donated by the artist.

Paris is crowned and dethroned at the same time. The Cobra movement of Copenhagen, Brussels, and Amsterdam chooses to be born there, as did Futurism in 1909. But this time the choice affirms the movement's Nordic particularism. Also this year, death comes to Antonin Artaud after many long years of hospitalization; to Schwitters, known especially for his Merzbau, and to Arshile Gorky, who decides to end his days when he is struck by a fatal illness. In the meantime, tireless Picasso has set himself up as a potter in Vallauris, creating a revival in that dying, ancestral craft.

1948

S U M M A R Y

MOVEMENTS

Cobra: a Revolutionary Surrealism
Asger Jorn: Intimate Banalities

AVANT-GARDE

Opening of the School "Subjects of the Artists"
Gorky Cuts Short His Suffering

GREAT MASTERS

The Solitude of Kurt Schwitters

DEVELOPMENTS

Picasso Becomes a Potter

ART NEWS

Dynaton in San Francisco
Debate on Painting in the USSR
The Siren of Warsaw
Exhibition of French Art in Germany
Rouault Burns 315 of His Works
In Brief

OBITUARIES

Antonin Artaud the Maniac
The Miserabilism of Gruber

WRITINGS AND THEORIES

Pierre Francastel: Art and Language

LITERATURE

ARGENTINA
Publication of The Outsider *by Ernesto Sábato.*

UNITED STATES
Ezra Pound, imprisoned for high treason, writes Pisan Cantos.

FRANCE
Nathalie Sarraute publishes a novel, Portrait of a Man Unknown.
  Michel Leiris publishes the essay Biffures.
Jacques Prévert publishes his Paroles.

JAPAN
Publication of The Makioka Sisters, *a novel by Jun'ichiró Tanizaki.*

MUSIC

UNITED STATES
Appearance of cool jazz. Miles Davis is typical of its mellow sound.

ITALY
Luigi Dallapiccola composes Four Poems by Machado *for soprano.*

THEATER

FRANCE
Three important plays are performed in Paris: State of Siege *by Albert Camus,* The Tidings Brought to Mary *by Paul Claudel, and* Dirty Hands *by Jean-Paul Sartre.*

MOTION PICTURES

UNITED STATES
Premiere of The Treasure of the Sierra Madre *by John Huston with Humphrey Bogart.*
  In Hollywood, "witch hunt" for Communist sympathizers.

ITALY
Premieres of The Bicycle Thief *by Vittorio De Sica and* The Earth Shakes *by Luchino Visconti.*

ASGER JORN
THE FACE OF THE EARTH. 194
Paris. Private Collecti

COBRA: A REVOLUTIONARY SURREALISM

PARIS

A new international art movement was born on November 8 that considers itself revolutionary. Reacting against the Parisian intelligentsia, which likes "isms" so much, it has chosen to call itself "Cobra."

Cobra is an acronym of the first letters of *Co*penhagen, *Br*ussels and *A*msterdam, the capitals of the three countries to which its founders belong: the Dane Asger Jorn, the Dutchmen Karel Appel, Constant Nieuwenhuis (called Constant), Cornelius Van Beverloo (called Corneille), and the Belgians Christian Dotremont and Joseph Noiret.

These six artists and poets decided to launch (with a "resolution" in French, typewritten, and entitled *The Cause Has Been Heard)* an appeal to creative artists all over the world, but one that rejected all doctrine. They did it at the Café Notre Dame on the Quai Saint-Michel; but they established the headquarters of the movement in Brussels, at 32 Rue des Éperonniers.

Rejecting all dogmatism and all theoretical influence, from which only sterile works would emanate, they define their association as "an experimental, organic collaboration," because "it is in a spirit of efficiency that we add to our respective national experiences the dialectic experience of our groups." Their watchword is: to experiment! There will be no leader. But the

The Cobra group.

oldest among them, Asger Jorn, enjoys, at the age of thirty-six, a prestige that derives not only from his paintings but from his writings, notably from what he had published in May 1941 in the second issue of the magazine *Helhesten.*

Even if it formulates its rejections (esthetics, the cultural industry) more easily than its choices, the movement cannot deny obvious affiliations: Surrealism, Abstractionism as it has evolved with Hartung and Wols, and, finally, Art Brut as Jean Dubuffet has defined it. The paintings of the group are characterized by the use of frank colors and flowings that often resemble children's drawings or primitive art, as in Karel Appel's *The Cry of Freedom.* As for its roots, if they are clearly Nordic, they go back to prewar Paris. It is in Paris that the painter Egill Jacobsen, fascinated by Picasso, sought to rediscover the life of popular art and that Asger Jorn, after working with Kandinsky, then with Léger and Le Corbusier, discovered Klee and Surrealism. Jorn and Constant met at the Miró exhibition at the Galerie Pierre in 1946. The Icelandic Svavar Gudnason, who had also worked in Paris, formulates this dual nature very well: "To be Nordic is to believe in oneself and in everyone. French art has been the most important. But it was up to us, as Scandinavians, to react against what

IT WAS UP TO US, AS SCANDINAVIANS, TO REACT AGAINST WHAT HAD BECOME THE PARISIAN MYTH

had become the Parisian myth." Through Jorn, Cobra owes much to Denmark and to its spirit of freedom. One of the sources of the new movement is the Expressionism of Edvard Munch. The Danes could see an exhibition of two hundred of his works in Copenhagen after his unexpected death in 1944. In the art of Munch, the founders of Cobra discovered how internal tensions and conflicts can determine the intensity of plastic motifs. To this we may add the influence of the Danish group Hùost, which since 1941 has been practicing a deliberately avant-gardist manner of abstract painting.

During the international Surrealist conference that took place in Brussels last year in the face of the French and the Bel-

KAREL APPEL: THE CRY OF FREEDOM. 1948. Denmark. Private Collection

ASGER JORN: INTIMATE BANALITIES

gians who cannot seem to break loose from their Communist allegiance, Jorn said, expressing what everyone felt: "For ten years we have been waiting in vain in Copenhagen to hear cries of alarm from Prague or Paris, from Brussels or Rome, in response to our questioning, and to hear of other solutions than the ones we have come up with to relieve our anxieties."

Christian Dotremont has perhaps formulated the best response: "The desire for an indivisible creative force, neither organized nor disorganized, where form and content go together, as do the means and the end, ugliness and beauty, design and color, subjective powers and references to external reality—all dualities maintainted since the Renaissance by aristocratic, then by bourgeois art" . . .

Cobra wants to be defined as liberation from a Surrealism that is dying through its own esthetic, as well as from the Socialist Realism of the Communist party. While there is no esthetic here, there is a moral standard: "Experimental, organic collaboration that avoids all theory and dogma." Jorn explains further that it is a question of putting art back to where it was at the beginning, on the foundation of the senses.

What Cobra wants is clear: to be reconnected with what Jung calls the collective unconscious, to have another culture re-emerge from it, one that is hidden, anonymous, but authentic.

If we are to try to understand the situation of art today, we must try to understand the conditions that determined the evolution of our artistic intuition and our notion of the relationship between man and society. The artist actively participates in the struggle to deepen what knowledge we have of the vital undercurrent that makes artistic creation possible. The artist's zone of interest, however, does not allow itself to be limited to this area alone. He must seek the ultimate awakening in everything and in the details of everything. Nothing is sacred for him, for everything has become important to him.

In no way can a choice be involved, but rather it is a question of penetrating the entire

KARL-HENNING PEDERSEN: UNTITLED. Around 1941. Silkeborg. Kunstmuseum

cosmic system of laws that govern the rhythms, the energies, and the substance that make up the world's reality, from the ugliest to the most beautiful, everything that has a character and an expression, whether it be the coarsest and most brutal or the finest and most tender thing, everything that cries out to us, for this is life itself.

And in order to express everything, we must know everything.

The esthetic principle must be abolished. We are not disillusioned, because we have no illusions. We never had any.

What we possess, and what represents our strength, is that life makes us rejoice,

that life in all its amoral aspects arouses our interest. And that is also what represents the foundation of art today. We do not even know the laws of esthetics, and the old idea of choice according to the principle of beautiful and ugly, in keeping with what is ethically noble or blameworthy, is dead for us, us for whom beautiful is also ugly, for whom everything that is ugly also has beauty in it . . .

There is no such thing as different styles, and there never was. Style is the expression of a bourgeois content, and its various nuances are what we call taste.

The rigid distinction between sculpture and painting does not exist. We cannot isolate any kind of artistic expression on the basis of its form, for there are only different means put to use for a common artistic goal. Sandpaper and absorbent cotton are forms of expression that are every bit as noble and every bit as usable as oil painting and marble.

ASGER JORN
HELHESTEN, May 1941
(Excerpt)

455

OPENING OF THE SCHOOL "SUBJECTS OF THE ARTISTS"

NEW YORK

This autumn, four artists from among the most active have opened an unusual sort of school. The artists are William Baziotes, David Hare, Robert Motherwell, and Mark Rothko. The school is located on East 8th Street. No formal teaching will be dispensed there, but the students will be able to benefit from painters who have had frequent contact with the Surrealists and with those European artists who are in New York.

The fact that last year Peggy Guggenheim closed her famous gallery Art of This Century encouraged these painters to try to create a new intellectual and artistic gathering place. At the

WILLIAM BAZIOTES: DWARF. 1947. New York. MOMA

present moment, all of them are exhibiting in the two galleries most open to contemporary art: those of Betty Parsons and Samuel Kootz.

The painting of the artists who, founded "Subjects of the Artists" was born of two sources that could seem antithetical but whose fusion is a completely original contribution of young New York painting. These two sources are the Cubist space and the psychic Automatism of Surrealism. These founding artists also rebel against the social and regional art that predominated in America during the thirties.

Calling their school "Subjects of the Artists," although most of them have styles close to Abstractionism, indicates a desire to give to art a philosophical dimension that it has never had in America. "For us," said Mark Rothko and Adolph Gottlieb in 1943, "art is an adventure and an unknown land that can only be explored by those who are ready to take risks."

GORKY CUTS SHORT HIS SUFFERING

SHERMAN

The painter Arshile Gorky has committed suicide in his studio in Connecticut. Born in Armenia in 1904, he was expelled by Turkish persecution and emigrated to the United States at the age of fifteen. He has left behind a body of work of great sensitivity whose quality and rigor have served as a model for young American painters.

His "Armenian portraits" are austere and moving images that emerged from his memory, especially portraits of his mother who died during their flight. While still painting in a representational mode, Gorky worked on monumental frescoes for the Federal Art Project. Thanks to this collaboration, he met a number of the painters who made up the heart of contemporary art in New York.

Yet the most important aspect of his work is his evolution toward Abstractionism. The linear rhythms and poetic space of Joan Miró influenced him, but even more so did the colors and organic forms of André Masson. A friend of Breton, of Matta, and of the other Surrealists in exile in New York during the war, he communicated his most intimate perceptions through his paintings and created "an interior infinity" revealing a strong feeling for nature, for vegetation, for the gardens of his childhood, and for the countryside in Virginia that he loved so much.

In the catalogue for Gorky's exhibition at the Julien Levy Gallery in 1945, André Breton wrote that Gorky was the only one who maintained a direct contact with nature. Two years ago, a fire in his studio des-troyed a great number of his paintings. Then serious health problems and certain private tragedies added up to a tragic end.

ARSHILE GORKY: BETROTHAL II. 1947. New York. Whitney Museum

THE SOLITUDE OF KURT SCHWITTERS

KENDAL

On January 8, the painter, sculptor, and poet Kurt Schwitters, who had escaped to England on June 8, 1940, after being in exile in Norway, died at the age of sixty-one in great solitude near Ambleside. The man who had wanted to kill traditional and stuffy art by ridicule assured us that "everything that the artist spits out is art."

He had intended to spur on the emancipation of artists by this provocative formula, implying by it that the materials of creation have little importance, because it is their imaginative arrangement that raises them to the rank of a work of art.

Having gone through the schools of fine arts in Hanover and Dresden, then having painted landscapes and academic portraits, Schwitters had already invented in 1917 Cubo-Expressionist painting and, under the influence of Synthetic Cubism, devoted himself to compositions in which he mixed scraps from wastepaper baskets, labels, tickets, pieces of wood, iron, and rubber, and shirt buttons, all of which he enhanced with paints.

Assemblages and collages were the two poles of his plastic genius, which evolved toward gigantic, heterogeneous sculpture. In 1922 he joined the Dada movement in Weimar.

He decided to label his production *Merz*, a syllable extracted from the German word *Kommerz* (commerce), which he had come across on a torn piece of newspaper where only one part of the word *Kommerz* appeared. Thus in 1923 he founded the review *Merz*, whose first issue was to be devoted to Dadaist activities in Holland, where he had traveled with Théo and Petro Van Doesburg. *Merz* works run the gamut from children's albums to the publication of functional architecture or abstract art. There were dozens of *Merz* publications, books, catalogues, poems, paintings, all the way to Schwitters's most remarkable accomplishment, his

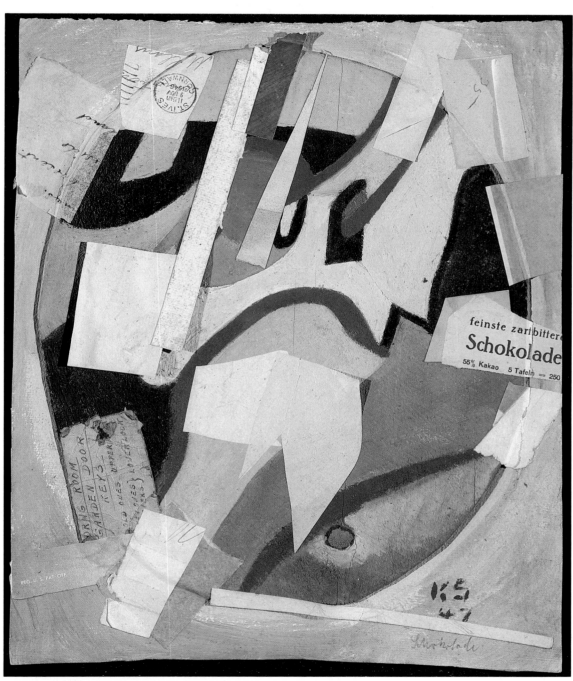

KURT SCHWITTERS: CHOCOLATE. 1947. Private Collection

first *Merzbau*, an environment that ended up occupying every bit of his home in Hanover before being completely destroyed in an Allied air raid during the last war.

Indeed, *Merzbau* was his great work. Each piece was entirely "merzed," that is to say, shaped into cut sections, into spaces that fit together, into geometrical stalactites whose entanglement was pursued through four stories up to the roof from which prismatic columns and pyramids were thrust into space. He emigrated to Lysaker, near Oslo, on January 1, 1937, and there undertook the construction of a second *Merzbau*, which he was to abandon to flee to England.

Persuaded that art "is not learned, but is deserved," he was erecting his third *Merzbau* when he died. A typical example of this artist's poetic humor is his invention of a musical and onomatopoeic language that he called the "language of the birds," in which he would greet his visitors from his perch on a tree in front of his house, in Hanover.

PICASSO BECOMES A POTTER

VALLAURIS

During the feast of Vallauris on July 26, 1946, Picasso met Georges and Suzanne Ramié, the owners of the Madoura ceramic factory. They invited him to visit it. Once there, he took two balls of clay and, with a few turns of the hand, modeled a faun and two bulls, which they immediately had fired.

The Ramiés saw him again in the summer of 1947. Accompanied by Françoise Gilot, with whom he was spinning out love's sweet dream, he showed them about ten rough sketches of projects involving ceramics and told them: "If you give me a worker to take care of the technical problems, I will come back to work."

Having obtained a great deal of information on methods of glazing and firing ceramics, Pablo Picasso was seized by a passion for pottery, and, after seeing the potters of Madoura at work, he astounded them by executing some doves with a practically innate skill. "Look, it's simple: To make a good pigeon you have to twist its neck," he explained to them. During the entire winter of 1947-1948, he worked at the Ramiés', where he spent nearly every afternoon, producing almost two thousand pieces. One hundred and fifty of them were exhibited in November at the Maison de la Pensée Française. When he went there with Françoise Gilot the day before the opening, he was pleasantly surprised by the effect produced by his amphoras in the shape of a woman.

Criticism was tinged with admiration. It emphasized Picasso's return to origins, his happiness in working with clay as if he had extracted a new energy from it. But many visitors saw the exhibition without getting excited, which made Picasso say, "They had hoped to be shocked and terrorized. If the monster is content to smile, they are disappointed."

(See also 1904, 1905, 1907, 1909, 1912, 1921, 1927, 1937, 1945, 1946, 1953, 1954, 1958, 1973.)

PABLO PICASSO:
LADY WITH MANTILLA.
1948. Paris.
Musée Picasso

PABLO PICASSO: THE SIREN OF WARSAW. 1948

Dynaton in San Francisco
Lee Mullican, Gordon Onslow-Ford, and Wolfgang Paalen, who make up the Dynaton group, are exhibiting their visionary works at the San Francisco Museum of Art. Onslow-Ford and Paalen were closely linked with the Surrealists before they went to live in Mexico. Paalen, however, continues to publish his journal *Dyn* in New York. Onslow-Ford, fascinated by Indian mythology, has developed an idiom based on "interior worlds." Since 1938 he has used the "flow" technique, pouring paint directly on the canvas.

Debate on Painting in the USSR
While recognizing that Naturalist art in the style of *Stalin's Arrival at the First Cavalry Army* or *The Sailors of the Black Sea* was a magnificent way to glorify the Red Army, Soviet art critics believe that it is time to think about other objectives in order to avoid stagnation in Russian painting. *Les lettres françaises* echo these criticisms, which appeared in a newspaper of wide circulation, *Komsomolskaya Pravda*, and which dismissed both Formalism and Naturalism. However, we must not have any illusions about the ability of the USSR to free itself from the weight of Socialist Realism.

"The Siren of Warsaw"
In the middle of the summer, Picasso left Vallauris to go to Wroclaw, Poland, to attend the congress of intellectuals for peace. His friends, the writers Éluard and Ilya Ehrenburg, convinced him to accept the invitation of his "Polish comrades." He was given to understand that he would be the star of the congress and that his intervention before intellectuals from all over the world would aid in freeing his friend, the poet Pablo Neruda, now imprisoned in Chile. Picasso, who flew in an airplane for the first time, wished to visit the ruins of the Warsaw ghetto, Auschwitz, and Kraków. It seems, however, that the violent attacks against Sartre directed at the rostrum and the campaign led by Lysenko against the Soviet biologists weakened his Communist convictions.

Exhibition of French Art in Germany
For the past two years, art exhibits have multiplied in the French occupation zone of Germany. In September 1946, an outstanding presentation of modern French painting from Impressionism to Picasso took place at Baden-Baden and Berlin. In 1947, a traveling exhibit brought together sixty paintings from private collections, including works by Cézanne, Braque, and Matisse, as well as Wols and Hartung, whom the German public saw for the first time. A new traveling exhibition organized by Ottomar Domnick is devoted to French abstract art. The poster announcing it shows a painting by Soulages, done last year.

Rouault Burns 315 of His Works
Following a lengthy legal process, first with Ambroise Vollard and then with his heirs, Georges Rouault has succeeded in reclaiming three hundred and fifteen of his paintings that he considered unfinished and that he thought should be destroyed. He burned the objects of the litigation in public himself. This auto-da-fé will certainly shock a lot of art lovers and dealers who are more sensitive to the market than to the spiritual needs of the artist. This court ruling creates a precedent in that it recognizes the sole right of the artist to make decisions about the perpetuation of his art.

GEORGES ROUAULT: LEGENDARY FIGURE. 1940

ANDRÉ MASSON:
PORTRAIT OF ANTONIN ARTAUD.
1925. Paris. Galerie Louise Leiris

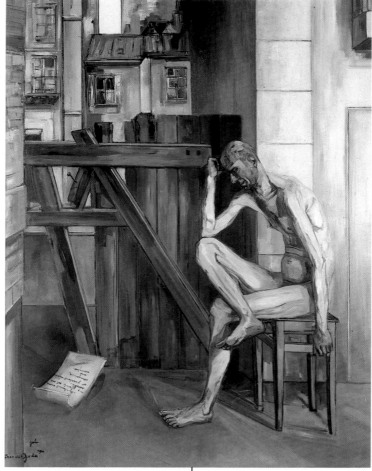

FRANCIS GRUBER: JOB.
1944. London. Tate Gallery

ANTONIN ARTAUD THE MANIAC

PARIS

Antonin Artaud died on March 4 at the age of fifty-two in the hospital at Ivry, ending a life of anguish and genius. Simultaneously a writer, draftsman, and man of the theater, he was one of the artists who expressed most forcefully the spiritual disaster of the world in which we live. In July 1947, at the gallery Pierre Loeb, he exhibited a series of drawings that were like so many exorcisms in their deranged inspiration. "Woe betide whoever might consider these drawings to be works of art . . . I have, moreover, definitively broken with art, style, or talent," warned the author in the preface of the catalogue.

Artaud was born in Marseilles in 1896, and his youth was marked by signs of a serious nervous imbalance. Associated with the Surrealist group, he published two collections of poems in 1925 and 1927, *L'ombilic des limbes* and *Le pèse-nerfs*, before collaborating as an actor with Dullin, Pitoëff, Jouvet, and Dreyer; in 1932 he wrote his *Manifesto of the Theater of Cruelty*. Drawing became for him an essential medium for expressing the furious despair of his tortured soul only in 1939-1940, following his trip to Mexico and during his confinement at the psychiatric hospitals of Ville-Évrard and Rodez.

In June 1946, barely six months after his discharge from the mental institution, a gala was organized in his honor, but he did not attend it. The lecture he gave at the Vieux-Colombier on January 13 proved to be a pathetic one. The event was announced in these terms: A "tête-à-tête" by Antonin Artaud with three poems recited by the author.

The room was filled to bursting. The first row included Jean Paulhan, André Breton, Albert Camus, Jean-Paul Sartre, and Pablo Picasso. The lecture began at about eight o'clock and ended at midnight with Artaud's precipitous departure. He had lost his glasses, misplaced his papers . . . André Gide and Adamov then got up onto the stage to ease a tension that had become unbearable.

There was not a laugh in the room; there was already the silence of death, enfolding a physically ruined artist around whom a legend was born.

THE MISERABILISM OF GRUBER

PARIS

Francis Gruber has passed away at the age of thirty-six at the Boucicaut Hospital in Paris. Born in Nancy in 1912, he had very early developed a passion for Bosch, Grünewald, Dürer, Callot, and his contemporary and friend Giacometti. He leaves behind paintings illuminated by a pale day full of poetry, whose themes are familiar: the interior of studios, adolescent nudes closed up in a world of great sadness but expressed with delicacy of nuance, glazes and reflections of exceptional lightness. Last year he received the national prize for painting. His skills as a draftsman and his deep understanding of the problems of art have placed him on the first rung of contemporary painting.

PIERRE FRANCASTEL: ART AND LANGUAGE

A professor at the École Pratique des Hautes Études and formerly at the universities of Strasbourg and Clermont-Ferrand, Pierre Francastel, forty-eight, has made a distinguished entry into the exclusive field of art history. He is suggesting that at last we learn to read figurative works instead of merely describing them or placing them in historical context as has too frequently been the case until now. The excerpts below are taken from a study that appeared in *Année sociologique*. In it, Francastel shows how the image is, as much as language, a capsule of meaning and how a better understanding of the image has become essential at a time when it is ever more prevalent in our modern society.

The recognition of the symbolic and representative nature of a work of art is certainly nothing new. Artists themselves have been keenly aware of it for half a century. With the discovery of photography and equally as much as a result of the brilliant studies of Cézanne, painting became seemingly the most original and most complete form of expression in our time . . .

I have decided, however, that the limitations and difficulties are inherent in the fact that the reading of a plastic—or musical—document is less common than the reading of a material fact or a written document. Everyone learns to read, and everyone feels more or less capable of reasoning on the basis of material facts or figures. Far fewer express themselves, at least in our society as it is now, with brush strokes or sounds. That does not mean, however, that brush strokes and sounds are not signs that are as capable of expressing ideas and sensations as are letters and words . . .

We must be aware of the fact that art, the figurative mode of expression, is as natural and necessary to societies as speech and writing. It is a mistake to think that only certain restricted classes of human beings, with special talents and inclinations, make up the artistic public. The predominance of different forms of expression has varied with the times. In antiquity, during the Renaissance, art had a special status. We have just lived through an age when, with the discovery of the book, all of civilization has been dominated by not only the written, but the printed, sign.

I, for one, am virtually convinced that we are moving toward a time when the figurative sign and artistic techniques will again take precedence over the written sign. Film, posters, ads, painting and architecture—wherever we turn, man is summoned visu-

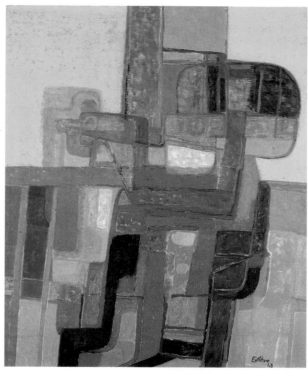

MAURICE ESTÈVE:
GLASS BLOWER.
1948. Paris.
Galerie Louis Carré

ally by abbreviated signs that demand rapid interpretation.

More than ever, people communicate with each other by looks. Understanding images, their origin, their laws, is one of the keys to our time. In order to understand them and express ourselves, we must have an in-depth knowledge of the workings of the signs we use.

PIERRE FRANCASTEL
Art et Sociologie *(Excerpt)*

Baron Ensor is dead at the age of eighty-nine, and is given a national funeral. But the man who was the great precursor of Expressionism at the end of the last century dies twice, for after his youth he had created nothing of importance. Abstract art, on the other hand, continues its ascendancy with Soulages, who has his first one-man exhibition at Lydia Conti's gallery, and with the much-noted appearance of Herbin's book Nonfigurative, Nonobjective Art, *also at Lydia Conti's. And finally, the retrospective of the sculptor Henry Moore in Paris is an event of great importance, given that it has never been easy for a British artist to cross the Channel.*

1949
S U M M A R Y

SCULPTURE

Moore: the Secret Soul of Things
In Moore's Words

AVANT-GARDE

Fontana: the First Perforated Canvases
Soulages: First Exhibition

ART NEWS

The Erector-Set Houses
Motherwell Inspired by García Lorca
Picasso's *Dove*
Delvaux's Pygmalion
Wols, Michaux, Mathieu at the Prospective Gallery
In Brief

GREAT MASTERS

The Second Death of Baron Ensor

WRITINGS AND THEORIES

Auguste Herbin: Art and Nature

HENRY MOORE:
MOTHER GETTING HER CHILD READY
FOR A BATH. London. Private Collection

MOORE: THE SECRET SOUL OF THINGS

PARIS

He had his first retrospective in New York three years ago. The Biennale of Venice awarded him its first prize for sculpture last year. France, of course, has heard of this Englishman who, since the thirties, has been quietly revolutionizing the art of sculpture. But France had not yet taken full measure of a work that was already gigantic. Today, she has done so thanks to the retrospective in the Musée National d'Art Moderne in Paris.

The work is gigantic first of all by the size of the sculptures, which are often cramped in the museum space. It is gigantic especially by virtue of the will that animates it, renewing a connection with the most ancient traditions of universal art such as neolithic, ancient Egyptian, Etruscan, Cycladian, and South American Indian art, and establishing a bridge between these so-called primitive arts and the avant-garde

experiments of the beginning of the century such as Cubism and Surrealism. It is made even more gigantic by the spirit, in the biblical sense of the term, and the inner power that animate the work, neither having anything to do with the play of influences or with the weight of the artistic and intellectual context of the moment. Henry Moore is one of those few truly inspired artists of our times.

He was born in 1898 in a small industrial city of Yorkshire. The countryside where he lived is one of mine pits, factories, a country of moors and hills. He owes his first contacts with the world of art to the visits he was obliged to make to the Gothic churches of his area when he was a child. The enormous trunks of the beech trees covering the Yorkshire moors, the harmonious curves of the hills and the monumental Gothic statuary are all probably at the source of his vocation as a

sculptor and of the predilection that he shows for great dimensions and for raw material. A Freudian recollection is added to all of this: the young Moore experiencing one of the strongest sensations of his life one day when his mother asks him to massage her back. The volume of the shoulder blade under his fingers, the feminine skin rolling over the bone whose strange geometric form he feels, the consistency, the density almost . . . These bones and that skin sud-

denly remind the young child of the earth of his countryside and the stones that show at its surface. In the same visual and tactile image, stone, humus, and woman, earth and mother, see their common destiny sealed in the mind of the future artist. The great theme of the *Reclining Woman* and the immemorial theme of *Mother and Son* unfurl freely, with a powerful lyricism. Grafted onto the nourishing earth, the imposing maternal figure, symbol of fertility, rises

HENRY MOORE:
RECLINING FIGURE.
1938. London. Tate Gallery

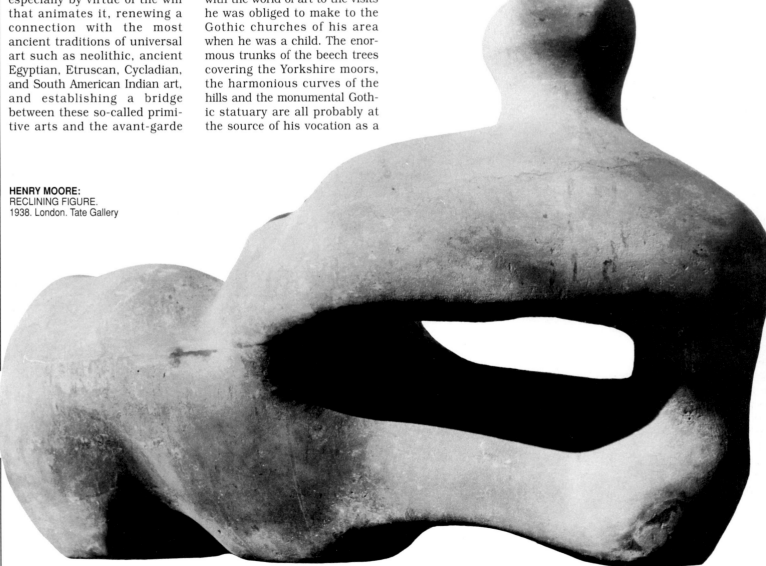

up, begins to levitate under the fingers of Henry Moore, the shaman.

His first works, produced at the beginning of the twenties, still remain prisoners of the ideology of "material." Under the influence of the sculptors Epstein and Gaudier-Brzeska, Moore believes that material, through its shape, its consistency, its accidents (a knot in the wood, a crack in the stone); predetermines the work.

He must not consider, then, molding clay or plaster; Moore allows himself nothing but the "direct cut." He works on his shapes while being inspired by the strange aspects of nature. One of his first works, *Woman and Child*, influenced by Cubism and Mexican art, is a massive block that maintains the original particularities of the stone. The woman is still soldered to the earth. As the years pass, as he completes nonrepresentational compositions, Moore develops his experiment with the "geometrization" of the human form.

Paradoxically, the more he "geometrizes" and the more he works in monumental proportions, the more his forms become lighter, suppler, and the more the stone becomes flesh and life. This is because the artist has made two major discoveries: the hole, and the body constituted of detached elements. Moore had been wishing for a long time to be able to treat sculpture like a landscape and the landscape like a sculpture. "Sculpture is an outdoor art. The light of the day is, for me, its best frame, and its complement is nature," he was to write. How can one integrate one into the other? Sculpture with holes, pierced or fragmented, allows for that marriage between sculpture and the surrounding space, between art and the world.

Moreover, it is not without reason that the man responsible for this happy wedding jealously prevents anyone, besides, himself from photographing his sculpture.

(See also 1940.)

In Moore's Words

Observing nature is part of an artist's life. It heightens his knowledge of form, enables him to preserve his freshness, spares him from having to work from formulas alone, and provides him with sources of inspiration.

The human form is what interests me most, but I have found shapes and rhythms in natural objects I have observed, like pebbles, rocks, bones, trees, and plants, etc.

In the bones there is a structure of astonishing vigor, a form of taut hardness, a subtle transition from one form to the next, and their cross section offers enormous variety.

In trees (in the trunks) we discover the elements of growth and the strength of knots, the easy passage from one section to the other. Their upward twisting movement lends itself ideally to wood sculpture.

Henry Moore.

The head is the most expressive part of the human being, and that is why it has always been treated as an independent theme in art. The artist may use the theme of the head in a variety of ways: for a portrait, to give expression to an imaginary head, or for a study as part of a larger work.

I will not betray the nature of stone in order to make it imitate soft flesh.

Pebbles and rocks reveal the way in which nature works on stone. Pebbles rolled in by the sea show the process of erosion, and friction of stone, and assymetrical elements.

Rocks reveal the treatment suffered by chipped and broken stone and have the rhythm of an angular, quivering block.

Shells represent the hard but hollow form of nature (metal sculpture) and possess the marvelous completeness of a single shape.

I cannot explain what gives a thing its monumental proportions. I think it is an inner vision, something that is in the mind rather than the material itself. The real size is not the question.

Knowledge of our own bodies, the bodies of others, and the human face is what makes the difference between a sculpture and an architect.

I would rather see my sculpture in a landscape, however uninspiring, than in the most beautiful building.

FONTANA: THE FIRST PERFORATED CANVASES

MILAN

Denying the limits of the pictorial surface by piercing it with strong blows from an awl is what the painter and sculptor Lucio Fontana is doing currently, in his concern with introducing a new spatial dimension.

"I don't want to make a painting, I want to open space, to create a new dimension for art," he declares, "to attach it to the cosmos that extends, infinite, beyond the flat surface of the image."

Born in 1899 in Argentina, of Italian origin (he is the son of the sculptor Luigi Fontana), Lucio Fontana passed progressively from representation to abstraction, and in 1935 in Paris, joined the group Abstraction-Creation. In 1946 in Buenos Aires, he published the *White Manifesto*, in which he advocates the "abandoning of the use of forms known to art for the development of an art based on the unity of time and space." The following year, in Milan, he signed a *Spatial Manifesto*, in which he declared that art must be "a function of new techniques and new means," that is to say, "evolutionary," and that "spatial art is the art of today: neon, Wood's light, television, therein lies the fourth ideal dimension of architecture." As for canvas, Fontana henceforth rejects its flat surface, and the dynamic role of the holes is to give to it the dimension it lacks.

With the exception of those who find in them a liberation of artistic expression, these perforated canvases are generally poorly received. Fontana affirms with lucidity: "Well beyond perforations a newly won liberty waits for us, but, just as obviously, the end of art waits for us as well."

(See also 1946.)

PIERRE SOULAGES: PAINTING. 1948. Paris. MNAM

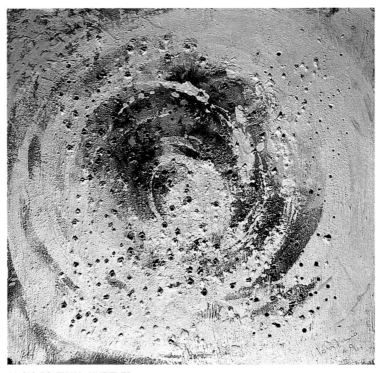

LUCIO FONTANA: UNTITLED.1948

SOULAGES: FIRST EXHIBITION

PARIS

Pierre Soulages is thirty years old. His first one-man show has taken place at the gallery Lydia Conti. His canvases are resolutely abstract. Their powerful graphic style is animated by marks grouped together by a large brush stroke. Their somber harmonies are warm, the "pastes" are generously handled. One feels a relationship with Celtic or Gallic engraved stones, the austere upstrokes of Roman sculpture, the structure of naked trees on a background of deserted plateaus . . .

This abrupt nature has always been a subject of fascination for this child of Aveyron, more so than the charming villages of his region or delicate Renaissance bas-reliefs. What he already loves in a wash drawing of Claude Lorrain or an ink drawing of Rembrandt is the brush stroke: its free and abstract line when the eye frames a detail, eliminating the representational subject in its unity. One day during his adolescence, in the nave of the cathedral of Sainte-Foy-de-Conques, a space housing a heated dialogue between shadow and light, Soulages decided to be a painter. At the age of eighteen he discovered Cézanne and Picasso in Paris. But he hid near Montpellier during the German occupation.

Only in 1946 was he able to settle down in Paris and paint. Refused entrance to several Salons, he exhibited in 1947 with the Ultraindependents. Picabia encouraged him: "It won't take you long to have a lot of enemies." Last year, Ottomar Domnick noticed him at the Third Salon des Réalités Nouvelles and selected him for the first abstract exhibition in Germany since Nazism. Its poster reproduced a painting of Soulages. His large signs are read with a single gaze. He strikes a chord, holds it, and creates a rhythm, a space, light . . .

The Erector-Set Houses

The Case Study Program initiated by the Los Angeles magazine *Arts and Architecture* has the objective of promoting modern architecture in California. It has recently presented its greatest accomplishment: a house built by the designer Charles Eames, a student of Saarinen, entirely from prefabricated elements. It is the first time in history that a house has been conceived from catalogued pieces and assembled on site like an erector set.

Motherwell Inspired by García Lorca

Robert Motherwell was profoundly influenced by European, especially Spanish, culture. Between 1941 and 1944, he executed *The Little Spanish Prison*, an extremely severe canvas, composed of vertical bands, which is devoid of any Automatism. His most recent painting, *At Five in the Afternoon*, notable for its almost brutal simplicity, opposes three oval forms among enormous bars. The title of this austere work clearly refers to a poem by Federico García Lorca, "A las cinco de la tarde." There is a strong connection between the painting and the poem.

Picasso's "Dove"

April 20 was a happy day for Picasso: Françoise Gilot gave him a daughter, Paloma ("dove"), and his painting *Dove*—the symbol of the World Peace Congress that opened at the Salle Pleyel—was to be seen all over the walls of Paris. Picasso let Aragon choose the ad hoc design from his already completed works. The choice was a lithograph executed in January at Mourlot's. It is said that Picasso could not resist making a little fun of his Party comrade Aragon: "The poor fellow. He doesn't know anything about pigeons! The sweetness of the dove, what a joke! No animals are more cruel!" It can be seen that Picasso's militant spirit has not caused him to lose his sense of humor, or his causticity.

Delvaux's "Pygmalion"

A confidential source informs us that during the Biennale of Venice last year a "confidential note" from Vatican authorities forbade members of the clergy to visit, under any circumstances, the Belgian Pavilion where Paul Delvaux's *Pygmalion* was displayed, as its sensuality was offensive to sight and thought. "I am horrified by scandal," commented the painter on his way to Paris, "and, of course, this decision makes me sad. Doesn't a church concerned with the misery and suffering of the world have other subjects to be concerned about?" And the artist also remarked that in the museums of Italy and the world there are other paintings at least as sensual as his. For, in fact, the essential characteristics of his painting are its novelty and hallucinatory qualities.

PABLO PICASSO: DOVE (POSTCARD ISSUED BY THE PEACE MOVEMENT). 1949

Wols, Michaux, and Mathieu at the Prospective Gallery

Three artists living in Paris are now being exhibited in New York: Wols, the young originator of Informal Art; Michaux, who is obsessed by the imprecise forms of his larval world; and above all Mathieu, who, at the age of twenty-eight, is acting as party leader. Less than two years ago, there was no indication that this self-taught artist, who regarded Salvador Dali as a model and idol, would take the lead in nonrepresentational, nongeometric painting, which in France seems to correspond to what in New York is called Gestural Painting. Mathieu, for whom "gesture precedes meaning," seeks what he calls "non-form" by means of rapidly brushed-on writing, which is sometimes very similar to Oriental calligraphy. It is artists like these who open today's art to totally new possibilities.

PAUL DELVAUX: PYGMALION. 1939. Brussels. Musée des Beaux-Arts de Belgique

JAMES ENSOR: THE ENTRY OF CHRIST IN BRUSSELS. 1888. Private Collection

THE SECOND DEATH OF BARON ENSOR

OSTEND

James Ensor died on November 19, in his good city of Ostend, at almost ninety years of age. His tragedy was that he was born too soon. The solitary precursor of Expressionism, his exploratory work was several years ahead of that of modern painters. Early on, his professors at the school of fine arts stigmatized his "boorish daydreams" because he demanded an unheard-of thing: a portrait's right to be ugly. Life, in his eyes, was nothing but a bitter farce that was best to be

laughed at. This is what made him the precursor of Expressionism and this is what, at the time, was disturbing.

An infallible instinct pushed Ensor to detect under appearances what was troubling in each face. From this derives his obsession with masks, which are present in almost all of his work. Ensor produced his most famous painting, *The Entry of Christ in Brussels*, in 1888, when he was only twenty-eight years old. This gift, which he said had been given to him mys-

teriously in 1879, was taken away from him just as mysteriously fifteen years later. Indeed, the man who has just died laden with honors, on whom nobility was conferred in 1930 by a king whom he had covered with sarcasm, this man loved and respected by all his countrymen, survived by a half-century the inspired painter he was during his youth, without adding anything significant to his work.

Critics today honor his remains as those of the greatest artist that Belgium has known

since Rubens, the last incarnation of Flemish genius with its excessive imagination, by turns sensual and diabolical. They agree to emphasize the unusual impression that the old white-bearded painter made on all who approached him, he who had accomplished his best paintings in another century, in the midst of the shells and Chinese curios of his studio.

Described in detail by all the newspapers of the country, the funeral services of Ensor were royal. Nothing was to be spared him; neither military fanfares nor flags, neither bishops nor tolling bells. The entire city, with its important figures at the head of the line, wanted to accompany the artist to his last resting place.

The creative activity of the artist was translated as a constant dialogue between the self and death, a choreography, a going back and forth between self-portraits and skeletons shown in all possible positions and all possible conditions. It is therefore not astonishing that a macabre irony is hidden in almost all of his canvases, even in his impassive and often implacable still lifes.

Ensor's funeral was the belated justification of his pessimistic vision of creatures and things, a grotesque parody of all parades and of all popular celebrations, a burlesque carnival, a zoomorphic paraphrase; nothing was lacking of what appears in his cavases. It is rare that an artist experiences fifty years of silence after such dazzling beginnings. And Ensor is perhaps the only great painter to have passed away prematurely. Thus the venerable baron who has just been buried at Ostend could well have died twice.

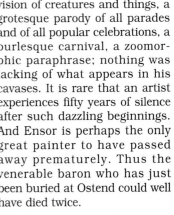

Funeral ceremony for James Ensor.

As supreme irony, and as a reprobate's ultimate nose thumbing at his posthumous admirers, his exit from life evokes irresistibly *The Entry of Christ in Brussels*, as though his masterwork had been a dress rehearsal.

AUGUSTE HERBIN: ART AND NATURE

For a long time, Auguste Herbin attempted to find himself through Cubism—he was Picasso's neighbor in the Bateau-Lavoir—and later by returning to a kind of Realism. But only now, at sixty-seven years of age, has he begun to blossom fully. The publication of his work *Nonfigurative, Nonobjective Art* at Lydia Conti places him squarely in the ranks of such theoreticians of abstract art as Mondrian or Kandinsky. Basing himself on Goethe's theory of color and Rudolf Steiner's theosophical thought, he creates a vocabulary that, poles apart from any type of Formalism, explains the creative force of his recent works. Below are his thoughts on the relationship between artist and nature.

There can be no work of art that is not, to some degree, related to external or internal nature. The degrees of these relationships are many and varied. From the faithful, strictly and immediately objective, superficial reproduction to the freest interpretations and transposiions and the most caricatural distortions, the nuances are endless. In these categories, there are very few works that could be considered living creations. These can be attributed to a few great artists who had intuition or a knowledge of the laws.

Creation is the product of the relationships of art not with aspects of the visible world but with the profound laws of nature, the fundamental laws. The relationships of art with aspects of the world engender still images only, which are greatly inferior to the living reality of those aspects. The relationships of art with the profound laws of nature create an original, spiritual reality, which enhances the richness of the visible world.

"Return to nature!" This piece of advice so often given to artists means nothing when put so simply. The artist does not exist outside nature. He does not leave it as one leaves a room and come back to it at his whim. We are nature itself, we are an integral part of nature, we do not have to return to it for we should not be leaving it.

Artists, perforce, always remain within the bounds of nature, which is at times only external, at other times only internal, or else in many more or less balanced combinations of external and internal nature. We have only to recall the recent example of Cézanne's and Van Gogh's teachings. Cézanne recommended translating external nature by geometrical volumes, cylinders, cones, pyramids, and so fort, in perspective and using blue for air. Van Gogh taught that color in itself expresses something, that

painting tends to become more subtle, more like music and less like sculpture. From Cézanne to Van Gogh, the idea of moving away from the external to the internal has made considerable progress.

A movement from external to internal and from internal to external must therefore be considered. This movement represents a long, sometimes painful struggle. In the process of this struggle, we can, by continually perfecting, achieve mastery of external and internal nature. This is the highest state, rarely attained by the artist, and the point at which the work expresses the purest reality.

AUGUSTE HERBIN
L'art non figuratif non objectif *(Excerpt)*

AUGUSTE HERBIN: AIR FAIRE. 1944. Paris. MNAM

The major event of the decade is the emergence of the United States as the star of the international art world, thanks to painters such as Pollock, De Kooning, and Rothko. This is a turning point in the history of world art, all the more radical in that the great creators of the beginning of the century die in rapid succession: Matisse in 1954, Brancusi in 1957, Rouault in 1958. Thus the

	1950	**1951**	**1952**	**1953**	**1954**
ARTS	• The "Irascibles," in New York, demand to be recognized by the American avant-garde • Matisse is awarded the grand prize at the Biennale in Venice	• The Catholic church turns to modern art • *Massacre in Korea* by Picasso • Nehru commissions Le Corbusier to build Chandigarh	• Harold Rosenberg defines new American painting as "Action Painting" • Inauguration of La Cité Radieuse by Le Corbusier in Marseilles	• Scandal over Picasso's *Portrait of Stalin* • Buckminster Fuller's geodesic dome • Braque's ceiling painting in the Louvre	• Death of Matisse • Jasper Johns paints the American flag • Arp, Ernst, and Miró: grand prizes at the Biennale in Venice
LITERATURE	• Bertrand Russell is awarded the Nobel prize in literature • *Canto general* by Pablo Neruda	• *REQUIEM for a Nun* by William Faulkner • *The Conformist* by Alberto Moravia	• *The Old Man and the Sea* by Ernest Hemingway • *East of Eden* by John Steinbeck	• *The Crucible* by Arthur Miller • *Writing Degree Zero* by Roland Barthes	• *A Ghost at Noon* by Alberto Moravia • *Lord of the Flies* by William Golding • *The Lord of the Rings* by J.R.R. Tolkien
MUSIC AND THEATER	• *The Bald Soprano* by Eugene Ionesco • *Symphony for a Lonely Man* by Pierre Henry and Pierre Schaeffer	• *The Devil and the Good Lord* by Jean-Paul Sartre • Gérard Philips in Kleist's *The Prince of Homburg* • Igor Stravinsky directs his *Rake's Progress* in Venice	• *Oedipus Rex* by Igor Stravinsky and Jean Cocteau • *Spiel für Orchester* by Karlheinz Stockhausen	• *Four Illustrations for Piano* by Giacento Scelsi • Death of Sergey Prokofiev	• First Jazz Festival in Newport, Rhode Island • *The Turn of the Screw* by Benjamin Britten • *Déserts* by Edgar Varèse
MOTION PICTURES	• *Rashomon* by Akira Kurosawa • *The Asphalt Jungle* by John Huston	• *An American in Paris* by Vincente Minnelli • *Strangers on a Train* by Alfred Hitchcock • *A Streetcar Named Desire* by Elia Kazan, with Marlon Brando	• *The Golden Helmet* by Jacques Becker • *The Quiet Man* by John Ford • *Limelight* by Charles Chaplin	• *Roman Holiday* by Roberto Rossellini • *Tales of a Hazy Moon after the Rain* by Kenji Mizoguchi	• *On the Waterfront* by Elia Kazan • *La Strada* by Federico Fellini • *The Seven Samurai* by Akira Kurosawa • *Rear Window* by Alfred Hitchcock
SCIENCE AND TECHNOLOGY	• Antihistamines are introduced for allergies and colds • Brooklyn-Battery Tunnel opens in New York	• First color-television broadcast, in the United States	• Test explosion of the first H-bomb • Mass production of IBM computer 701	• Discovery of DNA structure by Crick, Watson, and Wilkins • *Sexual Behavior in the Human Female* by Alfred C. Kinsey	• Polio vaccine developed at the Pasteur Institute • Linus Pauling is awarded Nobel prize in chemistry for work on molecular forces
POLITICS AND DAILY LIFE	• Beginning of the Korean War • Klaus Fuchs is found guilty of betraying atomic secrets	• 22nd Amendment to the U.S. Constitution, limiting the Presidency to two terms • Death sentence for Julius and Ethel Rosenberg for espionage	• Elizabeth II succeeds George VI • Dwight D. Eisenhhower is elected President • The "Iron Curtain" divides Berlin	• Death of Stalin • Armistice in Korea • Hillary and Tenzing are the first to climb Mount Everest	• Colonel Nasser seizes power in Egypt • U.S. Supreme Court rules that segregation by color is illegal in public schools

1959

panorama of art undergoes deep change in these post-war years. In Paris, painters in the French tradition gather around Bissière; the battle of Realism rages, troubling the best minds; and Mathieu proclaims the liberation of signs from meaning. With a view to securing the future, André Malraux, minister of culture, launches the Biennale des Jeunes in 1959.

1955	1956	1957	1958	1959
• Clement Greenberg defines "Color-Field Painting" • The first Documenta • *Yellow Manifesto* by Vasarely	• Death of Jackson Pollock in a car accident • *Cysp I* by Nicolas Schöffer, the first autonomous cybernetic sculpture	• Death of Constantin Brancusi • Hans Hartung exhibitions throughout West Germany • Ad Reinhart publishes *Twelve Rules for a New Academy*	• Inauguration of the UNESCO Building in Paris, which includes works by Picasso, Calder, and Miró • Expo 58 in Brussels: return of metal architecture	• First Biennale des Jeunes in Paris • Allan Kaprow invents the Happening • Frank Lloyd Wright's Guggenheim Museum in New York opens
• *Lolita* by Vladimir Nabokov • *Tristes Tropiques* by Claude Lévy-Strauss • *Cat on a Hot Tin Roof* by Tennessee Williams	• *The Fall* by Albert Camus • *The Roots of Heaven* by Romain Gary • Death of Bertolt Brecht	• *On the Road* by Jack Kerouac • *Two Women* by Alberto Moravia	• *Moderato Cantabile* by Marguerite Duras • *The Leopard* by Guiseppe Tomasi di Lampedusa • *Doctor Zhivago* by Boris Pasternak	• *Zazie* by Raymond Queneau • *Las armas secretas* by Julio Cortázar • *Henderson the Rain King* by Saul Bellow
• *Metastasis* by Iannis Xenakis • Maurice Béjart creates a ballet based on Symphony for a Lonely Man by Pierre Henry and Pierre Schaeffer	• *Gesang der Jünglinge* by Karlheinz Stockhausen • Faulkner's *Requiem for a Nun* is adapted to the stage by Albert Camus	• *Third Sonata for Piano* by Pierre Boulez • *Pulcinella*, a ballet by Maurice Béjart with music by Igor Stravinsky	• *Artic Meet*, ballet by Merce Cunningham, with music by John Cage and scenery by Robert Rauschenberg	• Performance of *The Resistible Rise of Arturo Ui* by Bertolt Brecht in Berlin • *The Condemned of Altona* by Jean-Paul Sartre
• *Rebel without a Cause* by Nicholas Ray • *Night of the Hunter* by Charles Laughton • *Diabolique* by Henri-Georges Clouzot	• *The Seventh Seal* by Ingmar Bergman • *The Silent World* by Jacques-Yves Cousteau	• *The Bridge over the River Kwai* by David Lean	• *Mon Oncle* by Jacques Tati • *Ashes and Diamonds* by Andrzej Wajda	• *Orfeu negro* by Marcel Camus • *Hiroshima, mon amour* by Alain Resnais • *The 400 Blows* by François Truffaut • *Suddenly, Last Summer* by Joseph L. Mankiewicz
• Death of Albert Einstein	• Atomic reactors opened at Marcoule in France and at Calder Hall in Great Britain • The neutrino is produced, and the antineutron is discovered	• The USSR launches the first satellites, *Sputnik I* and *II*.	• The United States launches its first satellite, *Explorer I* (31 pounds); the USSR, its third *Sputnik* (3,000 pounds) • Creation of NASA	• The USSR rocket Lunik reaches the moon • Launching of the first American nuclear-powered merchang vessel, Savannah
• Bus boycott against racial segregation in Montgomery, Alabama • *Why Johnny Can't Read* by Rudolf Flesch	• Egypt nationalizes the Suez Canal • The USSR crushes the Hungarian uprising • Martin Luther King emerges as a leader against racial segregation	• Six European nations sign the Rome Treaty, forming the European Market • Segregation crisis in Little Rock, Arkansas	• De Gaulle returns to office • Fidel Castro begins his war against the Batista government	• Khrushchev visits the United States • Castro become premier of Cuba • Alaska and Hawaii become the 49th and 50th states

Will European painting put up a long resistance to the American offensive? While Barnett Newman commands attention in New York, Bissière and Bazaine, two artists of the "sacrificed generation," set their work on a new course, making a complete break with the great movements of the early century. Bissière, after a long period of solitude, makes a particularly impressive showing as a first-rate painter with numerous disciples. But, an inevitable result of events, while Matisse and Villon receive important national prizes, it would be silly to hide the fact that the Parisian School, after reigning over the world of art for almost a century, is put to the test everywhere.

1950

S U M M A R Y

GREAT MASTERS

Bissière, Visionary Brother
In Bissière's Words

AVANT-GARDE

The Irascibles Revolt
Franz Kline's First Exhibit
The Faraway Light of Barnett Newman

AWARDS

Villon: the Carnegie Prize
Matisse: Grand Prize at the Biennale of Venice

ART NEWS

Picasso's *Man with a Sheep*
The New Künstlerbund
Mies van der Rohe in Chicago
Fluorescent Lighting Permitted in Museums
Clyfford Still at the Betty Parsons Gallery
In Brief

DEVELOPMENTS

The Bernard Buffet Event
A Studio without Models

WRITINGS AND THEORIES

Jean Bazaine: the False Quarrel of "Abstract" Art

LITERATURE

CHILE
Publication of Pablo Neruda's Canto general.

FRANCE
Roger Nimier publishes The Blue Hussar.
  Marguerite Duras publishes her first novel, Un barrage contre le Pacifique.

IRELAND
Publication of Insurrection, *a novel by O'Flaherty.*

MEXICO
Octavio Paz publishes The Labyrinth of Solitude.

MUSIC

FRANCE
Pierre Henry and Pierre Schaeffer compose Symphony for a Lonely Man.

THEATER

FRANCE
Premiere of The Bald Soprano *by Eugene Ionesco.*

DANCE

GREAT BRITAIN
The dancer and choreographer Vaslav Nijinsky dies at 60.

MOTION PICTURES

UNITED STATES
Premiere of John Huston's The Asphalt Jungle.

JAPAN
Akira Kurosawa presents his Rashomon.

CZECHOSLOVAKIA
Premiere of Prince Babaya, *an animated film by Jirí Trnka.*

ROGER BISSIÈRE
YELLOW AND GRAY.1950
Paris. MNAM

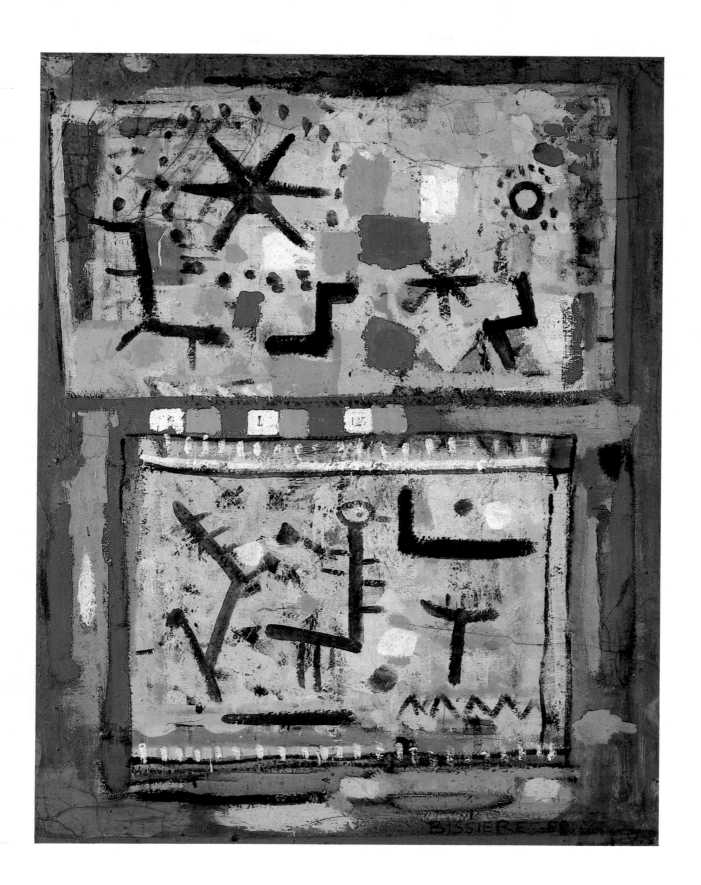

Roger Bissière.

BISSIÈRE, VISIONARY BROTHER

PARIS

The supreme horror for a painter: the loss of his sight, as happened to Claude Monet, in 1922, when he was working on the completion of the *Waterlilies*, now in the Orangerie. "My eyes continue to cause me concern; they aren't improving; on the contrary, my sight is diminish-

in the press, revealed one of the masters of contemporary French painting.

Bissière had not exhibited for twenty years. More in love with work than with fame, he retired in 1932, to Boissiérette in the Lot. He also gave up teaching at the Ranson Academy. "Now I am more or less settled. I have

"PAINTING IS NO LONGER ANYTHING TO ME EXCEPT A DESIRE FOR POETRY"

ing gradually, but continually," Roger Bissière writes to a friend at the beginning of the year. In July, he has an operation for glaucoma: "An operation has saved my eyes. But something that I cannot analyze has taken place in me . . . The material world has disappeared to make room for a marvelous world . . . Painting is no longer anything to me except a desire for poetry."

To listen to him, one would think that Bissière had to fear losing his sight to become suddenly, at the age of sixty-four, the visionary brother that everyone had been waiting for since Paul Klee. His exhibition at the gallery Drouin two years ago, even if it had few repercussions

received my twenty packages, my goats, my rabbits, my pigeons, and the whole bazaar. I have begun to dig my garden. Moreover, life conceived in this manner does not completely lack charm, it even has a certain sweetness." This was not the first time that he had cut himself off from the world. In 1914, he took up beekeeping, for a period of a year.

However, the artist is very far from being one of those that paint animals in the manner of Courbet, from whom art emerges at the simple unleashing of instinct. The monograph that he devoted to Braque in 1919 and his studies on Seurat, Ingres, and Corot come from a subtle

ROGER BISSIÈRE: LARGE COMPOSITION. 1947. Private Collection

and cultivated mind. But after being a fine-arts student in Bordeaux and in Paris, from 1905 to 1910, he rejected whatever culture contained that was conventional and required.

Like many other artists of this century, Bissière is fascinated with African statuary and children's drawings, and even more

so by Oceanic tapas. His paintings owe their enigmatic writing and even their particular matting to the latter. The artist obtains his matte finish by egg painting; the yolk allows water and oil to mix. Bissière paints willingly on poor supports, such as cardboard, small boards, and paper, as though he wished to preserve the modesty of an experimenter who doesn't want to fix anything in a definitive manner.

Perhaps his painting also proceeds from the stained-glass window, whose lead ribs support the multicolored elements. Like the artist, they sing the mornings of the world with many tones. One finds in both the same awe, the same spirituality.

If the artist likes to use waste materials, it is, however, never with the goal of derision, which is the opposite of Dada. After he came out of the war, Bissière accomplished with the help of his wife, Mousse, sumptuously sewn and embroidered hangings. Their themes are the sun, the moonlight, the goatherd. They are made out of sack canvas and old ends of cloth. Mud is transmuted into gold. This is the genius of the alchemist.

Bissière is not representational, but not abstract. In the artist's own words, he is used to being attached to "the sacrificed generation," which had the bad luck to come into the world at the tail end of the last century and close on the heels of the great creators of modern art. This generation comes to painting "too late," when it seems that nothing can be added to the discoveries of Fauvism and Cubism.

This misfortune has mainly the effect of making painting more difficult. "Good God, this struggle with the material is exhausting. And these days spent working—with the impression in the evening that one would have done better to stay in bed," Bissière writes to his son. "Nevertheless, I ought to be used to it, considering that I have known these despairs for thirty years, but I don't believe one ever gets used to it, and it's always just as discouraging."

Difficulty, fortunately, is not the enemy of achievement. After the success of his operation, Bissière is a visionary more than ever. One of his recent paintings, *Homage to Angelico,* is a masterpiece of innocence. After years of solitude, this work goes to explain his influence and his numerous disciples.

IN BISSIÈRE'S WORDS

Painting , if we truly wish to contemplate its essence, is a living geometry of forms and colors, a sort of new and more complex geometry in which colors and shapes would be inseparable and would react each upon the other, according to laws in which the elements of shape and of color would form one continuous whole.

In art, mathematics must be subordinate to phantoms. The good painter is the painter who buries a color every day.

The hand must venture into the unknown, it must remain alive to the danger it is courting, it must sense the brink.

A painting is the image of someone, a projection of the person in his entirety, devoid of lies or hesitation, with his flaws and his assets alike. Painting can brook no lies.

I do not go into a museum or to an exhibit to see paintings, but to meet people.

As we make one discovery, we already sense that we are about to make another, and hence the idea is ever ahead of achievement. Whence your torment, my torment, and the torment af all those who will struggle all their lives with the certainty of defeat.

The views we hold are of little importance. They are, moreover, limited. However inci-sive they may be, they have long been commonplace. The only way to awaken them is to find another angle from which to look. That rejuvenates them and makes them original, a result of being distorted in some unexpected manner through the prism of certain human minds.

I think that in order to attain self-fulfillment one must be brave enough to hover at the brink and to fall at times. It is by paying this price, and through dangerous undertakings that one emerges sufficiently original to be able to see the way clearly and stick to it without faltering.

I do not like masterpieces. There is something terribly boring about masterpieces. The painters who evoke a response in me have never been the creators of masterpieces. They have not exactly made pictures; but rather they have made mirrors in which their own image was reflected with an unsettling candor.

Cows in Paris—that does not mean much. For me, it is different. I do not disdain their company, and I have never become bored around them. They have large bright eyes; they are silent, gentle and pensive. They are simple and elementary like the Earth on which they stand and the grass on which they tread.

ROGER BISSIÈRE: HOMAGE TO ANGELICO. 1949. Amsterdam. Stedelijk Museum

THE IRASCIBLES REVOLT

NEW YORK

For several years, a number of New York artists have been expressing their discontent with the most important art institutions in the world, which, in their opinion, are scarcely concerned with new American painting, often preferring to exhibit European art. This year, eighteen painters send an open letter expressing their discontent to the president of the Metropolitan Museum of Art, Roland Redmond.

In fact, the famous museum is planning an exhibition entitled "American Painting Today—1950." But the eighteen painters maintain that the exhibitees are selected by juries "notoriously hostile to avant-garde art," and they refuse to submit their works. The most famous among the protesting artists are Adolph Gottlieb, Robert Motherwell, William Baziotes, Hans Hofmann, Barnett Newman, Clyfford Still, Ad Reinhardt, Jackson Pollock, and Mark Rothko. They constitute the heart of new Expressionist American painting.

The *New York Herald Tribune* devotes an editorial to the protest entitled "The Irascible Eighteen." It accuses the artists of distorting the facts. *The New York Times* and a number of magazines publish articles on the subject. It is an indication of the fact that the press and the public are beginning to be interested in true and authentic American creation. This preoccupation connects to a truth that has been imposing itself bit by bit since 1945: the shifting of the world's center of the arts from Paris to New York.

The fact is that these painters think of themselves as modern above all. As Jackson Pollock expressed it two years ago in the avant-garde review *Possibilities:* "It seems to me that modern painting cannot express our era (the airplane, the atomic bomb, the radio) through forms inherited from the Renaissance or from any other culture of the past. Each era finds its own technique."

The "Irascibles." 1951. From left to right and top to bottom: De Kooning, Gottlieb, Reinhardt, Sterne; Pousette-Dart, Baziotes, Pollock, Still, Motherwell, Tomlin; Stamos, Ernst, Newman, Brooks, Rothko.

FRANZ KLINE'S FIRST EXHIBIT

FRANZ KLINE: WOTAN. 1950

NEW YORK

Franz Kline differs from the other New York painters—he is not influenced by Surrealism. Born in Pennsylvania, in 1910, he was marked by the industrial landscapes of his youth. The cranes and the metallic towers of mining cities seem to have inspired his recent drawings and abstract paintings, done with ink or with black paint. His works seem to spurt forth with a purely spontaneous gesture, yet sketches do precede them. Eleven impressive paintings in black and white constitute his exhibition at the Eagen Gallery.

THE FARAWAY LIGHT OF BARNETT NEWMAN

NEW YORK

This first exhibition of Barnett Newman at the Betty Parsons Gallery represents a discovery even for his friends who had considered him to be more of a theoretician than a painter. Since 1944, however, his drawings and oil paintings have borne witness to preoccupations that are similar to those that he had been expressing in his articles and his prefaces. What is obvious here is his interest in Surrealism, and even more in primitive cultures. By the act of painting, he seeks to relearn the original gesture. "The first man was an artist" is the title of one of his articles.

The works from 1944 and 1945 evoke a gestating world in which are found shapes such as an egg on the point of being fertilized and suns in fusion. Soon, a vertical organization of the surface of the painting appears in which is discerned something like a faraway light pushing at the edges of a fissure, an opening toward the beyond. Bit by bit, space is made more austere. Newman abandons the Surrealism of his first works and attains, with *Onement One*, a symmetrical and unequivocal outline. Henceforth, he explores dimensions without depth of his

"WE MUST LISTEN
TO THE IMMOBILITY OF THE PAINTING"

vertical, rectangular canvas. *Onement One* is a small, flat, brown painting. It has a band covered in bright orange stuck in the middle of it. Cubist space is not what is found here; no object comes to punctuate it, as with Joan Miró. This is a major work and the point of departure of the current exhibition.

Betty Parsons has known the artist for several years. He was her closest consultant when she opened her gallery, and she willingly acknowledges that he

taught her more about art and esthetics than anyone. He has organized exhibits for her, for example, three years ago, "The Ideographic Picture," in which the works of Clyfford Still, Hans Hofmann, Mark Rothko, Ad Reinhardt, and Theodore Stamos were presented. In the preface of the catalogue, he said of the painters: "Here is a group of artists who are not abstract artists, even if their style is what people are used to labeling as abstract." This distinction is important, because for Newman "these artists create a truly abstract world . . . which can only be discussed in metaphysical terms."

The current exhibit surprises and shocks the artists and critics who are the most open to the pursuits of the New York

Expressionists. The canvases are generally large, almost monochromatic, and punctuated by one or two bands, most often vertical. *Onement III* is a variation on the first work. *End of Silence, Concord,* and *The Promise,* from 1949, are paintings of simple composition, with little gesture or texture, posing problems of proportions and the internal scale of the painting. This is all the more important because the color is often dark. The term metaphysical, surprising for canvases apparently all but empty, must be understood in the context of an article that Newman published in 1948: "The Sublime Is Now." A text by the critic Nicholas Calas dating from the same period confirms this point of view: "We must listen to the immobility of the painting with the same terror that causes us to hear the silence of deserts and of glaciers."

(See also 1955 and 1970.)

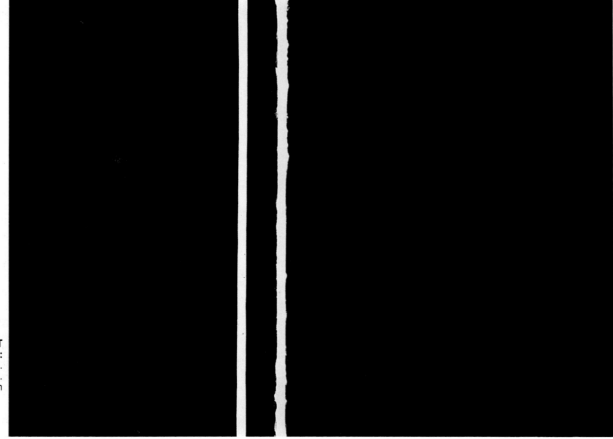

BARNETT NEWMAN: THE PROMISE. 1949. New York. Private Collection

VILLON: THE CARNEGIE PRIZE

JACQUES VILLON: WRESTLERS. 1937. Paris. Musée d'Art Moderne de la Ville

PITTSBURGH

"I believe this is the first time I have won a painting prize," Jacques Villon declares. His discreet career is made in the image of his modesty. At the age of seventy-five, he sees himself thrice honored: by an exhibit at the Venice Biennale, by a retrospective at the Musée National d'Art Moderne in Paris, and by the Carnegie prize, awarded in Pittsburgh.

The Carnegie is all the more prestigious because the jury decided to open it up to include Europeans for the first time since Hitler invaded the West. The new director of the Carnegie Institute, which was founded with the fortune of the philanthropic industrialist Andrew Carnegie, in fact noted that out of the three hundred and sixty paintings more than two hundred and fifty were of European origin. Great Britain and France were each represented by fifty-two paintings.

Jacques Villon was revealed to the United States in the early 1930s by an American critic, Walter Pach. Jacques is the brother of Raymond Duchamp-Villon and of the painters Marcel and Suzanne Duchamp, and the son of a notary. He was born in 1875 at Damville in Eure and named Gaston Duchamp. Sponsored by Frantz Jourdain, he participated in the Salon d'Automne from its beginning, in 1903. He was influenced by Fauvism and then by Cubism, and adopts Leonardo's principle of "pyramidal vision" in order to give to the painting "a thickness in which the colored echoes will play in depth" like a "perpetual motion device."

It was due to Villon's instigation that the group of artists in Puteaux organized and took the name Section d'Or (the golden section). His painting owes its peaceful influence mainly to the serenity of his inspiration. It is agreed that Villon's work remained in the background for much too long. It is appropriate to honor him with this international celebration.

MATISSE: GRAND PRIZE AT THE BIENNALE OF VENICE

VENICE

The 25th Biennale of the City of the Doges, which takes place from June 8 to October 15, awards its grand prize, one million lire, to Henri Matisse. At the age of eighty-one, the artist, who presents at the Maison de la Pensée Française the model and the plans for his Chapel of Vence, with a catalogue prefaced by Aragon, seems at the zenith of his genius. In spite of the assaults of age, he has never felt so free: "I hope that, as old as we may live to be, we will die young," he writes to a friend in the spring.

For the painter of *Joie de Vivre*, hell would be no longer being able to create. "Do I believe in God? Yes, when I work," he affirms. He aspires only to infinity! "Space has the extent of my imagination." It is to that henceforth serene imagination that Father Couturier appeals to erect the chapel, which absorbs him entirely. "Today, I am attached to its construction as to the definitive culmination of what I have been pursuing for years." He wants "to sum it all up in complete freedom."

Having exhausted the prestige of jubilant colors and found a live feeling, thanks to the freest expression, Matisse arrives at the most naive contemplation. He abridges the drawing and purifies the color in order to collect his thoughts in illumination. With generous cuts of the scissors, he fashions his own celestial spaces in the paper.

HENRI MATISSE: LARGE RED INTERIOR. 1948. Paris. MNAM

Picasso's "Man with a Sheep"

Picasso has been twice honored in Vallauris, where he has been working for the past several years. His Communist comrades on the municipal council have made him an honorary citizen, and on August 2 his sculpture *Man with a Sheep,* which he gave to the town, was dedicated in the main square. Among the friends of the painter who were present were Paul Éluard, Tristan Tzara, Jean Cocteau, and the poet André Verdet, who read a long poem in honor of the artist. The Communist party sent its "officer in charge of intellectuals," Laurent Casanova, who recalled the essential theses of the Communist esthetic in his speech. The bronze sculpture of almost classical construction—which, however, owes nothing to the "esthetic" of Socialist Realism—now stands in the main square of Vallauris, which is indebted to Picasso for the revival of its pottery industry and a new prosperity since he came to live there.

PABLO PICASSO: MAN WITH A SHEEP. 1944. Paris. Musée Picasso

The New Künstlerbund

During the month of June 1945, the Art Academy of Charlottenburg reopened its doors. The new director was the painter Karl Hofer, who had been forbidden to exhibit and was suspended from his teaching duties by the Nazis. A year later, in October 1946, Karl Hofer's first exhibit took place at the Berlin Academy. The artist, whose studio was bombed in 1943, resulting in the destruction of one hundred and fifty paintings and a thousand drawings, presented seventy-five of his recent works. Also in 1946, he founded, with Oskar Nerlinger, a new journal devoted to the plastic arts: *Bildende Kunst.* Today, with the painters Karl Schmidt-Rottluff and Karl Hartung, he has put the former Künstlerbund back on its feet, and was elected its president. The first exhibition of this association is scheduled for 1951, and will take place at the Art Academy.

Mies van der Rohe in Chicago

On the shores of Lake Michigan, near the historic center of Chicago, Ludwig van der Rohe, the pioneer of the glass skyscraper who has found in the United States, since 1937, the chosen land of his architecture, is building his Lake Shore Drive Apartments. The two twenty-six-story apartment buildings rise as parallelepipeds covered by a curtain of glass walls. Each section of façade was assembled on the roof of the buildings, then lowered and put in place on the steel structure. It is the first time in the world that buildings have been built almost entirely of glass and steel.

Fluorescent Lighting Permitted in Museums

The scientific consulting committee of the National Gallery in London, after studying the system of fluorescent lighting now installed in the museum, has just concluded that the paintings have not undergone any deterioration from ultraviolet radiation or from any other radiation emitted by this lighting. ICOM, the international organization that represents museums all over the world, came to the same conclusion in the latest issue of its journal: "The amount of natural daylight is at least twenty times greater than the maximum illumination supplied by fluorescent tubes in normal use."

Clyfford Still at the Betty Parsons Gallery

More than any other American painter, Still wishes to separate himself from the weight of history of European art and to create his own universe and his own history. He sees in painting an "unqualifiable act" that must break "with the illustration of worn-out myths or the various alibis of our contemporary world," and for which the artist "must assume complete responsibility." He spent his youth in the American West, moving to New York only in 1945. Since his representational beginnings, his work has been characterized by the vast prairie landscape and by the importance of the way it is affected by lighting. This explains in large part his present abstractions. Clyfford Still is forty-six years old.

BERNARD BUFFET: THE NET MENDER. 1948. Paris. Galerie Maurice Garnier

THE BERNARD BUFFET EVENT

PARIS

He is only twenty-two years old and already famous. The critical prize that Bernard Buffet received in 1948 (with Bernard Lorjou, twenty years his senior) immediately brings celebrity.

This year, in addition to the February exhibition at the gallery Drouant-David which stupefies art critics, Buffet exhibits at the gallery Motte in Geneva, the Kleemann Gallery in New York, the Bettie Thommen Gallery in Basel, the Apollo Gallery in Brussels, and the Tokanten Gallery in Copenhagen. The art world discovers his acid and ascetic work, stripped down to the cruelest and most expiatory detail. Journalists compare this skinny, timid young man to Rimbaud or to Lautréamont.

Buffet was discovered by Pierre Descargues in December 1947 at his very first exhibition. The artist seems born of the war, like the poet who, emerging from his *Season in Hell,* admits that he lost his life through being delicate. Or like the poet of *The Songs of Maldoror,* who announces, "I serve my genius by painting the delights of cruelty."

Even a single Buffet is enough to haunt the viewer. Everything is depopulated. His audacious timidity gets to the bottom of everything. Even his colors are the accomplices of his helpless confusion.

Buffet suffers from deep depression. He admits cruelly: "Painting is not supposed to make you laugh." He frays his environment as one patches a spider's web, taking parsimonious inventory of the little he finds there.

He cannot be consoled for having seen his mother die in July 1945, as he was vacationing with her. His dealer, Emmanuel David, takes him to the Vaucluse this summer. He comes back with a painting he presents to the gallery Charpentier: Two naked twin men in a desert of hills give evidence of the artist's desperate egotism.

A STUDIO WITH-OUT MODELS

PARIS

An upheaval in the "republic of the arts!" Two avant-garde artists decide to compete with the Beaux-Arts. Following Hayter, Friedlaender, and Flocon, two young abstract painters, Jean Dewasne and Edgard Pillet, take over the management of a teaching studio on the Rue de la Grande-Chaumière and devote it entirely to abstract art. The studio will have no models, obviously, and it decides that between its walls abstraction exclusively will be taught. The students will be made familiar with new materials, such as Formica and plexiglass.

"Our effort," says Dewasne, "depends on the notion of abstract painting. We will teach the students to strip themselves of all reminiscence and of all habits of thinking like Realistic painters in their paintings. And that is one of the least of the difficulties they will encounter. For example, we will compose a canvas with only three tones. Color will summon form. The students will apply themselves to finding well-defined colors, so that there will be no doubt as to what is on their canvases. They will learn to think and to paint without mystery; there is an obvious system linked to abstract painting. Pillet and I will be in the studio every day by rotation. Every two weeks, another abstract painter will come to confirm corrections. Historical and technical lectures will be given by artists and critics. We hope to make known, as much by the opinions expressed as by our collective work, the power and the rigor of a new art."

We wish good luck to this new studio. May it never become either an academy or an Academism. What developments are the new approaches to the theory of pictorial practice going to bring along?

Jean Dewasne in his workshop for abstract art.

JEAN BAZAINE: THE FALSE QUARREL OF "ABSTRACT" ART

At forty-six, Jean Bazaine is one of the masters of the new Parisian School. His work borders on Abstractionism, where the quarrel dividing artists and critics is, in his eyes, a false problem. Neither figurative nor allusive, his paintings seek to express the profound forces governing all of reality, such as what can be done now that the plastic arts have come full cycle. He expounds upon that admirably in his *Propos sur la peinture d'aujourd'hui* (thoughts on contemporary painting), published two years ago, which quickly sold out and has just been republished by Éditions du Seuil in a new, revised, and expanded version.

It is difficult to make sense of this false argument over "abstract" art that rests on such confusion of words and ideas. Its obvious success—the fact that hundreds of painters in the world have abruptly given up creating apples or sunsets to embark on what they see as an adventure—is not sufficient to justify it. But abstract art no doubt deserves better than its phony name, all the misunderstandings to which it has given rise, and this avant-garde Academicism of which it bears the seeds.

What is abstract art? It is, we are told, the utter rejection of "imitation, reproduction, and even the distortion of forms from nature." It is the refusal to let in the outside world and the striving to build, outside the realm of any "external" influence, the drama of line and color. It is what, in the language of today, is called "nonfigurative."

This temptation to draw forth from oneself what for the world is shapeless and unsettling, the very signs, the scars of one's most secret inner movements, has been the painter's raison d'être since painters have existed. But it cannot mean that forms (and combinations of forms) from nature are to be rejected, for the forms on the canvas, as nonfigurative as they may be, even when they pass through us and leave us, have to come from somewhere . . .

It is a tremendous error to continue speaking of the object, the "real" object, as if it had at one time been the "end" of the work of art and had not always been the means: Art, in every age, has always been nonfigurative. There is nothing new in that, and it is odd that it should have to be repeated.

As for the idea of I know not what progress in art that would make nonfigurative art the only means of attaining the universal, let us simply say that that idea has been put forward. It would amount to nothing less than denying all painting because

JEAN BAZAINE:
THE DIVER. 1949. Cologne.
Ludwig Museum

painting would be valuable only as an abstraction . . .

These passing thoughts merely cast a revealing light on the twisted thinking that tends to associate creation with a logical, incremental progression, with the distinct phases characteristic of intelligible knowledge, seemingly ignorant of the fact that things are sensed in a totally different fashion, by a sort of blossoming of sensation, radiating within itself . . .

JEAN BAZAINE
Propos sur la peinture d'aujourd'hui
(Excerpts)

481

After turning their backs on each other, the church in France and modern art now join hands, thanks to the perseverance of Father Couturier. In Assy, in Audincourt, in Vence, in Ronchamp, everywhere religious buildings are being built or planned. Most of the great names in painting and architecture of the twentieth century collaborate, including Matisse, Léger, and Le Corbusier. This coincides with André Malraux's publication of The Voices of Silence, *picking up the ideas of Elie Faure where they left off. As to the avant-garde, the works and writings of Georges Mathieu renew the notion of the sign in its relation to meaning, and Dewasne, with his Apotheosis of Marat, leads Abstract Geometric art in an unanticipated direction.*

1951

S U M M A R Y

ARCHITECTURE

The Church Calls upon Modern Art

WRITINGS AND THEORIES

Father Couturier: Sacred Art

ART AND POLITICS

The Apotheosis of Marat
Massacre in Korea

ART NEWS

Death of Dr. Barnes
Zadkine's Cry
Rauschenberg at Betty Parsons
From Van Gogh and Seurat to Children's Drawings
Le Corbusier in the Punjab
In Brief

WRITINGS AND THEORIES

Georges Mathieu: Sign Comes before Meaning
André Malraux: from Museum to Imaginary Museum

LITERATURE

UNITED STATES
William Faulkner publishes Requiem for a Nun.
William Styron publishes Lie Down in Darkness.

FRANCE
André Gide dies at 81.

ITALY
Publication of The Conformist *by Alberto Moravia.*

MUSIC

UNITED STATES
Arnold Schönberg, the creator of the twelve-tone system and the theory of atonality, dies in Los Angeles.

THEATER

FRANCE
The main event is the performance of The Devil and the Good Lord *by Jean-Paul Sartre, directed by Louis Jouvet, with scenery by Félix Labisse.*
In Avignon, Gérard Philipe is applauded in Heinrich von Kleist's Prince of Homburg.

MOTION PICTURES

UNITED STATES
Premiere of Alfred Hitchcock's Strangers on a Train *and Vincente Minnelli's* An American in Paris.

FRANCE
Robert Bresson films Journal d'un curé de campagne.

HENRI MATISSE
STAINED-GLASS WINDOWS OF VENCI
(DESIGN). 1949. Paris. MNAN

THE CHURCH CALLS UPON MODERN ART

FRANCE

"History will list January 20, 1951, as the date of renewal of Christian art. On this day, a diocesan commission met under the chairmanship of the arch-bishop and unanimously ap–proved seventeen sketches by Fernand Léger, the model of a large mosaic by Bazaine, and the drawings of Le Corbusier for the church in Ronchamp," Father Marie-Alain Couturier writes in the November issue of his maga-zine, *L'art sacré* (sacred art). Enthusiastically he adds: "If such projects, which represent what are now the purest and strongest works of modern art, can be approved without diffi-culty by high church authorities, it means that something has changed in the French church!"

What changes! In fact, what a revolution from the Gothic and Byzantine pastiches that the church has glorified in Lourdes, Fourvière, and Lisieux! The French church is finally asking the greatest creators of modern art to build and decorate churches and chapels. It is all far removed from the art it patronized throughout the nine-teenth century.

Notre-Dame-de-Toute-Grâce, Plateau d'Assy.

The French church? Let us rather say a Dominican Father. Aristocrat and artist, Father Couturier has adopted this motto of Delacroix: "We must always bet on genius." Being interested in renovating stained-glass windows, he spent the war years in America. With Léger, Ozenfant, and Chagall, he opened the French Institute of Modern Art at the French School in New York. He returned to France in 1945 and appealed to the greatest artists, whether or not they were religious, to con-vince them to convert the clergy to modern art. For two years now, religious works have been coming out of their studios and flourishing . . .

Last August 4, the church of Notre-Dame-de-Toute-Grâce was consecrated on the Plateau of Assy, a resort in Haute-Savoie. The architect was Maurice Nova-rina. "Here is Léger! Here is Lurçat! Here is the first time that Rouault is admitted to a church! Here, in the twilight, is Pierre Bonnard! Here is this altar of the sacred host where Christ receives the double, silent homage of Braque and Matisse," the Dominican proudly writes in *Art sacré*. Another church by Novarina is the church of the Sacré-Cœur in Audincourt, in Doubs, for which Bazaine made a mosaic on the theme of the Eucharist and Léger, Bazaine, and Le Moal made the stained-glass windows, and Léger an Aubusson tapestry. Isn't it a

The church at Audincourt, Doubs.

miracle that an unbeliever like Léger could produce such a religious work? Father Couturier is happy, for he sees that his audacity bears fruit: "He who always by conviction and taste recognizes his solidarity with the fate of the workers finds instinctively in a church a language they understand." He was touched by the volunteers who participated in building their new church, assisting with the structure, making the benches and liturgical appurtenances, to make up for the lack of funds.

But isn't it also an amazing reciprocal conversion, that of Matisse and the church?

The message of Matisse, which was conceived in its entirety for the Dominicans of Vence, the chapel of the Rosary, is clear: "I want those who enter my chapel to feel purified and released from their burdens." It is understood. Monsignor Rémond, the bishop of Nice, and the nuns inaugurate this admirable chapel in silent joy on June 14. Matisse is able, as he says, to endow it "with infinite dimensions by the simple play of colors and lines."

Matisse was fascinated in 1933 by the frescoes of Giotto in the chapel of the Annunciation in Padua. Convinced by his dear nurse and seductive model, Monique Bourgeois, who entered the Dominican order under the name of Sister Jacques-Marie in 1946, he first created the windows for the shed that served her community as a chapel, then undertook the creation of the whole chapel. Matisse was able to find a unique spiritual dimension in the clear light of his windows, shaped as stylized olive leaves, and under the immense silhouette of his Saint Dominic, inspired by the person of Father Couturier. It is nothing if not a prayer of adoration.

FATHER COUTURIER: SACRED ART

Three years after his return from the United States, Father Couturier resumed his post, in 1948, as director of *L'art sacré,* which he had founded in January 1937 at Éditions du Cerf with Father Régamey, who was also a Dominican, who disagreed, however, over the role the magazine should play. Father Régamey would have it pedagogical, while Father Couturier wanted it to be solely "poetic" for he wanted first of all to restore taste in the people of the church. Below are two excerpts of articles expressing his ideas.

The history of art proves irrefutably that for one hundred and fifty years no work has lasted, no work has survived other than those in which the preeminence of the beauty of forms as such as has been—consciously or unconsciously—absolute. Absolute, in other words without any concessions to moral, social, or apostolic purposes exterior to the work. The moment such concessions are made, we effectively leave the realm of art proper for the realm of propaganda, a realm in which the means are essentially temporary. And the work, discredited after a few years, loses all its effect, while pure relationships of color and lines preserve forever that miraculous power to purify, calm, or exalt not even sought by their creators. For beauty, in and of itself, is already a gen-

GERMAINE RICHIER:
CHRIST. Church on the
Plateau d'Assy

uine asset: Diffusum *sui (which spreads by itself) . . .*

That is why we are presenting images here that will be nothing but pure, beautiful images and, if possible, without legends or explanations. This is so that no rational activity comes between what should remain a very simple and very direct intuition of the senses . . ."

"Devant l'art profane,"
L'art sacré, *January-February 1950*

Is it possible to look to the great modern artists? . . . Great people are meant for great things . . . Is there a cathedral to be built? We will say to ourselves: Somewhere in the world, there must be an architect who is the greatest architect in the world. he is the one who is worthy and capable of it . . . The same is true for a great work of painting or sculpture. Let us recall that France has the greatest living painters and sculptors. Today they are covered with glory, universally known. We will turn to them. On principle...

They will not do what we want, we may tell ourselves. But, thank God! For often what one wants, what one likes, is vastly inferior to what they would do, left to their own inspiration. And, in any case, experience has proved that even when thus left to his own devices, what a great artist can come up with on his own has infinitely more worth than the inevitable platitudes of docile mediocre types, who are generally as mediocre as they are yielding.

Genius does not impart faith, but between mystical inspiration and the inspiration of heroes and great artists, the analogy is too deep not to be prejudiced in their favor.

"Le prêtre et la création artistique,"
L'art sacré, *May-June 1950*

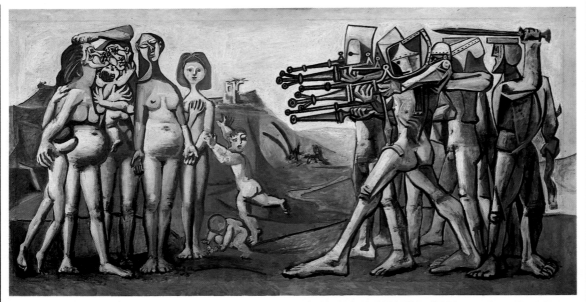

PABLO PICASSO: MASSACRE IN KOREA. 1951. Paris. Musée Picasso

THE APOTHEOSIS OF MARAT

PARIS

When David, during the Revolution, painted the assassinated Marat in his bathtub, with his poor body abused by work and sickness, art was Neoclassical, descriptive, and hagiographic, and historical painting was at its apex.

What Jean Dewasne is showing today, however, is the apotheosis of the Friend of the People, defender of widows and orphans, transported to the Pantheon with the ceremony due a revolutionary hero. Furthermore, his painting is abstract. "Last year, I read a selection of texts by Marat. I was carried away by their power and truthfulness. Marat analyzes the treason of Mirabeau before even thinking of betrayal . . ."

Dewasne's painting is an intellectual painting of the fiery tribune. It is also a feast of pure tints, a dynamic play of curves and right angles affecting the eye directly. It is proof that abstraction is not limited to expressing spiritual values, as in Malevich or Mondrian, but, like figurative painting, can evoke a historic or political event. Last year, Dewasne opened a school, with Edgard Pillet, devoted entirely to abstract art. His *Apotheosis of Marat* should prove that the school is not condemned to mere decoration.

MASSACRE IN KOREA

PARIS

The Communists are not happy and do not hide the fact. The reaction of the militants has been unanimous: Why does Picasso, the Communist, not remain faithful to Party directives on "art for the masses"? Why is he permitted—although he wishes to be known as a militant, like the others—to continue to paint in an illegible, incomprehensible, repulsive style?

Daniel-Henry Kahnweiler, Picasso's agent, who sees the contested painting in Vallauris before it is shown in the exhibition in May, finds it "overwhelming with human pity." Its title is *Massacre in Korea.* It was inspired by the American intervention in South Korea last year, after armed forces of Communist North Korea crossed the 38th Parallel and occupied the capital city of Seoul.

This again is "Picasso furioso" whose *Guernica,* in 1937, denounced the bombing of the Basque town by the Condor Legion. Like *Guernica,* the *Massacre in Korea* is monochrome, light steel gray with slight yellow and green shading. As in *Guernica,* innocent, resigned victims fall under enemy fire. The scene could take place anywhere, at any time: Robot men shooting a group of naked men and women as children flee—the action belongs to all times.

In *Les lettres françaises* Jean Marcenac is asked to speak out. Auguste Lecœur, the secretary of the Communist central committee, asks that as little mention as possible be made in Party papers of *Massacre in Korea.* How long will Picasso have to swallow insults to "save the revolution"?

(See also 1904, 1905, 1907, 1909, 1912, 1921, 1927, 1937, 1945, 1946, 1948, 1953, 1954, 1958, 1973.)

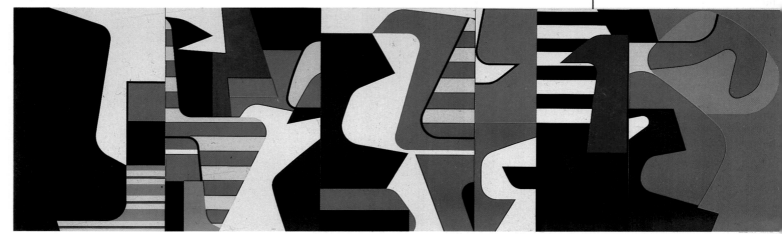

JEAN DEWASNE: THE APOTHEOSIS OF MARAT. 1951. Paris. MNAM

Death of Dr. Barnes

Albert C. Barnes recently died in an automobile accident near Philadelphia, at the age of seventy-eight. He leaves a collection of modern art valued at fifty million dollars. Barnes was the discoverer of the drug Argyrol, from which he made a fortune, allowing him to create a foundation in Merion that made him famous. He began his collection when he walked into the gallery Paul Guillaume in Paris one day and was soon the owner of two hundred Renoirs, seventy-five Matisses, thirty-five Picassos, and innumerable old masters. Conceived as a museum for public education, the Barnes Foundation was essentially reserved for students and workers. He refused admission to rich art lovers and even critics who came in the hope of contemplating Cézanne's famous painting *The Game of Cards*, for which he paid seven million prewar francs. According to his will, the collection is to remain intact.

Zadkine's Cry

Since 1948 the sculptor Ossip Zadkine had been working on the monument that he recently erected in Rotterdam. He wished to commemorate the destruction of the city by the *Luftwaffe* at the beginning of the last war with a cry, a little like Picasso when, with *Guernica* in 1937, he let out a cry of sorrow after the annihilation of the Basque town by the same forces. It is a complete success, for it was difficult to express human despair with such a great economy of means. It is the crowning achievement of this sixty-year-old sculptor who, starting with Cubism in his youth, has today achieved full maturity. And perhaps it was even more difficult to make his monument for the street, placing it in the midst of the immense concrete and glass buildings of rebuilt Rotterdam. It was no small challenge.

Rauschenberg at Betty Parsons

An important figure in the artistic life of New York, Betty Parsons comes from an old American family; one of her ancestors founded Yale University in the eighteenth century. Born in 1900, Betty Parsons came to Paris at the age of twenty to study sculpture. She worked beside Giacometti in the studio of Antoine Bourdelle before returning to the United States in the 1930s. In 1946, she began her career as an art dealer when she opened her own gallery, where she exhibited Hans Hofmann and the first "drip paintings" of Jackson Pollock. In recent years, she has regularly shown the paintings of Mark Rothko, Ad Reinhardt, and Clyfford Still. And more recently, Barnett Newman . . . She is now showing the paintings of the young Robert Rauschenberg. Her gallery has become a popular spot with the avant-garde.

From Van Gogh and Seurat to Children's Drawings

Exhibitions of children's drawings are multiplying. Each time, we are struck by the charm, the spontaneity, and the ingenuity that emerge from them. They are compared to works of art. But once the exhibition is over, everything is dispersed. That is why Dr. Françoise Minkowska has proposed to the Pedagogical Museum in Paris to take another look at the miracle of childhood, using Rorschach tests and drawing to attempt to approach the miracle of creativity that is manifested in the child from a young age. In this way, drawings by children of different ages, conditions, and ethnic backgrounds have been compared to Van Gogh and Seurat. From the healthy child to the sick one, up through the adult and the artist, Françoise Minkowska makes us travel the same road in two directions: We "go back" to the genius of childhood in order to return to the childhood of genius.

OSSIP ZADKINE: THE DESTROYED CITY. 1951. Rotterdam

Le Corbusier in the Punjab

Since the plans of the American Albert Mayer were not satisfactory, the realization of Chandigarh, the future capital of the Punjab and the city Nehru wishes to build as a symbol of modern India, has been entrusted to a team headed by Le Corbusier. The city will be laid out on a rectangular grid, with a monumental center marked by spectacular buildings: the assembly, the capitol, the secretariat, and the high court of justice, which will be designed by Le Corbusier. The principal buildings of Chandigarh will be reflected in a vast expanse of water, like the Taj Mahal.

GEORGES MATHIEU: SIGN COMES BEFORE MEANING

A youthful, cavorting master of Lyrical Abstractionism, Georges Mathieu, at age thirty, is also a brilliant theoretician whom no modern scientific, psychological, or linguistic notion escapes. Skipping over the Renaissance, he belives that painting today is undergoing its most radical revolution since the time of classical Greece in that, from now on, the sign will precede meaning—something never before seen in the history of art. Descriptive or allusive figuration is over, gone are the days of Automatic Writing so dear to the Surrealists and later adopted in the United States by Hans Hofmann and Jackson Pollock. We must start all over on different premises. The text that follows has never been published before.

GEORGES MATHIEU:
GREAT WHITE
ALGORITHM. 1951.
The Artist's Private
Collection

Just as there are approximations such as empty and full, permeable and watertight, light and dense, which are of some convenience in communication, so, it seems, there are two possible and rather decisive aspects of the means of expression: poetic and significant.

Through an almost total devaluation of the poetic, these two aspects, which were once intimately bound up, are in certain extreme current approaches completely separated.

The poetic, being irrepressible, had to take refuge in a sort of atonal superpoetic in order to find, in our Western mentality, a few traces of justification. It allowed the signifier to invade almost every area (even its own) at the expense of any secondary gratuitousness. This signifier, for its part, can no longer merely signify; it attempts to transcend meaning in order to attain effectiveness.

It has been stated elsewhere how much potential had been restored to the sign by the Gestalt theoreticians: There is no longer any need to make references to a previous sign in order to explain effectiveness—the fact that it existed is sufficent. The phenomenon of meaning is bursting forth: From now on, effectiveness would issue from the sign and not the signified. If this theory can be applied to figurative works, it is the only one to recognize the power of nonfigurative signs to convey meaning.

Indeed, in a figurative work, effectiveness enters into in the relationships of the signified, as signs are tainted with references that prevent them from acting autonomously and directly. In the nonfigurative work, on the contrary, the signs are not charged with resonances of "departure" or acquired resonances. Therefore, if they are effective, they have only themselves to thank . . .

The laws of semantics are suddenly reversed: Until now, given a thing, a sign was invented for it. From now on, given a sign, it will be viable and hence a veritable sign if it finds its incarnation.

GEORGES MATHIEU
Note sur le poétique et le signifiant
(Excerpt)

ANDRÉ MALRAUX: FROM MUSEUM TO IMAGINARY MUSEUM

André Malraux owes the title of his work *The Voices of Silence*, published by Gallimard, to Elie Faure. Like Faure in *The Spirit of Forms*, Malraux juggles with centuries and civilizations, criticizes, compares, deduces. His book—fascinating and dazzling like the author himself—has not always been well received by art historians, with whose method and customary ideas he takes issue. But it seems clear that from now on this will be an important text, which will have its place in history. Below we are reprinting a portion of his first chapter, which sets the tone. In it, Malraux ponders the meaning of the institution that we call a museum.

The role of museums in our relationship with works of art is so great that we can hardly conceive of the fact that there are none and never were any where modern European civilization is or was unknown, and that they have existed in France for less than two centuries. The nineteenth century lived off of them, and we still do, forgetting that they imposed a whole new relationship between viewer and work of art. They helped deliver the works of art they housed from being functional, to transform them into paintings, even portraits. While the bust of Caesar or horseman Charles V may still be Caesar and Charles V, the duke of Olivares is no longer anyone but Velásquez. Of what is the identity of the man with the helmet or the man with the glove? Their names are Rembrandt and Titian. The portrait ceases to be first and foremost the portrait of someone. Until the nineteenth century, all works of art were the images of something that did or did not exist, before being—and in order to be—works of art. Only in the painter's eyes was painting painting; often, it was even poetry as well. And the museum deprived almost all the portraits (even if they were of a dream) of almost all their models at the same time that it stripped works of art of their function. It no longer knew palladium, saint, or Christ, or object of veneration, likeness, imagination, décor, possession: but rather images of things, different from the things themselves, which from this specific difference derived their raison d'être . . . The museum separates the work from the "profane" world and brings it closer to opposing or rival works. It is a confrontation of metamorphoses . . .

Art's voyage completes it in the nineteenth century. But rare was the person at that time who had seen all of the great works of Europe. Gautier had seen Italy without seeing Rome, at thirty-nine; Edmond de

Visitors at the Picasso exhibition in Rome.

Goncourt, at thirty-three; Hugo, as a child; Baudelaire, Verlaine, never . . .

Today's student has a color reproduction of most of the masterly works, discovers many secondary paintings, archaic art, and the Indian, Chinese, and pre-Columbian sculpture of the major periods, knows some Byzantine art, Roman frescoes, and tribal and popular art. How many statues were reproduced in 1850? In our albums, sculpture—which black and white reproduced more faithfully than it did paintings—appears to be the preferred mode. We knew the Louvre (and some of its annexes), which we remembered as best we could. For an imaginary museum has opened, which will drive to an extreme the incomplete confrontation imposed by the real museums: In response to their cry, the plastic arts have invented their printing press.

ANDRÉ MALRAUX
The Voices of Silence *(Excerpts)*

The great offensive of the New York School begins, with first-rate artists like De Kooning and Pollock, who assert themselves at once as artists of international scale. For his part, the critic Harold Rosenberg invents the term "Action Painting" to designate their new way of painting, and the term seems to catch on. And, since one good thing leads to another, Black Mountain College also distinguishes itself when it stages a wild evening, orchestrated by John Cage.

In France, *Art of Another Kind*, an important work by Michel Tapié, is published. At the Salon de Mai, Picasso charms the crowds with his *Goat*, while silence greets Pignon's painting *The Dead Worker*, a work by an artist who goes against the grain of every style, abstract as well as Socialist Realist.

1952

S U M M A R Y

AVANT-GARDE

The Triumph of Abstract Expressionism
Harold Rosenberg: the American Action Painters
Black Mountain College

WRITINGS AND THEORIES

Michel Tapié: Art of Another Kind

POLEMIC

Breton: "Why Are They Hiding Soviet Painting from Us?"
Picasso Challenged by the Communists

ART NEWS

Mixed Reactions to Pignon's *Dead Worker*
Ellsworth Kelly's Monochrome Panels
Canvas Slashers Caught at the Musée d'Art Moderne
The de Chirico Brothers
Picasso's *Goat* at the Salon de Mai
In Brief

EXHIBITIONS

Germany Rediscovers Modern Art
**The Eternal Character of Fantastic Art
and Its Metamorphosis**

ARCHITECTURE

The Mirror on Park Avenue
The Incredible "Maison du Fada"

LITERATURE

ARGENTINA
Jorge Luis Borges publishes Other Inquisitions.

UNITED STATES
Publication of The Old Man and the Sea *by Ernest Hemingway, and* East of Eden *by John Steinbeck.*

FRANCE
Raymond Queneau publishes his collected poems as Si tu t'imagines.

MUSIC

GERMANY
Karlheinz Stockhausen composes Spiel für Orchester.

FRANCE
Performance of Oedipus Rex *by Igor Stravinsky and Jean Cocteau.*

MOTION PICTURES

UNITED STATES
Premiere of The Quiet Man *by John Ford, with John Wayne and Maureen O'Hara, and* The Greatest Show on Earth *by Cecil B. De Mille.*

FRANCE
Jacques Becker presents his first film, The Golden Helmet, *with Simone Signoret and Serge Reggiani.*
   Premiere of Forbidden Games *by René Clément, a beautiful film performed by children, with Brigitte Fossey.*

WILLEM DE KOONING:
WOMAN I. 1950-1952.
New York. MOMA

JACKSON POLLOCK: ECHO. NUMBER 25. 1951. New York. MOMA

THE TRIUMPH OF ABSTRACT EXPRESSIONISM

NEW YORK

Abstract Expressionism or Action Painting? The painters of the New York School are not always abstract and not always Expressionist. Perhaps the name Action Painting, proposed by the poet and critic Harold Rosenberg in a resounding article in the September issue of *Art News*, is not satisfying, either. It seems to fit only artists like Jackson Pollock and the older Hans Hofmann, who has been using the "dripping" technique since 1940: dripping paint, without direct use of the brush, on a canvas placed horizontally.

The label is irrelevant. The event is elsewhere: in the fact that two shows, one last year, one this year, in the Museum of Modern Art and several shows abroad have propelled American painting to the forefront of the international art scene.

Its fully original character is beginning to become evident to all, even though it has identifiable European origins, such as Cubism, which Willem De Kooning never wholly abandons, and Surrealism, which greatly influences Pollock. The Abstract

Expressionists have renovated the language of these origins in the assurance that painting, ancient or modern, is an empty form, without hold on a world in decline.

Many of the artists have known one another for a long time, having worked in the WPA, which President Roosevelt creat-

ARSHILE GORKY: THE LEAF OF THE ARTICHOKE IS AN OWL. 1944. New York. MOMA

ed during the Depression, hiring unemployed artists to decorate bus stops, schools, and other public buildings throughout the United States. Many have fallen under the influence of the Mexican muralists José Orozco, Diego Rivera, and Alfaro Siqueiros, all of whom worked in New York; this was the monumental

inspiration for their works which, even when they are not huge, differ from the intimate nature of easel painting.

Other circumstances also played a part. After Hitler defeated France, in 1940, several European painters fled to America: Dali reached New York that year. Léger, Max Ernst, and Masson, who had initiated Automatic Drawing in 1924, arrived in 1941; Mondrian came, too, and died here in 1944—not to forget André Breton, the pope of Surrealism, who became a close friend of Arshile Gorky and introduced the exiled artists to the American painters. Then there was Peggy Guggenheim, whose gallery Art of This Century, from its opening in 1942 to its close in 1947, exhibited all the artists in New York, and attracted critics and dealers interested in new things.

The Abstract Expressionists had neither a manifesto nor a program or comprehensive theories, but they knew how to bring artistic activity to incandescence, to the extent that each put his entire "metaphysical substance" into play, as the

HAROLD ROSENBERG: THE AMERICAN ACTION PAINTERS

The term Action Painting is such a perfectly apt designation that it appears to be assured a long and healthy life. It was coined by the erudite poet and prose writer Harold Rosenberg, forty-six years old. He used it for the first time in the December issue of *ARTnews*, to characterize painters for whom the canvas is first and foremost an arena for action.

writer Harold Rosenberg describes it in his article in *Art News*. This was true of Arshile Gorky, whose works, based on Surrealism and on his desire to leave the field free for the unconscious, are a type of internal landscape. The trend was accentuated by Pollock, Kline, and De Kooning.

After Hans Hofmann, Pollock began using "dripping" in 1947, with a passion unknown until then: "I don't work from drawings or sketches. My painting is direct. My method of painting grows out of a natural need. I want to express my feelings rather than illustrate them." This is indeed how his vast apocalyptic, lacerated, dizzy hangings are made.

The only equivalent is the "terribilità" of the *Women* of Willem De Kooning, with their greedy, carnivorous mouths, worn bodies, and menacing sexual attributes. They are straight-line descendants of the ghouls Picasso was painting at the end of the 1920s and, even more remotely, of his *Demoiselles d'Avignon.* "I have cut out many mouths. First I thought that everything must have a mouth," said De Kooning. But he is not an abstract artist, as he has proclaimed several times and as was evident until his *Excavation* in 1950. It is one of his most hermetic canvases. It was inspired by the incessant earth-moving work transforming New York into a permanent construction yard.

Although they are not Expressionists, other painters such as Mark Rothko, Ad Reinhardt, and Clyfford Still also belong to the New York School.

(See also 1956 and 1983.)

{A} vanguard assumption taken up by Action Painting with the fullest intensity was that which demanded the demolition of existing values in art. The revolutionary phrase "doing away with" was heard with the frequency and authority of a slogan. The total elimination of identifiable subject matter was the first in a series of moves—then came doing away with drawing, with composition, with color, with texture; later, with the flat surface, with art materials . . . In a fervor of subtraction art was taken apart element by element and the parts thrown away. As with diamond cutters, knowing where to make the split was the primary insight . . .

The content of Action Painting is the artist's drama of creation within the blind alley of an epoch that has identified its issues but allowed them to grow unmanageable. In this situation it has been the rule for creative performance to be a phase in a rhythm of confusion, misery, letting go, even self-destruction—as the formula of Thomas Mann had it, of the alliance of creation with sickness, at once moral and physical . . .

The happy fiction that the art of our time is a fulfillment of the art of the ages thus finds itself at war with the fiction that our time could find a fulfillment if it were not for the perversity of contemporary artists—a conflict of echoes in a vacuum. Art criticism is probably the only remaining intellectual activity, not excluding theology, in which pre-Darwinian minds continue to affirm value systems dissociated from any observable phenomena . . .

The idea of this "trans-formal" art was never a simple one, nor would it be wise to attempt, as is often proposed, a very close description of it. An action that eventuates on a canvas, rather than in the physical world or in society, is inherently ambiguous . . .

To literal minds the presence of a contradiction invalidates either the description or the object described. Yet it is precisely its

contradictions, shared with other forms of action (since all action takes place in a context by which its purpose may be reversed), that make Action Painting appropriate to the epoch of crisis. It retains its vigor only as long as it continues to sustain its dilemmas: if it slips over into action ("life") there is no

Jackson Pollock in his New York studio, working on a "dripping."

painting; if it is satisfied with itself as painting it turns into "apocalyptic wallpaper."

HAROLD ROSENBERG
The Anxious Object: Art Today and Its
Audience *(Excerpts)*

BLACK MOUNTAIN COLLEGE

EDEN LAKE

Who knows Black Mountain College? A few people in avant-garde art circles. But there is no doubt that this small college, nestled in the heart of mountains in North Carolina, will remain a site of choice for contemporary creation.

It was founded in 1933, during the Depression, by nine professors and twelve students with idealistic, egalitarian views. No educational system suited them. From the beginning, the community was almost entirely self-sufficient. It grew its own vegetables, raised poultry and cattle. Its first buildings were near Asheville. After 1940, it was on the shore of Eden Lake, built by students and professors, the professors contributing more than half their salary toward the new buildings.

The painter Josef Albers and his wife, Anni, were the first to join the group in 1933. They had had to leave the Bauhaus, because Hitler closed it. This explains why Black Mountain College is in many ways the spiritual heir of the celebrated German school. Its democratic organization, its active interest in contemporary ideas, and the intense, demanding personality and remarkable pedagogic gifts

IN MANY WAYS THE SPIRITUAL HEIR OF THE BAUHAUS

of Albers, himself, soon made it a leader in modern art. Over the years, the college has been visited by such personalities as Henry Miller, Anaïs Nin, Fernand Léger, and Albert Einstein. The summer sessions are particularly popular, because they offer high-quality courses and many special events, such as concerts and shows, which draw an art-loving public to Eden Lake.

During the summer of 1948, the dymaxion Buckminster Fuller made a first attempt at

At Black Mountain College, the tradition of Bauhaus parties and performances is resumed. Above, Buckminster Fuller and Merce Cunningham performing Erik Satie's *Raft of the Medusa.*

Black Mountain at building his geodesic dome. He failed, because the college could not provide sufficiently solid material for this new type of construction. (Fuller was not discouraged.) During the same summer, the composer John Cage organized an Erik Satie Festival and gave several lectures; one of them, "Contra Beethoven," created a scandal.

Cage returns to Black Mountain this year and gives his piece called *4' 33"*—four and a half minutes of silence. It was inspired by the blank paintings of Robert Rauschenberg. He organized an evening called "Event," during which he lectured from the top of a ladder for forty-five minutes, with interspersed silences. And while Cage lectured, Charles Olson and Mary Caroline Richards on top of another ladder read their poems, David Tudor played the piano, Rauschenberg wound up a phonograph, and Merce Cunningham and other dancers performed.

Albers left Black Mountain College three years ago. He now directs the art school of Yale University. People who know his painting, which is based on strict organization of color, may well wonder how much he appreciated that mixed-up evening.

The cast of the *Raft of the Medusa.* From left to right: Alvin Charles Few, Buckminster Fuller, John Cage, Elaine De Kooning, Bill Shrauger, and Merce Cunningham.

MICHEL TAPIÉ: ART OF ANOTHER KIND

Born on February 28, 1909, at the Château de Mauriac, Michel Tapié was a younger cousin of Henri de Toulouse-Lautrec, a bassist in the nightclubs of Saint-Germain-des-Prés, a friend of Dubuffet, and a great admirer of Tobey, Pollock, and De Kooning. He was at odds with his Jesuit teachers and passionately interested in mathematics and automobiles. In his spare time, he sculpted. His essay entitled *Art of Another Kind* will undoubtedly be long remembered. The author's thesis is that we must break with the past, abandoning even apparently revolutionary movements such as Fauvism and Cubism, which did not radically break with traditional art. What is the new road for painting to follow? The passage below deals with this issue.

One may say that Impressionism raised questions regarding the notions of beauty, form, space, and esthetics. The more daring works attacked them, turning their back on them, and even denying their existence. In all cases, they took a contrary position to these notions, which still meant taking them into account. But contemporary works exist in a completely separate sphere, with a total indifference to their ever having existed. Dada represented the major rupture. In the preceding movements, including Cubism, all the classical criteria were still at play, though in totally anarchic appearances. Order, composition, balance, and rhythm were in keeping with a humanism that was at the point of exhaustion, but which stayed alive because certain routines were still being followed by artists and collectors. Until Dadaism, all "isms" (except for the great German Expressionist movement, the importance of which is just beginning to be suspected) were only superficially revolutionary. They departed from accepted laws in their spectacular sacrilegious denials, but did not go so far as to ignore completely these useless laws.

Everything was put into question following the avalanche of revolutions from Impressionism to Dadaism and Surrealism. We are barely beginning to realize the full significance of this, and to what extent this questioning has made the epoch in which we live a particularly exciting one. For centuries, if not millennia, evolution could not be perceived for the slowness of its pace, artistic (and ethical-esthetic) problems were of no concern, nothing arose unexpectedly, and one was sure to know the direction one was moving in. Then, the entire system of décor, based on certitudes, collapsed, and the ossified and ossifying false order of the past gave way to a fruitful and exhilarating anarchy that, having gained momentum, is now moving toward a new order, a new sys-

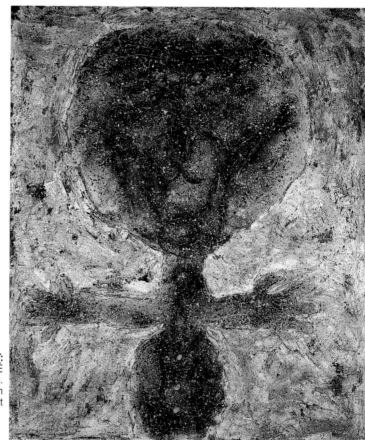

JEAN DUBUFFET: MICHEL TAPIÉ SOLEIL. 1946. Paris. Fondation Dubuffet

tem of notions commensurate with our potential. It is unheard-of to know that one is headed toward the unknown (which should always be the case for creators). In the words of Saint John of the Cross, "To reach the unknown, you must pass through the unknown." Academicism—finished for good, isn't it?

MICHEL TAPIÉ
Art of Another Kind
(Excerpts)

"Handsomer than he thinks he is . . ." Michel Tapié de Céleyran as the master of Art Brut sees him.

BRETON: "WHY ARE THEY HIDING SOVIET PAINTING FROM US?"

PARIS

André Breton, who spent the Second World War in the United States, could see for himself that freedom of expression and creativity are not dead letters there. He who once thought that Surrealism and the proletarian revolution could march hand in hand cannot castigate enough what is happening in the realm of art in the Soviet Union. He begins a polemic against Moscow's dictates in the weekly magazine *Arts*. He writes: "It is upsetting to see that what religious persecution and absolute power could not do has now been successfully accomplished for all its subjects by a regime backed by police power. It suffices to ask what has happened to the great poets and artists whose creative energy passed through the Russian Revolution for a short moment: Mayakovski, Lissitsky, Malevich, Rodchenko, Tatlin. Chagall and Kandinsky were fortunate enough to have fled.

"We see with dread the signs of oppression in the USSR, not only of artists but of intellectuals in general. Criticism is striking in its stylistic indulgence and in the use of the policeman's tone: 'After successfully overcoming the corrupting influence of Formalism and placing themselves solidly on the plane of Realism indicated by the great Stalin, Soviet painters are becoming increasingly demanding.'

"As regards the general views on art, we agree with the comments by Sunday strollers at the 'fair of bad pictures,' and as regards the moral and human condition, we stand precisely halfway between the janitor's desk and the commissariat. All this shrieks of bewilderment, it reeks of terror. Publicity in the USSR and abroad on the nature of art has long ceased to mislead us.

"The truth, carefully concealed, is that contemporary Russian painting, within the laughable limits allowed it, has been incapable of producing anything better than old images of department-store calendars or village prints. The color reproductions are atrocious: No harmony, no balance in tone has been attempted; in general, they have returned to the style of the official Preimpressionist salons. I don't know what will predominate in this amateur horror, grandiloquent foolishness or totally impersonal art.

"On May 24, 1949, Zamuchekin, director of the Tretiakow Gallery in Moscow, the pride of Russia, proclaimed, 'Cézanne must be condemned, Matisse cannot draw, Picasso is putrefying; any artist who does not follow the example of Soviet art is an enemy of Socialism.' The question is if in countries where art is not subjugated one can bear the idea that this royal road may be popularized to the extent that its monuments and even their memory are abolished, delivered up to a mob of plodders and mercenaries."

And Breton quoted Marx: "My property is the form, it constitutes my individuality. The style is man." This has become a seditious saying on the other side of the Iron Curtain. Who could have imagined that the Pope of Surrealism, a militant in the Communist cell on the Rue Fontaine during the lovely interwar years, would become so angry?

PICASSO CHALLENGED BY THE COMMUNISTS

PARIS

Six years ago, Jdanov, the Soviet minister of culture, in a long speech to the Supreme Soviet, affirmed the primacy of the theory of Socialist Realism in literature, music, and painting. In France, the deputy Laurent Casanova and Louis Aragon were put in charge by the Party of the "control of intellectuals," watching over the implementation of new directives.

With a group of Communist painters, sculptors, and art critics, they discussed the case of Picasso and of all the artists in the Party who reject Photographic Realism. Will Picasso subject himself to the demands of his censors? Salvador Dali, temporarily in Paris, states, "Picasso must leave the Communist party for the sake of his own mental hygiene. He would thus remain true to his mission, which has been to purge by violence the colossal mediocrity of twentieth-century painting."

It would be surprising if the creator of *Guernica* were to follow the advice of his compatriot, a fervent admirer of General Franco.

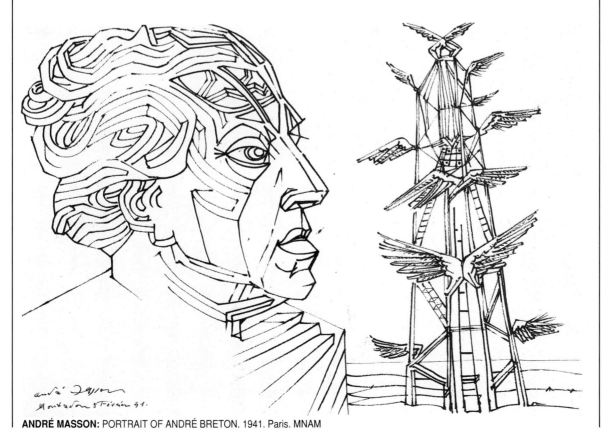

ANDRÉ MASSON: PORTRAIT OF ANDRÉ BRETON. 1941. Paris. MNAM

Mixed Reactions to Pignon's "Dead Worker"

On exhibit this year is Édouard Pignon's unclassifiable painting *The Dead Worker*, bringing a negative response from critics. It is questioned not only by the abstract school, which challenges the social theme, but by supporters of Socialist Realism, who find its forms "disturbing." While the artist's intention was to depict a childhood memory of the Clarence mine disaster, admiring visitors to the Salon view the scene as an entombment. Which is not displeasing to Pignon, a Communist.

Ellsworth Kelly's Monochrome Panels

One of many artists who went to Paris after the war to study art, Ellsworth Kelly had a personal show at the gallery Arnaud in 1951. He is one of the rare artists of his generation to be free of the influence of Abstract Expressionism. His forms are flat and clearly defined; he has more in common with Piet Mondrian. Kelly has just produced a startling series of paintings composed of monochrome panels, each a different color.

Canvas Slashers Caught at the Musée d'Art Moderne

Two young persons were stopped by a guard at the Musée National d'Art Moderne, where an exhibit of twentieth-century masterpieces is taking place. They had already used a razor blade to slash Bonnard's *Self-Portrait*, Renoir's *Bather*, and *La repasseuse* (woman ironing) from Picasso's blue period when they were apprehended while defacing works by Cézanne and Gauguin. The incident is the sixth since the theft of the *Mona Lisa* on August 22, 1911, by Vincenzo Perugio, an Italian who wanted to "avenge Italy for Napoleon's looting"!

The de Chirico Brothers

Andrea de Chirico died in Rome on May 5 at the age of sixty. As a painter, writer, and musician, he was known as Alberto Savinio, a name he chose forty years ago to sign articles he wrote in Apollinaire's magazine *Les soirées de Paris*. Rumors circulated that while the paintings were done by Giorgio de Chirico's hand, the ideas belonged to his younger brother, Andrea. The rumors were unfounded, however: When Alberto Savinio began painting in the 1920s, it became clear that, in spite of a common love for mythology, there were many differences in their style. Although they had not been on speaking terms, Giorgio now displays a photo of his deceased brother in his studio.

Picasso's "Goat" at the Salon de Mai

We were expecting a painting, but Pablo Picasso instead exhibited a sculpture. His *Goat* has a wicker basket for a belly, a palm frond for a back, and teats fashioned from small terra-cotta jars—all held together with plaster. Cast in bronze, it is an impressive piece, at once naturalistic and unreal. Picasso's goat is very much an expression of its creator's inventiveness, and will take its place among the other masterpieces of this painter-sculptor.

ÉDOUARD PIGNON: THE DEAD WORKER. 1952. Paris. The Artist's Private Collection

PABLO PICASSO: GOAT. 1950. Paris. Musée Picasso

GERMANY REDISCOVERS MODERN ART

WEST BERLIN

For twelve years, from 1933 to 1945, the German avant-garde was lifeless under the Nazi regime, after producing internally important movements, such as the Blue Rider, in 1911, and the Bauhaus, in 1919. During the dark Hitlerian years, art was propagandistic, mediocre, and academic, celebrating the native soil and the "healthy" mentality of the people.

This is why the Franco-German exhibition in the Neue Galerie is drawing curious crowds. They come to see the free play of shapes and colors.

Some thirty artists are represented, including Bazaine, Manessier, Hartung, Ubac, Singier, Schneider for the French, Theodor Werner, Fritz Winter, Ernst Wilhelm Nay for the Germans. Nay's canvases are based primarily on the search for color harmonies. He had been forbidden to paint in 1937, then served as a cartographer in the army of occupation in France.

The painter most people find attractive without doubt is Jean Bazaine. Much of his work is reminiscent of Nay. And each is reminiscent of Kandinsky. The most striking success is Hans Hartung's. He exercises a growing influence on young painters, who are sensitive to the originality of his graphics, which make him totally dissimilar from previous movements such as Expressionism or Abstractionism.

ERNST WILHELM NAY: JACOB'S LADDER. 1946. Cologne. Ludwig Museum

BALTHUS: THE ROOM. 1952. Rome. Private Collection

THE ETERNAL CHARACTER OF FANTASTIC ART AND ITS META- MORPHOSIS

BASEL

Fantasy in art is nothing new. But from antiquity to Hieronymus Bosch, it often has consisted of nothing more than terrifying allegories or sets of odd objects on a canvas. The exhibit in the Kunsthalle shows how, among contemporaries, it is the expression of an anxiety born of scientific progress, coupled with the anguish it brings.

The modern artist, to repeat Paul Klee's comment, knows that there is a world that "in its present form is not the only possible one." From this notion comes the multiplicity of universes that he invents. Klee, Miró, Tanguy—these are the great voyagers with whom the Basel exhibition invites us to travel through the invisible world not covered by any scientific treatise.

But one should not believe that the most extravagant fantasy is enough to achieve the fantastic. More than before, the great successes in this genre come from deep impulses in the personal or collective unconscious. They express archetypes going back through the ages. They obey precise laws as rigorous as those of formal logic but function according to different, more complex rules. There must be added a minutia and technical acumen that owe nothing to the traditional craft, as can be seen in Basel in the works of Salvador Dali, Max Ernst, and, in the new generation, Balthus.

For the public at large, modern art is often synonymous with improvisation, sloppiness, even imposture. Here is a group of works that should convince everybody of its capacities of invention and perfect technique.

THE MIRROR ON PARK AVENUE

NEW YORK

The renowned firm Skidmore, Owings & Merrill of Chicago, under the direction of architect Gordon Bunshaft, is asked to take the message of Ludwig Mies van der Rohe into the center of Manhattan, on majestic Park Avenue. The new headquarters of Lever Brothers has a shiny blue-green curtain wall barely relieved by a pattern of aluminum joinery. It is a method of uniform façade treatment, appearing as though enlivened with Scotch plaid. This parallelepiped is suspended above a square representing the latest fashion in office buildings. People are betting on its permanent influence, all the more so as the city is expanding. It is a solution to the problems of planning that the New York City zoning law had left pending.

Visually, Lever House satisfies the passerby: The glass façade reflects the city, replacing the vermiculations and cornices of older architecture with an ever-moving image. Raymond Loewy, the industrial designer of French origin, creates the interiors in his sober, elegant style.

Park Avenue reflected in the Lever House.

THE INCREDIBLE "MAISON DU FADA"

MARSEILLES

The "Maison du Fada" (the crackpot house). This is the name given by the locals to the residential unit designed by Le Corbusier and inaugurated on October 14 by Claudius Petit, minister of reconstruction. "I thank the government of France," Le Corbusier said, "for having given occasion for such an experience." The minister praised the qualities of this exceptional construction, and awarded the decoration of a commander of the Legion of Honor to the architect. The reactions of press and public have been divided.

The immense building is a revolutionary concept. Almost one hundred feet long and one hundred eighty-four feet high, it contains three hundred fifty apartments for one thousand six hundred people. Its polychrome mass rises above ground on forty solid concrete pylons, which fit into the landscape like tree trunks without obstructing space. Communal facilities are built on the roof terrace: a gym, a running track, an open-air theater, a kindergarten with a pool, and a playground for children. All facilities are supplemented by stores. A bakery, a butcher shop, and a produce store are located on the third level, so that housewives can do their shopping inside the building, without wasting time.

Le Corbusier gives his residential unit the name "La Cité Radieuse" (radiant city) because it is like a city. Each split-level apartment is slipped into the whole structure in staggered fashion, completely isolated from the others. It seems that the concept came to him before the war, on board the French liner *Normandie* taking him to the United States. He noticed the concentration of services and appreciated the on-board facilities.

It is easy to understand why the liner anchored at the edge of the Boulevard Michelet is not to everyone's taste. It cuts across the traditional concepts of a dwelling. The residential unit is judged by some to be "aggressive and inhuman," its apartments "narrow and suffocating." Le Corbusier has been called "blind" and the inspector of reconstruction a "waster of public funds."

Le Corbusier has withstood other tempests and again remains firm in his position. He comments, not without irony, "It would be an ideal place for Marie Antoinette, because the ceilings are as high as in the Petit Trianon."

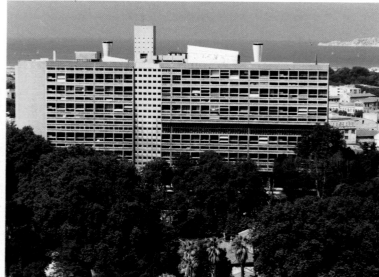

La Cité Radieuse in Marseilles, built by Le Corbusier, also nicknamed the "House of Fada".

The abscess was bound to burst. The affair of Picasso's Portrait of Stalin *shows the whole world how impossible it is for Stalinism to accept modern art insofar as it stands above all for nonconformism and liberty. The quarrel over Realism that began in 1936 ends in such total failure that its uselessness and emptiness should be absolutely clear to everyone. How genuine seem the problems art poses in the United States in comparison with what is happening in France, where many of the best are hampered by Socialist Realism. Braque "the inspector" happily perseveres. His ceiling for the Etruscan Room in the Louvre is an incomparable masterpiece, as well as a stunning first that weds ancient and modern art.*

1953

SUMMARY

ART AND POLITICS

The Scandal of Stalin's Portrait
L'humanité, **March 18**
Letters to the Editor of *Les lettres françaises*
Fougeron against Atlantism

AVANT-GARDE

Ad Reinhardt Simplifies Painting
Liebermann Does a Statue over the Phone

ART NEWS

Picabia Dead at Seventy-Four
Dufy Dead at Seventy-Six
Comic Strips and Art
German Art in Lucerne
In Brief

GREAT MASTERS

Braque's Birds in the Sky of the Louvre

ARCHITECTURE

Buckminster Fuller's Dome
Le Corbusier Builds in the Punjab

LITERATURE

UNITED STATES
Publication of The Adventures of Augie March *by Saul Bellow, and* The Crucible *by Arthur Miller.*

FRANCE
Alain Robbe-Grillet's first novel, The Erasers.
Roland Barthes publishes Writing Degree Zero.

GREAT BRITAIN
Publication of Lucky Jim *by Kingsley Amis.*

MUSIC

FRANCE
Olivier Messiaen composes Le réveil des oiseaux *for piano and orchestra.*

ITALY
Giacento Scelsi composes Four Illustrations for Piano.

RUSSIA
Death of Sergey Prokofiev.

MOTION PICTURES

FRANCE
Premiere of Les Vacances de Monsieur Hulot *by Jacques Tati.*

ITALY
Roberto Rossellini films Roman Holiday.

JAPAN
Tales of a Hazy Moon after the Rain *by Kenji Mizoguchi.*

PABLO PICASSO:
PORTRAIT OF STALIN. 1953

THE SCANDAL OF STALIN'S PORTRAIT

PARIS

Art and politics have rarely mixed well. Since the beginning of this century, successive generations of artists have had to suffer this painful experience for the fact finally to be understood. But memory is fallible. Who remembers the vexation that Marinetti, Kandinsky, Chagall, and Nolde had to endure when they wanted to meddle in affairs of state and deal with mankind's happiness? Perhaps the scandal that broke out at the end of last winter in Paris will finally open artists' eyes.

One of the cultural weeklies published by Louis Aragon, *Les lettres françaises*, of March 12, fans the flames. Stalin has just died, and the editors must quickly improvise an issue paying homage to the "well-loved comrade." The Communist magazine orders Picasso to paint a portrait of Stalin. A set of photographs of "the father of peoples" is sent to the painter, who sets to work in his house in Vallauris, where he has been residing since February. The whole publishing staff waits with bated breath for Picasso's sketch. Anything might come from the hands of the creator of *Guernica*.

Picasso's relations with the French Communist party and the partisans of Socialist Realism are not healthy. Furthermore, Maurice Thorez, the Party chief and usually Picasso's supporter, is not in France. He is under medical care in the Soviet Union. The sketch finally arrives, at the last moment; the magazine must be printed in three hours. Imagine the surprise of the publisher! Instead of the august old "man of steel" who has just died, he sees the portrait of a young blade with a moustache, in good health but a little pale. *Les lettres françaises* is published. The scandal bursts out immediately in the building where both Aragon's weekly and *L'Humanité* are published.

Astonishment gives way to anger. Soon, the whole party, down to the last corner of the provinces, is aflame. How can such a lack of respect for the "great Stalin" be shown? Who is this "zazou" who stretches his big mug between the articles by comrade Aragon and comrade Joliot-Curie? Letters of protest pour in. They denounce Picasso as a "bourgeois painter" and accuse Aragon and the entire editorial staff of *Les lettres françaises* of irresponsibility and culpable negligence. The Soviet embassy protests vehemently.

The leaders of the French Communist party officially condemn the portrait.

The enemies of the painter triumph—those who condemn him for his political commitments and those who always have hated his work. Picasso is at first annoyed, then seems to take it all philosophically. He is said to have said recently to Pierre Daix, the editor in chief of *Les lettres françaises,* during a private conversation, "I brought my bouquet of flowers to the funeral. They did not like it. That happens, but usually one does not abuse people because their flowers are not pleasing."

Les lettres françaises believes it must give in to the injunctions of the Party and publish all the letters that condemn Picasso, sometimes rudely.

As for Aragon's self-criticism, published in the magazine on

Louis Aragon.

LETTERS TO THE EDITOR OF "LES LETTRES FRANÇAISES"

The portrait drawn by Picasso was a profound shock to my sentiments of gratitude and love for our greatest leader.

Comrade Picasso, in my view, totally overlooked the workers who would be affected by the unfortunate publication of this portrait. But it would seem much more serious that the directors of Les lettres françaises *had allowed the inclusion of this work.*

Pierre L., Wagram cell

I hesitated before writing, but I feel I must tell you how shocked I was in opening the last issue of Les lettres françaises.

No, this is not the face of Stalin. His is a good face, strong, expressive, honest, and inspiring confidence. My fourteen-year-old son shares my opinion.

Colette B., Maisons-Alfort

Having an inadequate understanding of painting in general, especially painting that departs from a realist style, that is , from a style that assimilates the positions of the working class and is able to be understood and favorably accepted by them, I would never permit myself to criticize one of Picasso's works.

But now one sees that Picasso, in drawing a portrait of Stalin after his painful disappearance, threatens ot disseminate midunderstanding and confusion.

P. A., Alfortville

April 2 and April 9, it is a disavowal of Picasso, not only of the work that had been ordered from him, but a condemnation of all modern art: "It is clear now that the discussion at this point goes beyond and must go beyond a work by Picasso and even, more generally, beyond problems that Picasso's method may pose, and tackle the real problem. That problem is that of all creative people, including painters, who must resolutely take their position in the working class if they want to participate fully in its great combat at the head of the French people . . ."

He who in 1936 during the famous debates about the "quarrel of Realism" took the part of Socialist Realism against artists like Léger, Gromaire, and Delaunay, is now blindly backsliding, much to the surprise of many. Under the pretext that art must speak to the people, does he want to restrict creativity to the nineteenth-century rules of the Academy? In self-justification, Aragon claims, but with some embarrassment, that he had only one minute to look at the incriminating drawing before sending it to the printer: "My mistake was that, having been accustomed all my life to looking at Picasso's work, I lost sight of the reader who looks at it without thinking of the characteristics, of the technique . . ."

(See also 1904, 1905, 1907, 1909, 1912, 1921, 1927, 1937, 1945, 1946, 1948, 1954, 1958, 1973.)

ANDRÉ FOUGERON: ATLANTIC CIVILIZATION. 1953. The Artist's Private Collection

FOUGERON AGAINST ATLANTISM

PARIS

André Fougeron wants to make a great hit with his presentation of the *Atlantic Civilization* at the Salon d'Automne. The painting has in its center an enormous Cadillac, the symbol of Yankee capitalism. In the Cadillac is a German soldier with an SS helmet, an allegory of the "reactionary" alliance between America, the "imperialist power that oppresses the peoples of the world," with a "revanchist" Germany populated by Nazis. Around the center is exploitation of the people: a couple of poor old people, children playing among the noxious fumes of industrial plants, a mother and child without a roof over their heads, coffins containing the corpses of young soldiers killed in "dirty" colonial wars, an electric chair, a disgusting capitalist, a depraved alcoholic immersed in a pornographic magazine . . . In a word, all the corruption of diabolic America and its Western allies. Fougeron is in the direct line of official Soviet painters. One is horrified looking at the picture. Not by its subject, but by the painting itself.

AD REINHARDT SIMPLIFIES PAINTING

NEW YORK

Ad Reinhardt has often been seen in exhibits and events of the New York School. But he differs from other painters in that the origin of his Abstractionism is Cubism and the Neoplasticism of the 1930s. He thinks in the beginning that the only possible goal for art is geometric abstraction, the logical evocation of the "pure" and the "universal." His first private showing ten years ago of canvases reduced to a simple arrangement of horizontal and vertical lines and the use of primary colors illustrated his admiration of the "division of space, intensely, dramatically emotional," that is so dear to Piet Mondrian.

Reinhardt subsequently changes, and creates a manner of composition "without relationships" that emphasize color, not surface. It is the birth of Chromatic Abstraction. He pushes Abstractionism to *its* logical conclusion. After simplifying the composition into one single indivisible image, he manages to abstract the idea that is the finality of Mondrian's art. According to Reinhardt, politics, religion, ambition, and greed corrupt art, so he reduces art to silence in order to liberate it.

The critic Thomas Hess, in 1949, understands his taste for purity and the absence of expression when he writes, "Reinhardt seems to be an

"PAINTINGS WITHOUT BREATH, OUTSIDE OF TIME, WITHOUT STYLE, WITHOUT PURPOSE, WITHOUT DEATH, WITHOUT LIFE"

inventor of motifs, not shapes."

Like his friends Newman, Rothko, and Still, Reinhardt wants to create absolute art, but he takes away all traces of his own presence. For two or three years, his paintings have been organized very simply into cruciform motifs in similar colors, blue on blue, with imperceptibly different shades, vivid red, and now brown and dark green, colors that cannot be distinguished from one another without patient observation.

Reinhardt has begun a series of "Black Paintings," which in everybody's opinion can only be the last step in a process that the artist himself describes as "without breath, outside of time, without style, without purpose, without death, without life."

Need it be added that artists and art lovers are greatly upset by such radical declarations?

AD REINHARDT: ABSTRACT PAINTING. RED. 1952. New York. MOMA

LIEBERMANN DOES A STATUE OVER THE PHONE

UNITED STATES

Alexander Liebermann, since his move across the Atlantic, has become the champion of "Anonymous Art," which can be reproduced by assistants, as is the case, it seems, of several of his paintings, including the famous *Minimum,* made in 1949. He "orders" a sculpture, limiting himself to specifying "by phone," the material, the color, and the desired dimensions. Liebermann says that he is "anti-art" and is "anti-painter," and he joyfully proclaims that the "ego is detestable."

Born in Kiev, Russia, in 1912, the artist has been fascinated by the geometric, industrial shapes and constructions that he discovered at the Exhibition of Decorative Arts in Paris when he was only thirteen years old. In Paris, in the 1930s, he follows the career of the painter and theoretician André Lhote. He is a pupil of the architect Auguste Perret and works for the poster artist Cassandre. Three years ago, Liebermann begins to draw with a compass, and to use commercial art and plywood panels, industrial enamel, and aluminum panels. His "circles" are conceived to be permutable.

His antiindividualist concept of art explains why galleries generally hesitate to show his work. He really pushes anonymity to extreme consequences.

Picabia Dead at Seventy-Four

He was, up until the last, the *enfant terrible* of modern art and a prodigious agitator of ideas. Francis Picabia, dead in Paris on November 30 following a lengthy illness, shot through his time like a meteor. Born of a Cuban father and a French mother, he was first an Impressionist, then a Cubist with the group Section d'Or, and a Dadaist in 1915. In 1921, he had a falling-out with André Breton and his friends during the rise of the Surrealist movement. In 1924, he exhibited his works along with André Masson, Miró, Max Ernst, and Dali, returning to academically inspired figurative painting. He was one of the first to presage abstract painting with *Caoutchouc* (rubber) in 1909. A sense of mischief pervaded his art until the very end.

Dufy Dead at Seventy-Six

Raoul Dufy died on March 23 in Forcalquier of a heart attack. Born in Le Havre in 1877, he went to Paris in 1900 to work in Léon Bonnat's studio. But it was Matisse's *Luxe, calme et volupté,* which he discovered in 1905 at the Salon des Indépendants, that proved to be the greatest revelation for him. Freed from the influence of Fauvism, he produced works so full of color and light that he was dubbed "the painter of joy." For the 1937 International Exposition in Paris, he painted *La fée électricité,* an immense composition two hundred feet long and sixty feet high, the largest painting ever. Dufy will be remembered as a marvelous musician of color.

Comic Strips and Art

San Francisco is seething with activity. While places like The Cellar echo with the sounds of West Coast jazz, the King Ubu Gallery is also a site for innovation. Jess Collins, a thirty-year-old Californian who signs his work "Jess," has set the art world on its ear with his Necrofacts or Dead Art—comic-strip collages he has cut and edited. He makes a series of Tricky Cad word games that are both absurd and poetic, and uses Dick Tracy's name for an anagram.

RAOUL DUFY: THE MODEL. 1933. Paris. MNAM

According to Jess, the idea came from the collages of *Une semaine de bonté,* shown to him by poet Robert Duncan. Max Ernst would not be embarrassed by such an heir, whatever purists may think.

German Art in Lucerne

An exhibit of contemporary German art opened on July 4 for three months at the Kunstmuseum in Lucerne. Under the direction of Ludwig Grote of the Nationalmuseum of Nuremberg, the emphasis of the exhibit is on the period from 1900 to 1925. Not including Impressionists, among those represented are Expressionists Nolde, Beckmann, and Feininger, friends of Matisse such as Rudolf Levy and Hans Purrmann, and all the contradictory schools—abstract, Socialist Realist—from the 1930s. The works of many of the artists shown are not in their usual medium: Käthe Kollwitz, known especially as a painter, is represented at the exhibit by a series of her sculptures, and Otto Dix by watercolor portraits.

MAX BECKMANN:
PROMENADE DES ANGLAIS IN NICE.
1947. Essen. Folkwang Museum

GEORGES BRAQUE: THE BIRDS (CEILING OF THE HENRI II ROOM). 1949-1951. Paris. Louvre

BRAQUE'S BIRDS IN THE SKY OF THE LOUVRE

PARIS

He wants "the sky to rise gently" so that people might "see the sky without looking at it." It is done. The ceiling that André Cornu, the state secretary of art, orders from Georges Braque for the Henri II room in the Louvre, which houses a collection of Etruscan vases and objects, is inaugurated late in April with the artist on hand.

The subject chosen by the painter—black birds on a blue background—fits the room perfectly. Even people not favorable to the idea of mixing modern and ancient art are enchanted when they see the decoration on the ceiling.

Like other artists of his generation, Braque is influenced more by so-called "primitive" art than by the art of the Renaissance, from which he turns away. The theme of the bird, to which he has been committed for several years, is certainly best adapted to a ceiling. His birds are flying with outstretched wings, a fascinating expression of movement. They recur in many of his paintings, particularly in his series of "Studios," which push Cubism to the limits of sumptuousness. The series, made between 1949 and 1951, like the Analytical Cubist canvases of the early part of the century, accumulates a set of chairs, tables, and jugs, to which are added the palette and the painter's easel reduced to symbols difficult to identify at first sight. They are thick, obscure canvases, evoking a fluid, almost aerial ambience within which the objects emerge and dissolve by turns.

"ALL MY LIFE, MY GREAT AMBITION WAS TO PAINT SPACE"

"All my life, my great ambition was to paint space," Braque says. Not only to paint it but to express its substance, to have it touch the eyes. The bird born in space poses quite naturally in certain versions of the "Studios" before flying to the ceiling of the Henri II room.

Painters in the past depicted large, didactic spectacles, from a battle scene to the wedding at Cana. Braque always took the opposite road. He never feels inspiration from great subjects. He wants to transpose an intimate subject onto a monumental plane. He solves the problem by using color tints that give the whole the force of simplicity.

Modern art has long been mistrusted. It is known how difficult it is for the public to allow it to be exhibited in museums. The fact that Braque was asked to decorate the most prestigious museum of all seems to indicate a profound change. The artist made it by working flat on the ground with long brushes at a site placed at his disposal by the Louvre. Maybe it is the secret of the great success.

(See also 1908, 1912, 1963.)

BUCKMINSTER FULLER'S DOME

MICHIGAN

Engineer, mathematician, utopian, writer, poet—Richard Buckminster Fuller could well be called an American Leonardo. For twenty years, he has been astonishing the public with his creations. During the war, he perfected cylindrical huts for use by the Army in the Pacific. He is the creator of the Wichita House of aluminum and steel. It is suspended on a central mast and anchored to the ground by cables, and structured around seven metal tubes. It can support the weight of a hundred and twenty persons.

Henry Ford, Jr., faced with the problem of covering his Rotonda, of a diameter of one hundred feet, with a steel structure, calls on the man of the hour. Fuller quickly realizes that his geodesic dome is perfectly suited to the problem. His dome of aluminum and synthetics is ninety-two feet high and has a diameter of one hundred feet. It weighs only eight and a half tons, compared with the one hundred and sixty tons of the standard structure. Once the skeleton is in place, a synthetic skin is stretched over it. The task is finished in thirty days! The modular elements are made in a factory with minimum tolerances using techniques tested by the aeronautical industry. Buckminster Fuller is not just a technician. This is confirmed by his words, better understood in the presence of his dome: "Vectorial balance is never visible to man, for it is as pure as God."

Richard Buckminster Fuller with a model of his geodesic dome.

LE CORBUSIER BUILDS IN THE PUNJAB

CHANDIGARH

What great architect has not dreamed of building an ideal town where his ideas would flourish? Le Corbusier has this exceptional opportunity. The adventure began three years ago when two government commissars of the Punjab visited Le Corbusier in his studio. They asked him to build all of Chandigarh, the future administrative capital of the country. Le Corbusier did not hesitate a single second: "Your capital will be planned here. We, at 35 Rue de Sèvres, can solve this problem." In November 1950 an agreement was signed by the government of India with Le Corbusier, who was appointed general consultant for the building of the capital and the architect of the capitol buildings.

Three architects living in Chandigarh are attached to Le Corbusier. One is his cousin, Pierre Jeanneret. The three manage a local architectural firm and will build the residences, schools, clinics, and hospitals. The town plan was completed in spring of 1951, and work began immediately. With the Himalayas as the background, Le Corbusier imagines the five elements that constitute the capitol: the secretariat, the assembly, the governor's palace, and the superior court now under construction. What is more, Le Corbusier wants to adapt his theories to the climatic and cultural conditions of the Punjab. The town stretches horizontally. The houses have been planned with consideration of the fact that in order to take advantage of the cool of the night, people often sleep on the grass in front of their house or on the roof.

The first stage of the construction of Chandigarh provides shelter for 150,000 people, the second for 500,000. On the highway, on the main street, and on the neighborhood streets, it separates automobiles from pedestrians.

LE CORBUSIER: SKETCH FOR THE PALACE OF THE GOVERNOR OF CHANDIGARH. 1956

With Matisse, who dies in Nice at the age of eighty-five, covered with honors by the press the world over, and Picasso, honored in Vallauris for the inauguration of the temple of "War and Peace," France is in the center of international art news this year. Do we really recognize the importance of Matisse? With his death, the greatest colorist of the twentieth century leaves us. The deaths of Derain and of the architect Auguste Perret, moreover, unfortunate as they are, are cast into the shadows. Yet they all pointed art as well as architecture in a new direction. Only Picasso remains and, following him, the difficulty European artists will have in carrying the torch.

1954

SUMMARY

GREAT MASTERS

Matisse Goes Back to Color
In Matisse's Words

DEVELOPMENTS

Arp Is Honored
Derain Sequestered

ART NEWS

Alberto Burri: between Dada and Art Brut
A New Museum in São Paulo
Paris Is Losing Its Americans
Perret: the Master of Concrete
Foundation of the Gutai Group
In Brief

AVANT-GARDE

Rauschenberg Introduces Reality into Painting
Jasper Johns Paints the American Flag

DEDICATIONS

The Fiesta for Picasso

LITERATURE

FRANCE
Death of Colette.

GREAT BRITAIN
William Golding publishes Lord of the Flies.

ITALY
Alberto Moravia publishes A Ghost at Noon.

MUSIC

FRANCE
The performance of Edgar Varèse's Déserts *at the Théâtre des Champs-Élysées creates a scandal: The composer inserted tape recordings in his instrumental music.*
Pierre Boulez composes Le marteau sans maître, *based on René Char's poems, for contralto and six instruments.*
Iannis Xenakis composes Metastasis *for orchestra.*

GREAT BRITAIN
Success of Benjamin Britten's opera The Turn of the Screw, *from Henry James' ghost story.*

MOTION PICTURES

UNITED STATES
Premieres of On the Waterfront *by Elia Kazan, and* Johnny Guitar *by Nicholas Ray.*

ITALY
Federico Fellini completes La Strada.

JAPAN
Premiere of Seven Samurai *by Akira Kurosawa.*

HENRI MATISSE:
VIEW OF NOTRE DAME. 1914.
New York. MOMA

508

MATISSE GOES BACK TO COLOR

HENRI MATISSE:
LE LUXE, I. 1907.
Paris. MNAM

NICE

When Henri Matisse was tempted to leave France in 1940, he felt it would be desertion. He settled in the Hotel Regina at Cimiez. He wrote that he was going to "leave for painting."

He did so, using the last years of his life for his swan song, his chapel in Vence and the enchanted, primal, and primordial spaces of his cut and glued gouaches that seem to be removed from all heaviness.

"You cannot realize to what point, at that time of paper cutting, the sensation of flight within myself guides my hand when it traces the course of my scissors. It is hard to explain, I would say that it is a sort of linear, graphic equivalent of the sensation of flight," he explains to André Verdet. He sees in it the supreme achievement, the mastery, at last, of all the creative faculties of his brain, "a type of hierarchy of all my feelings," enabling him to "end" his life in apotheosis.

The final accord is reached on November 3. His heart submits to his passion. While the doctors are troubled because of the seri-

"WE MUST SEE ALL OF LIFE AS IF WE WERE CHILDREN"

ousness of his cardiac crisis, he says, "Please tell these gentlemen that they are wasting a lot of time discussing an illness that does not exist." Matisse, who during sixty-five years "drew color" without relaxation or let-up, does not have time to waste. He can afford only the "luxe, calme et volupté"—the luxury, the serenity, and the voluptuousness—to enter the purest color. He dies for love of it.

A few hours later, he comes back to the future to which he headed in 1889 at the age of twenty, a young lawyer's clerk in Saint-Quentin. He began to paint in order to place his ideas in order. He imposed on colors his passion for their beauty. He becomes less tormented and more specific as he progresses from Fauvism, of which he was a master, to Oriental and Oceanic splendors inspired by his trips to Morocco and Tahiti until finally, in Provence, near friends Renoir, Bonnard, and Picasso, he retains absolute truth alone. A truth on which his eyes close. In bed, on October 15, he has a rose window placed on the ground in order to organize the composition of a chapel for Mrs. Nelson Rockefeller. It is the last thing he sees.

In sum, Henri Matisse throughout his life merely follows the prediction of Gustave Moreau, his art teacher: "You will simplify painting."

In October last year, he gives Régine Pernoud an interview. He defines himself through his creation. These statements, collect-

HENRI MATISSE:
THE KING'S
SADNESS. 1952.
Paris. MNAM

ed in the *Courrier de l'UNESCO*, may be considered a spiritual testament. He begins by affirming that creation begins with vision. To see is to create. But it requires an effort to shed all prejudice. Great courage is needed by the artist to succeed in seeing everything as if he were seeing it for the first time. Matisse often asks visitors who come to him in Vence, "Did you see the acanthus on the hills along the highway?" He notes that no one sees them. "They all recognized the acanthus leaf on a Corinthian capital, but outdoors, the memory of the capital prevents them from seeing the acanthus."

He concludes that the first step toward creation is to see everything in its true state: "We must see all of life as if we were children." This was the secret of his art: his innocence, not subjected to his learning, which was great, but which he forgot in the moment of creation. His "dances," his "musicians," his "views from a window," his "still lifes," his "odalisques," his "monochrome nudes," his simple "cutouts" create an extraordinary impression of spontaneity, naivete, and freedom that are his alone. He confesses later that he had merely "put his nose to the grindstone," obsessed as he was by his parents' order, "Hurry up!"

To the inauguration in November 1952 of the Henri Matisse Museum, in Cateau, his native town, he sends this message: "I was only a medium." But what a medium! He is the only contemporary artist whom Picasso ever envied. All twentieth-century art changed through the eyes of the most French of painters.

(See also 1905, 1908, 1910, 1916, 1933, 1951.)

IN MATISSE'S WORDS

The artist has but one idea. He is born with it, and spends a lifetime developing it and making it breathe.

A painter is completely whole in his first works.

I believe that the personality of the artist develops and asserts itself by the struggles that it must wage against other personalities.

Being an artist is a matter of learning, and

Color attains its full expression only when it is organized, when it corresponds to the intensity of the artist's emotions.

What counts most in coloring a picture is relations. Because of these relations and only because of them, a drawing can be intensely colored without having to use any colors.

My drawing is the direct and purest translation of my emotion.

Henri Matisse in Vence.

perhaps relearning, the language of writing by lines.

Artistic creation acquires quality only when it comes up against difficulties.

Art imitates nature. By virtue of creative action, a work of art takes on a living quality. Thus, the work will appear fruitful and endowed with that same internal energy and vibrant beauty that can be seen in works of nature.

When I use green, that does not mean grass. When I use blue, that does not mean the sky.

Color helps to explain light. I do not refer to the physical phenomenon of light but, rather, the only kind of light that truly exists, that of the mind of the artist.

An avalanche of colors never has any force.

As soon as my emotionally charged line has channeled the light of my white sheet of paper, without sacrificing its touching quality of whiteness, I cannot add anything to it or take anything from it. The page is written; no correction is possible. If it is inadequate, I can only begin again as an acrobat would.

Someone once told me there was a difference between the way I saw women and my depiction of them. I answered by saying that if I ever in real life saw such women as I represented in my pictures, I would be terrified. I do not create a woman; I draw a picture.

I basically work without a theory. I am aware only of the forces I use, and I move along the course of the picture's creation, pushed by an idea that I come to know only gradually as it develops.

ANDRÉ DERAIN: THE BANKS OF THE SEINE. 1904. Paris. MNAM

DERAIN SEQUESTERED

CHAMBOURCY

André Derain dies on September 10, at the age of seventy-four, as a result of an accident. He is buried in Chambourcy, where he had been living since 1935. This refined painter was one of the first and greatest Fauves. Apollinaire said, "Archaism was his Cubism." Derain's last year is saddened by the action of his wife, who demands, with her divorce, that his studio be sequestered. Interviewed shortly before his death, Derain explains: "My wife demanded the separation of assets; she called the sheriffs, who came to me while I was ill and sealed everything . . . My paintings are in prison. This is unbelievable . . ."

This bold innovator of modern art, after Fauvism, drew the attention of Vlaminck and Picasso to African art. He had for a long time been uninterested in shows of his works; he made an exception for the show of "Masters of Contemporary Art" in the Petit Palais, in Paris in 1937, to which he sent thirty canvases.

Since then, he has been increasingly blamed by critics for "allowing himself to be dominated by past centuries while he had wanted to give so much to his own times."

Out of love for his vocation, he states that "every time we take up the brush, we must face again all the problems of painting," but his real ambition remained to become "a master in the great French tradition."

He broke with Vlaminck, who, considering only his own instincts, blamed him for wasting time in "cemeteries," meaning museums. If he gladly mentioned the great masters, such as Raphael, Leonardo, Poussin, Corot, he was just as capable of improvisation as of virtuosity. After the First World War, he cut copper masks from shell casings, which gave him a taste for sculpture. Perhaps he was most original in his illustrations, particularly his woodcuts for *L'enchanteur pourrissant* by Guillaume Apollinaire and Rabelais' *Pantagruel,* for which he invented a coloring technique that restores an astonishing vibrancy to xylography.

ARP IS HONORED

VENICE

At the age of sixty-eight, Jean Arp is being honored. The Biennale awards him its grand prize for sculpture.

The Alsatian painter, poet, and sculptor, the first Dadaist, has received the award for his redoubled activity during these last years. Orders are coming to Arp more and more often; the death of his wife, the sculptor Sophie Taeuber, in 1943, prevented him from working for several years.

He is back at work. Two years ago, he acted with Dada friends in the film by Hans Richter, *Rêves à vendre* (dreams for sale). Last year, his art crossed the Atlantic with great pomp, with an order for the University of Caracas. *Le berger des nuages* (the shepherd of clouds) is the first monumental work by an intimate sculptor who still pursues his search on small models, as is shown by his *Ptolemy*. For the first time, massive form contains empty spaces.

JEAN ARP: PTOLEMY, I. 1953. Nuremberg. Germanisches Nationalmuseum

Alberto Burri: Between Dada and Art Brut

He was a doctor before he became an artist. During the war, Alberto Burri began to create works of art using found objects. Living in Rome since 1948, Burri continues to incorporate cast-off bits of daily life in his paintings: worn-out burlap, charred wood, and paper. His works are at once sumptuous and dreary, akin to both Dada and Art Brut (raw art). Because of his constant inventiveness, Burri is considered among the best contemporary Italian artists. At thirty-nine, he has achieved international recognition.

A New Museum in São Paulo

Dr. Assis Chateaubriand, who runs several large newspapers in Brazil, has chosen to give his city, São Paulo, a museum of modern art worthy of Brazil's vast cultural heritage. Five years and 2.5 billion francs later, the result is what many consider to be the perfect museum of modern art. As an example to others, Chateaubriand used profits from his chemical companies, which he established specifically for the purpose, to fund a museum for his people. Through a well-organized press campaign, he convinced Brazilian businessmen of the advantage of making Brazil a "country of art." Some of the greatest names in Western painting are already represented: Lautrec, Renoir, Sisley, Gauguin, Manet, Rembrandt.

Paris Is Losing Its Americans

In the postwar years, hundreds of young American painters and sculptors went to Paris to study and soak up the atmosphere that had inspired their elders of the Lost Generation such as F. Scott Fitzgerald, Ernest Hemingway, and Gerald Murphy, and artists such as Man Ray and Calder. Many came through the GI Bill which allowed them to study in Europe after serving in the Army. Some chose to study at Beaux-Arts Academy, like Norman Bluhm, Ellsworth Kelly, and Jack Youngerman; others went to the Julian Academy, like Robert Breer, or the Fernand Léger studio, like

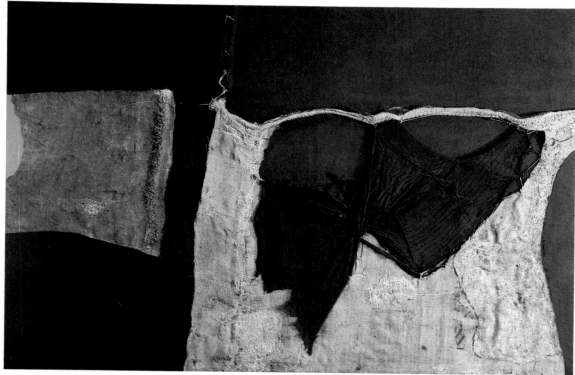

ALBERTO BURRI: SACKCLOTH WITH BLACK. 1954. The Artist's Private Collection

Seymour Boardman and Sam Francis. They all chose to live in Paris while the New York School triumphed. But after these calm and productive Parisian years, they are now returning to the intense pace of New York.

Perret: The Master of Concrete

Auguste Perret, who just died at the age of eighty, was the son of a Communard mason in exile. It is interesting to note that he never received an advanced degree in architecture, and executed his works through the family business, which he ran with his two brothers. His genius as a builder can be seen in his use of concrete with a remarkable restriction of means. Among his most notable structures: the apartment house on the Rue Franklin, the Théâtre des Champs-Élysées, the Museum of Public Works (1937), and, in the postwar years, the Saclay nuclear center, the reconstruction of the Old Port of Marseilles, the Perret building in Amiens, and Le Havre's urban development.

Foundation of the Gutai Group

In Japan's astonishing postwar period, Pollock attracted a devoted following. Now, the Gutai Group, established in the traditionalist province of Kansai, joins young artists who are meeting the challenge of Western modern art. The movement was started by a "master" painter, theorist, strategist, and precursor of abstract art in Japan, Jiro Yoshihara. Gutai means "concrete." The group's first paintings—using thick media, layers of pasted and torn paper, charred wood—will undoubtedly lead to yet more jarring works. This group has already made a statement.

IN BRIEF...

GERMANY
A traveling exhibition of the works of Joan Miró makes him known in the main cities of West Germany.

UNITED STATES
The second Jackson Pollock exhibition at the Sidney Janis Gallery in New York disappoints critics.

The French painter Pierre Soulages exhibits at the Kootz Gallery of New York.

The prize of the Art Institute of Chicago is awarded to the Japanese painter Kenzo Okada.

FRANCE
Duchamp's sketch Chess Players (1911) is bought by the Musée National d'Art Moderne in Paris: the first work by Duchamp in a public collection.

Erection in St. Cloud park of a "spatiodynamic cybernetic" tower by Nicolas Schöffer.

ITALY
Personal exhibition of the Danish painter Asger Jorn at the gallery Dell'Asterisco in Rome.

JASPER JOHNS: FLAG. 1954. New York. MOMA

JASPER JOHNS PAINTS THE AMERICAN FLAG

NEW YORK

There have always been flags in pictures, fluttering in the wind or reduced to spots of bright color as in Manet, Van Gogh, and Dufy. But Jasper Johns, twenty-four years old and newly arrived in New York from his native Georgia, has a stroke of genius. He entirely reworks the theme, creating on his canvas a flag perfectly adapted to the two-dimensional plastic screen, without any perspective or *trompe l'oeil.* It is not a "ready-made" of the Duchamp type, meant to push art off its pedestal.

If he had wanted to be a Duchamp, it would have been enough for Johns to go to any store and buy an American flag and depict it without changing anything. But his flag is both a flag and a painting, although neither can be identified with or dissociated from the other. To make it, the artist made a collage of newspaper covered with liquid wax and in which he dissolved pigments. Johns likes the fact that wax dries quickly and retains the traces of its working.

The work is particularly upsetting, for several reasons, during these years of triumphal Abstractionism. First of all, it represents an object everybody knows, or, rather, it represents it

out of context as object without integration in a narrative or a description. It deprives the very symbolic object of its symbolism. The image of America is overturned by brutality, power, and extreme subtlety. This is what makes of Johns's flag a superb illusion of the spirit.

RAUSCHENBERG INTRODUCES REALITY INTO PAINTING

NEW YORK

During the New York-style Christmas season, a show of large paintings with red dominant opens at the Egan Gallery. It is Robert Rauschenberg's, the *enfant terrible* of the new generation of artists. The show so pleases Egan that he calls it "Merry Christmas."

But it attracts little favorable criticism. Only the poet Frank O'Hara sees an exceptional lyrical talent in these amazing collages. The most outstanding of the four great paintings is the moving *Charlene,* ten feet long and seven feet tall. The variety and inventiveness of all sorts of elements demonstrate Rauschenberg's interest in the diverse techniques and objects made into "Combine Paintings." *Charlene* has everything: scarves, umbrellas unfolded in the shape of a rose window, old photos, even a T-shirt, a little like the *Merzbau* of Kurt Schwitters but integrated, mixed by and with painting.

Rauschenberg shared freedom and the absence of prejudice with a small group of artists formed around Black Mountain College, when Josef Albers was teaching there at the end of the 1940s. It is where he met the composer John Cage, the pianist David Tudor, and the choreographer Merce Cunningham, for whom Rauschenberg has created sets and costumes.

Rauschenberg had been known until now for his "White Paintings"—completely white abstracts on which shades of spectators or objects are playing—and for his "Black Paintings"—collages of newspapers dipped in black paint, which the artist repaints black. The recent "Combine Paintings" are meant to close the breach that separates painting from reality.

ROBERT RAUSCHENBERG: CHARLENE. 1954. Amsterdam. Stedelijk Museum

PABLO PICASSO: WAR. 1952. Vallauris. Temple de la Paix

THE FIESTA FOR PICASSO

VALLAURIS

The "Temple of Peace" was an old project. Picasso wanted to build it near Céret, on the top of Montfrède—a wonderful view that takes in Spanish and French Catalonia. But it is erected in Vallauris, in the restored priory chapel. "I had filled entire notebooks with sketches and details," Picasso writes, "but I never had a sketch of the whole. I started with war. What came to me first was the awkward, bumpy progress of one of those shabby and squeaky provincial hearses we see in the streets of small towns. I started on the right and everything else was built around this image."

Out of Picasso's notebooks arose two great compositions: One shows humanity at peace, enjoying life, the other shows assassination and death. Following the curve of the chapel, they are complemented by a third composition, which celebrates the reconciliation of races. The two large panels, 16 1/2 x 33 feet, that make up the essentials of war and peace were created two years ago in the hall of Hôtel Martinez in Cannes, rented by the artist during the last period of winter closing. As usual, Picasso excels in depicting war: It is symbolized by a hearse drawn by four horses, which trot over the books of civilization and culture; in the back are the silhouettes of assassins, a hideous procession against a nocturnal background.

The panel depicting peace, with its dancing women, playing children, and fish swimming in a bird cage, is less successful. Picasso seems to have found in Vallauris the same serenity as he did in Antibes in 1946. He worked in the large rooms of the castle Grimaldi. To add to his happiness, the town of potters holds its first bullfight.

It begins with a procession of gypsies, women from Arles, and bullfighters in a sky-blue coach, which Picasso decorates with huge bull horns. He follows in the orchestra car. He plays the trumpet, performing a tune in which some recognize the influence of military music and others that of the *pasodoble*.

The fiesta then officially opens. For two days, there is dancing and drinking. Françoise Gilot, Picasso's companion, is admired for her demonstration on horseback. Among the aficionados are Jacques Prévert, Édouard Pignon, Hélène Parmelin. They attend a burlesque bullfight. Three thousand people fill the improvised arena.

(See also 1904, 1905, 1907, 1909, 1912, 1921, 1927, 1937, 1945, 1946, 1948, 1953, 1958, 1973.)

Pablo Picasso in Vallauris, playing the trumpet.

The New York School is a topic of conversation again, this time with the Color-Field Painters, aptly named by the critic Clement Greenberg. He had wanted to differentiate them from the proponents of Action Painting, such as Pollock, who have other objectives. In Europe, art news is also in the headlines as newspapers report the suicide of Nicolas de Staël, one of the most gifted painters of the new generation, and the death of Fernand Léger, one of the great creators of the beginning of the century. But European painting is not dead for all that. In Kassel, an enormous exhibition entitled Documenta renews Germany's ties to modern art after Hitler had led the country away from it.

1955

SUMMARY

AVANT-GARDE

The Color-Field Painters
Clement Greenberg: the Picture as Field
Works in Motion, Free Beings

WRITINGS AND THEORIES

Victor Vasarely: the *Yellow Manifesto*

GREAT MASTERS

The Vertigo of Nicolas de Staël
Léger, a Modern Primitive

DEVELOPMENTS

The First Documenta
The School of Ulm

ART NEWS

Bernard Buffet's Works Scream Horrors of War
Vive la Différence Américaine!
Death of Yves Tanguy
Dali at the Sorbonne
Prize-Winning Posters
In Brief

WRITINGS AND THEORIES

Hans Sedlmayr: the Revolution of Modern Art

ARCHITECTURE

The Magnificence of General Motors
Inauguration of Notre-Dame-du-Haut

LITERATURE

UNITED STATES
Publication of Lolita *by Vladimir Nabokov, and* Cat on a Hot Tin Roof *by Tennessee Williams.*

FRANCE
Claude Lévy-Strauss publishes Tristes tropiques.
Death of Paul Claudel, diplomat and playwright.

GREAT BRITAIN
Evelyn Waugh publishes Officers and Gentlemen.

JAPAN
Publication of Snow Country *by Yasunari Kawabata.*

MUSIC

GERMANY
Iannis Xenakis directs his Metastasis *in Donaueschingen.*

FRANCE
Maurice Béjart revolutionizes ballet with Pierre Henry and Pierre Schaeffer's Symphony for a Lonely Man.
Death of the Swiss composer Arthur Honegger, a member of the Group of Six.

MOTION PICTURES

UNITED STATES
Rebel without a Cause *by Nicholas Ray is a great success in New York, while its hero, James Dean, is killed in a car accident.*
Premieres of The Seven Year Itch *by Billy Wilder and* Night of the Hunter *by Charles Laughton.*

FRANCE
Premiere of Diabolique *by Henri-Georges Clouzot.*

MARK ROTHKO
MAGENTA, BLACK, GREEN ON ORANGE. 1949
New York. MOMA

THE COLOR-FIELD PAINTERS

NEW YORK

The artists grouped together as Abstract Expressionists have gained an international audience since the end of the Second World War. Some of them are more Expressionistic than others, namely, those whom Harold Rosenberg in a famous 1952 text called Action Painters. Others are also abstract, although their style is not a direct expression of the character and emotions as customarily understood by the term Expressionism. They are the Color-Field Painters, as the critic Clement Greenberg calls them in an article in the *Partisan Review.* For them, the color field—a field saturated with color—becomes the silent but intense expression of their feelings about the world. The greatest of them are Mark Rothko, Barnett Newman, Clyfford Still, Ad Reinhardt, Adolph Gottlieb, and—less characteristic but close intellectually to their concerns—Robert Motherwell.

The Action Painters and the Color-Field Painters have been on the New York scene since Peggy Guggenheim began showing them in 1942 at the gallery Art of This Century. All of them have manifested their dissatisfaction with the American art establishment, which in their eyes is too conservative, too timid. The "Subjects of the Artists" school in 1948 and the manifestation of the "Irascibles" in 1950 were their way of separating their esthetic positions,

Mark Rothko, 1949.

which in *their* eyes have a future, from that of the American museums.

The heroic sentiment evident in this direction of painting is due as much to each' individual's life and personality as to the work itself. Both the Action Painters and the Color-Field Painters arose during a dark period in American history, the Depression. Many of them met and forged bonds of friendship in the 1930s when they worked on art projects for the New Deal and concluded there was a need for new American painting. The Depression shook the faith of Americans in the liberal, capitalist economic system and, even more, their confidence in the position of the intellectual and the artist in society.

The war convinced them that contemporary tragedy could not be expressed in the language of the old school. A new language had to be created. They were influenced by Cubism, Neoplasticism, and Surrealism, but it is undeniable that what they are saying and their manner of saying it are fundamentally new. They have also undertaken a mission, as Motherwell wrote: "In this world, modern artists are a sort of spiritual underground."

During the blackest period of solitude and uncertainty,

Rothko, Still, Newman, and Gottlieb still found a reason for living and creating in eternal human myths. In his preface to a Still catalogue, Rothko wrote, "Still expresses the tragic, religious drama that is the foundation of myths of all times." More meditative than the Action Painters, the Color-Fields have expressed their anguish and their faith in ways that embody all sensation and emotion. The sensuality of Rothko's colors, fine and translucent, applied layer by layer and slowly building mysterious depths . . . this is a concept, perhaps unexpected, of heroism, attempting to approach the essential in a materialistic, superficial time.

The term "sublime," often used by Newman and Still, is more apt; the text of Newman's, "The Sublime Is Now," published in 1948, in *Tiger's Eye,* introduces this notion of art. He says it is romantic, exalted, and a "revelation." The light that seems to emanate from the sumptuous paintings by Rothko and the light that shines from the vast monochrome fields of Newman—an intense midnight blue or red, with vertical "zips"—this light is energy, it attracts and radiates at the same time, enveloping the viewer.

The large size of their paintings is of prime importance: "If I

CLYFFORD STILL: UNTITLED. 1953. London. Tate Gallery

painted very large paintings," Rothko says, "it is because I want to be intimate and human. Painting a small painting means placing oneself outside the experience. When we paint a large painting, we are in it." Light is omnipresent as well in the work of Newman. He finds in Genesis a symbolism of artistic creation. Gottlieb opposes terrestrial and human activity to spiritual quietness by contrasting active planes with immobile disks suspended in a field that could be the sky.

The visionary quality of the work of the Color-Field Painters demands close attention: The frequent references by Newman to the Bible, the long time one must allow for being enveloped by Rothko's colors, the exaltation of vast, cut spaces by Still, the impenetrable abstraction of Ad Reinhardt are suitable to meditation . . .

These artists make a novel use of pure color. The work of Still is an example of the sumptuous use of color. His splendid beaches of intense yellow or flaming red approach the intensity of a Rothko.

In our troubled, shaken world, the Color-Field Painters speak of being. This is what causes the resistance they meet—and creates their chance to endure.

(See also 1945, 1950, 1952, 1953, 1957, 1961, 1970, 1971.)

CLEMENT GREENBERG: THE PICTURE AS FIELD

Under the title "American-Type Painting," the art critic Clement Greenberg has published a noteworthy article in the spring issue of *Partisan Review*. To label the painters Barnett Newman, Ad Reinhardt, Mark Rothko, and Clyfford Still, he proposes a new term—Color-Field Painters. It was three years ago that Harold Rosenberg coined the label Action Painting, primarily to characterize the work of Jackson Pollock. These two new terms prove helpful in distinguishing between the two important movements of the New York School, which often were collectively grouped under the ambiguous name of Abstract Expressionism.

Turner was actually the first painter to break with the European tradition of value painting. In the atmospheric pictures of his last phase he bunched value intervals together at the lighter end of the color scale for effects more picturesque than anything else. For the sake of these, the public soon forgave him his dissolution of form— besides, clouds and steam, mist, water, and light were not expected to have definite shape or form as long as they retained depth, which they did in Turner's pictures; what we today take for a daring abstractness on Turner's part was accepted then as another feat of naturalism. That Monet's close-valued painting won a similar acceptance strikes me as not being accidental. Of course, iridescent colors appeal to popular taste, which is often willing to take them in exchange for verisimilitude, but those of Monet's pictures in which he muddied—and flattened—form with dark color, as in some of his "Lily Pads," were almost as popular. Can it be suggested that the public's appetite for close-valued painting as manifested in both Turner's and Monet's cases, and in that of late Impressionism in general, meant the emergence of a new kind of taste which, though running counter to the high traditions of our art and possessed by people with little grasp of these, yet expressed a genuine underground change in European sensibility? . . .

A concomitant of the fact that Still, Newman, and Rothko suppress value contrasts and favor warm hues is the more emphatic flatness of their paintings. Because it is not broken by sharp differences of value or by more than a few incidents of drawing or design, color breathes from the canvas with an enveloping effect, which is intensified by the largeness of the picture itself. The spectator tends to react to this more in terms of

BARNETT NEWMAN: ADAM. 1951-1952. London. Tate Gallery

decor or environment than in those usually associated with a picture hung on a wall . . .

The easel picture will hardly survive such an approach, and Newman's huge, calmly and evenly burning canvases amount to the most direct attack upon it so far. And it is all the more effective an attack because the art behind it is deep and honest, and carries a feeling for color without its like in recent painting. Mark Rothko's art is a little less aggressive in this respect. He, too, was stimulated by Still's example. The three or four massive, horizontal strata of flat color that compose his typical picture allow the spectator to think of landscape—which may be why his decorative simplicity seems to meet less resistance.

CLEMENT GREENBERG
"American-Type Painting," Partisan Review, Spring (*Excerpts*)

WORKS IN MOTION, FREE BEINGS

JEAN TINGUELY: METAMECHANICAL AUTOMOBILE. 1954. Paris. MNAM

PARIS

"Please touch!" The poster greeting visitors to the show of "Le Mouvement" (motion) on April 6 to April 30 at the gallery Denise René and requesting their participation gives the tone to this event, which has aroused laughter, enthusiasm, or anger in critics and the public, but never indifference.

At 124 Rue La Boétie, Denise René, who for several years has been an active defender of abstract art, has assembled eight artists: Agam, Bury, Calder, Duchamp, Jacobsen, Soto, Tinguely, and Vasarely. They all pursue the same goal, but through different artistic expressions. They all want to introduce motion into painting or sculpture.

Incontestably, the forerunner of this Kinetic Art was Marcel Duchamp. In 1913 he created an animated "ready-made": A

Another precursor was Alexander Calder, whose mobiles are now famous. He invented them in 1932. They are composed of metal tubes and painted sheets held in unstable equilibrium. The least breath of air moves the mobiles like the leaves of a tree.

Apart from Tinguely, Agam and Vasarely may be the most interesting in the new generation. They actually make use of the viewer's movement inside the gallery. Agam shows, among his transformable objects, a polymorphous painting with abstract elements. It makes up different figures, depending on whether it is viewed frontally, from the left, or from the right. Vasarely exhibits a "profound kinetic work," composed of two vertical glass plates spaced from five to six inches apart like the double windows of his native Hungary. Networks of lines in infinite combinations are traced

WORKS OF ART WITH A KINETIC RHYTHM THAT IS NEVER REPEATED

bicycle wheel and its fork were attached to a high stool. In 1920 Man Ray helped Duchamp to make an optical device driven by an engine with glass blades; it almost killed Ray. The blades flew apart to the four corners of his studio under the effect of their speed of rotation.

Duchamp is represented at the gallery by his *Rotative Demisphere*, made in 1925 at the request of the stylist and collector Jacques Doucet, and by his *Rotoreliefs*, revolving disks that form spirals of various sizes.

The Swiss Jean Tinguely, thirty years old, shows strange wire sculptures driven by an engine. He calls them "metamechanics." One of them hops on meeting the visitor. Another makes drawings all by itself, an unsettling reminder of Automatic Writing so dear to Surrealists.

on the glass. He expresses his ideas in the *Yellow Manifesto*.

"Le Mouvement" introduces a wonderful novelty—the possibility for a work of art to recreate itself indefinitely. Its appearance is as great an innovation in art as was the rise of perspective in the fifteenth century, which fixed figures in space. More than even Cubism or Futurism, the artists brought together here have broken totally with perspective. This is what makes this show so fascinating. As Pontus Hulten wrote in his presentation of the show, "A work with a kinetic rhythm that is never repeated is one of the freest beings one can imagine, a creation that, escaping from all systems, lives on beauty."

VICTOR VASARELY: THE YELLOW MANIFESTO

At forty-seven years of age, Victor Vasarely is a master of Geometric Abstraction, which he is leading in an original direction. Aware of the entirely new image that we have of the world by virtue of its contemporary physical makeup, his goal is to create an art in agreement with the dematerialized idea we now have of matter. In his *Yellow Manifesto* he attempts to understand what contemporary painting must accomplish as it becomes the painting of tomorrow, in the age of transparencies and industrial multiproduction. What he says is new and intellectually stimulating as can be seen in the following passages from the *Yellow Manifesto*.

Artistic creations range from the "pleasant and useful" to "art for art's sake," from the "tasteful" to the "transcendent." Thus, there is a vast gradation of activities involving plastic arts: decorative art; style; pictorial advertisement and propaganda; the décor used in major industry, shows, celebrations, and sporting events; polychrome model factories; roadsigns and urbanism; documentary films on art; museum recreations; art editing; the synthesis of plastic arts; and, finally, the search for an authentic avant-garde. In these various disciplines, a personal accent does not necessarily indicate authenticity. Moreover, we are not qualified to decide whether these different manifestations of the plastic arts will be of a major or minor character for our time. We can effectively evaluate the past; not foresee the future.

But neither a work of value, be it immutable or reactionary, nor an advanced work that is mediocre can be adequate for future generations. The effect of artistic creation on us will range from minor pleasure to awe before dazzling beauty, with varying intensity and quality. These sensations will originate in us as emotions and will give rise to a sense of well-being or of tragedy. In so doing, art will have realized its goal to a certain extent. Analysis and comprehension of a message depend on our knowledge and degree of culture. Because only artistic entities of the past are intelligible, and because not everyone can engage in a profound study of contemporary art, we advocate, in the place of its "comprehension," its "presence." Sensitivity being a characteristic faculty of human beings, our message will reach ordinary mortals by the natural means of their emotive receptiveness.

Indeed, we cannot leave the enjoyment of a work of art to the elite of connoisseurs. Current art is moving toward more comprehensive forms, re-creatable at will. The art

VICTOR VASARELY: GIXEH. 1955. Paris. Private Collection

of tomorrow will be a common treasure, or it will not exist . . . It is a sad but necessary thing to abandon old values in order to possess the new ones. Our condition has changed, and, in turn, our ethics and esthetics must change. If the notion of plastic work has thus far been seen as a process of handicraft, and if it has been locked within the "single entity" myth, this is no longer so. It has come to imply re-creation, multiplication, and expansion . . . That great shackle of the two-dimensional fixed image constrains every work from Lascaux to abstract art. Our fortune lies in the future, in the new, touching beauty of the plastic arts.

VICTOR VASARELY
Yellow Manifesto *(Excerpts)*

THE VERTIGO OF NICOLAS DE STAËL

ANTIBES

Art has its martyrs. Long is the list of writers and painters who lived their creative adventure like a passion. The name of Nicolas de Staël must be added to this prestigious martyrology, near those of Nerval and Van Gogh. On March 16 he jumps out of the window of his studio. His body is found at the foot of the city walls. He had lived and worked in Antibes for a year.

Was it because of his Russian origin, the Dostoevski-type depth of his personality? De Staël was full of contradictions, dramas that all painters have had to face to the breaking point during these last fifty years. The void had always fascinated him. He now precipitates himself into it. "Contact with canvas," he wrote a short time before his suicide, "I lose it all the time, I find it again, and I lose it . . . Because I believe in chance, I can advance only from chance to chance."

This son of the governor of the Peter and Paul Fortress in what was St. Petersburg, a page of Czar Nicolas II at the age of two, journeyed through a career in painting with meteoric speed. He spent twenty years in misery during which he rarely used anything other than tablecloths and the sheets from his own bed to create polychrome compositions. Barely ten years of fame and wealth were his before he died at the age of forty-one.

His first real contact with canvas occurred in 1940; he painted still lifes and the *Portraits of Jeanine,* his wife. He had a unique mastery of line and color, which quickly prompted him to abandon figurative painting for abstract works, not without going to extremes. His *Compositions* of a network of open geometric surfaces, often of a thick substance, gradually became more cheerful, less austere, more colorful. The shapes become calmer. Soon, blue dominates. De Staël finds interior harmony. But success does not fully satisfy him.

Nicolas de Staël in Léger's studio.

NICOLAS DE STAËL: FIGURES AU BORD DE LA MER. 1952.
Düsseldorf. Kunstsammlung Nordrhein-Westfalen

At a time when Abstractionism is in fashion, and dominates the market, de Staël returns to the figure. Bottles, apples, roofs . . . But turning from a seascape or a quickly sketched musical instrument—what skill of construction! De Staël likes jazz, and paints "it" magnificently on canvases—the orchestra of Claude Luter and of Sidney Bechet. Living in the South, but fascinated by the musicians, he does not hesitate to make the ten-hour ride to a concert in Paris. His last painting, the large black shadow of his piano in the back, the baroque scrolls of his double bass among the brasses and woodwinds, is an exceptional masterpiece.

Another source of inspiration: soccer players. One evening de Staël goes to the Parc des Princes to watch a soccer game. It was like a stroke from the blue. He who worked at night, under electric light, discovers in "real life" the violent pyrotechnics of green grass and the spots of red and blue uniforms. Another subject: bathers on the beach, whom he reduces to blocks of color, in direct descent from his teacher Fernand Léger. The paintings issued from these experiences are difficult to understand at first. They are at the antipodes of abstract painting.

De Staël writes in January to a friend, the collector Douglas Cooper: "We harmonize heavy, fine, and very fine lines and direct, indirect, and opposite color relations. It has to be right, that's important. Always."

Shortly before being snatched into the void, he calls out, "God, how difficult life is! We must play all the notes, and play them well." De Staël had the absolute eye, like Léger. It is a pity that unlike the great cubist, who also dies this year, he does not believe that he can play his score to the end!

FERNAND LÉGER:
SPARE-TIME
ACTIVITIES
—HOMAGE TO LOUIS
DAVID. 1948-1949.
Paris. MNAM

LÉGER, A MODERN PRIMITIVE

GIF-SUR-YVETTE

Fernand Léger is drawn south by Vallauris and ceramics. He settles in Biot, where he buys the farmhouse Saint-André on July 31. He is tired and decides to return to Gif-sur-Yvette. On August 17, he succumbs to a cardiac crisis in the arms of his secretary, Georges Bauquier, who hears him murmur his last words: "It's hard! It's hard!"

This "builder of art," this "hefty character," who made the world of work the main subject of his art, was born in 1881 (as was Picasso). His father was a robust beef merchant in Argentan. Now Léger cannot bear the idea that he has to rest. He writes in the preface to a monograph by Pierre Descargues that "the artist, the poet, the creator of beauty are dedicated to this heroic fatality: to act in freedom. This cherished freedom, this day of glory, must be paid for dearly with incessant, daily risk. These living works have been conceived and forged standing up, at war with society."

Léger admires Henri Rousseau, with whom he goes to see an exhibition on David. He is enamored of the Italian Primitives and is close to Robert Delaunay, and is an important figure in Cubism. It was during the war of 1914, in the trenches, that he meets "people" and decides "to be very close to them while remaining demanding of myself and my art." He wants to be a "witness to his times." Seeing in the machine its dynamic necessity, he transcribes the optimistic images of our technological—and fraternal—civilization into a bold, clear, and joyful language.

There is no doubt that on his return in 1946 from the United States, to which he flees during the Second World War, Léger renders his most accomplished works. He was struck by the polychrome lights of Broadway to the point of projecting "the human body in space" in a mottled, aerial fashion. Magnificent last year was his *Great Parade*.

He is a member of the Communist party, but avoids the errors of Socialist Realism. His style is perfected. His theory of the figure-object, fashioned during the 1930s, prevents him from falling into pathos and laboring sentimentalism.

This is shown, among other paintings, in Léger's *Homage to David*. Only he could express "paid vacation" so joyfully; the lone exception may be Cartier-Bresson, with his 1936 photos of the Popular Front. Léger is the only one in the whole history of art who could draw with the callused hand of a laborer.

(See also 1917, 1933, 1946.)

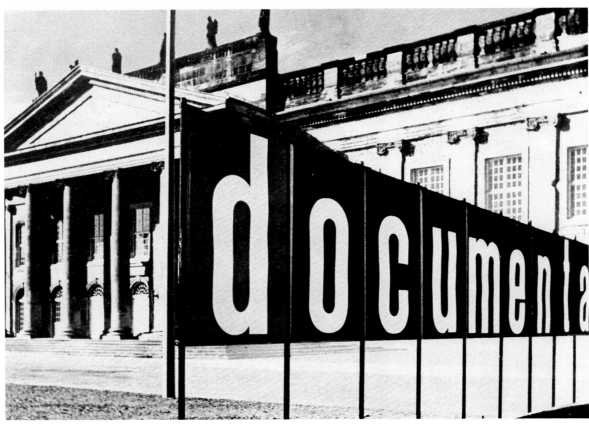

The first Documenta, in Kassel.

THE FIRST DOCUMENTA

KASSEL

The war is still prowling around. You feel it in the Fridericianum Museum, destroyed by Allied bombs and rebuilt hastily two years ago. For a long time, it had no windows. Its huge rooms still have no doors. It is ironic that

GERMANY, DEFLECTED BY HITLER'S FOLLY, HAS RETURNED TO MODERN ART

this classical building, erected between 1769 and 1779, now houses the greatest collection of modern art since the war. This is due to the initiator of the show, the painter Arnold Bode, a professor at the Academy of Kassel.

The selection of works was mainly inspired by the art historian Werner Haftmann, the author of a basic book on painting in the twentieth century. Five hundred and seventy paintings and sculptures are spread over fifty-four thousand square feet. Most of the artists are Ger-

man: thirty-five painters and fourteen sculptors. The French are present in good numbers, about forty. There are also about twenty Italians. Other European countries are poorly represented: Spain, Holland, Belgium, and Great Britain together have

only twelve painters and eight sculptors.

Werner Haftmann explains the purpose of Documenta (at least of its first show, for others are already planned). To some extent it is educational. According to the initiators, they want to show to the young generation the development of art in Europe since the beginning of the century. This is why the great movements early in the century, Fauvism, Expressionism, Cubism, and Futurism, are represented by "the European phalanx of old

masters": Kandinsky, Klee, Léger, Chagall, Beckmann, Morandi, and Rouault. Also more recent artists such as Max Ernst and Henry Moore, discovered around the 1930s, are included.

The visitor to Kassel finds some gaps. He sees little of Matisse and Picasso and no Brancusi, no Archipenko. But the whole presents an interesting diversity. Germany, deflected by Hitler's folly, has returned to modern art. In this sense, the first Documenta attains perfectly the goal set by its organizers.

(See also 1959, 1964, 1968, 1972, 1977, 1982.)

THE SCHOOL OF ULM

ULM

The great crowd on the Kuhberg on Sunday, October 2, inaugurates the Advanced School of Industrial Arts. This school would never have seen the light without the efforts of Inge Scholl, sister of the antinazi martyrs Hans and Sophie Scholl, who were beheaded by the Nazis in Munich. Her husband, Otl Aicher, a professor of design, has fully supported her in opening this institution.

Renaissance of the Bauhaus? The speeches at the inauguration make it appear so. The director is a former student of the Bauhaus, Max Bill. In Ulm, as in Dessau, all of man's environment—habitat, furniture, carpets, everyday utensils—must be studied. Also an initiation into psychology, sociology, and economics is planned. This does closely resemble the Bauhaus.

Bernard Buffet's
Works Scream Horrors of War

At the gallery Drouant-David in February, the young Bernard Buffet exhibits several drawings and three large paintings on the theme "The Horror of War." Completed last summer in Haute-Provence, these works shock the public with violent scenes both cruel and allegorical. "The first painting," he explains, "shows the angel of war, the second, a group of trees from which four people hang. Around them are houses and scenes of massacres. The third painting is the image of war behind closed doors because it's a concentration camp." Bernard Buffet emphasizes that his works know no particular place or time: This impressive series was simply inspired by his own feelings, and Henri Rousseau's *War*.

Vive la Différence Américaine!

New York's Museum of Modern Art celebrates its twenty-fifth anniversary with a dazzling exhibit covering works from Manet to Picasso. On the occasion, the well-known art critic and historian John Rewald talks about museums in the United States. Unlike French or other European museums, American museums are private foundations, and, as such, their curators enjoy certain freedoms. They may, for example, sell works that don't fit in with their collections and use the money from their sale to acquire more relevant works. Private collectors may buy a work because they fall in love with it and later donate it to a museum for tax purposes. These are the two factors, according to John Rewald, that make American museums so great.

Death of Yves Tanguy

Yves Tanguy, who died recently in Woodbury, Connecticut, was born in Paris in 1900. He left for the States in 1939, choosing to live on an isolated farm in Connecticut. He became an American citizen in 1948 and was married to Surrealist painter Kay Sage. A former sailor in the merchant marine, he became a painter after being moved by a work by de Chirico. His style affirmed itself right from the start: He seems to have invented a realm combining animal, vegetable, and mineral. He painted minutely detailed imaginary objects made of stone, shell, and bones in a marine atmosphere—a surreal universe of mineral hardness set in a dreamlike background.

Dali at the Sorbonne

He arrived in a white Rolls-Royce decorated with cauliflower. Salvador Dali gave a talk at the Sorbonne on the paranoiac-critical method. He gave this explanation: "I had artistic talent when still an infant. I had a bed with two boards to keep me from falling out, and these boards were completely covered with drawings. There was always some alchemy about them: If I drew a dog, it had a human face or a woman's breasts. I drew with crayons to capture the excessively colored intrauterine images that, for me, contained a paradisiac meaning. I later found this meaning again while reading a book on the trauma of birth, which gave me the key to very clear memories that I quickly identified as coming from my intrauterine period."

Prize-Winning Posters

The exhibit of graphic art currently on display at the Marsan Pavilion in Paris is attracting crowds of people. "One is struck by the enormous influence of abstract art on contemporary posters," stated André Maurois, adding that an amateur "who does not understand Braque" will be amused, charmed, and struck by a Carlu poster. "The trends of modern art are not arbitrary. They correspond to a profound movement that is also felt and expressed by our poster artists," concluded Maurois, who emphasized that in advertising, mistakes are not allowed.

YVES TANGUY: LE PALAIS AUX ROCHERS DE FENÊTRES. 1942. Paris. MNAM

HANS SEDLMAYR: THE REVOLUTION OF MODERN ART

When Ernesto Grassi was put in charge of a series of books to be called RoRoRo paperbacks (at the Rowohlt publishing house), he chose, as the first in the series, *The Revolution of Modern Art* by Hans Sedlmayr, a university professor of fifty-nine years of age. He knew that the work would cause a scandal in Germany. Indeed, the author contends that, ever since the avant-garde movements of the beginning of this century, "art is no longer art," which harkens back to theories that circulated during the Third Reich. Sedlmayr taught art history at the University of Vienna from 1934 to 1951. An excerpt from the concluding part of his work follows.

The transformations that have taken place in "modern art" can be seen as a revolution of an entirely new kind. Given the upheaval in the intellectual, social, and living conditions, it would indeed be unusual for art to remain unaffected. This revolution is a fait accompli. And it implies not only a rupture with all of European history but with all of past art. This fact has been far from overlooked by the leaders of this revolution. They have acknowledged it, hoped for it, advocated it, and, in their exaltation of the victorious world revolution, made themselves heard in no uncertain terms. For example, Le Corbusier says that "everything must be started over again, from scratch." Aragon, one of the two fathers of Surrealism, claims that "we are the defeatists of Europe." Hilla von Rebay, director of The New York Museum of Nonobjective Art, who thus has an official position in the worldwide artistic revolution, says that "still not enough bombs have been dropped on our old museums." All analyses emphasizing the "antinaturalist" elements of modern art miss its profound character. If this was all there was to modern art, it would be nothing more than a change of style as has occurred in past epochs, for example, in late antiquity.

This revolution is, however, characterized by the fact that art has either yielded to external forces or asserted its own autonomy and, consequently, has sunk into the nonartistic. No comparable examples of this phenomenon can be found in any other epoch. In extreme cases, modern art has submitted itself to an external entity, be it science, critical thinking, geometry, technology, risk-taking (as in Dadaism), the chaos of the unconscious, or an external world of dementia (as in Surrealism).

But what all this means is the following: To the extent that modern art submits itself to external forces and renounces the human element in favor of esthetic forces that are less artistic (such a submission having openly occured in the second, extremist phase of the revolution), it is no longer art. This cannot be denied; it is the necessary result of an orientation that is its own and which it has freely chosen.

The kind of modern art that truly deserves this designation is art that is born in the context of the previously described revolution and in the struggle against the type of art that no longer deserves to be called art. Through an artistic transformation and refinement of ideas, points of view, and forms engendered by this revolution, this true modern art is born of the substance and spirit of ancient and eternal art. It is recognizable by the fact that it takes seriously the profound difference between apparent representation and meaning, between form and goal. It is recognizable by the fact that it refuses to submit itself to nonartistic forces, that it does not renounce its human basis, that it acknowledges a system of values and adheres to it. If a modern art exists, it exists as the result of the struggles of the one art against the modern world, struggles in which art does not bend to contemporary totalitarian exigencies. Rather, it asserts its natural, inalienable right and appropriates the new, so far as it is capable, by transforming it.

HANS SEDLMAYR
The Revolution of Modern Art *(Excerpt)*

THE MAGNIFI-CENCE OF GENERAL MOTORS

DETROIT

Ten years ago, the preliminary studies for a General Motors technical research center were entrusted to Eliel and Eero Saarinen, father and son. The project was shelved. But the postwar boom and the prominence of the automobile makes it possible to resume plans and to carry them out on an even larger scale.

The center is inaugurated this year, six years after the death of Eliel Saarinen. It is said to cost at least one hundred million dollars—this includes the cost of the land and equipment. Eero was able to convince the client to erect a building that would be "an expression of the great precision and capacity for mass production of the metal industry."

The purity of the glass and metal structures designed by Eero Saarinen constitutes a radical change for industry. He is the first modern architect who has been offered the opportunity to work on such a large scale, and with little budgetary constraint.

A huge expanse of water serves as a mirror to the five divisions of the building, which demonstrate the purity of the architectural line. Industry dominates and is sumptuous, to such an extent that writers have given the whole the name of the "American Versailles."

General Motors research center, by Saarinen.

Le Corbusier with the church Notre-Dame-du-Haut at Ronchamp.

INAUGURATION OF NOTRE-DAME-DU-HAUT

RONCHAMP

Claudius Petit, minister of reconstruction, and the archbishop of Besançon preside on June 25 over the inauguration of Notre-Dame-du-Haut. "This," the minister says, "is an event eagerly awaited by the friends and the equally zealous enemies of Le Corbusier. I do not believe that any of his friends have been or will be disappointed. I have even seen skeptics and opponents conquered by the religious work of the greatest architect of our time."

The preparatory studies for Notre-Dame-du-Haut were undertaken five years ago. The chapel has an interior nave that can accommodate two hundred persons. The large canopy covering an altar and an outside pulpit make it possible on pilgrimage days to celebrate mass outdoors for three thousand of the faithful. The roof is concave. Three towers more than seventy feet tall collect light from three directions. The purple, black, and red robes of the prelates, priests, and choir boys are beautifully offset by brilliant white, grainy walls.

As part of the great revival of religious art launched by the French church at the end of the Second World War, Le Corbusier creates an incomparable masterpiece. He declares, "In building this chapel, I wanted to create a place of silence, of peace, and of internal joy. The feeling of the sacred animated our effort. Our workers have made this difficult, meticulous, and rough work. The cross—the true cross of torment—is installed in this ark. The Christian drama has taken possession of this place. I am giving you this chapel of true concrete, fashioned perhaps with audacity but certainly with courage, in the hope that it will find in you and in those who will climb the hill an echo of what all of us have inscribed there."

Le Corbusier is a nonpracticing Protestant. But art is the offspring of the sacred. From their meeting, an ardently religious building is born.

A myth is born when forty-four-year-old Jackson Pollock, at the height of his fame, is killed in a car accident on an East Hampton road. Through his life as well as his work, he shifted modern art from Europe to the United States. Everything in his work speaks of power and release, in the image of the American continent. Yet perhaps for that reason, he is already outmoded. In May, Nicolas Schöffer had presented Cysp I at the Théâtre Sarah Bernhardt in Paris. The work is the first cybernetic sculpture ever created, and it consciously moves around, reacts, and spins by means of an electronic brain concealed in its pedestal. Art and technology have always gone hand in hand with important periods in history. If the desperate Pollock carried painting to its extreme incandescence, Schöffer points the way to an outstanding new Classicism.

1956

S U M M A R Y

LITERATURE

FRANCE
Henri Michaux publishes a study of his drug experiences, Miserable Miracle.
   Publication of The Fall *by Albert Camus.*

HUNGARY
Tibor Dery publishes Niki.

MUSIC

GERMANY
Karlheinz Stockhausen composes Gesang der Jünglinge *for electroacoustic music and voice.*

MOTION PICTURES

FRANCE
Documentary by Jacques-Yves Cousteau, The Silent World.

SWEDEN
Premiere of The Seventh Seal *by Ingmar Bergman.*

JACKSON POLLOCK
NUMBER SEVEN. 1952

Jackson Pollock.

JACKSON POLLOCK THE MYTH

EAST HAMPTON

Jackson Pollock plans to attend a concert on the Ossorio property with his friends Ruth Kligmann and Edith Metzger, driving them there. He changes his mind about staying and drives home alone. He loses control of his car and crashes into a tree. He is killed instantly.

It is 10:15 p.m. on August 11. America loses one of its greatest painters, the one who doubtless best personifies the energy and the power of feeling that made this country the center of the art world since 1945. He is an artist out of the ordinary. He becomes a myth during his lifetime. He is a taciturn man of the West, with a genius close to the forces of the earth.

Jackson Pollock is born on the Watkins ranch in Cody, Wyoming, in 1912. He moves to New York in 1930. He takes courses in mural painting with Thomas Hart Benton, a regionalist painter with a strong personality, who greatly encourages his young student. During these years, Pollock is especially interested in the mural painting of the Mexicans Orozco and Siqueiros. But his work also reflects his admiration for Albert P. Ryder, whose dark, romantic seascapes are among the most original works in America at the end of the nineteenth century.

Pollock is inspired by the motifs of the Surrealists he meets in Peggy Guggenheim's

A TACITURN MAN OF THE WEST, WITH A GENIUS CLOSE TO THE FORCES OF THE EARTH

circle. He owes much to the example of André Masson, who invented Automatic Drawing in the mid-1920s: scattered sex organs and breasts in free fall, footprints, hybrids thrown on paper in a few seconds without prior plan. When André Breton publishes these drawings in *La révolution surréaliste*, Masson's Communist comrades of the cell on the Rue Fontaine find them pornographic. In New York, Breton later has several shows in the Museum of Modern Art, which buys his works. But in Paris no one wanted them. That is where Pollock saw them.

He owes to Masson, and to other influences, his invention of the "dripping" technique toward the end of the 1940s. It makes him famous almost from day one. "New needs require new techniques," he says. The feeling he wants to transmit is, however, much more than a formal invention. The unceasing energy in his paintings, covered entirely with networks, is a reflection of his internal rhythm.

Around 1951, Pollock begins to abandon dripping. He often reverts to the use of knife and brush, a more traditional painting technique. He makes innumerable splendid drawings on paper and on canvas, traces of enamel paint in brown or black—movement and suggestion.

Born of graphism, a shape appears in dark strokes on a plain canvas; sometimes it is entirely abstract, sometimes it is a face that contrasts with the "all over" and draws the viewer's attention. Some paintings, such as *The Deep* of 1953, exploring a new materiality of paint, are of a more intimate dimension and size. During these last years, Pollock resumes giving titles to his works—such as *Ocean Grayness*—using names that evoke the sea, light, the seasons, forces of nature which had inspired his excess.

The most exceptional successes may be his works in black and white with a population of swarming fallen titans. They usually are titled with numbers: *Number Five, Number Fourteen, Number Twenty-Two* . . . but they are mere reflex knots, flashing lightning. They write a letter of condolence to the age of the H-bomb, just as Picasso reminded the world of the air raid on Guernica, in Spain, in 1937.

One very long canvas, no doubt his masterpiece, *Portrait and a Dream*, retraces the artist's development. On the right, a powerful face, clearly legible; on the left, his dream, or rather his nightmare: a tangle of lines in which we recognize feverish, interlaced bodies. All of Pollock is in this one painting: his drama, his laceration between sense and nonsense, his inability to choose between representational art and ab-

JACKSON POLLOCK: PORTRAIT AND A DREAM. 1953. Dallas. Museum of Art

stract art, his confusion in spite of invigorating cauterizations from Jungian psychoanalysts.

Pollock seems to us to be the great successor of Picasso, whose universe of life and death fascinated the American. Maybe he is closer to Michelangelo.

When Michelangelo at the end of 1509 climbed down from the scaffold on which he had spent four years fighting with the ceiling of the Sistine Chapel, his back muscles, it is said, were so atrophied he could hardly stand. Like Michelangelo, Pollock was a slave of painting. From the time he studied live models in his youth, Pollock filled notebooks with sketches for the Pietà. Like the immense biblical crowd falling on the soul of the visitor to the Sistine Chapel, Pollock's vast apocalyptic hangings oppress one's personal or collective unconscious.

(See also 1943 and 1952.)

IN POLLOCK'S WORDS

All cultures have had means and techniques of expressing their immediate aims—the Chinese, the Renaissance, all cultures. The thing that interests me is that today painters do not have to go to a subject matter outside of themselves. Most modern painters work from a different source. They work from within.

. . . the modern artist is working with space and time, and expressing his feelings rather than illustrating.

Abstract painting is abstract. It confronts you. There was a reviewer a while back who wrote that my pictures didn't have any beginning or any end. He didn't mean it as a compliment, but is was. It was a fine compliment.

I'm very representational some of the time, and a little all of the time. But when you're painting out of your unconscious, figures are bound to emerge. We're all of us influenced by Freud, I guess. I've been a Jungian for a long time . . . painting is a state of being . . . Painting is self-discovery. Every good artist paints what he is.

I approach painting in the same sense as one approaches drawing; that is, it's direct. I don't work from drawings, I don't make sketches and drawings and color sketches into a final painting. Painting, I think, today—the more immediate, the more direct—the greater the possibilities of making a direct—of making a statement.

My painting does not come from the easel. I hardly ever stretch my canvas before painting. I prefer to tack the unstretched canvas to the hard wall or the floor. I need the resistance of a hard surface. On the floor I am more at ease. I feel nearer, more a part of the painting, since this way I can walk around it, work from the four sides and literally be in the painting. This is akin to the method of the Indian sand painters of the West.

When I am in my painting, I'm not aware of what I'm doing. It is only after a sort of "get acquainted" period that I see what I have been about. I have no fears about making changes, destroying the image, etc., because the painting has a life of its own. I try to let it come through.

. . . it seems to be possible to control the flow of the paint, to a great extent, and I don't use . . . the accident: I deny the accident.

BALTHUS AT MOMA

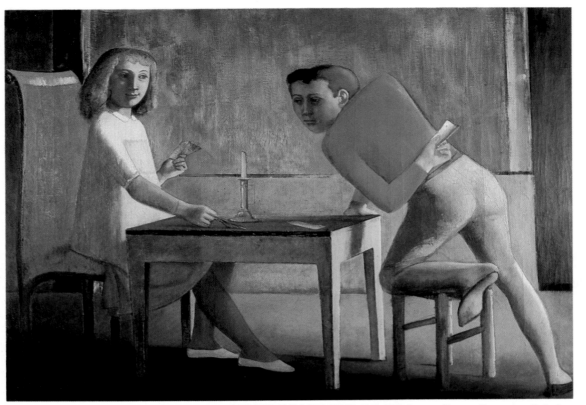

BALTHUS: THE CARD GAME. 1948-1950. Lugano. Thyssen-Bornemisza Collection

NEW YORK

Will the second half of this century be abstract, lyrical, or absolutely geometric? It does not seem to be the latter. A show installed early in December at the Museum of Modern Art could well prove the opposite. The artist is a forty-four-year-old French painter of Polish origin, Count Balthazar Klossowski de Rola, called Balthus.

Classical, unusual, the paintings show a world of pubescent girls, card players, and pensive pedestrians. A street in Paris, an interior with a black fireplace, a bank of light across the intimacy of a room—they form the background on which is played the sweet and diabolic melody of the unconscious.

GEORGES BRAQUE FLIES AWAY

LONDON

"A good picture never stops giving of itself." So says Georges Braque, whose migrating birds, which this year are invading his work, fly to the Edinburg Festival before landing at the Tate Gallery, where the British Arts Council organizes Braque's first official exhibition.

The eighty-nine canvases are distributed over three spacious rooms. They attract a large British and international public, which discovers that Braque is captivated by the traverse of space by swiftly flying birds, where he once was attentive to static forms in space.

Braque made his curvilinear, winged paintings in Varengeville, his Normandy harbor. "The wind, the clouds, lights, flux and reflux, everything changes in an instant. This is the country of mobility! This is what Braque has chosen and for which he renounced the Provence with its static light," says the writer Georges Limbourg.

GEORGES BRAQUE: THE STUDIO, IX. 1952-1956. Paris. MNAM

Le Corbusier —Maybe, Maybe Not

Le Corbusier agreed to participate in rebuilding Berlin and submitted, in particular, a project for a fifteen-story building. Divided into three hundred apartments, it would be based on the same model as the Cité Radieuse, which he built in Marseilles. Unfortunately, his ceiling height of seven and a half feet is below the eight-foot minimum set by German housing authorities. A Berlin newspaper held a poll for its readers, in which two thousand out of five thousand readers said they would accept the Le Corbusier plans. The other three thousand, however, were against the project and said it was up to the German people to decide. The famous architect himself thinks that his buildings are suitable for any of the world's cities, Marseilles, Berlin, or elsewhere.

Lyonel Feininger, Precursor of the Comic Strip

Lyonel Feininger died in New York, his birthplace, on January 13. He was eighty-five years old. Born of German immigrants, he studied in Hamburg, Berlin, and Liège, and stayed in Paris in 1892, 1906, and 1911. There he met Delaunay and discovered Cubism, which influenced his carefully composed works. In 1919, Walter Gropius asked him to teach at the Weimar Bauhaus. He worked there actively until the famous school left for Dessau. He returned to New York for good in 1937, fleeing Nazi attacks against "degenerate art." The Museum of Modern Art gave him a retrospective in 1944. His strangely dreamlike illustrations for *The Chicago Tribune* at the turn of the century placed him as one of the precursors of the comic strip.

work, along with the poster art of Chéret with their amiable casualness. But it is above all a brilliant demonstration of Seurat's optical theories, using the diffraction of light at the Montmartre circus. His clever composition shows the arabesques of the circus rider, the acrobat, and Monsieur Loyal's whip, all viewed by a delighted clown pulling the curtain shut—as Seurat thumbs his nose at death.

GEORGES SEURAT: CIRCUS. 1891. Paris. Musée d'Orsay

title *Just What Is It That Makes Today's Homes So Different, So Appealing?* But even before 1955, the Pop spirit was in the air in England, with Peter Blake, Peter Phillips, Allen Jones, and David Hockney, and in the United States with Robert Rauschenberg, Jasper Johns, Jim Dine, Roy Lichtenstein, and Andy Warhol.

IN BRIEF...

GERMANY
Emil Hansen, called Emil Nolde, dies at Seebüll. He had been a wood engraver and lithographer before coming to painting.

UNITED STATES
The greatest names of Cubism are reunited at the Sidney Janis Gallery for "Cubism 1910-1912": Delaunay, Villon, Picasso, Herbin . . .
Advised by Marcel Duchamp, the director of MOMA, Alfred Barr, buys a series of canvases from Frantisek Kupka.
The Cincinnati Museum of Art presents sculptures by Georges Braque.

FRANCE
Fernand Léger retrospective at the Musée National d'Art Moderne.
Henri Georges Clouzot creates The Mystery of Picasso, a feature film, which for the first time presents the actual process of artistic creation on the screen.

GREAT BRITAIN
At the Tate Gallery, "One Hundred Years of German Painting."

JAPAN
Creation of the Minami gallery in Tokyo, which exhibits the engravings of Komai Tetsuro.

The "Circus" Acquired by the Jeu de Paume

Executed between 1890 and 1891, Seurat's last masterpiece, *Circus,* was acquired by the Jeu de Paume museum. The inventor of Neoimpressionism died prematurely while his painting was being displayed at the Salon des Indépendants. The influence of Toulouse-Lautrec's humor and dazzling lines can be seen in this

The Birth of Pop Art

Pop Art was born last year during an exhibit organized by the Institute of Contemporary Art in London entitled "Man, Machine, and Motion." But it was not until this year that the name Pop Art appeared, during another historic exhibit called "This Is Tomorrow," presented at the Whitechapel Gallery. It appears in a collage by Richard Hamilton with the curious

Satan Is Dead

Giovanni Papini died in Florence, where he was born in 1881. Son of an atheist Garibaldian, he was considered a devil in Italy. A hotheaded polemicist, he said of himself, "I am the man who does not accept the world." His essay *Il Diavolo* (the devil), in which he developed the idea that God had pardoned Satan, was nearly prohibited in the Index. In 1951, he

published *The Black Book,* a series of imaginary interviews. He had Picasso say, for example, that he painted his works to mock his contemporaries—an apocryphal vow falsely attributed to that artist and used against him by enemies of modern art.

Cysp I **by Nicolas Schöffer with Maurice Béjart's dancers at the first avant-garde festival, on the roof of La Cité Radieuse in Marseilles.**

ELECTRONICS IN THE SERVICE OF SCULPTURE

PARIS

A statue that turns on its creator, hunts him, and tries to kill him! This is not a sensational horror movie. It is the reality that happened on May 28 during a "Night of Poetry," at the Théâtre Sarah Bernhardt.

This is what happened. Artists and poets come on the scene one after another. Georges Mathieu takes only a few minutes to paint a huge abstract painting. The evening's high point appears: *Cysp I,* the first cybernetic statue ever made, the work of Nicolas Schöffer, a forty-four-year-old Hungarian who has been living and working in Paris since 1936.

It is an orthogonal structure about ten feet high that can change freely. A microphone and a photoelectric cell connected to an electronic network hidden in its pedestal make it sensitive to noise, colors, and light in the environment. This evening, after turning its polychrome disks

and moving around and stretching out its steel and duralumin arms, it is no doubt overexcited by the applause of the public and suddenly pursues the "Dr. Frankenstein" who gave it life. Incapable of reasoning with the sculpture, Schöffer has to flee.

He became known two years ago at the public works and buildings show in the Park of Saint-Cloud. With the aid of the Philipps firm, he presents *Cybernetic Tower,* a gigantic tubular construction a hundred sixty-five feet high, which emits sound signals by the use of five electronically mixed magnetophones. The tower is fixed on the ground. *Cysp I* is mounted on four wheels propelled by small engines. Thus the danger of a work of art going wild.

Once a student at art institutes in Budapest and Paris, Schöffer cut his links to the past. The time had passed, at least for him, when a sculptor could work with chisels and

burins. He must use the new techniques of his time. Two years ago, under the auspices of the French Esthetic Society, at the Sorbonne, he gave a long explanatory lecture on "spatio-dynamism," a term he uses to characterize his work.

Cysp I is examined and repaired by Philipps engineers and returns to service on the roof of Le Corbusier's habitation unit in Marseilles. It is invited, as a "canvas-robot," to the avant-garde festival there and executes a perfect pas de deux choreographed by Maurice Béjart to music by Maurice Henry.

A SCULPTURE ANIMATED BY SURROUNDING NOISES, COLORS, AND LIGHTS

Cysp I, **the first cybernetic sculpture, on the stage of the Théâtre Sarah Bernhardt in Paris.**

WALTER GROPIUS: APOLLO IN A DEMOCRACY

Walter Gropius is well known for having founded the Bauhaus in Weimar, Germany, in 1919, which through its principles gave rise to Functionalism in architecture and design. Today, he seems to be reevaluating the intransigency of his earlier views. In the speech he gave in Berlin two years ago upon receiving the Goethepreis, he did not hesitate to reintroduce the notions of beauty and humanism, notions that had previously been looked down upon. These are the words of a revolutionary who could not foresee the crimes that would be perpetrated in his name. This speech is included, along with some of his writings, in a volume that has appeared under the Connaissance imprint in Brussels. A passage from the speech follows.

Over a long period of time, I came to realize that creation and love of beauty not only enrich man by granting him a large measure of happiness, but also make his ethical faculties evolve.

An age in which such a sentiment is not given much priority remains underdeveloped in a visual sense. Its perception remains imprecise, and its individual artistic manifestations have such a weak effect as to give almost no indication of any overall evolution.

Man is born with two eyes but needs an extended period of education in order to learn to see. Intense observation and a sharpened inner vision strengthen the imagination so as to enable him to create original forms and, by successive elimination, arrive at criteria of artistic values. Today's bookish system of education is obstructing the development of sensory perception and of a sense of beauty. There is a wide gap between the public and the creative artist, whose intrinsic value is misunderstood and underestimated as if he were a luxury item that society could do without.

The triumphant and unprecedented march of the exact sciences has chased away all magic in our life. The poet and the prophet have become the pauperized parents of positive-minded, materialistic man who, dazzled by the success of a mechanized civilization, breaks away from them. Einstein spoke forcefully of the consequences of this one-sided evolution, saying that "our age is characterized by perfected tools but imprecise goals." Tolstoy, before him, had foreseen this cultural dilemma. He accused science of deliberately trying to study "everything"; by moving in hundreds of directions at once, we would completely scatter ourselves, rather than choosing with precision

Harvard Graduate Center, 1949-1950.

what was closest to our heart and making it the target of our highest aspirations. Tolstoy's exhortation can undeniably be seen as an appeal in favor of a system of cultural values. Thus far, we have been unable to agree on such a system.

WALTER GROPIUS
Speech on receiving the Goethepreis
(Excerpts)

The greatest of modern sculptors leaves this world. It is difficult to see who might be placed on equal footing with Brancusi—his work is one of the most accomplished and beautiful ever created. He was not only an incomparable artist, but also possessed an exceptional moral conscience. Perhaps it is Ad Reinhardt who has taken up where Brancusi left off.

He, too, wants art to be first and foremost an activity of the mind, as demonstrated both by his painting and his Twelve Rules for a New Academy, a true profession of faith of a person in search of the absolute. Art is not only the mirror of society. It is truly great when it shows us the right path to follow.

1957
S U M M A R Y

GREAT MASTERS

Brancusi: the Passion for Shape
In Brancusi's Words

WRITINGS AND THEORIES

Ad Reinhardt: Twelve Rules for a New Academy

AVANT-GARDE

Hartung's Calligraphy

SCULPTURE

David Smith at MOMA

ART NEWS

Calder: from Mobiles to Stabiles
Yves Klein Presents His Blue Period
Mathieu in Japan
Trouble at the École de Paris
In Brief . . .

DESIGN

Danish Modern

ARCHITECTURE

The Return to a Synthesis of the Arts
Henry Van de Velde Dies

CONSTANTIN BRANCUSI
ENDLESS COLUMNS
Paris. MNAM

BRANCUSI: THE PASSION FOR SHAPE

PARIS

"Let's go, let's go, my boy." They are the last words spoken by Constantin Brancusi as he dies during the night of March 15 to March 16. He was eighty-one years old.

A religious service according to the Orthodox rite is held in the church on Jean-de-Beauvais street. During the funeral service punctuated by Gregorian chants, the question of heaven is raised. As for the earth that receives the body of the great sculptor from Romania, it is in the cemetery of Montparnasse.

Heaven and earth, the two obsessions, the two main motifs of the artist. A great work is a work that is measured directly in extremes. It tries to embrace all reality. By an ever more stringent and detailed analysis, it reduces the world to the elementary forces that move it. Brancusi very early becomes convinced that sculpture alone, by the unceasingly working on shape, can demonstrate the fundamental energy in matter.

To think of the world was for Brancusi to think of sculpture and its history, its development and its revolutions. Brancusi was not the intuitive, poorly

Constantin Brancusi.

trained, naive peasant, as some would have it. He not only mediated the lesson of Auguste Rodin, he was interested in the avant-garde movements of his time, in the Fauves and Cubists in particular. By means of his art, he sought to define the absolute singularity of sculpture.

How can a sculptured object be distinguished from any other object in the environment? A simple question, but one no one before Brancusi thought to pose so directly. The answer: As the frame delimits the picture, the pedestal isolates and makes the sculpture. Because it is the pedestal that makes the sculpture, efforts should be concentrated on the pedestal. The sculpted volume grows out of the ground. Like Antaeus, it draws its strength from earth in

CONSTANTIN BRANCUSI:
THE SEAL II. 1943.
Paris. MNAM

IN BRANCUSI'S WORDS

order to rise as high as possible and to reach Heaven.

The idea of the *Endless Column* was born in Brancusi's mind: an entirely autonomous pedestal that devours its sculpture and proliferates indefinitely in the vertical. It is known that Brancusi was busy throughout his life on this goal: an endless column, a beautiful, sober symbol of immortality. He made several such columns, of plaster, wood, cast, copper, and steel. The most impressive is the one that has been standing since 1938 in the small Romanian town of Targu Jiu: sixteen modules threaded one above the other, almost one hundred feet high, twenty tons. The idea that haunted Brancusi—placing sculpture in relation to and in connection with its environment—here found its most radical development.

His sculptures borrow their shapes from organic life. Among the first ones are *The Kiss*, the *Prayer*, *The Newborn*, the *Sleeping Muse* . . . Bodies of men, women, torsos, heads, sexual organs. Brancusi keeps repeating these shapes, he simplifies them, he purifies them, he gradually leads them back to a sort of original state and shape: the Orphic egg.

The importance and influence of Brancusi is hard to measure. He is still affecting young artists. Probably Americans will again "take advantage" of Brancusi, as they have done with Cézanne and Matisse. Once again the incorrigible French have allowed the best pieces, about eighty in number, to be shipped to the United States, while his adopted country keeps only three. To prevent complete dispersal of his works, Brancusi is said to have decided one year before his death to will the contents of his studio at the Impasse Ronsin to France. He stipulated that France must pledge to reproduce the studio faithfully in a museum.

(See also 1913, 1928, 1938.)

Ever since Michelangelo's time, sculptors have wanted to create the grandiose. They have only succeeded in creating the grandiloquent. There is no need to cite names. In the nineteenth century, sculpture was in a hopeless situation. Then Rodin came and transformed everything. Because of him, man once again became the measure according to which the statue was patterned. Sculpture once again became human in its dimensions and significance. Rodin's influence on the world of sculpture was, and still is, immense.

What use is there in tearing down a mountain and carving the stones into cadavers or enraged pieces of steak?

Beauty is absolute equity.

One fine, a bird flew into my attic. He wanted to get out but lost his way, frantically flying into walls, windows, and fanlights. Another bird flew into my attic, rested a few minutes on a ledge and then flew off, easily finding his way back to the sky. It is the same with artists.

CONSTANTIN BRANCUSI:
TORSO OF A YOUNG MAN. 1917. Paris. MNAM

To see is one thing; to go ahead is another. Only action counts.

Things are not difficult to do. The difficult thing is putting ourselves in the state to do them.

People do not get along with each other because they arrange their communal existence on the basis of a fatal pyramid. They all try to reach the top, relentlessly pushing each other aside when it would be more natural to live like flowers in a field, each one finding its own spot and being provided rain, sunshine, the freshness of a cool breeze, the blessing of the sky, and the violence of storms. When will people learn to follow the marvelous example of nature?

Reality lies in the essence of things and not their external forms. Hence, it is impossible for anyone to produce anything real by imitating the external form of an object.

Simplicity is not an objective in art, but one nevertheless arrives at simplicity by approaching the true meaning of things.

When you see a fish, you do not think about his scales. You think about his glittering body, seen swiftly gliding through the water. This is what I wanted to express. If I had depicted his fins, eyes, and scales, I would have sacrificed his movement, and I would have come up with a mere sampling of reality. I wanted to seize the radiance of his spirit.

What good is there in using models? You only end up sculpting cadavers.

Do not forget that you are an artist! Do not lose courage, fear nothing and you will be successful! Create like a God, command like a king, and work like a slave! I am no longer of this world. I am far from myself, detached from my person. I am in the realm of the essential.

AD REINHARDT: TWELVE RULES FOR A NEW ACADEMY

Ever since Malevich and Mondrian published their theories on art, we have known that art can be ascetic and dialectic, analogous to the spirit of denial we find in religious mystics. But the American painter Ad Reinhardt seems to go beyond all this in his disavowal of objective reality of any kind. There is nothing academic about his "Twelve Rules for a New Academy," in which he stipulates, point by point, what creation is allowed to be and what it must definitely not be. His rules are laid down with a mental vigor that seems to close—and simultaneously open—all the ancient and modern doors of meditation on the artistic process.

Tradition shows the artist what not to do. "Reason" in art shows what art is not . . . "The way to know is to forget."

The first rule and absolute standard of fine art, and painting, which is the highest and freest art, is the purity of it. The more uses, relations and "additions" a painting has, the less pure it is. The more stuff in it, the busier the work of art, the worse it is. "More is less."

The less an artist thinks in nonartistic terms and the less he exploits the easy, common skills, the more of an artist he is. "The less an artist obtrudes himself in his painting, the purer and clearer his aims." The less exposed a painting is to a chance public, the better. "Less is more."

The Six Traditions to be studied are:

1. the pure icon

2. pure perspective, pure line and pure brushwork

3. the pure landscape

4. the pure portrait

5. the pure still life

6. pure form, pure color and pure monochrome

"Study ten thousand paintings and walk ten thousand miles." "Externally keep yourself away from all relationships, and internally, have no hankerings in your heart." "The pure old men of old slept without dreams and waked without anxiety."

The Six General Canons or the Six Noes to be memorized are:

1. No Realism or Existentialism. "When the vulgar and commonplace dominate, the spirit subsides."

2. No Impressionism. "The artist should once and forever emancipate himself from the bondage of appearance." "The eye is a menace to clear sight."

3. No Expressionism or Surrealism. "The laying bare of oneself," autobiographically or socially, "is obscene."

4. No Fauvism, primitivism or brute art. "Art begins with the getting rid of nature."

5. No Constructivism, sculpture, plasticism or graphic arts. No collage, paste, paper, sand or string. "Sculpture is a very mechanical exercise causing much perspiration, which mingling with grit, turns into mud."

6. No "trompe l'oeil", interior decoration or architecture. The ordinary qualities and common sensitivities of these activities lie outside free and intellectual art.

AD REINHARDT
ARTnews, May *(Excerpts)*

AD REINHARDT: ABSTRACT PAINTING. 1956. New York. Marlborough Gerson Gallery

HARTUNG'S CALLIGRAPHY

PARIS

The shows of works by the painter Hans Hartung keep coming and keep demonstrating the public's great interest in the work of this man who is considered one of the masters of abstract art, close in importance to Kandinsky and Mondrian.

The present itinerant show in Germany—in Hanover, Stuttgart, Hamburg, Cologne, Nuremberg—follows the retrospective organized last year in Paris, in the gallery Craven, which covered drawings from the period of 1921 to 1938, jointly with the Galerie de France, which showed the recent paintings. For three years, Hartung has pursued research into figures, and developed an increasingly personal cursive script. Pushing his studies into the informal, he paints with rapid, supple strokes of the brush.

He arranges on modulated backgrounds signs that read like a semantic field, their nuances varying under the effect of shimmering light. On first viewing, it is tempting to draw a parallel with Far Eastern calligraphy, with which his art has a stylistic affinity due to the purity of the sign void of all references to reality. But if the comparison is pushed too far, interpretation of his works would be faulted.

If Hartung confesses his taste for calligraphy, he does not make it an end in itself. Mastery and reflection support the composition that functions on dynamics and instincts. His networks of vibrant, flexible lines, together with the refinement of his palette, enable the artist to introduce an invisible universe holding immense poetic power. In 1946, Hartung confessed to the critic Charles Estienne, "An emotional state impels me to draw, to create certain shapes in order to try to transmit and induce a similar feeling in the viewer. Then I enjoy working on a canvas. This is what urges me on, the wish to leave the trace of my work on canvas or paper. It is the action of painting, drawing, tracing, stamping."

HANS HARTUNG: T-1956-25. 1956. Paris. Galerie de France

This passion for graphics is reflected in the drawings and etchings he does simultaneously. From a young age, he enjoyed these instantaneous notations, and today seems preoccupied with the problem of speed as a motivating element of expression. The painter often recalls a childhood memory. During a thunderstorm, he sat on a window sill in order to copy the zigzags of lightning. As an adolescent, he was interested in astronomy and built a telescope for himself. Such memories may help explain his work.

Hans Hartung was born in Leipzig in 1904. German but fiercely anti-Hitler, he fought on the side of the Allies during the Second World War. He was seriously wounded on November 20, 1944, in Buc near Belfort; a leg was amputated. In 1946 he was made a French citizen. He pursued his work in a studio on the Rue Cels, which he shared with his wife, the painter Anna-Eva Bergmann. Last year, he was elected to the Academy of Fine Arts in Berlin. At the age of fifty-three, Hartung is being enthusiastically received by the public, which has long been ignorant of his seductive modernity.

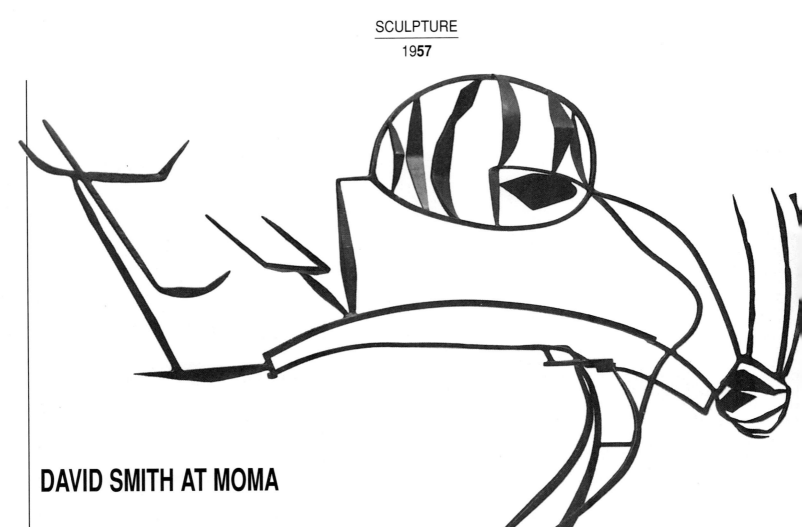

DAVID SMITH:
AUSTRALIA. 1951.
New York. MOMA

DAVID SMITH AT MOMA

NEW YORK

At the age of fifty-one, David Smith, in the opinion of many people, is the greatest living American sculptor. He redefines the approach to sculpture as to volume, material, and color. His free work in metal, using elements found or recycled, may be compared to the spontaneity and Surrealist inspiration of the Action Painters.

He is a descendant of a long line of blacksmiths from Indi-

siders himself a painter rather than a sculptor, and gladly admits that his sculpture is born of design. Using metal cuttings, he paints with steel. "I don't see sculpture under five different aspects at once, only a single one," he says.

The very supple, linear charm of *Australia* and the famous *Hudson River Landscape* illustrate his concept of sculpture along harmonized planes, viewed from the front, against a

*A FREE WORK IN METAL
THAT MAY BE COMPARED TO THE SPONTANEITY
OF THE ACTION PAINTERS*

ana. He worked as a welder while and after he studied painting at the Art Students League and during the Second World War. This familiarity with physical labor and his lack of prejudice against metal prepared him for a discovery that was of capital importance to him: the reproductions of the welded metal sculptures of Picasso and González he saw in the magazine *Les cahiers d'art.*

Strangely enough, Smith con-

wall, or against the sky, as the artist likes to show his work.

One of Smith's many series was begun six years ago: the *Agricola* sculptures, in which he put together fragments of machines or farm tools. The theme and the elements of the series were undoubtedly inspired by the Midwest of his youth: The machine was making its debut in the countryside, and building of large metallurgical plants was disturbing the life of

small towns. The sculptures also reflect his present environment: He left New York City in 1940, and ever since has been living in Bolton Landing, in the Adirondacks, Upstate New York. He calls his farm, fields, and studios "Terminal Art Works."

In other series, such as *Sentinels* and *Tanktotems* and last year's *Five Units Equal*, he stresses verticality with a clear anthropomorphic connotation. It appears that Smith is inaugurating a new method: the repetition of the same element—a parallelepiped rectangle, organized vertically, providing a more sys-

tematic, less action-oriented appearance.

The quality of his designs and the wealth of their invention are attractions at each of his exhibits. Designs have been inspired by Surrealism, Constructivism, and Cubism from the end of the 1930s and by political drawings from the 1940s. Interest in color has always been evident in his habit of painting his sculptures. All is displayed in an exhibition at the Museum of Modern Art.

ALEXANDER CALDER: HORIZONTAL MOBILE.1956

Calder: from Mobiles to Stabiles

American sculptor Alexander Calder seems to be permanently settled in France. After living in Touraine for the past four years, he has just bought a house in Brittany. And, as he sets down his roots, his works continue to spring forth. After the mechanical mobiles that started his career in the 1930s, he now creates large outdoor pieces that move in the wind. Alongside these creations, Calder is building more and more "stabiles." It was Jean Arp who suggested giving this name to Calder's stationary sculptures. In contrast to the light and airy aluminum mobile, the steel stabile suggests the earth's gravity. Whether from the air or the earth, this jovial artist is inspired by the forces of nature.

Yves Klein Presents His Blue Period

Yves Klein exhibits eleven monochrome panels from his "Blue Period" at the gallery Apollinaire in Milan. The panels, identi-cal in size and painted in a flat ultramarine blue, which the artist has patented, present the ultimate in abstract expression. Compared with these works, Malevich's famous *White Square on White* seems wildly baroque! Keenly interested in the occult, Klein said that he was trying to "conceptualize" color by taking it back to its primal energy. Pierre Restany, who is presenting the exhibit, calls it "cosmogenesis." Two years ago, the Salon des Réalités Nouvelles had refused to take Klein's *Orange Monochrome*. Yves Klein has been creating monochromatic paintings since 1946.

Mathieu in Japan

Georges Mathieu painted twenty-one canvases on Japanese television in Tokyo over the course of three days. One of the pieces was a fifty-foot-long fresco. We have come to expect this of Mathieu, who admits he would not mind becoming a Daliesque figure. Mathieu met Dali, his model and idol, when he was director of public relations for United States Lines, of whom Dali was a regular client. Mathieu becomes totally and physically involved in the execution of gestural paintings. Which is why he works on immense surfaces in public places, as he did last year on stage at the Théâtre Sarah Bernhardt.

Trouble at the École de Paris

With a hundred and fifty participants, the exhibit "L'École de Paris 1957" at the gallery Charpentier resembles a broad selection of artists working in France rather than a cohesive expression of a movement. The term "école de Paris"—"Parisian School"—includes the great pre- and post-World War I artists who started the modern art movement. This exhibit attempts to show the state of the art of this famous "school" during the generation that followed. Everyone is represented, from Soulages and Hartung to Singier, Pignon, and Bissière, all in the hall of honor. In adjoining rooms are run-of-the-mill painters such as Chapelain-Midy, Brayer, or Carzou—an incomprehensible choice that does nothing to help the Parisian School which is beleaguered from all sides.

GUSTAVE SINGIER: MARINE WINDOW. 1957. Paris. Galerie de France

DANISH MODERN

Danish design triumphs as Arne Jacobsen, fifty-five, receives the grand prize of the Triennale of Milan. Jacobsen's work is characterized by a concern for form, function, and adaptability to mass production. This philosophy has built the reputation of objects and furnishings created by Scandinavian designers.

Danish tableware in stainless steel or silver is world-renowned for its beauty and simplicity. This set, designed by Henning Koppel for Georg Jensen, fills a double role of form and function that is the basis for the new art of the table.

Karl Gustav Hansen focuses on simple forms with reflective surfaces. The careful finishes of his pieces show to their best advantage the color and shine of the metal. This pitcher is made to contain a precise measure of water; the handle is shaped to fit the hand.

These three- and four-legged chairs were designed by Arne Jacobsen of laminated wood and chrome steel. They were intentionally designed for mass production.

THE RETURN TO A SYNTHESIS OF THE ARTS

Campus of the University of Caracas, by Villanueva.

CARACAS

Synthesis of the arts—architecture, sculpture, painting—as practiced in Rome and Florence during the Renaissance is what the Venezuelan architect Villanueva wanted for the campus of the University of Caracas. Work began five years ago. With the inauguration of its main feature, the Aula Magna, the project is complete.

Villanueva was born in 1900 in Croydon, England. He is the chief artisan of architectural renewal in Venezuela. His hand shows in his buildings and in his activity at the Banco Obrero, the agency that supervises construction in Venezuela. Inspired by the architecture of the colonial period in Latin America, he visited the studio of Le Corbusier in Paris. There, he discovered Functionalism used in the age of reinforced concrete and the new art of building that saves space for beauty.

The university campus built by Villanueva includes the Aula Magna, lecture halls, a library, an amphitheater, a clubhouse, a clinic, and an Olympic stadium. Unlike Le Corbusier, a painter and sculptor himself, who never thinks it necessary to call on other great artists to decorate his buildings, Villanueva gives commissions to Arp, Vasarely, Calder, and Léger.

The complex is a perfect success, because Vasarely created a metal portal according to the concept of his profound kinetic works and Léger applied his principles of monumental art. They resulted in an admirable complement to the architecture. Villanueva's powerful shapes, in full harmony with the grandeur and roughness of the countryside, disprove the notion that modern architecture does not tolerate nationalist expression.

What will be the impact of the new campus on professors and students? It is difficult not to envy those who live and work in an environment worthy of magnificent times.

HENRY VAN DE VELDE DIES

ZURICH

The Belgian architect Henry Van de Velde, who had been living in Switzerland since 1947, dies in this city on the Limmat at the age of ninety-four. His first vocation was painting; he then turned to applied arts. He built his own house in Uccle in 1896. But his celebrated achievements took place in Germany. He was a leader of the School of Decorative Arts in Weimar until the First World War and an active member of the Werkbund.

The fact that he stayed in "enemy territory" until 1917 caused him some difficulties.

Yet, when he returned to Belgium, King Albert appointed him Director of the Advanced Institute of Decorative Arts in la Cambre. He held the position until 1935, at the same time pursuing his architectural work and building many country homes.

His most important work is the Kröller-Müller Museum in Otterlo, for which he drew the plans in 1921. Building was completed only in 1938. He built the Werkbund Theater, in Cologne, which was finished in 1914.

Theater for the Werkbund exhibition in Cologne in 1914, by Henry Van de Velde.

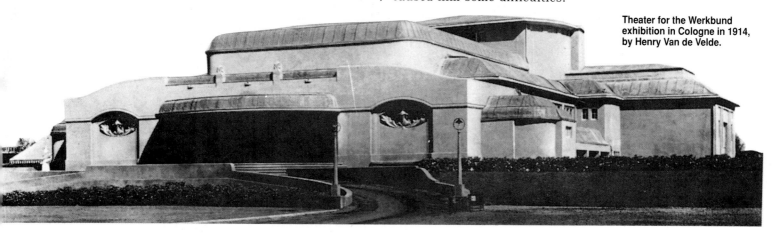

Death takes Georges Rouault from our midst. In an atheistic century, his work found a way to make us hear the voice of the first Christians, as few painters before him were able to do. But art, like life, moves onward by nature. Young Bernard Buffet's philosophy of misery draws crowds to the gallery Charpentier. And two events of worldwide importance capture attention. "Expo 58" in Brussels marks the unexpected return of metal architecture, and a new UNESCO building is opened in Paris. Painters, sculptors, and architects have worked in consort, just as they did in the Renaissance, toward a superb new synthesis of the arts.

1958

S U M M A R Y

GREAT MASTERS

Rouault Rediscovers His "Sweet Obscurity"
In Rouault's Words

SYNTHESIS OF THE ARTS

***The Fall of Icarus* at the UNESCO Building**

EXHIBITIONS

Bernard Buffet Consecrated

DEVELOPMENTS

Tàpies: a Room at the Biennale
Congo at Festival Hall

ART NEWS

The Guggenheim Collection at the Arts Déco
Dada: a Defused Fireball
Yves Klein: Down to the Bare Walls
Record Bids for a Cézanne
Picasso Restored
In Brief

ARCHITECTURE

The Return of Metal Architecture
The Pirelli Skyscraper
The Jewel of Park Avenue

LITERATURE

FRANCE
Publication of Moderato Cantabile *by Marguerite Duras.*

ITALY
Posthumous publication of Giuseppe Tomasi di Lampedusa's novel The Leopard.

RUSSIA
Boris Pasternak, whose Doctor Zhivago *was published abroad with great success, is forced to decline the Nobel prize in literature.*

MUSIC

GERMANY
György Ligeti performs the electronic piece Artikulation *in Cologne.*

BELGIUM
Edgar Varèse has composed an Electronic Poem *for Le Corbusier's pavilion at Expo 58 in Brussels.*

DANCE

UNITED STATES
Merce Cunningham stages the ballet Artic Meet, *with music by John Cage and scenery by Robert Rauschenberg.*

MOTION PICTURES

FRANCE
Great success of Mon Oncle *by Jacques Tati.*

POLAND
Premiere of Ashes and Diamonds *by Andrzej Wajda.*

GEORGES ROUAULT
THE FLIGHT TO EGYPT. 1945
Paris. Private Collection

Georges Rouault, 1953.

GEORGES ROUAULT: THE HOLY FACE. 1933

ROUAULT REDISCOVERS HIS "SWEET OBSCURITY"

PARIS

"How I miss my sweet obscurity . . ." Georges Rouault used to say to his dear daughter Isabelle toward the end of his life. Before dawn, on February 13, the famous painter of the *Miserere*, who suffered a good deal, dies in his apartment on the Rue Émile-Gilbert, near the Gare de Lyon. Those around him include his son, his daughters, and his wife, with whom he celebrated their golden anniversary two weeks earlier. His deathbed is then covered with violets whose color he loved so much. These flowers delicately perfumed his biblical landscapes, his ageless bouquets, and the sacrificed and sacred faces in which he finally saw nothing but *The Holy Face* . . .

Veronica's veil, the ideal model for all true icons, and the Shroud of Turin, the first human painting but a participant in divine reality, were cynosures for the image-making, iconic, sovereign art of this son of a cabinetmaker of Breton origin. He was born during the Commune in a cellar in Belleville. For

"I NEVER ACKNOWLEDGE ANYONE'S FANCY CLOTHES, BE HE KING OR EMPEROR"

a while, he was an apprentice of a glass cutter. In 1903, Rouault wrote to Schuré: "I have the bad habit—perhaps bad habit, but at any rate it's an abyss of suffering—of never acknowledging anyone's fancy clothes, be he king or emperor. The man I see

before me: It is his soul that I want to see, and the greater he is, or the more he is glorified by others, the more I fear for his soul."

Rouault had just been named curator of the Musée Gustave-Moreau, who had been his master at the Beaux-Arts Academy and from whom he had "learned to respect a certain inner vision" (thanks to which, however, he failed to receive the coveted Prix de Rome). Bound in friendship to Léon Bloy, then to Jacques and Raïssa Maritain, he derives from his Christian faith the

"immeasurable pity" that makes of his art a work of caritas, visible particularly in his stained-glass windows for the church on the Plateau d'Assy or his enamels of the Abbey of Ligugé.

When in 1917 Ambroise Vollard bought from him all the works he found in his studio, Rouault told him, "I shall have my whole life to finish my works." Whether he scrutinizes poverty, the anguish and remorse of aged prostitutes, of dancers beyond their prime, of tormented clowns, of bourgeois that are bored stiff, or of judges victimized by their tragicomical role, it is always the *Christ in Outrage*—whom he lets humbly be present like a watermark under their portraits, which show the Expressionist influences of Daumier, Goya, or Toulouse-Lautrec, and the mysteries of Rembrandt and the miracles of Gothic stained glass.

For many years, Georges Rouault—who through his lawsuit against Vollard's heirs in 1947 had eight hundred of his paintings returned to him so that he could burn most of them before court officials—hardly ever left his studio anymore. His surgeon's garb, white blouse and cap, corresponded to his maniacal obsession with perfection and to his sacrificial and sacral vocation to probe "the depths of the soul" under the strokes of his scalpel-brushes. Rouault painted himself in the guise of *The Worker Apprentice*—an admirable self-portrait that carries to perfection the velvet-smooth yet dramatic art of this master.

On June 6, 1951, the Catholic Center of French Intellectuals, on the occasion of the artist's eightieth birthday, organized a triumphal homage to Rouault at the Palais de Chaillot, including a showing of Abbot Morel's film on *Miserere*, which had premiered at the Galerie des Garets in 1948. These illustrations, inspired by the First World War and by the passion of Christ, and offered to Ambroise Vollard as of 1917, "were primitively executed," explained Rouault, "in the form of India ink drawings, later changed into paintings at the request of Ambroise Vollard. Vollard had someone do a transfer to copper of all the subjects . . . Starting from there, and with much difficulty, I have tried to preserve the rhythm and the initial design."

Armed with files, scrapers, chisels, and sandpaper, he would tell his dealer, "You give me copper, and I go full blast." Doing this, Georges Rouault, who said his eyes were wandering between "oasis and mirage," executed a new "Divine Comedy" in which, coming from hell, from suffering and misery, he created the most religious visions that twentieth-century art has seen. He had only one model: "Christ—obedient to the end, to the death on the cross."

IN ROUAULT'S WORDS

If today there were beautiful stained-glass windows like those of the Middle Ages, I would perhaps not have become a painter.

Art is deliverance, even in suffering. But for those outcasts who do not appreciate freedom of thought, art is a crime.

Greatness lies in conception, in the eye, the heart, and the hand of the artist, and not in the geometric dimensions of the work.

Blessed artist, even if your art is one of misfortune, pick up your load and move

like a trowel, that we give quality to a painting.

We must defend ourselves essentially through our work.

Under the pretense of liberty, what shams, what superficiality, what a miserable parody! And under the pretense of traditional order, what sorry substitutes for the masters of the past!

Knowing everything is of no use to the artist unless he can leave his own living

GEORGES ROUAULT: "QUI NE SE GRIME PAS?" 1923. Paris. Private Collection

along on your pilgrimage, following any road.

Being an artist is a matter of offering one's self as payment, without fear of being accused of fanatical individualism. It is a matter of digging one's own furrow, in joy or in suffering, never providing for one's self, instead of always looking to the past or the present for guaranties and stuffing one's self with science.

Certain works of art are made to give rise to vociferous disapproval. I never intended for my work to cause scandal.

We are born alone and we die alone, neither wanting nor seeking to do so.

Painting lightly can produce magnificent results. It is not always by doing "masonry" to the canvas, by wielding the palette knife

mark of greatness on what he sees and loves.

Ugliness is not always what the good apostles of unchanging beauty assume it to be. Rather, it is the copying of a successful mediocrity a hundred thousand times over.

A drawing is the gushing forth of an awakening spirit.

I would like to have created with colors as pure as flames.

A painter who loves his art should carefully avoid spending too much time with critics and literary people. These individuals, probably unintentionally, deform things by trying to explain everything, taking thought, will, and artistic sensitivities and shearing them just as Delilah sheared Samson.

"THE FALL OF ICARUS" AT THE UNESCO BUILDING

PARIS

The work of a school of architects including Marcel Breuer, Pier Luigi Nervi, and Bernard Zehrfuss, the new headquarters of UNESCO is inaugurated in November in the presence of René Coty, President of the Republic. Much administrative harassment had delayed the work; the project had been refused by the Landmark Commission as too modern before the building permit was at last granted in 1954.

Coincidentally, Bernard Zehrfuss is also the builder of the CNIT—National Center for Industry and Technology—at La Défense whose unique arch covers seven hundred fifty thousand square feet of floor space, also inaugurated this year.

But while the press unanimously emphasizes the extremely clean lines and the vast size of the CNIT—twice that of the Grand Palais at the Champs-Élysées—what is most striking about the new buildings of the UNESCO are the commissions given to artists. Five paintings, three sculptures, two ceramics, and one photograph at a total cost of $291,000 were chosen by an international committee under the chairmanship of Georges Salle, director general of the museums of France. The artists selected are among the most prestigious in contemporary art—names like Picasso, Miró, Moore, Calder, Appel, Matta, Tamayo.

Henry Moore, the greatest English sculptor today, has produced a monumental work, a reclining woman, *The Silhouette at Rest*. A major difficulty was to avoid that the sculpture be "crushed" by the immense façade. Moore, we know, has always been animated by a respect for his material. "The human figure is what interests me the most deeply, he wrote. However, it is while studying the nature of pebbles, stones, bones, trees, plants that I discovered the principles of shapes and rhythms." This, perhaps, is his

The UNESCO building.

PABLO PICASSO: THE FALL OF ICARUS. 1958

secret, *The Silhouette* integrating itself perfectly with the architecture, as well as with the two ceramics of Miró and Artigas, *The Wall of the Moon* and *The Wall of the Sun*, located in the gardens.

However, the chief attraction is no doubt *The Fall of Icarus*, a composition of almost one thousand one hundred square feet by Picasso. When the Secretary General of UNESCO wanted to visit the artist, he first refused: "I am no longer twenty years old, it's impossible," he said. Picasso, as a matter of fact, is seventy-seven years old. But his friend Georges Salle convinced him to admit the visitor.

Placed in the great lobby of UNESCO, called the Delegates Lounge, the huge work—an assembly of plywood panels painted flat on the ground—was inspired by flight in outer space, which both fascinated and terrified Picasso. Over the fixed blue of the sea, a burnt skeleton, surrounded by its own shadow, falls from the sky. On the right, two metaphorical bathers are tanning in the sun. Near them, a male bather, hands crossed on his abdomen, remains indifferent to the fall, which he does not see or feigns not to see. On the left, an odd feminine suggestion springs up from the water.

It is Georges Salle who gave the work its title, conferring on it a symbolic significance. As always when Picasso undertakes a large-scale work he makes many preliminary studies, but now that this huge painting is in place, it seems to have sprung from his brain spontaneously.

All the artists summoned have surpassed themselves. Above the door of the committee room we see a fresco by Tamayo. On the eighth floor we find works by Karel Appel, by Matta, by the Italian Afro, and by Brassai. In the garden there are a sculpture by Arp and a mobile by Calder, thirty-three feet high, the tallest he has created in Europe.

BERNARD BUFFET: THE HORROR OF WAR, THE ANGEL OF WAR. 1954. Paris. Galerie Maurice Garnier

BERNARD BUFFET CONSECRATED

RAMATUELLE

On December 12, to the great surprise of his friends, Bernard Buffet married Annabel in Ramatuelle, immediately after he had taken her to his beautiful residence at Château l'Arc, near Aix-en-Provence, where he has been living since 1956. A marriage of passionate love, crowning a rich year for him.

In January he triumphed in Paris with a retrospective of one hundred and fifty paintings, organized by the gallery Charpentier across from the Élysée Palace. Over one hundred thousand paying visitors were stunned by the integrity and the morbidity of his tragic paintings. They are bare but exalted, including three donated by Dr. Girardin to the city of Paris—*The Mender, The Seated Drinker,* and *The Artist and His Model*—also naked and emaciated self-portraits, a horrible *Woman with Chicken,* pitiless crucifixions, and his epic work *The Horror of War.* The enthusiastic preface to the catalogue was written by his friend Jean Giono.

In February he exhibited, at the gallery David et Garnier in Paris, seven large frescoes relating vividly the life of Joan of Arc: *The Voices, Recognition, The Siege of Orleans, The Annointing of Charles VII, The Trial, Prison, The Stake.*

In May he created, for the cover of the American magazine *Time,* the portrait of General de Gaulle, hailed as "Man of the Year" on the occasion of his return to power . . .

Critics don't quite know what to make of this genius. When Pierre de Boisdeffre saw the series *Scenes of New York,* which Buffet had painted for his next show at David et Garnier, he wrote, "Whether you like it or not, we must acknowledge in Bernard Buffet an essential witness of our times." What severity and what austerity in his dehumanized, vertical, purely architectural evocations of Manhattan, of the Empire State Building, of the Flat Iron Building, of Park Avenue, of the Brooklyn Bridge! "He imposes a vision of the linear world, laid bare . . . This painter of the vertical is a solitaire with whom it is difficult to establish rapport," writes Georges Hourdin in an essay published by Cerf, *The Hell and the Heaven of Bernard Buffet.*

In these times when Abstractionism contends with extensions of Surrealism, Bernard Buffet is a phenomenon that afflicts, irritates, surprises by the obstinacy of his ascetic and pessimistic Realism. He is a pitiless moralist who seems to accuse man only because he denounces the inhuman condition, as did Daumier. More than any other painter, Bernard Buffet is an outraged child of the Second World War! But he is also heir to the great French Realist painters of the nineteenth century. An admirer of David, Gros, Géricault, and Courbet, Buffet is also indebted to the primitives and to Japanism in the rigor of a hieratic style that makes his painting a work of "lèse-mortalité."

Bernard Buffet.

TÀPIES: A ROOM AT THE BIENNALE

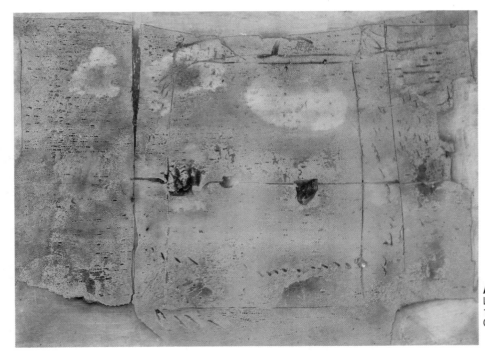

ANTONI TÀPIES:
LARGE PAINTING.
1958. New York.
Guggenheim Museum

VENICE

The Spanish Pavilion devotes an entire room to the painter Antoni Tàpies, who had already participated in the Biennales of Venice in 1952 and 1954. On the occasion of this show, the young Catalan artist was awarded the prize of the David F. Bright Foundation, reserved to a painter under the age of forty-five, as well as the UNESCO prize. It is a successful year for Tàpies, who also had received the first prize of the Carnegie Institute in Pittsburgh.

The Tàpies works on exhibit cover a period of a little less than ten years. They present strange similarities with mural graffiti; in fact, his plastic universe has justifiably been compared to "walls." Tàpies evokes archaeological collections, fossilized remains, elements that have withstood the ravages of time. Hence the relief effects: folds, scars, grainings that alternate in his composition with thick textures and with smooth surfaces.

Mainly through the influence of his painting on Spanish art today, the thirty-five-year-old Tàpies is one of the most important artists of his generation.

CONGO AT FESTIVAL HALL

LONDON

The big-circulation dailies just snicker, while other publications come to the conclusion that someone is trying to discredit modern art! The reason for this hubbub is the creative work of Congo, a talented chimpanzee two and one half years old, a boarder at the London Zoo, whose paintings will be on display during the month of September side by side with those of renowned informal artists at Festival Hall.

Congo has achieved, under the direction of Desmond Morris, several hundred drawings and paintings by using various techniques: brush, scratching with fingernails, finger painting. His pleasure is painting, his sense of color, the variations of his style are undeniable. The biologist Julian Huxley, recalling the enigma posed by the sudden blossoming of art during the paleolithic period, wrote, "This becomes more comprehensible if it is true that our ancestors, morphologically close to monkeys, possessed, in a primitive state, such esthetic aptitudes."

This is not the first show by Congo. Last year, a presentation of his paintings was held at the Institute of Contemporary Art in tandem with the works of Betsy, a five-year-old female chimpanzee who works in Baltimore.

What interests Desmond Morris is to explore—beyond children's drawings and beyond works produced by the mentally ill—the biological origins of art.

At the present time, worldwide, some thirty monkeys are painting. Among them is Rosa at the Moscow Zoo, whose drawings are the only abstract works not yet subject to Soviet Union censorship.

Work by Congo, a chimpanzee.

The Guggenheim Collection at the Arts Déco

A sampling from the Solomon Guggenheim collection is ending its tour through Europe with a stop at the Museum of Decorative Arts in Paris. It will then make its permanent home in the Guggenheim Museum in New York, built by Frank Lloyd Wright. The seventy-five paintings shown represent a panorama of twentieth-century painting from Cézanne and Henri Rousseau to the Abstract Impressionists. In between, Kandinsky, Klee, Mondrian, Malevich, Larionov, and Miró illustrate the early movements: Suprematism, Rayonism, Geometric Abstractionism. The Cubists are represented mainly by Picasso, Braque, and Léger, the "poetic" trend by Chagall, the Munich School by Franz Marc. There is, however, no example of the new Parisian School. Is this a sign of American disinterest?

Dada: a Defused Fireball

Does Dada shock anyone anymore? Has Dada, which denied art, become art? These are questions being raised at an exhibit at the Kunsthalle in Düsseldorf devoted to the movement created by Tzara, Arp, Ball, and Huelsenbeck in 1916. The organizers wanted to show the extent of its influence: from Zurich to Berlin, Hanover, and Cologne, and its attraction in Paris and New York. The exhibit not only shows paintings but photos, posters, and reviews. Max Ernst and Jean Arp are represented, of course, but so are Baargeld's montages, Seiwert's engravings, and works by other minor Dadaists. More puzzling is the presence of works by Kurt Schwitters, whom Berlin Dadaists found unworthy of participating in their happenings! "Dada was a fireball!" said Max Ernst. This exhibit, in its attempt to cram everything in, may have defused the fireball for good.

Yves Klein: Down to the Bare Walls

"Iris Clert invites you to honor, with all your emotional presence, the lucid and positive coming of a certain realm of the senses. This show of perceptive unification will allow Yves Klein to seek the pictorial expression of an ecstatic and immediately communicable emotion. Opening at 3 Rue des Beaux-Arts, Monday, April 28, from 9 p.m. until midnight." Such was the enigmatic invitation sent to anyone who is someone in Paris by the artist's dealer. Yves Klein, for the first time in the history of art, exhibited only empty space. The show was a considerable success: More than two thousand people jammed the Iris Clert Gallery's two hundred square feet. The walls were painted white, a large canopy and the windows in IKB, or "International Klein Blue," the artist's absolute color.

Record Bids for a Cézanne

Record bids were made on October 15 at Sotheby in London for seven Impressionist paintings from the Jacob Goldschmidt collection. The total amount bid was 916 million francs. Manet's *The Rue de Berne,* bought in 1878 for 500 francs, was sold for 133 million. Cézanne's *Large Apples,* found in a junk shop in 1900, reached 105 million. Van Gogh's *Le jardin public,* painted by the artist to decorate a room he had rented in Arles, fetched 155 million. Cézanne's *Boy in a Red Vest,* which the artist had wanted to destroy, commanded the highest price: 258 million. All the paintings were sold at sums considerably higher than on the market. None of the buyers wanted their identities revealed; they were represented by dealers.

Picasso Restored

For the first time, a painting by Picasso has been given to the Tate Gallery's restoration service in London, the best-equipped paint clinic in Europe. The name of the work will not be given out; restorer Stefan Slabezynski indicated only that the painting's surface was cracked and that the paint was peeling. Two other canvases by modern artists, a Rouault and a Chagall, are also being treated at the Tate. In the history of the gallery, it is the first time that paintings have come for restoration while the artists are still living.

PAUL CÉZANNE: BOY IN A RED VEST. 1894-1895. Zurich. Private Collection

The Atomium at the Expo 58 in Brussels.

In the French Pavilion at the Expo 58 in Brussels.

THE RETURN OF METAL ARCHITECTURE

BRUSSELS

Belgium is the country that proportionally to its size has the most often played the trump card of international exhibitions. Witness Antwerp, Ghent, Liège, and particularly Brussels, whose "Expo 58," which closed on October 19, is the fifth international exhibition in sixty years.

Like the preceding events, it is leaving behind tangible marks: the Antwerp turnpike, the model city, and, at Place de Brouckère, the information pavilion of the city with its wooden structure of the "horse-saddle" type resting on concrete supports, and, hanging in the sky at the Heysel plateau, the Atomium which delighted forty-two million visitors.

With its nine spheres, each sixty feet in diameter and connected with the others by tubes, the Atomium may be an attraction without architectural consequences, but it has strong sym-

bolic meaning. It was built to celebrate the peaceful use of the atom, on the occasion of the birth of the Euratom. But for the moment it is steel that triumphs in Brussels.

Expo 58 marked, in effect, the return to metal architecture, notably with the gigantic French Pavilion, covering a hundred and

ONE CAN SEE CONSTRUCTIVE SOLUTIONS FOR TOMORROW

thirty thousand square feet on the ground, by the architect Guillaume Gillet. "Metal today permits thin veils, the stretched vault that pulls and relieves what used to be a wall," he explained. After Eiffel, in 1889, the pace of iron had slackened, having a reputation of being more expensive than concrete, but the recent manufacturing processes have made it competitive once again. "Suspended

architecture" with a metal "skin": The French Pavilion creates a sensation among specialists.

More subdued, the pavilions of West Germany and of the Netherlands, as well as the general pavilion of Transportation, which is to be rebuilt at Juville, are revolutionary in their own

rights. Beneath modest appearances—here a cloth over steel cables, there a large flat roof resting on slim pylons—can be seen constructive solutions for tomorrow, based on simple structures, with light alloys.

As usual for him, and doubtlessly more by choice than in 1925 at the International Exhibition of Decorative Arts and in 1937 at the International Exposition, Le Corbusier again goes

his own way. The pavilion he designed for the Philipps Company is a pure masterpiece. Occupied with the construction at Chandigarh and at the convent of Sainte Marie de la Tourette, the great architect had left a free hand, starting from a scale model, to his close collaborator Iannis Xenakis, who is a mathematician and a musician.

Since the completion of Notre-Dame-du-Haut at Ronchamp in 1955, Le Corbusier covered the distance from a country chapel to a Futuristic manifestation. But he did more than that: He gave to Expo 58, which almost seemed to get lost in the diversity of the current prosperity, some sort of conscience. The destruction of the pavilion will be regretted all the more once the exhibition is over.

THE PIRELLI SKYSCRAPER

MILAN

Like a prow, it projects itself, two steps from the Mussolini-era central station, into the Milan sky. The Pirelli tower is a lesson in architecture four hundred and seven feet high. The large Italian tire company wanted to have a headquarters that would reflect the technological side of the firm. It seems to have gotten what it wanted. The building is the result of a close collaboration between engineers and architects.

The prime contractor was Gio Ponti, while Pier Luigi Nervi and Arturo Danusso worked on the structural studies. The edifice owes its beauty to an identification of the architecture with the structure. The thirty-four stories of the tower rise from a base of irregular outline that takes up only one seventh of the ground. This base, which descends about forty feet into the ground, leaves space for parking, a heating plant, and an auditorium.

As to the elevation itself, it has four façades that spread out progressively beginning with the second floor, narrowing toward the top as the weight decreases. The interior is characterized by a maximum use of floor space and by its flexible allocation through movable partitions.

Thus the Pirelli tower, conceived and built between 1955 and this year, affirms itself as a manifesto of European architecture: It is possible to build skyscrapers on the old continent without copying the American models.

The Pirelli tower in Milan.

THE JEWEL OF PARK AVENUE

NEW YORK

The spectacular skyscraper on Park Avenue by Ludwig Mies van der Rohe, in collaboration with Philip Johnson, is completed! There is no doubt that it will be seen as one of the masterpieces of architecture in the international style that has blossomed since the Second World War. Its high glass and steel tower occupies only half of the site on which it is built. It rests on pillars, set off from a slightly elevated terrace, which is open to the prestigious avenue. The Seagram Building—as it is called—faces the Lever House by Skidmore, Owing and Merrill, built between 1950 and 1952. Characteristic of Mies's style is the purity of line, which contrasts with the skyscrapers of the 1920s, whose summits taper as they rise and which are loaded with decorative elements. Here is a construction that cannot fail to be noticed on the famous New York skyline.

It confirms, in the heart of the city, the presence of the architect who was the director of the Bauhaus from 1930 to 1933, had immigrated to the United States in 1937, and since then has been directing the school of architecture of the Illinois Institute of Technology in Chicago, where his teaching, his precision, has marked new generations. The Seagram Building is a tower thirty-nine stories and about five hundred twenty feet high. Its verticality is especially emphasized by a structure that is held by bronze ribs.

Architectural Forum, in the July issue, calls it "the most luxurious skyscraper ever built."

The Seagram Building in New York.

Paris, the capital of art, challenged, attacked on all sides throughout the world, must take up the gauntlet! That is the sense of the First Biennale des Jeunes, the brainchild of Malraux, minister of culture under General de Gaulle. A complete success, the exhibition brings together artists under the age of thirty-five from forty different countries. There are two revelations: the Swiss Jean Tinguely and the Austrian Friedrich Hundertwasser. Along with others, such as Fontana, the eldest among them, who lacerates his paintings with a paper cutter, they send art, each in his own way, on stimulating new ventures. Germaine Richier, a forceful, vital sculptor, dies prematurely.

1959

S U M M A R Y

AVANT-GARDE

**The First Biennale des Jeunes
The Scandal of the Infinite Spiral**

DEVELOPMENTS

**Fontana and Cutter Painting
Klapheck's Scheming**

ART NEWS

**Fate of Rothko Frescoes Undetermined
Debate Continues over the Guggenheim
Rauschenberg's Combine Paintings
Eighteen Happenings in Six Parts
In Brief**

EXHIBITIONS

**The Panorama of Documenta II
A Portrait of Vieira da Silva**

SCULPTURE

Farewell to Germaine Richier

LITERATURE

ARGENTINA
Julio Cortázar publishes Las armas secretas.

UNITED STATES
Publication of Goodbye, Columbus *by Philip Roth.*

FRANCE
Uderzo and Goscinny publish the comic strip Asterix the Gaul.
Raymond Queneau publishes Zazie.

MUSIC

FRANCE
Death of the American jazz musician Sydney Bechet.

GERMANY
Theodor Wiesengrund Adorno publishes Klangfiguren.

THEATER

GERMANY
The Berliner Ensemble performs The Resistible Rise of Arturo Ui *by Bertolt Brecht.*

MOTION PICTURES

UNITED STATES
Premiere of Joseph L. Mankiewicz's Suddenly, Last Summer.

FRANCE
Orfeu negro *by Marcel Camus is awarded the Golden Palm prize at the film festival in Cannes.*
Alain Resnais tells a touching love story of a Frenchwoman and a Japanese man in Hiroshima, mon amour.
Premiere of The 400 Blows *by François Truffaut.*

Jean Tinguely and his *Meta-Matic 17* at the promenade of the Palais de Tokyo in Paris.

THE FIRST BIENNALE DES JEUNES

PARIS

How to restore to Paris the position of capital of the arts, which it had held until World War II and which, since the recent emergence of the New York School, is more contested with each day? It is to remedy this anguishing situation that André Malraux, minister of culture under General de Gaulle, has inaugurated, on October 2, the first youth biennale, which was held until the 25th of the month at the Palais de Tokyo.

experience, a place open to incertitudes and to hopes," writes the art critic Raymond Cogniat, general manager of the exhibition, in the foreword to the catalogue.

Malraux's idea was novel, even if his opening speech, sententious and ardent, did not take notice of the fact that Dada, today, is slowly coming back— in a generation that is little inclined to bet on the eternal values of art.

Among the painters, sketch-

TO RESTORE TO PARIS
THE POSITION OF CAPITAL OF THE ARTS

Artists, from forty countries, had to be under thirty-five to be allowed to participate. "Unlike the prestigious exhibits of Venice and of São Paulo, which pay homage to artists who have already established their reputation and whose works have made their mark, we have chosen to make of the Paris biennale a place of encounter and

ers, etchers, and sculptors, chosen by various juries and grouped in sections reflecting current trends, many belong to Lyrical Abstractionism, which, to tell the truth, is not very new. But many other individualities, temperaments, and orientations have been included, among them the Frenchmen Paul Rebeyrolle and Yves Klein, who

JEAN TINGUELY: META-MATIC 17 (IN THE ACT OF EXPLODING). 1959. Paris

FRIEDRICH HUNDERTWASSER: THE TOWER OF BABEL PUNCTURES THE SUN. 1959. Private Collection

displays a monochrome painting, the Austrian Friedrich Hundertwasser, the Americans Robert Rauschenberg and Jasper Johns, the Swiss Jean Tinguely.

Tinguely, who has been living and working in Paris since 1955, is far from being unknown. His *Meta-Matic* series, whose painted sheet steel and wire organs stamp and shake, has been arousing controversy ever since the gallery Denise René had a group show on the theme of motion. Now exhibited at the promenade of the Palais de Tokyo, outside the sacred enclosure of the museum, his strange machines attract a delighted public, which does not easily appreciate the ambitious speculations of modern art.

Especially built for the biennale is a drafting machine, the *Meta-Matic 17*. The invention, tall and slender, has turned out, within three weeks, some forty thousand abstract designs that simulate Automatic Drawing. They are never the same, and are not dependent on the person using it. It is a meeting of sculpture, painting, mechanization, sound effects, drama, and dance. Even Malraux, who came down from his pedestal for a minute, had a good time.

"Everything moves," said Tinguely when visiting Düsseldorf last spring. "Immobility does not exist . . . Forget hours, minutes, seconds. Do not resist the metamorphosis . . . Breathe deeply. Live in the present: Live in harmony with the times and live for a marvelous and absolute reality!" At thirty-four, he had become famous overnight.

Also remarkable is the Viennese painter Friedrich Hundertwasser, whose colored labyrinths in vivid hues seem to issue from Klimt, Schiele, Klee, and abstract art. The artist is the initiator of Transautomatism, which seeks to create by bringing to light the layers of the unconscious, images that enter into competition with the world and the visible reality. Hundertwasser's universe, spell-casting and narcissistic, has an incontestable power of fascination.

Will this newly created Biennale des Jeunes succeed in drawing Paris out of its present isolation? No doubt other initiatives, other efforts will be required for Paris to regain its position. There are many critics and artists who have not forgiven her for having reigned for too many years over the creation of art. "We have not brought about this gathering in order to defend one esthetic over another, but in order to get to know those who are coming, and to get a glimpse, if possible, of the face of the world of tomorrow," added Cogniat in his foreword.

At the end of the show, an international jury made up of museum curators and artists, among whom were Henry Moore, Ossip Zadkine, and Édouard Pignon, awarded prizes for each discipline, accompanied by grants.

THE SCANDAL OF THE INFINITE SPIRAL

HAMBURG
"Beware of the straight line and of the drunk line, but above all of the straight line. The straight line leads humanity to perdition." Friedrich Hundertwasser is the Austrian painter who initiated Transautomatism, which claims it is generated by the H-bomb and Jackson Pollock. Hundertwasser has new ideas all the time. Among other "miracles," he invented the rainbow- or multicolored typewriter ribbon, which lets the typist give unexpected coloring to personal and business letters. This year, he decides to make another breakthrough.

Soon after being invited to teach at the Hamburg School of Applied Arts, he proceeds to draw an endless "spiral" that starts from the walls of his classroom and is supposed to unwind through the whole building. In order to pick the most propitious moment to start, Hundertwasser consults Wulff, the astrologer who served both Hitler and Himmler; near the defeat of the Third Reich, he was thrown into a concentration camp by his masters. Wulff tells Hundertwasser the exact date and hour, December 18, 3:11 p.m.—and the precise starting point for his infinite line.

Hundertwasser at the School of Applied Arts in Hamburg.

After sending out invitations to attend, Hundertwasser, helped by his friends Bazon Brock and Herbert Schult and a few students, starts "spiraling." Things soon go sour. The curious public is physically contained by the school administration, and fistfights break out. The students are forbidden to remain in the classroom overnight—which they vowed to do—and are to be dismissed if they disobey. The administration cuts off the electricity, but Hundertwasser continues his artistry by candlelight. The principal, who was in Rome, learns about the event from newspapers and takes the first plane home. Abandoned by all, and exhausted, Hundertwasser gives up after two days and two nights, when the spiral is not much more than eight feet high.

His freedom has been limited. He hands in his resignation to the culture senate of Hamburg, which had nominated him to the teaching position. He expresses his regrets: "The line should have been a high sun around my students, who would have found the force for prodigious creation at its core." Jesus on the Mount of Olives! In his opinion, the time just is not ready to recognize its prophets!

Hundertwasser's spiral painted on the walls of his classroom at the School of Applied Arts in Hamburg.

FONTANA AND CUTTER PAINTING

Fontana lacerates a canvas.

MILAN

After the holes, here come the cuts! Lucio Fontana takes a new step in his researches into Spacialism: He cuts monochrome canvases with a razor blade, knife, or cutter. The artist recounts how, last winter, he discovered, by chance and through anger, this new form of expression. He was preparing an exhibition for the gallery Stadler in Paris. Furious because he ruined a painting he had been trying to improve, he slashed it with a knife. He immediately "realized the potential of this gesture."

Ten years ago, Fontana made perforated paintings. In 1951, for the Triennale of Milan, he created a light-space decoration made of a huge neon-tube sculpture.

He continues to reject traditional art forms. He is beyond figurative art and beyond abstraction, which he both rejects. He finds his support in space and stretches surface into three dimensions. He paints on raw canvas, or colors it in red, blue, gray, white, or yellow; a variation led to the *Quanta* series, small triangular, round, or square paintings with cuts and holes and mounted on the same panel. Fontana's cuts do not leave the viewer indifferent. Some people shout he is a genius; some shout it is a scandal and angrily rebuff what they view as an insult to art, symbolizing its destruction or, worse, its denial.

KLAPHECK'S SCHEMING

DÜSSELDORF

The American novelist Henry James loved his Remington typewriter so much that, on his deathbed, he asked that it be brought to him and that its keys be operated, so that he could hear its beloved music. Konrad Klapheck, who is very much alive, was born in Düsseldorf in 1935, and studied at the Academy of Fine Arts of his native city. But when his painting teacher, Bruno Goller, replaced the traditional female model with a typewriter, it was love at first sight. He had found his mechanical fiancée.

In 1955, the experience was repeated with a sewing machine. He was in France for a year, and his landlady, in Versailles, lent the machine to him. His girlfriend, Lilo, had stayed in Germany, and he missed her very much. The lines of the machine became alive, undulating like a woman's shape. The title of the painting is *The Mortified Fiancée.*

His machines look unusual, sometimes monstrous. Their almost too-perfect symmetry is stressed by the empty space surrounding them, which acts as though it were an analytical description of the apparatus.

They prompt the viewer to recall Kafka's device in *In the Penal Colony:* Piercing needles write on the condemned man's skin the commandment he violated—a monstrous, torturing inscription. Unlike Futurists or Léger, whom Klapheck resembles and who had an ironic attitude toward mechanisms, Klapheck undeniably shows machinery under a somber light.

Is Klapheck in reaction against Informal Art and Tachism? It is at least refreshing to many to see a twenty-four-year-old artist at odds with the modernist disarray that currently dominates German galleries.

KONRAD KLAPHECK: WILL TO POWER. 1959. The Artist's Private Collection

Fate of Rothko Frescoes Undetermined

A series of paintings that Mark Rothko has been working on for the past year will not be displayed in the Seagram Building as planned. They were to be hung in the restaurant of this spectacular new building on Park Avenue, but the artist felt that his meditative works should be contemplated in silence, not in the chatty, clinking milieu of an eatery. Rothko limited his palette to two colors per canvas, starting the series with bright orange, and ending with a somber reddish brown. He might donate his works to the Tate Gallery, unless he finds another location for them in the United States.

Debate Continues over the Guggenheim

The Guggenheim Museum had been the focus of endless disputes between its architect, Frank Lloyd Wright—who died this year—and the City of New York. Even though it has been completed, heated debates continue over this cylinder with its spiraling ramp. Critics unanimously condemn the building, which can hold some three hundred paintings, especially for its lighting. "If Wright had intentionally created this building to annihilate painting, he could not have succeeded more," said *The New York Times.* "The building could have been used for anything, except a museum," stated *The Baltimore Sun.* But James Rorimer, director of the Metropolitan Museum, enthusiastically exclaimed: "Moving, astonishing, it's an adventure."

Rauschenberg's Combine Paintings

"When he was eight, he had a toad, a goat, a rooster, and two dogs with nine puppies," his sister recalled. Today, this childhood memory is evoked by a stuffed angora goat wearing a tire around its middle. The work is entitled *Monogram,* the third phase in five years of work, and is being exhibited at the Castelli Gallery in New York. As in his other "Combine Paintings," the introduction of three-dimensional elements blurs the distinction between painting and sculpture: The foreground is gone; there is, instead, a base from which the image is projected toward the viewer. In *Monogram,* the pasture is the base. Collages and brush strokes unify the different parts. One cannot help but think of Picasso's famous *Goat!*

ROBERT RAUSCHENBERG: MONOGRAM. 1955-1959. Stockholm. Moderna Museet

Eighteen Happenings in Six Parts

Allan Kaprow, thirty-two, has just presented *18 Happenings in 6 Parts* at the Reuben Gallery in New York. Films and slides are projected on the walls while two protagonists—usually artists Alfred Leslie and Lester Johnson, but sometimes Robert Rauschenberg and Jasper Johns—paint a canvas. Public participation is an important part of this Happening, where the work of art itself becomes the action. The first event of this kind took place at Black Mountain College in 1952.

Guggenheim Museum.

MARIA-ELENA VIEIRA DA SILVA:
THE BIG CONSTRUCTIONS.
1958. Private Collection

A PORTRAIT OF VIEIRA DA SILVA

KASSEL

Maria-Elena Vieira da Silva has numerous works in the Documenta. In the wake of her retrospective in Hanover last year, Germany honors Portugal. It is only just. Vieira da Silva, who is fifty-one years old, is one of the best current painters.

Born in Lisbon in 1908, in a rich liberal family. Studies music, drawing, and sculpture early on. Arrives in Paris in 1928. Studies with Bourdelle, then Despiau. Learns engraving at Atelier 17. For several months, attends Fernand Léger's academy.

Her career took a decisive turn when she visited an exhibition by Bonnard at the gallery Bernheim-Jeune. While critics saw him as a kind man, a lover of nature, fascinated by the slimmest ray of sun or a trembling leaf, she was fascinated by the artist's plaid tablecloths and the slight shifting of space implied. Bonnard wanted to express "what one sees when one enters a room suddenly, at first glance." He was interested in first-second perceptions, as they are formed in the eye and mind. The same interest, pushed to vertigo, can be found in Vieira da Silva.

Her paintings are composed of squares, rectangles, and diamond shapes, slightly deformed, combined on the surface of the canvas and stretching space. Like Bonnard, she creates an obsession, but more visibly so, because her vision of the world is deeply disturbed.

She fled to Rio de Janeiro with her husband, Arpad Szenes, in 1942. Soon after her return seven years later, Pierre Loeb gave her an exhibition. It was the beginning of a fame that reaches its peak this year.

THE PANORAMA OF DOCUMENTA II

KASSEL

Is Documenta becoming a kind of commercial institution? After its popular success four years ago, when the German public suddenly discovered the great creators of modern art, this summer's exhibition proposes something entirely different.

The theme is vague: "Art Since 1945." The art historian Werner Haftmann chose it. In his view, art of the second half of the century will be abstract and informal. Therefore, these trends dominate the exhibition. The artists range from Jackson Pollock to Jean Fautrier.

Most of the painters were discovered during the past fifteen years, but some of their famous elders are represented as well: Klee, Mondrian, Beckmann, Kandinsky, Picasso. The last two have separate halls.

Sculpture, this time, has its own space. Some works, by Arp, Laurens, Lipsi, Heiliger, for instance, are exhibited out-of-doors, in the ruins of the Orangerie, which was all but completely destroyed by Allied bombardments during the Second World War. They offer some of the strongest achievements in this Documenta.

On the whole, the exhibition worries art specialists. Most of the works come from private collections in Germany, France, and the United States. They fear that Documenta risks becoming a store window for major art dealers who are trying to impose an international taste—to their own benefit.

FAREWELL TO GERMAINE RICHIER

MONTPELLIER

Three years after the important retrospective of her "metamorphic" sculptures at the Musée National d'Art Moderne in Paris, Germaine Richier dies after a long illness. She was born in Grans, near Arles, in 1904, and dies on July 31.

She had been the student of one of Rodin's collaborators, then of Bourdelle's. She first exhibited strong classical nudes in 1934, in Paris. From 1940 on, her subjects were animals and insects. She seemed fascinated by the obstinate strength of spiders, ants, and grasshoppers, whose shapes she stressed and stretched.

She liked to amplify their anatomic characteristics. She went even further in the Expressionistic description of mythic entities such as *Storm, Hurricane, Hydra and Pentacle.* Their fantastic disintegration and congenital decay led her to her most celebrated and impressive work,

AN ASTONISHING POWER OF INVENTION, LINKING HER TO THE CONTROLLED DELIRIUMS OF A HIERONYMUS BOSCH

which provoked a scandal: the *Christ* for the church of Plateau d'Assy. In spite of the sustained support by Father Couturier, who denounced "a strange alteration of the sense of Christian cult and its dignity, which makes us reject anything that doesn't look opulent," her *Christ* had to be withdrawn from the altar. Traditional Catholics hated it; they were shocked by the chafed, filiform, worm-eaten shape of this poor Jesus, which is comparable to Giacometti's skeleton forms.

This process of flesh deterioration and body decay characterized Germaine Richier's entire production—obsessive and mysteriously anarchistic. Eight years ago, she took up works of "lead with painted backgrounds," in cooperation with Hartung, Vieira da Silva, and Zao Wou-ki: gilded granulated bronze sculptures, enamel and glass inserts, and painted plasters with fabulous coloring.

Faithfully exhibiting at the Salons de Mai and actively participating in international group shows, Richier manifested an astonishing power of invention. Her art linked her to the controlled deliriums of a Hieronymus Bosch, James Ensor, or Max Ernst, but she did not become a Surrealist, properly speaking. She combined animal, mineral, and vegetal realms, as though she would have liked to have recovered the haunted world of her childhood in the South of France.

GERMAINE RICHIER:
LE GRIFFU. 1952. Arles.
Musée Réattun

The United States continues to lead as Rauschenberg receives the grand prize at the Biennale in Venice in 1964. This tips the art market away from Paris toward New York. At the same time, the Pop Art of Lichtenstein and Warhol replaces Abstract Expressionism. But Europe is far from having lost the game. Dubuffet asserts himself as one of the new masters of

1960

	1960	1961	1962	1963	1964
ARTS	• Birth of Pop Art in the United States • Birth of the New Realism • Inauguration of Brasilia, Brazil's new capital	• Retrospective by Jean Dubuffet and Mark Tobey at the Museum of Decorative Arts in Paris • Exhibition "The Art of Assemblage" at MOMA in New York	• Tàpies gains worldwide recognition • Death of Yves Klein	• Death of Georges Braque • Bacon retrospective in the United States • Birth of the New Figuration	• Robert Rauschenberg is awarded the grand prize at the Biennale in Venice • Kenzo Tange builds the Olympic stadium in Tokyo
LITERATURE	• Albert Camus dies in a car accident • *After the Banquet* by Yukio Mishima • *The Magician of Lublin* by Isaac Bashevis Singer	• Ernest Hemingway commits suicide	• Death of William Faulkner • *One Day in the Life of Ivan Denisovich* by Alexandr Solzhenitsyn	• *The Clown* by Heinrich Böll • *The Sailor Who Fell from Grace with the Sea* by Yukio Mishima • *Requiem* by Anna Akhmatova	• Jean-Paul Sartre refuses the Nobel prize • *Herzog* by Saul Bellow
MUSIC AND THEATER	• *Rhinoceros* by Eugène Ionesco	• *Silence* by John Cage • *Intolleranza* by Luigi Nono	• *War Requiem* by Benjamin Britten	• *Happy Days* by Samuel Beckett • Joan Baez and Bob Dylan are the most popular singers in the United States	• The Beatles gain worldwide fame • *Who's Afraid of Virginia Woolf?* by Edward Albee
MOTION PICTURES	• *La dolce vita* by Federico Fellini • *À bout de souffle* by Jean-Luc Godard • *Rocco and His Brothers* by Luchino Visconti	• *Jules and Jim* by François Truffaut • *Last Year in Marienbad* by Alain Resnais • *West Side Story* by Robert Wise	• *The Trial* by Orson Welles • *The Exterminating Angel* by Luis Buñuel	• *8 1/2* by Federico Fellini • *Le mépris* by Jean-Luc Godard • *The Birds* by Alfred Hitchcock	• *Dr. Strangelove: Or, How I Learned To Stop Worrying and Love the Bomb* by Stanley Kubrick
SCIENCE AND TECHNOLOGY	• First meterological satellite, launched by the United States • First French atom bomb	• The first human in space, orbiting the earth, Yuri Gagarin • Alan Shepard is the first American to ascend into space	• John Glenn is the first American to orbit the earth • Telstar, the first communications satellite, is launched from Cape Canaveral	• First Instamatic cameras, by Kodak • Valentina Tereschkova: the first woman in space	• First satellite in geostationary orbit • The Verrazano-Narrows Bridge in New York opens to traffic, as the world's longest suspension bridge
POLITICS AND DAILY LIFE	• John Fitzgerald Kennedy is elected President • Independence of former Belgian Congo, followed by civil war	• Erection of the Berlin Wall • The United States breaks off diplomatic relations with Cuba • The UN General Assembly condemns apartheid	• Cuban missile crisis • End of the war in Algeria • U Thant is elected UN Secretary-General	• Assassination of President John F. Kennedy • 250,000 black and white Freedom Marchers descend on Washington • Profumo crisis in England	• Martin Luther King, Jr., is awarded the Nobel Peace Prize • Khrushchev is stripped of his titles

1969

modern art; Tàpies triumphs just about every-where; Giacometti dies in 1966, universally acclaimed; France finds another avant-garde with the New Realists; Germany is born again with Beuys and the Fluxus movement; in Italy, Arte Povera gives a new definition of art. This is the time of unlimited daring. The rupture with the first years of the century is complete.

1965	1966	1967	1968	1969
• State funeral in Paris for Le Corbusier • Dominance of Op Art	• Formal exhibitions of Minimal Art • Death of Alberto Giacometti • Numerous "Happenings" in the United States and Europe	• Birth of Arte Povera • Birth of Land Art • Exhibition of Kinetic Art in Paris	• Death of Marcel Duchamp • Exhibition "Art and the Machine" at MOMA in New York	• Theft of the Penrose Collection in London • Vasarely exhibits in Budapest • Warhol resumes painting
• *An American Dream* by Norman Mailer • *Les choses* by Georges Perec • Death of T. S. Eliot	• *In Cold Blood* by Truman Capote • *The Green House* by Mario Vargas Llosa	• *One Hundred Years of Soli-tude* by Gabriel García Márquez • *The Joke* by Milan Kundera • *Alternating Current* by Octavio Paz	• *The Abyss* by Marguerite Yourcenar • *Cancer Ward* by Alexandr Solzhenitsyn	• Samuel Beckett is awarded Nobel prize in literature • *Portnoy's Complaint* by Philip Roth
• *The Beard* by Michael McClure	• *Variations V*, a ballet by Merce Cunningham with music by John Cage • *L'éloge de la folie*, a ballet by Roland Petit	• *Messe pour le temps présent* by Maurice Béjart • *Hymnen* by Karlheinz Stockhausen	• *Stimmung* by Karlheinz Stockhausen • Varèse, Zenakis, Berio, and Henry are honored at the inter-national music festival in Paris	• Woodstock music festival • Week-long Stockhausen festival in France
• *Pierrot le fou* by Jean-luc Godard • *The Love Life of a Blonde* by Milos Forman	• *Blow-Up* by Michelangelo Antonioni • *A Man and a Woman* by Claude Lelouch • *Andrei Rublev* by Andrei Tarkovski	• *Bonnie and Clyde* by Arthur Penn • *La guerre est finie* by Alain Resnais	• *2001: A Space Odyssey* by Stanley Kubrick • *Theorem* by Pier Paolo Pasolini	• *Z* by Costa-Gavras • *The Damned* by Luchino Visconti • *Fellini Satyricon* by Federico Fellini
• First spacewalk, by the Russian astronaut Leonov	• Michael E. DeBakey implants the first artificial heart • A Russian spacecraft, then an American one, make soft landings on the moon	• DNA produced synthetically, at Stanford University • First human heart transplant, by Christian Bernard	• *Apollo 8*, first staffed craft orbiting the moon • *The Double Helix* by James D. Watson	• Armstrong and Aldrin: the first humans walking on the moon • Two Mariner space probes transmit pictures of the surface of Mars
• Death of Winston Churchill • Assassination of Malcolm X • American intervention in Vietnam escalates	• Cultural Revolution in China • First American bombs on Hanoi • Kwame Nkrumah goes into exile after a military coup • Indira Gandhi becomes prime minister	• Six-Day War between Israel and Arab nations • Assassination of Che Guevara	• Assassination of Martin Luther King, Jr. • Assassination of Robert F. Kennedy • Czech uprising crushed by Russian tanks • Police riot at the Democratic convention in Chicago	• Massive protest against the war in Vietnam throughout the United States • Trial of the "Chicago Eight" • Georges Pompidou is elected president of France

Art becomes spectacle, thanks to a young man from Nice, Yves Klein, known up to now for his monochrome pictures. This time, instead of painting his pictures, Klein has used naked women, coated with color, as brushes during a memorable evening attended by guests in formal attire. This year also sees the creation of the New Realism by the critic Pierre Restany, who groups together artists from various horizons, Yves Klein included, all of them responding to the call for defiance of established values. But art can also be a descent into darkness, as it is for Henri Michaux who puts an end to four years of dangerous work under the influence of mescaline.

1960

SUMMARY

AVANT-GARDE

Yves Klein's Brush-Women
Pierre Restany: the New Realists
Sculptor Jasper Johns
Frank Stella's Aluminums
The Vertical Torrent of Henri Michaux

DEVELOPMENTS

Atlan Confides
Poliakoff, a Great Colorist

ART NEWS

Figurative Art in California
First Compression by César
Arman Overfloweth
Inauguration of the Musée Léger
Tinguely in New York
In Brief

GREAT MASTERS

The Last Word of Herbin

ARCHITECTURE

The New Capital of Brazil

YVES KLEIN: ANTHROPOMETRY OF THE BLUE PERIOD (DETAIL). 1960. Paris. MNAM

YVES KLEIN: ANTHROPOMETRY OF THE BLUE PERIOD. 1960. Paris. MNAM

YVES KLEIN'S BRUSH-WOMEN

PARIS

It is an astonishing event! It takes place on March 9, precisely at ten in the evening, at the beginning of a solemn ceremony organized by Count Maurice d'Arquian, with the help of Pierre Restany, at his International Gallery for Contemporary Art, at 253 Rue Saint-Honoré. In formal evening clothes, Yves Klein, inventor of "monochrome painting," walks onto a floor covered with white paper. He has in tow three young nude women and some pails of blue paint.

Three hundred guests, chosen among the most "in," surround a chamber-music orchestra playing Klein's *Symphony Monotone Silence,* one chord held for twenty minutes, followed by twenty minutes of total silence. One guest is heard uttering a parody of Sacha Guitry's witticism on Mozart, "Oh, privilege of the genius! After a piece by Klein, the silence that follows is also signed by him!"

During the forty-minute performance, and in an advanced state of nervous tension, Yves Klein guides, like a director, the creative ritual of the three "brush-women." With indescribable composure, they copiously smear their busts and hips with blue paint, and roll on the floor, and press their bodies against a vertical partition, imprinting their "anthropometries" on large white sheets of paper. Under a sidereal lighting, the spectacle of the three blue graces, mesmerized by their guru and marking the paper with their feminine phantomlike and "cosmic" shapes, has a strange poetic quality.

After the show is over, Restany explains that the audience had just seen one of the most ancient rites of creation. Did it not evoke the cave imprints of prehistoric man? "Rite is okay, but where is the myth?" the painter Georges Mathieu asks Yves Klein, who responds, "Myth

Yves Klein with one of his models.

is in art." "But what is art for you?" "Art is health!" the director of pictorial rituals replies, to the great amusement of the public.

The ceremony was the first manifestation of the New Realism. The trend revolves around Restany and Klein, Tinguely, Hains, Arman, and Dufrêne, joined later by Raisse and Spoerri. Their mottoes could be "Surpass Fiction by Reality" and "The Most Direct Expression," as Restany explains in a manifesto published on April 16, before a joint exhibition in the gallery Apollinaire in Milan.

These artists' new perceptive approach to reality can only be personal. It, therefore, is not surprising that they are so diverse, even so contradictory. Thus, Arman decides to fill Iris Clert's gallery with a heap of various objects in order to create a "filled-out space," where Klein had exhibited a void.

To justify Klein's monochrome painting, which some see as a mere gimmick, Restany does not hesitate to call dialectic and phenomenology, even Husserl, to the rescue. But he does not consider that Klein's artistry could just as well spring directly from the French humorist Alphonse Allais, the initiator of "monochroidal" painting more than a half century ago. In his April Fool's album published in 1897, there is a monochrome blue painting called *Stupeur de jeunes recrues apercevant pour la première fois ton azur, Oh Méditerranée!* Neither Klein nor his fans have ever mentioned the Côte d'Azur as a probable source of his art. He was born in Nice in April 1928, and his first vacation was on the beach; the sea we always return to.

(See also 1962.)

PIERRE RESTANY: THE NEW REALISTS

Wise academicians and brave individuals may be alarmed at the rate at which the history of art is progressing and at the extraordinary power of the modern world to wear away at things. But they would try in vain to stop the sun in its tracks or make time stand still by moving counterclockwise.

We are witnessing the draining and ossification of all established vocabularies, languages, and styles. Individual endeavors, still scattered over Europe and America, have responded to this exhaustion of traditional means. These projects, regardless of their range, all tend to define the normative bases for a new expressivity. It is not a question of a new formula for another oil or enamel-based medium. Easel painting, like any other classic means of painting or sculpture, has served its term. Still sublime at times, it is approaching the end of a long monopoly.

What is being proposed? The exciting adventure of the real seen for what it is and not through the prism of conceptual or imaginative transmission. What is the determining feature of this new perception? The introduction of sociological reinforcement at the critical stage of communication. Sociology comes to the aid of consciousness and hazard, whether it is in the posting or the tearing down of a sign, the physical appearance of an object, the rubbish from a house or living room, the unleashing of mechanical affectivity, or the expanding of sensitivity beyond the limits of its perception.

Sociological reality in its entirety, the work of individuals for the common good, the grand republic of our social exchanges, of our social commerce—this is what is being called on. Its artistic mission would not be doubted were it not for so many individuals who still believe in the eternal validity of certain genres held to be noble, such as painting . . .

At this stage where the creator steps outside of himself and attains full expression, and through the baroque appearance of certain experiences, we are making progress toward a New Realism of pure sensitivity. This is at least one of the roads of the future. With Yves Klein and Tinguely, Hains and Arman, Dufrêne and Villeglé, a variety of projects have been started in Paris. The work will be fruitful, its full consequences are still unpredictable, and, because of the existence of icons and the foolishness of their adorers, it will definitely be iconoclastic.

We find ourselves immersed up to our necks in direct expressivity at forty degrees below Dadaist zero, without any aggressivity complex, without any particular controversial desire, looking to nothing but to our realism for justification. And that produces positive results. People, if they succeed in reintegrating themselves with what is real, will identify it with their own transcendence, which is emotion, feeling, and, ultimately, poetry.

PIERRE RESTANY
First Manifesto (Extracts)
Milan, April 16

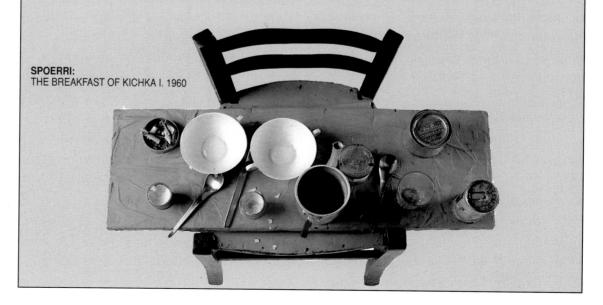

SPOERRI:
THE BREAKFAST OF KICHKA I. 1960

SCULPTOR JASPER JOHNS

NEW YORK

Jasper Johns uses the most common objects from his familiar universe as subjects for his paintings: American flags, targets, maps, and numbers and letters . . . He has turned to sculpture, using the same principle. One of his recent works, *Painted Bronze (Savarin)*, is a faithful reproduction of the coffee can he uses to dip his brushes. Another one, *Painted Bronze*

(Ale Cans), is made of a pedestal on which stand two Ballantine beer cans. Two years ago, the first attempts by Jasper Johns in the field of sculpture had the theme of a flashlight and a bulb. Then last year's *The Critic Smiles* had an ironic note: the cunning smile of the art critic flashing through a toothbrush, which is also mounted on a base. The question that interests Johns is one of illusion: perfect reproduction of an object that has been cast in bronze and is now useless, and on which the artist leaves his thumb print.

JASPER JOHNS: PAINTED BRONZE (ALE CANS). 1960. Basel. Kunstmuseum

FRANK STELLA'S ALUMINUMS

NEW YORK

The painter Frank Stella has his first solo exhibition, from September 27 to October 15 at the Leo Castelli Gallery. He shows his new series, *Aluminum.*

He was born in 1936, in Massachusetts, and studied at Princeton University. Like all painters of his generation Stella was at first influenced by Abstract Expressionism. He was simultaneously discovered last year by Leo Castelli and by Dorothy Miller and Alfred Barr of the Museum of Modern Art, who immediately invited him to participate in several exhibitions. Stella was then painting his *Black Series*, a group of paintings composed of straight or diagonal parallel black bands arranged around a central pattern. In spite of this color, which could have particular connotations, Stella said that he finds nothing poetic or mysterious in these paintings. He is interested in their formal aspect. *Aluminum* has the same concerns.

His beautiful *Aluminum* is organized around an initial form, a slit or cutting, and around the serial progression of bands generating the final form of the canvas. This results from the systematic repetition of the inner motive of the painting. In this manner the artist reaches a "shaped" canvas on which the classic rectangle is cut afterward.

He uses an aluminum paint of a light cold tone. Brush strokes are hardly discernible. The ensemble exhibited at the Castelli Gallery is both unexpected and elegant. Let us hope the critics will receive it better than they received Stella last year, when the artist was strongly criticized.

The names of the paintings have various inspirations: for instance, *Luis Miguel Dominguin,* the matador, *Avicenna,* the Arab philosopher, or *Newstead Abbey,* a celebrated place.

FRANK STELLA: NEWSTEAD ABBEY. 1960. Amsterdam. Stedelijk Museum

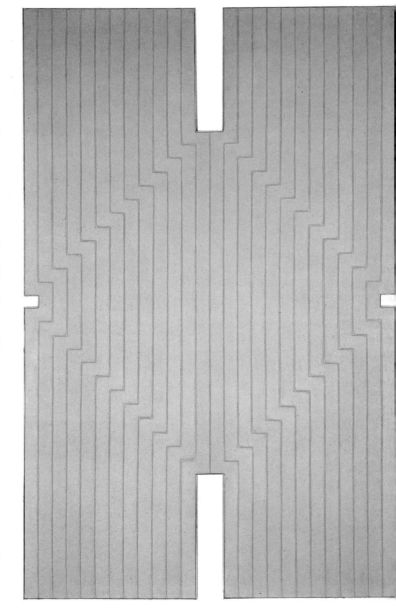

HENRI MICHAUX:
UNTITLED. 1959. Paris.
MNAM

THE VERTICAL TORRENT OF HENRI MICHAUX

PARIS

These last four years have been crucial for Henri Michaux. At his own risk and peril, he descended to a place from which many do not come back: the abyss of himself, through the use of hallucinogens, specifically mescaline, a drug obtained from a cactus that grows in Mexico. Mescaline alters the perception of time, dilates or contracts the internal image of the body, and creates visual hallucinations: "That's how it was," the artist writes. "But more violent, more electrical, more fantastic. For hours, especially in the beginning, the most vivid images. Eyes closed, as in a vision, I saw a sort of vertical torrent descend."

In 1925, when he discovered Klee, Max Ernst, and de Chirico, Michaux was amazed to see, at last, a style of painting that no longer tried to "repeat reality." The Automatism dear to the Surrealists showed him the essential role of spontaneity and chance in artistic creation. The result had to be fantastic, monstrous creations: nightmarish

"EXCESS IS THE TRUE MEASURE OF MAN, OF UNSUSPECTED MAN"

beasts, faces grimacing in anguish. Later, he created watercolors—imaginary landscapes and shapes barely outlined in an opaque black.

Now, at the age of sixty-one, and thanks to experiences with mescaline, Michaux finds himself turning out graphics of the first rank. The spots and runs of ink express directly on paper his maddened rhythms and memories. A whole latent world comes out: swirling lines that merge, accelerating movements, proliferating thin lines—it is as if his entire nervous system were suddenly exposed.

Michaux is certainly not the only artist or the first one to go to the edge of his being. In 1924, André Masson executed Automatic Drawings, the first in our century to seek the sources of the unconscious. It is well known to what apocalyptic lengths Jackson Pollock was able to bring the viewer's organic impulses. But what is striking in Michaux's work is the "mental," almost Cartesian, character of his picture-writing; the final product is not so much chaos but a sort of internal infinite of transcendence, a unity found again. "Excess is the true measure of man," he wrote, adding "of unsuspected man." Measure and excess: the two poles between which lie each of his drawings.

Michaux, who was a writer and a poet before becoming a painter, has written about his experiences in several works: *Miserable Miracle*, published in 1956, *Turbulent Infinity*, published in 1957, and chiefly *Paix dans les brisements*, published last year. "The deeper the trance," he explains, "and the stronger the dose taken, the greater was the force of the apparition, the transformation, the successions in the phenomenal stream (perhaps witness to another flux, for I would not swear that it ran)."

ATLAN
CONFIDES

MEUDON

There are painters who cannot be assigned to a particular school, for they are jealous of their freedom. Jean Atlan, who dies of generalized cancer at the age of forty-seven, was one of them. He came from Constantine, in Algeria, and studied at the Sorbonne while living a Bohemian life in the Latin Quarter and being passionately involved in political battles.

"In 1941, after finishing my studies in philosophy, I started to paint and to write poetry," he said to critic Jean Cathelin, who came to see him eight days before Atlan died at his farm in Bourguignon. "I was at that time obsessed with the mythic side of my native town, Constantine, which for me is as much Mexican as African."

Active in the Resistance and sought by the Gestapo, he escaped capture by the Germans by having himself shut up at Sainte-Anne after simulating madness. The importance for modern art of the pictorial activity of mentally ill people had influenced Klee and more recently has been an inspiration for Dubuffet. *Was* Atlan touched by insanity? The fact is that in his art there is something crude and brutal that puts him in contrast with any estheticism, both figurative and abstract. It is surely no accident that it was during his stay at Sainte-Anne that he threw himself into painting and drawing.

But his art is striking above all for its African content. "For me, the world of the Mediterranean and of Africa go together," he said before dying. "Africa is magic totality, rhythmic, poetic, vital, explosive, very young, and very old. The world of Africa leads me to related myths, the gypsy myths, the mythology of jazz. I believe in the necessity for violent joy because of my taste for movement, for dance."

ATLAN: LA KAHENA. 1958.
Paris. Musée d'Art Moderne de la Ville

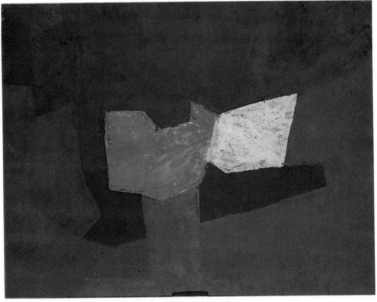

SERGE POLIAKOFF: COMPOSITION. 1955. Paris. Musée d'Art Moderne de la Ville

POLIAKOFF,
A GREAT
COLORIST

PARIS

Serge Poliakoff, a Muscovite who landed in the French capital in 1923, serenely continues his abstract work which he began before the war started. It can be seen in the galleries Bergman and Knoedler. He is now a recognized artist, but for many years he survived only because of his talent as a musician. He went to Russian restaurants in the evening to play the balalaika.

Poliakoff works with equal facility in oil, gouache, and watercolor. Squares, rectangles, triangles, and polygons overlap like pieces of a puzzle. But the contours that outline them—diagonals, verticals, horizontals—exist only in relation to color.

Color unites the articulated shapes whose outlines are changing continually. "Every figure has two colors, an internal one and an external one. The egg is white outside and yellow inside. This goes for everything else," he explains. This subtle geometric arrangement originates in a principle that Poliakoff calls his "canon."

His preoccupation with such principles reinforces his colors that give rhythm and life to the canvas. He obtains the density of his palette by cultivating his material: When he becomes aware of the limits of industrial colors in tubes, he makes his own colors. Following the example of the ancients, he chooses his pigments, grinds his powders according to processes that he improves progressively, using a whole alchemy that enriches his pictorial substance. He takes liberties, superimposing tones, red under blue, for instance, thereby reinforcing their luminous intensity. He plays with textures, some granular, others more fluid, in a desire to make each shade more vivid. A born colorist, Poliakoff shows in his recent work that at the age of sixty he has reached a splendid maturity.

Figurative Art in California

The painters in the Bay Area Figuration School in San Francisco have greatly contributed to the development of figurative painting in California in recent years. The best-known among them, Richard Diebenkorn, has moved away from the influence exerted on the California School of Fine Arts by Abstract Expressionism, mainly through Clyfford Still and Mark Rothko, and is once again including the human figure in his compositions. Along with David Park and Edmer Bischoff, Diebenkorn created the group in 1955 through U.C. Berkeley. The precision of their subjects, in a portrait or still life, sets the Figuration School apart from other West Coast art movements.

First Compression by César

The Compression chosen by César to be exhibited this year at the Salon de Mai will continue, no doubt, to draw applause and hisses. The work—if it can be called that—is a parallelepiped of crunched metal, an auto body crushed at the junkyard. The artist did not change it in any way; he simply "decided" it as a "ready-made" piece, as Duchamp would do. Perhaps this is an example of the New Realism created by critic Pierre Restany in Milan on April 16, when he changed the course of César's work. Renouncing the School of Fine Arts where he studied until the age of thirty-five, César seems to be off on a totally new adventure.

Arman Overfloweth

Two years ago, Yves Klein exhibited . . . nothing at the Iris Clert Gallery. Against a backdrop of bare white walls, visitors on the exhibit's opening day lifted glasses full of . . . nothing to their lips. Today, Arman has monopolized the same space, cramming it so full of junk that it is impossible to enter—a "filled-out space." He explains the origin of his obsession: "One day, I opened a great, mysterious trunk belonging to my grandmother. Inside was an incredible number of miscellaneous objects. I was fascinated then, and still am."

Inauguration of the Musée Léger

The Musée Fernand Léger, designed by the architect Svetchine, was inaugurated in Biot on the same site where the artist, in his later years, liked to devote his time to such work as ceramics, windows, and mosaics. The museum is above all the expression of a certain conception of art that began with Cubism and led to a Realism that is in sync with today's machine society and a sign of the new humanism for the masses. Léger, who considered himself the primitive of a future age, now has his own temple in the clear light of the Mediterranean, the light of the spirit.

Tinguely in New York

Jean Tinguely presented his self-destructing construction No. 1, entitled *Homage to New York,* in the garden of the Museum of Modern Art. The Museum gave him full use of the Buckminster Fuller dome near the garden. Assembly of the immense work, a machine composed of various objects and materials, lasted three weeks. Parts for the piece came from junkyards: bicycle wheels, chamber pots, washing-machine drums, electric motors, oil barrels. Motors were programed to set off a hundred different motions. "Meta-Matics" drew designs with sponges, typewriters clacked, a jack tipped things over, engines moved sideways, colors spilled over, and odors wafted forth. *Homage to New York* finally self-destructed in thirty minutes.

IN BRIEF...

GERMANY
Soulages retrospective at the Museum of Hanover.

UNITED STATES
Yves Tanguy and Max Ernst exhibition at the Bodley Gallery.

FRANCE
Some writers and the Surrealist group sign the Manifesto of the 121 *against the Algerian war.*

GREAT BRITAIN
The Tate Gallery has received more than 500,000 visitors for the great Picasso exhibition, which has now ended.

ITALY
In Milan, First Manifesto of the New Realism.

Henri Michaux receives the Einaudi Prize at the Biennale in Venice.

Alfred Manessier executes scenery and costumes for the Human Comedy, *a ballet drawn from the* Decameron *and staged at Nervi.*

Musée Fernand Léger.

THE LAST WORD OF HERBIN

PARIS

It is hard to believe, but cursed artists, as was true in the days of Van Gogh, still exist in a society where communication is universal and the revolution in modern art appears to be accepted. Auguste Herbin, who dies in his apartment on the Boulevard Pasteur at the end of January at the age of almost eighty, was able to make a living from his painting only during his last years. Thanks to Denise René, the enthusiastic supporter of abstract, geometric art, who regularly showed his work in her gallery, he finally gained his first real commission—when he was sixty-five years old.

He was born in 1882 in Quiévy, in Nord. After a period in the Art Institute of Lille, he lived in the Bateau-Lavoir, when Picasso and Gris were there, and participated in the Cubist adventure. But it was much later, during and immediately after the Second World War, that he was able to be entirely original. In the area of geometric abstraction, he is equal to a Malevich or a Mondrian.

During the last twenty years, from the object in order to arrive at an autonomous pictorial expression.

He summarized his ideas in an astonishing book, *Nonobjective, Nonfigurative Art,* published in 1949: "When the sap no longer rises, blue is absent, it stays yellow, that is fall. When in the dark, life leaves the grain, it

HIS PALETTE EXPRESSED
A SPIRITUAL VISION OF THE UNIVERSE

Herbin painted words: *Friday, Sanctity, Steel* . . . Each corresponds to the arrangement of a simple geometric shape: triangle, rectangle, circle, or square, and a color. It is the conclusion of a long process of reflection according to which it was necessary above all to separate painting manifests itself as white, the opposite of black." And, "In the plant, the transformation of energy occurs under certain conditions; in man, the transformation of the same energies is produced under opposite conditions." On the subject of his plastic alphabet: "B: reddish purple; a combination of spherical and rectangular shapes; sonority do, si. R: light blue; a combination of hemispheres and triangles; sonority sol, fa, mi." Rimbaud is not far away.

Herbin frequently retreated to the Goetheanum in Dornach, in the canton of Basel, in Switzerland. A disciple of Rudolf Steiner, he had a theosophic conception of the world and tried to express a spiritual vision of the universe by means of the geometrical order in his works.

Herbin was also a painter by temperament. To a critic who asked, not without skepticism, according to what rule were isosceles triangles usually yellow in his paintings, the artist replied, "It is obvious that yellow is sharp-pointed."
(See also 1949.)

AUGUSTE HERBIN:
FRIDAY I. 1951.
Paris. MNAM

The cathedral of Brasilia.

The congressional palace of Brasilia.

THE NEW CAPITAL OF BRAZIL

BRASILIA

An entirely new capital, in a circular arc, where there once were only savanna and a few herdsmen's huts. More than six hundred miles inland, President Juscelino Kubitschek inaugurates Brasilia on April 21. The schemes and buildings of the totally new town were designed by the urban planner Lúcio Costa and the architect Oscar Niemeyer.

President Kubitschek met Niemeyer some years ago, when he was mayor of Belo Horizonte. He commissioned the as-yet-little-known architect to build a series of prestige houses in the Pampulha quarter. The project, which lasted from 1941 to 1944, enabled Niemeyer to create original buildings with an architecture marvelously integrated with painting and sculpture. It was also the beginning of a profound understanding between the politician and the architect— Brasilia is the finest product.

Niemeyer created the buildings on Three-Power Square and the surrounding ministries. In the heart of the city are the halls of congress, the seat of the legislature, the Planalto, the residence of the head of state, and the supreme court, located each sixteen hundred feet apart from any of the other buildings. The principle of separation of powers is thus symbolized through space.

The city now has about ninety thousand inhabitants, and more than two hundred thousand live in the outskirts, in satellite towns. Brasilia is a genuine federal capital. Everywhere are government officials and a battalion of physicians, teachers, and professors for the hospitals, schools, colleges, and university. Trade and banking meet or will meet the needs of the population, but it *is* difficult to create a city out of nothing. It appears that, for the time being, life is more active and pleasant in the lodgings of the engineers and workmen who built Brasilia than in its long avenues and at its immense concrete buildings. But Niemeyer distinguished himself among architects of the current generation by his esthetic sense, which contrasts with the Functionalism of his colleagues.

His hall of congress and his cathedral are already among the

AN ALLIANCE OF SOLUTIONS BORROWED FROM THE PAST AND THE MOST MODERN METHODS

great mid-century successes. The construction of the hall of congress marks the successful marriage of Functionalism and Symbolism. The hall, which houses the chamber of deputies and the senate, is composed of two blind-flattened domes, across from two twin towers three hundred and thirty feet tall, isolated in a vast rectangular basin. The senate sits under the smaller of the two domes, and deputies, under the larger. In both chambers, the rows of the members are dominated by concentric public galleries, so that the politicians debate under the eyes of citizenry.

In most of the government buildings that he planned, Niemeyer revived the old Mediterranean principle of a building with a portico. He demonstrates the remarkable result that can be obtained from an alliance of solutions borrowed from the past and the most modern methods.

The urban planner Costa, for his part, invented crossovers at crossings, and he arranged some roads in such a way as to force automobile drivers to slow. A problem in all capitals has always been traffic jams. They have been famous in a city like Paris since the seventeenth century and are aggravated today by motorized vehicles. Will Brasilia function? It is the first town planned more for the car than for the pedestrian.

At the age of sixty, Dubuffet has his first museum exhibition. Even his detractors are concerned: It may be that the initiator of Art Brut, the enemy of the cultural values he incessantly vilifies, is the greatest French painter of the day, the only one of international standing. With Tobey and Rothko in the United States, also fully matured now, the public at large comes to know a new generation, as important as the generation that, from Matisse to Picasso and Braque, opened the doors to modern art. The die now seems cast. The "second" twentieth century, complete with its own problems and realizations, has definitely begun.

1961
S U M M A R Y

LITERATURE

ARGENTINA
Publication of Alexandra *by Ernesto Sabato.*

UNITED STATES
Ernest Hemingway commits suicide in Ketchum, Idaho.

FRANCE
The poet Guillevic publishes Carnac.

MUSIC

UNITED STATES
John Cage presents Silence.

ITALY
Luciano Berio composes Epiphany.
   Luigi Nono's opera Intolleranza, *with scenery by Emilio Vedova, creates a scandal when performed in Venice.*

MOTION PICTURES

SPAIN
Luis Buñuel shows his Viridiana.

UNITED STATES
Rivalry between white Americans and Puerto Ricans is treated in a great musical by Robert Wise, West Side Story.

FRANCE
The event of the season is Last Year in Marienbad *by Alain Resnais, with a script by Alain Robbe-Grillet.*
   François Truffaut's Jules and Jim *tells the story of an impossible love among two men and one woman.*

JEAN DUBUFFET
METAFIZYX. 1950
Paris. MNAM

DUBUFFET: THE PROVOCATION AT THE MUSEUM

PARIS

Charlatan or genius? The retrospective of four hundred paintings, gouaches, drawings, and sculptures of Jean Dubuffet, which took place at the Museum of Decorative Arts from December 16 to February 25, propels into the foreground of the international art scene this most controversial and admired French artist of the postwar era. In Dubuffet's own words, "Art should always induce some anguish and some smiles." Or consider the remark of Gaëtan Picon, author of the exhibition catalogue's foreword, "He is probably the only artist still provoking scandals." The exhibition, grouping his work from 1942 to the present, is *the* event of the beginning of the season.

In the glowing flow of Dubuffet's thoughts, at once intense and provocative, all the periods of his work are embraced: the *Hautes pâtes*, which transforms the traditional conception of landscape; the *Corps de dames*, in which the human figure is shown in a totally unique and revolutionary way; the *Phenomena* and the *Texturology*, which venture to the limits of abstraction; the *Tableaux d'assemblages*, wherein a straight path is bordered by untended wilderness.

The exhibition is, on the whole, complete. It represents an overall impression, not of Dubuffet's style, for this intriguing man is versatile, but of his many styles. His works stress the disconcerting opulence, the mutations and metamorphoses of an astounding creative power, and different techniques, exhausted always to the maximum of their possibilities.

Some people want to see another Picasso in Dubuffet. And indeed, the two artists share a constant renewal of their means of expression. Both of them adopted the same procedure, which later became very popular, of creating series or cycles dealing with the same subject over and over again: bullfights and bathing women for Picasso, earth structures, grotesque landscapes, and thistles for Dubuffet. While the sixty-year-old Dubuffet found his means of expression only about the age of forty, after having twice given up painting and after destroying practically all of his initial work, Picasso was a boy-wonder, realizing some of his masterpieces when he was barely past adolescence.

These important biographical differences no doubt explain to a large extent the differences in procedures. Picasso, set in tradition, concentrates on destroying, on taking apart the mechanism piece by piece. His inspirations are Titian, Velásquez, Delacroix, and Goya. He admires Renaissance painting, and always measures himself against it. Dubuffet, on the other hand, produces mainly noncultural art: graffiti,

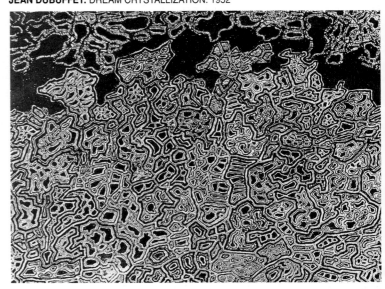

JEAN DUBUFFET: DREAM CRYSTALLIZATION. 1952

JEAN DUBUFFET: BUSTLING LIFE. 1953.
Paris. Fondation Dubuffet

bleak paintings, drawings of children and lunatics. He creates the Art Brut (raw art) with which his name will remain closely linked.

Where graphic art and the invention of plasticity remain the main purpose for Picasso, Dubuffet searches for his means of revival in the natural substances of common matter. He questions their stability, the opaque colors. As a result, his "Materiologies," thoroughly firm or viscous, are elaborate to an extent that seems beyond the control of either spirit or hand.

In Dubuffet's work, a return to the physical source of life can be recognized. This creates the strength and sanity of his work. To the magazine *Le peignoir de bain*'s question "Why don't you believe in God?," he answered, in 1954, "I am much more inspired by the fluid in my veins that relates to elements as marvelous as sea water or the sap of trees, and that is capable of crystallizing like brimstone or basalt, than by the thought of a contriving and rigid gentleman in love with grace, justice, and other notions that are not my forte. I don't have the mentality to want adding to life a foreign ingredient used only to beautify matters."

In Dubuffet's work, the image of man is reduced to that of a poor abandoned creature, vague to such a degree that René Huyghe, in *his* work, is not totally wrong to refuse a break with traditional values. The age of man, as a measure of all things, the pride of Renaissance, is over. Thus the debate between his fierce critics, who are upset by his rejection of humanity, and his fascinated followers.

(See also 1944, 1945, 1973, 1985.)

IN DUBUFFET'S WORDS

Art is a source of great enchantment. The need for art is as basic as the need for bread, perhaps even more so. Without bread, one dies of hunger. But without art, one dies of boredom.

Long live marvelous inventions, the enchanting sources of inspiration! Artists that we find boring are like professional inventors that have never invented anything.

Wise art—what a stupid idea! Art is nothing more than a product of exhilaration and folly!

Everyone is a painter. To paint is like to speak or to walk. For the human being it is just as natural to draw on any surface available and to make some kind of image as it is to speak.

When one really thinks about it, museums are nothing more than temples where the worshipers of the Mona Lisa, *Raphael, The* Gleaners, *and* The Raft of the Medusa *all come to celebrate. One visits a museum as one does a cemetery, on a Sunday afternoon, with the whole family, walking softly and speaking in hushed tones.*

As for myself, I hold in high estime the values of savagery: instinct, passion, capriciousness, violence, and delirousness.

Painting is a much more spontaneous and direct language than spoken words. It is nearer to a cry or a dance. That is why painting is much more effective than words as a means of expression for our inner voice.

Ideas are a but a faint puff of air. It is when visions disappear that ideas emerge along with the blind fish of their waters, the intellectual.

Art should not announce itself. It should emerge unexpectedly, by surprise. Otherwise, it will be much less effective.

JEAN DUBUFFET: THE EXEMPLARY LIFE OF THE SOIL. (TEXTUROLOGY L XIII). 1958. Paris. Fondation Dubuffet

A TOBEY RETROSPECTIVE

PARIS

The Museum of Decorative Arts dedicates an extremely beautiful retrospective to the American painter Mark Tobey, whose first one-man exhibition in France took place at the gallery Jeanne Bucher six years ago. For a long time, this aloof man led a secluded life in Seattle, Washington, removed from the world of art and his own restlessness. However, on the occasion of his exhibition at the Willard Gallery in 1944, the critic Clement Greenberg had already called Tobey's work "one of the first original contributions to today's American art."

Ever since his travels in China and Japan, in 1934, Tobey has been influenced by Oriental philosophy. The "white writing" that he invented became more ample, as in the *Forms Follow Man,* of 1942, in which swiftly sketched silhouettes become successively more abstract. But the tension, created by such graphic portrayal, covering nearly the entire canvas, was sometimes hard to maintain. In a letter to a friend, Tobey wrote, "I am not sure that I will be able to continue this 'white writing' for long. The style is too tense and too demanding for a nervous man like me."

In the 1950s, Tobey lived for some time in New York. His pictures of the city express its intensity and restlessness. Yet simultaneously he created his most lyrical and serene work, *Meditative Series,* embracing poetry of cosmic dimensions.

Since settling in Basel, Switzerland, a year ago, Tobey leads a solitary existence in an old house, at 69 Saint Alban Vorstadt. His sequestered life obviously agrees with him; never before has he worked as much.

The exhibition shows work characteristic of the style of these last years, with titles often revealing the preoccupation of this seventy-seven-year-old artist for whom spiritual quests have always been of primal

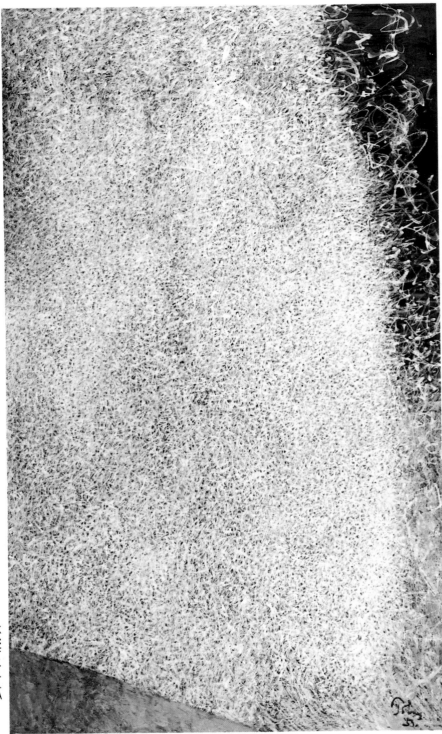

MARK TOBEY: EDGE OF AUGUST. 1955. New York. MOMA

importance. Among these, *Moment in Space, Space Ritual,* and *The Claws of Orion* are, at the same time, evocations of nature and of the forces that rule it.

The Bah'ai belief he has adopted is the nucleus of his life and work. One of the pieces exhibited, *Edge of August,* was described by Holger Cahill: "The intricate scroll to the right strongly resembles a page of Ts'ao-tzun, the Chinese way of writing 'on herbes.' The vibrant effect of Tobey's paintings depends on a subtle play between elusive structures and a dark background, a creation of implied forms and inter-weaving light, always bordering on infinity."

Greenberg was not wrong. Because of his inventiveness, his intelligence, and his originality, Tobey is counted among today's great American painters.

(See also 1934 and 1944.)

ROTHKO AT MOMA

NEW YORK

A retrospective at the Museum of Modern Art finally does justice to a great painter, Mark Rothko, who these last few years has had little exposure in New York. He did have one-man exhibitions at the Biennale in Venice in 1958 and at the Philipps Collection in Washington.

Rothko is one of the major artists of the "Color Field" that shapes the young American generation so much. His huge frontal shapes seem to be made entirely of pure light, translucent, flowing, but nevertheless with a remarkable presence. The shapes seem to quiver and invite the viewer to get lost within. It is painting that is utterly personal and embraces a poetry emanating from the depths of the artist's feelings. "I am not an abstract painter," Rothko says. "I am not interested in the relationship between form and color. The only thing I care about is the expression of man's basic emotions: tragedy, ecstasy, destiny . . ."

Mark Rothko is a quiet and sensitive man. His evolution is symbolic for that of many painters of his generation. In the 1930s, he painted strangely still and unreal landscapes. They were followed, in New York, by watercolors and paintings with mythological and archaic themes influenced by Surrealism: works like *Ritual, Vibration of Dawn, Totemic Sign, Incantation, Baptismal Scene* which are now on view. The sketched forms are absorbed by a luminous atmosphere becoming itself the mien of the pictures of the post 1947-1948 period.

Color has become the most important element of his creative expression. But especially noteworthy is his power of expansion, which he admires so much in Matisse's work. Since his "multiforms" of the 1940s, Mark Rothko uses only names of colors or numbers to title his works, with one exception: the

MARK ROTHKO: HOMAGE TO MATISSE. 1954. New York. Private Collection

splendid *Homage to Matisse*, painted this year with a clearly spiritual dimension.

Rothko's coloring is of an intensity, a sensuality, and a lyricism unequaled in today's art. But there is also another quality of importance to this pondering painter: a great depth that leads to meditation.

Lately, his painting has become more somber, especially since his commission of paintings for the Seagram Building on Park Avenue. They often exude an atmosphere of doom. Awaited with great impatience are the works for the Holyoke Center of José Luis Sert in Cambridge, Massachusetts, which Professor Wassily Leontief of Harvard University commissioned.

(See also 1945, 1955, 1971.)

LICHTENSTEIN, COURBET'S RIVAL

Roy Lichtenstein with his painting *Look Mickey.*

NEW YORK

Thirty-eight-year-old Roy Lichtenstein was painting cowboys *Guernica*-style when his son challenged him to paint the boy's favorite heroes, Mickey Mouse and Donald Duck. The artist painted *Look Mickey.* Foolish Donald pulls hard at his fishing rod, believing all the while he is reeling in a huge fish when all he has done is hook his own jacket.

Humor and pranks are means to supply the consumer society with a fantasy reflecting our beliefs and imaginations. Last century, Courbet was inspired by the popular etchings of Franche-Comté to stifle exaggerated formality. Today, Lichtenstein finds in the comic strip a measure to break with an estheticism that all too often impairs Abstract Expressionism.

THE ART OF ASSEMBLAGE

NEW YORK

In the last few years, there has appeared in America a new sculpture without the form, mass, or unity of the traditional. It is a "mixed-media" sculpture, made of objects, fragments of objects, assorted materials. An exhibition in the Museum of Modern Art confirms that this new art is practised by many, the most famous among them being Joseph Cornell.

Artists have traditionally borrowed from their immediate surroundings, somehow adapting and integrating them into their work: collages of Braque, Picasso, Hausmann, and Schwitters; Futuristic, Surrealistic, and "ready-made" objects of Duchamp; and the "Combine Paintings" of Robert Rauschenberg. Often, these elements are indus-

EDWARD KIENHOLZ: ROXY'S. 1961.

trial materials, like the metal cylinders used by John Chamberlain, Lee Bontecou, and Richard Stankiewicz, or wood in many shapes and of varied origins transformed by the sensitive

imagination of Louise Nevelson.

Rejects or waste from the consumer are used in a distinctive way by California artists Wallace Berman and Wally Hedrick, who are close to the California School

of Fine Arts and the Beat poets of San Francisco, and, above all, by Edward Kienholz, who created for the Modern Art show an assemblage of surprising liberty, *The Nativity.*

Niki de Saint-Phalle's Rifle Shot

First there was brush painting, then knife painting, and, more recently, "Action Painting," as practiced by Jackson Pollock. Now there is "rifle painting." On the Impasse Ronsin, where Brancusi used to live, four avant-garde artists—Jean Tinguely, Robert Rauschenberg, Larry Rivers, and Niki de Saint-Phalle—shot one of Saint-Phalle's paintings. Hidden among plaster and miscellaneous objects were packets of paint that burst open upon impact, running esthetically down the canvas. Since Picasso, color running has played a certain role in modern art; now it has been brought to the forefront of pictorial creation. Is Tinguely, who is Swiss like another famous marksman, William Tell, at the bottom of this?

Henri Rousseau's Secret

Eighty paintings by Henri Rousseau on exhibit at the gallery Charpentier tell the astonishing tale of this untaught customs clerk who painted both instinctively and with skill. Apollinaire declared him a great painter, but it is because of his true talent that he has remained great. Who exactly was Rousseau? Yann Le Pichon, who has spent five years studying the life of the artist, tells about it in the magazine *Arts.* His life was full of wonder, like a magic lantern through which both fantasy and real life are projected. Inspired by an album for children that he had bought, *The Wild Beasts,* Rousseau found his way and became known as an "exotic painter." He hid that book carefully, pretending to work from real, extraordinary adventures. Now the truth about Rousseau is out—an event for lovers of his art.

Ever-Popular Constructive Art

In late 1961, the gallery Denise René exhibited the works of sixty-nine artists under the title "International Abstract Constructive Art." These "modern-day pioneers" display the "constructive lines of abstract art." On view are works by Mondrian, Van Doesburg, Malevich, Kandinsky, Moholy-Nagy, Pevsner, and Lissitsky, who

NIKI DE SAINT-PHALLE: RIFLE FIRING. 1961. Paris. Galerie Beaubourg

paved the way with their spare, architectonic works. Of the next generation, represented by Agam, Schöffer, Mortensen, Costa, Gilioli, and Vasarely, Michel Seuphor wrote: "The architectural does not eliminate lyricism but rather channels and strengthens it."

Avant-Garde Artists Charged

"Art is the last domain of freedom, and we will defend it in every possible way," declared the Spur group in its 1958 manifesto. The group includes young artists in Munich and Berlin. Unfortunately, their freedom has been taken away. Under the pretext that it was spreading immoral and blasphemous ideas, six issues of the magazine *Spur* were seized, and five members of the group were charged and sentenced. Helmut Sturim received five months in prison, Dieter Kunzelmann, Heimrad Prem, and H. P. Zimmer each received two additional weeks. Then the court of appeals decided to give one uniform sentence and made it five months for all.

Night of Pandemonium

Two young students of West Berlin's Academy of Fine Arts, Georg Baselitz and Eugen Schönebeck, invite the public to see their work at their studio during a "night of pandemonium." They have also published a strange manifesto, handwritten and illustrated with a few drawings, recalling the Surrealists' colorful invectives against bourgeois society.

New Museum in Le Havre

An immense sculpture by Adam entitled *Signal* adorns Le Havre's "flexible museum." Facing the sea, it is Europe's most modern museum, capable of holding one thousand paintings on movable panels. The museum is a veritable cultural center for cinema, theater, concerts, and conferences. The second museum to be built in France since the war, it has a roof of reinforced glass and is a remarkable example of modern museology. Reynold Arnould, its director, back from the United States, where he spent several years, is himself an excellent painter and craftsman.

DAVID HOCKNEY:
PAINTING OF TEA IN ILLUSIONIST
STYLE. 1961. Private Collection

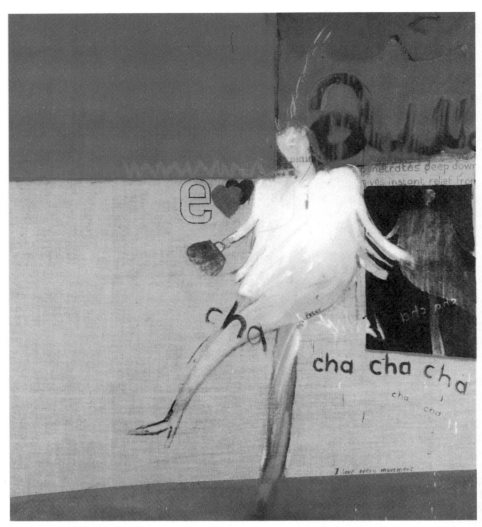

DAVID HOCKNEY: THE CHA-CHA AS DANCED IN THE EARLY HOURS OF MARCH 24. 1961. Private Collection

HOCKNEY RECEIVES THE GUINNESS PRIZE

LONDON
David Hockney, a twenty-four-year-old English painter, is awarded the Guinness prize for etching. Since becoming a member of the Royal College of Art two years ago, he has been wavering between his much-admired abstracts and his propensity for figurative art which, as he recognizes, generates more spontaneous interest from the public, because it is so easily recognized. The influence of abstract artists such as Jackson Pollock and Allen Davie marked his initial work, but Cubism, his love for poetry, and some friendly advice from his American fellow artist R. B. Kitaj induce Hockney to introduce words into his pictures.

Admiration for the poet Walt Whitman, illustrated in the first etching, *Me and My Heroes,* led him to the use of inscriptions, as in last year's *Adhesiveness* and *Third Painting of Love.*

In addition to the reference to Dubuffet for his use of graffiti, there is the example of Francis Bacon, a great inspiration to the young artist. Considering the human form to be the most beautiful subject in painting, Hockney admires the forceful composition and originality of Bacon's figures. The body of the figure in *The Cha-Cha As Danced in the Early Hours of March 24* owes a great deal to Bacon, who was the first to resist the trend toward abstract art.

On the other hand, there is Hockney's affinity with Pop Art, especially in his *Paintings of Tea.* The third canvas of this series shows a tea can changed to give the impression of a greater volume. All his works relate simultaneously to advertising posters and to children's drawings. But what will become of this "fake-naive" style, now that Hockney, with the one hundred pound sterling of the Guinness prize, has gone overseas to discover the New York School?

(See also 1974.)

DALI'S CHRIST IS WOUNDED

GLASGOW

Atheism or vandalism? Or both? One of Salvador Dali's masterpieces, *The Christ of Saint-Jean-de-la-Croix*, was discovered by one of the guards at the Art Gallery of this Scottish city, where the painting is on exhibition, to have been vandalized. It is a mystery when, why, or by whom the crime was committed.

The picture, painted ten years ago, is part of the period of "atomic mysticism" which coincides with Dali's return from the United States in 1948. The artist, an ardent reader of popularized works of science, created his own, following the discoveries of physics and its notions of vagueness and immaterialism, which represent a total break with last century's positivism. He saw, as many others do nowadays, a possibility for a new spiritualism and a different kind of belief, which is expressed in this painting.

Is this Christ, who tears himself away from the earth and is suspended above the Bay of Port Lligat, the man who escapes his own wretched carnal shape as it is affirmed by religion and as modern physics seems to permit to postulate anew?

The state of levitation in which Christ is portrayed is a typical interpretation of purity. Dali presents a poised Christ, free of all fears and infamy, as opposed to Grünewald's, who is torn by terror. Is that why people are troubled? Or is it Dali's scrupulous way of doing things which on occasion causes friction between him and other painters? Or is it the glaring publicity around his eccentric personality, so carefully nurtured by the artist?

An able restorer was needed to repair the damage, traces of which are still faintly visible to the right of the foot of the cross.

(See also 1929, 1934, 1935, 1936, 1938, 1964, 1974, 1979.)

SALVADOR DALI: THE CHRIST OF SAINT-JEAN-DE-LA-CROIX. 1951. Glasgow. Art Gallery

CHAGALL'S WINDOWS

PARIS

The Jardin des Tuileries is holding an exhibition of Marc Chagall's windows for the medical center of the Hadassah University in Jerusalem. There are twelve windows in groups of three, according to the four cardinal points. They represent the twelve tribes of Israel. Judah and Zebulun are flamboyant in red shades, Issachar, Gad, and Asher breathe tranquillity and abundance from green pastures. The Sun floods Levi, Naphtali, Joseph . . .

"Together, they will resemble a crown. Every color must induce prayers," the visibly satisfied artist declares, but adds, "I don't want to pray, I simply work!" Around 1957, the painter met the glass blowers Brigitte and Charles Marq, heirs of a many-centuries-old tradition in Reims. With them, he creates stained-glass windows for a variety of denominations and cults, demonstrating simultaneously his ecumenism and the spiritualism of his art.

Though the avant-garde was a stranger, challenged and mocked at the beginning of the century, now it is immediately exhibited in museums and scooped up by the art market. Antoni Tàpies, who, at the age of thirty-nine, wears the medals of a master, is not the only one to ask if an avant-garde is still possible. The New Realists themselves, like Arman and Christo, also seem unable to resist success. Can it be that this second half of the century, better informed, is more perceptive than the first, and can it be that modern art is now a fixture of our mentality? The question is impossible to answer, so unpredictable are changes in taste.

1962

S U M M A R Y

LITERATURE

UNITED STATES
Death of William Faulkner.

FRANCE
René Char publishes La parole en archipel.

GREAT BRITAIN
Critics praise the reemergence of George Oppen—author of Matters—*after almost 30 years of silence.*

RUSSIA
Publication of One Day in the Life of Ivan Denisovich *by Alexandr Solzhenitsyn, on conditions in Russian deportation camps.*

MUSIC

GREAT BRITAIN
Benjamin Britten composes War Requiem.
   Performance of Michel Tippett's opera King Priam.

THEATER

GREAT BRITAIN
Harold Pinter's The Collection and the Lover *is performed in London to a mixed press.*

MOTION PICTURES

UNITED STATES
Marilyn Monroe dies from an overdose of barbiturates.

FRANCE
Premiere of The Trial *by Orson Welles.*

JAPAN
Premiere of An Afternoon in Autumn *by Yasujiro Ozu.*

MEXICO
Luis Buñuel creates The Exterminating Angel.

ANTONI TÀPIES:
ULTRAMARINE COMPOSITION. 1958.
Eindhoven. Van Abbe Museum

Antoni Tàpies.

ANTONI TÀPIES: GRAPHIC OCHRE.
1960. Hanover. Landesmuseum

TÀPIES'S WORLD TOUR

BARCELONA

Antoni Tàpies enjoyed honors during his teenage years in Barcelona. His father enrolled him in the "Organizaciones Juveniles." With a few other students, he was chosen to stand guard at a monument built on Catalogna Place on May 2, in memory of the popular mutiny against the French occupation of 1808. All of Spain could see him in a military helmet on the cover of *La Vanguardia;* his parents were surprised, shy, and proud all at the same time.

Twenty-three years later, he is making news again. He is not a colonel or a general. He *is* the most celebrated painter of his generation. The occasion is his double retrospective, at the Kestner-Gesellschaft in Hanover and the Guggenheim Museum in New York, coming after various distinctions also obtained in

Europe and the United States.

Tàpies is not, and has never been, a follower of Franco. One can imagine his surprise when he saw the inscription "propaganda material" stamped on one of the cases of works he was sending to an international Biennale! It is a known fact that Franco is shrewder in the politi-

cal game than either Hitler or Mussolini. Now he is using the revolution of modern painting to his advantage.

Tàpies is not a "subject" painter. His work will never glorify the defenders of the Alcazar of Toledo in large compositions, nor will he paint a *Guernica.* His paintings, arising from "the other art" much loved by Michel

Tapié and from the "Materiologies" of Dubuffet, are graffiti, imprints, sketches, and glyphs. They are like metaphysical walls arising, as he says, from dust, ashes, earth, destruction, cataclysm, cosmic contemplation, and inner meditation.

During his high school studies, Antoni disrupted classes

INSPIRED BY "THE OTHER ART," BY DUBUFFET, AND BY ORIENTAL MYSTICISM

and scorned religion lessons but was all ears during philosophy courses. Heraclitus and the idea that everything changes and yet stays identical; Plato and the allegory of the cave; the skepticism of Berkeley and Hume, seemingly demonstrating that things may not have a corporeal existence: Everything troubled him and gave him feverish

visions. As an adult, he discovers Zen and Japanese sand gardens.

He seems to owe to Oriental mystique his fascination with matter as a means of reaching unusually acute mental states, hence his thick paste that he scratches and lacerates in order to suggest better the mineral aspect of his work, hence his use of new materials, such as latex, emulsion, and tar applied in thick layers inscribed with graphic signs and symbols. Triangles, circles, and crosses give his paintings an inner significance, setting them apart from the informal painting hung on walls all around the planet.

On the other hand, Tàpies represents an obligatory tour of the time's knowledge and ideas: Marxism, Surrealism, psychoanalysis, and the new physics. He reads Freud, although the

588

IN TÀPIES'S WORDS

good doctor is not recommended or even prohibited in Spain, and discovers the concept of archetypes in Jung. Like Dali, he is enthralled by the discussions between determinists and nondeterminists, by the quantum theory and by the uncertainty principle, which give us a totally different image of the world than did classical science.

In 1950-1951, he had a scholarship in Paris, and was tempted by Socialist Realism. But all of a sudden, he returned to Barcelona and shut himself for forty days in his small studio. He obsessively tested shapes, tried new instruments and materials in a state of extreme spiritual tension. He came out of this ascetic period with silence and humility, and with the fundaments of his art such as it is today.

At the end of January 1939, when Barcelona was conquered by Franco's troops, Tàpies' father, who was a lawyer, warned the family, "From now on, we have to censor our acts and words if we don't want to make mistakes and expose ourselves. We must start a new life and try to adapt as best we can."

This happened twenty-three years ago. It was difficult to get used to it. That same year, a priest came and asked Tàpies to support the congress of the Partisans of Peace. Shortly after leaving the painter, he was arrested and imprisoned. "Propaganda material." How much longer will Tàpies be able to put up with this situation?

Unless an artist locks himself in an ivory tower, he cannot consider himself as independent of other intellectual disciplines such as philosophy, science, and politics, and the progress of these disciplines.

We all agree that art is a product of profound reflection. But if that reflection is not accompanied by a struggle with the subject matter, the so-called artist will not be seen as having advanced a step, and his work will be but a sterile diversion, just like any formula or theory.

When a work of art is incapable of assail-

The plastic arts constitute the most direct and universal bridge between people and ideas.

The artist is a person of the laboratory, and has nothing to do with offices commissioned to spread propaganda or arbitrary judgments.

Since we have to construct a new vision of reality and push back the darkness that surrounds us, we can never be satisfied with the manipulation of worn-out, dated forms. A new content must inevitably make use of a new form.

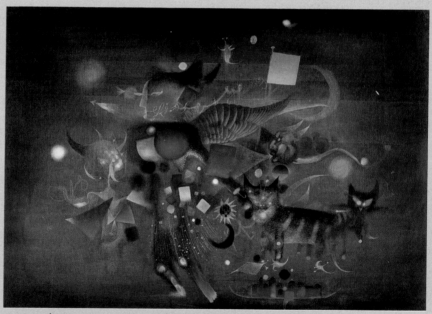

ANTONI TÀPIES: DREAM GARDEN. 1949. Private Collection

ing the society to which it is exposed, disturbing it, moving it to reflect, making it see how much distance it has to catch up with and breaking away from this society, then it is not authentic art.

If we come up with a new conception of reality, this is not just a whim. It is due to certain concrete things happening around us.

There is, as there always should be, a parallel progression between the work of the artist and that of other intellectuals, a progression enriched by constant dialogue.

It is useless to claim that certain classical forms are relevant for any age. The art and ideas of archaic defenders of so-called Classicism are completely lacking in substance.

They answer none of today's questions. They satisfy none of our needs.

If painting today did not make us tremble or at least disturb some of us, it would mean we have failed.

I cannot conceive of an artist that is not in the midst of an adventure . . .

THE NEW REALISTS ATTACK THE UNITED STATES

NEW YORK

There is not an artist or a movement today that doesn't try to gain recognition from New York critics and to become a value on the American market.

This was accomplished when Pierre Restany met the important art dealer Sidney Janis several months ago. In October, the New Realists debark in force in America, for a confrontation between European and American artists. Arman, Christo, Klein, Hains, Raysse, Rotella, Spoerri, and Tinguely face the young Americans of Pop Art: Jim Dine, Rauschenberg, Oldenburg, Lichtenstein, Warhol, Segal, Wesselmann, and Rosenquist.

Under the label "The New Realism," the exhibition's goal is to show the spiritual community and the feasibility of a true esthetic dialogue between the new generation on both sides of the Atlantic. In the catalogue, Pierre Restany writes of a gap between Paris and New York, and defends his flock with pathos: "Through cut-up posters, accumulations or 'caging' of objects, compressed metal, or monochrome statements, we see a new poetic art being born."

American Pop Art artists, whom he calls Neodadaists, seem to him less well armed to face the complex reality of tomorrow. He seems to be very sure of himself, as always.

Comparisons don't have to be true. Pop Art appears to be a more coherent and stronger movement than the New Realism which consists of contrasting personalities that are joined together only by the will of enterprising critics. In any case, the competition is open, and everybody may choose sides.

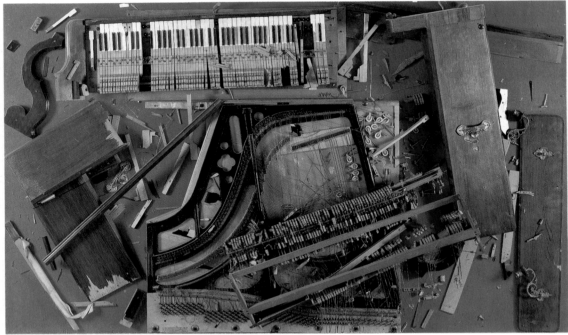

ARMAN: CHOPIN'S WATERLOO. 1962. Paris. MNAM

CHRISTO ON THE RUE VISCONTI

PARIS

On June 27, there is a gigantic bottleneck that lasts for several hours on the Rue Visconti. Student protest? Traffic accident? No, a work of art.

The narrow street linking the Rue de Seine to the Rue Bonaparte is completely blocked on its entire width by two hundred and forty oil barrels piled twelve feet high.

The author of this creation called *Wall of Oil Barrels—Iron Curtain* is Christo Javacheff, a Bulgarian émigré who took refuge in the West. The comments on the meaning of the work abound. Some think it is France cut in two, others that it is a finger pointed at the dangers of consumer society.

But it seems that Christo intends to denounce the building of the Berlin Wall last year.

Why does he choose Paris? Maybe the Wall belongs in the City of Light and with the same rights as the Arch of Triumph and the Eiffel Tower!

CHRISTO: WALL OF OIL BARRELS—IRON CURTAIN. 1962

THE IMMATERIAL PEVSNER

PARIS

Anton Pevsner, the French sculptor of Russian origin, dies on April 12, at the age of seventy-six. When he came to live in Paris, in 1923, he became a sculptor. He used to paint. His first abstract painting was done in 1913. He came to sculpture by associating himself with the experiments of his brother, Nahum Gabo.

Pevsner studied art in Kiev, then at the Fine Art Academy of St. Petersburg, which expelled him after a few months. This son of an engineer liked to say that his two greatest artistic emotions were the discovery of the Eiffel Tower, in 1911, when he first came to Paris, and that of an icon in Novgorod. He used to say that the eyes of that icon followed him, alternately appearing hollow, then in relief.

In both cases, Pevsner was moved by the play of the hollow and void. Both in the icon and in the tower, a suggested and actual void defined an esthetic of space, which he developed in his later researches.

Pevsner followed the same path as many other Russian artists of his generation: Western painting, Impressionist and Fauve, seen in the collections of Morosov and Shchukin, icons, love for modern art and ancient Oriental forms, theoretic research and the Revolution, which he saw not as a rupture but as field for accomplishment and growth.

Gabo and Pevsner were the authors of the Realist Manifesto, out of which Constructivism arose. It was printed by the Soviet state and posted in the streets of Moscow, in 1920, but forbidden three years later. Its authors, now art professors, were forced to leave the country. Emigration allowed Pevsner to apply his Constructivist credo of which time and space are the two basic elements.

Initially, he does transparent constructions of metal ribbons and celluloid. Later, bronze laminated into thin wires allows him to build a system of unlimited spaces where matter becomes line and color is born out of the spectral reflections of light in the metallic net. Light deforms mass, hollows it out into shells and volutes; the hollow suggests relief, while fullness suggests a void. The use of oxidation modifies the work in time, depending on humidity.

A great artist has died. His sculptures announced a new esthetic, that of the ephemeral and immaterial.

(See also 1920.)

ANTON PEVSNER:
SPATIAL CONSTRUCTION.
1961. Paris. MNAM

THE IMPERSONAL ELLSWORTH KELLY

ELLSWORTH KELLY: RED, YELLOW, BLUE. 1962. Private Collection

NEW YORK

Minimal painting or "hard edge"? Seeing the impeccable and totally impersonal paintings of Ellsworth Kelly, made with simple and often primary colors, it is all but impossible to believe that he studied for four years at the ultraconservative Beaux-Arts Academy in Paris. He returned to New York eight years ago and participated in the movement against "lyrical painting."

Kelly, at the age of thirty-nine, is one of the very few artists in his generation who is not influenced by Abstract Expressionism. His flat neat shapes show him, rather, as Mondrian's heir. However, his painting is different from Geometric Abstractionism because he uses few shapes on the same canvas, sometimes only two or three colored shapes without structural and "hierarchic" relationship.

He goes on the lines of Alexander Liebermann and Al Held, who are also "hard-edge" artists. Like Kelly's, their color shapes impose their presence, deliberately without breaking the unity of the ensemble.

On the other hand, considering the simplicity of his forms, Kelly undoubtedly remembers Matisse's collages and the extreme purity of the Frenchman's lines.

MORRIS LOUIS' RIVULETS OF COLOR

WASHINGTON

Morris Louis has died at the age of fifty. He was one of the main painters of Post-Painterly Abstraction.

He used diluted paint that impregnated the fine unprimed cotton of his canvases and mixed itself with the texture in "stains" or spots unified with the support. In *Veils,* a series started in 1954, close tonalities weave "veils" in a painting as transparent as watercolor. Louis' work becomes more dense, especially in the series of *Unfurleds,* in which different parallel "rivulets" cross the lower corners of the painting, opening up the white space above them. Louis considered this series to be his best, because it is completely devoid of intermingling color and of atmosphere.

By reinventing the techniques of Jackson Pollock and Helen Frankenthaler, Louis searched for a totally free color that would not suggest depth and for shapes that would be impossible to distinguish from the canvas itself. On a canvas hung on his studio wall, he poured diluted acrylic paint, which ran down the surface. The result was his series *Columns.* Bands of pure color align themselves one next to the other in the center of the naked canvas, vertically, diagonally, or horizontally.

Morris Louis was surnamed "the Washington painter" because of the great preponderance of color that could be seen in the painting of this city in recent years.

MORRIS LOUIS:
ALPHA PHI. 1961.
London. Tate Gallery

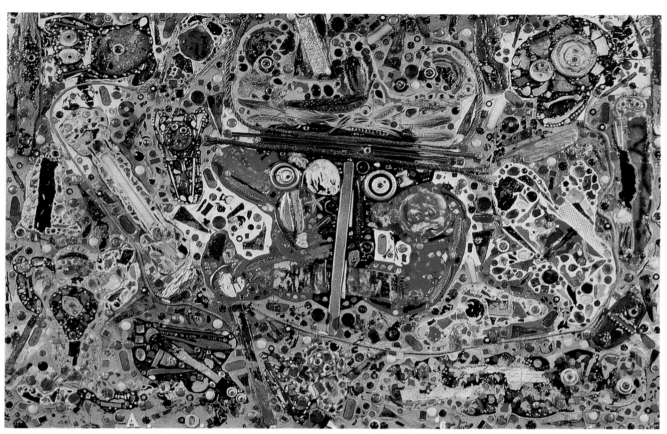

ALFONSO OSSORIO: LA BALANCE. 1961. New York. Whitney Museum

OSSORIO, PAINTER AND COLLECTOR

EAST HAMPTON, NEW YORK Jean Dubuffet decided to repatriate the Art Brut collection and install it on the Rue de Sèvres in Paris. It consists of a thousand drawings, paintings, objects, and sculptures, mostly produced by mentally ill persons. Since 1952, it was kept in six rooms on the third floor of Alfonso Ossorio's property in East Hampton, on Long Island, New York. The town is one of the high places of modern art in the United States.

Ossorio and Dubuffet met in 1949. Ossorio went to Paris to meet the famous Dubuffet, see more of his paintings, and talk to him. Ossorio was thirty-three years old. Dubuffet was flattered that a young and talented American painter, fifteen years younger than he, was so interested in his work. A solid friendship resulted.

At the time, Ossorio, whose family was wealthy, wanted to buy a property on Long Island, and asked Lee and Jackson Pollock to find one for him. He was in the Philippines when the Pollocks cabled that "The Creeks," the luxurious estate of the late portrait painter Albert Herter, had been put on the market here. The Creeks was a jewel. On nearly sixty acres of wooded land, it included a main building and a terrace on the Atlantic Ocean and two houses for guests and for the guard. Its vast studio with northern exposure was an artist's dream. The high-ceilinged music hall was the ideal space for hanging large paintings. It was at The Creeks that Ossorio helped his artist friends—the New York School

was still far from being recognized by art lovers and museums.

In 1949, he bought *Lavender Mist,* one of Pollock's main works, and organized Pollock's first exhibition in Paris, at the studio of Paul Facchetti, in March 1952. Besides Pollock,

HIS ALTRUISM AND HIS GENEROSITY OBSCURED OSSORIO'S OWN WORK AS A PAINTER

the main building of The Creeks contained works by Clyfford Still, Willem De Kooning, Lee Krasner, Wols, Fautrier, and Dubuffet, acquired at a time when they could hardly find buyers.

Ossorio organized, in 1957 and 1958, several important exhibitions in East Hampton. When artists had difficulties making ends meet, art dealers might not always help. Without

Ossorio's caring friendship and constant help, many might have stopped painting.

Dubuffet warned Ossorio that his altruism and generosity were obscuring his benefactor's own work as a painter. Indeed, Ossorio's work is not as well known as it should be. His paintings combine various elements, such as plastics, horns, and mirrors, which he saws, cuts, and sometimes paints in vivid colors and assembles on the canvas. In his studio the materials are arranged according to genre, on tables. He goes from one to the other, observes, chooses, and mixes them like paints on a palette. Gustave Caillebotte, also a painter, a collector, and a rich man, used to tell his Impressionist friends, "Nobody wants it, I buy it!" This is what happens with Ossorio. When will the world recognize that this Maecenas is also a great painter?

YVES KLEIN: A FAREWELL TO BLUE

PARIS

Yves Klein, "the Monochromist," dies on June 6 after his third heart attack of the year. He had one at the festival of Cannes, then at the opening of the exhibition "Donner à voir," organized by Pierre Restany, with whom he had founded New Realism in his apartment at 14 Rue Campagne-Première two years ago. He was not to know his own child: Rotraut Uecker, whom he married on January 21, gives birth to their son, Yves, two months after Klein's death. The child was born in Nice, where his father had been born thirty-four years ago.

Yves Klein was an expert in judo, a sportsman, and a charmer, as well as an inventive and challenging man. In 1959, he wrote an essay, *Dépassement de la problématique de l'art.* Although he was a founder of New Realism, he wanted to overcome reality and reach the cosmic horizon of infinity.

"Blue," he used to explain, "evokes the sea and the sky; after all, these are the most abstract things in the tangible and visible nature." He dived into this abyssal color and used it in his paintings and large murals decorated with sponges for the opera house of Gelsen-Kirchen. He exhibited *Le vide.* He used wind, rain, gold, and fire to compose cosmogonic art. He sold "areas of immaterial pictorial sensitivity." In short, he tried to demonstrate that art is nothing if it is not thoroughly unrealistic. It was his passion. Was his work finished, or was it just beginning? His premature death leaves the question unanswered forever.

(See also 1960.)

YVES KLEIN:
IMPRINT. 1961.
Life Size Visual Arts Library

Yves Klein hurling himself into space.

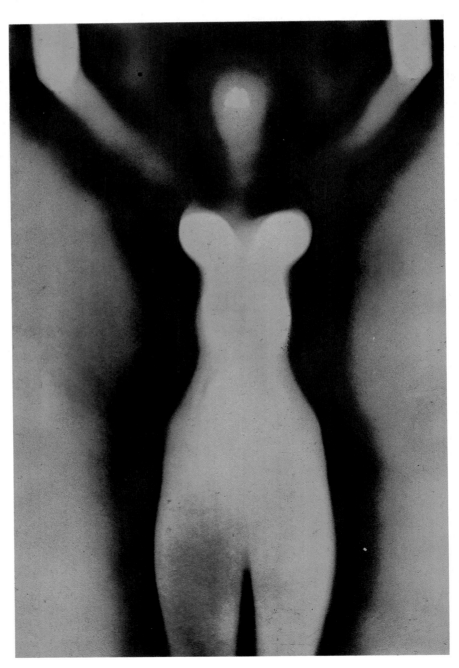

Sale of Maugham's Collection

The news that Somerset Maugham was selling his collection of paintings on June 10 at Sotheby's in London created quite a sensation. Most of the two thousand five hundred people who crowded the famous auction house had to participate in the bidding by way of closed-circuit television. The English novelist, who now lives in Saint-Jean-Cap-Ferrat, in France, removed the paintings that decorated his villa, "La Mauresque," wishing proceeds of the sale to go to a British writers' society so that needy writers would not have to do "small-time" work. One of the most exciting moments at the auction took place when Lord Beaverbrook, the British press magnate, and the American millionaire Huntington Hartford battled for Toulouse-Lautrec's *The Polisher.* Hartford topped the bids at 27,000 pound sterling. The paintings sold that afternoon attested to Maugham's good taste and intuition: Gauguin's *Tahitian Woman Standing* was bought by the writer in Tahiti for two hundred francs in 1916—and fetched 13,500 pound at the auction. Maugham's reaction to the 523,000-pound profit was typically cool: "It's more than I had expected."

REMBRANDT: SELF-PORTRAIT. 1629. Munich. Alte Pinakothek

Antagonisms 2 at the Museum of Decorative Arts

After Antagonisms 1, organized two years ago by the Museum of Decorative Arts in Paris, here is part 2. The museum's director, François Mathey, writes: "In order to create this exhibit, we asked sculptors and a few painters of very varied styles to express a new art of living through an object." Many artists strived to bring down the barriers separating the industrial society and daily life from art. Bernard Baschet's enormous machines produce "sound structures"; Bryan Gysin's "dream machines" are supposed to do just that; Yves Klein builds "architecture in the air." One can even sleep in Mathieu's formless bed.

Rembrandt's Third Eye

"Rembrandt was blind, but he had a third eye"—such is Salvador Dali's view, which he presented at a conference in Holland. "No one has noticed that one of Rembrandt's favorite themes, one that was almost an obsession for him, was the eye. There is the *Portrait of Homer*, the most sublime blind man in history, and the *Torment of Samson,* whose eyes were put out. No one has ever realized that Rembrandt's archetypal work is the blind man before God; all the master's works are somber except for the luminous circle, which is exactly what an ailing eye sees." Dali had no doubts that Rembrandt suffered from a double cataract; that he had a distorted vision of the world, leading him to create an inner eye that produced some of his finest works.

Informal Art Began in 1910

Does Informal Art go back to 1910, when Picasso was painting portraits of fragmented faces? This idea is being advanced in a short essay by Jean Paulhan under the title *Informal Art.* As usual, the well-known critic's writing is incisive and paradoxical, and puts an end to the pointless debate about whether it was Fautrier, Tobey, or Wols who invented the movement that is currently at the forefront of the international art scene.

Iris Clert in Venice

Art dealer Iris Clert, known for launching Yves Klein, Arman, and Tinguely, is, for a change, organizing her own Piccola Biennale at the palazzo Papadoli in Venice. Gondolas and motorboats jammed the canals as crowds came to the opening of this parallel biennale on June 15. Takis' "tele-lights" beneath the crystal chandeliers, and Fontana's "lacerations" under Tiepolo's painted ceilings were indeed striking. The event had been announced in the narrow streets of the city with banners proclaiming "Iris Clert in Venice."

Sonja Henie.

MAURICE ESTÈVE: FRESSELINE. 1960. Hovikodden. Henie-Onstad Foundation

SONJA HENIE COLLECTS THE PARISIAN SCHOOL

PARIS

Everything has been said about her blondness, her figure resembling that of a Scandinavian fairy, her silver ice skates, her Olympic successes, and her sixteen Hollywood films. But almost nothing is remarked on her careers as sportswoman and movie star, which, like Esther Williams, she tried to mix together. If Miss Williams, an excellent swimmer but a mediocre actress, succeeded in becoming "Hollywood's mermaid," people speak today about Miss Henie for another reason. At the age of fifty, she is the soul of one of the most important private institutions: the Sonja Henie-Niels Onstad Foundation.

She has gathered one of the most impressive private collections of modern art. The new Musée de la Ville de Paris presents a convincing ensemble.

One may be surprised that a foundation of such importance

THE FORMER OLYMPIC CHAMPION HAS BECOME AN ASTUTE MAECENAS

did not wait to have its own building in Sonja Henie's native Norway. The foundation, now one year old and owner of about a hundred works, originates many traveling and international manifestations. The Paris exhibition is the eleventh in a year, after others in London, Basel,

Hamburg, Frankfurt, and Stuttgart, besides numerous Scandinavian shows.

Sonja Henie's collection is received everywhere with an enthusiasm that seems to be lacking in Paris, judging by the first comments of the specialized press. The French reaction is surprising, considering that French art has an important place in the art world. It is true, however, that since the war, American art is praised the most everywhere.

The Parisian School is well

represented in the Henie collection. It includes Picasso, Matisse, and Braque, plus Léger and, more modestly, Gromaire and Bonnard. There is an exceptional concentration of artists of the second generation of this school. Fortunately, even though its momentum was slowed by the trend toward America, it is still strong in Scandinavian countries. Indeed, Miss Henie owns a group of paintings by Fautrier, Dubuffet, Bazaine, Estève, Lapicque, Manessier, Singier, and Nicolas de Staël. They glow in spite of the presence of Edvard Munch and of the Cobra group with its stars: Alechinsky, Corneille, Appel, and Asger Jorn.

UMBERTO ECO: THE FORM OF THE INFORMAL

A professor at the University of Bologna, Umberto Eco is, at thirty years of age, one the leading minds of the day. His book *L'œuvre ouverte* (the open work), released as a Bompiani edition, was an attempt to identify the structure common to various modern genres including modern musical compositions that leave the constituent parts to be connected freely by the interpreter, mobile sculpture, the semantic games of certain poets, and Informal Art. Eco also wonders to what degree a work's form can be left open without negating its essence. The passages that follow contain some of his reflections on these matters.

In the most spontaneous manifestations of Action Painting, the multitude of forms that assaults the viewer, allowing a complete freedom of interpretation, has nothing to do with the recording of an everyday earthly event. It is a gesture that is recorded. That is, a linear entity possessing a spacial and temporal direction rendered in a precise manner by a pictorial sign. We can glance the sign over, following it in all directions, but it is a field of (reversible) directions that have been imposed on it by a gesture (that is irreversible once it has been made). Thus, through the sign, we are being guided by the original gesture. We move along the lines, and we stop at the point of rediscovery of the gesture, which is also the discovery of the communicative intent . . .

In this sense, Informal Art is a rejection of classical forms with an equivocal direction, but not an abandonment of form as a fundamental precondition for communication. The formless, or informal, like any "open" work, does not lead us to proclaim the death of form, but to forge a more flexible notion, conceiving of form as a range of possibilites.

As an example, we can take a painting of Jackson Pollock. The disorder of the signs, the disintegration of contours, and the explosion of figures incite the observer to set up his own network of relations. But the original gestures indicated by the signs constitute orientations and enable one to determine the artist's intent. This is because the gesture is not external to the sign; it is not a point of reference to which the sign will refer us through convention. In other words, it is not a piece of hieroglyphics that could be reproduced repeatedly, evoking in a conventional manner the idea of a "free explosion." Gesture and sign find here a unique balance that is impossible to duplicate. This balance is the result of fusion of inert mate-

JACKSON POLLOCK: PAINTING. 1948. Paris. MNAM

rials under the action of formative energy. Our attention is directed beyond the relationship of forms (signs) to determine the relationship of gestures (intentions). Thus, a fusion of elements takes place, similar to the one that takes place in traditional poetic language in those rare moments when there is a unity of sound and meaning, of the conventional value of sound and its emotional value. This fusion is what Western culture considers to be art's distinguishing characteristic: the esthetic factor . . .

Once it is realized that the arrangement of signs has full control over the work's associations, these associations become an integral part of the work and take their place among the elements that the work incorporates, with all its creative dynamics.

UMBERTO ECO
L'oeuvre ouverte (*Excerpts*)

Braque the boss, as Jean Paulhan baptized him, Braque the inspector, is dead at the age of eighty-one, and so we lose the man who, along with Picasso, created Cubism. After Matisse and Léger, we lose another of those who brought about the revolution of modern art. Meanwhile, various trends are confronting each other as the Nihilists in Germany, grouped around Fluxus, claim art is useless, think it should be destroyed, and endlessly reinvent Dada. Opposite them stand those artists who, from Bacon to Prassinos and Saura, are convinced that Abstractionism has become academic, and who want to renew "figuration."

1963

S U M M A R Y

GREAT MASTERS

Braque's Last Flight
In Braque's Words

AVANT-GARDE

The Painters Join Fluxus

ART NEWS

Segal's Art in Paris
The Museum That Dare Not Speak Its Name
Paris Underwater
Record-Breaking Cargill Sale
In Brief

EXHIBITIONS

Birth of the New Figuration
Bacon at the Guggenheim

MANIFESTO

Jean-Louis Ferrier: the Idea of the New Figuration

GEORGES BRAQUE:
SWIFTLY, WINGS OUTSPREAD.
1956-1961. Paris. MNAM

BRAQUE'S LAST FLIGHT

PARIS

"His place is in the Louvre, just as the place of the angel of Reims is in the cathedral." These are the words of the minister of culture, André Malraux, in his eulogy for Georges Braque, on September 3, in the Carrée Court of the Louvre. The funeral is in Varengeville, Normandy.

It is a very solemn homage that is rendered by France to the most French of all painters, who dies at the age of eighty, in Paris, on August 31. The nation's greatest poet, Saint-John Perse, dedicates to him his *Oiseaux* (birds), the magnificent work published by Gallimard. This is what Perse writes about birds: "From the tragic banks of reality to this place of peace and unity, drawn in silence like a median point or a geometric place, the bird, escaped from its third dimension, cannot forget that it was first a volume in its ravisher's hand." One could not find a better definition either for Braque's favorite subject, the good-omen bird crossing the ceiling of the Henri II hall at the

"EACH OF HIS PAINTINGS IS A MONUMENT TO AN EFFORT UNEQUALED BY ANYONE BEFORE HIM"

Louvre to change into stained glass or jewelry, or for the spatial, yet deeply rooted, itinerary followed by Braque. As Malraux puts it, Braque's art joins "a brilliant and proclaimed freedom to the mastering of the means by which this freedom is obtained, unparalleled in contemporary painting."

While dreaming of blue birds, Braque did not forget his native Normandy. During his last years, he painted chariots, a *Sarcleuse* (mechanical weeder) left unfinished in her barely explored land. In his bedroom at 6 Rue du Douanier, in Paris, not far from the Montsouris Park, Braque kept and admired two old treasures: a landscape painted by his father, a building contractor in *Le Havre*, and a still life by Paul Cézanne, who had inspired him all his life. "Manet," Braque used to explain, "has nothing but the flower; Cézanne has both the flower and the root.

And what counts is the way from the root to the flower, where an entire life is concentrated."

His was the sober and withdrawn life of a painter-monk. He used to say that he was not seeking exaltation; fervor was enough for him. Under the arks of his interior shrine, built during his pilgrimage following in Cézanne's tracks in l'Estaque in 1908, he painted as monks pray in a Cistercian monastery. "Georges Braque never rests. Each of his paintings is a monument to an effort unequaled by anyone before him," Apollinaire wrote during Braque's exhibition at the Kahnweiler gallery. These were geometrical paintings à la Cézanne, about which the critic Vauxcelles used for the first time the description "cubes." It was the beginning of Cubism, which

Braque in his studio, 1949.

GEORGES BRAQUE: TOILETTE AT THE WINDOW. 1942. Paris. MNAM

Braque and Picasso led to the most poetical sense of the inner self.

The entire Braque genius was in this confession he made to Richardson: "I made a great discovery. I don't believe in anything anymore. Objects do not exist for me, except that there is a harmonious relationship among them, and also between them and myself. When one reaches this harmony, one reaches a sort of intellectual void. This way, everything becomes possible, everything becomes legitimate, and life is a perpetual revelation. This is true poetry."

Freeing himself from metaphor, that is from painting by comparisons and allusions, he reaches the metamorphosis and transfer of things "lit only by the poetic ray" in true bliss. It is a "methodical adventure," as the title of an essay by Reverdy on Braque defined it. It is demonstrated by the entire series of *Studios* started in 1949. They are "visions of mirages." The painting itself seems surprised by its mutation from gray to brown and from white to black. If Braque could say that "the vase gives void its shape," his monochrome painting, by absorbing colors, seems to annihilate them in order to exalt them better.

From Apollinaire to René Char, all the poets were sensitive to it. Char, who admired the *Studios,* writes to the painter, "You accumulate and crowd in them, with a genius' ingratitude, the eminent and useful forces of your dream and work. They take momentum from one another."

While painting remained for his friend Picasso a means of exorcising the most arduous ghosts, it was an end in itself for Braque. He used to say, "Painting knows the pictures better than the painter does."

(See also 1908, 1912, 1953.)

IN BRAQUE'S WORDS

When I begin to work, it is as though I already have my picture before me, only covered by that white powder, the canvas. All I have to do is dust it off. I have a small brush to dust off the blue areas, and I have other brushes to dust off the green and yellow areas. When everything is dusted off, the picture is complete.

It is not enough for what you paint to be visible. It must also be tangible.

There is art of the people and art for the people, the latter having been invented by intellectuals. I doubt that it was ever the intention of Beethoven or Bach, in drawing from popular airs, to establish a hirarchy.

Limited means bring about new forms. They invite creation and make style.

I like the rule that keeps emotion in check.

One cannot always hold one's hat in one's hand. This is why hangers were invented. As for myself, I have found painting to be a means of hanging up my ideas. This enables me to change them and to avoid any fixed idea.

Writing is not describing, just as painting is not representing. And verisimilitude is not trompe l'oeil.

When all is said and done, I prefer those who exploit me to those who follow me. The latter do not know me as well as they should.

The picture is complete when the idea is obliterated.

Reason is a pathway for the mind and a tumult for the soul.

Keep your mind free of concepts. One becomes obsessed by them. It did not require any profound meditation for man to drink from the hollow of his hand, from a hollow shell, or, ultimately, from a glass.

A remembrance of 1914: Joffre had no other concern than to redo the battle scenes of Vernet.

The artist who no longer encounters any resistance approaches perfection. But only a technical perfection.

With age, art and life become one.

GEORGE BRAQUE:
SMALL HORSE. 1939.
Paris. MNAM

THE PAINTERS JOIN FLUXUS

COLOGNE

Wiesbaden music lovers had the privilege last year of witnessing something new in the realm of concerts. Before some fifty listeners, the musicians broke the silence and . . . their piano.

The author of this musical event was an American, George Maciunas, founder of *Fluxus* magazine and a layout artist for United States Air Force publications in Germany. He gave an explanation, if it can be called that, in a conference at the gallery Parnass in Wuppertal, of the transformations that he wants in music. A sound is really concrete, he said, when it is closely related to the material that produces it. For instance, hammer blows on the keys of a piano do not only make sounds, they also express the toughness of the hammer. He added, "For the same reason, human language or eating noises are more concrete than artistic singing."

The entire questioning of traditional musical concepts by the Fluxus movement is contained in that statement by Maciunas. He is surrounded by American students of the composer John Cage: foremost among them George Brecht, Jackson Mac Low, Dick Higgins, and Al Hansen.

Music is the main concern of Fluxus, but John Cage considers that the notion of artistic specialization is completely obsolete. In his opinion, the contemporary world is a universal motherland where everything coexists and communicates. Maciunas and his friends, like Duchamp and the Dadaists before him, concluded that all art must be turned upside down.

This means that the production of paintings and objects has to end. In their manifestations, Fluxus members do antimusic, antipoetry, and "nonart." They make the public participate, especially in theater and music, but participation is duly conducted and channeled.

This year's event, which marks the true foundation date of Fluxus, is Beuys's joining the movement. In Cologne, on a warm July night, during a conference at the gallery Zwirner, Allan Kaprow exhibits a voluminous piece of fat. Beuys wants to bring an element of interrogation into the debate on culture and sculpture. The paradox is that fat, lard in this case, is essential for life, not a material used by the arts. Why not join these separate worlds of life and art? In Kaprow's opinion, lard may even be considered a symbol of Fluxus: It follows the double path adored by its fans—construction and destruction. It overcomes the will of its creator, because it is sensitive to temperature changes and melts.

Beuys's modest act tells a lot about the meaning of Fluxus: The events of this movement, which become international, celebrate the ephemeral. Because the birth of Fluxus is not accompanied by a manifesto, it greatly risks disappearing without a trace. On the other hand, because the practitioners try to preserve the unpreservable, Fluxus may get into the museums. People *are* talking about Fluxus.

A lively moment at the concert organized by George Maciunas, the founder of Fluxus.

Segal's Art in Paris

The gallery Ileana Sonnabend is organizing sculptor George Segal's first exhibit outside the United States. While he was in Paris to prepare the exhibit, the artist, born in 1924, created his first work off American soil. Entitled *Gottlieb's Wishing Well,* it is a plaster figure standing at a pinball machine. These figures first appeared in Segal's work in 1958; in 1960 he began placing them among elements of the real environment. The show will also include other recent works.

The Museum That Dare Not Speak Its Name

The discreet inauguration of Barcelona's Picasso Museum took place on March 10 in the absence of municipal officials. Only three hundred guests were on hand to view the wide selection of works, in particular the *Meninas* series after Velásquez. From his home in Mougins, Picasso oversaw work on the museum with a model of the building and photos of all the works to be displayed. He directed the hanging of the paintings and the lighting, and decided on the positions for panels and cases. A last-minute problem arose when it was found that there was no sign announcing the museum on the façade of the Berenguer de Aguilar palace, where the paintings hang. Picasso, who has sworn never to return to Spain while Franco is in power, is proud of his role as an "official opponent," which he is playing from afar.

Paris Underwater

The Seine runs under the famous Mirabeau bridge, and under the Seine runs . . . a highway? Paul Maymont, the creator of spatial urbanism, has just proposed building a highway along the path of the river that would cross Paris from east to west without the need to tear down buildings. Seven parking levels would accommodate five hundred thousand cars. Five other levels would be created for the expansion of department stores along the riverbank as well as for banks, swimming pools, movie houses, theaters, art gal-

GEORGE SEGAL: CINEMA. 1963. Buffalo. Art Gallery

leries, post offices and telephone companies. This underground city seems to be the solution of the future for overpopulation and traffic jams. Will Paris be the first city to have an underwater network?

Record-Breaking Cargill Sale

The art collection of William Cargill, an Irishman who, during his lifetime, collected Impressionist paintings, was sold at Sothe-

by's in London on June 11. The sale totaled over one million pound sterling, a new world record for Impressionist art. The previous record was in 1958 for the sale of the Goldschmidt collection. The event of the day was the auctioning of an 1889 Degas pastel, *The Dress Rehearsal.* The work was sold at 105,000 pound sterling before a roomful of art dealers from all over the world.

TANGUY DE REMUR: ILLUSTRATION FOR PAUL MAYMONT'S PROJECT "PARIS UNDER THE SEINE." About 1963

BIRTH OF THE NEW FIGURATION

FRANCIS BACON: RECLINING PERSON WITH HYPODERMIC SYRINGE. 1963.
Berkeley. University Art Museum

FLORENCE

Enough of the spots and the signs, contraptions of simple geometric shapes and monochrome paintings! Fifty years after its birth, abstract art becomes the most decaying of all academicisms! Yesterday, this accusation may have seemed backward or risky. Today, it drives the international exhibition at Strozzina, from June 11 to July 6, under the title "The New Figuration," joining thirty-four artists of ten nationalities.

It is organized under the patronage of Hugo Latira, the enterprising mayor of Florence, by three local artists, Antonio Bueno, Silvio Loffredi, and Alberto Moretti. Last year, they were the authors of the *New Figuration Manifesto*, which was much talked about in Italy. But the first shot was fired by the German painter Hans Platschek, in 1959, in an essay titled *New Figurations;* and in the same year, Jean-Louis Ferrier, art critic of *Les temps modernes,* published a long polemic study on painting figuration, in issue number 158 of the magazine.

The painters exhibited at Strozzina have the common idea that, after a period of lightweight avant-garde movements, the time has come for painting to become serious again.

They do not propose an impossible return to tradition and "fine art." Their idea is that art should make people see themselves and reality. Great creators such as Prassinos, Saura, Arroyo, Dufour, and Pignon are on hand to prove it. The idea is also expressed by Jean-Louis Ferrier in the catalogue of the exhibition.

"It is always around the human figure that all art revolves," Proudhon wrote in his time. The Florence exhibition, seen by many people, confirms it: Things have not changed.

BACON AT THE GUGGENHEIM

NEW YORK

The Solomon R. Guggenheim Museum on upper Fifth Avenue presents, for three months starting in October, a Francis Bacon retrospective. It is the first American one-man exhibition of the British painter. However, New York has known him since 1950, from group exhibitions. In the preface of the catalogue, Laurence Alloway writes that it is perhaps time to say about Bacon that he is a painter rather than an allegorist of fear, and about his work that it is painting rather than documents on the problems of the twentieth century and its difficulties and crisis. Bacon, who rejects abstract painting, which he judges merely decorative, often explains the meaning of his art. Far from repeating the patterns of traditional, objective, figurative art, he tries to project his own nervous system onto the canvas. Since his beginnings, his images suffer violent transformations. Most often, he paints after photographs clipped from newspaper. They are centered on horror and violence.

Bacon's characters reflect the anxiety and moral misery of the human condition; such are his figures of drug addicts and his studies for *Crucifixion,* a theme he repeats incessantly. They are symbols of a suffering that the artist tries to exorcise through painting.

MARIO PRASSINOS:
MELTEM. 1959. Saint-Rémy-de-Provence. Fondation Prassinos

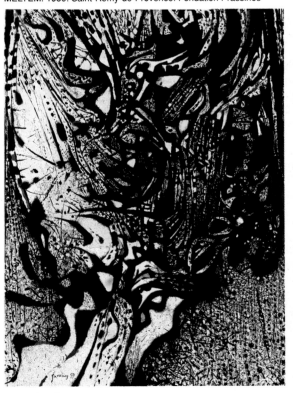

JEAN-LOUIS FERRIER: THE IDEA OF THE NEW FIGURATION

On the ruins of abstraction, a new form of representation is beginning to define itself, not by drawing from the past but by striving to create new structures capable of providing our world with a new and meaningful perspective.

It is important, however, to specify the terms of this new representation. Too many people, critics in particular, imagine that painting was once anecdotal, limited to describing grand events of public and private life, that it turned away from this anecdotal aspect during a half century in order to develop its strength, and that it must now begin once again to recount events. The problem lies elsewhere. Traditional representation is more complex and differential than imagined in our modern point of view, deluded by the scientific objectivism of the end of the last century. The individuals of the fifteenth century, in particular, never conceived of art as a passive means of recording external nature. On the contrary, for them it was a proposal concerning nature, a choice within nature, a creation and an action. Painters who currently try to unveil the new face of reality do not proceed with any less resolve. What they create on the canvas comes entirely from their imagination. But its validity comes from the fact that, rather than closing in on itself, it opens our eyes to ourselves and reality . . .

The walls of our museums and galleries are covered with narrative abstract paintings that amount to nothing more than poor imagery. Markings, smatterings, smudges, blots, squares, and triangles have undoubtedly replaced the shepherds and shepherdesses. But, as during the last century, these paintings use a pictorial language to tell a story, to speak wrongly about the absolute, nothingness, absurdity, contingency, and abandonment. Signs hover indeterminantly and pretend to encompass being while they are deprived of the most basic substance. Only philosophical discussion has, over the past few years, allowed for a sufficiently serious appearance of monochrome painting, a self-proclaimed New Realism that contents itself with torn-down signs, the different manifestations of a testimonial type of art ignoring anything

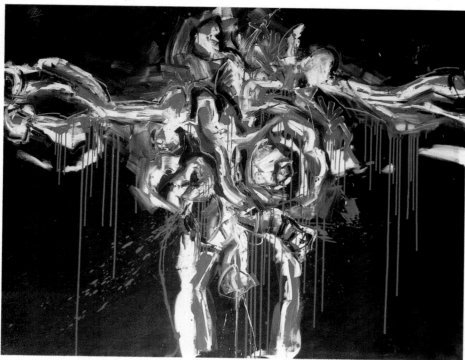

ANTONIO SAURA: LARGE RED AND WHITE CRUCIFIXION. 1963. Rotterdam. Boymans Van Beuningen Museum

having to do with the compromise necessary to language. . .

Moreover, one can clearly see the mistake of Socialist Realisms that consider art purely as a means of reproduction. Apart from the fact that the least little smattering by Pollock, with all of the energy behind it, is worth more than any of their stillborn works, it is indeed paradoxical that they intend to halt an image at a bygone point in the course of its history while calling for a historicism that is supposed to be geared toward the future. Their project, ridden with contradictions, is to copy a reality that has never been anything more than an approximated reality.

The only possible Realism today is a critical Realism that definitively situates painting and makes the universe revolve around it, an all-enveloping Realism of a sufficiently wide range. Some people may seek to impose upon modern painting the choice of being either traditionally representational or abstract, but this is a false dilemma.

JEAN-LOUIS FERRIER
The Idea of the New Figuration
(From the catalogue to the Strozzina exhibition of June 11 to July 6)

A storm breaks over the Biennale in Venice when that venerable institution, which has crowned universally known artists such as Braque and Matisse since the end of the Second World War, awards this year's grand prize to Robert Rauschenberg, a thirty-nine-year-old American artist. Does this distinction mean the end of European art, as certain people think, or wish? Another American event, this time in New York, is the publication of Marshall McLuhan's Understanding Media, a book as new as Pop Art. But the beginning of L'hourloupe, a new series by Dubuffet, and the death of Fautrier, initiator of Informal Painting, should be convincing evidence that art, making a mockery of nationalism, goes its own way.

1964

S U M M A R Y

AVANT-GARDE

Rauschenberg Triumphs at the Biennale
In Rauschenberg's Words
Dubuffet Changes His Style
Daily Mythology

WRITINGS AND THEORIES

Marshall McLuhan: The Medium Is the Message

GREAT MASTERS

Angry Fautrier

ART NEWS

Vedova's *Plurimi*
Oldenburg's Food Art
Documenta III: Quality, Not Quantity
Death of Roger Bissière
Chaissac: the Shoemaker Painter
In Brief

FOUNDATIONS

The Ideal Gallery of Aimé and Marguerite Maeght

ARCHITECTURE

Japan in Tange's Time

LITERATURE

UNITED STATES
Publication of several important books: Cassandra by John Hawkes; Nova Express by William Burroughs; Herzog by Saul Bellow; 7 Dream Songs by John Berryman.

FRANCE
Publication of Critical Essays *by Roland Barthes and* Le cru et le cuit *by Claude Lévi-Strauss.*

MUSIC

FRANCE
Maria Callas has a triumphant success as both a singer and an actress in Bellini's Norma *at the Paris Opera.*

THEATER

UNITED STATES
Premiere of Who's Afraid of Virginia Woolf? *by Edward Albee.*

FRANCE
Ariane Mnouchkine creates the cooperative Théâtre du Soleil.

MOTION PICTURES

FRANCE
Georges Franju presents Judex, *a homage to Louis Feuillade.*

UNITED STATES
Premiere of Dr. Strangelove: Or, How I Learned To Stop Worrying and Love the Bomb *by Stanley Kubrick.*

JAPAN
Hiroshi Teshigahara presents Woman in the Dunes.

ROBERT RAUSCHENBERG:
INTERVIEW. 1955
Private Collection

606

Robert Rauschenberg

ROBERT RAUSCHENBERG: CANYON. 1959. Pasadena. Art Museum

RAUSCHENBERG TRIUMPHS AT THE BIENNALE

VENICE

The 32nd Biennale quietly goes its way in the June sun, under the trees of the Giardini, then comes the American thunderbolt: the grand prize goes to Robert Rauschenberg, thirty-nine years old. The prize had always been given to veteran masters of the Old Continent. The organizer of the American participation makes no bones about it. "Anybody can see that the center of international art has shifted from Paris to New York," he declares to the press, immediately after the announcement. Thus, the first Pop Art generation is made official. The star of the day is surrounded by the Americans Jim Dine, Jasper Johns, and Claes Oldenburg.

Pop Art tries to express today's consumer society. Indeed, modern reality no longer identifies with the flowering meadows loved by Impressionists. It leads to the crowded metropolis, full of neon signs, Coca-Cola bottles, mounds of garbage, and the brutal images produced by the media and occupying our minds.

"ANYBODY CAN SEE THAT THE CENTER OF INTERNATIONAL ART HAS SHIFTED FROM PARIS TO NEW YORK"

Rauschenberg shows it quite well: Coca-Cola bottles, drifting pieces of wood, umbrellas, tires, and stuffed animals, shown not in paintings or sculptures but in "Combine Paintings"; the American flag by Johns, various objects by Dine and Oldenburg.

From an esthetic point of view, Rauschenberg is linked to Cubism, Dada, and Kurt Schwitters. From Cubism, he inherits the unclear plans and the rupture of space. From Dada, the idea of using any common object as a work of art. While Dada was essentially destructive, Rauschenberg's work seems an art of joy and exaltation, or at least the expression of a tender irony towards the American way of life.

"My works have the value of reality," the artist explains. "At a certain moment, perspective was a reality. Today, we know it is an illusion. In the same way, my Combine Paintings are actual." There is another declaration that explains his activity: "Painting is at the junction of art and life; I try to act in the gap between them."

IN RAUSCHENBERG'S WORDS

Rauschenberg studied at Black Mountain College, with the composer John Cage, who encouraged the introduction of life's casual items, city noises, and silence into art work. At the time, Rauschenberg painted white canvases on which only the spectator's shadow was reflected. He then made black canvases with crushed, pasted, and painted newspapers. Rags, ropes, chickens, eagles, photographs of President Kennedy, of the rockets about to be launched that we see in his Combine Paintings owe a lot to Cage's influence.

In turn, Jasper Johns works with simple everyday objects: letters, figures, targets, and maps: He is much like Charles Demuth who, in the 1930s, painted the figures and letters that had started to invade the city. As Johns puts it, he wants to show the "things that we see but never watch." His famous *Flag*, in 1954, moved people so much because it was a flag and an abstract painting at the same time, at the common limit between object and art sign.

Rauschenberg and Johns are great artists, both by the new world they reflect and by their artistic sensitivity. They are different from the new French Realists such as Arman or César, who often limit themselves to accumulations or compressions of garbage. Their work is poetic: Combine Paintings like *Canyon* or *Buffalo II*, shown in Venice, are masterpieces with a place in the history of contemporary art.

The greatness of the Parisian School has always stemmed from the century-long light that attracts energies from the whole world to Paris. Yet, in Paris, critics and art dealers were never so active as they are now in the United States. This should not turn art lovers away from Rauschenberg's huge originality. *(See also 1959.)*

I always thought of [my paintings] as being not passive but very hypersensitive, so that any situation that they were in one could almost look at the painting and see how many people there were in the room, by the number of shadows cast, or what time of day it was, like a very limited kind of clock.

I was very hesitant to just arbitrarily design forms and select colors that would achieve some preconceived result, because it seemed to me that I didn't have any ideas that would support that.

I had nothing for them [for colors and shapes] to do, so I wasn't going to hire them.

ROBERT RAUSCHENBERG:
TRACER. 1964. Altoona, Pennsylvania. Altoona Museum

. . . I didn't want painting to be simply an act of emphasizing one color to do something to another color, like using red to intensify green, because that would imply some subordination of red.

And then I became disturbed [by] the outside assumptions, the prejudices around the colors being black and white . . . The next move was obvious—to pick some other color. So I picked the hardest color I found to work with, which was red.

I was more interested in working with them than in their working for me.

In one painting I have a brick . . . it tended to look less like a brick because it looked like an architectural form of the particular material, and the only way I was able to let it look as BRICK as possible was to suspend it.

DUBUFFET CHANGES HIS STYLE

VENICE

At the very moment when Rauschenberg triumphs at the 32nd Biennale, Dubuffet shows his recent paintings at the Palazzo Grassi, on the banks of the Grand Canal.

This is new Dubuffet. He gives up the weather elements and landscapes that made him famous and goes to the city and its traffic jams, crowds strolling on the sidewalks, small-fry perpetrators, and street thieves.

Dubuffet called his new series *L'hourloupe*, a word minted from "loup" (wolf) and "entourloupette" (swindle). The sound of the word tells a lot about the artist's intentions. Unlike his previous paintings, these have paths crossing the space in a tight network around the characters, deforming and transforming them,

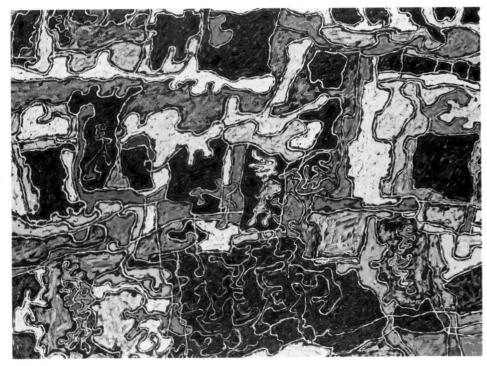

JEAN DUBUFFET: LÉGENDE DE LA RUE. 1963

expressing what a person feels when trapped in a crowd.

There is more. While his weather paintings have a telluric force that attracts the eye like a magnet, the shapes intermingled like a puzzle in *L'hourloupe* are

flat, tough, desperate. In Dubuffet's work, the next morning is always a disappointment. The artist does not believe in the progress of history, he does not believe in the benefits of culture.

The colors are essentially red

and blue, with some purple, thickly laid out. This, too, is new for Dubuffet. Although these works have some humor, the motto of this human, perhaps too-human, exhibition could well be "Man is a wolf to man."

DAILY MYTHOLOGY

PARIS

The exhibition at the Musée de la Ville on the topic of daily mythology is seen by some critics as a response to the American offensive at the Biennale in Venice. The exhibition, prepared a long time ago by a committee led by Gérald Gassiot-Talabot, excluded all "hasty Americanism." In fact, an attempt toward "Americanism" would have been useless anyway.

There is little in common between Robert Rauschenberg's "Combine Paintings" and the sexual demonology of Bettencourt or the collages of Réquichot. Perhaps only the Mediterranean dream of Martial Raysse has something in common with the American dream.

MARTIAL RAYSSE: SUDDENLY, LAST SUMMER. 1963. Paris. MNAM

Paris has its daily mythology. It invades the newspapers and television screens, and it gives the exhibition its theme. But the painters shown, namely, Rancillac, Télémaque, Cremonini, and Monory, even when they use comic strips or show life on

glossy paper, criticize the consumer society, while pop stars lovingly exalt it. As for confirmed artists such as Kalinowski, Niki de Saint-Phalle, Dado, and Faahlströn, their work has absolutely nothing to do with the archetypes of American society.

MARSHALL MCLUHAN: THE MEDIUM IS THE MESSAGE

The important fact about communication is not the message that is communicated, but the communication itself. Marshall McLuhan, the fifty-three-year-old professor from Toronto, has burst onto the contemporary scene like a cyclone. He rethinks everything: television, art, movies, clothing, money, books, telephone . . . all under the perspective of an electronic societ that is fast becoming ours. He is known, above all, through his much repeated motto, "The Medium Is the Message." The following passages are from his recent book *Understanding Media*.

In a culture like ours, long accustomed to splitting and dividing all things as a means of control, it is sometimes a bit of a shock to be reminded that, in operational and practical fact, the medium is the message. This is merely to say that the personal and social consequences of any medium—that is, of any extension of ourselves—result from the new scale that is introduced into our affairs by each extension of ourselves, or by any new technology . . .

To a highly literate and mechanized culture the movie appeared as a world of triumphant illusions and dreams that money could buy. It was at this moment of the movie that Cubism occurred, and it has been described by E.H. Gombrich (Art and Illusion) as "the most radical attempt to stamp out ambiguity and to enforce one reading of the picture—that of a man-made construction, a colored canvas." For Cubism substitutes all facets of an object simultaneously for the "point of view" or facet of perspective illusion. Instead of the specialized illusion of the third dimension on canvas, Cubism sets up an interplay of planes and contradiction or dramatic conflict of patterns, lights, textures that "drives home the message" by involvement. This is held by many to be an exercise in painting, not in illusion.

In other words, Cubism, by giving the inside and outside, the top, bottom, back, and front and the rest, in two dimensions, drops the illusion of perspective in favor of instant sensory awareness of the whole. Cubism, by seizing on instant total awareness, suddenly announced that the medium is the message. Is it not evident that the moment that sequence yields to the simultaneous, one is in the world of the structure and of configuration? Is that not what has happened in physics as in painting, poetry, and in communication? Specialized segments of attention have shifted to total field, and we can now say "The medium is the message" quite naturally. Before the electric speed and total field, it was not obvious that the medium is the message. The message, it seemed, was the "content," as people used to ask what a painting was about. Yet they never thought to ask what a melody was about, nor what a house or a dress was about . . .

Our conventional response to all media, namely that it is how they are used that counts, is the numb stance of the technological idiot. For the "content" of a medium is like the juicy piece of meat carried by the burglar to distract the watchdog of the mind. The effect of the medium is made strong and intense just because it is given another medium as "content."

The effects of technology do not occur at the level of opinions or concepts, but alter sense ratios or patterns of perception steadily and without any resistance. The serious artist is the only person able to encounter technology with impunity, just because he is an expert aware of the changes in sense perception.

Marshall McLuhan
Understanding Media (*Excerpts*)

JEAN FAUTRIER: MY LITTLE YELLOW BASKET. 1956

ANGRY FAUTRIER

CHÂTENAY-MALABRY

Irony of fate? The man whom Jean Paulhan called the "angry Fautrier" in a famous essay, dies of anger at the age of seventy in his home in Seine-et-Marne. The reason for the artist's fury: His daughter, born of a first marriage, refuses to be present at his second wedding.

He is the most Japanese of French painters, excessive and sweet at the same time. His game is to lead the viewer, in thought, to the most secret worlds of the human being.

He was born in Paris on May 16, 1898. His parents were from Béarn. He was raised in London and, like Picasso, he was an infant prodigy. He was admitted to the Royal Academy at the age of thirteen and exhibited and sold his still lifes at sixteen.

He painted skinned rabbits, cut-up wild boars, convulsive flowers, and, notably, the *Hostage* series of 1943, when he was hiding from the Gestapo. He knew periods of success, but didn't always make a living with his painting. There was a time, during the Depression, that he was an innkeeper, then a ski instructor, painting at night. The people who dealt with him in business knew nothing about his painting.

After the Second World War, he became one of the masters of Informal Art, loved and shown everywhere. He was instantly identifiable by the richness of his paste, better than the best enamel, with a range of tender pinks, poisonous greens, opal blues, sulphurous yellows, wine reds, snowlike whites, and crushed purples. He was never separated entirely from nature or the objects he studied. Matchboxes, fruits, landscapes, and naked women were pretexts for lyrical creation.

Fautrier thought that painting should perpetually destroy and reinvent itself, and he practiced his creed. Before anyone else, he used rich materials and colored powders. He thought that our eyes had changed, that our needs were different. He wondered why it was enough not so long ago to paint a black fish or a red tree to be considered an innovator.

Commenting on Fautrier's work, Jean Paulhan wrote, "It started in Saint-Christophe-de-Noissant with a gray lusterless mountain lake; a thin birch tree tried to cheer it up, but it was so weak that its color had a hard time staying on it." That was, the director of *La nouvelle revue française* believed, why the angry man, now dead, loved black and white. That was true at first, up to the 1920s, when the artist painted only figurative works. But once freed from subject, he became a wonderful colorist.

(See also 1943.)

Vedova's "Plurimi"

The Italian painter Emilio Vedova, a forty-five-year-old workaholic, has been invited to Berlin to work in Arno Breker's former studio for a year. There he created his *Plurimi*, assemblages of painted boards and pages from an "absurd Berlin newspaper." The piece he created for Kassel's Documenta is forty-six feet in diameter and almost forty feet high. A vehement pacifist, he has caught the attention of the Jerusalem Museum. Among those who have visited Vedova in his studio are the Surrealist André Masson, the Dadaist Hannah Höch, and critic Will Grohmann.

EMILIO VEDOVA: IMAGE OF TIME. 1951. Venice. Peggy Guggenheim Collection

Oldenburg's Food Art

The youngest of the American-influenced Pop artists is having a show at the gallery Ilena Sonnabend entitled "The European Table." Claes Oldenburg was born in Stockholm in 1929 but has become more American than some American artists. While in the States, his creations take the form of hamburgers, hot dogs, and ice cream made of painted plaster, but he has changed his menu for the Paris show. There one can drool over poached eggs and omelettes, *charcuterie*, fish with mustard sauce, loaves of French bread. It may not be filling, but it is fun to see.

Documenta III: Quality, Not Quantity

Unlike the first Documenta, which was a historical panorama, or the second, an overview of contemporary art, the third Documenta is narrowing its scope. There will be no "pseudomodern commercial phenomena," only quality work. Sculpture will dominate the scene at the Orangerie, with works by Henry Moore and Vedova. A vast area at the Fridericianum Museum will be given over to the Group for Visual Art Research of Paris, under the title "Light and Motion."

Death of Roger Bissière

Roger Bissière died at the age of seventy-six on his property at Boïssiérette, in Lot. Like Klee, he was the poet of the world's mornings. At the start of his career in 1908, he moved naturally into Cubism, decomposing the object, breaking up space, and fragmenting surfaces. This led to seemingly abstract works made up of patterns of squares with flat colors woven between, works that plumb the depths of the tangible universe. In 1958, he produced the stained-glass windows for the Cornol church in the Jura, a large eighteenth-century building. Bissière's windows rival those of medieval craftsmen in their grandeur.

Chaissac: the Shoemaker Painter

Gaston Chaissac, dead at the age of fifty-four, was an original figure in the art world. Neither his modest background or trade as a shoemaker predisposed him to art, but in 1937 he met Otto Freundlich by chance while on a trip to Paris. Freundlich introduced him to drawing and painting. Then Chaissac met André Lhote, who in turn had him meet Paulhan, Queneau, and Dubuffet. In Sainte-Florence-de-l'Oie and in Vix, where he lived with his wife, Chaissac led the life of a village shoemaker, while in the art world he was known for his paintings, collages, and painted wood pieces, all done with expressive verve.

GASTON CHAISSAC: PERSONAGE. 1961-1962. Paris. MNAM

THE IDEAL GALLERY OF AIMÉ AND MARGUERITE MAEGHT

SAINT-PAUL

The Maeght Foundation, the youngest of France's museums, and the first to be financed exclusively with private funds, is inaugurated on July 28 by André Malraux, minister of cultural affairs. "Thousands of years from now, somebody may put a plaque on the ruins of this spot, indicating that a moment of the history of spirit took place here," the minister declares.

A long path led Aimé Maeght, the rich art dealer, and his wife, Marguerite, to planning, building, and financing this museum. In 1936, the Maeghts opened, on the Rue des Belges in Cannes, a small store selling Clarville radios. Monsieur Maeght, who had graduated from the art school of Nîmes with a diploma of designer-lithographer, added, in the back room of the store, what today would be called an advertising agency. For the Maeghts' own satisfaction, they sometimes exhibited and sold works by local painters.

Things started getting serious in 1945 when the gallery Maeght opened at 13 Rue de Téhéran in Paris. The first exhibition was dedicated to Matisse, who had lost his dealer, Martin Fabiani, arrested for collaboration with the Germans. Then came Braque, Léger, and Giacometti, all without contracts.

The talent of the Maeght couple was knowing how to establish deep links with their artists. Bonnard loved Aimé like his own son, and Braque was part of the family. On the other hand, as a great admirer of Kandinsky, Aimé Maeght is said to have given the artist's wife, Nina, who was poor and coquettish, a taste for designer clothes in order to make her part with her husband's works.

Still, success was not fast. The paintings of Fernand Léger had no buyers, even at ridiculously low prices. Matisse didn't sell at all. Miró, Chagall, and Calder did not do any better. But in 1947, a Surrealist exhibition

The Maeght Foundation at Saint-Paul-de-Vence.

attracted the crowds. Two years later, an Abstractionist exhibition made the reputation of the gallery. Success was assured at the beginning of the 1950s.

The Foundation has two buildings linked by a lobby and opening on a vast terrace. It was built by the architect Josep Lluis Sert, author of the Pavilion of Republican Spain, where Picasso's *Guernica* was shown at the International Exposition of 1937 in Paris. Aimé Maeght has always been opposed to "closed museums, a labyrinth where you must pass in front of all the others if you want to see a painting."

Besides its private collection, which includes Léger, Bonnard, and Giacometti, the Foundation owns a few monumental works: mosaics by Braque, Chagall, and Tal Coat, stained-glass windows by Ubac, ceramics and sculptures by Miró. "I didn't get any work for nothing, I paid all the artists. I didn't call just the painters and sculptors of my gallery," Aimé Maeght specified.

Braque was really the initiator of the Foundation. The Maeghts had a son, Bernard, who died of leukemia in 1953, at age eleven. Braque advised them to try and forget their pain by building an "ideal gallery" on the twenty acres they owned in Saint-Paul. The initial plans, made in 1960, indicated that building would take ten years. Afraid of losing his gravely ill wife, Aimé Maeght had it finished in only three and a half. He wanted Marguerite to be able to see their Foundation.

Aimé Maeght, André Malraux, and Marc Chagall at the Maeght Foundation.

The Olympic area in Tokyo, built by Kenzo Tange.

JAPAN IN TANGE'S TIME

TOKYO

There have been fifteen Olympic games since that Friday in November 1892 when Baron Pierre de Coubertin, speaking in the grand amphitheater of the Sorbonne, proposed their revival. The sixteenth Olympiad gets underway on October 10 in the Japanese capital with the usual pomp: athletes' parade and oaths, lighting of the flame, the flight of pigeons.

It was expected that these 16th Olympic games would break records. And one was during the architecture competition, by Kenzo Tange, a fifty-one-year-old Japanese.

He is a prophet in his own country, where he cops many prizes, as well as in Europe, where he is honored by the Berlin Academy of Fine Arts. Tange is far from being unknown. Between 1950 and 1956, he built the Peace Center in Hiroshima, at the spot where

the first atomic bomb was dropped, on August 6, 1945. He then made a daring project: a new city on the bay of Tokyo. Tange was a challenger to architects like Frank Lloyd Wright, Walter Gropius, and Le Corbusier. The Olympic games made

A FUNCTIONALISM TRANSCENDED BY A THOROUGH KNOWLEDGE OF ANCESTRAL ARCHITECTURE

him an international champion.

The two stadiums, one large, one small, were designed for specific events. One is for the swimming competition, the other for events such as boxing and basketball. Both are exceptional successes. They seat sixteen thousand and five thousand people respectively thanks to roofs of canvas, made by a procedure developed in the 1950s and used to perfection here.

Stretched between two huge

reinforced concrete pillars, the roofing of the larger stadium has the longest span ever achieved in this kind of building. It is made of a prestressed steel net to which soldered and painted metal plaques are attached. The canvas of the smaller stadium is

suspended spectacularly on a single off-center mast from which it stretches radially.

However, Tange's architecture is not a slave to technology. He does want to be modern because he considers tradition incapable of creating anything, but his knowledge of ancient Japanese architecture is thorough. His memorial in Hiroshima is inspired by the ancestral shapes of Haniwa houses, which were built as tombs for the emperors

of old Japan. His perfect mastery of technique goes beyond Functionalism and reaches true poetry of space.

Tange believes that the artist must recover his rightful place in architecture. He asks, "Will current technology be able to move man's feelings?" He sees the need to recreate a synthesis of the arts rejected by a machinist society.

He is a daring city planner, as demonstrated by his project for the extension of Tokyo. He declares that the theories dear to Le Corbusier—namely, a place to live, a place to work, a place to relax, a street to walk—are obsolete. They do not respond to the needs of real life. He seeks "a new dwelling mode" taking into consideration the historic, economic, human, and political data of each place without which nothing can be built.

1965

SUMMARY

Le Corbusier, along with Frank Lloyd Wright the most famous architect of the twentieth century, dies of a heart attack on August 27 while swimming in the ocean off Cap Martin. Condolences pour into Paris from around the world. He is given a state funeral in the Louvre's Carrée Court, with André Malraux, minister of culture under General de Gaulle, presiding. But art goes on. Op Art is all the rage in the United States and Europe, and even penetrates the supermarkets, while Pop Art continues to be a topic of conversation. And, amazing revelation, Salvador Dali discovers what astrophysicists never even suspected—the Perpignan train station is the center of the Universe, which is finite but only on one side.

GREAT MASTERS

National Funeral for Le Corbusier
André Malraux: Le Corbusier Changed Architecture

DEVELOPMENTS

Dali: the Perpignan Railway Station
Ligabue Emulates Van Gogh

ART NEWS

School of Nice in the News
New York: New Capital of the Art Market?
Baselitz's Pornography
Alain Jacquet's *Luncheon on the Grass*
Calder: a Breath of Fresh Air
In Brief

AVANT-GARDE

Op Art Triumphs in America
Wesselmann's Fake Realism
Rosenquist's Artifices

LITERATURE

UNITED STATES
Norman Mailer publishes An American Dream.

FRANCE
Publication of Au cœur fantastique *by Roger Caillois and* Les Choses *by Georges Perec.*

THEATER

UNITED STATES
Controversial performance of The Beard *by Michael McClure in San Francisco.*

MOTION PICTURES

FRANCE
Jean-Luc Godard presents Pierrot le fou.

HUNGARY
Premiere of Miklós Janscó's film The Hopeless.

CZECHOSLOVAKIA
Premiere of Milos Forman's film The Love Life of a Blonde.

LE CORBUSIER
THE SECRETARIAT AT CHANDIGARH
Ind

NATIONAL FUNERAL FOR LE CORBUSIER

PARIS

Le Corbusier dies on August 27 of a heart attack, while swimming against his doctor's advice, at Cap Martin, in his beloved Mediterranean. The man who designed Chandigarh dies in the modest hut he had built between the railway and the gulf where he spent his summer holidays. The beachgoers who bring his body out of the water used to see him every day on his way to the beach. They called him "the old man." They did not know he was Le Corbusier.

On August 31, at 8 p.m., the Dominicans of La Tourette put his cask on the altar of their church. He had built their convent and used to say, jokingly, that he would have liked to end his days there as an auxiliary brother in charge of repairs.

Le Corbusier with his mother.

woman cut into pieces by her jealous husband. The press did not hesitate to accuse Le Corbusier. They charged that the crime was due to the blinding light pouring through the large bay windows, which, they said, rendered the killer crazy. It was a heinous accusation. All his life, Le Corbusier thought only about making beautiful "inhabitable poems" for modern man. In 1946, he was commissioned to build a housing unit that some still call the "Maison du Fada" (the crackpot house) on the Boulevard Michelet in Marseilles. When the commission was questioned, following the Geneva ruckus of 1932, Le Corbusier responded angrily to the authorities: "My patience has been tried for over twenty years. This accusation made me lose

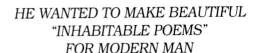

HE WANTED TO MAKE BEAUTIFUL "INHABITABLE POEMS" FOR MODERN MAN

On September 1, his body rests at 35 Rue de Sèvres, near his studio, before one of his tapestries. At 9 p.m., in the Carrée Court of the Louvre, in the presence of thousands of Parisians, André Malraux, minister of culture under General de Gaulle, renders the last homage. It is a beautiful official ceremony. A vase with sacred water from the Ganges and a handful of earth from the Acropolis are deposed at the foot of his catafalque.

Few artists are so much honored, and few were so much attacked, hated, and insulted. In 1916, in La Chaux-de-Fonds, in the canton of Neuchâtel in his native Switzerland, the town poked fun at one of the first houses he built. Because of its flat roof, they baptized it "the Turkish villa." Several years later, in an apartment of the Clarté, designed by Le Corbusier in Geneva in 1932, the police discovered the remains of a

all middle-class or capitalistic enterprises where my talent had been recognized. I think this comedy has gone far enough. This will perhaps explain the gesture I am going to make before so much ugliness and biased passion: I will leave France and take the offers that have been made to me for some time abroad."

He didn't hide his contempt, although he loved France enough to live there and become a citizen. "The French do not cross their borders, and they think themselves the most intelligent people; they would do better to find out what the others think," he wrote in a furious state to Malespine, director of social hygiene, who had opposed his conception with the results of a poll on the population's wishes regarding housing.

Like Michelangelo and Brunelleschi, Le Corbusier was also a painter and a sculptor. He would have dedicated himself to

LE CORBUSIER: COMPOSITION. 1942. Private Collection

ANDRÉ MALRAUX: LE CORBUSIER CHANGED ARCHITECTURE

painting if Charles L'Epplatenier, his teacher at the art school of La Chaux-de-Fonds, had not discouraged him. As it was, he dedicated half of each day to painting right up to the day he drowned. All his buildings, including the rigorous Villa Savoye in Poissy and the baroque Notre-Dame-du-Haut in Ronchamp and his palaces for Chandigarh and Ahmedabad, stemmed from the rhythms, proportions, and shapes first tried out in his paintings.

Glory arrived in 1923, after the publication of an iconoclastic book, *Vers une architecture*, which unsettled the art of building. From there on, he had shingle manufacturers against him because of his love for flat roofs, stone quarry operators because of his use of façades made of glass and visible concrete, and decorators because of his abhorrence of exterior decoration.

In Roquebrune, in the small marine cemetery on the side of a mountain, on a tomb designed by Le Corbusier for himself, an enamel plaque reminds the visitor: "Here rest Charles-Édouard Jeanneret, called Le Corbusier, born on October 6, 1887, deceased on August 27, 1965, in Roquebrune-Cap-Martin, and Yvonne Le Corbusier, née Jeanne Victorine Gallis, born on January 1, 1892, deceased on October 5, 1957, in Paris."

Le Corbusier's studio, at 35 Rue de Sèvres, where so many masterpieces were created and where so many prestigious architects learned their art, closes its gates in the autumn.

(See also 1923, 1931, 1943, 1951.)

While the Government decided that France should pay solemn tribute to Le Corbusier, it received the following telegram:

"The Greek architects, with profound sadness, decided to send their president to Le Corbusier's funeral to place earth from the Acropolis on his grave."

And yesterday:

"India—location of several of Le Corbusier's masterpieces and the capital he built, Chandigarh—will come to pour water from the Ganges on his ashes as an act of supreme homage."

Here, then, is the eternal recompense.

How beautiful that Greece is present in this illustrious coutryard which Henry II, Richelieu, Louis XIV, and Napoleon ordered by turns; and that this evening the pensive goddess is slowly tilting her lance over this coffin. How beautiful that the emissaries of the giant temples and the sacred grottoes are present, too, and that this homage is the homage of the elements. For these symbols are surely crying out to a fraternal symbol. Le Corbusier had bitter rivals, some of whom have honored us with their presence and some of whom are dead. But no one signaled the architectural revolution with such force, for none was so long and so patiently insulted.

He had been a painter, a sculptor, and, more secretly, a poet. He did not do battle for painting or for sculpture or for poetry: he did battle only for architecture. With a vehemence that he felt for nothing else because architecture alone responded to his confused and passionate hope of what could be done for man.

His famous phrase "A house is a machine to be lived in" does not depict him at all. What does depict him is: "The home should be the jewel case of life." The happiness machine. He always dreamed of cities, and the plans for these "radiant cities" are towers rising from gardens. This agnostic built the most arresting church and convent of the century. At the end of his life, he said: "I worked for what people today need most: silence and peace . . ."

LE CORBUSIER: AHMEDABAD HOUSE

This sometimes involuntary nobleness lent itself very well to often prophetic and almost always aggressive theories, to an enraged logic, which are part of the ferments of the century. All theories are doomed to become masterpieces or to sink into oblivion. But those theories have charged architects with the grandiose responsibility that is theirs today, the conquest of suggestions from the earth through the mind. Le Corbusier changed architecture—and the architect . . .

O Le Corbusier, whom I have seen so moved by Brazil's filial homage, here is the world's homage . . .

And here, finally is France—who so often misunderstood you, who was in your heart when you chose to become French again after two hundred years—saying to you, through the voice of her greatest poet: "I greet you at the stern threshold of the tomb."

"Adieu, my old master and my old friend. Good night . . ."

ANDRÉ MALRAUX
Funeral oration at the Louvre (*Excerpts*)

DALI: THE PERPIGNAN RAILWAY STATION

PERPIGNAN

The Perpignan railway station is the center of the universe! This is Salvador Dali's latest critical-paranoiac discovery.

"I live the reality of Riemann's curved-space geometry," the artist explains. "I feel in all my organs that a generalized relativity, everything that comes from the infinite, can make a loop and land at the Perpignan railway station. I collaborated with Einstein. I had another revelation, too. I got the certainty that the Universe is finite, but only on one side."

Curiously, the sources of Dali's discovery are the electric cables of the streetcar. They make a perfect circle. The machines turn around in front of the station before setting out on the boulevard again.

At the end of each summer, Dali and his wife, Gala, take their black Cadillac and travel from their home in Port Lligat to the Perpignan station. From there they ship to the United States his latest paintings. He experiences a feeling of intense jubilation every time he approaches Perpignan.

To make sure, he hails a taxi and asks the driver to motor around the station slowly. It is sunset. The yolk-yellow golden red light crosses the building and bursts like a flame from the windows of the surrounding façades. He raises his head and sees the electric cables. The universe reveals its secret—to him. As the confident of his discovery, Salvador Dali chooses the writer Louis Pauwels.

The yolk-yellow golden red light, Dali and Gala in a state of cosmic levitation, a streetcar symbolizing both the Perpignan railway station and the yearly sending of his paintings to the United States—the canvas is the culmination of the revelation.

"The only difference between a madman and me," Dali swears, "is that I am not a madman." Of course.

SALVADOR DALI: THE PERPIGNAN RAILWAY STATION. 1965. Cologne. Ludwig Museum

LIGABUE: SELF-PORTRAIT WITH DOG. Private Collection

LIGABUE EMULATES VAN GOGH

GUALTIERI

Fifty-six-year-old Antonio Licabue, nicknamed Ligabue, a schizophrenic, a tramp, a painter of genius, dies in Gualtieri, on the plains of the Po River. He was a savage man, with a tragic existential feeling visible in his self-portraits, which are similar to Van Gogh's *Man with an Ear Cut Off*. Fifteen years ago, the Italian press made him a hero. The price for a Licabue rose. He bought motorcycles that he drove without a license. He had a car with a chauffeur; he made the driver take off his cap when he opened the door. Licabue felt the need to be acknowledged and loved. He was fascinated by women. He had a brief romance with the daughter of his landlord, but rumor has it that he died never having been kissed.

School of Nice in the News

A Gaumont newsreel devoted to the School of Nice: quite an event, but one well deserved by the innovative institution. The School of Nice was started in 1947 by Yves Klein and Arman when they gathered artists who were tired of the Parisian School's Academicism. They looked toward the United States, toward the Dadaists and Marcel Duchamp. The involvement of Benjamin Vauthier, called "Ben," was the catalyst: He transformed his shop in Nice into a meeting place and an ever-changing work of art. His role as an agitator and his showman's flair have made him a pillar of the school. Arman, Robert Malaval, Robert Filliou, Gilli, George Brecht, Jean Claude Fahri, and Bernar Venet have won over the United States with their irreverent audacity.

New York: New Capital of the Art Market?

Those who thought that Sotheby's takeover of Parke-Bernet last year was a mistake were themselves mistaken. On April 14, the two allies gave a demonstration in New York of the soundness of their deal: They organized a dual art auction that was a financial and social success. At 6:30 p.m. was a sale of Impressionist and modern paintings whose eighty-seven lots brought a total of $2,345,000. Next, four hundred hand-picked guests dined on the third floor of the building at 980 Madison Avenue. The interior was transformed into a Parisian bistro from the 1870s, like the café Nouvelle Athènes where Manet and Degas met. After the meal, forty-three paintings from the Philippe Dotremont collection were put up on the block. Works by Rauschenberg, Picasso, Pollock, and Calder brought a total of $510,000. The last surprise of the evening was a preview of Mr. and Mrs. Charles Zadock's collection, to be auctioned in London.

Baselitz's Pornography

The painter Georges Baselitz has obtained a recovery of judgment: His paintings will at last be returned to him. His first private show took place in 1963 at the gallery Werner in West Berlin. Immediately, the press attacked his work as "painted trash" and "obscene paintings." An unknown until that moment, Baselitz was suddenly in the public spotlight, and crowds came to his exhibit. Legal and police authorities also went down to have a look, and the next day confiscated two paintings. The gallery owners and the artist were fined for "displaying obscene material in a public place," but on March 23 the court overturned the ruling in favor of the defendants, who had appealed.

Alain Jacquet's "Luncheon on the Grass"

At the gallery Rémy Audouin in Paris, Alain Jacquet is exhibiting a painting with a sense of déjà vu. His Luncheon on the Grass is, of course, a parody of Manet's painting. Three years ago, this twenty-six-year-old painter began to create "camouflages": maculating a photo of a famous work with road signs. This time, he has gone even further by photographing four young people in poses similar to the Manet, then blurring the image with colored dots by enlarging the photogravure. The resulting picture has little in common with the first photo taken. The idea of parodying a piece is not quite original; Picasso did it with Las meninas by Velásquez, and the same goes for this Luncheon on the Grass. Jacquet added a visual gag by placing a box of Jacquet-brand crackers in the foreground.

Calder: a Breath of Fresh Air

At the Alexander Calder exhibit at the Musée National d'Art Moderne, Jean Cassou quoted Baudelaire's statement that toys were "a child's first contact with art." Calder has retained the freshness of childhood in his contemporary art "toys." Over two hundred sculptures, paintings, watercolors, objects, and prints are on display, as well as parts of the famous Circus. Calder was noticed by Surrealists André Breton and Marcel Duchamp, who baptized his sculptures "stabiles" and "mobiles." Calder's works let us ride the wind of dreams.

IN BRIEF...

BRAZIL
The Biennale of São Paulo has the theme "Surrealism and Fantastic Art."

UNITED STATES
The Belgian painter René Magritte arrives in the United States, accompanied by his wife, on the occasion of a retrospective at MOMA.

At the Smith College Museum in Northampton, first retrospective of Willem De Kooning with paintings from 1939 to 1964.

FRANCE
At the gallery Kriegel, in Paris, exhibition of the young Spanish sculptor Berrocal.

With the Walt Disney Series of Bernard Rancillac at the gallery Fels, the comic strip enters French painting.

Foundation of the International Group of Prospective Architecture (GIAP), of which Yona Friedman, partisan of a mobile architecture, is an influential member.

ITALY
The gallery Marlborough in Rome exhibits the English sculptor Henry Moore.

ALAIN JACQUET: LUNCHEON ON THE GRASS. 1964. Canberra. Australian National Gallery

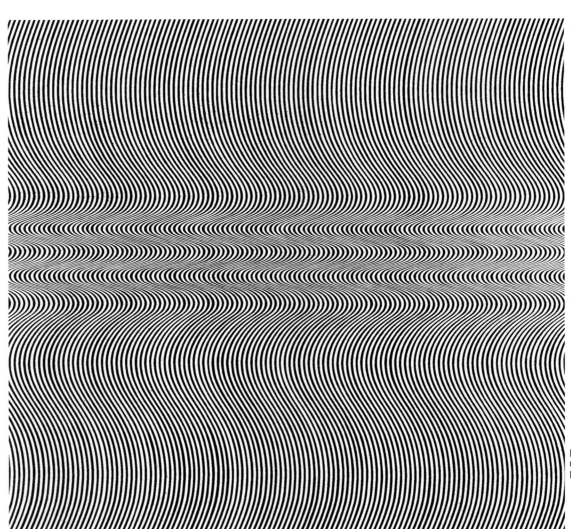

BRIDGET RILEY:
CURRENT. 1964.
New York. MOMA

OP ART TRIUMPHS IN AMERICA

NEW YORK
At the Museum of Modern Art, the exhibition "Responsive Eye" brings together artists representing an increasingly popular trend: Optical Art. It is painting played on visual illusions, such as line interferences, cross-hatching, scintillation, interchangeable images, and reversible perspectives that successively recede and advance, making it impossible for the eye to fix them in space. Among the originators of Optical Art are Vasarely, the inventor of Kinetic Art, and Albers. Contemporary as it is, the style has its origins in Geometric Abstractionism at the beginning of the century, Malevich's Suprematism, and Mondrian's Neoplasticism.

Besides "historic" artists, other participants in the exhibition are the Britisher Bridget Riley, the French Morellet, and the Americans Kelly, Liebermann, Louis, Noland, and Stella. The Americans are particularly interested in the juxtaposition of pure color surfaces that animate the canvas. They try to create a precise science of colored relations. Other artists, such as the Europeans and South Americans, use black and white color or plastic materials; with three-dimensional elements, they create optical effects that change when the viewer shifts his position. The paintings of Bridget Riley are significant. They are composed of precise weaves or graphs in black and white, dazzling the eye, creating a vertiginous feeling of malaise.

The public was captivated by the exhibition because of the care and precision of Op Art, in contrast with the "randomness" of Action Painting. To the amazement of artists and critics, the style has extended rapidly to diversified fields, such as commercial graphics, publicity, fashion, and magazines such as *Vogue* and *Harper's Bazaar* and even *Scientific American*. They have adopted and analyzed Op Art, for it seems to symbolize speed, the love of games, technology, and joy. In general, artists deplore the vulgarization of a creation that, in their view, is debased by "commercialism and the search for hysterical sensations." Vasarely doesn't think so. He believes in the social vocation of art, and is happy to see elements of his work being reproduced on dresses and shirts sold in supermarkets.

WESSELMANN'S FAKE REALISM

NEW YORK

There is no doubt that Modigliani would have liked Tom Wesselmann's painting. He detested Renoir. He used to say that he liked Pernod posters better than Renoir's pink, fat nudes!

Wesselmann has become known by his *Great American Nudes*, to which he devotes a series of many works. Like no other, his modern woman is tanned by lengthy sunbathing, kept trim by a strict diet, and is polished like a glossy fashion plate. It is not easy for a painter to push flesh modernism so far.

This thirty-five-year-old modernist, who has never left his native continent, could well be the remote heir of European Mannerists. In his recent works, illusion and palpable concrete objects are mixed, wiping out the gap between reality and the imaginary. The subject is the same: the American woman, standing in her tub, surrounded by radiators, curtains, towels, and towel holders. In a Wesselmann, the phone rings, the radio blasts information and music, the television is on. The effect is guaranteed: The viewer no longer knows where art starts and the space we inhabit ends.

The Mannerists, in the sixteenth century, accomplished this when they extended sculpture into the sky of a painting in an attempt to cancel the limit between the here-now and the space-beyond. But Wesselmann doesn't care about theology or religion. He turns the method upside down: He is trying to introduce perceptive doubt into our consumer society.

Rumor had it that the artist wanted to introduce live nudes

TOM WESSELMANN:
BATHTUB COLLAGE NO. 3. 1963.
Cologne. Ludwig Museum

into his paintings. He gave up the notion as too realistic! But it is additional evidence that, like the Mannerists before him, he tries—above everything else—to mislead the eye.

ROSENQUIST'S ARTIFICES

NEW YORK

Is he a Neodadaist? A Surrealist? A Cubist? A "Magritte of the Midwest"? Or even a "Kitschnik," as his detractors have labeled him? In April, Pop Artist James Rosenquist exhibited at the Castelli Gallery his *F111*, a life-size reproduction of the American fighter plane. There was plenty to surprise the unsuspecting viewer.

Rosenquist's admiration for Mexican Muralists explains the size of his work. He is also extremely well served by his professional experience in publicity graphics. There he learned technique and a precise, effective style.

Nonetheless, his painting is the opposite of publicity images, which he mocks. Rather than flattering the advertised object, Rosenquist plays on an assembly of random elements: razor blades, a comb, fragments of a face, a huge orange, and a field of spaghetti, all in the glimpse caught by the driver or the pedestrian of the posters of our urban landscape. For this reason, his *F111*, in spite of its size, is not his best work. Paintings such as *Sightseeing* or *The President-Elect* go much further in derision and the Symbolism of modern life.

JAMES ROSENQUIST:
THE PRESIDENT-ELECT. 1960-1961.
Paris. MNAM

Modern art can be divided into two camps. On the one side stands Giacometti, dead at the age of sixty-five after immortalizing sculpture. On the other side is a newcomer, the Happening. Giacometti is inscribed in the lineage of Rodin and Brancusi, whom he so brilliantly succeeded. For its part, the Happening, born in the United States, has triumphed in Europe and France. The contrast between the two poles is striking. The problem is to know where art stands today, to know if what is materializing these days is actually art. Warhol outlines one possible solution through lack of constraint and a sense of drama; Pignon offers another in creative reflection.

1966

SUMMARY

LITERATURE

UNITED STATES
Truman Capote publishes In Cold Blood.

FRANCE
Publication of Ouï-dire *and* Actes *by Michel Deguy, and* The Major Ordeals of the Mind and the Countless Minor Ones *by Henri Michaux.*

PERU
Mario Vargas Llosa publishes The Green House.

THEATER

FRANCE
Performances of Jean Genet's The Screens *at the Odeon are marred by demonstrations.*

DANCE

FRANCE
Premiere of Roland Petit's ballet L'éloge de la folie, *with Rudolf Nureyev.*
   Merce Cunningham presents the ballet Variations V, *with music by John Cage, at the International Dance Festival.*

MOTION PICTURES

FRANCE
Premiere of Fahrenheit 451 *by François Truffaut, and* A Man and a Woman *by Claude Lelouch.*

GREAT BRITAIN
Roman Polanski presents Cul-de-sac; *Michelangelo Antonioni presents* Blow-Up.

RUSSIA
Premiere of Andrei Rublev *by Andrei Tarkovski*

ALBERTO GIACOMETTI
DIEGO. 1952-1953
Paris. MNAM

GIACOMETTI, SCULPTOR AND PAINTER

COIRE

Alberto Giacometti, who at the end began resembling his work, reduced to the simplest forms, dies on January 11 of lung and heart failure, in Coire, France. He had been hospitalized for a month. He was buried next to his parents, who had died two years before. He used to travel every year to Switzerland to see them. He was sixty-five.

Giacometti was born on October 10, 1901, near Stampa, Val Bregaglia, in the canton of Grison in Switzerland. His father was a well-known Postimpressionist painter, and his godfather was the Fauve painter Cuno Amiet. In an interview by Michel Butor on the origin of his vocation as a sculptor and a painter interested only in the essential inner part of the soul, hidden under the appearance of bodies and faces, there was a significant revelation of a childhood spent in the mountains: "When my fingers feel clay, I see myself on the paths of Stampa, coming home from school, with mud on my shoes. The mountains start to undulate around me again. I see their ravines, calling me to the balconies of abysms, and their rock stairs, all stone and clouds. Mountain springs flow through my hands, echoes resound in my head, and birds of prey fly over all the carcasses of my life." When his fingers molded plaster, he was looking for the bones under the skin, the skull, the vertebrae, the entire inner body of man.

His main model was his brother Diego, himself a sculptor and decorator. They worked together in a seedy little studio in Paris, at 46 Rue Hipollyte-Maindron. Alberto did not pursue resemblance but an image of man reduced to a thread by the carelessness of the modern, absurd, faithless world—an upside-down world. "Drawing is the basis of everything," he used to say.

He was demanding, always

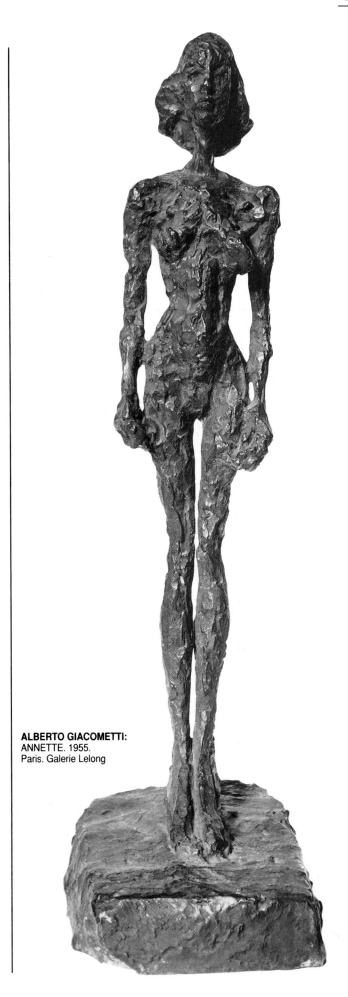

ALBERTO GIACOMETTI:
ANNETTE. 1955.
Paris. Galerie Lelong

Alberto Giacometti.

dissatisfied with his work. He tried to give the head an intimate precision and build the bronze figure like elongated, skeletal sentinels. In his modesty, he said, "But only the Byzantine knew how to draw. And Cézanne. That's all!"

If drawing was "the honesty of art," as Ingres defined it, it was true for Giacometti. He had an obsession with drawing that led him to the deepest anxiety. "It doesn't work!" he used to say. "If I try to analyze only the tip of a nose, it's enough to drive me crazy!"

After going along with Surrealism for a time, Giacometti came to consider it simply an attempt to fool the public. He also came to consider the dreams and desires, as well as the personal or collective unconscious that inspired his art for several years, as falsely profound; he decided they were much less enriching than the lessons of reality. He still gave Surrealism some of its most powerful and strange dream objects.

Giacometti reduced the human figure to its simplest expression. It has been claimed that his work in Geneva during the Second World War could be contained in a few match boxes.

He was admired by writers and philosophers such as Jean Genet and Jean-Paul Sartre. His petrified figures, haunted by the abysms of death, exert a deep fascination on them. One of the greatest artists of the century has expired.

(See also 1928 and 1935.)

JEAN GENET: ON GIACOMETTI

Giacometti's work makes our universe even more unbearable for me, so much it seems that this artist was able to distance what was troubling to his gaze and discover what would remain of man when the pretenses had been removed.

Beauty has no origin but the hurt, unique, different for each of us, hidden or visible, that everyone keeps inside himself, which he preserves, and where he retreats when he wants to leave the world behind for temporary but profound solitude. It is therefore very far removed from that brand of art that

tance between them and me has suddenly opened up. Where are they going? While their image is still visible, where are they?

It is hard for me to understand what they call an innovator in art. Is it by future generations that a work is to be understood? But why? And what will that mean? That they can use it? For what? I don't understand. But I understand much better—albeit very dimly—that every work of art, if it hopes to attain grandiose proportions, must, with infinite patience and application from the time of its creation, go back through the millenia

ALBERTO GIACOMETTI:
PORTRAIT OF JEAN
GENET. 1953. Paris. MNAM

we call "Miserabilism." Giacometti's art, it seems to me, wants to discover that secret hurt in every being and even in every thing, in order to illuminate them.

His statues evoke that curious feeling in me: They are familiar, they walk in the street. And yet, they go back into the depths of time, to the origin of everything, they draw near and pull away ceaselessly, in sovereign immobility. As my gaze attempts to tame them, to draw near to them, they —but without fury, without wrath or condemnation, merely because of a distance between them and me that was so compressed that I had not noticed it and so small that it made them think they were very close—fade from view: For that dis-

and re-enter, if it can, the immemorial night peopled with the dead who will recognize themselves in this work.

No, the work of art is not meant for the generations of children. It is offered up to the innumerable people of the dead. Who approve it. Or reject it. But those dead people of whom I have been speaking have never been alive. Or I am forgetting. They were alive enough to be forgotten, and for the purpose of crossing that tranquil shore where they await a sign—from here—that they recognize.

JEAN GENET
"L'atelier d'Alberto Giacometti" *(Excerpt)*
L'Arbalète, 1958

MINIMAL ART AT THE JEWISH MUSEUM

NEW YORK
A new trend of American art has affirmed itself in the wake of Abstract Expressionism and Pop Art. Characteristically, it concentrates on sculpture.

In an article published last year, "Specific Objects," Donald Judd, a theoretician and leader of this so-called Minimalist school, explained why he had left painting and taken up sculpture: The surface of the painting, regardless of how abstract, cold, and void of depth it is, always carries an irresistible illusionism; hence, the idea of creating a more radical art, based on the simplicity of geometric volumes in their most extreme formal rigor.

The title of the Jewish Museum's exhibition is significant: "Primary Structures." Variations are important, as are combinations and series starting from elementary figures whose formal potential is developed almost mathematically.

A work of art is thus defined by its visible material qualities and by nothing else. No metaphysical innuendos. For the Minimalist artist, sculpture is nothing but a certain number of volumes in space, rendering the space dynamic. His ambition is to define, through the most rudimentary materials, such as plywood, galvanized iron, aluminum, plastic, and wood, a new order of the space. The environment is just as important as the object itself.

"My works," explains Robert Morris, another leader of this school, "are not appropriate for all places, because the building surrounding them has a decisive role in the life of the object."

Minimalist works are characterized by huge dimensions,

SOL LEWITT: STRUCTURE. 1966

coldness, and absolute esthetic neutrality. Look no further than Tony Smith's black cubes, Carl André's metal plates lying on the floor, Dan Flavin's colored neon tubes, and Donald Judd's three-dimensional structures . . .

Certain artists, such as Sol Lewitt, with his combinations of geometrical elements—the cube is paramount—push the purge even further. Matter, with its weight, density, and energy, is superfluous. The only important thing is the logical mental operations leading to the placement of the object. Lewitt appeals more to the spirit than to the eye. His favorite sentence is, "Only ideas can be works of art." Other artists, even more radical, may reduce art to a mere concept. The Yankee Puritanism still surrenders to the demons of asceticism. Will Minimal Art, like Pop Art, invade Latin countries that have a Catholic and baroque tradition?

To define a new spatial order.
DONALD JUDD: STARK. 1965

THE HAPPENING: TOTAL ART OR CHEAP STRIPTEASE?

NEW YORK

Marcel Duchamp likes to tell about a Happening he saw at the Waldorf-Astoria Hotel in New York City. Two hundred people of high society, in tuxedos or evening gowns, did not hesitate to go down to a flooded basement of the hotel and stand in four inches of stagnant water in order to see a naked woman in various poses on a mound of coal. The most extraordinary detail, the Dadaist said, was that the woman was ugly, really ugly.

The first Happening took place in 1952. It was *Event* by John Cage, at Black Mountain College, in North Carolina. Cage gave a speech, standing on a ladder, while Charles Olson, on another ladder, recited poetry, and Robert Rauschenberg wound up a phonograph. In 1959, *18 Happenings in 6 Parts*, at the Reuben Gallery, wasn't boring, either: Allan Kaprow, a master of the genre, mixed up films, slides, and collages while several characters did assorted things at random.

But one could wonder whether the current fashion of the Happening, besides its jokes and tricks, is not linked—in Puritan America—to the discovery of the human body. There is almost no Happening without male and female nudity, of a young generation that eats too much, parading in front of an astonished public.

On the other hand, the Happening has to do with the games cherished by Boy Scouts and military patrols. On Long Island, Kaprow organized a Happening called *Gas*. The participants, coming from various places and fitted with precise instructions as to what to do, moved around like army troops.

Kaprow, who is forty years old, was an Abstract Expressionist painter. Later, he incorporated everyday objects into his paint-

ALLAN KAPROW: MONTAUK BLUFFS. 1966. Long Island, New York (Party of the collective Happening *Gas*)

ANN HALPRIN: PAPER DANCE. 1963

ings. Then he opened up his art so much that he was able to place live people into it. In the beginning, he used professional actors for his Happenings, making them rehearse. He soon realized that they were often stiff and awkward. He started to use improvisation and the audience itself.

Happenings are fashionable in Europe, too. The manifestations of the Fluxus group in Wiesbaden, West Germany, these past years, are of the same type. In Paris, Jean-Jacques Lebel organized a Happening in a theater on the Rue Fontaine. Standing on a ladder, Lebel urinated into some vials while a man in a hockey uniform glided on ice; there was also, of course, a more or less pretty nude. Besides the possible therapeutic virtues of the thing, it wasn't very interesting.

THE GRAV GROUP: ART IN THE STREETS

GRAV: a day in the street, 1966.

PARIS

On April 19, GRAV, a visual-art research group, an acronym of "Groupe de Recherche d'Art Visuel" made up of García Rossi, Le Parc, Morellet, Sobrino, Stein, and Yvaral, organized "a day in the streets." From morning till night, from one neighborhood to the next, the group asked passersby to experiment with the most heteroclite objects: a spring stool, a giant kaleidoscope, a sculpture that could be assembled and disassembled. The event was secretly filmed from a van that GRAV had borrowed from the post office for the occasion.

GRAV, in the tradition of both the Russian avant-garde of the beginning of the century and agitprop, has been trying for years to do away with the work of art that is reserved for privileged people and enclosed in places usually inaccessible to the population at large. One of the members of GRAV, Joël Stein, explains that he "wants to get out of the traditional circuit of galleries and maintain the closest possible contact with the public."

Founded in 1960, GRAV wants to fight the art market and artistic stardom. It is a partisan of art anonymity. It expressed itself with a kind of painting called "programed"; it is a research of surfaces, reliefs, optical effects, and mechanical constructions in space. Then GRAV created environments in casinos and public places. Each event is intended as a "collective feast," a prelude to the "free society" to which art is supposed to give birth.

NIKI DE SAINT-PHALLE'S LARGE BROAD

STOCKHOLM

Niki de Saint-Phalle sculpts as Arman accumulates, as César compresses, as Spoerri digests his diner leftovers in epoxy resin, as Christo packages, as Hains and Villeglé glue, tear up, and unglue, as Tinguely solders and disassembles.

She is a self-taught artist: "I dream of creating huge monsters to decorate gardens with. Today, sculptures are made of bronze and stone, and it's sad and boring. I propose color and variety in an architectural order. We must try and make life funnier. It's our role, as women."

The fattest and best of her women, Hon was recently presented at the Moderna Museet, a museum of modern art, in Stockholm. Niki de Saint-Phalle signed it in cooperation with

NIKI DE SAINT-PHALLE: HON. 1966. Stockholm. Moderna Museet

Jean Tinguely and Per Olof Ultvedt. Hon is seventy-seven feet long and twenty feet high. She weighs six tons. Hon is magnificent, and literally open to the public. She houses an aquarium, a bottle-smashing machine, and a bar in her left breast and a planetarium in the other. An exhibition of phony Dubuffet paintings is in her left hip. A red-velvet-covered toboggan is mounted on the generous curves of the lady. There is a lover's bench in her right leg. The visitor can watch Greta Garbo's first movie in a theater in one of the arms.

So far, two thousand visitors have come to live these astonishing minutes in the charms of Hon.

Theater According to Ben

Ben Vautier, a record dealer by profession and a crowd pleaser à la Marcel Duchamp along the Promenade des Anglais, has invented a new type of theater. Vautier, who in 1962 exhibited himself as art with a sign that read "Look at me, that's enough," sent a curious invitation to his guests: "You are hereby informed that the center for total art will present, on June 16, 1966, at the Artistique, 22 Boulevard Dubouchage in Nice, a piece of total Fluxus art entitled *No One*. The curtain will rise at precisely 9:30 p.m. and fall at precisely 10:30. Absolutely no one will be allowed to attend."

Barnett Newman's First One-Man Show

Barnett Newman is at last having his own show with fifteen black-and-white paintings. The title of the exhibit, "The Stations of the Cross," seems to evoke Newman's lonely years in New York. Explains the artist: "Jesus cried 'Lema sabachtani, why have you abandoned me?' It's the original question." But Newman is not pre-occupied by the metaphysical; his extreme austereness is explained thus by Lawrence Alloway: "Man is at the center of Newman's pictorial world, and it is from man that art comes."

Ben talking to a visitor.

use of color. Hofmann brought with him to the States the science of modern German and French painting at a time when little was known about it in this country. He was the only teacher to exert a strong influence on the American Abstract Expressionist generation.

Farewell to a Great Teacher

Painter Hans Hofmann is dead at the age of eighty-six. He immigrated to the States in 1930, where he opened the Hofmann School in New York in 1933 and the Summer School in Provincetown in 1934. Hofmann painted much in his youth, particularly during his years in Paris, from 1904 to 1914. More recently, he spent most of his time teaching. His courses were famous, and many of his students also became teachers and spread his theories. He emphasized the technical aspect of painting and gave fascinating talks on Picasso's drawings or Matisse's

The New Whitney Museum

The Whitney Museum is changing its address again, but will it be for the last time? Gertrude Vanderbilt Whitney's goal to present the American avant-garde to the public is a laudable one that has not changed since 1930. But while the number of works has steadily increased, the space for exhibiting them has not. The Whitney's first move was to 22 West 54th Street. Now it is on its way to new quarters on Madison Avenue. Marcel Breuer built the new museum, in collaboration with H. Smith.

The new Whitney Museum.

WARHOL SHOOTS LIFE AT THE CHELSEA HOTEL

Andy Warhol.

NEW YORK

Masterpieces do not take shape in heavenly places such as the parthenon or Niagara Falls, but in modest places: the bistro at the corner, a miserly studio, a humble hotel room. In France, they have been born in the Bateau-Lavoir in Montmartre, at La Ruche in Montparnasse, in old buildings full of penniless painters and poets. In the United States, many initiatives originated at discreet Black Mountain College, in North Carolina, and in the seedy Chelsea Hotel on West 23rd Street in Manhattan.

Chelsea Hotel in New York.

The elegant but now poorly maintained Chelsea was built in 1883 by ten rich art-loving New Yorkers. It was one of the first co-ops. It has always attracted celebrities: Mark Twain organized meetings with his friends there. In room 829, novelist Thomas Wolfe wrote *The Web and the Rock* and *You Can't Go Home Again* not long before his death, in 1938. In room 205, Welsh poet Dylan Thomas died in 1953 in an alcoholic coma. Arthur Miller wrote *After the Fall* there; he lived at the hotel after his separation from his wife, Marilyn Monroe.

Painters, both European and American, have worked, made contacts, exchanged ideas, thrown parties, and experienced existential anxiety there. Now Andy Warhol makes the hotel known to even more people through his movie *Chelsea Girls*, released in September

The move reinforces the fact that Warhol is not only Pop Art's *enfant terrible* but a caustic moviemaker as well. There are twelve separate episodes, filmed in as many rooms of the hotel,

without identifying them by numbers, probably out of fear of being sued by the management. There are scenes of drugs, sex, and, of course, violence, supposedly happening in the hotel, and depicted in three long hours of projection. However, like Léger's *Mechanical Ballet* whose main characters are mass-produced industrial objects, *Chelsea Girls* is a painter's film above all. The close-up faces, the projection on a double screen, and the almost complete absence of a script show the same quest and the same universe as his paintings.

Just as Warhol's paintings capture everyday life through serigraphic blowups of newspaper photographs colored with thin layers of paint, in the movie, too, Warhol shows an artist's life as absurd, dull, without interest in the romantic sense of the word. He is biased, but opposed to myth. Life in the Bateau-Lavoir or La Ruche wasn't all roses, either. In any case, the film is the opposite of how the subject is invariably treated in Hollywood.

(See also 1969.)

ÉDOUARD PIGNON: EVERY PAINTING IS AN ANSWER TO A QUESTION

By turns an underground miner, cement- and ceiling-maker, and skilled laborer at the Citroën factories before becoming a painter and a close friend of Picasso, Édouard Pignon, sixty-one, did not follow a dull itinerary. A great and tireless commentator on modern or traditional painting, he committed his thoughts to tape. Deciphered, but preserved in their original form, they were later published under the title *La quête de la réalité* (the quest for reality) in Denoël's Bibliothèque Médiations. Astonishingly lively, intelligent, and penetrating, they stand in stark contrast to the gobbledygook of the usual discourse on art, as the reader will discover in the passages that follow.

For me, the experimentalist does not exist. Or else he is not a complete man. We do not have these people who run experiments on one side and the people who benefit from them on the other. There is no point in the pioneer being merely a pioneer—he must make the entire voyage . . .

In the same way, or in much the same way, an artist is not a man who sees one way, understands in another, and paints in yet another. He is a man who understands the pencil or the paint brush. In attempting to express what he sees, he understands how things happen. He alone can conduct his visual experiment. And he must rely only on himself.

We notice that in our attempt to look, carrying in us all the knowledge, all the cares that are the products of the age we live in, we see things as no one else has seen them. Reality can please the entire world, for everyone puts a new face on it. I have perceived cockfights in that way, because in the second half of the twentieth century, I could see in them what would have escaped from my view, my knowledge, at any other time. The time had come for me to look at them. There are moments of perception which we are given by the times.

Potential for such moments already exists in space, in society. The truth appears to you at a certain instant, because you are prepared to receive it. For example, I went toward those cocks in the midst of an intense atmosphere in painting, of heated discussions, of extremely interesting battles of ideas, in the midst of an ocean of abstraction. In my childhood, I had seen cockfights like everyone else. But at that time, I had come to ask of them something that had to do with the pictorial restlessness of my times and my own restlessness.

Every painting is an answer to a question.

ÉDOUARD PIGNON: COCKFIGHT. 1960. Paris. MNAM

Every painting is my part in the dialogue between me and the painting of my time. These are answers that are more or less affirmed, more or less unambiguous, more or less sensitive. But they are the only genuine language. Obviously, it is possible to be deaf to these answers. But they cannot be prevented from existing. It is also possible to be deaf to the answers of Cézanne, of Van Gogh, or of others. The fruit of the painter's cares, borne by the times, will never be understood. None of that is in the air. The artist's work is steeped in the pictorial anxiety of his time, but at the same time in other anxieties, which are also political, musical, economic, literary. It is the complete language of his time that he speaks. A language common to all humans.

ÉDOUARD PIGNON
La quête de la réalité *(Excerpt)*

Which is it to be: Arte Povera or technological art? An exhibition of Arte Povera (poor art) in Genoa sees the only hope for salvation in a return to the earthly origins of life. In Paris, on the other hand, the official recognition of Kinetic Art and Lumino-dynamism at the Musée d'Art Moderne de la Ville points resolutely toward the future. The United States, for twenty years in the forefront of the world's avant-garde tradition, begins to look like the guardian of Classicism. One comes away with that feeling after the two retrospectives of Nevelson and Cornell in New York, while Motherwell's Elegy to the Spanish Republic series appears in all its beauty and gravity.

1967

S U M M A R Y

LITERATURE

COLOMBIA
Gabriel García Márquez publishes One Hundred Years of Solitude.

UNITED STATES
Publication of The Confessions of Nat Turner *by William Styron.*

FRANCE
André Malraux publishes his Anti-Memoirs.
Michel Tournier publishes Friday.

MEXICO
Publication of Alternating Current *by Octavio Paz.*

CZECHOSLOVAKIA
Publication of The Joke *by Milan Kundera.*

MUSIC

GERMANY
Karlheinz Stockhausen composes Hymnen, *playing electronically on various national anthems.*

FRANCE
Music award for Henri Dutilleux, whose mature talent is recognized more and more.

DANCE

FRANCE
Presentation of Maurice Béjart's The Temptation of Saint Anthony, *after Flaubert, and Pierre Henry's* Messe pour le temps présent.

MOTION PICTURES

UNITED STATES
Premiere of Bonnie and Clyde *by Arthur Penn.*

RENÉ MAGRITTE:
THE CALL OF THE SUMMIT. 1942.
Private Collection

MAGRITTE, THE MAGICIAN OF THE IMAGINARY

SCHAERBEEK

His last work remains unfinished, but it leaves us a message: a hand cut off on a closed book whose secret pages it will never turn. Belgian Surrealist painter René Magritte dies on August 15, in Schaerbeek. He was sixty-nine. Was his last work a premonition?

Almost his entire output, which sometimes depicted enigmatic casks, illustrates the conviction that he expressed quite clearly: "The idea that death is an absolute void is not contradicted by the idea that we live in mystery." He searched for the strange and the unusual. He joined an apple with granite. He put a glass of water on an umbrella. He did not trust dreams; they were too vague. When he was a child, his mother committed suicide by throwing herself into the Sambre. One day, a barrage balloon fell on the roof of his house. The world was inscrutable. It didn't take much to convince Magritte that the unreal was the mold of reality.

His "Esthetic Futurism" stage started in 1915. The encounter with de Chirico's *Metaphysical Interiors* led him to Surrealism. Through unusual visions, he

HE WAS CONVINCED THAT THE UNREAL WAS THE MOLD OF REALITY

wanted to express the unforeseeable and upsetting "forbidden images," the ineffable isolation that allows man to hear "the silence of the world." One night, in 1936, he woke up in a room where there was a cage with a sleeping bird. A "magnificent error" made him see an egg instead of the bird: "I had a new poetical secret." It dawned on him that a fact long buried in

René Magritte.

memory could burst out "in the light of coincidences." This was the recognition and the exploration of the unconscious due to the uprooting and the transposition of imagination. The duality of the perception of the world made it recover its mystery.

For years, Magritte had an advertising agency. He hated it, but it allowed him to earn a living. When success came late in life, he continued to paint in his dining room, as he always had done. If Dali is a mad Surrealist, Magritte was a Surrealist indifferent to precise, meticulous images and impersonal technique. "I would like my paintings to become unnecessary for someone to think about what they show," he used to say. He sought the self-effacement of the

RENÉ MAGRITTE: THE FIRE LADDER. 1949. Private Collection

IN MAGRITTE'S WORDS

"creative hand," so that nothing would distract the eye. His "loose" images did not lead the viewer to anything but the void of all things.

Magritte sometimes created or adopted archetypes, that is, mental images related to the depths of the personal or collective soul. "In short, one puts a dove on the bottom of a railway stationmaster," Picasso had said, mocking Surrealist painting and irritating Magritte. Surrealists try to "disturb," that is, trouble and scandalize the common person, to Picasso's annoyance.

Magritte was not simple. If he never took to the streets with a burning lion, he still knew how to make blue cubes fly in the sky and cultivate birds on their stems. Mixing up realms, opposing the natural to the artificial, he went back into the ages of the spirit—that's what made him so great, unique.

One day, someone asked Magritte whether he was ever commissioned. He answered, "No, I have to commission myself every time." He meant that the paintings came from his inner depths. He used to say, "Like a child, a work of art cannot be born before its body is complete; otherwise, it is aborted." The exceptional poetic force of his works stems from the extraordinary contradiction between the unlikeliness of their subjects and the resemblance of their objects. He succeeded in capturing the imaginary in the traps of reality.

(See also 1936 and 1983.)

In art, as in everything, there is evolution. The contemporary public prefers the mechanical saw to the silex saw which, in its time, was an ingenious find, the utmost, perfection; but this public will not concede or will barely concede that art evolves.

Invalids justify Cubism.

I am for a rupture with ancient or modern art.

When Rimbaud says he prefers idiotic, naive paintings, he is knowingly rebelling against an official, petrified art. But at the time, he was the only one to speak out that way. Since the time that everyone realized he had a similar preference, it is no longer possible to tolerate such a leaning toward painting.

It is difficult to think by thinking about nothing.

RENÉ MAGRITTE: THE BETRAYAL OF IMAGES. 1929. Los Angeles. LACMA

All things unknown that come to light make me think that our happiness, too, depends on an enigma associated with man and that our sole duty is to try to divine it.

An object is not so dependent on its name that another, more suitable for it, cannot be found.

The real value of art is a function of its power of liberating revelation.

The use of Automatism for psychoanalytic purposes is still of great value, like the use of the microscope in biology. But, as a poetic device, it has been made most ineffective through familiarity and its singularly indifferent effects, devoid of all charm.

The purpose of the art of painting is to make the gaze function perfectly.

He who sees is necessary to the vision of the world. He is a vision of the world.

Too often, by a twist of thought, we tend to reduce what is strange to what is familiar. I endeavor to restore the familiar to the strange.

The image of resemblance is what must be painted—if thought is to become visible in the world.

The mysterious is not just one of the possibilities of the real. The mysterious is what is absolutely necessary for the real to exist.

I always try to make painting something that will not be noticeable, something that is the least visible possible.

THE BIRTH OF ARTE POVERA

GENOA

This September, at the Bertesca gallery, Italians witnessed—astonished and perplexed—an event called "Arte povera IM spazio." Organized and presented by the art critic Germano Celant, it shows the works (many hesitate to call them art) of a new generation of artists!: Artistic creation is dissociated from the idea of culture. The exhibition is accompanied by Celant's manifesto. It is the birth certificate of this avant-garde movement, which does not hide its affinity with American Neodadaism and French New Realism.

By simplifying analysis, Arte Povera (poor art) wants to elevate the banal to the status of art. Its cult of poverty becomes the absolute criterium. Its logo is poverty of materials, means, and effects. As Celant says, it is an artistic and existential praxis whose language is designed to remove, eliminate, degrade things to a minimum and to impoverish signs, reducing them to archetypes. He adds, "Iconographic conventions are canceled, and so are symbolic and traditional languages." Art lovers are amazed. Five Italians—Alighiero Boetti, Luciano Fabro, Pino Pascali, Paolini, Prini—and a Greek, Iannis Kounellis, are the purveyors of this innovative movement.

They use a personal mythology sharing in universal knowledge through gratuitous gestures and acts often difficult to explain. Arte Povera bases its action on the surrounding space and solicits the spectator to participate. The demonstrations are organized with objects made of organic materials. In perpetual change, they reinforce the unstable character of intuition. Individual subjectivity and collective unconscious are both subordinated to the historic objectivity of the object in a complex situation whose only goal is to trouble the viewer's thoughts and contemplation.

Creation must be ephemeral (as opposed to consumer goods)

IANNIS KOUNELLIS: DAISY WITH FIRE. 1967

and a refusal to assimilate art to a product. These esthetic principles involve ridicule and parody based on metaphors. Pascali's playful sculptures of white plastic illustrate this aspect of Arte Povera. When he wants to evoke earth and water, he takes them directly from the natural world and literally puts them in the sculpture. Daily items are made into an autonomous language. Kounellis, in a different mood, introduces natural elements such as charcoal. He uses it for a purpose different from what nature had intended. He uses it to make the fire of the flower, in order to recreate a landscape where fire and charcoal are mixed in a symbolic dialectic based on the material as a mode of being. Mario Merz does not participate in the exhibition, but one cannot speak of Arte Povera without mentioning the thirty-two-year-old Milan painter. His researches are parallel to the movement. He is considered as one of its inventors.

Because plastic reality must reflect visual reality, an inventory of accessories, gestures, images, and facts is rendered commonplace by repetition, in order to expose the artifice and arbitrary character of the intellectual art language, which of course is considered to be merely speculative. This is what Paolini seems to say with his "painting of painting," a sort of theatrical setup where the image becomes alive and requires the presence of the object and subject. Fabro and Prini go further; they recreate the environment of their life. The public wonders about the future of such manifestations.

MARIO MERZ:
PREHISTORIC WIND OVER
FROZEN MOUNTAINS. 1962.
Paris. MNAM

GERMANO CELANT: BANALITY ELEVATED TO THE RANK OF ART

What has happened is that the commonplace has penetrated the sphere of art. The insignificant has begun to exist—in fact, it has imposed itself on its own. Physical presence and conduct have become art.

The instrumental sources of language have become the subject of a new philological analysis. Their renaissance has given rise to a new brand of humanism.

Film, theater, and the plastic arts spurn pretense, they tend to deal exclusively with reality and the present. Their intention is to abolish the conceptual by a pure presence. They reject any rhetorical complication and semantic convention. They want to observe and analyze the uniqueness of what is real and not its ambiguity as in the past. They eliminate from their scope anything that might resemble mimesis a representation, or a linguistic habit, in the aim of attaining a new type of art that might be called, in Grotowsky's words, "impoverished art"—"poor art."

Film—for example, Warhol's Sleep *and* Empire *and Andersen's* Melting—*is reduced to its simplest term: a single image that moves. It has become cinema again, as opposed to the movie. It reproduces the action and the present without cuts or montage. There is no subjective effect, no intellectual elaboration or narration. From a philological point of view, it rediscovers Muybridge, Dickonson, Lumière and leaves the field wide open for the language of action.*

The theater does the same thing. It eliminates written dialogue or reduces it to a simple voice-over, as in Ricci's Sacrificio edilizio. *It destroys any linguistic artifice and returns to the roots, to elementary situations. It arrives at phonic silence and gestural silence. Thus it rediscovers the art of mime and gesture. Gestural language replaces the written text. Elementary human situations acquire the value of a sign. The need arises for a real semiology based on the language of action. The body is raised to the status of a ritual altar, as in the work of the Living Theater. The text is constructed using the gestures of life.*

The linguistic process now consists of removing, eliminating, degrading things to the utmost, impoverishing signs in order to reduce them to their own archetypal dimension. We are in a period of deculture. Iconographic conventions are falling apart, and symbolic and conventional languages are crumbling.

Thus, in the plastic arts, visual reality is seen as it is, as it happens. They are reduced to their linguistic artifices. The image that is not connected to the essence of the object is rejected. Language is reduced to a purely visual element, devoid of any historical and narrative superstructure. The empirical quality of the artist's quest is given preference over its specula-

GIOVANNI ANSELMO: COMPASS ON STONE. 1967. Paris. MNAM

tive aspect. The accent is placed on the raw fact and the physical presence of an object or the attitude of a subject. Hence the painting of a painting by Paolini, his identification with an instrumental image, the amalgam of image and idea, and his analysis of visual and verbal language.

The takeover by the prop, by painting, and by space (space having become the space of the world) is the rule. They are returning to the essential primitivism of any visual operation. Visual insignificance, the language of the elements devoid of symbols that assails the beholder, whether he is specialized or not, awakens the horror of cultural reality.

GERMANO CELANT
L'Arte Povera *(Excerpt)*

CORNELL AT THE GUGGENHEIM

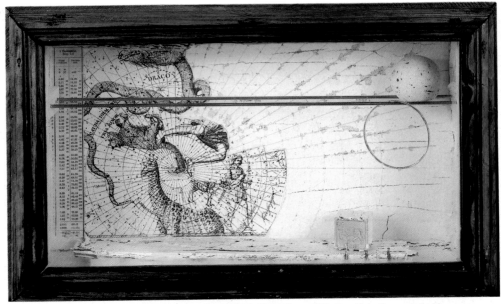

JOSEPH CORNELL: SPACE OBJECT BOX: "LITTLE BEAR, ETC." About 1960. New York. Guggenheim Museum

NEW YORK

Joseph Cornell has been known in artistic circles since his first one-man exhibition at the Julien Levy Gallery in 1932. Four years later, he was one of the few Americans in the famous show organized at the Museum of Modern Art by Alfred Barr: "Fantastic Art, Dada, and Surrealism." Today, at sixty-four, he again gains fame with his retrospective at the Solomon Guggenheim Museum on upper Fifth Avenue. His precious "boxes" framed in wood enclose a mysterious universe on backgrounds of sky or old prints. A discreet artist, Cornell lives in Queens and does not get involved in the hectic life of Manhattan across the East River. When he does journey to Manhattan, it is to seek out small objects in antique shops, including old photographs, souvenirs of unknown lives. In his studio on Utopia Parkway, he composes in his "boxes" a time he did not know

and countries he will never visit.

Hotel brochures inform Cornell of trips and remote places that he prefers to know only in dreams. His universe is without boundaries: His use of sky maps, such as the one enclosed in *Space Object Box*, reflect his fascination with the constellations of the celestial system.

NEVELSON AT THE WHITNEY

NEW YORK

Louise Nevelson is sixty-seven years old, but her exhibition at the Whitney Museum is the first retrospective dedicated to her work. Nonetheless, her importance is generally acknowledged. She was one of the first artists to extend the concept of sculpture to the concept of environment.

She started in the early 1950s the series that made her famous. The *Royal Voyage* was her first environment, *Moon Garden-One* her first wall of black boxes. *Dawn's Wedding Feast*, in 1959, was her first white environment, *Royal Tides* her first golden environment.

Nevelson was born in Kiev in the last year of the last century and came to the United States when she was five. Her family settled in Rockland, Maine. She returned to Europe to study painting with Hans Hofmann in Munich, Germany. She was an assistant to Diego Riviera. Her environments made her famous in her own right. They are composed of vertically accumulated compartments filled with cut or assembled objects, and they look like pieces of magic, useless furniture ascending from the depths of time. Which may account for their mystery and strange beauty.

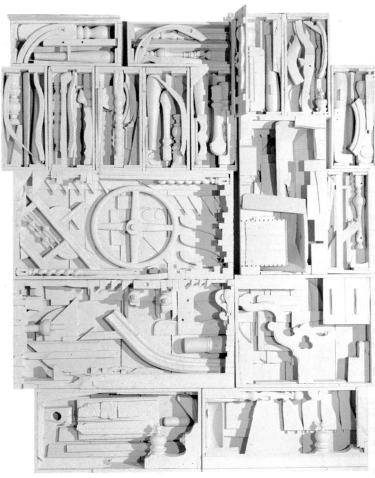

LOUISE NEVELSON: WEDDING CHAPEL IV. 1960. Paris. Private Collection

ROBERT MOTHERWELL: ELEGY TO THE SPANISH REPUBLIC. 1965-1967. New York. MOMA

MOTHERWELL, VARIATIONS ON THE REPUBLIC OF SPAIN

NEW YORK

Will Robert Motherwell be remembered for a single series of paintings with a constantly repeated theme? In his retrospective at the Museum of Modern Art two years ago, which featured *Pancho Villa, Dead and Alive* and *Mallarmé's Swan*, the most striking work was the series *Elegy to the Spanish Republic*. He had worked on it for twenty years. He now adds to it a new masterpiece, which seems to be its culmination.

The theme is the same, as are the shapes, or almost: large void spots contained between vertical bars, black on white, sometimes with a discreet color—hardly sketched reds or greens.

This series began in 1948 with an ink study, *Elegy No. 1*, an illustration to a poem by Harold

Rosenberg, the poet and critic who coined the term Action Painting. Or did it get underway a year later with *At Five in the Afternoon*, which was inspired by a poem by García Lorca—

THE SENSE OF THE TRAGIC IS INTIMATELY LINKED WITH THE EXALTATION OF CREATION

Motherwell here linking the funerary song in the memory of the bullfighter Sànchez Majías and the burial of a great culture after the advent of the Franco regime.

But the roots of his theme may go back even further in time. In 1937, after obtaining a degree in philosophy from Stanford University, in California, the artist was deeply moved by a speech given by André Malraux in San Francisco. The French cultural

writer was seeking financial and moral support for republican fighters in the Spanish Civil War. Motherwell's inspiration crystallized around Spain.

The *Elegies* are a metaphor with which an entire generation identifies. The sense of the tragic is intimately linked with the exaltation of creation. The presence of death and the faith in life appear in the works and thinking of all Abstract Expressionists. In the early 1950s, Motherwell generically named his works *Elegies* and placed them in the universal cycle of creation and destruction. The black and the white stress the hierarchism of his paintings. Their monolithic

architecture reminds the viewer of a mausoleum or a prison. Their crushed ovals are the symbols of sexuality and castration.

The *Elegies* are a relative of Action Painting, but their Automatism is much more controlled than Jackson Pollock's. Motherwell makes small ink drawings, then magnifies them by grids, as do traditional painters. The canvas is painted on the floor with long-handled brushes. This lengthy elaboration nevertheless gives an unexpected, exceptional feeling of spontaneity.

Motherwell's arduous work is comparable to a form of asceticism. He has the intensity with which Jackson Pollock and Mark Rothko explore both the same format and the same sentiment: the game of life and death. When is it going to end?

A PORTRAIT OF LEO CASTELLI

NEW YORK

The Leo Castelli Gallery celebrates its tenth anniversary this year. Who doesn't know this champion of Pop Art, which propelled its artists onto international stages? Jackson Pollock once exhorted Castelli never to become an art dealer: "You are not greedy enough."

The intelligent and cultured Italian opened a gallery in Paris

Rosenquist. On the occasion of the tenth anniversary of the gallery, the critic Barbara Rose remembered that Leo Castelli was one of the very first American dealers to pay a monthly salary to some of his artists, allowing them to paint instead of wasting time earning a living in other pursuits.

He also drew the attention of the country to contemporary art,

HE DREW THE ATTENTION OF THE COUNTRY TO CONTEMPORARY ART

in 1939, in time for a successful Surrealist exhibition. The war started, and Castelli sailed for the United States. In 1957, with his wife, Ileana Sonnabend, he opened a gallery at 4 East 77th Street, exhibiting Willem De Kooning, Delaunay, Dubuffet, Léger, and David Smith. He encouraged young talent, such as Jasper Johns, Robert Rauschenberg, Marisol Escobar, Frank Stella, Cy Twombly, Roy Lichtenstein, Andy Warhol, and James

thanks to continuous contacts with museum curators, art critics, and writers. Barbara Rose wrote that Leo was influenced, like almost all the artists of his gallery, by the ideas of Cage and Cunningham, ideas opposed to the metaphysics of anxiety and crisis of Abstract Expressionism.

The Castelli Gallery became the heart of the anti-Expressionistic feelings of the 1950s.

MARISOL ESCOBAR: RUTH. 1962. Massachusetts. Rose Art Museum

One of the many artists launched by Leo Castelli.

THE LEGROS AFFAIR

DALLAS

Naive trust, esthetic inexperience and the lure of good business! If the Algur Hurtle Meadows collection had been authentic, it would have been worth at least three million dollars. But surely he didn't pay more than two hundred fifty thousand dollars for all of it.

Meadows, an oil magnate, a director of Republic National Bank and a benefactor of

Methodist University of the South, contacted the Parisian art dealer Alex Maguy last year. He wanted to buy Fauve paintings, but found them too expensive. So he made an arrangement with another dealer, Fernand Legros, who sold him works by Derain, Modigliani, Vlaminck, and Marquet, all certified. They are all fakes.

The affair exploded at the beginning of the year, during a second-rate sale organized in Pontoise by Martinot, auctioneer. Legros had offered two watercolors by Dufy and one by Vlaminck and one painting from Derain's Fauve period. The four

were certified, and Martinot, delighted to present the Derain, published it on the cover of his catalogue. The Derain was quickly denounced as a fake by other dealers, and all the works sent by Legros had to be withdrawn from auction. And so Fernand Legros, an ex-dancer from the ballets of the Count de Cuevas, sporting cowboy hats, black glasses, loud necklaces, and a chauffeured Rolls, was exposed.

At the same time, in the United States, the Association of American Art Dealers estimated that the entire Meadows collection was counterfeit. American

law allows taxpayers to deduct from their taxable income art donated to museums. Many people buy an indistinct painting of the Parisian School for a hundred dollars and donate it to their town museum, which then places a much higher value on it. Perhaps Algur Hurtle Meadows knew what he was doing.

But the affair is serious because Legros supplied modern paintings to many collectors. Two questions are raised: How could reputable experts certify counterfeits? Who is the counterfeiter?

Picasso Plebiscite

The citizens of Basel voted to decide if the Kunstmuseum should keep *The Two Brothers* and *Sitting Harlequin* by Picasso, which had been stored there for several years. The paintings belonged to Peter Staelin, the owner of Balair, a small airline. One of its craft had recently been damaged, and Balair needed money to compensate the victims' relatives. The city council had approved a six-million-Swiss-franc credit line to buy the two paintings, but a garage owner thought other expenses were more pressing. He was able to get the one thousand votes necessary for a referendum. The people of Basel still voted thirty-two thousand for and twenty-seven thousand against keeping the works of art. The day before the vote, the Kuntsmuseum had organized a big fair; schoolchildren went through the streets, asking for donations to meet the cost of the purchase. Declared Picasso: "This is the first time that the people have imposed their will in an artistic and cultural matter."

PABLO PICASSO:
SITTING HARLEQUIN. 1923.
Basel. Kunstmuseum

Birth of Land Art

Rejection of the museum as the center of artistic activity; rejection of traditionally conceived works of art: Such was the message being spread by Duchamp fifty years ago, and it was later repeated by Walter De Maria. In 1960, De Maria organized a happening called *Art Yard,* the goal of which was to dig an enormous hole. Today, a group of artists is attempting to interact with nature itself. Denis Oppenheim just poured a red dye into the sea, plus gasoline which he set on fire. Carl André of Minimal Art fame is piling rocks on top of one another in Aspen, Colorado. Are they communing with nature, or protesting?

César's Expansions

César drew notice at the 1960 Salon de Mai with his three compacted auto bodies, and critic Pierre Restany saluted a brilliant new proponent of New Realism. Today the sculptor is discovering the "explosive" possibilities of plastic, which is the stuff of his latest creation. Entitled *Orange Expansion,* it is a sixteen-foot-long piece of poured polyurethane. "After mechanical quantitative language, chemical quantitative language; after scrap metal, plastic; after compression, expansion," stated Pierre Restany, satisfied that no Neodadaist would have dared to go so far.

César creates an "Expansion."

IN BRIEF...

UNITED STATES
Sam Francis retrospective at the Houston Museum.
The Knoedler Gallery presents an exhibition of the designs and sculptures of Raymond Duchamp-Villon.
At the Pierre Matisse Gallery, Joan Miró exhibits The Sun Bird, The Moon Bird, *and* Sparks.

FRANCE
The Maeght Foundation of Saint-Paul-de-Vence holds an exhibition on "Ten Years of Living Art, 1955-1965."
In Paris, the gallery Rive Gauche presents "22 Painters of a Different Kind of Figuration," including works by Ljuba.

ITALY
Valerio Adami exhibits at Milan at the studio Marconi and at the gallery Schwartz.

SWITZERLAND
Death of Johannes Itten. Professor at the Bauhaus before founding his own school in Berlin, he later directed the School and the Museum of Arts and Trades in Zurich.

BMPT: the Group of Four

On June 2, they had an exhibit in the conference room of the Museum of Decorative Arts. Four artists—Daniel Buren, Olivier Mosset, Michel Parmentier, and Niele Toroni, known collectively by their initials as BMPT—hung four paintings facing the public. Buren's had vertical lines; white with a black circle in the middle for Mosset; wide horizontal stripes for Parmentier; dots for Toroni. With the public sitting quietly, a text was distributed containing a precise and strictly neutral description of the works. Marcel Duchamp was there and gave his opinion as he left: "For a frustrating happening, you couldn't do better."

LIGHT AND MOTION

PARIS

The Musée d'Art Moderne de la Ville presents the first Kinetic Art exhibition ever organized by a French museum: Under the title "Light and Motion" it shows works "created by actual motion and artificial light" by artists working in Paris. For the past ten years, this city has been the capital of this new art form.

The conception of the exhibition, which tries to be a manifesto of the trend, explains its origins. For the longest time, artists have been trying to "sculpt light." In the eighteenth century, Father Castel, a Jesuit, invented the color organ. In 1910, the composer Aleksandr Scriabin introduced a "light piano" into a score. Vladimir Baranoff-Rossiné presented his *Optophonic Piano*. Marcel Duchamp, the American Franck Malina, and the sculptors Gabo and Moholy-Nagy provided continuity to this endeavor until the end of the 1950s.

SINCE THE EIGHTEENTH CENTURY, ARTISTS HAVE BEEN TRYING TO "SCULPT LIGHT"

It is impossible to list everything on display at the museum. The best known artists are Agam, Bury, Le Parc, Takis, Tinguely, and Vasarely.

Among the most original and spectacular works is Kramer's chair. It is made of various elements. Water flows through. Bulky parts move on wheels and pulleys. The chair is after the image of machines made by Tinguely and presented in a film. As for Takis, he uses the invisible force of electromagnetism. It creates around his works an atmosphere of mysterious communication, taken from railways signals. Nicolas Schöffer, inventor of "Luminodynamism" and creator of *Cysp I*, the first "autonomous cybernetic sculpture," presents his series *Lux*. These works are large prisms whose interiors are decorated with mirrors projecting light effects into space. Carrera uses the force of an air turbine. The artists attracted by architecture—Soto, Duarte, and Cruz-Diez—present "vibration walls" and "colored atmospheres."

The exhibition invites the public to act and cooperate in creations. The visitor can enter booths, push buttons, and even pass through the field of a photoelectric cell that triggers light sources. Some effects are realized only via speech. Kinetic Art promotes the integration of art into society and man into the work. For its devotees, it represents the century of light that is entered, in their opinion, a little more every day.

In Nicolas Schöffer's studio. From left to right: *Prism, Chronos Sculpture,* and a model for the *Cybernetic Tower.*

"TERRE DES HOMMES" ON THE ST. LAWRENCE

MONTREAL

The international Expo 67 on the topic "Terre des hommes" (Man and His World) opens in late April. It covers the impressive surface of nearly one thousand acres and is built "on" the St. Lawrence River. Doubling the surface of St. Helen's Island, another island was created ex nihilo: Notre-Dame, on which the main pavilions are built.

Modern-art lovers enjoy subject or national exhibitions; for a change, they are not behind contemporary creation. The expected fifty million visitors see a stabile by Alexander Calder (sixty tons, eighty-two feet in height) and, in the French Pavilion, an eclectic ensemble featuring Mathieu, Arman, Miró, Debré, and Dubuffet, as well as Tinguely and Niki de Saint-Phalle. The machinery and the *Nanas* of the latter lead a humorous confrontation on the roof of the building. The central shaft of the French Pavilion around which the various stories are built is animated by an audiovisual show composed by the musician Iannis Xenakis. Le Corbusier is represented for the first time in a national pavilion with—surprise—a tapestry.

The dominant trend in Expo

The United States Pavilion, by Buckminster Fuller, at Expo 67.

67 is the fashionable "building-envelope." Its two main representatives are the German Pavilion, by Frei Otto and Rolf Gutbrod, and the pavilion of the United States, by R. Buckminster Fuller, the most "utopian" among American architects. The German Pavilion is a simple plastic tent planted on columns and covered by a steel-thread net. The American one is a huge geodesic dome: a round tubular structure resembling a spiderweb; it is the realization of the concept of a climatic envelope that is independent of its internal traffic and services.

This innovative, gravity-free architecture shelters an odd collection bordering on the ridiculous—objects of "the good old days" of pioneers and Hollywood productions; a space capsule, half-charred on its reentry into the atmosphere; a simulated landing on the moon.

Visitors are charmed by the work of the Israeli architect Moshe Safdie. His Habitat 67 is made of prefabricated dwellings arranged in fives in a random order, a reminder of the volumes of a Cubist canvas. It is a new solution to the problem of large ensembles, and undoubtedly the most interesting one since Le Corbusier's Cité Radieuse in 1947 in Marseilles.

Habitat 67 by Moshe Safdie, at Expo 67.

Duchamp, "the great agitator," as André Breton called him, is able to see, just before he dies, the students of the May revolution agitate the consumer society he himself so disliked. While Dali takes part in the cultural revolution in a most astounding manner, a graphics studio is set up at the Beaux-Arts Academy of Paris and turns out pitiful posters full of working-class allusions and nostalgia for the past. It is one more lost opportunity. Meanwhile, in the United States, art continues to rise to ever greater heights, particularly with Kienholz's environments.

1968

S U M M A R Y

LITERATURE

GERMANY
Siegfried Lenz publishes
The German Lesson.

UNITED STATES
*Unauthorized publication of
Alexandr Solzhenitsyn's books*
The First Circle *and* Cancer
Ward.

FRANCE
Marguerite Yourcenar's work
The Abyss *is awarded the
Prix Femina.*

MUSIC

FRANCE
*Premiere of Olivier Messiaen's
opera* Turangalia, *with choreography by Roland Petit.*
*During the international
music festival in Paris, one
day each is devoted to the
works of the four composers
Varèse, Xenakis, Berio, and
Henry.*

SWITZERLAND
Continuum for Harpsichord
*by the Hungarian composer
György Ligeti is performed
in Basel.*

MOTION PICTURES

BELGIUM
Premiere of An Evening, a
Train *by André Delvaux.*

UNITED STATES
Two important releases: The
Vampires *by Roman Polanski,
a parody of horror films, and*
2001: A Space Odyssey *by
Stanley Kubrick, a science-
fiction film whose hero
(or villain) is a computer.*

FRANCE
Jacques Rivette presents
L'amour fou.

MARCEL DUCHAMP
GIVEN (1) THE WATERFALL, (2) TH
ILLUMINATING GAS. 1946-196
Philadelphia. Museum of A

MARCEL DUCHAMP: FEMALE FIG LEAF. 1950. New York. Mary Sisler Collection

clearly: "Once the artist makes something, it gains recognition through the intervention of the public, the intervention of the spectator: That is how it subsequently passes to posterity. There is, in sum, an inevitable reaction between two poles, one being the maker of a work, the other being the viewer. I consider the viewer just as important as the maker."

There are those who do not hesitate to call Duchamp a modern Leonardo da Vinci. As evidence, they cite his *Large Glass* sketches. The feminine musculature is conceived as a machine, with its levers, pulleys, and retorts distilling hidden essences. There is the fact that painting, "una cosa mentale" (a mental thing) to Leonardo, in the eyes of Duchamp should be

DUCHAMP'S WORLD

NEUILLY

Last year, in an interview with the art critic and historian Pierre Cabanne, Marcel Duchamp confided he had lived as happily as a café waiter. The quip sheds light on his personality. It is like Valéry's deathbed utterance, "What a gross charade!" Or Kant's last words, "All is well!"

Duchamp dies October 2, at the age of eighty-one, in Neuilly. He had refined irony to the point of ambiguity, and nothing could be more biting than his intellectual detachment. He was determined that the notary's son, who he always remained, would not go down in history without leaving a posthumous work. He had been occupied with it in secret for twenty years. Mysteriously titled *Étant donnés—Given*—it will be exhibited in the Philadelphia Museum of Art, which owns his celebrated *Large Glass* or *The Bride Stripped Bare by Her Bachelors* and a number of his paintings and "ready-mades." Those few who have been privileged to see *Given* describe it as an old broken-down barn door

with peepholes through which can be seen, beyond a breech in a brick-walled enclosure, a nude, sexually immature woman sprawled out in tall weeds, with her legs spread apart, exposed to voyeurs.

Duchamp's visual testament is neither painting nor sculpture, but a setting, or, in his own words, a "separable approximation," which can be taken down and reassembled anywhere. As in some Mannerist works, a landscape and a waterfall are visible in the distance, and one cannot tell where reality ends and illusion begins. What has happened? A crime? Foul play? Is she a bather drying off in the sun, or is she sleeping in her garden? Is this a young woman who has been raped, or is she a nymphomaniac? No one knows, thus everyone can form a personal interpretation, fulfilling one of Duchamp's basic ideas: that it is less the artist than the beholder who creates a work of art.

In the interview with Pierre Cabanne, Duchamp said it

Marcel Duchamp descending a staircase.

placed "anew in the service of the mind." Devotees also point out Duchamp's interest in science: "Introducing the exact and precise side of science interested me. It had not been often done, or at least not mentioned much."

"The great agitator," as André Breton called him, was above all a skeptic, who came to doubt even his own doubt. In this way he preeminently became the incarnation of the spirit of the times. It shows that in these last few years nothing has been done in the field of art that does not pass through or cross or derive from Duchamp. The poet and essayist Octavio Paz, one of the best minds of the present era, recently observed that modern art has lived between two extremities—Marcel Duchamp and Pablo Picasso. And yet, Duchamp's work has been paradoxical. Would his ready-mades exist without the museum they were intended to destroy and without the art market from which the artist thought he had escaped?

Duchamp, who often lived in straits, considered the ready-mades so unsalable that most of them have been lost or destroyed. But in 1966, Arturo Schwarz, a Milanese dealer, scenting profitable business, had eight major ones reconstructed and asked the aging artist to sign them. They are worth their weight in gold.

Although it is true that the only way to be faithful to the spirit that animated Duchamp would be to acquire his *Fountain*, that famous urinal, and have it installed in a public restroom, or to use his *Bottle Rack* in a cellar. That would make them reciprocal ready-mades. Duchamp has many followers, but few disciples. It is a safe bet that the café waiter in him would have been delighted. *(See also 1913, 1917, 1920, 1923.)*

IN DUCHAMP'S WORDS

The danger is always in pleasing the most immediate public, the one that surrounds you, that welcomes you, that finally consecrates you and confers success on you . . . and all the rest. On the contrary, you may have to wait fifty or one hundred years in order to reach your real public, but that is the only one that interests me.

Painting must not be exclusively visual or retinal.

I think that art is the only form of activity in which man as such comes across as a veritable individual. Through art alone, he can transcend the animal stage because art opens out onto regions where neither time nor space dominates.

Since Courbet, we have believed that painting appeals to the retina; that was everyone's mistake. The retinal thrill! Before, painting had other functions, it could be religious, philosophical, moral.

Men are mortal, so are paintings.

A picture that does not shock is not worth creating.

The viewer makes the museums, gives the museum its elements. Is the museum the final form of comprehension, of judgment?

I would have liked to work but in me was an undercurrent of enormous laziness. I would rather live, breathe, than work.

I do not attribute to the artist the type of social role in which he feels obligated to do something, in which he must consider his public. I abhor all such considerations.

Life is more a matter of expenditure than gain. You just have to know what you want to live with.

I believe strongly in eroticism because it is truly a rather general thing throughout the world, something people understand.

The word "belief" is also an error. It is like the word "judgment." They are dreadful givens on which the world is based. I hope it will not be like that on the moon!

MARCEL DUCHAMP: BICYCLE WHEEL. 1913

I do not believe in the word "being." The concept of being is a human invention.

I understand nothing of politics, and I have noticed that it is really a stupid activity that leads to nothing.

Metaphysics: tautology; religion: tautology, everything is a tautology except black coffee because it is controlled by the senses.

ART IN OUTRAGE

PARIS

May 12: About twenty artists participating in the first Biennale Internationale de l'Estampe (international engravings show) appear spontaneously at the lithography shop and create the first "revolutionary posters." Fifty sets are pulled, stamped by UNEF, the French National Students Union, and sold two days

May 24: Sixty painters and sculptors sign a statement: "We accuse society of making the arts a source of prestige rather than an avenue of communication among people. We denounce all measures inhibiting creative freedom. We will henceforth use all means within our power to bring about true integration of art into society."

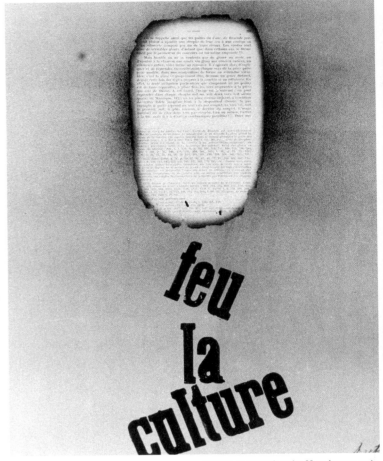

feu la culture

**Poster announcing the May-June events
(the three words mean "The Deceased Culture").**

WE WANT TEACHERS WHO ARE WITH IT AND KNOW HOW TO TEACH

later at the Odéon and La Hune for the benefit of the students.

May 14: Occupation of the Beaux-Arts Academy. The strike committee decides to make it a "discussion and information center" open to all. The doors are heavily guarded. Leaflets spread the message: "We want no more of these overseers who spend fifteen minutes a week inspecting the work of the student painters. We want teachers who are with it and know how to teach."

May 20: Closing of the national and municipal museums. A plastic-arts committee is formed. It sets up headquarters in the Beaux-Arts Academy and calls on the galleries that exhibit paintings to join the movement. Students at the Sorbonne call for specialists to remove the immense Puvis de Chavannes décor from the walls of the great amphitheater. Critics ask themselves: "Would the proposed reforms amount in the end to propping up mediocrities? Haven't we had numerous artists urge seriously an outright embargo on French participation in the Biennale in Venice?"

May 27: The curators of the national and municipal museums of Paris meet in the Guimet Museum. Working committees are set up to try to formulate a policy statement concerning mainly the operation and management of their museums.

June 4: Another meeting, of the heads of the Salons and the artists unions, at the Grand Palais. Twelve representatives are appointed for "the defense of their rights of participation" in the inner workings of all artistic committees under Beaux-Arts jurisdiction.

June 7: The Louvre reopens its doors. The tourists flock in.

Pierre Gaudibert, Silberman, Michel Troche, Cueco, Roberto Matta, and Shamai Haber at the Sorbonne.

650

SALVADOR DALI: MY CULTURAL REVOLUTION

One can be apostolic Roman Catholic, a monarchist, and nonetheless feel the wind of History blowing. For some time, Salvador Dali has been putting his checks and bills in a wallet bearing the double effigy of Lenin and Mao, to make them bear interest. And now the big day has come, and with the countenance he hoped it would have—playful, nonconformist, antibourgeois. He had to be there, too, through his manifesto, as a way of bringing his stone to the May revolution. It embraced none of the usual political and social demands, but since imagination was in power, why worry? Below are some excerpts.

I bring to the new revolution what is mine: that is, my paranoid method of criticism, uniquely adapted, it seems to me, to the felicitously irrational nature of the events unfolding. In the light of this method, I offer the following suggestions:

Color

The color of modern cultural revolutions is no longer red, but an amethyst color, evoking the air, the sky, fluidity. This is the color that corresponds to a change in era. The age of Aquarius, which will determine the next millenium, will see the disappearance of bloodshed. For the time being, we have just assassinated The Fish ("God is dead!"), and the blue sea is tinted by his blood, giving the waves this amethyst color.

Structure

Bourgeois culture can only be replaced vertically. Culture will be disembourgeoised only by deproletarizing society and turning the functions of the mind upward, by redirecting them toward their transcendent and legitimate divine origin. An aristocracy of the mind must emerge . . .

Quantified Institutions

Add a quantum of libido to antipleasure organizations such as UNESCO. Make UNESCO a ministry of public Cretinization, so that we will not lose what has already been done. Blend in some laudable folkloric prostitution, but add to it a strong dose of libidinal and spiritual energy. Thus transform this center of superboredom into a genuine erogenous zone under the auspices of Saint Louis, chief legislator of venal love.

Justice

Activation of cybernetic-research commissions for the resurrection and glorification of great thoughts that have fallen victim to materialism. Examples: the combinative wheels of Raymond Lulle, the natural theology of Raymond de Sebonde, the treatise of Paracelsus, Gaudi's architecture of Mediterranean Gothic inspiration, Francesco Pujols' hyperaxiology, Raymond Roussels' anti-Jules Verne poetics, the theoreticians of traditional mystical thought, all those who are genuinely inspired . . .

Note: *Where the cultural revolution goes, the fantastic should sprout up.*

Paris, Saturday, May 18, 1968

SALVADOR DALI (Excerpt)

Salvador Dali coming out of the Bastille metro station.

THE ART OF THE REAL AT MOMA

NEW YORK

Let us disregard the title of this Museum of Modern Art exhibit, which is scheduled to be shown at the Grand Palais in Paris. The term "Art of the Real" is misleading. It does not refer to realistic art. One could search in vain among the nonobjective works in the exhibit for the slightest trace of Realism—a steel cube by Tony Smith, a white circle on a black background by Alexander Liebermann, a composition of parallel lines by Franck Stella, and so forth.

What, then, is one supposed to understand by "Art of the Real"? The organizer of the exhibit, E. E. Goosen, is an eminent critic of American art. He explains that "it presents the viewer with facts rather than symbols. What was formerly disguised in the field of art—the technical means employed by the artist—is now openly shown." In short, the point is not to indulge any longer the inclination to make things "that seem real," but to produce objects as "real as reality itself." It explains the importance given to material, to structure, to technical methods used in painting, to simple, geometric forms.

A notable change is definitely underway in American art. It would be astonishing if Europe were not affected.

One of the rooms of Documenta IV, in Kassel. Center: *Giant* by Claes Oldenburg; left: Marilyn Monroe series by Andy Warhol; right: graphical works by James Rosenquist.

A DOCUMENTA THAT IS MODERN AT ALL COSTS

KASSEL

No more galleries of ancestors! The Dutch architect Jan Leering, who succeeded Werner Haftmann, exerts his influence to favor Minimalist Art in the selections for the paintings section of the fourth Documenta. As a third of the exhibits are from Americans, many artists have protested against what they call the "Documenta Americana."

Curator Werner Schmalenbach and the painter Fritz Winter resigned from the organizing committee. They were advocates of a broader accessibility, and did not want to endorse an expansion of novelty at any price.

What is shown at this Documenta is the negation of the museum. The accent has been placed on the treatment of space, on the artist as creator of an environment. Robert Rauschenberg, for instance, propounds a phantasmagoria of light, color, and motion. The work becomes an object of immediate consumption, an ephemeral phenomenon requiring spectator participation. As the ancestor of conceptual art, Marcel Duchamp, once said, it is the viewer that makes the picture. His followers surely understand the lesson. The fourth Documenta, in any case, tries to reflect the new tendencies faithfully.

FRANCK STELLA: AGBOTANA II. 1968. Saint-Étienne. Musée d'Art et d'Industrie

First Resort Town for Languedoc-Roussillon

La Grande-Motte is the first resort town to be built in Languedoc-Roussillon. Construction on two of the pyramid-style residences, begun in 1967, is finished. The town, which has five thousand residents, and attracts sixty thousand in the summer, stretches over a hundred and ten acres. Architect Jean Balladur gave careful thought to the residences: "I wanted them to be cheerful, free of both past and present influences. The pyramids are dune-shaped with open-work concrete balconies to add beauty and privacy."

Boo Hiss

A group of young Action Painters has decided to shake up Austrian society. Their predecessors, Arnulf Rainer and Fritz Hundertwasser, had paved the way with their Dadaist derision, Exhibitionism, and Happenings. This June, Günter Brus, Otto Mühl, and poet Oswald Wiener entered a university amphitheater under the pretext of giving a lecture. Instead, they booed the authorities. The three were sentenced to two months in prison. After an appeal, Wiener was let off on probation, while Brus and Mühl received four additional months. Brus, however, managed to leave the country!

Raynaud Sells 300 Flowerpots

Jean-Pierre Raynaud lines up flowerpots as Warhol does with his boxes of Brillo, or Don Judd with his cubes. As a participant at Prospect, a large international art exhibit in Düsseldorf, the artist lined up three hundred flaming-red pots, most of which were bought by visitors. Why flowerpots? Of course, Raynaud was a gardener at the Truffaut nurseries before becoming an artist. But the pots seem well-suited for Pop Art, where the ordinary is elevated to art. "My goal," stated Raynaud, "is to create maximum tension with a minimum of materials . . . I set up the explosives; the spectator lights the match."

Building "Le Provence" at La Grande-Motte, by Jean Balladur.

Sun Has Set for Foujita

Tsugouharu Léonard Foujita is dead in Zurich at the age of eighty-two. Arriving in Paris in 1913, he became one of the stars of Montparnasse. His 1928 self-portrait shows him watchful. Born in Tokyo in 1886, he became a French citizen in 1953. When he converted to Catholicism, he took as his baptismal name Léonard, in honor of Leonardo da Vinci, whom he admired. His paintings contain elements of both Western and traditional Japanese art, with smooth, ivorylike surfaces. He pleased the cosmopolitan tastes of his admirers with his precious but sharp-edged nudes, his cats, and his unsettling paintings of small girls. He was buried in Reims.

Factory Work for Mathieu

"French industrialists are out of touch with art," stated painter Georges Mathieu two years ago in the magazine *Galerie des arts*. Yves Biraud, chief executive officer of BC transformers, responded by asking Mathieu to design buildings and gardens for BC's new factory in Fontenay-le-Comte. To those who found the assignment surprising, the artist replied: Michelangelo, Leonardo, and Le Brun did not limit themselves to painting." Mathieu did a splendid job of translating his pictorial energy into architecture.

"ART AND THE MACHINE" AT MOMA

NEW YORK

Crowds flock to the Museum of Modern Art to see the exhibit "Art and the Machine," which opens November 25.

The vast and varied theme did not intimidate Pontus Hulten, the Swedish organizer of the exhibit. It traces the relationship of art and the machine historically by reviewing inventions of artists such as those of Leonardo da Vinci and Vaucanson. Artists and inventors are indeed close relatives. Alongside inventions by artists there are artisanal and industrial artifacts that are true works of art, for example, Cugnot's dragnet and the Ettore Bugatti vehicle. But the heart of the exhibit is a retrospective on the concept of the machine in modern art.

Connecting rods and cogwheels inspired the Dadaists; to Picabia, the machine was associated with woman, to Duchamp, standardized material constituted the actual work. And the Italian Futurists were inspired by Dadaism and by the Russian avant-garde. The machine, stripped, disassembled, vies with pictures for exhibit space. Sculpture becomes machine. Duchamp, Nahum Gabo, Tatlin led the way toward contemporary kinetic sculpture. The omnipresence of sculpture in the rooms that are dedicated to recent work is manifest. If Tinguely suggests "Meta-Matic" drawing machines, the machine itself becomes both work of art and its creator. Tinguely, who pays homage to New York with a monumental work, is much honored. He has emerged as one of those who push mechanistic mockery to the ultimate. This is apparent on opening the catalogue, whose riveted metal cover and hinges evoke the machine idea. The subtitle of the exhibit is significant: "Aspects of the end of the mechanical age." The idea of the "end" seems to haunt numerous young artists. The dawn-of-the-century enthusiasm becomes stifled, the machine intimidates, the artist protests. César compresses a car as though to combat technical civilization. Claes Oldenburg uses a soft but gigantic fan to ridicule it. Even among the most "technological" researchers, the traditional machine, like the artist, is being displaced by computer science.

An exhibit like this could be mere bric-a-brac, but that danger has been avoided. By producing this inspiring variation on a difficult theme, Pontus Hulten has opened the way for others of the same type. The MOMA exhibit will travel to the Moderna Museet in Stockholm. Going beyond the traditional showing of pictures and sculpture, it puts into perspective, like anthropologists, the art and the collective imagination of society.

CÉSAR: THE YELLOW BUICK. 1961. New York. MOMA

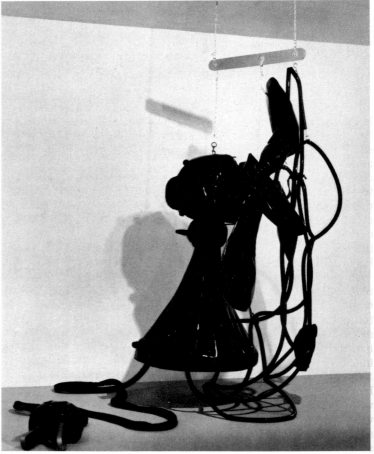

CLAES OLDENBURG: GIANT SOFT FAN. 1966-1967. New York. MOMA

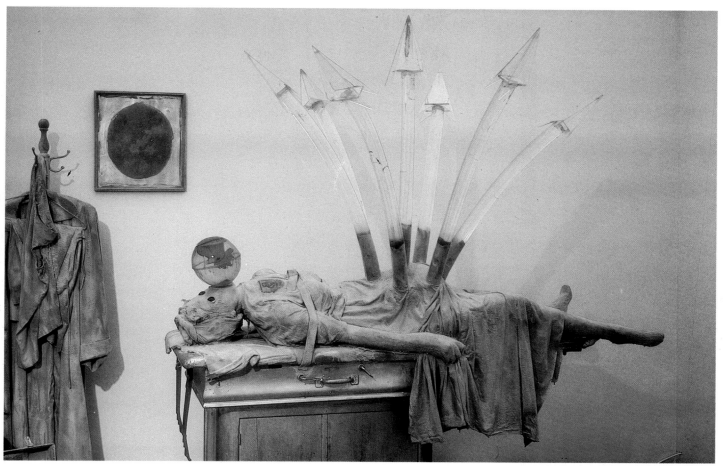

EDWARD KIENHOLZ: THE BIRTHDAY. 1968

THE PROVOCATIONS OF KIENHOLZ

PARIS

Is Edward Kienholz provocative? He certainly is, and intentionally so. But with him, nothing is arbitrary. In a time when America seems prosperous and content, he creates life-size environments that are bitter denials of a civilization that ignores its castoffs. His showing at CNAC, in the Rue Berryer, struck the Parisian public like a bomb.

Kienholz, born in 1927, grew up in a family of farmers on the border of the states of Washington and Idaho. He tried innumerable lines of work, experiencing first-hand the suffering and injustice that are the essence of his work. In 1953, he found himself in Los Angeles at a time when "underground" artists were turning their backs on a society of conspicuous consumption and uniting with adherents of a student and intellectual counterculture that frequently proclaimed the mystical and even occult traditions of Oriental thought. It was a unique period in the literary and artistic life of the United States—the Beat and funk generations, and the hippies.

ASSEMBLAGES THAT DENOUNCE THE WRONGS OF AMERICAN SOCIETY AND POLITICS

Kienholz became busy. With Walter Hopps, and later with Irving Blum, he opened the Ferus Gallery and exhibited the city's most creative artists. Kienholz himself created dense, colored bas-reliefs, paintings to which he glued or nailed pieces of wood, scraps of wire, and bits of junk. Subsequently, he included mannequin or doll parts, bones, skulls, stuffed animals, strips of cloth or metal, contributing to the development of the new genre called Assembly Art. In the early sixties, a series of totally stupefying features began to emerge. He reacted to the horror of mental hospitals in *State Hospital,* to Puritan hypocrisy in *Back Seat Dodge,* to the falsehood of the abortion issue in *The Illegal Operation,* to the loneliness and abandonment of the aged in *The Wait.* Kienholz has never again shrunk from denunciation.

Several of his works created a scandal, especially *Roxy's,* which, in a brutal and explicit manner, evokes a notorious Los Angeles bordello of the 1940s, and *The Birthday,* which displays the solitary childbirth labor of a woman left alone with her pains—luminous rockets springing from her abdomen. On examining *The Birthday* closely, one notices, in the mother's disheveled clothing, a letter. It accentuates the meaning of the work: It is a joky little note from "Dick," undoubtedly the father, to explain his absence in these circumstances.

Sometimes Kienholz takes a political stand. His recent *Portable War Memorial,* inspired by the famous photograph of a band of Marines raising the American flag on Mount Suribachi in the Pacific island of Iwo Jima, shows Marines raising the Stars and Stripes over the centerhole in a garden table—to serve as a parasol. It is the artist's commentary on the absurdity of the Vietnam war.

A Vasarely retrospective in Budapest reviews the ensemble of his work, and, for the nations of the East, it is a grand premiere for modern art, which pierces the Iron Curtain with a single stroke. Vasarely receives a warm welcome from an enthusiastic public that comes from all over Hungary for the occasion. Of a lesser historical magnitude, twenty-six masterpieces of twentieth-century art belonging to the Penrose collection are stolen in London. The collection could easily have been destroyed by the loss of these paintings that are saved at the last moment. And Warhol recovers slowly from the attempt on his life in June 1968.

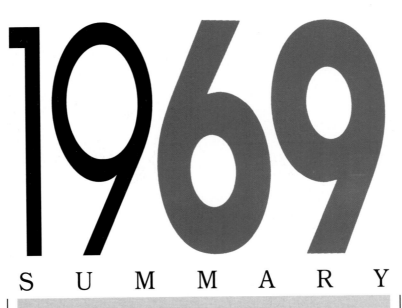

1969

S U M M A R Y

AVANT-GARDE

**Warhol, Image Maker for the Mass Media
In Warhol's Words**

EVENTS

Theft of the Penrose Collection

ART NEWS

**Andréou's Work Brutal, Archaic
Trémois: Variations on Love
Hélène Parmelin Invents the Anartist
Paris Discovers Paul Delvaux
Helen Frankenthaler Retrospective at the Whitney
Lipstick by Oldenburg
In Brief**

GREAT MASTERS

The Space of Sam Francis

EXHIBITIONS

Vasarely Went East

**ANDY WARHOL:
THE TWENTY MARILYNS. 1962.
Paris. Private Collection**

WARHOL, IMAGE MAKER FOR THE MASS MEDIA

NEW YORK
Andy Warhol recovers slowly from the serious gunshot wounds he suffered in an assassination attempt last year. Doctors had given the Pop artist only a fifty-percent chance for survival, after a lengthy four-hour operation.

He was returning late in the afternoon on Monday, June 3, to the Factory, his headquarters at 33 Union Square West, northeast of Greenwich Village. He was accompanied by Valerie Solanas, twenty-eight years old, who suddenly pumped two bullets into his abdomen. She had been a protagonist in his film *I, a Man.* In her statement to the police, she said, "He had too much influence over my life." It is possible that she was acting on behalf of SCUM, the one-person feminist movement she had founded. She held that the male

is a biological accident . . . an incomplete female that needed to be destroyed.

The *enfant terrible* of Pop Art, nicknamed "the guy of the Campbell Soup cans," is more than a biological accident. He is an ingenious image maker for the consumer society, which swallows not only its mass-produced goods but also its sham goods, namely, advertising. Warhol declares that he adores America and that his paintings represent a documentary on it, that his image is a mirror held up to these impersonal products, to the materialistically flashy objects upon which the United States builds itself today—a projection of whatever there is that can be bought or sold, and from whose pragmatic and ephemeral symbols we derive our nourishment.

When photography made its

ANDY WARHOL: SELF-PORTRAIT. 1966. Private Collection

ANDY WARHOL: THE ELECTRIC CHAIR. 1966. Paris. MNAM

appearance toward the middle of the last century, some painters seized on the new possibilities by introducing into petit-bourgeois homes the photographs of members of the family, enlarged to life size, to which the artists added color by hand—here's grandfather with his moustache, here's that adorable little niece, for all to admire. Andy Warhol, today, does more or less the same thing. The difference is, though, that his works are collective pictures of our society.

Typical of his technique are the silk screens of the late Marilyn Monroe, which, with their reddish, bluish, and greenish tints, promote and at the same time ridicule the myth of the actress, who had been made into a divinity by the mass media, or his treatment of other stars such as Elizabeth Taylor, Jacqueline Kennedy, and Elvis Presley—all fantasies and products of today's consumer. As for the Campbell Soup cans, Warhol

IN WARHOL'S WORDS

stated, impertinent as always, "I have eaten from them habitually. I have eaten the same meal every day for the last twenty years, always eating the same thing." In a more serious vein we can say that he has reinvented the nature of the still life. But his work, in which his detractors want to see a "capitalistic reality," is far from being a celebration of the "American way of life." The dogs and the police who attack the crowd in *Pink Race Riot*, the person hanging from a tree and the demolished car in *Green Accident*, and above all his *Electric Chair* series in orange, blue, or red, are terrifying accusations. Contrasting opposites of shadow and light, shapes looming from the sickly sweet or acidulous chrome of the canvas, the repetitious themes, sometimes carried to obsessiveness, have no other aim than to make art the basis from which to gauge the truth of violence and death.

In this era of mass media, it can be said that Warhol holds the event right before everyone's eyes: He forces the viewer to read it and to meditate. He puts out a fixed image that the speed of the media event, in its glut of data, cannot help but make banal.

Many of his silk screens are produced by assistants recruited among the regular crowd of hangers-on who frequent the Factory. This Neodada side, deeply provocative in its relations with the art market and the public's bourgeois taste for the master's works, permits comparison with Marcel Duchamp's shenanigans. In fact, his *Brillo Boxes* seem to be directly related to Duchamp's "ready-mades." Warhol's films, with their out-of-focus images, defy Hollywood; *Chelsea Girls* was made for $1,500 three years ago. But while Duchamp was a skeptic, Warhol may have tragedy in his bones.

(See also 1966.)

If you want to know who I am, look at the surface of my pictures and my films. There is nothing behind.

I only read the texture of words. I see everything in this way, the surface of things, a kind of mental Braille.

Business art is the step that comes after Art. I started as a commercial artist, and I want to finish as a business artist. After I did the thing called "art" or whatever it's called, I went into business art. I wanted to be an Art Businessman or a Business Artist. Being good in business is the most fascinating kind of art.

people always paint the same painting.

What's great about this country is that America started the tradition where the richest consumers buy essentially the same things as the poorest. You can be watching TV and see Coca-Cola, and you can know that the President drinks Coke, Liz Taylor drinks Coke, and just think, you can drink Coke, too. A Coke is a Coke and no amount of money can get you a better Coke than the one the bum on the corner is drinking. All the Cokes are the same and all are good. Liz Taylor knows it, the President knows it, the bum knows it, and you know it.

A Warhol exhibition at the Stable Gallery.

So on the one hand I really believe in empty spaces, but on the other hand, because I'm still making some art, I'm still making junk for people to put in their spaces that I believe should be empty: i.e., I'm helping people waste their space when what I really want to do is help them empty their space.

As soon as you have to decide and choose, it's wrong. And the more you decide about, the more wrong it gets. Some people, they paint abstract, so they sit there thinking about it because their thinking makes them feel they're doing something. But my thinking never makes me feel I'm doing anything.

I think every painting should be the same size and the same color so they're all interchangeable and nobody thinks they have a better or a worse painting. And if the one "master painting" is good, they're all good. Besides, even when the subject is different,

An actress should count up her plays and movies and a model should count up her photographs and a writer should count up his words and an artist should count up his pictures so you always know exactly what you're worth, and you don't get stuck thinking your product is you and your fame, and your aura.

I never particularly wanted to make simply sex movies. If I had wanted to make a real sex movie I would have filmed a flower giving birth to another flower.

The movies make emotions look so strong and real, whereas when things really do happen to you, it's like watching television—you don't feel anything.

THEFT OF THE PENROSE COLLECTION

LONDON

Modern art is one masterpiece short, for a spell. *Weeping Woman*, painted by Picasso in 1937, immediately after *Guernica*, is stolen.

The canvas was part of the prestigious collection of Roland Penrose. He had bought it directly from Picasso at his studio in the Rue des Grands-Augustins. It is stolen on the Monday following Easter Sunday, as are twenty-five other famous paintings, from Penrose's apartment in London. Another was *A Poet's Incertitude* by de Chirico, as well as other Picassos from his Cubist period and a painting by Magritte.

Here are the facts. Penrose is spending a few day's vacation in his Sussex home with his wife, Lee Miller, and his son, Tony, when Elsa, their governess, phones, urgently suggesting the Penroses hurry back to the apartment in Kensington where the most beautiful pieces of his collection are kept. The collector is horrified to find police and journalists present. Apparently, a burglarly has occurred, because the ground is covered with glass debris and empty picture frames. It is a catastrophe. The paintings had been insured far below their value. In recent burglaries, thieves have had the habit of cashing in on their spoils with various insurance companies, which then return the booty to the owners for a handsome profit.

Penrose's paintings were found by a Scotland Yard team in the basement of a building about to be demolished, in Ealing, a suburb of London. It had taken three months to crack the case. The loot had gotten away. The thieves, feeling they were being tracked down, had unloaded the paintings in the cellar, which some workers were about to clean out. The workers were going to burn the frameless paintings, which they thought had no value, but two people had some doubts. One took a canvas to a friend who lived

PABLO PICASSO:
WEEPING WOMAN. 1937.
London. Private Collection

nearby. The friend immediately identified it as a genuine Picasso and urged that the authorities be informed. The canvas turned out to be *Weeping Woman*. Twenty-six priceless works of art were saved from the flames.

Roland Penrose, himself a painter, began his collection in 1936, with some Surrealist paintings from René Gaffé, a Belgian collector looking to resell some canvases; at the time, nobody was buying. Two years later, for 1,500 pound sterling, Penrose bought eighty-two paintings: six de Chiricos, ten Picassos, forty Max Ernsts, three Dalis, and one Klee, from the poet Paul Éluard, who always needed more money than he could ever get for his verse.

Penrose has said that his collection was assembled for the sole purpose of helping friends emerge from financial difficulties. His property of over two thousand acres of grazing land, wheat, and forest was bought through the sale of a single painting: the *Portrait of Wilhelm Uhde*, an Analytical Cubist work by Picasso, painted in 1910.

After the April theft, Penrose dreams of putting his most precious paintings into museums. The *Weeping Woman* ends up in the Tate Gallery.

Photographs of the stolen paintings appear in various English newspapers, such as *The Times* of April 8. The *Evening Standard* of July 2 gives front-page coverage to this "incredible adventure."

GIORGIO DE CHIRICO:
A POET'S INCERTITUDE. 1913.
London. Private Collection

Andréou's Work, Brutal, Archaic

Some fifty sculptures by Constantin Andréou, some of them very large, are being shown this summer at the Athens Gallery. Andréou, at fifty-one, is the best of the contemporary Greek sculptors. His first themes were birds, bulls, and horses. There was a curious mermaid with the head of a fish and a woman's body. His recent works, more abstract, are made from soldered brass-leaf to which he occasionally applies color. His style is brutal and archaic, as if he is grappling with wild forces in the depths of life.

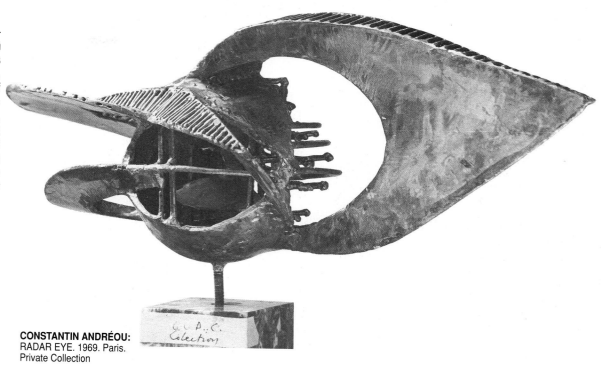

CONSTANTIN ANDRÉOU:
RADAR EYE. 1969. Paris.
Private Collection

Trémois: Variations on Love

Faithful friendship binds Pierre-Yves Trémois to Jean Rostand, whose *Bestiaire d'amour* he illustrated in 1957 with one hundred and fifty monotypes. Trémois, who received the grand prix in Rome in 1943, has turned his talents to illustrating. This year, he completes provocative drawings to accompany Verlaine's *Parallèlement*, and Ovid's *Metamorphoses,* with notes by a specialist on the fertilization of frogs. Jean Rostand states that Trémois lives his own version of Darwinian evolution.

Hélène Parmelin Invents the Anartist

Under the title *Art and Anartists,* Hélène Parmelin publishes an attack of everything that in recent years, under the pretext of being avant-garde, is nothing more than approximations, assemblages, montages, and accumulations of garbage. "Absence of thought, of research and creation; absence of knowledge," she wrote, "and, especially, absence of lucidity and humility." She also chastises the critics for collaborating with so much hot air. Her book is gritty and refreshing, and her coining of the word "anartist" has already been noticed in Parisian art circles. It will undoubtedly find its way into the dictionary one day.

Paris Discovers Paul Delvaux

Now that the abstraction-versus-figuration debate has died down, Paul Delvaux is coming into his own. That is the opinion of François Mathey, head curator of the Museum of Decorative Arts in Paris. The museum is having its first retrospective of the Belgian painter's work, which, until now, has never really been recognized in France. Delvaux, along with Magritte, is one of the best representatives of "Magic Realism" which, between the wars, brought Surrealism from lunacy to dreamlike statements, taking on, in Delvaux's case, a melancholy eroticism. His works are filled with young nudes, sleepwalking toward unknown, possibly violent, destinations. Delvaux is seventy-two.

Helen Frankenthaler Retrospective at the Whitney

At forty-one, Helen Frankenthaler is having a retrospective at the Whitney, which will then travel to London, Hanover, and Berlin. While distancing herself early on from Abstract Expressionism, she has remained a talented colorist whose immense canvases cannot be easily classified. Wide stretches of color suggest the range of colors found in nature; there is a feeling of wind and water, and organic growth. Her painting is lyrical at a time when rigid forms and cold colors are predominant. As early as 1953, the gifted young artist was called, by Morris Louis, "the bridge between Pollock and all possibilities."

Lipstick by Oldenburg

Are lipsticks protesting the war in Vietnam? Claes Oldenburg's latest piece, erected on the campus of Yale University, seems to be making such a statement. The giant lipstick, mounted on caterpillars, is an ordinary object transformed into a metaphorical monument, a missile, a phallic symbol. It sits between the flag and a war monument!

IN BRIEF...

CANADA
Exhibition organized by the Beaux-Arts Museum of Montreal: "The Common Man: Works of Jean Dubuffet."

FRANCE
More than two hundred and fifty works by Hans Hartung at the Musée National d'Art Moderne. The exhibition will move on to Houston, Montreal, and Quebec.
  At the gallery Maeght, Paul Rebeyrolle exhibits his Guerilleros, *inspired by his recent trip to Cuba.*
  Erro has an exhibit at the ARC.

ITALY
Retrospective of André Masson works from 1923 to 1968 at the Civic Gallery of Modern Art, with a catalogue of Daniel-Henry Kahnweiler.

SWITZERLAND
In Bern, a large exhibition of Land Art: "When Attitudes Become Shapes."

SAM FRANCIS: IN LOVELY BLUENESS. 1955-1957. Paris. MNAM

THE SPACE OF SAM FRANCIS

BERLIN

A new Pollock or a new Monet? Sam Francis, commissioned by the Nationalgalerie of Berlin to make a monumental work, is inspired by Action Painting. He recognizes that going beyond Automatism can be transfomed into a special sensitivity toward space and light. During the last few years, it has become the essence of his work.

The artist was intimate with light while in California, where he was born in 1923. He studied medicine and psychology at the University of California-Berkeley and served in the Air Force during the Second World War. He was wounded in his spinal column, and hospitalized. While recuperating, he began to paint. He made his first abstract painting in 1947. A little later, he moved to Paris, where he lived and studied for the next decade. He became good friends with Jean-Pierre Riopelle, the Canadian artist, and with several American artists: Norman Bluhm, Al Held, Ruth Francken, Shirley Jaffe, Joan Mitchell, and Kimber Smith.

In Paris, Sam Francis had a showing at the Salon de Mai, at the gallery du Dragon, and at the gallery Rive Droite. He par-

AN INSPIRATION COMING FROM THE TINTS OF SUNRISE AND THE FORMATION OF CLOUDS

ticipated in the exhibitions "Signifiants de l'Informel" and "Art of a Different Kind," organized by Michel Tapié. In 1952, Mrs. Henri Matisse bought one of his paintings. He made a series of white paintings that brought to mind the sunlit Mediterranean—the wondrous light that he had discovered when spending summers at the home of the Duthuits in Aix-en-Provence.

Sam Francis has always been fascinated by the Orient, and has visited Japan many times. Two of his wives were Japanese. In Tokyo, he worked in ceramics, and executed a marvelous mural painting for the Sogetsu School. In 1966, he had the idea of having five helicopters trace designs in the sky—a Francis!

He continued to live on three continents, with studios in California, France, Switzerland, and Japan. He stayed in New York a good deal. In 1959, he put in six months on a mural for the Chase Manhattan Bank. He was included by Clement Greenberg in the prestigious exhibition "Post-Painterly Abstraction" at the Los Angeles County Museum of Art in 1964. The show brought together the colorist painters whom the celebrated critic and theoretician had helped launch.

Sam Francis has also made beautiful lithographies, especially at the Tamarind Gallery in Los Angeles. Lithography and watercolor are perfectly suited for the fluid and subtle manner that is the artist's way: From a milky white and the blackest black, mysterious spaces arise from the paper in which the areas of white become more and more vast, and silent.

From Francis' exhibition at the Museum of Fine Arts in Houston two years ago, James Johnson Sweeney discerned the tints of sunrise and sunset, the colors, the light, and the formation of clouds, the depth, the space, the infinite distances, above and below the clouds that break through, for a glimpse— sources of inspiration for Francis.

Similar terms were used forty years earlier by Georges Clemenceau to describe *Waterlilies* when the Monet was exhibited for the first time at the Orangerie in Paris.

VASARELY WENT EAST

BUDAPEST

Victor Vasarely once again discovers his native soil. He is now sixty-one years old. A retrospective of his works, at the Fine Arts Palace, brings out almost all of socialist Hungary. After twenty-five years, one of the masters of postwar abstract art is cheered by compatriots. The exhibition is open less than a month and is acclaimed enthusiastically by the tens of thousands who arrive from districts and regions throughout the country.

Vasarely has called his work Kinetic Art because it has, by analogy with the kinetic theory of gas, both movement and the immaterial. His paintings, in fact, are based on optical illusions, squares that advance and recede successively, spheres that swell and deflate. The spectator's eyes cannot remain fixed in space. It is this mobility of perception that transfixes the visitors. They are intrigued because they don't know that geometry can live within its own mystery.

The origin of Vasarely's Kinetic Art was his *Homage to Malevich*, of which he did several versions between 1952 and 1958. He presents it as a play of rhombuses and squares turning slightly on their cross-brace and impossible to fix with the eye in the two dimensions of the plane. The inspiration may have been both the famous *White Square on White*, which Malevich painted in 1918, and the play of light filtering through the skylight of Vasarely's summer studio in Gordes. The thickness of the studio wall had in fact the ability to transform what was square into an obsessive rhombus shape as the sun was setting.

Vasarely was a student of the Bauhaus in Budapest, created by Sandor Bortnyk, before establishing himself in 1930 in Paris, where he began to work in advertising. Vasarely had the peculiarity of not doing the actual painting himself. He put onto

VICTOR VASARELY: INFLATING

graph paper all kinds of partitions which he called "start-up prototypes." They were then enlarged and colored by assistants according to a range of strictly marked tints. He thought it unnecessary that the creator also bury himself in the tasks of a craftsman, thereby hindering his freedom of spirit. Vasarely's works have the severity and precision of a theorem.

He has always had a passion for modern scientific theories and for the new nondeterminist image of matter, as well as for astronomy and astronautics. Many of his paintings bear the names of stars. One is *Laika*, the name of the dog who was on one of the Sputniks and who died in space.

(See also 1944 and 1955.)

One of the rooms of the Vasarely retrospective in Budapest.

Late twentieth-century eclecticism begins with Land Art, Hyperrealism, and the emergence of Francis Bacon, long ignored, then honored in 1971 as the best painter of the year—art takes off in opposite directions simultaneously. But the event of the decade is, without doubt, the death of Picasso in 1973 at the age of ninety-two. He left his mark on the entire century from beginning to end, having tried everything,

1970

	1970	1971	1972	1973	1974
ARTS	• Deaths of Rothko and Newman • "Expo 70" in Osaka • The Support-Surface Group exhibits	• Inauguration of the Rothko Chapel in Houston • Francis Bacon retrospective in Paris • Exhibition on the metamorphosis of the object, in Brussels	• Soulages retrospective in the United States • Trouble at the "72/72" exhibition in Paris • Still lifes by Claes Oldenburg	• Death of Picasso • Jorn retrospective in Berlin • Record auction prices for the New York School	• Worldwide success of Hyperrealism • Inauguration of the Dali Museum in Figueras • Joseph Beuys performs in New York
LITERATURE	• Alexandr Solzhenitsyn is awarded Nobel prize in literature	• *Group Portrait with Lady* by Heinrich Böll	• *No Name in the Street* by James Baldwin • *A Sorrow beyond Dreams* by Peter Handke • Heinrich Böll is awarded Nobel prize in literature	• *Triptych* by Clause Simon • *Gravity's Rainbow* by Thomas Pynchon	• *La tête d'obsidienne* (Picasso's mask) by André Malraux
MUSIC AND THEATER	• Concerto for Violoncello by Witold Lutoslawski • 500,000 attend a music festival on the Isle of Wight	• Deaths of Igor Stravinsky and Louis Armstrong	• Premiere of *Jesus Christ Superstar* by Tim Rice and Andrew Lloyd Weber	• *Concerto for Two Pianos and Orchestra* by Luciano Berio	• Death of Duke Ellington
MOTION PICTURES	• *Dodes'ka-den* by Akira Kurosawa	• *Clockwork Orange* by Stanley Kubrick • *Death in Venice* by Luchino Visconti	• *Last Tango in Paris* by Bernardo Bertolucci • *Cries and Whispers* by Ingmar Bergman	• *State of Siege* by Costa-Gavras • *Sleeper* by Woody Allen	• *Chinatown* by Roman Polanski • *Lacombe Lucien* by Louis Malle
SCIENCE AND TECHNOLOGY	• First complete gene synthesis, at the University of Wisconsin • Completion of the Aswan High Dam	• Russia launches the first habitable space station • Russia soft-lands a space capsule on Mars	• Russia's *Venus 8* soft-lands on Venus • Discovery of the Tasaday "stone-age" tribe in the Philippines	• America's *Pioneer 10* transmits pictures from the vicinity of Jupiter • Konrad Lorenz is awarded Nobel prize in medicine	• A Russian space probe lands on Mars and finds water vapor • Death of Charles A. Lindbergh
POLITICS AND DAILY LIFE	• American incursions into Cambodia • Salvador Allende becomes president of Chile	• China joins the UN • Famine in Bangladesh • Lt. Calley found guilty in Mylai massacre	• President Nixon visits China • Terrorism at the Olympic games in Munich • Beginning of the Watergate affair	• Cease-fire in Vietnam • Watergate crisis • Oil crisis • Salvador Allende in Chile overthrown	• President Nixon is forced to resign • Severe gasoline shortage in the United States

664

1979

invented everything, succeeded at everything, reexamined everything, while the whole world watched. His death leaves an immense void, yet it is also a liberation. From now on, the masters of modern art, after Bacon and Duffet, are the artists born in the twenties, such as Soulages, Jasper Johns, Lichtenstein. It is they who stand in the forefront of the international artistic scene and take up its cause.

1975	1976	1977	1978	1979
• Lichtenstein retrospective in Paris • Muralism makes a comeback in the United States • Spain opens up to contemporary art	• Christo builds *The Running Fence* in California • Vasarely Foundation in Aix-en-Provence • Art Brut Museum in Lausanne • Jasper Johns at the Whitney Museum in New York	• Inauguration of Georges Pompidou Center, and exhibition "Paris-New York"	• Calder at La Défense • Exhibition "Paris-Berlin" at Georges Pompidou Center	• Dali retrospective at Georges Pompidou Center • Beuys at the Guggenheim Museum in New York
• *The Autumne of the Patriarch* by Gabriel García Márquez	• *The Gulag Archipelago* by Alexandr Solzhenitsyn • Death of André Malraux	• *Terra Nostra* by Carlos Fuentes • *A Lover's Discourse: Fragments* by Roland Barthes	• *Rumors of Rain* by André Brink • *Rue des boutiques obscures* by Patrick Modiano • Isaac Bashevis Singer is awarded Nobel prize in literature	• *The Executioner's Song* by Norman Mailer • *If on a Winter's Night a Traveler* by Italo Calvino
• *Locus* by Trisha Brown	• Wagner's tetralogy *The Ring of the Nibelung* in Bayreuth, under Pierre Boulez and Patrice Chéreau • *Einstein on the Beach,* opera by Robert Wilson and Philip Glass, in Avignon	• *Tetralogy* by Carolyn Carlson at the Paris Opera	• *Notre-Dame de Paris* at the Palais des Sports, directed by Robet Hossein	• *Lulu* by Alban Berg, in its entirety, at the Paris Opera
• *One Flew over the Cuckoo's Nest* by Milos Forman • *Dersu Uzala* by Akira Kurosawa • Murder of Pier Paolo Pasolini	• *Fellini's Casanova* by Federico Fellini • *In the Realm of the Senses* by Nagisa Oshima	• *Network* by Sidney Lumet • *Star Wars* by George Lucas • Death of Charlie Chaplin	• *The Duellists* by Ridley Scott • *Annie Hall* by Woody Allen	• *Apocalypse Now* by Francis Ford Coppola • *The Tin Drum* by Volker Schlöndorff
• American and Russian spacecraft link up above the earth • Invention of Bic disposable razor	• American craft soft-lands on Mars and sends first close-up photographs • The Concorde flies from Paris to Washington in less than four hours • Death of Werner Heisenberg	• First staffed flight of space shuttle *Enterprise*	• Birth of the first "test-tube baby" • Two Russian astronauts orbit the earth for 140 days	• Development of the compact disk
• End of the war in Vietnam • Genocide in Cambodia • Andrei Sakharov is awarded Nobel peace prize	• Deaths of Mao Tse-Tung and Chou En-lai • Israeli raid on Entebbe	• Egyptian President Anwar Sadat visits Israel • U.S. Department of Energy is established	• Camp David peace treaty; Menachem Begin and Anwar Sadat share Nobel peace prize • Mass suicide (of over 900) in Jonestown, Guyana	• Islamic revolution in Iran • Soviet intervention in Afghanistan

"What if the earth were a work of art?" wonder the Land Artists in the United States. In the aftermath of Arte Povera, these artists decide to go even further, and act on nature itself. The most recent form of Romanticism, it is also the urge of creative young artists to escape museums and the imperatives of the art market. Inversely, members of the Parisian group Support-Surface find a way to prolong Conceptual Art, while making it clear that they too hope to escape the capitalist system. In fact, challenging the establishment is the best thing to do in our mass-media society—where everything is swept up and enlarged upon—to become an instant success.

1970

S U M M A R Y

ROBERT SMITHSON:
SPIRAL JETTY. April 1970.
Rozel Point, Great Salt Lake, Utah

THE NATURAL FORCES OF LAND ART

UNITED STATES

They are no longer satisfied with the space in the museums and galleries. They get choked in the cities. They need vast spaces in order to feel free to be creative. So they choose the deserts in which they can hollow out elongated trenches or trace lines a half mile in length. They shift blocks of granite weighing many tons and tip them into trenches. Or they trace wide rings into the snow of New England. They are young. They are American. They are "earthworkers" or—"Land Artists."

Of course, they are not the first people to be interested in the earth. Many others before them have used it to create their compositions. They have dumped it on the floors of exhibition halls, making the floor part of the material used in Arte Povera (poor art). But these new artists show earth in its pure state, crude, heaped up together with pieces of rock—Robert Smithson has done that—or, better yet, made use of it *in situ*. Out there, in the middle of open spaces, there is a nonorganized, undetermined environment, a field for action. There, right in the heart of the desert, nobody can buy the works, or collect them, or amass them. They don't have to be assessed. The bourgeois, who get wrapped up in worshiping a painting or a sculpture, do not have to cogitate about them. In a society full of overconsumption, these artists refuse to create objects that are there merely to be added to other objects. They want to create something without manufacturing it, unlike all those who are subservient to industrial technologies.

Michael Heizer, twenty-six years old, began in 1967 to work in the heart of the desert in Nevada, then in a dried-up lake of the Mojave Desert in California. He was assisted by the art

ROBERT SMITHSON: CAYUGA SALT MINE PROJECT. 1965

collector Robert Scull. This year, he finishes *Double Negative*, an enormous trench scooped out by bulldozers on the side of the Mormon Mesa Plateau overlooking a valley. Heizer knows that the ground will eventually reclaim the land, that the wind-driven earth and the rains will one day fill up the trenches,

making the sides of his works crumble away. But it is the fascination of the earth that makes him do what he does.

Robert Smithson, who is thirty-two years old, looks with delight at the deposits of salt and sulphur on the sides of his *Spiral Jetty*, a large artificial spiral that he constructed in Utah

that extends into the Great Salt Lake. He was attracted by this lake when he heard that it was full of microorganisms that turn the color of the water to red. The arid, desolate site also fascinated him.

The *Circles* of Dennis Oppenheim melt in the snow, the desert tracings of Walter De

Maria become obliterated. It is not just the act itself that creates an interest in undertaking this avant-garde artistry. The builders keep photographic archives of their works and of the works' decomposition—of everything that constitutes the work in its totality.

Some film their works, even going as far as making a film that illustrates their ideas. Charles Simonds made a short film in which he is seen emerging naked from the mud, a Happening that evoked the mists of time. It was, of course, called *Birth*.

One cannot dissociate Land Art from the philosophical preoccupations and politics of the current era. In fact, America is becoming aware of the precariousness of its natural resources and the fragility of a continent that everybody has mindlessly assumed is a cornucopia. In addition, young people are leaning toward Oriental philosophy, a kind of wisdom that has attracted American intellectuals for the past twenty years.

The Land Artists have been attracted by the vast naked and deserted spaces where they can experience the "sense of space" intensely, the all but sacred sense of a place evoked by a Barnett Newman, a timeless place where the immensity of nature places the human being into another time.

Heizer is particularly sensitive to this notion of timelessness: His father is a well-known archeologist. Smithson, who had observed Heizer working on his first "earthworks" in the West, was quickly seduced by places which rekindled his interest in the slow transformation and decomposition of life and material things.

Many eagerly await the photographs that document the evolution of the work of the Land Artists, who themselves wait out the continuing transformation of the works that will go on for many years.

WALTER DE MARIA:
LAS VEGAS PIECE. 1969.
Mormon Mesa, Nevada

A one-mile-long straight line traced through the desert in southern Nevada.

"I am interested above all in physical properties, in density, volume, mass, space. For example, finding a granite block measuring twenty feet along one edge. Now that's mass. It already is a sculpture as it is . . . My work is the antithesis of a sculpture, which implies shaping, welding, sealing, polishing one's matter. Also, I want my work to live, to destroy itself, to disappear while I myself am still alive."— MICHAEL HEIZER

MICHAEL HEIZER:
MASS—REMOVED AND PUT BACK IN PLACE. 1969.
Silver Springs, Nevada

CARL ANDRÉ:
EQUIVALENT VIII.
1966. London.
Tate Gallery

CARL ANDRÉ: THE MINIMALIST SCULPTURE

NEW YORK

Never has art, since the advent of the century seven decades ago, reached such a degree of stripped-downness, severeness, geometric austerity. Never has the paradoxical been pushed so far.

Carl André is a sculptor. For hundreds of years, a sculptor was somebody who elevated mass in space, a sculpture being a vertical object that is placed on something horizontal, usually a pedestal.

Carl André, however, turns the displaying of sculpture on its head. He has invented the flat sculpture. Almost two-dimensional, no bulk, horizontal on horizontal. The Guggenheim Museum has several sober structures, pieces of square metal on which the visitor is invited to walk.

Works of art that can be trampled! The need to desacredize art springs from a pragmatic viewpoint: Carl André wishes to be a consistent materialist. But, in reality, he does not break new ground. Who does not remember having walked with shoes on the steles of tombs in Italian churches?

Of course, the Guggenheim also exhibits other "pieces" by Carl André: wooden sculptures in simple geometric shapes, dating from 1958-1959, influenced by Brancusi; strips of aluminum with random shapes; and brick structures. "Shape = structure = place"—that is Carl André's formula. The emphasizing of the pedestal at the expense of the statuary itself, begun by Brancusi, reaches its ultimate limits with Carl André. Does this signify the end of the art of the idol?

THE BLACK OLYMPIA OF LARRY RIVERS

NEW YORK

It is because the critics had reproached Manet somewhat for placing a black woman and a black cat in his *Olympia* that Larry Rivers paints, as a sort of protest, a "Black Olympia"—entitled *I Like Olympia in Black Face*? Manet's bas-relief became one of the most famous paintings of French art, a pleasant, and unusual, surprise—it can currently be seen at the Marlborough Gallery.

Larry Rivers, who is forty-seven years old, began his first three-dimensional work in 1957: sculptures made from fused metals. He then began to create paintings in which his artistry as a sculptor could be perceived. In Egypt and ancient Mesopotamia, bas-reliefs were already made in color. Rivers reinvents them, with today's ways and symbols.

Rivers became totally dedicated to painting in 1946, and he studied it until 1948. His first one-man exhibition took place the following year; he was twenty-six. After a short phase of Abstract Impressionism, under the influence of Jackson Pollock and Willem De Kooning, he reintroduced figuration into postwar American art.

His Realism came directly from the iconic universe of the mass media. He employed advertising images and typeset letters, a practice that made him a forerunner of Pop Art. Manet in his *Olympia* was inspired by Titian's *Venus of Urbino*. Did the artist realize this? Larry Rivers, Venetian painter of a later date. From what we can tell from his playfulness, he just might like this label.

LARRY RIVERS:
I LIKE OLYMPIA IN
BLACK FACE. 1970.
Paris. MNAM

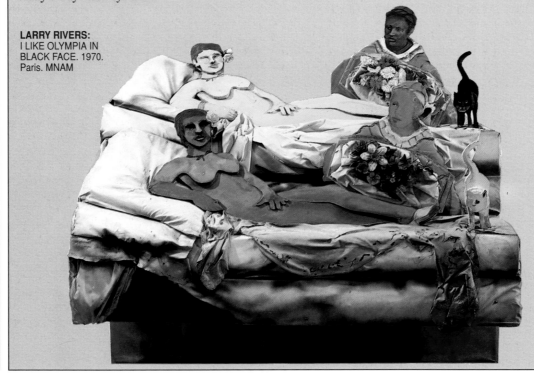

JIM DINE: THE HOUSECOAT

JIM DINE RECOGNIZED

LONDON

Jim Dine has been famous in the United States since the early sixties, ever since he was close to the center of some Happenings that he had helped create. As were Allan Kaprow and Robert Whitman, Dine was influenced by Abstract Impressionism, but moved somewhat away from it through these Happenings, which were a very personal matter to him, like those of Claes Oldenburg. Dine felt that the rapport between his artistic life and his personal life was too intense, and so he began to make his works from assorted objects, tools, and clothes that had no apparent connection to him personally.

Because Dine took objects from the current materialistic life, he quickly became linked to Pop Art. There was total freedom in working with the object, which had been rediscovered after many years of dealing with abstraction. The cutters or the palettes that Dine integrated with or attached to his works had an air of playfulness or detachment about them. Some of his works were aggressive, disturbing, when he added to them unusual objects like plumbing, clothing, and even a lawn, as though reality itself was being made questionable.

Jim Dine's interest in today's current objects must, however, not be equated with that of the Pop Artists, which is much more publicity-oriented. Dine asserts that Pop Art is mainly interested in the outside aspect of the structure of the objects or the materials, while he himself uses objects as metaphors for his feelings. The saws and other tools that he affixes to his works derive from childhood memories—from the hardware business of his grandfather. They are, on the other hand, instru-

WORKS CREATED WITH DISTURBING OBJECTS, AS THOUGH REALITY ITSELF WAS BEING MADE QUESTIONABLE

ments of the painter and the sculptor, an allusion to physical work that makes him feel good. What he wishes to do is to explore his own sensitive experiences and express them in physical and material terms.

The heart is a recurring theme in his paintings and his sculptures, and he refers frequently to his wife, Nancy, for example, in the giant straw heart entitled *Nancy and I at Ithaca (Straw Heart)*. As for his famous *House-coat*: One could think it is insignificant if it were not known that he saw it in a magazine and, imagining himself in it, made a kind of self-portrait. It is not the kind of housecoat that an Andy Warhol or a Tom Wesselmann might have painted, with publicity in mind. Neither is it an "essence" of clothing, a timeless symbol, like the sculpture of an electrical bulb by Jasper Johns. Dine's housecoat has, with other works, become a way of expressing the humor and the state of mind of the artist, sometimes somber and dramatic, sometimes light and cheerful.

Dine felt isolated among the New York artists because he did not find any other artist with his kind of sensitivity. He left with his family three years ago to live in London, where, in 1956, Pop Art was born!

671

THE VICTORY OF TINGUELY

MILAN

The British novelist Graham Greene should think twice before suggesting, as he does in *The Third Man*, that the Swiss were incapable of inventing anything but the cuckoo clock! The party organized on November 28 by Jean Tinguely, from Fribourg, is so lavish that it can be compared to the grandest extravaganzas put on by the Medicis and the Sforzas.

Tinguely came to Milan to help celebrate the tenth anniversary of the New Realism. The first celebration was held in Milan as well, in 1960. Tinguely and his assistant, Niki de Saint-Phalle, surpass themselves for the occasion.

The two artists constructed, in Dome Square, a gigantic monument entitled *Victory*, and draped it in a red cloth with the letters NR stamped on it, evoking the Christian "INRI." Eight thousand people gather for the event. The poet and writer Jacques Dufrêne addresses the crowd in an imaginary Italian composed mainly of vowels and reminiscent of a speech by Mussolini. A band makes several turns around the square playing military marches. During the interval, a group of Maoists play the *International* on a variety of instruments. Fifty police guard the monument. Three television crews film the event.

Tension rises to a dangerous level when, once the drape falls from the monument, a gigantic red phallus with two gold testicles decorated with bananas and raisins appears, set right between the two towers of the cathedral. The top of the phallus explodes, ejaculating fiery projectiles toward the sky. During the fireworks display, loudspeakers play *O Sole Mio* sung by a drunkard. Dada is not dead yet. But is it still possible to create a scandal? When Max Ernst and Baargeld exhibited works that were judged to be pornographic in the back room of the Winter Brasserie in Cologne, in 1920, the exhibition was immediately shut down by the police. Here, the police are in attendance and other Milan authorities merely close their eyes.

The day after, the newspaper *Corriere della Sera* speaks modestly of "a vertical statue of a symbolic character, reminiscent of the Greek god of fertility." Was the god, at the same time he exploded, being cuckolded? The uproar was so great in Dome Square that we will never find out.

JEAN TINGUELY: VICTORY, NOVEMBER 28. 1970. Milan. Dome Square

THE ANIMALIST LALANNES

LALANNE: SHEEP. 1965

PARIS

No, the gallery Iolas has not become a sheep farm. No, François-Xavier Lalanne and Claude Lalanne are not gentle shepherds playing their pipes amidst their herd. We are in an art gallery exhibiting the work of two artists. The two are unlike other artists, to be sure, subjecting the visitor to the undulations of their strangely silent mammals. It was four years ago, at the Salon of young painters, that their animals were shown for the first time.

There they stand on all fours, so dignified, even hieratic, not escapees from some rural enclosure but from an Egyptian or Assyrian room of the Louvre where, it has been said, François-Xavier worked as a guard. The Lalanne's material is neither wood nor stone. This couple, dreamers and fantasizers, are all-out modern. In order to make their sheep stand out, they used the most sophisticated techniques and materials, including electroforming and aluminum—and real sheepskins.

The originality of the Lalannes consists in not making a distinction between so-called noble art and the applied arts. They want their works to be placed in private or domestic places, not in museums. Their ideal is to reconcile the medieval concept of the artisan with the concept of the inspired modern artist.

Gnoli's Close-Ups

Domenico Gnoli, an Italian painter of the new generation, dies prematurely in New York at the age of thirty-seven. His imposing paintings, rather like those of Léger in his time, bring us close up to such objects as shirt collars, buttons, shoes, and hairstyles. These unusual views of usual objects create a dreamlike universe. His style, now unclassifiable, grew from Pop Art and Hyperrealism, and shows his great talent as a painter. Gnoli stands out among other artists today for his remarkable technique, as well as a taste for the bizarre that quickly brought him international attention. His passing came at a time of full artistic development.

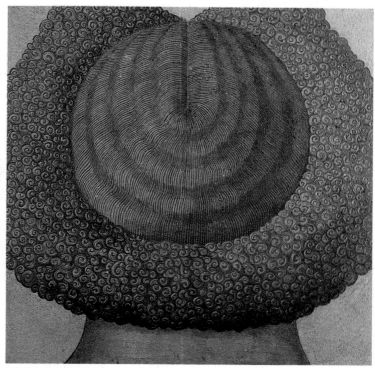

DOMENICO GNOLI: PERMANENT WAVE. 1964. Paris. Galerie Isy Brachot

Heavy Crowds at Dali Retrospective in Rotterdam

There are long lines at the Boymans Museum in Rotterdam despite chilly winter weather. Salvador Dali had hesitated for a long time before accepting the museum's offer of a retrospective, secretly fearful of seeing all his paintings together. He has told young artists: "Don't be afraid of perfection; you'll never reach it!" One is struck, upon viewing the exhibit, by both the exceptional technical qualities and inventiveness of the artist. The creative impulse is evident everywhere among the paintings, drawings, sculpture, objects, and jewelry of this most extravagant of the modern painters. The surprise at Rotterdam is discovering that Dali's genius is evident, not only in his surrealist art, but in his works done in the past twenty years. Through their precisely detailed mysticism they are the crowning glory of the show.

Happening and Fluxus Festival in Cologne

The Kuntshalle in Cologne is "exhibiting" ten years of activity by the "Happening and Fluxus" movement, presented by Harald Szeemann in the form of a festival. In the words of Allan Kaprow, who coined the word "Happening," "We have to learn to play again!" But it depends on the game, and,

in the case of Otto Mühl, the game may have gone too far. Mühl, naked except for an artificial phallus, threw cow's blood and intestines at two young women, also naked. Then the three rolled themselves in the bloody feathers of a goose whose head had just been cut off before the spectators. The tone of the festival was set by Vostell, who had tried, without success, to bring in a cow ready to give birth. The object was to lead it near a television set that was sitting on a pile of bones. The message? "A cow is to people what bones are to television!" The only message the public got was that the festival was a pathological display of provocation and scandal.

Color-Field Painters Are Dead

Mark Rothko took his own life in his studio this year. The famous painter had felt misunderstood in recent years, and his palette grew darker as his solitude increased. His last paintings look like night landscapes; he who was a poet of light left us in a shadowy place. The top half is dark, the bottom, light, like a stormy, oppressive sky. Another passing in New York: Bar-

nett Newman. His art, too, had changed, but toward, rather than away from, color. His last paintings were much larger; he often used acrylic paint in audacious chromatic combinations, reconciling with the physical reality absent in his early works.

Reconstruction of the "Merzbau"

In 1922, Schwitters had the idea to build a gigantic sculpture in the same spirit as his paintings. He worked for six years on the ever-growing column that had invaded his house in Hanover. Nazism forced him to stop, and it was destroyed by an Allied bombing in 1943. Two other attempts—in Lysaker, Norway, where he had sought refuge, and later in England—did not come to fruition, either. No *Merzbau*—as he called his structure—survived, but there has been a resurrection of sorts: A *Merzbau* has been built in Hanover. This "totem of banalities," to use Dadaist Raoul Hausmann's words, has conquered history to take its place in the eternity of art.

IN BRIEF...

UNITED STATES
Retrospective of the works of László Moholy-Nagy at the Guggenheim in New York.

FRANCE
The gallery Templon in Paris holds an exhibition of Gérard Titus-Carmel: "The Road of the Giants."

In Avignon, Yvonne and Christian Zervos organize an exhibition of recent Picasso works at the Palace of the Popes.

The inauguration of the ceramic sculpture 20th Century by Édouard Pignon, at the cultural center of Argenteuil, raises lively controversy.

JAPAN
The French painter Olivier Debré executes, for the CEE pavilion in Osaka, a wall of ceramics fifty-four feet long and over nine feet high.

The artist Kudo sculpts, on one of the seventy-two saw-tooth peaks of Mount Nikogiri, in Tokyo Bay, a Monument of Metamorphoses, *showing a hybrid form, half chrysalis, half phallus.*

SUPPORT-SURFACE AT THE MUSEUM

PARIS

The BMPT group and the group that exhibits their art at the ARC show for the first time this fall under the name "Support-Surface," after doing parallel work since 1966 on the concept of "the support."

BMPT—an acronym of their founders, Daniel Buren, Olivier Mosset, Michel Parmentier, and Niele Toroni—exhibited in January 1967, at the Salon de la Jeune Peinture, a canvas that was divided into twenty-nine red and white vertical stripes, another canvas that was white with a black ring in the center, and another with alternating with the markings of a flat paint brush in a quincunx pattern. Theirs is a calculated approach as to how to reconcile artistic sensitivity and the painter's individuality and role in society.

In fact, these works, which evoke the American Minimalists, are the products of a radical and violent breakaway from traditional art. The painting no longer has to give a message or represent anything else except its own material reality, that is to say, canvas, pigments, and shapes.

The Support-Surface artists exhibiting at the ARC for the first time—Vincent Bioulès, Marc Devade, Daniel Dezeuze, Patrick Saytour, André Valensi, and Claude Viallat—are systematically questioning the traditional concept of art. According to them, this art is the fruit of a bourgeois and capitalist society. In response, they are creating an abstraction that goes far beyond the formal limits of a work of art.

Thus, Viallat refuses to work with a frame. He uses cloth, then tissue, which he bends, ruffles, rolls up, "or floats in space," thanks to its suppleness. He tints rather than paints it, and applies indefinitely repeated markings. He also aims at "organizing the space without moving it, by showing knotted threads and ropes. Dezeuze is only interested in a frame that can

become mobile, changing into a trellis or into long flexible ladders of thin lath. The erect batons of Saytour and the ropes placed on the floor by Valensi reflect, too, a "zero degree" of painting.

Some of the critics and the public cry out that they see genius at work. Others remain indifferent, or wonder what it really is that these young talents have done to be talked about. Anyway, as perfect revolutionaries they do not hesitate to take full advantage of the museum —the bourgeois institution they want to destroy.

CLAUDE VIALLAT:
REPETITION. 1970.
Private Collection

VINCENT BIOULES:
UNTITLED. 1966.
Paris. CNAC

ENCHANTMENT AND SPACE AT EXPO 70

OSAKA

Expo 70 opens, on eight hundred and fifteen acres, on March 15. The general concept was executed by the architects Kenzo Tange and Noburu Kawazooe. Their basic idea was a new harmonious urban design, employing new techniques. Thirty-five industries and forty-seven nations participate. The exhibition can accommodate close to two and a half million visitors per day. Sundry means of transportation are available: electric minibuses, escalators, and moving sidewalks. Suspended bridges lead whole families into various pavilions.

The most remarkable construction is the "Space-Frame" of Koji Kamiaya, which covers the Festival Plaza and serves as a support for the light and sound equipment used for various shows. It was conceived as a homage to the French engineer Eugène Freyssinet, who is famous for having constructed, in the 1930s, hangars for dirigibles at Orly Airport, in Paris. The metallic structure dominates the Expo's main entrance, foreshadowing orbiting cities. Soaring above its transparent roof of 320,000 square feet, which shelters several panoramic restaurants, is an elongated spire rising a hundred and thirty feet, called the "Sun Tower" by Taro Okamato, the designer.

At ground level, the "Symbol Zone" runs north to south and is almost five hundred feet wide and over three thousand feet long. With its artificial lake, several water fountains, and traditional Japanese gardens, it neighbors the "Expo Tower" of Kikutake. Erected on a hill to the south is Expo's observatory. The foreign pavilions seem modest compared with the monumental metallic frames that dominate the site. Japan is indeed looking to the future. Without a doubt, the fair clearly reflects that inspiration.

The Canadian Pavilion at Expo 70.

Expo 70, at Osaka.

Many people thought our period was sworn to abstract art. But art follows its own calling, and now Paris discovers a great figurative painter in Francis Bacon, a sixty-two-year-old Englishman. His work is powerful, pitiless; the magazine Connaissance des arts has named him the finest living artist. In Brussels, a huge exhibition is devoted to the object, from Cubism to our day. The exhibition makes a new genre official, placing it on the level of painting and sculpture, and its indisputable possibilities, plastic as well as poetic, burst into bloom in full view here for the first time.

1971
SUMMARY

GREAT MASTERS

Francis Bacon: the Dedication
In Bacon's Words

DEVELOPMENTS

The Rothko Chapel
Resurgence of Prints in America

ART NEWS

Buren Removed from Guggenheim Show
Chef Spoerri
Ernest Pignon—Ernest's Recumbent Statues
Paik's Tele-Cello
Marcuse Defends "Bourgeois" Art
In Brief

AVANT-GARDE

The Metamorphosis of the Object
On the Object
The Doll-Woman Enters the Museum

LITERATURE

ALBANIA
Publication of Chronicle of the Town of Stones *by Ismaïl Kadaré.*

GERMANY
Heinrich Böll publishes Group Portrait with Lady.

MUSIC

UNITED STATES
Deaths of Igor Stravinsky and Louis Armstrong.

THEATER

FRANCE
Death of Jean Vilar.
Premiere of Prodiges *by Jean Vauthier.*

MOTION PICTURES

GREAT BRITAIN
Premieres of The Go-Between *by Joseph Losey, and* A Clockwork Orange *by Stanley Kubrick.*

ITALY
Thomas Mann's Death in Venice *is brought to the screen by Luchino Visconti, with subtle actors and sumptuous scenery.*

POLAND
Andrzej Wajda presents The Birch Forest.

FRANCIS BACON:
STUDY AFTER A PORTRAIT OF POPE INNOCENT X BY VELÁSQUEZ. 1953. New York. Private Collection

Francis Bacon.

FRANCIS BACON:
TWO PERSONS LYING ON
A BED WITH WITNESSES.
1968. New York. Marlborough
Gallery (Left panel of triptych)

FRANCIS BACON: THE DEDICATION

PARIS
Why did he choose permanent residency in Berlin in 1926? "Because it's the capital of vice!" And why doesn't he put more than one person in his paintings? Is it to express the solitude of contemporary man? "No, because as it is so difficult to paint just one person, why do two!"

This Englishman of sixty-two years, born in 1909 in the green land of Ireland, does not have the habit of being indirect. Neither in his life nor in his works. His father bred race horses near Dublin; the son began by being a manservant, then was a designer of modern furniture, before he turned to painting just before reaching the age of thirty. He went on to become one of the most expensive living painters of our time. And the magazine *Connaissance des arts*, which every five years publishes a list of the ten best painters worldwide,

classed him as being at the head of today's creative geniuses.

But he had to wait a long time for success; right up into his fiftieth year his paintings did not sell easily, his London agent had a full vault of things that he could not dispose of. This may seem amazing when visiting the important and magnificent exhi-

*IN AN AGE OF ABSTRACTION,
BACON DEPICTS REALITY IN ALL ITS CRUELTY*

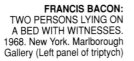

bition that the Grand Palais has dedicated to him.

It was said, forgetting about Gainsborough and Turner, that England had never produced great painters. At that time, the fashion for Abstractionism, Tachism, or Informal Art, reigned supreme. But Bacon was going against this stream and never attempted to do any abstract art. "Look at the Pollocks," he said, "when one looks

at them now, it's the same as old lace." Instead, what stirred up Bacon was a not very tenable reality: figures with glaring faces, women and men with terribly disjointed, ugly, wild bodies.

Curiously enough, his first paintings dealt with Eisenstein's *Battleship Potemkin*, and in particular the sequence of the Odessa staircase with the nanny who cried and shrieked. Then one day, passing through Paris, he bought a little book with illustrations of skin diseases. "I adore the shine and the color that comes from a mouth, and I have always hoped that I could paint a mouth as good as the sunsets of Manet." This is where it began.

After that, Bacon's paintings did not change much. One still

continues to see the same themes, the same dissections, the same cruelty. "I believe that man understands now that he is an accident, that he is a being devoid of all meaning." We are far from "man is the measure of all things" so dear to the Italian Renaissance. Neither realistic nor classic, nor both together, that is what Bacon has always tried to put on canvas. His works are meant to act directly on our nervous system, not on our spirit. In this he has had total success.

His references to the history of art are very revealing. Of the *Crucifixion* of Cimabue, regarded as one of the principal works of the Beatification, he wrote, "The image that I always carry in my head is that of a worm crawling to the foot of the cross." And, in a Degas found in the National Gallery in London, showing a woman at her wash basin sponging her back, he sees only torsions, as though the spinal column "was almost breaking through the skin."

But his first model seems to be Vincent Van Gogh, to whom Bacon dedicated many a painting showing poor Vincent, his painting material on his back, roaming through desolate places just outside Saint-Rémy-de-Provence. Like Van Gogh in his lifetime, Bacon had an accursed life as an artist for many years; like Van Gogh, he is a vagabond in a modern society he does not like; like Van Gogh, he is also fascinated by color through which he expresses "the terrible human passions." Above all, Bacon is a great colorist who knows how to find the right dissonance, precisely the opposite of all coarse Expressionism.

The artist tells us about the difficulty he has crossing the threshold of a butcher's shop because, like other animals, we are meat; and if he does go to a butcher, he finds it surprising that he, too, is not hung up by his feet amidst the quarters of beef. Rembrandt, and more recently Soutine, expressed the tragedy of meat in famous paintings. Today Bacon goes even further: It is man who is now hanging like a skinned live animal in his paintings.

How is it that such a difficult painter is included in the honor list of the painters of the year? Looking further than the pictorial qualities of Bacon's paintings, much truth can be found in his works that we don't find elsewhere. "I think," he says, "that now that we have at our disposal the mechanical means of recording, such as the movies, the camera, and the tape recorder, one should, in one's painting, plunge only into the most elementary and fundamental things."

While art has shown, during many hundreds of years, man as he is seen but not as he is, Bacon shows us the way we are in the depth of our being. Maybe that is what makes him so fascinating.

(See also 1963.)

IN BACON'S WORDS

Art is a method of opening up areas of feeling rather than merely an illustration of an object . . . A picture should be a recreation of an event rather than an illustration of an object; but there is no tension in the picture unless there is the struggle with the object.

I would like my pictures to look as if a human being had passed between them, like a snail, leaving a trail of the human presence and memory trace of past events as the snail leaves its slime.

FRANCIS BACON:
STUDY FOR A PORTRAIT
OF VAN GOGH, II. 1957.
Private Collection

painting, they were still, whatever their attitude to life, slightly conditioned by certain types of religious possibilities, which man now, you could say, has had canceled out for him. Man now can only attempt to beguile himself, for a time, by prolonging his life—by buying a kind of immortality through the doctors. You see, painting has become, all art has become a game by which man distracts himself. And you may say it has always been like that, but now it's entirely a game. What is fascinating is that it's going

One thing that has never been really worked out is how photography has completely altered figurative painting. I think Velásquez believed that he was recording the court at that time and certain people at that time. But a really good artist today would be forced to make a game of the same situation. He knows that particular thing could be recorded on film; so this side of his activity has been taken over by something else.

Also man now realizes that he is an accident, that he is a completely futile being, that he has to play out the game without reason. I think that even when Velásquez was painting, even when Rembrandt was

to become much more difficult for the artist, because he must really deepen the game to be any good at all, that he can make life a bit more exciting.

In my case all painting—and the older I get, the more it becomes so—is an accident. I foresee it and yet I hardly ever carry it out as I foresee it. It transforms itself by the actual paint. I don't in fact know very often what the paint will do, and it does many things that are very much better than I could make it do. Perhaps one could say it's not an accident, because it becomes a selective process what part of the accident one chooses to preserve.

THE ROTHKO CHAPEL

BARNETT NEWMAN:
BROKEN OBELISK. 1966. Houston. Rothko Chapel

HOUSTON

The inauguration of the chapel built by Jean and Dominique de Ménil took place on February 27. The chapel was built to house the last paintings of Mark Rothko, who died last year. In front of the chapel, reflected in the waters of an ornamental pond, the splendid *Broken Obelisk* has been erected—the ingly broken obelisk, symbolizing that which is tragic and yet eternal in human nature.

Inside the narrow and silent chapel one can contemplate the testament of Mark Rothko. His fourteen canvases, of very large dimensions, monochrome and extremely somber, induce meditation. Upon entering, still blinded by the bright light of the

FOURTEEN MONOCHROME AND EXTREMELY SOMBER PAINTINGS

work of Barnett Newman, who died just a few months after Rothko.

Monsieur and Madame de Ménil wanted to dedicate this obelisk to the memory of Martin Luther King, but the town refused to be a part of the project. In fact, it was the money of local patrons that purchased this great work and placed it here. The shape of the obelisk can be found in the most ancient of religions and corresponds entirely to Newman's aims: to establish a place where everyone can experience the heroic and sacred character of humanity, an unfinished, seem-

Texan sky, one very strongly gets used to the relative darkness of the building, whose interior is illuminated by a glass dome. When building this chapel, the de Ménils wanted to evoke what they had felt upon visiting Matisse's chapel in Vence and the church of Audincourt with the stained-glass windows of Léger. Overwhelmed by the works of Rothko, they requested the most somber of those he had ever painted, the ones he painted just before his death.

The Rothko chapel is open to all denominations.

(See also 1945, 1950, 1955, 1961, 1970.)

RESURGENCE OF PRINTS IN AMERICA

UNITED STATES

Prints, forgotten for a good many years, have found a new popularity thanks to Pop Artists. One of the first artists to work in this field, Tatiana Grosman, opened a lithography shop in 1957 called Universal Limited Art Editions. On the West Coast, June Wayne opened Tamarind Lithography Workshop where a new generation of engravers developed their skills. Tatiana Grosman brought Robert Rauschenberg, Jasper Johns, Barnett Newman, and numerous New York artists into ULAE

and enabled them to become familiar with and then use new lithographic techniques. This is how Jasper Johns became one of the most sought-after lithographers in the United States.

Kenneth Tyler, technical director of the Tamarind workshop, established the Gemini shops in Los Angeles as well; modern studios, disseminating the works of Stella, Kelly, Lichtenstein, and others. Silk-screen printing, made popular again by Andy Warhol, has even been reintroduced at universities.

Buren Removed from Guggenheim Show

Twenty artists were invited to exhibit their works at the Guggenheim Museum (among them, Lewitt, De Maria, Serra, Flavin, Judd, André, Morris and . . . Buren) for the Sixth International Exhibition. Paintings were to be hung in "boxes" set up along the spiraling walls. Buren instead hung an immense, striped, sixty-six-by-thirty-three-foot canvas from the ceiling that reached down to the second level. A second canvas was hung outside the building, stretching across the street. It was a fine example of the avant-garde artist's desire for total freedom, but a hue and cry went up to remove the painting from the inside space. Buren, his point made, took down both works and left the exhibit.

Chef Spoerri

Last year the New Realism movement had its tenth birthday party in Milan, an event organized by Spoerri. The public was invited to a "funeral banquet," where artists, dressed as the foods they thought symbolized them the most, offered themselves up. Arman was easy to spot under an "Accumulation" of eels in a sorbet shape; César wore a "Compression" of liquor-soaked pralines. This year, Daniel Spoerri is at it again at the Stedelijk Museum in Amsterdam. It is not exactly a banquet, but the risks of indigestion are the same. Moreover, Spoerri has just opened an "Eat-Gallery" in Frankfurt, where edible works are signed César, Arman, and Georges Brecht, who creates portraits of Spoerri in licorice.

Ernest Pignon-Ernest's Recumbent Statues

How do you celebrate the one hundredth anniversary of the Commune? It would be difficult to paint a picture without falling into the trap of the old Socialist Realism. That is why Ernest Pignon-Ernest, thirty-five, decided to commemorate the event in a different way, bringing together art and politics. Between Sacré-Coeur and the Charonne metro station, he laid down two thousand paper statues, like a human wave swept by the winds of history. A graduate of the May 1968 unrest, Pignon-Ernest feels that art must take to the streets. Agitprop? Provocation? The idea for the event was new and forceful and has made its organizer better known than artists his age who exhibit their work in more conventional ways.

Paik's Tele-Cello

Now here's something really new: a tele-cellist. Her name is Charlotte Moorman, and she is a specialist in contemporary repertoire. Nam June Paik met her for the first time in 1964 in New York where he had gone to meet G. Maciunas, the theorist of the Fluxus movement. When Moorman plays, the television screens surrounding her instrument show images that have been prerecorded or broadcast live and then transformed by a Paik/Abe synthesizer. The vibrations of each note are doubled by the vibration of the visual image. It is a conceptual and humorous piece that expresses the artist's feelings: "I am a poor man from a poor country; I must always be amusing."

Marcuse Defends "Bourgeois" Art

Art theory, which, according to Bazon Brock, boils down to the issue of contemporary creation, was the focus of debate during a five-day conference in Cologne. Among the eminent personalities present, Herbert Marcuse made a splash by defending so-called "bourgeois" art, invoking "moderation" and the "laws of beauty." This was to the great surprise of many, who no longer recognized behind these words the philosopher of *Eros and Civilization* and the pope of the student protests of the 1960s.

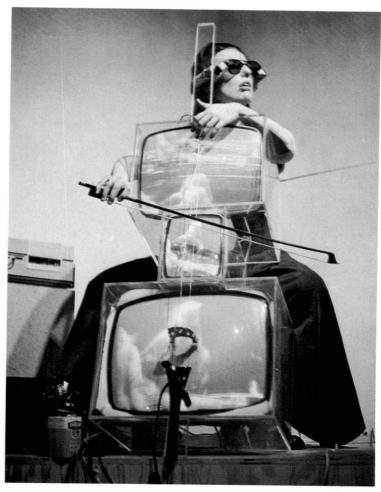

NAM JUNE PAIK:
THE TELE-CELLO. 1971.
(With the cellist Charlotte Moorman)

IN BRIEF...

GERMANY
In Düsseldorf, exhibition of the group "Zero," created ten years ago in reaction against Tachism.

Inauguration of the new Kunsthalle of Tübingen, with a Willi Baumeister exhibition.

BELGIUM
Exhibition of the Swedish Ballet at the National Theater of Belgium in Brussels. The collection—models, posters, costumes—was loaned by the Museum of Dance in Stockholm.

FRANCE
Clovis Prévost has made a short film on Joan Miró, Lithography of a Poster, showing the artist at work.

The CNAC holds an exhibition of Hans Bellmer, a French painter of German origin.

The artists' residence La Ruche in Paris, threatened by developers, is declared a landmark, and will be restored.

GREAT BRITAIN
The editor Anthony Blond opens Art Laboratory. This environment, intended for all creative activities, is located in King's Street in an old and immense underground hangar; it will hold, among other things, a bookstore, a theater, and an auditorium for pop music.

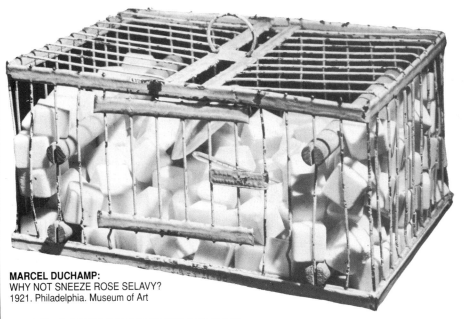

MARCEL DUCHAMP:
WHY NOT SNEEZE ROSE SELAVY?
1921. Philadelphia. Museum of Art

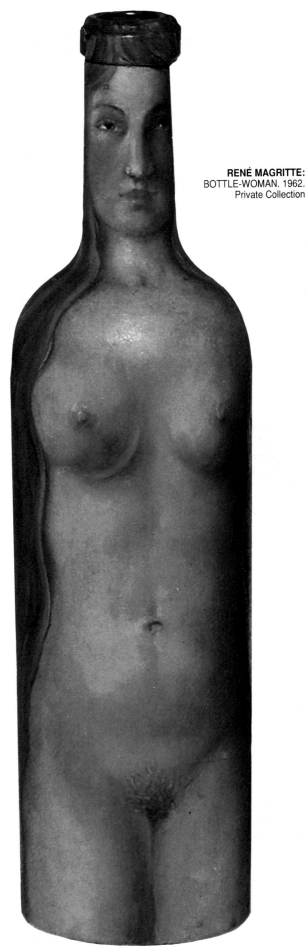

RENÉ MAGRITTE:
BOTTLE-WOMAN. 1962.
Private Collection

THE METAMORPHOSIS OF THE OBJECT

BRUSSELS

Starting April 22, the Palais des Beaux-Arts is presenting an imposing exhibition that is dedicated to the object and entitled "Art and Anti-Art, from Cubism through Today." The peregrinations of the object will be traced back in two parts, one historical, the other contemporary, both showing the metamorphoses of the commonplace.

The Cubist object, to begin with. Cubists stick to a limited repertory, newspapers and guitars being the most common objects. And the glass and the bottle. Simple, commonplace objects. However, this makes them the ideal subjects for study. Léger, for example, isolated the object, developing it out of context, making it a simple surface of color that contrasted with the other objects, as in *Mona Lisa with Keys* of 1928, in which Mona Lisa is portrayed next to a bunch of keys and a can of sardines.

For the Futurists, the object appears as relating to space, time, and movement. This cannot be expressed within a well-defined setting. With Analytical Cubism we come to the destruction of the object, as in the cases of Giacomo Balla and Boccioni.

The Dadaists, for their part, considered that the esthetic values of the standard object were already established. Duchamp chose any type of object for his "ready-mades," his only choice being that of bestowing on it the value of a work of art. And, paradoxically, the viewer of today, when looking at the bottle rack bought by Duchamp at a second-hand shop at a town hall bazaar in 1914 or at his urinal of 1917, perceives them as almost classic works of art now that the utilization of random objects and waste has pushed anti-art to an extreme.

Surrealism, too, has dedicated a large place to the object, both in paintings that show subjects in all sorts of unusual relationships, as in the creation of objects that lose their original attributes by taking on new characteristics, such as the *Bottle-Woman* of Magritte. These do away with their functionality in the sense of animism and fetishism.

But perhaps only now, in the present era of consumerism, does the art of the object come fully into its own. With the New Realism and Pop Art or, more recently, Land Art, the object reigns supreme. It exists as an artistic genre on the same level as painting and sculpture. It had to be shown. That is the major concern of this exhibition.

ON THE OBJECT

THE CUBIST OBJECT

The first Cubist objects were created by Picasso: They were guitars made of bits of string and roughly cut wood. The Cubists then put such things as pieces of newspaper, tobacco wrappers, and paper cutouts in their paintings. By the end of Cubism's analytic period, it was a means of proving that art could be created with anything, and of placing real elements in a painting.

THE FUTURIST OBJECT

The difference between the Futurist and the Cubist object is not always clear. However, the notion of the object in Futurism gives way to notions of speed, motion, and energy. The object cannot have a finite structure: It is dependent upon the domain of signification. Boccioni's wood and metal object representing a racehorse, is, by virtue of its concise lyricism, a perfect example of Futurist art.

THE DADA OBJECT

The typical Dada object is one like Duchamp's "ready-mades": an ordinary object such as a wine rack, a urinal, a snow shovel, presented as a work of art. Dada objects work on the principle of the ordinary, of the beauty of indifference, of ultimate neutrality. However, the boundaries between the Dada and Surrealist object are difficult to discern. Duchamp himself has created few "ready-mades." An object such as the one entitled *Why not Sneeze?*, composed of sugar cubes of white marble in a birdcage, is closer to Surrealism than to Dada.

THE SURREALIST OBJECT

Surrealism brings together two unlikely elements. The movement is inspired by Lautréamont, who said: "Beautiful like the chance meeting of a sewing machine and an umbrella on a dissecting table." Surrealist objects are based on the same principle. Meret Oppenheim's fur-lined teacup, Magritte's nude painted on a bottle—the point is to surprise and disturb. The effect is unsettling and dreamlike.

THE POP OBJECT

Pop Art makes frequent use of objects. There is Jasper Johns' American Flag, his lightbulb, his beer bottle, or Andy Warhol's Coke bottle. These objects mark the advent of the consumer society, which in the words of Arman "secretes" large quantities of new objects. The Pop object, rather than destabilizing art, as was the goal of Dada, strives to create a new standard of beauty.

THE DOLL-WOMAN ENTERS THE MUSEUM

LEVERKUSEN

Bellmer has initiated a school. Its now famous *Doll*, which may be disassembled, manipulated, and transformed at will, was the first object-woman in art, in the 1930s. Almost forty years later, the Museum of Leverkusen has dedicated an important exhibition to the glory of *The Doll* and, at the same time, to the derision of woman.

museum here, there are effigies of brothels dominated by the phantasms of desire.

The *Marilyn* series by Andy Warhol—simple silk-screens in vivid colors—also express the myth of the object-woman, but with the offhand manner and irony of this *enfant terrible* of Pop Art. The same qualities are found in *Cosmetic Ladies* by Richard Hamilton and in the

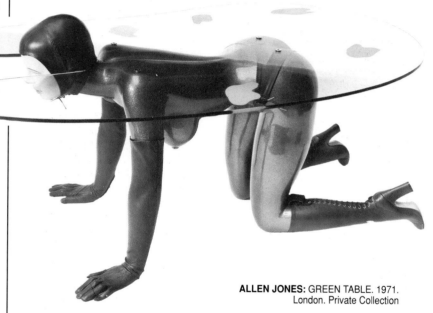

ALLEN JONES: GREEN TABLE. 1971.
London. Private Collection

Indeed, what are all these table-women, chair-women, armchair-women, monster-women, and star-women if not an image of mocked and even enslaved woman?

The notion was introduced by the Surrealists. Not only Bellmer, but also Magritte, Dali, and Max Ernst, for whom women were simultaneously idols and foes. Today, it is striking to reencounter the entire ambiguity of that time in the sadomasochist furniture of Allen Jones, as well as in Wesselmann's nudes: depersonalized and prefabricated, often obscene with their unexpected pubic hair on synthetic skin. It was said that Titian's paintings of Venus, in commercially hedonistic Venice, were bedroom paintings. In the

bare-breasted pinups leaning on toothpaste tubes by Mel Ramos. Here, woman is funny, attractive, playful, as images coming straight from advertising should be. They are the opposite of Niki de Saint-Phalle's *Nanas*, full of teeth and claws, ready to bite, although—they, too—not without *some* humor and playfulness.

Art is a long way from the time when André Breton wrote that beauty should be convulsive, erotic-veiled, exploding-fixed, and magic-circumstantial, or there is no art. At the Museum of Leverkusen, it is erotic-*un*veiled, hence both the interest and the vulgarity of the exhibition. It can be seen as a document of the period.

Cries, insults, and blows greet the preview of the "72/72" Exhibition at the Grand Palais in Paris. The creature of President Pompidou, it regrettably expresses the discomfiture of artists in regard to political power, as the richness and diversity of creative activity in France over the past twenty years is now revealed. A retrospective of Soulages at the University of Maryland, and the reissue of an important essay by Nicolas Schöffer, The Cybernetic City, seem proof enough that the current Parisian School is not as anemic as some people would like to make it seem.

1972

SUMMARY

GREAT MASTERS

**Soulages: the Severity of Black
In Soulages's Words**

AVANT-GARDE

**The Trees of Dubuffet
The Pseudo-Living Figures of George Segal
Oldenburg Reinvents Still Life**

POLEMIC

The Blows of the 72/72 Exhibition

ART NEWS

**Agam's Illusions
Christo's Valley Curtain
An Airy Stadium for Munich
A School of Vision
Catherine Millet on Conceptual Art
In Brief**

DESIGN

Italian Innovation

WRITINGS AND THEORIES

Nicolas Schöffer: the Prospective and Art

LITERATURE

AUSTRIA
Peter Handky publishes A Sorrow beyond Dreams.

UNITED STATES
Publication of No Name in the Street *by James Baldwin.*

THEATER

FRANCE
The Royal Shakespeare Company presents, at the Théâtre de la Ville, A Midsummer Night's Dream, *staged by Peter Brook.*

DANCE

FRANCE
Maurice Béjart and Les Ballets du XXe Siècle present, at the Palais des Sports, Nijinsky, clown de Dieu, *with music by Pierre Henry.*

MOTION PICTURES

AUSTRIA
The avant-garde film festival in Vienna includes propaganda films of 1935-1945: German, British, American, and Russian documents.

UNITED STATES
Premiere of Savages *by James Ivory.*

FRANCE
Bernardo Bertolucci's Last Tango in Paris *is released amidst much controversy.*

SWEDEN
Three women and Death are the protagonists in Ingmar Bergman's Cries and Whispers.

PIERRE SOULAGES:
PAINTING MAY 14, 1968. 1968.
Paris. MNAM

PIERRE SOULAGES: PAINTING APRIL 14, 1956. 1956. Paris. MNAM

SOULAGES: THE SEVERITY OF BLACK

ANNAPOLIS

The black trees are added to the ruins of Sainte-Foy de Conques. If childhood is sufficient to explain the works of an artist, this could well be the two sources of the paintings of Soulages, to which the Art Gallery of the University of Maryland has dedicated an important exhibition.

At the age of twelve or fourteen, Pierre Soulages visited the famous ruins for the first time, taken by a Rodez schoolteacher on a school outing. And that was when he was struck. Bowled over by the architecture and the sculpture, he thought that "it was the only thing that one should really do . . . the only thing worth one's pains and dedicating one's life to." The nave of Sainte-Foy, its columns with their severe lines, the coarse material of the stones, the changing tones of the semidarkness that cut the rays of light coming from the narrow win-

dows, it was there, at the core of these overpowering Roman monuments, that he realized that he would be an artist.

And then, the black trees. "When I was a child," he confided to his biographer, the art critic and historian James Johnson Sweeney, "I trimmed trees in

Pierre Soulages.

winter. I have never painted trees with their foliage or things like that . . . I begin with a tree but I transform the shapes of the branches. After all, a tree is a kind of abstract sculpture. What interested me at that time was the layout of the branches, their movement in space."

With his strong childhood impressions, his short passage through the Beaux-Arts Academy of Paris in 1938, where the teaching left him disappointed and surprised, was of little importance. A few visits to the Louvre made him understand why his first one-man exhibition in 1949 at Lydia Conti's gave the critics and the Parisian public a sense of his having found his own particular style very quickly.

Soulages was molded by contact with worn materials, such as the Roman stone, the earth, the pebbles. But he kept the architecture of the trees. The main characteristic in his painting is found in his lines, in displaying them vertically and horizontally, within a rhythm, play, and articulation of the theme.

In an era where his generation, just after the war, was marked by painting what it witnessed in the war, he was one of the few who refused to be anecdotal or documentary. And even though he was not figurative, he seemed to have passed over the influences of the fashionable Abstractionism in which many artists of his era remained adrift. It is equally impossible to attribute to abstract painting the fact that his art was never based on intellectual research, because he was always moved by a rush of creativity, by emotion, and by poetry.

In trying to define him, one sees that Soulages is above all a craftsman. He discovered progressively what he needed. For example, when he thought it useful, he took a piece of walnut shell for his composition. He gave up paintbrushes for a scraper and a spatula, for he wanted to flatten and display the painted parts in a more distinct fashion. He claimed that the work of an artist is strongly determined by his choice of materials, by its consistency, perhaps thick, viscous, or liquid, and by the tool that allowed him to work. This is also something "gestural" to the degree that painting is, in his eyes, essentially the trace of a gesture.

Some of his works of the 1950s contain browns, blues, ochres, and even reds, which most of the time came out transparent. But Soulages got more and more to using a single color. Black became his preferred means of expressing himself. Internal needs? He explained that he had always been attracted to black, with its tone of absoluteness. A return to childhood? In his designs, not only the trees but also the snow was painted black.

Some have compared Soulages to Rembrandt because of the chiaroscuro. Perhaps this is going too far. As to his predilection for things Roman, he is not sure that an occasional concern with elegance is necessarily a contradiction to his art. In any case, Soulages was born, on December 24, 1919, in Rodez. Before the Roman era, Rodez was a Celtic or Gallic center. Within this painter there is something of Celtic ancestry that now seems to seduce the frontier spirit of America.

IN SOULAGES' WORDS

If the involuntary figurative anecdote is not to be found in my painting, no doubt it is because of the importance given in it to rhythm, to that throbbing of forms in space, to that cutting up of space by time.

Time seems to me to be one of the preoccupations expressed in my painting; time seems to me to be at the center of my approach to painting, time and its relationships with space.

The artist's intentions, like the viewer's explanations, are always false keys. They

ing that is not figurative introduces other relationships: For viewer and painter alike, the world is no longer looked upon, but lived, it has become part of the experience they have of it.

There is no human faith more exalting than that which draws a great deal of humble attention to what is born rather than attempting to codify the past only to invent a future just like it.

The things I found fraternal, the earth, old wood, stone, rusted iron, all of these worn

PIERRE SOULAGES: PAINTING APRIL 30, 1972. 1972. Paris. Galerie de France

approach only one side of a work, they do not even begin to penetrate the enigma it represents: A painting, like an entire work, borrows and then sheds the meanings we lend it.

I have always thought that the more limited the means, the stronger the expression: That may explain the choice of a small palette.

Because painting is an adventure into the world, it signifies the world. Because it is a synthesis, it signifies it in its totality.

If by figuration a painting introduces reciprocal relationships with the world, the paint-

things have surely left their mark on me. I have always preferred them to pure and lifeless materials.

For me, my painting has always stood apart from the figurative-versus-nonfigurative dilemma. I do not start out from either an object or a landscape, later to distort them, nor, conversely, do I seek to conjure them up in my painting.

It seems to me that what happens in a painting, which, from an object in the making, suddenly comes alive, defies description.

JEAN DUBUFFET:
GROUP OF FOUR
TREES IN NEW YORK.
1972. New York City

GEORGE SEGAL:
TIMES SQUARE. 1970.
Omaha. Joslyn Art
Museum

THE TREES OF DUBUFFET

THE PSEUDO-LIVING FIGURES OF GEORGE SEGAL

NEW YORK

The petrified Happening! This, it seems, is what George Segal has invented. For it cannot be said that these are sculptures as such when one thinks in terms of those created by Michelangelo or Rodin, these personalities made of plaster mixed in with one's daily life on the pavement on Times Square or sitting on a public bench in Central Park. The artist, one is told, discovered his path by chance in the summer of 1961. He was then a painter and gave courses in painting, inviting his pupils to use the most unusual materials when telling them to put something together. One day, a young woman who was in his class arrived carrying a box of dress-ing gauze. Segal got the idea of plunging this gauze into plaster, then asked his wife to apply it directly onto his body. After the gauze had dried and been cut off and reconstructed, he thought the result was startling. His path

*HE MAKES FIGURES OF PLASTER
AND MIXES THEM IN WITH OUR DAILY LIFE*

had been found. The main interest of the work for Segal, however, does not lie in the cast or mold but in the distortions brought about by it. In fact, after wrapping them in their bandages, his figures have to wait for about forty minutes until the plaster is dry, something they cannot do without moving a lit-tle. Their minute movement, their becoming more limp, and eventually their mental attitudes are retained by the plaster, con-serving the impression as does a track or a mirror. This explains how Segal managed to avoid the danger of ending up in the Grévin wax museum. One is reminded of Rembrandt's *Beth-sheba*, for which X-rays demon-strate that his model, in the var-ious sessions of posing, was slowly "collapsing." The environ-ment does the rest. Segal's works are the pseudo-living.

NEW YORK

Although they are dominated by the inflexible and vertiginous skyscrapers of New York that surround them, the *Four Trees* that Jean Dubuffet planted in July on the square in front of the Chase Manhattan Bank look like giant mushrooms. And one could almost find them poi-sonous if the initiator of Art Brut would not assert that he is not provocative at all. "My position," he states, "is that of celebration, and whoever thinks he can rec-ognize sardonic and satirical intentions, or bitterness or abuse, has totally misunder-stood them." Created in epoxy in his studios in Périgny-sur-Yerres, and painted with poly-urethane, his phytoform trees, none taller than forty feet, seem to suggest the desire of an ir-rational reconquering of this harsh and arrogant space that is the island of Manhattan.

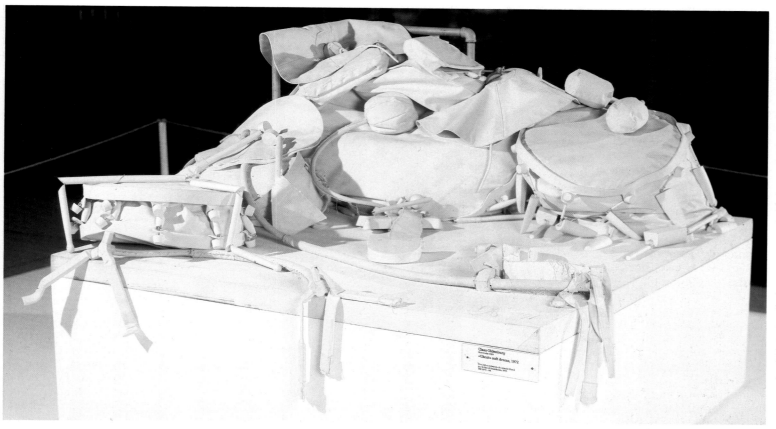

CLAES OLDENBURG: "GHOST" DRUM SET. 1972. Paris. MNAM

OLDENBURG REINVENTS STILL LIFE

NEW YORK

Claes Oldenburg seems to have lost the sense of measure. What should one call his works? Paintings? Sculptures? Monuments? Already in the 1960s, finding that painting is too limited, he wanted to play with "total space" in his Happenings. Then came the introduction of pliant, nonfitted objects. Who does not remember his exhibition at the Green Gallery in 1962, which showed his very first vinyl objects and where the visitors could amuse themselves by changing the shapes?

Today, since the earth is itself a work of art in his eyes, he is becoming more and more inclined toward monumental art. Besides the *Triple Electric Outlets,* presented in March at the Sidney Janis Gallery, he continues to enlarge his earlier works: *Geometric Mice; Fagends, Clothespins, Correction Key,* and so on.

The themes have very little variety. Oldenburg has always had a passion for cheeseburgers and ice cream. And with Dubuffet he shares a taste for cheap-looking materials and repulsive objects. Or maybe he just practices the confusion of the era around him. His motors and telephones have the consistency of human organisms, and his pliers have the elegance of women's legs, in accordance with a sort of generalized animism. While Rauschenberg integrates the object, as in his Combine paintings, Oldenburg modifies it morphologically, obtaining in this fashion "a work of art and an object, both at the same time."

Given their dimensions, his gigantic works have necessitated help from people in industry. Lippincoat, Inc. of New Haven, Connecticut, has replaced the help of his wife who usually assisted him in his work. He sees himself as being in the mechanistic spirit characteristic of twentieth-century America. At the same time, the conjuring-up of objects that have disappeared from the market makes him state that he is creating "an industrial-objects cemetery." Besides, he thinks that the cooperation of workmen and

"MY THOUGHTS ARE MORE AMERICAN THAN SURREALIST"

engineers creates a new sort of Happening, as when construction of a giant project takes on a theatrical aspect.

But perhaps Oldenburg is, at forty-three, one of the masters of still life, and is rekindling this kind of art. This type of art, as we know, consists historically of paintings of hunting guns, game pouches, game birds with and without feathers, all arranged in a certain order. Then it became painting of objects which, as did the works of Chardin and our own Morandi, took on a secret life. Oldenburg wanted to "rework" his objects, "relate to their death," and that is precisely what he did with his typewriters and his washbasins when he made them collapse lifelessly, or in his most recent work *"Ghost" Drum Set,* with its flaccid drums, as if it were slowly melting around us.

This approach, if it owes something to Cubism, to Constructivism, and to Surrealism, is mainly experimental. "My thoughts are more practical, more American than Surrealist . . . I am not an abstract artist. I am a Realist . . . In my way of looking at things, abstraction does not delve into one's everyday life." No doubt this is why Oldenburg wishes to replace the statues of anachronistic American heroes with what is truly America: the objects currently being used, such as fans or lipstick, on gigantic lips.

(See also 1964.)

THE BLOWS OF THE 72/72 EXHIBITION

PARIS

The exhibition "72 years of contemporary art in France," which opened in May at the Grand Palais, will go down in history for the difficult relationship between art and power. President Georges Pompidou, anxious to restore the Parisian School to its old prestige, wanted this exhibition. A commission presided over by François Mathey, avant-garde curator from the Museum of Decorative Arts, had chosen seventy-two names that represented, according to him, the current trends among French painters and among foreign painters currently working in France. Now, on the day of *vernissage*, the law, and not the critics, came out in force to calm things down.

The Malassis cooperative, which gathered together, painters such as Tisserand, Parré, and Cueco, followed by others, decided to take down their works at the same time that other artists were putting up theirs along the length of the picture rail. Cries, insults, clashes with the law took place. François Mathey justified his choice of a jury by stating that he did not choose its members from an honors list but from a selection of major artists whose works had contributed to the

The Malassis cooperative withdraws its paintings from the Pompidou exhibition at the Grand Palais. At left, Tisserand holding a painting.

Parisian artistic climate over the past ten years. The opponents retorted that once an artist is officially recognized by the powers that be, he will inevitably produce into kitsch. "No exhibitions, but good galleries for the artist; more orders, less mundane hot air." 72/72 started off rather badly.

And yet, the large numbers that turned up were able to find richness and diversity in the works on display, such as those of Bettencourt, who makes extremely erotic paintings with unusual materials such as bits of tissue paper, slates, and egg shells. Or those of Réquichot,

who committed suicide in 1961; or the works of Kalinowski, Velickovic, and perhaps above all of Dado for his incredibly violent fantasmagorical inspiration.

Born in Montenegro, thirty-nine years old, Dado has lived in France since 1956. His real name is Miodrag Djuric; Dado was the nickname given to him by his mother. Flayed and maimed alive, the beings in his works change, are transformed, become mineralized. Daniel Cordier, a dealer of Dado's works and a member of the commission, speaks on his behalf when he writes, "I am astonished that they criticize his works as being

morbid. The works disclose reality, what surrounds us. But we don't want to see it, being ashamed of our health, our comforts, and our indifference." Almost all of the works of Dado are in blue, the eternal blue of a summer sky that frays one's nerves as does a very long winter. Every stump talks about our terrible truth. One cannot see how the powers that be could recover from this.

It is said that in France everything ends with songs. This time, and it is a great pity, all has begun with blows!

DADO: LARGE BLUE BEACH. 1969. Paris. MNAM

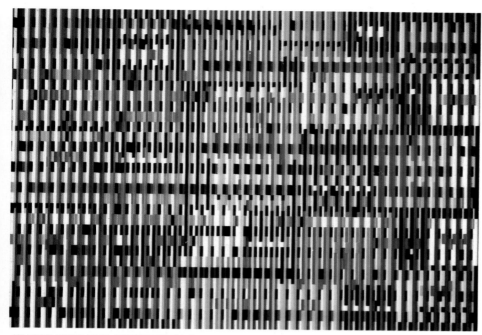

YAACOV AGAM: DUAL METAMORPHOSIS III. 1968-1969. Paris. MNAM

Agam's Illusions

"What is art? In my opinion, it must rival God." Yaacov Agam is the ambitious, forty-four-year-old son of a rabbi. A retrospective of his works at the Musée National d'Art Moderne in Paris covers almost twenty years of activity, from the first works to his current *Metamorphoses*. Since his arrival in Paris in 1951, Agam has continually used the most modern artistic techniques. There is, for example, his recent oil on aluminum entitled *Dual Metamorphosis III,* completed in three years. The work seems to change, depending where one stands in relation to it. These "plastic themes," as the artist calls the seeming movements, present an ever-changing view to the spectator, who thus participates in the artistic creation.

Christo's Valley Curtain

The Great Wrapper's latest dream: a curtain made of more than twenty thousand square yards of orange nylon drawn across highway 325, seven miles north of Rifle, Colorado. Thirteen hundred feet long, almost five hundred feet high. On August 10, around thirty workers were still scrambling to attach the last of twenty-seven ropes needed to hold up the gigantic piece of synthetic fabric. It took nearly thirty months of work and the advice of specialists to pull off this latest stunt of Christo's, who is not exactly an amateur at this kind of thing. He has already wrapped a tower and a fountain at Spoleto, then the Kunsthalle in Bern, and even a seven-thousand-cubic-yard "air column" at the Documenta in Kassel. His sense of the monumental comes from his native Bulgaria, where, during his years of study at the School of Fine Arts in Sofia, one of his jobs was to arrange agricultural machinery in fields near the tracks of the Orient Express in order to impress foreign travelers aboard the trains.

An Airy Stadium for Munich

International athletes left the gigantic, one-hundred-thousand-seat Aztec amphitheater in Mexico City for the 17th Olympic games at Munich's new stadium. It is the work of the German architect Günther Behnisch, known for his elegant structures. The frame of the stadium is the logical development of new structures begun by Freyssinet and continued by Nervi. The use of prestretched canvas and beams of tubular steel make it possible to cover large surfaces and make the stadium's roof lightweight and translucent, adding to the beauty of the games.

A School of Vision

For the last Documenta, responsibilities had been split up within a general organizing committee. This year, Harald Szeemann alone is in charge. This former director of the Kunsthalle in Bern wanted to turn the famous event into an antimuseum. The proposed program is enormous. It is based on the idea that our everyday world is dominated by images; the Documenta should thus be a sort of school of vision. Which is why one can find artwork from psychiatric wards alongside "photorealist" paintings and "personal mythologies." As for Socialist Realism, with its heavy emphasis on imagery, it should have been represented, too, but neither the Soviet Union nor China would send any works.

Catherine Millet on Conceptual Art

We suspected that Conceptual Art was tied to linguistics; now we have proof. Catherine Millet, director of Art Press, has collected some of her previously published studies into a single book. The chapter titles read "Conceptual Art As Semiotics of Art," "The Use of Language in Conceptual Art," etc. She tells the reader in the preface that the collection of studies, which were written for various occasions, are not to be viewed as a whole. They do, nonetheless, comprise a remarkable critical ensemble. *Conceptual Art:* Do read it carefully.

ITALIAN INNOVATION

The postwar era made Italy a center for design and a laboratory for innovation. Most Italian designers receive degrees in architecture from Milan's polytechnical school. This rigorous training gives their work its distinct style. But these designers are children of the Renaissance, and their rigorous standards never exclude a sense of playfulness.

The Italians have a special flair when it comes to sofas and chairs. Just after the famous Sacco was designed in 1968 by Gatti, Paolini, and Teodora for Zanotta, Poltronova launched its Joe sofa. This giant baseball glove of a chair was inspired by Claes Oldenburg's sculptures.

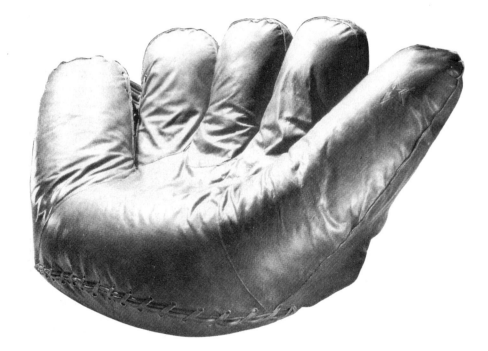

The "Pipistrello" (bat, as in the animal) lamp, created in 1965 by the Milanese designer Gae Aulenti, is one of a series of imaginative lamps. Aulenti's designs are mostly for the home, with somewhat of an Art Deco influence.

It started fifty years ago when Olivetti, an industrialist, asked Nizzoli, an architect, to design a typewriter. Then came Ettore Sottsass, who designed the latest Olivetti Valentine in 1969. This bright red, Pop Art style machine received Italy's coveted Compasso d'Oro award for beauty in design.

NICOLAS SCHÖFFER: THE PROSPECTIVE AND ART

What will be the future conditions of artistic creation? This serious question is at the heart of the work and writings of Nicolas Schöffer, sixty years old, initiator of Luminodynamism. As far as he is concerned, there will not be any future for art if art does not take root in technology and prospective thought. In 1956, Schöffer created *Cysp I,* the first "cybernetic sculpture." He widens his concerns to architecture and urbanism which must be rethought, according to him, on a new basis. The passage that follows is from *La ville cybernétique,* his last book, published two years ago and republished today.

The question can be raised: Why try to forecast the future of the art? We know that because of a permanently accelerated evolution of the various branches of human activity it has become absolutely necessary to forecast the conditions of this evolution, stages of this evolution following one another faster and faster. Without a certain foresight we run the risk of being overtaken by the events or to become disoriented. One useful technique—prospective—has been with us for the last few decades. It uses more and more improved and complex scientific methods to establish lines of interaction and the best conditions for evolution. Prospective has developed in various key sectors—economy, industry, political strategy—and especially in the organization of production and distribution-consumption, that is, in the socialization of products. It matters little whether this technique is used in a capitalist or a socialist system, because both systems must increasingly objectivize their economy to obtain solutions that will eventually be similar.

The only sector that still escapes completely from organized prospective is the art sector (including architecture). This exception is all the more paradoxical as art is the field of avant-garde par excellence; and it is, in fact, in art that prospective has first appeared, and continues to rule, but in an intuitive way, nonorganized and relatively ineffective.

We can say that art is, and must be, prospective in a permanent manner. When art ceases to be prospective, it becomes redundant, folkloric, or commercial.

But while the prospective character of art hardly was noticeable in the rhythm of the past, today, with an accelerated rhythm of evolution, this prospective character becomes evident.

Permanent prospective demands constant effort. From now on, the artist's work must be directed toward a vision and a concept that are instantly future-oriented, and which forbid the artist any retrospective attitude, and even any stagnation.

The artist's work will take place with decreasing intellectual comfort. The artist must be the fulcrum of universal conscience.

The more or less gratuitous appearance of art will disappear as its role will become more visible and more important.

The artist must cease to practice an art of the image and must create an art of conditioning. It will no longer be enough to give the public certain impressions; the public must be impressed profoundly. To reach this goal, the products of artistic creation must enter into the vital circuits of society.

The totality of information networks, of interchange systems of any kind, must be opened up to true esthetic products. But this demands a new artistic technology, and a total transformation of the relationship of the producing artist and the consuming public.

We have brought up the problem of immateriality. When the artist uses the information networks that we are in the process of improving constantly, the immateriality and uniqueness of the object are no longer sufficient for the distribution of esthetic products through these networks. On the other hand, the esthetic products, which are linked to the primordial problem of conditioning and are thus destined to impress in depth, must not fascinate in a hazardous, gratuitous, and ephemeral manner, but must become integrated into the basic program that determines the rhythm of daily life and must become the stimulating ferment of our actions, the preparatory elements of our cyclical decontractions, thus creating an optimal, omnipresent, and quasi-permanent environment for the human being.

NICOLAS SCHÖFFER
La ville cybernétique *(Extract)*

The century belongs to Picasso. In the history of art, the twentieth century will doubtless be known by his name. Indeed, he saw all, tried all, succeeded before anyone else did, so much so that few artists except Duchamp or Matisse can be compared to him. The demiurge of painting, he dies at the canonical age of ninety-two. Another irreparable loss comes a few days later with the premature death of the Danish painter Asger Jorn—great colorist and founder of the Cobra movement in 1948—just as he was becoming known.

1973
S U M M A R Y

GREAT MASTERS

**Picasso, the Genius Who Was Struck Down
In Picasso's Words**

THE MARKETPLACE

Contemporary Art on the Auction Block

ART NEWS

**The Political Comic Strip
Saree Is Dead
Japanese Galleries Come to Paris
Chagall Museum Inaugurated
Two Million Dollars for a Pollock
In Brief**

AVANT-GARDE

Coucou Bazar
Ben's Boutique

GREAT MASTERS

The Jorn Miracle

LITERATURE

GERMANY
Publication of Lenz *by Peter Schneider.*

FRANCE
Publication of Triptych *by Claude Simon, and* Giants *by J.-M. Le Clézio.*

MUSIC

FRANCE
Rolf Liebermann assumes the direction of the Paris Opera.

ITALY
Luciano Berio composes Concerto for Two Pianos and Orchestra.

MOTION PICTURES

UNITED STATES
The Western loses John Ford, its foremost producer.

FRANCE
Costa-Gavras is awarded the Louis Delluc prize for State of Siege.
    Premiere of Day for Night *by François Truffaut.*

PABLO PICASSO:
WOMAN'S HEAD. 1962
Paris. Musée Picasso

PICASSO, THE GENIUS WHO WAS STRUCK DOWN

MOUGINS

Picasso is no more. This giant, this genius, consummated his wondrous destiny. His legend begins. And already we ask: How will his work fare in the future? Only this era, our era, could be so suitable for him, an era without tradition, without faith, always on the launching pad, creative, in shock, feverishly adolescent, changeable. By the sheer power of his passion, Picasso became both the Balzac and the Rimbaud of modern art. He died on Sunday, April 8, following a heart attack that came just after a pulmonary edema. He was ninety-two years old.

In the preceding days, nothing led one to believe that this would happen so quickly. On Saturday night, the eve of his death, he had had his attorney, Monsieur Antebi, and his wife over for dinner. During the night things got worse as Picasso, feeling that he was suffocating, was gasping for breath. His private physician

incredible act. He gave an enormous pull on his cigar and blew it into the face of the baby, who then grimaced and started to cry.

Could we discern in this trauma the violence, the ravaging, the tragic dimensions of his work—his showing the difficulty of being, from the beginning, in his paintings of the blue and rose period; his reducing the world of objects to scraps during the Cubist period; and, later, his dislocating and contorting of the human body?

Talking to Malraux one day about his first visit to the Trocadero Museum during the summer of 1907, where he discovered African art, he was vociferous about his fascination and horror when he found himself unexpectedly stopping in front of what were then called "fetishes." "I understand. I myself, too, am against things. I, too, think that the unknown is the enemy. Everything, not just details like women, children, animals, tobac-

PABLO PICASSO: THE THREE DANCERS. 1925. London. Tate Gallery

DURING THREE QUARTERS OF A CENTURY, HE MADE A TEMPEST BLOW THROUGH THE WORLD OF ART

gave him injections to calm him down, then called a cardiologist from Paris. When the specialist arrived, Picasso was dozing; from time to time, he muttered semiintelligible phrases. Everybody, including his wife, Jacqueline, who was seeing an abyss of loneliness opening up, understood that the end was near.

His birth on October 25, 1881, in Malaga, came under very strange circumstances. He who was destined to become the most famous painter of the century, an equal to the Michelangelos and the Tintorettos of another era, refused to be born. In spite of being patted and smacked, not a breath was coming forth from his tiny icy lips. Then the obstetrician, Salvador Ruiz, who was his uncle on his mother's side, distressed at seeing the tiny inert body, did not hesitate to perform an

Pablo Picasso.

co, playing. Everything! I came to understand why I am an artist."

This unknown, the enemy! Picasso never ceased to repeat that. Ever since the Spanish Civil War he defined his painting as an offensive and defensive weapon against the enemy. Later on he spoke of the fact that each of his paintings was an epitome of destruction. Picasso cut up, distorted, broke, and dislocated his works. During three quarters of a century, he made a tempest blow through the world of art.

Nevertheless, if Picasso gave forms of violence to his works, he also had another side, love and tenderness. Save for the Cubist period, which was essentially an enormous struggle with the world of objects, in each artistic stage he went through in his life there was a different woman. There was the conventional Olga Koklova, a petite dancer with the Russian ballet. He met her in Rome in 1917. She, for a while, made him paint in a traditional and prudent style. Then there was the blonde and buxom Marie-Thérèse Walter, who corresponded to the era of women-flowers and metamorphoses. And there were others, including the tortured Dora Maar, who cries those bitter tears in *Guernica*; Françoise Gilot during the brilliant period of Antibes; and above all his wife, Jacqueline, who was at the center of the series of works on *The Painter and His Model*, where he gave free rein to his carnal desires.

Picasso identified over and over again, through his love of shepherds, satyrs, and minotaurs, with the figures of ancient mythology, which he took from the shadows and flooded his paintings with. And his Spanish atavism made him love bullfights; being face to face with death always fascinated him.

A television newsflash announced his death on April 8. He was buried privately on Tuesday, April 10, at the foot of the stone stairs that lead to the main entrance of the Vauvenargues Château, which he had acquired in 1958 and which lies at the foothills of Mount Sainte-Victoire.

(See also 1904, 1905, 1907, 1909, 1912, 1921, 1927, 1937, 1945, 1946, 1948, 1953, 1954, 1958.)

IN PICASSO'S WORDS

Terrible is that one is one's own eagle of Prometheus, at the same time the one that devours and the one that is being devoured.

As for me, I cannot do anything else but what I do.

Painters and ambition. That's fine. Why not? What annoys people is that it's painters. When someone is ambitious in the office, it is fine. One ends up as a department head. The annoying thing for the painters is that they

one is the true one? And what is that truth, is it the one that I use as a model or the one that I paint? No, it is the way it is with everything else. Truth does not exist.

Freedom—we must be very careful with it. In painting and in everything else. What ever you do, you find you bear chains: The freedom not to do one thing requires doing something else. This means chains.

What I am looking for at the present time is

PABLO PICASSO: THREE LADIES ON THE SHORE OF THE SEINE, AFTER COURBET. 1950. Basel. Kunstsammlungen

become—what?. . . And in the end they are not even painters anymore.

Imagine, for example, a hunter that's abstract. What could he do, this abstract hunter? In any case, he'd kill nothing.

How lucky to be an Impressionist! It is the painter innocent of being a painter.

Nine times out of ten when a painter tells you: no, this canvas is not completely finished . . . it lacks a little something . . . it must still be finished . . . nine times out of ten you can be sure that in trying to finish it he is surely going to kill it. You know—just as you finish off the victim by firing squad. Or with a revolver shot in the head.

The interior me is necessarily present in my canvas since I am the one who is doing it. This requires no effort. Whatever I do, it will be there. Too much of it may be there . . . The problem is everything else.

What truth? Truth cannot exist. If I am trying for truth in a canvas, I can make one hundred canvases with this truth. Then, which

the word saying "nude" on my canvas, all at once, without anything leading up to it.

If one knows exactly what one is going to do, what is the sense of doing it? Since one knows it, it has no value. Better do something else.

If Raphael would return now, with exactly the same canvases, nobody would buy a single one.

What is terrible today is that nobody speaks ill of anyone. If we believe what we read, everything is fine. Nobody kills anybody anymore, everything is equivalent, nothing is thrown on the ground, and nothing is a flag. Everything is on the same level. Why? Surely not because it is true.

Remarks written down by
Hélène Parmelin

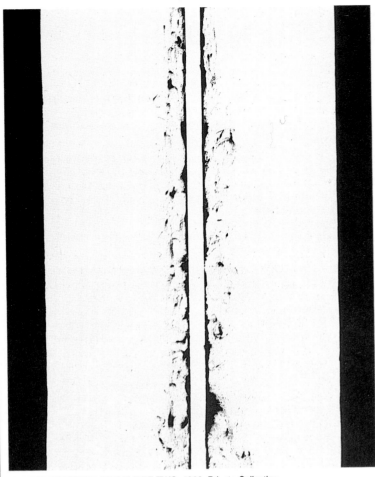

BARNETT NEWMAN: WHITE FIRE TWO. 1960. Private Collection

JASPER JOHNS: DOUBLE WHITE MAP. 1965. Private Collection

CONTEMPORARY ART ON THE AUCTION BLOCK

NEW YORK

Robert C. Scull: There are names that become synonymous with the word "collection." Not only is Robert Scull the owner of a flourishing taxi company, he is known in the art world as one of the shrewdest collectors of contemporary art. At the sale held at Sotheby's Parke-Benett on October 18, Mr. Scull chose his fifth painting for his collection. An event! Because so many of the fifty paintings and sculptures on sale were among the most remarkable works coming from the New York School. Nobody was mistaken about the interest created by these sales; the Japanese, German, English, and even Italian buyers were present in number at 89 Madison Avenue.

Robert Scull does business, he says, in order to have cash on hand to invest in young artists. Before the sale began, the more audacious forecasters were predicting record prices at Sotheby's. In fact, from this point of view the auction was remarkably successful at $2,242,900. Never

THE COLLECTOR ROBERT SCULL IS CHALLENGED IN THE STREET

in the history of sales of contemporary American artists had such an amount been achieved. The biggest seller was without a doubt Jasper Johns. His enormous canvas *Double White Map*, painted in 1965, made him the most expensive living American artist of the moment. It sold for $240,000! In addition, one of his sculptures, *Painted Bronze*,

raised the sum of $90,000, also a record for a sculpture from a living American artist. Other artists, such as De Kooning, Kline, Rauschenberg, Poons, and Rosenquist, also had never had their works sold for so much. Two paintings by Barnett Newman, *Errance* and *White Fire Two*, sold for $140,000 and $155,000 respectively.

The sideshows at the Parke-Benett sale were no less interesting than the sale itself. In fact, two things happened that disturbed the opening of the auction and made it start late. There was a noisy group of taxi drivers who accused Mr. Scull of

getting rich from their labors. They had chosen this particular day to take advantage of the presence of television cameras and the publicity that their demonstration would receive. The second happening, also a colorful one, was created by representatives of the movement "Women in the Arts." This militant association, which demands that women in the arts be recognized for the same things as their male colleagues, protested against the fact that only one female artist was represented in this sale: Lee Bontecu, who had put a work up for auction, a piece constructed in steel. In spite of the unexpected publicity, it sold for only $7,500, even though its estimated minimum was put at $8,000.

The Political Comic Strip

At forty-five, Swedish artist Öyvind Fahlström exhibits his work at the Sidney Janis Gallery in New York, as well as in Philadelphia and Wisconsin. America forgives him for being so down on her in his comic strips. The comic strips of Jess Collins and Roy Lichtenstein are esthetic, but with such French artists as Rancillac and Télémaque, and Swedish artists such as Erro and Fahlström, the comic strip carries a political message. Fahlström, by far the most severe critic, uses his *Column No. 2: Picasso* to depict the United States' recent actions and addresses a letter to Picasso, asking him to remove *Guernica* from such a brutally imperialistic country.

Saree Is Dead

Günther Saree, who died recently in Munich, was, along with Schult, one of the main protagonists of the "Actionist Movement," which had taken over in Germany in the late sixties, after the Happening and Neodadaism. Saree, to protest the wastefulness of a consumer society, had once transformed an entire Munich street into a trash heap. Saree's obsession with rotting and death pursued him. At the Documenta V last year, he handed visitors a questionnaire asking if they had already planned for their burial. It was a cruel twist of fate that, ten months later, Günther Saree would die of a cancer spreading throughout his body.

Japanese Galleries Come to Paris

First there were the galleries Tamenaga and Yoshii on the Avenue Matignon. Now the gallery Nichido—the largest in Japan—is opening its doors on the Rue du Faubourg-Saint-Honoré. It was founded in 1927; today, its owner, Tokuchi Hasegawa, has nine branches, including two other galleries in Tokyo. One hundred and ten people work on Hasegawa's staff. He has his own art review, called *Painting*, and a museum near Tokyo. Last year he bought the collection of Edward G. Robinson, the famous American actor.

Hasegawa speaks of the influence of Japanese art on French Impressionists and emphasizes that Japanese painters have always gone to Paris to study. He is a specialist in Impressionism, but also exhibits Modigliani, Rousseau, Rouault, Chagall, Miró, Braque, Picasso, Vlaminck, Kisling, Dunoyer de Segonzac, and Marie Laurencin.

Chagall Museum Inaugurated

The Musée du Message Biblique (the museum of the biblical message) was inaugurated in Nice this July. A gift to France from Chagall, it contains windows by the artist as well as numerous paintings with biblical themes. What is striking is the feeling of love, and perhaps also of sensuousness, that pervades the museum. Chagall is best known for the poetry and fantasy of his work: the red calf inside a blue cow; the fiddler who flys through the sky while playing. Here we have the earthly Chagall, life with all its joys, sorrows, hopes, and miracles. At eighty-six, Marc Chagall has taken his place alongside Rouault as one of the great masters of faith, which he expresses with innocence and spirituality.

Two Million Dollars for a Pollock

How high will art prices go? *Blue Poles*, a painting by Jackson Pollock from 1953, has been bought by the Museum of Canberra in Australia for the unheard-of sum of two million dollars. It is the highest price ever paid for a modern painting, even more than for a Picasso or a Matisse. The work belongs to the artist's series of drippings, and is particularly characteristic of his style. Originally purchased for $6,000, it was sold several years later at $32,000 to art collector and dealer Ben Heller before jumping to the current price. Pollock, who died in an automobile accident in 1956, was undoubtedly an artist of great talent, but isn't two million dollars a bit much for a painting only twenty years old?

The Chagall Museum in Nice.

BEN'S BOUTIQUE

NICE

Only Ben can talk about Ben, and this he surely does. "I am the most famous anonymous artist in the world," he declares. And if this is true in the way it is intended, he is not demanding anything. "If I have arrived," he states again, "it's because I have copied others." He copied under his nickname "Ben" from works from almost everywhere. (He was born Benjamin Vautier, in Naples in 1935.) He even did not hesitate to copy "ideas," such as a Ping-Pong ball containing— God. He even went so far as to sign his own body and exhibit himself in the window of a London gallery.

Ben's Store, the "boutique" that he is currently showing in Nice, is both a paraphrase and a compilation of all his affirmations, declarations, and definitions. At the same time it is a sort of incredible bric-a-brac of objects ranging from a coffee grinder to a chair or to the inevitable "Ben Is a Genius"— carefully written on a blackboard.

But Ben, in spite of a more or less simulated paranoia, is too

BEN VAUTIER: BEN'S STORE. 1958-1973. Paris. MNAM

intelligent not to have, like Dali, a critical method. His "boutique" is a modern rejoinder to the "curio cabinets" that existed in large number during the sixteenth and seventeenth centuries. It is different, however, in that the banalities that he shows and juxtaposes originate, more than do Dada and the *Merzbau* of Kurt Schwit-ters, from the provocative and derisory in their content rather than from a concern for illuminating our consciousness.

"COUCOU BAZAR"

NEW YORK

Jean Dubuffet has shown for the very first time, in the exhibition of his works from May to July at the Guggenheim Museum, his "animated painting" entitled *Coucou Bazar*, an astonishing sculptural and pictorial ballet.

With music by Miramoglu and staging choreographed by McFaddin, the creator of the *L'hourloupe* series introduced a sort of commedia dell'arte in which the actors proper are sculptures of white, red, and blue encircled by black, who are slowly dancing the pavane for a defunct society.

Is it because of the parasite bird who leaves his own egg in the nest of others that he makes allusion to "playing a dirty trick" on his dancers by disguising them as "practicable" stereotypes, which makes them seem as though they have movement? *Coucou Bazar* is compared to a giant sculpture made human, as were the medieval *danses macabres* or the masked ceremonial dances of Africa or the representations of the Japanese No theater that appear to be inanimate animations.

"Painting can be a subtle machine for conveying philosophy," declares Jean Dubuffet, whose work wants to be a reanimation of the static arts.

JEAN DUBUFFET: COUCOU BAZAR. 1971-1973

THE JORN MIRACLE

AARHUS

A large exhibition opened in April in Berlin, after having been previewed in Brussels and in Copenhagen: Works of Asger Jorn, who was on his way to great fame when he died just before reaching his sixtieth birthday.

He was born in 1914 at Vejrum, in Jutland, and began painting in 1932. He came to Paris before the war and worked at Fernand Léger's, and then at Le Corbusier's, and at the International Exposition of 1937 he participated in the decoration of the New Age Pavilion. But the war sent him back to occupied Denmark, where he spent the war years in total isolation.

Actually, his career did not really begin until 1945. He returned to Paris and lived there from 1947 until 1950. In 1948 he was one of the founder members of the Cobra group, of which he became the prime mover. Unfortunately nobody was interested in his paintings, and he went through a period of physical and emotional misery. In 1951, he found himself convalescing in a sanitarium, where

LIFE ITSELF IS SO CRUDE, SAVAGE, PRIMITIVE

he spent eighteen months.

He traveled a great deal, to Lapland, Tunisia, Cuba, and the Far East, for he had an inborn curiosity for all forms of creation. As one of the founding fathers of the Internationale Situationniste, he did not content himself with merely painting. He loved to write, and his essays on art, entitled *Pour la forme* (for form), were collected in 1958.

The title of this work was quite surprising, considering the content of Asger Jorn's works! Reacting against Geometric Abstraction, as did his fellow members of Cobra, he often gave the impression of painting in a state of fury, of an uncontrolled violence. His works are blocks of color projected with rage onto the canvas, whirlwinds, scrawls, all sorts of tones that crawl all over each other.

Asger Jorn had a lot of anguish. But he managed to liberate himself from his nightmarish visions, and, paradoxically, he did this with bright colors. As if he laughed at his own tragic humor! He was also quite poetic in the titles he gave to his works: *Chéri-Bibi*, *The Abominable Snow Man*, *The Shabby Warrior*. For him painting was an outlet, a type of exorcism.

The forms in his work remain imprecise. What counts is the movement of strokes, of colors, of lines: Life itself is so crude, savage, primitive. It also brought irreparable heartbreak.

In the August-September issue of *L'art vivant*, René Micha cites a letter he had received from Christian Dotremont, giving a wonderful portrait of his old cofounder of Cobra: "He always wanted to go far in winning by something like deliberate failure. He did everything possible not to create masterworks or works that taken together would be a masterpiece." Success came at this price—but the artist who has left us was one of the major creators of the second half of this century, the equal of a Pollock, of a Dubuffet.

(See also 1948.)

ASGER JORN: KYOTOSMORA-MA. 1969-1970. Paris. MNAM

1974

SUMMARY

People thought modern art was destined to be nothing but smears and graffiti, and now, suddenly, against all expectations, it turns photographic. The appearance of Hyperrealism in the United States contradicts every prediction of the best experts on the future of art. The movement marks the unexpected return of meticulous representation and compulsive craft. Fantastic Art, also figurative, triumphs with artists such as Ljuba and Roland Cat, who place painting in the service of dreams and the archetypal. They align themselves with Salvador Dali, whose opening of a theater-museum in Figueras reveals a kind of gigantic Surrealist object.

DUANE HANSON
TOURISTS. 197●
New York. Private Collectio●

HYPERREALISM, REALER THAN REAL

**PARIS/
BRUSSELS/HELSINKI**

American Hyperrealism spontaneously emerges in California and in New York under names that are as different as their appearance is simultaneous: Hyperrealism, Radical Realism, Photo-Realism, New Realism, Superrealism, Sharp-Focus Realism. It is displayed to the interested—and critical—eyes of Europe. Indeed, a series of related exhibitions provides Europeans with an opportunity to discover this new realistic art, which is purely descriptive, often anecdotal. It is a fiercely traditional art form based intentionally on photography in its most objective form possible. It can be described as new *trompe l'oeil.*

The recent wave of these young Superrealistic painters crosses the Atlantic and arrives in Paris at the Musée d'Art Moderne de la Ville, the Centre National d'Art Contemporain, the Canadian Cultural Center, and in about a half dozen private galleries, as well as in Brussels and in Helsinki. It generates an infatuation that has led critics to wonder about its origins and causes. What are the painters seeking? Why has the

RALPH GOINGS: AIRSTREAM TRAILER. 1970. Vienna. Museum Moderner Kunst

glass and aluminum, chrome motorcycles, neon signs, airports starkly outlined against the California sky . . . Everything must be predictable and without defect, without risk of human error, and more real than reality itself.

If, properly speaking, this Superrealism does not yet constitute a school, it is certainly a reaction to the Abstract Expressionism of Action Painting. It is clearly a return to that highly

EVERYTHING MUST BE MADE PREDICTABLE AND WITHOUT DEFECT, WITHOUT RISK OF HUMAN ERROR, AND MORE REAL THAN REALITY ITSELF

world of art dealers become so interested in this phenomenon since the Whitney Museum in New York, in 1970, presented "22 Realists" and the gallery owner Sidney Janis in 1972 proposed a "Sharp-Focus Realism" show?

Infatuation with this Realism—which seizes and presents American civilization closely—is so great in the United States because the country finally recognizes itself in a contemporary art form. It reassures the country with the kind of perfect, impeccable, shiny reflection that it imagines for itself. Gleaming cars, cafeterias, supermarkets of

traditional American art form of figurative Realism inaugurated by the first portrait painters and the landscape painters of an imaginary Far West and later confirmed by the champions of the Ash Can School at the beginning of this century.

Drawing on the recent lessons of Pop Art, which reminds people how much they are being invaded by objects, Hyperrealism places the accent more particularly on the profusion of photographic images in society. Everyone knows the story of the mother and the neighbor who admires the baby, whereupon the mother replies, "He's even

RICHARD ESTES: GROSSINGER'S BAKERY. 1972

THE FLAT WORLD OF HOCKNEY

PARIS

From the beginning of October and through the end of the year, the Museum of Decorative Arts gives Parisians the opportunity to discover the painter David Hockney. At the age of thirty-seven, he is, with Francis Bacon, one of the two greatest English painters of the day.

Hockney's art falls between Pop Art and Superrealism. He uses graffiti, children's drawings, adhesive paper, and advertising images, juxtaposing them with drawings and paintings. His canvases have a make-believe naive quality, which contrasts with his extremely refined technique.

His world is flat, artificial,

DAVID HOCKNEY: PORTRAIT OF AN ARTIST (POOL WITH TWO PEOPLE). 1971

immobile, almost frozen. A perfect illustration of this is his series of *Beverly Hills Swimming Pools*; several of the canvases are presented in the show. At the same time, Hockney is an exceptional draftsman. His work drew attention at the Third Bien-

nale of Young Artists in 1963, where he participated in the graphics section.

(See also 1961.)

KLASEN: REALITY WITH A SCALPEL

PETER KLASEN: KEEP OUT. 1974. Private Collection

PARIS

Peter Klasen, who is forty-four years old, trained at the Academy of Fine Arts in Berlin and has lived in France since 1956. He could be considered a new Léger. Like Léger, Klasen has as his main subject the technical aspect of civilization, with its cars, trains, and planes. Like Léger, he favors close-ups and flat color surfaces. Like Léger, he is a classic painter who uses the object itself as the point of departure.

Yet, he differs from Léger, perhaps because of his nationality

preparing a book on Klasen, mentions an exchange of letters between the management of the chemical company Bayer and the commander of Auschwitz. The correspondence makes reference to the purchase of one hundred and fifty women for one hundred and seventy marks each; every one of the women dies as the result of experiments with a new soporific. There is mention of a second order at the same price. Hitler committed suicide in his bunker, but that did not settle the accounts. This is not just an anecdote; we know

THE PURCHASE OF ONE HUNDRED AND FIFTY WOMEN FOR ONE HUNDRED AND SEVENTY MARKS EACH

and the historic era of which he is a part. Léger loved factories, and considered agricultural machines in the fields as beautiful as butterflies. He was touched by scraps of iron, preferring them to sunsets. He thought that machinery and the better living conditions it provided would bring happiness and good fortune to everyone.

Klasen, on the other hand, belongs to a generation that has lost its illusions. His friend the writer Pierre Tilman, who is

that scientific and industrial societies can be monstrous.

Klasen paints from photographs, which he takes himself or cuts out of magazines. He projects the forms on a canvas to define the general layout. He selects certain shapes, masking others, then paints them over with an airbrush, which he manipulates with the precision of a scalpel. After the death of God, we are witnessing the death of man. Herein lies the difference with Léger.

PEGGY GUGGENHEIM SHOWS HER COLLECTION

PARIS

The Musée de l'Orangerie shows part of Peggy Guggenheim's collection, one of Europe's most important in the areas of Cubism, Surrealism, and abstract art. A daughter and a niece of copper magnates, Peggy Guggenheim has always been an anticonformist. She worked as a nurse for two dollars a day and

tion together, because the war had broken out in Poland, and it was important to prevent major works from falling into Nazi hands. Léger told her, "Peggy, you should entrust them to the Louvre." But the Louvre did not want them. They were hidden in the stables of a friend's château in the center of France. She whisked them to the United

Peggy Guggenheim in Venice.

ONE OF THE MOST BEAUTIFUL COLLECTIONS OF CUBIST, SURREALIST, AND ABSTRACT WORKS BROUGHT TOGETHER SINCE 1939

as a library employee in Greenwich Village, in New York, before opening in 1934 a gallery in London where she showed works by Tanguy, Arp, Laurens, Kandinsky, Klee, Miró, Moore, and Dali.

She started her collection in Paris in 1939. "We were offered paintings at every street corner," she says. "I decided to buy one each day, and did so throughout the winter of 1940, and until the arrival of the Germans." She wanted to put a historical collec-

States in 1941, traveling with Max Ernst, who became her husband for a short spell.

The Guggenheim collection also contains works by painters of the New York School whom she was the first to exhibit, in 1942, in her famous Art of This Century Gallery. She thus owns works by Pollock, De Kooning, Rothko, Gorky, and Clifford Still; she knew the artists personally. She has said: "I wanted to create a museum in New York for my collection. Kiesler, a fine theater

architect, designed it. He thought that each painting should be lighted separately. There was a timing device that allowed only three minutes to

view a painting, so one had to rush through a room to see something. Finally, I couldn't take that museum any more. I went to Venice for the Biennale and I stayed. Ever since, I have been taking it easy here, with my sacred dogs from Tibet, it's very pleasant."

The year was 1948. She was looking for a palazzo on the Grand Canal. She ended up purchasing the Palazzo Venier di Leoni, between La Salute and the Accademia delle Belle Arti. Her collection consists of two hundred works by one hundred artists. Besides Picasso, Braque, Juan Gris, Léger, and the new generation of Americans, it contains many Surrealist works. Among young artists, she chooses works by artists of the Cobra group, including Asger Jorn, Appel, and Alechinsky.

(See also 1942, 1946, 1947.)

PIERRE ALECHINSKY:
BATHROBE. 1972. Venice.
Peggy Guggenheim
Collection

A Display of Bulldozers

Modern art and Soviet totalitarianism have never been good bedfellows. Once the Revolution was over, repression against avant-garde artists began. Then, when Stalinism went out, artists hoped for a more liberal attitude on the part of the authorities. The dogma of Socialist Realism, however, remains all-powerful. Since nonofficial painters in the Soviet Union have no shows or galleries for exhibiting their work, a number of them decided to show their work outside. On the morning of September 15, they went to an empty lot to hold an exhibit that had been neither prohibited nor authorized, simply "not recommended." Word got out, and a crowd came to see. But police bulldozers appeared suddenly and moved the public out while plainclothes police threw the crushed paintings into disposal bins. So much for modern art in the Soviet Union, in 1974.

California Ceramics

For the past ten years, ceramics, an art long looked down upon, has become increasingly important in California. In New York, the Whitney Museum, recognizing ceramics' rebirth, is organizing an exhibit with five of the most important artists in the medium: Peter Voulkos, Kenneth Price, Robert Arneson, David Gilhooly, and Richard Shaw. A retrospective at the Pasadena Museum of Modern Art is devoted to the work of the famous ceramist James Mason. In 1959, Peter Voulkos had started a ceramics studio at the University of Berkeley. Little by little, the Bay Area, traditionally open to this form of art, became a center of intense creative activity, in particular at Mills College, at the San Francisco Art Institute, and at San José State College. Through these artists, ceramics has become a means of expression for contemporary sensibilities.

Jean-Pierre Raynaud: Hospital or Bathroom?

Jean-Pierre Raynaud is having an open house at the outskirts of Paris. The outside of his home resembles a cement cube, and the interior is entirely covered—walls, floors, and ceilings—with white tile reminiscent of hospitals or bathrooms. Even the furniture, which is all stationary, is covered with the stuff, so that the visitor has the impression of floating in a shiny white space. Only the grid created by the squares of tile brings the eye back to reality. Raynaud, in recent years, has caught the art world's attention with his flowerpots, his traffic signals, his crutches, coffins, and other more or less gloomy outpourings. He admits that his house is sometimes difficult to live in; so from time to time he goes to live with friends.

Interior of Jean-Pierre Raynaud's house at La Celle-Saint-Cloud.

The Solid Walls of Louis Kahn

Architect Louis Kahn died at the age of seventy-three in New York, on March 17. He had left Estonia with his parents at the age of four to go to the United States. He did not gain popularity until the 1960s. In 1958, he designed the Institute of Medical Research at the University of Pennsylvania; it was there that his massive style first became known, a style that makes use of large masses and simple geometric forms. The Institute, built of brick and cement, has something medieval about it, with its towers and thick walls. The following decade provided many opportunities for Kahn to display his talent. In 1962, urban planning in Dacca, Eastern Pakistan's capital, allowed him to bring together his architectural and urban ideas in one project.

IN BRIEF...

FRANCE
Dorothea Tanning retrospective at the Centre National d'Art Contemporain.

At the Grand Palais, centenary exhibition of Impressionism.

Dual exhibition of Monory and Boltanski at the Centre National d'Art Contemporain.

Plans are made definite to establish the Musée Picasso at the Salé Mansion.

GREAT BRITAIN
An important Lucien Freud retrospective at the Hayward Gallery.

Sale of Picasso's Woman with Mandolin, dated 1910, for three million francs.

SWEDEN
The director of the Moderna Museet of Stockholm, Pontus Hulten, is named to head the museum of the future Georges Pompidou Center.

UNITED STATES
The MOMA acquires Card Tower by André Masson, a canvas dating from 1923.

Cologne, Avant-Garde City

The one-hundred-fiftieth anniversary of the Wallraf-Richartz Museum provided the occasion for an enormous international exhibit that will spotlight "Projekt 74, Art of the 1970s." Seventy-five participants were chosen and divided into three sections corresponding to the major themes of the decade: time and perception, formal systems, and conceptual systems. Among the artists are Palermo, Gerhard Richter, Klaus Rinke, Richard Serra, Christian Boltanski. There are few paintings; the artists are using "performances" or "environments" as their means of expression.

CAT: DREAM AND NIGHTMARE

PARIS

A waiting list for the right to buy a painting! Previously, this happened only with Picasso, whose collectors, in the last years of his life, had to wait their turn at his dealer, Daniel-Henry Kahnweiler. Today, the same is true for Roland Cat, a thirty-one-year-old artist whose works are sold before they even go on exhibit at the gallery Braumüller.

It is indeed a fact that his work does not go unnoticed. Cat is a visionary artist whose approach seems to be inspired by the verses of René Char: "Man has already withdrawn from the terrestrial scene, all that remains is to listen to the tale of what he sees." Man is not to be seen in Cat's overflowing, or deserted, strange landscapes,

ROLAND CAT: THE REFLECTED BUILDING. 1973. Private Collection

though there are a few traces. The cities either are dead or seem to have emerged from a dream. They are formed by amazing accumulations: a half-submerged skyscraper surrounded by mammoths; a labyrinth that unwinds its infernal circle in a deserted universe; a monster from prehistoric times, the sole "escapee" from an infinity of water and rocks.

The degree of precision of Cat's creations is all the more striking in that he slants and deforms reality: for example, when none of the meticulously detailed vegetation corresponds to any real plants, or when the color details tip a canvas simultaneously into a realm of dreams and a realm of nightmares. In 1967, Roland Cat received the Prix de la Critique, and in 1971, the first prize for drawing from the Weill Foundation. He surpasses Symbolism and Surrealism. Each Cat is "a contraption that staggers the mind."

THE FANTASTIC WORLD OF LJUBA

NEW YORK

Between God and Satan—this is certainly the realm of the works that Popovic Alekes Ljubomir, better known as Ljuba, puts up for view at the Aberbach Fine Arts Gallery. Satan is present in the sulfureous yellow and the burned shadows, God in the superterrestrial blue blazes. Ljuba was born in Tuzla, Yugoslavia, of Serbian parents, in 1934. He studied at the Fine Arts Academy in Belgrade, then settled in Paris, in 1963, where he still lives and works. He is the painter of hybrid beings—partially plantlike, partially animallike—with characteristics of both genders: pallid faces with large feverish eyes, a fragile slenderness, all on the verge of disintegration. There is no doubt

LJUBA: VENUS AND DEATH (A GARDEN FOR VENUS). New York. Julian Aberbach Collection

that Ljuba is obsessed with the idea of pulverization, though in his work it is closer to metamorphosis than to destruction. He links alchemy with dreams about the most modern aspects of sciences. The painter draws us into this vision by juxtaposing elements of futuristic settings, horned animals, arched windows, and other baroque allusions. Ljuba is the spiritual heir of Monsu Desiderio and his exploded colonnades, and the heir of both Füssli and Dali. He claims that Dali provides evidence that in these turbulent times, painting remains possible. He belongs to the same family. Ljuba throws the prisons of the mind wide open.

THE FABULOUS DALI THEATER-MUSEUM

FIGUERAS

When evening falls on September 28, under the blows of the tramontane wind bearing down from the Pyrenees, an unlikely parade files festively through the narrow streets of Figueras toward the ancient municipal theater, which has become,

THE FIRST AND ONLY "READY-MADE" MUSEUM

thanks to Dali, a museum for Dali. Folklore groups, dwarfs and giants, and witchlike majorettes are preceded by a young elephant, trunk in the air, and followed by serious-looking officials from the provinces, from Madrid, and from Montpellier. The Catalans and the Figuerases celebrate and pay homage to their most famous prodigal son, now seventy years old, "Salvador Dali, the genius," who honored them by being born in this straggling town on the Ampurdan plain, in northern Catalonia, on May 11, 1904.

They magnify the self-glorification that the mythical father of Surrealism bestows on himself by offering them, with a royal gesture, his "sanctuary museum." Dali arrives from his fisherman's house in Port-Lligat and installs himself on a gilded throne. He receives the gold medal of his native town from the hands of the mayor, and Gala, his wife and Egeria, is covered with flowers.

In a staccato voice, which makes the antennas of his waxed mustache vibrate, the delirious painter of *Leda Atomica, Corpus hypercubicus, The Dream of Christopher Columbus,* and many other magnificently dreamlike paintings declares, "Our Caudillo told me that this museum will become the mecca of contemporary art. I want it to be the spiritual center of Europe! From today onward, this spiritual center will be located under the geodesic dome that dominates the museum. Pérez Pinero and I dedicate this cupola to the princes of Spain!" While

Franco's illness drags on, Dali claims himself to be "Roman Catholic, apostolic, and monarchist." Like someone who, as noted by André Breton, has the incomparable gift of putting himself in center-stage he points to the divine nature of the cupola, designed by the architect Pinero and based on Fuller's *Biosphere* of the international Expo 67 in Montreal.

In the courtyard of his museum, Dali has placed a replica of *Le taxi pluvieux* (rainy taxi), which he had presented at the 1938 International Exhibition of Surrealism. It includes a female mannequin with platinum hair, a driver with the head of a shark, and green plants. When a fifty-peseta coin is inserted into a slot, a fine rain begins to fall inside the cab. If museums are often somber places where people move about as if on felt slippers, Dali's is a kind of artistic theme park.

It is the first and only "ready-made" museum, weird and conventional at the same time. Strangely mixed in with baroque furniture and décors, with paintings by Bouguereau, with anamorphoses, and with arrangements of optical illusions are Surrealist works of the artist: paintings, sculptures, and tapestries, including a homage to Velásquez. In the frescoes painted on the ceiling of the lobby, the artist ascends with Gala—their feet are shown in close-up—toward a heaven of irresistible glory.

Once again there is confirmation that Dali's tyrannical self exults in creative hallucinations: a tumescent self, always in pursuit of an impossible universal orgasm from which his pride derives vengeance, dollars, and gold. Oh, this damned "Avida Dollars!" That's what André Breton called him—an anagram of his name. It was to bring Salvador Dali not only fame but also a constant downpour of bank notes!

(See also 1929, 1934, 1935, 1936, 1938, 1968, 1974, 1979.)

The Dali Museum in Figueras.

Lichtenstein paints comic strips the way others paint still lifes or landscapes. Those who thought his experiment was doomed to failure and accused him of anti-art in 1961, when they saw that he had used Mickey Mouse and Donald Duck as themes in his painting, are paying the price now. He gives expression to our new reality, just as other pop stars do. But at the same time, art leaves the museum for the obscure façades of our cities. In the United States as in Europe, Muralism recreates a rapport with the public that should never have been interrupted.

1975

S U M M A R Y

GREAT MASTERS

Lichtenstein Paints Comic Strips
In Lichtenstein's Words

DEVELOPMENTS

The Miró Foundation
Spain: Artistic Life Reemerges

ART NEWS

Hundertwasser at the MNAM
The Soho Phenomenon
The Opening of Artcuriel
Dubuffet's Follies
American Realism
In Brief

MURALISM

Muralism: Return to *Trompe l'oeil*?

SCULPTURE

César's Battles

ROY LICHTENSTEIN
TEMPLE OF APOLLO. 1964
Los Angeles. Private Collection

ROY LICHTENSTEIN: WHAAM! 1963. London. Tate Gallery

LICHTENSTEIN PAINTS COMIC STRIPS

PARIS

Aggression against art? Nonculture? Childishness? Or nationalism, or even a perversion to the extent that comic strips are a medium of violence, of lechery, of everything that morality finds reprehensible and makes a society rot and sink into capitalist decadence? The critics were not soft when the American Roy Lichtenstein, who is now fifty-three years old, showed his paintings of comic strips for the first time at the gallery Leo Castelli thirteen years ago.

At the time, New York was overflowing with Abstract Expressionism, a movement that had conquered the world. In the middle of the hustle and the bustle, a young, elegant gentleman who until then had painted cowboys in the style of *Guernica* started spoiling things for those fascinated with Abstractionism.

Now Paris is discovering him—Lichtenstein has become a pop star—at the Centre National d'Art Contemporain, 11 Rue Berryer, with a retrospective of his work.

Legend has it that when Lichtenstein's son was small, the boy had no taste for his father's paintings and challenged him to paint a large picture of Mickey Mouse, his favorite hero. However, reality is both simpler and more serious: After many years of "apprenticeship," during which he came up against insurmountable obstacles, Lichtenstein found in comic strips the means of zeroing in on mass culture.

Indeed, comic strips are one of the favorite tools for expressing the American dream. From both sociological and psychological points of view, the comic strip has always exercised considerable influence in the United States, in private as well as in public life.

One day, when Dagwood and Blondie could not agree on a name for their second child, four hundred thousand readers wrote in spontaneously with suggestions.

When a candidate for high political office had the idea of composing speeches based solely on quotes of Andy, another famous comic-strip character, who vents the recriminations and desires of the average citizen, he was elected by an overwhelming majority.

Zeus and Aphrodite were the delight of many painters throughout the centuries. A new mythology is replacing the old one, which is no longer applicable anyway. Today's gods are called Marilyn Monroe, Superman, Eddie Diptych, Donald Duck . . . Comic strips are at the same time a caricature and an immense reservoir of collective desires, and they serve Lichtenstein in renewing the painted image, as Andy Warhol has done through advertising images.

It would be an error to assume that the artist is satisfied with merely making copies. He has stated repeatedly that what interests him is to paint comic

Roy Lichtenstein in his studio.

strips the way others paint still lifes or landscapes. In his paintings. Lichtenstein preserves the characteristics of cheap mass reproduction, for example, the rough typographical screen, the black lines surrounding the forms, the clashing colors. What fascinates Lichtenstein in comic strips is not the "hand" of the artist but the intervention of the machine that denies work by hand. To him, *that* is where the creative act lies.

His interpretations of Picasso have no other objective. Whatever remains of the original—a touch or modulation—crumbles when it is made subject to the comic-strip style. By painting originals like reproductions of originals, Lichtenstein operates, pictorially, as if he were executing a kind of cleaning with a sweep of the void. He does the same with his copies of Mondrian, which he combines with a typographical grid to reduce their spiritual claim.

"What interests me is to paint the kind of antisensitivity that impregnates modern civilization," the artist says. "At the same time, I believe that comic strips possess great strength, aggressiveness, and energy." He emphasizes this notion with "balloons," the typical cartouches of comic strips. They enclose a burning word, often onomatopoeic, for example, "Wham," "Ratata," "Blam," "Pow." They constitute a kind of primitive infralanguage whose phonetic vigor strikes the viewer with full force.

In 1963, Lichtenstein painted a large diptych, which is appropriately called *Whaam*. It depicts a war scene: A fighter plane shoots down another plane with a rocket. It is his masterpiece. There is no reason to be surprised. The artist was in Europe, with the American Army, during the Second World War. No GI plunged into battle without Flash Gordon or Joe Pallooka at his side.

(See also 1961.)

IN LICHTENSTEIN'S WORDS

I want my painting to look as if it has been programed. I want to hide the record of my hand.

I think art since Cézanne has become extremely romantic and unrealistic, feeding on art; it is utopian. It has less and less to do with the world, it looks inward—neo-Zen and all that. This is not so much a criticism as an obvious observation. Outside is the world; it's there. Pop Art looks out into the world; it appears to accept its environment, which is not good or bad, but different —another state of mind.

"How can you like exploitation?" "How can you like the complete mechanization of work? How can you like bad art?" I have to answer that I accept it as being there, in the world.

I suppose I would still prefer to sit under a tree with a picnic basket rather than under a gas pump, but signs and comic strips are interesting as subject matter.

I paint directly—then it's said to be an exact copy, and not art. probably because there's no perspective or shading. It doesn't look like a painting of something, it looks like the thing itself. Instead of looking like a painting of a billboard—the way a Reginald Marsh would look—Pop Art seems to be the actual thing. It is an intensification, a stylistic intensification of the excitement which the subject matter has for me; but the style is... cool. One of the things a cartoon does is to express violent emotion and passion in a completely mechanical and removed style. To express this thing in a painterly style would dilute it; the techniques I use are not commercial, they only appear to be commercial—and the ways of seeing and composing and unifying are different and have different ends.

I often transfer a cartoon style into an art style. For example, the Art Nouveau flames at the nozzle of the machine gun. It is a stylistic way of presenting the lights and darks. In the Drowning Girl the water is not only Art Nouveau, but it can also be seen as Hokusai.

I think that in these objects, the golf ball, the frankfurter, and so on, there is an anti-Cubist composition. You pick an object and put it on a blank ground. I was interested in non-Cubist composition. The idea is contrary to the major direction of art since the early Renaissance which has more and more symbolized the integration of "figure" with "ground."

{I think I am anti-experimental} and anti-contemplative, anti-nuance, anti-getting-away-from-the-tyranny-of-the-rectangle, anti-movement-and-light, anti-mystery, anti-paint-quality, anti-Zen, and anti all of those brilliant ideas of preceding movements which everyone understands so thoroughly.

ROY LICHTENSTEIN:
SPRAY II. 1963. Turin.
Private Collection

SPAIN: ARTISTIC LIFE REEMERGES

MADRID

For the last three or four years, the explosion of Spanish art has been drawing attention. Ten years ago, there were maybe ten or twelve galleries in Madrid; now, there are more than two hundred, and some areas of the city have taken on a special character because of their presence. There are at least eight art magazines whose luxurious presentations command prices of forty to one hundred twenty-five pesetas. The phenomenon has spread over the whole of Spain. In Barcelona, there are now more than one hundred galleries, about thirty in Valencia, sixteen in Bilbao, twelve each in Santander, Seville, and Valladolid, and eight in Saragossa. To these galleries should be added many auction houses, including Christie's and Sotheby's, and a growing number of competitions, biennales, and exhibitions of all kinds.

ANTONI TÀPIES: THE INVERTED HAT. 1966. Paris. MNAM

Prices are higher in Spain than in the French market. Auction houses are receiving surprising bids. Most galleries are geared toward the "national production." On the official side, more than one hundred traveling exhibits have been organized. They have attracted over three million visitors in more than four hundred cities and towns and have generated sales of three hundred thirty thousand catalogues and several thousand art books. Spanish artists already have received numerous international prizes, for example, at the Biennale in São Paulo, the Biennale in Venice (Chillida, Tàpies), the Biennale in Alexandria, the International Fair in Tokyo, and the International Biennale of etchings in Kraków. The political, economic, and cultural life of Spain is undergoing a thorough transformation.

THE MIRÓ FOUNDATION

BARCELONA

The Miró Foundation in the Catalan capital opens its doors to the public on June 10. It was designed by the artist himself, who wanted to give the city where he was born in 1893 a permanent exhibition of his work. At the same time, the Foundation is to function as a center of contemporary art, exposing his compatriots to the avant-garde and stimulating young artists.

The project dates back to 1971, when Miró asked his friend, the architect Josep-Lluis Sert, to execute a first model. The city, realizing the importance of such an institution in Barcelona, agreed to collaborate on the project. In a gesture of great generosity, it offered land, leaving the choice of the site to the painter and the architect. Miró and Sert chose Montjuïc Park. The city contributed to the building expenses and agreed to give the Foundation all of Miró's works that he had donated to Barcelona.

Sert, who also designed the Fondation Maeght, in Saint-Paul-de-Vence, created a building in which the spacious layout favors clarity and order. The exhibition rooms were designed as a function of the works to be shown. The patios and terraces include peaceful havens and are enlivened with olive and locust trees.

The Foundation, dedicated to the study and the distribution of Miró's work, includes a substantial collection of paintings, sculptures, drawings, and etchings donated by the artist. But there are also rooms where shows by recognized contemporary artists can alternate with those of young talent, in accordance with Miró's wishes. The Foundation has a specialized library and an auditorium. Miró is one of the great creative artists of the twentieth century. A long life is wished for such a project dedicated to art, poetry, and dreams.

A hall of the Miró Foundation with works by the artist.

716

Hundertwasser at the MNAM

Hundertwasser's watch is permanently set to New Zealand time—he likes to sail there in *Regentag,* his boat. But he manages to arrive on time at business meetings in Vienna, New York, or Paris. At the moment, he is at the Musée National d'Art Moderne in Paris with a retrospective of essential pieces from his work. Hundertwasser is the well-known initiator of Transautomatism, which he sees as an outgrowth of Jackson Pollock and the H-bomb. The exhibition shows the public an inspired painter, who stands at the crossroads between Klimt and Klee. But Hundertwasser is also a militant ecologist, an architect, and an amateur stripteaser—he has been known to appear nude in public to defend his ideas. One of these was a nonpolluting toilet that had no flusher, which he claimed made it possible to save humanity from ecological disaster.

FRIEDRICH HUNDERTWASSER:
IRINALAND OVER THE BALKANS. 1971. Private Collection

The Soho Phenomenon

Since the end of the 1960s, New York's Soho has become one of the centers of contemporary art. It has welcomed successive influxes of artists and writers, drawn by the low rents in this neighborhood of warehouses and old workshops, whose vast spaces and ironwork architecture are not without charm. Art dealers moved in soon after, Paula Cooper being among the first to open a gallery there in 1968. She showed Donald Judd, Dan Flavin, Robert Mangold, and Robert Rymn, among others. Then Ivan Karp featured all the Hyperrealists in his gallery, the O.K. Harris. In 1973, a few prestigious dealers such as Leo Castelli and André Emmerich, whose reputations had been built on Pop Art, Minimal Art, and Color-Field Painting, descended on Soho. Most recently, several "alternative spaces" have opened their doors in the neighborhood, such as the Kitchen, Artists Space, and the well-known P.S. 1 (Public School Number 1).

The Opening of Artcurial

On the strength of its outstanding commercial success, L'Oréal opens the Artcurial center for the promotion of contemporary art. Located at 9 Avenue Matignon, the center occupies twenty-seven thousand square feet. On view are an environment by Kandinsky, *The Music Salon,* a carbon copy of the models the painter had completed for Mies van der Rohe for the architecture exhibition in Berlin in 1931. Artcurial has commissioned works by Agam and Schöffer, and is planning to develop the sale of multiple works, sculptures by Dali or Berrocal, as well as everyday objects and jewelry designed by artists such as the Lalannes or Sonia Delaunay. This new kind of gallery will attempt to bring the public into contact with the creative arts as they are currently practiced.

Dubuffet's Follies

Dubuffet as an architect? It was to be expected, so much does this incredible artist enjoy the endless challenge of new projects. Yet he simply cannot do things the way everyone else does. His architecture, for example, has nothing in common with the international style of Gropius and Le Corbusier. What he has created are "follies," passions, in the sense this term had in the eighteenth century. Influenced by the arborescences of his *L'hourloupe* series, these creations turn a cold shoulder to straight lines but also to large bay windows. So far, no takers have come forward, but Dubuffet has built one of these "follies" to house his foundation in Périgny-sur-Yerres, where his studios are located. The name of this "folly" can be seen on a sign in the middle of its enamel garden: Villa Falbala.

American Realism

If American art between 1945 and 1965 was dominated by abstraction, figurative art is now experiencing a new creative surge. This time the surge is related to the classical tradition, and is quite different from Hyperrealism. One of the most important representatives of this tendency is the former abstract painter Philip Pearlstein, whose portraits are treated in the same direct manner as the décor in his work. Jack Beal, on the other hand, dehumanizes bodies, drowning them in draperies and wildly colored accessories. As for Alfred Leslie, he dramatizes his figures with Caravaggesque lighting. Also noteworthy in the context of this new tendency are Alex Katz and Jack Yougerman.

Dubuffet's Villa Falbala at Périgny-sur-Yerres.

WARREN JOHNSON: TUNNEL VISION. Columbia, South Carolina

A wall painting in Los Angeles.

MURALISM: RETURN TO TROMPE L'OEIL

UNITED STATES

Murals are rare in France. Here, across the Atlantic, they have become a general feature, especially in New York City, San Francisco, and Los Angeles, where they have become part of the daily scene. They are happy solutions for hiding the ugliness of decrepit walls, while giving artists an opportunity to add an unusual touch to a bland, functional urban background.

The original murals were militant and political in nature. They date back to the 1930s in Mexico, where Diego Rivera and José Clemente Orozco put their walls at the service of the revolution. They created enormous historical and allegorical scenes in a colorful language and with a consistent simplicity, which contrasted with the art in the museums, which in those years had often become obscure and full of allusions.

Muralism is rarely anonymous or collective, and it has its own stars: formerly Rivera and Orozco in Mexico, now Warren Johnson in the United States. But always it is addressed to the masses. While on occasion it may still be the expression of some militant action, its aim is mainly to surprise or to entertain. Most often, the muralist will draw a false opening on a

TO HIDE THE UGLINESS OF DECREPIT WALLS AND TO ENTERTAIN THE PUBLIC IN THE STREETS

façade and create a landscape in the middle of a block. Sometimes, façades are replaced by an illusion from nature, conjured up like a challenge. For example, in Columbia, South Carolina, a road tunnel with rocks and a setting sun has been created on the wall of a bank with such convincing

detail that, the story goes, an absent-minded driver tried driving his car into it. In Los Angeles, the cataclysmic end of California is depicted on the façade of an insurance company.

Contemporary architecture is often terribly dreary because of its theoretical rigor. Where have the vermiculations gone, the ornamental foliage, the cornices that used to give sparkle to

houses? It was inevitable that one day, on the flesh of the façades, there would be a reappearance of redundant, resounding, overflowing décor. It is probably not by accident that this happened on the concrete walls of the New World.

Nevertheless, Muralism has nothing to do with what is com-

monly known as "the revolution of modern art"—Cubism, Fauvism, Abstract Expressionism. Neither is it connected to the ancestral art of the fresco or to its latest embodiment found in Fernand Léger. Muralism has links to perspective drawing, narrative depiction, and *trompe l'oeil*. And it has roots in advertising.

The noninformed public finds it hard to accept that smears, lines, circles, triangles, and squares in some kind of arrangement or, worse, just monochrome surfaces can be works of art. The public continues to want images, as it has traditionally. Muralism meets this need. Besides advertising posters, it is a new kind of street art, with its own subjects, rules, and theatricality. From now on, the walls will talk.

(See also 1932.)

CÉSAR'S BATTLES

PARIS

Narcissistic? Undoubtedly, but not any more than many other artists. César Balduccini owes his reputation to the fact that ten years ago, for a collective exhibition with the hand as subject, he had a mold made of one of his thumbs, which was then enlarged to enormous proportions. In reality, César, born in 1921, the son of Italian immigrants in Marseilles, is one of the best French sculptors of this generation. He is internationally known and appreciated.

As a child, seated at a table in his parents' bistrot, he made drawings continuously, and the customers would agree he was gifted. After obtaining the customary secondary-school diploma, he attended the Academy of Fine Arts, first in his native city, later in Paris, where they made him professor five years ago. All this has led to an exclusive agreement linking him, since October, with the newly created gallery Beaubourg, with the prospects of numerous and major retrospectives throughout the world.

His first personal exhibition dates back to 1956, to the Biennale in Venice, where his work was presented at the French Pavilion. He was thirty-five years old, and it proved to be the end of the lean years. He was the oldest student in France, having reached the age where he was no longer entitled to eat in the cafeteria of the university. Two years earlier, he had discovered industrial waste—scrap metal, sections of tubing, rusty iron— and arc welding in a factory in Villetaneuse. César was totally penniless. Although he would have preferred working in marble or bronze, he had to satisfy himself with industrial leftovers, which he started to sculpt with passion, creating shapes of birds, insects, fish, and even nudes. His *Venus of Villetaneuse,* a giant female whose anatomy consists of metal scraps, is one of his most famous pieces.

Joining the New Realism

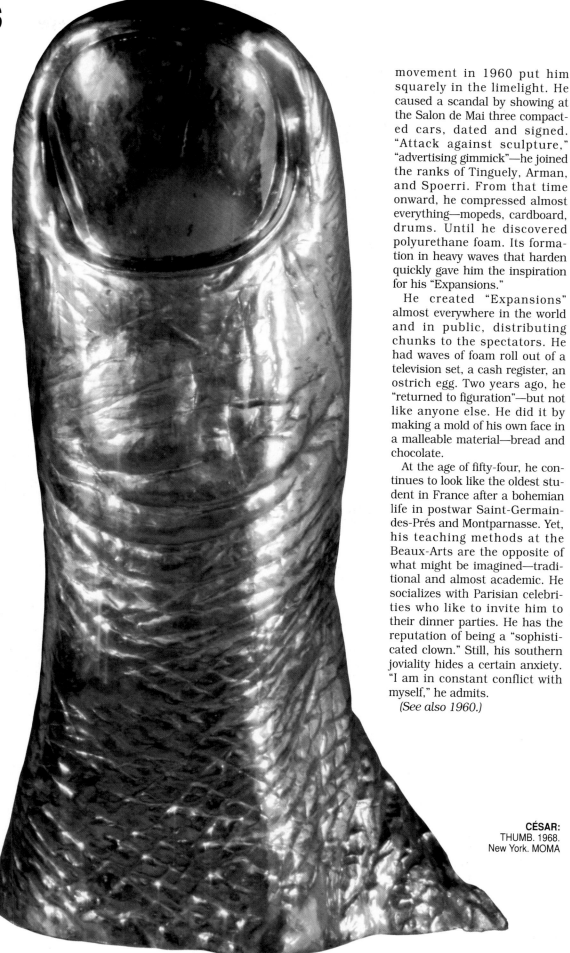

movement in 1960 put him squarely in the limelight. He caused a scandal by showing at the Salon de Mai three compacted cars, dated and signed. "Attack against sculpture," "advertising gimmick"—he joined the ranks of Tinguely, Arman, and Spoerri. From that time onward, he compressed almost everything—mopeds, cardboard, drums. Until he discovered polyurethane foam. Its formation in heavy waves that harden quickly gave him the inspiration for his "Expansions."

He created "Expansions" almost everywhere in the world and in public, distributing chunks to the spectators. He had waves of foam roll out of a television set, a cash register, an ostrich egg. Two years ago, he "returned to figuration"—but not like anyone else. He did it by making a mold of his own face in a malleable material—bread and chocolate.

At the age of fifty-four, he continues to look like the oldest student in France after a bohemian life in postwar Saint-Germain-des-Prés and Montparnasse. Yet, his teaching methods at the Beaux-Arts are the opposite of what might be imagined—traditional and almost academic. He socializes with Parisian celebrities who like to invite him to their dinner parties. He has the reputation of being a "sophisticated clown." Still, his southern joviality hides a certain anxiety. "I am in constant conflict with myself," he admits.

(See also 1960.)

CÉSAR:
THUMB. 1968.
New York. MOMA

Gigantism! With The Running Fence, an ephemeral wall stretching over hill and dale for twenty-five miles, Christo realizes his most ambitious work. Composed of multiple pieces of nylon, the wall required the collaboration of several hundred engineers, workers, and students, and costs two million dollars. Long gone is 1962, when the artist used gasoline barrels to block the Rue Visconti in Paris. When Vasarely opens a foundation in Aix-en-Provence for the contemplation of the various relationships of painting, architecture, and urbanism, it is quite clear that art, in the last quarter of this century, aims at integrating itself into everyday life.

1976
S U M M A R Y

ENVIRONMENTS

Christo Builds His Own Great Wall

DEVELOPMENTS

**The Vasarely Foundation
A Museum for Art Brut**

ART NEWS

**Subway Art
Death of a Photographer-Painter
Farewell to the Square
Frank Stella Retrospective
Nina Kandinsky's Fabulous Donation
In Brief**

GREAT MASTERS

Max Ernst: Genius without a Passport

ARCHITECTURE

**A Portrait of Alvar Aalto
The Olympic Stadium of Montreal**

LITERATURE

UNITED STATES
Publication of The Gulag Archipelago *by Alexandr Solzhenitsyn.*

FRANCE
Death of André Malraux.

MUSIC

GERMANY
At the centenary of the Bayreuth festivals, performance of the tetralogy The Ring of the Nibelung, *directed by Patrice Chéreau, under the musical direction of Pierre Boulez.*

GREAT BRITAIN
Peter Maxwell Davies creates his first symphony.

ITALY
Luigi Nono composes Sofferte onde serene *for piano and recording tape.*

FRANCE
At the 30th festival of Avignon, performance of the avant-garde opera Einstein on the Beach *by Robert Wilson and Philip Glass, staged by Benno Besson.*

MOTION PICTURES

UNITED STATES
Premiere of Marathon Man *by John Schlesinger, and* Taxi Driver *by Martin Scorsese.*

ITALY
Death of Luchino Visconti. Premiere of Fellini's Casanova *by Federico Fellini.*

JAPAN
Nagisa Oshima presents In the Realm of the Senses.

CHRISTO:
THE RUNNING FENCE. 1972-1976.
Northern California

720

CHRISTO BUILDS HIS OWN GREAT WALL

CALIFORNIA

Since the beginning of September, a nylon ribbon twenty-five miles long has run through the green California countryside, between the Pacific coast and the town of Petaluma. The gigantic curtain—a modern-day Great Wall of China—is the work of the sculptor Christo. It is called *The Running Fence*.

TWENTY-FIVE MILES LONG, TWENTY FEET HIGH, "THE LARGEST PICTURE IN THE WORLD"

The Running Fence consists of two thousand fifty pieces of white nylon, each twenty feet wide, carried by steel poles and cables anchored in the ground. The fence winds its way from east to west, circling houses, ranches, and villages until it reaches the ocean, into which it disappears. From April to September, sixty-five workers put in sixty hours a week manipulating the poles and the cables with the help of twenty vehicles and bulldozers. During the last week of August and the first week of September, three hundred sixty students installed the immense canvas, which was often difficult to attach because of violent winds at the site. The cost amounted to two million dollars, all paid by Christo. It is a short-lived phenomenon. The

The Running Fence disappears into the Pacific Ocean.

fence must be dismantled by October 31.

It is not surprising that *The Running Fence* triggers a lively controversy. Christo is of Bulgarian origin. His real name is Christo Javacheff. He was born in 1935. After a stay of several years in Paris, where he joined the New Realists in 1961, he started making a name for himself in New York as a "wrapper" of objects. The objects kept

The fabric swelling in the wind.

growing in size until they included monuments and, finally, landscapes. In a vein similar to *The Running Fence*, he closed off a valley in Colorado with a gigantic orange curtain four years ago.

The idea of such colossal undertakings came to him in a rather curious way during his years as a fine-arts student in Sofia. Only acknowledged artists were allowed to paint portraits of the masters of the regime. As for students, they were sent in summer to an area along the route of the Orient Express to embellish the landscape around the harvesters, tractors, and other agricultural machinery in order to impress Western travelers.

In capitalistic America, on the other hand, people question Christo about the useless, futile, gratuitous, and spectacular aspects of *The Running Fence*, whose budget bore little relationship to the idea people generally have of a work of art. Another problem was whether an individual—even an artist—has the moral right to close off a corner of nature for a certain length of time by means of a nylon curtain. At any rate, the officials of the two counties that *The Running Fence* was to cross realized that during the existence of the project the increase in tourism and added temporary employment might not be bad for a cattle region with high unemployment. Economic interest soon prevailed over moral concerns.

With regard to the actual organization of the operation, apparently nothing would have succeeded without Christo's wife.

She was the organizer, the planner, the pillar on which her husband leaned. She is French. They met during Christo's Paris years. Planning is in her genes: She is the daughter of General Guillebon, who was General Leclerc's chief of staff in the Second World War.

With his twenty-five-mile fence, Christo has created "the largest picture in the world." But it was not only destined for the *Guinness Book of World Records.* Christo's goal was to make an inhabited sculpture. It crisscrosses the area with minimal disturbance to the life and the customs of the region. Besides preliminary studies, a strict report was drawn on the impact of *The Running Fence* on the environment. Christo insisted on preserving a perfect harmony between the work and nature. He did everything possible to achieve this aim.

The gigantic fence links two symbols of infinity—the ocean and the highway—in a country where time seems frozen in eternity. However, the work itself is ephemeral, and will live on only in souvenirs. A transitory aspect and instantaneousness are among the principal impressions provoked by *The Running Fence.* After the shock of the first encounter with the unbroken line, which cuts through the green hills, underscoring the immensity of nature, the next sensation is one of momentariness created by the shimmer of the ribbon, by the play of low light intercepted by the white nylon canvas swaying in the landscape.

Nothing will remain but a few pictures, which the local merchants hope will bring in some money. *The Running Fence* will collapse without a trace. The poles will be offered to the people on whose land they were erected. The fasteners of the cables will be buried three feet below the prairie, to satisfy the curiosity of future archaeologists.

(See also 1962.)

A steel cable being unrolled at the entrance of the Spirito Ballatore ranch. Total length of cable (upper, lower, lateral) used is nearly 90 miles.

2,050 white nylon sheets, each measuring 20 X 68 feet, are attached to the cables. The upper cable is stretched between 21-foot metal poles that are secured in the ground by 11,000 steel anchors.

The nylon sheets are held by 350,000 hooks above and below. Over a length of 25 miles, *The Running Fence* forms an immense terrestrial sail, billowing in the wind.

THE VASARELY FOUNDATION

AIX-EN-PROVENCE

To the "Didactic Museum" in Gordes, which has been displaying his best pictorial creations for the past six years, Victor Vasarely now adds a Foundation with emphasis on architecture.

A fervent disciple of the Bauhaus, whose principles have seduced him since his youth, Vasarely considers the artist to be the conscience of society. In creating furniture, apartments, and houses, the artist perforce becomes involved in city planning, politics, and philosophy. Vasarely himself has designed the layout of the Foundation, an enormous building of 360 x 165 feet. It is in the immediate vicinity of the Boufan farm where Cézanne used to live.

The complex consists of sixteen hexagonal units. Seven halls have forty-foot-high ceilings, showing examples of architectural integration emanating from his paintings. The other nine are divided into three levels. There are a conference room, a library, a workshop for research, a room with more than one thousand polychromatic studies for public viewing, apartments for the director and the guard, and an area housing the air-conditioning facilities. Construction costs amount to twenty-five million francs and are paid entirely by Vasarely himself.

Each year, colloquia are organized on various subjects; for example, on new materials and colored cement. There is something fascinating in watching a man launch a gigantic undertaking to impose beauty, "his" beauty, on everyone. But the proof is here. The Aix Foundation shows that even magnified one hundred times a work by Vasarely loses none of its power.

The Vasarely Foundation.

GASTON DUF: "PÂÛLÎHINÊLE GÂNSTHÊRS VITRÊS-HE."
Lausanne. Collection de l'Art Brut

A MUSEUM FOR ART BRUT

LAUSANNE

Since Jean Dubuffet, in 1962, returned to France his collection of Art Brut from the house of his friend Alfonso Ossorio in East Hampton, New York, he has been looking for a place to exhibit it. He has one. From now on, the collection will be on display at the Beaulieu Château in Lausanne. The opening on February 26 is attended by city officials.

Besides the Prinzhorn collection in Heidelberg, the collection is the most complete in Europe. In contrast to the collection in Heidelberg, the Lausanne collection does not consist only of works by mental patients. Dubuffet has tried to gather works by autodidactic artists who, sane or not, are free of cultural contamination. These include works by a mailman, Raphaël Lonné, whose Automatic Drawings were dictated to him during spiritual séances, and the "scribblings" by Palanc, who applies to his artwork the sugar ornaments that he uses in his trade as a pastry chef.

The core of the collection, nevertheless, is drawings, paintings, and sculptures by residents of mental hospitals. There are, for example, the colorful works of Aloïse, who spent more than forty years at the Rosière Asylum in Gimel, a small town in the Jura Mountains of the Vaud, and the broad paintings on paper of Gaston, the "zoologist," who was locked up at the age of twenty with the following medical assessment: "mental alienation; refuses to eat; claims his parents are trying to poison him." Also included are creations by Gaston Duf, Jeanne Tripier, Auguste Forestier, and many others.

The collection, which is the property of the Art Brut company founded by Dubuffet in 1948, should have remained in Paris. The city was eager to have the collection, but when Dubuffet was faced with unkept promises and procrastination by the administration, he shipped the collection to Lausanne, where there are ideal conditions for the preservation of a treasure to which—as he has never denied—his own art owes a lot.

Subway Art

The most sinister subway in the world belongs to New York; the most pretentious is in Moscow. But then, there is not much to boast about in Western Europe, either. In London, Eduardo Paolozzi has been commissioned to decorate one of the subway stations, though tangible results have yet to come. The cleverest in this regard are the Belgians, who have systematically entrusted subway-station decoration to artists. Certainly the greatest success is the Hankar Station by the Brussels artist Roger Somville. It opens on September 20, after two and a half years of work. On nearly six thousand five hundred square feet, *Our Times* offers a stunning synthesis of anguish (crazed motorcyclists, the dictator) and hope (the crowd, the beach).

Death of a Photographer-Painter

A photographer and painter whose painting was not photographic, Man Ray was among the few Americans who, like Pascin and Alexander Calder, were successful in Paris, where he died at the age of eighty-six. As the inventor of "Rayographs" in 1922, he made photographic portraits of his Surrealist friends. His painting plays on surprising juxtapositions, and is more amusing than disturbing. Half Max Ernst, half Magritte, his most celebrated work shows scarlet, Daliesque lips floating in a peculiar firmament. "I have always envied those for whom a work of art is a mystery," quipped the old dauber toward the end of his life.

Farewell to the Square

He was a teacher without peer, and his name will always be associated with those hallowed places of twentieth-century art, the Bauhaus and Black Mountain College. Josef Albers is dead in New Haven, Connecticut, at the age of eighty-eight. A remarkable painter, he was obsessed, especially in his last years, with the power of color on the eye and mind. His series *Homages to the Square,* which brought him international fame, is an exemplary realization of Abstract Geometric Art. His graphic art—dry points, woodcuts, linocuts, and lithographs—is based on a strict Constructivism.

Frank Stella Retrospective

At the Museum of Art in Baltimore, Frank Stella exhibits the works from two series, *Protractors* and *Saskatchewan.* Discovered in 1959 by Leo Castelli, Dorothy Miller, and Alfred Barr, Stella quickly initiated his *Black Series,* black paintings composed of rectilinear bands parallel with the frame, then displayed diagonally. The fine paintings in the *Aluminum* series followed, giving rise to the "shaped canvas," with its multiple cutouts of symmetrical form, which, in the 1960s, became irregular polygons of increasingly vivid and finally phosphorescent colors.

Nina Kandinsky's Fabulous Donation

Madame Kandinsky has donated fifteen important paintings that show the artist's development between 1908 and 1942 to the Musée National d'Art Moderne in the Georges Pompidou Center. The first stage, called the Muscovite period, is illustrated notably by *Improvisation 3, Black Arc,* and especially *Red Spot,* all of which are among the artist's first masterpieces. The Bauhaus period, characteristic of what Kandinsky called "Lyric Geometrism," is magnificently represented by works such as *Yellow, Red, Blue with Hyphens Between* and *Sur les pointes.* Five other paintings belonging to Kandinsky's Parisian period, from 1933 to his death in 1944, complement the collection, along with some fifteen watercolors and gouaches, including the celebrated first *Abstract Watercolor,* painted in 1910.

IN BRIEF...

GERMANY
At the Künstlerhaus in Munich, a retrospective of Wassili Kandinsky: the most complete overview ever in Germany.

BRAZIL
Retrospective in São Paulo of the painter Emiliano Di Cavalcanti, who died this year.

UNITED STATES
At the Whitney Museum, an Alexander Calder exhibition (which opened several days before his death), showing the great diversity of his work.
  Soviet sculptor Ernst Neizvestny opens a sculpting school in New York.

FRANCE
At the Orangerie, a Dunoyer de Segonzac retrospective.
  Leon Zack retrospective at the Musée National d'Art Moderne. He was one of the figures of Lyrical Abstractionism.

JOSEF ALBERS:
AFFECTIONATE.
1954. Paris. MNAM

MAX ERNST:
CAPRICORN. 1948-
1964. Paris. MNAM

MAX ERNST: GENIUS WITHOUT A PASSPORT

PARIS

Max Ernst didn't like to be called "Master." "Picasso is a master," he said, "not me!" He preferred to consider himself a bird, on account of his sharp profile and transparent eyes, and because birds were a frequent subject of his paintings. He also identified with Loplop, a little guy who was simultaneously his creative genius and the double with whom he would have ongoing internal dialogues. Now Loplop has left us—as has Max Ernst, at the age of eighty-five. He died on April 1.

As a child, Ernst was indignant when his father, a teacher of deaf mutes and an amateur painter, depicted Max as little Jesus in a small painting on plaster. He had the feeling that some kind of blasphemy was being committed, because he secretly felt more like a devil.

Max—neither angel nor devil. This could be the leitmotif of an *oeuvre* that borrowed from many trends and that is viewed as one of the most important in Surrealism (together with the works of Magritte and Dali).

When he came to France, illegally, in 1922, on the passport of the French poet Paul Éluard, who had gone to Germany to visit him, the thirty-one-year-old, uncompromising pacifist, who had been in the artillery in the First World War, already had a weighty past. As soon as the war was over, he plunged into Dada with a style all his own. The 1920 show, which he organized with his friend Baargeld in the back of Winter Brasserie in Cologne, remains one of the high points of the Dadaist revolution.

Ernst never stopped painting. Works like *The Elephant of Celebes* and *Ubu Imperator* are ironic masterpieces. He played on unusual combinations: The elephant looks like a cooking pot . . . the man has the shape of a top . . . there are plenty of strange and hallucinatory elements. They are in contrast with Ernst's other direction—hallucinations of perception, especially in his frottages and decalcomania work.

A German living in France, Ernst was a pacifist who turned against Hitler. In 1940, after the defeat of France, he decided to go into exile in the United States, where he became a sculptor. Sculpture is the least known part of his *oeuvre*, though certainly not the least significant.

When he returned to France in 1948, he belatedly became famous, and for twenty-eight years was counted among the artists of international significance.

(See also 1924, 1926, 1928, 1936, 1941, 1942.)

The house that Alvar Aalto built for Louis Carré, 1956-1959.

A PORTRAIT OF ALVAR AALTO

HELSINKI

At the age of seventy-eight, Alvar Aalto, the famous Finnish architect, dies. He was born in Kuortane. He started out on his career in a democratic country, where secular Protestant individualism imposes a lifestyle geared toward a type of home design which, though open to modern technology, remains closely linked with traditional and popular values.

Aalto always retained an intimate relationship with the social, ecological, and economic conditions of his nation. Therein lay the uniqueness of this authentic creator, whose guiding principles were the adaptation of the design to the building site and the purpose and function of interior spaces. These fundamental concerns underscore the permanent gap that exists between Aalto's work and the rationalism promoted by the Bauhaus.

With the Païmio Sanitarium (1929-1933), commissioned after a contest among architects, Aalto placed himself, at the age of thirty, in the front ranks of his contemporaries. His many administrative, religious, and sports creations, as well as his industrial, cultural, and apartment complexes in Helsinki, Sunila, and Vuoksenniska, unified the architectural image of Finland. His reputation crossed national borders. He designed buildings in Germany, the Middle East, the Scandinavian countries, and France, where the art dealer Louis Carré engaged him to design his country house.

To define interior spaces better, Aalto often used asymmetrical layouts and bent shapes, which frequently included curved walls. His concern with human values led him to design vases and furniture. Whenever questioned, he replied, "I build."

THE OLYMPIC STADIUM OF MONTREAL

MONTREAL

The largest building site on the planet is the largest Olympic stadium. The creator is a fifty-year-old French architect, Roger Taillibert. He also designed the Olympic center in Font-Romeu, a swimming pool in Deauville, and the Parc des Princes in Paris.

The stadium is elliptical. It evokes the image of a gigantic shell. Under usual circumstances, the stadium can accommodate fifty thousand spectators; during the Olympics, this figure goes up to sixty-five thousand. It has six horizontal levels, where the spectators can circulate. The structure includes thirty-four bases consisting of one thousand five hundred elements, prefabricated, mounted, assembled, poststressed. Cantilevered sections rise to a height of a hundred sixty-five feet. The structure contains four hundred thousand cubic yards of concrete and thirty thousand tons of steel.

The stadium will be protected against adverse weather by a twenty-thousand-square-foot removable awning, weighing twenty tons and supported by a five-hundred-fifty-foot-high tower. On top of the tower will be a revolving restaurant. Diners will enjoy a super view of the athletic fields. The complex includes a swimming center and an athletic track eight hundred and twenty feet long.

The ambitious stadium came about through the support of the mayor of Montreal, Jean Drapeau. Construction, which took three years, did not go smoothly. The choice of a French architect caused an uproar. The site was the scene of union fights and sabotage on such a scale that the Canadian government formed a committee to examine union behavior. Strikes inflated the budget by fourteen million dollars. Notwithstanding these troubles, the stadium is ready for the games. Its esthetic impact proves that architecture has had the last word.

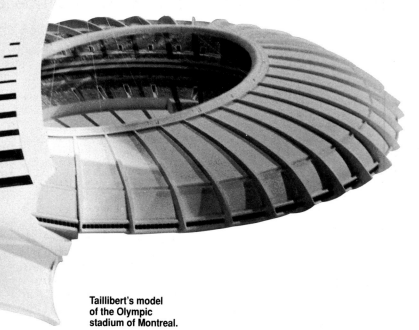

Taillibert's model of the Olympic stadium of Montreal.

As soon as Valéry Giscard d'Estaing has presided over its opening in the presence of guests from all over the world, the Georges Pompidou Center draws endless crowds. The deceased president, for whom it had been named, had wanted it to be built to help bring France out of its artistic isolation. Its objectives are both to mount large international exhibitions and to open the door to exhibitions from other countries that would not have come to Paris before this. Already the center has shown a large collection entitled Paris-New York, demonstrating the kinds of artistic exchanges between the two cities since the beginning of the century. Also on view is an exhibit on François Topino-Lebrun, an artist of the Revolution, guillotined in 1801. This show poses the problem of the possibilty of historical painting today.

1977

S U M M A R Y

MUSEUMS

The Inauguration of Pompidou Center
Paris-New York

DEVELOPMENTS

Monumental Pignon
An Executive Enamored of Painting

ART NEWS

Daily Mythologies II
De Maria: *The Lightning Field*
Baby Beuys's Bathtub
Documenta VI
Pattern Painting at the MOMA
In Brief

EXHIBITIONS

The Return of Historical Painting

SCULPTURE

Kowalski: Games of Art and Science
Pol Bury's Fantasies in Metal

The Georges Pompidou Center.

VICTOR VASARELY:
PORTRAIT OF GEORGES
POMPIDOU. 1977. Paris.
Georges Pompidou Center

**Detail of the Georges
Pompidou Center
facing the Rue
Beaubourg.**

THE INAUGURATION OF POMPIDOU CENTER

PARIS

On January 31, the president of the Republic, Valéry Giscard d'Estaing, inaugurates the Centre Georges Pompidou in the presence of Madame Pompidou, Prime Minister Raymond Barre, Secretary of Culture Françoise Giroud, and four thousand guests. The president pays homage to Georges Pompidou, recalling that he was "a man greatly appreciative of contemporary art, who worried about the risk of our creative forces going abroad, overseas, forces that Paris used to protect and that he wanted to keep here."

Pompidou decided in 1969 to build a contemporary-art center. He had dreamed about it for years. He found a site on the

Beaubourg plateau, a vacant area in the 4th *arrondissement*—where a small island had been destroyed for health reasons in 1936. What he hadn't done as prime minister under General Charles de Gaulle, that is, "give the capital an architec-

Pompidou planned an international competition, for which he appointed an international jury. It consisted of ten members, who studied six hundred and eighty-one projects and voted, nine to one, for the submission of two young foreign architects, Renzo

Four years ago, it was decided that the center would include four departments: a department of plastic arts, including the Musée National d'Art Moderne (MNAM) and the Centre National d'Art Contemporain (CNAC); a center for industrial design; a public library; and a center for acoustical research. The president appointed Robert Bordaz to be manager of the project. He in turn chose the Swede Pontus Hulten to manage the plastic-arts department. Hulten was known for the many exhibitions he had organized in Europe and the United States.

"AN ARCHITECTURAL AND URBAN CENTER REPRESENTATIVE OF OUR TIME"

tural and urban complex typical of our time," Pompidou achieved as president. He stipulated that the center should contain "a large museum of painting and sculpture, also special facilities for music and records, and later also for film and theater research, completed by a library."

Piano, aged thirty-three, and Richard Rogers, aged thirty-seven. The design was "functional, flexible, multiuse." When it was disclosed to the public, it came under fire immediately for constituting a complete break with its surroundings, one of the oldest neighborhoods of Paris.

When Pompidou died on April 2, 1974, the fate of the center appeared threatened, though its infrastructure was in place. The

PARIS-NEW YORK

administrative tribunal of Paris announced that work would be halted. An appeal was filed by an association of architects for the defense of important sites. The work was forty percent complete, with ninety percent of the subcontracts awarded. There is no doubt that without the aggressiveness of Jacques Chirac, an ardent supporter of the project, construction would not have resumed. On December 12, 1974, the law creating the Centre National d'Art et de Culture Georges Pompidou was adopted by the National Assembly; the Socialist and Communist deputies abstained.

But it did not mean the end of the center's troubles. In January 1975, as the metal framework was being erected—it was referred to as "the refinery," "the machine," "the monster"—the "revolt of the donors" erupted. The heirs of Rouault, Matisse, Chagall, Picasso, Laurens, and Braque refused to release the works of these masters, which were stored in the Musée National d'Art Moderne at the Palais de Tokyo. Even more than the "dismembering" of collections, they feared that the new center could not guarantee the dignified atmosphere of a traditional museum. Françoise Giroud, appointed secretary of culture in August 1976, dropped another bombshell: "The Pompidou Center cannot be made profitable." At the unveiling of his project, Pompidou had declared, "All this is expensive, I frankly admit it. But over a number of years it will finally be no more than a drop in the bucket of the government. If our goal is achieved, it will be an achievement without precedent."

And so: What will happen to what the Left calls "a bureaucratic, centralist, and scandalously elitist undertaking" and what the Right describes as "an ocean liner of the future grounded in our silted-up ports"?

(See also 1987.)

PARIS
The Paris-New York Exhibition, which opened on June 1 on the fifth floor of the Georges Pompidou Center, is met with great expectations. For three months, the most significant works of artists who have worked in France and the United States in search of avant-garde works. The exhibition's first display is, appropriately, the reconstruction of the salon of Leo, Michael, Sarah, and Gertrude Stein, with the works of Gauguin, Cézanne, and Maurice Denis purchased from 1904 onward and the famous portrait of Miss Stein

THE MOST COMPLETE SUMMARY OF ARTISTIC EXCHANGES BETWEEN THE TWO COUNTRIES

since the beginning of the century are on display: several hundred paintings, drawings, sculptures, and documents. This fascinating and impressive show constitutes the most complete summary of artistic exchanges between the two countries.

These exchanges began with the highly acclaimed Armory Show in 1913, in New York City.

However, American collectors had arrived years earlier in Paris painted in 1906 by Picasso and lent by the Metropolitan Museum for the occasion.

Before Picasso, Matisse had an influence on American painters. They assiduously visited his studio and turned it into an academy. Seventy years later, paintings of Bruce, Dove, and Schamberg returned to the city where they were made. During the Second World War, Europeans fled to America. Léger, Mondrian, Chagall, Matta, Ernst, and Masson sought refuge in New York. Their arrival generated the first American artistic movement of international significance. Peggy Guggenheim's gallery, Art of This Century, where so many artists, such as Giacometti, Pollock, Rothko were shown, is also reproduced. During the fifties and sixties, many European artists, including Arman, Christo, Dubuffet, Raysse, and Tinguely, lived in New York, some for extensive periods of time.

Some claim that in the Paris-New York Exhibition there are too many juxtapositions of masterpieces and secondary works. Still, this extraordinary artistic panorama—the first of its kind in the new Georges Pompidou Center—goes far in illustrating the adventure of modern art.

JEAN-PAUL RIOPELLE: UNTITLED. 1953. Paris. Private Collection

MONUMENTAL PIGNON

LILLE

The ceramic wall Pignon has created for a building here is a masterpiece of its kind. It covers a side wall at an intersection close to the railroad station and measures 66 x 33 feet. It is called *Man and Child*, and deals with a favorite subject of the artist. He has given it monumental proportions.

The theme has surfaced in his paintings since 1953. The previous year, Picasso had invited Pignon to work with him in Vallauris for part of the winter. At the end of the day, the two painters, sometimes accompanied by Picasso's daughter Paloma, would walk from their respective studios in the little village to the hill where they lived.

One evening, Paloma had a hard time keeping up with her father and his guest. Pignon lifted the child to his shoulders. Paloma fell asleep at once, her head on Pignon's head, her legs

ÉDOUARD PIGNON: MAN AND CHILD. 1976-1977. Lille

around Pignon's neck, her hands in Pignon's hands. Pignon experienced a strange sensation. Their breaths intermingled in the night air. This was the origin of the intertwined rhythms, the flat color surfaces, and the creative deformations of *Man and Child*.

The ceramic wall here reflects another of Pignon's favorite subjects, cock fighting, which he shows next to the man. It derives from Pignon's attempts to capture in similar fights that he has observed and drawn for a long time the proximity, the

movement of adversaries in the pit: he tries to throw the expression of speed on the canvas.

Street art is an old revolutionary form of expression. Everyone coming to Lille can see a magnificent example.

AN EXECUTIVE ENAMORED OF PAINTING

TROYES

Pierre Lévy, a sixty-eight-year-old industrialist from Troyes, has donated to France his collection consisting of eight hundred fifty paintings, three thousand two hundred drawings, dozens of sculptures, glass objects, items from Africa, the Pacific, Egypt, and China, rugs, and nineteen hundred pieces of ceramic and Louristan bronzes. His collection reveals a passion rather than a concern for investment. "No acquisition was made for reasons of speculation or fashion,"

ROBERT DELAUNAY: THE RUNNERS. 1926. Troyes. Musée des Beaux-Arts

Pierre Lévy explains. His first buys were in 1937, three paintings by Vlaminck, Friesz, and Utrillo. The collection reflects Lévy's taste, which requires works of art to be a source of joy.

Monsieur Lévy was initiated to modern art by the painter and glass artist Marinot. In 1946, he purchased most of the collection of the art critic Félix Fénéon. In the same year, he met and befriended André Derain, from whom he would buy seventy-nine paintings, fifty-three drawings, and seventy-one pieces of sculpture.

The industrialist spends fifteen to twenty percent of his income on his passion for art. He bequeaths his collection on condition that it not be dispersed, that it be presented in accordance with its spirit. The bishop's palace in Troyes, a magnificent building from the sixteenth and seventeenth centuries, will be refurbished. In the meantime, the collector continues to collect "with his heart."

Daily Mythologies II

Thirteen years after the 1964 exhibition "Daily Mythologies," in which Rauschenberg, crowned by the Venice Biennale, made Europe conscious of Pop Art, a new exhibition opened in April on the same theme. Called "Daily Mythologies II," it brings together ninety artists for three months at ARC 2 in the Musée d'Art Moderne de la Ville in Paris. The selections, made by Gérald Gassiot-Talabot, Jean-Louis Pradel, Rancillac, and Télémaque are divided into two groups. On the one hand, there is a response to the critical analysis of Roland Barthes, according to whom myths are a "stolen language" that "transforms history into nature." On the other hand, there is the response to the opinion of Gillo Dorflès who sees in myth a positive force that functions as a "testing ground for all human values." Among those exhibited are Adami, Pommereule, Aillaud, Arroyo, Cremonini, Erro, Klasen, Kudo, Monory, Moninot, Vostell, Fahlström, Voss, and Velickovic.

De Maria: "The Lightning Field"

Land Artist Walter de Maria completes his latest monumental landscape in New Mexico. *The Lightning Field* is located far from civilization in the heart of a semi-arid state. At the center of a vast, barren plain ringed with mountains, it is composed of four hundred thick steel poles, about twenty-three feet high, set into the ground according to a precise geometric plan. These regularly spaced poles form a quadrilateral, one mile long from east to west, and two-thirds of a mile long from north to south. The zone where *The Lightning Field* is set experiences frequent storms, and the work invites people by day and by night to look at reality through the creative power of art.

Baby Beuys's Bathtub

The collector Lothar Shirmer, who sued for damages plus interest for destruction of a work of art, has received one hundred eighty thousand German marks. For the traveling exhibition Realität, he had loaned Joseph Beuys's *Bathtub*, the sanitary apparatus in which the artist made his ablutions as a child. Beuys had completed his work in 1960, with a few additions: adhesive plaster and gauze soaked in grease to emphasize the birth trauma. But on the occasion of a meeting held in the Leverkusen Museum, where it had been installed, the precious apparatus had been used to cool beer. It was then cleaned, reducing Joseph Beuys's work to nothing.

Documenta VI

Documenta VI has had an auspicious opening. Harald Szeemann has been replaced by Manfred Schneckenburger, and now the whole town is part of the project. Bazon Brock has opened a school to introduce visitors to the visual arts, following the exhibition at the Orangerie "Forms and Functions of Drawing in 1969 and 1970."

That exhibit had brought together more than seven hundred works by some two hundred artists of the old generation, such as Picasso and Henry Moore, as well as works by the new generation, including Botero, Christo, Beuys, and Serra. For the first time, the German Democratic Republic is represented in Kassel.

Pattern Painting at the MOMA

The MOMA exhibition "Pattern Painting at P.S. 1" brings together artists who only a short time ago would have been dismissed as "decorative." But after years of Minimal Art, the public is obviously pleased by the rediscovery of a symphony of colors and textures. Among the artists exhibited, Alain Shields was the first to be inspired by Indian crafts during the hippie period, integrating feathers and pearls in his ragged compositions. Sam Gilliam's canvases, painted like baldachins, give proof of a deep sensitivity to color. Cynthia Carlson, Kim McConnel, Rodney Ripps, and Miriam Schapiro also exhibit works bursting with joyous, floral motifs.

WALTER DE MARIA:
THE LIGHTNING FIELD.
1971-1977. Quemada,
New Mexico

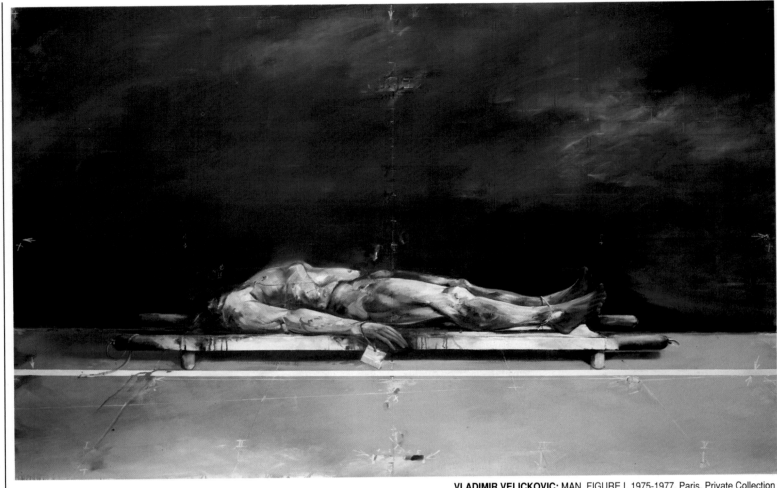

VLADIMIR VELICKOVIC: MAN. FIGURE I. 1975-1977. Paris. Private Collection

THE RETURN OF HISTORICAL PAINTING

PARIS

Everyone expected the Georges Pompidou Center to draw France out of its artistic isolation. From that point of view, the major "Paris-New York" exhibit has been a first, and overwhelming, success. In addition, the enormous "machine" built by the architects Piano and Rogers permits several exhibitions at the same time; in June, there is the simultaneous homage to François Topino-Lebrun.

He was a disciple of David, who was beheaded by the guillotine at the Place de Grève on January 31, 1801. To rescue him from oblivion, seven painters and an author have formed an association. They have made thirty paintings for the purpose of reinventing historical painting.

"No one wanted to assume the ultimate risk, which in cultural circles means going against the tide," Alain Jouffroy, the author and founder of the association, declares. The main painting of Topino-Lebrun, *The Death of Caius Gracchus*, which inspired the exhibit, tells the story of Caius' escape from the accomplices of Optimus and his tragic end in a forest dedicated to the Goddess of Fury, killed there by his slave Philocratus. The painting bears the inscription "The law of which Caius Gracchus is the author prohibits anyone to own more than three hundred fifty acres of land." Topino-Lebrun's intention is clear. The publicist Gracchus Babeuf had recently advocated the abolishment of private property in favor of collective property. Shortly before the 1798 Salon, for which Topino-Lebrun had to complete his painting, Babeuf committed suicide. Through the association of both men and both names, and the similarity between their struggles and their deaths, the artist linked history and social demands. Can painting do the same today?

"FRAGMENTS OF A WORLD IN THE PROCESS OF KILLING ITSELF"

For the seven friends of Topino-Lebrun, it was the main obstacle because there is no question of turning to Socialist Realism. They had to find something new.

Fromanger and Monory have painted images of cops and neon lights—cold reality that strikes like a guillotine blade. Erro has used the sharp language of the comic strip to depict the killing of Allende. Recalcati and Chambas have opted for buffoonery. On the subject of "fragments of a world in the process of killing itself," Dufour has created an impressive painting. Velickovic's is a corpse without a head and with bound ankles, abandoned on a stretcher in the sad light of dawn.

At the age of forty-two, Velickovic is one of the best contemporary painters. He has everything: technical virtuosity, rapid execution, a sense of tragedy. His works are black, gray, and white, and most often they derive from Muybridge's chronophotographs. In this form and with this kind of inventiveness, historical painting is still possible. The show is worth a visit, if only for Velickovic.

KOWALSKI: GAMES OF ART AND SCIENCE

PIOTR KOWALSKI: NOW. 1965. Long Beach. University of Southern California

PARIS

Because he knows the technology from the inside, and because he has the soul of an artist, Piotr Kowalski never indulges in redundancy or facileness. Recently, he proposed a project for Les Halles involving a lake of Symmetry and a Lake of Perspective, a Cone of Gravitation and a Planetarium, offering everyone the possibility of becoming familiar with the laws governing earthly existence.

He also initiated sculpting with dynamite: "Everything started with a project I had been nurturing for several years, the instant molding of metal by means of dynamite. The method is not new. About sixty years ago, an American, I believe, used it to make cuspidors. I wanted to experiment with 'free forming' that is, getting rid of the mold by substituting it with an excellent, instantaneous, and natural container: water. I felt that, under the effect of dynamite, metal would show the same flexibility and the same suppleness as the plastic materials I commonly use in my sculpting."

Kowalski studied mathematics in Poland and received a degree in architecture in the United States. At the age of fifty-five, he divides his time between Paris and the Massachusetts Institute of Technology, the famous M.I.T.

The underwater explosions that created his Dynamite Sculpture took place at North American Aviation in Los Angeles where the workers normally concentrate on the Gemini and Apollo spaceship projects. The resulting work is surprisingly graceful.

An exhibition of Kowalski's work at the Georges Pompidou Center is announced.

POL BURY'S FANTASIES IN METAL

PARIS

"I often show in America," Pol Bury explains. "The enthusiasm, openness, and interest of the public are very encouraging." But the artist is not unknown in France. In recent years, his work has been on display a bit everywhere, for example, at Denise René, Iris Clert, and the gallery Maeght.

A former Surrealist, Bury at the age of fifty-five is an artist who defies classification. His pieces fluctuate between dream and technology. Masses of rising balls turning and turning, chirping like insects; small wooden cylinders that align and then suddenly rearrange themselves; "erectile punctuations," where the word "erectile" should be seen in both the architectural and physiological senses. "The speed of the snail combined with the slowness of the elephant"— this is how Bury characterizes motion in his sculpture.

Like Schöffer and Kowalski, Pol Bury is one of the sculptors who have put hammer and chisel aside in order to embrace the techniques of the industrial age. He believes that in our time, when everything is brought into question, neither painting nor sculpture can be what it has been since the Renaissance. The son of a car mechanic from Haine-Saint-Pierre, in Belgium, Pol Bury became an artist so as not to spend his life behind a desk or a wheelbarrow. He is also a remarkable polemicist and the author of several books. When necessary, he does not hesitate to make mincemeat of certain aberrations of modern art.

POL BURY: 4087 ERECTILE CYLINDERS. 1972. Paris

Metaphysical Painting mourns a great loss. Giorgio de Chirico dies in Rome at the age of eighty. His work, which had inspired Surrealism and was then rejected by André Breton during the twenties when the artist returned to a kind of Classicism, now seems to be one of the strangest of the century. When we compare it with that of Jasper Johns, who figures today among the great American artists, we can appreciate the distance covered in three generations by the revolution of modern art. In the domain of art, nothing now is as it was in the past, and what shocks us today becomes our standard of beauty tomorrow.

1978

SUMMARY

GREAT MASTERS

**Jasper Johns: Implosion of Perception
In Johns's Words**

DEVELOPMENTS

**Kenneth Noland Draws Plans in Color
The Death of Lindner**

ART NEWS

**Ipoustéguy Dramatizes His Sculpture
Paris-Berlin
Realism and Aluminum
The Von Hirsch Sale in London
Alberto Savinio in Rome
In Brief**

OBITUARIES

The World of Metaphysical Painting Is in Mourning

ENVIRONMENTS

Artists Defend La Défense

JASPER JOHNS: IMPLOSION OF PERCEPTION

NEW YORK

When Jasper Johns showed his first *Flags*, in 1957, at the Leo Castelli Gallery, they were met with a storm of protest. A sad example of chauvinism, people said, he dreams of the American flag and then paints it! Abstract Impressionism was on the point of conquering the planet, and here was this character of twenty-seven who produced figurative paintings. And in the most vulgar way, too, by copying the Star-Spangled Banner.

Italian genius in depth. He also reads Wittgenstein, loves philosophy, psychology, and poetry. No wonder he is not limited to painting a patriotic dream.

A final *Flag*, dated 1965, reveals what has unified Johns's work. The painting shows the flag in green, orange, and black in such a way that after the viewer stares at the false American flag for a minute, an after-image appears on his retina with the correct red, white, and blue colors when looking at a second

A FALSE AMERICAN FLAG, GREEN, ORANGE, AND BLACK

Today, at the age of forty-eight, Johns is seen all over the world. He has become a respected artist among the young generation of American painters. Wesleyan University organized a retrospective of his graphic work; it is touring the United States. Johns is an admirer of Picasso, Duchamp, Cézanne, and Leonardo. As a student, he studied this

flag, almost monochrome, which is painted below the green, orange, and black one. Johns plays knowingly with what is known about the mechanisms of perception. At the same time, he replies to attacks by the Dadaists, who accuse him unjustly of extending unnecessarily the excessive list of "ready-mades."

JASPER JOHNS: ZERO THROUGH NINE. 1961. London. Tate Gallery

In fact, what the artist always aims for is to subject the eye to a tour de force. This is particularly clear in his *White Flag* from 1954. The canvas shows thin, horizontal, parallel red stripes covering a molded white surface and a flat blue rectangle strewn with small stars occupying the top left corner. It is a beautiful abstract painting, executed with artistry, offering the eye all that is needed to charm and elevate us. But at the same time, the elaborate finish and the sparkle of the colors stand apart from the American flag itself, with all its historical, political, and economic connotations. The charm is broken.

As fascinating as the game of perception may be, the *Flag* series does not come close to

Jasper Johns with a painting of his target series.

IN JOHNS'S WORDS

My idea has always been that in painting, the way ideas are conveyed is through the way it looks and I see no way to avoid that, and I don't think Duchamp can either. To say that you don't care how it looks suggests something that I think is not quite possible, if what you're doing is making something to be looked at . . . I tend to think that the one object that is being examined is what's important.

Transformation is in the head. If you have one thing and make another thing, there is

not very long ago they changed the design. . . . It turns out that actually the choice is quite personal and is not based on one's observations at all.

I try to pick something that seems to me typical, undistinguished by its peculiar esthetic or design qualities. I am interested in things that suggest the world rather than suggest the personality. I'm interested in things that suggest things that are, rather than in judgments.

JASPER JOHNS: END PAPER. 1976. Private Collection

no transformation, but there are two things. I don't think you would mistake one for the other.

I had this image of a flashlight in my head and I wanted to go and buy one as a model. I looked for a week for what I thought looked like an ordinary flashlight, and I found all kinds of flashlights with red plastic shields, wings on the sides . . . and I finally found one that I wanted and it made me very suspicious of my idea, because it was so difficult to find this thing I had thought was so common. And about that old ale can that I thought was very standard and unchanging,

I think one is ready to accept the illusionistic painting as an object, and it is of no great interest that an illusion has been made. I think the object itself is perhaps in greater doubt than the illusion of an object.

I think the object itself is a somewhat dubious concept . . . The canvas is object, the paint is object, and the object is object. Once the canvas can be taken to have any kind of spatial meaning, then an object can be taken to have that meaning within the canvas.

summing up the *oeuvre* of Jasper Johns. Perhaps inspired by Charles Demuth's 1928 painting *I Saw the Figure 5 in Gold*, Johns has produced numerous paintings in which figures are superimposed or juxtaposed on the surface of the canvas. For the American Pavilion at Expo 67 in Montreal, he painted *Map*, a large-sized work modeled after Buckminster Fuller's planisphere.

Since Johns's idea is never to dissociate art and object, he was obliged to start sculpting when he wanted to apply three dimensions to his objects. This is clear in the moldings superimposed on some of his *Targets* and in the electric bulbs, beer boxes, and toothbrushes that he used in his *Painted Bronze* series—wanting to identify common items and their esthetic enjoyment, but only to allow this enjoyment to implode.

In recent years, Johns has created works that are vaguely reminiscent of Cubism and the "Exquisite Cadavers" favored by the Surrealists. They retain from Cubism a taste for a canvas effect and for structures that are visually broken and rebuilt, and from Surrealism, the notion of mirrors, as if it were impossible to distinguish for certain between reality and its reflection.

His friendships of twenty years with Robert Rauschenberg, John Cage, and Merce Cunningham have naturally affected his art. Yet, more than Rauschenberg and Cage, Johns opens the door to Pop Art. Artists like Andy Warhol, who incorporates advertising techniques into painting, and Roy Lichtenstein, who finds inspiration in comic strips, also act from a full-blooded Americanness. Like Johns, they have entered the realm of Abstract Expressionism.

(See also 1954.)

KENNETH NOLAND DRAWS PLANS IN COLOR

NEW YORK

The Kenneth Noland retrospective held at the Guggenheim Museum last year travels this year to museums in Toledo and Denver, while new Nolands are on display at the André Emmerich Gallery in New York.

The new show supports and increases the attention given this American painter, who was born in North Carolina in 1924 and was a student of Josef Albers at Black Mountain College and of Zadkine in Paris, where he had his first one-man show at the gallery Greuze twenty-nine years ago. He is one of the most influential practitioners of Chromatic Abstraction. Wanting to use pure color, he aims above all at optical effects created by the geometric interaction of color surfaces, for example, of concentric circles or patterned stripes. He allows the pigments to penetrate the canvas without priming. It yields flexible and soft tones. The simplicity of his paintings and his use of white spaces to bring out colors in their pure state draw even greater attention because they please the eye with their highly natural vibrations.

Noland uses acrylic paint; it allows him to work faster and to give greater spontaneity to his series of paintings and to explore their methodical forms relentlessly. They involve "shaped canvases," canvases whose shapes are determined by the symmetrical motifs defining their composition. This way, Noland makes sure that his paintings depend on what supports them, and in doing so he delivers a traditional lesson: He draws new plans in color.

KENNETH NOLAND:
EARTHEN-BOUND. 1960.
Paris. Private Collection

RICHARD LINDNER: MOON OVER ALABAMA. 1963. Lugano. Thyssen-Bornemisza Collection

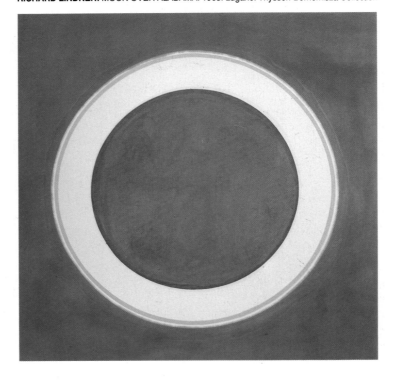

THE DEATH OF LINDNER

NEW YORK

Like so many others, Robert Lindner, German-Jewish, is forced to leave his home when Hitler comes to power.

In 1933 he leaves Munich for Paris. In 1939 he gets to know the internment camps for foreigners in France. In 1941 he manages to escape. He joins the Foreign Legion and is later in the French army. He is arrested by the Germans and condemned to death. He escapes again! He hides in Marseilles. He manages to get to Lisbon, and from there to the United States. He is forty years old.

His discovery of New York determines his career as a painter. The spectacle of the city becomes his source of inspiration. He observes the city from an inner distance, with humor, as if it were only a stage. He paints loneliness the way people experience it in New York. He paints the bright suits, the incongruous clothes, the most incredible accessories—belts, buckles, buttons—as he sees them in the streets. He paints human beings who look like robots, automatons, puppets.

A critic in his own way, Lindner wants to be a witness to the American consumer society, a society in search of enjoyment, where pleasure is a commodity. This explains his provocative portraits of women-machines, with exuberant shapes, and his aggressive colors, which make him a precursor of Pop Art. They are simply the colors of American jukeboxes, movie commercials, advertising posters, and magazines!

In his last years, Lindner divides his time between New York and Paris, where Liliane François shows a selection of his lithographs and Aimé Maeght a collection of his paintings. Lindner is one of the last artists of a generation that is educated in Europe and comes to full artistic bloom in contact with American culture. Lindner dies in New York City at the age of seventy.

Ipoustéguy Dramatizes His Sculpture

After receiving the Grand Prix National des Arts de la Ville de Paris last year, Ipoustéguy now presents fifty sculptures and seventy color-tinted drawings at the Fondation Nationale des Art Plastiques on the Rue Berryer in Paris. This retrospective offers the opportunity to observe the sculptor's development. He started off as an abstractionist in 1949, and since the sixties has been involved in a dramatized anatomical approach to the human figure, as his revolutionary *Val-de-Grâce*, completed in 1977, shows. His baroque, Expressionist works take hold of the human body, distort it, and cut it into pieces.

Paris-Berlin

The "Paris-Berlin 1900-1933" exhibition at the Georges Pompidou Center is declared the major cultural event in Paris this season. In the domain of the plastic arts, Werner Spiess is in charge of Germany, Jean-Hubert Martin is responsible for France. The literary part of the exhibit is in the hands of Serge Fauchereau. The French public is sure to be surprised to find out what German painting really was during the twenties, more particularly its Expressionist current, exemplified by a generous selection of works by Beckmann, Dix, Nolde, and Schad. All the arts are involved here, architecture in particular in the form of utopian projects nurtured by plans of Expressionist architects and of the Bauhaus in Dessau.

Realism and Aluminum

At the age of forty-five, Alex Katz makes a decisive breakthrough at the Marlborough Gallery in New York. Until now, he had been one of those Realist painters, like Fairfield Porter and Jane Freilicher, who, surprisingly, were noted by Jasper Johns and John Ashbery of *ARTnews*. Katz painted portraits and landscapes. At the end of the fifties, in his search for clear contours, he sometimes cut figures out of his paintings and affixed them by lamination. Now

JEAN-ROBERT IPOUSTÉGUY: VAL-DE-GRÂCE. 1977. Paris. Private Collection

he has begun to paint life-size figures on aluminum. No, this has nothing to do with the painting on metal associated with the Italian Michelangelo Pistoletto or the Frenchman Jean-Louis Bilweis, for Katz's figures have abandoned the supporting wall and stand alone, painted on both sides.

The von Hirsch Sale in London

On November 1 of last year, Robert von Hirsch died at the age of ninety-four in Basel. Of German birth, this wealthy industrialist went to Switzerland in 1933 when Hitler came to power. At his death, von Hirsch left an extraordinary collection, begun in 1907 with the purchase of Toulouse-Lautrec's *Redheaded Woman in a White Jacket* in Paris. Over the course of time, the collection grew to such an extent that when it came time to auction it off it took Sotheby's in London six days to disperse the ceramics, Meissen porcelains, old paintings, and works by modern masters from Van Gogh to Matisse. The result of the sale exceeded all previous records, totaling twenty million five hundred thousand pound sterling. The biggest buyers were the German museums.

Alberto Savinio in Rome

For the first time since the death of Alberto Savinio in 1952, Rome is organizing a retrospective of his work that is worthy of the artist. At the exhibition hall, over two hundred items have been assembled, including oil paintings, graphic art, even books, screens, and ballet scenery. An unusually active man, Andrea de Chirico was first a musician; later he turned to literature, publishing idiosyncratic texts under the name of Alberto Savinio in *Les soirées de Paris*, edited by Apollinaire. Following the example of his older brother, Giorgio de Chirico, he finally began painting, but in contrast to his brother he was never tempted to return to Classicism. In his work, mythology gives rise to disturbing objects, hybrid beings, people with the heads of animals, creations that Surrealism could not disown.

Giorgio de Chirico.

GIORGIO DE CHIRICO:
THE DISQUIETING MUSES.
Around 1962. Private Collection

THE WORLD OF METAPHYSICAL PAINTING IS IN MOURNING

ROME

What needs to be seen can only be looked at with closed eyes! This was the opinion of Giorgio de Chirico, the founder of Metaphysical Painting who died in Rome at the age of eighty.

De Chirico, born the son of an Italian engineer in Volo, in Thessalia—the ancient Iolkos, where the Argonauts embarked in search of the Golden Fleece —had been attracted since childhood by Greek mythology. His lifelong quest for an inexpressible surreality is over.

A fervent fan of Nietzsche and Schopenhauer and an admirer of Böcklin, de Chirico discovered in Turin the key that gave him access to his enigmatic future. One autumn afternoon, while walking in the city, he had the impression that the statues on their low pedestals were strolling

through the streets. He was overwhelmed by their shadows, which were laden with an uncertain melancholy and a fatal resignation.

He wrote, "The shadow is the reflected life of the statue, its magic mobility." Having discovered the unrealistic dimension of

his art, he arrived in Paris on Bastille Day in 1911. He was soon exhibiting his *Enigmas* at the Salon d'Automne. His mysterious views of the Montparnasse railway station were shown at the Salon des Indépendants. Apollinaire, confronted with de Chirico's fleeting foregrounds, lunar illuminations, and the spatial tensions of his architec-

tural deserts, wrote in *Les soirées de Paris* of "metaphysical landscapes."

Did de Chirico's *oeuvre* come to a halt around 1920 when he changed his style and assumed the title "Pictor Classicus"? When he was younger, he depicted himself in the manner

of Nietzsche, a fine hand supporting the heavy brow of a thinker. In his maturity, he painted himself in full length, wearing a Renaissance costume, standing in a park, his left hand resting on a sword. This difference was an indication of his metamorphosis, but though his craft was traditional and the subjects were totally different

from those of his youth, the spirit remained the same.

In the last years of his life, the painter returned to a so-called Neometaphysical period. Once again the mannequins, inclined planes, precarious—though this time Realistic—spaces rendered with a freshness that he did not possess at the age of twenty. Fundamentally, de Chirico did not change.

The artist lived in Athens, Munich, Paris, Ferrara, Turin, and Florence before settling in Rome in 1938. In his eyes, man was only a mannequin and the world a puppet theater whose background de Chirico lit but left deserted. Few artists have expressed so precisely our "human, all-too-human" disenchantment.

(See also 1914, 1926, 1969.)

THE WORLD IS A PUPPET THEATER WITH A DESERTED BACKGROUND

ARTISTS DEFEND LA DÉFENSE

PARIS

After a crisis of five years, due to the oil embargo and President Giscard d'Estaing's lack of enthusiasm for the incongruous Manhattan rising across the Seine, the government has decided to finish the urban development of La Défense.

The construction of a business center west of Paris dates back twenty years, to 1958. At that time, La Défense was an area of decayed houses, on which an enormous dome would be erected: an exhibition center double the size of the center at the Porte de Versailles. The plan was to build a complex of over ten million square feet of office and residential space according to the principles of Le Corbusier's Charte d'Athènes—traffic ways for pedestrians and cars again would be separated. It became the largest building site in Europe and at the same time a major artistic endeavor, especially in conjunction with concrete and steel architecture.

In fact, since the Renaissance, cities have not been built with the architecture, sculpture, and painting in harmony, as they were in Rome or Florence. The scale has changed. How can we today achieve a synthesis of the arts, how can we erect sculptures that do not look ridiculous at the foot of five-hundred-foot-tall buildings?

From this point of view, Calder's enormous *Stabile*, installed two years ago on the esplanade—seventy-five tons of steel beams painted red—certainly opens new perspectives. Since 1932, Calder has made a name for himself with his mobiles, which react to the slightest breath of air like leaves in the wind. At about the same time, he started designing stabiles that—as their name indicates—are different from mobiles in that nothing can make them move. The *Stabile* at La Défense is reminiscent of some kind of sinister crab or spider. It counterbalances another major work, issued from the

mythic and archaic imagination of the Catalan artist Miró.

The new business center hosts the First Biennale of Street Art. About thirty works are shown. The show proves a great popular success, and the residents of La Défense protest the eventual removal of the works which, to them, have become part of the urban landscape. It has been announced that works by César, Kowalski, Takis, and Rieti will take their place.

The greatest attraction is probably the *Fountain*, by Agam, a rectangular basin covering about twenty-two thousand square feet and a spillway two hundred and forty feet long lined

with enamel in eighty-six different color tones. At lunch time, people gather around the fountain to admire its sixty-six water jets, whose flow and height are computer-controlled. Indeed, everyone is aware of the ability of water to animate architecture. Witness the Villa d'Este or the gardens of the Château de Versailles.

About ten years ago, the first artist to "adopt" La Défense to the point of taking up residence was Raymond Moretti. To those who express amazement that he can live happily in such a bare spot, he replies that life there involves neither anxiety nor traffic lights . . . he looks out at the

sky. . . the moon shines through his windows . . . he hears birds singing. At an underground level near Agam's *Fountain*, Moretti has installed his famous *Monster*, an enormous sculpture in perpetual flux, consisting of wood, metal, plexiglass, Formica, and glass—which he goes on making larger and more complicated.

In the seventeenth century, Le Nôtre dreamed of extending the axis of the Tuileries to what was then called the Butte Chantecoq. He would be very surprised to see how his wishes have taken shape today.

ALEXANDER CALDER: STABILE. 1978. Paris. La Défense

1979

SUMMARY

The event of the year is the retrospective devoted to Salvador Dali under the auspices of the Georges Pompidou Center in Paris. After a brief strike that prevents the official preview from taking place smoothly, the public is able to discover one of the great creators of the twentieth century, the equal of a Picasso and a Matisse, who, too concerned with promoting his personality, tended to cause his work itself to be neglected. At the same time, Paris also discovers Picasso's donation, on view at the Grand Palais. Quite by chance, then, we become aware of Spain's impact, in keeping with its great pictorial tradition, on modern art. As we approach the Third Millenium, the question put to us by the critic and theorist Pierre Restany is: What will painting be like by the year 2000?

GREAT MASTERS

Dali Censured by a Strike
Dali Grades Painters

DEVELOPMENTS

Picasso's Estate
The Art Market Is Doing Well

ART NEWS

The Death of Sonia Delaunay
Beuys in New York
Vibrations by Soto
The Parsimony of Titus-Carmel
In Brief

AVANT-GARDE

Baselitz: a Subjective and Expressive Style
Impetuous Painting

WRITINGS AND THEORIES

Pierre Restany: between Now and the Year 2000

LITERATURE

UNITED STATES
Norman Mailer publishes The Executioner's Song.

FRANCE
Publication of La soupe aux choux *by René Fallet, and* The Book of Laughter and Forgetting *by the exiled Czech writer Milan Kundera.*

GREAT BRITAIN
V. S. Naipaul publishes A Bend in the River.

ITALY
Publication of If on a Winter's Night a Traveler *by Italo Calvino, and* Candido; or, A Dream Dreamed in Sicily *by Leonardo Sciascia.*

MUSIC

FRANCE
Alban Berg's Lulu *is performed for the first time in its entirety at the Paris Opera, directed by Patrice Chéreau, under the musical direction of Pierre Boulez.*

THEATER

FRANCE
Ariane Mnouchkine presents Mephisto *at the Cartoucherie, an adaptation of Klaus Mann's work.*

MOTION PICTURES

GERMANY
Volker Schlöndorff presents The Tin Drum.

UNITED STATES
Premiere of Francis Ford Coppola's Apocalypse Now.

SALVADOR DALI: CORPUS HYPERCUBICUS (CRUCIFIXION). 1954. New York, Metropolitan Museum

744

DALI CENSURED BY A STRIKE

PARIS

Salvador Dali is received by a rain of multicolored butterflies bearing the word "strike," which flutter down on his Cadillac and force him to turn back! The opening of his retrospective does not take place as planned on Tuesday, December 18, at 11 o'clock, because of a work stoppage by workers of every kind at the Georges Pompidou Center. No one knows when the show will open.

This is all the more regrettable as it is the most important exhibition ever dedicated to Dali's *oeuvre*. The one hundred and ten paintings and about two hundred drawings include most of the works that have brought fame to their author—the limp clocks indicating the flabby hours of life that Dali painted one night while suffering from headaches and after eating a runny Camembert; the incandescent *Burning Giraffe*, with sliding-box-women convulsing in the melancholy light of the setting sun; *The Enigma of William Tell*, showing Lenin's shirt tails, his anamorphous, disproportionately long buttocks supported by crutches—the painting for which Dali was almost expelled from the Surrealist movement.

The viscosity and turgidity of flesh is an almost constant theme of his first phase, in which Dali's technique is already the technique of an old master. In his youth, Dali created works inspired by Impressionism. There was a quick detour into Cubism—a few examples of this time are scheduled for the exhibition. He soon came to believe that bearing the name of Salvador ("the Savior") meant that the Heavens expected him to save the art of painting in a century in which people no longer knew how to paint or draw.

He defined his way of painting as follows: "Instant photography, in color and by hand, of superfine extravagant and unexplored images of concrete irrationality." His secret was critical paranoia, an actual nervous influx of the work and persona of Dali, which he described as "a spontaneous method of irrational knowledge based on the interpretative-critical association of delirious phenomena."

As early as 1929, he could feel its presence, and it was confirmed during the visit of a young psychiatrist three years later. His name was Jacques Lacan. He had recently completed his doctoral thesis on paranoia. The central figure was a thirty-eight-year-old woman, Aimée A. A self-taught secretary, she declared herself to be "a woman of letters and sciences" in love with the Prince of Wales, to whom she sent passionate letters. She once tried to stab a celebrated actress because, she claimed, the actress defied her publicly. A magnificent case of megalomania!

The Dali exhibition at the Georges Pompidou Center.

SALVADOR DALI: THE ENDLESS ENIGMA. 1938. Private Collection

This canvas is a good example of the double, triple, multiple images so dear to Dali. Six different subjects can be seen here: a landscape, a reclining figure, a greyhound, a face, a still life with fruit dish, a mythological creature.

Dali's attention was caught by the fact that though Aimée A. possessed perfectly intact physical and intellectual faculties, she at will reinvented reality according to a systematic, flawless form of exaltation. Aimée A. confirmed Dali in his paranoia, though his was "critical," that is, triggered *on purpose*, in a controlled way—and maybe even simulated.

Dali's passion shifted toward contemporary science, especially physics, with all the spiritualist speculations that accompany it. In several of his paintings, glasses and bottles fly around and tigers float in space like astronauts, while the corpuscular face of his wife, Gala, pulls loose from the yoke of determinism.

The artist's final period is the so-called nuclear-mystic period, starting in the 1950s—several of its canvases are at Beaubourg. This period includes, in particular, the *Christ* of the Glasgow Art Gallery, a Christ suspended in a void by a mysterious principle of levitation; and *Corpus hypercubicus*, one of Dali's masterpieces—Gala watches in ecstasy as an androgynous Christ rises above Cape Creus in a hallucinatory stripped landscape.

Dali sold his first painting, a still life with three lemons, for five hundred pesetas. He was six years old! Today, the prodigy is in his seventies and "criminally rich," as he likes to put it. Besides Picasso, he is the most famous painter of the twentieth century. It is sufficient to draw his fine moustache on a letter or a postcard with the notation "España" and he will receive it at his home in Port-Lligat.

Between eight hundred thousand and one million visitors are expected when the retrospective opens at Beaubourg. The strike can't go on indefinitely—can it?

(See also 1929, 1934, 1935, 1936, 1938, 1968, 1974.)

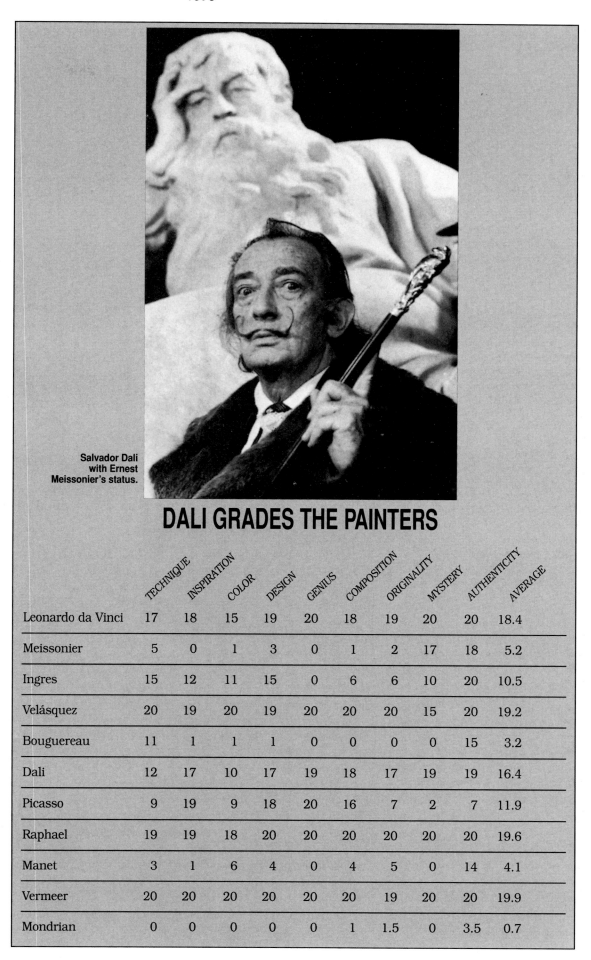

Salvador Dali with Ernest Meissonier's status.

DALI GRADES THE PAINTERS

	TECHNIQUE	INSPIRATION	COLOR	DESIGN	GENIUS	COMPOSITION	ORIGINALITY	MYSTERY	AUTHENTICITY	AVERAGE
Leonardo da Vinci	17	18	15	19	20	18	19	20	20	18.4
Meissonier	5	0	1	3	0	1	2	17	18	5.2
Ingres	15	12	11	15	0	6	6	10	20	10.5
Velásquez	20	19	20	19	20	20	20	15	20	19.2
Bouguereau	11	1	1	1	0	0	0	0	15	3.2
Dali	12	17	10	17	19	18	17	19	19	16.4
Picasso	9	19	9	18	20	16	7	2	7	11.9
Raphael	19	19	18	20	20	20	20	20	20	19.6
Manet	3	1	6	4	0	4	5	0	14	4.1
Vermeer	20	20	20	20	20	20	19	20	20	19.9
Mondrian	0	0	0	0	0	1	1.5	0	3.5	0.7

PICASSO'S ESTATE

PARIS

As soon as the president of the Republic inaugurated, on October 11, the show of Picasso's works inherited by the government, lines formed in front of the Grand Palais. The show is a preview—before it goes to New York—of eight hundred paintings, sculptures, etchings, and drawings that will be on display a few years from now in the future Musée Picasso in the Salé Mansion, one of the most beautiful houses in the Marais, now undergoing restoration.

The eight hundred works, gathered for three months at the Grand Palais, represent the donation by which the artist's heirs paid the inheritance tax due after the artist's death on April 8, 1973. Because Picasso had kept most of what he considered his best work, and because he had kept all of his sketchbooks and draft drawings, the inventory of the inheritance drawn by the attorney Maurice Rheims is fabulous: 1,876 paintings, rugs, and illustrated books estimated at 801,925,352 francs; furthermore, 7,089 drawings, 149 sketchbooks, 18,095 etchings, 6,112 lithographs, 3,181 linocuts, 1,355 sculptures, and 2,880 works in ceramics, for a grand total of 1,251,663,200 francs. To this can be added the value of Picasso's real estate: the farm Notre-Dame-de-Vie in Mougins, the villa La Californie in Cannes, and the two châteaux in Vauvenargues and Boigeloup—their combined worth is estimated at 10,000,000 francs.

The collection put together by a commission of experts includes some of the most significant of Picasso's works. His various periods are represented, such as the blue period, when the artist lived in poverty in the Bateau-Lavoir in Montmartre, the Cubist phases, and the so-called time of metamorphoses when, on contact with Surrealism, he began distorting the human figure. Thus it is possible to follow the path of one of

PABLO PICASSO: CAT WITH BIRD. 1939. Paris. Musée Picasso

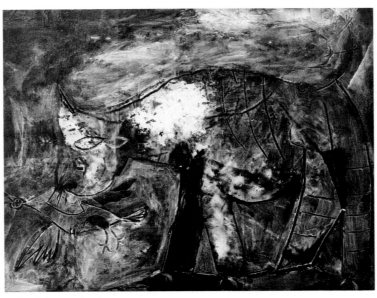

The same picture in infrared light.

the greatest creative geniuses of all time.

To avoid that fake Picassos be included among the works, and to check their condition, they have been examined by the Laboratoire de Recherches des Musées de France. Materials have also been analyzed, so that certain stylistic conclusions could be made. For example, in a painting entitled *Cat with Bird*, of 1939, infrared light revealed three successive strokes aimed at capturing with maximum precision the curve of the cat's back, indicating that Picasso worked conscientiously—contrary to what detractors continue to believe.

Jacqueline Picasso and Paulo, his legitimate son who has died in the meantime, declared four days after Picasso's death that in accordance with the artist's wishes they would give France the collection of other artists' works he had assembled: thirty-nine canvases and fourteen drawings by Chardin, Corot, Henri Rousseau, Le Nain, Matisse, and others.

This collection is also at the Grand Palais; it, too, will reside in the Musée Picasso. The state has never received such treats.

(See also 1904, 1905, 1907, 1909, 1912, 1921, 1927, 1937, 1945, 1946, 1948, 1953, 1954, 1958, 1973.)

THE ART MARKET IS DOING WELL

LONDON/NEW YORK

This is another good year for speculators in modern art. Notwithstanding a slight downward trend in the fall, prices continue to soar. The weakness of the dollar has made New York the most interesting center, ahead of London. Three sales in particular mark the year.

On April 2, the collection of Sidney Barlow was sold at Sotheby's Parke-Bernet: mainly Impressionist paintings. The auction marked two records: Monet's *Bridge at Argenteuil* for 3,700,000 francs, followed by Corot's *Bathing Venus* for 2,100,000 francs.

The most exceptional sale of the year took place at Sotheby's in London on July 3. It involved the collection of the famous Parisian dealer Paul Rosenberg. Braque, Gris, and Léger got consistently high prices, but the uncontested winner was Picasso. His *Wine Bottle* sold for 4,300,000 francs. The total intake was 30,000,000 francs. During the same week, Christie's sold the collection of Hans Mettler, a Swiss textile industrialist, for 24,200,000 francs. *La grande loge* by Toulouse-Lautrec established the day's record, fetching 3,200,000 francs.

It still happens that lost masterpieces come back to light. A painting by the American artist Frederick Church, *The Icebergs*, was discovered in a boys' school in Manchester. The painting, which dates back to 1861, was sold for 13,800,000 francs at Sotheby's in October. Consequently, Church occupies the enviable place of the artist whose painting has fetched the third highest price ever at public auction. These record prices continue to be the monopoly of the two great English auction houses. They seem to have no competition for the time being.

The Death of Sonia Delaunay

Sonia Delaunay, last representative of the Cubist adventure, died in her studio on the Rue Saint-Simon in Paris on December 5. Active until her death at the age of ninety-four, she worked on several projects at once. Born in 1885 in St. Petersburg, she survived her husband, the painter Robert Delaunay, by thirty-eight years, devoting the second part of her life to making his work better known. She was an excellent painter in her own right, an assiduous decorative artist who wanted to bring art into the street and make it more alive and accessible to all. She was equally successful as a fashion artist, and designed furniture, rugs, carpets, and wallpaper, creating surroundings that were a hymn to life.

Beuys in New York

Since November, the Guggenheim Museum has played host to the largest exhibit ever devoted to Joseph Beuys. It is a two-month show, organized in twenty-four stations similar to the hours of a day. Most noteworthy are four hundred drawings executed from 1936 to 1972, and his "sculptures," including the famous *Honey Pump*. Given its spiral interior, the Guggenheim hardly lends itself to the "environments" that made Beuys famous in Europe. Four containers, shipped by air and boat, were required to bring the materials for this exhibit to New York. Moreover, special precautions were taken so that the works would not be damaged, and their handling was entrusted only to experts.

Vibrations by Soto

Organized around four big sequences, *Les carrés virtuels*, *Les écritures*, *Les lignes immatérielles*, and an environment of six thousand yellow and white poles entitled *Suspended Progression*, the exhibition of works by Soto at the Georges Pompidou Center honors one of the masters of Kinetism. A fifty-six-year-old Venezuelan, Jesús Raphael Soto was profoundly influenced in his early years by the work of artists

SONIA DELAUNAY: COLOR RHYTHM. 1969. Private Collection

such as Malevich, Kandinsky, and Mondrian. But he soon became interested in "moirages," a technique of reversible perspectives and optic vibrations that associates him with Le Parc, Agam, and Vasarely. Situated between painting and sculpture, his art is meant to be essentially monumental, and is best expressed in architecture.

The Parsimony of Titus-Carmel

Presented at the Georges Pompidou Center, then at the Kunsthalle in Düsseldorf, the Gérard Titus-Carmel exhibit brings the public at large into contact with an artist who defies classification. He was twenty-three when he appeared at the Biennale of Paris in 1965, the same year in which he published an album of linocuts, *For Bramm*. In 1968 and 1969, he showed his *Grande bananeraie culturelle*: several dozen plastic bananas and one real banana, which was rotting. In 1970, his *Road of Giants* at the gallery Templon was

an "olfactory operation," an empty room smelling of seaweed and wet sand. At this time, he began showing very precise drawings, sometimes accompanied by collages. Since then, adding color with great parsimony, he has been drawing tattered containers, long loaves of bread, and rags knotted together.

JESÚS RAPHAEL SOTO: SUSPENDED PROGRESSION. 1978-1979. Paris. Georges Pompidou Center

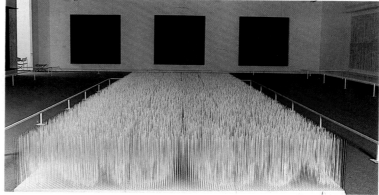

GEORG BASELITZ: READING WOMAN. 1978

BASELITZ: A SUBJECTIVE AND EXPRESSIVE STYLE

BERLIN

There was a time when Georg Baselitz was a scarecrow to the bourgeois. He used to scandalize the decent citizen. In the course of his first show in Berlin, at the gallery Michael Werner, two of his canvases were confiscated following a court decision, and he was sued on grounds of pornography. One of the seized paintings was *Naked Man*; the other one, *Big Night in the Bucket*, was viewed as being particularly obscene because it showed a masturbating child with an enormous penis.

The scandal, or at least the amazement, was not any less in the enlightened circles of art critics and dealers. Though for different reasons. This elite did not understand how, with Informal Art the order of the day, anyone could have the audacity to create figurative paintings with vaguely social pretensions. Indeed, *Big Night in the Bucket* is a metaphor for solitude in a dehumanized society.

Baselitz paints in an exalted way. The colors and shapes are carried with a moving vehemence. What is important to him is the gesture of painting itself. This is why for some years now he has painted reversed images of traditional subjects, so that vision retains the pictorial act, not the object represented.

Like Anselm Kiefer, he is often compared to the Expressionists of the 1920s. But he rejects all labels. He admits that he applies his brush with brutality, but he believes that this way of working is more German than typically Expressionist. At the age of forty-one, he is one of the masters of new German painting.

IMPETUOUS PAINTING

BERLIN

The fashion of Conceptual Art has spread all over Europe in recent years. A reaction was inevitable. It is on display here in the form of a figurative movement that has rediscovered the power of images as a reaction against artistic dematerialization. At the same time, this movement has rediscovered the violence of Expressionist colors.

Public evidence of this trend was first apparent two years ago. The occasion was the opening of a gallery in the popular Berlin district of Kreuzberg, home to many Turks. The special feature of the gallery is that it is controlled by the artists themselves—Rainer Fetting, Salomé, Bernd Zimmer, and Helmut Middendorf.

These painters haven't published any manifesto. Nor do they make claims regarding carefully labeled esthetic positions. They haven't created any new "ism." As it turns out, they are former students of the Academy of Fine Arts where one of their professors was the figurative painter Karl Horst Hödicke.

Their first show, a group exhibition, was held last year. Their gallery, Am Moritzplatz, caught the attention of the punk-rock generation, whose interest continues.

These Neoexpressionists practice a vehement form of painting, with aggressive shapes and colors. Many of Salomé's paintings are self-portraits and nudes. Fetting, for his part, exhibited in 1977 a series of images of the city. This year, he takes up the same theme; in collaboration with Zimmer, he creates an immense work entitled simply *New York*.

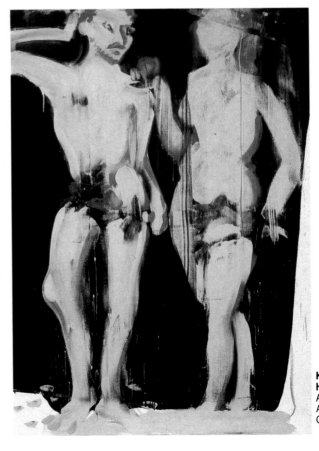

KARL HORST HÖDICKE: ADAM AND EVE. 1977. After Lucas Cranach

PIERRE RESTANY: BETWEEN NOW AND THE YEAR 2000

Initiator of the New Realism, indefatigable globe-trotter, curious about everything that is made and that seeks its identity, Pierre Restany remains, at age forty-nine, one of the main theoreticians and movers of the current art scene. His book, *L'autre face de l'art* (the other face of art), which was just published by Éditions Galilée, retraces the main phases of what the author calls "the deviant function" that, from Duchamp to Dada to Beuys, has produced so many new works that do not conform to the traditional idea of beauty. We are excerpting below the conclusion of his work in which he asks what this "deviance" will be from now to the dawn of the third millenium.

This decade seems to have produced a lot of stars and very few planets, you will tell me. But, let's be careful! The sixties and seventies have seen the extraordinary consecration of Joseph Beuys, talented draftsman and "assemblist," great lord of Arte Povera and yoga master of the Happening, art-world champion of all classes, a Picasso of the concept . . . Magnificent Vice-Chancellor of the Free University. What offices, titles, functions: an impressive honors list worthy of Dada chieftain Baader, but which corresponds to a well-oiled and faultlessly efficient and deliberate mechanism . . . The man with a hat that seems eternally screwed onto his head is given to the solitude of the greats, on the pedestal that was erected for him in postwar Germany, happy to find in himself all the contrasts and contradictions of our chaotic modernity . . .

All that remains for us from now until the year 2000 is to watch for the advent of symptoms of a revenge of the spirit against the form, of the alchemists against the mathematicians, for the advent of a kind of humanism that can synthetically maintain the dual meaning of things.

The deviant function must use new words and new objects to rediscover the immemorial applications of the game of life and chance. The European soil is not the most arid in this matter . . . Let's pay attention to what is happening under the hippie uniform of a Jacquet or under the bourgeois motto of an Asnaghi: The road of Tao goes through the poverty of the rich world and the wealth of the poor world, through the scrap metals of a Tinguely and through the tropical lianas of a Frans Krajcberg. Vicenzo Agnetti dopes the calculation by means of literature and restores the silence by inverting the sound. He reminds us also very appropriately that the ethics of indifference goes over into the world's wisdom, and that this

JOSEPH BEUYS: HOMOGENOUS INFILTRATION FOR GRAND PIANO. 1966. Paris. MNAM

kind of humor is an initiation code. The other face of art at the end of this century will have a symbolism that is endlessly exacting in its deep idealism.

A symbolism of effusion, liberated and liberating: Idealistic symbols, beyond the yoke of metaphors, will try to push their roots deeper and deeper in the real. Neither Surrealism nor a Realism a fortiori is the real, but they are nature, in its foundation and its essence. On the horizon of the third millenium we perceive a neospiritualist intuition of an integral Naturalism, a gigantic catalyst and accelerator of our faculties of smell, of thinking, of acting: a pantheism of sensitivity, an ultimate refuge of synthetic humanism, and soon its demise. The Judeo-Christian civilization will then cease to have all the answers.

PIERRE RESTANY
L'autre face de l'art *(Excerpts)*

The avant-garde is no more—nothing shocks us, anything that is daring is immediately absorbed by the media and the art market. The Italian Trans-avantgarde, appearing for the first time at the Biennale in Venice in 1980, is most indicative of this new situation. It is marked by a return to individual sensitivity as well as to traditional themes and craft. A period that began with Fauvism in 1905

1980

1980	**1981**	**1982**	**1983**	**1984**
ARTS				
• The Biennale in Venice celebrates the Transavantgarde	• International recognition of the new German art • Exhibition "Moscow-Paris" at the Pushkin Museum in Moscow	• Arman erects *Long-Term Parking* in Jouy-en-Josas • New French painters in New York • Video Art at the Whitney Museum in New York	• Schnabel's great success • Balthus retrospective at Georges Pompidou Center	• Exhibition "Primitivism" at MOMA in New York • Garouste revives mythology
LITERATURE				
• *The Name of the Rose* by Umberto Eco • *Sophie's Choice* by William Styron	• *Chronicle of a Death Foretold* by Gabriel García Márquez	• *Monsignor Quixote* by Graham Greene	• *Enfance* by Nathalie Sarraute	• *The Penitent* by Isaac Bashevis Singer • *L'amant* by Marguerite Duras
MUSIC AND THEATER				
• *Don Giovanni* staged by Maurice Béjart in Geneva	• Maurice Béjart organizes "Danza Europa 81" in Venice	• *Amadeus* by Peter Schaffer, with Roman Polanski and François Périer	• *Saint Francis of Assisi* by Olivier Messiaen at the Paris Opera	• *Fifth Quartet* by Giacinto Scelsi, commemorating Henri Michaux
MOTION PICTURES				
• *The Last Metro* by François Truffaut • *Kagemusha* by Akira Kurosawa	• *Raiders of the Lost Ark* by Steven Spielberg • *The Elephant Man* by David Lynch	• *Yol* by Yilman Güney • *E.T.* by Steven Spielberg	• *And the Ship Sails On* by Federico Fellini • *The Ballad of Narayama* by Shohei Imamura	• *Amadeus* by Milos Forman • *Brazil* by Terry Gilliam • *Hail Mary* by Jean-Luc Godard
SCIENCE AND TECHNOLOGY				
• Dramatic close-up color photographs of the rings around Saturn	• AIDS cases begin to show up in New York	• First permanent artificial-heart operation	• *Pioneer 10* leaves the solar system, 11 years after it was launched, and continues to radio information back to earth	• Baby given baboon heart, in California
POLITICS AND DAILY LIFE				
• Lech Walesa creates "Solidarity" • Ronald Reagan is elected President	• Sandra Day O'Connor is the first woman to be appointed to the U.S. Supreme Court • Assassination of Anwar Sadat	• Falkland war between Great Britain and Argentina • Israel invades Lebanon	• Soviets shoot down Korean commercial airliner, killing all 269 passengers • Lech Walesa is awarded Nobel peace prize • Chicago gets its first black mayor	• Chemical-plant leak in Bhopal, India, kills 2,500 and injures 200,000 • Assassination of Indira Gandhi

1988

draws to a close, especially with the death of André Masson in 1987, which marks the passing on of a last survivor. The battle of modern art now seems to have won over the vast majority of people. Wherever we go, any newspaper we read, each museum we enter—modern art is there. This is where the future begins.

1985	1986	1987	1988	
• Inauguration of the Musée Picasso at the Salé Mansion • Pignon retrospective at the Grand Palais in Paris • The Immaterialists at Georges Pompidou Center	• Death of Beuys • Rediscovery of Futurism in Venice • Inauguration of the Ludwig Museum in Munich	• Death of André Masson • Chagall exhibition in Moscow • Tinguely retrospective in Venice	• Emergence of Computer Art • Pei's pyramid rises at the Louvre • The *glasnost* of the arts	
• *Perfume* by Patrick Süskind • *Palomar* by Italo Calvino	• Death of Jean Genet • *The Cider House Rules* by John Irving	• *The Privileges of Perspective* by Octavio Paz • *The Bonfire of the Vanities* by Tom Wolfe	• Naguib Mahfouz is awarded Nobel prize in literatue • *The Satanic Verses* by Salman Rushdie • *Cat's Eye* by Margaret Atwood	
• *Carmen*, ballet with Cristina Hoyos and Antonio Gadès	• *A Chorus Line*, a Broadway success	• *Prometheus* by Luigi Nono in Paris	• Posthumous premiere of Beethoven's *Tenth Symphony*, completed by Barry Cooper	
• *The Purple Rose of Cairo* by Woody Allen • *Ran* by Akira Kurosawa	• *Out of Africa* by Syndey Pollack • *Ginger and Fred* by Federico Fellini • *The Sacrifice* by Andrei Tarkovski	• *Empire of the Sun* by Steven Spielberg • *Fatal Attraction* by Adrian Lyne • *Good-bye, Children* by Louis Malle	• *The Last Temptation of Christ* by Martin Scorsese • *Little Vera* by Vassili Pitchul	
• *Titanic* wreck found, through use of underwater robots	• Explosion of the space shuttle *Challenger* • Explosion at the Chernobyl nuclear plant, in Russia	• The Russian astronaut Romanenko sets record of 326 days in space	• DNA fingerprinting revolutionizes forensics and paternity testing • Revival of the American space-shuttle program with the launch of *Discovery*	
• Mikhail Gorbachev takes office • Death toll of South African blacks mounts, as apartheid continues • Greenpeace ship sunk	• American bombing raid on Libya • Corazon Aquino replaces Marcos as Philippine president • Haitians overthrow Duvalier	• Iran-*contra* hearings in Washington • U.S. stock market collapses • Gorbachev's *glasnost* and *perestroika*	• George Bush is elected President • Devastating earthquake in Armenia • The Dalai Lama rejects China's offer to return to Tibet	

The Venice Biennale had been dozing since 1964 when it awarded its grand prize to Rauschenberg. Now it suddenly wakes up with the appearance of the Transavantgarde, whose talented mentor is the critic and theoretician Achille Bonito Oliva. With this movement, the art of the end of the century has its starting point, Mannerist and eclectic. It also marks the return of Europe to a position of competition with the United States, which had been in control of the art market and museums since the end of the Second World War. Beyond the avant-garde movements, which are often hermetic, the public renews ties with painting that accepts once more, this time without second thoughts, the invitation to be pleasant, figurative, and narrative. It, too, is a revolution.

1980

S U M M A R Y

AVANT-GARDE

The Biennale Establishes the Transavantgarde

MANIFESTO

Achille Bonito Oliva: an Art without Ideology

EXHIBITIONS

The Return of the Realisms

ART NEWS

The Humanism of the Eighties
Botta's Casa Rotonda
Death of a Great Colorist
The Ford Sale
In Brief

DEVELOPMENTS

The Mentally Handicapped Visit Chomo

SCULPTURE

Berrocal's Combinations
Kienholz the Misogynist

LITERATURE

FRANCE
Death of Jean-Paul Sartre. Publication of Désert *by Jean-Marie Le Clézio.*

UNITED STATES
William Styron publishes Sophie's Choice.

ITALY
Umberto Eco's novel The Name of the Rose *is an instant success.*

PERU
Publication of Aunt Julia and the Scriptwriter *by Mario Vargas Llosa.*

MUSIC

GREAT BRITAIN
Last performance of Jesus Christ Superstar *by Tim Rice, music by Andrew Lloyd Weber (performed since 1972).*

MOTION PICTURES

UNITED STATES
Bob Fosse presents All That Jazz.

FRANCE
François Truffaut's film The Last Metro *is received enthusiastically. Premiere of* My American Uncle *by Alain Resnais.*

GREAT BRITAIN
John Boorman presents Excalibur.

JAPAN
Premiere of Akira Kurosawa's Kagemusha.

SANDRO CHIA:
THE INCENDIARY. 1980.
Private Collection

THE BIENNALE ESTABLISHES THE TRANSAVANTGARDE

VENICE

The fortieth celebration of the Biennale marks the establishment of the Transavantgarde. Its five members—Nicola de Maria, Sandro Chia, Enzo Cucchi, Francesco Clemente, Mimmo Paladino—make a resounding entrance into the international art scene.

This new movement values figurative painting, the imaginary, "the cultural territory" of the transgression of the rules governing the artistic system and the overall social order. Now, however, the system simply digests any attempt at something new, whether it involves direct gestures, as in politics, or indirect gestures in a cultural context.

According to Bonito Oliva, there is no longer an avant-garde, because thinking in those terms means entertaining an

A REAPPROPRIATION OF MYTHS AND IMAGES

individual who digs into the memory of his past, and the reappropriation of myths and images. It now finds itself recognized by one of the most prestigious art forums. This signifies the rise to officialdom of a trend that emerged from the seventies but has been neglected by the critics and the art market. The Transavantgarde is orchestrated by a mastermind—the mind of its brilliant theoretician and mentor, Achille Bonito Oliva.

The movement involves a return to the individual, to national values, and to classical iconography, and is supported by a new reading of art history, with focus on the figurative renewal of the period between the two World Wars. The violent reactions of the press, with references to a "return to order" and a "regression," provide a notion of the incongruity of the movement relative to the revolution of modern art.

Bonito Oliva believes that at this point the term "avant-garde" has lost its meaning because it implies the notion of rupture. Bonito Oliva says that is impossible in this time.

At the beginning of the twentieth century, when history still gave the artist the illusion that art could be used as a tool for social struggle and transformation, the avant-garde was urged into existence by the facts themselves. A scandal was an actual

evolutionary—therefore an optimistic—concept of history, as if art evolved in a coherent and progressive manner beyond the realm of contradictions. Bonito Oliva traces the origins of the Transavantgarde to the Yom Kippur War, of 1973. The oil crisis tolled the bell for the consumer society as a model, after Marxism had shown its own failings to one and all. Freed from ideological illusions, the artist from now on can dedicate himself to creative work, without dialectic concerns.

ENZO CUCCHI: CACCIA MEDITERRANEA. 1979. Paris. Galerie Templon

The Transavantgarde is not wholly Italian. Painters like Anselm Kiefer and Georg Baselitz in Germany and Gérard Garouste in France are evidence of the importance of the movement in Europe, and it is further supported by the increasing fame of Julian Schnabel in the United States. All of them cultivate the "genius of the site" so dear to Bonito Oliva. Reconciled with the museums, they offer the public—isolated for a long time by the hermitism of the avant-gardes—once more images that do not reject the pleasure of representation or narration. Bonito Oliva believes that present-day painting is "reterritorialized" in the south, as it was during the Renaissance, and that it

FRANCESCO CLEMENTE: SELF-PORTRAIT. 1978. Paris. Galerie Templon

centers especially on the artists whose advocate he is. Sandro Chia, the most promising in the group, explains his approach: "From 1972 to the middle of 1975, I concentrated on Magic Conceptualism. I tried to go all the way to the roots of the creative phenomenon. I wanted to find the zero point of creation. That zero does not exist." Chia, a native of Florence, emerges from his bad dream by creating a gigantic pictorial theater, in which, painting after painting, shepherds and shepherdesses telescope from modern poets in suits, while antique acts exult in sexual subversion.

Enzo Cucchi transcribes hallucinatory scenes with colossi and magic mountains, perhaps as a remembrance of Jules Romain. Francesco Clemente paints self-portraits and intimate compositions. Nicola de Maria approaches the formal naiveté of children, and Mimmo Paladino creates large canvases of mythological inspiration.

Quotes of de Chirico, Carlo Carrà, Picasso, and even Chagall force the eye to scrutinize a reality that is reviewed and corrected by subjectivity and metaphor. Apart from any concern for originality, the artists of the Transavantgarde evoke an almost timeless universe, which is also the ambition of the advocates of the "pittura colta" (cultivated painting), who also accumulate pictorial quotes, and who are represented in Venice as well.

Soon, Achille Bonito Oliva will present in Modena the exhibition "Avanguardia/Transavanguardia" to better situate the work of young Italian artists. But art history will remember the resounding arrival of the Transavantgarde at the fortieth Biennale. The avowed intention of Bonito Oliva and his followers is to provide proof that from now on it will be possible to dethrone the supremacy of American painting with the help of international galleries and museums. It looks as if they are on the right track.

ACHILLE BONITO OLIVA: AN ART WITHOUT IDEOLOGY

To do art means henceforth to control the levels of the cortical matter of art. After the self-flagellation of these last years, the artist has rediscovered his own specific role as well as the pleasure to exercise creative activity without obligation to invent something new.

To requalify the role of art means for the artist to reconquer its own territory, to transfer its own practice within specific frontiers of an operation that does not measure itself against the world, against its own history, and against the history of its own expressions. The artist of this generation rediscov-

Art becomes again direct expression, leaving behind it the feeling of guilt for being permanent, which was a symptom of contact with the world. The artist becomes again maniacal and Mannerist in his own mania.

The opposition moved toward the perspective of a possible reconciliation with the world. The dialectic was the symptom of an ideology that thought it could continue using its old tricks in the face of a henceforth impregnable reality. The young artists have ceased to practice such tricks because there is no longer any direction toward which they can steer the creative experience . . .

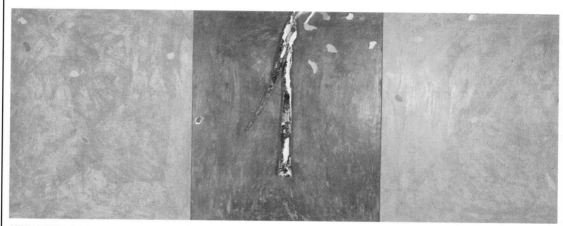

MIMMO PALADINO: PIERO DI STELLA. 1980. Paris. Galerie Templon

ers the privilege of enclosure in the sense of reserve, concentration, and focus point of a biology of art. Behind this experience broods a great humility that consists in beginning anew from the narrow and laborious territory of a manual production, not limiting itself to thinking or indicating but devoted to a uniting, to visible facticity—as it appears in the terminal of the work—and to a mental index. The mentality that licensed techniques and materials is being replaced by a mentality licensing the tangibility of a product. The missing pride of the conceptual artist's work, the elitist behavior of the artist who was playing on the amazement of the public and on the element of surprise, are being replaced by the humility of creative, accessible, and real work.

The Transavantgarde is born precisely from this condition, unfolding like a fan, open not only toward a mythical future but also toward the renewal of a minor past, namely, a past removed from the rhetoric of the great traditions. This "minority" is one more value that is recovered by the new art mentality, which moves with feminine gestures and with a feminine and subterranean sensitivity.

Transavantgarde artists who practice this other-than-art feeling belong to this generation and are part of a great creative expansion.

ACHILLE BONITO OLIVA
La Transavantgarde italienne *(Excerpts)*

THE RETURN OF THE REALISMS

PARIS

The prevailing feeling at the exhibit that opened at the Georges Pompidou Center on December 20 may be that the strongest works are from two countries that were tragically hit by Fascism, Italy and Germany.

When Jean Clair, who is in charge of this abundant show, started to look for these works two years ago, he learned that many had been moved to museum basements. Curators were ashamed of them, and some refused to lend them even after hearing of their undeniable interest. In the introduction to his catalogue Jean Clair puts it clearly: The paintings he gathered are not Fauves or Cubist, Futurist, Expressionist, Dadaist, Surrealist, or abstract, even if their authors belonged occasionally to one or the other of these movements. Their common denominator is the imitative rendering of the exterior aspect of reality, the diligence, the craftsmanship. Under the title "Les Réalismes, entre Révolution et Réaction, 1919-1939" (the Realisms, between Revolution and Reaction, 1919-1939) they embody the "return to order" that many artists experienced in the thirties.

Giorgio de Chirico's return to Classicism in 1920 marks the point of departure for the exhibition. De Chirico was the inventor of Metaphysical Painting: spaces without atmosphere or oxygen, where blind façades rise, façades behind which no one lives. His feverish disquiet freed the way for Surrealism and simultaneously influenced Achille Funi, Mario Sironi, and Ubaldo Oppi—all, more or less, painters of the Fascist regime. De Chirico also painted self-portraits with great verisimilitude and Roman ruins in a style he derived from Tintoretto and Raphael.

On the other hand, and curiously, Nazi Germany, which employed technology that had

RUDOLF SCHLICHTER: BLIND FORCE. 1937. Berlin. Berlinische Galerie

never been equaled, chose to dwell artistically in pastoral and moral nonsense. Poorly painted pictures adhered to the same principles as Socialist Realism, which, by the way, is absent from the Georges Pompidou Center. Hitler despised modern art. He judged it "contrary to the dignity and health" of Aryan man. From 1937 on, he had shows of "degenerate art" circulate through Germany. They included—from Gauguin to Klee—the most creative work produced by the various avant-gardes in fifty years.

Realism, however, could not become imitative or traditional without turning into trifling Realism—copying, narrative, and overly finished—as is often the case with works in this show. There are a few exceptions: Ivan Le Lorrain Albright, an eccentric American specializing in medical drawing, who thought nothing of dedicating years of effort to a single canvas; Albert Carel Willink, whose imaginary castles are worth their weight in flaming ruins; and Rudolf Schlichter, one of the masters of New Objectivity. For them alone it is worth visiting the Georges Pompidou Center.

SUZAN ROTHENBERG: BLACK IN PLACE. 1976. Private Collection

The Humanism of the Eighties

For years, people have been saying that painting is dead, and the critic and historian Barbara Rose is tired of hearing it. She decided to visit several studios and galleries in New York's Soho, then chose a certain number of artists who are, in her opinion, the talented creators of the eighties. She writes that these are the artists who want to preserve painting as an art that is superior, transcendant, universal, humanist and that they are trying to bring back the pleasure of texture and the optical qualities of painting. Among the chosen few are Suzan Rothenberg, Sam Gillian, Nancy Graves, Robert Moskovitz—all excellent painters.

Botta's Casa Rotonda

The thirty-nine-year-old Swiss architect Mario Botta has completed plans for the Casa Rotonda. A cylinder measuring forty feet in diameter and constructed of bondstone, the house is sure to surprise viewers. Is it architectural Minimalism? Botta is fascinated by simple shapes, and has been attracted to them since he designed his first houses in the sixties. His round house is to be built outside the village of Stabio, in the canton of Tessin. It will be organized around a central opening overhung by a skylight, separating the façade from the mass. The staircase serving the four floors will occupy the central axis. Built for Liliana and Ovidio Medici, the house is to be entirely visible to the passerby, who can take in its lines at a glance.

Death of a Great Colorist

His friends called him O.K. He was born in Pöchlarn, Austria-Hungary, in 1886, and he died at the age of ninety-four in Montreux, on the shores of Lake Leman, where he had lived and worked for years. Oskar Kokoschka belonged to a generation battered by Hitlerism and two World Wars. He was one of the masters of Expressionism and, in fact, one of the great colorists of the century. Unappreciated in France, where his lyricism had always seemed a bit shocking, he leaves behind a large body of work scattered throughout the great museums of the world. He also drew exceptionally well, continually evolving, each time able to grasp the intimate character of his model. He wrote of his stormy affair with Alma Mahler, as well as of other adventures, in his autobiography, *My Life*.

The Ford Sale

On May 13, Christie's in New York sold off ten paintings that were part of the collection of Henry Ford II. Works by Degas, Cézanne, Gauguin, Van Gogh, Matisse, Monet, Picasso, Renoir, Signac, and Toulouse-Lautrec were practically all masterpieces. So it is hardly a surprise that the total sale should amount to $18,390,000. Held in Christie's four sale rooms on Park Avenue, nearly one thousand people attended the auction. The greatest sensation was the sale of a painting by Van Gogh, *The Poet's Garden in Arles*, for $5,720,000, the second-highest price ever paid for a painting at a public sale. Persistent rumors attribute the purchase of the canvas to the Greek shipping magnate Stavros Niarchos, despite denials by David Bathurst, president of Christie's New York.

OSKAR KOKOSCHKA: YOUNG WOMAN WITH HAND ON HIP. 1921

759

THE MENTALLY HANDICAPPED VISIT CHOMO

FRANKIE G.: VISITING CHOMO

FRANCIS L.: PORTRAIT OF JEAN REVOL AND JOËLLE RICOL

ACHÈRES-LA-FORÊT

The mentally handicapped visit Chomo, a meeting organized by Jean Revol, a fifty-year-old painter with a Gallic moustache who has several of the handicapped under his artistic wing.

Chomo is a hermit, a wise man who lives in seclusion on his sacred domain near Achères-la-Forêt, a microcosm of which he is surveyor, architect, mechanic, chemist, philosopher, musician, and, above all, painter and sculptor. After a final show at the gallery Camion at the very end of the Second World War, Chomo chose to flee cultural society. He has lived here for about thirty years. Access to his estate is via a long, winding road, which runs through a universe of his sculptures, signs, and sanctuaries—*The Church of the Poor, The Sanctuary of Bois-Brûlé* housing his first works which bear the same name. Visitors cross not just a gate but a border.

Among the mentally handicapped under Revol's artistic guardianship is Marie-Jo, who is severely troubled. The first time she touched paint, she threw herself on it and carried on a Dionysian dance with cries of joy. In a few years she painted, on the floor, dozens and dozens of pictures. Then there is Béatrice, less handicapped, who invents birds traveling swiftly through space, comparable to those painted by Braque at the end of his life. And there is

"IF YOU LOOK FOR ART, YOU WILL FIND THERAPY"

Jean-Luc, whose blind genius does "Klees" flawlessly.

Revol started his work with the mentally handicapped in New York, where he collaborated with Ionel Rappaport, a physician at Staten Island Hospital and the chairman of the American Society of Psychopathology until his death in 1972. Rappaport had gathered a small collection of works by the mentally handicapped. When Revol returned to France, he wanted to take up the torch and go even further by creating real studios for the mentally handicapped.

He does not try to occupy or to distract his students. He wants them to express their "personimage" hidden in the recesses of their being. He'll say, "If you look for therapy, you will find nothing. If you look for art, you will find therapy." It is sufficient to see him surrounded in the Ménilmontant studio by his protégés to realize that though he does not want to influence them he nevertheless acts as a master who congratulates and criticizes, and does not let them get away with anything.

Revol wants them to cause themselves to "be born." While the mentally alienated—the paranoiacs and the schizophrenics—suffer from a hypertrophied ego, the feebleminded have an ego that has been totally crushed but which can be progressively liberated by artistic activity. Their work emerges from the abyss of the collective unconscious. It is based on archetypes, for example, the house that they never had and which they know they never will have, and the figure symbolizing the mother and the father that—in their immense need for love—they call the tree of life, the mandala.

The encounter of Chomo's hypertrophied "ego" and the buried egos of the handicapped is successful. Chomo addresses them in his polished and imaginal speech. He talks to them about his one hundred and fifty-three reincarnations. He evokes the mystery of their previous lives as the sole explanation for their precarious condition, for which they shouldn't suffer except to turn their suffering into creation and, therefore, into joy.

How well his message is received! On the way home, the mentally handicapped—so dear to Revol—talk only about Chomo. It was a happy day in their sad lives.

BERROCAL'S COMBINATIONS

VERONA

The Spanish sculptor Miguel Berrocal continues to produce his series of detachable sculptures in the luxurious house where he has been living and working for several years. At the origin of his vocation was his fascination with his great precursors, Gargallo, González, and Chillida, who directed him toward metal work, and his studies: "My sculpture was born from my training as architect-engineer. What I wanted was to create recognizable forms."

One kind of development led to the creation of monumental pieces for which he "imagines working the parts one by one so that the components can be manipulated individually . . . The parts must be separate like stones in a wall." Berrocal's sculptures consist of several dozen interlocking components like puzzles—the element of play is never absent. They can be taken apart and put back together at will.

The principle is the interaction of external and internal shapes combined with the manipulation of parts that permits their structural analysis: "I draw the details of every part in such a way that I can afterward assemble the pieces scientifically. My taste for the baroque leads me to multiply the combinations. It's an exciting game, the stakes being the design of each shape."

The foundry in Verona where the artist works looks like Vulcan's den. The works coming out of it make the art lover an accomplice in the act of creation, because for Berrocal "the person who assembles or disassembles a piece will be more interested in it than a person who merely looks at it." On the other hand, the nature of his work allows him to make a certain number of copies of each of his sculptures, leading to a reduction in cost and in price. He thus fights the charge of elitism and makes his art accessible to a greater number of people.

MIGUEL BERROCAL: CLEOPATRA. 1968. Private Collection

EDWARD KIENHOLZ:
THE BRONZE PINBALL MACHINE
WITH WOMAN AFFIXED ALSO. 1980

KIENHOLZ THE MISOGYNIST

PARIS

Feminists are furious everywhere that Edward Kienholz has left his mark. Few people can disagree entirely with them. The focus of their present resentment is a piece of sculpture with the long title *The Bronze Pinball Machine with Woman Affixed Also*, which shows a woman's open legs attached to the front of a pinball machine. Her vagina is open to the manipulations of the players. It is difficult to find anything more misogynist.

This is not the first work of Kienholz, an artist now around age fifty, who looks like a lumberjack and divides his time between Berlin and the Rocky Mountains. The woman as sexual object bought, mistreated, impregnated, and abandoned by the male has long been at the center of his work. This new sculpture brings his fantasies to the boiling point, as can be seen in his exhibition at the gallery Maeght.

The show reveals that there are other explosive subjects in the artist's *oeuvre*. For example, there is an "environment" entitled *The Art Show*, a biting satire of the art world with its life-size mannequins uttering banalities lost in the general brouhaha of an opening. There is his series *Volksempfänger*—radio assemblages evoking Nazi Germany, its radio propaganda, and its use of music by Richard Wagner.

At the core of most of Kienholz's works lies loneliness: the loneliness of old age, of poverty, of madness, of alcoholism, and now of just any man alone in the crowd.

First Italy, now Germany wakes up. These two countries, which Mussolini and Hitler had emptied of artistic activity, now find themselves in the forefront of the international scene, after an eclipse of almost a half century. Between Düsseldorf, Cologne, and Berlin, one loses count of the painters, such as Baselitz and Kiefer, who proudly take up the torch of the German Expressionist tradition. Nor is it possible to enumerate the sculptors, from Beuys to Vostell, who alone are capable of measuring up to the great Americans. In the meantime, Paris continues its program of historical retrospectives with "Paris-Paris," closing the cycle begun four years ago at the Georges Pompidou Center with "Paris-New York."

1981
SUMMARY

AVANT-GARDE
**The New Masters of German Art
In Baselitz's Words**

EXHIBITIONS
**Paris-Paris
The Art of the West**

ART NEWS
**Raffray, Art, and Its Double
An American in Paris
Trotsky? Never Heard of Him
Millions for a Braque
Guernica at the Prado
In Brief**

SCULPTURE
Vostell's Cruel Art

ARCHITECTURE
**The Return of Eclecticism
Texas Architecture**

LITERATURE

SPAIN
Publication of Chronicle of a Death Foretold *by Gabriel García Márquez.*

FRANCE
Marguerite Yourcenar is the first woman to be elected to the French Academy.
Claude Simon publishes Georgics.

GREAT BRITAIN
Publication of Earthly Powers *by Anthony Burgess.*

THEATER

FRANCE
Peter Brook stages Chekhov's Cherry Orchard *at the Bouffes du Nord.*

MUSIC

GERMANY
Premiere of Répons *by Pierre Boulez in Donaueschingen.*

DANCE

ITALY
Three weeks of dance with "Danza Europa 81" in Venice, organized by Maurice Béjart.

MOTION PICTURES

UNITED STATES
Steven Spielberg revives the genre of the adventure film with Raiders of the Lost Ark.

GREAT BRITAIN
Premiere of The Elephant Man *by David Lynch.*

POLAND
For his film Man of Iron, *Andrzej Wajda has cast an unusual actor: Lech Walesa.*

ANSELM KIEFER:
RESURREXIT. 1973.
Amsterdam. Sanders Collection

THE NEW MASTERS OF GERMAN ART

PARIS

Hitler created a void, and the rebirth of German art took a long time. In the ARC at the Musée d'Art Moderne de la Ville, an exhibition under the name "German Art Today" shows the vigor and the diversity of artistic creation in the German Federal Republic.

Movements like Expressionism

cials." This attitude seems to be highly favorable for creativity, because Germany for some years has had talents on the level of the Kirchners, Dixes, and Beckmanns—possibly the best it has ever had.

The best known among them is Joseph Beuys, who is sixty years old. He is considered the most famous German artist

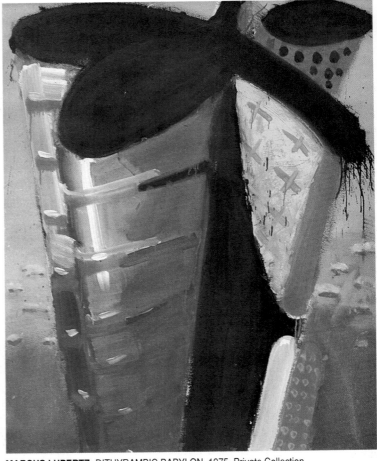

MARCUS LUPERTZ: DITHYRAMBIC BABYLON. 1975. Private Collection

A GENERATION
IN SEARCH OF ITS IDENTITY

and the Blue Rider made pre-Nazi Germany a vigorously active center of European art. After a hiatus lasting almost a half century, the country has regained that status, due this time, however, to individuals more than to collective movements.

Undoubtedly, the reason is that there is no longer a cultural center east of the Rhine comparable to Berlin or Munich of yore. The new generation of artists live and exhibit in Cologne, Düsseldorf, Hamburg, and all over, yet they do not think of themselves as "provin-

since Dürer, but his status is not completely uncontested. Charlatan or genius? The question remains open in Germany itself. The weekly magazine *Der Spiegel* headlined this question in connection with his retrospective two years ago at the Guggenheim Museum in New York.

The distinguished specialty of the former *Luftwaffe* pilot is "actions." In 1965, he sat on a footstool for three hours with powdered gold in his hair and a dead rabbit in his arms and undertook to explain the trend of art. An indefatigable speaker, he gave his opinion on every-

thing—love, the economic crisis, ecology, fat, copper, honey, the felt he uses in his sculptures, and the nature of his fantasies. He had, until then, disliked

Paris, and had never been there. His abruptness and arrogance kept the opening-day audience enthralled, as though by a Medusa.

The other big name in contemporary German art is Anselm Kiefer, age thirty-nine. He lives in the Odenwald, south of Frankfurt, and, unlike Beuys, shrinks from openings and publicity. He draws his inspiration randomly from Germanic ancestral mythology, alchemy, his native land, and the recent history of his country. Because he has been moved to juxtapose such great names from German philosophy and literature as Fichte, Goethe, and Hölderin with Horst Wessel, the Nazi cult-figure of the early 1930s, he is sometimes suspected of having neo-Nazi leanings. But, above all, he is searching for his identity.

Aside from retailers of ridicule like Dieter Roth, who depicts Hegel's *Collected Works* as twenty sausages, and Andrea Tippel, whose slices of cake form roller skates, the new German artists

A. R. PENCK: MEN II. 1981

IN BASELITZ'S WORDS

are serious. This is evident not only in the works of Beuys and Kiefer but also with Vostell, one of whose "environments" consists of barbed wire and piles of teaspoons evoking death camps. Immerdorf, Baselitz, Lupertz, and Penck are also highly talented artists.

Their canvases are strongly colored, powerful compositions. They may be classed as International Post-Avant-Garde, for these artists subscribe to the idea that art today is not so much a phenomenon of breaking away from the modern tradition, which has been evolving since the beginning of this century, as a sort of *slipping away* from it. This is equally true of Baselitz, who paradoxically rejects any compromise with Expressionism; of Lupertz, whose aggressive figures sport reminders of the Picasso period of metamorphoses; and of Penck, whose pictograms resemble enlargements of Klee's handwriting. The same applies to the visionary fever and elevating concepts of Immerdorf, who is rebuilding the framework of the genre, albeit on new foundations.

The Schuldfrage (the question of guilt) was the title of an important book of the period immediately after the war. In it, the philosopher Karl Jaspers raised the question of the responsibility of the German people for the horrors of Nazism. The question is thought no longer relevant, for who today would dream of reproaching the new generations of Germans for anything? Yet, it seems to haunt their collective subconscious, if one can judge by the works of the artists at the "German Art Today" exhibition.

(See also 1905, 1911, 1912, 1920, 1925, 1932, 1979, 1986.)

The artist is responsible to no one. His social role is asocial. His sole responsibility lies in his position in relation to the work that he completes.

The work begins to exist in the artist's head, and it remains in the artist's head. Communication with the public does not exist. The artist asks no question, ascertains nothing; he does not give information, neither message nor opinion.

The painting has nothing in common with the wall upon which it is hung or with the room in which it is placed. Firstly, because it

can be changed at will; next, because the decorative function of the painting can be fulfilled by any other thing.

I am of the opinion that a museum should only be considered a place where art works are kept and where it is possible to simply look at them, without impediment and without pretense.

Works of art have an existence independent from the place where they find themselves and from the fact of being seen. They exist solely by virtue of their very own qualities and of the artist's intention. As for the artworks and the museums that house

them, I feel that it is incorrect to speak of political intentions, of principles of selection, or of didactic methods, all ideas that overload the art object and, in fact, concern only the public.

The goal is to assimilate art, to enroll it in bourgeois society. The direct contemplation of the objects themselves does not seem sufficient. The work of art is watered down.

Contemporary works no longer need to incorporate any idea of function whatsoever, they are isolated, autonomous . . .

The inability to find one's measure in art

GEORG BASELITZ: THE GIRLS OF OLMO. 1981. Paris. MNAM

can only be overcome by imposing upon it a role in the media or by making it a commonplace. Art contains no information, at least not any more than it has ever held. It can be used for nothing other than to be looked at.

The isolation of the artist in the heart of bourgeois society has never been greater, his work has never been more anonymous. This serves, obviously, to develop the madness of the artist. It is only the finished product that counts—in my case, the painting.

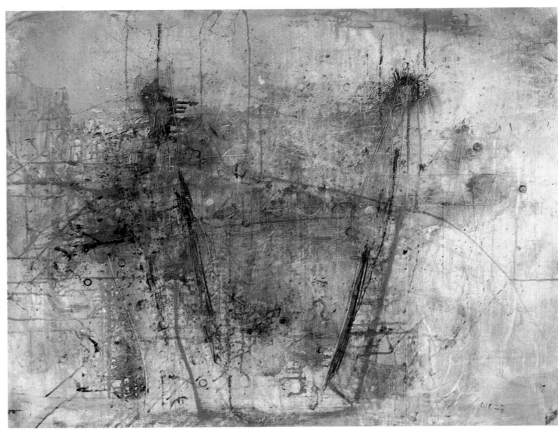

WOLS: YELLOW COMPOSITION. 1946-1947. Berlin. Nationalgalerie

PARIS-PARIS

PARIS

A multidisciplinary retrospective designed to recall an epoch crowded with events, artists, and works! The exhibit, which opened May 28, was planned to conclude the first series of great historic panoramas presented at the Georges Pompidou Center since its opening four years ago—"Paris-New York," "Paris-Berlin," "Paris-Moscow," "Realisms"—and also to trace twenty years of artistic production by a creative arsenal whose output has spread throughout the world.

Comment is animated, because every artist of the past fifty years or more may rightly, or wrongly, feel entitled to be included. The contemporaneity of the period, the fact that it deals with France, and that many of the observers and practioners are still living, generate frustrations and reactions. Controversy peaked with respect to the proposal to show works of Arno Brecker, Hitler's official sculptor.

To say "exhibition" is to say "selection," not a "replay of the period," complains Germain Viatte, chief curator and organizer of "Paris-Paris": "An exhibition is an exploration of a period, and if ten more exhibitions are held in order to explore what I overlooked, well and good."

"Paris-Paris" assembles a series of forty sequences, portfolios, or personal appearances. We can see paintings and sculptures, from Matisse to Pignon and Wols, but also the creations of architects, like Perret's *Public Works Museum* of 1937 and the *House of the People at Clichy* of 1939 by Beaudoin, Lotz, and Prouvé, plus political and advertising posters, including Carlu, Collin, and Savignac, as well as international news—the war, Pétain, the assassination of Trotsky, or Hiroshima.

The exhibition covers twenty years of cultural life in Paris, as it can be visualized in 1981. It is like a freeze-frame photo of a period of intense creativity in France.

THE ART OF THE WEST

COLOGNE

Ten times as large as "Paris-Paris" at the Georges Pompidou Center, "Westkunst" is one of those didactic undertakings to which the Germans seem to have the secret. The exhibition covers everything truly revolutionary in modern art that the

EVERYTHING TRULY REVOLUTIONARY IN MODERN ART

West has produced, from Matisse and Picasso to the present. The principal interest lies in the juxtaposition of Europe and America, which strikes the viewer's eye at almost every turn.

On the one side is Jackson Pollock: A whole room is reserved for him. In the center is one of his masterpieces, *Portrait and a Dream*. Then Willem De Kooning, the world's most expensive painter, and Roy Lichtenstein, Jasper Johns, and Mark Rothko, the mystic who is

ill-served by fluorescent lighting. On the other side are Wols, Dubuffet, Giacometti, Asger Jorn, who started the Cobra movement thirty-three years ago. The comparison is fascinating. Even though it is true that since the end of the Second World War the United States has produced art of the greatest international significance, this has by no means obliterated its European counterparts.

But it may be that the eye-opener of "Westkunst" is, once again, Francis Bacon. His seven great paintings in homage to Van Gogh are rounded up for the occasion. They show poor Vincent wandering along the roads of Provence with knapsack and easel on his back, in a wheat field near Auvers-sur-Oise, and with tormented visage shortly before his suicide. Bacon validates for himself alone the viability of figurative painting today, even though art quite often swears only by "performances" or "environments."

Raffray, Art, and Its Double

At the age of fifty-six, André Raffray specializes in painting places immortalized by the grand masters: Étretat at sunset, a favorite of Monet; the church at Dombourg studied by Mondrian; the spring in Lison painted by Courbet; and the church in Auvers, dramatized by Van Gogh. Returning to the exact spot where the masters had placed their easels, Raffray photographs what his illustrious predecessors saw and painted. Then on his return to his studio, he sets about repainting the painting, attempting to synthesize in his own work the masterpiece and the photograph, as if striving to erase the distance between art and reality.

An American in Paris

One can almost count on the fingers of one hand the American painters of the new generation who have settled in France, though to make this move was at one time the dream of many. Shirley Jaffe is an exception. Born in 1923 in New Jersey, she moved to Paris in 1949, when her husband took advantage of the GI Bill, as did many Americans at the time, studying where they wished. She became part of the American community then in France, joining members such as Jules Olitski, Sam Francis, and Kimber Smith. Her canvases are huge, composed of abstract, brightly colored cutouts, like Matisse's paper art, giving the impression of serene joy. Her work could be seen at a recent exhibit in Chambéry.

Trotsky? Never Heard of Him

The counterpart of the "Paris-Moscow" show, presented in Paris two years ago, is being mounted in Moscow, and the Franco-Russian team has been working since the end of May in an atmosphere that is reported to be stormy at times. Some team members have a penchant for Petrov-Vodkine, Gorki, and Yves Alix, others prefer Filonov, Khlebnikov, and the Surrealists. At the *vernissage* ceremonies, Pontus Hulten was openly crabby, while Jean-Hubert Martin and Serge Fauchereau, commissioners of the second part of the exhibit, went out for a walk. Later,

ANDRÉ RAFFRAY: THE CHURCH OF DOMBOURG, AFTER MONDRIAN

Fauchereau held a news conference that ABC News was only too happy to broadcast, in which he denounced the suppression of Trotsky's name in the catalogue, despite promises from the Russian authorities. They were willing to show all the French Surrealists, all the Russian Futurists, mention Gide, Mandelstam, and even Goumilev, but the name of Trotsky remains unpronounceable.

Millions for a Braque

In 1921, the French government auctioned off the art collection of the dealer D. H. Kahnweiler. As he was a German citizen, all his property was confiscated during the war. Among the works that were liquidated, a painting by Georges Braque, *Man with a Guitar*, was sold for the ridiculous sum of two thousand eight hundred twenty francs. This masterpiece, painted in 1914, and an admirable conclusion to the period of Analytical Cubism, has just been purchased by the Georges Pompidou Center for an unknown amount, although rumor has it that the price was fifteen million francs. The Musée National d'Art Moderne had to rely on special credit from the government and on the Scaler Foundation to make this key painting a part of its collection. Thanks to this purchase, it is now possible to view side by side *Man with a Guitar* and its mate, *Woman with a Guitar,* which Braque had painted one year earlier.

"Guernica" at the Prado

Picasso's *Guernica* is in Madrid since September 10, strengthening Spain's status as a democracy. *Guernica* had been stored at the Museum of Modern Art in New York since 1939, but Picasso had stipulated in his will that the painting could be turned over to Spain when the conditions of democracy prevailed there once again. Spaniards may view the painting at the Casón del Buen Retiro, an annex to the Prado. It is to be exhibited behind bullet-proof glass, in a specially protected, patrolled room.

The arrival of *Guernica* at the Prado.

WOLF VOSTELL:
BLOCKED CIRCULATION. 1969.
Cologne, Domstrasse

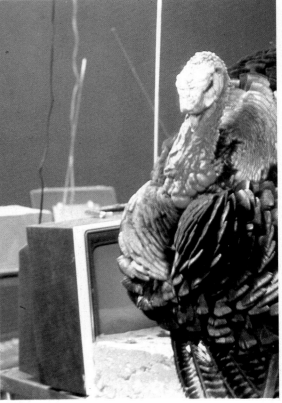

WOLF VOSTELL:
ENDOGENOUS DEPRESSION. 1980. Paris.
Musée d'Art Moderne de la Ville

VOSTELL'S CRUEL ART

COLOGNE

Cruel Wolf Vostell! When he put a gas mask on a female nude or concealed her genitalia behind a block of concrete, it could not be said that he was particularly gentle. But he was no harder on women than on, well, turkeys.

It is really astonishing that his latest arrangement, *Endogenous Depression,* did not perturb the SPCA. A collection of television sets more or less out of order, emitting electronic flashes, static, and inane programs based on a half-dozen poultry sounds, it is a prison without pity.

All of us are turkeys! What the artist means to decry is our collective alienation in the mass-media era. He likes to speak of "art as a philosophy, as thought, and not as a precious object." Philosophy with hammer, one might add, alluding to Nietzche.

Vostell is indebted to Paris, where he lived in the 1950s, for

his having become the "life engineer" who has since organized demonstrations, happenings, and exhibitions as often in Europe and the United States as in Germany. It was when he was going almost every day to the Louvre or to the Bibliothèque Nationale to scrutinize the engravings of Goya with a mag-

nifying glass that a headline in *Le Figaro,* of September 6, 1954, attracted his attention: "Super-constellation Crashes into the Shannon River Shortly after Takeoff." Reality and Goya meshed: Vostell had found his path. "I began making a point of focusing on reality, on the complex phenomena of the epoch and the environment in which I was living," he would write later. "That gave birth to the com-

pelling necessity of integrating, in my art, all I saw and heard, all I had a presentiment of, or learned, starting from the literal meaning of 'Take/off' (French: 'dé-coll/age')—a separation, or 'coming unglued'—and applying this concept to open forms, torn from mobile fragments of reality, from events, that is."

TO DECRY OUR COLLECTIVE ALIENATION

He would literally call his work, for a considerable period thereafter, "décoll/ages," which originates from unglued and torn posters on walls. From this, it follows that the term "décoll/age" applies to an action that is incomplete or fragmented, For example, in 1962, at the first Fluxus concert in Wiesbaden, Vostell planned a "Kleenex décoll/age." Two hundred light bulbs were hurled

from the stage and exploded in the auditorium to attack the audience and compel it to be responsive.

But the term "décoll/age" can also be applied to what he calls his "action sculptures." In 1969, Vostell packed an automobile in cement in front of the Cologne Art Gallery, apparently without causing any objection. But when the cement pouring began, the police insisted that the work be removed on the grounds that its lack of warning signals was a traffic hazard. Under the name *Blocked Circulation* this automobile then occupied a space in the parking lot of the gallery.

"Décoll/age" also applies to the turkeys of *Endogenous Depression.* There were complaints that the cruel Vostell planned to replace the turkeys with turtles, which are less sensitive to electric light.

THE RETURN OF ECLECTICISM

NEW YORK

Hugh Hardy, Malcolm Holzman, and Norman Pfeiffer are three New York architects who started an office together in 1967. Their work, which might be described as "functionalism with a human face," due to its eclecticism and unusual use of contemporary materials, quickly drew attention.

The three renovated and transformed with great elegance old structures, such as the Madison Civic Center, the Cooper-Hewitt Museum, and the St. Louis Art Museum. In Minneapolis and in Denver, they built two splendid, much-admired concert halls in which their use of glass and metal harmonizes perfectly with their sober design. Their Best Stores office building combines the same elegance, luminance, and cheerfulness.

In their succession of schools, theaters, cultural centers, residences, and medical centers, Hardy, Holzman, and Pfeiffer, with their freedom and humor, are forerunners of the Postmodernist movement.

Head office of the Best Products Corporation in Richmond, Virginia, by Hardy, Holzman & Pfeiffer.

TEXAS ARCHITECTURE

HOUSTON

Houston, deep in the heart of Texas, amid vast spaces and ranches, has become a spectacular and bold city that can pride itself on having the most handsome skyscraper architecture in the United States.

Today's city was born out of the extraordinary prosperity of the 1960s and 1970s and the unprecedented economic growth of the state. Each corporation wanted to build more handsomely than the next, and this stimulated ingenuity and creativity. The next new building had to be the highest. The skyscrapers multiplied and surpassed one another, each becoming a towering symbol of the company for which it stood.

The greatest architects have put them up. The so-called "local boys," Texas architects like Howard Barnstone and Eugene Aubry—who designed the Rothko Chapel and the recently built CRS office. Philip Johnson, who built the Jean and Dominique de Ménil residence, did his first large buildings here: the splendid Pennzoil Plaza, the Post Oak Central, the Transco Tower, and the future Republic Bank —the two latter with Burgee. Other famous architects have built in Houston: I. M. Pei, Skidmore Owings and Merrill, Stanley Tigerman, and Michael Graves.

But in the absence of any legislation or planning, the city grows in a chaotic manner. Daily life, especially auto traffic, is a critical problem, finally beginning to concern municipal authorities.

While architecture has made great progress, it must be emphasized that it is urbanism that remains a major task.

Tower of the Commerce Bank in Houston, Texas, by I. M. Pei.

There were those who claimed that art in France could only be meek, petty, and small. But now, in Jouy-en-Josas, near Paris, Arman puts up Long-Term Parking, a sculpture sixty-four feet high composed of a pile of fifty-nine cars immobilized in a gigantic cement parallelepiped. Barely unveiled, it arouses protests and polemics, while in Avignon the exhibition of recent paintings by Rebeyrolle shows a work of equal strength, though drawing on totally different means. The part of France that belongs to art is doing very well indeed. Regaining confidence in itself, the country goes off to conquer America in a series of shows presented in New York under the title of "Statements One."

1982
S U M M A R Y

AVANT-GARDE

Arman's Great Pyramid
In Arman's Words

EXHIBITIONS

Rebeyrolle, the Broken Transcendency

DEVELOPMENTS

The French Are Coming, the French Are Coming
Bram Van Velde: Opulent and Restless
Walls for the Painters
Seventy-Two Government Measures for Artistic Creation

ART NEWS

Bofill in Marne-la-Vallée
London Opens Its Cultural Center
Video Art at the Whitney
Documenta VII: between Art and Life
The Naïf Artists Get Their Museum
In Brief

MUSEUMS

Paul Delvaux Opens His Museum

SCULPTURE

The Dwellings of Étienne-Martin

ARMAN'S GREAT PYRAMID

Arman burning a violin in public, in Nice, 1965.

ARMAN:
PROUD IN
DESPITE OF. 1980

JOUY-EN-JOSAS

It is sixty-four feet high and twenty feet wide, and it has automobiles on all "floors." Arman, fifty-four years old, an artist from Nice, who spends most of his time in the United States, carries off near Paris his most astounding work. He became known many years ago for his "Accumulations": piles of irons, saws, and coffeepots. Now he moves into high gear: Fifty-

Baron Oberkampf. Jean Hammon, founder of the club and a modern-art patron, commissioned it. Arman is jubilant: "I feel like the architect of a pyramid when I am at the top, I feel the joy of having created something out of nothing." Cheops, Khephren, Mykerynos . . . now the automobile seems to have found its modern pharaoh.

Arman has been known for "Accumulations" since the

THE MODERN OBJECT,
TRANSLATED INTO THE DIRECT LANGUAGE
OF THE CONSUMER

nine brightly colored Buicks, Renaults, and Citroëns are parked for eternity among century-old trees—in 1,600 tons of concrete. The work is called *Long-Term Parking* and is a jeering monument to a triumphant consumer society. In a sense, it is like the statues that were dedicated to the condottieri in another time.

The monument is inaugurated, on November 7, in the presence of the usual crowd of curious people and crews from the three American television networks. It is built in the middle of Montcel Park, a club for the rich and the former property of

evening of October 23, 1960, when he filled the gallery Iris Clert with garbage. However, he is also a destructor. In April 1975, at the John Gibson Gallery in New York, he enacted one of his most memorable "angers": the destruction, in public, in twenty minutes, with ax and hammer, of a bourgeois room created for the occasion. It was a Happening of furious Neodadaist inspiration, and also, seemingly a psychoanalytic act—his father was an antique-furniture dealer.

Arman stopped painting in 1965, after he had studied at the decorative-arts school in his

IN ARMAN'S WORDS

native town and at the Louvre school. Very impressed with the collages of Kurt Schwitters and the drippings of Jackson Pollock, which he had seen at Studio Fachetti in Paris, Arman made a series of paintings with ink stamps on primed paper. At the time, he made his living by selling furniture and by harpoon fishing.

His original name was Armand Fernandez. The typesetter for an exhibition catalogue amputated the "d" in his given name. "Born out of an error." A change of identity. The moment had come to find something else.

His mentor, the critic and theoretician Pierre Restany, the founder with Arman and others of the New Realism, wrote about Arman's "Accumulations": "Arman opened our eyes to modern nature. So much so that we have identified him with the feeling of modernism. His adventure follows exactly that of the modern object: a new language about the world, translated into the simple and direct language of the consumer."

Arman became notorious for the violins he broke, burst, and cut into fine slices. He likes the finished shape of the violin. It reminds him of the body of a woman, an idol of the Cyclades, an insect: "By maltreating a perfect object, I render it a homage, because a perfect object can only give perfect debris or ruins, pregnant with its perfection in a different order."

For the time being, the residents of the neighborhood, shocked by *Long-Term Parking*, consider suing to have it dismantled. It doesn't bother Arman. He is thinking of making another pyramid, higher and prettier: a monument to peace, an accumulation of tanks from various countries that participated in the Second World War, put to rest symbolically in a block of concrete.

(See also 1960 and 1962.)

I did not discover the principle of accumulation; it discovered me.

It has always been obvious that this society demonstrates its need for security by its mania for piling up, as can be seen in its store windows, its assembly lines, and its garbage heaps. As a witness to the society in which I live, I have always been involved in the pseudobiological production cycle of consumption and destruction. And for a long time, I was anguished by the fact that its most obvious material result is the invasion of our world by rejects and discards.

My great shock was Dadaism and Surrealism and the use of the object as directly integrated into the work of art.

The violin is a very easy object to reproduce because the violin is a finished form that has not been improved upon since the eighteenth century and which shall not be improved upon; the violin as finished product, charged with identity and with correspondence, is final.

The art object: a trompe l'oeil, *Arcimboldo's head made of vegetables, nineteenth-century* trompe l'oeil, *or, for instance, an explosion—because an explosion becomes an object in a church by Monsu Desiderio—are for me objects because they escape from the formal conditions of their era and of plastic dimensions, to present either an event or an object out of context.*

As a canoe is an extension of the Eskimo, the car is an extension of its user, as if it were an orthopedic device, like a thing that grows on him and which he can get rid of easily.

The inside of a coffee grinder is a divine thing: You can lose yourself in the meanders of a simple but efficient architecture; it is the hidden side of the moon that has remained unchanged—it is the same thing as the other side.

I show the inside simply to show the inside.

I have never been able to keep myself from collecting things; everything that falls into

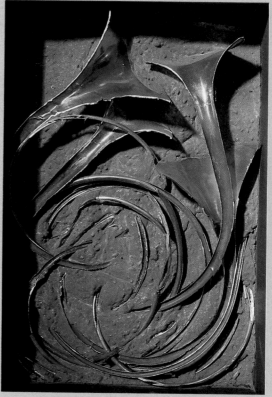

ARMAN:
LE COR DE L'UN, LE COR
DE L'AUTRE. 1971-1974.
Paris. MNAM

my hands, from plants to stamps to seashells, primitive art, and even modern paintings, even books, everything that falls into my hands—I conceive of it as a whole; I have always been suffering from a sickness that could be called the squirrel syndrome; the appetitive value a well-filled showcase has for me—I redo the showcase that I admired in my childhood.

When my father took me to exhibits such as a Paris Trade Fair or a World's Fair, I was extremely fascinated seeing the inside of an engine, the inside of a very complicated electric device to be used for a boat, any cross section, I found incredible things, marvelous entrails that would explain to me the workings of everything, therefore of God.

The artist is an informer.

PAUL REBEYROLLE:
PRAY FOR US. 1981. Private Collection

REBEYROLLE, THE BROKEN TRANSCENDENCY

AVIGNON

He did not dismantle the Vendôme column, but in another time he would have. Like Courbet during the Commune, he could be pictured leading the artists' federation; like Courbet, he would have opposed the Communards who wanted to burn down the Louvre. Like Courbet, he never stops being torn between art and politics, never stops trying to unite them. It is time that one of the greatest current French painters—Paul Rebeyrolle—be recognized.

This fifty-six-year-old artist, born to Leftist parents, is nothing like a Marxist lecturer, and makes no concessions to Social-ist Realism. But he paints bloody bodies, paintings that are hard to stomach, like the silence of the martyrs. This is visible in his exhibition this summer, where he shows some fifty works

PAINTINGS THAT ARE HARD TO STOMACH, LIKE THE SILENCE OF THE MARTYRS

in the former premises of Saint-Louis Hospital.

In the past, his works had the weight of the earth, the scope of nature, the blood of animals. Now he paints violence: remains, failed escapes, bruised nudes, men stabbed in the back, tied up, hanged men with bleeding wounds, suicides—above all suicides, with gasping twitching flesh.

Rebeyrolle remarks: "People spoke of Courbet when they commented on my previous paintings. Now I begin to agree, because of his knowledge of greens, light, and the intimate structure that superficial Realism only sees and treats from the outside." The artist said this twenty years ago. Since then, he has fully justified the observation. His ardent desire to paint is an expression of our modern destitution.

Transcendency was for him his Communist faith, which he, like so many others, lost in 1956, when the Russians smashed the Hungarian uprising. In Rebeyrolle, it takes the shape of a poor kneeling zek (Soviet camp prisoner) contemplating Baroque paintings lying flat on the floor and watching pious images in the style of El Greco and Zurbarán with his lost glance. Another, with his laceless boots at his side, dreams of green pastures. In our faithless society, what has become of the angels and saints of yesteryear?

THE FRENCH ARE COMING, THE FRENCH ARE COMING

NEW YORK

The French are debarking in force on United States soil, in spite of American protectionism, and occupy New York galleries. The official initiative belongs to the art critic Otto Hahn. The "Statements One" exhibition, with twenty-one artists, fills fifteen galleries. It is a panorama ranging from Debré and Hantaï, the master of folding, to the latest trends, represented by Blanchard, Garouste, and Combas, and including Ben, Boltanski, the Poirier couple, Venet, Le Gac, and Messagier.

It is a group of painters belonging to different generations and often conflicting tendencies. Indeed, this is a time of cultural packaging, with Americans, Germans, and Italians imposing a new wave of painters with national character. But is this really the best way for French painting to recover an international place?

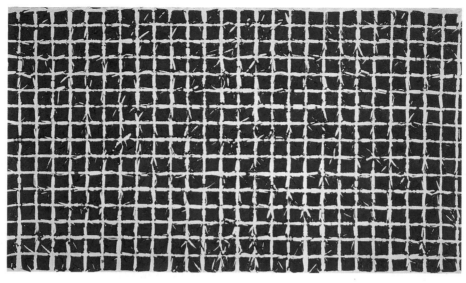

SIMON HANTAÏ: PAINTING. 1974. Saint-Étienne. Musée d'Art et d'Industrie

BRAM VAN VELDE: OPULENT AND RESTLESS

GRIMAUD

There were two brothers, Bram and Geer Van Velde, the former an Expressionist, showing violence and using harsh colors, the latter Geometric and almost translucent. They moved from their native Holland to Paris in the 1920s. Geer, the younger brother, died in 1977, and Bram died on December 28 of last year, at the age of eighty-seven. His friend Samuel Beckett wrote, "He was the first to admit that being an artist means failing like nobody else dares to fail, and that failure is his universe." It was a description of this great artist's fate as an "impossibility to paint."

Indeed, Bram Van Velde's entire life was a merciless struggle. He was born in Zoeterwoude, near Leiden in 1895. Forced to work as a youth, he became an apprentice in a Hague decoration company. He taught himself drawing and easel painting. Before going to Paris, in 1924, he was influenced by Impressionism. He eventually composed his style, freeing himself of any influence.

Yet, the "impossibility to paint" described by Beckett was truer in his art than in his life. Rejecting figurative painting, as well as the Geometric Abstractionism fashionable after the First World War, Van Velde concentrated on the closed universe of his own mystery. While other artists went through periods and styles, he continued in his mature years with the same ovals, triangles, drippings, and unfinished shapes, always in search of a lyricism bordering on pictorial opulence and restlessness.

Van Velde was a painter for subtle art lovers. He isolated himself, avoiding noise. In 1923, he tried lithography. Later, when he went back to it, he imposed himself as a master of this technique. He is honored this year by two exhibitions, in New York and Amsterdam.

BRAM VAN VELDE: COMPOSITION. 1966. Paris. MNAM

WALLS FOR THE PAINTERS

FRANCE

For the first time in the cultural history of the country, thirteen municipalities agree to conduct a campaign of painted walls: "13 walls for 13 cities painted by 13 artists."

The operation mobilizes enthusiasm and talent. In four months, eighteen thousand square feet of wall are turned over to decorative painters to show "the free and diversified expression of an entire people," in the words of Jack Lang, minister of culture. The event was launched by Gilles de Bure, journalist and the author of a recent book, *Des murs dans la ville* (city walls).

The artists for each city are chosen by their artistic and social interest in the project, as well as by their fame. Eleven have their first public commission. The thirteen—eight Frenchmen and five foreigners living in France—are as follows: Chambas in Albi, Cueco in Limoges, Fromanger in Dreux, Pignon-Ernest in Hyères, Pommereulle in Antony, Bouillé in Montbéliard, Mahé in Le Mans, Messager (the only woman) in Bordeaux, Arroyo in Grenoble, Erro in Angoulême, Fanti in Chambéry, Ségui in Boulogne-sur-Mer, and Télémaque in Rennes.

Painters have few occasions to present their work beyond consecrated places, where the small circle of art lovers and high society get together. Therefore, this initiative, due to the Association for the Development of Artistic Environment, is saluted. Half of the cost is carried by the ministry of culture. The operation "Walls in France" will leave its mark, even though its idea is somewhat utopian. It affirms an art that tries to free itself from the monopoly of the few.

Inauguration of Eduardo Arroyo's wall in Grenoble by Jack Lang, minister of culture.

SEVENTY-TWO GOVERNMENT MEASURES FOR ARTISTIC CREATION

PARIS

Jack Lang, the minister of culture, announces the creation of a Committee for Visual Arts, which will sponsor a public institution: the Centre National des Arts Plastiques, or CNAP. It is a brand-new team: Claude Mollard, Gérard Gassiot-Talabot, Geneviève Gallot, Michel Troche, and Bernard Anthonioz.

The minister proposes seventy-two measures in accord with his new lines of action: creation, decentralization, public commission, training, information. CNAP will be responsible especially for the plants of Gobelins and Sèvres, national furniture centers, national and regional art schools, and tasks designed to extend the scope of action by the committee: drawing, comic strips, art films, history of costume, art collection, photography, typographical arts, posters, even cooking. One of CNAP's tasks will be to improve the level of the so-called secondary arts. The CNAP budget for the acquisition of art works triples, going from three million francs to nine million francs, with a projection of thirteen mil-lion in 1983. The one-percent commissions that have been for the decoration of schools and art buildings will be extended to all public buildings. The budget earmarked for the construction of artists' studios, for aid for first exhibitions, and for the encouragement of artistic professions will grow. The ministry will develop its relations with art salons and galleries.

The main measures regard decentralization through the establishment of Fonds d'Incitation à la Création (funds for the stimulation of creation), or FIACRE, a new organism serving the various regions, the artists, and the public, but not replacing present mechanisms for the purchase of art works. Permanent regional art councils will be implanted in all regions. At the same time, the ministry of culture has decided to create, with the cooperation of the regions, twenty-two Fonds Régionaux d'Art Contemporain (regional funds for contemporary art), or FRAC, and twenty-two Fonds Régionaux d'Acquisition pour les Musées (acquisition funds for museums), or FRAM, with a credit of thirty billion francs for this year.

Bofill in Marne-la-Vallée

At the age of forty-four, Ricardo Bofill has become a specialist in the construction of new towns in the Neoclassical style. In 1963, the Catalan architect had put together a team of young collaborators, creating the Taller de Arquitectura (architecture workshop). After building the Arcades du Lac, a neighborhood in Saint-Quentin-en-Yvelines, between 1974 and 1980, he has just completed Abraxas, a neighborhood in Marne-la-Vallée. The village is a U-shaped palace, with a semicircular "theater," a triumphal arch, and a court of honor. The columns, entablature, and capitals are of exaggerated, Piranesi-like proportions.

London Opens Its Cultural Center

Queen Elizabeth II opened the Barbican Arts and Conferences Center on March 3. Designed twenty-one years ago by the architects Chamberlin, Powell, and Bon, the center houses an art gallery, a library, a theater for the Royal Shakespeare Company, conference rooms, concert halls, three movie houses, and several restaurants. The Barbican Center is intended to play a role in London's cultural life similar to the role played by New York's Lincoln Center or the Georges Pompidou Center in Paris. Critics of the center's enormous cost—about three hundred million dollars—abound. Also under fire are its remote location at the northern end of the city, and especially its dated esthetic, resembling an international-style grand hotel.

Video Art at the Whitney

An exhibit of the works of Nam June Paik is held this summer at the Whitney Museum in New York. The artist, aptly nicknamed "the pope of video," was born in Seoul in 1932, and studied music and composition in Germany. In 1961, he took part in the activities of the Fluxus group, and became interested in television. After moving to New York, he presented his first videotape, *Global*, in 1965, at the Café à Go-Go. At the Whitney exhibit, television sets are piled up to a dizzying height, and several

RICARDO BOFILL: PALACE AND THEATER. Marne-la-Vallée

are even hung from the ceiling. Paik's inventiveness, his liberty, and his humor are accompanied by true technical tours de force.

Documenta VII: between Art and Life

"Olympiad of the Arts"—a gigantic international "visual machine," this year's Documenta—put together by Rudi Fuchs, curator of the Eindhoven Museum, gives eloquent testimony to the revolutionary effect of the new painting of today. But the event also presents works by the older generation. The central theme remains the dialogue between art and daily life. At the same time, the exhibit is also designed to reflect the latest Happenings. David Salle and Dan Graham, James Lee Byars and Martin Disler, Bruce Nauman and Keith Haring illustrate the remarkable contrast between the Formalist avant-gardes of the seventies and the new wave. Documenta VII thus preserves its original character in dealing with these self-assured young stars.

The Naïf Artists Get Their Museum

The Musée International d'Art Naïf Anatole Jakovsky (Anatole Jakovsky international museum of Art

Naïf) in Nice is opened in the Château Sainte-Hélène, a large Italianate building once owned by Coty, the perfume manufacturer. The town of Nice restored this superb dwelling to house the Jakovsky donation, which includes more than six hundred paintings and drawings, as well as a large collection of archives. Works from twenty-seven countries are on view, from the eighteenth century to the present. Anatole Jakovsky,

writer, art critic, collector, and a defender of Gaston Chaissac, published the first *Dictionnaire mondial des peintres naïfs* (international dictionary of Naïf Artists). It includes over one thousand biographies. He had suggested to the city of Nice, where Guillaume Apollinaire had written his first articles on Art Naïf in *Hérésiarque et* Cie (heresiarch and company), that it be the recipient of his collection.

LOUIS VIVIN: THE PANTHEON. 1930. Nice. Musée International d'Art Naïf Anatole Jakovsky

PAUL DELVAUX: WHERE THE CITY BEGINS. 1940. Saint-Idesbald. Delvaux Museum

PAUL DELVAUX OPENS HIS MUSEUM

SAINT-IDESBALD

At the end of June, the Delvaux Museum opens its doors in a typical Flemish house covered with rose vines.

Twelve years ago, when he was eighty-two years old, Paul Delvaux, who had already donated his drawings to Belgium, was seriously concerned with making available to the public his personal collection of paintings and watercolors. Yet, the Museum of Modern Art of Brussels was far from being completed. Delvaux's nephew, Charles van Deun, and some friends suggested he create a foundation.

The artist thought of building a house in Saint-Idesbald, where he lives and works. Instead, the Delvaux Foundation bought there the "Vlierhof," an old fishermen's house renovated as a hotel and restaurant. It is now a museum.

The restricted space is not well suited to viewing all those young women in Delvaux's paintings rising from their beds or wandering about in railway stations, in alleys, in old cities, in lethargic neighborhoods.

The artist, who comes to the museum often, is amazed that

SUSPENDED FAIRY TALES, WHOSE END WILL NEVER BE KNOWN

so many people ask him about his inspirations and the reasons for his obsession with young virgins waiting for mysterious and ritual love. And why all those locomotives and parked railway cars? "But they are to look at, that's all!" he declares to *Le Soir* on August 20. It seems like a banal answer, but it does explain his art, with its poetic dream. The erotic motivation is

oddly devoid of any libertine implication. The ineffable young women and boys are narcissistic, introverted, or narcotic.

Delvaux sees these images, but does not interfere. Everything is in this way of seeing, similar to that of the entomologist, who sometimes appears in his paintings. It is also the way of seeing of his boys, surprised and moved, rather than tempted, by the painter's sleeping beauties and vestals with ethereal graces and temples that are railway stations and dormant cities whose inhabitants are nowhere to be seen or reduced to skeletons.

Paul Delvaux ou les rêves éveillés (Paul Delvaux or the

wakened dream) is the title of a monograph that accurately describes the eerie ambience of his compositions. They are suspended fairy tales, whose end will never be known, because the painter is afraid to find it out. "When I was a child," he says, "I used to put my ear on the telephone poles and listen to the vibrations." He listened without deciphering. He heard the trains whistle without knowing where they were going.

The Delvaux Museum lets the visitor see and dream. It is already too small for the crowds that gather, and there are plans for expansion.

(See also 1949.)

THE DWELLINGS OF ÉTIENNE-MARTIN

PARIS

The recent work of Étienne-Martin, the white-bearded sculptor, who is sixty-nine years old, is displayed in a book by Dominique Le Buhan and in an exhibition at the gallery Artcurial. The key to his work could be the poetic art of space so dear to Gaston Bachelard, with its hidden corners, tiny quirks, uprootings, and layers.

THE OBSESSIVE MOVEMENTS OF HIS INNER LIFE

For a quarter of a century, most of Étienne-Martin's sculptures represent his parents' house in Loriol, in Drôme, a town between Valence and Montélimar. The house was divided into two parts by a wall. One had to pass through a communication door, on the ground floor or in the attic to go from one part to the other. "In a way, the house was two houses," the artist says. The day he realized this, his future as a sculptor was decided.

However, it should not be deduced that he sculpts and re-sculpts his native house in an anecdotic manner. Recurrent is a psychologic form and structure, enhanced by the remembrance of a dormer window opening to the surrounding landscape: "I loved to play next to this window, located at the top of a staircase in the attic. It was like the hinge between fullness and void." Étienne-Martin's *Demeures* (dwellings) are cut in wood and molded in plaster, and are alternately large and small. Some are made of fabric decorated with string, because the coats designed by the sculptor and sometimes worn by him also belong to the *Demeures* series. They are plastic poems, repeating the obsessive movements of his inner life.

In 1929, at the age of sixteen, he enrolled in the Fine Arts School in Lyon. From 1933, he studied at the Ranson Academy with Charles Malfray. There, he became friends with Manessier, Le Moal, and Bertholle. He was always concerned with drawing, which, in his opinion, is linked naturally to sculpture: "Drawing is a very obvious initial element. If you sculpt, drawing is in space. On paper, it occupies a flat surface, but the pencil will contour and define the place of the volumes in light—this is what drawing means." In his work, drawing and sculpture are joined in a common movement. Through drawing, space incarnates his impulses and remembrances.

No less important than the topology of his native house were, as of 1947, his friendship with Brancusi and his visits to the community created by Georges Ivanovich Gurdieff. The latter, a philosopher and writer from the Caucasus, advocated a knowledge of one's ego through a joint effort of feeling, body, and thought. It is to Gurdieff that Étienne-Martin seems to owe a certain mysticism.

The artist's work is not limited to the *Demeures*. He makes busts, couples embracing and in other poses, multilimbed tree trunks, and a twenty-six-foot-high Virgin sculpted during the war on the bank of Beauvallon, but now gone. He won the prize of the Bill Copley Foundation in 1963 and the Grand Prix National des Arts. He has exhibitions worldwide.

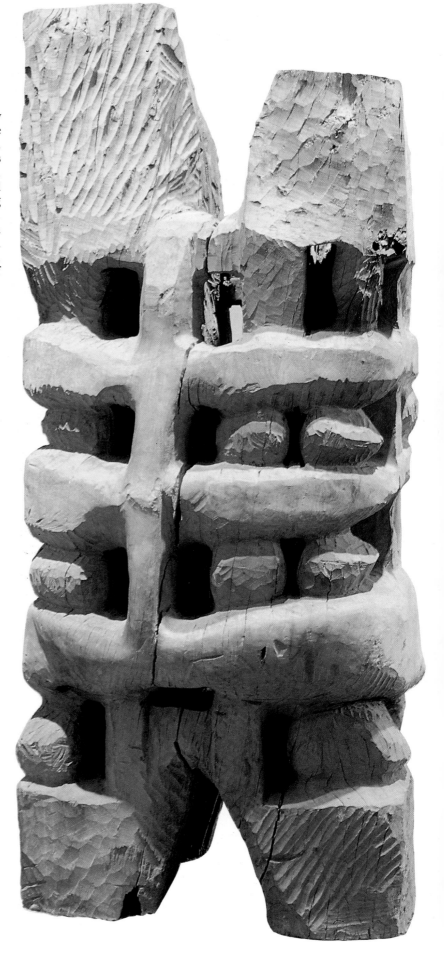

ÉTIENNE-MARTIN:
PASSAGE. 1969

After much Neodadaist puttering about, painting had begun to stage a comeback several years earlier. With the birth of the Transavantgarde and of Free Figuration, it had appeared in Italy, France and Germany. Now it comes from the United States in the person of Julian Schnabel, the most European of American painters, who emerges practically overnight in the forefront of the international art scene. This return of painting is accompanied by the return of the institution designed to contain it, the museum. In the last few decades, many artists, sociologists, and critics had predicted its slow death, but now, throughout the world, new museums open daily, and others are under construction.

1983

S U M M A R Y

AVANT-GARDE

Schnabel, the Omnivorous Painter
French Artists Exhibit in London

GREAT MASTERS

De Kooning or Pictorial Lightning
The Mysteries of Balthus

PORTRAITS

The Dynamite of Monory
Erro Makes Picasso's Portrait

MUSEUMS

A Museum around a Collection
An Art Lover's Passion

DEVELOPMENTS

Magritte and Publicity

ART NEWS

Donizetti Renews Ties with the Renaissance
The *Fountain* by Jean Tinguely and Niki de Saint-Phalle
Art despite the War
Inauguration of the Monument to Picasso by Tàpies
In Brief

SCULPTURE

The Return to Mythology
Richard Serra at the Tuileries

WRITINGS AND THEORIES

Jacques Henric: the Museum As Incubator

JULIAN SCHNABEL:
VITA. 1983.
New York. Private Collection

SCHNABEL, THE OMNIVOROUS PAINTER

NEW YORK

Julian Schnabel was presented to the public last year through several exhibitions, the big ones being at the Stedelijk Museum in Amsterdam and the Museum of Contemporary Art of Los Angeles. This year, his exhibitions in New York, Rome, Paris, Zurich, and Tokyo confirm the place assumed by this young artist, born in New York in 1951. He is considered to be the standard-bearer of the new painting. He symbolizes American success. His solo show at the gallery Dezember in Düsseldorf in 1978 and his show at the Mary Boone Gallery in New York made him a celebrity and—controversial. Each one of his exhibitions revive the polemic on the originality of his art.

He has been searching for an identity a long time. He went to Paris and Milan, he lived several months in Tuscany, he traveled to Germany, and he found his vocation in Spain. In July 1978, he was stuck in Barcelona because he had lost his passport. For five days, he waited in a seedy hotel. It was an obsessive tête-à-tête with the imposing wardrobe standing in his room, the Goyas discovered at the Prado, and Gaudí's Güell Park, with its mosaics made of porcelain shards. Such glazed ceramic tiles appeared even in some restaurants. It was a decisive moment for his future. It was the starting point of his *Plate Paintings* that made him famous overnight.

Indeed, as soon as he returned to New York, Schnabel started a series of paintings. *The Patients and the Doctors* became all the rage. The work consists of fragments of dinner plates incorporated and glued, together with other materials, on a wooden background. Its heterogeneous elements are linked by rapid brush strokes. Certain fragments are convex, others concave, their edges jut out, cut at a

Julian Schnabel in 1982.

JULIAN SCHNABEL:
PORTRAIT OF GOD.
1981. Private Collection

straight angle. If the *Plate Paintings* are derived from the mosaics of Güell Park, they have a violence and aggressiveness of their own.

Schnabel explains the sense of his work: "The use of preexisting materials gives my art an ethnographic character. I mean, it places the esthetic work in a precise place and time. It allows identification of a cultural, familiar, or exotic place, which comes out of my fantasy or is inspired by outside influences. It is a kind of mental and physical platform for my painting." If his paintings are set flat on the floor, they become ruins, reminiscent of archaeologic sites and long-vanished worlds, such as *The Sea*, a huge composition in which the blue plaster holds not only plate shards but also pieces of amphoras and deer antlers.

FRENCH ARTISTS EXHIBIT IN LONDON

Like the entire European Transavantgarde, he is an eclectic who reunites all myths, present and past, and the themes of all cultures. His reputation is that of an imitator, a devourer, an "omnivore." It is true that nothing scares him, no topic, no technique, no style.

Far from limiting himself to his *Plate Paintings*, he painted, two years ago, on a large canvas, a *Portrait of God* made of a blue shape that did not look like anything and whose title is its most original feature. The painting is especially representative of our agnostic time, which hardly acknowledges Michelangelo's venerable bearded old man on the ceiling of the Sistine Chapel.

Like many other artists of his generation, Schnabel loves theatrical effects. This love is reflected in his work in a series of paintings on velvet, named *Velvet Paintings*. They have an alchemy and substance different from the *Plate Paintings*, a substance that let the artist be sweet, luxurious, and opulent. A product of this love are his four paintings dedicated to Maria Callas. They are close to Informal Painting.

It is said that Schnabel is the most European among American painters, and it is true. His work is similar to Jackson Pollock's "drippings" and Robert Rauschenberg's "Combine Paintings" in which he partially has his roots. In addition to Gaudí, he is especially influenced by the Germans Sigmar, Polke, and Beuys.

Is Schnabel successful because of his eclecticism? There is no painting by him on the market for less than five hundred thousand francs. The time of the cursed artists seems quite far in the past.

LONDON

The traveling exhibition "New French Painting," the first manifestation abroad of the new generation of outstanding French painters, opens at Riverside Studio. It is well received. At a time when the Americans, the Germans, and the Italians are conquering the planet, the goal of the exhibition is to show that France, too, has international-class painting which unjustly has been ignored. It has several points in common with other European schools, namely a questioning of avant-gardes, a revival of the painting of everyday activities considered minor or far afield, a rejection of the old debate of figurative versus abstract, not for the sake of a return to figuration but for the sake of Free Figuration unconcerned with Realism or resemblance.

The exhibition at Riverside Studio is a comprehensive review of certain artistic view-

THE DIVERSITY OF FRENCH PAINTING IN ALL ITS DYNAMICS AND MODERNITY

points. It presents a group of various personalities that do not make a group per se, even though they have certain affinities and some, such as Combas, Boisrond, and Blanchard, are all inspired by comic strips, the mass media, rock music, or color photographs in a swift and deliberately simple style. It is especially Boisrond who knows how to invent designs by starting from any object: glasses, ashtrays, plants, television sets, just people. If one were to find him a "father" in painting, one would have to think of Matisse because of the roses he arranges with a certain tenderness or of Picasso in the 1930s for his black-eyed "closed" faces.

Others, such as Alberola, Garouste, and Laget, use quotations while playing on the ambiguity of newness and on the reality value of a story. That is what Blais does with his poster paintings, Frize with his perpetual search, Poivret with his airplanes, and Rousse, the painter-photographer, as well as Antonuicci and Corpet. The range of approaches demonstrates the diversity of French painting in all its dynamics and modernity.

FRANÇOIS BOISROND: UNTITLED. 1983. Bordeaux. CAPC Entrepôt Lainé

DE KOONING OR PICTORIAL LIGHTNING

Willem De Kooning and his wife, Elaine, in 1980.

NEW YORK

On May 5, *Two Women*, one of the most terrifying paintings by Willem De Kooning, was sold at Christie's for the record amount of $1,200,000. It was the largest sum ever paid for a painting by a living artist. And yet, De Kooning, who is seventy-nine and the recognized master of the New York School, with a retrospective at the Whitney Museum, had to wait until he was fifty to be able to live on his painting.

His path was that of the immigrant immortalized by Charlie Chaplin. He came to Manhattan on August 15, 1926, aboard the *Shelley*, on which he worked as a sailor. He debarked illegally. At an art school in his native Rotterdam, he had obtained an arts and crafts diploma. He did all kinds of small jobs, such as wall painting, because he knew how to use a brush. Until the Russian-German pact of 1939, he flirted with the union of Communist artists, decorating floats for the May 1 parade.

The painting that brought him critics' applause in 1950 is a large biomorphic canvas. Its title, *Excavation*, reminds us of the endless demolitions and reconstructions that, at the time, had transformed Manhattan into a vast pit. Barbara Rose, the great priestess of the new American painting, wrote that in *Excavation* De Kooning makes line give birth to a group of organic shapes soldered among themselves, often adjoining and sometimes overlapping. In accordance with the fashion of the time, she dwelled on the speed of execution characteristic of De Kooning. Speed, indeed, but that didn't stop the artist from spending eighteen months on *Woman I*.

De Kooning's subject had obsessed him for twenty years: the representation of a sitting woman. He worked as hard as he could, then tore the canvas off the stretcher and threw it aside. But then, his friend, art historian Meyer Shapiro, asked to see the abandoned painting. De Kooning retrieved it and looked at it again. After a few retouches, it was declared finished, that is to say "not to be destroyed." It is his most celebrated work, and the origin of the painting that reached a record sum.

"Many artists and critics have attacked my *Women*, but that is their problem, not mine," De Kooning declares. "I don't feel comfortable in the shoes of an abstract painter." It is known that Rembrandt, toward the end of his life, struggled to produce a self-portrait showing him as a wrinkled old man. Would it be De Kooning's Dutch origin? Aggression or rape of the resisting flesh, his *Women* are a sort of pictorial lightning, like Rembrandt's old man.

Did the devil grant De Kooning only one expression? One could think so, because his other series, usually abstract landscapes, do not have the same force or the same degree of inspiration.

"I have slit open many mouths," the painter remarks. "At the beginning, I used to think that everything must have a mouth." Of course, without ever forgetting the teeth. It looks exactly like the famous *vagina dentata* of the celebrated Doctor Freud. Apparently, a well-ingrained obsession is enough to inspire an outstanding work.

(See also 1950 and 1952.)

WILLEM DE KOONING:
TWO FIGURES IN A LANDSCAPE. 1967. Amsterdam. Stedelijk Museum

BALTHUS: THE GOOD DAYS. 1944-1946.
Washington. Hirshhorn Museum

THE MYSTERIES OF BALTHUS

PARIS

The critics are pulling out their hair: Not one interview, no biographical information, just the year of birth, 1908, and the fact that, as a child, he had met the poet Rainer Maria Rilke, who encouraged him to become a painter. That's all they know about the man who, as of November 5, occupies the floor of "great exhibitions" at the Georges Pompidou Center. The mystery of Balthus is complete! The limelight of artistic news focuses on a work that is no less of a secret than its author.

Indeed, it would be difficult to imagine a painter who is less in the mainstream, more stubbornly against the grain, than this "figurative artist." His world is troubled and shady—familiar objects, prepubertal girls in ambiguous poses, streets in the Paris of yesteryear, and sweetish cherry trees. A priori, there is

nothing spectacular. On the contrary, a first glance could put Balthus in with those painters of cute bouquets. But Balthus—whose real name is Count Balthazar Klossowski de Rola—is the last of the aristocrat painters.

THE NOSTALGIC SEARCH FOR THE LOST PARADISE OF CHILDHOOD

Despising easy success and the beaten path, he preferred to perfect a know-how derived from the fresco painters of the Renaissance. The apparent banality of his compositions and the falsely commonplace gestures of his characters hide a tragic universe of silence and solitary despair. Antonin Artaud was right when he suggested that Balthus was a brother of his own "théâtre de cruauté" (theater of cruelty); Pierre-Jean

Jouve was right, too, when he said that this kind of painting "reminded one of Bluebeard."

Expressing an inaccessible happiness and the nostalgic search for the lost paradise of childhood, with remembered images that are drowned in the faint light of the past, Balthus' paintings allow a glimpse into the timeless. The young girls before their mirrors, reading, or sleeping on sofas, seem to come from a world in violent contrast with ours.

But the aristocratic remoteness of the painter, his predilection for neat colors and precise drawing, his choice of a simple, almost banal, pictorial language—all these elements trans-

form this gap into a revelation. The public swarms to the exhibition.

Balthus, one of the few French painters exhibited at the Museum of Modern Art in New York, one of the few to have had a retrospective at Beaubourg during his lifetime, one of the most sought-after and most highly priced painters in the world, held in esteem by a group of collectors who fight over his paintings, seems to be a prophet in his own country. "Different from so many painters tempted by the void and refusing to pursue their work to the limit on behalf of an illusory 'going beyond,' Balthus is the painter of slow advancement and a secret and profound maturation; he is 'the one who believes in incarnation,'" Jean Clair, curator of the exhibition, observes.

(See also 1956.)

THE DYNAMITE OF MONORY

GRENOBLE

Rumor has it that Jacques Monory, who confesses to be forty-nine, is actually ten years older. This is legal, because the law allows artists to change their age if they deem it prejudicial to their career.

But why did Monory need this artifice? He is one of the few French artists whose work, dedicated almost completely to Rembrandt blue, is comparable to British or American Pop Art. Everybody knows the series that made famous this outstanding representative of narrative figuration, so much loved by the critic Gérald Gassiot-Talabot: *Murders*; *New York*; *Faces*; *Skies, Nebulas, Galaxies*.

The paintings are cold and impersonal, principally because of the transfer of the photographic image to the canvas. Yet, "each painting is a story, and a man's life is the life of his way of seeing," writes one of the painter's admirers. "Between 'nowhere' and the place of a catastrophe, the distance is not great. It is the eternal story of the senses, of their displacements, and of fiction. If all of Monory's paintings were to come to life, the novel would become the lyrical film full of gaps that he resembles."

In "Dynamite," the exhibition at the Cultural House of Grenoble, the painter continues his analysis of actuality, using shades of pink and yellow. But the image of a world that is drowning, where confusion and madness reign, is not fundamentally modified.

Even if he is ten years older (supposing it is true), Jacques Monory remains one of the youngest in spirit in current French painting.

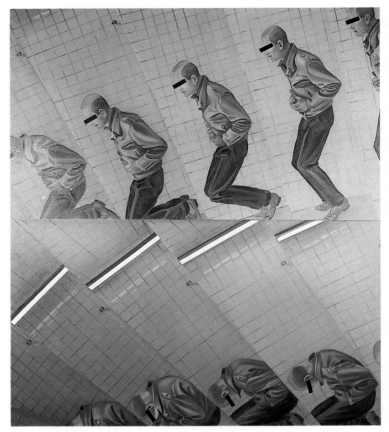

JACQUES MONORY: MURDER II. 1968. The Artist's Private Collection

ERRO MAKES PICASSO'S PORTRAIT

ANTIBES

There is justice! Whenever Gertrude Stein came to see Picasso at the Bateau-Lavoir, before the First World War, she always brought him the latest episode of the adventures of the *Katzenjammer Kids,* a cartoon she received from home in the United States. She loved its heroes, Hans and Fritz, who struggled against all authority.

And now, Icelandic painter Gudmundur Gudmundson, who is fifty-one years old and better known by the name Erro, does Picasso as a cartoon character. He was commissioned by Danièle Giraudy, curator of the Musée Picasso in Antibes. She had the idea of asking ten painters of the new generation to paint a tribute to the artist. Erro had already used the cartoon style for portraits of Galileo, Wagner, and Stravinsky, and in order to point out the absurdity of politicians.

He shows Picasso as Picasso saw himself at different ages. The main image is that of one of Picasso's caricatures: arriving in Paris, in 1905, wearing a large-rimmed hat. Behind the multiple portrayal is a small reproduction of some of Picasso's paintings of the Antibes period—they were made at the close of 1946 on the very spot where the Musée Picasso is located.

Erro has also made a series called *Birdscape,* which is a sequel to his *Carscape, Foodscape, Lovescape,* and *Fishscape.* By accumulating bird images, he creates a kind of visual hallucination. A "Gargantua of painting," Erro is one of the masters of narrative figuration.

ERRO:
PICASSO-ANTIBES.
1982. Antibes.
Musée Picasso

A MUSEUM AROUND A COLLECTION

VILLENEUVE-D'ASCQ
Conceived in 1975 to house the Dutilleul-Masurel Collection, the Musée d'Art Moderne of Villeneuve-d'Ascq, near Lille, opens to the public on November 19. It is the donation of Geneviève and Jean Masurel: two hundred masterpieces from the beautiful collection gathered during his lifetime by Roger Dutilleul, the unmarried corporate administrator who was Jean Masurel's uncle.

At the beginning of the century, Roger Dutilleul was one of the few Frenchmen deeply interested in Picasso and Braque, and he bought several of their works. In 1908, he bought *Houses and Trees* by Braque, which had been refused at the Salon d'Automne because the jury saw only "little cubes" in it. Dutilleul had his portrait made by Modigliani, whose misery moved

ANDRÉ BAUCHANT: THE STYX. 1939. Villeneuve-d'Ascq. Musée d'Art Moderne

him, and he bought eleven other paintings by the artist. His portrait was also painted by Van Hecke and by Lanskoy. With his eclectic taste, he was as interested in the Naïfs Bauchant and Vivin as in Van Dongen, Derain, Miró, Klee, Léger, and Herbin. But he had no Matisse. "He doesn't move me," Dutilleul used to say.

In his apartment on the Rue Monceau in Paris the walls disappeared under the paintings, and he ended up putting his "children," as he called them, on the floor.

Jean Masurel, who had loved to look at his uncle's paintings since he was ten, continued his work when Dutilleul died in 1956. Thus he faithfully bought

a *Sitting Nude* by Picasso and several paintings by Léger. With his uncle, he had bought paintings by Buffet since 1948. By the donors' wishes the museum is also open to contemporary art: Several halls are dedicated to temporary exhibitions by young artists of the North and elsewhere. Roger Dutilleul would surely have approved.

AN ART LOVER'S PASSION

DUNKIRK
A scheme was needed. Gilbert Delaine, forty-eight years old, a civil engineer and a great art lover, found it. It was a scheme called "acquisition-donation," so that Dunkirk could have what it had never had, namely a museum of contemporary art. In 1974, Delaine started to knock on artists' doors. With the money he obtained from industrialist friends, he bought a painting from each artist, and asked that each donate another. At the time, Delaine had nowhere to exhibit the paintings; he did not even know whether he would have a space one day. The artists trusted him, and the scheme worked.

Vasarely, who was always generous, donated a trunk of serigraphs, then a large canvas.

Pignon and Kijno, both from the North, fell in love with the project. Arman made a twenty-three-foot-high sculpture out of ship anchors. Hartung, Prassinos, Vieira da Silva, Messagier, Alechinsky, Klasen, Velickovic, and many others joined in. Today, Dunkirk has seven hundred paintings, sculptures, objets d'art, and drawings of the best contemporary artists.

And the museum? Since the collection existed, it was logical to build a place to house it. Twenty-five million francs were contributed by the municipality and the state. In the middle of a garden adjoining a shipyard with its crafts and cranes, there is now a building of forty-three thousand square feet, inaugurated last December. It is the perfect setting for the paintings.

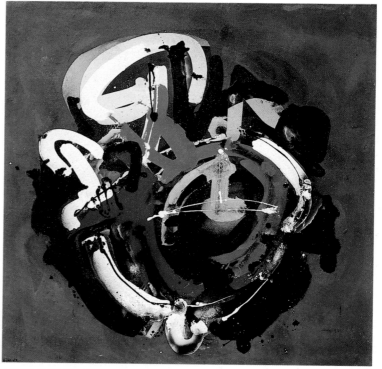

LADISLAS KIJNO: HOMAGE TO GALILEO. 1963. Dunkirk. Musée d'Art Moderne

MAGRITTE AND PUBLICITY

PARIS

Of all painters, Magritte influences publicity the most. This becomes obvious at the exhibition that opened May 4 at the Musée de l'Affiche et de la Publicité. The initiative belongs to a young CNRS researcher, Georges Roque, a collector of Magritte. For the occasion, he has published a book with a significant and ironic title: *Ceci n'est pas un Magritte* (this is not a Magritte).

Roque has plenty of ideas on generating publicity. The most stimulating one is that Magritte is not an artist in the manner of Matisse and Picasso: He looks for the effacing of the "creating hand" so as to let the eye look unhindered. "I would like my paintings to be unnecessary for anyone's thinking of what they represent," Magritte used to say. This thought contains the secret desire of every commercial artist who wishes his advertisement to be as inconspicuous as possible, so that only the product it promotes is seen. In Magritte's art, objects have an unusual presence that enhances their mystery. This makes them sell better when they are placed in the field of advertising.

Certain paintings of the artist, such as *False Mirror* or *The Betrayal of Images*, would be perfect logos for an optician or a tobacconist. Sabena Airlines bought an oil painting from Magritte—a bird landing—for its ads. The ambiguity is total. The circle is closed.

Magritte, who did not have a studio, and used to make in his dining room the paintings that are worth a fortune today, once owned an advertising agency. "Stands—Counters—Publicity Objects—Posters—Drawings—Photocollages—Advertising Copy," his letterhead said. He used to draw Neocubist dresses and fur coats. His clients included the best of the fashion designers, milliners, and jewelers of Brussels. But he was unhappy. He hated advertising.

Thus, it is a paradox that his paintings give rise to so many advertising masterpieces. The

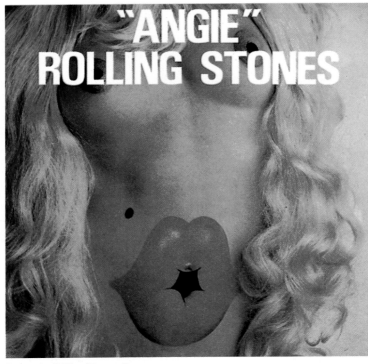

Cover of a Rolling Stones album.

jacket of a Rolling Stones record, inspired by Magritte's *Rape*, with its female body transformed into a face, is as striking as its original. The image of John Players Special cigarettes, with its transparent geometry raised to the heavens, is as troubling as Magritte's strangest compositions. And what can one say about the image created for Crédit Agricole on the basis of *La belle captive*?

As is often the case in Magritte's paintings, the latter shows a canvas on an easel, the landscape behind it: A small village hides among trees. In the advertisement it inspired, there is a villa with a garage on the easel, because when one says villa, one also says car to get there; and there is a doghouse, because when one says private property, one also says fence and dog for protection. This house, which is now just an architectural drawing, extends naturally into reality. The dream is subtly incarnated. The effect is immediate. Magritte's paintings are "detached" images. They do not refer the viewer to anything. They are neutral. They do not deliver any message. That's why it is so easy for advertisers to insert their own message.

In addition, Magritte is an outstanding creator of archetypes. Almost every one of his paintings causes a short circuit and opens a hole under our feet. The ancients believed in their myths. Sometimes they doubted a little, but only better to believe. As for us, we are pleased that the apple eats up the nose of the gentleman with the bowler hat—it's a pleasure to see. That is the reason why Magritte is so good for advertising.

(See also 1936 and 1967.)

RENÉ MAGRITTE:
RAPE. 1934.
Houston.
Ménil Foundation

Donizetti Renews Ties with the Renaissance

Mario Donizetti, fifty-one-year-old descendant of the composer by the same name, and also from Bergamo, is a happy man. What is happening to him is indeed out of the ordinary: The Ambrosian Gallery in Milan is holding an exhibit of his work, including some thirty paintings and about a hundred drawings. One of the oldest museums in the world, it houses the *Codex Atlanticus*, in which Leonardo da Vinci put his sketches of flying machines and other mechanical wonders. There is also the life-size sketch of Raphael's *The School of Athens*. And now Mario Donizetti's striking portraits of famous actors and actresses, his paintings of young women, renderings of flowers placed on a marble fragment, and pictures of old men, are exhibited in the shadow of these masterpieces. Donizetti uses techniques that were developed during the Renaissance, having taken over twenty years to rediscover the secrets of that period.

The "Fountain" by Jean Tinguely and Niki de Saint-Phalle

Niki de Saint-Phalle and Tinguely have created the *Fountain* for Place Igor-Stravinsky, between the Georges Pompidou Center and Saint-Merri Church. The square occupies an area above Ircam, the underground kingdom of Pierre Boulez. *Fountain* is simultaneously a mechanical ballet, a circus production, and a carnival of colors. A delighted, obviously enchanted public continually files past the *Nanas* by Niki de Saint-Phalle, which act as water spouts, and past the "metamechanical" devices by Tinguely, which find unusual application here. The animated and poetic water play in the fountain on Place Igor-Stravinsky adds the dynamics of its modernity to this privileged place in the center of Paris, where culture is queen. The magic of movement was all that was lacking here, and now that, too, has become a reality with this monumental fountain.

MARIO DONIZETTI: OLD MAN IN WHITE. Private Collection

Art despite the War

Incomprehensible Lebanon! While Beirut burns and bleeds, Lebanese developers are not only building but are commissioning mural art from artists. Two enamel-on-steel walls, each measuring 43 X 8 feet, created by the fifty-five-year-old Swiss painter Jean Coulot, who lives in Paris, are installed at the Faraya-Mzar ski resort. The two works are a free interpretation of Mount Lebanon and the surrounding mountains, as seen from the ski slope.

Inauguration of the Monument to Picasso by Tàpies

Ten years after Picasso's death, Barcelona pays homage to him with a monument entitled *Le passage Picasso* by the painter and sculptor Antoni Tàpies. Unveiled on March 19, the monument rises up from a dip in the terrain. Encased in a plexiglas block, it is composed of a sofa covered with a huge sheet. Water runs off its surface, forming a fluid, transparent curtain.

JEAN TINGUELY AND NIKI DE SAINT-PHALLE: FOUNTAIN. Paris. Place Igor-Stravinsky

THE RETURN TO MYTHOLOGY

PARIS

We thought that the battles of giants had been relegated to prop storage forever. But they are coming back. Rocks roll down the slopes of Olympus . . . celestial fire . . . temples smashed . . . pillars broken. The main characters are back, too: Enceladus, on whose head Sicily fell; Mimas, buried under the fires of Vesuvius. The place it all happens? The Salpêtrière Chapel, where the fools and derelicts of Paris paraded for centuries.

The mythographers are Anne and Patrick Poirier. They have always worked together. Both are forty-one years old. They are among the best French artists of the new generation. How can their works, inaugurated on October 4, be described? Are they architectural models, are they environments? Anne Poirier speaks of "installations." What matters is the return of intelligence in current art.

Enceladus, the first piece visi-

ANNE AND PATRICK POIRIER:
MIMAS. 1983.
Paris. Galerie Templon

ble from the entrance, embodies the spirit of the exhibition. It looks like the result of an explosion. It incorporates architectural elements of various sizes and two huge marble eyes, which are pierced by an enormous arrow of polished bronze. The Poiriers divide their activi-

ties between Italy and France. One thinks of the *Apennines* by Jean de Bologne, whose mass sits in the gardens of the Villa Medicis, in Pratolino. It is a pulverized, monumental statue. Another work on exhibit, *Mimas*, has a huge eye dominating a pond whose waters bathe an

archaeological site stricken by the gods' anger.

The Mannerist art is deliberately symbolic, cataclysmic, and extravagant. Symbolism and extravagance are the means by which the Poiriers bring the myths of another time into the reality of today.

RICHARD SERRA AT THE TUILERIES

PARIS

Richard Serra celebrates his first official exhibition in France. He was seen here once before, in 1976, at the gallery Daniel Templon. Two prestigious places host this important forty-four-year-old American sculptor: the contemporary art galleries of the Georges Pompidou Center and the Jardin de Tuileries.

The exhibition at the Georges Pompidou Center offers a panorama ranging from the first rubber pieces of 1966, which are characteristic of the so-called "Process Art," where the traces of the manufacturing process are as important as the finished work, to the "Prop," which is the origin of his entire work. His series questions the very nature

of sculpture by playing on antagonisms: stability versus unbalance, and mobility of forms versus rigidity of materials. Without a stand, or soldering, or any other support, these works are like card castles made of thick tin plates that look as

though anything could make them crumble.

This is especially obvious in the large pieces. At the Tuileries, *Clara-Clara*, one hundred and twenty feet long and eleven feet high, made of two immense curved plates of steel, plays with

the landscape that is marked by Le Nôtre's ramps and the obelisk of the Concorde. Its presence in this historic place is incongruous, but Parisians may sleep in peace. *Clara-Clara* is there for a limited time only.

RICHARD SERRA:
CLARA-CLARA.
1983. Paris.
Jardin des Tuileries

JACQUES HENRIC: THE MUSEUM AS INCUBATOR

Jacques Henric was born in 1938. His book *La peinture et le mal* (painting and evil), just published by Grasset, is less the work of an art critic or an essayist than that of a writer. Outside of styles and of schools, Henric inquires into the sense of artistic creation at this end of the century where it seems that anything can henceforth be explained, legitimized. In particular, he inquires into the ambiguous bond between the avant-garde and the museum, which immediately absorbs and digests it. His thoughts are disturbing because they question the history of contemporary art as it is constructed by the media today—as we will see in the excerpt that follows.

Dealers, collectors, brokers are all indispensable Simon-the-Magicians. Perhaps they will end up in hell, as do all the simoniacs and those guilty of misappropriation, but they will be there for the purpose of demonstrating the example.

As for the garbage can of history, and particularly art history, if there absolutely has to be one, there's a convenient one: the museum. The museum, that is to say, the extraordinary heap of works resulting from the European revolutions during which —especially in France, as pointed out by André Chastel—the dispersions of illustrious galleries, the secularization of convents, the confiscations by the Republic and the looting by the Empire have fed the voracious ghoul of Paris, as well as the provinces. Should we complain about it? Just as money, the museum is the truth of painting. It is the outcome of innumerable sales and deals, of a fabulous hubbub, the moment of stasis, of rest. It is also the possibility that the accumulation of wealth is offered for contemplation.

Bataille, after having brought the guillotine and museums closer together, compares the latter to the lung of a large city where the crowd would flock and from which it would come out purified and fresh, like blood. A lung, a liver, a kidney—a filter! A place of transformation, of mutation of substances, of drainage, a kind of chic toilet. This should obviously imply a new, not standardized, practice by the museum. For instance, to consider not only the gallery but the paintings as the "containers," certainly not idols before which one prostrates oneself, but "dead surfaces," and in this way it would be in the crowd that "the outbursts, the games, the flooding of light" would occur. The museum according to Bataille? "A colossal mirror in which man contemplates himself in all his faces, finds himself truly admirable, and abandons himself to ecstasy." It's the very definition of the toilet.

To go there, you need extreme mobility, inner distance, a sense of play, and humor, without which you, in turn, are caught in the reflection of the mirror, sent back to your initial inconsistency, to the misery of narcissism, to the anguish of volatile heaviness, trembling with fear at the idea of seeing the feathers drop one by one, to the state of pure dejection that the museum gut will never cease to spill all through the centuries.

What is puzzling is the anxious precipitation with which the painters of the young generation throw themselves into said garbage can. Unload, quick! unload! Fleeing from the demanding circuit of the trade, of the competition, our barely hatched cute little cockerels dash under the warm protective wind of Museum-Mommy. Garbage can or incubator. They arrive before having left. Retrospectives, fat catalogues as tomb stones . . .

This is what it means when naive fowls take the museum for a church, whereas the museum ought to be used as one uses a shit house, or, following St. Ambrose's suggestion, to be turned into an immense whorehouse. This is what it is to have forgotten that Simon was a magician, that is to say, a sex manipulator. It isn't Picasso who wants it! A perverse market has captured you like little chickens. You have swallowed the hook. The great "Matouse" has struck. On the moldings we can see an alignment of stillborn chicks.

JACQUES HENRIC
La peinture et le mal *(Excerpt)*

The twentieth century, it seems, has unfolded under the sign of Primitivism, be it African, North American, or Oceanian, replacing the ancestral reference to the Renaissance and Greco-Roman antiquity. Its influence cuts across almost the entire period, from Gauguin to Picasso to the Surrealists. The immense interest of the MOMA exhibition in New York, "Primitivism in Twentieth-Century Art," is that it shows this influence more completely than it had ever been shown before. But what will the future of art consist of? If Anselm Kiefer, the German painter who is the most inspired artist of the new generation, is abrasive, violent and primitive, the young French painters, notably artists such as Rouan and Garouste, seem to be trying to renew ties with Western tradition.

1984

S U M M A R Y

MBUYA MASK.
From Pende, Zaïre. Tervuren.
Musée Royal de l'Afrique Centrale

IONIAKÉ MASK. From Tusyan, Burkina Faso. Geneva. Musée Barbier-Müller

MAX ERNST:
HEAD-BIRD. 1934-1935.
Basel. Galerie Beyeler

A CENTURY
OF PRIMITIVISM

NEW YORK
Newly installed in expanded quarters, the Museum of Modern Art attracts crowds with a red-hot exhibition, "Primitivism in Twentieth-Century Art: Affinity of the Tribal and the Modern." Since its opening on October 24, the show hasn't stopped dividing critics. On display are two hundred masks, sculptures, and other objects from Africa, Oceania, and North America, as well as one hundred and fifty works by Gauguin, Matisse, Picasso, Brancusi, Modigliani, Klee, Giacometti, and Ernst. "Primitivism" raises the eternal question of the relationship between modern art and "uncivilized" art during this century.

Both in the galleries and in the catalogue, the pairing-off is often striking, such as the juxtaposition of *Portrait of Madame Matisse* by her husband and a Gabon mask; *The Mask of Fear* by Klee and a god of war from the Southwest United States; *The Nose* by Giacometti and a mask-helmet from New Britain in the Bismarck Archipelago; a bronze by Max Ernst, *Head-Bird*, and a mask from Burkina Faso.

Before Picasso's *Demoiselles d'Avignon* of 1907—which is partly due to a visit made by the artist to the Museum at the Trocadero—Gauguin had left the land of the Renaissance for the Marquesas Islands and Maori beauty. But it has never been a matter of simple formal or visual games.

William Rubin and Kirk Varnedoe, the curators of this exceptional confrontation, say that the main goal of the exhibition is not to find direct influences of tribal arts on modern works, that this is only one theme among others. Speaking of the *Demoiselles d'Avignon*, Varnedoe explains that Picasso showed us that his conception, beyond the formal lessons he learned from tribal art, was modified by the spirit of their view and their powerful magic, which transforms the object rather than imitates it.

Much later, Picasso confessed to André Malraux, who recounts it in *Picasso's Mask*, that he found African art repulsive and fascinating at the same time, and that it seemed hostile and alien. He did not say "sculpture" but "fetishes." Most artists who, like Derain and Vlaminck, were influenced by it saw it that way. They couldn't even differentiate between Africa and Oceania.

They did not know what is known today, namely that African sculpture has its masters, schools, and tendencies, as was demonstrated by Jean Laude, one of the leading specialists in the subject. This was also felt by Carl Einstein, who wrote *Negerplastik* (African sculpture), the first book on African art, written during the

THE RENEWAL OF AMERICAN MUSEUMS

First World War, after visiting the Congo Museum in Tervuren.

The main attraction of the MOMA exhibition is not so much the revelation of the relationship between African Primitivism and Fauvism, Cubism, and German Expressionism, but rather the fact that it shows its influence on Surrealism. Indeed, who would have thought that Giacometti in his Surrealist period and Max Ernst in the 1930s were deeply touched both by Primitivism and the unconscious?

On May 10, 1931, the ethnographic and linguistic Dakar-Djibouti mission left Paris. It was led by Marcel Griaule, a young and brilliant specialist in African studies. His team was also brilliant; the poet Michel Leiris was a member. Two years later, the mission returned with significant material, covered in detail by the magazine *Minotaure*: three thousand five hundred ethnographic objects, six thousand photos, two hundred sound recordings, plus notations in thirty languages and dialects that were mostly unknown in the West until then.

Africa stopped being exotic; Europeans started seeing it as a civilization and a culture, with its own customs, rites, beliefs, and mental attitudes. That is what made it so attractive to the Surrealists.

Primitivism has something supernatural and magic. So it is understandable that our troubled times find deep resonances in it.

The so-called fetishes cherished by artists at the beginning of the century are a thing of the past. The West is exhausted by two thousand five hundred years of Greco-Roman tradition. We owe to Primitivism a new technique, new blood. This is what people take away from the MOMA exhibition.

(See also 1905, 1906, 1907.)

UNITED STATES

The year is particularly successful for American museums. One of the major cultural events is the reopening of the Museum of Modern Art, whose 1939 building was completely transformed by César Pelli. The museum was able to finance the doubling of its space with proceeds from the fifty-two-story luxury apartment tower that was built on its land. The layout of the new MOMA will calm the fears of those who liked the old building, which was small and intimate. The halls are large, and the famous sculpture garden is not shaded by the tower.

The Miami Center for the Fine Arts, designed by Philip Johnson, opens in Miami. In Dallas, the spectacular museum by Edward Larrabee Barnes exhibits a collection of beautiful contemporary American works. Barnes also designed the Museum of New Mexico in Santa Fe

ART IS BECOMING PART OF A CERTAIN LIFESTYLE

and the Art Museum of Fort Lauderdale. Museums are multiplying all over the country, and they all are of top quality. Richard Meier's High Museum of Art, built last year in Atlanta, is hailed. The same purity and elegance of shape is found in Meier's Des Moines Art Center. The postmodern architect Charles Moore is remodeling the museum in Hanover, New Hampshire.

The flourishing of American museums reflects, for the most part, the development of the Sunbelt cities, in the southern regions. Artistic life there used to be strictly local. It is now fascinated by contemporary art. Actually, aspiration toward cultural development is growing across the country. In New York, besides the expansion of MOMA and the Metropolitan Museum of Art, there are plans to extend the Guggenheim and the Whitney museums.

Art is becoming part of a certain lifestyle, especially in large cities. Thousands of young people go to museums as they would have gone for a day in the country in another time. Educational programs are being developed. The museums are organizing children's activities and adult art courses, movies, and conferences.

Cultural and educational programs are offered by the Walker Art Center of Minneapolis and the Brooklyn Museum. There is a long tradition of voluntary work in the United States. Good-willed volunteers are trained by the museums and in turn help conduct workshops. Most museums are private and financed by Maecenases who usually are members of the boards of directors and consultant committees.

The Garden Hall at MOMA.

ANSELM KIEFER: UNTITLED. 1983. Private Collection

ANSELM KIEFER CONQUERS PARIS

PARIS

A crowd gathers at the gallery ARC for Anselm Kiefer. Born into a Catholic family in Donaueschingen in 1945, the artist was marked by his childhood in the Black Forest. He has a tendency toward dreaming and a deep love of nature.

During his studies in Fribourg, then in Düsseldorf, where he was Beuys's student, he was obsessed by the relation between art and crime. He was interested in such figures as Nero and Hitler. He didn't try to identify himself with them, but he wanted to interiorize their madness in order to understand them better. He also tried to relive the Nazi mentality from the inside. During his trips abroad, he shocked people, especially in France, by saluting with the Nazi salute.

Provocation? It seemed that he wanted to assimilate German history in order to better reject it, to get rid of it through catharsis. He said he worked with symbols. He claimed to be the dramatist of German myths. In 1975, he painted *Siegfried Forgetting Brunhilde*, and in 1980, for the Venice biennale, *Germany's Spiritual Heroes*.

Kiefer used, and combined, his senses, imagination, and intelligence. On his canvases he would use various materials: wood, sand, metal, and paper. He did so in *Marching Sand*, which reconstructs battlefields of Prussian wars.

He tries to make people see and think. His paintings, generally large, are like stage spaces. Kiefer is a powerful creator of archetypes. Through his familiarity with certain decors (landscape, woods, paths, itineraries), he follows the great romantic tradition.

THE AFFAIR OF THE FAKE MODIGLIANIS

LEGHORN

During the entire month of July, municipal employees feverishly search the port to find the sculptures that Amedeo Modigliani, unhappy with his work, is said to have thrown into the channel seventy-five years ago. A miracle occurs: Three are found. The most eminent specialists confirm they had indeed come from the hand of the master.

Véra Durbé, director of the local museum of modern art, brims with happiness. Having heard the local legend, she initiated the search. The plan is to use the found pieces in the exhibition "The Other Modigliani," in celebration of the centenary of the artist's birth.

Officially authenticated, the three heads are supposed to be put in the catalogue when events take a dramatic turn. Three art students claim the paternity of the pieces, with proof. They had a videotape showing them making the pieces. Art historians and the newspapers take hold of the affair. The three students create a copy of the Modiglianis before Italian television cameras. The municipal government of Leghorn threatens to resign. Véra Durbé has to be hospitalized. That's how modern art goes . . .

ROGER CHASTEL:
CARD TOWER.
Private Collection

Chastel Unappreciated

A hundred and fifty paintings and drawings born of the marriage between Cubism and Gaston Bachelard are featured in a retrospective on the old fairgrounds in Saint-Germain-en-Laye. Like Bonnard, who took Impressionism to the limits of its fruitfulness, Roger Chastel went to the limit of the possibilities opened up by Picasso and Braque at the beginning of the century. His death in 1981 at the age of eighty-four is ignored by the media, though he was hardly ignored during his lifetime. Chastel was known as the laureate of the 1951 biennale in São Paolo, but, above and beyond the honors, he is revealed here for what he really was: one of the very great painters of his generation. Chastel's themes were those of daily life: humble people making merry, drinkers gathered at the bar in a bistro, still-life compositions with lamp or pitcher.

Beckmann Celebrated

Max Beckmann was already famous in the twenties. Even in France he had his admirers. Moreover, he had lived for more than three years in Paris. In 1931, an exhibit devoted to his work was held at the gallery La Renaissance. With the rise of Nazism, he emigrated to Holland, where he encountered difficulties and was forced to live in semiclandestine circumstances. In 1947, he left for the United States where he taught until his death in 1950. In the two Germanies, then in the United States at the Saint Louis Art Museum and at the Los Angeles County Museum of Art, the centenary of his birth was celebrated this year by retrospective exhibits. Expressionist Realism is apparent throughout his work. Noticeable in his work after 1932 is his increasingly pronounced recourse to a cold, hard personal mythology.

CHARLES DELHAES:
METAPHOR OF THE LAST JUDGMENT
AFTER R. DE LA PASTURE.
Polyptich of Beaune. 1984.
The Artist's Private Collection

Art by Invitation

Before going into retirement, François Mathey, who, in 1960, became the first curator to mount a retrospective of Dubuffet's work, decided to receive two hundred artists of every persuasion "by invitation only" at the Museum of Decorative Arts. Neither a demonstration nor a statement about the present state of affairs, this exhibit is an attempt to respond to the commercial and media overkill that is the current rage in the domain of art. He claims he has gathered "ten percent of the worst and ten percent of the best, but the important thing is that the worst and the best are not necessarily the same for every visitor." An anticonformist to the very end, Mathey did not hesitate to select artists as young as Delhaes or Eugène Leroy.

Modern Art Underground

King Baudouin has revealed a superb underground architectural success, giving Brussels the Museum of Modern Art that it has been waiting for since 1959. The new museum includes sixty-five thousand square feet of floor space arranged "in the form of a Japanese sun," around a light well that is sixty feet deep. Philippe Roberts-Jones, curator of the Royal Museums, and his architect, Roger Bastin, had hoped to erect a building representative of our time. However, the moment it was made public, the project became controversial: It was forbidden to disrupt the urban fabric in a spot laden with memories. Thus evolved the Ali Baba cave, hollowed out of the earth, then filled to overflowing with works by Ensor, Delvaux, Permecke, and Magritte.

IN BRIEF...

UNITED STATES
The Three Nymphs, *in bronze, and* The River, *in lead, by Aristide Maillol are sold for about nine million francs each at Sotheby's in New York.*

FRANCE
At the Musée National d'Art Moderne, a Pierre Bonnard exhibition, organized jointly with the Philipps Collection in Washington and the Dallas Museum of Art, receives five hundred thousand visitors in three months.
   An exhibition of Camille Claudel sculptures at the Rodin Museum.
   The donation by Nina Kandinsky to the Musée National d'Art Moderne is the basis of the exhibition on view at the present. Added to the donation are fifty works borrowed from the most prestigious collections.

SWITZERLAND
An important exhibition of the works of Georg Baselitz from 1960 to 1983 is presented at the Kunsthalle of Basel after having been to London and Amsterdam.

GERMANY
A Sandro Chia exhibition at the Kestnergesellschaft of Hanover.

GAROUSTE RENEWS MYTHOLOGY

PARIS

Who would think, when looking at his paintings, that his master was Marcel Duchamp? Gérard Garouste, at the age of thirty-nine, is the most celebrated French painter of his generation. He stepped on the international stage suddenly, after being selected for "Statements One," the exhibition of the new French painting two years ago in New York.

At the end of the 1960s, after Garouste had graduated from art school, art was replaced by speeches on art. An end had to be put to that situation. Indeed, if art was everywhere, in a bottle rack, a bike wheel, a public toilet, it wasn't anywhere. That is why Garouste returned to tradition.

He could be slotted in the Neoclassic lines of de Chirico in the 1920s, and, further back, of Tintoretto. He mainly paints mythological scenes, but as reviewed by Freud and Lacan. "We cannot escape our culture, but we must know how to outsmart it," he said. "When I paint, I return to Delacroix's soft tones and to Ingres' thin layers. At that point, I do my best to avoid them."

When Garouste paints a reclining man, he doesn't want the viewer to know whether he rests, sleeps, is dead, or is injured. He does not look for narration or description, but for ambiguity, like Alfred Hitchcock's movies, where a cloud of milk darkening a teacup lets the audience in on the drama—or prevents it from being discovered. The story of the movie lets another story be discovered. It is what Garouste tries to suggest anyway.

GÉRARD GAROUSTE: ORION THE MAGNIFICENT, ORION THE INDIAN. 1981-1982. Paris. MNAM

FRANÇOIS ROUAN: UNTITLED. 1966. Paris. MNAM

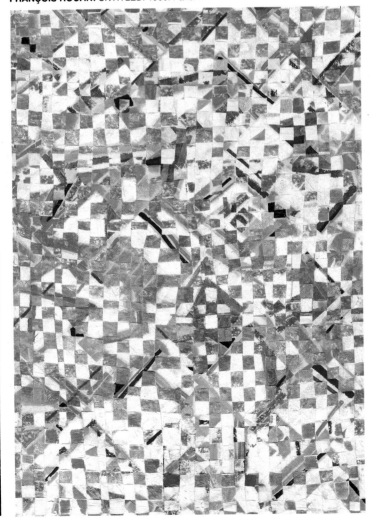

ROUAN'S WEAVINGS

PARIS

From October 27 to January 2, François Rouan, who is forty-one years old, exhibits at the contemporary galleries of the Georges Pompidou Center. His "weavings"—painted cloth ribbons woven diagonally, where every motif is covered in panels and forms a complex rhythmic figure—have not been shown in Paris since 1975.

Acknowledged worldwide, he exhibits at the Pierre Matisse Gallery in New York and is commented on by Jacques Lacan. The psychoanalyst sees the structure of modern thinking in the weaver's work. Rouan is praised by the fans of "cultivated" art as well as by French painting traditionalists. He has returned to work in France after living for several years at the Villa Medicis in Rome: "I want, somewhat foolishly, to paint closer to my real experience, a fragmented and burst reality. What actually counts is the effect of concentration."

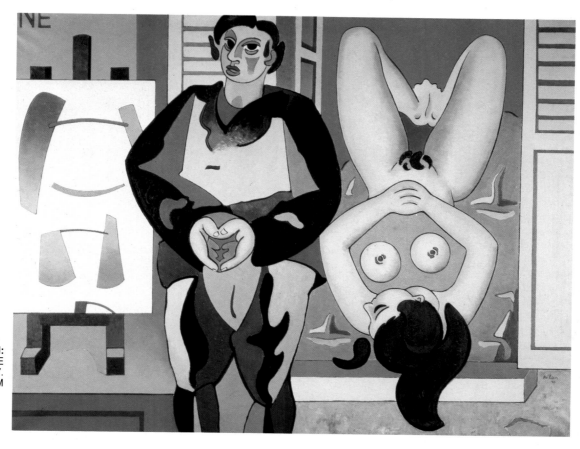

JEAN HÉLION:
AGAINST THE
GRAIN. 1947.
Paris. MNAM

HÉLION: FROM ABSTRACTION TO FIGURATION

PARIS

After years of abstract painting in the style of Mondrian, Jean Hélion knows more than anyone else about fruits and vegetables, how to clean a soup bowl, how to pull a hat over one's eyes. The most impressive feature in his painting may be his division into two parts, unequal in interest and value.

He has always denied that he is divided. Undoubtedly, his abstract period allowed him to learn the trade. But how boring it was! We must have the courage of saying it. In turn, Hélion at the age of eighty is one of the major painters of the day. His figurative work can be seen once more in his retrospective at the Musée d'Art Moderne in Paris, where some two hundred canvases and drawings are exhibited.

Was it youthful pride or a metaphysical mistake? In the 1930s, when he was friends with Théo Van Doesburg, Hélion only spoke of the universality of art, composition, and the primacy of the spirit. True depth came to him one summer when he fell in love with a cabbage: "What is a cabbage? What type of creation does it define? Today, August

"WHEN I FALL IN LOVE WITH AN OBJECT, I SEE THE ENTIRE CREATION"

15, I admit that I had never noticed that the leaves turn around themselves to form a heart. I only had eyes for the gaps between them." Later he said, "When I fall in love with an object, I see the entire creation."

There is no doubt that Hélion is one of the innovators of still life. We have only to look at his cabbages—"roses under a different name"—and his pumpkins, herrings, vegetable-store scales, and shoes of all descriptions. They are poetic and attractive. And his beloved French bread! While Magritte converts it into a blimp sailing through the skies, Hélion simply puts it on a table or a chair with infinite mystery.

However, it seems that he reaches his true greatness in a subject that touches us all: the man in a business suit. There are some magnificent figures in the exhibition: lighting a cigarette, going up steps, riding a bike, looking out the window, reading the paper: "The simplest coat makes a superb column for the head, a stern draped support. I love the work of the scissors, the V in the lapel, at an angle from the region where the tie goes down." And his women!

Their breasts are hard as weights under their dresses. It is just the opposite of the characters of the maddening Dubuffet, who are all yellow teeth and stomachaches.

Hélion goes to the United States often, sometimes staying a while, at a time when painters usually cross the Atlantic in the opposite direction. Between the World Wars, he lived in New York and Virginia. He loves streets, which he considers the paragon of all shows. He loves markets, a feast for the eye. "Deep down, you are a naturalist," Mondrian told him at the height of Hélion's abstract period. The Dutch painter knew what he was talking about; before being consumed with the rectangle and the square, he painted cows grazing in the field.

Pignon is recognized, at the age of eighty, as one of the greatest living French painters. His retrospective at the Grand Palais in Paris hallows a work that, for almost half a century, has not once ceased to run counter to all styles, no matter where they come from, and that now proclaims its liberty for all to see. The event coincides with the death of Dubuffet, a recognized artist for many years now. What will the future of art be? The question is asked once again in the last years of the century at an exhibition unlike any other, "The Immaterialists," held at the Georges Pompidou Center.

1985
SUMMARY

ÉDOUARD PIGNON:
THE BLUE OF THE SEA
(LA COUDOULIÈRE). 1978.
Private Collection

PIGNON: THE VICTORY OVER REALITY

PARIS

Édouard Pignon says, "I was lucky to have Picasso in my life. For me, Picasso was like a holiday." They became friends in 1936, but their friendship flourished in 1951, when Picasso invited Pignon to "live a painter's life" in Vallauris.

As of February 22, Pignon, who is eighty years old, can be seen at the Grand Palais, on three floors and sixteen thousand square feet—in the very halls where Picasso exhibited in 1966. One hundred and fifty-five large paintings cover forty years of painting, from the Ostende period to the recent work *The Ladies of the Sun*. There are also watercolors, posters, sketchbooks, books, and drawings. The ensemble is huge, colorful, exalting, magnificent.

His love for painting must have started in the bar run by his mother while his father worked in the mines. It was during the First World War, when British troops arrived in Marles-les-Mines. Little Édouard had red hair. A British soldier who came by for a beer in the bar noticed the child and drew his portrait in colored pencils. The magic of resemblance was to change his life.

Not immediately, however, because Pignon engaged in thirty-five occupations. He was a "pit boy": "I worked in the mine myself. Not for long, I hated it. When it was sunny outside, going down in the dark pit was terrible." He was a ceiling plasterer; unemployed; an employee at the Citroën plant; a layout artist: a walk-on with Dullin and Artaud. Only later could he live, albeit poorly, on his art. He had the school of hard knocks and evening courses. He suffered injury to his pride: One Saturday evening, in one of the galleries on the Left Bank, he was leafing through some prints when he was called to account by the dealer, who was suspicious of Pignon's rough worker's hands. Pignon was the opposite of intellectualism and snobbery.

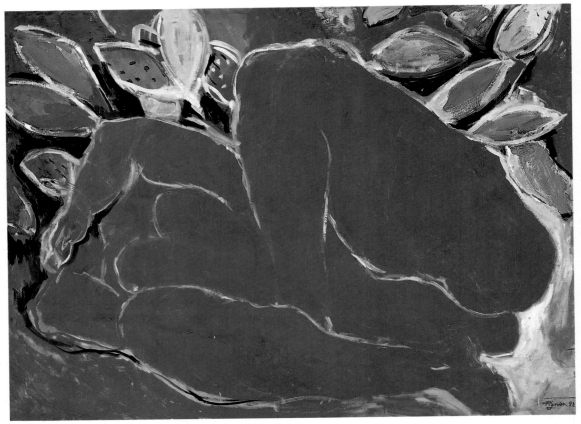

ÉDOUARD PIGNON: GREAT SCARLET NUDE WITH CACTUSES. 1982

Édouard Pignon and Pablo Picasso at Vallauris in 1951.

In his youth, he could go up a ladder with a two-hundred-and-twenty-pound sack on his back. He knew the difficulties of life. In his paintings, he said, he tried to "make reality yield."

This search for reality is found in each one of his series. Immediately after the Second World War, he painted fishing boats trapped in ice in Ostende at twenty-five degrees centigrade below zero. When he arrived in the South, he took on the olive tree. One of the main paintings of the exhibition is *Trunk of an Olive Tree*, an enormous tree he found on a summer's day on the Bandol highway. Later, he went back to the land of the mines, to see the cockfights, to peek through the grille, his hands as sensitive as an oscillograph, there amidst the blood of the victims and the crowd of bettors.

This painter who came from the North was particularly fond

of beach scenes. In the series *Divers*, men with small heads between stretched arms step into the water with their huge feet. The series *Waves* made him confess, "I am afraid of the wave, when I am alone facing it, when I see the rock and this huge, grumbling thing." He is fascinated by its explosions during mistrals or on stormy days. Hokusai would have loved it. Then the *Nudes*: upside down, bending over, crouching, crumpled, asleep, white, red, burning.

His space is close to us, a palpable, open space, in contrast to the illusionist space of tradition. Pignon lets us see the invisible that seems so real. There are no representations, in the theatrical sense, in his work, or descriptions, but something much more complete that tries, above all, to function.

Today, the artist, freer than ever, does not hesitate to paint his bathing women blue, to put his long-dead friend Picasso in a boat next to him in Antibes, or to transform sun shades into chandeliers. It is clear why the little pit lad detested the black hole of the mine. He didn't know it, but he was a clairvoyant. In 1966, during an important exhibition of his work at the Musée National d'Art Moderne, a self-appointed Neo-neo-neo-Dadaist critic said that Pignon's was the kind of painting that entitled an artist to break Pignon's brushes. But not everybody thinks that way. As soon as he became minister of culture, Jack Lang wanted this exhibition arranged. The National Center for Plastic Arts organized it. At the same time, the gallery Beaubourg exhibits a tribute to Picasso by Pignon.

(See also 1952, 1966, 1977.)

IN PIGNON'S WORDS

Art is not cumulative, additive. One cannot say that one picks up Matisse and carries on. Matisse said all there was to say about Matisse. He did open certain doors, but he said all there was to say in his own creative work. One cannot say that one takes Picasso and is going to continue him. That is impossible. He gives some direction, but you have to start all over again.

The artist is not a destroyer, he is a builder. In other words, art takes a positive position; otherwise, there is no art.

There is no law that determines whether a painting has been completed or not. There is been exhausted makes no sense. It is an idealistic position that may bear some fruit, like certain nihilist ideas in the past. But with no vital force.

Truth is what the canvas says. It is not only intentions. Intentions are true only if they are realized.

When material alone guides the artist, that's not good. The artist must dominate materials. His role is to make something rare out of this material, because the mind takes possession of it. Materials in themselves are nothing. Whether it is plastic or gouache or watercolor, materials are at the service of

ÉDOUARD PIGNON: WHITE LADIES. 1984

the artist's evidence. The esthetic of the times is something quite profound that has nothing to do with taste. It is a different understanding of the world.

One engages in the art of the present, not of the future.

When I speak of nature, I am not speaking just of forests, animals, and grass, but also of people's work and thought processes. What one thinks is part of nature, part of the world.

What can you gain in a single lifetime? Nothing better than the desire to fight.

Looking at things will always be different. To say that the forms of this world have what the artist wishes to say. One can be a perfect "traditionalist," or even less than a "traditionalist," and yet use ultramodern materials.

The artist does not know what he is doing. He wants to attain something he vaguely perceives. He works his way toward a solution.

More than anything else, there is the question of work, of people who are capable of carrying a heavy workload more easily than others because they have learned how to work, and because, for them, work is a necessity.

It is a question of knowing at first. That's the hardest part.

THE IMMATERIAL ARTISTS AT BEAUBOURG

PARIS

What will the art of the future be? An exhibition that opens on March 28, occupying the entire fifth floor of the Georges Pompidou Center, tries to show it.

The exhibition was to be called "New Materials and Creation." But that didn't mean much, and there was a risk of eclecticism and confusion. Jean-François Lyotard, the sixty-two-year-old philosopher from the former university of Vincennes who organized the exhibition, suggested calling it "Les Immatériaux"— "The Immaterials."

"This title came by itself: I thought that, in fact, what is interesting is that it is the new technology that is the substitute for mental operations and not, as in the past, for physical operations." Indeed, for Lyotard, this is the *post*modern age, the modern age having been born two centuries ago—the modern age: encyclopedic, materialistic, historicist. "The distinction between mind substance and matter substance becomes obsolete, it is unable to express our way of living and thinking," he says. In his view, the transformation is so complete that painting is not able to express it.

Modulatory Sequence-Language Labyrinth at the exhibition "The Immaterials" at the Georges Pompidou Center.

Therefore, there are few paintings in the exhibition. It is divided into twenty-five sites, or zones. The walls are covered with a monotonous gray. Photographs of the cosmos, metals seen under an electronic microscope, images exploding or rephotographed, holograms, interactive programs, voice fragments linking the public with today's reality, of which it sometimes loses track—some show!

The stunning innovation of "The Immaterials" is that it addresses the ear as well as the eye. At the entrance, the visitor is handed a pair of earphones. A recording plays a site-by-site narration. The texts are from Plato, Proust, Artaud, Michaux. Lyotard is familiar with the classics. It is a pity that his visual culture is less extensive. With the exception of Duchamp, he unfortunately exhibits only inferior imitators while ignoring artists such as Schöffer or Kowalski, who are the only great Immaterials in today's art.

The Pont-Neuf packaged by Christo.

CHRISTO PACKAGES THE PONT-NEUF

PARIS

From September 23 to October 7, the Pont-Neuf was wrapped in a huge fireproof canvas of forty-three thousand square feet, held in place by seven miles of cables. A team of technicians, including mountain guides from Chamonix, performed the delicate operation. A hundred students explained to passersby the enormous effort made by Christo, a fifty-year-old American of Bulgarian origin, who is celebrated in art circles worldwide. Before taking on the Pont-Neuf, the artist made other monumental packagings. In Little Bay, Australia, he covered a portion of a rocky coast with canvas. The cost of the Pont-Neuf operation, paid by the artist, was nineteen million francs. The procedure, however, is not entirely new. As early as 1920, Man Ray packaged "an enigmatic object."

JEAN-FRANÇOIS LYOTARD: WHAT IS POSTMODERN?

Jean-François Lyotard, sixty-two-year-old philosopher and art theoretician, is curator of the "The Immaterials," an exhibition he designed and mounted for the Georges Pompidou Center. In his recent works, Lyotard has focused on the Postmodern, a concept he explained in *La Condition postmoderne,* published in 1979. More recently, he has explained the term in *Réponse à la question: "Qu'est-ce que le postmoderne?"* (answer to the question: "What is the Postmodern?" We have reprinted the conclusion of that article here, so that the exhibition at Beaubourg might be better understood. In fact, the Postmodern does not take its place in the aftermath of the "modern," nor in opposition to it, as does the Transavantgarde. What is Postmodern is already a part of the modern. We simply cannot see it.

Postmodern is that which, in modernism, alleges the unpresentable within the presentation. The Postmodern is that which rebels against the consolation of good manners, against the concensus of a taste allowing people a mutual feeling of nostalgia for the impossible. It is that which seeks new ways of being presented, not for the enjoyment of it, but to make the existence of the unpresentable more apparent. A Postmodern artist or writer is in the same situation as a philosopher: the work the artist completes, or the text the writer creates, is not governed in principle by preestablished rules. The work or the text cannot be judged by a determinant judgment, by the application to this work, to this text, of known categories. These rules and categories are precisely what the work and the text are seeking. Therefore, the artist and the writer work without rules. Their job is to establish the rules of what will be created. That is why the work and the text have the properties of an event, and that is why they occur too late for their author. Rather, saying the same thing another way, their realization begins too soon. Postmodern would be understood as the paradox of the future (post) anterior (modo). It seems to me that the essay (Montaigne) is Postmodern, while the fragment (the Atheneum) is modern.

It must be clear once and for all that it is not for us to supply reality, but to invent allusions to the conceivable, which cannot be presented. It should also be clear that we must not expect this task to reconcile in any way the "language games," which, under the name of faculties, Kant knew to be separated by an abyss, and which only the transcendant illusion (Hegel's) can hope to encompass in true unity. But Kant also knew that terror was the price for this illusion. The nineteenth and twentieth centuries have given us our fill of terror. We have paid enough for nostalgia for

Medusa by Takis at the exhibition "The Immaterials" at the Georges Pompidou Center.

the whole and the singular, for the reconciliation of concept and feeling, of transparent and communicable experience. Beneath the clamor for a relaxation of discipline and pacification can be heard the muttering of the desire to begin terror anew, to realize the hallucination of grasping hold of reality. Our answer to that is: Let us do battle against the whole, let us bear witness to the unpresentable, let us activate differences, let us save the honor of that which we call by name.

JEAN-FRANÇOIS LYOTARD
Réponse à la question: "Qu'est-ce que le postmoderne?" *(Excerpt)*

ART ON THE ISLAND

LAC DE VASSIVIÈRE
The miracle of the Île-aux-Pierres! Two years ago, nobody believed it would be possible when Marc Sautivet, a teacher of mathematics in Limoges and a modern-art devotee, launched an international art competition. Fifteen sculptors were selected to make works of granite, the traditional stone of the area.

Not only are the fifteen sculptures in place, but they are perfectly integrated into the site. Vassivière-en-Limousin is a twenty-five-hundred-acre artificial lake with sloping banks built in 1947. People spend their summer vacation here. The sculptures are part of the scene. Newly married couples have their picture taken with *The Shepherd* by Pierre Digan. Swimmers hang their towels to dry on the archaic arcs of Linder.

JEAN-FRANÇOIS DEMEURE: SCULPTURE. Lac de Vassivière-en-Limousin

The huge metaphysical table by Prentice, looking like something between an altar and a reclining woman, is used for picnics. On June 21, people celebrate St. John next to a minimalist sculpture by François Bouillon, which is decorated with thirty-two cups with burning oil.

Jung regretted that modern man, with his verbose and rationalistic nature, forgot how to hide eggs in the grass at Easter or to decorate a Christmas tree without trying to know why he does it. Jung saw it as a serious danger for the future of civilization. Vassivière is the link with our common irrational core. It is like in the Neolithic, when there was a fairy stone or a druid table. One says "art on the island" as one would say "art in the streets." It is proof that there is no final gap between modern creators and the public.

PABLO PICASSO: STUDIES. 1920. Paris. Musée Picasso

PICASSO AT THE SALÉ MANSION

PARIS
The city where Cubism was born now has a Picasso museum. Installed at the Salé Mansion, one of the most beautiful Marais houses, which was totally renovated, it is inaugurated on September 23 by François Mitterand, president of the Republic.

The collection contains, on a thirty-two-thousand-square-foot surface, two hundred and three paintings, one hundred and fifty-eight sculptures, twenty-three reliefs, eighty-eight ceramics, over three thousand drawings and prints, plus sketches and manuscripts, all donated as payment against their inheritance tax by the heirs of the artist, who died on April 8, 1973. All of his periods are represented, from the blue and the "metamorphosis," which was influenced by Surrealism, to the works of his last years.

At the end of the Second World War, the state only owned three works by the genius. Two years later, in 1947, Picasso donated a dozen paintings to the Musée National d'Art Moderne, which are now at Beaubourg. *The Muse* and *Enameled Saucepan*, pure masterpieces, are among them. Thanks to the heirs' donation and a few complementary gifts, the museum is richer than the Picasso Museum in Barcelona. Restoration and installation at the Salé Mansion cost fifty million francs. When the legacy tax was calculated, in 1974, the heirs' donation was estimated at two hundred ninety million francs, that is, about a quarter of the painter's personal assets. Today, the value of the collection is impossible to calculate.

As soon as it opens, the museum attracts crowds of tourists and art lovers. Over one thousand visitors a day walk through the portals.

Mason Exhibit at Beaubourg

At the age of sixty-three, Raymond Mason, a native of Birmingham who had always lived in Paris, affirms his status as one of the greatest contemporary sculptors, as much for the originality of his style as for the originality of his well-known themes, reminiscent of Pop Art. The exhibit devoted to his work at the Georges Pompidou Center is proof of this. Whether pleasant or threatening, his themes are an attempt to reflect the most characteristic features of our society. His *Departure of Fruit and Vegetables from the Heart of Paris* is, in his opinion, "the last image of the natural in our cities." His *Barcelona Tramway* is not just any old tramway, but probably the one that killed Gaudí in 1926. Mason is one of the rare artists of today who has succeeded in renewing the image of reality, and he means to make people think as well as see.

The Gentle Violence of Émile Hecq

He considers himself "misunderstood" but not "unknown," and he is right. The retrospective that Mons devotes to the sixty-one-year-old Émile Hecq reveals a painter whose importance should no longer escape anyone. It is striking to see how Hecq uses his brush to chop, incise, excise, and slash the human form and face, as few artists today can do with such passion. He could be placed with the Expressionists, and his works bear affinities to the Cobra esthetic. But there is a "gentleness" in his painting, and it is difficult to know whether it emanates from the way he handles the human form or rather from his use of color, or from both at once. To depict the gourds he observed growing in his garden, Hecq assembled patches of color with the same vitality he used in painting the human body.

German Art since 1960

Prince Franz von Wittelsbach has donated his collection of contemporary German art to the regional state of Bavaria. The collection, exhibited at the National Gallery of Modern Art in Munich, gives a representative overview of artistic development in the German Federal Republic over the last twenty

RAYMOND MASON: THE DEPARTURE OF FRUIT AND VEGETABLES FROM THE HEART OF PARIS ON FEBRUARY 28, 1969. 1969-1971

years. Thus the city of Munich has inherited one of Beuys's most significant works, *The End of the Twentieth Century,* composed of forty-four scattered blocks of basalt, each one of which has had a chip removed, then replaced and covered with a piece of felt. As far as painting is concerned, the entire Neofigurative movement is there, from Baselitz, Schönebeck, and Penck to Polke, Kiefer, and Blinky Palermo. The Austrian Arnulf Rainer has been added to this group with works from the fifties.

Saatchi, a Great Patron

The recent opening of the fabulous Saatchi collection to the public, at 98A Boundary Road in the northern section of London, shows Charles Saatchi to be a great patron. He had begun in 1970, when he and his brother Maurice started Saatchi Saatchi, an advertising company that became one of the foremost agencies in the world. That same year, Charles acquired a drawing by Sol Lewitt, the beginning of a collection that now includes five hundred works by about fifty artists. Charles Saatchi has followed the bent of his passions in his purchases. Notable among the works he has bought are eighteen canvases by Baselitz, fifteen by Warhol, twenty-three by Kiefer, and twenty-seven by Schnabel.

SIGMAR POLKE:
CAMELEONARDO
DA WILLING. 1979.
Paris. MNAM

ART BRUT LOSES ITS GENIUS

SAINT-PAUL

The man was difficult, irritable, pedantic. He quarrelled with most of his fans. Jean-Louis Prat, director of the Maeght Foundation, worked for three years on this retrospective. For much of the time, there were doubts that it could be held —because of the changing moods of the artist. But on May 12, Jean Dubuffet dies, in his eighty-eighth year. From now on, only his *oeuvre* counts. The one

boiled water. Without roots. Without attachments. Losing his sight." Well, here he is the opposite. The most amazing feature of this great lecturer is, first and foremost, his pictorial quality.

It is so much more astonishing because Dubuffet's genius manifested itself late in life, around 1943-1945, when he was already over forty, after various failures and after he had given up several times. Not that he was without talent—in his adolescence, he

HE WAS INSPIRED BY THE ART OF THE MENTALLY ILL

hundred and fifty paintings, sculptures, and drawings brought together for the summer at Saint-Paul-de-Vence are an invitation to the first overall view of his art.

The exhibition is impressive. It is feared that Dubuffet's art would be intellectual, because no contemporary painter has written, commented, and lectured more. His opinion of the intellectual is known: "A person without horizon, opaque, without vitamins, a swimmer in

painted his grandparents in the manner of Watteau—but he did not want merely to create more "museum art."

"It is naive to think that the poor facts and works of the past that are preserved are necessarily the best of that time. They have been preserved only because a small group chose and applauded them, eliminating all the others," Dubuffet wrote. He was interested by high fever, the fight against fate, and savage values. He liked art by

Jean Dubuffet.

the mentally ill, made by "people unspoiled by artistic culture," and which he called "Art Brut" (art in the rough). The mentally ill were *his* African artists without whom Cubism would not have been possible. They allowed him to reach the same breakthrough that Picasso reached through a Dogon mask.

This search for physical beginnings is everywhere in Dubuffet's work. It is in his desertlike and cataclysmic "Materiologies" and in his rustic assembled paintings, and in his stumbling characters, closer to the atheist, indifferent, modern bum than to Monsieur Bertin's portrait by Ingres. And in the endless *L'hourloupe* series. Dubuffet was one of the rare French painters of his generation with an international reputation. A very great artist is dead.

(See also 1944, 1945, 1961, 1973.)

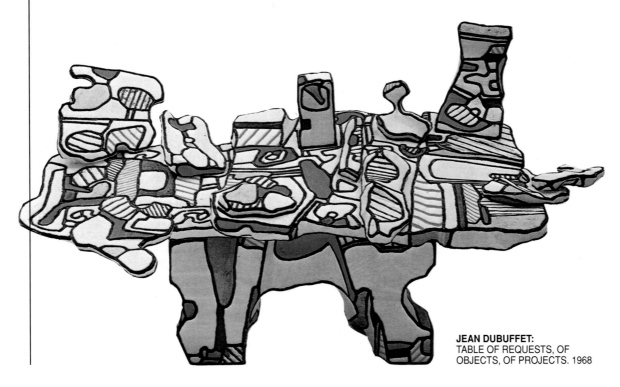

JEAN DUBUFFET: TABLE OF REQUESTS, OF OBJECTS, OF PROJECTS. 1968

MATHIEU AT THE PALACE OF THE POPES

GEORGES MATHIEU: THE MASSACRE OF THE 269. 1985. The Artist's Private Collection

AVIGNON

He is the one who launched the shocking credo "Freedom is the void!" He is the one who claimed that Lyrical Abstractionism, which he initiated, is the greatest revolution since Aristotle. He became famous through a sleight of hand: He made a painting in three seconds, in front of an audience, a record never surpassed. His name is Georges Mathieu, sixty-four years old, painter, poster artist, glazer, decorative artist, architect, medal maker, and, to top it off, a member of the Beaux-Arts Academy.

One hundred of his works are exhibited at the Palace of the Popes in Avignon—thirty years of signs, spots, calligraphy, culminating with *The Massacre of the 269,* made in June just before the exhibition.

The painting exposes the savage destruction by a Soviet fighter plane of a Korean Air Boeing 747 thousands of feet above Sakhalin Island, the night from August 31 to September 1, 1983. Better than any lecture or photograph, the painting ex-

presses the burning of the skies, torn apart by two hundred and sixty-nine senseless deaths. Because the disaster took place at the border of the visible, it can only be denounced with sufficient force by an artist who knows everything about the linguistics and embryology of signs, as well as topology and modern mathematics.

AN OEUVRE *THAT SPEAKS THE LANGUAGE OF THE SECOND HALF OF THE CENTURY*

The painting reflects Mathieu's indignation generated by the bloodshed. He is the same in *The Quartering of François Ravaillac* except that the murder of so many people is a current event. We deal with an act of a dictatorship that believes that everything it does is permissible. A half century ago, Picasso's *Guernica* denounced another massacre of the innocent. It may be an absolute novelty that an artist dares to point a finger at a slaughter perpetrated by a Marxist country.

The Avignon exhibition is not limited to this success. As long ago as 1954, Mathieu wrote, "With Lyrical Abstractionism, semantic laws are reversed. For ages, for any given thing a sign was invented; therefore, when a sign is given, it would be viable and true if it finds its incarnation." While signs in a figurative work are pregnant with references to reality, which prevents them from acting autonomously and directly, Mathieu wants signs to be efficient by themselves in his work. He did not hesitate to attack Jackson Pollock; for the American's Automatism, springing from Surrealism, "encloses" an incipient figuration.

André Malraux said that Mathieu was the first Western calligrapher. The reference to Oriental calligraphy, with its rapidity of execution, tense graphism, and supreme elegance

is patent throughout his work. He shares with Mark Tobey the description of "best Japanist." But Mathieu is completely devoid of exoticism. Moreover, he has no tenderness for philosophers. He finds them sophistic and vain. He grasps the most daring contemporary scientific accomplishments and the process of spiritualization that issues from them in arts. "In the world that turns around things," he writes, "the artist is the last person who can recenter humanity on humans, if he succeeds in attracting his brothers and reassembling them on the front of spiritual forces."

Painting is to be signs, writing, or nothing at all. It is a difficult position, and this is obvious in Avignon, where many works are merely decorative. Yet, the exhibition leaves the impression of an *oeuvre* that speaks the language of the second half of the century. Mathieu's acrobatics and provocations sometimes obscure this fact.

(See also 1951.)

Charlatan or genius? Joseph Beuys, whom some unhesitatingly call the greatest German artist since Dürer, is dead in Düsseldorf at the age of sixty-five. It is difficult at this point to give a definitive judgment of him and his work. But no one in our century was as criticized, adored, and abhorred, except perhaps Salvador Dali. Daniel Buren, another shocking artist, erects columns, or cylinders, in the courtyard of the Palais-Royal in Paris, and is the talk of town: "Shameful!" "We are being ridiculed!" The great battles of the beginning of the century are still being waged today, though they have been moved elsewhere. All this comes at the very time when new museums are opening everywhere. It is a sign that art, more diverse than ever before, is doing fine.

1986

S U M M A R Y

GREAT MASTERS

**Joseph Beuys: Charlatan or Genius?
In Beuys's Words**

DEVELOPMENTS

**The Scandal of Buren's Pillars
Prassinos' Way of the Cross**

ART NEWS

**Braque Beats His Own Record
Michel Tourlière: the Woven Works
Futurismo, Futurismi
Lukaschewski, the Portraitist
In Brief**

AVANT-GARDE

**Giacometti between Yesterday and Tomorrow
Recondo, Painter and Sculptor**

MUSEUMS

**A Museum for the Ludwig Collection
MOCA Challenges MOMA**

JOSEPH BEUYS:
CHAIR WITH FAT. 1964.
Darmstadt. Hessisches Landesmuseum

Joseph Beuys during the *7000 Oaks* "action" at the 1982 Documenta in Kassel.

JOSEPH BEUYS:
FLOWER AND SUN. 1947.
Gand. Museum van
Hedendaagse Kunst

JOSEPH BEUYS: CHARLATAN OR GENIUS?

DÜSSELDORF
The Lehmbruck prize of the city of Duisburg was awarded to Joseph Beuys last year, but it was handed to him officially only this January 12. It is his last public appearance. He dies nine days later in Düsseldorf at the age of sixty-five. For many years, he was a major figure of contemporary art, acknowledged as such worldwide. He was considered to be the most famous German artist in almost five hundred years, since Dürer. He is the only German artist of this generation whom America, whose Guggenheim Museum staged a Beuys exhibition in 1979, envied Europe for.

On the occasion of the Lehmbruck ceremony, Beuys delivers a speech that in a way is his last will and testament. He explains that his chance discovery, dur-

ing the last war, of a catalogue of the work of Wilhelm Lehmbruck determined his orientation. Through this catalogue he came to understand what sculpture could be. In 1947, on his return from the Crimea, where his Stuka dive bomber was shot down during the war, he enrolled at the Fine Art School of Düsseldorf.

ALCHEMIC RESONANCES ARE FOUND AT THE CORE OF HIS WORK

He said he knew nothing about plastic arts. Lehmbruck gave him what no other sculptor could have given him: artistic intuition. Lehmbruck, whose work resembles Expressionism, pushed the expression of the artist's inner necessity to its limits.

In the 1960s, Beuys raised a

scandal with the motto "Everybody is an artist!" He was teaching in Düsseldorf. The slogan was unacceptable to traditionalists because it denied the usefulness of artistic training. Beuys became the embodiment of provocative irresponsibility.

He did love to provoke. His every exhibition was accompanied by declarations and discussions. He delighted in holding forth on theories on life, human, religion, and politics, and ended up by making his thinking seem confused.

He became famous more by his "actions" than by his work. In 1965 he explained art for three hours, with his face pow-

dered with gold and holding a dead rabbit in his arms. His omnipresent overcoat and his hat perpetually attached to a sad-clown face enhanced the spectacular side of his character.

In his sculpting, Beuys introduced lard, margarine, brass, felt, and honey, perhaps as a consequence of deep obsessions caused by being a prisoner during the war, but also of his being a disciple of Rudolf Steiner, the initiator of anthroposophy, who died in 1925. Unlike Duchamp, Beuys not only handled concepts but the very matter, rich with alchemist resonances, that is found at the core of his work. The animal was for him the archetype of the natural forces from which humans should have never become estranged.

In the December 23, 1978, issue of the daily *Die Frankfurter*

IN BEUYS'S WORDS

Rundschau, Beuys, who was also an ecologist, published "An Appeal to Alternatives," in which he expressed his ideas for the reform of society. Capitalism and Communism, he thought, led humanity to a dead end. The relationship between industrial society and nature is completely perverted. A third path must be found: "social sculpture, which molds humans as an artist."

His sculptures and drawings reached exorbitant prices. Yet, the art object as finished product did not interest him, and he condemned the art trade. He said that his "works" were mere documents and traces of his "life acts." They were made merely to reconstitute the creative process. Hence, he acted like a sorcerer or shaman, as though inspired by the origins of the creative spirit.

At the time of the exhibition in the Guggenheim, in 1979, the weekly *Der Spiegel* featured Beuys on the cover of the November 5 issue. It was an unusual honor for a living artist. *Der Spiegel* asked, "Is Beuys a charlatan or a genius?" It is not possible to know what the future will answer. Yet, the "action" that he staged at Kassel's Documenta in 1982 is perhaps the most significant for his spirit.

In front of the Fredericianum Museum, where the famous exhibition is held each year, Beuys unloads a mountain of heavy basalt blocks. They are withdrawn, one by one, as seven thousand oak trees are planted instead. A symbolic fight against the transformation of the planet into a desert, it is a union of ecology and art, a joining of the mineral and vegetal reigns that obsessed the artist. It is the best expression of Beuys' belief that the artist intervenes between history and nature in order to reestablish what is separated and torn apart.

(See also 1981.)

The error begins the minute you take it into your head to buy a painting and a frame.

In every human there exists a potential creative faculty. This does not mean that each person is a painter or a sculptor, but that there is latent creativity in every domain of human effort.

I keep coming back to this expression: In the beginning was the Word. The Word is a form. It is, quite simply, the principle of evolution. This principle of evolution can now come forth, emerge from humankind; the old

My sole aim is to show, in a constructive manner, the monstrously undeveloped possibilities that are within us, possibilities that we unfortunately use so rarely, and which we ought to use.

For me, the necessary condition in the evolution of a sculpture is that an inner form first appear to the mind and to the skilled eye, and then that it be expressed in the modeling of material.

We need the soil of this earth, on which every person feels himself, and knows him-

JOSEPH BEUYS: PALAZZO REGALE. 1985. Naples. Museo de Capodimonte

evolution is over. That is the reason for the crisis. Anything new that happens on this planet must be brought about by humans. But it cannot come about if the source has dried up, that is to say, if the beginning has no form. So I am calling for a better form of thought, of feeling, of willpower. Those are true esthetic criteria. But they should not be judged solely on the basis of their exterior forms. They lend themselves to judgment while they are still within the individual where they can be observed. That is when we suddenly become aware that we are spiritual beings.

self, to be a creative being, acting upon the world. The slogan "Everybody is an artist," which has aroused such anger, and which people continue to misunderstand, refers to the transformation of the social body. Each of us can, even must, take part in this transformation so that we can bring it about as quickly as possible. That is why I create expressions that, though they may have other meanings when translated, have the same basic principles.

Creativity is solely that which can de defined and justified as the science of freedom.

Daniel Buren's pillars in the Cour d'Honneur of the Palais-Royal in Paris.

THE SCANDAL OF BUREN'S PILLARS

PARIS

Isn't it a shame? Are they mocking us? That's what people say at the courtyard of the Palais-Royal, where the pillars created by the sculptor Daniel Buren are finally accepted, by decision of François Léotard, the minister of culture. The pillars had been commissioned by Monsieur Léotard's predecessor, and the site had been opened without filing an official declaration to the mayor of Paris.

At one time, the work was almost discontinued. It is a monumental ensemble, with a surface of thirty-two thousand square feet and composed of two hundred and sixty striped pillars, or cylinders of white and black Pyrenean granite marble. Their heights differ. Some sit in three trenches which are covered with a grating and have a small spring flowing at the bottom. Visitors can rest on the lower pillars and walk on the grating as on a subway grating. At night, luminous rays, red at one side, green at the other, sweep the ground like beacons at an airport.

Although the critics are for the most part horrified, the public seems to enjoy walking through this sculpture garden. The courtyard has become a social center, a salon where people talk and stroll.

Buren sees that his work integrates well with the site and asks why it causes so many polemics. The courtyard used to be a parking space for the clerks in the Rue de Valois. If Buren's work is compared with Pol Bury's metallic sphere installed not far away around two fountains and perfectly integrated with the spirit of the site, a question can be raised as to whether the columns are in the right place.

PRASSINOS' WAY OF THE CROSS

SAINT-RÉMY-DE-PROVENCE

Mario Prassinos died last year at age sixty-nine. This year, his series of eleven mural paintings was installed at Notre-Dame-de-Pitié, a small sixteenth-century church renovated for the occasion. Notre-Dame-de-Pitié (Our Lady of Mercy) used to be invoked whenever calamities occurred. The faithful came seeking protection against the plague, drought, and hunger. Prassinos' eleven paintings here include a *Shroud* and a *Martyr*, surrounded by vast foliage eaten by the night. He had finished the last painting only fifteen days before he succumbed to the cancer that was torturing him.

The tree shoving its roots into the earth and stretching its foliage into the sky is a symbol of life. Prassinos transforms the symbol into its opposite. The trunks are bodies of crucified men. Branches penetrate the bark like arrows or lances into the sides of a martyr saint. Notre-Dame-de-Pitié is one of those high places where the Spirit seems to hover, as in Vence in Matisse's chapel, or in Le Corbusier's chapel in Ronchamp. But in this ancient church, charged with pain, man is not promised Paradise, but the way of the cross, expressed in the last suffering of the artist.

The chapel of Notre-Dame-de-Pitié in Saint-Rémy-de-Provence with the eleven murals by Mario Prassinos.

Braque Beats His Own Record

Georges Braque becomes one of the exclusive number of artists whose works command high figures. On December 2, Sotheby's of London auctioned off the most important piece of his work from a private collection, *Reading Woman*, for the record price of 6.6 million pound sterling. The canvas was part of the collection of Raoul La Roche, a well-known collector of Cubist art who kept his paintings in a Parisian home built by Le Corbusier. The work had been valued at 2 million to 2.7 million pound sterling, and was auctioned off in a highly competitive atmosphere. It was finally bought by the London merchant Thomas Gibson on behalf of an anonymous client believed to be the Greek shipping tycoon Basile Goulandris, a resident of Lausanne.

Michel Tourlière: the Woven Works

Michel Tourlière, sixty-one years old, presents a retrospective of his tapestries at the Paris Art Center at 36 Rue Falguière. He is one of the modern masters of the art of tapestry, and is known for his characteristic use of themes associated with wine, grape plants, vineyards, and the valleys of his native Burgundy. But Tourlière's works are not truly figurative. Composed of large swaths of color that play off each other, they suggest soil, light, land. Lurçat had renewed the art of tapestry, and now with Tourlière and a few others it again becomes the great mural art it had once been.

Futurismo, Futurismi

The Futurists, who detest Venice so much they would like to see it bulldozed to the ground, ironically find themselves on the Grand Canal. "Futurismo, futurismi" (Futurism, Futurisms), an exhibition devoted to them at the Palazzo Grassi, retraces the entire history of the movement from its inspired sources, including Seurat, Munch, Picasso, Marey's photography, and the images by Méliès, to its international posterity in "Futurismi," notably Chagall,

GEORGES BRAQUE: READING WOMAN. 1911. Private Collection

Duchamp, and Kandinsky, which comes as a surprise for some. Conceived by Pontus Hulten, the exhibition is strong in works by Boccioni, Balla, Severini, and Carrà, founding fathers of the movement.

Lukaschewski, the Portraitist

His universe is one of prostitutes with disproportionate thighs and breasts, gangster-faced men, bullies in felt hats and leather coats. But Rolf Lukaschewski, a thirty-eight-year-old German who is better known in Paris than in Cologne or Berlin, is equally fascinated by the circus world of clowns, trapeze artists, jugglers, and wild-animal trainers of whom he draws multi-colored caricatures, freely likened to political figures. As his painting develops, he shows himself to be a great portraitist who knows how to scrutinize the most minute features of a face. His *Portrait of the Art Critic Jean-Louis Ferrier with Gini (The Good Shepherd)* is a masterpiece of psychological insight.

ROLF LUKASCHEWSKI: PORTRAIT OF THE ART CRITIC JEAN-LOUIS FERRIER WITH GINI (THE GOOD SHEPHERD). 1986. Paris. Private Collection

GIACOMETTI BETWEEN YESTERDAY AND TOMORROW

MARTIGNY

Modern times and antiquity join each other in a magical encounter. A filiform Waggoner is next to the ruins of a Gallo-Roman altar . . . a hungry dog looks for food on a stone podium . . . an ageless arm hangs in the void, vibrating, like the needle of a compass, between yesterday and tomorrow. We are in Martigny, in French Switzerland, a town of twelve thousand inhabitants at the foot of the Great Saint Bernard, and in a high place of art: the Pierre-Gianadda Foundation. From the end of May to the beginning of November, it is host to an exhibition of some two hundred drawings, paintings, sculptures, and engravings by Alberto Giacometti.

The history of the foundation is worth recounting. Léonard Gianadda, Pierre's brother, architect and engineer in Martigny, had bought a sixty-eight-thousand-square-foot lot on the outskirts of town on which he planned to build a sixteen-story apartment tower. But preliminary tests of the soil uncovered the ruins of an antique temple dedicated to Mercury and a large number of coins and other objects, such as votive offerings, jewels, utensils, and tools. And then a tragic event: Pierre Gianadda was burned alive in a plane accident on July 31, 1976, near Bari.

Léonard Gianadda decided to discard his plans for a tower and instead he would build a museum around Mercury's temple: "Compared with the Parthenon, this building is nothing but dust, yet it is ours." It was an occasion both to preserve a portion of the local patrimony and to celebrate the memory of his brother. In summers past, there were exhibitions by Rodin, Klee, Picasso, and Goya, as well as Giacometti. All of them were challenges. All were successes.

Giacometti, whose filiform characters express the solitude of modern man, is one of the greatest artists of the century. The exhibition at the Gianadda Foundation commemorates his death twenty years ago. It shows his work like it has never been shown before.

RECONDO, PAINTER AND SCULPTOR

COPENHAGEN

Since November 6, mysterious creatures haunt the Brix Gallery in Copenhagen. Disquieting characters, with heavy glances and clad in distended skin that folds on them like an awkward trap. Characters worrying about their swollen, hardened bellies and bearing fetuses to which they will never give birth. Such are the personages of Félix de Recondo: elongated, oppressed by their own weight, stretched to the breaking point.

Until now, the fifty-four-year-old Recondo worked in silver etching. The works exhibited in Copenhagen show that he found new ways of embodying his characters. His means, such as pencil drawing, are very simple, capable of exploring all the nuances of the play of shade and light. The bodies are prisoners of a gray mist from which they cannot break out, in spite of efforts. By their large size, 5 x 4 feet, as well as by their quality, these Recondos are a decisive stage in the history of drawing.

Color appears in pastels: Large panels where the characters, big, flabby, savor their cigars while passively watching the smoke taking over the painting and their body dissolving. In the pastels, as in the drawings, the shapes and figures are threatened with disappearance into nothingness.

Recondo surprises us still. In the center of the gallery, odd motionless visitors stand, strangely resembling the artist's characters: beings whose bodies are bronze, with wrinkles and folds like the mold of a skeleton. They are escapees from the paintings. They stand there, paralyzed by the surrounding space. They are brilliant sculptures. Recondo's mastery and art have found a new accomplishment.

FÉLIX DE RECONDO: SEATED PERSON. 1983. The Artist's Private Collection

ALBERTO GIACOMETTI: CHIAVENNA. 1964. Geneva. Private Collection

A MUSEUM FOR THE LUDWIG COLLECTION

COLOGNE

In September, the city of Cologne inaugurates the Wallraf-Richartz Museum-Museum Ludwig. The collection, presented under this double name (the most expensive in the world, 252 million marks), is referred to as a "Rhenish Beaubourg." This true refuge of European patrimony is a guardian of six hundred years of art history.

Hanging are masterpieces inherited by the city: baroque paintings, great masters of the Flemish and Dutch schools of the eighteenth century, paintings by Franz Hals and Ruisdael—and the jewel of this section of the exhibition, the famous 1668 *Self-Portrait* by Rembrandt. Several halls are dedicated to the Impressionists and to the French School of the nineteenth century: Claude Monet and Vincent Van Gogh are there.

The museum also houses part of the famous Peter Ludwig Collection. This industrialist, aided by his wife, whom he met while both were studying art, is one of the great collectors worldwide. These last years, he has become interested in contemporary art. Among the eight hundred pieces of Ludwig's eclectic collection, numerous works by Picasso follow the artist's career and periods. One hall is occupied completely by Cubists: Braque, Juan Gris, Gleizes. Another contains Surrealists, such as Magritte, Dali, de Chirico, Tanguy, and Labisse, and the principal Futurists. There is a good collection of the 1960s and 1970s: Pop Art and the Germans Baselitz, Lüpertz, Richter, and Polke, bought by Peter Ludwig when the artists were first starting out.

Ludwig Museum in Cologne.

MOCA CHALLENGES MOMA

LOS ANGELES

The worldwide museum-building fever finds the perfect terrain in California. Los Angeles deals a severe blow to the cultural imperialism of the East Coast. A spectacular extension of the LACMA—the Los Angeles County Museum of Art—is unveiled: the Robert Anderson Building, dedicated to twentieth-century art. Two weeks later, the Museum of Contemporary Art, MOCA in short, is inaugurated.

The decision to build MOCA was made in 1979, and it started out under the auspices of Pontus Hulten, in the buildings of the Temporary Contemporary Museum. It finally was put up at California Place, an elegant silhouette of red stone. It is somewhat exotic, perhaps because it was designed by the most cosmopolitan of Japanese architects, Arata Isosaki. Some four hundred works illustrate the great trends of American painting from 1940 to the present, from Abstract Expressionism to Minimalism, passing through Pop Art. Many are donated by the Count Panza di Biumo.

Certain critics underline the somewhat artificial character of the enterprise. "Are we getting empty shells?" asked Robert Fitzpatrick, president of the California Institute of Arts. "One must start somewhere," replied Richard Koshalek, the MOCA curator. Koshalek seems confident about the brilliant future of his institution. California has myriad collectors. The state is a magnetic pole for artists and dealers. After the eclipse of the 1960s, which was marked by the bankruptcy of the Pasadena Art Museum, Los Angeles decided to reconquer lost ground. From now on, MOCA will be a challenge to the famous MOMA in New York.

An artist in his century: So does André Masson seem to us, now that death has brought his work to a close. The initiator of Automatic Drawing in 1924, then creator of Sand Painting in 1927, he was present at the birth of practically everything created during the last forty years, from Jackson Pollock's "drippings" to "Materiologies." Masson's death comes at the very moment when the USSR, welcoming Chagall, timidly opens itself to modern art.

The booming art market attests to the seemingly insatiable popular appetite for art. Has the Establishment taken over as the arbiter of cultural advancement? Pol Bury the sculptor, scathing as always, answers the question in an editorial in Le Figaro significantly called "The Rear End of the Avant-Garde."

1987
S U M M A R Y

LITERATURE

FRANCE
350th anniversary of René Descartes' Discours de la méthode.
Marcel Proust falls into the public domain.

UNITED STATES
Publication of The Bonfire of the Vanities *by Tom Wolfe, and* Beloved *by Toni Morrison.*

MUSIC

FRANCE
The opera Prometheus *by the Italian composer Luigi Nono is performed in Paris.*

THEATER

FRANCE
The 41st festival in Avignon opens with Paul Claudel's The Satin Slipper, *directed by Antoine Vitez.*

MOTION PICTURES

GERMANY
Premiere of Wings of Desire *by Wim Wenders.*

DENMARK
Gabriel Axel presents Babette's Feast.

UNITED STATES
Premiere of Stanley Kubrick's Full Metal Jacket.

FRANCE
Louis Malle presents Good-bye, Children.

ANDRÉ MASSON:
THE LABYRINTH. 1930.
Paris. MNAM

André Masson in 1965.

ANDRÉ MASSON: AUTOMATIC DRAWING. 1927. Paris. MNAM

MASSON, A PAINTER IN HIS CENTURY

PARIS

Soon after Picasso's death, in April 1973, a friend visiting André Masson said ironically on the threshold of his studio: "Victor Hugo is dead, make place for Beaudelaire." One day when he was talking with Picasso about borrowing from other artists, Picasso looked Masson straight in the eye and admitted, "I borrow from everywhere, even from the worst." Picasso was becoming famous while Masson was emerging from the psychiatric hospital where he recovered from the First World War.

André Masson died on October 27 at the age of ninety-one. He was a misunderstood artist, like Beaudelaire, like Moreau, like Cézanne in their days. Like them, he was an artist for whom the future came unnoticed by his contemporaries.

Indeed, without Masson's Automatic Drawings, the art of the twentieth-century would not have been the same. The first was made in 1924. The artist spoke of "spontaneous" drawing. It was the time of the Bal Nègre at the Rue Blomet, of the boxing lessons that Ernest Hemingway gave Masson and Miró, of psychics, of the derangement of all senses. " Surrealism: n. Pure psychic Automatism by which one undertakes to express, verbally, in writing, or by any other form, the true functioning of thought."

This was exactly what Masson did, going straight to the roots like no other painter before him.

Masson was severely wounded at Chemin des Dames in 1917. He remained a whole night in a bomb crater immobilized on a

FEVERISH DREAMS SEIZED IN THE MADNESS OF THE MOMENT

stretcher. The sky went mad. The earth was torn by explosions, with luminous smoke. It was a riot of color. It was a nerve-racking experience. His drawings became nerve-racking.

Masson explained his work: "Materially, a little paper, a little ink. Psychologically, one must void oneself; automatic drawing, rising from the unconscious, must emege like an unforeseen birth . . . I do not know any sure means to obtain this state. It is a little like grace in theology." Heads look for their bodies. Breasts and genitals fall all around. Severed hands, traces, remains, ruins, hybrid forms. Feverish dreams seized in the madness of the moment. Different from the orthodox Surrealists, such as Magritte or Dali, who merely copied their dreams.

André Breton, who published Masson's Automatic Drawings in *The Surrealist Revolution,* did not like them at all. He preferred more finished drawings. But when the painter exiled himself to New York, in 1941, he was surprised to find some at the Museum of Modern Art. The filiation is well known. The vast

IN MASSON'S WORDS

apocalyptic canvases of Jackson Pollock owe Masson a lot. Pollock used to drip car paint on his canvases laid flat on the ground, but the procedure was identical. The hallucination-like weavings of Masson, made fifteen years earlier in almost complete solitude, were to transfer the future of art from Europe to the United States.

His Sand Paintings should be mentioned as well. They were also made amidst general indifference, and they also had decisive consequences. The year was 1927. Masson was looking for a way of expressing spontaneity in painting, the flashing speed of his drawings. He found the solution by throwing glue onto parts of the canvas, then covering it with sand, which adhered only to the parts smeared with glue. In his own way, he was recreating Leonardo's hypnotic wall. These were the first "Materiologies" of this century. Later there would be others.

The artist was always fascinated with myths and mythology. His first paintings, although Neocubist in nature, are full of symbols: open tombs, horses becoming celestial signs, branches undulating like snakes. At the end of the 1930s, the Minotaur appeared, the derelict of its race, the illegitimate child of Pasiphaë and a white bull.

Masson consecrated to it paintings in which tibias became Doric columns and guts became mazes, in a mixture of the mineral and animal kingdoms. Then came his massacres, his erotic series, and his calligraphies. In the works of his old age, such as the last series, called *Lansquenets*, a synthesis of lines and colored surfaces appeared.

Beaudelaire was scandalous and a calamity. People avoided him like the plague. But we know the outcome: With Masson, the most incisive of modern creators has left us.

(See also 1924 and 1927.)

The keen sensation, sharp as a knife, followed by the flush of emotions, the burning desire to express the unexpressed. Neither "realism" nor "fantasy" exists any longer, there is only the unlimited.

It is an obsession. If you were to ask me what sort of light I would like to express in my paintings, my answer would be: a torrential light.

The student takes a giant step forward when he realizes that what goes on between objects is as important as the objects themselves.

ANDRÉ MASSON: MASQUERADE WITH THE THEME OF EROS AND THANATOS. 1964

Shake the canvas or any surface—cover it here and there with ink or light colors. Shake it from top to bottom, from left to right, using the body's flexibility to its utmost.

Spit ink out or breathe it in.

Why renounce nature and mythology? In the name of what taboo am I forbidden to find and impose the symbols of blossoming and germination? In the name of what commandments, in the name of what ethics, am I to abstain from painting the certain signs of life: that which is impregnated, and that which is devoured?

A visual meditation, without the intervention of thought, can enliven the moment. Things reveal themselves suddenly; what appeared inert becomes rich with the mystery of a smile, the heat of a growing flame, or the explosion of a celebration. What was a given becomes the unknown. Absolutely.

Zen is the contrary of an escape from time. An awakening and the profound presence of being is the very essence of the inward light.

There are neither shapes nor objects. There are only events—sudden sightings —appearance.

Let us hear no more about fantasy. What is fantasy is being here—existing—a tragicomic surprise, a reality so overwhelming that, when you really think about it, many paintings classified as fantastic are but mediocre "realities."

Painting has no true destination as it had in the past; it no longer finds its "victory and repose" in answering to the spiritual needs of peoples. It lives on itself. The brief pleasure that painting can still give us should leave no illusions: It no longer has any effective necessity.

THE RACE FOR ART

Auction at Christie's of Van Gogh's painting *Sunflowers*, in March 1987.

NEW YORK

What suspense! On November 11, over two thousand art lovers from all over the world participated in the auction of Vincent Van Gogh's *Irises* at Sotheby's. This oil painting, 39 x 28 inches, a bush of irises vibrating with the Duchman's passion, had belonged to Père Tangui, a dealer from Montmartre who was a friend of Vincent's, and the first to buy paintings from the Impressionists when they were unknown. In 1947, it was bought for eighty-four thousand

recounting. The tremors and the admiring whispers of the attendees gained momentum quickly. The auctioning advanced by lots of five hundred thousand dollars. Fifteen million dollars soon became twenty-five. And then, only two foreigners were left in the bidding. They were represented via telephone by the auctioneer's associates Géraldine Nagger and David Nash, who took turns in raising their fingers: 28, 30, 41, 42, 45, 46, 47, 48, 49 . . . Nash again raised a finger. Nagger, her ear glued to

"TODAY'S PRICES WILL SEEM CHEAP IN A FEW YEARS"

dollars by the American billionaire Joan Whytney Payson. It was inherited by her son John.

The fantastic flames of Van Gogh's *Sunflowers* sold last March at Christie's for two hundred twenty million francs, which raised the hopes of John L. Marion, Sotheby's president, and his seven associates, who were backed up by a hundred muscular guards. They expected a new world record.

This exceptional event is worth

her phone, motioned that her party had given up. In three and half minutes, *Irises* had reached the unbelievable sum of $53,900,000, or 320,000,000 francs.

How much longer are prices going to rise? In five years, Impressionists' prices boomed four hundred percent. Van Gogh alone went up twice that figure. The moderns, such as the Cubist Georges Braque, reached sixty-six million francs last year

at Sotheby's. Rarity does not explain everything. This race for art, accelerated by the uncertainties of the stock market, could be a campaign to possess the only durable values, namely universal masterpieces.

Considering the fact that for the nouveaux riches ten million dollars represents more or less a day's work, as Maurice Rheims puts it, it seems that nothing is going to stop speculators. "Today's prices will seem cheap

in a few years," John Lumley, a former director of the painting department at Sotheby's London, declared cooly after the sale of *Sunflowers*.

These are wagers on the future. It is so much more significant because it is impossible to know how tomorrow, with its changing fashions and opinions and posthumous rehabilitations, will rearrange things. Today, Van Gogh is considered one of the greatest masters of all time. Who would have believed it a century ago, when he was all but unknown? There are all the misunderstood of the beginning of the century—Matisse, Picasso, Léger, Modigliani, Mondrian, all now at the top. In this age of international uniformity of lifestyle, dwelling style, furniture, and mode of thinking and feeling, it is the originality of art that makes its value soar.

VINCENT VAN GOGH:
IRISES. Private Collection

THE CITY OF THE DOGES CONSECRATES TINGUELY

VENICE

Who would have thought, a few years ago, that the world's number-one "anartist" would become a great religious artist, the equal of a Grünewald and a Bosch? An artist burning up with the panic obsession of Dame Death?

This is the revelation and the surprise of this magnificent retrospective of Jean Tinguely, organized for the summer at the Palazzo Grassi. It is made of a hundred "Metamachines" from his various periods that turn, grate, pant, crowd, and tremble in a mixture of sounds and colors, born out of the tricks of a Till Eulenspiegel become engineer. To top it off, there are fabulous arrangements of pulleys, swings, cams, and tumblers that open and shut as disproportionate jaws of cows, dogs, and ducks.

If we are to believe Tinguely, the origin of these last works can be found in two recent experiences. A year and a half ago, his lungs refused to process the smoke of the tons of cigarettes he had been smoking for forty years. He was six weeks in a coma, his feet and hands bound. And then a nightmarish sight: For three days and three nights, the farm next to his own burned down, hit by lightning. Dame Death had called on him twice. It was too much.

Does this double experience really explain everything? Fifteen years ago, for the Salzburg Festival, Tinguely made the props for Jacob Bidermann's *Cenodoxus*. It is a baroque play in which angels and devils fight on stage over the souls of the poor deceased. A consequence was a retable with a sheep's head, a death skull, and turning, luminous ramps. That was in 1981. Another consequence was the *Inferno* of 1984, animated and shaken by infinite pains. Or *Snow White and the Seven Dwarfs or The Witches* of 1985, a magnificent capharnaum in which white bones and rusty irons decompose together. The stake is Thanatos. At the age of sixty, Tinguely himself is

JEAN TINGUELY: SNOW WHITE AND THE SEVEN DWARFS OR THE WITCHES. 1985

amazed: He looks at his recent works without pleasure. He rejects them after creating them. What he has always liked in his art is the process.

For the biennale of young artists in 1959 he built *Metamatic 17*, a frail, gracious drawing machine. It enchanted the crowds by producing, in three weeks, forty thousand drawings simulating the Automatic Writing so dear to the Surrealists. Then Tinguely conceived a series of motorized works that mimicked Malevich, Mondrian, and Kandinsky, reproducing exactly their circles, triangles, and squares. They can be seen in the upper halls in Venice. Tinguely quickly established a worldwide reputation. He won the wager.

Is Tinguely's sculpture a condemnation of our technological society, or, on the contrary, its praise, as some thought, considering him dangerous? "Jean Tinguely and his supporters threaten humanity and civilization, in the spirit of the maniacs of atomic war, wearing the uniform of American generals," *Izvestia* wrote in 1963. Tinguely a war criminal? This is not the feeling gained from the Venice retrospective of the "anartist" in blue overalls, the genius amateur mechanic, the tragic sexagenarian.

(See also 1955, 1959, 1970.)

CHAGALL EXHIBITS IN MOSCOW

MOSCOW

An official public exhibition of eighty paintings and two hundred graphic works by Marc Chagall is inaugurated on September 2 by Irina Antonovna, curator of the Pushkin Museum. Vava, the painter's widow, assists. The Soviet and international press are on hand. Is this exhibition the sign of a true opening of the USSR to modern art? Is it a revision of its antisemitic and antireligious policies?

Most Western art critics who come to Moscow for the occasion doubt that the current Russian leaders, even with Gorbachev's more flexible line, really forgive Chagall's Judeo-biblical inspiration and his modernism. Be that as it may, three days after the opening, the supply of catalogues is gone. Every morning, hundreds of Muscovites are in line at 5 a.m. to be sure to be able to see the paintings, unknown to them until now. (The exiled Chagall died two years ago, in Vence.)

Mrs. Antonovna expects four hundred thousand visitors if

MARC CHAGALL:
THE MARRIAGE.
1918

good weather holds, "only" a quarter of a million if the autumn is harsh. *Pravda* praises Chagall, and condemns mistakes of the past, noting that the paintings are at last in the artist's native country, after years of interdiction.

"We should turn, since the Earth turns. We should fly, and we don't," Chagall once said regretfully. Although he was inspired by the mystical rites of Hasidic doctrine, his works are devoid of any materialistic heaviness, thanks to his dreamlike and spiritual detachment from the terrestrial attraction. Perhaps this explains the fascination he exerts on the Soviet public, amazed, with some delay, by such opposition to overused, exhausted, Socialist Realism.

Chagall, whose works include *Biblical Message,* notes that "without the Bible and Mozart, life would not be worth living." And André Malraux thought that the next century would return to religion. Does the success of the Moscow exhibition show that Malraux was on track? "If the culture of the eighteenth century revived everything that reinforced its rationalism, our century revives everything that reinforces our irrationalism." he once wrote in *Money and the Absolute.*

At this hour, when Chagall's genius shines for all, France waits to receive its own inherited collection, from Vava Chagall, from Ida Chagall, a daughter

HIS DREAMLIKE PAINTING AMAZED THE SOVIET PUBLIC USED TO SOCIALIST REALISM

born from his first marriage to Bella, and from David McNeil, an illegitimate son born in America. The collection is fabulous. Its inventory is being made by the Maeght Foundation.

An exceptional colorist and painter-poet, Chagall was the last representative of the astounding modern-art creators at the beginning of the century.

He had to die before the masters of the Kremlin could accept, on the centenary of his birth in Vitebsk, this son of their land, to which he owed so much. He never forgot that it was in this land that his father used to get up early every morning to invoke God in the synagogue.

(See also 1918 and 1931.)

The opening of the exhibition with Madame Chagall and Irina Antonovna.

Leroy Crowned at Last

An artist who works at each of his paintings ten years or more has become a rarity in this century of high speed. But Eugène Leroy, seventy-seven years old, is just that kind of artist. His exhibit of sixty-nine paintings at the Musée d'Art Moderne in Villeneuve-d'Ascq reveals one of the masters of current art who is recognized as such throughout Europe and the United States, though France has yet to fully appreciate him. At first glance, his canvases seem to be nothing but colorful chaos, their subject matter emerging slowly from the depths of the picture. Leroy concentrates on nudes, who seem to be nothing more than intense vibrations of flesh, as if the female body were appearing from beneath the ashes of art. Baselitz, the German painter, has been one of his fervent collectors for several years.

Botero in Madrid

The Centro de Arte Reina Sofia in Madrid hosts a retrospective of paintings and drawings by the Colombian artist Fernando Botero. His generously enlarged figures are famous in the United States as well as in Europe, where Paris discovered him at the 1967 Biennale. Adopting a naive style, Botero presents his single figures or groups as though they were posing for a photographer. Beneath his barely disguised humor, one senses a tenderness for, and complicity with, the figures in the picture, bringing us closer to them. A similar inflationary characteristic marks his still-life compositions in which fruits and vegetables are offered up to us in a rich, at times acid, profusion of colors. Botero's training as a fresco artist at the Academy of Saint Mark in Florence from 1954 to 1955, when he was twenty-two, explains his undeniable pictorial strengths.

Paul Klee Retrospective in New York

From February 12 to May 5, a large retrospective of three hundred works by Paul Klee is held at the Museum of Modern Art in New York, before traveling to Cleveland, then to Bern. Accompanied by a richly documented catalogue,

FERNANDO BOTERO:
THE ORCHESTRA. 1979.
Private Collection

the exhibit finally gives the public a chance to appreciate Klee's genius, as well as the varied development of his art from beginning to end. Born in 1879 in Münchenbuchsee, he died in Muralto-Locarno in 1940, pursued by the Nazis. His works as well as his pedagogical gifts give testimony to one of the most unfettered minds of the first half of the century. At his inaugural lecture at the Bauhaus, where he taught from 1921 to 1930, Klee surprised his pupils by asking them to paint the explosive encounter of two comets.

Milshtein in Denmark

Odense, pearl of the island of Fyn in Denmark, discovers Milshtein, a forty-year-old Israeli who lives and works in Paris. His works, generally of generous dimensions, vascillate between anger and humor. They are wild compositions of grandiloquent, blustery figures who reinvent the world in their own exaggerated image. One of the artist's favorite subjects is a bed rendered as a dreamlike home to strange collections of people. Milshtein uses a broad stroke, monotonous or grating colors, and outlines as sharp as his mind. He is rarely shown in Paris, although François Mathey invited him to exhibit in his farewell show at the Museum of Decorative Arts three years ago.

EUGÈNE LEROY: WOMAN. 1981.
Villeneuve-d'Ascq Musée d'Art Moderne

FASHION WITH-OUT PASSION

PARIS

The Georges Pompidou Center was inaugurated ten years ago by President Giscard d'Estaing, who didn't like it at all. To celebrate its anniversary, there is an exhibition called "Our Time, Fashion, Morals, Passion, Aspects of Today's Art, 1977-1987." It seems that the title is derived from Beaudelaire. As far as fashion is concerned, those who came after the departure of Pontus Hulten, and who revel in it, can be trusted. There is no point in dwelling on morals, a hot subject. But where is the passion?

It seems that the organizers of the exhibition have selected, from the storage rooms of international museums, the most "in" and the most boring works of all. Roaming the halls are only a few lost visitors. This is far from the great events, like the "Paris-New York" and "Paris-Moscow" exhibitions, that made "Beaubourg" an equal of the famous New York MOMA.

The worst doesn't always happen. There are some quality artists, such as the Germans Anselm Kiefer, who never disappoints, and Georges Baselitz, a magnificent painting machine; the French Gérard Garouste, whose recent paintings show a successful evolution, and, above all, Jean-Michel Alberola, a newcomer.

Alberola was born in Saida, Algeria. He is thirty-four years old. He takes up some of the great themes of the Renaissance, such as *Suzanne and the Old Men* or the myth of *Actaeon*, which he analyzes, digs, and undermines from within. Sometimes, he opposes them to the figures of his native, phantom-like Africa, in an impossible dialogue. Cultivated, intelligent, a profound colorist, Alberola saves the exhibition single-handedly. He deserves better than this tasteless ambience.

JEAN-MICHEL ALBEROLA: BEHIND SUZANNE. 1983. PARIS. MNAM

THE EUROPE OF THE PAINTERS

STRASBOURG

Are the readers of news magazines better informed then the decision makers in the world of art? In May, the magazine *Eighty,* dedicated, as the name suggests, to the art of the 1980s, asked thirty newspapers from sixteen European countries to invite their readers to designate their eighty preferred artists.

The exhibition resulting from the poll, titled "Painters of Europe Today" is seen in Strasbourg. After the end of the year, it is to tour Europe. The three hundred magnificent works demonstrate that the art of the Old Continent is as good as the American, and that France has its place in it.

In the French selection, the dominant figure is fifty-one-year-old Guy-Rachel Grataloup, chosen by the readers of the weekly *Le Point* among artists that included internationally acclaimed names such as Buren, Blais, and Viallat. His four paintings do not resemble anything we know. With Grataloup there are the remarkable Rouan and Alberola.

Italy, once more, sends its Transavantgarde: Chia, Clemente, and Cucchi. Spain sends two of its masters, Saura and Arroyo, as well as a newcomer, Broto, who is a discovery for many. Germany sends young artists who follow the triumphant generation of Baselitz and Kiefer but who are not devoid of certain modernist banality.

Although it sometimes confirms official choices, this exhibition is, in may aspects, nonconformist. It does reach its goal: enlarging the panorama of current art by appealing to the judgment of the public.

GUY-RACHEL GRATALOUP:
THE FALL OF THE BIRD
MAN.1987. Private Collection

POL BURY: THE REAR END OF THE AVANT-GARDE

Is it avant-garde or new Academicism? Though the question is not new, it is asked with more urgency than ever today, as can be seen in the following text from *Le Figaro* of September 15 by the internationally renowned sculptor Pol Bury. Bury, a brilliant polemicist with an incisive style and a biting wit, is known for his writing. This article is addressed to all those who believe all the paths of contemporary art have been blazed, and it deserves our attention for questioning what we had assumed were certainties.

The nineteenth century was strict about the virtue of its daughters, who, when they lost theirs, were promptly allocated to the trash heap. The twentieth century is just as strict about its avant-gardes in the fine arts: At the pinnacle of success for the duration of a single season, rejection awaits them when they lose their novelty.

But what can be said of the scholasticism that has emerged from these multiple avant-gardes? What is to be done when a student in fine arts has to adopt the strategy of a weather vane so he can adapt himself to the specials of the day?

It has been a century since pictorial impertinences began. When Cézanne's painting gained admission to art galleries and later to museums, aspiring painters tried to paint like Cézanne. Followers, we all know, exaggerate the faults of their model, as is evident in certain landscapes by Vlaminck. It did not take long for the followers to gain their own following. It is said that Monet, toward the end of his life, commented with a sigh as he left that year's Salon and its army of pale paintings watered down in Impressionist fashion, "Sometimes I would like to paint nothing but black."

From plagiarists to plagiarism, painting was simplified, becoming a smooth, monochromatic surface. You might have thought it had gone as far as it could go. In fact, it "started from scratch." Everything was erased, and art began again. The market economy and cultural commentators did the rest.

Nowadays, esthetic fashions have adapted themselves to the era of jet planes. Yesterday, stringiness stiffened with resin was all the rage; today, tree branches grow wrapped in clay or cotton. For tomorrow, people leaf through the latest art magazines.

Totally at a loss when confronted by so many transient and contradictory models, students tend toward the least constraining, the most rapid . . .

If it were permissible to be radical, it could be stated that the abandonment of Academicism (perspective, anatomy, etc.) results in the abandonment of the teaching of fine arts. The purpose of Thomas Couture has been taken up by the cinemascope of Cecil. B. DeMille.

Academicism, thanks to its strict rules, was necessarily pedagogical, and therefore transmissible. It is contrary to the very essence of the avant-garde to allow itself to be codified and transmitted by teaching.

The force of habit, the fear of what people might say, annulled all the questions that were being asked. The teaching of fine arts adapted itself to the fashions of the day, to the climate of the time with a fair degree of flexibility. In its consequences, it has not changed much. As had happened in the past, it follows official art: that which is shown and seen in museums.

Faced with this tourniquet of esthetics, you can well imagine the confusion of students. The moment they take their place at their easels, the models begin to follow one another on the podium: Impressionism, Neoimpressionism, Postimpressionism, Cubism, Fauvism, Expressionism, Surrealism, Dadaism, Constructivism, Neoconstructivism . . . the waiting room is full, and still more keep coming: Minimalism, Conceptualism, Pop Art, Arte Povera, Body Art, Land Art, not to mention the negation of art, which was also a scholastic model.

This enumeration is enough to show how amusing the situation is. To adapt oneself fully to the circumstances, it is of the utmost urgency to replace the treatises on perspective and anatomy with manuals on dot, gesture, and monochrome painting. At least it would be entertaining.

Today, the garbage cans are full of obsolete avant-gardes. Less space-consuming than radioactive waste, they should at least make us understand that esthetics pass, but that technique remains.

For lack of anything better.

Pol Bury
Le Figaro

As the decade nears its close, the avant-garde no longer commands the outsider position. Thanks to media attention and a burgeoning art market, vanguard painters, sculptors, and architects are quickly absorbed into the mainstream. It remains for the technological revolution to provide the framework in which radical new concepts of creativity can flourish, with the computer acting as th catalyst of innovation. Politics, too, play a significant role, as the Soviet Union emerges from decades of self-denial to acknowledge its past contribution to Modernism and to compete for a position on the contemporary scene. New attitudes of openness are evident on many fronts, calling into question long-held ideas about both the history and the future of art.

1988
S U M M A R Y

COMPUTER ART

The Computer-Art Revolution
An Artwork That Creates Art

ART AND POLITICS

Glasnost
Wyeth and the Mystery Woman

EXHIBITIONS

Georgia O'Keeffe Retrospective

SCULPTURE

Isamu Noguchi

ART NEWS

Auctions: Everybody Is Stunned
Pollock-Krasner House and Study Center
Picasso: Inhuman? Human?
In Brief

MUSEUMS

The New Museum in Saint-Étienne
The Ménil Collection in Houston

ARCHITECTURE

Pei Has Won the Battle of the Louvre

LOUISE NEVELSON: DAWN SHADOWS. 1982 New York. The Pace Gallery

NAM JUNE PAIK : NOVEMBER. 1985.
New York. Holly Solomon Gallery

DENNIS ASHBAUGH:
BLACK SONIC BATH. 1989.
New York. Kasmin Gallery

THE COMPUTER-ART REVOLUTION

NEW YORK

Rapid advances in electronic technology are breaking down the practical and ideological barriers that have long existed between the artist and the computer. New developments in software and the wide availability of home computers with graphics capabilities have opened up a field once limited to those artists who were willing and able to master the often daunting problems of programing, and who had access to the expensive, sophisticated equipment at the few research centers where artists can work under the guidance of scientists and engineers.

The introduction of the microprocessor has enabled manufacturers to produce inexpensive computer graphics systems for the mass market. Just as the camera evolved from being a large, costly, and complicated piece of equipment that required expert handling into a small, cheap, and simple device that even an amateur can operate, so the computer has become accessible to expert and layperson alike. And like the camera, the computer challenges cherished beliefs about the appropriate-

ness of applying technological process to making art.

Technology's impact on the fine arts has never been more widespread or more apparent, affecting not only those artists whose imagery is generated directly by electronic media, but also those who use the new tools to interpret ideas and images conceived independently of such systems. The question is no longer whether the computer is capable of, or even suitable for, artistic expression, but how it can best be adapted to each artist's individual needs.

Many painters and sculptors use the computer to work out design concepts or to test structural ideas in preparation for finished works in traditional media. The English painter John Pearson constructs his compositions according to complex mathematical calculations. Using a custom-made computer program, he experiments with various permutations, generat-

ing visual data that serve as the basis for his pastel drawings and painted constructions. Similarly, sculptors such as the American Ruth Leavitt and Peter Struycken of the Netherlands design their three-dimensional objects with the aid of computer-imaging systems that analyze their proposals from all possible angles and plot their structures for fabrication.

Environmental artists and creators of site-specific pieces

A GROWING NUMBER OF ARTISTS VIEW THE COMPUTER AS A CREATIVE MEDIUM IN ITS OWN RIGHT

explore options in configuration, construction, and placement prior to execution. CAD/CAM computer programs that simulate both design and manufacture allow artists to resolve problems at the conceptual stage, without the need to manipulate bulky materials or to undertake expensive building projects. The ECOSITE program, developed by the American sculptor Robert Mallary, devises strategies for land reclamation.

An extension of this process

involves the adaptation of conventional artwork to expression by computer. Among those active in this area, Alan Saret in the United States, Manfred Mohr in Germany, and Manuel Barbadillo in Spain base their imagery on geometric and mathematical constructs that lend themselves naturally to computerization. Britain's Howard Hodgkin and David Hockney, and Australia's Sidney Nolan, together with numerous American artists, including Kenneth Noland, Jennifer Bartlett, and Larry Rivers, are experimenting with paint-box programs, creating digitized hybrids of characteristic painting styles as diverse as the linear, graffitilike approach of Keith Haring and the naturalistic, fully modeled technique seen in Philip Pearlstein's nudes.

Dennis Ashbaugh's abstract stripe paintings, converted by computer into digital code, are transformed by the intervention of a "virus" that attacks, breaks down, and reorganizes data according to its own whims. Deliberately allowed to invade the program, this unpredictable force introduces an element of

AN ARTWORK THAT CREATES ART

risk and chance analogous to the unplanned, intuitive quality of Action Painting, except that the machine replaces the artist as the agent of image evolution.

A growing number of artists view the computer as a creative medium in its own right, rather than as a research and development tool alone. The computer's memory allows artists to make changes in design and color without destroying the previous stages, which can be recalled on demand from the databanks, thus encouraging experimentation. Both customized programs and over-the-counter software can generate imagery that is unique to the system, and can produce either still pictures or animated sequences. A variety of hard-copy techniques, from color photography to inkjet printing, translate computer imagery into independent artworks that are suitable for exhibition and sale. Animations are recorded on videotapes and disks that are broadcast or distributed on the market.

Artificial intelligence also enables artists to program sequential works in other media, such as electronic signboards and kinetic sculpture. In New York, the computer-controlled Spectacolor billboard in Times Square is a vehicle for artists' animations, sponsored by the Public Art Fund. The pioneering video artist Nam June Paik incorporates television monitors into his automated constructions and multimedia installations, and the performance artist Laurie Anderson uses a battery of electronic devices to generate a broad spectrum of aural and visual special effects.

The widespread acceptance of computer technology in communications, broadcasting, film, and information processing, the development of ever more sophisticated and adaptable programs, and the increasing availability of "user-friendly" systems that can be mastered by nonspecialists, offer exciting opportunities for artists accustomed to thinking of electronic media as limited, arcane, and alien to the creative process.

SAN DIEGO, CALIFORNIA
Most artists regard electronic technology as simply another tool, but beginning some twenty years ago, the British painter Harold Cohen (who has been on the faculty of the University of California at San Diego since 1968) recognized that the computer offered a new way to answer some questions about the nature of freehand drawing that have intrigued artists for years.

He began with simple questions—for example, the minimum number of marks that function as an image for the human viewer—and translated his speculations into a computer program, which then executed drawings accordingly. These drawings served to test his ideas in immediate visual terms, permitting modification of his understanding, and of the program, as needed. Thus the questions grew more and more ambitious, addressing not only evocation and form but also meaning and their relationships to modes of representation in freehand drawing, most recently including figuration.

The result has been a computer program called AARON, which has been under continuous development since the early 1970s: It is an autonomous generator of drawings that behaves according to general rules that Cohen has derived from his own experience as an artist and has "taught" to the program. Using the techniques of artificial intelligence, AARON calls on knowledge about making art, knowledge about the real world, and knowledge about methods of representation, and makes drawings without human intervention. It produced some 7,000 drawings during an exhibition in Japan while the human artist was himself in California. No two drawings are ever identical. Occasionally Cohen hand-colors some of these in oils or water colors, preparing for the time when he can teach AARON how to color as well as draw.

In AARON, Cohen has created an artistic double that makes decisions about drawing in much the same ways he himself does. He describes his relationship with this elaborate electronic double as symbiotic rather than as toolmaker to tool. AARON enacts what Cohen believes about making art (or even what the literature of art suggests that artists believe): AARON's drawings confirm or deny those beliefs, forcing Cohen to ask new questions about the nature of representation in art.

Cohen has created a work of art that creates works of art.

Harold Cohen in Studio, 1989.

GLASNOST

MOSCOW

For the first time since the late 1920s, important exhibitions inside the Soviet Union itself are devoted to the art of Constructivists, Rayonists, Suprematists, and Cubo-Futurists, who for so long have been officially ignored and whose work has been hidden from public view. Kazimir Malevich, who was once reviled as a "decadent" and "bourgeois" formalist, is honored at public ceremonies. Plans are made to erect a memorial near his burial site outside Moscow, and a major traveling exhibition of his work opens at the Russian Museum in Leningrad. The names of avant-garde artists have now been returned to the art-historical canon, and their works are being resurrected from obscurity in the storerooms of provincial museums.

"Art and Revolution," a large exhibition mounted in the temporary quarters of Moscow's Tretiakow Gallery, brings together many works of the pre- and postrevolutionary vanguard that were suppressed under Stalin's imposition of Socialist Realism. The latter is also represented, in what one Western critic describes as a "grand hodgepodge."

Paintings by Malevich, Chagall, and other avant-garde figures hang in the company of Socialist Realist canvases by Nikolai Terpsikhorov and Alexander Samokhvalov, among others. The exhibition illustrates the new openness that is exposing Russian audiences to artists revered in the West but little-known in their own land.

There is also a greater willingness on the part of the Soviets to share their modern and contemporary works with the West. The Malevich show travels to Amsterdam, and another "Art and Revolution" exhibition, which premiers in Budapest, goes on to the Austrian Museum of Fine Arts

A NEW OPENNESS TO EXPOSING AUDIENCES TO WESTERN ART, AND TO SHARING RUSSIAN ARTISTS WITH THE WEST

in Vienna, where visitors marvel at outstanding avant-garde works from provincial Russian museums exhibited for the first time outside the Soviet Union. At least one other Eastern-bloc country capitalizes on the relaxation of cultural-exchange restrictions. Following a survey show of contemporary West German painting sent to East Berlin and Dresden last year, East Germany mounts an exhibition of works by fifty contemporary sculptors, which travels to Bonn and Mannheim. West German audiences, accustomed to thinking of sculpture in terms of abstract form, are surprised by the dominance of figurative work. "The human being is central to East German art," Klaus Honnef, the Rheinisches Landesmuseum's director, explains. Yet observers note that the work has nothing in common with the stereotypic characterizations of Socialist Realism; it expresses instead the humanistic tradition that runs through much of modern European art.

Talks between representatives of the Soviet government and Peter Ludwig, the renowned West German collector and museum benefactor, further demonstrate the Soviet Union's new openness to contemporary art. Ludwig, whose name already graces several European institutions, now proposes to establish a museum in Moscow devoted to international contemporary art. The project is sanctioned by the Soviet Ministry of Culture and the Union of Artists, as well as by the General Secretary of the Communist Party, Mikhail Gorbachev. With the blessing of the Bonn government, Ludwig proposes to donate fifty contemporary paintings from his vast collection, including contemporary Soviet works, and to contribute a further one hundred pieces on permanent loan.

Perhaps the most surprising example of cultural openness is the Soviet Union's first international art auction, held in Moscow on July 7 and conducted by Sotheby's. Brisk competition among European and American bidders brings the sum of $407,166 for Grisha Brushkin's painting *Fundamental Lexicon,* setting a record price for work by a living Soviet artist. The top lot is Alexandre Rodchenko's *Line of* 1920, which fetches $556,632, according to a report in *ARTnews.* The magazine notes that, "under the new policy of *glasnost,* the ministry of culture no longer distinguishes between 'official' and 'unofficial' art," making it possible for younger artists, unrecognized and without a market in their own country, to offer their works. Several, including Svetlana Kopystianskaya and Ilya Kabakov, sell well to Western buyers.

(See also 1908, 1910, 1915, 1918, 1922, 1930, 1935.)

ANDREW WYETH: CROWN OF FLOWERS. 1974. New York. The Brooklyn Museum

WYETH AND THE MYSTERY WOMAN

NEW YORK

"The Helga Pictures," a controversial exhibition of paintings on paper, watercolors, and drawings by Andrew Wyeth, travels from the National Gallery of Art in Washington, D.C., where it opened last year, to museums in Boston, Houston, Los Angeles, San Francisco, and Detroit, and will finish its national tour next year at the Brooklyn Museum in New York. The show provokes heated debate, both on the quality and character of Wyeth's art and over the participating museums' motives in presenting it to the public.

The "Helga" series, executed between 1970 and 1985, comprises two hundred and forty studies of Helga Testorf, a neighbor of the artist, who lives in Chadds Ford, Pennsylvania. The entire suite was bought in 1986 by a collector, Leonard E. B. Andrews, for a sum that he described as "multimillions of dollars." Reports of the sale note that Wyeth had kept his obsessive devotion to his model secret, even from his wife, causing a sensation almost as great as that generated by the staggering purchase price.

The heavily promoted show of selections from the series, accompanied by a lavish book, takes on the air of a media event, with outspoken detractors

GEORGIA O'KEEFFE:
RED POPPY. 1928. Private Collection

and equally vociferous defenders eager to score points in the press. The National Gallery's deputy director, John Wilmerding, describes Wyeth as "one of the two greatest American Realists in the twentieth century"—the other being Edward Hopper—while Hilton Kramer, editor of *The New Criterion*, a conservative cultural journal, denounces Wyeth's art: "It's provincial, it's sentimental, it's illustration, and it's without substance."

Critics assess that the show is a mere crowd pleaser, pandering to lowbrow taste and the desire to attract crowds. Several prominent museums, including the Metropolitan Museum of Art in New York, decline to participate in the tour. Andrews's involvement in promoting the collection is viewed as self-serving, as demonstrated by his statement in the book that the series is "a national treasure," and by his characterization of Wyeth as a "genius . . . far ahead of any other living artist."

But what of the pictures themselves? How do they rate as expressions, both of the individual depicted and of the artist's interpretation of that singular being? As a subject of Wyeth's relentless probing, Helga emerges as remarkably unyielding, her protective façade intact. One reviewer describes her personality as "curiously absent," writing that "Wyeth does not set out to represent Helga, but through the act of painting to partake of what she represents to him." She is less a subject than an object, manipulated according to the artist's needs, observed but never revealed, interpreted while scarcely being understood.

GEORGIA O'KEEFFE RETROSPECTIVE

WASHINGTON, D.C.
At the National Gallery of Art, a retrospective exhibition surveys the career of Georgia O'Keeffe (1887-1986), a painter associated with the early Modernist Movement in the United States. She is perhaps best known for her sensuous treatment of flowers and her landscape paintings of the American Southwest, where she lived for many years.

A protégé and later the wife of Alfred Stieglitz, who exhibited and promoted her work at his avant-garde galleries in New York, O'Keeffe was influenced by the contemporary photographers Paul Strand and Edward Weston, whose work Stieglitz also championed. Many of her canvases and pastels zero in on her subjects—such as flowers, plants, bones, and other natural objects—as if they were seen through the close-up lens of a camera.

Her voluptuous floral studies are often described as sexual metaphors, but O'Keeffe always dismissed this interpretation as motivated by the viewer's own erotic imaginings. You [hang] all your own associations with flowers on my flower," she once wrote in exasperation, " . . . as if I think and see what you think and see of the flower—and I don't."

(See also 1917 and 1929.)

ISAMU NOGUCHI

NEW YORK

As the year ended, so too did an era in modern sculpture, with the death on December 30 of Isamu Noguchi. Revered as a master whose outdoor sculptures and environmental projects occupy prominent sites around the world, Noguchi synthesized a personal idiom from influences as diverse as Zen gardens, Constantin Brancusi, and Social Realism.

Noguchi was born in Los Angeles in 1904, the son of a Japanese poet and an American writer. The family moved to Japan when the boy was two years old, and it was there that he began to develop the sensitivity to natural materials that characterizes much of his work. As an adolescent, he was sent to school in the United States and was briefly apprenticed to Gutzon Borglum, the sculptor of the Mount Rushmore Presidential memorial, who belittled Noguchi's artistic ambitions. Later, with his mother's encouragement, he studied sculpture at the Leonardo da Vinci Art School in New York, and in 1927 was awarded a Guggenheim Fellowship, which enabled him to travel to Paris. There he worked for six months as a studio assistant to Brancusi, from whom he received a grounding in modernist form, and who reinforced his respect for the innate character of wood and stone.

Noguchi's output was remarkably diverse, including many public commissions worldwide, as well as furniture, lighting, and stage décor, in addition to conventional sculpture. His intellectual interests were equally varied, and led him to travel extensively in Europe and the Far East.

His longstanding friendship with the visionary engineer R. Buckminster Fuller and the architect Gordon Bunshaft contributed to this interest in structure, and led him to conceive works on an architectural and environmental scale.

Noguchi's first public sculpture was executed in Mexico City in 1935-1936. A mural relief fashioned in colored cement, its bold, Expressionistic style echoed that of the "socially conscious" Mexican painters. During the 1930s, most of his proposals for playgrounds and sculptures for public housing and community buildings were unrealized; but he did execute a garden sculpture for the Ford pavilion at the 1939-1940 New York World's Fair, and received a prestigious commission to decorate the façade of the Associated Press building at Rockefeller Center, for which he created *News,* a monumental bas-relief in stainless steel.

A deep concern for the environment and its influence on human sensibilities led Noguchi to make a lifelong study of the concept of leisure. Many of his projects for public gardens and playgrounds drew on his interest in creating interactive spaces, in which the visitor experiences sculpture as an environment of forms, rather than as isolated objects. The expressive possibilities of such interaction were most fully exploited in his settings for the dances of Martha Graham, the pioneering modern dancer-choreographer, with whom he began collaborating in 1935. In such works as Graham's *Appalachian Spring* (1944), *Cave of the Heart* (1946), *Judith* (1950), and *Phaedra* (1962), Noguchi's interactive décor functions almost as a character in the unfolding drama of the dance.

The poles of Oriental and Occidental culture exerted strong and sometimes conflicting influences on Noguchi, who sought resolution through synthesis. Following the Second World War, he designed two bridges titled *Tsukuru* (to build) and *Yuku* (to depart), at the entrance to the Peace Park in Hiroshima (com-

ISAMU NOGUCHI: NARROW GATE. 1981. New York. Isamu Noguchi Garden Museum

pleted in 1952), as a "gesture of expiation," both in atonement for the atomic bomb and in promotion of the cultural unification that he, as a Japanese-American, symbolized in his own person. Although he set up a studio in Kamakura, he continued to travel widely and to spend part of each year in New York. His brief marriage to the Japanese actress Yoshiko Yamaguchi ended in divorce in 1955.

During the next three decades, Noguchi solidified his reputation as one of the foremost contemporary sculptors. Among his many outstanding public projects are the UNESCO gardens in Paris (1956-1958), sunken plazas at the Chase Manhattan Bank in New York and the Beinecke Rare Book and Manuscript Library at Yale University (both completed in 1964), the Billy Rose Sculpture Garden at the Israel Museum in Jerusalem (completed in 1965), fountains for Expo '70 in Osaka (1970), and *Landscape of Time* for the U.S. Federal Building in Seattle, Washington (1975). He experimented with many materials, and though he is renowned for his work in stone, he was equally adept at handling cast and direct metal, wood, and ceramic. Important exhibitions of his work have been held throughout the United States, Europe, and the Far East. Most recently, Noguchi represented the United States as the featured artist of the 1986 Biennale in Venice.

His most personal creation is the Isamu Noguchi Garden Museum, established in Long Island City, New York, in 1985. There, in a building complex, a retrospective collection of his work, along with documentation of his site-specific and environmental projects, is displayed in galleries and a garden designed by the artist. This environment expresses the spirit of Noguchi, whose last sculptures involved "the unique confrontation with matter" which he felt when working with the primal shapes of natural boulders.

Auctions: Everybody Is Stunned

Astronomical auction prices for modern and contemporary paintings continue to provoke controversy. At Christie's London salesroom on November 28, Picasso's *Acrobat and Young Harlequin,* a 1905 gouache from his rose period, sold for $38,450,000, setting an auction record for a twentieth-century painting. Among the modern masters, only Van Gogh's prices exceed those of the two latest Picassos to come on the block. Even more stunning to the contemporary art market is the seventeen million dollars paid at Sotheby's November 10 New York sale for Jasper Johns' *False Start,* a 1959 canvas that sets a record for the work of a living artist and breaks the Johns record established only the previous day with the sale of his *White Flag* at Christie's for seven million dollars. Johns represented the United States at this year's Venice Biennale, where he received the coveted Golden Lion award, and the resulting media attention may have stimulated the market. Members of the audience at the November 10 sale rise to their feet and cheer as the gavel falls on the Johns. Observers later express amazement at the price. "Everybody is stunned," according to Thomas Amman, a Zurich dealer, who calls the record "a victory for American painting."

Pollock-Krasner House and Study Center

In a modest, 625-square-foot studio in the eastern Long Island hamlet The Springs, Jackson Pollock created the "drip" paintings that established his reputation. In June, the studio and the nearby farmhouse, where Pollock lived with his wife, the painter Lee Krasner, from late 1945 until his death in 1956, are dedicated as the Pollock-Krasner House and Study Center. The center's primary attraction is the studio, which boasts a floor bearing the evidence of Pollock's celebrated Action Painting method. The wooden boards are embellished with dribbles, spatters, layerings of poured color, and linear ara-

besques made as the painter's arm swept past the edge of the canvases laid on its surface. Visitors, wearing foam slippers to prevent damage to the painted boards, stand where Pollock stood while such masterpieces as *Autumn Rhythm, Blue Poles,* and *Lavender Mist* took shape. The center's director, Meg Perlman, points out that the floor is not comparable to a "lost" Pollock painting, but that it is a valuable record of Pollock's creative process. "We've tried to present it as a document of the artist's palette, gesture, and energy, and not as a work of art in itself," she says.

Picasso: Inhuman? Human?

The human—some would say, inhuman—side of the twentieth century's most celebrated artist is the focus of *Picasso: Creator and Destroyer,* a scathing biography

JASPER JOHNS:
FALSE START. 1959.
New York. Leo Castelli Gallery
Photo: VAGA New York 1989

by Arianna Stassinopolous Huffington. The book is received cooly by the art press, which accuses the author of dwelling on Picasso's personal frailties and ignoring his creative genius. Admitting that Picasso's was a fascinating personality, Huffington nevertheless judges him harshly as a selfish lover, thoughtless parent, and unfaithful friend, accusing him of failing to rescue the poet Max Jacob from death at the hands of the Nazis. In her interpretation, Picasso's abstract distortions of the human—especially female—body are tantamount to mutilation. Avis Berman, in her review of the book, acknowledges the artist's private shortcomings but echoes the opinion of most critics with her observation that "Huffington bristles with so much indignation that we forgive Picasso everything out of exasperation with this hectoring and tiresomely prejudiced voice."

IN BRIEF...

THE NETHERLANDS
Three paintings by Vincent van Gogh, including a version of The Potato Eaters, *are stolen from the Kröller-Müller Museum in Otterlo.*

GREAT BRITAIN
The Tate Gallery in London mounts an exhibition of Beatrix Potter's illustrations for such classic children's tales as Peter Rabbit.

SPAIN
The Spanish government announces that approximately half of the renowned Thyssen-Bornemisza Collection of Lugano, Italy, will be on loan for ten years to the Prado.

UNITED STATES
Louise Nevelson, a sculptor known for her boxed constructions of found wooden objects, dies at the age of eighty-eight.

The industrialist Armand Hammer shocks the Los Angeles County Museum of Art by withdrawing his promised major donation and announcing plans to build a private museum for his famous collection.

The brief, meteoric career of twenty-seven-year-old Jean Michel Basquiat ends tragically with his death from a drug overdose.

GERMANY
Elevations for Mies, a steel sculpture by Richard Serra, is installed at the Mies van der Rohe villa Hans Esters, in Krefeld.

CANADA
Moshe Safdie's spectacular granite and glass building for the National Gallery of Canada opens in Ottawa.

THE NEW MUSEUM IN SAINT-ÉTIENNE

The museum housing the Ménil Collection in Houston, Texas.

THE MÉNIL COLLECTION IN HOUSTON

HOUSTON

Everybody likes the new museum, inaugurated here last year. It houses the Ménil Collection, which Parisians admired at the Grand Palais four years ago. Built by Renzo Piano, coarchitect, with Richard Rogers, of the Georges Pompidou Center, the new museum is a long, low building of white and gray. It is discreetly integrated among the houses of the so-called "Ménil Strip," that is, Montrose Avenue. Saint Thomas University, built by Philip Johnson, is nearby, as is the Rothko Chapel, both commissioned by Jean and Dominique de Ménil. The neighborhood is said to be an "oasis of humanity" in the heart of this city of the future.

The main building is simple, enhanced by its delicate structure of white metal, which sustains a shady platform surrounding gray walls. The distribution of the halls and the interior gardens, and, above all, the extraordinary quality of light, a combination of natural and artificial, does not allow sunlight to enter the exhibition halls directly. It gives the museum great refinement.

Once more, the Ménil family advances art and architecture. Indeed, when Jean and Dominique de Ménil came to

Houston in the 1940s, contemporary art was virtually unknown here. The couple learned slowly, during trips to New York, thanks to Couturier and the dealer Alexandre Iolas, who aroused their interest in Surrealism. With a sure taste, the Ménils started to collect classic antique pieces and works from Oceania, Africa, and the Middle Ages. Their fine eye showed in the precocity of some of their choices. They were among the first admirers of Max Ernst, then hardly known in America, as well as of artists such as Joseph Cornell and Yves Klein.

SAINT-ÉTIENNE

A new museum opens in the world every week. It is a phenomenon of the end of the twentieth century. Yet, France had to wait until these last few years to see the creation of truly modern contemporary-art museums. The new museum of Saint-Étienne was inaugurated on December

Guichard was erected. It contains the three thousand works acquired during four decades.

Conceived for an ever-growing collection dominated by contemporary works, the seventy-seven thousand square feet of the new building permit great flexibility of presentation. The curator and his team wanted the ensemble,

CONCEIVED AS A STEP FORWARD ONTO THE EUROPEAN STAGE

10 last year in the presence of François Léotard, the minister of culture.

Thanks to Maurice Allemand, who became curator in 1947, and Bernard Ceysson, his successor since 1967, the collection was constantly enriched. It includes works by Léger, Kupka, Dubuffet, Giacometti, and Baselitz. The old and dusty Musée d'Art et d'Industrie, where it was housed, became too small.

In 1983, a location was chosen: a thirteen-acre park in the northern end of the city. With the help of the municipality, the state, the region, and the department, the building designed by the architect Didier

which contains a library and several meeting halls, to function also as a training, research, and documentation center.

The new Musée d'Art et d'Industrie—located in the heart of the dynamic region of Rhône-Alpes—is supported by four local corporations. It was conceived as a step forward onto the European stage. Its inaugural exhibition is "Art in Europe, the Decisive Years 1945-1953," presenting Picasso, Bonnard, Poliakoff, Pignon, Staël, Corpora—the best produced by the Old World after the war. The catalogue for the occasion is the first work of such importance on this major period.

The Musée d'Art et d'Industrie in Saint-Étienne.

Model of the Louvre with Ieoh Ming Pei's pyramid.

PEI HAS WON THE BATTLE OF THE LOUVRE

PARIS

Tourists and Parisians watch the rise of an astonishing structure in the Napoleon Court of the great Louvre: the glass pyramid of the Chinese-American architect Ieoh Ming Pei. When the design was announced four years ago, many were outraged by what they saw as an intrusion into their classical Paris. Ever since, much ink has spilled in "the battle of the pyramid."

Judging by most reactions to the brilliant diamond tip, seventy feet high and one hundred and eight feet wide, it can be believed that Pei has won the battle. As Napoleon fought ten thousand Mameluke riders, so, Pei resisted an equal number of antimodern letter writers. "From the height of these pyramids, forty centuries watch you!" the Corsican general once said. "On this pyramid, people will see the moving reflex of the clouds and the stars," the great architect promised. "Paris is made fun of!"

art historians Bruno Foucart and Antoine Schnapper protested in a brochure on *The Great Illusion of the Great Louvre.* "It is an admirable jewel; it is only the first stage of an even more beautiful adventure: turning the Louvre into the most beautiful museum in the world," the former minister of culture Jack Lang proclaimed. Ricardo Bofil, who considers Mitterand a

*"ON THIS PYRAMID,
PEOPLE WILL SEE THE MOVING REFLEX
OF THE CLOUDS AND THE STARS."*

genius of city planning, agreed. "He placed a window on the greatest view of the world by enlarging the history of French architecture."

What does the most interested party have to say? Born in China seventy-one years ago, Pei studied in the United States. A graduate of Harvard (1946), he became a professor at the Uni-

versity's school of architecture and was influenced by Gropius. But Pei was affected more by the theories of Marcel Breuer. He adopted the "importance he gave to light, texture, sun, and shade." That was Pei's goal with the pyramid. In an interview to *Connaissance des arts* he said: "I studied Le Nôtre very closely during the entire period when I dealt with the great Louvre.

There is the geometry, the use of the landscape, of the sky, of water. There will be a sheet of water next to the pyramid. Our solution is that of the landscape, the only one we can use to obtain continuity with the past . . . I did not use the shape of the pyramid because of Napoleon's conquest of Egypt but because it was the simplest geometric

shape, the best. It will give light to the basement. The basement will become the heart and the core of the Louvre. At the same time, the pyramid gives it space and therefore importance . . . We must have an architectonic body that tells people, 'Yes, this is the Great Louvre.' "

The pyramid comprises six hundred and sixty-six reflecting glass panels, each four feet wide, inserted and glued on silicon, held by a network of cables and tubes. It will contain services that the Louvre lacked: a bar, a restaurant, an art bookstore, a gift shop, an auditorium for lectures, and four audiovisual spaces explaining the collections of the museum.

How is Pei's design going to integrate with this place pregnant with history? Next year's opening of the new Louvre with its pyramid may be too early to judge it without passion. Time will tell.

ABSTRACT EXPRESSIONISM

The movement had its origins in New York during the forties, but really took off in the early fifties. Some of the artists who are grouped under this name had become famous when they worked on the Work Projects Administration, which was created by President Roosevelt to put unemployed artists to work during the Depression. But it is to the Second World War that they owe the conditions for their total innovativeness. In 1940, because of the conflict raging in Europe, the artistic center moved from Paris to New York, to which many artists, from Masson to Max Ernst, Dali, and Mondrian, came as refugees. This concentration of talent, never seen this side of the Atlantic, would exercise a great influence on American painters, who for the most part had been limited to regional confrontations. It was the Surrealists in particular—Jackson Pollock and Robert Motherwell and others—who had continued contact with them.

Abstract Expressionism is sometimes known as the New York School, although the latter term has a broader meaning and also encompasses artists from the next generation. Nonetheless, Abstract Expressionism, which was never a structured group like Cubism or Futurism, is subdivided into two major currents.

Action Painting is one of those currents, and Jackson Pollock was its most important artist. Abstract Expressionism would probably not have attained the stature that enabled it to expand worldwide without his strong personality. Beginning in 1946, he made his first "drippings," seething psychological labyrinths that were never organized around a central point, consisted rather of an upheaval of matter in fusion. Alongside Pollock are other equally important artists like Willem De Kooning, Philip Guston, and, in some respects, Robert Motherwell and Adolph Gottlieb. Like him, they were Gestural painters, sometimes even violent; some of them used the "All-Over" technique, which consisted of covering the canvas uniformly. De Kooning held a special place among the Action Painters, as he never stopped practicing figurative painting. De Kooning's figurative work, like that of other Action Painters, nonetheless had a violent aspect to it, an unbridled aggressiveness in his attack of the canvas.

The other current is Color-Field Painting, which has a more lyrical, meditative inspiration, and in which color is laden with emotion. The most important artists of this group are Mark Rothko, Barnett Newman, Clyfford Still, and Ad Reinhardt. Their canvases are rigorous and simple. They have less to do with the expression of the personal or collective unconscious than with the expression of eternal metaphysical truths, to which they introduced meditation, as if those truths were so many materials. Paradoxically, not all the Abstract Expressionists were abstract, and this is particularly true of De Kooning. They did, however, have in common the use of large canvases, which took them away from easel painting and to a powerful use of the material and of color.

ABSTRACTION-CREATION

Abstraction-Creation, an international association of artists, was founded in Paris February 15, 1931. Its president was Auguste Herbin; Georges Vantongerloo, vice-president; Jean-Hélion, secretary-treasurer. Other members of the board of directors were Arp, Gleizes, Kupka, Tutundjian, and Valmier. The purpose of the association was to bring together abstract painters of all leanings, and in fact almost all the noteworthy painters of abstract art belonged to Abstraction-Creation during its brief existence.

The association was preceded by Circle and Square (Cercle et Carré), founded by Michel Seuphor and Joaquín Torrès-García in 1930. Among its members were such first-rate abstract artists as Arp, Le Corbusier, Gropius, Kandinsky, Léger, Schwitters, and Mondrian. But Circle and Square did not last more than a year, just enough time for a beautiful exhibition and for two issues of a revue. Abstraction-Creation, which Vantongerloo created from the ashes of Circle and Square, lasted longer and was more active.

The drive to form a common front of all abstract artists against the return to Realism in painting, and also against Surrealism, reappeared after the demise of Abstraction-Creation in such guises as "Abstract Art," a 1938 exhibition at Amsterdam's Stedelijk Museum, and the revue *Circle*, (1937), published in Great Britain. Abstraction-Creation broke up in 1936 after nearly six years of existence.

ART BRUT

Jean Dubuffet (1901-1985) first defined the concept of Art Brut (rough art, raw art) as follows; "Productions of any type that are spontaneous and highly inventive, and that weaken traditional art and cultural stereotypes as little as possible. Their creators are obscure people, outside professional artistic circles." Himself a collector of such creations, which he said were "free from artistic culture," Dubuffet in November 1947 opened a Foyer of Art Brut in the cellars of the gallery René Drouin, on the Place Vendôme in Paris; and in June 1948 he created the Compagnie de l'Art Brut (Art Brut company) in order to increase and publicize the collections that had been left to the city of Lausanne in 1971, which included more than five thousand works by two hundred different creators. Beginning in 1964, the company published *Cahiers de l'Art Brut* (Art Brut notebooks), which presented such exceptionally original creators as Aloïse, Joseph Crépin, Augustin Lesage, and Adolf Wölfli.

ARTE POVERA

The beginnings of Arte Povera (poor art), an Italian movement, go back to 1967. Arte Povera was named by the critic Germano Celant during an exhibition at the Galleria La Bertesca, in Genoa. A manifesto accompanied it, in which Celant explained the purposes of the movement and introduced its principal figures. Arte Povera endeavored to go beyond the sixties, as Pop Art had done, and to be associated with certain concepts from earlier years, without attempting to hide its debt to French Realism and American Neodadaism in its refusal to make a consumer product out of the work of art. It made a cult of "poverty," raising banality to the stature of art. Arte Povera was also part of a broader international phenomenon, the main variations on which were Land Art and Conceptual Art.

The work of the Arte Povera group is ephemeral, and demands the viewer's participation, which reinforces the endless mutation of the works. Derision, parody, and metaphor add to the unexpected quality of the artistic process. Boetti, for example, favored the human body. By multiplying its gestures, he accumulated signs that are so many perceptions of surrounding space. In the work of Pascali and Kounelis, by contrast, physical presence is relayed by borrowing from nature, specifically the elements of earth, fire, and water. As to Merz, for several years he has been updating his reflections by using the theme of the igloo.

Turin and Rome are the two centers in which these studies were pursued, but the movement spread rapidly beyond Italy. Arte Povera exhibitions have been mounted in New York, at the Castelli and Sonnabend Galleries, and later in international museums and exhibitions, such as the 1968 Documenta in Kassel, the Kunsthalle in Bern in 1969, and the 1970 Biennale in Paris.

ART NAÏF

If there have always been Naïfs, they owe the adoring spotlight of art lovers, and the speculative interest of dealers, to the great posthumous fame of Henri Rousseau (1844-1910). Their success, which became increasingly commercial, kept growing after the 1937 exhibition "Popular Masters of Reality," organized in Paris, thanks to their first great collector, Wilhelm Uhde. The art critic Anatole Jakovsky would later be their foremost discoverer.

While the Naïfs are known especially for their ingenuousness, spontaneity, and independence, it is paradoxical that the most famous Naïfs, such as Bauchant, Bombois, Rimbert, Séraphine, and Vivin, formed a school in spite of themselves. Different currents of Art Naïf (naive art) prospered in several Eastern European countries, particularly Yugoslavia, and in Haiti and West Africa, where its cultural traits are found.

The vogue for Art Naïf, which reached its heyday in the sixties, led to the rediscovery of nineteenth-century American Art Naïf and of ex-votos from chapels in the rural and coastal areas of Latin countries. It also resulted in the creation of several Art Naïf museums, notably in Laval (where Henri Rousseau was born), Nice, and Montmartre, while the opening of many specialized galleries caused most of the art of that style to lose its authenticity, as it could not be truly naive if it did not retain its original candor.

COBRA

The name Cobra is an acronym of *Co*penhagen, *Br*ussels, and *A*msterdam. Ten issues of a revue called *Cobra* appeared between 1948 and 1951. Bibliothèque de Cobra (Cobra library), a monograph series devoted to the group's principal artists, was also created. Cobra's first exhibition in Paris took place in a bookstore on the Boulevard Saint-Michel in February 1951. A second exhibition a few months later was held at the gallery Pierre. The Parisian School was the prevailing force at the time, so the exhibitions received little attention. Although it did not really have an agenda, Cobra presented itself as the heir to primitive and popular arts, to Expressionism, and to Dadaism, as shown in its painting, which was aggressive, wild, disorderly, and violently colorful. Cobra was opposed to French traditionalism, Academicism, and Geometric Abstractionism.

Behind the group was Asger Jorn, a Dane who was impassioned by ethnology. The Belgian poet and painter Christian Dotremont played the role of arts patron. Early members of Cobra included Karel Appel, Egill Jacobsen, Corneille, Constant, and Carl-Henning Pedersen; they were later joined by Alechinsky. Eventually, others became part of the group to varying extents, such as Atlan, but the only French member was Doucet.

Beyond several faithful followers, the Cobra painters aroused little interest until the sixties, when their audience expanded in both Europe and the United States. The work of each member evolved in accordance with his temperament, Alechinsky moving toward fantasy-ridden calligraphy, and Jorn—the greatest Cobra artist—toward action convulsed by increasingly elaborate color. But their work bore the indelible mark of what they had discovered together: exuberance, a sense of humor, and fierceness.

CONCEPTUAL ART

Conceptual Art (Art Conceptuel) is a trend that first appeared in the late sixties, bringing together artists from varied backgrounds rather than from a single movement. It was first of all a question asked of art, its self-analysis and self-criticism, in the aftermath of Dada and, more recently, of Minimal Art, which in many senses prefigures it. "Conceptual Art does not mean reducing the work to an idea, to a concept, but rather to an 'idea' of art, or a 'concept' of art," wrote Catherine Millet. In other words, it was not a question of creating a new repertoire of forms, as had been done by Cubism, abstract art, and Pop Art, all of which—even if they started out by jolting our ways of thinking—eventually became acceptable, and annexed, by our society through the system of galleries and museums. Conceptual artists attempted, rather, to conceive of the artistic phenomenon in terms of wholly new standards in order to make any subsequent retrieval of art by the public impossible. That was not easy since there was not any art—not even Duchamp's ready-mades—that had not been retrieved by critics or art historians. Even though Duchamp wished his ready-mades to be perfectly neutral, the critics and art historians overload them with various meanings.

This explains why, for one of the most famous figures of the trend—Joseph Kosuth—the elimination of all connotation was the highest goal. His conception of art led him to exhibit not just different objects, such as a chair, but also photographs of them, as banal as possible, as well as their definitions in the dictionary. In so doing he thought he could suspend the viewer's esthetic reaction—a suspending that in his opinion was a prerequisite to any exploration of the nature of art.

Linguistics was preeminent in Conceptual Art in that all art derives from and returns to language in a sort of intangible circle. That, however, meant aligning artistic activity with linguistic structures as if those structures were applicable to all systems of signs—an idea that was contested by such prominent linguists as André Martinet and Georges Mounin. Barry, Weimer, and Huebler should also be mentioned in association with Kosuth. Ben (Vautier), who for two weeks in 1962 put *himself* on display in a London window, also belonged to Conceptual Art.

CONSTRUCTIVISM

Shortly after the Russian Revolution, creators felt that, in a world they wished to change completely, art could no longer be the affair of allimited number of people, intended solely for the esthetic pleasure of a few art lovers. In December 1918, in the revue *Communist Art*, Vladimir Mayakovski made the following peremptory statement: "We do not need an art mausoleum in which to adore dead works, but living factories of the human mind: in the streets, on troley cars, in factories, workshops, and the homes of workers." However, far from rejecting what had been discovered at the time of Futurism and Suprematism, it was on the contrary a question of getting more out of those discoveries for the greater good. During the twenties, the revue *Lef*, published by Mayakovski, put all its energies into the service of those ideas.

Pevsner and Gabo's *Realist Manifesto*, which came out in Moscow in 1920, separated art from everything connected to fantasy, automatism, and the unconscious in favor of reason and calculation. Artists must "construct objects like an engineer building a bridge, with the precise frame of mind of a compass." In 1922 Alexis Gans' *Constructivism* would go further still, challenging all distinction between pure and applied art: "The end of 'pure' and 'applied' has come! The social and rational is at hand . . . Nothing fortuitous, uncalculated; no blind taste or arbitrary esthetics. Everything must be thought through on a technical, functional level. Our Constructivism—that is, the Constructivism of the Soviet Union—differs radically from Western Constructivism; at the meeting point between the two are our painters of Leftist art."

That distinction applied to El Lissitsky, Van Doesburg, Hans Richter, and several others who, in the West, then considered themselves Constructivists. Actually, Constructivist publications appeared throughout Europe, including *De Sikkel* in Antwerp, *7 Arts* in Brussels, *Contimporanul* in Bucharest, and *Blok* in Warsaw. It was in order to avoid any Western deviance, which had not occurred to the writers of the *Realist Manifesto*, that Rodchenko and Varvara Stepanova drafted their *Program of the Group of Productivists*, in which Communist ideological reflection took precedence over any artistic work.

That was the context in which Tatlin and Rodchenko, for example, created functional pieces of furniture for collectives, and alevich his dishwashing models for state factories. Of greatest importance were the Vkhoutemas (higher workshops of art and technology), founded in the late twenties: In charge of the metallurgy faculty, Rodchenko designed railroad cars and trolley cars there; in the textile faculty, where Exter, Popova, and Stepanova

taught, new clothes were proposed and new motifs for fabric.

Bastardized and in decline because it was, after all, not an efficient propaganda tool at the service of the people and of the Socialist Revolution, Constructivism died out around 1925.

CUBISM

The term Cubism covers the revolution in painting that was instigated in 1914 by Picasso, Braque, Léger, and Gris. It started with *Les demoiselles d'Avignon*, a huge canvas by Picasso that was inspired by African art and Iberian sculpture, which the artist painted in two phases during the first half of 1907. The term Cubism did not, however, surface until the following year, and was coined by the critic Louis Vauxcelles when reviewing for the magazine *Gil Blas* a Braque exhibition at the gallery Kahnweiler. The development of Cubism is generally divided into three phases: the Cézanne period (1907-1909), the Analytical period (1910-1912), and the Synthetic period (1913-1914).

The painting of Cézanne, who died in 1906, made a strong impression on young artists. The great painter exercised considerable influence on Cubism. At first put off by *Les demoiselles d'Avignon*, which he saw in Picasso's studio, Braque soon painted a nude that was intended to compete with it, and in the summer of 1908 did *Houses at L'Estaque*, in which trees and houses are interpreted geometrically as a reference to Cézanne. Picasso worked in the same spirit. During that first period, perspective was lopsided and the skyline done away with, and it was the articulation of volumes between them that provided the depth of space.

From 1910 on, landscapes lost all but the most limited place in the works of Picasso and Braque. Shut up in their studios, they did innumerable still lifes and some figures and portraits. The image of the visible explodes; faces and objects—guitars, glasses, violins, and pitchers—are fragmented into myriad facets. It became almost impossible to distinguish between the canvases of the two artists, so much were they based on joint research. Tones are deliberately reduced to the range of ochres and grays.

After the Analytic period, which led to the explosion of the image of the visible, came the Synthetic period. This began with the progressive introduction into the painting of stenciled letters, fake wood made by the technique used by building painters, and glued paper. These elements brought to the canvas bits and pieces of reality in the rough, such as newspaper clippings and even, in the work of Juan Gris, bits of mirror. Léger, in turn, who was never Analytical in the strict sense of the term, played on interlocking pieces and contrasts of forms while introducing the three primary colors—red, yellow, and blue—to Cubism.

Cubism was first codified in 1912 in the book *About Cubism* (Du cubisme), by Gleizes and Metzinger, neither of whom was among the founders of the movement. At that time, everyone practiced a synthesized, bastardized form of Cubism. This was, at the outbreak of the First World War, both the triumph and betrayal of the work of Braque and Picasso, whose two versions of *Three Musicians* of 1921 can be considered as the conclusion of his

Cubist period. Also at this time, in 1912, the Section d'Or (Golden Section) was being created around the Duchamp brothers, Jacques Villon, Raymond Duchamp-Villon, and Marcel Duchamp; this group was concerned above all with the mathematical aspects of artistic creation. Delaunay, on the other hand, who also started out as a Cubist, ended up doing nonobjective painting during this period.

DADAISM

While it is difficult to say exactly who coined the term Dada, since each member of the group claimed that honor for himself, the uncontested birthplace of the movement is Zurich. Several Germans had become refugees in that city during the First World War, including the poet Hugo Ball and his companion Emmy Hennings. On February 5, 1916, they opened a literary and artistic cabaret, the Cabaret Voltaire. A few days later, Ball and Richard Huelsenbeck, a fellow German; Romanian émigrés Tristan Tzara and Marcel Janco; and the Alsatian Jean Arp gave birth to the Dada movement. In May 1916, the word Dada appeared in print for the first time, in the "literary and artistic collection" published in Zurich by Hugo Ball, entitled *Cabaret Voltaire*. That same year, a Dada collection had its debut with two works, *Mr. Antipyrine's First Celestial Adventure*, by Tristan Tzara, and *Fantastic Prayers*, by Richard Huelsenbeck, the latter with illustrations by Jean Arp. A Dada gallery was founded in Zurich in March 1917.

The Dada movement was marked more than anything else by the personality of Tzara, who gave it its true theoretical expression, particularly in the *Dadaist Manifesto* published in 1918. It was Tzara too who, after moving to Paris in 1919, did everything to publicize it in international avant-garde milieux. He did not avoid provocations and scandals; on the contrary. Dada was antitradition, antilogic, antiinstitutions; in short, antieverything. That attitude was what caused, after a period of joint delirium, the break between Tzara and André Breton who, with his adherents, founded a constructive movement: Surrealism.

Francis Picabia, who lived in Zurich during 1919, is responsible for Dada's impact on the arts. That impact is also due in large part to the iconoclasm of Marcel Duchamp. In Germany much more than in France, Dadaism was manifested by political opposition and by certain techniques, such as collage (Max Ernst in Cologne, and Johannes Baargeld's revue *Der Ventilator*, and photomontage (John Heartfield and Raoul Hausmann).

The Dada movement died out around 1923. But after 1945 it reappeared in the United States and Germany under different forms, through the influence of Marcel Duchamp: Pop Art, Fluxus, the Happening, and anti-art are all reminiscent of Dadaist provocations.

EXPRESSIONISM

There are two groups that are generally considered to be representative of Expressionism in painting: Die Brücke (the bridge) in Dresden, from 1905 to 1910, and the Blue Rider (Der Blaue Reiter) in Munich, from 1911 to 1913. The term Expressionism was coined in Germany in reaction to the term Impressionism. While the idea of Expressionism had always been around, it became widespread through the revue *Der Sturm* (thunderstorm), which did not hesitate to extend Expressionism to all the avant-garde movements that emerged between 1910 and 1920.

The common denominator of Expressionism is Antinaturalism. No longer was it a question, in the strict sense, of imitating nature or copying it, but rather of creating, of giving the artist the prerogative of his role as creator. There were outstanding Expressionists, such as Nolde and Kirchner or Kokoschka in Vienna. Kokoschka, during the years when Freud was coming up with psychoanalysis in that city, executed a striking series of portraits in which he dove into the depths of the unconscious.

Unlike Fauvism, Cubism, and Futurism, which were all concerned to different degrees with providing an image of the visible, Expressionism explores the most violent and intense aspects of the inner world, which explains why it is never better manifested than in times of social crisis and spiritual disarray. Such painters as Munch and Ensor were its precursors; in their work the difficulty of existence, and a fascination with death, are paramount. Their influence on Expressionism was comparable to Cézanne's impact on Cubism. While the Fauves had a constructive and emotive conception of color, the Expressionists dreamed only of dissonances, of tearing things up. They demanded that colored accents translate "the terrible human passions," as Van Gogh had written to his brother Theo, and were concerned only with shouting out. They did not express themselves solely through the exacerbation of color but also through the destruction of forms and graphism.

Considering how violent the twentieth century is, some theoreticians have tried to extend the term Expressionism to everything that is most constant and most fecund in modern art. That point of view is, however, an exaggeration, since Expressionism no longer means anything very specific. It is probably no accident, nonetheless, that the New York School, which emerged during and immediately following the Second World War, came to be known as Abstract Expressionism—which is rather inappropriate for some of its members. Such artists as Willem De Kooning, Franz Kline, and Jackson Pollock are, in fact, more or less directly affiliated with Expressionism, as well as being contemporaries of the concentration camps and the atom bomb.

FAUVISM

An early, ephemeral, twentieth-century avant-garde movement, Fauvism was born in Paris in 1905 and died out in about 1908. Based on the exaltation of pure color, Fauvism was not a school in the strict sense of the term, with a manifesto, agenda, and theories, but a group of painters motivated by shared concerns. At its heart lay the dominant personality of Matisse, and around him gathered artists from very different backgrounds: Marquet, Manguin, Camoin, Puy, from the Gustave Morau studio and the Académie Carrière; Derain and Vlaminck, who worked in Chatou; and Braque, Dufy, and Friesz, from The Haque. Some independents, including Valtat, Von Dongen, and Rouault, were also Fauvists.

Fauvism got its name from the critic Louis Vauxcelles in a review of the Salon d'Automne that appeared in a supplement to *Gil Blas* on October 17, 1905. Writing about a small bronze piece of Florentine inspiration by the sculptor Marquet, which appeared in the same room as the work by Matisse and his friends, Vauxcelles said: "Donatello among the Fauves" (among wild beasts). The word spread like wildfire, and under the generic term Fauvism it came to express the revolt of the young artists against the Academicism of the officially accepted Masters. The Fauves claimed as their sources Delacroix, Manet, Van Gogh, Gauguin's Tahiti series, the Neoimpressionism of Seurat, Signac, and Cross, and Henri Rousseau, who exhibited in the same Salon his painting *The Hungry Lion Jumps on the Antelope, Devours It, the Panther Anxiously Waits for the Moment When It Can Have Its Share . . .Sunset,* the title of which might have been the unconscious basis for Vauxcelles' use of the term "fauve." From those forebears the Fauves acquired the taste for pure tones, the arabesque, and the simplification of means. The shock of African sculpture, which the Fauvists discovered for the future Cubists, would be added later.

Once it became a phenomenon, Fauvism began arousing infatuation not only in salons, but also in galleries. Berthe Weill and Ambroise Vollard organized exhibition after exhibition of the works of Matisse, Valtat, and Van Dongen. The collectors Gertrude and Leo Stein, Morosov, and Chukin bought many of their paintings and carried their fame as far as Russia and the United States. However, beginning in 1908, the Fauves broke up. Braque moved abruptly to Cubism, and the others continued to work independently and in solitude. Matisse alone would take Fauvism to its last stages without ever deviating, ending up with the admirable cutouts he did late in life. To a certain extent, Van Dongen also did not stray, although he often indulged in mundane, more descriptive painting. Derain, in turn, flirted with Cubism and then went back to the traditional manner out of concern for a "return to order," and in this respect he was followed by Vlaminck, of whose debuts as a powerful colorist little now remains. Georges Rouault moved increasingly toward painting of religious inspiration, while the "little" Fauves, such as Manguin and Camoin, repeated themselves without much innovation.

FLUXUS

This group made its first appearance in Wiesbaden, Germany, in 1962. The event was organized by George Maciunas, an American. Its major participants were disciples of the musician John Cage, including George Brecht, Jackson MacLow, Dick Higgins, and Al Hansen. Basically, Fluxus was concerned with music: pianos and violins broken in public, concerts consisting of noise.

In 1963, at the Fine Arts School of Düsseldorf and with the participation of Beuys, Fluxus became active in the plastic arts as well. Events or "performances" were staged by means of provocations reminiscent of the Dadaists, and so-called "environments" were set up. The classic notion of painting, sculpture, or a work of art in general was rejected. There must be identification between art and life. The idea of performance, very closely allied with Fluxus, can be understood through the following explanation by Wolf Vostell: Fluxus, he said, shows how the group conceives of "all life as a piece of music, a musical process."

In 1964, the Fluxus Festival was held at the Technical Academy of Aachen. From then on, certain names were always associated with the movement, including the Korean Nam June Paik (smitten with electronic music, he worked in Germany), Tomas Schmit, Wolf Vostell, Joseph Beuys, and Ludwig Gosewitz. Fluxus events were held in London, Copenhagen, and Paris. Two Frenchmen are particularly representative of the movement's vitality: Robert Filliou and Ben (Vautier).

FUTURISM

An Italian avant-garde movement launched by the poet and lampooner Filippo Tommaso Marinetti, Futurism's most active period was between 1909 and 1914, but it lasted longer in individual countries. There were five founders in addition to Marinetti: four painters—Balla, Carà, Russolo, and Severini—and a sculptor-painter, Boccioni.

On February 20, 1909, the readers of the docile newspaper *Le Figaro* were startled by the outrageous text of the *Futurist Manifesto* on page one, written by Marinetti. Marinetti, who wrote perfect French, had decided to express his ideas in a Paris daily because at the time Paris was, in his opinion, the capital of all artistic audacities. Among other outrages, he proclaimed the beauty of speed, lay claims to courage and rebellion in the name of young artists, and demanded the demolition of museums and libraries. *The Futurist Manifesto*, which was followed by many other manifestos signed by all the members of the group, brought provocation to art several years in advance of Dada. Founded by a poet, Futurism claimed to be not only pictorial but also literary, musical, architectural, social, moral, and political. It attempted to encompass all human activity, but its primary goal was to fight Academicism and the slavish devotion to the past that at the time shackled all creativity in Italy.

In formal terms, Futurism is above all an outgrowth of Cubism, from which it borrowed many of its characteristics; it also owes a debt, albeit more remote, to Neoimpressionism. For a group that was basically concerned with speed and movement, the chronophotographs of Muybridge and Marey, which for the first time revealed the secrets of animal movement, played a decisive role. The very clear positions adopted in the 1909 manifesto predated the appearance of Futurist works at a time when Balla, Boccioni, and their peers were still involved in a form of painting that vacillated between late Impressionism and sentimentality. Futurism was a school with an agenda, and that distinguished it completely from such movements as Fauvism and Cubism, which were much more pragmatic and which owe their names more or less to chance.

Futurism lasted until after the First World War, but now cramped by its exacerbated chauvinism and nationalism, which would later make Marinetti into an ardent supporter of Mussolini. This hot-headed poet carried his polemics to every country he visited for debates and lectures. Late Futurists were found in every corner of the globe, and the impact of Futurism was great, particularly in the Soviet Union. The Vorticists of Great Britain and the Stridentists of Mexico have been associated with Futurism. Long neglected because of the pro-Fascist inclination of its members, the influence of Italian Futurism was not fully appreciated until the eighties.

HYPERREALISM

A pictorial movement that was defined during the seventies in New York and on the West Coast of the United States, Hyperrealism was a reaction against Abstract Expressionism and Conceptual Art. While works of Pop Art contained objects from everyday manufactured reality, such as cartoons, rubbish, and Coca-Cola bottles, the Hyperrealists made faithful reproductions. Those reproductions, as perfect as possible, brought a new sensation to viewers: While they were looking at a Hyperrealist work of art, reality was unfolding before their eyes according to an image.

To the Hyperrealists, no object or theme was unworthy of attention, from Kacere's women in panties to Estes's building façades, Salt's and Don Eddy's cars, and the famous *Airstream Trailer* of Goings, which have the precision of snapshot photos. A special place must be reserved alongside Hyperrealist painting for the mannequins of Hanson and De Andrea, which add surroundings to the image of a man and a woman captured at a specific movement in their existence—facts attempting to present an event exactly as it occurs.

Without pretending to adopt a political or psychological stance, the Hyperrealists devoted themselves exclusively to becoming acquainted with actuality, depicted with a maximum of objectivity.

Hyperrealism has also been referred to as Radical Realism, Photo-Realism, Sharp-Focus Realism, Superrealism, and—confusingly—even New Realism.

INFORMAL ART

The term "informal" refers less to a school than to a trend that included artists who happened to be together for a time. Among the most important were Fautrier, who supported Jean Paulhan; Mathieu, whom André Malraux called the greatest calligrapher of the West; and the unclassifiable Wols.

During a 1951 exhibition that included six painters—Mathieu, Riopelle, Serpan, Fautrier, Dubuffet, and Michaux—the critic Michel Tapié formulated a name for them all: Signifiants de l'Informel (personifiers of the informal). At the time, abstract art was at the peak of its popularity. There were many varieties of Informal Art in France, where Lyrical Abstractionism prevailed; and in the United States, where a new current called Action Painting, or Gestural Painting, had just emerged. The exhibition organized by Tapié was intended to be one variation of that movement; its goal was to promote a language of "new signs."

Everything would have gone without a hitch if the Machiavellian Tapié had not, as Mathieu reproached

him for, put three nonfigurative artists together with three figurative ones: Fautrier, Dubuffet, and Michaux. A polemic ensued that had to do with the ambiguousness of the adjective "informal". In retrospect, one can laugh at the rigidity of the classifications used then: Fautrier and Michaux could just as well be considered to represent Lyrical Abstractionism, without misconstruing them to a great extent. In any case, until the late fifties, Informal Art was able to keep some specific traits that distinguished it from Tachism (from "tache," blot) or pure abstraction. It managed to be open to new artists as well as to cross oceans. Its fertile contagion reached as far as Japan.

KINETIC ART (OP ART)

Kinetic Art—motion and light art—has many origins: Duchamp's wheel and rotating plaques; the mobile structures of Tatlin, Pevsner, and Gabo; Viking Eggeling's "Diagonal Symphony"; the experiments of Moholy-Nagy; Calder's mobiles; and so forth. These were the acknowledged forebears of the fundamental exhibition, "Le Mouvement"—"Motion"—presented at the gallery Denise René in Paris, April 1955. Eight artists of different age groups and backgrounds took part, each with his own interest in mobility and variability of a work of art: Agam, Bury, Calder, Duchamp, Jacobsen, Soto, Tinguely, and Vasarely. Vasarely published his "Notes for a Manifesto" in the exhibition catalogue. Endowed with motion that was either autonomous (Tinguely, Bury) or variable, depending on the whim of the viewer (Vasarely, Agam), the work of art henceforth acquired the right to move actually or visually.

In France, many Kinetic artists followed in Vasarely's footsteps, and several of them in 1963 founded the Groupe de Recherche d'Art Visuel (group of Op Art research) in Paris. Kinetic Art was introduced to the United States by Josef Alberts, much of whose work centered on the retina's animation by means of superimposed polychrome squares. Kinetic Art became also known as Op Art in this country and in Great Britain, where its most gifted adherent was Bridget Riley. Compared to an antiestablishment movement like Dada, Kinetic Art was, in the age of science, the affirmation of a new Classicism.

LAND ART

The movement called Land Art appeared in the United States in 1967. The artists who represented it, who are also called Earthworkers, refused to produce for collectors and dealers objects that would find their way into the consumer circuit. In the aftermath of the powerful rush toward nature of the sixties, and after frequent use of earth, stone, and salt in works executed in galleries, these artists decided to abandon the too-confining framework of the studio and go work in the countryside or even the desert. Michael Heizer, who dug enormous trenches on the Nevada plateaus, is one of the pioneers of Land Art, while Walter De Maria, Robert Smithson, and Dennis Oppenheim also acted on nature or evoked the expanses of the continent. But the ultimate achievement of the Earthworkers also comprises the slow process by which their work is transformed over time, as well as preparatory drawings, photos, texts, and films that document them and preserve their history.

A cousin of Arte Povera, Land Art represented its radicalization and prolongation. It questioned the notion of durability attached to the modern or traditionalist work of art, while at the same time being a kind of new Romanticism, abandoning itself to the forces and beauty of the virgin universe not yet tainted by civilization. Their works were frequently realized in places inaccessible to the public. And, like the adherents of Arte Povera, the Land Artists sought most often the ephemeral, for example, when Oppenheim drew concentric circles in the snow. Christo can be associated with this movement, particularly his use of mountainous reliefs, and, more conceptual, the Britons Richard Long and Hamish Fulton.

MURALISM

The Muralist movement developed in Mexico around Diego Rivera beginning in 1921. Shortly after the Mexican Revolution, Minister of Culture Vasconcelos wanted a public art accessible to all, which led to the idea of covering the walls of public buildings with frescoes. Even though it is specifically Mexican, Muralism has always included foreign-born artists, since Rivera worked not just with his compatriots, Alva de la Canal, Fernando Leal, and Fermín Revueltas, but also with the Frenchman Jean Charlot and the Guatemalan Carlos Merida. Orozco and Siqueiros became part of the first group, proposing a figurative art with a clear message but scholarly in origin.

The renown of the Muralists extended across all America. They were invited to paint in the United States, but their political beliefs sometimes caused them difficulties, as for example in the Rockefeller Center scandal of 1934. In the late sixties, the Chicano and black artists painting the walls of their ghettos acknowledged Rivera, Orozco, and Siqueiros.

NEOPLASTICISM

Mondrian defined this theory, which was his own, in a work published in Paris in 1920 by the gallery Léonce Rosenberg, entitled *Neoplasticism.* In it Mondrian called for a geometric purpose, insisting on the very strict play of horizontals and verticals cutting each other at right angles and compartmentalizing the white surface of the painting, as well as on the variations of relationships among the squares of pure color: red, yellow, and blue. In architecture, the consequences of Neoplasticism were a return to order, clarity, and spareness. These principles are visible in several works of the time: the Schröder House in Utrecht, for example, which dates from 1924, or the furniture dreamed up by Rietweld.

An outgrowth of the Cubism Mondrian had discovered in 1912 and whose simplicity of construction he had immediately grasped, Neoplasticism pushed Cubism to its logical extreme, supported by theosophical conceptions of a great moral rigor that made a system out of it,

at once totalizing and rigid, and which left no room for improvisation or fantasy. Mondrian hated the color green and curves, which he ultimately left out of his paintings, as they reminded him of nature; he judged them to be incompatible with the absolute order he sought in his desire to bring about a purer world in which human relations would themselves become works of art. But his extreme rigor was difficult to follow for anyone who did not share his metaphysical assumptions; also, it was not long before Mondrian drew the hostility of his colleagues at the revue *De Stijl,* founded in October 1917.

The architects J.J.P. Oud, Wils, and Van't Hoff reacted most of all to the principles they felt were ossifying, considering that it was impossible to imprison the creative imagination in geometric relations limited to squares and rectangles. Van Doesburg himself, one of the pillars of *De Stijl,* revolted in 1924 against Mondrian's Neoplasticism. In a 1927 article, he opposed "Elementarism" to the "excessively dogmatic and frequently narrow application" of Neoplasticism. Elementarism was based on the "introduction of inclined surfaces, dissonant surfaces, in opposition to heaviness and static architectonic structure." Against the stasis evident in Mondrian's principles, Van Doesburg proposed a dynamism of forms.

However, the flawless rigor of Neoplasticism is, along with Malevich's Suprematism, the major source of Abstract Geometric Art, as it would eventually develop during the course of the century.

NEW FIGURATION

This trend emerged in about 1960, when gestural abstraction was collapsing both artistically and commercially. In fact, New Figuration had always existed in twentieth-century painting: Dubuffet's little men, Baco's swollen popes, and Pignon's miners all express, each in their own way, the new relations of modern humanity with the new reality surrounding it on all sides.

Actually, it is inaccurate to imagine a clean break according to which painting in the past is viewed as having been content simply to copy or record the visible world, while contemporary painting purely and simply renounces it. Relations between the artist and reality are more complex; in every era, various elements enter into those relations, such that any painting becomes a sociocultural montage in accordance with the way the world is viewed by different ages.

However, Hans Platscheck was undoubtedly the first among the painters of the new generation to become aware of the phenomenon and to express it in a 1959 essay entitled *Neue Figurationen* (new figurations). Three painters from Florence—Antonio Buono, Silvio Loffredo, and Alberto Moretti—in 1962 signed a manifesto, *Nuova Figurazione*—New Figuration—which caused a great stir in Italy. The manifesto was what inspired an exhibition the following year, at the gallery Strozzina in Florence, which brought together the work of some thirty painters from all over Europe, including Jan Lebestein (Poland), Antonio Saura (Spain), and Hans Platscheck (Germany). A new installment of the manifesto was published on that occasion, also entitled *Nuova Figurazione,* with a preface by Jean-Louis Ferrier, then an art critic for the magazine *Les temps modernes,* accompanied by articles by various Italian and foreign critics. Two exhibitions, "New Figuration I" and "New Figuration II," were also organized at the gallery Fels in Paris, with catalogue prefaces written by Jean-Louis Ferrier and Michel Ragon.

Eventually, New Figuration triumphed just about everywhere once it became clear that abstraction, of which the major acquisitions had taken place before or during the First World War, had largely become a kind of new Academicism.

NEW OBJECTIVITY

Under the name Neue Sachlichkeit (New Objectivity), a whole current that touched on all arts and literature surfaced in Germany as of 1923. It was marked by a recourse to the act or document of the times, by a drive to illustrate sociological phenomena. It corresponds to the period of so-called economic stability and is characterized by faith in technology on the American model. Opposed to Expressionism, which was in its death agony after 1918, New Objectivity returned to order, rigor, and a Realism that encompassed two branches: a corrosive and denouncing left wing, called Verist—represented by George Grosz and Otto Dix, among others—and a Neoclassical or Neonaturalist right wing, including such painters as Kanoldt and Mense. These distinctions arose from the exhibition organized by museum curator and art historian Gustav Friedrich Hartlaub in Mannheim, 1925. The term New Objectivist applied to all those who, during the preceding ten years, were not Impressionists, Expressionists, or Constructivists, but who had "remained true to positive, perceptible reality," or who had "come back to their faith" in that reality.

In fact, the categorization is rather artificial. The only traits that the painters grouped under the heading New Objectivity had in common were a rejection of Expressionist "chaos" and of the destruction of traditional forms, and return to the values of craftsmen, withh an admiration of the techniques of medieval and Renaissance craftsmen. Later, the Nazis were unfortunately able to bring about a division: They condemned all those who appeared to be socially dangerous because of their critical Realism—Otto Dix, for example—and kept the inoffensive painters of still lifes, such as Kanoldt and Mense.

NEW REALISM

Founded by the critic Pierre Restany, New Realism took shape in a manifesto published in April 1960 in Milan, on the occasion of an exhibition of its early adherents at the gallery Apollinaire. It included Arman, César, Dufrêne, Hains, Klein, Raysse, Rotella, Spoerri, Tinguely, and Villeglé. In search of a "new expressiveness," of an "adventure of the real as perceived within oneself," and unconcerned with conceptual or imaginative transcriptions, the New Realists "considered the world as a painting from which they appropriated fragments endowed with universal meaning."

The New Realists made several appearances in 1960 and 1961, benefiting from the fame of their most audacious figure, Yves Klein, who had a talent for provoking media happenings—such as his 1960 exhibition of empty space at the gallery Iris Clert, or his "brushwomen" at the Galerie Internationale d'Art Contemporain in 1960—in order to make "pure appropriative gestures" esthetic and to give creation an absolute objectivization. Shortly thereafter, Niki de Saint-Phalle, Deschamps, and Christo joined the New Realists, whose theoretician, Pierre Restany, tried to prolong the worldwide influence of the movement beyond the death of Yves Klein in 1962 until 1970, the tenth anniversary and date of the breakup of the movement.

POP ART

Pop Art is not actually a movement, born at a specific time and place, nor is it an easy concept to define. The term first appeared in Great Britain during the fifties, when it referred, particularly in the decorative arts, to an inclination to go back and imitate the stereotyped images of the mass media: film, advertising, cartoons, and other popular consumer products.

The first appearance of the Pop spirit preceded the mid-fifties, as for example in California, with the collages of Jess Collins, the naive kitsch paintings of Bill Copley, and even in Europe, with the assemblages of Enrico Bey. Its immediate precursors were Eduardo Paolozzi, who organized the 1953 exhibition entitled "Parallel between Life and Art" at London's Institute of Contemporary Arts; Robert Rauschenberg, whose New York exhibition that same year caused a scandal; Jasper Johns, who in 1955 presented his *Targets* and *Flags*; and the Englishman Richard Hamilton, whose exhibition "Man, Machine, and Motion" was also held in 1955.

From that point on it was clear that a new mood was prevailing in the art world, which would predominate during a time that saw the globalization of pop music, from Bill Haley's 1955 hit *Rock around the Clock* to the triumph of the Beatles in 1963; it is symptomatic that the singer Elvis Presley should appear as a symbolic figure in the work of both the American Andy Warhol and the Briton Peter Blake, who in fact illustrated several of Presley's album covers.

Among the early Pop Artists were Robert Rauschenberg, Jasper Johns, Claes Oldenburg, Roy Lichtenstein, Andy Warhol, James Rosenquist, Jim Dine, Larry Rivers, and Tom Wesselman; later Pop Artists included Richard Hamilton, Peter Blake, Allen Jones, Richard Smith, and Patrick Caulfield. In the English School, the names of David Hockney and the American R. B. Kitaj—who has lived in London since 1958, where his influence has been considerable—can also be added. If the artists have chosen to magnify the most matter-of-fact and transiently flashy aspects of consumer society (Warhol's Brillo boxes and Campbell's Soup cans, Jones's inordinately high heels, and Lichtenstein's comic strips); if they have sometimes done so with humor (Oldenburg's flabby telephone and plaster cakes), generally their attitude has remained formalistic, ruling out any commitment. Even Warhol's *Electric Chair* does not have a more explicit message than the portraits of Marilyn Monroe he made at the same time (1963). It was not until the sixties that a violent denunciation of the social order occurred, with the Californian Peter Saul and later with several similarly inspired Europeans.

In France, such artists as Bernard Rancillac and Hervé Télémaque were quickly labeled Pop Artists, but in most cases the affiliation was not accepted without reluctance. In Germany, Konrad Klapheck and Peter Klasen have been associated with Pop Art; in Italy, Valerio Adami and Antonio Recalcati; in France, Martial Raysse and Jacques Monory; in Switzerland, Samuel Buri and Peter Stämpfli; Rober Raveel in Belgium; and elsewhere, Erro, Sarkis, Öyvind Fahlström, Tetsumi Kudo, and others. In the seventies, Pop Art provoked two reactions in the United States, as violent as they were contradictory: Minimal Art and Hyperrealism.

RAYONISM

Rayonism, developed by the Russian painters Mikhail Larionov and Natalia Gontcharova in around 1910, did not make an appearance in public until 1912. A manifesto was published the following year. Rayonism derived from the studies of Larionov just after the turn of the century—his painting *Rain,* for example. Forms were to be distributed according to the diffusion of light, and not according to "lines of strength," as the Italian Futurists would have it. Rayonist paintings caused their subject to explode in beams of color at sharp angles, becoming almost abstract.

Several Russian painters followed the lead of Larionov and Gontcharova, especially Mikhail Ledentu. If the scope of their work appears in retrospect to be rather limited, that of the *Rayonist Manifesto,* by contrast, remains indisputable. It is, in fact, at the origin of an awakening of Slavic individualism on the subject of artistic creation, and there is no doubt that, during a time of great change, it facilitated the birth of Suprematism and Constructivism.

SUPPORT-SURFACE

A movement that emerged primarily from the leanings of Buren and the BMPT Group, Support-Surface was founded in the fall of 1970 almost entirely by artists from the South of France. Two exhibitions were held under that name in 1971, one in the Théâtre de la Cité International in Paris, the other at the Théâtre Municipal in Nice. The key idea that drove the painters Devade, Cane, Bioules, Dezeuze, Saytour, Valensi, and Viallat to start a movement together was to reaffirm painting as such, that is, after the Neodadaism of the sixties and in reaction to the vogue of Conceptual Art, to return to such sadly neglected facts as that painting is colored matter placed on a surface and on a support, the canvas, whether or not the canvas is framed.

It is not surprising that these young artists found their theoretical inspiration in dialectical and historical materialism. The political involvement of some of them, who were grouped together around the revue *Peinture, cahiers théoriques* (painting: theoretical notebooks), caused a schism within the movement. All of them considered Cézanne and Matisse to be their great tutelary forebears. Other emphatic idols were Malevich and American Abstract Expressionism. Cane and Devade were involved with the revue *Tel quel.* Writer and critic Marcelin Pleynet closely followed the work of Support-Surface, particularly that of Viallat.

SUPREMATISM

Suprematism is a movement born of the reflections of the Russian painter Kazimir Malevich who, under the title *From Cubism and Futurism to Suprematism,* launched the idea in Petrograd (now Leningrad) in 1915. Also that year, he had exhibited his *Black Square on White,* which caused a real sensation.

For Malevich, the painter must be concerned only with painting and must reject any external considerations: "All painting prior to Suprematism, past and present (sculpture, verbal arts, music), was enslaved by the form of nature and awaits its liberation to speak in its own language and avoid dependence on reason, common sense, logic, philosophy, psychology, various laws of causality, and technical changes in life." More than Kandinsky's *About the Spiritual in Art,* this was the foundation for an art that was radically nonfigurative. Malevich would later state that painters must "reject subject and objects if they wish to be pure painters." He himself practiced what he preached by putting nothing but two-dimensional geometric figures on his canvases. An outgrowth of Cubism and Futurism, Suprematism was also a translation to the plastic arts of "Zaoum" studies—transmental language—consisting of neologisms and imaginary words, which the poets Khlevrickov and Kruchernykh, friends of Malevich, had been involved in for several years.

Beginning in 1916, several major painters rallied around Suprematism, including Olga Rozanova, Ivan Klioun, Liubov Popova, Alexandra Exter, Nadejda Oudalstova, and Ivan Pougny. After the Russian Revolutuion, Malevich taught his own theories at the Unovis studios in Vitebsk. With his students Nicolas Suetin and Ilya Chachnik, he used Suprematism in the applied arts, particularly industrial ceramics. Thus, despite the opposition of the Constructivists Tatlin and Rodchenko, Suprematism had a real impact on the Soviet Union. It became known abroad in 1922 thanks to El Lissitsky, who became involved with the Bauhaus through Moholy-Nagy and with the Stijl group through Van Doesburg. Suprematism reached its extreme with *White Square on White,* Malevich's most famous painting, which he executed in 1919. Deliberately aggressive, the Suprematist conceptions created a considerable stir. Beyond their frequently anarchistic inspiration, these conceptions evinced a rare sense of the absolute. And even though the studies to which they led finally reached an impasse on both the plastic and theoretical levels, Suprematism's goal of wiping the slate clean of the past and placing the art of our century on entirely new foundations is not present with so much intransigence in any other movement.

SURREALISM

Following Dadaism, as revolutions tend to take over from rebellions, Surrealism is above all a movement of the conquest and deepening of the unconscious. Dada, the negation of everything, contained its own demise, whereas the exploitation of Freud's discoveries opened a new, practically unlimited path for artistic studies to Surrealism. Published in 1924 by André Breton, *Surrealist Manifesto*, which stressed psychic Automatism as a creative principle, constitutes the founding of the movement.

Nonetheless, it was several years earlier that Breton, Aragon, Soupault, and Éluard had undertaken, pen in hand, the defense of the artists they loved: Duchamp, Picabia, Ernst, Masson, Arp, and Man Ray, several of whom were naturally, after Dada, in the Surrealist group. Automatism and objective chance had already been utilized by the Dadaists, it is true, but without any theory to back them, while Surrealism threw itself into a systematic prospecting through various techniques that had been discovered over the years: Masson's Automatic Drawing and Sand Painting, Max Ernst's frottages, Oskar Dominguez's decalcomania, Wolfgang Paalen's "fumages," Salvador Dali's "paranoid-critical" method, Jean Arp's torn and crumpled papers, and so forth.

In his own search for a definition of Surrealism, Max Ernst explained in 1934 why it took painters so long "to achieve poetic objectivity, in other words to banish reason, taste, and conscious will from the process of producing a work of art. All theoretical research could not, under the circumstances, be of any use to them. On the contrary, nothing but practical tests and their outcome could help them." It was, however, a sort of theory and history in which Breton would involve himself from 1925 on, with a series of aritcles that eventually became *Surrealism and Painting*, in 1928. After welcoming the Cubism of Picasso and Braque in its disarticulation of reality, Breton studied the work of de Chirico and paused briefly at Picabia before considering former Dadaists-turned-Surrealists—Ernst, Man Ray, and Arp—and newcomers Masson, Miró, and Tanguy.

By the time of the *Second Surrealist Manifesto* (1929), new artists had come into contact with the movement, including Pierre Roy and Georges Malkine, while others, from all over, would decide to join later: the Catalonian Dali, the Swiss Giacometti, Brauner from Romania, and Toyen from Czechoslovakia, living proof of how vast the influence of Surrealism had been. Surrealist groups emerged in several countries as far as Japan, but the most important group was the Belgians, who included not only some excellent poets but, with René Magritte and Paul Delvaux, two outstanding figures of Surrealist painting on an international level.

Whether it was rejecting the conventions of academic art, as Ernst and Arp did, or adopting those conventions in order to pervert them all the better, as Magritte and Dali did, Surrealism ended up affecting a broad public by entering into daily life, such as advertising. It is never absent, as can be seen when we look for the origins of many of the movements that followed it, such as Art Brut, Cobra, and Pop Art.

TRANSAVANTGARDE

Transavantgarde is a movement created in 1979 under the auspices of the Italian critic Achille Bonito Oliva and made public in 1980 at the Biennale in Venice, when three of its representative figures, Chia, Cucchi, and Clemente, became known. They were later joined by Paladino and Nicola de Maria. A 1982 exhibition in Rome assured Transavantgarde of an international audience. It is the only European movement to have conquered New York and the American market since the years immediately after the Second World War.

In reaction to the Conceptual Art of the seventies, and to the avant-gardes associated with progressive political ideologies, the Transavantgardists reaffirm the powers of subjectivity and of national origins. They reject everything about Marxism, psychoanalysis, and the ascendancy of linguistics, and renew their ties with turn-of-the-century Expressionism as well as with the Italian past; Chagall, Malevich's figurative work, Masson, Picabia, de Chirico, and the Fauves are also not far removed. The ideas of a craft once again comes into fashion. Techniques are meant to be traditional: charcoal, pencil, pen-and-ink, stencil, perspective, shadows, and varnish. Nothing matters but the invention of intimate, symbolic signs.

But Transavantgarde, although it originated in Italy, extends beyond that country. In Germany, such artists as Baselitz and Kiefer can be considered to represent it; in France, Garouste has many affinities with the movement, as do the painters known under the label of Free Figuration; in the United States, Schnabel's painting seems closer to European Transavantgarde than such primarily American movements as Pop Art and Hyperrealism, from which he completely differs.

According to Bonito Oliva, the word avant-garde has become pathetic and meaningless since it suggests the possibility and claim of rupture and of newness. In the early years of the twentieth century, when the historical situation gave the artist the illusion that he could make art into an instrument of struggle and of the transformation of society, the existence of the avant-garde was actually legitimized by the facts themselves. Scandal demonstrated that the work of art could become an effective transgression of the rules governing both the artistic system and social system as a whole. Today, by contrast, galleries informed by the media immediately digest all ruptures and all newness, which have thereby become inoperative. In time, the public has acquired a musclelike ability to absorb the blows art has given it below the belt, and has learned not to be frightened by it anymore, accepting exhibitions of rubbish, piles of stones, and other expressions of an art devoid of all capacity for contention, even in museums.

The role of cultural promotion and social identification that the avant-garde used to play has become an illusion, a deception, at the same time as it was being drained by its immediate absorption by the marketplace. Nothing remained but to return to the traditional qualities of the work of art: universality, necessity, and authenticity, all of which are found in the Transavantgarde.

AALTO
ALVAR

Finnish architect; born in Kuortane, 1898; died in Helsinki, 1976. After studying at the Helsinki polytechnical school, in 1923 he opened his own firm and in 1925 married Aino Marsio, who became his most important collaborator until her death in 1949. He was a regular participant in the CIAM (Congrès Internationaux d'Architecture Moderne—international congresses of modern architecture); his friends included such artists as Brancusi, Léger, Moholy-Nagy, Braque, and Calder. His architecture is characterized by extreme simplicity and by the use of wood, brick, and glass, as well as concrete. Scandinavia's greatest contemporary architect, Aalto was also an urbanist, sensitive to the psychological problems posed by cities, and a talented designer, to whom we are especially indebted for his chairs and other pieces of furniture. His major achievements include the Helsinki Cultural Center, 1955-1958, and the Maison Carré in Bazoches-sur-Guyonne, France, 1956-1959.

ALBERS
JOSEF

A German-American painter, born in Bottrop, Westphalia, 1888 died in New Haven, Connecticut, 1976. He studied at the Bauhaus from 1920 to 1923 and later taught there, and in 1933 went into exile in the United States, chairing the art department at the experimental Black Mountain College in North Carolina. Albers confined himself to the strict geometry of the square as the principal motif of his paintings, and created infinite and subtle variations on that theme; in his work he achieved a rare economy of means. Under his impetus, Black Mountain College became a major center of avant-garde activities in the United States during the forties. Robert Rauschenberg and Kenneth Noland were among his students. Because of Albers's research on the interaction of

The twentieth century, one of the richest in the history of art, abounds in geniuses and great talents. They appear in the Index at the end of this work. Several of them, however, have been more influential than others, and they are listed here with a brief biographical sketch, followed by museums where their work is on display.

colors, he is considered one of the fathers of Op Art.

New York: Museum of Modern Art;
   Whitney Museum
London: Tate Gallery
Amsterdam: Stedelijk Museum

APPEL
KAREL

Dutch painter; born in Amsterdam, 1921. He studied at the academy in Amsterdam and had his first show in Groningen, 1946. His early work was influenced by Picasso, Matisse, and Dubuffet. In 1948, with Corneille and Constant, he founded the experimental group and magazine *Reflex*, which soon thereafter merged with the Cobra movement. It was in Paris, where he had an exhibition in 1949 and took up residence in 1950, that Appel truly mastered his creative powers. He worked freely with color, which he applied in thick blotches as a reaction against the geometric Academicism inherited from neoplasticism, and his subject matter was both broad-ranging and powerful. A trip to the United States in 1957, where he was introduced to Action Painting, ushered in a new period for Appel, as his work became more dynamic: *Two Heads in a Landscape*, 1968. He also created polychrome sculptures, stained-glass windows, and mural paintings.

Amsterdam: Stedelijk Museum
Paris: Musée National d'Art Moderne

ARCHIPENKO
ALEXANDER

Russian sculptor; born in Kiev, 1887; died in New York, 1964. After studying at the fine-arts school in Kiev, he moved to Paris in 1908 and became passionately interested in the research of Picasso and Braque. His *Torso* (1909) is considered the first Cubist sculpture, and his work from 1911 on puts him in the forefront of innovators. Archipenko's work is characterized by its disarticulation and perforation of volumes that are subsequently penetrated by space. In 1913, he took part in the Armory Show, and, after directing an art school in Berlin from 1921 to 1923, he moved to the United States, where he taught at Washington University, the New Bauhaus in Chicago, and New York. His sculptopaintings from the important *Medrano* series, combining painted wood, metal, and glass, are among his most distinctive work.

New York: Museum of Modern Art
Paris: Musée National d'Art Moderne

ARMAN
(ARMAND FERNANDEZ)

A French-American sculptor; born in Nice, 1928. Member of the School of Nice and cofounder of the New Realists group in 1960. Arman is universally known for his "Accumulations," consisting of heaps of common utensils such as jugs, irons, coffeepots, saws, or even rubbish enclosed in plexiglass boxes. Arman's *Colères* (anger) series, with dismembered violins, cellos, and other musical instruments, is famous. Also

noteworthy are his *Combustions*. But his greatest work to date is *Long-Term Parking*, a sixty-six-foot-tall monument made from the Accumulation of sixty automobiles imprisoned in concrete. Arman is planning a monumental Accumulation comprising World War II combat tanks from different countries.

New York: Museum of Modern Art
Paris: Musée National d'Art Moderne
Jouy-en-Josas: Fondation Cartier

ARP
JEAN

French painter and sculptor; born in Strasbourg, 1886; died in Basel, 1966. He studied first at the academy in Weimar, then at the Julian Academy in Paris. After moving to Weggis, Switzerland, in 1911, he took part in the activities of the Blue Rider and the magazine *Der Sturm*. Later, in Paris, he met Apollinaire and Picasso. The war overtook him in Grasse, and he moved to Zurich as a refugee; there, starting in 1916, he became well known as the cofounder with Tristan Tzara of the Dadaist movement. During his Dadaist period, he worked primarily on collages, painted wood, and reliefs. In 1930 Arp, who had been playing with the laws of chance and was interested in anti-art of every sort, became part of the Circle and Square group and was increasingly diligent in his devotion to sculpture. The elegant curves and frequently hollowed-out volumes of his marbles and bronzes are pure and concise. He also created monumental sculptures for the Caracas university campus, 1953; the UNESCO building in Paris, 1956; and the university of Bonn, 1961.

Paris: Musée National d'Art Moderne
Basel: Kunstmuseum
Clamart: Fondation Arp

BACON
FRANCIS

English painter; born in Dublin, 1909. Self-taught, he made frequent trips to England, France, and Germany. In 1930, he painted his first self-portraits, which for the most part he destroyed. The following year, he began his studies for *Crucifixion*, a subject that obsessed him for years. Later subjects were often based on a preexisting iconography: photography, film, current events, or a work of art; in 1953, for example, he was inspired by Velásquez' *Portrait of Innocent X* and by one of Van Gogh's self-portraits. His aim was to agitate the spectator; never being one for traditional representation, he interpreted the human figure stripped of both beauty and repose, in pained and compact poses. With dramatic intensity, he revealed the arcane secrets of his anguished soul. Major retrospectives of Bacon's work were held in 1971-1972 at the Grand Palais, Paris, and the Kunsthalle, Düsseldorf.

New York: Museum of Modern Art
London: Tate Gallery
Paris: Musée National d'Art Moderne
Marseilles: Musée Cantini

BALLA
GIACOMO

Italian painter; born in Turin, 1871; died in Rome, 1958. Self-taught, he went to Paris in 1900, discovering Impressionism and divisionism. It was the working world that inspired his early paintings, such as *A Worker's Day*, 1904. Severini and Boccioni were frequent visitors to his studio. In 1909, Marinetti won him over to the Futurists' theories: He then painted *The Street Light*, showing the decomposition of light, and in about 1910 he analyzed motion and reproduced the mechanics of walking in *Dynamism of a Dog on a Leash*, 1912. He later developed extreme theories of Futurism and composed a series of canvases, one of which—*Mercury Passes before the Sun*, 1914—attained a degree of nonfiguration that made him a precursor of abstract painting. After the First World War, Balla continued to paint highly cadenced pictures, and in 1925 he participated in the "International Exhibition of Decorative Arts" in Paris, with two large tapestries: *Sea, Sail, and Wind* and *The Futurist Spirit*. After 1930 he returned to figurative painting. The Galleria Nazionale d'Arte Moderna in Rome did a major retrospective on him in 1972.

Rome: Galleria Nazionale d'Arte Moderna
New York: Museum of Modern Art

BALTHUS
(COUNT BALTHAZAR KLOSSOWSKI DE ROLA)

French painter; born in Paris, 1908, to a family of artists who introduced him to Bonnard, Russel, and Derain. He had shows in Paris starting in 1934, and slowly his favorite subjects took shape: street scenes, interiors, portraits. Under the influence of Surrealism, Balthus created a sort of Realism of the dream, and his paintings are laden with the heavy tensions of innuendos. Since 1933 and throughout his life, he has painted the street in all its many aspects: silent, filled with mysterious echos, magical unreality, and anguish all at once. His language is extremely simple; his colors are light and delicate. From 1961 to 1976, Balthus was the director of the Villa Medici in Rome. He has had few exhibitions, but a number of major retrospectives have been devoted to him: in 1966, at the Museum of Decorative Arts in Paris; in 1968, at London's Tate Gallery; in 1973, at the Musée de Marseille; and in 1983-1984, at the Georges Pompidou Center in Paris and at the Metropolitan Museum in New York.

Paris: Musée National d'Art Moderne
New York: Museum of Modern Art
Zurich: Kunsthaus

BAZAINE
JEAN

French painter; born in Paris, 1904. After studying sculpture at the Beaux-Arts Academy in Paris, he took up painting, and had his first show in 1932. During the German occupation, he surrounded himself with the young set of artists who in 1941 had a group show at the gallery Braun, entitled "Vingt Peintres de Tradition Française" (twenty painters in the French tradition). It was not until after the war, however, that Bazaine turned to nonfiguration, although he never stopped questioning nature, translating the profound impressions it evoked in him: *La clairière* (the clearing), 1951; *L'arbre et la vague* (tree and wave), 1953. His rhythms unfolded over the entire surface of the painting, and while he has gone through a number of different periods and subjects, the rhythms have barely changed. Bazaine also wrote theoretical treatises, such as *Notes sur la peinture d'aujourd'hui* (notes on the painting of our time), 1948. In 1951 he created stained-glass windows for the baptistery in the church in Audincourt as well as the mosaics adorning the church façade; most recently, he decorated the Cluny metro station in Paris.

Paris: Musée National d'Art Moderne
Eindhoven: Van Abbenmuseum
Saint-Paul: Fondation Maeght

BECKMANN
MAX

German painter; born in Leipzig, 1884; died in New York, 1950. From early youth, he was drawn to Gothic painting, one of several revelations from a 1903 trip to Paris, where he saw the exhibition of the French Primitives. He was also influenced by El Greco and painted a number of canvases inspired by religion or mythology: *The Calling of the Holy Spirit*, 1910, and *Battle of the Amazons*, 1911. The many horrors of the war he lived through marked a turning point for his work. Death and the hellishness of large cities then became his favorite subjects. During the thirties, he was committed to the New Objectivity, but his Realism could not be separated from philosophical concerns and Symbolism. In 1933, he lost his professorship at the academy in Frankfurt, and in 1937 emigrated to the Netherlands, where he remained for ten years. He then lived in the United States, and throughout his American period he protested irrationality and the evils of modern society, exalting the individual and the spiritual life.

Paris: Musée National d'Art Moderne
Munich: Neue Pinakothek
New York: Museum of Modern Art

BEUYS
JOSEPH

German artist; born in Krefeld, 1921; died in Düsseldorf, 1986. As a child, he lived in Rindern and Cleves, in Lower Rhineland, and graduated from the Cleves *gymnasium* in 1940. A copilot in the *Luftwaffe*, he was shot down over Russia, where he remained as a prisoner of war until late 1946. In 1947 he registered at the Düsseldorf Academy of Fine Arts, taking sculpture classes from Josef Enseling and Ewald Mataré. He was named professor of sculpture at the Academy in 1961. After taking part in the Fluxus movement, he turned to politics, and in 1970 founded the "organization of non-vothers." Dismissed from his teaching post in 1972, he contested the decision, which was declared nul and void by the federal work tribunal in Kassel on April 7, 1978. In the meantime, he had acquired international fame, capped by a major retrospective at New York's Guggenheim Museum in 1979. His most recent honor was the Wilhelm Lehmbruck prize from the city of Duisburg, 1986.

Paris: Musée National d'Art Moderne
Darmstadt: Hessisches Landesmuseum
Munich: Städtische Galerie im Lenbachhaus
New York: Museum of Modern Art
Basel: Kunstmuseum

BISSIÈRE
ROGER

French painter; born at Villaréal in Lot-et-Garonne, 1886; died in

Boissiérette in Lot, 1964. A friend of Braque, he was fascinated by Cubism and taught at the Ranson Academy from 1925 to 1938. During the Second World War, he hid out in Lot and stopped painting to lead the humble life of a farmer. He returned to his canvases in 1945, endowed with a profound lyricism and a free interpretation of his emotions. He spiritualized and enriched his subject matter; his colored textures, painted with a full brush in vivid yet modulated tones, earned the unanimous veneration of his young contemporaries. He abandoned figurative painting, but not before finding his inspiration in nature, which he depicted from his own inner perspective. He was awarded the Prix National des Arts in 1952, and was given a retrospective at the Musée National d'Art Moderne in Paris in 1959.

Paris: Musée National d'Art Moderne

BOCCIONI
UMBERTO

Italian painter and sculptor; born in Reggio, Calabria, 1882; died in Verona, 1916. From 1898 to 1902, he was a frequent visitor to Balla's studio in Rome. He admired the Impressionists and Seurat. He became allied with the Italian Divisionism of Privati and Pelizza, adopting their social theories aimed at the renewal of society and art: *The City Rises,* 1911. His Divisionist research led him to a dynamism akin to Futurist ideas. His affiliation with the poet Marinetti and the painters Carrà and Russolo began in 1910, and from it Futurism took shape. Boccioni's writings, painting, and sculpture made him that movement's most active proponent. *Unique Shape of Continuity in Space,* 1913, is his masterpiece. His dynamic conception of volume was utterly remarkable.

Milan: Galleria d'Arte Moderna
New York: Museum of Modern Art
Zurich: Kunsthaus

BONNARD
PIERRE

French painter; born in Fontenay-aux-Roses, 1867; died in Cannet, 1947. He attended the Julian Academy, where in 1889 he joined forces with Maurice Denise and Paul Ranson to create the Nabi group under the influence of Paul Sérusier. Seduced by the synthetic forms of Japanism, his boldness was apparent in his layouts, in which space was reduced to the flat surface; *Le peignoir* (housecoat), 1890. From 1893 to 1898, he painted scenes from the daily life of Paris, which have been described as "Verlainesque": In them, light and perspective are reversed. Later, he increasingly lightened his palette after the manner of the Impressionists, while still maintaining a rigorous composition, such as in *La barque* (the boat), 1906. His *Nus au bain* (bathing nudes) represented the opportunity to play with an inexhaustible variety of reflections and to change his attitude towards reality. From 1930 on, his chromaticism became more and more dazzling, and his work broke free from reality, expressing space through the simple juxtaposition of tones: *Nu prenant son bain* (the bathing nude) or *Atelier au mimosa* (mimosa studio), 1939. He painted these in his house at Cannet, where he died.

Paris: Musée du Petit Palais
Minneapolis: Institute of Arts
London: Tate Gallery

BRANCUSI
CONSTANTIN

Romanian sculptor; born at Targu-Jiu, 1876; died in Paris, 1957. He left home at age eleven, received no schooling, and in 1899 enrolled at the fine-arts school in Bucharest. After wandering throughout Europe, he reached Paris in 1904. There, he was fascinated by Rodin, who suggested Brancusi come to work for him. Brancusi, however, refused, preferring his freedom to search for absolute, primordial form and to perfect the sleek and glossy surfaces he felt were the essence of his art. In

The Seal, 1924-1936, he evoked the idea of the seal, rather than representing its Naturalist reality. His vocation was a constant thirst for the absolute and the eternal. In some of his wood sculptures, such as *Adam and Eve,* 1921, the influence of African art is fully apparent. He conceived of an order that ruled nature and that found its expression in perfect, simplified forms. His most significant work is the monumental group he executed in 1937 for the city of his birth, which included the famous *Endless Column.*

Paris: Musée National d'Art Moderne
New York: Museum of Modern Art
Zurich: Kunsthaus

BRAQUE
GEORGES

French painter; born at Argenteuil, 1882; died in Paris, 1963. He learned decorative painting and was later very impressed by Fauve painting. Soon, however, his art underwent a transformation: *Les maisons à l'Estaque* (houses at l'Estaque), 1908, along with Picasso's *Les demoiselles d'Avignon,* is one of the founding canvases of Cubism. He then worked closely with Picasso; until the outbreak of the First World War, the two of them lived out one of the most fabulous adventures of modern art. Wounded in the war, after a long convalescence he returned to painting and took Cubism along a Synthetic path, sumptuous and personal at the same time. Braque began executing sculptures in about 1943, and painted large canvases, including *Le salon, Le billard,* 1944. In 1948 he received the grand prize at the Biennale in Venise. From 1949 to 1956, he painted his *Ateliers* (studios) series, which combined the research and themes of his entire opus. In 1953, he painted the ceiling of the Etruscan room in the Louvre on the theme of the bird, which became the symbol of his later work. He designed several ballet sets for Diaghilev and also designed jewelry.

Paris: Musée National d'Art Moderne

New York: Museum of Modern Art
Basel: Kunstmuseum

BUFFET
BERNARD

French painter; born in Paris, 1928. He took courses at the Beaux-Arts Academy and at Darbefeuille. Later, he was influenced by the great Realist painters of the nineteenth century, as well as by Gruber. His first exhibition was in 1947, at a bookstore in the Latin Quarter, where he was noticed by Pierre Descargues. In 1948, he received the Prix de la Critique, and Emmanuel David, who became his dealer, was impressed by the rigor of his Miserabilist style and the asceticism of his angular, vertical traits, reduced to their simplest expression. In 1955, at the gallery Drouant-David, he exhibited his *Horreur de la guerre* (the horror of war), a denunciation of concentration camps. Each year from 1955 on, he exhibited thematic series: *Le cirque* (circus), *Jeanne d'Arc* (Joan of Arc), *Les oiseaux* (birds), *Le museum, La corrida* (bullfight), *Les folles* (madwomen), and so on. In 1958, when he married Annabel, he had a highly successful retrospective at the gallery Charpentier. He illustrated books by Giono, Cyrano de Bergerac, and Cocteau, among others, and designed ballet sets for Roland Petit. In 1973, the Bernard Buffet Museum opened at Surugadaira, Japan, where his popularity is skyrocketing.

Paris: Musée d'Art Moderne de la Ville;
      Musée National d'Art Moderne

CALDER
ALEXANDER

American sculptor; born in Lawton, a suburb of Philadelphia, 1898, died in New York, 1976. He studied engineering, took drawing classes at night, and had an extremely vaied career. Calder moved to New York in 1923, where he made his first sculptures out of wood and wire. In 1931 he again moved, this-time to Paris, where he joined the Abstraction-Creation group and befriended Arp, Léger, Miró, and Mondrian. His first bronze sculptures were created in this period, as well as animated constructions. It was Marcel Duchamp who gave the name "mobiles" to Calder's sculptures, which were set in motion by hand or electricity, and eventually only by air; later, Jean Arp dubbed his massive, static sculptures "stabiles." Through his imagination, combined with his mechanic's skill, Calder was able to create a completely free and rhythmic universe in a state of constant renewal. There have been several Calder retrospectives, particularly in New York. After the Second World War, he lived in both France and Connecticut. He published his *Autobiography* in 1972.

Paris: Musée National d'Art Moderne
Zurich: Kunsthaus
New York: Museum of Modern Art

CÉSAR
(CÉSAR BALDACCINI)

French sculptor; born in Marseilles, 1921. The son of humble Italian immigrants, he studied first at the Academy of Fine Arts in Marseilles and, beginning in 1943, at the Beaux-Arts Academy in Paris. Lacking the funds to purchase marble, he made his early works by soldering scrap metal. That experience attracted him to scrap heaps, the "authentic quarries of modern society." His sculpture is akin to that of Picasso and Germaine Richier. In 1960, he showed a compressed automobile at the Salon de Mai, causing a sensation. He would later compress motorcycles, cardboard, and jewelry. After the Compressions came Expansions of polyurethane, which he poured in generous quantities over the floor. He also executed mechanical enlargements, by pantograph, of his own thumb. César thought of himself in all seriousness as a traditional sculptor, enamored of work well done, at the opposite extreme from Dada.

Paris: Musée National d'Art Moderne
Marseilles: Musée Cantini
New York: Museum of Modern Art

CHAGALL
MARC

Russian-French painter; born in Vitebsk, 1887; died in Saint-Paul-de-Vence, 1985. He came from a modest Jewish family and studied first at the arts school in Leningrad; he was later a student of Léon Bakst. In 1910, in Paris, he became a friend of the poet Blaise Cendrars and lived in La Ruche with Modigliani, Soutine, Léger, and Lipchitz. Using the precepts of Cubism, he transformed his memories of Russia and imaginary visions: *Moi et le village*, 1911. When the First World War broke out, he returned to Russia, and during the Revolution was named fine-arts commissioner for the province of Vitebsk. He went back to France in 1923, where he illustrated Gogol's *Dead Souls*, the *Fables* of La Fontaine, and the Bible. A trip to Palestine, Syria, and Egypt left a deep impression on him. Shortly before 1940, the anguish of war emerged in his paintings: *La chute de l'ange* (the fall of the angel). He became a refugee in the United States in 1941, designing sets and costumes for Stravinski's *Firebird*. Back in France in 1948, he produced ceramics and stained-glass windows for the church at the Plateau d'Assy, the Metz cathedral, and the synagogue of the Hadassah Medical Center in Jerusalem. In 1964, he painted the ceiling of the Paris Opera. In 1973, the Musée Chagall opened in Nice, primarily to house the *Message biblique* (biblical message), which was executed between 1954 and 1967; one hundred and five plates of the engraved Bible; and seventy-five lithographs.

Nice: Musée Chagall
Paris: Musée National d'Art Moderne
New York: Museum of Modern Art; Guggenheim Museum
London: Tate Gallery
Amsterdam: Stedelijk Museum

DALI
SALVADOR

Spanish painter; born in 1904 in Figueras, Catalonia, where he died in 1989. Trained at Madrid's school of fine arts, he was drawn simultaneously to Academicism, Impressionism, Futurism, and Cubism; after reading Freud, his passions turned to dreams and the unconscious. In 1928, he met Picasso and Breton and joined the Surrealists. He also met Gala Éluard, who became his companion and muse. In 1929, he began formulating the "paranoid-critical" method, which would provide the foundations for most of his paintings: *Construction molle avec haricots bouillis; prémonition de la guerre civile* (soft construction with boiled beans; premonition of civil war), 1936; *Girafes en feu* (burning giraffes), 1936-1937. After a stay in the United States from 1940 to 1948, where his influence was felt on fashion, advertising, and ballet sets, he went back to Spain to undergo a religious crisis: *Le Christ de Saint-Jean-de-la-Croix*, 1951, and returned to the baroque traditions and landscapes of his youth, in harmony with his temperament. His rich and complex personality was revealed through his writings: *The Secret Life of Salvador Dali*, 1941; *Journal of a Genius*, 1954. Two enormous retrospectives have been done on him, in the Boymans Van Beuningen Museum of Rotterdam (1970-1971), and at the Georges Pompidou Center in Paris (1979-1980). In 1974 he created his own museum in Figueras. Another museum, in Cleverland, houses the Reynold Morse Collection. He was elected to the Beaux-Arts Academy of Paris in 1979.

Figueras: Théâtre-Musée Dali
Paris: Musée National d'Art Moderne
New York: Metropolitan Museum of Art; Museum of Modern Art
Cleveland: Museum of Art
Basel: Kunstmuseum
London: Tate Gallery

DE CHIRICO
GIORGIO

Italian painter; born in Volos, Thessaly, 1888; died in Rome, 1978. De Chirico received his artistic training in Munich, from the visionary painters Arnold Böcklin and Max Klinger. In 1911, he met Appolinaire and Picasso in Paris. He was the principal founder of Metaphysical Painting, advocating the role of the imagination while rendering a solid, precise reality. The object, arbitrarily transposed in a fantastic setting, expresses a dreamlike Surrealism: *The Philosopher's Conquest*, 1914. During this period, his paintings featured the dressmakers' faceless mannequins that had frightened and fascinated him in childhood. After 1915, he moved to Ferrare. Back in Paris in 1924, he took part in the first exhibition of the Surrealists. He made a final break with them in 1928, embracing tradition and devoting himself to deliberately Classical painting inspired by ancient culture. Towards the end of his life, he returned to the Metaphysical Painting of his origins, repeating his old discoveries but bringing nothing new to them except great technical mastery.

Paris: Musée National d'Art Moderne
New York: Museum of Modern Art

DE KOONING
WILLEM

Dutch-American painter; born in Rotterdam, 1904. He came to the United States in 1926 and, in 1935 and 1936, worked as a Muralist in the Federal Arts Project. He taught at Black Mountain College, North Carolina, and at Yale University. Influenced, as was his friend Arshile Gorky, by Picasso, he always kept to Cubist space but tackled figuration. He had his first personal exhibition in 1948, a recognition that was as belated as that accorded his friends in the New York School. Almost overnight he was acknowledged as one of Gestural tendency, on the basis of the beautiful abstractions in black and white he exhibited there. Nonetheless,

De Kooning's work is not exclusively abstract, as he has always been drawn to the human figure. His numerous *Women* are the image of violence that De Kooning found in life and in the heart of the American city. His vehement gestures contrast with the pastel colors used in his handsome, although rare, abstract landscapes, as well as in the work of his later years.

New York: Museum of Modern Art;
  Whitney Museum; Metropolitan
  Museum of Art
Paris: Musée National d'Art Moderne
Amsterdam: Stedelijk Museum

DELAUNAY
ROBERT AND SONIA

Both born in 1885, Robert Delaunay, a Frenchman, died in Montpellier, 1941, and Sonia Terk (of Russian origin) in Paris, 1979; they were married in 11910. Impassioned by problems of light, Robert Delaunay followed in the footsteps of Seurat before joining the Cubist movement. Following a similar path when she arrived in Paris, Sonia Terk was shocked by Fauvism at the 1905 Salon d'Automne. The meeting of these two young people precipitated their respective studies. For this pair, enamored of color, colorful structure became both the form and subject of their art. Beginning in 1914, this new plastic language led to Inobjective Painting that sought to express the pace of modern society in the terms of our perceptual awareness of it. In 1934, they executed the Air Palace and the Railways Palace for the Paris International Exposition. Sonia, who outlived her husband by many years, had her own style, full of skillful freshness. She used color-forms to create also dresses, fabrics, and various objects of daily use.

Paris: Musée National d'Art Moderne;
  Musée d'Art Moderne de la Ville
New York: Guggenheim Museum

DERAIN
ANDRÉ

French painter, born in Chatou, 1880; died in Chambourcy, 1954. At age nineteen, he enrolled in the Académie Carrière, where he met Vlaminck. He worked in the Louvre, attracting the attention of Matisse with the freedom and strength of his copies. After military service, he devoted himself completely to painting, and exhibited at the 1905 Salon d'Automne as part of the famous "Cage aux Fauves," Then, at the suggestion of Vollard, he went to London, painting Hyde Park with striking colors and simple lines, but always with a readable composition. In 1907 he moved to Montmartre, near the Bateau-Lavoir and his new friends Braque, Apollinaire, Van Dongen, and Picasso. Relentlessly curious, he was one of the first to discover African Art and popular imagery. Although he was not a total adherent of Cubism, he introduced an increasingly strong structure into his canvases: *Baigneuses* (bathers), 1908. After the First World War, he began examining the arts of the past and embraced tradition to some extent through his use of perspective, shape, and chiaroscuro, as can be seen in his series of *Tables garnies* from 1921-1923.

Grenoble: Musée de Peinture et de
  Sculpture
Paris: Musée National d'Art Moderne
Troyes: Collection Pierre Lévy
Washington: National Gallery of Art
London: Tate Gallery

DIX
OTTO

German painter; born in Untermhaus, Thuringia, 1891; died in Hemmenhofen, 1969. In 1910, he enrolled in Dresden's school of decorative arts, one of the earliest centers of Expressionism, where he assimilated the innovations of the Blue Rider, Die Brücke, and Futurism. He enlisted during the First World War, which provided him with the major theme of his art; his engravings are full of appalling hallucinations. After the war, Dix's essentially graphic, lively, and aggressive style emerged, heightened by an intense palette of cold, strident color: *Trench Warfare*, 1920-1923. He set himself up as a pitiless judge of his times, depicting them with sarcastic ferocity. He is considered the leader of New Objectivism, whose first exhibition took place in Manheim, 1925. After 1930, Dix softened his style somewhat and borrowed his themes from ancient masters, as in the *Temptation of St. Anthony*, 1944, infusing his painting with a strange, Cranachian poetry.

New York: Museum of Modern Art
Düsseldorf: Kunstmuseum
Stuttgart: Staatsgalerie

DUBUFFET
JEAN

French painter; born in The Hague, 1901; died in Paris, 1985. He trained at the fine-arts school in The Hague, and attended the Julian Academy in 1918 before deciding to work on his own. It was not until he was about forty that he finally chose the artist's career. From his first exhibition in 1944, he caused a scandal with his ferocious, destructive verve, but he was noticed by such writers as Paulhan and Éluard. Interested in the plastic expression of mental illness, he created in 1948 the Compagnie de l'Art Brut. He introduced "Materiologies" into painting, including tar and coal, transforming his canvases into bas-reliefs marrying hollows with bumps or comprising grotesque characters: *Sols et terrains*, 1952; *Fleur de barbe*, 1960. From 1962 on, Dubuffet began the cycle of the *L'hourloupe*, in which familiar characters or motifs are composed as in a fantastic puzzle: *J'accours*, 1964. Later, the surface of the wall was no longer enough for him, and he applied the same esthetic to architectural plans and polyester sculptures: *Table porteuse d'instances, d'objets et de projets* (table of requests, of objects, of projects), 1968.

Paris: Musée National d'Art Moderne;
  Musée des Arts Décoratifs
New York: Guggenheim Museum;
  Museum of Modern Art
Zurich: Kunsthaus
London: Tate Gallery
Venice: Peggy Guggenheim Collection
Cologne: Ludwig Museum

DUCHAMP
MARCEL

French-American artist; born in Blainville-Crévon, Eure, 1887; died in Neuilly-sur-Seine, 1968. In Paris he met up with his brothers, Jacques and Raymond, taking classes at the Julian Academy. His first portraits and landscapes were painted under the influence of Neoimpressionism and the Nabis: *Maison rouge dans les pommiers* (red house among apple trees), 1908, and then of Cubism: *Joueurs d'échecs* (portrait of chess players), 1911. At the New York Armory Show of 1913, he showed his *Nu descendant un escalier* (nude descending a staircase), which caused a sensation. The same year, he decided on his first "readymade," which was a bicycle wheel attached to a stool by means of its fork, an everyday object turned into a work of art. He then began to design his famous glass, composed of fragments of cut, painted tin: *La mariée mise à nu par ses célibataires, même* (the bride stripped bare by her bachelors), which was finally left "uncompleted" in 1923. Moving to New York after the Armory Show, Duchamp, along with Picabia, brought Dadaism to that city, and published the revue 291 with Man Ray. In 1918, he executed his last canvas, *Tu m'as* his farewell to painting. He became a professional chess player, participating in a number of tournaments in France and the United States. His last work, *Étant donnés ...(given ...),* which was not seen until after his death, evokes both the erotic and the initiatory.

Philadelphia: Museum of Art
New York: Museum of Modern Art
Paris: Musée National d'Art Moderne

DUFY
RAOUL

French painter; born in The Hague, 1877; died in Forcalquier, 1953. Beginning in 1892, he took night classes at the municipal school of fine arts in The Hague, where he met Othon Friesz. He went to Paris in 1900, getting into fine arts in the Bonnat studio, and became interested in the Impressionists and Postimpressionists. In 1906, he painted *Affiches à Trouville*, whose colors and themes align him with the Fauve movement. Dufy's art subsequently became more severe, especially after he met Matisse and Braque. He brought the xylograph back into fashion, illustrating Apollinaire's *Bestiary* (1910) and designing fabrics for Paul Poiret and the sets for Jean Cocteau's *Bœuf sur le toit*. Time spent in southern France and Italy liberated his art; his brush stroke became extraordinarily sharp, and his pure colors spread out in flat tints. He executed *La fée électricité*, the largest painting in the world, which told the story of electricity on about seventy thousand square feet, for the Palace of Light at the 1937 International Exposition. At the end of his life, Dufy went in for more ambitious studies, demonstrating a great faculty for invention, vitality, and youth.

Paris: Musée d'Art Moderne de la Ville; Musée National d'Art Moderne

ERNST
MAX

German-French painter; born in Bruhl, Rhineland, 1891; died in Paris, 1976. He studied philosophy in Bonn, where he met August Macke and Jean Arp. After the First World War, he joined the Dada movement in Cologne. In France between 1924 and 1938, he was a member of the Surrealists. He began his early "collages" in 1920. Then, in 1925, he discovered "frottage," which consisted of rubbing graphite on a piece of paper placed on a piece of wood with tortuous veins, from which a barbaric bestiary emerged.

Next he extended his technique to all sorts of materials, including leaves and frayed canvas, to express his Surrealistic reveries. He is the inventor of the "romans-collages"—Collage Novel: *The 100-Headed Woman*, 1929, and *Une semaine de bonté*, 1934. In his sculpture, Ernst gives form to the creations of his own personal mythology: *The King Playing the Queen*, 1944; *Capricorn*, 1948. He went to the United States as a refugee during the Second World War, after which he returned to France. In 1954 he received the grand prize in painting at the Biennale in Venice.

Paris: Musée National d'Art Moderne
New York: Museum of Modern Art
London: Tate Gallery
Venice: Peggy Guggenheim Collection

FAUTRIER
JEAN

French painter; born in Paris, 1889; died in Châtenay-Malabry, 1964. At age fourteen, he was admitted to the Royal Academy of London, where his mother took him after the death of his father. He was drafted into military service, gassed, and then given a medical discharge; after the First World War, he moved to Paris. He began exhibiting in 1921, and thereafter his painting quickly moved toward allusive figuration, using a scale of quite sombre colors and incisive design in his still lifes and landscapes, such as *Le sanglier*, (the boar), 1926-1927. In 1928 he executed a series of lithographs to illustrate Dante's *Inferno*, presaging Informal Art. He then abandoned oil painting, seeking a more impulsive expression of reality through watercolors, pastels, and a lighter graphic touch. He began his series of *Otages*, (hostages) in 1943, finding his style and technique at last by stressing the subject matter that was his first source of inspiration. He developed a reproduction process, "multiple originals," which were shown in Paris in 1950 and in New York in 1956. In 1960 he received the

painting prize at the Biennale in Venice.

Paris: Musée National d'Art Moderne; Musée d'Art Moderne de la Ville
New York: Museum of Modern Art

FONTANA
LUCIO

Italian sculptor and painter; born in Santa Fe, Argentina, 1899; died in Varese, 1968. He studied at the Brera School in Milan, and took classes from the Sumbolist sculptor Adolfo Wildt in 1928. He began working in enameled clay: *Torso italico*, 1931. In 1934 he took part in the Abstraction-Creation movement, although he never completely adopted "geometrism." He published his *White Manifesto* in 1946, in which he set out the principle that the work of art should synthesize the "four dimensions of existence": color, sound, movement, and space. He founded Spatialism in Milan, 1948, while working with ceramics, the material that best enabled him to deepen his study of space. His first *Buchi* (holes) were executed in 1949, made of pierced paper and canvas, which were intended to represent the demise of traditional painting. These were followed in 1959 by his "lacerations," or canvases lacerated by a cutter. In 1962, the Städtisches Museum of Leverkusen organized a retrospective of his work. He had his own exhibition at the 1966 Biennale in Venice.

Paris: Musée National d'Art Moderne
Rome: Galleria Nazionale d'Arte Moderna
Amsterdam: Stedelijk Museum

FRANCIS
SAM

American painter; born in San Mateo, California, 1923. He studied medicine and psychology at Berkeley and was an army aviator from 1943 to 1945. Wounded and given a medical discharge, he exhibited in San Francisco in 1948 and received his B.A. in 1949. He left for France in 1950 and made

numerous trips to the Far East, returning to California in 1962. Since 1956, Francis has been considered one of the "signifiants de l'informel" (personifiers of the informal), with "un art autre" (art of a different kind). He brought a new dimension to space, a place with an effusion of light, using the "dripping" technique and applying his colors with a sponge to create a new space of air and water. He likes to modulate large surfaces with big, vibrant blotches of bright or delicate color: *Other White*, 1952. He has had a number of successful exhibitions in various countries: New York, 1956; London, 1957; Tokyo; Osaka. In 1956 he painted an enormous diptych mural for the Basel Kunsthalle, and has had a number of his own exhibitions, particularly in Bern and Düsseldorf. All of Francis's work is permeated by color, which is its absolute point of departure.

Paris: Musée National d'Art Moderne
New York: Museum of Modern Art
London: Tate Gallery

FULLER
RICHARD BUCKMINSTER

American creator; born in Milton, Massachusetts, 1895; died in Los Angeles, 1983. He constructed buildings in which the technical fittings and dwelling areas were his sole concerns, going far beyond esthetics and the poetic depiction of the industrial era: His *Dymaxion House*, 1927, meant dynamism plus a maximum of efficiency. He then created geodesic domes, or hemispheric structures, constructed from steel ribs joined together by surfaces of different materials: metal, plastic, or even padded cardboard. The immense success of these domes was assured by their lightness, solidity, and speed of assembly. The first was built in 1952, in Woods Hole, Massachusetts, measuring fifty-nine feet in diameter. Subsequent domes were larger still, up to three hundred ninety-four feet in diameter (Union Tank Co., Baton Rouge, Louisiana, 1968). There are now more than five thousand geodesic domes of various sizes, used for a variety of purposes: radar shelters, community centers, and emergency shelters. Fuller—perhaps the only such "comprehensivist" of our time—was also a mathematician, a philosopher, a cartographer, a choreographer, a poet, and a tireless lecturer on nearly any subject.

GIACOMETTI
ALBERTO

Swiss sculptor and painter; born in Stampa, 1901; died in Coire, 1966. A student at the École des Arts et Métiers in Geneva in 1919, he went to Paris in 1922, taking classes from Bourelle at the Grande Chaumière. In 1927 he moved into a tiny studio at 46 Rue Hippolyte-Maindron. He started creating imaginary, symbolic sculptures of succinct volumes, such as *Femme cuiller* (spoon woman), 1926. In about 1930, he joined Surrealism: *Boule suspendue, ou l'heure des traces* (suspended ball), 1930. A long period of study ensued: he worked from nature, and then from memory; his sculptures became smaller and smaller. After a stay in Geneva during the war years, he turned to elongated, spindly figures fixed on enormous pedestals, imprinting them with movement and thereby reinforcing their transitory aspect: *L'homme qui marche* (walking man), 1960. Giacometti retrospectives have been held in Basel, 1950; New York, Chicago, London, Copenhagen, Bern, Zurich, and Paris, 1951-1955, and 1965. In 1962 he won the Carnegie prize for sculpture and the grand prize for sculpture at the Biennale in Venice. The Alberto Giacometti Foundation opened in Zurich the year of his death.

Paris: Musée National d'Art Moderne
Cologne: Ludwig Museum
Venice: Peggy Guggenheim Collection

GRIS
JUAN (JOSÉ VICTORIANO GONZÁLES)

Spanish painter; born in Madrid, 1887; died in Boulogne-sur-Seine, 1927. He gave up his engineering studies in 1904 to learn painting. Disillusioned by the Jugendstil, in 1906 he joined his compatriot Picasso in the Bateau-Lavoir in Paris. He made humorous drawings for *L'assiette au beurre* and *Charivari* in order to earn a living. He did not devote himself completely to painting until 1912, when his Hommage à Picasso, exhibited in the Salon des Indépendants, showed the public his personal interpretation of Cubism. After signing an exclusive contract with the dealer Daniel-Henry Kahnweiler, he became intensely involved in his studies, incorporating bands of glued paper into his paintings and even fragments of mirrors: *Table de toilette*, 1912. In about 1914, he moved toward a more synthetic technique that no longer divided the object into infinity but recreated it in an organized synthesis. His health began deteriorating in 1920. Gris's theories are set forth in lectures and articles.

Paris: Musée National d'Art Moderne
New York: Museum of Modern Art
Chicago: Art Institute

GROPIUS
WALTER

German-American architect; born in Berlin, 1883; died in Boston, 1969. He studied in Munich and Berlin. In 1911, he built the Fagus shoe factory in Alfeld an der Leine, the walls of which consisted of glass-encased steel sheaths, with the building's interior transformed into the major supporting element. He founded the Bauhaus in Weimar in 1919, and directed it until 1928; the movement was transferred to Dessau in 1925. He thought of himself not only as an architect and "industrial designer"—bringing together in his building designs all of the plastic arts, crafts, and industry—but also as a sociologist: His idea was to preserve the dignity of humanity, which was threatened by industry and mechanization. In 1934, after the Nazis came to power,

Gropius emigrated to England, and in 1937 he chaired the department of architecture at Harvard University. He created an agency in 1945, the Architects Collaborative, with young American architects, designing private dwellings and official buildings, notably in Berlin, Athens, and Boston.

GROSZ
GEORGE (GEORG)

German-American designer and painter; born in 1893 in Berlin, where he died in 1959. After studying at the Academy of Fine Arts in Dresden, he was drafted during the First World War, describing its absurdity in his drawings of 1916. In 1918, he took part in the Dada movement in Berlin, illustrating the magazine *Der Dada* with his satirical drawings. In 1925, he joined the New Objectivism group, or more specifically its Left wing, which was called "Verist." His paintings of the hypocrisies and foibles of bourgeois society were grim, pessimistic, and violent. In 1932 he was asked to teach at the Art Sudents League of New York. He then began depicting American society with watercolor and oil, turning his satire against the materialism of the middle classes. He exhibited at New York's Museum of Modern Art in 1941. After the Second World War, Grosz produced the series of *Stick Figures*, a vision of nightmares, hallucinations, and fantasies. He died shortly after his return to Berlin in 1959.

Berlin: Nationalgalerie
Stuttgart: Staatsgalerie
New York: Museum of Modern Art
Düsseldorf: Kunstsammlung
   Nordrhein Westfalen

HARTUNG
HANS

German-French painter; born in Leipzig, 1904. His earliest abstract drawings and watercolors date to 1922. He studied philosophy and art history at the university of Leipzig and attend the fine-arts academies

of Dresden and Leipzig. He became interested in the old masters, the Expressionists, and the theories of Kandinsky. From 1926 to 1935, he traveled throughout Europe, notably in the Balearic Islands, where he spent a few years. In 1939 he enlisted in the Foreign Legion; gravely wounded in 1944, he had his right leg amputated. Hartung then moved to Paris and participated in the Salon des Réalités Nouvelles of 1946. Later, widespread interest in his purely calligraphic expression developed as a result of numerous exhibitions. Hartung also does drawing, engraving, lithography, and photography. He received the painting prize at the 1960 Biennale in Venice, and the Musée National d'Art Moderne in Paris honored him with a retrospective in 1968.

Paris: Musée National d'Art Moderne
New York: Museum of Modern Art

HÉLION
JEAN

French painter; born in Couterne, in the Orne, in 1904; died in Paris, 1987. After studying engineering and architecture, he met Torrès-García and Van Doesburg; in 1929 he exhibited his first nonrepresentational canvases. He took part in the creation of the Concrete Art group and, from 1932 to 1934, collaborated with the Abstraction-Creation group, and painted *Equilibrium*, 1934. His works were shown at the "Thesis, Antithesis, Synthesis" exhibition in Lucerne, 1935, and in 1937 he left for the United States, where his work evolved towards representation: *For a Cyclist*, 1939. Drafted in 1940, he was captured and escaped. In 1947, he painted *Against the Grain*, a canvas that sums up the transition from his previous abstraction to the representation of everyday scenes and still lifes. He moved to Neuilly, France, developing a Realistic style and choosing to show events and men in action; he chronicled the events of May 1968 by sketching real-life situations. The Musée d'Art Moderne de la Ville in Paris did a retrospective on him in 1984.

Paris: Musée National d'Art Moderne
New York: Guggenheim Museum
Chicago: Art Institute

HERBIN
AUGUSTE

French painter; born in Quiévy, 1882; died in Paris, 1960. His painting, at first highly colorful, was influenced by Cézanne and then by Cubism, which led him to simplify his compositions. In 1917, he attained a personal form of "synchronetic" Cubism and began moving towards abstraction, which he finally adopted in 1927. He founded the Abstraction-Creation group in 1931 with Vantongerloo. At that time his forms were purely geometric, and his pure tones set in flat tints. He was concerned with creating a simple plastic vocabulary, and he had considerable influence on the young abstract French painters following the Second World War, especially after the appearance in 1949 of his book *Nonfigurative, Nonobjective Art*, in which he showed, in the manner of Goethe, that colors had a spiritual significance.

Paris: Musée National d'Art Moderne
Cateau-Cambrésis: Musée Matisse
New York: Museum of Modern Art;
 Guggenheim Museum

HOPPER
EDWARD

American painter; born in Nyack, New York, in 1882; died in New York, 1967. Hopper studied with Realist artists at the New York School of Art before beginning a fine career as an illustrator and commercial artist. His magazine covers from the twenties are famous. Periods of residence in Paris had a decisive impact on his painting, particularly on the most important element of his art: light. He never left the United States again after 1910, spending his summers on the New England coast, which he proceeded to paint tirelessly: luminous land-scapes, seasides, and deserted villages, lighthouses rising up against the sky. The main subject of his work is, however, New York, where he lived on Washington Square. Empty streets, cafeterias, bars at night, his scenes are illumined with a strange light. The solitary or isolated characters in their inner world seem to reflect the silence of the years when America turned inward and which became the universe of Hopper, one of the best-loved painters of his country.

New York: Museum of Modern Art;
 Whitney Museum

HUNDERTWASSER
FRIEDRICH (FRITZ STOWASSER)

Austrian painter; born in Vienna, 1928. He lost his father when he was one year old. Self-taught, he began drawing and painting in 1943 and took many trips from 1949 on, especially to Italy and France. He lived in Paris during 1950-1951 and returned to Vienna until 1953. In January 1953, he had his first exhibition, at Vienna's Art Club. In the introduction to the catalogue, he wrote: "We are no longer able to give form, to interpret the signs around us and within us." It was the beginning of a quasi-religious quest in which he is still involved. He fought against convention, so-called traditions, Academicism, against anything that stifled the creative potential of the individual. In 1953-1954, during another stay in Paris, he launched Transautomatism, with a messianic zeal. He acquired international fame between 1960 and 1966, thanks to his success at the 1962 Biennale in Venice. He became passionately interested in architecture in 1973, and fought to integrate dwellings with the natural setting.

Vienna: Österreichische Galerie
Amsterdam: Stedelijk Museum
Paris: Musée National d'Art Moderne

JAWLENSKY
ALEXEI VON

Russian painter; born in Torschok, near Tver, in 1864; died in Wiesbaden, 1941. He started a military career, then studied at the fine-arts academies in Leningrad and Munich. The colors of van Gogh left a strong impression on him. He went to Paris in 1905, met Matisse, and discovered the Fauves, who influenced his painting between 1905 and 1913: *Jeune fille aux pivoines* (young woman with bullfinches), 1909. He founded, in 1909, the New Association of Munich Artists with Kandinsky. A brilliant colorist, Jawlensky expressed his emotional reactions to the great symbols of humanity, which allied him with Expressionism. The influence of Cubism helped darken his palette and make his forms geometrical. He painted schematic faces with black rings under their eyes: *Woman with Blue Hat*, 1912; *Medusa*, 1923. Crippled by arthritis in 1929, he was increasingly inspired by mysticism and painted sad, nostalgic faces.

Paris: Musée National d'Art Moderne
Most of the German museums,
 including Düsseldorf, Cologne,
 Munich, Stuttgart, Wiesbaden,
 Wuppertal

JOHNS
JASPER

American painter; born 1930 in Augusta, Georgia. Johns moved to New York in 1951, where three years later he met Robert Rauschenberg and John Cage. He was noticed by the curator of the Museum of Modern Art and by Leo Castelli, who arranged his first exhibition in 1957. Johns and his friend Rauschenberg quickly became the inspiration for a new avant-garde. Admirers of Abstract Expressionism, they did not repudiate it but turned it into the basis for a work that was oriented toward the real world, incorporating elements of daily life into their paintings. The work that drew the attention of art connoisseurs was *Flag*, 1954, a pure and simple American flag, two-dimensional but rich and thick in texture, as is most of Johns's work. He and Rauschenberg thus opened the way to a completely new language, that of the Pop Artists. Johns's subjects are obvious, impersonal, repetitive; they are, in addition to flags, targets, maps, numbers, and letters. The elements from his studio were less obvious: paint brushes and beer bottles melted into bronze and painted. Abstract motifs, such as networks and hatchings, appear in his works of the seventies. His prints, engravings, and especially his lithographs are extremely refined.

New York: Museum of Modern Art
Houston: Ménil Collection
Paris: Musée National d'Art Moderne

JORN
ASGER (ASGER OLUF JOGERSEN)

Danish painter; born 1914 in Verjum; died in Aarhus, 1973. He began painting small landscapes and portraits in 1930. He studied the publications of Kandinsky, worked with Léger and Le Corbusier, and was then influenced by Jacobsen, Miró, Klee, and Ensor. During the war, he founded the magazine *Helhesten* in Copenhagen. At that time he was painting colorful, dynamic watercolors: *Didaska*, 1944. Between 1948 and 1951, he dominated the Cobra movement he had helped found, and participated in the "International Situationist" movement, 1957-1960. His early work was inspired by Viking mythology, but his later painting is increasingly violent Expressionist work, and in 1959 and 1962 he exhibited his *Disfigurations*, chromos charged with aggressive signs. Jorn later associated the real with the dreamlike, showing suppleness and fluidity: *Quiet Look*, 1971. He also executed engravings, immense decorative ensembles, ceramics, and tapestries.

Denmark: Museums of Louisiana,
 Aalborg, Sikeborg
Paris: Musée National d'Art Moderne
Cologne: Ludwig Museum
New York: Guggenheim Museum

KANDINSKY
WASSILI

Russian-French painter; born in Moscow, 1866; died in Neuilly-sur-Seine, 1944. He studied law and political economics, began a university career, and did not begin to paint until age thirty. He conceived of the possibility of a "pure painting," whose language would be based on the "primary values of color," and became the creator of Abstractionism in 1910. With Franz Marc, he founded in 1911 the Blue Rider and published *About the Spiritual in Art*. The First World War sent him running back to Moscow: After the Revolution, he was named to the fine-arts section of the commissariat for public education. Walter Gropius called him to Weimar in 1922 to teach at the Bauhaus, where he was put in charge of theoretical teaching in the framework of the "introductory course," and where he directed the mural-painting studio until 1933. His work, intense at the time, made use of geometric forms: *Composition VIII*, 1923. In 1931, he executed large mural panels in ceramic for the music salon of Mies van der Rohe at the international exhibition of architecture in Berlin. He emigrated to Paris in 1933, where his international stature as one of the geniuses of twentieth-century art solidified.

Paris: Musée National d'Art Moderne
Munich: Städtische Galerie
New York: Guggenheim Museum

KIRCHNER
ERNST LUDWIG

German painter; born in Aschaffenburg, 1880; died in Frauen-kirch, near Davos, 1938. As an architectural student, he discovered in the Nuremburg mus-eum the engravings of Dürer in 1898, when he made his first xylograph. In 1901 he enrolled in the Technical Academy of Dresden and studied painting in Munich. His work was shaped by a series of encounters with art: Japanese prints, Neoimpressionism, Fauvism (through Kandinsky), and sculptures from Palau and Africa. In 1905, he drafted the program of Die Brücke with Erich Heckel, Karl Schmidt-Rottluff, and Fritz Bleyl, calling on young artists to "unite to win freedom of action and life." His *Self-Portrait with Model* was painted in 1907, its colors set in flat tints and its atmosphere erotic. His art reached its peak in Berlin, where he moved in 1911: *Bare-Breasted Woman with Hat*. After the First World War, shocked by what he had witnessed, he had difficulty readapting to normal life. He moved to Switzerland, near Davos. The Nazi government confiscated six hundred and thirty-nine of his paintings in 1937. Devastated, he committed suicide a few months later.

Cologne: Wallraf- Richartz Museum
Basel: Kunstmuseum
New York: Museum of Modern Art
Paris: Musée National d'Art Moderne

KLEE
PAUL

German-Swiss painter; born in Münchenbuchsee, near Bern, in 1879; died in Muralto-Locarno, 1940. Born into a family of musicians, he vacillated between music and painting. He was trained at the Munich Academy. In 1910-, the Bern museum presented his first exhibition, featuring his "under-glass" watercolors. He met Macke, Kandinsky, and Marc in 1911 and with them took part in the Blue Rider exhibition. A trip to Tunisia in 1914 exposed him to color: "It has me in its grip, color and I are but one"; *Red and White Cupolas*, 1914. In 1920, Gropius proposed that he teach at the Bauhaus. The "geometricization" of his subjects, the incessant search for perfection in substance, and color, were all sublimated by his primordial concern for preserving the role of intuition: *Around the Fish*, 1926. Klee accepted a post at the Düsseldorf Academy of Fine Arts in 1931, but he was dismissed by the Nazis and returned to Bern in 1933. He was overcome by sorrow and suffering from scleroderma; his painting took on a symbolic, metaphysical tone *Full Moon over the Garden*, 1934. Klee's genius places him beyond all the movements of modern art.

Bern: Fondation Paul Klee
Düsseldorf: Kunstsammlung Nordrhein Westfalen
Paris: Musée National d'Art Moderne
New York: Museum of Modern Art

KLEIN
YVES

French painter; born in Nice, 1928; died in Paris, 1962. He studied for the merchant navy as well as oriental languages, and had several careers. Beginning in 1946, he executed his *Monochromes*, panels covered uniformly with a layer of pure color. In 1958, at the gallery Iris Clert, he presented an exhibition entitled "Le Vide" (the void), with absolutely bare walls. He then decorated the Gelsenkirchen opera house, in the German Ruhr district, with blue monochromes and reliefs in laminated sponges. Klein's next undertaking was his "Anthropometrics," paper prints of nude models coated with blue paint, and his "cosmogonies," using the elements of rain, wind, and thunder. In 1961, with the aid of incandescent gas, he created "peintures de feu"—"fire paintings." And in 1962, he made a plaster cast of his friend Arman's body for a *Portrait relief d'Arman*. His search for the impossible conquest of the immaterial appears today to be a synthesis of doubts common to his time.

Paris: Musée National d'Art Moderne
New York: Museum of Modern Art
London: Tate Gallery

KLIMT
GUSTAV

Austrian painter; born in 1862 in Vienna, where he died in 1918. Klimt was trained at Vienna's School of Decorative Arts. Along with his brother Ernst and Franz Matsch, he founded a workshop that executed a number of mural paintings for museums and theaters in the historical tradition of the Vienna School. In 1897 he became the first founding member and president of the Viennese Secession, in the spirit of Art Nouveau. He was given many fresco commissions: the Aula Magna of the university of Vienna, a cycle whose eroticism caused a sensation leading to its destruction; and the dining room of the Stoclet Palace in Brussels, 1905. At the same time, he drew and painted almost exclusively erotic themes celebrating the seductiveness of women: *Danae*, 1907. In his landscapes, color is applied in Pointillist strokes: *The Park*, 1910. His work is laden with symbolism.

Vienna: Österreichische Galerie; Österreichisches Museum
London: National Gallery
New York: Museum of Modern Art

KOKOSCHKA
OSKAR

Austrian painter; born in Pochlarn, 1886; died in Villeneuve, Switzerland, 1980. He studied at the School of Decorative Arts in Vienna. Influenced by Van Gogh, the art of East Asia, and Klimt, he collaborated with the Vienna Ateliers and published his first book, *Children Who Dream*, in 1908, along with eight lithographs. Adolf Loos provided him with commissions for portraits, in which Kokoschka stressed the anxiety and suffering of his models. A stay in Italy revealed to him the light and colors of Venetian painting: *The Betrothed of the Wind*, 1914. Called up to fight in 1914 and wounded in 1915, he moved to Dresden, where he became a professor at the academy. He then divided his time among Paris, Vienna, Prague, and London before retiring finally to Switzerland in 1953. Primarily urban landscapes be-came his favorite subject: *The Charles Bridge in Prague*, 1934. Generally he favored a high vantage point, which called for a "visual plunge" in his composition; his colors became increasingly pale and his lines dashing and nervous. In addition to portraits and landscapes, he painted some allegories, imbuing his subjects with philosophical intentions. He published his autobiography, *My Life*, in 1971.

Stuttgart: Staatsgalerie
Basel: Kunstmuseum
New York: Museum of Modern Art

KUPKA
FRANTISEK

Czech painter; born in Opocno, Eastern Bohemia, 1871; died in Puteaux, France, 1957. He studied at the fine-arts schools in Prague and Vienna before moving to Paris in 1894. In order to earn a living, Kupka did satirical drawings for *L'assiette au beurre* and illustrated books. He moved to Puteaux, where Jacques Villon also lived, and took part in the Section d'Or. At the 1910 Salon d'Automne he showed his work *Le grand nu* (large nude), the body of which was cut up into luminous zones following a rigorous composition, and in 1911 he painted his first abstract work, *Fugue en rouge et bleu* (fugue in red and blue). He foreshadowed the Italian Futurists in his struggle to translate movement and light by dividing his canvases into thin parallel bands: *Madame Kupka parmi les verticales* (Mrs. Kupka among verticals), 1911. In 1931, Kupka joined the Abstraction-Creation movement. A large show at the Jeu de Paume Museum in 1931 brought together his different creations, including *Circulaires, Verticales,* and *Diagonales*. A retrospective was organized in 1946 in Czechoslovakia, where a Kupka museum was created.

Paris: Musée National d'Art Moderne
New York: Museum of Modern Art
Prague: Národní Galerie V Praze

LAPICQUE
CHARLES

French painter; born in Taize, Rhône, 1898. Lapicque was drafted in 1917 and studied at the École Centrale before under-

talking a career in engineering. He spent his Sundays painting landscapes of Brittany until Jeanne Bucher finally convinced him to put all his efforts into painting. While spending time with Jacques Lipchitz and Pierre Chareau, he did scientific research on color and luminosity. He won a medal of honor at the International Exposition of 1937 for his panel, *La synthèse organique* (organic synthesis). In May 1941, he took part in the exhibition "Twenty Young Painters of the French Tradition" at the gallery Braun. He invented a blue structure that was both figurative and abstract and which "allowed glimpses of color to show through." Later, he rediscovered the sea: *L'Orage sur Lanmodez* (storm over Lanmodez), 1948. Major series were devoted to horses, races, Venetia, zoos, and music. In 1964, Lapicque became enthralled with Greece and ancient mythology. The Musée National d'Art Moderne did a retrospective on him in 1967. In 1979 he received the Grand Prix National for painting.

Paris: Musée National d'Art Moderne
Dijon: Musée des Beaux-Arts

LARIONOV
MIKHAIL

Russian-French painter; born in Tiraspol, Bessarabia, 1881; died in Fontenay-aux-Roses, 1964. By the turn of the century, he was painting in bold colors. In 1900 he met Natalia Gontcharova, who would be his lifelong companion. In 1907 he became a close friend of the Bourliouk brothers. This was the Primitivist stage of his work, in which he did brutal executions from daily life in the style of popular Russian art: his series of *Soldiers and Hairdressers*, 1907-1910. The first Rayonist works of Larionov and Gontcharova appeared in 1910-1911, and the *Rayonist Manifesto* appeared in 1913. The two painters, who had been exhibiting in Paris since 1914, finally left Russia for good in 1915 to join the ballets of Diaghilev. Larionov moved to Paris in 1918 and

abandoned painting to take up theatrical set design.

New York: Guggenheim Museum

LAURENS
HENRI

French sculptor; born 1885 in Paris, where he died in 1954. The son of a working-class family, Laurens was self-taught. He took night classes and sculpted stone at construction sites. In 1905 he moved to Montmartre, where he was influenced by Rodin. He met Braque in 1911 for what would be a lifelong friendship. With his *Constructions*, 1915-1918, he applied the procedures of Cubism to sculpture. Through Picasso he met the dealers Léonce Rosenberg and Daniel-Henry Kahnweiler, who later proved quite helpful. Laurens returned to sculpture "in the round" beginning in 1917, and from 1932 on his creations of women, nymphs, and ondines became elongated, swollen, or coiled around imaginary spirals: *Autumn*, 1948. Lauren sketched, illustrated books, and designed sets: Diaghilev's *The Blue Train*, 1924. In 1935 he received the Helena Rubenstein prize, and in 1953, the prize from the São Paulo Biennale. In 1951, the Musée National d'Art Moderne did a retrospective on him.

Paris: Musée National d'Art Moderne
Amsterdam: Stedelijk Museum
New York: Museum of Modern Art
Venice: Peggy Guggenheim Collection

LE CORBUSIER
(CHARLES-ÉDOUARD JEANNERET)

Swiss-French architect; born in La Chaux-de-Fonds, 1887; died in Roquebrune-Cap-Martin, 1965. Between 1907 and 1911, he traveled to Italy, Germany, Austria, Hungary, the Balkans, and France, familiarizing himself with different architectural styles. He moved to Paris for good in 1917. In 1920 he began publishing articles in the magazine *L'esprit nouveau*, which he founded with Amédée Ozenfant. *Vers une architecture* (toward an

architecture) followed in 1923, which made him famous. In 1929, Le Corbusier founded the CIAM (Congrès Internationaux d'Architecture Moderne), and thereafter he devoted himself to studies of urbanism and regional development, setting forth his theories in *La charte d'Athènes* (the Athens charter), 1943. Just after the war, he developed the "Modulor," a system of proportions based on the designation for gold ("or") and human measure, and built enormous housing complexes in Marseilles and Nantes. Between 1951 and 1956, he worked on plans for the city of Chandigarh, as well as executing religious structures: the chapel of Notre-Dame-du-Haut in Ronchamp, 1950-1955, and the convent of Sainte-Marie-de-la-Tourette near Lyons, 1957-1959. An exceptional creator of forms—he was also a painter—Le Corbusier tried to bring architecture into harmony with industrial civilization by proposing a new way of life.

LÉGER
FERNAND

French painter; born in Argentan, 1881; died in Gif-sur-Yvette, 1955. He studied architecture for two years in Caen before moving to Paris, where he enrolled in the school for decorative arts and spent time at the Julian Academy. Drawn by the work of Cézanne, and a friend of Robert Delaunay, he took part in the first Cubist exhibition of 1911 with his *Nus dans la forêt* (nudes in the forest). *Les contrastes de formes* (contrasts of forms), 1913, was characteristic of his bare, massive style. Drafted in 1914, he sketched from real life, resulting in *Partie de cartes* (the game of cards), 1917. He then became fascinated by industrial civilization, making humans a part of his mechanical universe: *Le grand déjeuner* (three Women), 1921. Later, he worked on his concept of objects at liberty, putting unlikely elements together within the space of the canvas: *La Joconde aux clés* (Mona Lisa with keys), 1930. He also became involved with film: *Ballets mécaniques* (mechanical ballet), 1924. He fled to the United States during the Second World War, and after his return to Europe worked on large paintings from popular inspiration on the themes of *Loisirs* (spare-time activities) and *Constructeurs* (constructors).

Biot: Musée Fernand Léger
Paris: Musée National d'Art Moderne
New York: Museum of Modern Art
Basel: Kunstmuseum

LICHTENSTEIN
ROY

American painter; born in New York, 1923. He studied with the Realist painter Reginald Marsh at the Art Students League and then at Ohio State University, where he later taught. His first one-man show was at the Leo Castelli Gallery in 1962; Castelli organized regular shows for him from then on, as he did for other Pop Artists. After several years devoted to Abstract Expressionism, Lichtenstein became interested in the comic strip. In 1961, Mickey Mouse, Donald Duck, and Popeye began appearing in his paintings, followed by all sorts of images from everyday life. Beginning in 1962, Lichtenstein took part in a number of exhibitions. His famous *Whaam!* of 1963 is characteristic of a deliberately visual style, painted on stencil to imitate the plotted appearance of printed images. A golf ball filling up an entire canvas, a Greek temple stripped of all historical reference and lyricism, a close-up of the barrel of a gun, an exploding fighter plane, and so forth—evocative of contemporary life and its violence, but especially of images generated by the media—are depicted without emotion, as social phenomena. Irony is a frequent aspect of his work, which attacks myths and masterpieces: Lichtenstein painted canvases after Monet, Mondrian, Picasso, and Pollock.

New York: Whitney Museum; Museum of Modern Art
London: Tate Gallery
Cologne: Ludwig Museum

LIPCHITZ
JACQUES

Polish-French sculptor; born in Druskieniki, Lithuania, 1891; died in Capri, 1973. He studied architecture in Vilna and went to Paris in 1909, where he took classes at the Beaux-Arts Academy and the Julian Academy. He lived on the Rue Montmartre from 1913 to 1941, when he fled to New York. Lipchitz's work approached Cubism, and much of his sculpture consisted of spirals wound around a central axis: *Marin à la guitare* (sailor with guitar), 1914. He also did a series of works that could be taken apart, suggestive of volume without the help of any mass whatsoever: *Figure démontable*, 1915. In about 1925 the "transparents" ap-peared, which were open-work sculptures in strips of bronze: *Arlequin et guitare* (Harlequin with guitar), 1926. He made several monumental works: Figure, 1930. His art tended to be baroque and intensely personal, based on mythological and biblical themes: *Prometheus*, 1936; *Theseus*, 1942; and *Notre Dame de Liesse*, 1948.

Paris: Musée d'Art Moderne de la Ville

LURÇAT
JEAN

French painter and decorator, master of contemporary tapestry; born in Bruyères, in the Vosges, 1892; died in Saint-Paul-de-Vence, 1966. He gave up his studies of medicine and worked with Victor Prouvé in Nancy. He moved to Paris and completed most of his painted work between 1919 and 1936, strongly influenced by Cubism and Surrealism. His mother began executing his first tapestries for him in tapestry stitch in 1917. In 1933, the Aubusson workshop did *L'orage* (the storm), and in 1936 the Govelins workshop made *Illusions d'Icare* (the illusions of Icarus). Lurçat discovered the *Apocalypse of Angers* in 1938. He fought in the underground during the Second World War and had *Liberté* (freedom) woven, based on the poem by Éluard. He received monumental commissions for the church at the Plateau d'Assy and the museum of Beaune. In 1956, he began *Le chant du monde* (song of the world), a huge hanging in ten pieces (five thousand four hundred square feet), which today looks like the apocalypse of the twentieth century. Lurçat renovated the art of tapestry weaving, using fresh tones, eliminating perspective, and reviving the use of tapestries as mural decoration.

Paris: Musée d'Art Moderne de la Ville
Angers: Ancien Hôpital Saint-Jean

MAGRITTE
RENÉ

Belgian painter; born in Lessines, 1898; died in Brussels in 1967. He was trained at the fine-arts academy of Brussels, and in 1922 discovered the metaphysical painting of de Chirico, whose *Chant d'amour* (song of love) he had seen reproduced in a magazine. He became the principal founder of Belgian Surrealism. The meaning of his paintings lay in the coming together of people and objects, in which common logic was abandoned: *Les marches de l'été*, 1938. Detached from their fate, thrown into an existence out of all proportion, and rigorously figurative, these objects became so many mental traps. In Magritte's eyes, nothing is certain and anything is possible: Under a scrupulously drawn pipe, he carefully wrote the words "This is not a pipe." Magritte's paintings tried to express freedom and the "magnificent mistakes" provided us by dreams. Extremely gifted at provocation, he courted irony by living a petit-bourgeois existence, donning a bowler hat as if to hide the tempests raging inside his skull.

Brussels: Musées Royaux des Beaux-Arts
New York: Museum of Modern Art
Paris: Musée National d'Art Moderne
Vienna: Museum des 20. Jahrhunderts

MALEVICH
KAZIMIR

Russian painter; born in Kiev, 1878; died in Leningrad, 1935. Trained at the fine-arts academy of Kiev, he began painting in the Impressionist style, was influenced by the Fauves, and be-came interested in Cubist and Futurist studies, executing brightly colored canvases: *The Return of the Harvests*, and *Morning in the Country after the Rain*, 1912. In 1913, he took part in the exhibition "Target" in Moscow, and in 1915 showed his *Black Square on White* at the "0,10" exhibition in Petrograd, (now Leningrad), along with thirty-seven abstract paintings that marked the birth of Suprematism. In search of supreme color, in 1918 he produced *White Square on White*, in which he achieved the "boundary of color." In 1927, during a stay in Germany, he was recalled to Russia, where he returned to figurative painting in order to meet the demands of the regime: *Running Man*, 1930. He was extremely active during the Russian Revolution, teaching at the fine-arts academies in Moscow and Vitebsk, but later fell into disgrace. In 1958 and again in 1970, Amsterdam's Stedelijk Museum organized several retrospectives of his work.

Amsterdam: Stedelijk Museum
Bern: Kunsthalle
Paris: Musée National d'Art Moderne

MARQUET
ALBERT

French painter; born in Bordeaux, 1875; died in Paris, 1947. He and Matisse studied under Gustave Moreau at the Beaux-Arts Academy. After a long period of study, making copies, and meeting people, he painted landscapes turned into pure colors, presaging Fauvism. In 1905 he took part in the "cage aux fauves" at the Salon d'Automne. Within the group, he used brutal colors but also evinced a need for order and structure: *Le Quatorze Juillet au Havre* (the Fourteenth of July, Le Havre), 1906. After Fauvism, he did nothing but landscapes and views of Paris and Algiers. Canvases painted during his many trips boasted concise lines, shimmering colors, and a nonchalant charm: *Le Pont-Neuf la nuit* (the Pont-Neuf at night), 1935. He did a number of thumbnail sketches of street people.

Paris: Musée National d'Art Moderne
Besançon: Musée des Beaux-Arts
Bordeaux: Musée des Beaux-Arts

MASSON
ANDRÉ

French painter; born in Balagny, Oise, 1896; died in Paris, 1987. In 1912 he enrolled in the Beaux-Arts Academy; later he enlisted, was wounded and was discharged. Masson flirted briefly with Cubism, after which his first symbolic painting—*Les quatre éléments* (the four elements), 1923—was purchased by André Breton. He then joined the Surrealists, making the first Automatic Drawing in 1924 and Sand Paintings in 1927. He began working on the magazine *Minotaure* in 1933. In 1941 he fled to the United States for the duration of the war, and had a decisive influence on such painters as Gorky and Pollock, who were drawn to his Automatic approach. He pursued his work back in France, replacing Automatism with a colorful lyricism that frequently took him to the limits of abstraction. In 1965 he painted the ceiling of the Odéon in Paris. His first retrospective took place in Paris, 1965, at the Musée National d'Art Moderne; it was followed by many others worldwide. Extremely cultured, particularly in literature and philosophy, Masson always remained faithful to his need to achieve the heights of expressiveness.

New York: Museum of Modern Art
Paris: Musée National d'Art Moderne

MATHIEU
GEORGES

French painter; born in Boulogne-sur-Mer, 1921. Ma-thieu studied law and philosophy and took up painting in 1942. In 1947 he organized the exhibition "The Imaginary," as a reaction against the Geometric Abstractionism that had just resurfaced in Paris and to publicize his concept of "psychic non-figuration" or "Lyrical Abstraction." From 1945 to 1948, his canvases were composed of blobs of paint, drippings, and projections. In improvised works, canvases completed in the space of a few minutes, Mathieu developed in 1949-1950 an "esthetic of speed and risk." In 1954, he made his brilliantly decorative *Batailles* (battles), inspired by history, as well as *Les Capétiens partout* (Capetians everywhere). In 1956, he painted *Hommage aux poètes du monde entier* (homage to poets of the whole world) in public, an experience that he later repeated in Düsseldorf, Stockholm, Vienna, New York, and Tokyo. Mathieu published a milestone book, *Au-delà du tachisme* (beyond Tachism), in 1963. There was a major Mathieu retrospective in 1986 at the Palace of the Popes in Avignon. He was interested in every aspect of creativity, from architecture and posters to numismatics and tapestry-weaving.

Paris: Musée National d'Art Moderne
New York: Museum of Modern Art
Montreal: Musée d'Art Contemporain

MATISSE
HENRI

French painter; born in Cateau-Cambrésis, 1869; died in Nice, 1954. The son of grain merchants, Matisse studied law and then moved to Paris to study fine arts in the studio of Gustave Moreau. He then became interested in Neoimpressionism: *Luxe, calme et volupté*, 1904. His colors became increasingly bright, and he was soon thought of as the master of Fauvism, 1905-1908. His first sculptures were executed in 1907. From 1908 to 1917, he took several trips to Germany, Algeria, and Morocco, hoping to express space by finding more rhythmic structures, linear forms, and more violent colors: *La leçon de musique* (music lesson), 1916. In 1917, Matisse moved to the South of France, where his art acquired greater decorativeness, purity, and tranquillity. He completed the two versions of *La danse* (dance) for the Barnes Foundation in Merion, Pennsylvania. Towards the end of his life, Matisse achieved a perfect synthesis of brush stroke and color in his large cutout gouaches: *La piscine* (swimming pool), 1952, and in his decoration of the Dominican chapel in Vence. In 1952, Matisse museums opened in Cateau and in Cimiez.

Paris: Musée National d'Art Moderne
New York: Museum of Modern Art
Moscow: Pushkin Museum
Leningrad: Hermitage Museum

MIES
VAN DER ROHE LUDWIG
(LUDWIG MIES)

German-American architect; born in Aachen, 1886; died in Chicago, 1969. A student of Peter Behrens in Berlin, he quickly moved away from Classical forms and in 1920 submitted plans for a glass skyscraper that demonstrated his definite orientation towards the "international style," in which the rigor of lines at right angles, harmonious proportions, and the luminosity of surfaces predominated. He created the famous "curtain wall," a surface free of all support, which he designed in 1922 for an office building. In 1929, he built the German Pavilion at the International Exposition in Barcelona, and the next year he became head of the Bauhaus, which shut down with Hitler's rise to power in 1933. Success came quickly after he moved to the United States in 1938, especially in Chicago, where he taught at the Institute of Technology he had rebuilt. Everywhere, he attained a total stripping of form. He also created furniture in the Bauhaus style.

MIRÓ
JOAN

Spanish painter; born in Barcelona, 1893; died in Mallorca, 1983. He did not particularly enjoy Classical studies, and entered Barcelona's school of fine arts at the age of fourteen. His first works, from around 1915, were a synthesis of Cubism and Fauvism: *Portrait of E.C. Ricart*, 1917, followed by a Detailist period in which he minutely analyzed landscapes: *The Farm*, 1921. In Paris, he came into contact with Picasso, the poet Reverdy, Dadaism, and Surrealism, which totally transformed his painting. In *Terre labourée* (tilled soil), 1924, he completed the transition from poetic Realism to systematic fantasizing, which reached its peak in *Le carnaval de Venise* (Venetian carnival), 1924. As the threat of war loomed near, he sought refuge in the garden of his dreams, celebrating women, birds, and starry nights: *Constellations*, 1940-1941. In 1944, he produced his first ceramics, which led him to large-scale paintings: *Peinture pour la cellule d'un prisonnier* (painting for a prison cell), 1968. Miró's sculpture transformed found objects—*Horloge du vent* (clock of the wind), 1967—and in 1979 he executed an immense sculpture for La Défense in Paris. The Grand Palais in Paris did a major retrospective on him in 1974. In 1975, the Joan Miró Foundation opened in Barcelona.

Barcelona: Joan Miró Foundation
Paris: Musée National d'Art Moderne
New York: Museum of Modern Art
Baltimore: Museum of Art
London: Tate Gallery

MODIGLIANI
AMEDEO

Italian painter; born in Leghorn, 1884; died in Paris, 1920. At an early age, he began taking drawing lessons in Leghorn, Florence, Rome, and then Venice. He went to Paris in 1906, moved to Montmartre and then Montparnasse. Modigliani first exhibited his work in 1908 at the Salon des Indépendants after meeting his first buyer, Paul Alexandre, in 1907. Influenced by Cézanne and Toulouse-Lautrec, his layout became stronger and his line more accentuated: *Le joueur de violoncelle* (the cellist), 1909. That same year, he met Brancusi, who encouraged him to sculpt: Modigliani's *Têtes* (heads), 1912, were inspired by the same ideal of timeless purity. He then spent most of his time on portraits of his wife, Jeanne Hébuterne, and friends, in search of an abstract, ideal beauty. In 1917, a series of his nudes on exhibit at the gallery Berthe Weill was closed for "indecency." Sensitive to rhythm and to the poetry of line, Modigliani expressed the personality of his models: *Jean Cocteau*, 1916; *Soutine*, 1917. His precarious health and excesses got the better of him, and he died at age thirty-six.

Paris: Musée National d'Art Moderne;
    Collection Walter Guillaume
New York: Guggenheim Museum

MOHOLY-NAGY
LÁZLÓ

Hungarian painter and sculptor; born in Bácsborsód, 1895; died in Chicago, 1946. Strongly influenced by Neoplasticism and a fervent admirer of Mondrian, Moholy-Nagy was one of a group of creators who for several years were part of the Bauhaus, and whom the Nazis turned into martyrs. Keenly interested in Gabo's studies on the mechanical form of motion, he made his own important mobile with his own hands: *Modulateur lumière-espace* (space-light-modulator), 1922-1928, which foreshadowed Kinetic Art. After leaving the Bauhaus, where he taught the introductory course and then the metal workshop, he went to Berlin and later took many trips before settling in London for two years. In 1937, like many others in search of a country that would take them in during the war, Moholy-Nagy arrived in Chicago, where he founded the New Bauhaus. Forty years after his death, he is looked upon as an important precursor of today's young artists.

Essen: Folkwang Museum
Cambridge, Massachusetts: Busch-Reisinger Museum

MONDRIAN
PIET
(PIETER CORNELIS MONDRIAAN)

Dutch painter; born in Amersfoort, 1872; died in New York, 1944. Drawn to painting at a very young age, he studied at the fine-arts academy in Amsterdam. In 1908, he met Jan Toorop, with whom he did a show in 1909. He went to Paris in 1912, where his art, influenced by Cubism, underwent a profound transformation from figurative painting to abstract work: *Composition No. 7*, 1913. The magazine *De Stijl*, which he started with Van Doesburg, defended his "pure plastic," called "Neoplasticism"; eventually the form allowed nothing but horizontal and vertical lines, separating planes of primary colors into flat tints: red, yellow, and blue. His influence on architecture was considerable. In his last canvas, *Victory Boogie-Woogie*, painted in New York the year of his death, black is eliminated and replaced by many small, colored squares. After his death, several museums did Mondrian retrospectives: in 1945, the Museum of Modern Art in New York; the Stedelijk Museum in Amsterdam, 1946; a Basel museum, 1947; and the Oran-gerie in Paris, 1969.

The Hague: Gemeentemuseum
Amsterdam: Stedelijk Museum
New York: Museum of Modern Art

MOORE
HENRY

British sculptor; born in Castleford, Yorkshire, 1898; died in Much Hadham, near London, 1986. A miner's son, he studied sculpture at the School of Fine Arts in Leeds and at London's Royal College of Art. He quickly received commissions; in 1938, he became a Surrealist. The human figure was almost his only subject, as an expression of the interplay of the forces and tensions moving the universe. Going beyond Abstraction-versus-Figuration, Moore sought to express the sum of energy amassed in certain natural forms: *Reclining Figure*, 1925; *Mother and Child*, 1936. After the Second World War, his work evoked a tragic atmosphere: *Falling Warrior*, 1956. Moore introduced hollows into his sculpture through the interpenetration of planes in order to better define and magnify form. In 1948 he received the sculpture prize at the Biennale in Venice, and in 1957, the Carnegie prize. There have been a number of Moore retrospectives, notably in New York, London, and Paris.

Paris: Musée National d'Art Moderne
London: Tate Gallery
Toronto: Gallery of Ontario

MORANDI
GIORGIO

Italian painter and engraver; born in 1890 in Bologna, where he died in 1964. He studied at the fine-arts academy in his hometown at a time when Futurism was sweeping through Italy. Under the influence of Cézanne, he realized the limitations imposed by the Futurists, from whom he distanced himself. In 1915, he painted *The Bathers*, analyzing space and planes. His still lifes, being more than just formal studies, disclosed a universe in which objects escaped from their material reality. Between 1919 and 1922, he belonged to the group of Metaphysical Painters. His paintings at the time were spare and geometrical. Morandi then moved towards an even greater spareness: Some objects, always the same—cups, pitchers, vases, and bottles—were shown under different light. Through them the painter sought a personal artistic expression, which questioned the world of forms. He has been honored with numerous retrospectives, notably in Venice, 1948; Paris, 1971; and Rome, 1973.

Turin: Galleria Civica d'Arte Moderna
Paris: Musée National d'Art Moderne
New York: Museum of Modern Art
Düsseldorf: Kunstsammlung
    Nordrhein-Westfalen

MOTHERWELL
ROBERT

American painter; born in Aberdeen, Washington, 1915. He studied at the California School of Fine Arts, Stanford, and Yale. Very close to the Surrealists during their wartime exile in New York, Motherwell quickly became one of the important members of the New York School, both because of his writings, inspired by Mediterranean culture, and because of his free Expressionist paintings. His prolific work is organized around two lengthy series: *Elegies to the Spanish Republic* —vast, austere canvases in black and white, inspired by his love of Spain—and *Opens*, in bright colors. Collages, sketches, illustrations, and graphics round out his work, which is very characteristic of New York culture of the sixties.

New York: Metropolitan Museum of
    Art; Museum of Modern Art
Cambridge, Massachusetts: Fogg
    Art Museum

NEWMAN
BARNETT

American painter; born in 1905 in New York, where he died in 1970. Famous in the forties for his writings on Primitive Art and his esthetic polemics, Newman is among those artists whose work in the United States brought an entirely new language to painting: the Abstract Expressionists. He evolved very quickly from a Symbolism inspired by Genesis towards an extremely pure, austere style of painting, whose metaphysical connotations have to do with Jewish mysticism. His huge monochrome canvases are punctuated by "zips," thin, vertical strips that create a very physical place within the color. Throughout the development of Newman's painting, color becomes less modulated and lyrical, accentuating the materiality of the canvas. His sculpture is also full of allusions to sacred places, particularly his *Broken Obelisk*, a broken steel obelisk with an imposing presence. Newman's rigorous Abstractionism played a decisive role in the birth of Minimal Art.

New York: Museum of Modern Art
Houston: Ménil Collection
Amsterdam: Stedelijk Museum

OLDENBURG
CLAES

Swedish-American artist; born in Stockholm, 1929. He studied at the Art Institute of Chicago and came to New York in 1956, where he met Allan Kaprow, initiator of the Happening. Starting in the late fifties, his sculptures have been made of paper and cardboard and then of plaster, and are virtual inventories of the consumer society: *The Street, The Store, The Home*. His giant objects, disproportionately enlarged tools for everyday life, became caricaturelike idols of American prosperity. They are also piercing commentaries on violence: *Lipstick on Caterpillar Tracks*, 1969, at Yale University, is a monumental lipstick placed over caterpillars as a sort of derisory missile that denounces the Vietnam War. He also made sculptures from colored plaster or kapok-stuffed moleskins, which were intended as satire, to provoke laughter: *Pink Cap*, 1961. Since the seventies, Oldenburg has done plans for giant utopian monuments.

Paris: Musée National d'Art Moderne
Houston: Contemporary Arts Museum
New Canaan: Philip Johnson
   Collection

PEVSNER
ANTOINE

Russian-French painter and sculptor; born in Orel, 1886; died in Paris, 1962. He studied at the fine-arts schools of Kiev and St. Petersburg (now Leningrad). After moving to Paris in 1911, he became friends with

Archipenko, and in 1915 met up with his brother Nahum Gabo in Norway. The two returned to Moscow, where in 1920 they wrote the *Realist Manifesto*, expounding the theories of Constructivism. Back in Paris in 1923, he executed sculptures with metal blades and plastics: *Portrait de Marcel Duchamp*, 1926. In 1927, the two brothers designed sets and costumes for Diaghilev's *La Chatte* (the cat). In the thirties, Pevsner used bronze that had been hammered out into thin reeds and soldered, radiating from one axis of development: *Surface développable* (developable surface), 1938. At the same time, he was involved in the Abstraction-Creation group. After the war, he received commissions for large-scale monuments: *Envol de l'oiseau* (the bird flies off), 1955. All his work is intended to express space that has neither beginning nor end.

Paris: Musée National d'Art Moderne
Amsterdam: Stedelijk Museum
New York: Guggenheim Museum

PICABIA
FRANCIS
(FRANÇOIS-MARIE MARTINEZ-PICABIA)

French painter; born in 1879 in Paris, where he died in 1953. He studied drawing at the École des Arts Décoratifs and painting at the Beaux-Arts Academy. His canvases were Impressionist until 1908. Then he married Gabrielle Buffet, a young musician who drew him into the intellectual currents of the iera, and he became a part of the avant-garde movements: Cubism, Section d'Or, and Orphism. His canvases, gouaches, and pencil sketches evoke the studies of Cubism and Futurism: *Udnie*, 1913. In New York, 1915, he met Marcel Duchamp and joined the Dadaists. The machine takes on mythical values in his work, and poetic or absurd phrases accompany imaginary mechanisms: *Parade amoureuse* (amorous procession), 1917. In Paris, 1920, he and Tristan Tzara continued developing Dadaism until the movement ended. Picabia moved

first to the South of France and then to Paris, after which his painting again became academic and figurative.

Paris: Musée National d'Art Moderne
New York: Guggenheim Museum;
   Metropolitan Museum of Art
Philadelphia: Museum of Art

PICASSO
PABLO
(PABLO RUIZ Y PICASSO)

Spanish-French painter; born in Málaga, 1881; died in Mougins, 1973. He studied fine arts in Barcelona and moved to Paris in 1904. His early work, approaching Postimpressionism, is divided into his "blue period," in which his canvases are shrouded in sadness, and his "pink period," which leaves a more peaceful impression. *Les demoiselles d'Avignon*, 1907, marks the beginnings of Cubism, which he developed in close collaboration with Braque. Starting in 1913, he broke the object into planes rather than volumes—*Le violon et la guitare* (violin and guitar), 1913—and introduced collage elements into the canvas, such as glued fabric and paper: *Nature morte avec fruits et violons* (still life with fruit and violins), 1913. With *La danse* (dance), 1925, a period akin to Surrealism debuts, called the "period of metamorphoses," which lasted about ten years: *Femme assise* (seated woman), 1927. In 1937 he painted *Guernica*, after that Basque town was destroyed in a German bombardment during the Spanish Civil War. He moved to the South of France in 1948, after which his output became even more prolific and diverse. His work covers all genres, including lithography, sculpture *La chèvre*, (the goat, 1950), pottery, and ceramics, and until his death he demonstrated a vitality and fecundity of invention that left their mark on all of twentieth-century art.

Paris: Musée Picasso; Musée National
   d'Art Moderne
Antibes: Musée Picasso
Barcelona: Museo Picasso
Basel: Kunstmuseum
New York: Museum of Modern Art

PIGNON
ÉDOUARD

French painter; born in Bully-les-Mines, Pas-de-Calais, 1905. At first a miner, then a typographer in Paris, he took night classes. He began painting in about 1930. *L'ouvrier mort* (the dead worker), 1936, was a major theme of his work, one he returned to sixteen years later and always with the same sense of reality. His paintings of people, still lifes, and harbor views show extreme rigor, right up to the fifties: *Catalanes*, 1945; *Ostend*, 1947. Pignon became a close friend of Picasso in 1953, although they originally met before the war. His discovery of the South of France made his painting more rhythmic and exuberant: *Oliviers* (olive trees), 1955. Several major series followed: *Les combats de coqs* (cockfights), *Les dames du soleil* (the ladies of the sun), extremely colorful, with quick sketches that expressed the close ties between humans and nature. There was a major Pignon retrospective at the Grand Palais in Paris 1985.

Paris: Musée National d'Art Moderne

POLLOCK
JACKSON

American painter; born in Cody, Wyoming, 1912; died in East Hampton, 1956. He went to New York in 1930 and studied under Thomas Hart Benton. From the very start, his painting turned its back on traditionalism and used thickened material that was a first for its time. He met the Surrealists who were living in New York during the Second World War and was fascinated hby psychic Automatism. Impassioned by myths, Jungian symbolism, and the pictorial techniques of Native Americans, he forged a violent and intense style that is the very essence of Action Painting. Pollock was noticed by Peggy Guggenheim, who commissioned his first large mural work in 1943—a painting on canvas twenty feet long. His techniques are "All-Overs" (the brush-stroke covers the canvas without any centered structure) and "drippings," in which the canvas is placed on the ground and the paint dropped onto it from a brush or an open can of paint. After 1951, he returned to black-and-white figuration.

New York: Museum of Modern Art
Paris: Musée National d'Art Moderne
London: Tate Gallery

RAUSCHENBERG
ROBERT

American painter; born in Port Arthur, Texas, 1925. He studied at the Kansas Art Institute and Black Mountain College, where he met the composer John Cage; from then on, he worked frequently with the choreographers Merce Cunningham and Paul Taylor. From 1953 to 1955, he used a large variety of objects, from stuffed birds and radios to painted paper, for such works as *Charlene*, 1954, and *Rebus*, 1955, a technique he called "Combine Painting." That integration of objects into works of art had a great influence on the future Pop Artists. In 1960 Rauschenberg began using silkscreen printing to represent subjects from contemporary America: President Kennedy, the Vietnam War, the exploration of outer space, and so forth. Then, his art became more abstract: *Revolvers*, 1967, is composed of circular plates of plexiglass over which he placed large constructions of objects, as also in his *Venetian Series*, 1973. He won the painting prize at the 1964 Biennale in Venice.

New York: Guggenheim Museum;
    Museum of Modern Art
Amsterdam: Stedelijk Museum
Stockholm: Moderna Museet

REINHARDT
AD

American painter; born in Buffalo, 1913; died in New York, 1967. He studied art history at Columbia University and the Institute of Fine Arts of New York. During the fifties, criticizing both the conservatism of museums and the artistic milieux of the avant-garde, his search for the absolute was expressed in almost monochrome paintings and, beginning in 1960, in "Black Paintings," canvases with imperceptible repetitions of cruciform geometric shapes. Reinhardt hoped to create in this manner an opposition between the concepts of change and stability, and to realize the last paintings anyone could ever paint, as he put it. Extremely careful and purely realized, his paintings moved toward an increasingly ascetic, repetitive form of art. In 1972, Düsseldorf, Eindhoven, Zurich, Paris, and Vienna held major retrospectives on him.

New York: Museum of Modern Art;
    Metropolitan Museum of Art
Pittsburgh: Carnegie Institute

RICHIER
GERMAINE

French sculptor; born at Grans, near Arles, 1904; died in Montpellier, 1959. She studied at the fine-arts school in Grans and in 1925 went to Paris, where she studied under Bourdelle. A frequent subject of hers was animals: the spider, the owl, the bat, the toad. But animals never had anything but symbolic meaning in her work: neither she nor Brancusi was a true sculptor of animals. She was haunted by a feeling of the tragic precariousness of all things, which found its way into her decomposing bodies, such as the *Christ*, pitiable and barely able to support itself, which she executed for the church on the Plateau d'Assy in 1950. Like Picasso and Giacometti, she belongs among those artists who "disturbed," in the sense that their work at the time of the concentration camps and Hiroshima showed the true nature of humanity.

Paris: Musée National d'Art Moderne
Zurich: Kunstmuseum

RIVERA
DIEGO

Mexican painter; born in Puebla, 1886; died in Mexico City, 1957. Rivera studied at the Academy of San Carlos in Mexico City, and later in Spain. He moved to Paris in 1909. In 1912 he turned from Postimpressionism to Cubism. He spent time in Montparnasse with Picasso, Modigliani, Lipchitz, Mondrian, and Severini. From 1915 to 1918, he practiced an original Cubism and then went back to figuration. He returned to Mexico in 1921. In 1922 he began his first frescoes, along with Jean Charlot, Carlos Merida, Fermín Revueltas, and Alva de la Canal. Thenceforth, Rivera, Siqueiros, and Orozco would be the most important figures in Mexican Muralism. A highlight of his periods of residence in the United States with Frida Kahlo from 1930 to 1934 was the 1934 scandal of the Rockefeller Center frescoes.

Mexico City: Fine Arts Palace

ROTHKO
MARK

Russian-American painter; born in Dvinsk, 1903; died in New York, 1970. He emigrated to the United States in 1913 and studied fine arts at Yale, and with Max Wever at the Art Students League in New York. His early painting was Expressionist in style, and with Gottlieb he founded the group "the Ten" in 1935. After the Second World War, he was influenced by Surrealism, which drew him toward abstraction, and he became one of the masters of Abstract Expressionism. Then, in about 1950, the canvases of Rothko and other painters of the New York School, depicting imprecise rectangles, and infused with luminous, velvety colors, took on mural dimensions. In 1967-1969, he executed paintings for the Ecumenical Chapel in Houston. His colors then grew somber, tending toward grays and browns, attesting to a depression that culminated in suicide. In 1961, New York's Museum of Modern Art gave him a major retrospective.

Paris: Musée National d'Art Moderne
London: Tate Gallery
New York: Museum of Modern Art

ROUAULT
GEORGES

French painter and engraver; born in 1871 in Paris, where he died in 1958. At the age of fourteen, he was an apprentice glassmaker, and in 1890 he was admitted to the Beaux-Arts Academy in the studio of Élie Delaunay and later that of Gustave Moreau. After a serious illness, and his meeting with Huysmans, Rouault became a fervent Catholic. In about 1905, he was drawn to the Fauves, while at the same time being interested in the religious implications of his subjects. He painted social topics, prostitutes, and judges in a style reminiscent of Daumier's caricatures, abandoning chiaroscuros, nuances, and reliefs, and outlining his subjects in a large black stroke, like the lead of stained-glass windows. From 1917 to 1927, he illustrated books for Vollard: *The Reincarnations of Père Ubu*, and the plates for the *Miserere*. In 1929, he designed sets and costumes for Diaghilev's *Prodigal Son*. Subsequently, aside from clowns and pierrots, he painted nothing but religious subjects, such as *La sainte face* (the holy face), 1933. In 1945 he did the stained-glass windows for the church at Assy, and in 1949 the enamels for the abbey of Ligugé. Rouault himself felt he did not belong to modern times, and that his real life took place in the age of the cathedrals.

Paris: Musée National d'Art Moderne;
    Musée d'Art Modernde la Ville
New York: Museum of Modern Art
London: Tate Gallery

RUSSOLO
LUIGI

Italian painter; born in Portogruaro, 1885; died in Cerro di Laveno, 1947. He studied music rather than painting, and was a part of Milan's avant-garde literary circles. In 1909 he allied himself with Boccioni and, along with Balla, Carrà, and Severini, signed the first *Futurist Manifesto* in 1910. While dealing with most of the themes of the Futurists—riots, in *Revolt*, 1911; mechanical dynamism, in *The Dynamism of an Automobile*, 1912; and light, in *Power Paths of Lightning*, 1912—his style was very much his own, and very original: *Music*, 1911. Gravely wounded in 1917, he moved to Paris and devoted himself more to concerts than to painting. In 1938 he published a book on occultism, and in 1941 returned to painting, but to figurative work, without any hint of Futurism.

Paris: Musée National d'Art Moderne
Basel: Kunstmuseum
Milan: Mattioli Collection

SCHIELE

EGON

Austrian painter; born in Tulin, 1890; died in Vienna, 1918. He studied at the Vienna Academy of Fine Arts from 1906 to 1909 and met Klimt, whom he admired, and who influenced his early work, in 1907. An exceptional draftsman, much of his work—strikingly erotic and provocative—was realized in pencil, watercolor, and gouache. Schiele's line is sharp and carnal. He stressed the sexual organs, which he loved to reveal; cadaverous bodies; and complicated entanglements: *Dual Self-Portrait*, 1910; *Lovers*, 1913. Fascinated by Van Gogh, he also painted, in 1913, the miserable room where he himself lived in Neulangenbach. His landscapes, few in number, depicted nature in equally deathly, lacerated fashion. Schiele married in 1915, but he and his expectant wife succumbed to the epidemic of the Spanish influenza that ravaged Europe in 1918. His premature death left his work incomplete.

Vienna: Österreichische Galerie; Albertina
The Hague: Gemeentemuseum
New York: Guggenheim Museum

SCHÖFFER

NICOLAS

Hungarian-French sculptor; born in Kalocsa, 1912. After studying at the fine-arts academy in Budapest, he moved to Paris in 1937. He was the initiator of Spatiodynamics and of Luminodynamism. After many periods of experimentation, and after meeting Marcel Duchamp, Schöffer became convinced that art could not be an expression of its era unless it embraced the science and technology of its age, rather than turning from it. In 1956, he created *Cysp I*, the first cybernetic, autonomously acting sculpture, which moved self-controlled over the ground by reacting to sounds, noises, and colors. *Cysp I* followed a Spatiodynamic tower one hundred and sixty-five feet tall, built in the Park of Saint-Cloud in 1954, on the occasion of the Salon des Travaux Publics. A number of sculptures followed, including the series of *Chronos* and of *Luxes*, which were gigantic kaleidoscopes consisting of reflecting prisms. Schöffer erected monumental sculptures in many countries. His ideas are recorded in several books, including *Le nouvel esprit artistique* (the new artistic spirit), 1970, and *Tour-lumière-cybernétique* (cybernetic light tower), 1973. Schöffer has his own museum in Kalocsa.

New York: Museum of Modern *Art*
Cologne: Kunstmuseum
Paris: Musée National d'Art Moderne

SCHWITTERS

KURT

German painter; born in Hanover, 1887; died in Ambleside, Great Britain, 1948. He studied at the fine-arts academies of Hanover, Dresden, and Berlin, and began painting under the influence of Expressionism and Cubism. He then used castoffs, which led to the compositions he called "Merz paintings," a name that came arbitrarily from separating the syllable "Merz" from the word "Kommerzbank" (bank of commerce), a bank whose mutilated billboard he could see from his home. This was how he discovered the collage, or montage, to which he then devoted himself almost to the point of obsession, filling his canvases with all sorts of objects he collected: old theater stubs, rusty nails, bits of wire, and the like. He began elaborating the *Merzbau* (Merz construction) in his house at Hanover, 1923, based on the same principle, and worked on it for ten years. The *Merzbau*, acquired gigantic proportions before it was destroyed in an Allied air raid in 1943. Schwitters not only painted and worked in graphic arts, typography, and architecture, but was also a poet, prose writer, playwright, and theatrical essayist.

Hanover: Sprengel Museum
New York: Museum of Modern Art
Düsseldorf: Kunstsammlung Nordrhein-Westfalen

SEVERINI

GINO

Italian painter; born in Cortone, 1883; died in Paris, 1966. Severini took night classes and then met Boccioni, who introduced him to Balla. He went to Paris in 1906, where he lived for many years. At first he painted in the Divisionist style, but in 1910 he joined the Futurists Balla, Boccioni, Carrà, and Russolo, signing their *Manifesto*. In 1912, he painted *Pan-Pan at Monico* and several canvases inspired by dance and movement. He moved towards Cubism in 1915, and the next year exhibited his *Maternity*, which marked his return to Realism. Converted to Catholicism in 1923, he painted many sacred and profane frescoes, while publishing theoretical writings and recollections of his friends Boccioni and Matisse. From 1935 to 1946, he lived in Rome, and then returned to Paris. In 1952, he went back to Cubo-Futurist Abstraction.

New York: Museum of Modern Art
Paris: Musée National d'Art Moderne

SOULAGES

PIERRE

French painter; born in Rodez, 1919. He left the Roman monuments and megaliths of his native Rouergue region to move to Paris in 1946, discovering Cézanne and Picasso; he showed his work in 1947 at the Salon des Surindépendants. Extremely solitary in nature, his art at-tained a personal abstraction, and he painted on paper with walnut stain, gasoline, and oil. He worked almost exclusively in black, and rectilinear motifs form a dense, dramatic architecture in his painting; a profound strength lies behind his strokes of the spatula, knife, or even rubber sole. In 1949, he designed the sets and costumes for Roger Vaillant's *Héloïse et Abélard*, and in 1951 for Graham Greene's *The Power and the Glory*. His line and colors then began to soften, with more rhythm, white, and sometimes even color stealing into his canvases: *Painting April 27, 1972.* The approach he uses in his current work has not changed throughout the years.

Paris: Musée National d'Art Moderne
London: Tate Gallery
New York: Museum of Modern Art; Guggenheim Museum

SOUTINE

CHAIM

Lithuanian-French painter; born in Smilovitchi, near Minsk, in 1893; died in Paris, 1943. He studied at the fine-arts academy in Vilna, and went to Paris, where he became a friend of Chagall, Lipchitz, and Modigliani. He spent time at the Beaux-Arts Academy and the Louvre, and he especially admired Rembrandt and Cézanne. His early still lifes were Realistic and sober. His characteristic reds, blue-greens, and whites were first introduced in 1917-1918: *Auto-portrait*, 1918; *Le bœuf écorché* (side of beef), 1925. In 1923, the American collector Albert C. Barnes visited his studio, buying one hundred paintings all at once, which brought Soutine fame and put an end to his poverty. He then met Monsieur and Madame Castaing, who took him to their château at Lèves, near Chartres. His themes, associated with particular colors, followed one on the other: he used white, for example, for the *Pâtissiers* (pastry cooks), red for the *Chasseurs* (hunters), and blue and green for still lifes. Soutine was drawn to defenseless beings, and his paintings of children are deeply moving. He was tormented by the war, which caused his art to return to the dramatic: *Après l'orage* (after the storm), 1930-1940.

Paris: Musée National d'Art Moderne
Washington: Philipps Collection
New York: Museum of Moderne Art

STAËL
NICOLAS DE

Russian-French painter; born in St. Petersburg (now Leningrad), 1914; died in Antibes, 1955. He emigrated from Russia to Poland and then Belgium, studied at the Saint-Gilles Academy and the Royal Academy of Fine Arts in Brussels, and traveled widely throughout Europe and North Africa. In April 1944, he and Kandinsky took part in an exhibition of abstract painting. Then, between 1946 and 1947, his canvases, while abstract, showed pathos and emotion with the superimposition of solid impastos: *La vie dure* (the hard life), 1946. He acquired a large studio in 1949 and began to make monumental works with more luminous colors: *Composition,* 1950. Then, placing small brush strokes in a checkered pattern, he composed *Les toits de Paris* (the roofs of Paris), with a very similar motif. In spring 1952, the nighttime soccer match between France and Sweden inspired a number of colorful and turbulent paintings. Worn out and depressive, Staël threw himself from his studio window in 1955.

Paris: Musée National d'Art Moderne
Antibes: Musée Picasso
Dijon: Musée des Beaux-Arts
Chicago: Art Institute

TANGUY
YVES

French-American painter; born in Paris, 1900; died in Woodbury, Connecticut, 1955. Like his father, Tanguy started out as a sailor; he met Jacques Prévert, with whom he moved to Montparnasse in 1922. He took up painting after seeing a canvas by de Chirico, and was also strongly influenced by Max Ernst. In 1925, he joined the Surrealists and took part in all their exhibitions: *La Genèse* (genesis), 1926. He then painted deserted landscapes with deep blue skies: *Maman, papa est blessé* (Mommy, Daddy is hurt), 1927. In 1938, he met Kay Sage, an American Surrealist painter, with whom he moved to the United States. He did a number of characteristic canvases, in which he expressed his sense of a world independent of perceptible reality. His next-to-last work, *Multiplication of Arcs,* 1954, shows the horrifying eternity of mineral life invading the planet.

Paris: Musée National d'Art Moderne
New York: Museum of Modern Art
London: Tate Gallery

TÀPIES
ANTONI

Spanish painter; born in Barcelona, 1923. He studied law and commerce, and was deeply marked by the atrocities of the Spanish Civil War. In 1946, he made collages from newspapers, cord, paper, and aluminum. In 1948, along with Ponç, Tharrats, and Cuixart, he founded the group and magazine called *Dau el Set* (seven on the die). Influenced by Miró, he then went through a Surrealist period: *Desconsuelo lunar* (lunar disconsolation), 1949. In 1950 and 1951, he lived in Paris, discovering the Informal Art of Dubuffet and Fautrier and the writings of Michel Tapié. From 1954 on, he returned to his studies of materials, mixing oil, pulverized marble, and pigments in powder or latex, scraped onto the pictorial layer: *Negro y ocre* (black and ocher), 1955; *Grand triangle marron* (large maroon triangle), 1963. He also sculpted. Tàpies published several essays on painting including, in 1970, *La pratique de l'art* (art practice) and an autobiography, *Mémoire,* in 1981.

Paris: Musée National d'Art Moderne
New York: Guggenheim Museum

TATLIN
VLADIMIR

Russian artist; born in Kharkov, 1885; died in Moscow in 1953. Tatlin studied art and made a number of trips as a sailor until 1907. He began studying architecture in Moscow in 1909. Two years later, he met Malevich, and then Larionov, and took part in exhibitions arranged by the latter. During 1913, he spent time in Berlin and Paris, visiting Picasso. His work appeared in several exhibitions in Russia during the First World War, and in 1917 he, Jakulov, and Rodchenko were responsible for decorating Moscow's Café Pittoresque. In 1918, he became a professor at the Institute of Architecture. In 1919-1920, his model for the *Monument to the Third International* made him famous; it was presented in public in Moscow during the Third Communist International in 1920. After several years of teaching architecture, Tatlin turned to theatrical set design in 1933.

Leningrad: Russian Museum
Moscow: Tretiakow Gallery; Museum of Architecture

TINGUELY
JEAN

Swiss sculptor; born in Fribourg, 1925. He took painting classes at the school of fine arts in Basel, and in 1953 moved to Paris where, impassioned by movement, he made his first *Metamechanicals,* animated robots made of wire and sheet metal, which put geometric forms into movement. In 1959, at the Biennale in Paris, he presented his "Painting Machines," mechanized scorpions that were able to make abstract drawings. Then, in an attempt to be provocative, in 1959 he made his *Homage to New York,* an explosive construction designed to destroy itself which, in the garden of the Museum of Modern Art, caught fire and went up in smoke, illustrating his thought: "Who gives a damn about art!" Beyond art, his "Happening Machines" were intended to be "something that functions, that's never been seen before," using scrap iron that would come back to life in the museum. In his last period, Tinguely made altarpieces and various compositions in which he put animal skulls, making his work disturbing and poetic.

Paris: Musée National d'Art Moderne
New York: Museum of Modern Art
Basel: Kunstmuseum

TOBEY
MARK

American painter; born in Centerville, Wisconsin, 1890; died in Basel, 1976. After a brief time at the Hammond High School, he had several careers, becoming a fashion designer in Chicago and New York. In 1918, he converted to the Bahai faith, and Eastern religion. He began traveling extensively in 1930, and lived in China and Japan in 1934, including a month at a Zen monastery. On his return, his study of calligraphy resulted in his "White Writing," ia modern transposition of Chinese writing, which made him famous: Broadway Norm, a work of rapid, fluid calligraphy, symbolized the infinitely small. Tobey tried to synthesize East and West in his work, seeking a secret correspondence between internal impulses and rhythms of the universe: *Sumi Still Life,* 1957. He received the national prize from the Guggenheim Foundation in 1957, and the painting prize at the 1958 Biennale in Venice. Also that year, he was elected to the American Academy of Arts and Sciences.

Paris: Musée National d'Art Moderne
New York: Museum of Modern Art
London: Tate Gallery

UTRILLO
MAURICE

French painter; born in Paris, 1883; died in Dax, 1955. The illegitimate son of Suzanne Valladon, acknowledged by the Spanish artist Miguel Utrillo, he began drinking at an early age and underwent a series of detoxification treatments from 1900 on. After the first such treatment, his mother taught him drawing and painting. From 1903 to 1905, during his Montmagny period, he was fond of somber tones and thick textures. Then, in about 1908, Utrillo entered his white period, using a mixture of plaster and glue to represent snow with gray and pink reflections and creamy white walls: *Square Saint-Pierre sous la neige* (Saint Peter Square under the snow), 1908. Based on picture postcards, he then painted all the nooks and corners of Montmartre, such a the *Rue du Mont-Cenis*, 1914. His style became more colorful and fragmented. In 1923 he designed the sets of *Barabao*, for Diaghilev's Russian Ballet. His concept of space, with ascending and descending perspectives, and his leprous walls, attest to his anguish and his instinctive poetry.

Paris: Musée National d'Art Moderne; Musée d'Art Modern de la Ville

VAN DONGEN
KEES

Dutch-French painter; born in Delfshaven, near Rotterdam, in 1877; died in Monte Carlo, 1968. He studied only briefly at the academy in Rotterdam, then drew port scenes and prostitutes for *Groene* and the *Rotterdam Niewsblad*, causing a sensation. He arrived in Paris in 1897 and moved to the Bateau-Lavoir, did sketches for *L'assiette au beurre*, joined the staff of the *Revue blanche* in 1903, and was exhibited by Druet as of 1903 and by Vollard as of 1904. He took part in the Fauvism manifestation of 1905, but showed greater affinity for the German Expressionists. His relationships with the Marquise Casati in 1913 and with Leo Jasmy in 1916 gave his painting a worldly style for which Van Dongen became famous. His portraits of celebrities from both society and the Parisian demimonde were highly valued, despite their frequently cruel reality and insolent colors. Alternating with costume balls, he sought isolation in the countryside, bringing back spontaneous, sober, and apt landscapes. Van Dongen is one of the great colorists of the twentieth century.

Paris: Musée National d'Art Moderne
Grenoble: Musée de Peinture et de Sculpture
New York: Museum of Modern Art

VAN VELDE
BRAM

Dutch painter; born in Zaeterwoude, 1895; died in Grimaud, in the Var, in 1981. He did an apprenticeship as a decorator-painter at the age of fifteen. In 1922 he went to Worspwede, the famous painters colony near Bremen, Germany, where he stayed until 1924, undergoing the influence of Expressionism. He moved to Paris in 1925 where, except for a period in Mallorca from 1932 to 1936, he remained until 1965. His friends included Samuel Beckett. Thereafter, he divided his time between Paris and his residence in Geneva. A representative of Informal Art, he remained independent of all the movements, while nonetheless belonging to the Parisian School. His art is at once sensitive and powerful, and his colors are bright. Nearly all his works since 1945 have been entitled either *Gouache* or *Painting*.

Paris: Musée National d'Art Moderne
Amsterdam: Stedelijk Museum

VASARELY
VICTOR
(VIKTOR VASARHELYI)

Hungarian-French painter; born in Pécs, 1908. He attended the Muhely Academy in Budapest, which was modeled after the Bauhaus. He went to Paris in 1930. While working at an ad agency, he did graphic sketches in black and white. In order to go beyond the Geometricism of Mondrian and Malevich, he soon began playing with reversible perspectives and optical effects: *Homage to Malevich*, 1952-1958. In 1955 he participated in the "Motion" exhibition at the gallery Denise René and published his *Yellow Manifesto*, which marked the birth of Kinetism. In 1960 he started working with colors that exploded, fresh and serene, in his conception of a plastic alphabet he called *Planetary Folklore*. He moved from easel painting to mural decoration, using such new materials as aluminum and glass: *Sophia*, a mural painting of black and white ceramic, at the university of Caracas, 1954. In 1970, the Musée Didactique Victor Vasarely opened in Gordes, and a Vasarely Foundation was inaugurated in Aix-en-Provence in 1976.

Paris: Musée National d'Art Moderne
New York: Museum of Modern Art
Rotterdam: Boymans Van Beuningen Museum

VILLON
JACQUES
(GASTON DUCHAMP)

French painter and engraver; born in Damvillle, Eure, 1875; died in Puteaux, 1963. Villon was a notary's clerk in Rouen before going to Paris in 1894, where he adopted the name of his favorite poet and took up painting with his brother Raymond. His sketches appeared in humorous newspapers such as *Le rêve* and *L'assiette au beurre*, in which his skills as a draftsman are already evident. Drawn to Cubism, he founded the Puteaux Group of artists that included his brothers Marcel and Raymond, as well as Gleizes, Metzinger, Léger, Delaunay, and Picabia, who would later found the Section d'Or; he wanted to create a Cubism concerned with proportions that grew out of the golden number, beloved of Leonardo da Vinci. In *Les soldats en marche* (soldiers on the march), 1913, he created the impression of movement through the interplay of straight lines and colors, out of which his later work grew. After the somberness of the war years, he added light to his geometric vision: *Architecture*, 1931. His success continued to grow with such masterly compositions as *Les grands fonds*, 1945. He won the Carnegie prize in 1950, and in 1956 was given a commission to make the stained-glass windows for the Metz Cathedral. In his engravings, he developed a system of closely carved networks, infinitely faceting his volumes, and found in drypoint a soft brush stroke that balanced the rigor of his compositions.

Paris: Musée National d'Art Moderne
New York: Museum of Modern Art

VLAMINCK
MAURICE DE

French painter; born in Paris, 1876; died in Rueil-la-Gadelière, Eure-et-Loir, 1958. He had no academic training. Early on, he was impassioned by cycling and the violin, which enabled him to earn a living. In July 1900, he met Derain and decided to take up painting. Fascinated by Van Gogh, he joined the group of Marquet and Matisse, and exhibited at the 1905 Salon d'Automnee, in the "cage aux fauves." His *Le pont de Chatou*, the *Bateaux-Lavoirs*, and *Rue à Marly-le-Roi* date from this period. The retrospective that followed the death of Cézanne in 1906 had a great influence on him; his colors became more sober and his forms more robust: *Bougival*, 1910. His paintings are powerful, rich in color, and their subjects are generally the Seine and the Île-de-France. After the Second World War, Vlaminck's work became more Realistic and approached the German Expressionists and Dutch Naturalists.

Paris: Musée National d'Art Moderne

VUILLARD
ÉDOUARD

French painter; born in Cuiseaux, Saône-et-Loire, 1868; died in La Baule, 1940. A student at the Lycée Condorcet, he was supposed to enter the Saint-Cyr Military Academy when his fellow student K.-X. Roussel introduced him to his true calling. At the fine-arts school where he enrolled, he was quickly discouraged by the official form of instruction. He enrolled in the Julian Academy, where he met Sérusier and Bonnard, and then joined the Nabis. His sense of intimacy, reinforced by the use of painting on cardboard, which absorbed color, creates a padded atmosphere in his work: *Interior,* 1898. Under the influence of Japanese prints, which he admired, his paintings, confirming his taste for soft boudoirs and barely illumined by the filtered light of a lamp, are reminiscent of chamber music. He also created mural compositions: in the Théâtre des Champs-Élysées in 1913, the Palais de Chaillot in 1937, and the League of Nations Palace in Geneva in 1938.

Paris: Musée National d'Art Moderne
Saint-Tropez: Musée de l'Annonciade

WARHOL
ANDY

American painter and filmmaker; born in Pittsburgh, 1931; died in New York, 1987. His early career was as a commercial artist for ad agencies, after which, during the sixties, he painted canvases inspired by everyday images, labels, and comic strips. Then, in 1962, he presented *Campbell's Soup Can,* as well as portraits of Marilyn Monroe and Elizabeth Taylor, taken from magazines of the time and produced in series in his famous New York studio, by means of a silk-screen process on canvas. He said he wanted to be a machine, and that anyone should be able to execute his canvases in his place. In 1963 he depicted the hidden side of the "American way of life": riots, accidents, the electric chair, and the like. From 1968 to 1972, he devoted himself to film, making *Kiss, Empire,* and *Chelsea Girls,* in which he let the actor improvise in real time before an immobile camera. During the seventies, he returned to his pictorial activities, producing series based on Mao, Muhammad Ali, and commissioned portraits: *Ladies and Gentlemen,* 1975. Often dubbed the Pope of Pop, he was, indeed, at the forefront of Pop Art.

New York: Museum of Modern Art
Cologne: Ludwig Museum

WOLS
(ALFRED OTTO WOLFGANG SCHULZE)

German painter; born in Berlin, 1913; died in Paris, 1951. A brilliant student, gifted in music, mechanics, and geology, he studied at the Bauhaus of Dessau. Refusing to live under the Nazi regime, he moved to Paris, where he made his first drawings in India ink and watercolor. Imprisoned and then set free in 1940, he returned to Paris in 1945. In 1945 and 1947, René Drouin organized two exhibitions without Wols's consent, since he refused to be associated with galleries or art critics. With the help of blobs and signs, Wols depicted objects and people as expressions of the unconscious: *Blue Specter.* It was the beginning of Informal Painting. At the boundary of Expressionism and Surrealism, he sought to translate the shudders, vibrations, and teeming of life: *Champigny Blue.* He had a major influence on the later development of Lyrical Abstractionism.

Paris: Musée National d'Art Moderne
Cologne: Ludwig Museum
New York: Museum of Modern Art

WRIGHT
FRANK LLOYD

American architect; born in Richland Center, Wisconsin, 1867; died in Phoenix, Arizona, 1959. A student of Louis Sullivan in Chicago, 1887, attempting to reconcile the Rationalism of the machine with his own poetics, he rejected the traditional principle of the architectural box and designed his Prairie Houses, buildings with "free" plans, with large horizontal lines: Willits House, Illinois, 1902. He became interested in reinforced concrete, which he used in public buildings, such as the Larkin Building in Buffalo, 1904. In 1910, in an abrupt change of direction, he abandoned his family and his studio and left for Europe. During a stay in Japan, he built the Imperial Hotel in Tokyo in 1922. In 1936, he built the Kaufmann House, Falling Water, in Pennsylvania, which incarnated his ideal of life in nature, in which the interior spaces are projected outward like aspirations. Johnson Wax Company, in Wisconsin, then commissioned him for its administration building, whose volumes are undulating and fluid. His last great work was the Solomon R. Guggenheim Museum, 1956-1959, an im-mense spiral rising as a continuous ramp in which paintings and sculptures are displayed. He influenced a considerable number of architects, such as Gropius and Mies van der Rohe, although he had no real disciples.

ZADKINE
OSSIP

Russian-French sculptor; born in Smolensk, 1890; died in Paris, 1967. Sent to England in 1905, he was trained at Sunderland and London. He went to Paris in 1910, where he was admitted to the Beaux-Arts Academy. He was a part of early Cubism: *Femme à l'éventail* (woman with fan), 1918. But his poet's instinct did not fit well into the rigidity of Cubism; he transformed, for example, natural elements such as large tree trunks into women's bodies: *Torso,* 1928. His inspiration was then increasingly baroque, playing with curves and straight lines, full spaces and hollows: *Homo sapiens,* 1935. In about 1940, he lightened his forms by piercing them, thereby creating multiple viewpoints. Working against contemporary art movements, which tended toward abstraction, Zadkine realized an abstract idea by means of figurative elements: *La ville détruite* (the destroyed city), 1948, his masterpiece. He also made gouaches, aqua fortis, and engravings.

Paris: Musée National d'Art Moderne
Amsterdam: Stedelijk Museum

p. 22. John Ruskin. *The Seven Lamps of Architecture*. London: Smith, Elder, 1849 (pp. 185, 189, 190).

p. 23. Friedrich Nietzsche. *Werke in zwei Bänden*. Munich: Carl Hanser, 1967.

p. 41. Benedetto Croce. *L"esthétique comme science de l'expression et linguistique générale*. Paris: Gérard et Brière, 1904.

p. 45. Paul Gauguin.

p. 66. Guillaume Apollinaire. *Les peintre cubistes*.

p. 71. Paul Cézanne.

p. 76. Adolf Loos. *Wohnungswanderungen*. 1906.

p. 81. Pablo Picasso: André Malraux. *La tête d'obsidienne*. Paris: Gallimard, 1974.

p. 89. Mecislas Goldberg. *La morale des lignes*. 1908.

p. 94. Wilhelm Worringer. *Abstraction et Einfühlung*. Paris: Klincksieck, 1978.

p. 95. Henri Matisse. "Propos sur la peinture" in *Écrits et propos sur l'art*. Paris: Hermann, 1972.

p. 99. Filipo Tommaso Marinetti. "Manifeste du futurisme" in Giovanni Lista, *Futurisme*. Lausanne: L'Age d'Homme, 1973.

p. 117. Sigmund Freud. *Un souvenir d'enfance de Léonard de Vinci*. Paris: Gallimard, 1977.

p. 121. Wassili Kandinsky. *Du spirituel dans l'art et dans la peinture en particulier*. Paris: Denoël-Gonthier, 1969.

p. 131. Robert Delaunay. "Notes sur la construction de la réalité de la peinture pure" in *Du cubisme à l'art abstrait*. Paris: SEVPEN, 1957.

p. 133. Albert Gleizes and Jean Metzinger. *Du cubisme*. Paris: Figuière, 1912.

p. 145. Guillaume Apollinaire. *Les peintres cubists. Œuvres complètes*. Paris: Balland, 1965.

p. 149. Arthur Schopenhauer. *Essai sur les apparitions et opuscules divers*. Paris: Alcan, 1912.

p. 154. Umberto Boccioni. "Peinture et sculpture futuriste" in Giovanni Lista, *Futurisme*. Lausanne: L'Âge d'Homme, 1973.

p. 159. Kazimir Malevich. "Du cubisme et du futurisme au suprématisme" in *Écrits, I*. Lausanne: L'Âge d'Homme, 1974.

p. 167. Tristan Tzara. "Manifeste de Monsieur Antipyrine" in *Sept manifestes Dada*. Paris: Pauvert, 1967.

p. 175. Piet Mondrian. "Le néo-plasticisme" in Michel Seuphor, *Mondrian. Sa vie, son œuvre, ses écrits*. Paris: Flammarion, 1960.

p. 179. Marcel Duchamp. "Le cas Richard Mutt (Lettre ouverte aux américains)" in *The Blind Man*. 1917.

p. 183. Guillaume Apollinaire.

p. 191. Walter Gropius. "Manifeste du Bauhaus" in Jocelyn de Noblet, *Design*. Paris: Stock/Chêne, 1974.

p. 193. Gino Severini. "Symbolisme plastique et symbolisme littéraire" in Giovanni Lista, *Futurisme*. Lausanne: L'Âge d'Homme, 1973.

p. 197. Stanislaw Witkiewicz. *Les formes nouvelles en peinture et les malentendus qui en découlent*. Lausanne: L'Âge d'Homme, 1979.

p. 203. Léopold Zbroswki. Letter to Emmanuele Modigliani, January 31, 1920/ Gustave Coquiot. *Les indépendants*. 1920/ Francis Carco. "Modigliani" in *Éventail*. July 15, 1919/ Charles-Albert Cingria/ Paul Guillaume.

p. 205. Paul Klee. "La confession créatrice" in *Théorie de l'art moderne*. Paris: Denoël-Gonthier, 1964.

p. 209. Nahum Gabo and Antoine Pevsner. "Manifeste réaliste" in Jocelyn de Noblet, *Design*. Paris: Gallimard, 1964.

p. 229. Gaston de Pawlowsky. *Voyage au pays de la quatrième dimension*. Paris: Denoël, 1962.

p. 233. Le Corbusier. *Vers une architecture*. Paris: Crès, 1923.

p. 237. André Breton. "Manifeste du surréalisme" in *Manifestes du surréalisme*. Paris: Gallimard, 1963.

p. 243. Juan Gris. "Des possibilités de la peinture" in Daniel-Henry Kahnweiler, *Juan Girs. Sa vie, son œuvre, ses écrits*. Paris: Gallimard, 1946.

p. 258. Max Ernst. "Histoire d'une histoire naturelle" in *Écritures*. Paris: Gallimard, 1970.

p. 259. Wassili Kandinsky. *Point, ligne, plan*. Paris: Denoël-Gonthier, 1972.

p. 263. René Jean. *Comœdia*. December 6, 1926/ Arsène Alexandre. *Le Figaro*. December 10, 1926/ Jacques des Gachons. *Le National*. December 19, 1926.

p. 265. Elie Faure. *L'esprit des formes. Œuvres complètes*. Paris: Pauvert, 1927.

p. 273. André Breton. *Le surréalisme et la peinture*. Paris: Gallimard, 1965.

p. 275. Georges Hugnet.

p. 299. Louis Aragon. *La peinture au défi et la peinture*. Paris: Gallimard, 1965.

p. 303. Marc Chagall. *Ma vie*. Paris: Stock, 1931.

p. 311. Frank Lloyd Wright. *An Autobiography*. London: Longmans, Green, 1932 (pp. 170, 171, 193, 329, 365).

p. 317. Carl Gustav Jung. "Picasso" in *Problèmes de l'ame moderne*. Paris: Buchet-Chastel, 1961.

p. 327. Fernand Léger. "Le mur, l'architecte et le peintre" in *Fonctions de la peinture*. Paris: Denoël-Gonthier, 1965.

p. 335. Lewis Mumford. *Art and Technics*. New York: Columbia University Press, 1952 (pp. 70, 71, 107-109).

p. 339. Kazimir Malevich. *Écrits*. Paris: Champ Libre.

p. 342. Adolf Hitler. "Discours au congrès de Nüremberg" in Lionel Richard, *Le nazisme et la culture*. Paris: Masperio, 1978.

p. 343. Salvador Dali. "La conquête de l'irrationnel" in *Oui*. Paris: Denoël-Gonthier, 1971.

p. 357. Paul Éluard: Wallace Fowlie (ed.). *Mid-Century French Poets*. New York: Twayne, 1955.

p. 365. Walter Benjamin. "L'œuvre d'art à l'ère de la reproductibilité technique" in *Œuvres choisies*. Paris: Julliard, 1959.

p. 369. *L'Humanité*. January 18, 1938/ *Candide*. January 20, 1938.

p. 383. André Lhote. *Traité du paysage*. Paris: Librairie Floury, 1939.

p. 389. Paul Klee. *Théorie de l'art moderne*. Paris: Denoël-Gonthier, 1964.

p. 363. Jean-Paul Sartre. *L'imaginaire*. Paris: Gallimard, 1940.

p. 416. Le Corbusier. *Entretiens avec les étudiants des écoles d"architecture*. Paris: Denoël, 1943.

p. 417. Henri Focillon. *La vie des formes*. Paris: Alcan, 1934.

p. 421. Wassili Kandinsky. *Du spirituel dans l'art et dans la peinture en particulier*. Paris: Denoël-Gonthier, 1969.

T E X T S   Q U O T E D

p. 429. Piet Mondrian: Michel Seuphor. *Mondrian. Sa vie, son œuvre, ses écrits.* Paris: Flammarion, 1960.

p. 433. Jean Dubuffet. "Notes aux fins lettrés" in *Prospectus et tous écrits suivants.* Paris: Gallimard, 1967.

p. 437. Fernand Léger. "New York" in *Fonctions de la peinture.* Denoël-Gonthier, 1965.

p. 442. Lucio Fontana. "Manifeste blanc" in Michel Tapié, *Devenir de Fontanna.* Paris: Guy Le Prat, 1961.

p. 447. Pierre Bonnard: *Exposition Bonnard, Catalogue.* Éditions du Centre Georges Pompidou, 1984.

p. 447. Léon Werth. *Cahiers d'aujourd'hui.* 1919/ Charles Terrace. *Bonnard..* 1927.

p. 455. Asger Jorn. "Les banalités intimes" in Jean-Clarence Lambert, *Cobra, un art libre.* Paris: Chêne/Hachette, 1983.

p. 461. Pierre Francastel. "Art et sociologie" in *La réalité figurative.* Paris: Denoël-Gonthier, 1965.

p. 465. Henry Moore. *Henry Moore.* Paris: Cercle d'Art, 1984.

p. 469. Auguste Herbin. *L'art non figuratif non objectif.* Paris: Lydia Conti, 1949.

p. 475. Roger Bissière: Daniel Abadie. *Bissière.* Neuchâtel: Ides et Calendes, 1986.

p. 481. Jean Bazaine. *Propos sur la peinture d'aujourd'hui.* Paris: Le Seuil, 1950.

p. 485. Père Couturier. "Le prêtre et la création artistique" in *L'art sacré.* May-June. 1950.

p. 488. Georges Mathieu. "Note sur le poétique et le signifiant" in *Au delà du tachisme.* Paris: Julliard, 1963.

p. 489. André Malraux. *Les voix du silence.* Paris: Gallimard, 1951.

p. 493. Harold Rosenberg. *The Anxious Object: Art Today and Its Audience.* New York: Horizon Press, 1964 (pp. 41, 44-46).

p. 495. Michel Tapié. *Un art autre.* Paris: Stadler, 1952.

p. 502. *L'Humanité.* March 18, 1953.

p. 503. Letters to the editor of *L'Humanité.*

p. 511. Henri Matisse. *Écrits et propos sur l'art.* Paris: Hermann, 1972.

p. 519. Clement Greenberg. "American-Type Painting" in *Partisan Review.* Spring 1955 (pp. 191, 193, 194).

p. 521. Victor Vasarely. "Manifeste jaune" in *Vasarely.* Neuchâtel: Griffon, 1974.

p. 526. Hans Sedlmayr. *Die Revolution der modernen Kunst.* Munich: Rowholt, 1955.

p. 531. Jackson Pollock: Francis O'Connor. *Jackson Pollock.* New York: Museum of Modern Art, 1967 (pp. 40, 51, 73, 79-81).

p. 535. Walter Gropius. *Allocation prononcée lors de la réception du Hansische Goethepreis.* Brussels: Éditions de la Connaissance, 1969.

p. 539. Constantin Brancusi: Carola Giedion-Welcker. *Constantin Brancusi.* Basel and Stuttgart: Benno Schwabe, 1958.

p. 540. Ad Reinhardt. "Twelve Rules for a New Academy" in *ARTnews,* May 1957 (p. 38).

p. 549. Georges Rouault. *Sur l'art et sur la vie.* Paris: Denoël-Gonthier, 1971.

p. 569. Pierre Restany. "Premier manifeste" in *Les nouveaux réalistes.* Paris: Éditions Planète, 1968.

p. 579. Jean Dubuffet. *Prospectus et tous écrits suivants.* Paris: Gallimard, 1967.

p. 589. Antoni Tàpies. *La pratique de l'art.* Paris: Gallimar;d, 1974.

p. 597. Umberto Eco. *L'œuvre ouverte.* Paris: Le Seuil, 1964.

p. 601. Georges Braque. *Le jour et la nuit.* Paris: Gallimard, 1952.

p. 605. Jean-Louis Ferrier. "L'idée de nouvelle figuration" in *La nuova figurazione.* Florence: Vallechi, 1963.

p. 609. Robert Rauschenberg: Andrew Forge. *Rauschenberg.* New York: Harry N. Abrams, 1969.

p. 611. Marshall McLuhan. *Understanding Media.* New York: McGraw-Hill, 1964. (pp. 12, 13, 18).

p. 619 André Malraux. "Discours du Louvre" in Jean Petit, *Le Corbusier.* Paris: Forces Vives, 1967.

p. 627. Jean Genet. *L'atelier d'Alberto Giacometti.* Œuvres complètes, Vol. V. Paris: Gallimard, 1979.

p. 633. Édouard Pignon. *La quête de la réalité.* Paris: Denoël-Gonthier, 1966.

p. 637. René Magritte. *Écrits complets.* Paris: Flammarion, 1979.

p. 639. Germano Celant. "L'arte povera" in catalogue of *Qu'est-ce que la sculpture moderne?* Paris: Éditions du Centre Georges Pompidou, 1986.

p. 649. Marcel Duchamp: Pierre Cabanne. *Entretiens avec Duchamps.* Paris: Belfond, 1967.

p. 651. Salvador Dali. "Ma revolution culturelle" in *Oui.* Paris: Denoël-Gonthier, 1971.

p.659. Andy Warhol. *The Philosophy of Andy Warhol.* Harcourt Brace Jovanovich, 1975.

p. 679. Francis Bacon: John Russell. *Francis Bacon.* London:" Methuen, 1964.

p. 687. Pierre Soulages: Jean Grenier. *Entretiens avec dix-sept peintres non figuratifs.* Paris: Calmann-Lévy, 1953.

p. 693. Nicolas Schöffer. *La ville cybernétique.* Paris: Denoël-Gonthier. 1972.

p. 697. Pablo Picasso: Hélène Parmelin. *Secret d'alcôve d'un atelier.* Paris: Cercle d'Art, 1964, 1966.

p. 705. Chuck Close/ Tom Blackwell/ Linda Chase.

p. 715. Roy Lichtenstein: Tate Gallery, London, *Roy Lichtenstein.* 1968. 1969 (pp. 7, 9, 11-13).

p. 739. Jasper Johns: Max Kozloff. *Jasper Johns.* New York: Harry N. Abrams, 1967 (pp. 24, 30-32).

p. 751. Pierre Restany. *L'autre face de l'art.* Paris: Galilée, 1979.

p.757. Achille Bonito Oliva. *La transavantgarde italienne.* Milan: Gian-Carlo Politi, 1980.

p. 765. George Baselitz. "Entretiens avec Demosthène Davvitas" in *Art Press.* No. 123.

p. 773. Arman: Bernard Lamarche-Vadel. *Arman.* Geneva: Éditions La Différence, 1987.

p. 791. Jacques Henric. *La peinture et le mal.* Paris: Grasset, 1983.

p. 803. Édouard Pignon. *Contre-courant.* Paris: Stock, 1974.

p. 805. Jean-François Lyotard. *Le post-moderne expliqué aux enfants.* Paris: Galilée, 1986.

p. 813. Joseph Beuys.

p. 821. André Masson. *La mémoire du monde.* Geneva: Skira, 1974.

p. 827. Pol Bury. "L'arrière-train de l'avant-garde" in *Le Figaro.* September 15, 1987.

A C K N O W L E D G M E N T S

Editor in Chief	Jean-Louis Ferrier
Senior Editors	Yann le Pichon, Madeleine Deschamps, Serge Fauchereau, Lionel Richard
Associate Editors	Ulrike Aubertin, Agnès Barbier, Gérard Barrière, Véronique Bonamour, Nicolas Bourriaud, David Bouvier, Claire Bouvier-Oger, Isabelle Caziot, Frédérique Côme, Henri-François Debailleux, Jacqueline Delpech, Nathalie Glarner, Ariane Grenon, Lydia Harambourg, Jacques Henric, Pierre Jacquin, Rosa Laisné, Éric Lamoure, Béatrice Laurent, René Lesné, Claude Libert, Évelyne Mangin, Marie-Hélène Masson, Catherine Millet, Philippe Nourry, André Parinaud, Marie-Hélène Parinaud, Dominique de Pirey, Isabelle Poiraudeau, Jean Revol, Claude-Henri Rocquet, Jérôme Sans, Bénédicte Servignat, Sandra Silve, Catherine Trouiller
Managing Editor	Anne Souleau-Joffre
Assistant Editor	Lorraine Miltgen
Editorial Assistant	Brigitte Veillon
Art Director	François Huertas
Associate Art Director	Philippe Pierrelée
Layout	Pierre Chapelot
Illustrations	Claire Balladur
Proofreaders	Catherine Picard, Catherine Schram

We are grateful to all persons, institutions, and galleries who have assisted in the preparation of this work, but especially to Martine Briant, Pierre Cabanne, Valentina Chagall, Nicole Chamson, Michèle Collinet, Hélène Couza, Élisabeth Delaigue, Robert Descharnes, Nicole Duault, Sylvie Forestier, Pierrette Gargallo Anguerra, André Gomez, Pedro Guerrero, Otto Hahn, Hugues Joffre, Monique Le Pelley-Fonteny, Adrien Maeght, M. Maillet, Ingrid Parge, Catherine Prassinos, Michel Ragon, Antoinette Rézé, Isabelle Rouault, Robert Schmidt, Catherine Swan, André Verdet, Brigitte Vincent, Guy Weelen; to the galleries Adrien Maeght, Beaubourg, Claude Bernard, Isy Brachot, Jacques Fournier, Daniel Templon, Denise René, Karl Flinker, Lelong, Leo Castelli, Louise Leiris, Stadler; to Mr. and Mrs. Christo Javacheff, Mr. and Mrs. Nicolas Schöffer, the F. L. Wright Foundation; and to the many artists who have kindly provided material and whom it would be impossible to acknowledge here individually.

English-language edition edited by Walter D. Glanze with translations by Vicki Bogard, Lawrence M. Brunet, Suzanne DeCamp, Erica Meltzer, Susan L. Rosenstreich, Marie-Madeleine Saphire, Kenneth T. Simpson, Translation Company of America, Laurie A. Treuhaft, and Pierre Weill; and with the contribution of the year 1988 by Helen A. Harrison of the *New York Times*.

English-language edition produced by ST. REMY PRESS, *Montreal, Canada*

Managing Editor	Kenneth Winchester
Managing Art Director	Pierre Léveillé
Senior Art Director	Diane Denoncourt
Coordinating Editor	Nancy D. Kingsbury
Designers	Maryse Doray, Francine Lemieux, Nicolas Moumouris, Solange Pelland, Jean-Luc Roy, Odette Sévigny
Proofreaders	Gilles Humbert Jack Ognistoff Jane Pavanel
Coordinator	Michelle Turbide
Systems Manager	Shirley Grynspan
Systems Analysts	Daniel Bazinet Simon Lapierre

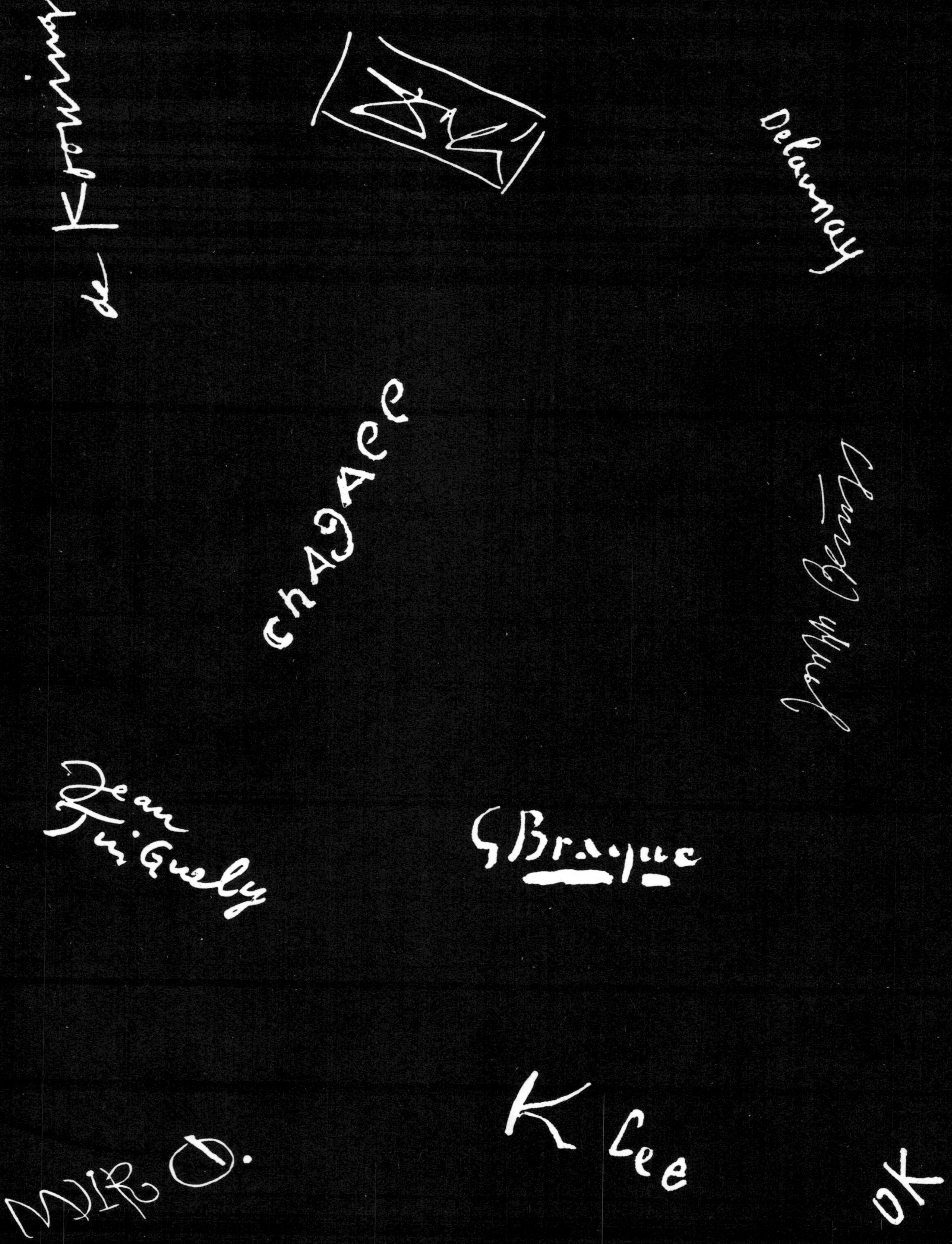

de Kooning

Delaunay

chAGAll

GBraque

Jean
Tinguely

MIRO.

K Lee

OK